Lecture Notes in Computer Science 5142

Commenced Publication in 1973
Founding and Former Series Editors:
Gerhard Goos, Juris Hartmanis, and Jan van Leeuwen

Jan Vitek (Ed.)

ECOOP 2008 – Object-Oriented Programming

22nd European Conference
Paphos, Cyprus, July 7-11, 2008
Proceedings

 Springer

Volume Editor

Jan Vitek
Purdue University
Department of Computer Sciences
West Lafayette, IN 47907, USA
E-mail: jv@cs.purdue.edu

Library of Congress Control Number: 2008930413

CR Subject Classification (1998): D.1, D.2, D.3, F.3, C.2, K.4, J.1

LNCS Sublibrary: SL 2 – Programming and Software Engineering

ISSN 0302-9743

ISBN 978-3-540-70591-8 Springer Berlin Heidelberg New York

Springer is a part of Springer Science+Business Media

springer.com

© Springer-Verlag Berlin Heidelberg 2008

Typesetting: Camera-ready by author, data conversion by Scientific Publishing Services, Chennai, India
Printed on acid-free paper   SPIN: 12512270   06/3180   5 4 3 2 1

Preface

It is a pleasure to present the proceedings of the 22nd European Conference on Object-Oriented Programming (ECOOP 2008) held in Paphos, Cyprus. The conference continues to serve a broad object-oriented community with a technical program spanning theory and practice and a healthy mix of industrial and academic participants. This year a strong workshop and tutorial program complemented the main technical track. We had 13 workshops and 8 tutorials, as well as the co-located Dynamic Language Symposium (DLS). Finally, the program was rounded out with a keynote by Rachid Guerraoui and a banquet speech by James Noble. As in previous years, two Dahl-Nygaard awards were selected by AITO, and for the first time, the ECOOP Program Committee gave a best paper award.

The proceedings include 27 papers selected from 138 submissions. The papers were reviewed in a single-blind process with three to five reviews per paper. Preliminary versions of the reviews were made available to the authors a week before the PC meeting to allow for short (500 words or less) author responses. The responses were discussed at the PC meeting and were instrumental in reaching decisions. The PC discussions followed Oscar Nierstrasz' Champion pattern. PC papers had five reviews and were held at a higher standard.

ECOOP owes is success to the efforts of many. I would like to thank the authors for their submissions; the Program Committee members and their subreviewers for the thoroughness of their reviews—on average 2.500 words per paper (but going all the way to 5.863 words!); our General Chair George A. Papadopoulos; the AITO executive board; Richard van de Stadt for his invaluable help with CyberChairPRO, and Susan Eisenbach and Sophia Drossopoulou for hosting the PC meeting at Imperial College.

May 2008 Jan Vitek

Organization

ECOOP 2008 was organized by the Department of Computer Science of the University of Cyprus, under the auspices of AITO (Association Internationale pour les Technologies Objets), and in cooperation with ACM SIGPLAN and SIGSOFT.

Executive Committee

Conference Chair

George A. Papadopoulos (University of Cyprus, Cyprus)

Program Chair

Jan Vitek (Purdue University, USA)

Organizing Committee

Workshop Chairs

Patrick Eugster (Purdue University, USA)
Costas Pattichis (University of Cyprus, Cyprus)

Tutorial Chair

James Noble (Victoria University, New Zealand)

Publicity Chair

Dave Clarke (CWI, The Netherlands)

PhD Symposium Chair

Mark Hills (UIUC, USA)

Exhibition Chair

Andreas Andreou (University of Cyprus, Cyprus)

Demonstration and Poster Chair

Anna Phillipou (University of Cyprus, Cyprus)

Student Volunteer Chair

Tobias Wrigstad (Stockholm University, Sweden)

Panel Chair

Tony Hosking (Purdue University, USA)

Workshops Review Committee

Benoit Garbinato (University of Lausanne, Switzerland)
Peter Müller (Microsoft Research, USA)
Friedrich Steimann (Fernuniversität Hagen, Germany)

Sponsoring Organizations

Gold

Silver

Program Committee

Elisa Baniassad (Chinese University of Hong Kong)
Gavin Bierman (Microsoft Research, UK)
Alex Buckley (Sun Microsystems, USA)
William Cook (University of Texas at Austin, USA)
Susan Eisenbach (Imperial College, UK)
Manuel Fahndrich (Microsoft Research, USA)
Pascal Felber (University of Neuchatel, Switzerland)
Robby Findler (University of Chicago, USA)
Kathleen Fisher (ATT Research, USA)
Jeff Foster (University of Maryland, College Park, USA)
Michael Haupt (Hasso Plattner Institute, Germany)
Matthias Hauswirth (University of Lugano, Switzerland)
Görel Hedin (Lund University, Sweden)
Richard Jones (University of Kent, UK)
Doug Lea (State University of New York at Oswego, USA)
Ondrej Lhotak (University of Waterloo, Canada)
Todd Millstein (University of California Los Angeles, USA)
James Noble (Victoria University, New Zealand)
Nathaniel Nystrom (IBM Research, USA)
Manuel Oriol (ETH Zurich, Switzerland)
Erez Petrank (Technion and Microsoft Research, Israel)
Frantisek Plasil (Charles University, Czech Republic)

Awais Rashid (Lancaster University, UK)
Michael I. Schwartzbach (University of Aarhus, Denmark)
Jeremy G. Siek (University of Colorado at Boulder, USA)
Mario Sudholt (EMN-INRIA, LINA, France)
Peter Theimann (Universität Freiburg, Germany)
Frank Tip (IBM Research, USA)
Eelco Visser (Delft University of Technology, The Netherlands)
Tobias Wrigstad (Stockholm University, Sweden)
Roel Wuyts (IMEC and K.U.Leuven, Belgium)

Referees

Jiri Adamek
Tristan Allwood
Jose Nelson Amaral
Malte Appeltauer
Pavel Avgustinov
Vlastimil Babka
Stephanie Balzer
Anindya Banerjee
Fred Barnes
Don Batory
Nelly Bencomo
Nick Benton
Annette Bieniusa
Steve Blackburn
Joshua Bloch
Bard Bloom
Noury Bouraqadi
John Boyland
Martin Bravenboer
Lubomir Bulej
Tomas Bures
Nicholas Cameron
Susanne Cech Previtali
Robert Chatley
Feng Chen
Juan Chen
Ilinca Ciupa
Dave Clarke
Charles Consel
Dave Cunningham
Maja D'Hondt
Martin Decky
Markus Degen

Benjamin Delaware
Dave Dice
Werner Dietl
Danny Dig
Remi Douence
Derek Dreyer
Sophia Drossopoulou
Stephane Ducasse
Torbjörn Ekman
Michael Engel
Erik Ernst
Matthias Felleisen
Fabiano Cutigi Ferrari
Sally Fincher
Matthew Flatt
Matthew Fluet
Cedric Fournet
Neal Gafter
Bas Graaf
Hervé Grall
Phil Greenwood
Dan Grossman
Khilan Gudka
Tim Harris
Jan Heering
Phillip Heidegger
Laurence Hellyer
Zef Hemel
Robert Hirschfeld
Martin Hirzel
Petr Hnetynka
Jippe Holwerda
Ali Ibrahim

Pavel Jezek
Lingxiao Jiang
Milan Jovic
Jaakko Järvi
Thomas Kühne
Tomas Kalibera
Lennart Kats
Shmuel Katz
Andrew Kennedy
Ron Kersic
Raffi Khatchadourian
Joe Kiniry
David Kitchin
Jan Kofron
Robert Krahn
Shriram Krishnamurthi
Peter Kropf
George Kuan
Ralf Lämmel
Patrick Lam
Ghulam Lashari
Andreas Leitner
Alan Leung
Jens Lincke
Jed Liu
Yanhong A. Liu
Brad Lushman
Donna Malayeri
Michal Malohlava
Jeremy Manson
Simon Marlow
Antoine Marot
Jacob Matthews
John Matthews
Jean-Marc Menaud
Ana Milanova
Oege de Moor
Peter Mueller
Anders Møller
Nomair Naeem
Luis Daniel Benavides Navarro
Iulian Neamtiu
Srinivas Nedunuri
Joost Noppen
Jacques Noyé

Klaus Ostermann
Johan Östlund
Pavel Parizek
Matthew Parkinson
Igor Peshansky
Alexis Petrounias
Andrew Pitts
Polyvios Pratikakis
Xin Qi
Etienne Rivière
Tom Rothamel
Jean-Claude Royer
Joseph N. Ruskiewicz
Claudio Russo
Chris Ryder
Matthew Sackman
Chris Sadler
Bernd Schoeller
Carsten Schwender
Ondrej Sery
Jeremy Singer
Doug Smith
Christian Spielvoegel
Alexander Spoon
Mathieu Suen
Alex Summers
Nikhil Swamy
Francois Taiani
David Tarditi
Max Troy
Petr Tuma
Ian Utting
Viktor Vafeiadis
Arnout Vandecappelle
Mandana Vaziri
Clark Verbrugge
Sander Vermolen
Joost Visser
Stefan Wehr
Ian Wehrman
Nathan Weston
Jan Wloka
Eran Yahav
Dmitrijs Zaparanuks

Table of Contents

Keynote

Session I

Session II

Session III

Session VIII

Session IX

The Return of Transactions

Rachid Guerraoui

School of Computer and Communication Sciences (LPD), EPFL
rachid.guerraoui@epfl.ch

Abstract. Major chip manufacturers have recently shifted their focus from speeding individual processors to multiplying them on the same chip and shipping multicore architectures. Boosting the performance of programs will thus necessarily go through parallelizing them. This is not trivial and the average programmer will badly need abstractions for synchronizing concurrent accesses to shared memory objects. The transaction abstraction looks promising for this purpose and there is a lot of interest around its use in modern parallel programming. This talk will investigate whether the "return" of the old transaction idea brings any interesting research question, especially for the programming language community.

J. Vitek (Ed.): ECOOP 2008, LNCS 5142, p. 1, 2008.
© Springer-Verlag Berlin Heidelberg 2008

A Model for Java with Wildcards

Nicholas Cameron[1], Sophia Drossopoulou[1], and Erik Ernst[2,*]

[1] Imperial College London
{ncameron, scd}@doc.ic.ac.uk
[2] University of Aarhus
eernst@daimi.au.dk

Abstract. Wildcards are a complex and subtle part of the Java type system, present since version 5.0. Although there have been various formalisations and partial type soundness results concerning wildcards, to the best of our knowledge, no system that includes all the key aspects of Java wildcards has been proven type sound. This paper establishes that Java wildcards are type sound. We describe a new formal model based on explicit existential types whose pack and unpack operations are handled implicitly, and prove it type sound. Moreover, we specify a translation from a subset of Java to our formal model, and discuss how several interesting aspects of the Java type system are handled.

1 Introduction

This paper establishes type soundness for Java wildcards, used in the Java type system to reconcile parametric polymorphism (also known as generics) and inclusion polymorphism [7] (subclassing). A *parametric* (or *generic*) type in Java, e.g., class List<X> ..., can be instantiated to a *parameterised type*, e.g., List<Integer>. Wildcards extend generics by allowing parameterised types to have actual type arguments which denote unknown or partially known types, such as List<?> where ? stands for an unknown actual type argument. With traditional generics, different actual type arguments to the same parametric type create unrelated parameterised types, but wildcards introduce *variance*, i.e., they allow for subtype relationships among such types; for instance, List<Integer> is a subtype of List<? extends Number>.

Wildcards have been part of the Java language since 2004, but type soundness for Java with wildcards has been an open question until now. There are several informal, semi-formal, and formal descriptions of Java wildcards [3,11,17,24] and soundness proofs for partial systems [5,14]. However, a soundness proof for a type system exhibiting all of the interesting features of Java wildcards has been elusive. Showing type soundness for Java with wildcards is difficult for a number of reasons: first, the Java wildcard syntax prioritises a concise notation for common

---

* Supported by the DRCTPS grant 95093428.

J. Vitek (Ed.): ECOOP 2008, LNCS 5142, pp. 2–26, 2008.

cases, but is not expressive enough to denote all the types which may arise during type checking; second, modeling wildcards with traditional existential types is not straightforward; and third, the inference of type parameters during a process known as wildcard capture requires careful treatment.

We show type soundness for Java with wildcards using a new formal model, TameFJ, which extends FGJ [13], which is a formalisation of Java generics. We use explicit existential types (such as $\exists$X.List<X>) to model Java wildcard types, but packing and unpacking of existential types is handled implicitly, in the rules for typing and subtyping. The implicit unpacking of existential types is used to model wildcard capture in Java. The use of an implicit approach (also found in Wild FJ [17]) contrasts with our recent previous work [5], where explicit packing and unpacking expressions were used. This approach created problems with expressiveness and, a soundness proof for Wild FJ is still missing, due in part to the complexity of creating existential types 'on the fly'. In this paper we provide a soundness proof without compromising expressiveness. In addition, we define a translation to TameFJ from a subset of the Java language that includes wildcards.

The main contribution of this paper is the new formal model and the soundness result, achieved via several technical innovations. Additionally, the translation supports the claim that TameFJ is a faithful model of Java with wildcards.

In Sect. 2 we outline the background for Java wildcards and their formalisation. In Sect. 3 we define and discuss TameFJ and its type soundness proof, and in Sect. 4 we present the translation from Java to TameFJ. Finally, in Sect. 5 we cover related work, and in Sect. 6 we discuss future work and conclude.

2 Background

In this section we give some background for the key concepts of this paper. We deliberately keep this section rather brief; more details may be found in [5]. In the examples here and elsewhere in the paper we make use of a class hierarchy of shapes: Shape is a subclass of Object, Polygon and Circle are subclasses of Shape, and Square is a subclass of Polygon.

2.1 Generics, Wildcards and Existential Types

Generics [3,11] add parametric polymorphism to Java. Classes and interfaces may be generic, i.e., they may have formal type parameters. Parameterised types are then constructed by applying generic types to actual type parameters. For example, a list class could be defined as class List<X>..., and we may then construct lists of strings and shapes using List<String> and List<Shape>, or more complex types like List<List<Y>>, where Y could be a type variable defined in the context. Similarly, methods may have formal type parameters and receive actual type arguments at invocation; e.g., the method walk has one formal type parameter, X, while walkSquares has none:

```
<X> List<X> walk(Tree<X> x) {...}

List<Square> walkSquares(Tree<Square> y) {
    return this.<Square>walk(y);
}
```

Wildcards. A *wildcard type* is a parameterised type where ? is used as an actual type parameter, for example List<?>. Such a type can be thought of as a list of *some* type, where the wildcard is *hiding* that type. Where multiple wildcards are used, for example Pair<?, ?>, each wildcard hides a potentially different type. Wildcards enjoy *variant subtyping* [14], so List<Shape> is a subtype of List<?>. This is in contrast to generic types that are *invariant* with respect to subtyping, so List<Circle> is not a subtype of List<Shape>. Wildcards may be given upper or lower bounds using the **extends** and **super** keywords, respectively. This restricts subtyping to be *co-* or *contravariant*. So List<Square> is a subtype of List<? extends Polygon> and List<Shape> is a subtype of List<? super Polygon>, but not vice versa.

Java wildcards have the property of *wildcard capture*, where a wildcard is promoted to a fresh type variable. This occurs most visibly at method calls: List<?> is not a subtype of List<X>, but the wildcard can be *capture converted* to a fresh type variable which allows otherwise illegal method invocations. Consider the following legal Java code (using the method **walk** declared above):

```
List<?> walkAny(Tree<?> y) {                          (example 1)
    this.walk(y);
}
```

At the method invocation, the wildcard in the type of y is capture converted to a fresh type variable, Z, and the method invocation can then be thought of as this.<Z>walk(y). In Sect. 3.4 we show how this example is type checked in TameFJ.

Wildcard capture may give rise to types during type checking that can not be denoted using the Java syntax. This is a serious obstacle for a direct formalisation of Java wildcards using the Java syntax, because type soundness requires typability of every step of the computation, and this may require the use of types that cannot be denoted directly.

In the next example we show how the type system treats each wildcard as hiding a potentially different type. The method invocation at 1 is type incorrect because the method **compare** requires a Pair parameterised by a single type variable twice. Pair<?, ?> can not be capture converted to this type because the two wildcards may hide different types. The invocation of the **make** method at 2 has a type which is *expressible but not denotable*. The type checker knows that the wildcards hide the same type (even though this can not be denoted in the surface syntax) and so capture conversion, and thus type checking, succeeds.

```
<X>Pair<X, X> make(List<X> x) {}                    (example 2)
<X>Boolean compare(Pair<X, X> x) {}

void m()
{
    Pair<?, ?> p;
    List<?> b;

    this.compare(p);             //1, type incorrect
    this.compare(this.make(b));  //2, OK
}
```

Again, we show how this example is type checked in Sect. 3.4. The example can be easily understood (and type checked) by using existential types to denote the types that are expressible but not denotable using Java syntax.

Existential Types. Existential types are a form of parametric polymorphism whereby a type may be existentially quantified [6,7,10,20,21,22]. For example, a function may be defined with type $\exists T.T \rightarrow T$, that is, the function has type T to T for some type, T. Existential types are a basis for data hiding and abstraction in type systems; an early practical use was in modelling abstract data types [20]. In our formalisation we use existential types in a Java like setting, and so are concerned with types of the form $\exists X.\texttt{List<X>}$. Values of existential types are opaque packages; usually they are created using a *pack* (or *close*) expression and then have to be *unpacked* (or *opened*) using another expression before they can be used; in our approach both packing and unpacking occur implicitly.

2.2   Formalising Wildcards

The correspondence between wildcards and existential types goes back to the work on Variant Parametric Types [14]. It has been integral to all formal work with wildcards since [24]. This correspondence is discussed in more depth in Sect. 4.

Wildcards are a strict extension of Java generics, and far more interesting to describe formally. A number of features contribute to this, but foremost among them is wildcard capture. Wildcard capture is roughly equivalent to unpacking an existential type [17,24], but an explicit unpack expression appears to be very hard to use to safely model wildcard capture [5]. Wildcards may have lower bounds, which also introduces problems. Indeed, they had to be omitted from our previous work [5] in order to show type soundness. Lower bounds can cause problems by transitivity of subtyping; a naïve formalism would consider a type variable's lower bound to be a subtype of its upper bound, even if there is no such relationship in the class hierarchy. This issue is addressed in Sect. 3.3. Furthermore, when an existential type is created (which occurs in subtyping in Java and TameFJ) we must somehow keep track of the witness type—the type hidden by the wildcard—in order to recover it when the type is unpacked. In [5] this is done in the syntax of close expressions. However, in a system without explicit packing of existential types it has proven very difficult to track the witness types. Therefore, we resort to following the Java compiler (and [17]) and infer the hidden type parameters during execution and type checking. This reliance on a simple kind of type inference can cause problems for the proof of subject reduction, as described in [17], and it is one of the contributions of this paper to handle it safely.

Wild FJ [17] is the first, and previously only, formalism that includes all the interesting features of Java wildcards. Our formal model is, in many ways, a development of Wild FJ. The syntax of Wild FJ is a strict subset of Java with wildcards, requiring explicit type arguments to polymorphic method calls as in our approach. However, Java types are converted to existential types 'on the fly', and this conversion of types makes the typing, subtyping, well-formedness, and auxiliary rules more complicated in Wild FJ. As a rough metric there are 10 auxiliary functions with 23 cases, nine subtyping, and 10 well-formedness rules in Wild FJ, compared with seven auxiliary functions with 15 cases, eight subtyping (11, counting subclassing), and eight well-formedness rules in our system. Type soundness has never been proven for Wild FJ.

3   Type Soundness for Java Wildcards

We show type soundness for Java by developing a core calculus, TameFJ, which models all the significant elements of type checking found in Java with wildcards.

e	::=	x | e.f | e.<$\overline{\text{P}}$>m($\overline{\text{e}}$) | new C<$\overline{\text{T}}$>($\overline{\text{e}}$)	*expressions*
Q	::=	class C<$\overline{\text{X}} \lhd$ T> $\lhd$ N {$\overline{\text{T f}}$; $\overline{\text{M}}$}	*class declarations*
M	::=	<$\overline{\text{X}} \lhd$ T> T m($\overline{\text{T x}}$) {return e;}	*method declarations*
v	::=	new C<$\overline{\text{T}}$>($\overline{\text{v}}$)	*values*
N	::=	C<$\overline{\text{T}}$> | Object<>	*class types*
R	::=	N | X	*non-existential types*
T, U	::=	$\exists \Delta$.N | $\exists \emptyset$.X	*types*
P	::=	T | $\star$	*type parameters*
Δ	::=	$\overline{\text{X} \rightarrow [\text{B}_l\ \text{B}_u]}$	*type environments*
Γ	::=	$\overline{\text{x:T}}$	*variable environments*
B	::=	T | $\perp$	*bounds*
x			*variables*
C			*classes*
X, Y			*type variables*

Fig. 1. Syntax of TameFJ

TameFJ is not a strict subset of the Java language. However, a Java program written in a subset of Java (corresponding to the syntax of Wild FJ) can be easily translated to a TameFJ program, as we discuss in Sect. 4. Part of that translation is to perform Java's inference of type parameters for method calls (except where this involves wildcards). As is common [17], we regard this as a separate pre-processing step and do not model this in TameFJ.

TameFJ is an extension of FGJ [13]. The major extension to FGJ is the addition of existential types, used to model wildcard types. Typing, subtyping and reduction rules must be extended to accommodate these new types, and to handle wildcard capture.

We use existential types in the surface syntax and, in contrast to Wild FJ, do not create them during type checking; this simplifies the formal system and our proofs significantly. In particular, capture conversion is dealt with more easily in our system because fresh type variables do not have to be supplied. We also 'pack' existential types more declaratively, by using subtyping, rather than explicitly constructing existential types. This means that we avoid obtaining the awkward[1] type $\exists X.X$, found both in [17] and our previous work[2] [5].

TameFJ has none of the limitations of our previous approach [5]; we allow lower bounds, have more flexible type environments, allow quantification of more than one type variable in an existential type, and have more flexible subtyping. Thus, together with the absence of open and close expressions, TameFJ is much closer to the Java programming language.

3.1 Notation and Syntax

TameFJ is a calculus in the FJ [13] style. We use vector notation for sequences; for example, $\bar{x}$ stands for a sequence of 'x's. We use $\emptyset$ to denote the empty sequence. We use a comma to concatenate two sequences. We implicitly assume that concatenation of two sequences of mappings only succeeds if their domains are disjoint. We use $\lhd$ as a shorthand for **extends** and $\rhd$ for **super**. The function $fv()$ returns the free variables of a type or expression, and $dom()$ returns the domain of a mapping. We assume that all type variables, variables, and fields are named uniquely.

The syntax for TameFJ is given in Fig. 1. The syntax for expressions and class and method declarations is very similar to Java, except that we allow $\star$ as a type parameter in method invocations. In TameFJ (and as opposed to Java) all actual type parameters to a method invocation must be given. However, where a

---

[1] There is no corresponding type in Java, so it is unclear how such a type should behave.

[2] Such a type is required in earlier work because the construction $\exists \Delta.T$ appears in the conclusion of type rules, where T is a previously derived type. Since T may be a type variable, one may construct $\exists X.X$; this can not happen in our calculus. Under a standard interpretation of existential types, types of the form $\exists X \lhd T.X$ have no observably different behaviour from T because Java subtyping already involves subclass polymorphism. Rigorous justification of this fact is outside the scope of this paper, but is part of planned future work.

type parameter is existentially quantified (corresponding to a wildcard in Java), we may use ⋆ to mark that the parameter should be inferred. Such types can not be named explicitly because they can not be named outside of the scope of their type. The marker ⋆ is not a replacement for ? in Java; ⋆ can not be used as a parameter in TameFJ types, and ? can not be used as a type parameter to method calls in Java. Note that we treat this as a regular variable.

The syntax of types is that of FGJ [13] extended with existential types. Non-existential types consist of class types (e.g., C<D<>>) and type variables, X. Types (T) are existential types, that is a non-existential type (R) quantified by an environment (Δ, i.e., a sequence of formal type variables and their bounds), for example, $\exists$X → [$\exists\emptyset$.D<> $\exists\emptyset$.Object<>].C<X>. Type variables may only be quantified by the empty environment, e.g., $\exists\emptyset$.X. In the text and examples, we use the shorthands C for C<>, $\exists$X.C<X> for $\exists$X→[⊥ Object<>].C<X>, and R for $\exists\emptyset$.R.

Existential types in TameFJ correspond to types parameterised by wildcards in Java. Using T as an upper or lower bound on a formal type variable corresponds to using **extends** T or **super** T, respectively, to bound a wildcard. This correspondence is discussed further in Sect. 4. The bottom type, ⊥, is used only as a lower bound and is used to model the situation in Java where a lower bound is omitted.

Substitution in TameFJ is defined in the usual way with a slight modification. For the sake of consistency formal type variables are quantified by the empty set when used as a type in a program ($\exists\emptyset$.X). Therefore, we define substitution on such types to replace the whole type, which is [T/X]$\exists\emptyset$.X = T.

A variable environment, Γ, maps variables to types. A type environment, Δ, maps type variables to their bounds. Where the distinction is clear from the context, we use "environment" to refer to either sort of environment.

3.2   Subtyping

The subclassing relation between non-existential types (⊏:), reflects the class hierarchy. Subclassing of type variables is restricted to reflexivity because they have no place in the subclass hierarchy. Subtyping (<:) extends subclassing by adding subtyping between existential types and between type variables and their bounds. Extended subclassing (⊏:) is an intermediate relation that expresses the class hierarchy (with the addition of a bottom type) and the behaviour of wildcards and type variables *as type parameters*; it is used mainly to simplify the proofs of soundness. All three relations are defined in Fig. 2.

The rule XS-ENV, adapted from Wild FJ [17], gives all the interesting variance properties for wildcard types. It gives a subtype relationship between two existentially quantified class types, where the type parameters of the subtype are 'more precise' than those of the supertype. The following relationships are given by this rule, given the class hierarchy described in Sect. 2 and using the shorthands described in Sect. 3.1:

$\emptyset$ ⊢ Shape ⊏: Shape
$\emptyset$ ⊢ List<Shape> ⊏: $\exists$X.List<X>

Subclasses: $\boxed{\vdash R \sqsubseteq: R}$

$$\frac{\texttt{class } \texttt{C<}\overline{\texttt{X}} \triangleleft \overline{T_u}\texttt{>} \triangleleft \texttt{N } \{\ldots\}}{\vdash \texttt{C<}\overline{\texttt{T}}\texttt{>} \sqsubseteq: [\overline{\texttt{T}/\texttt{X}}]\texttt{N}}$$
(SC-Sub-Class)

$$\frac{}{\vdash R \sqsubseteq: R}$$
(SC-Reflex)

$$\frac{\vdash R \sqsubseteq: R'' \qquad \vdash R'' \sqsubseteq: R'}{\vdash R \sqsubseteq: R'}$$
(SC-Trans)

Extended subclasses: $\boxed{\Delta \vdash B \sqsubseteq: B}$

$$\frac{\texttt{class } \texttt{C<}\overline{\texttt{X}} \triangleleft \overline{T_u}\texttt{>} \triangleleft \texttt{N } \{\ldots\}}{\Delta \vdash \exists \Delta'.\texttt{C<}\overline{\texttt{T}}\texttt{>} \sqsubseteq: \exists \Delta'.[\overline{\texttt{T}/\texttt{X}}]\texttt{N}}$$
(XS-Sub-Class)

$$\frac{}{\Delta \vdash \perp \sqsubseteq: B}$$
(XS-Bottom)

$$\frac{}{\Delta \vdash B \sqsubseteq: B}$$
(XS-Reflex)

$$\frac{\Delta \vdash B \sqsubseteq: B'' \qquad \Delta \vdash B'' \sqsubseteq: B'}{\Delta \vdash B \sqsubseteq: B'}$$
(XS-Trans)

$$\frac{dom(\Delta') \cap fv(\exists \overline{\texttt{X} \to [B_l\ B_u]}.\texttt{N}) = \emptyset \qquad fv(\overline{\texttt{T}}) \subseteq dom(\Delta, \Delta') \\ \Delta, \Delta' \vdash \overline{[\texttt{T}/\texttt{X}]B_l <: \texttt{T}} \qquad \Delta, \Delta' \vdash \overline{\texttt{T} <: [\texttt{T}/\texttt{X}]B_u}}{\Delta \vdash \exists \Delta'.[\texttt{T}/\texttt{X}]\texttt{N} \sqsubseteq: \exists \overline{\texttt{X} \to [B_l\ B_u]}.\texttt{N}}$$
(XS-Env)

Subtypes: $\boxed{\Delta \vdash B <: B}$

$$\frac{\Delta \vdash B \sqsubseteq: B'}{\Delta \vdash B <: B'}$$
(S-SC)

$$\frac{\Delta \vdash B <: B'' \qquad \Delta \vdash B'' <: B'}{\Delta \vdash B <: B'}$$
(S-Trans)

$$\frac{\Delta(\texttt{X}) = [B_l\ B_u]}{\Delta \vdash \exists \emptyset.\texttt{X} <: B_u} \qquad \frac{}{\Delta \vdash B_l <: \exists \emptyset.\texttt{X}}$$
(S-Bound)

Fig. 2. TameFJ subclasses, extended subclasses, and subtypes

$$\emptyset \vdash \texttt{List<Shape>} \sqsubseteq: \exists \texttt{X} \to [\texttt{Circle Object}].\texttt{List<X>}$$
$$\emptyset \vdash \exists \texttt{X} \to [\texttt{Circle Shape}].\texttt{List<X>} \sqsubseteq: \exists \texttt{X} \to [\texttt{Circle Object}].\texttt{List<X>}$$
$$\emptyset \vdash \exists \texttt{X}.\texttt{Pair<X, X>} \sqsubseteq: \exists \texttt{Y},\texttt{Z}.\texttt{Pair<Y, Z>}$$

That type parameters are 'more precise' is expressed in terms of a substitution, $[\overline{\texttt{T}/\texttt{X}}]$, where $\overline{\texttt{X}}$ are some of the parameters of the supertype and $\overline{\texttt{T}}$ are the corresponding parameters in the subtype. The subtype checks in the premises of XS-Env ensure that $\overline{\texttt{T}}$ are 'more precise' than $\overline{\texttt{X}}$; that is, that $\overline{\texttt{T}}$ are within the bounds of $\overline{\texttt{X}}$. The first premise ensures that free variables in the supertype can not be captured in the subtype, thus forbidding erroneous subtypes such as $\Delta \vdash \exists \texttt{X}.\texttt{C<X>} \sqsubseteq: \texttt{C<X>}$. The second premise ensures that variables are not introduced to the subtype which are not bound either in Δ or Δ'. This is a limited form of well-formedness constraint on the subtype, and is only used in the details of the proof of soundness.

Most of the type rules and lemmas are expressed in terms of subtyping, however, the standard object-oriented features of the language (such as field and method lookup) are defined around subclassing. We therefore need lemmas that link subtyping with subclassing. This is done in two stages: lemma 17 links subtyping to extended subclassing, and lemma 35 links extended subclassing to subclassing.

Lemma 17 (*uBound* **refines subtyping**). *If* $\Delta \vdash \mathtt{T} <: \mathtt{T}'$ *and* $\vdash \Delta$ OK *then* $\Delta \vdash uBound_\Delta(\mathtt{T}) \sqsubseteq: uBound_\Delta(\mathtt{T}')$.

This lemma states that if two types are subtypes then their upper bounds are extended subclasses. The *uBound* function (defined in Fig. 7) returns a non-variable type by recursively finding the upper bound of a type until a non-variable type is reached. The interesting cases in the proof are from the S-BOUND rule; where $\mathtt{T} = \exists\emptyset.\mathtt{X}$ and $\mathtt{T}' = \mathtt{B}_u$, then by the definition of *uBound*, we have that $uBound(\exists\emptyset.\mathtt{X}) = uBound(\mathtt{B}_u)$, and are done by reflexivity. The other S-BOUND sub-case is where $\mathtt{T} = \mathtt{B}_l$ and $\mathtt{T}' = \exists\emptyset.\mathtt{X}$, here we use $\Delta \vdash uBound(\mathtt{B}_l) \sqsubseteq: uBound(\mathtt{B}_u)$ from F-ENV and $uBound(\exists\emptyset.\mathtt{X}) = uBound(\mathtt{B}_u)$, again from the definition of *uBound*. A corollary to this lemma is that any two non-variable types, which are subtypes, are also subclasses.

Lemma 35 (Extended subclassing gives subclassing). *If* $\Delta \vdash \exists\Delta'.\mathtt{R}' \sqsubseteq: \exists\overline{\mathtt{X}{\to}[\mathtt{B}_l\ \mathtt{B}_u]}.\mathtt{R}$ *and* $\Delta \vdash$ OK *then there exists* $\overline{\mathtt{T}}$ *where* $\vdash \mathtt{R}' \sqsubseteq: [\overline{\mathtt{T}/\mathtt{X}}]\mathtt{R}$ *and* $\Delta, \Delta' \vdash \overline{\mathtt{T}} <: [\overline{\mathtt{T}/\mathtt{X}}]\mathtt{B}_u$ *and* $\Delta, \Delta' \vdash [\overline{\mathtt{T}/\mathtt{X}}]\mathtt{B}_l <: \mathtt{T}$ *and* $fv(\overline{\mathtt{T}}) \subseteq dom(\Delta, \Delta')$.

This lemma states that for any types in an extended subclass relationship, a substitution can be found where there is a subclass relationship between the

---

Well-formed types: $\boxed{\Delta \vdash \mathtt{B}\ \text{OK},\ \Delta \vdash \mathtt{P}\ \text{OK},\ \Delta \vdash \mathtt{R}\ \text{OK}}$

$$\frac{\mathtt{X} \in \Delta}{\Delta \vdash \mathtt{X}\ \text{OK}}$$
(F-VAR)

$$\frac{}{\Delta \vdash \bot\ \text{OK}}$$
(F-BOTTOM)

$$\frac{}{\Delta \vdash \mathtt{Object}{<}{>}\ \text{OK}}$$
(F-OBJECT)

$$\frac{}{\Delta \vdash \star\ \text{OK}}$$
(F-STAR)

$$\frac{\mathtt{class}\ \mathtt{C}{<}\overline{\mathtt{X} \lhd \mathtt{T}_u}{>} \lhd \mathtt{N}\ \{...\} \quad \Delta \vdash \overline{\mathtt{T}}\ \text{OK} \quad \Delta \vdash \overline{\mathtt{T} <: [\overline{\mathtt{T}/\mathtt{X}}]\mathtt{T}_u}}{\Delta \vdash \mathtt{C}{<}\overline{\mathtt{T}}{>}\ \text{OK}}$$
(F-CLASS)

$$\frac{\Delta \vdash \Delta'\ \text{OK} \quad \Delta, \Delta' \vdash \mathtt{R}\ \text{OK}}{\Delta \vdash \exists\Delta'.\mathtt{R}\ \text{OK}}$$
(F-EXIST)

Well-formed type environments: $\boxed{\Delta \vdash \Delta\ \text{OK}}$

$$\frac{}{\Delta \vdash \emptyset\ \text{OK}}$$
(F-ENV-EMPTY)

$$\frac{\Delta, \mathtt{X}{\to}[\mathtt{B}_l\ \mathtt{B}_u], \Delta' \vdash \mathtt{B}_l\ \text{OK} \quad \Delta, \mathtt{X}{\to}[\mathtt{B}_l\ \mathtt{B}_u], \Delta' \vdash \mathtt{B}_u\ \text{OK} \quad \Delta \vdash uBound_\Delta(\mathtt{B}_l) \sqsubseteq: uBound_\Delta(\mathtt{B}_u) \quad \Delta \vdash \mathtt{B}_l <: \mathtt{B}_u \quad \Delta, \mathtt{X}{\to}[\mathtt{B}_l\ \mathtt{B}_u] \vdash \Delta'\ \text{OK}}{\Delta \vdash \mathtt{X}{\to}[\mathtt{B}_l\ \mathtt{B}_u], \Delta'\ \text{OK}}$$
(F-ENV)

Fig. 3. TameFJ well-formed types and type environments

subtype and the substituted supertype. The difference between subclassing and extended subclassing is, essentially, the XS-ENV rule. This rule finds an extended subclass of an existential type by substituting away its existential type variables. This substitution corresponds to the one in the conclusion of the lemma.

3.3   Well-Formedness

Rules for judging well-formed types and type environments are given in Fig. 3. The rules for well-formed type environments are the most interesting. There are two motivating issues: we must not allow type variables which have upper and lower bounds that are unrelated in the class hierarchy; and we must restrict forward references.

The first issue can cause a problem where an environment could judge a subtype relation that does not reflect the class hierarchy. For example, an environment containing $Z \rightarrow$ [Fish Plant] could judge (by using rule S-Bound and transitivity) that Fish is a subtype of Plant, which is presumably incorrect. We therefore check that the bounds of a type variable are related by subtyping under an environment without that type variable. We also require the stronger subclass relationship to hold for the upper bounds of the type variable's immediate bounds. This ensures that subtype relationships judged by a well-formed environment respect the class hierarchy. We need this property to prove lemma 17, described in Sect. 3.2.

Method typing: $\boxed{\Delta \vdash \texttt{M OK in C}}$

$$\Delta' = \overline{\texttt{Y} \rightarrow [\bot \ \ \texttt{T}_u]} \qquad \Delta \vdash \Delta' \ \text{OK} \qquad \Delta, \Delta' \vdash \texttt{T}, \overline{\texttt{T}} \ \text{OK}$$
$$\texttt{class C<}\overline{\texttt{X}}...\texttt{>} \ \lhd \ \texttt{N} \ \{\ldots\}$$
$$\Delta, \Delta'; \overline{\texttt{x}:\texttt{T}}, \ \texttt{this}: \exists \emptyset.\texttt{C<}\overline{\texttt{X}}\texttt{>} \vdash \texttt{e} : \texttt{T} \mid \emptyset$$
$$override(\texttt{m}, \texttt{N}, \texttt{<}\overline{\texttt{Y} \lhd \ \texttt{T}_u}\texttt{>}\overline{\texttt{T}} \rightarrow \texttt{T})$$
$$\overline{\Delta \vdash \texttt{<}\overline{\texttt{Y} \lhd \ \texttt{T}_u}\texttt{>}\texttt{T m}(\overline{\texttt{T x}}) \ \{\texttt{return e}\} \ \text{OK in C}}$$

(T-METHOD)

$$\frac{mType(\texttt{m}, \texttt{N}) = \texttt{<}\overline{\texttt{X} \lhd \ \texttt{U}}\texttt{>}\overline{\texttt{T}} \rightarrow \texttt{T}}{override(\texttt{m}, \texttt{N}, \texttt{<}\overline{\texttt{X} \lhd \ \texttt{U}}\texttt{>}\overline{\texttt{T}} \rightarrow \texttt{T})}$$

(T-OVERRIDE)

$$\frac{mType(\texttt{m}, \texttt{N}) \quad undefined}{override(\texttt{m}, \texttt{N}, \texttt{<}\overline{\texttt{X} \lhd \ \texttt{U}}\texttt{>}\overline{\texttt{T}} \rightarrow \texttt{T})}$$

(T-OVERRIDEUNDEF)

Class typing: $\boxed{\vdash \texttt{Q OK}}$

$$\frac{\Delta = \overline{\texttt{X} \rightarrow [\bot \ \ \texttt{T}_u]} \qquad \emptyset \vdash \Delta \ \text{OK} \qquad \Delta \vdash \texttt{N}, \overline{\texttt{T}} \ \text{OK} \qquad \Delta \vdash \overline{\texttt{M}} \ \text{OK in C}}{\vdash \texttt{class C<}\overline{\texttt{X} \lhd \ \texttt{T}_u}\texttt{>} \ \lhd \ \texttt{N} \ \{\overline{\texttt{T f}}; \ \overline{\texttt{M}}\} \ \text{OK}}$$

(T-CLASS)

Fig. 4. TameFJ class and method typing rules

Forward references are only allowed to occur as *parameters* of the bounding type. In the well-formedness rule, this is addressed by allowing forward references when checking that the bounds are well-formed types, but not when checking the subtype and subclass relationships of the bounds. This reflects Java where (in a class or method declaration) <X◁ Y, Y◁ Object> is illegal, due to the forward reference in the bound of X; however, <X◁ List<Y>, Y◁ Object> is legal.

3.4 Typing

Method and class type checking judgements are given in Fig. 4 and are mostly straightforward. The only interesting detail is the correct construction of type environments for checking well-formedness of types and type environments. The *override* relation allows method overriding, but does not allow overloading.

Expression typing: $\boxed{\Delta; \Gamma \vdash e : T \mid \Delta}$

$$\frac{}{\Delta; \Gamma \vdash x : \Gamma(x) \mid \emptyset}$$
(T-VAR)

$$\frac{\Delta \vdash C<\overline{T}> \text{ OK} \quad fields(C) = \overline{f} \quad fType(f, C<\overline{T}>) = U \quad \Delta; \Gamma \vdash e : U \mid \emptyset}{\Delta; \Gamma \vdash new \ C<\overline{T}>(\overline{e}) : \exists \emptyset . C<\overline{T}> \mid \emptyset}$$
(T-NEW)

$$\frac{\Delta; \Gamma \vdash e : \exists \Delta'.N \mid \emptyset \quad fType(f, N) = T}{\Delta; \Gamma \vdash e.f : T \mid \Delta'}$$
(T-FIELD)

$$\frac{\Delta; \Gamma \vdash e : U \mid \Delta' \quad \Delta, \Delta' \vdash U <: T \quad \Delta \vdash \Delta' \text{ OK} \quad \Delta \vdash T \text{ OK}}{\Delta; \Gamma \vdash e : T \mid \emptyset}$$
(T-SUBS)

$$\frac{\Delta; \Gamma \vdash e : \exists \Delta'.N \mid \emptyset \quad mType(m, N) = <\overline{Y◁ B}>\overline{U} \to U \quad \Delta \vdash \overline{P} \text{ OK} \quad \Delta; \Gamma \vdash \overline{e} : \exists \Delta.\overline{R} \mid \emptyset \quad match(sift(\overline{R}, \overline{U}, \overline{Y}), \overline{P}, \overline{Y}, \overline{T}) \quad \Delta, \Delta', \overline{\Delta} \vdash \overline{T} <: [\overline{T/Y}]\overline{B} \quad \Delta, \Delta', \overline{\Delta} \vdash \exists \emptyset.\overline{R} <: [\overline{T/Y}]\overline{U}}{\Delta; \Gamma \vdash e.<\overline{P}>m(\overline{e}) : [\overline{T/Y}]U \mid \Delta', \overline{\Delta}}$$
(T-INVK)

Fig. 5. TameFJ expression typing rules

The typing rules are given in Fig. 5. Auxiliary functions used in typing are given in Figs. 6 and 7.

The type checking judgement has the form $\Delta; \Gamma \vdash e : T \mid \Delta'$, and should be read as

expression e has type T under the environments Δ and Γ, guarded by environment Δ'.

Δ' contains variables that have been unpacked from an existential type during type checking. These variables are used with Δ to judge some premises of a rule. Any free variables in T are bound in either Δ or Δ'.

T-SUBS is an extended subsumption rule; when Δ' is empty it allows an expression to be typed with a supertype of the expression's type in the usual way. The T-SUBS rule can also be used to 'remove' the guarding environment from the judgement. Type checking of a TameFJ expression is complete when a type is found using an empty guarding environment (non-empty guarding environments may only occur at intermediate stages in the derivation tree). This ensures that no bound type variables escape the scope in which they are unpacked. The scope covers the conclusions, some premises, and the derivations of these premises in the type rule in which the variables are unbound.

Auxiliary Functions: $\boxed{uBound_\Delta(\mathtt{B}) \text{ and } match(\overline{\mathtt{R}},\overline{\mathtt{U}},\overline{\mathtt{P}},\overline{\mathtt{Y}},\overline{\mathtt{T}}) \text{ and } sift(\overline{\mathtt{R}},\overline{\mathtt{U}},\overline{\mathtt{Y}})}$

$$uBound_\Delta(\mathtt{B}) = \begin{cases} uBound_\Delta(\mathtt{B}_u), & if\ \mathtt{B} = \exists\emptyset.\mathtt{X},\ where\ \Delta(\mathtt{X}) = [\mathtt{B}_l\ \mathtt{B}_u] \\ \mathtt{B}, & otherwise \end{cases}$$

$$\frac{\forall j\ where\ \mathtt{P}_j = \star : \mathtt{Y}_j \in fv(\overline{\mathtt{R}'}) \quad \forall i\ where\ \mathtt{P}_i \neq \star : \mathtt{T}_i = \mathtt{P}_i}{\vdash \mathtt{R} \sqsubset: [\overline{\mathtt{T}/\mathtt{Y}},\overline{\mathtt{T}'/\mathtt{X}}]\mathtt{R}' \qquad dom(\overline{\Delta}) = \overline{\mathtt{X}} \quad fv(\overline{\mathtt{T}},\overline{\mathtt{T}'}) \cap \overline{\mathtt{Y}},\overline{\mathtt{X}} = \emptyset}{match(\overline{\mathtt{R}},\overline{\exists\Delta.\mathtt{R}'},\overline{\mathtt{P}},\overline{\mathtt{Y}},\overline{\mathtt{T}})}$$

$$\frac{\mathtt{X} \in \overline{\mathtt{Y}}}{sift((\mathtt{R},\overline{\mathtt{R}}),\ (\exists\emptyset.\mathtt{X},\overline{\mathtt{U}}),\ \overline{\mathtt{Y}}) = sift(\overline{\mathtt{R}},\ \overline{\mathtt{U}},\ \overline{\mathtt{Y}})}$$

$$\frac{\mathtt{X} \notin \overline{\mathtt{Y}} \quad sift(\overline{\mathtt{R}},\ \overline{\mathtt{U}},\ \overline{\mathtt{Y}}) = (\overline{\mathtt{R}'},\ \overline{\mathtt{U}'})}{sift((\mathtt{R},\overline{\mathtt{R}}),\ (\exists\emptyset.\mathtt{X},\overline{\mathtt{U}}),\ \overline{\mathtt{Y}}) = ((\mathtt{R},\overline{\mathtt{R}'}),\ (\exists\emptyset.\mathtt{X},\overline{\mathtt{U}'}))}$$

$$\frac{}{sift(\emptyset,\ \emptyset,\ \overline{\mathtt{Y}}) = (\emptyset,\ \emptyset)} \qquad \frac{sift(\overline{\mathtt{R}},\ \overline{\mathtt{U}},\ \overline{\mathtt{Y}}) = (\overline{\mathtt{R}'},\ \overline{\mathtt{U}'})}{sift((\mathtt{R},\overline{\mathtt{R}}),\ (\exists\Delta.\mathtt{N},\overline{\mathtt{U}}),\ \overline{\mathtt{Y}}) = (\mathtt{R},\overline{\mathtt{R}'},\ \overline{\exists\Delta.\mathtt{N},\overline{\mathtt{U}'}})}$$

Fig. 6. Auxiliary functions for TameFJ

Typing of variables and 'new' expressions is done in the usual way. The lookup function $fields$ returns a sequence of the field names in a class, and $fType$ takes a field and a class type and returns the field's type.

The type checking of field access and method invocation expressions follow similar patterns: sub-expressions are type checked and their types are unpacked, then some work is done using these unpacked types, and a result type is found. The rule T-SUBS may then be used to find a final result type that does not require a guarding environment.

Lookup Functions

$$fields(\texttt{Object}) = \emptyset$$

$$\frac{\texttt{class } \texttt{C<}\overline{\texttt{X}\triangleleft\texttt{T}_u}\texttt{>} \triangleleft \texttt{D<}\ldots\texttt{>} \; \{\overline{\texttt{U f};} \; \overline{\texttt{M}}\} \quad fields(\texttt{D}) = \overline{\texttt{g}}}{fields(\texttt{C}) = \overline{\texttt{g}}, \overline{\texttt{f}}}$$

$$\frac{\texttt{class } \texttt{C<}\overline{\texttt{X}\triangleleft\texttt{T}_u}\texttt{>} \triangleleft \texttt{N} \; \{\overline{\texttt{U f};} \; \overline{\texttt{M}}\} \quad \texttt{f} \notin \overline{\texttt{f}}}{fType(\texttt{f}, \texttt{C<}\overline{\texttt{T}}\texttt{>}) = fType(\texttt{f}, [\overline{\texttt{T}/\texttt{X}}]\texttt{N})}$$

$$\frac{\texttt{class } \texttt{C<}\overline{\texttt{X}\triangleleft\texttt{T}_u}\texttt{>} \triangleleft \texttt{N} \; \{\overline{\texttt{U f};} \; \overline{\texttt{M}}\}}{fType(\texttt{f}_i, \texttt{C<}\overline{\texttt{T}}\texttt{>}) = [\overline{\texttt{T}/\texttt{X}}]\texttt{U}_i}$$

$$\frac{\texttt{class } \texttt{C<}\overline{\texttt{X}\triangleleft\texttt{T}_u}\texttt{>} \triangleleft \texttt{N} \; \{\overline{\texttt{U f};} \; \overline{\texttt{M}}\} \quad \texttt{m} \notin \overline{\texttt{M}}}{mBody(\texttt{m}, \texttt{C<}\overline{\texttt{T}}\texttt{>}) = mBody(\texttt{m}, [\overline{\texttt{T}/\texttt{X}}]\texttt{N})}$$

$$\frac{\texttt{class } \texttt{C<}\overline{\texttt{X}\triangleleft\texttt{T}_u}\texttt{>} \triangleleft \texttt{N} \; \{\overline{\texttt{U}' \texttt{f}};} \; \overline{\texttt{M}}\} \quad \texttt{<}\overline{\texttt{Y}\triangleleft\texttt{T}'_u}\texttt{>} \texttt{U m}(\overline{\texttt{U x}}) \; \{\texttt{return } \texttt{e}_0;\} \in \overline{\texttt{M}}}{mBody(\texttt{m}, \texttt{C<}\overline{\texttt{T}}\texttt{>}) = (\overline{\texttt{x}}; [\overline{\texttt{T}/\texttt{X}}]\texttt{e}_0)}$$

$$\frac{\texttt{class } \texttt{C<}\overline{\texttt{X}\triangleleft\texttt{T}_u}\texttt{>} \triangleleft \texttt{N} \; \{\overline{\texttt{U f};} \; \overline{\texttt{M}}\} \quad \texttt{m} \notin \overline{\texttt{M}}}{mType(\texttt{m}, \texttt{C<}\overline{\texttt{T}}\texttt{>}) = mType(\texttt{m}, [\overline{\texttt{T}/\texttt{X}}]\texttt{N})}$$

$$\frac{\texttt{class } \texttt{C<}\overline{\texttt{X}\triangleleft\texttt{T}_u}\texttt{>} \triangleleft \texttt{N} \; \{\overline{\texttt{U}' \texttt{f}};} \; \overline{\texttt{M}}\} \quad \texttt{<}\overline{\texttt{Y}\triangleleft\texttt{T}'_u}\texttt{>} \texttt{U m}(\overline{\texttt{U x}}) \; \{\texttt{return } \texttt{e}_0;\} \in \overline{\texttt{M}}}{mType(\texttt{m}, \texttt{C<}\overline{\texttt{T}}\texttt{>}) = [\overline{\texttt{T}/\texttt{X}}](\texttt{<}\overline{\texttt{Y}\triangleleft\texttt{T}'_u}\texttt{>}\overline{\texttt{U}} \rightarrow \texttt{U})}$$

Fig. 7. Method and field lookup functions for TameFJ

In the following paragraphs we describe unpacking and packing, followed by descriptions of type checking using T-FIELD and T-INVK, accompanied with examples.

Unpacking an existential type ($\exists\Delta.\texttt{R}$) entails separating the environment (Δ) from the quantified type (R). Δ can be used to judge premises of a rule and must be added to the guarding environment in the rule's conclusion. R can be used without quantification in the rule; bound type variables in R will now be free, we must take care that these do not escape the scope of the type rule.

If the result of type checking an expression contains escaping type variables (indicated by a non-empty guarding environment), then we must find a super-type (using T-SUBS) in which there are no free variables, and use this as the expression's type. In the case that an escaping type variable occurs as a type parameter (e.g., X in C<X>), then the type may be packed to an existential type (e.g., $\exists\texttt{X}.\texttt{C<X>}$) using the subtyping rule XS-ENV. In the case that the type variable is the whole type, i.e., $\exists\emptyset.\texttt{X}$, then the upper bound of X can be used as the result type by using S-BOUND.

Field Access. In T-FIELD, the *fType* function applied to the unpacked type (N) of the receiver gives the type of the field (T). Because T may contain type variables bound in the environment Δ', the judgement must be guarded by Δ'.

Example — Field Access. The following example of the derivation of a type for a field access expression demonstrates the sequence of unpacking, finding the field type, and finding a supertype that does not contain free variables. In the example, the type labelled 1 is unpacked to 2. The type labelled 3 would escape its scope, and so its supertype (4) must be used as the result of type checking. We assume that the `TreeNode<Y>` class declaration has a field `datum` with type Y and that $\Gamma = $ x:$\exists$X$\rightarrow$[$\bot$ Shape].TreeNode<X>.

$$\frac{\emptyset; \Gamma \vdash \text{x} : \exists\text{X}{\rightarrow}[\bot \text{ Shape}].\text{TreeNode<X>}^1 \mid \emptyset \qquad fType(\text{datum}, \text{TreeNode<X>}^2) = \text{X}^3}{\emptyset; \Gamma \vdash \text{x.datum} : \text{X}^3 \mid \text{X}{\rightarrow}[\bot \text{ Shape}]^2} \text{ (T-Field)}$$

$$\emptyset, \text{X}{\rightarrow}[\bot \text{ Shape}] \vdash \text{X}^3 <: \text{Shape}^4 \qquad \emptyset \vdash \text{X}{\rightarrow}[\bot \text{ Shape}] \text{ OK} \qquad \emptyset \vdash \text{Shape}^4 \text{ OK}$$

$$\frac{}{\emptyset; \Gamma \vdash \text{x.datum} : \text{Shape}^4 \mid \emptyset} \text{ (T-Subs)}$$

□

Method Invocation. In T-INVK, function $mType$ applied to the unpacked type (N) of the receiver gives the method's signature, <$\overline{\text{Y}\lhd \text{ B}}$>$\overline{\text{U}}{\rightarrow}$U. We use the unpacked types ($\overline{\text{R}}$) of the actual parameters and the *match* function to infer any 'missing' (actual) type parameters (denoted by $\star$ in our syntax, following Wild FJ). The (possibly inferred) actual type parameters are substituted for formal ([$\overline{\text{T}/\text{Y}}$]) in the method's type signature. After substitution, the actual type parameters ($\overline{\text{T}}$) must be within the formal bounds ($\overline{\text{B}}$), and the types of the actual parameters must be subtypes of the types of the formal parameters ($\overline{\text{U}}$). These checks are performed under the type environment $\Delta, \Delta', \overline{\Delta}$. Similarly to T-FIELD, we must guard the conclusion of the type rule with the environments extracted by unpacking ($\Delta', \overline{\Delta}$).

The substitution [$\overline{\text{T}/\text{Y}}$] is determined using the types of actual ($\overline{\text{R}}$) and formal parameters ($\overline{\text{U}}$). These types are filtered using the *sift* function before being passed to *match*. This ensures that where the type of a formal parameter is one of the formal type parameters (U$_i$ $\in \overline{\text{Y}}$), the formals and actuals at this position are not used for inference. Hence, we only infer the value of a type variable based on its usage as a type parameter in the formal type of a value argument.

Type parameter inference is done using the *match* relation (Fig. 6). All formal type parameters ($\overline{\text{Y}}$) are substituted by types $\overline{\text{T}}$. These types are either given explicitly, or are inferred if left unspecified (i.e., marked with $\star$). The first premise of *match* ensures that any unspecified type parameter can be inferred, i.e., it appears as a type parameter in a type of at least one of the method's formal value parameters. The second premise ensures that each specified type parameter is used in the returned sequence. The remaining premises find a substitution that allows subclassing between the formal and actual parameter types. Part of this substitution will be the substitution of actual type parameters for formals, and these actual type parameters are $\overline{\text{T}}$. The remainder ($\overline{\text{T}'}$) account for existentially quantified type variables in the formal parameter types. These are forgotten, since in T-INVK we use full subtyping which allows us to use the XS-ENV rule to fulfil the same role.

Examples — Method Invocation. *Example 1* from Sect. 2.1 demonstrates method invocation with a simple case of wildcard capture. The existential type

$\exists Z.\texttt{Tree<Z>}$ is unpacked to $\texttt{Tree<Z>}$, and $\texttt{Z}$ is inferred and substituted for $\texttt{X}$. The return type ($\texttt{List<Z>}$) is then packed to the existential type $\exists Z.\texttt{List<Z>}$. We show how the example can be type checked using the T-INVK and T-SUBS rules (the bounds of type variables are omitted for clarity); the type labelled 1 is unpacked to 2 and the type labelled 3 is packed to 4. We omit from the derivation tree the call to *sift* for clarity, note that $sift(\texttt{Tree<Z>}^2, \texttt{Tree<X>}, \texttt{X}) = (\texttt{Tree<Z>}^2, \texttt{Tree<X>})$

$$
\frac{
\begin{array}{c}
\emptyset; \texttt{this:C} \vdash \texttt{this} : \texttt{C} \mid \emptyset \\
mType(\texttt{walk}, \texttt{C}) = \texttt{<X> Tree<X>} \rightarrow \texttt{List<X>} \\
\emptyset; \texttt{this:C} \vdash \texttt{y} : \exists Z.\texttt{Tree<Z>}^1 \mid \emptyset \\
match(\texttt{Tree<Z>}^2, \texttt{Tree<X>}, \star, \texttt{X}, \texttt{Z}^2) \\
\hline
\dfrac{\texttt{Z}^2 \vdash \texttt{Tree<Z>}^2 <: \texttt{Tree<Z>}}{\emptyset; \texttt{this:C} \vdash \texttt{this.<}\star\texttt{>walk(y)} : \texttt{List<Z>}^3 \mid \texttt{Z}^2} \\
\text{(T-INVK)}
\end{array}
\qquad
\begin{array}{c}
\texttt{Z}^2 \vdash \texttt{List<Z>}^3 <: \exists Z.\texttt{List<Z>}^4 \\
\emptyset \vdash \texttt{Z}^2 \text{ OK} \\
\emptyset \vdash \exists Z.\texttt{List<Z>}^4 \text{ OK}
\end{array}
}{
\emptyset; \texttt{this:C} \vdash \texttt{this.<}\star\texttt{>walk(y)} : \exists Z.\texttt{List<Z>}^4 \mid \emptyset
}
$$

$$\text{(T-SUBS)} \qquad \qquad \square$$

Example 2 from Sect. 2.1 expresses types which can not be denoted using Java syntax. Using the syntax of existential types, it becomes clear why type checking fails at 1. Namely, for the expression at 1 to be type correct, a $\texttt{T}$ would need to be found so that $match(\texttt{Pair<U, V>}, \texttt{Pair<X, X>}, \star, \texttt{X}, \texttt{T})$. From the definition of *match* we see that $\texttt{T}$ would have to satisfy $\vdash \texttt{Pair<U, V>} \sqsubseteq: [\texttt{T/X}]\texttt{Pair<X, X>}$; no such $\texttt{T}$ exists, and hence *match*ing, and thus type checking, fails.

```
<X>Pair<X, X> make(List<X> x) {}
<X>void compare(Pair<X, X> x) {}

void m()
{
    ∃U,V.Pair<U, V> p;
    ∃Z.List<Z> b;

    this.<*>compare(p);                  //1, type incorrect
    this.<*>compare(this.<*>make(b));    //2, OK
}
```

$$\square$$

Type Inference. As is usual with formal type systems, we consider type inference to be performed in a separate phase before type checking. Due to the presence of existential types, some inferred type parameters can not be named and are marked with $\star$. These parameters must be inferred during type checking. In T-INVK we only allow the inference of types where they are used as parameters to an actual parameter type (e.g., $\texttt{X}$ in $\texttt{<X>void m(Tree<X> x)}\ldots$). This is enforced by the *sift* function (defined in Fig. 6), which excludes pairs of actual and formal parameter types where the formal parameter type is a formal type variable of the method.

Computation: $\boxed{\mathtt{e} \rightsquigarrow \mathtt{e}}$

$$\frac{fields(\mathtt{C}) = \overline{\mathtt{f}}}{\mathtt{new}\ \mathtt{C}\!<\!\overline{\mathtt{T}}\!>\!(\overline{\mathtt{v}})\,.\,\mathtt{f}_i \rightsquigarrow \mathtt{v}_i}$$

(R-FIELD)

$$\frac{\begin{array}{c}\mathtt{v} = \mathtt{new}\ \mathtt{N}(\overline{\mathtt{v}'})\qquad \mathtt{v} = \mathtt{new}\ \mathtt{N}(\overline{\mathtt{v}''})\\ mBody(\mathtt{m},\mathtt{N}) = (\overline{\mathtt{x}};\mathtt{e}_0)\qquad mType(\mathtt{m},\mathtt{N}) = <\!\overline{\mathtt{Y}\vartriangleleft\mathtt{B}}\!>\!\overline{\mathtt{U}} \to \mathtt{U}\\ match(sift(\overline{\mathtt{N}},\overline{\mathtt{U}},\overline{\mathtt{Y}}),\overline{\mathtt{P}},\overline{\mathtt{Y}},\overline{\mathtt{T}})\end{array}}{\mathtt{v}\,.\!<\!\overline{\mathtt{P}}\!>\!\mathtt{m}(\overline{\mathtt{v}}) \rightsquigarrow [\overline{\mathtt{v}/\mathtt{x}},\ \mathtt{v}/\mathtt{this},\ \overline{\mathtt{T}/\mathtt{Y}}]\mathtt{e}_0}$$

(R-INVK)

Congruence: $\boxed{\mathtt{e} \rightsquigarrow \mathtt{e}}$

$$\frac{\mathtt{e} \rightsquigarrow \mathtt{e}'}{\mathtt{e}.\mathtt{f} \rightsquigarrow \mathtt{e}'.\mathtt{f}}\qquad\qquad\qquad \frac{\mathtt{e} \rightsquigarrow \mathtt{e}'}{\mathtt{e}.\!<\!\overline{\mathtt{P}}\!>\!\mathtt{m}(\overline{\mathtt{e}}) \rightsquigarrow \mathtt{e}'.\!<\!\overline{\mathtt{P}}\!>\!\mathtt{m}(\overline{\mathtt{e}})}$$

(RC-FIELD)   (RC-INV-RECV)

$$\frac{\mathtt{e}_i \rightsquigarrow \mathtt{e}_i'}{\mathtt{e}.\!<\!\overline{\mathtt{P}}\!>\!\mathtt{m}(..\mathtt{e}_i..) \rightsquigarrow \mathtt{e}.\!<\!\overline{\mathtt{P}}\!>\!\mathtt{m}(..\mathtt{e}_i'..)}\qquad \frac{\mathtt{e}_i \rightsquigarrow \mathtt{e}_i'}{\mathtt{new}\ \mathtt{C}\!<\!\overline{\mathtt{T}}\!>\!(..\mathtt{e}_i..) \rightsquigarrow \mathtt{new}\ \mathtt{C}\!<\!\overline{\mathtt{T}}\!>\!(..\mathtt{e}_i'..)}$$

(RC-INV-ARG)   (RC-NEW-ARG)

Fig. 8. TameFJ reduction rules

3.5   Operational Semantics

The operational semantics of TameFJ are defined in Fig. 8. Most rules are simple and similar to those in FGJ. The interesting rule is R-INVK, which requires actual type parameters which do not include $\star$, these are found using the *match* relation. Avoiding the substitution of $\star$ for a formal type variable in the method body prevents the creation of invalid expressions, such as new C<$\star$>(). Since we are dealing only with values when using this rule, there will be no existential types and so all type parameters *could* be specified. However, there is no safe way to substitute the appropriate types for $\star$s during execution because each $\star$ may mark a different type. In this rule, *mBody* (defined in Fig. 6) is used to lookup the body (an expression) and the formal parameters of the method.

3.6   Type Soundness

We show type soundness for TameFJ by proving progress and subject reduction theorems [27], stated below. We prove these with empty environments since, at run-time, variables and type variables should not appear in expressions. A non-empty guarding environment is required in the statement of the progress theorem, because we use structural induction over the type rules; if this environment were empty, the inductive hypothesis could not be applied in the case of T-SUBS.

In the remainder of this section, we summarise some selected lemmas; we list most other lemmas in the appendix. We give full proofs in the extended version of this paper, available from:

http://www.doc.ic.ac.uk/~ncameron/papers/cameron_ecoop08_full.pdf

Theorem 1 (Progress). *For any Δ, e, T, if $\emptyset; \emptyset \vdash e : T \mid \Delta$ then either $e \rightsquigarrow e'$ or there exists a v such that $e = v$.*

Theorem 2 (Subject Reduction). *For any e, e', T, if $\emptyset; \emptyset \vdash e : T \mid \emptyset$ and $e \rightsquigarrow e'$ then $\emptyset; \emptyset \vdash e' : T \mid \emptyset$.*

To prove these two theorems, 40 supporting lemmas are required. These establish 'foundational' properties of the system, properties of substitution, properties of subtyping and subclassing (discussed in Sect. 3.2), which functions and relations always give well-formed types, and properties specific to each case of subject reduction and progress. Two of the most interesting lemmas concern the *match* relation:

Lemma 36 (Subclassing preserves *matching* (receiver)). *If $\Delta \vdash \exists \Delta_1 . N_1 \sqsubseteq: \exists \Delta_2 . N_2$ and $mType(m, N_2) = \langle \overline{Y_2} \rightarrow [B_{2l}\ B_{2u}] \rangle > \overline{U_2} \rightarrow U_2$ and $mType(m, N_1) = \langle \overline{Y_1} \rightarrow [B_{1l}\ B_{1u}] \rangle > \overline{U_1} \rightarrow U_1$ and $match(sift(\overline{R}, \overline{U_2}, \overline{Y_2}), \overline{P}, \overline{Y_2}, \overline{T})$ and $\emptyset \vdash \Delta$ OK and $\Delta, \Delta' \vdash \overline{T}$ OK then $match(sift(\overline{R}, \overline{U_1}, \overline{Y_1}), \overline{P}, \overline{Y_1}, \overline{T})$.*

Lemma 37 (Subclassing preserves *matching* (arguments)). *If $\Delta \vdash \overline{\exists \Delta_1 . R_1} \sqsubseteq: \overline{\exists \Delta_2 . R_2}$ and $match(sift(\overline{R_2}, \overline{U}, \overline{Y}), \overline{P}, \overline{Y}, \overline{T})$ and $fv(\overline{U}) \cap \overline{Z} = \emptyset$ and $\overline{\Delta_2} = \overline{Z \rightarrow [B_l\ B_u]}$ and $\emptyset \vdash \Delta$ OK and $\Delta \vdash \overline{\exists \Delta_1 . R_1}$ OK and $\Delta \vdash \overline{P}$ OK then there exists $\overline{U'}$ where $match(sift(\overline{R_1}, \overline{U}, \overline{Y}), \overline{P}, \overline{Y}, \overline{[U'/Z] T})$ and $\Delta, \overline{\Delta_1} \vdash \overline{U'} <: \overline{[U'/Z] B_u}$ and $\Delta, \overline{\Delta_1} \vdash \overline{[U'/Z] B_l} <: U'$ and $\vdash \overline{R_1} \sqsubseteq: \overline{[U'/Z] R_2}$ and $fv(\overline{U'}) \subseteq \Delta, \overline{\Delta_1}$.*

Lemma 36 states that if match succeeds with the formal parameter types of a superclass, then match will succeed where the formal parameter types are taken from the (extended) subclass (and the other arguments remain unchanged). Since overriding methods must have the same parameter types and formal type variables as the methods they override, the proof should be straightforward. However, it is complicated by extended subclassing of existential types; for example, if a method m is declared to have a parameter with type Z in the class declaration of class C<Z◁ Object>, then the type of m's formal parameter will have type X when looked up in ∃X.C<X> and A in C<A>. X may not be a subtype of A, even if C<A> is an extended subclass of ∃X.C<X>. We show in the proof that such issues do not affect $\overline{T}$, because these types are found only from the actual parameter types of the method call.

Lemma 37 performs a similar duty, but for the types of the actual parameters. The conclusion defines a 'valid' substitution which is given by lemma 35 (see Sect. 3.2). The types $\overline{T}$ in *match* are found from the actual parameter types and so, in contrast to lemma 36, these types are affected by the substitution in the conclusion of the lemma.

Lemma 31 (Inversion Lemma (object creation))
If $\Delta; \Gamma \vdash$ new C<$\overline{\texttt{T}}$>($\overline{\texttt{e}}$) : T $| \Delta'$ then $\Delta' = \emptyset$ and $\Delta \vdash$ C<$\overline{\texttt{T}}$> OK and fields(C) $= \overline{\texttt{f}}$ and $\overline{fType(\texttt{f},\texttt{C<}\overline{\texttt{T}}\texttt{>}) = \texttt{U}}$ and $\Delta; \Gamma \vdash \overline{\texttt{e} : \texttt{U} \mid \emptyset}$ and $\Delta \vdash \exists \emptyset.\texttt{C<}\overline{\texttt{T}}\texttt{>} <: \texttt{T}$.

Lemma 33 (Inversion Lemma (method invocation)). *If $\Delta; \Gamma \vdash$ e.<$\overline{\texttt{P}}$>m($\overline{\texttt{e}}$) : T $| \Delta'$ and $\emptyset \vdash \Delta$ OK and $\Delta \vdash \Delta'$ OK and $\forall \texttt{x} \in dom(\Gamma) :$ $\Delta \vdash \Gamma(\texttt{x})$ OK then there exists Δ_n where $\Delta', \Delta_n = \Delta'', \overline{\Delta}$ and $\Delta \vdash \Delta', \Delta_n$ OK and $\Delta; \Gamma \vdash$ e : $\exists \Delta''.\texttt{N} \mid \emptyset$ and $mType(\texttt{m}, \texttt{N}) = $<$\overline{\texttt{Y} \lhd \texttt{B}}$>$\overline{\texttt{U}} \rightarrow$ U and $\Delta; \Gamma \vdash \overline{\texttt{e} : \exists \Delta.\texttt{R} \mid \emptyset}$ and $match(sift(\overline{\texttt{R}}, \overline{\texttt{U}}, \overline{\texttt{Y}}), \overline{\texttt{P}}, \overline{\texttt{Y}}, \overline{\texttt{T}})$ and $\Delta \vdash$ $\overline{\texttt{P}}$ OK and $\Delta, \Delta'', \overline{\Delta} \vdash \texttt{T} <: [\overline{\texttt{T}/\texttt{Y}}]\texttt{B}$ and $\Delta, \Delta'', \overline{\Delta} \vdash \exists \emptyset.\texttt{R} <: [\overline{\texttt{T}/\texttt{Y}}]\texttt{U}$ and $\Delta, \Delta'', \Delta_n \vdash [\overline{\texttt{T}/\texttt{Y}}]\texttt{U} <: \texttt{T}$.*

The formulation of the inversion lemmas is made more interesting by the presence of the guarding environment (Δ') in the typing judgement ($\Delta; \Gamma \vdash$ e : T $| \Delta'$). In the case of object creation (lemma 31) we show that the guarding environment must be empty. Intuitively, this is because no existential types may be unpacked in the application of T-NEW, and T-SUBS can only shrink the guarding environment, but not add to it. This property of object creation is used heavily in the proof of subject reduction since values in TameFJ are object creation expressions.

Method invocation is more complex; the guarding environment of T-INVK is formed from the environments unpacked from the types of the receiver and arguments, but these may be re-packed by applying T-SUBS. The conclusion of lemma 33 is that there exists some environment, Δ_n, which, when concatenated with Δ' will be equal to the unpacked environments from the receiver and arguments.

Alpha Conversion and Barendregt's Variable Convention. As well as the standard use of alpha conversion to rename bound variables in existential types, we also need to be able to rename type variables in the guarding environment, as in the following lemma:

Lemma 7 (Alpha renaming of guarding environments)
If $\Delta; \Gamma \vdash$ e : T $| \overline{\texttt{X} \rightarrow [\texttt{B}_l \ \texttt{B}_u]}$ and $\overline{\texttt{Y}}$ are fresh, then $\Delta; \Gamma \vdash$ e : $[\overline{\texttt{Y}/\texttt{X}}]\texttt{T} \mid \overline{\texttt{Y} \rightarrow [[\overline{\texttt{Y}/\texttt{X}}]\texttt{B}_l \ [\overline{\texttt{Y}/\texttt{X}}]\texttt{B}_u]}$.

Lemma 7 guarantees that we can rename variables in Δ' and T and preserve typing. Thus, the guarding environment can be thought of as binding its type variables; the scope of the binding is T, the result of type checking. Note that we do not need to rename types in e. This is because any type variables in the domain of the guarding environment ($\overline{\texttt{X}}$) come from unpacked existential types, and so can not be explicitly named in the expression syntax; instead they would be marked with $\star$.

In order to reduce the number of places where we need to apply alpha conversion in our proofs, we make use of Barendregt's variable convention [2]; i.e., we assume that bound and free variables are distinct. For example, consider the proof of lemma 2:

Lemma 2 (Subsititution preserves *matching*). *If* $match(\overline{R}, \overline{\exists\Delta.R'}, \overline{P}, \overline{Y}, \overline{U})$ *and* $(\overline{X} \cup fv(\overline{T})) \cap \overline{Y}) = \emptyset$ *then* $match([\overline{T/X}]R, [\overline{T/X}]\overline{\exists\Delta.R'}, [\overline{T/X}]P, \overline{Y}, [\overline{T/X}]U)$.

We reach a point in the proofs where we have shown that $\vdash [\overline{T/X}]R \sqsubset: [\overline{T/X}][\overline{U/Y}, \overline{U'/Z}]R'$, $dom(\overline{\Delta}) = \overline{Z}$, and $(\overline{X} \cup fv(\overline{T})) \cap \overline{Y}) = \emptyset$; we wish to show $\vdash [\overline{T/X}]R \sqsubset: [[\overline{T/X}]U/Y, [\overline{T/X}]U'/Z][\overline{T/X}]R'$ and for this we require that $\overline{Z}$ are not free in $\overline{T}$. We would have used alpha conversion on $\overline{\exists\Delta.R'}$ to accomplish this; however, this would have required extensive renaming throughout the proof. Instead we use the variable convention and assume that $\overline{Z}$ are fresh at the point of becoming free and we can proceed with an elegant proof.

The use of Barendregt's variable convention is not always safe [25]. A sufficient condition is that all rules are equivariant and that any binders in a rule do not appear free in that rule's conclusion [25]. Since TameFJ satisfies these conditions, using Barendregt's convention *is* safe.

4   Translating Java to TameFJ

In this section we describe a possible translation from the Java subset which accommodates wildcards into TameFJ.

As said in the introduction, we work in a setting where we expect the first phase to have happened. Here we describe the second phase, and define it in Fig. 10. In Fig. 9 we give the syntax of the relevant subset of Java types, which are also those of Wild FJ.

N_s	$::=$	$C<\overline{T_s}>$	*Java class types*
T_s	$::=$	$C<\overline{P_s}> \mid X$	*Java types*
P_s	$::=$	$T_s \mid ? \mid ? \lhd T_s \mid ? \rhd T_s$	*Java type parameters*

Fig. 9. Syntax of Java types

The second phase is defined in terms of the functions $\mathcal{T}$, $\mathcal{P}$, and $\mathcal{M}$, where $\mathcal{T}$ translates Java types to TameFJ types; $\mathcal{P}$ translates a type parameter to an environment and a TameFJ type; and $\mathcal{M}$ gives the minimal types out of two. The function $\mathcal{T}$ maps each occurrence of a wildcard, ?, in a Java type onto an existentially quantified type variable. To do this, it uses the function $\mathcal{P}$, which maps any Java type onto an environment and a TameFJ type. $\mathcal{T}$ uses the collected environments to create an existential type, using the $\mathcal{M}$ function to find the appropriate upper bounds, and replaces each type argument by its image through $\mathcal{P}$. Note that, in order to reduce the notational complexity, the translation of non-wildcard type parameters introduces a type variable which is never used; this is harmless.

We now highlight some of the finer points of the translation in terms of examples.

$$\frac{\texttt{class } \texttt{C<X} \triangleleft \texttt{T}_s \texttt{>} \ldots \qquad \mathcal{P}_\Delta(\texttt{P}_s) = (\texttt{Y} \to [\texttt{U}_s\ \texttt{U}'_s], \texttt{T})}{\mathcal{T}_\Delta(\texttt{C<}\overline{\texttt{P}_s}\texttt{>}) = \exists \texttt{Y} \to\ \ [\mathcal{T}_\Delta(\texttt{U}_s)\ \mathcal{M}_\Delta(\mathcal{T}_\Delta(\texttt{U}'_s), [\overline{\texttt{Y/X}}]\mathcal{T}_\Delta(\texttt{T}_s))]\ .\texttt{C<}\overline{\texttt{T}}\texttt{>}}$$

$$\frac{}{\mathcal{T}_\Delta(\texttt{X}) = \exists \emptyset . \texttt{X}} \qquad \frac{\Delta \vdash \texttt{T} <: \texttt{T}'}{\mathcal{M}_\Delta(\texttt{T}, \texttt{T}') = \texttt{T} = \mathcal{M}_\Delta(\texttt{T}', \texttt{T})} \qquad \frac{\Delta \vdash \texttt{T} \not<: \texttt{T}' \quad \Delta \vdash \texttt{T}' \not<: \texttt{T}}{\mathcal{M}_\Delta(\texttt{T}', \texttt{T}) = \texttt{T}}$$

$$\frac{\texttt{X } is\ fresh}{\begin{array}{l} \mathcal{P}_\Delta(\texttt{?}) = (\texttt{X} \to [\bot\ \exists \emptyset . \texttt{Object}], \texttt{X}) \\ \mathcal{P}_\Delta(\texttt{? } \triangleleft \texttt{T}_s) = (\texttt{X} \to [\bot\ \mathcal{T}_\Delta(\texttt{T}_s)], \texttt{X}) \\ \mathcal{P}_\Delta(\texttt{? } \triangleright \texttt{T}_s) = (\texttt{X} \to [\mathcal{T}_\Delta(\texttt{T}_s)\ \exists \emptyset . \texttt{Object}], \texttt{X}) \\ \mathcal{P}_\Delta(\texttt{T}_s) = (\texttt{X} \to [\bot\ \exists \emptyset . \texttt{Object}], \mathcal{T}_\Delta(\texttt{T}_s)) \end{array}}$$

Fig. 10. Translation from Java types to TameFJ types

A wildcard that occurs as a type parameter is replaced by a quantified type variable. Bounds on the wildcard become bounds on the quantifying type variable. Where bounds are not given we use $\exists \emptyset . \texttt{Object}$ as the default upper bound and $\bot$ as the default lower bound. For instance, $\texttt{C<?} \triangleleft \texttt{Shape>}$ is translated to $\exists \texttt{X} \to [\bot\ \exists \emptyset . \texttt{Shape}] . \texttt{C<X>}$, and the translation of $\texttt{C<?} \triangleright \texttt{Shape>}$ amounts to $\exists \texttt{X} \to [\exists \emptyset . \texttt{Shape}\ \exists \emptyset . \texttt{Object}] . \texttt{C<X>}$. We must distinguish different occurrences of the wildcard symbol by translating them to distinct type variables. Hence, $\texttt{Pair<?, ?>}$ translates to $\exists \texttt{X}, \texttt{Y} . \texttt{Pair<X, Y>}$. Finally, nested wildcards are quantified at the immediately enclosing level, so $\texttt{C<C<C<?>>>}$ translates to $\exists \emptyset . \texttt{C<}\exists \emptyset . \texttt{C<}\exists \texttt{X} . \texttt{C<X>>>}$.

A subtle aspect of the translation is that wildcards can inherit their upper bound from the upper bound of the corresponding formal type variable in the class declaration. Since we want to avoid doing this in the calculus, we must take care of this in the translation, which is achieved as in the following example: for a class C declared as $\texttt{class } \texttt{C<Z} \triangleleft \texttt{Circle>} \ldots$, the type $\texttt{C<?>}$ is translated to $\exists \texttt{X} \to [\bot\ \exists \emptyset . \texttt{Circle}] . \texttt{C<X>}$.

When an upper bound is declared both for a wildcard and in the corresponding class declaration, then the 'smallest' type is taken as the upper bound, if the types are subtypes of each other ($\mathcal{M}$). Hence, $\texttt{C<?} \triangleleft \texttt{Shape>}$ is translated to the same type as in the previous example, and is *not* a type error. Finally, if the bounds are unrelated, then the bound from the declaration is taken as the upper bound of the wildcard, which means that even the type $\texttt{C<?} \triangleleft \texttt{Serializable>}$ is translated into the same type as the previous two examples.

This last behaviour implies that the Java type analysis uses a more general type for some expressions than it would have to in order to maintain soundness (in the example it could have used the intersection of `Circle` and `Serializable`, but it just uses `Circle`), and this means that some reasonable and actually type safe programs will be rejected by the Java compiler. However, it poses no problems for the soundness of Java, nor for our translation.

The most interesting aspect of the translation is where wildcards meet F-bounds. An F-bounded type is a type where the formal type variable is bounded by an expression in which the variable itself occurs. These types are crucial for modelling common idioms such as subject-observer in Java generics [23]. In the following example both instantiations of F using wildcards are legal.

```
class F<X ◁ F<X>> {...}
void m(F<?> x1, F<? ◁ F<?>> x2) {...}
```

The translation of the types `F<?>` and `F<? ◁ F<?>>` is not immediately obvious, because in Java there is no finite type expression for the least supertype of all legal type arguments to F, i.e., the upper bound of the type argument X is not denotable in Java. However, in TameFJ this upper bound *is*, in fact, denotable: it is just $\exists Y \rightarrow [\perp \text{ F<Y>}].\text{F<Y>}$. Indeed, our translation of `F<?>` gives this type. In the case of `F<? ◁ F<?>>` where the wildcard is translated to the fresh variable Y, the upper bound will be the least subtype of $\exists Z.\text{F<Z>}$ (the translation of the given bound; where Z is fresh) and `F<Y>` (the bound derived from the class declaration). Since the latter is more strict, it is used, even though this appears to contradict the rule of using fresh type variables for each wildcard; in fact it does no such thing, the second wildcard *is* translated to a fresh type variable, but is then forgotten.

5   Related Work

In this section we discuss related work. We distinguish three categories: the evolution of wildcards, formal and informal specifications of Java wildcards, and related systems with type soundness results.

Wildcards are a form of *use-site* variance. This means that the variance of a type is determined at the instantiation of the type. The first uses of variant generic types in object oriented languages were *declaration-site* variance, where the variance of a type is determined by the class declaration. Use-site variance was first expressed in terms of structural virtual types [23]. The concept developed into Variant Parametric Types [14] which were extended to give Java wildcards.

Wildcards in Java are officially (and informally) described in the Java Language Specification [11]. Wildcards and generics are described in detail in [3]. Wildcards were first described in a research paper in [24], again informally, but with some description of their formal properties and of the correspondence to existential types. The most important formal description of wildcards is the Wild FJ calculus [17], referred to throughout this paper. Wildcards have also been described in terms of access restriction [26] and flow analysis [8] (actually Variant Parametric Types).

Variant Parametric Types [14] could be thought of as a partial model for Java wildcards (notably missing wildcard capture, but different in several subtler ways also). The calculus in [14] was proven type sound and as such it can be regarded as a partial soundness result for wildcards. In [5] we describe a sound partial model for wildcards using a more traditional existential types approach. In particular, the calculus has explicit open and close expressions, as opposed to the implicit versions found in this paper and in other approaches [14,17]. Subtyping of existential types in [5] is taken from the full variant of System $F_{<:}$ with existential types [10], rather than the wildcards style subtyping, exemplified in the XS-ENV rule in this paper. The soundness result for that system follows those of FGJ and traditional existential types closely. However, it is only a partial result; the system lacks lower bounds amongst other restrictions.

6   Conclusion and Future Work

In this paper we have presented a formal model for Java with wildcards, TameFJ, and a type soundness proof for this formalism. To the best of our knowledge, this is the first type sound model for wildcards that captures *all* the significant features for soundness. We have shown through discussion and a formal translation that TameFJ is a satisfactory model for Java wildcards.

Future Work. We are investigating several directions for future work. The most straightforward is to extend our model to include imperative features. Previous work with existential types found issues that only occurred in an imperative setting [12]; although we do not believe these issues affect our result, a proof for an imperative system would settle this matter once and for all. To complete the argument for type soundness in Java, we would like to prove soundness for the translation described in Sect. 4, expanded to expressions. Another interesting property for Java wildcards would be the decidability of typing and type inference. Such questions have been investigated elsewhere [15,19], but there is no complete answer specifically for Java.

We would like to apply the tools developed for this work, i.e., existential types for variance, in other settings. For example, ownership types, where an 'any' or '?' parameter or ad hoc existential types often appear [1,4,16,28]; or virtual classes [9,18]. We would also like to further develop the use of existential types to give programmers a better understanding of how to use wildcards.

Acknowledgements. We are deeply grateful to Alex Summers for introducing us to Barendregt's variable convention, and to Christian Urban, Mariangiola Dezani-Ciancaglini, and again Alex Summers, for discussions on the convention. We had illuminating discussions with Alex Buckley about the Java language and spec and the implementation of Wildcards, with Atushi Igarashi about Featherweight Java and FGJ, and with Dave Clarke about existential types and other approaches. We thank the anonymous reviewers for their helpful comments.

References

1. Aldrich, J., Chambers, C.: Ownership domains: Separating aliasing policy from mechanism. In: Odersky, M. (ed.) ECOOP 2004. LNCS, vol. 3086, pp. 1–25. Springer, Heidelberg (2004)
2. Barendregt, H.: The Lambda Calculus. Revised edn. North-Holland, Amsterdam (1984)
3. Bracha, G.: Generics in the Java programming language (2004), http://java.sun.com/j2se/1.5/pdf/generics-tutorial.pdf
4. Cameron, N., Drossopoulou, S., Noble, J., Smith, M.: Multiple Ownership. In: OOPSLA 2007 (October 2007)
5. Cameron, N., Ernst, E., Drossopoulou, S.: Towards an existential types model for java wildcards. In: 9th Workshop on Formal Techniques for Java-like Programs (2007)
6. Cardelli, L., Leroy, X.: Abstract types and the dot notation. Research report 56, DEC Systems Research Center (1990)
7. Cardelli, L., Wegner, P.: On understanding types, data abstraction, and polymorphism. ACM Computing Surveys 17(4), 471–522 (1985)
8. Chin, W.-N., Craciun, F., Khoo, S.-C., Popeea, C.: A flow-based approach for variant parametric types. In: Proceedings of the 2006 ACM SIGPLAN conference on Object-oriented programming, systems, languages, and applications (OOPSLA 2006). ACM Press, New York (2006)
9. Clarke, D., Drossopoulou, S., Noble, J., Wrigstad, T.: Tribe: a simple virtual class calculus. In: AOSD 2007: Proceedings of the 6th international conference on Aspect-oriented software development, Vancouver, British Columbia, Canada, pp. 121–134. ACM, New York (2007), http://doi.acm.org/10.1145/1218563.1218578
10. Ghelli, G., Pierce, B.: Bounded existentials and minimal typing. Theoretical Computer Science 193(1-2), 75–96 (1998)
11. Gosling, J., Joy, B., Steele, G., Bracha, G.: The Java Language Specification Third Edition. Addison-Wesley, Boston (2005)
12. Grossman, D.: Existential types for imperative languages. In: Le Métayer, D. (ed.) ESOP 2002 and ETAPS 2002. LNCS, vol. 2305, pp. 21–35. Springer, Heidelberg (2002)
13. Igarashi, A., Pierce, B.C., Wadler, P.: Featherweight Java: a minimal core calculus for Java and GJ. ACM Trans. Program. Lang. Syst. 23(3), 396–450 (2001); An earlier version of this work appeared at OOPSLA 1999.
14. Igarashi, A., Viroli, M.: Variant parametric types: A flexible subtyping scheme for generics. ACM Trans. Program. Lang. Syst. 28(5), 795–847 (2006); An earlier version appeared as On variance-based subtyping for parametric types at (ECOOP 2002)
15. Kennedy, A.J., Pierce, B.C.: On decidability of nominal subtyping with variance. In: International Workshop on Foundations and Developments of Object-Oriented Languages (FOOL/WOOD 2007), Nice, France (January 2007)
16. Lu, Y., Potter, J.: On ownership and accessibility. In: Thomas, D. (ed.) ECOOP 2006. LNCS, vol. 4067, pp. 99–123. Springer, Heidelberg (2006)
17. Torgersen, M., Ernst, E., Hansen, C.P.: Wild FJ. In: 12th International Workshop on Foundations of Object-Oriented Languages (FOOL 12), Long Beach, California, ACM Press, New York (2005)

18. Madsen, O.L., Moller-Pedersen, B.: Virtual classes: a powerful mechanism in object-oriented programming. In: OOPSLA 1989: Conference proceedings on Object-oriented programming systems, languages and applications, pp. 397–406. ACM Press, New York (1989)
19. Mazurak, K., Zdancewic, S.: Note on Type Inference for Java 5: Wildcards, F-Bounds, and Undecidability (2006), http://www.cis.upenn.edu/~stevez/note.html
20. Mitchell, J.C., Plotkin, G.D.: Abstract types have existential types. In: POPL 1985: Proceedings of the 12th ACM SIGACT-SIGPLAN symposium on Principles of programming languages, pp. 37–51. ACM Press, New York (1985)
21. Pierce, B.C.: Bounded quantification is undecidable. In: POPL 1992: Proceedings of the 19th ACM SIGPLAN-SIGACT symposium on Principles of programming languages, pp. 305–315. ACM Press, New York (1992)
22. Pierce, B.C.: Types and programming languages. MIT Press, Cambridge (2002)
23. Krab Thorup, K., Torgersen, M.: Unifying genericity - combining the benefits of virtual types and parameterized classes. In: Guerraoui, R. (ed.) ECOOP 1999. LNCS, vol. 1628, pp. 186–204. Springer, Heidelberg (1999)
24. Torgersen, M., Hansen, C.P., Ernst, E., von der Ahé, P., Bracha, G., Gafter, N.: Adding wildcards to the Java programming language. Journal of Object Technology 3(11), 97–116 (2004); Special issue: OOPS track at SAC 2004, Nicosia/Cyprus.
25. Urban, C., Berghofer, S., Norrish, M.: Barendregt's variable convention in rule inductions. In: Pfenning, F. (ed.) CADE 2007. LNCS (LNAI), vol. 4603, pp. 35–50. Springer, Heidelberg (2007)
26. Viroli, M., Rimassa, G.: On access restriction with Java wildcards. Journal of Object Technology 4(10), 117–139 (2005); Special issue: OOPS track at SAC 2005, Santa Fe/New Mexico. The earlier version in the proceedings of SAC 2005 appeared as Understanding access restriction of variant parametric types and Java wildcards.
27. Wright, A.K., Felleisen, M.: A syntactic approach to type soundness. Information and Computation 115(1), 38–94 (1994)
28. Wrigstad, T., Clarke, D.: Existential owners for ownership types. JOT 6(4), 141–159 (2007)

A   Summary of Lemmas

For all lemmas and theorems we require the additional premise that the program is well-formed, i.e., for all class declarations, Q, in the program, $\vdash Q$ OK. Lemmas in the text have not been repeated, some lemmas have been omitted; full proofs of all lemmas can be downloaded from:

http://www.doc.ic.ac.uk/~ncameron/papers/cameron_ecoop08_full.pdf

Lemma 1 (Substitution preserves subclassing). *If* $\vdash R \sqsubset: R'$ *then* $\vdash [T/X]R \sqsubset: [T/X]R'$.

Proof is by structural induction on the derivation of $\vdash R \sqsubset: R'$.

Lemma 3 (Substitution on $\bar{U}$ preserves $sift$). *If* $sift(\bar{R}, \bar{U}, \bar{Y}) = (\bar{R_r}, \bar{T_r})$ *and* $(fv(\bar{T}) \cup \bar{X}) \cap \bar{Y} = \emptyset$ *then* $sift(\bar{R}, \overline{[T/X]U}, \bar{Y}) = (\bar{R_r}, \overline{[T/X]T_r})$.

Proof is by structural induction on the derivation of $sift(\bar{R}, \bar{U}, \bar{Y}) = (\bar{R_r}, \bar{T_r})$.

Lemma 4 (Substitution on $\overline{R}$ preserves $sift$). *If $sift(\overline{R}, \overline{U}, \overline{Y}) = (\overline{R_r}, \overline{T_r})$ and f is a mapping from and to types in the syntactic category* R.   *then $sift(\overline{f(R)}, \overline{U}, \overline{Y}) = (\overline{f(R_r)}, \overline{T_r})$.*

Proof is by structural induction on the derivation of $sift(\overline{R}, \overline{U}, \overline{Y}) = (\overline{R_r}, \overline{T_r})$.

Lemma 11 (Weakening of Typing).

If $dom(\Delta, \Delta', \Delta''') \cap dom(\Delta'') = \emptyset$ and $dom(\Gamma, \Gamma'') \cap dom(\Gamma') = \emptyset$ and $\Delta, \Delta'; \Gamma, \Gamma'' \vdash e : T \mid \Delta'''$ then $\Delta, \Delta'', \Delta'; \Gamma, \Gamma', \Gamma'' \vdash e : T \mid \Delta'''$ and

Proof is by structural induction on the derivation of $\Delta, \Delta'; \Gamma, \Gamma'' \vdash e : T \mid \Delta'''$.

Lemma 13 (Extension of type environments preserves well-formedness). *If $\Delta \vdash \Delta'$ OK and $\Delta, \Delta' \vdash \Delta''$ OK   then $\Delta \vdash \Delta', \Delta''$ OK.*

Proof is by structural induction on the derivation of $\Delta \vdash \Delta'$ OK.

Lemma 21 (Subsititution preserves typing).

If $\Delta; \Gamma \vdash e : T \mid \Delta''$ and $\Delta_1 \vdash T <: [\overline{T/X}]B_u$ and $\Delta_1 \vdash [\overline{T/X}]B_l <: T$ and $\Delta = \Delta_1, \overline{X \rightarrow [B_l \ B_u]}, \Delta_2$ and $\Delta' = \Delta_1, [\overline{T/X}]\Delta_2$ and $\overline{X} \cap fv(\Delta_1) = \emptyset$ and $\Delta_1 \vdash \overline{T}$ OK and $\emptyset \vdash \Delta_1$ OK and $\Delta_1, \overline{X \rightarrow [B_l \ B_u]} \vdash \Delta_2$ OK   then $\Delta'; [\overline{T/X}]\Gamma \vdash [\overline{T/X}]e : [\overline{T/X}]T \mid [\overline{T/X}]\Delta''.$

Proof is by structural induction on the derivation of $\Delta; \Gamma \vdash e : T \mid \Delta''$.

Lemma 22 (Superclasses are well-formed). *If $\vdash R \sqsubset: R'$ and $\Delta \vdash R$ OK and $\emptyset \vdash \Delta$ OK   then $\Delta \vdash R'$ OK.*

Proof is by structural induction on the derivation of $\vdash R \sqsubset: R'$.

Lemma 23 (Subclassing preserves field types). *If $\vdash N \sqsubset: N'$ and $fType(f, N') = T$ then $fType(f, N) = T$.*

Proof is by structural induction on the derivation of $\vdash N \sqsubset: N'$.

Lemma 24 (Subclassing preserves method return type). *If $\vdash N_1 \sqsubset: N_2$ and $mType(m, N_2) = <\overline{Y \lhd T_u}>\overline{T} \rightarrow T$ then $mType(m, N_1) = <\overline{Y \lhd T_u}>\overline{T} \rightarrow T$.*

Proof is by structural induction on the derivation of $\vdash N_1 \sqsubset: N_2$.

Lemma 25 (Expression substitution preserves typing). *If $\Delta; \Gamma, x:U \vdash e : T \mid \Delta'$ and $\Delta; \Gamma \vdash e' : U' \mid \emptyset$ and $\Delta \vdash U' <: U$ and $\Delta \vdash U$ OK   then $\Delta; \Gamma \vdash [e'/x]e : T \mid \Delta'$.   Proof is by structural induction on the derivation of $\Delta; \Gamma, x:U \vdash e : T \mid \Delta'$.*

Lemma 29 (match gives well-formed types). *If $\Delta \vdash \overline{P}$ OK and $\Delta \vdash \exists \overline{\Delta}.\overline{R}$ OK and $\emptyset \vdash \Delta$ OK and $match(\overline{R}, \exists \overline{\Delta'}.\overline{R'}, \overline{P}, \overline{Y}, \overline{T})$ then $\Delta, \overline{\Delta} \vdash \overline{T}$ OK.*

Lemma 30 (Typing gives well-formed types). *If $\Delta; \Gamma \vdash e : T \mid \Delta'$ and $\emptyset \vdash \Delta$ OK and $\forall x \in dom(\Gamma): \Delta \vdash \Gamma(x)$ OK then $\Delta, \Delta' \vdash T$ OK.*

Proof is by structural induction on the derivation of $\Delta; \Gamma \vdash e : T \mid \Delta'$.

On Validity of Program Transformations in the Java Memory Model

Jaroslav Ševčík and David Aspinall

LFCS, School of Informatics, University of Edinburgh

Abstract. We analyse the validity of several common program transformations in multi-threaded Java, as defined by the Memory Model section of the Java Language Specification. The main design goal of the Java Memory Model (JMM) was to allow as many optimisations as possible. However, we find that commonly used optimisations, such as common subexpression elimination, can introduce new behaviours and so are invalid for Java. In this paper, we describe several kinds of transformations and explain the problems with a number of counterexamples. More positively, we also examine some valid transformations, and prove their validity. Our study contributes to the understanding of the JMM, and has the practical impact of revealing some cases where the Sun Hotspot JVM does not comply with the Java Memory Model.

1 Introduction

Although programmers generally assume an interleaved semantics, the Java Language Specification defines more relaxed semantics, which is called the Java Memory Model [11,18]. The reasons for having a weaker semantics become apparent from the following example:

Initially, x = y = 0

x = 1	if (x==1) {
if (y==1)	x = 0
print x	y = 1
	}

The question is: can this program ever print 1? In the interleaved semantics, the answer is *no*, because if the program prints at all then all the instructions of the second thread must be executed between the statements x=1 and if (y==1) of the first thread. Hence, if the program prints, the write x=1 must be overwritten by the assignment x=0, and the program prints 0.

In reality, a modern optimising compiler, such as Sun HotSpot JVM or GCJ, will replace print x by print 1, because the read of x can reuse the value previously written to x. After this optimisation, the program can print 1, which was not a possible behaviour of the original program. One could argue that compilers should only perform optimisations that are safe for multi-threaded as well as single-threaded programs; however, most modern processors would perform optimisations like this. Preventing the hardware from optimising memory accesses

J. Vitek (Ed.): ECOOP 2008, LNCS 5142, pp. 27–51, 2008.

comes at much higher cost than a missed optimisation in a compiler—typical memory barrier instructions consume hundreds of cycles and should be avoided if they are not necessary.

Instead of guaranteeing sequential consistency for all programs, the Java Language Specification defines a semantics that guarantees sequential consistency (interleaved semantics) for data race free programs, while giving some basic security guarantees for programs with data races. The authors of the Java Memory Model claim that the JMM is flexible enough to validate commonly used hardware and compiler optimisations. They give a theorem in [18], which states that reordering of certain combinations of statements is a valid transformation. However, Cenciarelli et al. [9] discovered a counterexample, which shows that reordering of independent memory accesses is invalid in the JMM.

This raises several questions: What common transformations are valid in the JMM? Can we fix the memory model so that more or all these transformations become valid? We have made initial steps to address this question—in earlier work we suggested a subtle variation of the JMM definition and conjectured that their version allows reordering of independent statements.

Contribution. In this paper, we analyse several commonly used local optimisations and classify them by their validity in the Java Memory Model. We prove that removal of redundant reads after writes and writes after writes are valid transformations in the JMM. With the alternative definition suggested in [5] we also establish validity of reordering of independent statements. On the other hand, we demonstrate that some other cases of reordering, which [18] claims to be valid, are not generally valid transformations. For example, swapping a normal memory access with a consequent lock can introduce new behaviours, and thus is not a valid transformation. Another example of an invalid transformation is reusing a value of a read for a subsequent read, or an introduction of an irrelevant read. With this analysis, we establish that the JMM is still flawed, because these transformations are performed by hardware and compilers. Even Sun's Hotspot JVM [19] performs transformations that are not compliant with the JMM.

1.1 Introduction to the JMM

We illustrate the key properties of the JMM on three canonical examples (from [18]), given in Fig. 1. The programs show statements in parallel threads, operating on thread-local registers ($r1$, $r2$, ...) and shared memory locations (x, y, ...). We assume no aliasing, different location names denote different locations.

In an interleaved semantics, program A could not result in $r1 = r2 = 1$, because one of the statements $r1=x$, $r2=y$ must be executed first, thus either $r1$ or $r2$ must be 0. However, current hardware can, and often does, execute instructions out of order. Imagine a scenario where the read $r1=x$ is too slow because of cache management. The processor can realise that the next statement $y=1$ is independent of the read, and instead of waiting for the read it performs the write. The second thread then might execute both of its instructions, seeing initially x = y = 0

lock m1	lock m2
r1=x	r2=y
unlock m1	unlock m2
lock m2	lock m1
y=1	x=1
unlock m2	unlock m1

initially x = y = 0

r1 = x	r2 = y
y = 1	x = 1

initially x = y = 0

r1 = x	r2 = y
y = r1	x = r2

A. (allowed)   B. (prohibited)   C. (prohibited)

Is it possible to get r1 = r2 = 1 at the end of an execution?

Fig. 1. Examples of legal and illegal executions

the write y=1 (so r2 = 1). Finally, the postponed read of x can see the value 1 written by the second thread, resulting in r1 = r2 = 1. Similar non-intuitive behaviours could result from simple compiler optimisations, as illustrated in the introduction.

However, there are limits on the optimisations allowed—if the programmer synchronises properly, e.g., by guarding each access to a field by a synchronised section on a designated monitor, then the program should only have sequentially consistent behaviours. This is why the behaviour r1 = r2 = 1 must be prohibited in program B of Fig. 1. This guarantee for data race free programs is called DRF guarantee.

Even if a program contains data races, there must be some security guarantees. Program C in Fig. 1 illustrates an unwanted "out-of-thin-air" behaviour—if a value does not occur anywhere in the program, it should not be read in any execution of the program. The out-of-thin-air behaviours could cause security leaks, because references to objects from possibly confidential parts of program could suddenly appear as a result of a self-justifying data race.

2 Transformations and Traces

In this section we give an overview of the classes of program transformations that we have considered. Most common compiler transformations, such as common subexpression elimination, dead code elimination, and various types of loop optimisations can be expressed as a composition of our basic transformations. Similarly to [18], we will consider a transformation valid if it does not introduce any new behaviours. A valid transformation may reduce the possible behaviours. In Table 1 we classify the transformations by their validity under sequential consistency (column 'SC'), in the current Java Memory Model (column 'JMM'), and in the memory model modification suggested in [5] (column 'JMM-Alt'). Note that the JMM is in fact stricter than sequential consistency in terms of closure under some transformations, even though the JMM is more relaxed in the sense that any sequentially consistent execution is a JMM execution.

In the following subsections we describe the transformations and explain them through examples. The proofs and counterexamples for (in)validity in the JMM will follow in Sect. 4, after we have explained the mechanics of the JMM in Sect. 3.

Table 1. Validity of transformations in the JMM

Transformation	SC	JMM	JMM-Alt
Trace-preserving transformations	✓	✓	✓
Reordering normal memory accesses	×	×	✓
Redundant read after read elimination	✓	×	×
Redundant read after write elimination	✓	✓	✓
Irrelevant read elimination	✓	✓	✓
Irrelevant read introduction	✓	×	×
Redundant write before write elimination	✓	✓	✓
Redundant write after read elimination	✓	×	×
Roach-motel reordering	×(✓ for locks)	×	×
External action reordering	×	×	×

2.1 Traces

To describe some of the thread-local transformations we introduce the notion of memory traces, which also constitute the connection between the JMM and the sequential part of the Java language[1]. The memory traces are finite sequences of memory operations, which can be of the following kinds:

- *volatile read* $\mathrm{Rd}_v(v, i)$,
- *volatile write* $\mathrm{Wr}_v(v, i)$,
- *normal read* $\mathrm{Rd}(x, i)$,
- *normal write* $\mathrm{Wr}(x, i)$,
- *external action* $\mathrm{Ex}(i)$,

- *lock* $\mathrm{L}(m)$,
- *unlock* $\mathrm{U}(m)$,
- *thread start* St,
- *thread finish* Fin,

where x is a non-volatile memory location, v is a volatile memory location, i is a value, and m is a synchronisation monitor. In the spirit of the JMM, we consider an external action to be an output of a value. The meaning of a sequential program is then a prefix-closed set of the memory traces that can be performed by the program.

For example, assuming that v is a volatile memory location, x and y non-volatile locations, m a monitor, and r a thread-local register, the meaning of the program

```
v:=1; lock m; r:=x; y:=r; unlock m; print(r)
```

is the prefix closure of the set

---

[1] The JMM calls this connection intra-thread consistency.

$\{[\mathrm{St}, \mathrm{Wr}_v(v, 1), \mathrm{L}(m), \mathrm{Rd}(x, i), \mathrm{Wr}(y, i), \mathrm{U}(m), \mathrm{Ex}(i), \mathrm{Fin}] \mid i \text{ is a value}\}.$

All our transformations can be generalised as transformations on memory traces, and we will show this later in this paper when proving validity of some transformations (Subsect. 4.2 and App. B).

2.2 Transformations

In the following paragraphs we describe the transformations that we have considered in our analysis. Our transformations are local, i.e., they should be valid in any context.

Trace-preserving Transformations. Because the meaning of a program in the JMM is just the set of its traces, any transformation that does not change the set of traces must trivially be valid. E.g., if both branches of a conditional—whose guard does not examine memory—contain the same code, it is valid to eliminate the conditional, as illustrated by the transformation

```
if (r1==1)
     {x=1;y=1}              x=1
else {x=1;y=1}              y=1
```
$\rightleftarrows$

Reordering. Reordering of independent statements is an important transformation that swaps two consecutive non-synchronisation memory accesses. It is often performed in hardware [13,12,24], or in a compiler's loop optimiser [15,10]. The following program transformation shows a reordering of two independent writes.

```
x=1              y=1
y=1              x=1
```
$\longrightarrow$

Although Manson et al. claim this transformation to be valid in the JMM [18, Theorem 1], Cenciarelli et al. [9] found a counterexample to this. In earlier work [5], we suggested a simple fix and conjectured that it makes reordering of independent memory accesses valid. We state and prove this claim precisely in Subsect. 4.2 and App. B. Demonstrating a successful repair for this crucial property is one of the main contributions of this paper.

Redundant (Duplicated) Read Elimination. Elimination of a redundant read is a transformation that replaces a read immediately preceded by a read or a write to the same variable by the value of that read/write. This transformation is often performed as a part of common subexpression elimination optimisations in compilers. For example, the two examples of transformations below reuse the value of x stored in register r1 instead of re-reading x:

```
r1 = x            r1 = x            x = r1            x = r1
r2 = x            r2 = r1           r2 = x            r2 = r1
if (r1==r2)       if (r1==r2)       if (r1==r2)       if (r1==r2)
   y = 1             y = 1             y = 1             y = 1
     (read after read)                     (read after write)
```
$\longrightarrow$ $\longrightarrow$

Later we will show that redundant read elimination is valid in the JMM for a read after a write, but *invalid* for a read after a read.

Irrelevant Read Elimination. A read statement can also be removed if the value of the read is not used. For example, `r1=x;r1=1` can be replaced by `r1=1`, because the register `r1` is overwritten by the value 1 immediately after reading shared variable x, and thus the value read is irrelevant for the continuation for the program. An example of this transformation is dead code elimination because of dead variables. It is valid in the JMM.

Irrelevant Read Introduction. Irrelevant read introduction is the inverse transformation to the irrelevant read elimination. It might seem that this transformation is not an optimisation, but modern processor hardware often introduces irrelevant reads speculatively. For example, the first transformation in

```
if (r1==1) {        if (r1==1) {          r2=x
   r2=x                r2=x            ⇌ if (r1==1)
   y=r2       →        y=r2                 y=r2
}                   } else r2=x
```

introduces irrelevant read of x in the **else** branch of the conditional (assuming that r2 is not used in the rest of the program). In terms of traces, this is equivalent to reading x speculatively, as demonstrated by the program on the right. In Subsect. 4.1, we show that this is an *invalid* transformation in the JMM.

Redundant Write Elimination. This transformation eliminates a write in two cases: (i) if it follows a read of the same value, or (ii) if it precedes another write to the same variable. For example, in the first transformation in

```
r = x
if (r == 1)  ⟶   r = x          x = 1
   x = 1                         x = 3   ⟶   x = 3
(write after read)                 (write before write)
```

the write x=1 can be eliminated, because in all traces where the write occurs, it always follows a read of x with value 1. The other transformation shows the elimination of a previous overwritten write. This transformation is often included in peephole optimisations [4]. Similarly to the read elimination, it is valid in the JMM before a write, but *invalid* after a read.

Roach-motel Semantics. Intuitively, increasing synchronisation should limit a program's behaviours. In the limit, if a program is fully synchronised, i.e., data race free, the DRF guarantee promises only sequentially consistent behaviours. One way of increasing synchronisation is moving normal memory accesses into synchronised blocks, as in

```
x=1              lock m
lock m             x=1
  y=1      ⟶       y=1
unlock m         unlock m
```

Although compilers do not perform this transformation explicitly, it may be performed by underlying hardware if a synchronisation action uses only one memory fence to prevent the code inside a synchronised section from being reordered to outside of the section. Manson et al. [18, Theorem 1] claim that this transformation is valid. We show a counterexample to this in Subsect. 4.1, so unfortunately it is *invalid* in general.

Reordering with external actions. As well as reordering memory operations with one another, one may consider richer reorderings, for example, reordering memory operations with external operations. This seems more likely to alter the behaviour of a program, but it is valid for data race free programs under sequential consistency. For example, the exchange of printing a constant with a memory write: x=1;print 1 $\longrightarrow$ print 1;x=1. Theorem 1 of [18] incorrectly states that this transformation is valid in the JMM.

3   JMM Operationally

To reason about the Java Memory Model, we introduce an intuitive operational interpretation, based on some observations about the construction of the formal definition[2]. This re-interpretation will allow us to explain key counterexamples in a direct way in the next section. The formal definition of the memory model is used to argue about validity; our adjusted definition is given in detail App. A (the original is given in [11]).

Unlike interleaved semantics, the Java Memory Model has no explicit global ordering of all actions by time consistent with each thread's perception of time, and has no global store. Instead, executions are described in terms of memory related actions, partial orders on these actions, and a visibility function that assigns a write action to each read action. We first explain the building blocks of Java executions, then we show how Java builds *legal executions* out of simple "well-behaved" executions.

JMM actions and orders. An action is a tuple consisting of a *thread identifier*, an *action kind*, and a *unique identifier*. Action kinds were described in Sect. 2.1.

The volatile read/write and lock/unlock actions are called *synchronisation actions*. An *execution* consists of a *set of actions*, a *program order*, a *synchronisation order*, a *write-seen* function, and a *value-written* function. The program order ($\leq_{po}$) is a total order on the actions of each thread, but it does not relate actions of different threads. All synchronisation actions are totally ordered by the synchronisation order ($\leq_{so}$). From these two orders we construct a happens-before order of the execution: action a happens-before action b ($a \leq_{hb} b$) if (1) a synchronises-with b, i.e., $a \leq_{so} b$, a is an unlock of m and b is a lock of m, or a is a volatile write to v and b is a volatile read from v, or (2) $a \leq_{po} b$, or (3) there is an action c such that $a \leq_{hb} c \leq_{hb} b$. The happens-before order determines an

---

[2] Jeremy Manson made essentially the same observations in his description of his model checker for the JMM [17].

upper bound on the visibility of writes—a read happening before a write should never see that write, and a read r should not see a write w if there is another write happening "in-between", i.e., if $w \leq_{hb} w' \leq_{hb} r$ and $w \neq w'$, then r cannot see w.[3]

We say that an execution is *sequentially consistent* if there is a total order consistent with the program order, such that each read sees the most recent write to the same variable in that order. A pair of memory accesses to the same variable is called a *data race* if at least one of the accesses is a write and they are not ordered by the happens-before order. A program is *correctly synchronised* (or *data-race-free*) if no sequentially consistent execution contains a data race.

A thorny issue is initialisation of variables. The JMM says

The write of the default value (zero, false, or null) to each variable synchronises-with to the first action in every thread [11]

However, normal writes are not synchronisation actions and synchronises-with only relates synchronisation actions, so normal writes cannot synchronise-with any action. For this paper, we will assume that all default writes are executed in a special initialisation thread and the thread is finished before all other threads start.

Committing semantics. The basic building blocks are *well-behaved* executions, in which reads are only allowed to see writes that happen before them. In other words, in these executions reads cannot see writes through data races, and threads can only communicate through synchronisation. For example, programs A and C in Fig. 1 have just one such execution—the one, where $r1 = r2 = 0$. On the other hand, the behaviours of program B are exactly the behaviours that could be observed by the interleaved semantics, i.e. $r1 = r2 = 0$, or $r1 = 1$ and $r2 = 0$, or $r1 = 0$ and $r2 = 1$. In fact, if a program is correctly synchronised then its execution is well-behaved if and only if it is sequentially consistent [18, Lemma 2]. This does not hold for incorrectly synchronised programs (e.g., see the first counterexample in Subsect. 4.1).

The Java Memory Model starts from a well-behaved execution and *commits* one or more read-write data races from the well-behaved execution. After committing the actions involved in the data races it "restarts" the execution, but this time it must execute the committed actions. This means that each read in the execution must be either committed and see the value through the race, or it must see the write that happens-before it. Similarly, all committed writes must be executed in the restarted execution and must write the same value. The JMM can repeat the process, i.e., it may choose some non-committed reads involved in a data race, commit the writes involved in these data races if they are not committed already, commit the chosen reads, and restart the execution. The executions constructed using this procedure are called *legal executions*.

---

[3] For details, see Defs. 2, 4 and 7 in App. A.

The JMM imposes several requirements on the committing sequence:

1. All subsequent (restarted) executions must preserve happens-before ordering of all the committed actions. Cenciarelli et al. [9] observed that this requirement makes reordering of independent statements invalid. In our earlier work [5], we suggested that the happens-before ordering should be preserved only between a read and the write it sees. We showed there that this revision still satisfies the DRF guarantee; in this paper we further establish that validity of reordering is indeed rescued in this version.
2. If some synchronisation happens-before the committed data race(s), the synchronisation must be preserved in all subsequent executions[4].
3. All external actions that happen-before any committed action must be committed, as well.

This committing semantics imposes a causality order on races—the outcome of a race must be explained in terms of previously committed races. This prevents causality loops, where the outcome of a race depends on the outcome of the very same race, e.g., the outcome $r1 = 1$ in program C in Fig. 1. The DRF guarantee is a simple consequence of this procedure. If there are no data races in the program, there is nothing to commit, and we can only generate well-behaved executions, which are sequentially consistent for data race free programs.

In fact, the JMM, as defined in [11], actually commits all actions in an execution, but committing a read that sees a write that happens-before it does not create any opportunities for committing new races, because reads can see writes that happen-before them in a well-behaved execution. This is why we need to consider only read-write races and not write-write races. Similarly, committing synchronisation actions does not create any committing opportunities and can be always performed in the last step. Therefore, the central issue is committing read-write data races, and we explain our examples using this observation.

Example. An example should help make the operational interpretation clearer. First, we demonstrate the committing semantics on program A in Fig. 1. In the well-behaved execution of this program, illustrated by the first diagram in Fig. 2, the reads of x and y can only see the default writes of 0, because there is no synchronisation. This results in $r1 = r2 = 0$.

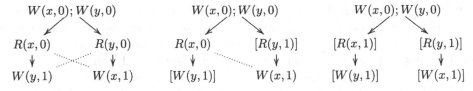

Fig. 2. Justifying executions of program A from Fig. 1

There are two data races in this execution (depicted by the dotted lines, the solid lines represent the happens-before order)—one on x and one on y. We can

---

[4] For a formal definition, see rule 8 in the list that follows Def. 8.

commit either one of the races or both of them. Suppose we commit the race on y. In the second diagram we show the only restarted execution that uses this data race; the committed actions are in brackets and the committed read sees the value of (the write in) the data race. The non-committed read sees the write that happens-before it, i.e., the default write. This execution gives the result r1 = 0 and r2 = 1. The JMM can again decide to commit a data race from the execution. There is only one such data race. Committing the data race on x gives the last diagram, and results in r1 = r2 = 1.

4   Validity of Transformations

This sections contains the technical explanations of validity and invalidity of the transformations. All invalidity arguments will be carried in the finite version[5] of the Java Memory Model as described in [11], but the same arguments apply to the alternative weaker memory model JMM-Alt. On the other hand, the validity argument will refer to the more permissive JMM-Alt. It is straightforward to simplify the argument to prove the valid transformations of the original JMM.

4.1   Invalid Transformations

In this subsection we show and explain our counterexamples for the invalid transformations. The examples follow the same pattern—at first we list a program where a certain behaviour is not possible in the JMM, and then we show that after the transformation the behaviour becomes possible (in the JMM). This shows that the transformation in question is invalid, because any run of the transformed program should be indistinguishable from some run of the original program. In the Java Memory Model, the behaviour of a program is essentially the set of external actions, such as printing, performed by the program[6]. In our examples, we will consider final contents of registers being part of the program's behaviour, because we could observe them by printing them at the end of each thread.

Redundant Write After Read Elimination

	initially x = 0	
lock m1	lock m2	lock m1
x=2	x=1	lock m2
unlock m1	unlock m2	r1=x
		x=r1
		r2=x
		unlock m2
		unlock m1

---

[5] We use the finite version, because the infinite JMM is inconsistent [5].

[6] The definition in [18] is slightly more complex because of non-terminating executions and ordering, see Def. 10 for details. Our examples are always terminating.

First note that no well-behaved execution of this program contains a read-write data race, so all legal executions of this program are well-behaved. Moreover, in all executions the read r2=x must see the write x=r1, because it overwrites any other write. As the write x=r1 always writes the value that is read by r1=x, we have that $r1 = r2$.

On the other hand, if a compiler removes the redundant write x=r1, the reads r1=x and r2=x can see different values in a well-behaved execution, e.g., we might get the outcome $r1 = 1$ and $r2 = 2$.

Redundant Read After Read Elimination. The counterexample for the elimination of a read after a read uses a trick with switching the branches of an if statement—in the first well-behaved execution we take one branch, and then we commit a data race so that we can take the other branch after we restart. Let us examine the program below.

x = y = 0

r1=x	r2=y
y=r1	if (r2==1) {
	r3=y
	x=r3
	} else x=1

The question is whether we can observe the result $r2 = 1$. This result is not possible in this program, but it becomes possible after rewriting r3=y to r3=r2.

First we show that this is not possible with the original program: With the initially empty commit set we can get just one well-behaved execution—the one, where $r1 = r2 = 0$. In this well-behaved execution, we have two data races: (i) between the actions preformed by y=r1 and r2=y with value 0, (ii) between the actions performed by r1=x and x=1 with value 1. If we commit (i), we are stuck with $r2 = 0$, because all subsequent restarted executions must perform the committed read of y with the value 0. If we commit (ii) and restart, we get an execution, where $r1 = 1$, so we can now commit the data race between y=r1 and r2=y with value 1. After we restart the execution, suppose we were to read $r1 = r2 = 1$. Then r3=y must read a value that happens-before it; the only such value is the default value 0, but then x=r3 must write 0, which contradicts the commitment to perform the write of 1 to x.

On the other hand, if JVM transforms the read r3=y into r3=r2, we can obtain the result $r2 = 1$ by committing the data race between r1=x and x=1, restarting, committing the data race between y=r1 and r2=y, and restarting again. As opposed to the original program, now we can keep the commitment to write 1 to x, because $r3 = r2 = 1$ in the transformed program.

Roach Motel Semantics. We demonstrate the invalidity of roach motel semantics on the program:

initially x = y = z = 0

lock m	lock m	r1=x	r3= y
x=2	x=1	lock m	z=r3
unlock m	unlock m	r2=z	
		if (r1==2)	
		y=1	
		else	
		y=r2	
		unlock m	

This program cannot result in r1 = r2 = r3 = 1 in the JMM: In all well-behaved executions of this program, we have r1 = r2 = r3 = 0, and four data races—two on x with values 1 and 2, then on y and z with value 0. If we commit the data race on y (resp. z, resp. x with value 2) we would be stuck with r3 = 0 (resp. r2 = 0, resp. r1 = 2), so we can only commit a race on x. However, if we commit the race with x=1 and restart, we are only left with races on z and y with value 0. Committing any of these races would result in r2 and r3 being 0.

However, after swapping r1=x and lock m the program offers more freedom to well-behaved executions, e.g., the read r1=x can see value 2 (without committing any action on x!), and we can commit the data race on y with value 1 (sec execution A from Fig. 3). After restarting, we can commit data race on z with value 1. After another restart, we change the synchronisation order so that the write x=1 overwrites the write x=2, and the read r1=x sees value 1 (see execution B from Fig. 3). In this execution, we have r1 = r2 = r3 = 1.

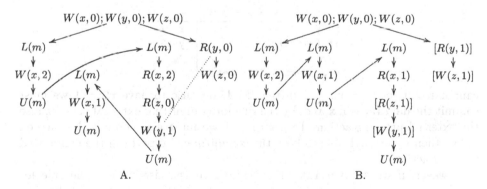

Fig. 3. Justifying and final executions for the roach motel semantics counterexample

Note that this committing sequence respects the rule that all the subsequent restarted executions must preserve synchronisation that was used to justify the previous data races, because our committing sequence only introduces new synchronisation that in effect overwrites the write x=2 with the write x=1. This problem seems to be hard to solve in a committing semantics based on well-behaved executions, because more synchronisation gives more freedom to well-behaved executions and allows more actions to be committed.

Irrelevant Read Introduction. The counterexample for irrelevant read introduction uses the trick with switching branches again. The program

```
              x = y = z = 0
r1 = z                    | x = 1
if (r1==0) {              | r2 = y
    r3 = x                | z = r2
    if (r3==1) y = 1      |
} else {                  |
    //r4 = x              |
    r4 = 1                |
    y = r1                |
}                         |
```

cannot result in $r1 = r2 = 1$: its only well-formed execution has data races on x with value 1 and z with value 0. We cannot commit the data race on z, because then r1 would remain 0. If we commit the data race on x and restart, we have a new data race between y=1 and r2=y. After committing it and restarting, we can try to commit the data race on z with value 1. However, after this commit and restart, we cannot fulfil the commitment to perform the data race on x.

On the other hand, if we introduce the irrelevant read r4=x by uncommenting the commented-out line, we can keep the commitment to perform the committed read on x, and the program can result in $r1 = r2 = 1$. This seems to be another deep problem with committing semantics—even introducing a benign irrelevant read may validate some committing sequence that was previously invalid.

Reordering with External Actions. The program

```
              x = y = 0
r1=y                      | r2=x
if (r1==1)                | y=r2
    x=1                   |
else {print "!"; x=1}     |
```

cannot result in $r1 = r2 = 1$ in the JMM, because to have $r2 = 1$ we must commit the data race on x and, by the rule for committing external actions, also the external printing action. To get $r1 = 1$ we must also commit the race on y, but then we are not able to keep the commitment to perform the committed printing action.

However, if we swap `print` "!" with x=1 in the else-branch, the rule for external actions does not apply, and we can commit the race on x, and then the race on y, resulting in $r1 = r2 = 1$.

4.2 Valid Transformations

In this subsection we outline the proof of the validity of irrelevant read elimination, read after write elimination, write after write elimination, and reordering of independent non-volatile memory accesses in the weaker memory model (JMM-Alt). Using the same method one could also prove that the first three of these transformations are valid in the standard JMM [11].

The validity of a transformation says that any behaviour of the transformed program is a behaviour of the original program. We prove the validity very directly—we take an execution of the transformed program that exhibits the behaviour in question, then we apply an 'inverse' transformation to the execution, and finally we show that the untransformed execution has the same behaviour as the one of the transformed program. Since the details of the proof are somewhat technical, we show a careful proof in App. B. In this section we only explain informally the main ideas, i.e., the construction of the inverse transformation, and the relationship between the transformations on programs and the memory traces. Note that our proof technique does not consider non-termination being a behaviour; we only prove safety of transformations. We leave the preservation of termination for future work.

The main idea of the proof is that we describe transformations using their 'inverse' transformations. We will say that P' is a transformation of P if for any trace $t' \in P'$ there is an *untransformation* in P. By the untransformation we mean a trace t of P together with an injective function f that describes a valid reordering of the actions of t'. Moreover, each action of t that is not in $\text{rng}(f)$ must be either (i) a redundant read after write, i.e., it must be a read of the same value as the last write to the same variable in the trace, and there cannot be any synchronisation or read from the same variable in between, or (ii) a redundant write before write, i.e., the write must precede another write to the same variable such that there is no read from the same location or synchronisation in between, or (iii) an irrelevant read, i.e., the value of the read cannot affect validity of the trace t in P. For formal details, see Def. 11. By induction on the operational execution of sequential programs, we can show that the program transformations on the syntax level implies the existence of an untransformed trace and an untransformation function for each trace of the transformed program.

For example, the program on the left in Fig. 4 can be transformed to the program on the right of the arrow, because for each trace of the transformed program there is its untransformation. For example, for the trace t' (on the right of Fig. 4) of the transformed program there is a trace t of the original program, and a function f that determines the reordering of the actions. Moreover, $\text{Wr}(x, 2)$ is a redundant write before write, $\text{Rd}(x, 2)$ is a redundant read after write, and $\text{Rd}(y, *)$ is an irrelevant read, i.e., t is a valid trace of P if we replace $*$ by any value.

Having this definition, the proof is technical, but straightforward—given an execution of the transformed program we construct an execution of the original program by untransforming the traces of all its threads, while preserving the synchronisation order (see the details in App. B). This is possible because the definition of program transformation preserves ordering of synchronisation actions, thus guaranteeing consistency of the program order with the synchronisation order.

We also observe that the untransformed execution is legal: if we take the committing sequence of data races and justifying executions, and untransform the justifying executions, we get a legal committing sequence for the untransformed program (Lemma 3). We conclude that any behaviour of the transformed program is a behaviour of the original program (Theorem 1).

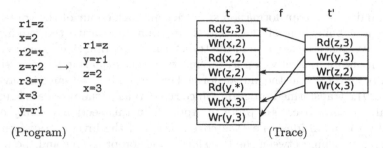

Fig. 4. Transformation of a program as a transformation on traces

5 Practical Impact

The flaw in the memory model is important in theory, but it is conceivable that it might not be manifested in practical implementations, because JVMs compile to stricter memory models than the JMM. It is natural to ask whether some widely used JVM actually implements optimisations that lead to forbidden behaviours. In fact, this is indeed the case! We have experimented with the Sun Hotspot JVM [19] to discover this. For example, the first program in Fig. 5 cannot print 1 under the JMM (for details, see the counterexample for redundant read after read elimination in Subsect. 4.1). A typical optimising compiler may reuse the value of y in r2 and transform x=(r2==1)?y:1 → x=(r2==1)?r2:1, which is equivalent to the second program from Fig. 5. Then it may reorder the write to x with read of y, yielding the last program in Fig. 5. Observe that this transformed program can print 1 using the interleaving x=1, r1=x, y=r1, r2:=y, print r2. After minor modifications to the program, Sun Hotspot JVMs will perform these transformations, so it does not comply with the JMM[7].

x = y = 0		x = y = 0		x = y = 0	
r1=x	r2=y	r1=x	**r2=y**	r1=x	x=1
y=r1	x=(r2==1)?y:1	y=r1	**x=1**	y=r1	**r2=y**
	print r2		print r2		print r2

Fig. 5. Hotspot JVM's transformations violating the JMM

The program in Fig. 5 is not data-race-free. Should we worry about behaviours of correctly synchronised programs after optimisations? We conjecture that any composition of the transformations from this paper applied to a correctly synchronised program can only yield a program that does not have any new behaviours. This means that Java implementations might be in fact correct, i.e., satisfy the DRF guarantee, and it is only the JMM specification that needs fixing.

---

[7] Tested on Java HotSpot(TM) Tiered VM (build 1.7.0-ea-fastdebug-b16-fastdebug, mixed mode), Linux x86. Further details are in a short technical report [25].

6   Conclusion

We have examined the most common software and hardware local program transformations and classified them by their validity in the Java Memory Model, and
its variation suggested by [5]. For each class of transformations we give either a
proof of its validity or a counterexample. Despite the JMM's main design goal
to enable common optimisations, we show that the JMM does not allow several
commonly used optimisations although some of these transformations are valid
under the natural strict memory model–sequential consistency. This is a serious
flaw in the Java Memory Model, which does not seem to have an easy fix, as
discussed in the explanations of the counterexamples (Subsect. 4.1).

Related Work. The computer architecture community has studied the problem
of weak memory models (MM) for a long time, for a detailed survey see [3,2].
However, the problems of MMs in programming languages seems to be more
complex [20]. Most of the work has focused on alternative definitions of memory
models and proving the guarantee of sequential consistency for data race free
programs [16,1,9,23]. E.g., Cenciarelli et al. [9] describe a subset of the JMM
using the theory of configuration structures. However, they do not attempt to
prove validity of compiler transformations or compliance with any hardware
memory model. Saraswat et al. [23] use denotations of commands as functions on
partial stores and transformations on them to describe a memory model for their
X10 language. Although their work is based on transformations of denotations, it
is hard to map their transformations to program transformations in a Java-like
language because they use a language with restricted control-flow constructs.
Moreover, both [9] and [23] use languages that do not have any general loops,
and we do not see any easy way of adding them. To our knowledge, the only
work dealing with a program transformation in a weak memory model is the
POPL paper about the JMM [18]. Our paper shows a corrected version of their
proof, together with counterexamples for cases that seem to be hard to fix.
Brookes [8] studied program transformations in interleaved semantics using a
trace semantics, but his technique uses traces of global states, which makes it
hard to use with weak memory models.

There is some previous work that points out defects in the current JMM.
While looking for an alternative description based on event structures, Cenciarelli et al. [9] observed that reordering of independent statements is an invalid
transformation. In our own previous work we found several minor flaws [5].

Future Work. Our main objective is to analyse the effects of the above transformations on programs. We conjecture that for data race free programs these
transformations cannot introduce new behaviours, and for programs with data
races they satisfy some form of out-of-thin-air guarantees. To analyse the transformations we intend to continue using the trace semantics, and employ ideas
from the trace semantics literature on shared memory and concurrency [7,22,14].
We believe that the JMM ought to be revised to admit all the transformations
considered in this paper.

Acknowledgements

The authors enjoyed discussions on some of the examples in this paper with P. Cenciarelli, M. Huisman, and G. Petri. We would especially like to thank G. Petri, who supplied a simpler counterexample for the read after read elimination transformation, and checked our counterexamples. The first author is supported by a PhD studentship awarded by the UK EPSRC, grant EP/C537068. Both authors also acknowledge the support of the EU project MOBIUS (IST-15905). Some of the content of this paper was first presented at the VAMP'2007 workshop [6].

References

1. Adve, S.: The SC- memory model for Java (2004), http://www.cs.uiuc. edu/~sadve/jmm
2. Adve, S.V., Aggarwal, J.K.: A unified formalization of four shared-memory models. IEEE Trans. Parallel Distrib. Syst. 4(6), 613–624 (1993)
3. Adve, S.V., Gharachorloo, K.: Shared memory consistency models: A tutorial. Computer 29(12), 66–76 (1996)
4. Aho, A.V., Sethi, R., Ullman, J.D.: Compilers: principles, techniques, and tools. Addison-Wesley Longman Publishing Co., Inc, Boston (1986)
5. Aspinall, D., Ševčík, J.: Formalising Java's data race free guarantee. In: Schneider, K., Brandt, J. (eds.) TPHOLs 2007. LNCS, vol. 4732, pp. 22–37. Springer, Heidelberg (2007)
6. Aspinall, D., Ševčík, J.: Java memory model examples: Good, bad and ugly. Technical Report EDI-INF-RR-1121, School of Informatics, University of Edinburgh (2007)
7. Brookes, S.: A semantics for concurrent separation logic. Theor. Comput. Sci. 375(1-3), 227–270 (2007)
8. Brookes, S.D.: Full abstraction for a shared variable parallel language. In: LICS, pp. 98–109. IEEE Computer Society, Los Alamitos (1993)
9. Cenciarelli, P., Knapp, A., Sibilio, E.: The Java memory model: Operationally, denotationally, axiomatically. In: De Nicola, R. (ed.) ESOP 2007. LNCS, vol. 4421. Springer, Heidelberg (2007)
10. Click, C.: Global code motion/global value numbering. SIGPLAN Not. 30(6), 246–257 (1995)
11. Gosling, J., Joy, B., Steele, G., Bracha, G.: Java(TM) Language Specification. In: Threads and Locks, 3rd edn. Java Series, pp. 557–573. Addison-Wesley Professional, Reading (2005)
12. Intel. A formal specification of Intel Itanium processor family memory ordering (2002), http://www.intel.com/design/itanium/downloads/251429.htm
13. Intel. Intel 64 architecture memory ordering white paper (2007), http://www. intel.com/products/processor/manuals/318147.pdf
14. Jeffrey, A., Rathke, J.: A fully abstract may testing semantics for concurrent objects. Theor. Comput. Sci. 338(1-3), 17–63 (2005)
15. Kennedy, K., Allen, J.R.: Optimizing compilers for modern architectures: a dependence-based approach. Morgan Kaufmann Publishers Inc., San Francisco (2002)

16. Maessen, J.-W., Shen, X.: Improving the Java memory model using CRF. In: OOP-SLA, pp. 1–12. ACM Press, New York (2000)
17. Manson, J.: The Java memory model. PhD thesis, University of Maryland, College Park (2004)
18. Manson, J., Pugh, W., Adve, S.V.: The Java memory model. In: POPL 2005: Proceedings of the 32nd ACM SIGPLAN-SIGACT symposium on Principles of Programming Languages, pp. 378–391. ACM Press, New York (2005)
19. Paleczny, M., Vick, C., Click, C.: The Java Hotspot(TM) server compiler. In: USENIX Java(TM) Virtual Machine Research and Technology Symposium (April 2001)
20. Pugh, W.: The Java memory model is fatally flawed. Concurrency - Practice and Experience 12(6), 445–455 (2000)
21. Pugh, W., Manson, J.: Java memory model causality test cases (2004), http://www.cs.umd.edu/~pugh/java/memoryModel/CausalityTestCases.html
22. Reynolds, J.C.: Toward a grainless semantics for shared-variable concurrency. In: Lodaya, K., Mahajan, M. (eds.) FSTTCS 2004. LNCS, vol. 3328, pp. 35–48. Springer, Heidelberg (2004)
23. Saraswat, V., Jagadeesan, R., Michael, M., von Praun, C.: A theory of memory models. In: ACM 2007 SIGPLAN Conference on Principles and Practice of Parallel Computing. ACM Press, New York (2007)
24. Sparc International. Sparc architecture manual, version 9 (2000), http://developers.sun.com/solaris/articles/sparcv9.html
25. Ševčík, J.: The Sun Hotspot JVM does not conform with the Java memory model. Technical Report EDI-INF-RR-1252, School of Informatics, University of Edinburgh (2008)

A   JMM Definitions

The following definitions are mostly from [11,18]; however, we have weakened the definition of execution legality as suggested in [5]. We use letters θ for thread names, m for synchronisation monitor names, and v for variables (i.e., memory locations, in examples, x, y, v etc.). The abstract type $\mathcal{V}$ will denote values.

The starting point is the notion of *action*.

Definition 1. *An action is a memory-related operation; it is modelled by an abstract type $\mathcal{A}$ with the following properties: (1) Each action belongs to one thread, we will denote it by $T(a)$. (2) An action is one of the following action kinds:*

- volatile read *of v,*   - normal write *to v,*   - thread start,
- volatile write *to v,*   - lock *on m,*   - thread finish,
- normal read *from v,*   - unlock *on m,*   - external action.

We denote the action kind of a by $K(a)$, the action kinds will be abbreviated to $\text{Rd}_v(v)$, $\text{Wr}_v(v)$, $\text{Rd}(v)$, $\text{Wr}(v)$, $\text{L}(m)$, $\text{U}(m)$, St, Fin, Ex. An action kind also includes the associated variable or monitor. The volatile read, volatile write, lock, unlock, start, finish actions are called synchronisation actions.

The JMM also defines thread spawn and join action kinds. We omit these for simplicity.

Definition 2. *An* execution *E is a tuple $E = \langle A, P, \leq_{po}, \leq_{so}, W, V \rangle$, where $A \subseteq \mathcal{A}$ is a set of actions; P is a program, represented as a thread-indexed set of memory traces; the partial order $\leq_{po} \subseteq A \times A$ is the program order, which is a union of total orders on actions of each thread; $\leq_{so} \subseteq A \times A$ is the synchronisation order, which is a total order on all synchronisation actions in A; $V :: \mathcal{A} \Rightarrow \mathcal{V}$ is a value-written function that assigns a value to each write from A; $W :: \mathcal{A} \Rightarrow \mathcal{A}$ is a write-seen function that assigns a write to each read action from A, the $W(r)$ denotes the write seen by r, i.e. the value read by r is $V(W(r))$.*

Definition 3. *In an execution with synchronisation order $\leq_{so}$, an action a synchronises-with an action b (written $a <_{sw} b$) if $a \leq_{so} b$ and a and b satisfy one of the following conditions:*

  − *a is an unlock on monitor m and b is a lock on monitor m,*
  − *a is a volatile write to v and b is a volatile read from v.*

Definition 4. *The* happens-before *order of an execution is the transitive closure of the composition of its synchronises-with order and its program order, i.e. $\leq_{hb} = (<_{sw} \cup \leq_{po})^+$.*

To relate a (sequential) program to a sequence of actions performed by one thread we must define a notion of *sequential validity*. We consider single-thread programs as sets of sequences of pairs of an action kind and a value, which we call *traces*. A multi-thread program is a set of single-thread programs indexed by thread identifiers.

Definition 5. *Given an execution $E = \langle A, P, \leq_{po}, \leq_{so}, W, V \rangle$, the* action trace *of thread θ in E, denoted $\overline{\mathrm{Tr}}_E(\theta)$, is the list of actions of thread θ in the order $\leq_{po}$. The* trace *of thread θ in E, written $\mathrm{Tr}_E(\theta)$ is the list of action kinds and corresponding values obtained from the action trace (i.e., $V(W(a))$ if a is a read, $V(a)$ otherwise).*

By writing $t \leq t'$ we mean that t is a prefix of t', $set(t)$ is the set of elements of the list t, $\iota(t, a)$ is an index i such that $t_i = a$, or 0 if $a \notin set(t)$. For an action kind-value pair $p = \langle k, v \rangle$ we will use the notation $\pi_K(p)$ for the action kind k and $\pi_V(p)$ for the value v. We say that a sequence s of action kind-value pairs is *sequentially valid* with respect to a program P if $t \in P$. A sequentially valid trace t is *finished* for P if there is no sequentially valid trace $t' > t$. The operator $+\!\!\!+$ stands for trace concatenation.

   To establish reasonable properties of concurrent programs we assume reasonable properties of the underlying sequential language:

Definition 6. *We say that program P is* well-formed *if sequential validity of trace t in P implies:*

  1. *any trace $t' \leq t$ is sequentially valid (prefix closedness),*
  2. *if the last action of t is a read with value v, then the trace obtained from t by replacing the value in the last action by v' is also sequentially valid in P (final read value independence),*

3. $|t| > 0$ *implies* $\pi_K(()t_0) = \text{St}$ *(start action first)*,
4. $\pi_K(()t_i) = \text{Fin}$ *implies* $i = |t| - 1$ *(finish action last)*.
5. $\theta = \theta_{init}$ *implies* $\forall i.\ 1 \leq i < |t| - 1 \rightarrow \exists v.\ \pi_K(()t_i) = \text{Wr}(v) \vee \pi_K(()t_i) = \text{Wr}_v(v)$ *and* $\pi_K(()t_{|t|-1}) = \text{Fin}$ *(initialisation thread only contains writes)*.

The well-formedness of programs should not be hard to establish for any reasonable sequential language.

The next definition places some sensible restriction on executions.

Definition 7. *We say that an* execution $\langle A, P, \leq_{po}, \leq_{so}, W, V \rangle$ *is well-formed if*

1. *A is finite.*
2. $\leq_{po}$ *restricted on actions of one thread is a total order,* $\leq_{po}$ *does not relate actions of different threads.*
3. $\leq_{so}$ *is total on synchronisation actions of A.*
4. $\leq_{so}$ *is consistent with* $\leq_{po}$.
5. *W is properly typed: for every non-volatile read* $r \in A$, $W(r)$ *is a non-volatile write; for every volatile read* $r \in A$, $W(r)$ *is a volatile write.*
6. *Locking is proper: for all lock actions* $l \in A$ *on monitors m and all threads* θ *different from the thread of l, the number of locks in* θ *before l in* $\leq_{so}$ *is the same as the number of unlocks in* θ *before l in* $\leq_{so}$.
7. *Program order is intra-thread consistent: for each thread* θ, *the trace of* θ *in E is sequentially valid for* P_θ.
8. $\leq_{so}$ *is consistent with W: for every volatile read r of a variable v we have* $W(r) \leq_{so} r$ *and for any volatile write w to v, either* $w \leq_{so} W(r)$ *or* $r \leq_{so} w$.
9. $\leq_{hb}$ *is consistent with W: for all reads r of v it holds that* $r \not\leq_{hb} W(r)$ *and there is no intervening write w to v, i.e. if* $W(r) \leq_{hb} w \leq_{hb} r$ *and w writes to v then* $W(r) = w$.
10. *The initialisation thread* θ_{init} *finishes before any other thread starts, i.e.,* $\forall a, b \in A.\ K(a) = \text{Fin} \wedge T(a) = \theta_{init} \wedge K(b) = \text{St} \wedge T(b) \neq \theta_{init} \rightarrow a \leq_{so} b$.

The following definition of *legal execution* constitutes the core of the Java Memory Model. In our work, we use a weakened version of the memory model that we suggested in [5] and which permits more transformations than the original version. In Tbl. 1, we label this version by 'JMM-Alt'.

Definition 8. *A well-formed execution* $\langle A, P, \leq_{po}, \leq_{so}, W, V \rangle$ *with happens before order* $\leq_{hb}$ *is legal if there is a finite sequence of sets of actions* C_i *and well-formed executions* $E_i = \langle A_i, P, \leq_{po_i}, \leq_{so_i}, W_i, V_i \rangle$ *with happens-before* $\leq_{hb_i}$ *and synchronises-with* $<_{sw_i}$ *such that* $C_0 = \emptyset$, $C_{i-1} \subseteq C_i$ *for all* $i > 0$, $\bigcup C_i = A$, *and for each* $i > 0$ *the following rules are satisfied:*

1. $C_i \subseteq A_i$.
2. *For all reads* $r \in C_i$ *we have* $W(r) \leq_{hb} r \iff W(r) \leq_{hb_i} r$, *and* $r \not\leq_{hb_i} W(r)$,
3. $V_i|_{C_i} = V|_{C_i}$.
4. $W_i|_{C_{i-1}} = W|_{C_{i-1}}$.

5. *For all reads $r \in A_i - C_{i-1}$ we have $W_i(r) \leq_{hb_i} r$.*
6. *For all reads $r \in C_i - C_{i-1}$ we have $W(r) \in C_{i-1}$.*
7. *If $y \in C_i$ is an external action and $x \leq_{hb} y$ then $x \in C_i$.*

The original definition of legality from [11,18] differs in rules 2 and 6, and adds rule 8:

2. $\leq_{hb_i} |_{C_i} = \leq_{hb} |_{C_i}$.
6. For all reads $r \in C_i - C_{i-1}$ we have $W(r) \in C_{i-1}$ and $W_i(r) \in C_{i-1}$.
8. If $x <_{ssw_i} y \leq_{hb_i} z$ and $z \in C_i - C_{i-1}$, then $x <_{sw_j} y$ for all $j \geq i$, where $<_{ssw_i}$ is the transitive reduction of $\leq_{hb_i}$ without any $\leq_{po_i}$ edges, and the transitive reduction of $\leq_{hb_i}$ is a minimum relation such that its transitive closure is $\leq_{hb_i}$.

The reasons for weakening the rules are invalidity of reordering of independent statements, broken JMM causality tests 17–20 [21], and redundancy. For details, see [5,6].

For reasoning about validity of reordering, we define observable behaviours of executions and programs. Intuitively, a program P has an observable behaviour B if B is a subset of external actions of some execution of P, and B is downward closed on happens-before order (restricted to external actions). The JMM captures non-termination as a behaviour in the definition of allowable behaviours.

Definition 9. *An execution $\langle A, P, \leq_{po}, \leq_{so}, W, V \rangle$ with happens-before order $\leq_{hb}$ has a set of observable behaviours O if for all $x \in O$ we have $y \leq_{hb} x$ or $y \leq_{so} x$ implies $y \in O$ or $T(y) = \theta_{init}$. Moreover, there is no $x \in O$ such that $T(x) = \theta_{init}$.*

The allowable behaviours may contain a special external *hang* action if the execution does not terminate. We will use the notation $\mathrm{Ext}(A))$ for all external actions of set A, i.e., $\mathrm{Ext}(A) = \{a \mid K(a) = \mathrm{Ex}\}$.

Definition 10. *A finite set of actions B is an allowable behaviour of a program P if either*

- *There is a legal execution E of P with a set of observable behaviours O such that $B = \mathrm{Ext}(O)$, or $B = \mathrm{Ext}(O) \cup \{hang\}$ and E is hung.*
- *There is a set O such that $B = \mathrm{Ext}(O) \cup \{hang\}$, and for all $n \geq |O|$ there must be a legal execution E of P with set of actions A, and a set of actions O' such that (i) O and O' are observable behaviours of E, (ii) $O \subseteq O' \subseteq A$, (iii) $n \leq |O'|$, and (iv) $\mathrm{Ext}(O') = \mathrm{Ext}(O)$.*

B   Proof

We prove validity of irrelevant read elimination, elimination of redundant write before write, elimination of redundant read after write, and reordering of non-volatile memory accesses to different variables.

The plan of the proof is straightforward—for any behaviour B of a transformed program P' we need to show that the original program P had the same behaviour. Given a legal execution E' of P' with behaviour B we build a legal execution of P with (almost) the same behaviour. Using this construction, we will prove that transformations do not introduce new allowable behaviours (Def. 10), except hanging. The issues with hanging are tricky—its definition does not correspond with the committing semantics.

Effects of Transformations on Traces. First, we define the notion of transformed program loosely enough so that redundant read/write elimination, irrelevant read elimination and reordering fit our definition. The idea is that for any trace of the transformed program there should be a trace of the original program that is just reordered with the redundant and irrelevant operations added.

To describe the effects of irrelevant read elimination formally we define *wildcard traces* that may contain star $*$ symbols instead of some values. For example, sequence $[\langle \mathrm{Wr}(x), 2 \rangle, \langle \mathrm{Rd}(y), * \rangle, \langle \mathrm{Rd}(x), 3 \rangle]$ is a wildcard trace. If $\hat{t}$ is a wildcard trace, then $[\![\hat{t}]\!]$ stands for a family of all (normal) traces with the $*$ symbols replaced by some values.

Given a wildcard trace $\hat{t}$, we say its ith component $\hat{t}_i = \langle a, v \rangle$ is

- *irrelevant read* if a is a read and v is the wildcard symbol $*$,
- *redundant read* if a is a read of some x and the most recent access of x is a write of the same value, and there is no synchronisation or external action in between; formally, there must be $j < i$ such that $\hat{t}_j = \langle \mathrm{Wr}(x), v \rangle$ and for each k such that $j < k < i$ it must be that $\hat{t}_k = \langle \mathrm{Wr}(y), v' \rangle$ or $\hat{t}_k = \langle \mathrm{Rd}(y), v' \rangle$ for some $y \neq x$ and some v',
- *redundant write* if a is a write to some x and one of these two cases holds: (i) the write is overwritten by a subsequent write to the same variable and there are no synchronisation or external actions, and no read of x in between, or (ii) $\hat{t}_i$ is the last access of the variable in the trace and there are no synchronisation or external actions in the rest of the trace.

Definition 11. *We will say that P' is a* transformed program *from P if for any trace t' in P' there is a wildcard trace $\hat{t}$ and a function $f :: \{0, \ldots, |t'| - 1\} \to \{0, \ldots, |\hat{t}| - 1\}$ such that:*

1. *all traces in $[\![\hat{t}]\!]$ are sequentially valid in P.*
2. *if t' is finished in P' then all traces in $[\![\hat{t}]\!]$ are finished in P,*
3. *function f is injective,*
4. *the action kind-value pair t'_i is equal to $\hat{t}_{f(i)}$,*
5. *for $0 \leq i \leq j < |t'|$ we have that $f(i) \leq f(j)$ if any of the following reordering restrictions holds:*
   (a) t'_i or t'_j is a synchronisation or external actions, or
   (b) t'_i and t'_j are conflicting memory accesses, i.e., accesses to the same variables such that at least one is a write,
6. *if there is an index $j < |\hat{t}|$ such that $f(i) \neq j$ for any i, then $\hat{t}_j$ must be a redundant read, a redundant write, or an irrelevant read.*

A multi-thread program P' is a transformed program of P if all single-thread programs of P' are transformed programs of single-thread programs of P with the same index. For space reasons we omit the link between the concrete syntax and the meaning in terms of traces. It is straightforward to establish by induction on derivation in operational semantics that if we obtain a program P' from a program P by a memory trace preserving transformation, or by an elimination of a redundant read after write, or by an elimination of a redundant write before write, or by an elimination of an irrelevant read, or by reordering of independent non-volatile memory accesses, then the set of traces of P' is a transformed program from the set of traces of P. The only non-trivial part is proving that reordering of independent non-volatile memory accesses on source level corresponds to a trace transformation if the trace of the transformed program ends in between the reordered statements. In this case we can consider the missing part of the statement as being eliminated (either as a redundant write or an irrelevant read), and finish the proof.

Transforming Executions. Let P' be a program transformed from P, and $E' = \langle A', P', \leq'_{po}, \leq'_{so}, W', V' \rangle$ be a legal execution of P'. Our goal is to construct a legal execution E of P with the following properties with the same observable behaviours.

The main idea of the construction is to take the memory trace of each thread in E' and use Def. 11 to obtain a trace of P, and mapping of actions and program order of E' to actions and program order of our newly constructed execution. We will also need to restore actions that were eliminated by the transformation and construct the visibility functions W and V for the reconstructed actions.

Given an execution $E' = \langle A', P', \leq'_{po}, \leq'_{so}, W', V' \rangle$ we construct *untransformed execution* E of P: for each thread $\theta \neq \theta_{init}$ let $\mathrm{Tr}_{E'}(\theta)$ be the trace of θ in E'. By the definition of transformed program (Def. 11), there must be a wildcard trace of P, let's denote it by $\hat{t}^\theta$ and corresponding transformation function f_θ.

For the initialisation thread θ_{init} we define

$$\hat{t}^{\theta_{init}} = [\langle \mathrm{St}, 0 \rangle] + \mathrm{Tr}_{E'}(\theta_{init})|_W + \mathrm{Init}_E + [\langle \mathrm{Fin}, 0 \rangle],$$

where $\mathrm{Tr}_{E'}(\theta_{init})|_W$ is the trace of the initialisation thread of E' restricted to (possibly volatile) write actions, and Init_E is any sequence of initialisation writes for all variables that appear in any component of $\hat{t}_\theta$ ($\theta \neq \theta_{init}$), but are not initialised in E'. We set $f_{\theta_{init}}(i) = i$ if $0 \leq i < |\mathrm{Tr}_{E'}(\theta_{init})| - 1$, and $f_{\theta_{init}}(|\mathrm{Tr}_{E'}(\theta_{init})| - 1) = |\hat{t}^{\theta_{init}}| - 1$.

From the traces $\hat{t}^\theta$ we build action traces t^θ of the same length. For $0 \leq i < |\hat{t}^\theta|$, we set the i-th component of t^θ to be

- $f_\theta^{-1}(i)$-th element of $\mathrm{Tr}_{E'}(\theta)$ if $f_\theta^{-1}(i)$ exists, or
- fresh action a such that $K(a) = \hat{t}_i^\theta$ and $T(a) = \theta$, if there is no j such that $i = f_\theta(j)$.

We use the action traces t^θ to construct our *untransformed* execution $E = \langle A, P, \leq_{po}, \leq_{so}, W, V \rangle$:

1. $A = \{t_i^\theta \mid 0 \le i < |\hat{t}^\theta|\}$,
2. order $\le_{po}$ is the order induced by the traces t^θ, i.e.

$$\le_{po} = \{(a,b) \mid T(a) = T(b) \wedge \iota(t^{T(a)}, a) \le \iota(t^{T(a)}, b)\}$$

3. order $\le_{so}$ is equal to $\le'_{so}$,
4. the write-seen function $W(a)$ is
   - $W'(a)$ if $a \in A'$,
   - most recent write[8] to x in $\le_{hb}$ if $a \notin A'$ and a is a read from x,
   - a otherwise, i.e., if a is not a read,
5. $V(a)$ is the corresponding value in the wildcard trace $\hat{t}^\theta$, i.e., $V(a) = \pi_V(\hat{t}^{T(a)}_{\iota(t^{T(a)},a)})$.

Lemma 1. *Let P' be a transformation of P, E' be a well-formed execution of P' with happens-before order $\le'_{hb}$ and E be the untransformed execution of P with happens-before order $\le_{hb}$. Let x and y be two actions from E' such that any of them is synchronisation action, or they are conflicting memory accesses[9], or $T(x) \ne T(y)$. Then $x \le_{hb} y$ if and only if $x \le'_{hb} y$.*

Proof. Observe that by point 3 of Def. 11 we have $x \le_{po} y$ iff $x \le'_{po} y$ for all x and y from E' such that x or y is a synchronisation or external action, or x and y are conflicting memory accesses. By induction on the transitive closure definition of $\le_{hb}$ we get that for any $z \le_{hb} y$ either $z \le_{po} y$ or there is a synchronisation action s such that $z \le_{po} s \le'_{hb} y$. With the observation above we conclude that $x \le_{hb} y$ implies $x \le'_{hb} y$ if x is in E' and x or y is a synchronisation action, or x and y are conflicting memory accesses, or $T(a) \ne T(b)$. On the other hand, we prove that $z \le'_{hb} x$ implies that either $z \le'_{po} x$ or there is a synchronisation action s such that $z \le'_{po} s \le_{hb} x$ by induction on the definition of $\le'_{hb}$. This implies the other direction of the equivalence.

Lemma 2. *Let P' be a transformation of P, E' be a well-formed execution of P' and E be the untransformed execution of P. Then E is a well-formed execution of P.*

Proof. Properties 1–8 and 10 of well-formedness (Def. 7) are satisfied directly by our construction. We prove property 9, the hb-consistency, i.e., that for all reads in E, $r \not\le_{hb} W(r)$ and there is no write w to the same variable as $W(r)$ such that $W(r) <_{hb} w \le_{hb} r$. There are two cases: (i) for r being an irrelevant read or a redundant read the hb-consistency is satisfied trivially by construction, (ii) for $r \in E'$, we get the result using hb-consistency of E' and Lemma 1.

Lemma 3. *Let P' be a transformation of P, E' be a legal execution of P' and E be the untransformed execution of P. Then E is a legal execution of P.*

---

[8] Note that the initialisation writes in thread θ_{init} happen-before any read action, so a most recent write always exists.

[9] I.e. a read and a write to the same variable, or two writes to the same variable.

Proof. Let $\{C_i\}_{i=0}^n$ be a sequence of committing sets and $\{E_i'\}_{i=0}^n$ the corresponding justifying executions for E'. Let E_i be the untransformed executions of E_i'. Let's define C_{n+1} as the set of actions of E and $E_{n+1} = E$. Then it is straightforward to show that the committing sequence $\{C_i\}_{i=0}^{n+1}$ with justifying executions $\{E_i\}_{i=0}^{n+1}$ satisfies the conditions (1), (3), (4) and (6) of Def. 8. To establish rules (2), (5) and (7) we use Lemma 1 and legality of E'.

In the following we will write $C_{\leq_{so},\leq_{po}}(X)$ to denote $\leq_{so}$ and $\leq_{po}$ downward closure of X without the initialisation actions, i.e.

$$C_{\leq_{so},\leq_{po}}(X) = \{y \mid \exists x \in X.\ y \leq_{po\cup so} x \wedge T(y) \neq \theta_{init}\},$$

where $\leq_{po\cup so} = (\leq_{po} \cup \leq_{so})^+$. We will often use $C_E(X)$ for $C_{\leq_{so},\leq_{hb}}(X)$, where E has synchronisation order $\leq_{so}$ and happens-before order $\leq_{hb}$. The set $C_E(X)$ is an observable behaviour of execution E with actions A for any $X \subseteq A$.

Lemma 4. *Let P' be a transformation of P, E' be a legal execution of P' with observable behaviour O', and E be the untransformed execution of P. Then $\mathrm{Ext}(C_E(O')) = \mathrm{Ext}(O')$.*

Proof. The direction $\supseteq$ is trivial, because $\mathrm{Ext}(-)$ is monotone and $C_E(O') \supseteq O'$.

On the other hand, if an external action $x \leq_{po\cup so} y \in O'$, then for any $z \leq_{po\cup so} y$ there is s such that $z \leq_{po} s \leq_{po\cup so}' y$ by induction on the transitive definition of $\leq_{po\cup so}$. By Lemma 1 we get $x \leq_{po\cup so}' y$, thus $x \in O'$.

The main theorem says that transforming a program using Def. 11 cannot introduce any new behaviour, except hanging.

Theorem 1. *Let P' be a program transformed from P. If B is an allowable behaviour of P' then $B \setminus \{hang\}$ is an allowable behaviour of P.*

Proof. By Def. 10, there must an execution E' of P' with observable behaviour O' such that $B = \mathrm{Ext}(O')$ or $B = \mathrm{Ext}(O') \cup \{hang\}$.

Let's take an untransformation E of E' and let $O = C_E(O')$. Using Lemma 4, we have $\mathrm{Ext}(O) = \mathrm{Ext}(O')$. Since O is an observable behaviour of E and E is a legal execution of P (Lemma 3), the set $B \setminus \{hang\} = \mathrm{Ext}(O)$ is an allowable behaviour of P.

Safe Cross-Language Inheritance

Kathryn E. Gray

Computer Laboratory, University of Cambridge, UK
kathryn.gray@cl.cam.ac.uk

Abstract. Inheritance is a standard means for reuse and for interfacing
with external libraries. In a multi-language software product, extending a class written in a statically-typed language with a dynamically-
typed class can require a significant number of manual indirections and
other error-prone complications. Building on our previous interoperability work, we introduce a technique that allows safe, easy inheritance
across languages. We demonstrate our technique for cross-language inheritance with a statically-typed object calculus and a dynamically-typed
object calculus, where a statically-typed class can extend a dynamically-
typed one and vice versa. We provide a proof sketch of soundness, as well
as a guarantee that dynamic type errors do not arise due to statically-
typed expressions.

1 Crossing Language Boundaries

Object-oriented libraries often require that clients extend a class. For a multi-
language product, extending the proper class may require developing a super-
fluous bridge between two languages with manual data marshaling, dispatching, and dynamic type-checking. Providing access to useful libraries can lead
to language developers manually building these bridges for each relevant class
(MrEd [1], Groovy [2], etc.), developing reflective APIs (MLj, Jython, JScheme,
Bigloo, etc.), or using an external tool. All of these techniques add complexity to developing programs in multiple languages and allow conversion/checking
omissions that violate language safety and cause obscure runtime errors.

In our previous work, Java+dynamic [3], we demonstrated a compiler technique for automatically inserting dynamic checks and data conversions in programs that connect two languages, namely Java and PLT Scheme. Runtime
type-errors report which value failed to match a required type specification and
blame the origin of this value for the program fault. The programmer should
expect a Scheme value, never a Java value, to be blamed for any dynamic type
fault. However, inheritance of a Java class from Scheme performed no data conversions and caused misallocated blame, and inheritance of a Scheme class from
Java carried the same problems while requiring an external type specification.

We expand our support for interoperability by modifying the dynamic dispatch mechanism of a class so that cross-language inheritance automatically
performs conversions and cannot result in dynamic type errors within typed ancestors or descendants. We present this in terms of a combined calculus, with

J. Vitek (Ed.): ECOOP 2008, LNCS 5142, pp. 52–75, 2008.

```
class Wizard extends Character {

  dynamic spellbook;

  Action response() {
    dynamic plan = scheme.control.analyze(items ...); ...
    if (plan.fire())
      return spellbook.invoke("fire");
    ...
  }
  Stat[] getStats(boolean current) { ... }
}
```

```
(module control
 (define (analyze items opponent partners)
   (send opponent get-stats #t) ... ))
```

Fig. 1. A partial Java+dynamic and PLT Scheme program

typed classes, untyped classes, and untyped functions. Our calculus also models the interoperability support from our previous implementation. We show the full model sound and we further show that dynamic type errors only arise from dynamic expressions, building on the work of Tobin-Hochstadt [4] and Wadler [5] and their proofs of blame assignment for functional language combinations.

1.1 Interoperability Background: Java+dynamic

Our Java+dynamic language extension allows programs to mix Scheme modules and Java classes without concern for data representations or dynamic checks. The extension allows Java programmers to import Scheme values and store them locally; it also allows Scheme programmers to interact with Java objects.

Our Java compiler automatically detects Java expressions that use Scheme values and annotates the program with conversions and dynamic checks based on the local context. An example program appears in Fig. 1 where a Java game framework interfaces with a Scheme agent.

The `Wizard` class imports function values from the `control` module using a 'scheme.' naming convention; this prefix directs the compiler to extract values from Scheme modules instead of Java packages. Since values exported from Scheme modules do not provide type information (and may not have valid Java types), Java+dynamic uses a **dynamic** keyword in place of a type specification for references to Scheme values. Java values may also be assigned to these variables, hiding their static type information.

During compilation, each use of `plan`, `spellbook`, or `analyze` is annotated with type expectations to be checked at runtime. The value returned from `plan.fire()` must be a (conversion of a) Java boolean value or violate Java's type safety. Therefore, the compiler inserts a runtime check (and data conversion) around this expression that isolates the point of failure if an incompatible value is produced. Similarly, the value returned by **response** must behave in all circumstances as an instance of the **Action** class; the compiler inserts another check and a conversion that contains the **Action** type signature. Failure to adhere to these type expectations causes an exception that reports a faulty value and the source location where the conversion was introduced; this informs programmers that the error lies at the language boundary and not within the typed portion of the program.

Within the **control** module, the **analyze** function invokes a method of the **opponent** parameter using **send** and provides (a Scheme representation of) a boolean. In our example, this object is an instance of a Java class, and its methods do not expect the Scheme representations of values. We cannot statically determine whether a Scheme program respects the Java type requirements and data expectations, nor should we expect Scheme programmers to perform necessary conversions that tie functions to Java. Therefore, our compiler inserts conversions for Java values used in dynamically typed expressions to Scheme representations.

Runtime checking is the key to safe interoperability; however, checking that the value returned by **response** fully complies with the **Action** type signature cannot occur immediately. Without static information, we cannot assess the behavior of higher-order values. Instead, we check that an object support fields and methods with the required names, then embed objects in higher-order wrappers that perform type-directed conversions and checks at method and field boundaries. Unaccessed members are never checked.

This example also illustrates the problem with extending classes while using multiple languages. Although the **Wizard** class does not require manual checks and conversions, it does separate the **Wizard** class into two implementations, increasing the difficulty of refining the class in the future. With safe inheritance, the **Wizard** class could be written in Scheme for flexibility while allowing future refinements in Scheme or Java.

Roadmap

We illustrate our technique to support multi-language class inheritance in Sect. 2. In Sect. 3, we present the formal representations of our language. Sections 4 and 5 demonstrate that our model, and therefore our style of interoperability, is sound and that dynamic type errors do not arise from typed expressions.

2   Safe Inheritance

An overridden method in Java always accepts the same number and type of parameters and always produces the same type of value. In PLT Scheme, the type and number of parameters and type of return for a method can change on each class extension. With type-checked subtype inheritance, statically maintaining

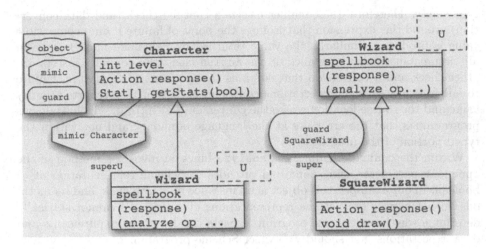

Fig. 2. Safe interactions along super calls

these invariants is expected by programmers and compilers; with dynamically-checked inheritance, the programmer may rely on the ability to modify the kind of value produced or expected. A cross-language inheritance system should support the static guarantees when considering a member of the class-hierarchy within typed definitions and support the lack of guarantee when considering a member within untyped definitions.

Figure 2 includes a section of a class hierarchy spanning typed and untyped languages; the `Character` and `SquareWizard` classes are implemented in the typed language, while `Wizard` is implemented in the untyped one. As an untyped object, an instance of `Wizard` may assign any value to `level` and `spellbook`; while as a typed object, an instance of `SquareWizard` must assign integers to `level`; similar constraints apply to the returned value of the stated methods.

In addition to the language boundaries discussed in Sect. 1.1, objects also cross language boundaries at super calls and self-dispatches within an object. As dynamically-checked languages may not support compile-time analysis and inspection, some wrapper insertions must now occur during evaluation.

2.1 Safety with Untyped Parent

Within `SquareWizard`, a compiler can inject wrappers on all super calls to convert typed parameters and checks to ensure that the returned value matches the stated return type. These inserted wrappers preserve the type expectations, and thus type safety, of any `SquareWizard` object when all methods are overridden. It is unlikely for a class to override every method of its parent and distant ancestors, yet without this property the inheritance is unsafe.

A `SquareWizard` object, s, may be passed to a method expecting a `Character`. If the `getStats` method is overridden in `Wizard` and not in `SquareWizard`, then any call to `getStats` on s does not pass through any wrappers and produces an untyped value. This can result in dynamic errors elsewhere in the program as the compiler did not anticipate the possibility of an untyped value within `Character`.

We resolve this by automatically overriding every method (not directly overridden) when a typed class extends an untyped one. The body of each inserted method contains only a super call forwarding the necessary parameters; the types of each inserted method reflect the original type specifications of the method, by examining the types of the nearest typed ancestor and using **dynamic** when no applicable ancestor is found. Thus all calls, including self-references, pass through a wrapper to perform conversions and checks. The `SquareWizard` extension now serves as a bridge between languages in the class hierarchy as well as serving as behavioral extensions.

2.2   Safety with Untyped Child

Some dynamic languages provide means of modifying code after compilation, whether through macros, dynamic evaluation, explicit method insertion, or mutable method bodies. While we do not model these features particularly, we respect the dynamic nature of our untyped language and do not statically analyze or annotate untyped methods or expressions. We do statically inspect untyped class definitions and insert class-hierarchy information; however, this process could be delayed until evaluation in a dynamic implementation.

The untyped `Wizard` class from our example also serves as a bridge between the typed ancestors and any untyped children. As with `SquareWizard`, problems can arise in `Wizard` objects calling inherited (non-overridden) methods from `Character` with untyped parameters and ill-formed primitive values. Therefore, we augment the untyped class definition with method declarations for each inherited (non-overridden) method, with a super call expression.

Wrappers are necessary when a `Wizard` instance invokes a super call as the parent class is statically-typed, however none are present in the method as no analysis has occurred. In order to inject wrappers dynamically, each untyped class must contain a runtime-representation of its parent's type. This type information is used by the super-call dispatch to insert checks and wrappers for parameters and returned values.

By embedding the parent type in the class while delaying wrapping values until runtime, we respect the typed class hierarchy's static guarantees and avoid static analysis of the dynamic class hierarchy's method implementations. This solution can support delayed method body definition and insertion, although our model does not support these features.

Figure 2 also demonstrates the insertion of wrappers on super calls through an untyped parent or child. The wrappers depicted are the conversion for the current object, i.e. `this`; a wrapped untyped-object conforms to the types of the immediate typed parent on super calls, and a wrapped typed object enforces its type expectations on its untyped parent. Type errors only occur within the untyped class body, even with a typed subclass instantiation.

def ::=
  | **class** *cid* { *field** *method** }
  | **class** cid_1 **extends** cid_2 { *field** *method** }
  | (**defineU** *id valueU*)
  | (**classU** *cid* (*fid**) (*methodU**))
  | (**classU-extends** cid_1 cid_2 (*fid**) (*methodU**))

Fig. 3. Definitions in J+S

J-forms

field ::= *type fid* ;

method ::=
  | *type mid*($type_0$ id_0, .. , $type_n$ id_n) { *exprT* }

exprT ::= **new** *cid* ($exprT_0$, .. , $exprT_n$)
  | **get-field** (*exprT*, *fid*)
  | **call** (*exprT* , *mid*, $exprT_0$ .. , $exprT_n$)
  | **super** (*mid*, $exprT_0$, .. , $exprT_n$)
  | **if** ($exprT_1$) $exprT_2$ **else** $exprT_3$
  | **instanceof** (*exprT*, *type*)
  | **cast**(*exprT*, *type*)
  | **app**(*exprT*, $exprT_0$ .. , $exprT_n$)
  | **this** | *id* | *valueT*

valueT ::= **trueT** | **falseT**

type ::= *cid* | **boolean** | **dynamic**

S-forms

methodU ::= (*mid* (id_0 .. id_n) *exprU*)

exprU ::=
  | (**newU** *cid* $exprU_0$ .. $exprU_n$)
  | (**get-fieldU** *exprU fid cid*)
  | (**callU** *exprU mid* $exprU_0$..$exprU_n$)
  | (**superU thisU** (*mid* : *cid*)
       $exprU_0$ .. $exprU_n$)
  | (**ifU** $exprU_1$ $exprU_2$ $exprU_3$)
  | (*exprU* $exprU_0$ .. $exprU_n$)
  | **thisU** | *id* | *valueU*

valueU ::=
  | **trueU**
  | **falseU**
  | (λ (id_0 .. id_n) *exprUA*)

Fig. 4. J+S language

3 J+S Language

In modeling cross-language inheritance, we combine a statically typed object-oriented calculus, J, with a dynamically-checked joint object-oriented and function calculus, S. Definitions in our language, see Fig. 3, are either typed classes with semantics similar to Java, untyped classes with semantics similar to Scheme, or function definitions. The typed J-forms, on the left of Fig. 4, may appear only in typed classes. The untyped S-forms, marked with a U on the right of Fig. 4, may appear only in untyped **classU**s and value definitions.

The J+S language builds on our previous model [6], represented in PLT Redex[7]. The PLT Redex model included a small-step semantics and annotation relation supporting typed class inheritance, and value conversion, but restricted the forms of cyclic dependencies, did not contain casts, nor cross-language inheritance. This extension supports these features and has been proven sound.

embeds ::=
| **guard** *exprA* |$_{(typeA, expr)}$
| **mimic** *exprA* |$_{(typeA, expr)}$

Fig. 5. Guards and mimics

A program in J+S consists of a sequence of *def*s followed by an *expr*, which is an *exprU* or *exprT*. Although we present one language, the J and S portions are syntactically disjoint to represent a single program written in two languages. Each class name, *cid*, in the *def* sequence must be unique, and we assume that ancestors precede descendants in the sequence. Within a class, the field, variable, and method names – *fid*, *id*, and *mid* – can intersect provided no duplicate fields, methods, or method parameters occur. Typed values cannot occur in untyped expressions, and vice-versa. We model different value representations, with suffixes, to demonstrate primitive value conversions. A **new** expression may only refer to a typed class name, while a **newU** expression may only refer to an untyped class.

A **superU** expression contains the current class name as a means of representing the source location. The **get-fieldU** expression's class name specifies a particular field definition to allow duplicate field names in a class hierarchy, this reflects existing models and dynamic class systems [8,9,10]. The **app** J-expression only applies untyped functions and produces untyped values.

We do not support higher-order classes or mutation. The first omission allows us to simplify evaluation; higher-order classes could be supported within our model by duplicating class annotation rules within the reduction rules. Modeling mutation adds complexity to the model that is not inherent in supporting interoperability; our representation and rules should support mutable fields.

3.1 Safe Interoperability – Mimic and Guard

Our compilation technique provides safe interoperability by expanding the source language to insert wrappers that transfer values between typed and untyped expressions. We use two wrappers: one that converts typed-values into untyped expressions – a **guard**; and another that converts untyped values into typed expressions – a **mimic**. Both wrappers contain an embedded expression, a type, and a source location (represented as an expression), see Fig. 5; reductions involving these expressions use the embedded type information to check and convert values during higher-order accesses.[1]

From our initial example, Fig. 1, the expression returned from **response** is embedded in a **mimic** with type **Action** and the expression **items** is embedded in a **guard** with type **Item[]**. A **mimic** injects a runtime check as well, so that only valid untyped values are converted. A failed mimic expression produces an error containing the source of the failure (the expression) and the incorrect value.

---

[1] These forms assume the role of mirrors and unmirrors, respectively, from Gray [3].

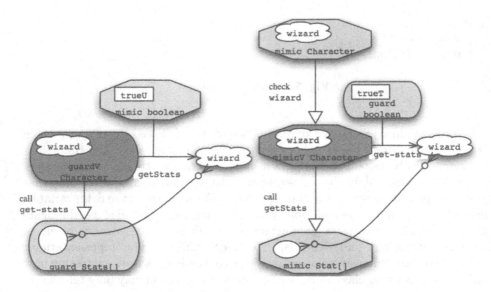

Fig. 6. Calling method getStats through embeddings

Guards. A **guard** is an interactive converter for typed to untyped values. No checking precedes the conversion, as the embedded value must be a subtype of the recorded type specification. Despite embedding a typed value, a **guard** expression is untyped. Conversions of primitive values occur immediately; thus a reduction of **guard trueT|boolean** produces **trueU**.

A guard on an object reduces to a special value containing the object and redirecting all future access to the object. The left side of Fig. 6 presents a method call to a guarded Wizard object (the dark oval). The guard injects a **mimic** expression (the light octagon) onto the parameters of the call using the embedded type information. These mimicked values pass to the embedded object's method and the resulting value is embedded in a new guard.

Mimics. A **mimic** checks that an untyped value satisfies the embedded type, and is then an interactive converter for untyped to typed values. A **mimic** expression is a typed expression, with the type matching the embedded specification. As with **guard**s, primitive values are immediately checked and converted while object values remain embedded.

Figure 6, on the right, illustrates the interaction of a call to a mimicked Wizard object. First, the mimic ensures that a Wizard satisfies the Character specification. An object satisfies a class specification when the value contains a superset of the specified class's fields and methods; we do not require that the object descend from the specified class as the object may itself be a **guard** or the languages may have differing object representations. When passing parameters, the mimic injects guards on the values to implement conversions and embeds the result in a new **mimic**.

4   Modeling Interoperability

Safe interoperability requires that compilation wrap expressions that cross from untyped contexts to typed contexts. We model this with a big-step annotation relation, which additionally confirms that a source program is well-typed, and a small-step evaluation-context relation. The reduction relation extends our previous evaluation-context relation [6]. Our previous model supported typed inheritance, object-instantiation, protected conversions for primitive and object values, and pure functions. The small-step context-based annotation relation did not support cyclic class references (i.e. a class could not include any descendent types), nor was the interaction between the annotations and evaluation relations shown to be sound. The model presented below removes the cyclic-reference restriction (preserving the common cyclic inheritance restriction) as well as adding support for casts and mutual inheritance.

4.1   Annotated Language

Our annotation relation expands a *prog* into a *progA*, key differences between the grammars are outlined in Fig. 7. Annotated class definitions include inheritance information, including the type signature of the super class. Annotated *field* and *fieldU* definitions include the name of their containing class; *methodAs* include an *exprTA*.

In addition to the new productions shown, the *exprA* grammar includes the *exprTA* forms and the *exprUA* forms. The *exprUA* grammar follows the *exprU* grammar exactly except that all *values* are allowed. Untyped methods are not expanded, but the body must be an *exprUA*.

Figure 7 contains the modified forms for typed expressions: a **super** call specifies the immediate parent and the implicit object; the **get-field** form specifies the containing class; and expressions can be embedded in **guards** or **mimics** with the annotated type. The error forms included in *exprA* are used to signal errors within the reduction rules and are not generated by the annotation. An object's tag, either **T** or **U**, indicates whether the object came from **new** or **newU**.

4.2   Type System and Annotations

Our annotation-type relation, Fig. 8[2], relies on a set of predicates that ensures 1) unique class names 2) acyclic inheritance 3) unique method/field names within each class and 4) unique top-level identifiers. Annotation proceeds when *prog* is well-typed; otherwise the relation is 'stuck' and the program is ill-formed. ANTPROG builds a tuple-environment, Γ, that maps *ids* to *typeAs* and *cids* to class types or **dynamic** (using **cMap**) and a definition map, Δ.

---

[2] We use the semantics specification tool, Ott, for our relations. In our rules, a line over an item indicates repetition; the tag on each line identifies the set of items.

$progA ::= defA^* \; exprA$

$defA ::=$
  | **class** cid { $ancestor^*$ $fieldA^*$ $methodA^*$ }
  | (**classU** cid ($ancestor^*$) ($fieldAU^*$) ($methodUAS$))
  | (**defineU** $id\;valueU$)

$fieldA ::= type\;fid\;cid$;

$ancestor ::= (cid\;typeA)$

$exprA ::= ...$
  | **badCast**
  | **mimicError** ($value$, $expr$)
  | **dynamicError**
  | $E\,[\,exprA\,]$

$typeA ::=$
  | **classT** $cid\,[\,cid^*\,]\,[\,fieldT^*\,]\,[\,methodT^*\,]$
  | **boolean**
  | **dynamic**

$exprTA ::= ...$
  | **get-field** ($exprTA$, fid, cid)
  | **get-field** ($exprTA$, fid, **dynamic**)
  | **super** ($exprTA$, mid, cid, $exprTA_0$, .., $exprTA_n$)
  | $value$
  | **guard** $exprA\,|_{(typeA,expr)}$
  | **mimic** $exprA\,|_{(typeA,expr)}$

$objValue ::=$
  | **obj** (cid, tag, $parents$, $fieldVals$)
  | **guardV** $value\,|_{(typeA,expr)}$
  | **mimicV** $value\,|_{(typeA,expr)}$

$value ::= valueU \mid valueT \mid objValue$

Fig. 7. Expanded language

$\vdash prog \rightsquigarrow progA$

$$\Gamma = \{\ \epsilon,\ \textbf{cMap}\,(\,def_1\,..\,def_m\,,\ \epsilon\,)\,\}\quad \Delta = def_1\,..\,def_m$$
$$\Gamma, \Delta \vdash def_1 \rightsquigarrow defA_1\quad ..\quad \Gamma, \Delta \vdash def_m \rightsquigarrow defA_m$$
$$\Gamma \vdash expr \rightsquigarrow_a exprA : typeA$$
$$\overline{\qquad\qquad def_1\,..\,def_m\;expr \rightsquigarrow defA_1\,..\,defA_m\;exprA \qquad\qquad}\;\;\text{AntProg}$$

Fig. 8. Program expansion

Class annotation embeds ancestor types, annotates methods, and also creates the stubs for non-overridden methods discussed in Sect. 2. Figure 9 contains the expansion of a typed class and the corresponding method creation. The **inheritMethod** function maps the **addMType** function over the inherited, non-overriden methods. The function inserts the correct type signature for methods inherited from the nearest typed ancestor, emitting **dynamic** when no information is available. Untyped class annotation proceeds similarly, with an **inheritMethodU** that maps over a function to strip the type information from inherited methods.

$$\boxed{\Gamma, \Delta \vdash def \rightsquigarrow defA}$$

$\Gamma(cida)$: **dynamic**

$\Delta(cida).\textbf{ancestors} \Rightarrow \overline{ancestor_i}^{\,i} \quad typeA = \textbf{typeAnc}(\overline{ancestor_i}^{\,i})$

$\Delta(cida).\textbf{fields} \Rightarrow \overline{fieldAU_j}^{\,j} \quad \Delta(cida).\textbf{methods} \Rightarrow \overline{methodUA_l'}^{\,l}$

$\overline{fieldA_j'}^{\,j} = \textbf{inheritField}(\overline{fieldAU_j}^{\,j}) \quad \overline{field_n \rightsquigarrow_{cid} fieldA_n}^{\,n}$

$\overline{methodUA_p}^{\,p} = \textbf{intersect}(\overline{methodUA_l'}^{\,l}, \overline{method_m}^{\,m})$

$\overline{method_p'}^{\,p} = \textbf{inheritMethod}(\overline{methodUA_p}^{\,p}, typeA)$

$\overline{\Gamma \vdash method_m \rightsquigarrow_{(cid,cida)} methodA_m}^{\,m} \quad \overline{\Gamma \vdash method_p' \rightsquigarrow_{(cid,cida)} methodA_p'}^{\,p}$

$$\frac{}{\begin{array}{c}\Gamma, \Delta \vdash \textbf{class } cid \textbf{ extends } cida \,\{\, \overline{field_n}^{\,n} \; \overline{method_m}^{\,m} \,\} \rightsquigarrow \\[4pt] \textbf{class } cid \,\{\, (cida \textbf{ dynamic}) \, \overline{ancestor_i}^{\,i} \\[2pt] \overline{fieldA_j'}^{\,j} \; \overline{fieldA_n}^{\,n} \; \overline{methodA_p'}^{\,p} \; \overline{methodA_m}^{\,m} \,\}\end{array}} \quad \text{CLASSE\textsc{u}}$$

$$\boxed{\textbf{inheritMethod}(\,methodUAS,\,typeA)}$$

$\textbf{inheritMethod}(methodUAS, typeA) \equiv \textbf{map addMType } methodUAS \; typeA$

$$\boxed{\textbf{addMType}(methodUA,\,typeA)}$$

$\textbf{addMType}((mid\,(id_1 .. id_n)\,exprUA),$

$\qquad \textbf{classT } cid[cid^*][fieldT^*][\overline{methodT_i}^{\,i}\;mid\;type\;[type_1' .. type_n']\;\overline{methodT_p'}^{\,p}]) \equiv$

$\qquad type\,mid(type_1'\,id_1, .., type_n'\,id_n)\,\{\textbf{super}(mid, id_1, .., id_n)\}$

$\textbf{addMType}((mid\,(id_1 .. id_n)\,exprUA), -) \equiv$

$\qquad \textbf{dynamic } mid(\textbf{dynamic } id_1, .., \textbf{dynamic } id_n)\,\{\textbf{super}(mid, id_1, .., id_n)\}$

Fig. 9. Class expansion

$$\boxed{\Gamma \vdash method \rightsquigarrow_{(c,a)} methodA}$$

$\Gamma = \{\epsilon, typeMap\} \quad \Gamma' = \{\overline{id_i : type_i ::}^{\,i} \epsilon, typeMap\}$

$\Gamma' \vdash exprT \rightsquigarrow exprTA_1 : typeA$

$\Gamma \vdash typeA \preceq_d type \quad \Gamma \vdash exprTA_1 : typeA \mapsto_{type, exprT} exprTA$

$$\frac{}{\Gamma \vdash type\,mid\,(\,\overline{type_i\,id_i}^{\,i}\,)\,\{\,exprT\,\} \rightsquigarrow type\,mid\,(\,\overline{type_i\,id_i}^{\,i}\,)\,\{\,exprTA\,\}} \quad \text{ANT\textsc{meth}}$$

Fig. 10. Method expansion

Method expansion, Fig. 10, expands Γ with the parameter bindings to annotate the body, which may be wrapped with an *embed* based on the expected and actual types, and ensures that the derived type is a subtype of the declared type. The $\rightsquigarrow$ relation is tagged with the current and parent class name, these do not change during expansion.[3]

---

[3] For simplicity, we omit these tags unless needed in the rule.

$$\boxed{\Gamma \vdash exprT \leadsto_{(c,a)} exprTA : typeA}$$

$\Gamma \vdash exprT \leadsto exprTA :$

$$\frac{\begin{array}{c} \mathbf{classT}\ cid\ [cid^*]\ [fieldT^*]\ \overline{[methodT_r}^{\,r}\ mid\ type\ \overline{[type_n}^{\,n}]\ \overline{methodT_{1\,p}}^{\,p}] \\[4pt] \overline{\Gamma \vdash exprT_n \leadsto exprTA_{1\,n} : typeA_n}^{\,n} \qquad \overline{\Gamma \vdash typeA_n \preceq_d type_n}^{\,n} \\[4pt] \overline{\Gamma \vdash exprTA_{1\,n} : typeA_n \mapsto_{type_n, exprT_n} exprTA_n}^{\,n} \qquad \Gamma(type) : typeA \end{array}}{\Gamma \vdash \mathbf{call}(exprT,\ mid,\ \overline{exprT_n}^{\,n}) \leadsto \mathbf{call}(exprTA,\ mid,\ \overline{exprTA_n}^{\,n}) : typeA} \quad \text{ANTCALL}$$

$$\frac{\begin{array}{c} expr = \mathbf{super}(mid,\ \overline{exprT_n}^{\,n}) \\[4pt] typeA' = \mathbf{classT}\ cidc\ [cid^*]\ [fieldT^*] \\[4pt] \qquad\qquad [\overline{methodT_i}^{\,i}\ mid\ type\ \overline{[type_n'}^{\,n}]\ \overline{methodT_l'}^{\,l}] \\[4pt] \Gamma(cidc) : typeA' \qquad \Gamma(cida) : \mathbf{dynamic} \qquad \Gamma(type) : typeA \\[4pt] \Gamma \vdash \mathbf{this} : typeA' \mapsto_{\mathbf{dynamic},\mathbf{this}} exprTA \\[4pt] \overline{\Gamma \vdash exprT_n \leadsto_{(cidc,cida)} exprTA_n' : typeA_n}^{\,n} \qquad \overline{\Gamma \vdash typeA_n \preceq_d type_n'}^{\,n} \\[4pt] \overline{\Gamma \vdash exprTA_n' : typeA_n \mapsto_{\mathbf{dynamic},exprT_n} exprTA_n}^{\,n} \\[4pt] \Gamma \vdash \mathbf{super}(exprTA, mid, cida, \overline{exprTA_n}^{\,n}) : typeA \mapsto_{\mathbf{dynamic},expr} \\[4pt] \qquad exprTA'' \end{array}}{\Gamma \vdash expr \leadsto_{(cidc,cida)} exprTA'' : typeA} \quad \text{ANTSUPERD}$$

Fig. 11. Type annotation rules

$$\boxed{\Gamma \vdash typeR \preceq_d typeR'}$$

$$\frac{}{\Gamma \vdash typeR \preceq_d typeR} \quad \text{SUBDREFLEX}$$

$$\frac{}{\Gamma \vdash \mathbf{dynamic} \preceq_d typeR} \quad \text{SUBDBOTTOM}$$

$$\frac{}{\begin{array}{c} \Gamma \vdash \mathbf{classT}\ cid_1\ [\,\overline{cid_{3\,m}}^{\,m}\ cid_2\ \overline{cid_{4\,p}}^{\,p}\,]\ [\,fieldT^*\,]\ [\,methodT^*\,] \preceq_d \\[4pt] \mathbf{classT}\ cid_2\ [\,\overline{cid_{5\,n}}^{\,n}\,]\ [\,fieldT_1^*\,]\ [\,methodT_1^*\,] \end{array}} \quad \text{SUBDCLASST}$$

Fig. 12. Subtype relation

Expression annotation typically follows a similar pattern to the treatment of a method body. Figure 11 contains a typical rule, ANTCALL, and an atypical one, ANTSUPERD. Like method annotation, the call rule checks that the parameters are subtypes of the specified types. Figure 12 contains the subtype relation for expansion, in which **dynamic** is a subtype for all types. The derived expression type and the specified type guide the embedding relation, Fig. 13, to insert guards and mimics.

The ANTSUPERD rule annotates a super call for an untyped parent. The implicit **this** parameter is inserted within a **guard** for the current class type, and the explicit parameters are embedded in appropriate **guards**. Each parameter's derived type determines the guarded expectation; however, each derived type must be a subtype of the specified parameter.

$$\boxed{\Gamma \vdash exprTA : typeA \longmapsto_{(type, expr)} exprTA'}$$

$$typeA \neq \mathbf{dynamic}$$

$$\overline{\Gamma \vdash exprTA : typeA \longmapsto_{\mathbf{dynamic}, expr} \mathbf{guard}\ exprTA\ |_{(typeA, expr)}} \quad \text{EMBGUARD}$$

$$\Gamma\ (\ cid\ )\ :\ typeA$$

$$\overline{\Gamma \vdash exprTA : \mathbf{dynamic} \longmapsto_{cid, expr} \mathbf{mimic}\ exprTA\ |_{(typeA, expr)}} \quad \text{EMBMIMICOBJ}$$

$$\overline{\begin{array}{c}\Gamma \vdash exprTA : \mathbf{dynamic} \longmapsto_{\mathbf{boolean}, expr} \\ \mathbf{mimic}\ exprTA\ |_{(\mathbf{boolean}, expr)}\end{array}} \quad \text{EMBMIMICBOOL}$$

$$\overline{\Gamma \vdash exprTA : \mathbf{dynamic} \longmapsto_{\mathbf{dynamic}, expr} exprTA} \quad \text{EMBDYN}$$

$$typeA \neq \mathbf{dynamic} \qquad type \neq \mathbf{dynamic}$$

$$\overline{\Gamma \vdash exprTA : typeA \longmapsto_{type, expr} exprTA} \quad \text{EMBREFLECT}$$

Fig. 13. Embedding Rules

$$\boxed{\Gamma \vdash exprT \rightsquigarrow_{(c,a)} exprTA : typeA}$$

$$\Gamma \vdash exprT \rightsquigarrow exprTA_1 : typeA_1$$
$$\Gamma\ |- typeA_1 \preceq_d type \lor \Gamma\ |- type \preceq_d typeA_1$$
$$exprTA_2 = \mathbf{cast}(exprTA_1, type)$$
$$\Gamma \vdash exprTA_2 : typeA_1 \longmapsto_{type, exprT} exprTA$$
$$\Gamma(type)\ :\ typeA$$

$$\overline{\Gamma \vdash \mathbf{cast}(exprT, type) \rightsquigarrow exprTA : typeA} \quad \text{ANTCAST}$$

Fig. 14. Cast annotation

The embedding rules in Fig. 13 determine the embedding of expressions in guards and mimics. Guards arise when an expectation, i.e. the declared type, is **dynamic**. Mimics arise when the declared type is not **dynamic** and the derived expression type is **dynamic**. Embeddings are not introduced in other circumstances.

Cast annotation, Fig. 14, embeds the cast value (where necessary) such that any embedding check occurs before the cast check, so that the value is properly embedded as well as ensuring that casts remain nominal.

4.3 Operational Semantics

The final *exprA* of a *progA* reduces to a value or an error using a small-step evaluation context reduction. The REDUCE rule, Fig. 15 constructs an environment, Γ, mapping class names to types and constructs Δ to represent the program

$$\boxed{\vdash progA \rightarrow progA'}$$

$$\Delta = defA_0 \,..\, defA_n \quad \Gamma = \{\epsilon, \mathbf{cAMap}(defA_0 \,..\, defA_n)\}$$
$$\Gamma, \Delta \vdash E \,[\, exprA \,] \rightarrow exprA'$$

$$\rule{8cm}{0.4pt}$$ REDUCE

$$\vdash defA_0 \,..\, defA_n \, exprA \rightarrow defA_0 \,..\, defA_n \, exprA'$$

Fig. 15. Program reduction

$$\boxed{\Gamma, \Delta \vdash exprA \rightarrow exprA'}$$

$$value = \mathbf{obj}(cid, \, tag, \, parents, \, fieldVals)$$
$$\Delta(cid) \Rightarrow \mathbf{class}\, cid\, \{ancestor^* \, fieldA^*$$
$$\overline{methodA_m}^m \, type\, mid(\overline{type'_n \, id_n}^n)\, \{exprTA\} \, \overline{methodA'_p}^p\}$$

$$\rule{10cm}{0.4pt}$$ CALL

$$\Gamma, \Delta \vdash E[\mathbf{call}(value, mid, \overline{v'_n}^n)] \rightarrow E[exprTA\{\mathbf{this} \models value\}\, \overline{\{id_n \models v'_n\}}^n]$$

$$typeA = \mathbf{classT}\, cid\, [cid^*]\, [fieldT^*]$$
$$[\overline{methodT_r}^r \, mid\, type\, [\overline{type'}^n]\, \overline{methodT'_p}^p]$$
$$\overline{\Gamma(type'_n) : typeA'_n}^n \quad \overline{\Gamma \vdash value_n : typeA'_n \mapsto_{\mathbf{dynamic}, expr} exprTA'_n}^n$$
$$\Gamma \vdash (\mathbf{callU}\, value\, mid\, \overline{exprTA'_n}^n) : \mathbf{dynamic} \mapsto_{type, expr} exprTA$$

$$\rule{11cm}{0.4pt}$$ CALLM

$$\Gamma, \Delta \vdash E\,[\mathbf{call}(\mathbf{mimicV}\, value\,|_{(typeA, expr)}, \, mid, \, \overline{value}^n)] \rightarrow E\,[exprTA]$$

$$typeA = \mathbf{classT}\, cid\, [cid^*]\, [fieldT^*]$$
$$[\overline{methodT_r}^r \, mid\, type\, [\overline{type'}^n]\, \overline{methodT'_p}^p]$$
$$\Gamma(type) : typeA' \quad \overline{\Gamma \vdash value_n : \mathbf{dynamic} \mapsto_{type'_n, expr} exprTA_n}^n$$
$$\Gamma \vdash \mathbf{call}(value, \, mid, \, \overline{exprTA_n}^n) : typeA' \mapsto_{\mathbf{dynamic}, expr} exprTA$$

$$\rule{11cm}{0.4pt}$$ CALLUG

$$\Gamma, \Delta \vdash E\,[\,(\mathbf{callU}\, \mathbf{guardV}\, value\,|_{(typeA, expr)}\, mid\, \overline{value_n}^n)] \rightarrow E\,[exprTA]$$

Fig. 16. Call reduction

definitions. The type environment is necessary for operations on mimics and guards.

Reduction of most expressions, such as conditionals and function application, is straightforward. Reduction of a method call for an object value, CALL in Fig. 16, uses Δ to extract the correct method body, then substitutes the parameter values into the body, denoted with $\models$. Method calls for guarded or mimicked objects require the insertion of appropriate wrappers on parameters and on the resulting value; CALLM demonstrates this for a mimicked object, while CALLUG demonstrates a guarded one. These rules dispatch to a method call in the alternate expression form using their embedded value directly.

Typed super calls follow the same pattern as standard method calls, extracting the specified expression body instead of using the object. Untyped super calls must insert wrappers to dynamically protect the language boundary when the immediate ancestor is typed. The SUPERUM rule, in Fig. 17, extracts the parent class's type and uses the method type information to dynamically embed the

$$\boxed{\Gamma, \Delta \vdash exprA \to exprA'}$$

$\Delta(cid).\mathbf{ancestors.first} \Rightarrow typeA_1$
$typeA_1 = \mathbf{classT}\ cid'\ [\overline{cid_l''}^l]\ [fieldT^*]$
$\qquad\qquad [\overline{methodT_i}^i\ mid\ type\ [\overline{type_n'}^n]\ \overline{methodT_j'}^j]$
$\Gamma(type) : typeA \qquad \overline{\Gamma \vdash value_n : \mathbf{dynamic} \mapsto_{type_n', expr} exprTA_n}^n$
$value' = \mathbf{mimicV}\ value\ |_{(typeA_1, \mathbf{thisU})}$
$expr = (\mathbf{superU\ thisU}\ (mid : cid)\ \overline{valueU_n}^n)$
$\Gamma \vdash \mathbf{super}(value', mid, cid', \overline{exprTA_n}^n) : typeA \mapsto_{\mathbf{dynamic}, expr} exprTA$

$$\rule{7cm}{0.4pt}$$
$$\Gamma, \Delta \vdash E[(\mathbf{superU}\ value\ (mid : cid)\ \overline{value_n}^n)] \to E[exprTA] \qquad \text{SUPERUM}$$

Fig. 17. superU reduction, with a typed parent

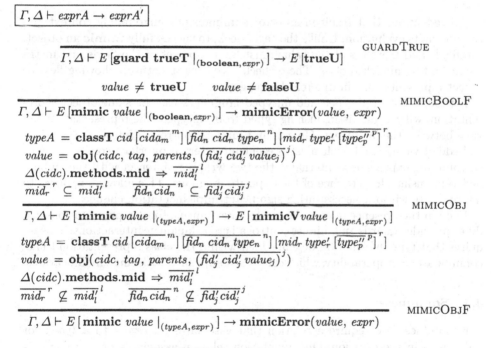

$$\boxed{\Gamma, \Delta \vdash exprA \to exprA'}$$

$$\text{GUARDTRUE}$$
$$\Gamma, \Delta \vdash E[\mathbf{guard\ trueT}\ |_{(\mathbf{boolean}, expr)}] \to E[\mathbf{trueU}]$$

$$value \neq \mathbf{trueU} \qquad value \neq \mathbf{falseU}$$
$$\text{MIMICBOOLF}$$
$$\Gamma, \Delta \vdash E[\mathbf{mimic}\ value\ |_{(\mathbf{boolean}, expr)}] \to \mathbf{mimicError}(value, expr)$$

$typeA = \mathbf{classT}\ cid\ [\overline{cida_m}^m]\ [\overline{fid_n\ cid_n\ type_n}^n]\ [\overline{mid_r\ type_r'\ [\overline{type_p''}^p]}^r]$
$value = \mathbf{obj}(cidc, tag, parents, \overline{(fid_j'\ cid_j'\ value_j)}^j)$
$\Delta(cidc).\mathbf{methods.mid} \Rightarrow \overline{mid_l'}^l$
$\overline{mid_r}^r \subseteq \overline{mid_l'}^l \qquad \overline{fid_n\ cid_n}^n \subseteq \overline{fid_j'\ cid_j'}^j$
$$\text{MIMICOBJ}$$
$$\Gamma, \Delta \vdash E[\mathbf{mimic}\ value\ |_{(typeA, expr)}] \to E[\mathbf{mimicV}\ value\ |_{(typeA, expr)}]$$

$typeA = \mathbf{classT}\ cid\ [\overline{cida_m}^m]\ [\overline{fid_n\ cid_n\ type_n}^n]\ [\overline{mid_r\ type_r'\ [\overline{type_p''}^p]}^r]$
$value = \mathbf{obj}(cidc, tag, parents, \overline{(fid_j'\ cid_j'\ value_j)}^j)$
$\Delta(cidc).\mathbf{methods.mid} \Rightarrow \overline{mid_l'}^l$
$\overline{mid_r}^r \not\subseteq \overline{mid_l'}^l \qquad \overline{fid_n\ cid_n}^n \not\subseteq \overline{fid_j'\ cid_j'}^j$
$$\text{MIMICOBJF}$$
$$\Gamma, \Delta \vdash E[\mathbf{mimic}\ value\ |_{(typeA, expr)}] \to \mathbf{mimicError}(value, expr)$$

Fig. 18. Mimic and guard reductions

method parameters, result, and current object. The actual call dispatches to the equivalent *exprTA* call using the now typed object.

Mimicking the current object in SUPERUG cannot fail. This is the only **mimic** embedding that cannot fail; a failed **mimic** contains the wrong primitive or an object lacking the correct interface, Fig. 18 presents **mimic** failure and success. Failed mimics halt evaluation with a **mimicError** containing the offending value and the expression which introduced the wrapper (to blame the source of the

$$\boxed{\Gamma, \Delta \vdash exprA \rightarrow exprA'}$$

$$\frac{typeA \ = \ \mathbf{classT} \ cid'[\overline{cida_m}^{\,m} \ cid \ \overline{cida_n'}^{\,n}][fieldT^*][methodT^*]}{\Gamma, \Delta \vdash E[\mathbf{cast}(\mathbf{mimicV} val \,|_{(typeA, expr)}, \ cid)] \rightarrow E[\mathbf{mimicV} val \,|_{(typeA, expr)}]} \quad \text{CAST MA}$$

Fig. 19. Cast of a mimicked object

error). Theorem 2 in Sect. 5 shows that this value cannot be a typed value, and therefore interoperability cannot lead to errors within typed programs.

Cast reduction for object values examines the *cid* list within the **obj** value for the target class name, resulting in a **badCast** when the list does not contain the name. With mimicked objects, as seen in Fig. 19, the reduction checks the *cid* list within the embedded type and preserves the **mimic**, performing a nominal cast.

All reductions that result in an error eliminate the surrounding context and thereby halts evaluation. Unlike the cast check, to successfully **mimic** an object, the fields and methods of the value must be a superset of the fields and methods from the mimicked class. These checks are thus structural, allowing flexible object representations in different languages.

Although both the typed and untyped languages use the same object representation, with a tag distinguishing typed from untyped, the representation can vary between the languages. Guards and mimics control all interaction to their embedded values, and each must present an external interface consistent with surrounding expressions. Internally, the two wrappers interact with the embedded value using the interface of the opposite language. This allows languages to interoperate without necessitating significant implementation changes.

Even in the presence of cross-language inheritance, object representations can differ provided guards and mimics control all cross-language interactions. This requires that type information be embedded within the class representation to accommodate interoperability, which can be accomplished with small modifications.

4.4 Soundness

For soundness, we require a relation that associates an *exprA* to a *typeA* for reductions in preservation. Our annotation relation associates *exprs* to *exprAs* and *typeAs* and is unsuitable. We therefore use a third relation that associates the annotated language to types and closely resembles the annotation relation without embedding expressions. Figure 20 presents the updated rule for checking super calls, as well as the rules for checking guards and mimics.

Due to dynamic typing, reductions can result in the errors **badCast**, **dynamicError**, and **mimicError**. The first indicates a cast failure within a typed expression; the second, an error in reducing an *exprU* or *app*; and the third, an error in transferring an untyped value into an *exprTA*. With these possible errors, soundness in our system says

$$\boxed{\Gamma \vdash_{(c,a)} exprTA : typeA}$$

$$\frac{\begin{array}{l} \Gamma(cidc) \; : \; \mathbf{classT} \; cidc[cid^*] \, [\mathit{field T}^*] \\ \qquad\qquad [\overline{methodT_i}^{\;i} \; mid \; type' \, \overline{[type_n}^{\;n}] \; \overline{methodT_l'}^{\;l}] \\ \Gamma(cida) \; : \; \mathbf{dynamic} \\ \Gamma \vdash exprTA : \mathbf{dynamic} \qquad \overline{\Gamma \vdash_{(cidc,cida)} exprTA_n : \mathbf{dynamic}}^{\;n} \end{array}}{\Gamma \vdash_{(cidc,cida)} \mathbf{super}(exprTA, mid, cidc, \overline{exprTA_n}^{\;n}) : \mathbf{dynamic}} \; \text{CHECKSUPERD}$$

$$\frac{\Gamma \vdash exprTA : typeA}{\Gamma \vdash \mathbf{guard} \; exprTA \mid_{(typeA, expr)} : \mathbf{dynamic}} \; \text{CHECKG}$$

$$\frac{\Gamma \vdash exprA : \mathbf{dynamic}}{\Gamma \vdash \mathbf{mimic} \; exprA \mid_{(typeA, expr)} : typeA} \; \text{CHECKM}$$

Fig. 20. Type checking annotated expressions

Theorem 1 (Soundness).
If $\Gamma \vdash exprA : typeA$ and $\Delta, \Gamma \vdash exprA \twoheadrightarrow exprA'$ and $FV(exprA) \subseteq dom(\Delta) \subseteq dom(\Gamma)$ then either $exprA' \in value$ or $\exists exprA''. \Delta, \Gamma \vdash exprA' \to exprA''$ or $\exists v, e. \; exprA' \in \{\mathbf{badCast}, \mathbf{mimicError}(v, e), \mathbf{dynamicError}\}$.

Proof. By lemmas 1 and 2.

Where FV returns the free *ids*, *cids*, and any **this** or **thisU** occurring in *exprA*.

Lemma 1 (Progress). *If $\Gamma \vdash exprA : typeA$ and $FV(exprA) \subseteq dom(\Delta) \subseteq dom(\Gamma)$ then either $exprA \in value$ or $\Delta, \Gamma \vdash exprA \to exprA'$.*

Proof. Proof by induction on the structure of *exprA*.

Cases for *exprTA* expressions proceed following standard case analysis with induction. Case splits occur for expressions containing an *objValue*, performing a different reduction on the possible forms. Three expressions can result in a **dynamicError**: **app**, when the first value is not a function; **get-field** and **call**, when for the first expression, e_1, $\Gamma \vdash e_1 : \mathbf{dynamic}$.

Cases for *exprUA* expressions proceed following standard case analysis with induction. Similar case splits occur for *objValue*; **mimic** values cannot occur based on the type relation precondition. Each expression can result in a **dynamicError**.

There are no cases for **mimicError**, **dynamicError**, or **badCast**, none of which derive a type. Neither are there cases for **this** or **thisU**, which are replaced by substitution, and do not occur within $dom(\Delta)$.

Lemma 2 (Preservation). *If $\Gamma \vdash exprA : typeA$ and $\Gamma, \Delta \vdash exprA \to exprA'$ and $FV(exprA) \subseteq dom(\Delta) \subseteq dom(\Gamma)$ then either $\Gamma \vdash exprA' : typeA'$ where $\Gamma \vdash typeA' \preceq_d typeA$ and $FV(exprA') \subseteq dom(\Delta) \subseteq dom(\Gamma)$ or $\exists v. \; exprA' \in \{\mathbf{badCast}, \mathbf{mimicError}(v), \mathbf{dynamicError}\}$.*

Proof. By case analysis of the → reduction relation with induction on E in each case.

Most cases follow a standard rule analysis showing that the constructed expression is either a subtype or same type as the original expression. Some cases rely on the unique-names contained in Γ, stated in Sect. 4.2. The method call and function application rules use a standard substitution lemma 3, including **this** and **thisU** as identifiers. Remaining identifiers use an identifier rule, TOPDEF, that extracts the value of **defineU** bindings from the program.

Cases for the rules reducing **guard** and **mimic** expressions show that the reduced expression always provides the same type as the type expectation. Cases for rules using method substitutions also rely on method preconditions for the CHECKPROG rule asserting that methods have unique ids and correctly override.

Lemma 3 (Substitution). *For any exprA, id, and value, if $\Gamma \vdash exprA : typeA$, $\Gamma(id) : typeA_1$, $\Gamma \vdash value : typeA'_1$, and $\Gamma \vdash typeA'_1 \preceq_d typeA_1$ then $\Gamma \vdash exprA\{id \leftarrow value\} : typeA'$ and $\Gamma \vdash typeA' \preceq_d typeA$.*

Proof. By a standard induction on the structure of *exprA*. J+S is a call-by-value language with closed terms. The λ-expression introduces only internal bindings. Therefore all cases follow a standard substitution proof.

5   Blaming Untyped Relatives

For a statically-typed language, soundness means that programs do not fail; in a combined system, soundness cannot provide this result as both dynamic type errors and conversion errors may occur. These errors are an inescapable result of combining languages with differing static guarantees; however, no dynamic errors should arise within a typed program, only within untyped programs and expressions that bridge the two languages. The value within the **mimicError** violates the type expectations of a typed program and the expression provides the program location where the value was introduced to the typed program. If the incorrect value is a typed value, then the program semantics allowed a typed expression to produce a type error. This violates our expectations for a typed program, but is not ruled out through a traditional soundness proof.

We strengthen the soundness claim to have a further safety property, eliminating the possibility that type errors arise due to typed portions of the program. Our proof follows insights from the works of Tobin-Hochstadt [4] and Wadler [5] to show that well-typed programs are not responsible for type errors in languages with combined semantics and only untyped expressions cause type errors.

We consider J+S to be *safe* as well as sound, meaning that

Theorem 2 (Safety).
*If $\Gamma \vdash expr \leadsto exprA : typeA$ and $\Gamma \vdash exprA : typeA$, and $typeA \neq$ **dynamic**, then $exprA \in value$ or $\Gamma, \Delta \vdash exprA \rightarrow exprA'$ and $exprA' \neq$ **dynamicError**.*
*If $\Gamma \vdash expr \leadsto exprA : typeA$ and $\Gamma, \Delta \vdash exprA \twoheadrightarrow$ **mimicError**(v, e), $dom(\Delta) \subseteq dom(\Gamma)$ then $\Gamma \vdash v :$ **dynamic**.*

Proof. The first statement shows that typed expressions cannot cause type failures; the second that typed values do not violate type expectations. We prove the two statements separately.

The proof of the first statement is by a case analysis on the rules of the $\rightarrow$ relation. We can inspect that each rule with **dynamicError** relates to an expression on the left that derives type **dynamic**; therefore, a typed expression cannot reduce to **dynamicError** in one step.

The proof of the second statement begins with a case analysis on the rules of $\rightarrow$ that relate to the **mimicError** expression. Each of these rules contain a **mimic** expression with an embedded value, related to the **mimicError**. With lemma 4, we show that for each of these rules, the embedded value must be untyped and therefore the type expectations from the enclosed expression were not failed by a typed expression.

Mimic reduction rules only apply when the context supplies a value; therefore lemmas 4 and 5 can ignore reductions resulting in errors and nontermination.

The following lemmas require two sets: *valueU+*, containing all untyped values, and *valueT+*, containing all typed values.

$v \in valueU+$ **iff** $v \in valueU \vee v \in objValueU$

$v \in objValueU$ **iff** $(v = \mathbf{guardV}v_1|_{(typeA, expr)} \wedge v_1 \in valueT+) \vee$
$$(v = \mathbf{obj}(cid, cid^*, \mathbf{U}, \overline{(fid_n\, cid'_n\, v'_n}^n)) \wedge \overline{v'_n \in valueU+}^n)$$

$v \in valueT+$ **iff** $v \in valueT \vee v \in objValueT$

$v \in objValueT$ **iff** $(v = \mathbf{mimicV}v_1|_{(typeA, expr)} \wedge v_1 \in valueU+) \vee$
$$(v = \mathbf{obj}(cid, cid^*, \mathbf{T}, \overline{(fid_n\, cid'_n\, v'_n}^n)) \wedge$$
$$\forall i.\, i \in n \implies (\Gamma(cid_i)(fid_i) : \mathbf{dynamic} \implies v'_i \in valueU+)$$
$$\wedge\; (\Gamma(cid_i)(fid_i) \neq \mathbf{dynamic} \implies v'_i \in valueT+))$$

Lemma 4 (Untyped values). *If* $\Gamma \vdash expr \rightsquigarrow exprA : \mathbf{dynamic}$ *and* $\Gamma, \Delta \vdash exprA \twoheadrightarrow v$ *for* $v \in value$ *then* $v \in valueU+$

Proof. Proof by induction on the structure of *expr*. Interesting cases are **newU**; **superU**; **callU, super, call**, and **get-field**.
case $e : (\mathbf{newU}\; cid\; \overline{exprUA_n}^n)$

Each *exprUA* derives **dynamic**, by $\rightsquigarrow$ rules; $\overline{exprUA_n \in valueU+}^n$ by inductive hypothesis. Therefore *e* reduces to a $v \in valueU+$ by NEWU.
case e: $(\mathbf{superU}\; exprU\; (mid : cid)\; \overline{exprUA_n}^n)$

Each *exprUA* derives **dynamic**, by $\rightsquigarrow$ rules; both $\overline{exprUA_n \in valueU+}^n$ and $exprUA \in valueU+$ by inductive hypothesis.

When referring to a typed parent class, *e* reduces to a guard, *g* by SUPERUM. We show that v_1 in *g* is a member of *valueT+*, by lemma 5 and thus $g \in valueU+$
case e: **callU, get-fieldU, get-field, call, super**

These five cases are similar, resulting in a **guard** expression *g*. In each $g \in valueU+$ when the embedded value v_1 is in *valueT+* by lemma 5. Additionally, both call expressions rely on type preservation during substitution using lemma 3.

Our value lemmas, 4 and 5 are mutually inductive; we separate them for clarity in the specifications.

Lemma 5 (Typed values). *If $\Gamma \vdash expr \rightsquigarrow exprA : typeA$ and $\Gamma, \Delta \vdash exprA \rightarrow\!\!\!\rightarrow v$, where $v \in value$, and $typeA \neq$ dynamic then $v \in valueT+$*

Proof. Proof by induction on the structure of $expr$, omitting $exprU$ forms due to type derivations. Most cases proceed like the corresponding untyped cases in lemma 4 with case splits for object values versus mimic values, where reduction to a mimic relies on the embedded value being in $valueU+$ by lemma 4.

The cases for **call** and **super** substitute values into typed expressions and require a typed expression as a result; however, substituted values can be subtypes of the declared parameter types and could therefore switch the type to be **dynamic**. We show by lemma 6 that the substituted values, although subtypes of the declared types, do not have type **dynamic** unless the specified parameter type was **dynamic**.

After annotation, correctly typed programs do not allow untyped expressions within typed expressions unless mimicked. We prove this using a variation of our type checking relation – $\Gamma \vdash exprA :_S typeA$. This relation uses a modified subtype relation $\preceq$, in which there is no SUBDBOTTOM rule, without other changes. Thus **dynamic** is related only to itself after annotation, as proposed by Wadler [5]. Using this lemma, we show that substitution cannot introduce untyped values during reduction.

Lemma 6 (Correct Annotations). *If $\Gamma \vdash expr \rightsquigarrow exprA : typeA$ then $\Gamma \vdash exprA :_S typeA$*

Proof. Proof by induction on the structure of $expr$. Cases where no $\rightsquigarrow$ relation rule use the embedding relation follow from the rules, as the type and representation cannot change.

Other cases are all similar, to illustrate we consider the call expression, **call**(e, mid, e_d). The e_d argument may be embedded in a **mimic** during annotation, to eA_d. This annotated subexpression does not impact the derived type during annotation, but it does during type checking. For the call expression to type check and derive the same $typeA$, the type of eA_d, tA, must be a subtype of the declared parameter, $tA \preceq t$. Lemma 7 shows that embedding preserves this property.

Lemma 7 (Embed). *If $\Gamma \vdash exprTA : typeA \mapsto_{type} exprTA'$ then $\Gamma \vdash exprTA' : typeA'$ where $\Gamma \vdash typeA' \preceq type$*

Proof. Proof by inspection of the $\mapsto$ relation. The top three rules embed expressions but do not modify the type, which is directly extracted CHECKM and CHECKG. The final two are identity relations on the expressions.

Removing the SUBDBOTTOM rule separates the type systems of our typed and untyped languages, allowing us to show that values crossing between typed and untyped expressions must pass through the appropriate wrapper. Theorem 1 relied on the original subtype relation for preservation; however, the $\preceq_D$ subtype relation is not necessary for preservation. We proved preservation using both subtype relations with no difference between the proofs.

This shows that in cross-language interoperability, **dynamic** must be the bottom subtype during annotation, to derive the insertion of appropriate expression embeddings; however, it must not be related after annotation so that strict boundaries between languages can be observed.

6   Implementing Inheritance

We implement our inheritance reduction relation in the PLT Redex system, as an extension of our previous reduction relation. We also extend our small-step annotation relation to annotate super calls and embed class types. This creates an executable model within the PLT Redex framework, where we can create specific cross-language class hierarchies and examine intermediate stages in the reduction to ascertain that values are properly converted. The Redex reduction relation differs from the presented model by eliminating the definition map and environment, instead our context rules use the program's context to extract method definitions and the embedded ancestor types.

This experience gives us insight into the steps necessary to extend our existing implementation with cross-language inheritance support. The primary change would be to embed type information for the parent class in the untyped representation; as the existing class system requires an elaboration phase, we can insert the type and redirect super calls during this phase. The embedded type could be stored either as a closure value or a new element in the class table – it is neither desirable nor necessary to institute a per-object overhead. We can insert the requisite stub methods while building the method table.

7   Related Work

Previous work on interoperability explores exchanging values safely between languages with different semantics and permitting execution of partially-typed programs; these projects did not directly address the concerns of permitting inheritance across language boundaries with value and type preservation.

The style of our language model draws heavily from previous object and function calculi; primarily ClassicJava [9] and Featherweight Java [8].

Siek and Taha [11] present a calculus for incorporating typed and untyped expressions within an object system, where a fully-typed program cannot produce a runtime type error. Their calculus, building on the Abadi and Cardelli $\mathbf{OB}_{<:}$ calculus, can encode structural inheritance of existing objects through copying. However, this does not preserve type guarantees across generations as subtyping is only structural and inheritance only behavioral. Our system is the first to support cross-language inheritance in this style with support for nominal subtyping and behavioral inheritance, conforming to the expectations of both languages.

The Siek and Taha work uses casts to confirm runtime-type compliance that provide higher-order wrappings for object values after type-erasure. While they show that fully-annotated programs are sound, their work does not take the additional step of showing that typed programs cannot be blamed for runtime errors. Their earlier work [12], connects the simply-typed lambda calculus to the untyped variant, and prove that their fully annotated calculus is equivalent to simply-typed lambda calculus.

Wadler and Findler [5] demonstrate a proof technique for proving safety in a language supporting different static guarantees, including untyped expressions, using contracts. This work shows that a well-typed program cannot be blamed for type inconsistencies introduced across a contract. Additionally, thy demonstrate that in a combined language, with full contract annotations, the dynamic type is neither a subtype nor super type of the statically-checked types. Our experience provides further evidence of this relationship for fully annotated programs.

Tobin-Hochstadt's and Felleisen's [4] work on integrating statically-typed functional modules, following the PLT Scheme module system, with untyped modules in the same language provide a proof showing that the typed modules cannot be blamed for any dynamic type errors. In this language, boundaries between typed and untyped implementations occur at module levels, so blame tracking reports the relevant module. Boundaries within our system can occur with finer granularity, complicating the source of the blame. However, both Tobin-Hochstadt's proof and our own demonstrate the necessity of proving that the source of type inconsistencies lies with untyped program fragments.

Matthews and Findler [13] propose models of combining multiple languages using guards to protect the type expectations of the different languages. Their semantics follows similar techniques as those presented in our model; however, neither language represented in this work supports object-oriented computations focusing on functional language interoperation.

A proposed extension to ML allows for a `Dynamic` type constructor [14,15], which is similar to the `dynamic` declaration. The `Dynamic` operators allow the explicit extraction of untyped data into programmer specified types; guards are not supported. This work demonstrates that within one language, such operations are sound.

7.1 Mixing Dynamic and Static Types

Some implementations also provide combinations of static and dynamic types.

Strongtalk [16] adds an optional static type system to Smalltalk [17]. On the boundary between typed and untyped expressions the compiler either assumes a type or relies on an annotation from the programmer.

The Amber programming language [18] also mixes static and dynamic type checking. Values with statically checked types can be placed into `Dynamic` wrappers, in which the static type information is disregarded. During program execution, interaction with these values is checked to conform to the static type knowledge. Like the Dynamic ML language, the programmer must explicitly cast the type.

Work on embedding languages by Benton [19] and Ramsey [20] provides connections between statically-typed languages and embedded dynamically-typed languages. For both systems, when a value from the dynamically typed language is passed into the statically typed language, the system performs an immediate check of the value but does not check higher-order properties. The expected type is derived from a specification either written by the programmer or provided by the system library.

8   Conclusions

While the J+S language does not support mutation, the **get-field** and **superU** semantics reflect the possibility of extending the model to include both mutable fields and mutable method implementations. Field accesses dispatch to the embedded object before inserting wrappers; in a system with mutable fields this ensures that the current value is always retrieved. Field updates require the same embeddings as method and object-instantiation parameters; the only missing pieces are the representation of a store and reference indirections.

By dynamically injecting wrappers during **superU** reduction, the untyped language could support the modification of method bodies without any variation in the insertion. Further, dynamically injecting additional methods into a leaf class should similarly cause no variation for interoperability. Injecting methods into a non-leaf class in a multi-language hierarchy can lead to the errors we describe for partially overriding classes. We suspect that a descendent class should consider its parent sealed at the point of extension, with any additions invisible, to alleviate this problem.

Using our technique, a program combining Java with Ruby, Groovy, Scheme, or Javascript, can provide safe interaction without the requirements of marshaling or checking values reducing the programmer overhead typically involved in these combinations. Our proof of safety confirms that only dynamically-typed expressions cause type failures. Further we provide evidence that the proof requirements presented by Tobin-Hochstadt [4] and the subtyping relations and blame assessment presented by Wadler [5] apply to any two interoperating languages, while providing similar safety assurances.

Our full semantics, their Ott-based specification, and an executable PLT Redex model are available from www.cl.cam.ac.uk/~keg29/inheritance-model.

Acknowledgements

We thank the anonymous reviewers for helping us improve the presentation of this work, as well as Alan Mycroft and Matthew Flatt; Matthias Felleisen and Scott Owens for helping us find flaws in our model; and the developers of PLT Redex and Ott for providing tools that simplify the specification of semantic models.

References

1. Flatt, M., Findler, R.B.: PLT MrEd: Graphical Toolbox Manual. Technical Report PLT-TR-2007-2-v370, PLT Scheme (2007)
2. Koenig, D., Glover, A., King, P., Laforge, G., Skeet, J.: Groovy in Action. Manning Publications (2007)
3. Gray, K.E., Findler, R.B., Flatt, M.: Fine-grained interoperability through mirrors and contracts. In: Proc. ACM Conf. on OOPSLA (2005)
4. Tobin-Hochstadt, S., Felleisen, M.: Interlanguage migration: From scripts to programs. In: Proc. of ACM Dynamic Languages Symposium (2006)
5. Wadler, P., Findler, R.B.: Well-typed programs can't be blamed. In: Proc. ACM Workshop on Scheme and Functional Programming (2007)
6. Gray, K.E.: A model of Java/Scheme interoperability. In: Findler, R.B., Flatt, M., Felleisen, M. (eds.) Designing, Developing, and Debugging Programming Language Models. MIT Press, Cambridge (to appear, 2008)
7. Matthews, J., Findler, R.B., Flatt, M., Felleisen, M.: A visual environment for developing context-sensitive term rewriting systems. In: van Oostrom, V. (ed.) RTA 2004. LNCS, vol. 3091. Springer, Heidelberg (2004)
8. Igarashi, A., Pierce, B., Wadler, P.: Featherweight Java: A Minimal Core Calculus for Java and GJ. In: Proc. ACM Conf. on OOPSLA (1999)
9. Flatt, M., Krishnamurthi, S., Felleisen, M.: A Programmer's Reduction Semantics for Classes and Mixins. In: Alves-Foss, J. (ed.) Formal Syntax and Semantics of Java. LNCS, vol. 1523. Springer, Heidelberg (1999)
10. Flatt, M.: PLT MzLib: Libraries manual. Technical Report PLT-TR-2007-n-v370, PLT Scheme (2007)
11. Siek, J.G., Taha, W.: Gradual typing for objects. In: Ernst, E. (ed.) ECOOP 2007. LNCS, vol. 4609. Springer, Heidelberg (2007)
12. Siek, J.G., Taha, W.: Gradual typing for functional languages. In: Proc. ACM Workshop on Scheme and Functional Programming (2006)
13. Matthews, J., Findler, R.B.: Operational semantics for multi-language programs. In: Proc. ACM Conf. on Principles of Programming Languages (2007)
14. Abadi, M., Cardelli, L., Pierce, B., Plotkin, G.: Dynamic Typing in a Statically Typed Language. ACM J. Tran. on Prog. Languages and Systems 13 (1991)
15. Duggan, D.: Dynamic Typing for Distributed Programming in Polymorphic Languages. ACM J. Tran. on Prog. Languages and Systems 21, 11–45 (1999)
16. Bracha, G., Griswold, D.: Strongtalk: Typechecking Smalltalk in a Production Environment. In: Proc. ACM Conf. on OOPSLA (1993)
17. Goldberg, A., Robson, D.: Smalltalk-80: The Language and its Implementation. Addison-Wesley, Reading (1983)
18. Cardelli, L.: Amber. In: Cousineau, G., Curien, P.-L., Robinet, B. (eds.) LITP 1985. LNCS, vol. 242. Springer, Heidelberg (1986)
19. Benton, N.: Embedded Interpreters. Journal of Functional Programming 15 (2005)
20. Ramsey, N.: Embedding an Interpreted Language Using Higher-Order Functions and Types. Journal of Functional Programming (to appear) Initial version in ACM Workshop on Interpreters, Virtual Machines and Emulators (June 2003)

Liquid Metal: Object-Oriented Programming Across the Hardware/Software Boundary

Shan Shan Huang[1], Amir Hormati[2], David F. Bacon[3], and Rodric Rabbah[3]

[1] Georgia Institute of Technology
[2] University of Michigan
[3] IBM Research

Abstract. The paradigm shift in processor design from monolithic processors to multicore has renewed interest in programming models that
facilitate parallelism. While multicores are here today, the future is likely
to witness architectures that use reconfigurable fabrics (FPGAs) as co-
processors. FPGAs provide an unmatched ability to tailor their circuitry
per application, leading to better performance at lower power. Unfortunately, the skills required to program FPGAs are beyond the expertise
of skilled software programmers. This paper shows how to bridge the
gap between programming software vs. hardware. We introduce Lime,
a new Object-Oriented language that can be compiled for the JVM or
into a synthesizable hardware description language. Lime extends Java
with features that provide a way to carry OO concepts into efficient
hardware. We detail an end-to-end system from the language down to
hardware synthesis and demonstrate a Lime program running on both a
conventional processor and in an FPGA.

1 Introduction

The end of the free ride from clock scaling has stimulated renewed interest in
alternative computer architectures. Due to the increased complexity of these architectures, there has also been a corresponding revival of interest in alternative
models for programming them.

Most of the attention has been focused on multicore chips, but many other
types of systems are being produced and explored: SIMD, graphics processors,
"manycore", and reconfigurable hardware fabrics. While multicore chips are the
most straightforward for chip manufacturers to produce, it remains an open
question as to which hardware organization is the most efficient or the easiest
to program. Furthermore, as power outweighs chip area, it seems likely that
systems will become increasingly heterogeneous.

Among these alternative architectures, reconfigurable fabrics such as field-
programmable gate arrays (FPGAs) have many compelling features: low power
consumption, extremely high performance for many applications, a high degree
of determinism, and enormous flexibility. Because FPGAs route and operate on
single bits, it is possible to exploit many different kinds of parallelism either
individually or in combination: at the micro-scale of bits or the macro-scale of
tasks, with pipelining or data parallelism, etc.

J. Vitek (Ed.): ECOOP 2008, LNCS 5142, pp. 76–103, 2008.
© Springer-Verlag Berlin Heidelberg 2008

Recently, chip manufacturers have begun providing interfaces to allow the kinds of high-bandwidth data transfer that makes it easier to connect accelerator chips to CPUs (for instance, AMD's Torenza and Intel's QuickAssist). Some motherboards come with an open socket connected to such a bus into which one can plug an FPGA. The increasing availability of systems with FPGAs offers an opportunity to customize processing architectures according to the applications they run. An application-customized architecture can offer extremely high performance with very low power compared to more general purpose designs.

However, FPGAs are notoriously difficult to program, and are generally programmed using hardware description languages like VHDL and Verilog. Such languages lack many of the software engineering and abstraction facilities that we take for granted in modern Object-Oriented (OO) languages. On the other hand, they do provide abstractions of time and a much more rigorous style of modular decomposition. In hybrid CPU/FPGA systems, additional complexity is introduced by the fact that the CPU and the FPGA are programmed in completely different languages with very different semantics.

The goal of the Liquid Metal project at IBM Research is to allow such hybrid systems to be programmed in a single high-level OO language that maps well to both CPUs and FPGAs. This language, which is backward-compatible with Java, is called *Lime*.

While at first glance it may seem that conflicting requirements for programming these different kinds of systems create an inevitable tension that will result in a hodgepodge language design, it is our belief that when the features are provided at a sufficiently high level of abstraction, many of them turn out to be highly beneficial in both environments.

By using a single language we open up the opportunity to hide the complexity of domain crossing between CPU and FPGA. Furthermore, we can fluidly move computations back and forth between the two types of computational devices, choosing to execute them where they are most efficient or where we have the most available resources.

Our long-term goal is to "JIT the hardware" – to dynamically select methods or tasks for compilation to hardware, potentially taking advantage of dynamic information in the same way that multi-level JIT compilers do today for software. However, many challenges remain before this vision can be realized.

In this paper, we present an end-to-end system from language design to co-execution on hardware and software. While some of the individual components are incomplete, significant portions of each part of the system have been built, and the overall system architecture is complete.

The system that we present in this paper consists of the components shown in Figure 1 (the components are labeled with the paper sections in which they are described). The system consists of a front-end for the Lime language which can generate either Java bytecodes or a spatial intermediate language suitable for computing on FPGAs. When compiling to hardware, a sequence of compilation steps is used to produce *bitfiles* which can be loaded onto the FPGA. The Liquid Metal Runtime system (LMRT) consists of portions that reside on both the

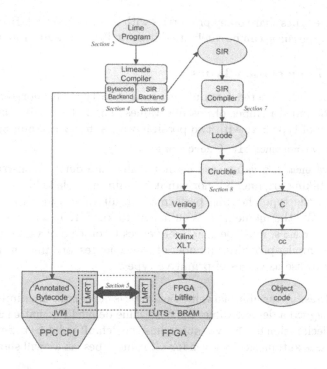

Fig. 1. The Liquid Metal Compilation and Runtime System

FPGA and on the CPU. LMRT handles communication and synchronization between the two domains, as well as loading of FPGA code.

The infrastructure also allows generation of C code, which could be used for compilation to either standard multicores or SIMD processors like Cell. However, we have not investigated the performance of this portion of the tool chain, so we do not discuss it in this paper.

2   Lime: Language Design

Lime is designed with two goals in mind: Programmers should be able to program with high-level OO features and abstractions; These high-level programs should be amenable to bit-level analysis and should expose parallelism. To achieve these goals, Lime extends Java with value types, value generic types, and enum-indexed arrays. In this section, we discuss these features and demonstrate how they can be used by the programmer. We will also highlight their implications for the compiler, particularly with respect to efficient synthesis to an FPGA.

A value type in Lime can be an enum, class, or interface, annotated with the modifier value. The defining characteristic of value types is that they are immutable. An object of a value type, once created, never changes. We begin our exposition with the building block of value types: value enum's.

Lime's value types share many properties with those of Kava [1]. However, they have simpler type rules, can be safely used in Java libraries, and support generics.

2.1   Value Enumeration Types

A value `enum` is a restricted form of the Java `enum` type. It represents a value type with a bounded number of possible values. The following is a user-defined representation of type `bit`, with two possible values, `bit.zero`, and `bit.one`:

```
public value enum bit { zero, one; }
```

Unlike Java `enum`'s, a value `enum` cannot define non-default constructors (i.e. constructors taking arguments), nor can it contain mutable fields. We elaborate in Section 2.5 the type checking performed on all value types to ensure their immutability. For the moment, it is sufficient to know that all fields of a value type, including `enum`'s, must be `final` references to objects of value types.

The Lime compiler provides a number of conveniences for value `enum`'s, making them as easy to use as values of primitive types.

Default Values. A variable of a value `enum` type is never `null`. If uninitialized, the variable is assigned a default value: the first value defined for that `enum` type. For example, in declaration `bit b;` variable `b` has the default value `bit.zero`. In fact, a default value is automatically given for *all* value types, as we will show shortly.

Compiler-Defined Operators. Arithmetic operators such as `+`, `-`, `++`, and `--`, are automatically defined for value `enum`'s. For example, `bit.one + bit.zero` returns `bit.one`. Similarly, `bit.one + bit.one`, returns `bit.zero`, akin to how integers wrap around when overflowing their range. Comparison operators are also defined for value `enum`'s. For example, `bit.one > bit.zero` returns `true`.

Lime also provides programmers an easy way to produce and iterate over a range of values. Lime introduces the binary operator, `::`. The expression `x :: y` produces an object of `lime.lang.Range<T>` or `lime.lang.ReverseRange<T>`, depending on whether `x < y`, or `x > y`, and where `T` is the least upper bound type of `x` and `y`. Both `Range<T>` and `ReverseRange<T>` are value types, implementing the `Iterable<T>` interface in Java. They are thus usable in the "for-each" style loops introduced since Java 5. For example, the following code defines a loop over the range of values greater than or equal to `bit.zero`, and less than or equal to `bit.one`:

```
for ( bit b : bit.zero :: bit.one ) { System.out.println(b); }
```

Furthermore, there is nothing required of the programmer to indicate whether a range is ascending or descending, even when the operands' values cannot be statically determined. For instance, in the code below, depending on the arguments used to invoke `printBits`, the object generated by `begin :: end` can be either `Range<bit>` or `ReverseRange<bit>`:

```
void printBits(bit begin, bit end) {
  for ( bit b : begin :: end ) { System.out.println(b); }
}
```

In Lime programs, programmers often need to iterate over the entire range of possible values of a value `enum`. A convenient shorthand is provided for iterating over this range. For example, `for (bit b) {...}` is equivalent to `for (bit b : bit.first :: bit.last) {...}`. Such a default range is always an ascending one.

The `::` operator is automatically defined for any value type supporting the operators `++`, `--`, `<` and `>`. Lime also supports the `::` operator for Java's primitive integral types, such as `int`, `short`, etc.

Compiler-Defined Fields and Methods. In addition to operators, static fields `first` and `last` are automatically defined to reference the smallest and largest values in a value `enum`'s range. For instance, `bit.first` returns `bit.zero`. These fields may seem redundant for a known `enum` type, but they become invaluable when we iterate over the range of an `enum` type *variable*, where the exact values of an `enum` are not known statically.

Methods `next()` and `prev()` are generated to return the value proceeding and preceding the value invoking the method: `bit.first.next()` returns `bit.one`.

Since objects of value `enum`'s (and in fact, all value types) do not have object identity at the Lime language level (i.e., all instances of `bit.zero` should be treated as the same object), the Lime compiler automatically generates `equals(Object o)` and `hashCode()` methods for these `enum`'s. The compiler also overloads the `==` operator for value `enum`'s to invoke `equals(Object o)`. (An exception to this case is when `==` is used inside the definition of `equals(Object o)` itself.) Note that this is exactly the opposite from what is in Java: the `equals(Object o)` method in Java defaults to invoking `==` and comparing object identity.

User-defined Operators. Lime also allows programmers to define their custom operators, or even override the automatically defined ones. For instance, we can define a unary complement operator for `bit`:

```
public bit ~ this { return this++; }
```

A binary operator could be similarly defined. For instance, the operator `&` for `bit` can be defined as follows:

```
public bit this & (bit that) { return this == one && that == one; }
```

Operator definitions are converted into compiler-generated methods, dispatched off of the `this` operand. For example, the `~` operator definition becomes: `public bit $COMP() { return this++; }`, and the definition for `&` thus becomes `public bit $AND(bit that) { ... }`.

2.2   enum-indexed Arrays

Lime also extends Java with `enum`-indexed arrays. For example, `int[bit] twoInts;` declares an `int` array, named `twoInts`. The size of `twoInts` is bounded by the number of values in the value `enum` type `bit`. Thus, `twoInts` has a fixed size of 2. Furthermore, only an object of the array size's `enum` type can be used to index into an enum-indexed array. The following code demonstrates the use of enum-indexed arrays.

```
int i = twoInts[0];        // ILLEGAL! 0 is not of type bit
int j = twoInts[bit.zero]  // OK
```

An enum-indexed array has space automatically allocated for it by the compiler. enum-indexed arrays provide a nice way to express fixed-size arrays, where the type system can easily guarantee that array indexes can never be out of bounds. Both of these are important properties for laying out the program in hardware – but are also valuable for writing exception-free software and for compiling it for efficient execution.

2.3   A More Complex Value Type: Unsigned

Using value enum's and enum-indexed arrays, we can now define a much more interesting value class, Unsigned32:

```
public value enum thirtytwo { b0,b1,...,b31; }

public value class Unsigned32 {
    bit data[thirtytwo];

    public Unsigned32(bit vector[thirtytwo]) { data = vector; }

    public boolean this ^ (Unsigned32 that) {
        bit newData[thirtytwo];
        for ( thirtytwo i)
            newData[i] = this.data[i] ^ that.data[i];
        return new Unsigned32(newData);
    }
    ... // define other operators and methods.
}
```

Unsigned32 is an OO representation of a 32-bit unsigned integer. It uses the value enum type thirtytwo to create an enum-indexed array of exactly 32 bit's, holding the data for the integer. The definition of Unsigned32 exposes another interesting feature of the Lime compiler. Recall that a value type must have a default value that is assigned to uninitialized variables of that type. This means each value type must provide a default constructor for this purpose. Notice however that there is no such default constructor defined for Unsigned32. Conveniently, the Lime compiler can automatically generate this constructor for value types. The generated constructor initializes each field to its default value. Recall that one of the typing requirements of value types is that all fields must be references to value types. Thus, each field must also have a default value constructor defined (or generated) for it. The base case of our recursive argument ends with value enum's. Thus, it is always possible for the Lime compiler to generate a default constructor.

Implications for the Compiler. Even though Unsigned32 is defined using high-level abstractions, the combination of value enum's and enum-indexed arrays exposes it to bit-level analysis. We can easily analyze the code to see that an object of Unsigned32 requires exactly 32 bits: each element of data[thirtytwo] is of type bit, which requires exactly 1 bit; there are 32 of them in data[thirtytwo].

This high level abstraction provides the Lime compiler with a lot of flexibility in both software and hardware representations of a value object and its operations. In software, Lime programs can be compiled down to regular Java bytecode and run on a virtual machine. We can choose to represent objects of Unsigned32 and thirtytwo as true objects, and iterations over values of thirtytwo are done through next() method calls on the iterator. However, without any optimizations, this would yield very poor performance compared to operations on a primitive int. We can thus also choose to use the bit-level information, and the knowledge that value objects do not have mutable state, to perform optimizations such as semantic expansions [2]. Using semantic expansions, value objects are treated like primitive types, represented in unboxed formats. Method invocations are treated as static procedure calls. These choices can be made completely transparent to the programmer.

The same analogy holds for hardware. Existing hardware description languages such as VHDL [3] and SystemC [4] require programmers to provide detailed data layouts for registers, down to the meaning of each bit. In contrast, Lime's high level abstraction allows the compiler to be very flexible with the way object data is represented in hardware. For instance, in order to perform "dynamic dispatch" in hardware, each object must carry its own type information in the form of a type id number. However, we can also strip an object of its type information when all target methods can be statically determined, and achieve space savings. The hardware layout choices are again transparent to the programmer.

The definition of Unsigned32 exposes bit-level parallelism when it is natural to program at that level. Even more performance speed up can be gained through coarser-grained parallelism, where entire blocks of code are executed in a parallel or pipelined fashion. Very sophisticated algorithms have been developed to discover loop dependencies and identify which loops can be parallelized or pipelined safely. The knowledge of immutable objects make Lime programs even more amenable to these techniques. Our eventual goal is to design language constructs that promote a style of programming where different forms of parallelism are easily discovered and easily exploited.

2.4 Generic Value Types

A closer inspection of Unsigned32 shows that its code is entirely parametric to the value enum type used to represent the length of the array data. No matter what enum is used to size data, the definitions for the constructor and operator ^ are exactly the same, modulo the substitution of a different enum for thirtytwo. A good programming abstraction mechanism should allow us to define these operations once in a generic way. Lime extends the type genericity mechanism in

Java to offer exactly this type of abstraction. The following is a generic definition of Unsigned<W>, where type parameter W can be instantiated with different value enum to represent integers of various bit width:

```
public value class Unsigned<W extends Enum<W>> {
    bit data[W];

    public Unsigned(bit vector[W]) { data = vector; }

    public Unsigned<T> this ^ (Unsigned<T> that) {
        bit newData[T];
        for ( T i )
            newData[i] = this.data[i] ^ that.data[i];
        return new Unsigned<T>(newData);
    }
    ... // similarly parameterize operator definitions
}
```

Thus, to represent a 32-bit integer, we simply use type Unsigned<thirtytwo>. Similarly, we could use Unsigned<sixtyfour> to represent a 64-bit integer where sixtyfour is defined as follows:

```
public value enum sixtyfour { b0,b1,...,b63; }
```

Note that type parameters to value type are assumed to be value types, and can only be instantiated with value types.

For notational convenience, Lime offers a limited form of type aliasing. A typedef declaration can appear wherever variable declarations are allowed, and are similarly scoped. For example, the following statement declares Unsigned32 as an alias for Unsigned<thirtytwo>:

```
typedef Unsigned32 = Unsigned<thirtytwo>;
```

We use the aliased forms of the Unsigned<W> class for the remainder of the paper.

2.5 Type-Checking Value Types

In order to ensure that the objects of value types are truly immutable, we must impose the following rules on the definition of a value type:

1. A field of a value type must be final, and of a value type. The keyword final is assumed in the definition of value types and is inserted by the Lime compiler. Compile-time checks make sure that assignment to fields only happen in initializers.
2. The supertypes of a value type must also be value types (with the exception of Object).
3. The type parameter of a value type is assumed to be a value type during the type checking process, and can only be instantiated by value types.
4. Objects of value types can only be assigned to variables of value types.

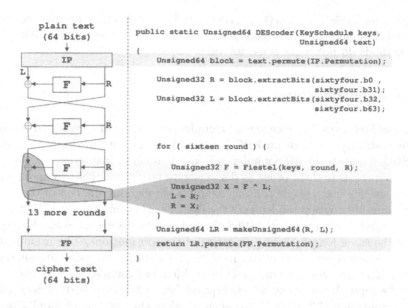

Fig. 2. Block level diagram of DES and Lime code snippet

The first three rules are fairly straight forward. The last rule requires a bit more elaboration. The Lime compiler imposes that value types can only be subtypes of other value types, except for `Object`. Therefore, the only legal assignment from a value type to a non-value type is an assignment to `Object`. In this case, we "box" the object of value type into an object of `lime.lang.BoxedValue`, a special Lime compiler class. The boxed value can then be used as a regular object. In fact, this is the technique used when a value type is used in `synchronized`, or when `wait()` is invoked on it.

Method `equals(Object o)` requires special treatment by these rules. The `equals` method must take an argument of `Object` type. It is inefficient to box up a value type to pass into the `equals` of another value type, which then has to strip the boxed value before comparison. Thus, the Lime compiler allows a value type to be passed into the `equals` of value types without being boxed. These `equals` methods have been type-checked to ensure that they do not mutate fields, it is thus safe to do so.

It is also important to point out that an array holding objects of value types is not a value type itself. Neither is an `enum`-indexed array holding objects of value types. The contents of the array can still mutate. A value array, then, is expressed as (`value int[]`) `valInts`. Similarly for value `enum`-indexed arrays.

A value array must be initialized when it is declared. All further writing into the array is disallowed. Our syntax does not allow multiple levels of immutability in arrays. It is not possible to express a mutable array of value arrays, for example. The `value` keyword at the outside means the entire array, at all dimensions, are immutable.

Finally, methods `finalize()`, `notify()`, and `notifyAll()` can never be called on objects of value types. Objects of value types have no storage identity, thus these methods do not make sense for value objects.

3   Running Example

The Liquid Metal system is somewhat complex, consisting of a front-end compiler that generates bytecode or an FPGA-oriented spatial intermediate representation (SIR), a high-level SIR compiler, a layout planner, a low-level compiler, and finally a synthesis tool. In order to demonstrate how all of these components fit together, we will use a single running example throughout the rest of the paper.

Our example program implements the Data Encryption Standard (DES). The program inputs plain text as 64-bit blocks and generates encrypted blocks (cipher text) of the same length through a series of transformations. The organization of the DES algorithm and its top level implementation in Lime are shown in Figure 2. The transformations occur in 16 identical rounds, each of which encrypts the input block using an encryption key. The plain text undergoes an initial permutation (IP) of the bit-sequence before the first round. Similarly, the

```
public value class Unsigned<T extends Enum<T>> {
    ...
    Unsigned<T> permute ( (value T[T]) permTable ) {
        bit newBits[T];
        for ( T i ) {
            newBits[i] = data[permTable[i]];
        }
        return new Unsigned<T>(newBits);
    }
    ...
}

// initial permutation (IP)
import static DES.sixtyfour.*;

public value class IP {
    public static (value sixtyfour[sixtyfour]) Permutation = {
        b57, b49, b41, b33, b25, b17, b9,  b1, b59, b51, b43, b35, b27, b19, b11, b3,
        b61, b53, b45, b37, b29, b21, b13, b5, b63, b55, b47, b39, b31, b23, b15, b7,
        b56, b48, b40, b32, b24, b16, b8,  b0, b58, b50, b42, b34, b26, b18, b10, b2,
        b60, b52, b44, b36, b28, b20, b12, b4, b62, b54, b46, b38, b30, b22, b14, b6
    };
    ...
}
```

Fig. 3. DES code snippets showing initial permutation

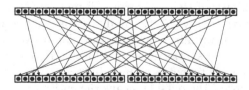

Fig. 4. Permutation pattern for IP

```
static Unsigned32 Fiestel(KeySchedule keys, Sixteen round, Unsigned32 R) {
    // half-block expansion
    Unsigned48 E = expand(R);

    // key mixing
    Unsigned48 K = keys.keySchedule(round);
    Unsigned48 S = E ^ K;

    // substitutions
    Unsigned4 Substitutes[eight];

    fourtyeight startBit = fourtyeight.b0;
    for ( eight i ) {
        // extract 6-bit piece
        fourtyeight endBit = startBit + fourtyeight.b5;
        Unsigned6 bits = S.extractSixBits(startBit, endBit);

        // substitute bits
        Substitutes[i] = Sbox(i, bits);

        // move on to next 6-bit piece
        startBit += fourtyeight.b6;
    }

    // concatenate pieces to form
    // a 32-bit half block again
    thirtytwo k;
    bit[thirtytwo] pBits;
    for ( eight i ) {
        for (four j) {
            pBits[k] = Substitutes[i].data[j];
        }
    }

    // permute result and return
    Unsigned32 P = new Unsigned32(pBits);
    return reversePermute(P);
}
```

Fig. 5. DES Fiestel round

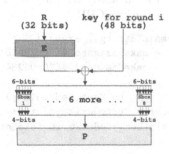

Fig. 6. Block level diagram of Fiestel round

bit-sequence produced in the final round is permuted using a final permutation (FP). The output of the initial permutation is partitioned into two 32-bit half blocks. One half (R) is transformed using a Feistel function. The result of the function is then exclusive-OR'ed (`xor`) with the other half (L). The two halves are then interchanged and another round of transformations occurs.

The initial and final permutations consume a 64-bit sequence and produce a sequence of bits according to a specific permutation pattern. The pattern for the initial permutation is illustrated in Figure 4. We implemented the permutations using a lookup table as shown in Figure 3. The `permute` method loops through the output bit indexes in order, and maps the appropriate input bit to the corresponding output bit. The enumerations and their iterators make it possible to readily name each individual bit, and as a result, bit-permutations are easy to implement. The ability to specify transformations at the bit-level provides several advantages for hardware synthesis. Namely, the explicit enumeration of the bits decouples their naming from a platform-specific implementation, and as a result there are no bit-masks or other bit-extraction routines that muddle the code. Furthermore, the enumeration of the individual bits means we can closely match permutations and similar transformations to their Verilog or VHDL counterparts. As a result, the compiler can command a lot of freedom in transforming the code. It has also been shown that such a bit-level representation of the computation leads to efficient code generation for conventional architectures and processors that support short-vector instructions [5,6]. There are also various benefits for a programmer. For example, the `permute` method can process the input or output bits in any order, according to what is most convenient. Similarly, off-by-one errors are avoided, through the use of `enum`-indexed arrays.

The `Fiestel` method performs the transformations illustrated in Figure 6. The 32-bit R half block undergoes an expansion to 48-bits, and the result is mixed with an encryption key using an `xor` operation. The result is then split into eight 6-bit pieces, each of which is substituted with a 4-bit value using a unique substitution box (`Substitutes[i]`). The eight 4-bit resultant values are concatenated to form a 32-bit half block that is in turn permuted. The `Fiestel` method and coding rounds run in hardware on the FPGA. The `main` method, shown below, runs in software on the CPU.

```
public static void main(String[] argv) {
    Unsigned64 key  = makeUnsigned64("0xFEDCBA9876543210");
    Unsigned64 text = makeUnsigned64("0x0123456789ABCDEF");

    KeySchedule keys   = new KeySchedule(key);
    Unsigned64  cipher = DEScoder(keys, text);
    System.out.println(Long.toHexString(cipher.longValue()));
}
```

The program exercises co-execution between hardware and software, and demonstrates the use of varying object sizes and object-oriented features in hardware.

4 From Lime to the Virtual Machine

Lime programs can be compiled to regular Java bytecode and executed on any Java VM. The Lime bytecode generation performs two additional steps than the

Java compiler. First, the Lime compiler generates bytecode to add "value" to value types:

- Default constructors, `equals(Object o)` and `hashCode()` methods are created for those value classes that do not define them.
- Uninitialized variables of value types are rewritten with default initializers.
- Operator definitions listed in Section 2.1 are added for value `enum`'s. Value types that support `++`, `--`, `<` and `>` operators have the range operator, `::`, defined for them.
- Operator expressions are converted to appropriate operator method calls. E.g., `x == y` is converted to `x.equals(y)`, assuming x is of value type.

For the purpose of separate compilation, all value types are translated to implement the `lime.lang.Value` interface. When loaded as a binary class, this interface indicates to the Lime compiler that it is a value class. Additional interfaces are added for value types supporting different operators. For example, all value types supporting operator `<` implement the interface `lime.lang.HasGT<T>`, where `HasGT<T>` contains one operator, `boolean this < (T op2)`.

Next, instantiations of value generic types must be expanded. Generics is a powerful abstraction tool for programmers. However, generic value classes also significantly complicate our compilation process. To see why, consider generating a default constructor for `Unsigned<W>`. This constructor needs to initialize the `data` field to a `bit`-array of size w, where w is the number of values defined for `enum` type `W`. However, the value of w changes for each concrete instantiation of `W`. We have no way of initializing this field without knowing what `W` is type-instantiated to. For this reason, the erasure-based compilation technique used by Java generics is not applicable. We must employ an expansion-based compilation scheme, where each instantiation of `Unsigned<W>` creates a different type.

Java generic classes not annotated with the `value` modifier are translated using the standard erasure technique, as long as they do not instantiate generic value types with their type variables. As a result, pure Java code that is compiled with our compiler remains backward compatible.

There are of course numerous optimizations that exploit bit-width information and the immutable properties of value types (see Section 2.3 for examples). Such optimizations are well studied and understood. In this paper, we primarily focus on the less understood parts of our language, such as translating Object-Oriented semantics down to the hardware fabric.

The Lime frontend compiler (source to bytecode or spatial intermediate representation) is implemented using the JastAdd extensible Java compiler [7].

5   Liquid Metal Runtime for Mixed-Mode Execution

A Lime program may run in mixed-mode. That is, some parts of the program will run in the virtual machine, and some parts will run in hardware (FPGA). An example mixed-mode architecture is a CPU coupled with an FPGA coprocessor, or a desktop workstation with an FPGA PCI card. Yet another example is an FPGA with processors that are embedded within the fabric. We use a Xilinx

Virtex-4 board as an instance of the latter. The Virtex-4 is also our evaluation platform for this paper. Programs that run in software use its embedded IBM PowerPC 405 which runs at a frequency of 300 MHz. The processor boots an embedded Linux kernel and can run a JVM.

The Liquid Metal runtime (LMRT) provides an API and a library implementation that allows a program to orchestrate its execution on a given computational platform. It simplifies the exchange of code and data between processing elements (e.g., PowerPC and FPGA), and automatically manages data transfer and synchronization where appropriate. The API calls are typically generated automatically by our compiler, although a programmer can make use of the API directly and manually manage the computation when it is desirable to do so.

The LMRT organizes computation as a set of code objects and buffer objects. A buffer is either an input buffer, an output buffer, or a shared buffer. A code object reads input data from an attached input buffer. Similarly it writes its output to an attached output buffer. Data is explicitly transferred (copied) between input and output buffers. In contrast, a shared buffer simultaneously serves as an input and output buffer for multiple code objects. All communication between code objects is done through buffers.

5.1 Code Objects

The LMRT assumes there is a master processing element that initiates all computation. For example, the VM running on the PowerPC processor serves as the master on our Virtex board. The VM can invoke the LMRT API through JNI. The master creates code objects, attaches input and output buffers, and then runs, pauses, or deletes the code object as the computation evolves.

A code object embodies a set of methods that carry out computation. It can contain private mutable data that persists throughout its execution (i.e., stateful computation). However, code objects are not allowed to maintain references to state that is mutated in another object.

A Lime program running wholly in the virtual machine can be viewed as a code object with no input or output buffers. A program running in mixed-mode consists of at least two code objects: one running in software, and the other running in hardware. Data is exchanged between them using buffer objects.

5.2 Buffer Objects

A buffer is attached to a code object which can then access the buffered data using read and write operators. The LMRT defines three modes to read data from or write data to a buffer.

- **FIFO:** The buffer is a first-in first-out queue, and it is accessed using push or pop methods. For example, code running in the VM can push data into the buffer, and code running in the FPGA pops data from the buffer.
- **DMA:** The buffer serves as a local store, with put operations to write data to the buffer, and get operations to read data from it. The put and get commands operate on contiguous chunks of data.

– **RF:** The buffer serves as a scalar register file, shared between code objects.

The LMRT makes it possible to decouple the application-level communication model from the implementation in the architecture. That is, a buffer decouples (1) the program view of how data is shared and communicated between code objects from (2) the actual implementation of the I/O network in the target architecture. Hence a program can use a pattern of communication that is suitable for the application it encodes, while the compiler and runtime system can determine the best method for supporting the application-level communication model on the architecture.

5.3   The LMRT Hardware Interface Layer

One of the main reasons for the LMRT is to automatically manage communication and synchronization between processing elements. In a mixed-mode environment, communication between the VM and FPGA has to be realized over a physical network interconnecting the FPGA with the processor where the VM is running.

In our current Virtex platform, we use the register file (RF) interface between the processor and the FPGA. The RF is synthesized into the fabric itself. It is directly accessible from the FPGA. From the processor side, the registers are memory mapped to a designated region of memory. The RF we use consists of 32 registers, each 32 bits wide. The 32 registers are portioned into two sets. The first is read accessible from the FPGA, but not write accessible. Those registers are read/write accessible from the VM. The second set is read accessible from the VM, but not write accessible. The registers in the second set are read/write accessible from the FPGA.

The FIFO and DMA communication styles are implemented using the RF model. The FIFO model maintains head and tail pointers and writes the registers in order. The DMA model allows for 15x32 bits of data transfer, with 32 bits used for tags. While we use a register file interface between the VM and the FPGA, other implementations are feasible. Namely, we can implement a FIFO or a DMA directly in the FPGA fabric, and compile the code objects to use these interfaces. This kind of flexibility makes it possible to both experiment with different communication models, and adapt the interconnect according to the characteristics of the computation.

6   From Lime to a Spatial Intermediate Representation

Compiling a Lime program to execute on the FPGA requires a few transformations. Some transformations are necessary to correctly and adequately handle object orientation in hardware. Others are necessary for exposing parallelism and generating efficient circuits. Performance efficiency in the FPGA is attributed to several factors [8]:

1. **Custom datapaths:** a custom datapath elides extraneous resources to provide a distinct advantage over a predefined datapath in a conventional processor.
2. **Multi-granular operations:** a bit-width cognizant datapath, ALUs, and operators tailor the circuitry to the application, often leading to power and performance advantages.
3. **Spatial parallelism:** FPGAs offer flexible parallel structures to match the parallelism in an application. Hence bit, instruction, data, and task-level parallelism are all plausible forms of parallelism. We refer to parallelism in the FPGA as spatial since computation typically propagates throughout the fabric.

In this paper we focus exclusively on the issues related to discovering spatial parallelism and realizing such parallelism in hardware. Toward this purpose, we employ a spatial intermediate representation (SIR) that facilates the analysis of Lime programs. The SIR also provides a uniform framework for refining the inherent parallelism in the application to that it is best suited for the target platform.

6.1   Spatial Intermediate Representation

The SIR exposes both computation and communication. It is based on the synchronous dataflow model of computation [9,10]. The SIR is a graph of *filters* interconnected with communication channels. A filter consists of a single *work* method that corresponds to a specific method call derived from a Lime program. A filter may contain other methods that are called *helpers*. The difference between the work method and the helpers is that only the work method may read data from its input channel or write data to its output channel.

For example, each static call to `permute()` in the DES example corresponds to a specific filter in the SIR. A filter consumes data from its input channel, executes the work method, and writes its results to an output channel. The input and output of the `permute` method that performs the initial permutation is an `Unsigned64` value. Hence, the work method for `permute` consumes 64 bits and produces 64 bits on every execution. The filter work method runs repeatedly as long as a sufficient quantity of input data is available. Filters are independent of each other, do not share state, and can run autonomously.

Filters have a single input channel and a single output channel. A filter may communicate its output data to multiple filters by routing the data through a *splitter*. A splitter can either duplicate the input it receives and pass it on to its siblings, or it can distribute data in a roundrobin manner according to a specified set of weights. The splitter's counterpart is a *joiner*. A joiner collects and aggregates data from multiple filters in a roundrobin manner, and routes the resultant data to another filter. The single-input to single-output restriction placed on filters, and the routing of data through splitters and joiners for fan-out and fan-in imposes structure on the SIR graphs. The structure can occasionally lead to additional communication compared to an unstructured graph. In DES, this

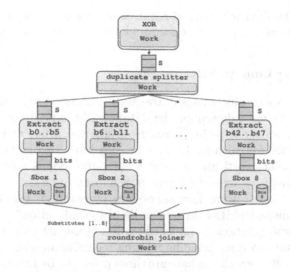

Fig. 7. SIR example for box substitutions in DES

occurs between **Fiestel** rounds where the values of L and R are interchanged[1]. However we believe that the benefits of a structured SIR outweigh its drawbacks, and prior work has shown that structured graphs can be practically refined to their unstructured counterparts [11].

The SIR graph in Figure 7 illustrates an example derived from the box substitutions (**Sbox**) that occur in the **Fiestel** rounds. In the Figure, the output of the **xor** operator is duplicated to eight filters labeled **Extract**, each of which implements the **extractSixBits** methods but for different bit indexes. For example, the left-most filter labeled **Extract b0..b5** inputs a 32-bit value and always extracts a value consisting of the bits at locations **b0..b5**. Similarly, the **Extract b42..b47** filter always extracts the bits **b42..b47**. The output of the former is the input to the **Sbox 1** filter which performs the appropriate bit substitutions for bits **b0..b5**. The **Extract** and **Sbox** filters make up a producer-consumer pair and are said to form a *pipeline*. Pipelines in the SIR graph expose pipeline parallelism that is readily exploited in hardware. The output of each **Sbox** is routed to a joiner that collects each of the 4-bit pieces in a roundrobin manner and outputs a 32-bit half block.

Filters, like objects, may have fields. The fields are initialized using an *init* method whose parameters must be resolved when the SIR is constructed. Each of the **Extract** filters is initialized with the start and end bits that it is responsible for. Similarly, each of the **Sbox** filters is initialized with a table that encodes the unique substitution pattern for the bits it is responsible for. The fields of a filter cannot be shared and are conceptually stored in a local memory that is exclusive to that filter. In the Figure 7, the cylinders labeled **Box 1..8** store the substi-

---

[1] Figure 2 illustrates unstructured communication. It is left as an exercise for the reader to determine the structured SIR equivalent.

tution boxes. The `Extract` method requires no storage since the initialization parameters are constant-propagated throughout the filter work method.

6.2   Compiling Lime to SIR

There are three key considerations in translating a Lime program into a spatial representation. We must determine the dataflow of the program: which objects (or primitive values) need to be passed from filter to filter, and which can be statically initialized (or calculated from statically initialized variables). We must also determine what constitutes a filter: what Lime code is a filter responsible for executing? Lastly, we must determine how important object-oriented features can be supported in hardware: how are objects represented? How do we support virtual method dispatch? How do we handle object allocation?

Answering these questions requires us to first construct a control flow graph from program entry to exit, including inlining recursive method calls[2]. The only cycles the control flow graph can have are those produced by Lime's looping primitives, such as `for` or `while`. The inlining of recursive method calls necessarily places a restriction on the type of programs that can be synthesized into hardware: programs involving recursive method calls that are not statically bounded are out of the reach of synthesis. The basic approach is to construct a dataflow graph of non-static data in a program. Methods that receive non-static data as input are conceptually mapped to filters. The flow of data between methods outlines the overall SIR topology.

Determining Dataflow. We use constant propagation to determine which variables have statically computable values. For example, in `for (eight i) { ... }` used in the box substitution in `Fiestel`, the variable `i` is statically initialized to be `eight.b0`, and subsequently updated by `i + eight.b1` during each iteration. This updated value can be computed from statically known values. Thus, `i` does not need to be an input to a filter work method. Instead, it is used as a filter initializer or mapped to a filter field. On the other hand, `bits` is initialized by expression `S.extractSixBits(startBit, endBit)`. `S` does not have a statically computable value—its value depends on the filter input to method `Fiestel`. Thus, the computation of `S.extractSixBits(startBit, endBit)` requires `S` as an input. (Note that the receiver of a method invocation is considered an input, as well.) Consequently, `bits` is not statically computable either, and must be the output of the filter/pipeline for the expression `S.extractSixBits(startBit, endBit)`. Using standard dataflow techniques, we can determine the data necessary at each point of the program.

Defining Filters. The identifying characteristic of filters is that they perform input or output (I/O) of data that is not statically computable. Once we determine what data is needed for input and output at each program location,

---

[2] There is no good way to deal with unbounded recursion in hardware.

we decompose the program into (possibly nested) I/O "containers", and then construct filters and pipelines from these containers.

The entry and exit of a Lime method form natural bounds for an outer-most I/O container. For example, an outermost I/O container is constructed for method `Fiestel`. Within these bounds, we identify two types of I/O containers.

First, an I/O container is indicated by a method or constructor invocation, where at least one of the arguments (including `this`, if method call is not static) has been identified as a filter input. For example, `S.extractSixBits(startBit, endBit)` in `Fiestel` becomes an I/O container, with `S` as its input. We then analyze the declaration of `extractSixBits`, and inline the I/O containers for the method declaration inside the container for the method invocation.

A second type of I/O container is formed from branching statements such as `for` loops, or `if/else`, where the body of a branch references filter inputs. Each branching container may include nested containers depending on the body of the branch. For example, the box substitution `for (eight i) { ... }` loop in `Fiestel` becomes a branching I/O container. Nested within it, are a series of containers, such as the one for method call `S.extractSixBits(startBit, endBit)`, as well as a container of `Sbox(i, bits)`.

Figure 8 illustrates the I/O containers identified for `Fiestel` in Figure 3. Note that expression `E^K` constitutes an I/O container because operator `^` is defined for `Unsigned`. Thus, `E^K` is turned into method invocation `E.$XOR(K)`. Also note that non-I/O statements, such as loop index update (e.g., `sIndex += fourtyeight.b6;`), become local to their enclosing I/O container. For space rea-sons, ... represents elided I/O containers.

SIR from I/O Containers. An I/O container has a natural mapping down to the SIR. An I/O container with no nested containers naturally maps to a filter. Its work method contains all the statements enclosed by the container. These are generally arithmetic computations that have a straight-forward mapping to hardware. If these statements involve any static references, the definitions of the referenced data or methods are declared as local fields in the filter or as local variables in the work method.

Filters (or pipelines) from I/O containers at the same nesting level are con-nected to form a pipeline. Thus, an I/O container with nested containers is mapped down to a pipeline formed by its children.

A branching I/O container that is formed by a `for` statement, creates a more interesting mapping to the SIR. First, the work statements or nested I/O con-tainers within the loop body are turned into a filter (or pipeline, respectively). If the loop iterations are independent of each other with respect to the filter input and output data, then the filter (pipeline) that makes up the loop body is considered data-parallel. It can be replicated once for each iteration of the loop. This basically translates the Lime code to a data-parallel representation in the SIR. A data splitter is added at the beginning of the `for` I/O container. The splitter *duplicates* the incoming data, and sends it down each replicated loop body filter (pipeline). Data that is not part of the filter input and that may

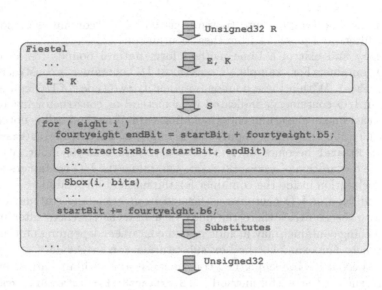

Fig. 8. I/O containers for Fiestel

depend on the loop index are used as *init* values for the filter construction. A joiner is then added at the exit of the `for` I/O container to assemble the output of each replicated filter (pipeline).

When we cannot determine that the loop iterations are independent, we have to explore an alternative mapping. In the case, the computation is considered stateful. In this case, we can statically unroll the loop and connect the unrolled loop body filter (pipeline) sequential to form longer pipelines. Alternatively, we can create a feedback loop such that the output of the loop body filter (pipeline) feeds back into itself. This second option, however, is untested in our SIR compiler.

Similar split/join structures are generated for other branching statement I/O containers. Applying these rules, it is easy to see how I/O containers from Figure 8 can be mapped to exactly the SIR structure in Figure 7.

Object Representation in Hardware. The most general way an object can be represented in hardware is by serializing it into an array of bits that is either packed into registers, or stored in memory. The kind of Lime programs most amenable for synthesis to hardware use data with efficient representations. Lime's language design is geared toward exposing such representations from a high level, as we illustrated in Section 2. Objects of value types have no mutable state, and thus can be safely packed into registers, instead of being stored in much slower memory.

Dynamic Dispatch in hardware. One of the defining features of object-oriented paradigms is the dynamic dispatch of methods. In order to perform dynamic dispatch in hardware, we assign a unique identifier to each type, which is then carried by the object of that type. Thus, object representation may require bits for the type identifier to be serialized, as well. When mapping an I/O container resulting from a virtual method invocation to SIR filters, we must generate a pipeline for each possible target method of the virtual call. All pipelines from target methods are then added to a *switch* connector. The condition for the switch is the type identifier that is carried by the incoming this object. A pipeline of the target method is only invoked if the type identifier of the input this object is equal to the type identifier of the method's declaring class, or one of its subclasses. We use analysis such as RTA [12] to reduce the number of potential target methods that need to be synthesized. If the target method of a virtual call can be statically identified, then the object does not have to carry a type identifier.

Object Allocation in Hardware. Lime programs can use the new keyword to create new objects. However, laying out a program in hardware means all memory needed must be known ahead of time. Thus, a program for synthesis must be able to resolve statically all new's, and space is allocated in registers or memory. Repeatedly new-ing objects in an unbounded loop, with the objects having lifetimes persisting beyond the life of the loop, is not permitted in synthesized programs.

7   SIR Compiler

The SIR that we adopt is both a good match for synthesis and also convenient for performing coarse-grained optimizations that impact the realized parallelism. We build heavily on the StreamIt compiler [13] to implement our SIR and our SIR compiler. The StreamIt compiler is designed for the StreamIt programming language. In StreamIt, programs describe SIR graphs algorithmically and programmatically using language constructs for filters, pipelines, splitters/joiners, and feedback loops. The latter create cycles in the SIR graph although we do not currently handle cycles.

7.1   Lowering Communication

The SIR compiler transforms the SIR graph to reduce the communication overhead and cost. In an FPGA, excessive fan-out and fan-in is not desirable. Hence the compiler attempts to collapse subgraphs that are dominated by a splitter and post-dominated by a joiner. This transformation is feasible when the filters that make up the subgraph are stateless. In a Lime program, methods of a value class are stateless. For example, the Extract and Sbox filters in the SIR graph shown in Figure 7 are stateless since neither of the two has any mutable state. However, since each of these filters is specialized for a specific set of bits, collapsing the subgraph results in at least one stateful filter, namely the Sbox filter in this case. The collapsed graph is shown in Figure 9. Each execution of the work method updates the state of the filter (shown as i in the Figure) so that

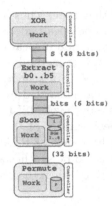

Fig. 9. Result of collapsing SIR shown in Figure 7

on the first execution it performs the substitution that correlates with **Sbox** 8, on its second execution it performs the substitution for **Sbox** 7, and so on until its ninth execution where it resets the state and resumes with **Sbox** 8.

The **Extract** filter does not need to keep track of its execution counts if the compiler can determine that each of the **Extract** filters in the original graph operated in order on mutually exclusive bits. Such an analysis requires dataflow analysis within the filter work method, and is aided by very aggressive constant propagation, loop unrolling, and dead code elimination. More powerful analysis is also possible when filters carry out affine computations [14,15,6]. The SIR compiler employs these techniques to reduce overall communication. The impact on the generated hardware can be significant in terms of speed (time) and overall area (space). We demonstrate the space-time tradeoff by synthesizing the SIR graphs in Figures 7 and 9. The results for these two implementations appear as **Sbox Parallel Duplicate** and **Sbox State** respectively in Figure 10. The evaluation platform is a Virtex-4 FPGA with an embedded PowerPC processor (PPC). The speedup results compare the performance of each hardware implementation to the implementation that yields the best results on the PPC.

We also performed two other transformations: **Sbox Parallel Roundrobin** and **Sbox Coarse**. The former uses dataflow analysis to determine that a roundrobin splitter can replace the duplicate splitter and the **Extract** filters in Figure 7. The latter eliminates the state from the **Sbox** filter in Figure 9 by substituting all 48 bits in one execution of the work method. The results are as one should expect. The fastest hardware implementation uses the roundrobin splitter and parallel **Sbox** filters. This implementation is roughly 3x faster than the duplicate splitter implementation and 100% more space efficient since the roundrobin splitter avoids needless communication and optimizes the datapaths between filters aggressively. The area overhead is 50% larger than that of the most compact implementation, namely **Sbox State** which is a pipelined implementation with an aggressively optimized datapath. The coarse implementation

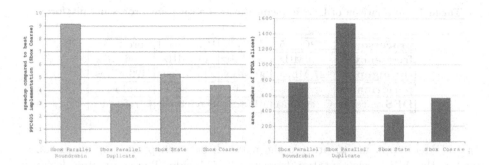

Fig. 10. Speedup and area results for different SIR realizations of Sbox

is the slowest of the four variants since it performs the most amount of work per execution of the work method and affords little opportunity for pipeline parallelism. It is however the best implementation for software although it is worthy to note that it does not use the natural width of the machine in this case. In other words, the version of Sbox Coarse that we benchmark in software uses the same granularity as the FPGA and runs the work methods at bit-granularity. This purpose of the performance comparison is to illustrate the space-time trade-off that exists. In Section 9 we compare our synthesis results to various optimized baselines.

7.2 Load Balancing

The SIR compiler also attempts to refine the SIR graph to realize a more load-balanced graph. This is important because it minimizes the effects of a bottleneck in the overall design. Toward this end, we currently use the heuristics and optimizations described in [11] and implemented in the StreamIt compiler. The compiler uses various heuristics to fuse adjacent filters when it is profitable to do so. The heuristics rely on a work-estimation methodology to detect load imbalance. In our case, work-estimation is a simple scalar measure of the critical path length through the filter work method. It is calculated using predefined latencies for individual primitive operations. We believe however that there are other ways of dealing with load imbalance on an FPGA platform but we have not yet thoroughly investigated alternatives.

8   Getting to Hardware

The last step in our toolflow is HDL code generation. It is accomplished using our SIR to Verilog compiler called Crucible. It compiles each filter in the SIR to a Verilog hardware module. It then assembles the modules together according to the dataflow edges in the SIR graph. The Crucible also generates the HDL interfaces used to exchange data between the processor and the FPGA in order to support mixed-mode execution. The interfaces work in conjunctions with the

Table 1. Comparison of DES implementation on different processing platforms

processor	PPC 405	FPGA	Pentium-II	Core 2 Duo
frequency	300 MHz	129 MHz	400 MHz	2.66 GHz
throughput	27 Mbps	30 Mbps	45 Mbps	426 Mbps
performance	1	1.11	1.69	16
DES version	C reference	Lime	C reference	C reference

Liquid Metal runtime to provide the network between processing elements, as well as the API implementation from the FPGA side. The completed design is finally synthesized using commercial synthesis tools to produce a bitstream that can be used to program the FPGA. We use the Xilinx synthesis tool (XST) for this purpose. FPGAs typically require vendor specific tools, so for other targets, the appropriate synthesis tool is used. The Crucible controls and guides the synthesis tool by setting appropriate synthesis parameters that impact resource allocation policies, arithmetic circuit implementation, the placement of objects in FPGA memory, etc. The Crucible is best suited to guide these policies since it has a global view of the application.

The Crucible address both micro-functional (intra-filter) and macro-functional (inter-filter) synthesis issues. It extends the Trimaran [16] compiler with optimizations and heuristics that are space-time aware. We leverage many of the existing analysis and optimizations in Trimaran to optimize the code within each filter. These optimizations include critical path reduction, region formation for instruction-level parallelism, predication, vectorization, and aggressive instruction scheduling algorithms. In addition, the Crucible is bit-width cognizant, and although the compiler can perform bit-width analysis, we primarily rely on the high level semantics of the Lime program to elide or augment the analysis where feasible.

In the micro-functional sense, the compiler operates on a control flow graph (CFG) consisting of operations and edges. Operations are grouped into basic blocks. Basic blocks are in turn grouped into procedures. Each procedure typically represents a filter. The code generation applies a bottom-up algorithm to the CFG, starting with the operations. It generates Verilog for each operation, then routes the operands between them. Basic blocks serve as a hierarchical building block. They are composed together with dataflow edges, eventually encompassing the entire procedure. Since procedures represent filters, it is also necessary to generate the FIFOs that interconnect them according to the SIR. The size of each FIFO is either determined from the SIR according to the data types exchanged between filters, or using a heuristic that is subject to space-time constraints. This is an example of a macro-functional optimization. If too little buffering is provided, then throughput decreases as modules stall to send or receive data; whereas too much buffering incurs substantial space overheads. Macro-functional optimizations require careful consideration of area and performance trade-offs to judiciously maximize application throughput at the lowest costs.

In addition to the buffering considerations, the Crucible also generates hardware controllers that stage the execution of the filters in hardware. The results presented in this paper use a basic execution model that executes the filter work methods when the input data is ready, and reads from an empty channel (writes to full channel) block the filter under the channel until other filters make progress.

A greater description of the Crucible and its optimizations are beyond the scope of this paper.

9   Experimental Results

We compiled and synthesized the DES Lime code from Section 3 to run in an FPGA. We measured the application throughput at steady state in terms of Mbits per second second (Mbps). We compare our results to an optimized implementation of DES (reference implementation) running on an Intel Pentium-II at 400 MHz, a Core 2 Duo processor with a frequency of 2.66 GHz, and a 300 MHz PPC 405 which is the embedded processor available in the Virtex-4 LX200. The frequency of the DES design generated from the Lime program is 129 MHz. The results are summarized in Table 1. The row labeled **performance** shows the relative throughput compared to the PPC 405. The PPC is a reasonable baseline since it is manufactured in the same technology as the FPGA fabric. Compared to the embedded processor, the FPGA implementation is 11% faster. It is 66% slower than a reasonably optimized DES coder running on a Pentium-II, and 14x slower than the fastest processor we tested.

The results show that we can achieve a reasonable hardware implementation of DES starting from a high level program that was relatively easy to implement. Compared to reference C implementations that we found and studied, we believe the Lime program is easier to understand. In addition, the Lime program is arguably more portable since computation is explicitly expressed at the bit-level and is therefore platform independent. This is in contrast to software implementations that have to match the natural processing width of their target platforms and hence express computation at the granularity of bytes or words instead of bits. We believe that starting with a bit-level implementation is more natural for a programmer since it closely follows the specification of the algorithm.

The FPGA implementation that we realized from the Lime program requires nearly 84% of the total FPGA area. This is a significant portion of the FPGA. The area requirement is high because we are mapping the entire DES coder pipeline (all 16 rounds) to hardware and we are not reusing any resources. The spatial mapping is straightforward to realize but there are alternative mapping strategies that can significantly reduce the area. Namely, sharing resources and trading off space for throughput is an important consideration. We showed an example of this kind of trade-off earlier using the Sbox code (refer to Figure 10). We believe that there is significant room for improvement in this regard and this is an active area of research that we are pursuing.

Our goal however is not to be the world's best high-level synthesis compiler. Rather, our emphasis is on extending the set of object-oriented programming features that we can readily and efficiently implement in hardware so that skilled

Java programmers can transparently tap the advantages of FPGAs. In the current work, we showed that we can support several important features including value types, generics, object allocation, and operator overloading. We are also capable of supporting dynamic dispatch in hardware although the DES example did not provide a natural way to showcase this feature.

10   Related Work

10.1   Languages with Value Types

Kava [1] is an early implementation of value types as lightweight objects in Java. The design of Lime is very much inspired by Kava. However, Kava was designed before `enum` types or generics were introduced into Java. Thus, Kava chose a different type hierarchy which put value types and `Object` at the same level. This design does not fit in well with the current Java design. Lime remedied this by using a `value` modifier. Lime also provides support for value generic types. Additionally, Kava value types are not automatically initialized, nor are default constructors generated.

C# [17] offers value types in the form of structs. One important difference between C# value types and Lime value types is that C# value types cannot inherit from other value types. Inheritance and dynamic dispatch of methods are key features of the OO paradigm. Value types should be able to take advantage of these abstractions. Furthermore, C# struct references must be manually initialized by the programmer, even though a default constructor is provided for each struct. Lime value type references are automatically initialized, similar to the way primitive types are treated.

Recent work by Zibin et al. [18] has shown a way to enforce immutability using an extra immutability type parameter. In this work, a class can be defined such that it can be used in a mutable or immutable context. In Lime, a value class and a mutable class must be separately defined. The method proposed in [18] is an interesting way to integrate a functional style with Java's inherently mutable core. We could incorporate similar techniques in Lime in the future.

10.2   Synthesizing High-Level Languages

Many researchers have worked on compilers and new high-level languages for generating hardware in the past few years. Languages such as SystemC [4] have been proposed to provide the same functionality as lower-level languages such as Verilog and VHDL at a higher-level of abstraction. SystemC is a set of library routines and macros implemented in C++, which makes it possible to simulate concurrent processes, each described by ordinary C++ syntax. Similarly, Handle-C [19] is another hardware/software construction language with C syntax that support behavioral description of hardware. SA-C [20] is a single assignment high-level synthesizable language. An SA-C program can be viewed as a graph where nodes correspond to operators, and edges to data paths. Dataflow graphs are ideal (data driven, timeless) abstractions for hardware circuits.

StreamC [21] is a compiler which focuses on extensions to C that facilitate expressing communication between parallel processes. Spark [22] is another C to VHDL compiler which supports transformations such as loop unrolling, common sub-expression elimination, copy propagation, etc. DEFACTO[23] and ROCCC[24] are two other hardware generation systems that take C as input and generate VHDL code as output. To the best of our knowledge, none of these compilation systems support high level object-oriented techniques.

Work by Chu[25] proposes object oriented circuit-generators. Circuit-generators, parameterized code which produces a digital design, enable designers to conveniently specify reusable designs in a familiar programming environment. Although object oriented techniques can be used to design these generator, this system is not intended for both hardware and software programming in a parallel system. Additionally, the syntax used in the proposed system is not appropriate for large-scale object oriented software designs.

11 Conclusion

In this paper, we introduce Lime, an OO language for programming heterogeneous computing environments. The entire Lime architecture provides end-to-end support from a high-level OO programming language, to compilation to both the Java VM, the FPGA, and a runtime that allows mixed-mode operation such that code can run on partly on the VM and partly on the FPGA, delegating work to the most optimal fabric for a certain task. Lime is a first step toward a system that can "JIT the hardware", truly taking advantage of the multitude of computing architectures.

Acknowledgments

This work is supported in part by IBM Research and the National Science Foundation Graduate Research Fellowship. We thank Bill Thies and Michael Gordon of MIT for their help with the StreamIt compiler, Stephen Neuendorffer of Xilinx for his help with the Xilinx tools and platforms, and the reviewers for their helpful comments and appreciation of our vision.

References

1. Bacon, D.F.: Kava: A Java dialect with a uniform object model for lightweight classes. Concurrency—Practice and Experience 15, 185–206 (2003)
2. Wu, P., Midkiff, S.P., Moreira, J.E., Gupta, M.: Efficient support for complex numbers in java. In: Java Grande, pp. 109–118 (1999)
3. IEEE: 1076 IEEE standard VHDL language reference manual. Technical report (2002)
4. IEEE: IEEE standard SystemC language reference manual. Technical report (2006)
5. Narayanan, M., Yelick, K.A.: Generating permutation instructions from a high-level description. In: Workshop on Media and Streaming Processors (2004)

6. Solar-Lezama, A., Rabbah, R., Bodík, R., Ebcioğlu, K.: Programming by sketching for bit-streaming programs. In: PLDI 2005: Proceedings of the 2005 ACM SIGPLAN conference on Programming language design and implementation, pp. 281–294. ACM, New York (2005)
7. Ekman, T., Hedin, G.: The jastadd extensible java compiler. In: OOPSLA 2007: Proceedings of the 22nd annual ACM SIGPLAN conference on Object oriented programming systems and applications, pp. 1–18. ACM, New York (2007)
8. Babb, J., Frank, M., Lee, V., Waingold, E., Barua, R., Taylor, M., Kim, J., Devabhaktuni, S., Agarwal, A.: The raw benchmark suite: Computation structures for general purpose computing. In: Proceedings of the IEEE Symposium on Field-Programmable Custom Computing Machines (1997)
9. Lee, E.A., Messerschmitt, D.G.: Static scheduling of synchronous data flow programs for digital signal processing. IEEE Trans. on Computers (1987)
10. Bhattacharyya, S.S., Murthy, P.K., Lee, E.A.: Software Synthesis from Dataflow Graphs. Kluwer Academic Publishers, Dordrecht (1996)
11. Gordon, M., Thies, W., Amarasinghe, S.: Exploiting Coarse-Grained Task, Data, and Pipeline Parallelism in Stream Programs. In: Proceedings of the 12th International Conference on Architectural Support for Programming Languages and Operating Systems (2006)
12. Bacon, D.F.: Fast and effective optimization of statically typed object-oriented languages. PhD thesis (1997)
13. StreamIt (2003), http://cag.csail.mit.edu/streamit
14. Lamb, A.A., Thies, W., Amarasinghe, S.: Linear Analysis and Optimization of Stream Programs. In: PLDI (2003)
15. Agrawal, S., Thies, W., Amarasinghe, S.: Optimizing stream programs using linear state space analysis. In: CASES (2005)
16. Trimaran Research Infrastructure (1999), http://www.trimaran.org
17. Hejlsberg, A., Wiltamuth, S., Golde, P.: C# Language Specification. Addison-Wesley Longman Publishing Co., Inc., Boston (2003)
18. Zibin, Y., Potanin, A., Ali, M., Artzi, S., Kieżun, A., Ernst, M.D.: Object and reference immutability using Java generics. In: ESEC/FSE 2007: Proceedings of the 11th European Software Engineering Conference and the 15th ACM SIGSOFT Symposium on the Foundations of Software Engineering, Dubrovnik, Croatia (2007)
19. Handle-C Language Overview (2004), http://www.celoxica.com
20. Najjar, W., Bohm, W., Draper, B., Hammes, J., Rinker, R., Beveridge, J., Chawathe, M., Ross, C.: High-level language abstraction for reconfigurable computing (2003)
21. Mencer, O., Hubert, H., Morf, M., Flynn, M.J.: Stream: Object-oriented programming of stream architectures using PAM-blox. In: FPL, pp. 595–604 (2000)
22. Gupta, S.: Spark: A high-level synthesis framework for applying parallelizing compiler transformations (2003)
23. Diniz, P.C., Hall, M.W., Park, J., So, B., Ziegler, H.E.: Bridging the gap between compilation and synthesis in the defacto system. In: Lecture Notes in Computer Science, pp. 52–70 (2001)
24. Guo, Z., Buyukkurt, B., Najjar, W., Vissers, K.: Optimized generation of data-path from c codes for fpgas. In: Design Automation Conference (2005)
25. Chu, M., Sulimma, K., Weaver, N., DeHon, A., Wawrzynek, J.: Object oriented circuit-generators in Java. In: Pocek, K.L., Arnold, J. (eds.) IEEE Symposium on FPGAs for Custom Computing Machines, pp. 158–166. IEEE Computer Society Press, Los Alamitos (1998)

Kilim: Isolation-Typed Actors for Java
(A Million Actors, Safe Zero-Copy Communication)

Sriram Srinivasan and Alan Mycroft

University of Cambridge Computer Laboratory,
Cambridge CB3 0FD, UK
{Sriram.Srinivasan,Alan.Mycroft}@cl.cam.ac.uk

Abstract. This paper describes Kilim, a framework that employs a combination of techniques to help create robust, massively concurrent systems in mainstream languages such as Java: (*i*) ultra-lightweight, cooperatively-scheduled threads (*actors*), (*ii*) a message-passing framework (no shared memory, no locks) and (*iii*) isolation-aware messaging.

Isolation is achieved by controlling the shape and ownership of mutable messages – they must not have internal aliases and can only be owned by a single actor at a time. We demonstrate a static analysis built around isolation type qualifiers to enforce these constraints.

Kilim comfortably scales to handle hundreds of thousands of actors and messages on modest hardware. It is fast as well – task-switching is 1000x faster than Java threads and 60x faster than other lightweight tasking frameworks, and message-passing is 3x faster than Erlang (currently the gold standard for *concurrency-oriented* programming).

1   Imagine No Sharing

Computing architectures are getting increasingly distributed, from multiple cores in one processor and multiple NUMA processors in one box, to many boxes in a data centre and many data centres. The shared memory mindset – synonymous with the concurrent computation model – is at odds with this trend. Not only are its idioms substantially different from those of distributed programming, it is extremely difficult to obtain correctness, fairness and efficiency in the presence of fine-grained locks and access to shared objects.

The "Actor" model, espoused by Erlang, Singularity and the Unix process+pipe model, offers an alternative: independent communicating sequential entities that share nothing and communicate by passing messages. Address-space isolation engenders several desirable properties: component-oriented testing, elimination of data races, unification of local and distributed programming models and better optimisation opportunities for compilers and garbage collectors. Finally, data-independence promotes failure-independence [1]: an exception in one actor cannot fatally affect another.

1.1   Motivation

The actor and message-passing approach, with its coarse-grained concurrency and loosely-coupled components is a good fit for split-phase workloads (CPU,

J. Vitek (Ed.): ECOOP 2008, LNCS 5142, pp. 104–128, 2008.

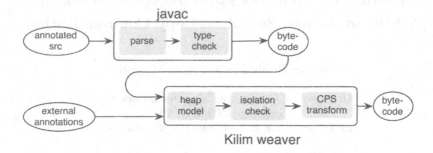

Fig. 1. `javac` output post-processed by Kilim `weaver`

network and disk) [4] and service-oriented workflows. With a view to immediate industrial adoption, we impose the following additional requirements: (*a*) no changes to Java syntax or to the JVM, (*b*) lightweight actors[1] (*c*) fast messaging (*d*) no assumptions made about a message receiver's location and implementation language (*e*) widespread support for debugging, logging and persistence.

1.2   The Kilim Solution

This paper introduces Kilim[2], an actor framework for Java that contains a bytecode post-processor ("weaver", see Fig. 1) and a run-time library. We list below some important features as well as the design points:

Ultra-lightweight threads. Kilim's *weaver* transforms methods identified by an @pausable annotation into continuation passing style (CPS) to provide cooperatively-scheduled lightweight threads with automatic stack management and trampolined call stack [3, 20]. These actor threads are quick to context-switch and do not need pre-allocated private heaps. The annotation is similar in spirit to checked exceptions in that all callers and overriding methods must be marked @pausable as well.

Messages as a special category. For the reasons outlined above, we treat message types as philosophically distinct from, and much simpler than other Java objects. Messages are:

– *Unencapsulated values* without identity (like their on-the-wire counterparts, XML, C++ structs, ML datatypes and Scala's case classes). The public structure permits pattern-matching, structure transformation, delegation and flexible auditing at message exchange points; these are much harder to achieve in the presence of encapsulation.
– *Not internally aliased.* A message object may be pointed to by at most one other message object (and then only by one field or array element of

---

[1] For example, threads are too heavyweight to assign per HTTP connection or per component in composable communication protocol state machines.
[2] Kilims are flexible, lightweight Turkish flat rugs woven with fine threads.

it). The resulting tree-structure can be serialized and cloned efficiently and effortlessly stored in relational and XML schemas. The lack of internal aliasing is less limiting in practice than would first appear, mostly because loosely-coupled components tend to have simple interfaces. Examples include events or messages in most server frameworks, windowing systems, the Singularity operating system [18] and CORBA valuetypes.

- *Linearly owned.* A message can have at most one owner at any time. This allows efficient zero-copy message transfer where possible. The programmer has to explicitly make a copy if needed, and the imperative to avoid copies puts a noticeable "back pressure" on the programmer.

Statically-enforced isolation. We enforce the above properties at compile-time. Isolation is interpreted as *interference-freedom*, obtained by keeping the set of *mutable* objects reachable from an actor's instance fields and stack totally disjoint from another actor's. Kilim's weaver performs a static intra-procedural heap analysis that takes hints from isolation qualifiers specified on method interfaces.

Run-time support. Kilim contains a run-time library of type-parametrised *mailboxes* for asynchronous message-passing with I/O throttling and prioritised *alting* [23]; SEDA-style I/O conditioning [36] is omnipresent. Mailboxes can be incorporated into messages, π-calculus [28] style. Space prevents us from presenting much of the run-time framework; this paper concentrates on the compile-time analysis and transformations.

The contribution of this work is the synthesis of ideas found in extant literature and in picking particular design points that allow portability and immediate applicability (no change to the language or the JVM).

1.3 Isolation Qualifiers and Capabilities: A Brief Overview

Drossopoulou *et al* [16] present in their brief survey the choices of syntactic representations for controlling aliasing. One issue they raise is the need to "develop lightweight and yet powerful [shape] systems". We have adopted "only trees may be transferred between actors" as our guiding principle.

The motivations given in Sec. 1.1 led us to choose a scheme with (i) a marker interface Message to identify tree-shaped message types which may contain primitive types, references to Messages and arrays of the above; and (ii) three qualifiers (@free, @cuttable, @safe) on method parameters, which we formalise within a calculus.

These qualifiers can be understood in terms of two orthogonal *capabilities* of an object in a tree: first, whether it is pointed to by another object or not (called a *root* in the latter case) and second, whether or not it is structurally modifiable (whether its pointer-valued fields are assignable). The latter is a transitive property; an object is structurally modifiable if its parent is.

Given this, an object is *free*[3] if it is the root of a tree and is structurally modifiable. A *cuttable* object may or may not be the root, but is structurally modifiable. An object with a *safe* capability cannot be structurally modified (transitively so), and does not care whether or not it is the root. These capabilities represent in decreasing order the amount of freedom offered by an object (in our ability to modify it, send to another actor, to placel on either side of a field assignment). We use the term *send* (*sent*) to mean that the message is effectively transferred out of the sender's space after which the sender is not permitted access to the message.

Clearly, in all cases, a node in our **Message** tree can have at most one other object pointing to it[4]; in Boylands' terminology [9], all fields of our **Messages** are *unique*, which *provides a system-wide invariant that permits an easy intuitive grasp of our isolation qualifiers as deep qualifiers*. The *cut* operator (see below) can be read as an explicit version of the notion of *destructive reads* [9]. The *cuttable* and *safe* capabilities can be seen as variants of Boylands' *borrowed*.

The relationship between qualifiers and capabilities is this: the qualifiers are specified on method interfaces and imply a interface contract between a method and its caller and, in addition, bestow the corresponding capability on the object referred to by the method parameter. Sec. 3 gives the specifics.

The *cut* operator performs a specific structural modification: it cuts a branch of a tree, severing a subtree from its parent. In addition, it grants the root of the subtree a *free* capability. Only *new* and *cut* can create *free* objects.

As an aside, we provide an additional (unchecked) escape interface **Sharable** that allows the programmer to identify classes that do not follow our message restrictions, yet can be safely transferred across to another thread. These may include immutable classes and those with internal aliasing.

2   Example

Fig. 2 shows a simple Actor class **TxtSrvr** that blocks on a mailbox awaiting a message, transforms the message and responds to a reply-to mailbox specified in the message itself.

TxtMsg is a message class identified as such with the marker interface **Message**. The programming model for actors (**TxtSrvr** here) is similar to that for Java threads – replace **Thread** with **Actor** and **run()** with **execute()**. Similarly, an actor is spawned thus: **new TxtSrvr().start()**;

The entry point of a Kilim task is **execute()**, the only method of the actor required to be public. Its other non-private methods may only have message-compatible parameters and results. The **@pausable** annotation on a method informs Kilim's **weaver** that the method may (directly or transitively) call other pausable methods such as **Actor.sleep()** and **Mailbox.get()**.

---

[3] Note: parameters have qualifiers, objects have capabilities; we write **@free** for the programmer-supplied qualifier and *free* for the corresponding object's capability.

[4] At most one *heap alias*. Multiple local variables may also have the same pointer value.

```
import kilim.*;                          class TxtMsg
class Mbx extends Mailbox<TxtMsg> {}        implements Message
                                         {
class TxtSrvr extends Actor {              Mbx replymb;
  Mbx mb;                                  byte [ ] data;
  TxtSrvr(Mbx mb) {this.mb = mb;}        }

  @pausable
  public void execute() {
    while(true) {
      TxtMsg m = mb.get();               // Sample driver code
      transform(m);
      reply(m);                          // spawn actor
  }}                                      Mbx outmb = new Mbx();
                                         new TxtSrvr(outmb).start();

  @pausable
  void reply(@free TxtMsg m) {           // Send and recv message
    m.replymb.put(m);                    Mbx replymb = new Mbx();
  }                                      byte [ ] data = ...
                                         outmb.put(new TxtMsg(replymb, data));
  // @safe is default, so optional       ... = replymb.get();
  void transform(@safe TxtMsg m) {···}
}
```

Fig. 2. Example Kilim code showing annotations for message and stack management. Kilim's semantic extensions are in bold.

The blocking call (to `Mailbox.get()`) in an infinite loop illustrates automatic stack management. A typical state machine framework would have the programmer rewrite this in a callback-oriented style and arrange to return to a main loop; this style is prevalent even in multi-threaded settings because threads are expensive and slow resources.

Kilim's mailboxes are type-specific and thread-safe message queues, and being sharable objects (see Sec. 5.2), they can be passed around in messages. They support blocking, timed-blocking and non-blocking variants of `get` and `put`. An actor may simultaneously wait for a message from one of many mailboxes using `select` (like CSP's *alt* [23]). Rudimentary I/O throttling is provided in the form of bounded queue sizes (default is unbounded), and the caller of `Mailbox.put()` is suspended if the queue is full (which is why `reply()`) must be marked as pausable in the example.

The isolation qualifier `@free` on the `reply()` method's parameter is a contract between the caller (`execute()`) and the callee. The weaver checks that the caller supplies an object with a *free* capability to the callee and subsequently does not use any local variables pointing to or into the message. In turn, `reply` cedes

---

$FuncDcl ::= free_{\text{opt}}\ m(\vec{p} : \vec{\alpha})\ \{\ (lb : Stmt)^{*;}\ \}$
$\quad Stmt ::= x := \mathbf{new}\ \ |\ x := y$
$\qquad\quad |\ x := y.f\ \ \ |\ x.f := y\ \ \ |\ x := \mathbf{cut}(y.f)$
$\qquad\quad |\ x := y[\cdot]\ \ \ |\ x[\cdot] := y\ \ \ |\ x := \mathbf{cut}(y[\cdot])$
$\qquad\quad |\ x := m(\vec{y})\ |\ \mathbf{if/goto}\ \vec{lb}\ |\ \mathbf{return}\ x$

$x, y, p \in$ variable names $f \in$ field names
$lb \in$ label names $m \in$ function names
$sel \in$ field names $\cup\ \{[\cdot]\}$ $[\cdot]$ pseudo field name for array access
$\alpha, \beta \in$ isolation qualifier $\{$*free*, *cuttable*, *safe*$\}$
null is treated as a special readonly variable

Fig. 3. Core syntax. All expressions are in A-normal form. Variables not appearing in the parameter list are assumed to be local variables.

all rights to the message after calling the mailbox's `put()` method (because the latter too has a `@free` annotation on its formal parameters).

The `transform()` method does not require its supplied arguments to be *free*. This means that `execute()` is permitted to use the message object after `transform()` returns. Note also that `transform()` is not marked with `@pausable`, which guarantees us that it does not call any other pausable methods.

3   Core Language

Fig. 3 shows our core syntax, a Java-like intra-procedural language. The language is meant for the isolation checking phase only; it focuses solely on message types and its statements have a bearing on variable and heap aliasing only. We confine ourselves to purely intra-procedural reasoning for speed, precision and localising the effect of changes to code (whole program analyses sometimes show errors in seemingly unrelated pieces of code).

Primitive fields and normal Java objects, while tracked for the CPS transformation phase, are not germane to the issue of isolation checking. A program in this language is already in A-normal form (all intermediate expressions named).

Isolation Qualifiers and Capabilities. We mentioned earlier that isolation qualifiers (α, β) are specified in the form of annotations on method parameters and return values. Like normal types, they represent the capabilities of the arguments expected (an object must be at least as capable). Internally to the method, the qualifiers represent the *initial* capability for each parameter object; the object's capability may subsequently change (unlike its Java type). Other objects' capabilities are inferred by a data-flow analysis (Sec. 5). In all cases, we enforce the invariant that there can be at most one heap pointer to any message object.

The list below informally describes object capabilities (Fig. 8 has the precise semantics). It bears repeating that they reflect a lattice composed of two boolean properties – root node or not and, whether or not its pointer-valued fields are assignable (structurally modifiable).

free: The *free* capability is granted to the root of a tree by *new* and by *cut*, and to a method parameter marked as @free. A *free* object is guaranteed to be a root, but not vice-versa. It is field-assignable to another non-*safe* object and can be used as an argument to a method with any qualifier.

cuttable: This capability is granted to an object obtained via a field lookup of another non-*safe* object, from downgrading a *free* object by assigning it to a field of another (it is no longer a root) and to a method parameter marked @cuttable. This capability permits the object to be cut, but not to be assigned to another object (because it is not necessarily a root). This capability is transitive: an object is *cuttable* if its parent is.

safe: The *safe* capability is granted to a method parameter marked @safe or (transitively) to any object reachable from it. A *safe* object may not be structurally modified or further heap-aliased or *sent* to another actor.

The qualifiers on method parameters impose the following interface contracts on callers and callees:

@free: This allows the method to treat the parameter (transitively the entire tree rooted there) as it sees fit, including *sending* it to another actor. The type system ensures that the caller of the method supplies a *free* argument, and subsequently forbids the use of all local variables that may point to any part of the tree (reachable from the argument).

@cuttable: The caller must assume that the corresponding object may be cut anywhere, and must therefore forget about all local variables that are reachable from the argument (because the objects they refer to could be cut off and possibly *sent* to another actor).

@safe: The caller can continue to use a message object (and all aliases into it) if it is passed to a @safe parameter. The callee cannot modify the structure.

The cut operator severs a subtree from its (*cuttable*) parent thus:

$$y = cut(x.sel) \qquad \stackrel{def}{=} \qquad y = x.sel; x.sel = null;$$

Crucially, and in addition, it marks y as *free*; ordinarily, performing the two operations on the right hand side would only mark y as *cuttable*. The cut operator works identically on fields and arrays. Because it is a single operation and because messages (and their array-valued components) are tree-structured by construction, the subtree can be marked *free*.

Remark 1. The most notable aspect of this calculus is that we amplify the requirement that at most one actor owns a given message into the stronger one that at most one dynamically active method stack frame may refer to a *free* message. This is justified by the requirements that (*i*) a *free* object is a root object and (*ii*) the rules on passing it to a method expecting a @free parameter cause all local variables pointing to it to be marked inaccessible. Therefore inter-actor communication primitives of the form *send* and *receive* are treated as simple method calls; in other words, all that is required of an inter-actor messaging facility like the mailbox is that they annotate their parameters and return values (for send and receive operations respectively) with *free*, thereby trivially isolating the intricacies of inter-actor and inter-thread interaction, Java memory model, serialization, batched I/O, scheduling etc.

Remark 2. One could readily add an intermediate qualifier between @cuttable and @safe, say @cutsafe, which permits all modifications except cutting. That is, it could allow additions to the tree and nullification, but not extraction via *cut* for possible transfer of ownership.

In addition to matching object capabilities with isolation qualifiers on method parameters, Kilim enforces a rule to eliminate parameter-induced aliasing: arguments to a method must be pairwise disjoint (trees may not overlap) if any one of them is non-*safe*, and the return value, if any, must be *free* and disjoint from the input parameters.

3.1   Why Qualifiers on Variables Are Not Enough

One might hope that a simple type system à la PACLANG [17] can be created by associating variables of Message type with isolation type qualifiers, which change with the program point. However, such type systems do not take relationships between variables into account. For example, if we know that x and y are aliases, or y points within the structure rooted at x, then passing x to a method accepting a *free* message (e.g. Mailbox.put()) must result in not only x but also y being removed from the objects accessible from the scope of the actor.

In other words, while it is convenient to think of *variables* as having a qualifier such as @free, it is really the *objects* that have such a qualifier. We need to analyse methods to infer variable dependencies; the next two sections expand on this subject.

We split isolation checking into two phases for exposition, although the implementation performs them pointwise on the control flow graph. These two phases are covered in Sec. 4 and Sec. 5.

4   Heap Graph Construction

A program may create an unbounded set of message objects at run-time. A compile-time analysis of such a program requires that we first create an abstract model of the heap, called a *heap graph*. Each *node* of this (necessarily finite) graph represents a potentially infinite set of run-time objects that have something in common with each other at a given program point, and different heap analyses differ on the common theme that binds the objects represented by the node.

We base our heap graph abstraction on a simple variant of shape analysis [37]; we claim no novelty. Our contribution is the set of design choices (isolation qualifiers, tree-structure, local analysis, the cut operator) that make the problem

$G : \langle L, E \rangle$	Heap graph is a pair of local var info L and edges E
$L \in \mathcal{P}(\langle Var, LNode \rangle)$	L = relation between local variable names and *nodes* (*LNode* is logically the nodes of the graph)
$E \in \mathcal{P}(\langle Node, sel, Node \rangle)$	E = a set of Node-Node edges labelled with field names
$LNode \in \mathcal{P}(Var)$	Heap Graph node; in this formalism the name of the node consists of the set of local variable names that may point to it. Well-formedness: $\langle x, N \rangle \in L \Leftrightarrow x \in N$
$Node \in \mathcal{P}(Var) \cup \{\emptyset\}$	Labelled nodes plus summary node.
Convenience: $L(x) \stackrel{def}{=} \{N \mid \langle x, N \rangle \in L\}$	set of *LNodes* to which a local variable might point.

Fig. 4. Heap Graph formalism following [37]

simpler and faster to reason about; it is a shape-enforcement rather than a general analysis problem.

A heap graph G (see Fig. 4) is a pair $\langle L, E \rangle$; L is the set of associations between variable names and nodes, and E represents the set of labelled edges between nodes. A node may be pointed to by more than one variable and is identified by a label that is merely the set of variable names pointing to it (a reverse index).

Fig. 5 shows example heap graphs at two program points. The sample heap graph l_1 is represented algebraically as follows[5]:

$L = \{ \langle a, \{a\} \rangle, \langle b, \{b, d\} \rangle, \langle d, \{b, d\} \rangle, \langle c, \{c, d\} \rangle, \langle d, \{c, d\} \rangle, \langle e, \{e\} \rangle \}$
$E = \{ \langle \{a\}, f, \{b, d\} \rangle, \langle \{a\}, f, \{c, d\} \rangle, \langle \{b, d\}, g, \{e\} \rangle, \langle \{c, d\}, g, \{e\} \rangle \}$

The common theme among run-time objects represented by a shape analysis node is that they are all referred to by the set of variables in the node's label, at that program point, for any given run of the program – a node is an *aliasing configuration*.

In addition to the labelled nodes mentioned thus far, there is one generic *summary* node with the special label $\emptyset$ that represents all heap objects not directly referred to by a local variable. When a node ceases to be pointed to by any variable, its label set becomes empty and it is merged with the summary node (hence '$\emptyset$'—by analogy with the empty set symbol).

Note that edges originate or end in labelled nodes only; the heap graph does not know anything about the connectivity of anonymous objects (inside the $\emptyset$ node)

The most important invariant in heap graph construction is that there cannot be an edge between two nodes whose labels are not disjoint. Without the invariant, an edge such as $\langle \{x, y\}, f, \{x, u\} \rangle$ would represent the following impossible situation. x and y point to the same set of run-time objects (at that

---

[5] Parallels to shape analysis [37]: G is their *static shape graph*, L is E_v with a layer of subscripting is removed; we write $\langle y, \{x, y, z\} \rangle$ for their $\langle y, n_{x,y,z} \rangle$.

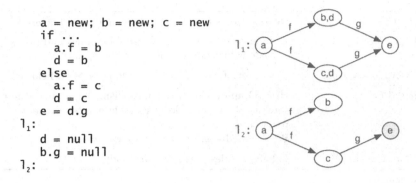

```
a = new; b = new; c = new
if ...
    a.f = b
    d = b
else
    a.f = c
    d = c
e = d.g
l₁:

d = null
b.g = null
l₂:
```

Fig. 5. Sample heap graphs at l_1 and l_2. Only edges E are shown; L is implicit.

program point, on any run of the program). These objects in turn are connected to another bunch of objects, referred to by x and u. This is clearly not possible, because x's objects have both an outgoing and an incoming edge while its aliasing partners (y and u) only have one or the other edge. Non-disjoint alias sets can coexist in the graph, as long as they do not violate this invariant.

Given the control flow graph CFG mentioned earlier, we use the following equations to construct the heap graph G after every program point. The analysis is specified in terms of an iterative forward flow performed on the lattice $\langle G, \subseteq \rangle$. We merge the heap graphs at control-flow join points to avoid the exponential growth in the set of graphs (like [37], unlike [29]). This means all transfer functions operate on a single heap graph (rather than a set of graphs).

$$G_{out}^{init} = \langle \{\}, \{\} \rangle$$
$$G_{in}^l = \bigcup \{G_{out}^{l'} \mid (l', l) \in CFG\}$$
$$G_{out}^l = [\![\cdot]\!](G_{in}^l)$$

The second equation merges the graphs from the CFG node's incoming edges (simple set union of node and edge sets). $[\![\cdot]\!]$ represents the transfer functions for each CFG node (Fig. 6). Note that *if_goto* and *return* do not have transfer functions; they are turned into edges of the CFG.

The transfer functions are simpler than the ones in shape analysis because they do not deal with sharing (attempts to share are faulted in the isolation checking phase). Note that the heap graph may have nodes with multiple incoming edges, but it reflects a may-alias edge, not an edge that induces sharing. The node labelled e in Fig. 5 represents two disjoint sets of run-time objects, one of which has incoming edges from the $\{b, d\}$ set of objects and the other from $\{c, f\}$.

The transfer function for $x := y.f$ deserves some attention. It associates x with all nodes T pointed to by $y.f$, which may or may not have been created as yet by the analysis procedure. Fig. 7 covers both possibilities. In the case where a node does not exist, it is treated as if it belongs as a discrete blob inside the summary node, implicitly referred to by $y.f$ (the grey region in Fig. 7). In

Notation: V (any Node), S (source Node), T (target Node)

$S_x \overset{def}{=} S \cup \{x\}$

$S_x^y \overset{def}{=} \begin{cases} S \cup \{x\} & \text{if } y \in S \\ S & \text{otherwise} \end{cases}$

$kill(G, x) \overset{def}{=} L' = \{ \langle v, V \rangle \in L \mid v \neq x \ \wedge \ V' = V \setminus \{x\} \ \wedge \langle v, V \rangle \in L\}$
$E' = \{ \langle S \setminus \{x\}, \ sel, \ T \setminus \{x\} \rangle \mid \langle S, \ sel, \ T \rangle \in E\}$

$[\![entry(mthd)]\!]\ G$	$\mathbf{L''} = \bigcup_i \{ \langle p_i, \{p_i\} \rangle \}$ where p_i is the ith parameter of $mthd$ $\mathbf{E''} = \{\}$
$[\![x := \mathbf{new}]\!]\ G$	$G' : \langle L', E' \rangle = kill(G, x)$ $\mathbf{L''} = L' \cup \langle x, \{x\} \rangle, \quad \mathbf{E''} = E'$
$[\![x := y]\!]\ G$	$G' : \langle L', E' \rangle = kill(G, x)$ $\mathbf{L''} = \{ \langle v, V_x^y \rangle \mid \{v, V\} \in L'\}$ $\mathbf{E''} = \{ \langle S_x^y, \ sel, \ T_x^y \rangle \mid \langle S, \ sel, \ T \rangle \in E'\}$
$[\![x.f := y]\!]\ G$	$E' = E \ \setminus \ \{ \langle S, f, * \rangle \in E \mid x \in S \}$ $\mathbf{E''} = \begin{cases} E' & \text{if } y \equiv null \\ E' \cup \{ \langle S, f, T \rangle \mid x \in S \wedge y \in T \} & \text{otherwise} \end{cases}$ $\mathbf{L''} = L$
$[\![x[\cdot] := y]\!]\ G$	$\mathbf{E''} = \begin{cases} E & \text{if } y \equiv null \\ E \cup \{ \langle S, \text{'}[\cdot]\text{'}, T \rangle \mid x \in S \wedge y \in T \} & \text{otherwise} \end{cases}$ $\mathbf{L''} = L$
$[\![x := y.sel]\!]\ G$	$G' : \langle L', E' \rangle = kill(G, x)$ $\mathbf{L''} = L'$ $\quad \cup \{ \langle t, T_x \rangle \mid \langle t, T \rangle \in L' \wedge \langle y, S \rangle \in L' \wedge \langle S, sel, T \rangle \in E'\}$ $\quad \cup \{ \langle x, T_x \rangle \mid \langle y, S \rangle \in L' \wedge \langle S, sel, T \rangle \in E'\}$ $\mathbf{E''} = (E' \ \setminus \ \bigcup \{ \langle y, sel, * \rangle \in E' \})$ $\quad \cup \{ \langle y, sel, T_x \rangle \mid \langle y, sel, T \rangle \in E'\}$ $\quad \cup \{ \langle T_x, sel, U \rangle \mid \langle T, sel, U \rangle \in E'\}$
$[\![x := cut(y.sel)]\!]$	$[\![y.sel := null]\!] \quad \circ \quad [\![x := y.sel]\!]$
$[\![x := m(\vec{v})]\!]\ G$	$G' : \langle L', E' \rangle = kill(G, x)$ $\mathbf{L''} = L' \cup \{ \langle x, \{x\} \rangle \}$ $\mathbf{E''} = E'$

Fig. 6. Transfer functions $[\![\cdot]\!]$ for heap graph construction. They transform $G : \langle L, E \rangle$ to $G'' : \langle L'', E'' \rangle$. '*' represents wildcards and *sel* represents field and array access.

this case, the node is *materialized* [37] out of the summary node and all edges outgoing from that node are replicated and attached to the newly materialized node. This replication is necessary because we do not have precise information about which portion of the anonymous heap (represented by the summary node) is responsible for the outgoing edges (the grey blob, or the non-grey portion). Note that we do not have to replicate the incoming edges because we know that nodes are not shared and that the newly materialized node is already pointed to by the $y.f$ edge.

Shape analysis provides *strong nullification* and *disjointness* [37], as illustrated in Fig. 5 by the transition from heap graph at l_1 to that of l_2. Unfortunately, shape analysis cannot do the same for arrays: setting "$x[i] = y$" tells us nothing at all about $x[j]$. However, cut performs strong nullification even on arrays, because our type system ensures that the array's components are disjoint both mutually and from the variable on the right hand side.

Remark 3. There is an important software engineering reason for having *cut*, instead of relying on shape analysis to inform us about disjointness: we want to make explicit in the code the act of cutting a branch from the tree and giving the subtree a *free* capability. Most methods do not need to cut; they can have the default @safe qualifier, which allows them to (transitively) modify the arguments, but not *cut* or *send* the object.

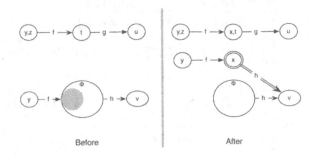

Before   After

Fig. 7. Example heap graph before and after transformation by $[\![x := y.f]\!]$. Double lines show the newly materialized node and edge. The grey blob is the portion of the anonymous heap that is the implicit target of $y.f$.

5   Isolation Capability Checking

Having built heap graphs at every program point, we now associate each labelled node n in each heap graph with a *capability* $\kappa(n)$, as mentioned earlier. All runtime objects represented by n implicitly have the same capability.

Fig. 8 shows the monotone transfer functions operating over the capability lattice in a simple forward-flow pass. At CFG join points, the merged heap graph's nodes are set to the minimum of the capabilities of the corresponding nodes in the predecessor heap graphs (in the CFG). For example,

```
a = new        // κ(a)  :=  free
if ...
    b.f = a    // κ(a)  :=  cuttable
               // join point. κ(a)  :=  min(free, cuttable)
    send(a)    // ERROR: κ(a) is not free
```

Assumption 1: the current method's signature is *free* $mthd(\vec{p}:\vec{\alpha})$.
Assumption 2: E and L used (e.g.) in *dependants* result from Heap Graph analysis for the current instruction.

$[\![entry(mthd)]\!]\ \kappa$	$=$	$[\vec{p}\overset{\kappa}{\mapsto}\vec{\alpha}]$
$[\![x := \mathbf{new}\ T]\!]\ \kappa$	$=$	$\kappa[x\overset{\kappa}{\mapsto}free]$
$[\![x := y]\!]\ \kappa$	$=$	$\kappa[x\overset{\kappa}{\mapsto}\kappa(y)]$

$precondition : \kappa(y) = free$

$$[\![x.f := y]\!]\ \kappa\ =\ \kappa[y\overset{\kappa}{\mapsto}cuttable]$$

$$[\![x := y.f]\!]\ \kappa\ =\ \kappa[x\overset{\kappa}{\mapsto}s]$$
$$s = \begin{cases} safe & \text{if } \kappa(y) = safe \\ cuttable & \text{if } \kappa(y) \in \{free, cuttable\} \end{cases}$$

$precondition : \beta_i \sqsubseteq \kappa(y_i)\ \wedge\ (\forall i \neq j)(disjoint(y_i, y_j) \vee \beta_i = \beta_j = safe)$

$$[\![x := m(\vec{y})]\!]\ \kappa\ =\ \kappa\begin{bmatrix} dependants(y_i) \cup \{y_i\} \overset{\kappa}{\mapsto} \bot, \text{ if } (\beta_i = free) \\ dependants(y_i) \overset{\kappa}{\mapsto} \bot, \qquad\ \text{ if } (\beta_i = cuttable) \end{bmatrix}\begin{bmatrix} x \overset{\kappa}{\mapsto} free \end{bmatrix}$$

(assumption: m's signature is *free* $m(\vec{\beta})$. Return value is always *free*)

$precondition : \kappa(y) \in \{free, cuttable\}$

$$[\![x := cut(y.f)]\!]\ \kappa =\ \kappa[x\overset{\kappa}{\mapsto}free]$$

$precondition : \kappa(x) = free \wedge \forall i(\alpha_i = cuttable \implies disjoint(x, p_i))$

$$[\![\mathbf{return}\ x]\!]\ \kappa\ =\ \kappa\ \text{(no change)}$$

where:

$\kappa(n) : LNode \mapsto Capability$ gives the Capability associated with a node $n \in LNode$

$(Capability, \sqsubseteq)\ =\ \bot \sqsubseteq safe \sqsubseteq cuttable \sqsubseteq free$

$\kappa(v)\ \overset{def}{=}\ min(\kappa(n)),\ n \in L(v)$

$\kappa[v\overset{\kappa}{\mapsto}c : Capability]\ \overset{def}{=}\ \kappa[n \mapsto c], n \in L(v)$

$dependants(v)\ \overset{def}{=}\ \{v' \mid n \in L(v) \wedge n' \in L(v') \wedge n' \in reachset(n)\}$
$\qquad\qquad\qquad$ where $reachset(n) = \bigcup_{\{n,\ \_,\ n'\} \in E}\{n'\} \cup reachset(n')$

$disjoint(x,y)\ \overset{def}{=}\ x \neq y\ \wedge\ (x \notin dependants(y)\ \wedge y \notin dependants(x))$

Fig. 8. Transfer functions for capability inference. Standard precondition: variables used as rvalues must be valid (i.e. $\sqsupset\bot$).

$\kappa(y)$	Isolation qualifier β		
	free	**cuttable**	**safe**
free	$\kappa' = \kappa[y \overset{\kappa}{\mapsto} \bot, \vec{z} \overset{\kappa}{\mapsto} \bot]$	$\kappa' = \kappa[y \overset{\kappa}{\mapsto} \bot]$	$\kappa' = \kappa$
cuttable		$\kappa' = \kappa[y \overset{\kappa}{\mapsto} \bot]$	$\kappa' = \kappa$
safe			$\kappa' = \kappa$

Fig. 9. Effect of the call $m(y)$ – where m's signature is $m(\beta\ p))$ – on the capabilities of y and on the dependants $\vec{z}$ of y. A blank indicates the call is illegal.

Note that the function κ has been overloaded to work for both variables and nodes; a variable's capability is the *minimum* capability of all the nodes to which it points.

The transfer function for method calls may be better understood from Fig. 9. The matrix matches capabilities of the argument with the corresponding parameter's isolation qualifier and each cell of the matrix reflects the effect on the capabilities of objects reachable from the argument.

5.1 Soundness

A formal proof of correctness is left to future work. Below, we outline the intuitions that justify our belief that the system is correct, and which we expect could form the basis of a proof.

Firstly, we require all built-in functions that can transfer a message (or a tree of such messages) from one actor to another do so via a `free` parameter or result. Therefore it is necessary to ensure that when an object is so transferred, no part of it remains accessible by the caller after the call – i.e. all local variables that can reference it can no longer be used. Of course, using conventional stack frames, there may remain pointers into the transferred structure, but the critical requirement is that all variables that may refer to these are marked with capability $\bot$. This effect is achieved by a combination of heap graph analysis followed by the capability dataflow propagation.

Secondly, we need to ensure that all operations in the language preserve the invariant that messages are tree-structured and that only the root of a message is ever marked as *free*. This requires a careful examination of each language primitive. Critical cases are:

- $x := \mathsf{cut}(y.f)$. If y is a well-formed tree, the modified y and x are also well-formed.
- $x.f := y$. This is the only form that can create heap aliases and its preconditions ensure that no more than one heap alias is created for any object. Further, y simultaneously loses the property of being a root and being *free*.

The correctness of the heap graph analysis rests on it being a special case of shape analysis (we can omit the "heap-sharing" flag).

Together, the argument is that each single step of evaluation preserves the property that only the root of a message can ever be *free*.

As a consequence each heap node is only accessible from at most one method in one actor as *free*, and therefore accessible from at most one actor.

5.2 Interoperation with Java

Java classes identified by the marker interface `Message` are treated as message types. We have treated Java objects and `Message`s as immiscible so far. This section describes the manner in which they can be mixed and the effect of such mixing on correctness.

Immutable classes such as `String` and `Date` already satisfy our interference-freedom version of isolation—even though, in the JVM they may be implemented as references shared by multiple actors, this sharing is benign. However, if the programmer wants to share a class between actors and is aware of the implications of sharing such a class (the mailbox is an example), he can have the class implement a marker interface `Sharable`. The weaver does not perform any checks on objects of such and therefore permits multiple heap-aliases. Clearly, this is a potential safety loophole. Objects derived from fields of `Sharable` objects are treated as regular Java objects, unless they too are instances of a `Sharable` class.

If a method parameter is not a message type, but is type compatible (upcast to `Object`, for example), then the absence of an annotation is treated as an escape into unknown territory; the weaver treats it as a compile-time error. For existing classes whose sources cannot be annotated, but whose behaviour is known, the programmer can supply "external annotations" to the weaver as a text file (Fig. 1):

```
class java.lang.String implements Sharable
interface java.io.PrintStream {
  void println(@safe Object o);
}
```

This scheme works as if the annotations were present in the original code. Clearly, it only works for non-executable annotations (type-qualifiers used for validation); `@pausable` cannot be used as it results in code transformations. Further, externally annotated libraries are not intended to be passed through Kilim's weaver; the annotations serve to declare the library methods' effects on their parameters.

The `@safe` annotation implies that the method guarantees that the parameter does not escape to a global variable or introduce other aliases (such as a collection class might), guarantees that are ordinarily given by message-aware methods.

Kilim accommodates other object types (needed for creating closures for the CPS transformation phase), but does not track them as it does message types. We take the pragmatic route of allowing ordinary Java objects (and their arrays) to be referenced from message classes but give no guarantees of safety. We do not implement any run-time checks or annotations or restrictions (such as a classloader per actor) on such objects.

Finally, the weaver limits static class fields to constant primitive or final `Sharable` objects and prevents exceptions from being message types.

6   Creating Scalable, Efficient Actors

Traditional threading facilities (including those available in the JVM) are tied to kernel resources, which limits their scalability and the efficiency of context switching. We map large numbers of actors onto a few Java threads by the simple expedient of rewriting their bytecode and having them cooperatively unwind their call stack. Unwinding is triggered by calls to `Actor.pause` or `Actor.sleep` (the mailbox library calls these internally).

A scheduler then initiates the process of rewinding (restoring) another actor's call stack, which then continues from where it left off. Much of the mechanics of transformation has been covered in an earlier paper [33]; this section summarises and highlights some of the important engineering decisions.

Unwinding a call stack involves remembering, for each activation frame, the state of the Java operand stack and of the local variables and the code offset to which to return. A call stack can unwind and rewind only if the entire call chain is composed of methods annotated with `@pausable`. Each pausable method's signature is transformed to include an extra argument called a *fiber* (of type `Fiber`), a logical thread of control. The fiber is a mechanism for a method to signal to its caller that it wants to return prematurely. The fiber also acts as a store for the activation frame of each method in the call hierarchy as the stack unwinds. The activation frame of a method consists of the program counter (the code offset to jump back to), the operand stack and the local variables. When the callee pauses (calls `Actor.pause()` or `mailbox.get()`), the caller examines the fiber, learns that it is now in a pausing state, stores its activation frame on the fiber and returns. And so on all the way up past the call chain's starting point, the actor's `execute()` method. This way, the entire call stack with its control and data elements is reified onto the fiber. The process is easily reversed: each method consults the fiber upon entry, jumps directly to the resumption point and restores its state where necessary.

This is conceptually equivalent to a continuation passing style (CPS) transformation; it is however applied only to pausable methods and produces single-shot continuations. The transform inlines local subroutines (reachable from the `jsr` instruction and used in try-finally blocks). Finally, the A-normal form of the CFG helps deal with the restriction imposed by the JVM that one cannot branch to an offset between `new` and the corresponding constructor invocation.

Transforming Java bytecode has the advantage that its format has remained constant while the source language has undergone tremendous transformations (generics, inner classes and soon, lambda functions and closures). It also allows us to perform local surgery and to `goto` into a loop without modifying any of the original code. Finally, it is applicable to other JVM-based languages as well (e.g. Scala).

Fig. 10 shows a sample CFG of a pausable method that makes a call to another pausable method, before and after the transformation performed by Kilim's weaver. The CFG shows extended basic blocks (multiple out-edges that account for JVM branching instructions and exception handlers), with the `invoke` instruction to a pausable method separated out into its own block. We will henceforth refer to this basic block as a *call site*.

The weaver adds one *prelude* node at entry, modifies each call site and adds two edges, one from the prelude to the call site to help recreate the stack and another from the call site to the exit to pause and unwind the stack. It also adds a node at the entry to every catch handler. None of the original nodes or edges

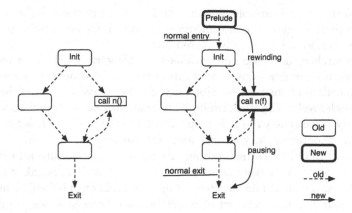

Fig. 10. CFG before and after transform

are touched, but the **weaver** maintains the JVM-verified invariant that the types and number of elements in the local variables and operand stack are identical regardless of the path taken to arrive at any instruction. This means that we cannot arbitrarily jump to any offset without balancing the stack first. For this reason, the stack and variables may need to be seeded with an appropriate number of dummy (constant) values of the expected type before doing the jump in the prelude.

6.1 Implementation Remarks

While the general approach is similar to many earlier approaches [5, 25], we feel the following engineering decisions contribute to the speed and scalability of our approach.

We store and restore the activation frame's state lazily in order to incur the least possible penalty when a pausable method does not pause. Unlike typical CPS transformations, we transform only those methods that contain invocations to methods marked @pausable. Our heap analysis phase also tracks live variables, duplicate values and constants. The latter two are never stored in the fiber; they are restored through explicit code. These steps ensure the minimum possible size for the closure. To the extent we are aware, these analyses are not performed by competing approaches.

In contrast to most CPS transformations on Java/C# bytecode, we chose to preserve the original call structure and to rewind and unwind the call stack. One reason is that CPS transformations also typically require the environment to support tail-call optimisation, a feature not present in the JVM. Second, the Java environment and mindset is quite dependent on the stack view of things: from security based on stack inspection to stack traces for debugging. In any case, the process of rewinding and unwinding the call stack turned out to be far less expensive than we had originally suspected, partly because we eagerly restore only the control plane, but lazily restore the data plane: only the topmost activation frame's local variables and operand stack are restored before resuming. If the actor pauses again, the intermediate activation frames' states are already in the fiber and do not need to be stored again.

Some researchers have used exceptions as a `longjmp` mechanism to unwind the stack; we use `return` because we found exceptions to be more expensive by almost two orders of magnitude. Not only do they have to be caught and re-thrown at each level of the stack chain, they clear the operand stack as well. This unnecessarily forces one to take a snapshot of the operand stack *before* making a call; in our experience, lazy storage and restoration works better.

We chose to modify the method signatures to accommodate an extra fiber parameter in contrast to other approaches that use Java's `ThreadLocal` facility to carry the out-of-band information. Using `ThreadLocals` is inefficient at best (about 10x slower), and incorrect at worst because there's no way to detect at run time that a non-pausable method is calling a pausable method (unless all methods are instrumented).

We have also noticed that the `@pausable` annotation makes explicit in the programmer's mind the cost of pausing, which in turn has a noticeable impact on the program structure.

7 Performance

Erlang is the current standard bearer for concurrency-oriented programming and sets the terms of the debate, from micro-benchmarks such as speed of process creation and messaging performance, to systems with an incredible 9-nines reliability [2]. Naturally, a comparison between Kilim and Erlang is warranted.

Unfortunately, no standard benchmark suites are yet available for the actor paradigm. We evaluated both platforms on the three most often quoted and much praised characteristics of the Erlang run-time: ability to create many processes, speed of process creation and that of message passing.

All tests were run on a 3GHz Pentium D machine with 1GB memory, running Fedora Core 6 Linux, Erlang v. R11B-3 (running HIPE) and Java 1.6. All tests were conducted with no special command-line parameters to tweak performance. Ten samples were taken from each system, after allowing the just-in-time compilers (JITs) to *warm up*. The variance was small enough in all experiments to be effectively ignored.

Kilim's performance exceeded our expectations on all counts. We had assumed that having to unwind and rewind the stack would drag down performance that could only be compensated for by an application that could make use of the JIT compiler. But Kilim's transformation, along with the quality of Java's current run-time, was able to compete favourably with Erlang on tasking, messaging and scalability.

Process creation The first test (Fig. 11(a)) measures the speed of (lightweight Erlang) process creation. The test creates n processes (actors) each of which sends a message to a central accounting process before exiting. The test measures the time taken from start to the last exit message arriving at the central object.

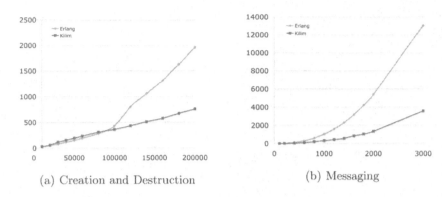

(a) Creation and Destruction   (b) Messaging

Fig. 11. Erlang vs. Kilim times. X-axis: n actors (n^2 messages), Y-axis: Time in ms (lower is better).

Kilim's creation penalty is negligible (200,000 actors in 578ms, a rate of 350KHz), and scaling is linear. We were unable to determine the reason for the knee in the Erlang curve.

Messaging Performance. The second test (Fig. 11(b)) has n actors exchanging n^2 messages with one another. This tests messaging performance and the ability to make use of multiple processing elements (cores or processors). Kilim's messaging is fast (9M+ messages in 0.54 μ sec, which includes context-switching time) and scales linearly.

Exploiting parallelism. The dual-core Pentium platform offered no tangible improvement (a slight decrease if anything) by running more than one thread with different kinds of schedulers (all threads managed by one scheduler vs. independent schedulers). We tried the messaging performance experiment on a Sun Fire T2000 machine with 32G total memory, eight cores on one chip and four hardware threads per core. We compared the system running with one thread vs. ten. Fig. 12 demonstrates the improvement afforded by real parallelism. Note also that the overall performance in this case is limited by the slower CPUs running at 1.4 GHz.

Miscellaneous numbers. We benchmarked against standard Java threads, RMI objects and Scala (2.6.1-RC1) (within one JVM instance). We do not include these numbers because we found all of them to be considerably slower: a simple binary ping-pong test with two objects bouncing a message back and forth has Kilim 10x faster than Scala's Actor framework [22] (even with the lighter-weight `react` mechanism), 5x faster than threads with Java's `Pipe*Stream` and 100x faster than RMI between collocated objects (RMI always serialises its messages, even if the parameters are non-referential types). Larger scales only worsened the performance gap.

Interpreting the results. One cannot set too much store by micro-benchmarks against a run-time as robust as that of Erlang. We are writing real-world applications to properly evaluate issues such as scheduling fairness, cache locality and

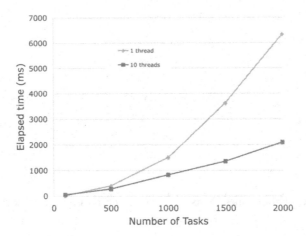

Fig. 12. Kilim messaging performance and hardware parallelism. (n actors, n^2 messages).

memory usage. Still, these tests do demonstrate that Kilim is a promising step combining the best of both worlds: concurrency-oriented programming, Erlang style, and the extant experience and training in object-oriented programming.

8   Related Work

Our work combines two orthogonal streams: lightweight tasking frameworks and alias control, with the focus on portability and immediate applicability (no changes to Java or the JVM).

Concurrent Languages. Most concurrency solutions can—on one axis—be broadly classified as a language versus library approach [11]. We are partial to Hans Boehm's persuasive arguments [6] that threads belong to the language, not a library. While most of the proposed concurrent languages notably support tasks and messages, few have found real industrial acceptance: Ada, Erlang and Occam. For the Java audience, Scala provides an elegant syntax and type system with support for actors provided as a library [22]; however, lack of isolation and aliasing are still issues. Scala has no lightweight threading mechanism, although the combination of higher-order functions and the react mechanism is a far superior alternative to callback functions in Java. JCSP [35], a Java implementation of CSP [23] has much the same issues.

The Singularity operating system [18] features similar to ours: lightweight isolated processes and special message types that do not allow internal aliasing. The system is written in a new concurrency-oriented language (Sing$^\#$), and a new run-time based on Microsoft's CLR model but with special heaps for exchanging messages. While ours is a more of an evolutionary approach, we look forward to their efforts becoming mainstream.

Tasks and Lightweight Threads. None of the existing lightweight tasking frameworks that we are aware of address the problems of aliased references.

The word "task" is overloaded. We are interested only in tasking frameworks that provide automatic stack management (can pause and resume) and not run to completion, such as Java's `Executor`, FJTask [27]) and JCilk [14]. That said, we have much to learn from the Cilk project's work on hierarchical task structures and work-stealing scheduling algorithms.

The Capriccio project [4] modified the user-level POSIX threads (`pthreads`) library to avoid overly conservative pre-allocation of heap and stack space, relying instead on a static analysis of code to infer the appropriate size and locations to dynamically expand heap space. They report scalability to 100,000 preemptively-scheduled threads.

Pettyjohn *et al* [30] generalise previous approaches to implementing first-class continuations for environments that do not support stack inspections. However, their generated code is considerably less efficient than ours; it relies on exceptions for stack unwinding, it creates custom objects per invocation site, splits the code into top-level procedures which results in loops being split into virtual function calls.

Many frameworks such as RIFE [5], and the Apache project's JavaFlow [25] transform Java bytecode into a style similar to ours. RIFE does not handle nested pausable calls. Kilim handles all bytecode instructions (including `jsr`) and is significantly faster for reasons explained earlier (and in [33]).

Static Analysis. Inferring, enforcing, and reasoning about properties of the heap is the subject of a sizable proportion of research literature on programming languages. We will not attempt to do this topic justice here and will instead provide a brief survey of the most relevant work. We heartily recommend [24], an "action plan" drawn up to address issues caused by unrestricted aliasing in the context of object-oriented programming languages.

Alias analysis concentrates on which variables may (or must) be aliases, but not on how sets of aliases relate to each other, an important requirement for us. We also require strong nullification and disjointness-preservation, something not available from most points-to analyses (*e.g.* [31]), because their method of associating abstract heap nodes with allocation points is equivalent to fixing the set of run-time objects that a variable may point to.

Shape analysis provides us the required properties because it accommodates dynamic repartitioning of the set of run-time objects represented by an alias configuration. However, the precision comes at the expense of speed. Our annotations provide more information to the analysis and pave the way for more modular inter-procedural analyses in the future.

Our approach is most closely related to Boyland's excellent paper on alias burying [10], which provides the notions of *unique* (identical to our *free*) and *borrowed*, which indicates that the object is not further aliasable (*cuttable* and *safe*, in our case). Boyland does not speak of safety from structural modifications, but this is a minor difference. The biggest difference in our approach is not the mechanics of the analysis, but in our design decision that messages be different classes and references to them and their components be unique. Making them different helps in dealing with versioning and selective upgrades (for example, one can have separate classloaders for actors and messages). Allowing free mixing of non-unique and unique references makes it very difficult to statically guarantee safety unless one extends the language, as with ownership types. This is an important software engineering decision; the knowledge that every message pointer is always unique and not subject to lock mistakes ensures that code for serialization, logging, filtering and persistence code does not need to deal with cycles, and permits arrays and embedded components to be exposed.

Type systems are generally monadic (do not relate one variable to another) and flow-insensitive (a variable's type does not change), although flow-sensitive type qualifiers [19] and quasi-linear types [26] are analogous to our efforts. Quasi-linear types have been successfully for network packet processing [17]; however packet structures in their language do not have nested pointers.

Ownership types [12, 7, 8] limit access to an object's internal representations through its owners. External uniqueness types [13] add to ownership types a linearly-typed pointer pointing to the root object. Each of these schemes offers powerful ways of containing aliasing, but are not a good fit for our current requirements: retrofitting into existing work, working with unencapsulated value objects and low annotation burden. An excellent summary of type systems for hierarchic shapes is presented in [16].

StreamFlex [32] relies on an implicit ownership type system that implements scoped allocation and ensures that there are no references to an object in a higher scope, but allows aliasing of objects in sibling and lower scopes. Their analysis relies on a partially closed world assumption. The type system is eminently suited for hooking together chained filters; it is less clear to us how it would work for long-lived communicating actors and changing connection topologies.

There are clearly domains where internal aliasing is useful to have, such as transmitting graphs across compiler stages. Although gcc's GIMPLE IR is tree-structured, one still has to convert it back to a graph, for example. A type system with scoped regions, such as StreamFlex's, permits internal aliasing without allowing non-unique pointers to escape from their embedded scope.

There are several works related to isolation. Reference immutability annotations [34, 21] can naturally complement our work. The Java community has recently proposed JSR-121, a specification for application level isolation; this ensures all global structures are global only to an isolate.

9   Conclusion and Future Work

We have demonstrated Kilim, a fast and scalable actor framework for Java. It features ultra-lightweight threads with logically disjoint heaps, a message-passing framework and a static analysis that semantically distinguishes messages from other objects purely internal to the actor. The type system ensures that messages are free of internal aliases and are owned by at most one actor at a time. This is in contrast to the current environment in all mainstream languages: heavyweight kernel threads, shared memory and explicit locking.

The techniques are applicable to any language with pointers and garbage collection, such as C#, Scala and OCaml.

Our target deployment platform is data-centre servers, where a user request results in a split-phase workflow involving CPU, disk and possibly dozens of remote services [15]; this application scenario helps distinguish our design choices from extant approaches to parallel and grid computing, which are oriented towards CPU-intensive problems such as protein folding.

Our message-passing framework lends itself naturally to a seamless view of local and distributed messaging. Integrating our platform with distributed naming and queueing systems is our current focus.

Another promising area of future work of interest to server-side frameworks is precise accounting of *resources* such as database connections, file handles and security credentials; these must be properly disposed of or returned even in the presence of actor crashes. We expect to extend the linearity paradigm towards statically-checked accountability of resource usage.

Acknowledgements. Thanks are due to Jean Bacon, Boris Feigin, Alexei Gotsman, Reto Kramer, Ken Moody, Matthew Parkinson, Mooly Sagiv, Viktor Vafeiadis, Tobias Wrigstad and the anonymous referees for their patient and detailed feedback. This work is supported by EPSRC grant GR/T28164.

References

[1] Armstrong, J.: Making Reliable Distributed Systems in the Presence of Software Errors. PhD thesis, The Royal Institute of Technology, Stockholm (2003)

[2] Armstrong, J., Virding, R., Wikström, C., Williams, M.: Concurrent Programming in Erlang. Prentice-Hall, Englewood Cliffs (1996)

[3] Adya, A., Howell, J., Theimer, M., Bolosky, W.J., Douceur, J.R.: Cooperative Task Management Without Manual Stack Management. In: USENIX Annual Technical Conference, General Track, pp. 289–302 (2002)

[4] von Behren, R., Condit, J., Zhou, F., Necula, G., Brewer, E.: Capriccio: Scalable threads for Internet Services. In: 19th ACM Symposium on Operating Systems Principles (2003)

[5] Bevin, G.: Rife, http://rifers.org

[6] Boehm, H.J.: Threads cannot be implemented as a library. In: ACM Conf. on PLDI, pp. 261–268 (2005)

[7] Boyapati, C., Lee, R., Rinard, M.C.: Ownership types for safe programming: preventing data races and deadlocks. In: Proc. of OOPSLA, pp. 211–230 (2002)

[8] Boyapati, C., Liskov, B., Shrira, L.: Ownership types for object encapsulation. In: Proc. of ACM POPL, pp. 213–223 (2003)

[9] Boyland, J., Noble, J., Retert, W.: Capabilities for sharing: A generalisation of uniqueness and read-only. In: Knudsen, J.L. (ed.) ECOOP 2001. LNCS, vol. 2072, pp. 2–27. Springer, Heidelberg (2001)

[10] Boyland, J.: Alias burying: Unique Variables Without Destructive Reads. Softw. Pract. Exper. 31(6), 533–553 (2001)

[11] Briot, J.P., Guerraoui, R., Löhr, K.P.: Concurrency and distribution in object-oriented programming. ACM Comput. Surv. 30(3), 291–329 (1998)

[12] Clarke, D.G., Potter, J., Noble, J.: Ownership types for flexible alias protection. In: Proc. of OOPSLA, pp. 48–64 (1998)

[13] Clarke, D., Wrigstad, T.: External uniqueness is unique enough. In: Cardelli, L. (ed.) ECOOP 2003. LNCS, vol. 2743, pp. 176–200. Springer, Heidelberg (2003)

[14] Danaher, J.S., Lee, I.T.A., Leiserson, C.E.: Programming with exceptions in JCilk. Sci. Comput. Program. 63(2), 147–171 (2006)

[15] DeCandia, G., Hastorun, D., Jampani, M., Kakulapati, G., Lakshman, A., Pilchin, A., Sivasubramanian, S., Vosshall, P., Vogels, W.: Dynamo: Amazon's Highly Available Key-value Store. In: SOSP, pp. 205–220 (2007)

[16] Drossopoulou, S., Clarke, D., Noble, J.: Types for Hierarchic Shapes. In: Sestoft, P. (ed.) ESOP 2006 and ETAPS 2006. LNCS, vol. 3924, pp. 1–6. Springer, Heidelberg (2006)

[17] Ennals, R., Sharp, R., Mycroft, A.: Linear types for Packet Processing. In: Schmidt, D. (ed.) ESOP 2004. LNCS, vol. 2986, pp. 204–218. Springer, Heidelberg (2004)

[18] Fähndrich, M., Aiken, M., Hawblitzel, C., Hodson, O., Hunt, G.C., Larus, J.R., Levi, S.: Language support for fast and reliable message-based communication in Singularity OS. In: Proc. of EuroSys (2006)

[19] Foster, J.S., Terauchi, T., Aiken, A.: Flow-sensitive type qualifiers. In: ACM Conf. on PLDI, pp. 1–12 (2002)

[20] Ganz, S.E., Friedman, D.P., Wand, M.: Trampolined style. In: ICFP, pp. 18–27 (1999)

[21] Haack, C., Poll, E., Schäfer, J., Schubert, A.: Immutable objects for a Java-like language. In: De Nicola, R. (ed.) ESOP 2007. LNCS, vol. 4421, pp. 347–362. Springer, Heidelberg (2007), http://www.cs.ru.nl/~chaack/papers/papers/imm-obj.pdf

[22] Haller, P., Odersky, M.: Event-based programming without inversion of control. In: Proc. Joint Modular Languages Conference. Springer, Heidelberg (2006)

[23] Hoare, C.A.R.: Communicating sequential processes. Communications of the ACM 21(8), 666–677 (1978)

[24] Hogg, J., Lea, D., Wills, A., de Champeaux, D., Holt, R.C.: The Geneva Convention on the treatment of object aliasing. OOPS Messenger 3(2), 11–16 (1992)

[25] JavaFlow: The Apache Software Foundation: http://jakarta.apache.org/commons/sandbox/javaflow

[26] Kobayashi, N.: Quasi-linear types. In: Proc. of ACM POPL, pp. 29–42 (1999)

[27] Lea, D.: A Java fork/join framework. In: Java Grande, pp. 36–43 (2000)

[28] Milner, R.: Communicating and Mobile Systems: the π-calculus. Cambridge University Press, Cambridge (1999)

[29] Nielson, F., Nielson, H.R., Hankin, C.: Principles of Program Analysis. Springer, Heidelberg (1999)

[30] Pettyjohn, G., Clements, J., Marshall, J., Krishnamurthi, S., Felleisen, M.: Continuations from generalized stack inspection. In: ICFP, pp. 216–227 (2005)

[31] Salcianu, A., Rinard, M.C.: A combined pointer and purity analysis for Java programs. In: MIT Technical Report MIT-CSAIL-TR-949 (2004)

[32] Spring, J.H., Privat, J., Guerraoui, R., Vitek, J.: Streamflex: High-throughput stream programming in Java, 211–228 (2007)
[33] Srinivasan, S.: A thread of one's own. In: Workshop on New Horizons in Compilers (2006), http://www.cse.iitb.ac.in/~uday/NHC-06/advprogram.html
[34] Tschantz, M.S., Ernst, M.D.: Javari: adding reference immutability to Java. In: Proc. of OOPSLA, pp. 211–230 (2005)
[35] Welch, P.: JCSP, http://www.cs.kent.ac.uk/projects/ofa/jcsp
[36] Welsh, M., Culler, D.E., Brewer, E.A.: SEDA: An architecture for well-conditioned, scalable internet services. In: SOSP, 230–243 (2001)
[37] Wilhelm, R., Sagiv, S., Reps, T.W.: Shape analysis. In: Watt, D.A. (ed.) CC 2000 and ETAPS 2000. LNCS, vol. 1781, pp. 1–17. Springer, Heidelberg (2000)

A Uniform Transactional Execution Environment for Java

Lukasz Ziarek[1], Adam Welc[2], Ali-Reza Adl-Tabatabai[2], Vijay Menon[2], Tatiana Shpeisman[2], and Suresh Jagannathan[1]

[1] Dept. of Computer Sciences
Purdue University
West Lafayette, IN 47907
{lziarek,suresh}@cs.purdue.edu
[2] Programming Systems Lab
Intel Corporation
Santa Clara, CA 95054
{adam.welc,ali-reza.adl-tabatabai,vijay.s.menon,
tatiana.shpeisman}@intel.com

Abstract. Transactional memory (TM) has recently emerged as an effective tool for extracting fine-grain parallelism from declarative critical sections. In order to make STM systems practical, significant effort has been made to integrate transactions into existing programming languages. Unfortunately, existing approaches fail to provide a simple implementation that permits lock-based and transaction-based abstractions to coexist seamlessly. Because of the fundamental semantic differences between locks and transactions, legacy applications or libraries written using locks can not be transparently used within atomic regions. To address these shortcomings, we implement a uniform transactional execution environment for Java programs in which transactions can be integrated with more traditional concurrency control constructs. Programmers can run arbitrary programs that utilize traditional mutual-exclusion-based programming techniques, execute new programs written with explicit transactional constructs, and freely combine abstractions that use both coding styles.

1 Introduction

Over the last decade, transactional memory (TM) has emerged as an attractive alternative to lock-based abstractions by providing stronger semantic guarantees (atomicity and isolation) as well as a simpler programming model. Transactional memory relieves the burden of reasoning about deadlocks and locking protocols. Additionally, transactional memory has also been utilized to extract fine-grain parallelism from critical sections. In particular, software transactional memory (STM) systems provide scalable performance surpassing that of coarse-grain locks and a simpler, but competitive alternative to hand-tuned fine-grain locks [3,10,12,25,30].

J. Vitek (Ed.): ECOOP 2008, LNCS 5142, pp. 129–154, 2008.

In order to make STM systems practical, significant effort has been made to integrate transactions into existing programming languages, virtual machines, and run-time systems. Since languages such as Java already provide concurrency control primitives based on mutual exclusion, seamlessly integrating transactions into these languages requires rectifying the semantics and implementation of the two constructs. Existing approaches that attempt to support different concurrency control mechanisms [10,30] do not provide a uniform implementation. Therefore, complex programs that make use of mutual-exclusion cannot be executed on a system providing transactional support without breaking composability and abstraction – to be assured that it is safe to execute a code region transactionally requires knowing that methods invoked within the dynamic context of this region do not make use of mechanisms that violate transactional semantics such as I/O or communication. Such disparities between different concurrency control mechanisms have prevented the integration of transactions into large, complex programs and limited mainstream deployment. As a result, programmers cannot easily compose transactions with other concurrency primitives.

In this paper, we describe a uniform transactional execution environment for Java programs in which transactions and other concurrency control constructs can be seamlessly integrated, interchanged, and composed. Programmers can run arbitrary programs that utilize traditional mutual-exclusion-based programming techniques, execute new programs written with explicit transactional constructs, and freely combine abstractions that use both coding styles. Our framework allows programmers to write modular transactional code without having to hand-inspect all calls within a transactional region to guarantee safety. The uniform transactional execution environment is composed of two mutually co-operating implementations, one for locks and the other for transactions, and allows for dynamic handoff between different concurrency control primitives.

Our paper makes the following contributions:

1. We describe how explicit transactional constructs can be seamlessly integrated into Java. We present a programming model which provides both *synchronized* and *atomic* primitives, and a uniform semantics for composing and interchanging the two.
2. We provide an in-depth exploration of how transactions can be used to support execution of lock-based synchronization constructs. Our study includes issues related to language memory models, and concurrency operators which inherently break isolation such as `wait` and `notify`. We explore properties that must be satisfied by a transactional implementation striving to address these issues. We present the theoretical foundations of such an implementation we call P-SLE (*pure-software lock elision*).
3. We present the design and implementation of the first fully uniform execution environment supporting both traditional (locks) and new (atomic blocks) constructs.
4. We evaluate the performance of our system on a set of non-trivial benchmarks demonstrating scalability comparable to programs using fine-grained mutual-exclusion locks, and improved performance over coarse-grain locks.

T1	T2

`synchronized(hmap1) {`
`  synchronized(hmap2) {`
 	
`    hmap2.move(hmap1);`
 	
`  }`
`}`
	`synchronized(hmap1) {`
	
	`  hmap1.get(x);`
	`}`

Fig. 1. An example program where locks can be elided, allowing for additional concurrency

Our benchmarks perform I/O actions, inter-thread communication, thread spawns, class loading, and reflection, exercising a significant portion of Java language features.

2   Motivation

Locks are the most pervasive concurrency control mechanism used to guard shared data accesses within critical sections. Their semantics is defined by the mutual exclusion of critical sections. In addition to providing *thread synchronization* and preventing interference between locked regions, lock operations act as *memory synchronization* points providing ordering and visibility guarantees [16]. Software transactional memory, advocated as a lock replacement mechanism, unfortunately provides different semantics. STMs guarantee *atomicity* and *isolation* of operations executed within critical sections (also known as *atomic regions* or *atomic blocks*) to prevent interference. The exact semantics provided by an STM is defined in terms of an underlying transactional implementation. For example, STMs with weakly atomic and strongly atomic semantics [4,26] are implemented differently. STM systems also typically define their own notions of ordering and visibility (e.g., closed vs. open nesting [21]). Due to differences in both semantics and implementations, locks and transactions cannot easily be composed or interchanged. For example, mutual exclusion may hinder extraction of additional scalability, whereas semantic properties of atomic regions may violate visibility guarantees provided by lock-based synchronized blocks.

To provide composability, differences in semantics and implementations must be rectified. The semantics of locked regions and atomic blocks must be consistent and their implementations uniform. Observe that the semantics of locks may be supported by an implementation different from mutual exclusion and, similarly, alternative implementations can be used to implement the semantics dictated by transactions. The following examples illustrate some of the issues that arise in defining a uniform implementation and consistent semantics for both constructs.

```
synchronized(m) {
  count--;
  if (count == 0) m.notifyAll();
  while (count != 0) {
    m.wait();
  }
}
```

Fig. 2. Barrier Example

Consider the example Java program in Figure 1 which consists of two threads operating over two different hashmaps hmap1 and hmap2. Although highly concurrent lock-based Java implementations of hashmap exist, exclusively locking the hashmap object to perform operations on the hashmap as a whole fundamentally limits scalability. In the example in Figure 1 thread T1 moves the content of hashmap hmap1 into hmap2, locking both hashmaps and thus preventing thread T2 from concurrently accessing hmap1. In some cases, as seen in the example in Figure 1, locks can be elided – their implementation, mutual exclusion of critical sections, can be replaced by a transactional one. This can be accomplished by rewriting source code to utilize transactions without changing the semantics of the original program. If locks were elided, thread T2 in Figure 1 would be able to perform its operations concurrently with thread T1. The underlying transactional machinery would guarantee correctness and consistency of the operations on hmap1 and hmap2. To summarize, in this example either transactions or locks may be utilized with no change to the underlying program semantics.

Lock elision, however, is not always possible. Consider an example program that spawns multiple worker threads that perform work over a collection of shared structures. Data computed by those threads is then collected and aggregated (SPECjbb2000 [29] is an example of such a program). Such programs use coordination barriers to synchronize the worker threads so that data may be compiled. Coordination barriers typically use a communication protocol that allows threads to exchange information about their arrival at the barrier point. Consider a simple counter-based Java implementation that notifies all threads waiting on the barrier when the counter (initialized to the total number of threads) reaches zero (Figure 2).

A naive translation of the synchronized block in Figure 2 to use transactions is problematic for multiple reasons. First, the execution of the wait and notify methods inside of atomic regions is typically prohibited by STMs [3,10]. Second, even if an STM defined meaningful behavior for the invocation of such methods inside atomic regions, the execution of the barrier would not complete. The update to the internal counter would never become visible because transactions impose isolation requirements on the code they protect.

A potential solution to translating the example in Figure 2 to use atomic regions must therefore not only support wait/notify but also allow updates to the

T1	T2

`atomic {`
`  synchronized(m) {`
 	
`    foo();`
`  }`
`  ...`
`}`
	
	`  synchronized(m) {`
	
	`    bar();`
	`  }`

Fig. 3. Composition of synchronized blocks and atomic regions

internal counter to become visible to other threads. One solution, suggested by [27], is to expose the value of the internal counter by explicitly violating isolation of the original atomic region – splitting the atomic region into multiple separate regions without altering the behavior of the program. Isolation would also have to be broken to support `wait/notify` primitives. Breaking isolation in such a manner creates a race condition on accesses to the shared counter because it is no longer protected within the same contiguous critical region. Alternatively, we can leave the synchronized block unmodified. Such a solution requires reasoning about all possible interactions between the synchronized blocks and the atomic regions present in the program.

Although it may be possible to translate the example code in Figure 2 with extensions to an STM, previous work [4] suggests that even with access to all source code a translation of synchronized blocks to atomic regions that retains the original program's semantics is not always feasible. At best, such a translation requires careful analysis of the original program's source code. However, source code may not always be available, might be complex, and may need to be re-engineered for transactions. Our own experience in translating lock-based versions of some well-known benchmarks into their transactional equivalents [26] mirrors these findings. Even with STM extensions, it is still unclear if certain synchronized blocks can even be translated at all, motivating the necessity of supporting composability between synchronized blocks and atomic regions.

Unfortunately, composability of different concurrency control primitives is not easily achieved. Since atomic regions and synchronized blocks provide different semantic guarantees on visibility and isolation, composition of the two constructs can yield non-intuitive and potentially erroneous behavior. Consider the program in Figure 3. In the common case, locks protecting synchronized blocks in both threads might be elided allowing execution to proceed fully under transactional control. However, consider a situation when method `foo()` executes a native call and prints a message to the screen. In order to prevent the message from being printed more than once, a possibility that could arise if the synchronized block is implemented transactionally, the block must be expressed using mutual exclusion semantics. Additionally, once thread T1 acquires lock m, the synchronized block executed by thread T2 must also be implemented using mutual exclusion. Moreover, an abort may still be triggered after thread T1 finishes executing its synchronized block but before it finishes executing the outer atomic region. As a result, the entire atomic region in thread T1 must also be prevented from aborting, and thus must be implemented using mutual exclusion.

To address these issues, this paper presents a uniform execution environment that allows *safe* interoperability between lock-based and transaction-based concurrency primitives. The execution environment *dynamically* switches between transactional and lock based implementations to provide consistent semantics for both constructs. This allows for arbitrary composition and interchangeability of synchronized blocks and atomic regions.

3   Programming and Execution Model

Our system supports concurrent programming in Java by offering two basic primitives to programmers: `synchronized` providing lock semantics and `atomic` providing transactional semantics. The system imposes no constraints on how the two primitives may interact. Programmers may utilize both primitives for concurrency control and can compose them arbitrarily. Additionally, there are no restrictions on what code can be executed within the dynamic context of a transaction, allowing support for I/O, legacy and native code.

Both primitives are realized using a transactional implementation. In our system, synchronized blocks are automatically and transparently transformed to implicitly use a transactional implementation we call pure-software lock elision (P-SLE), rather than an implementation based on mutual exclusion. We explore properties that the P-SLE implementation must satisfy in order to preserve lock semantics in Section 4. User-defined atomic regions are already implemented using transactions and thus require no additional support under P-SLE (details are given in Section 5).

Since transactions and locks differ in their semantic definitions, execution of lock-based critical sections using P-SLE may not always be possible. When such situations are detected, our system seamlessly reverts critical sections to use an implementation based on mutual exclusion. This is accomplished through a *fallback* mechanism discussed in Section 4. Fallback has a natural definition for transactions translated from critical sections: acquire the original lock as defined by the input program. User injected atomic regions, however, are not defined with regard to locks. Thus, we present a new mechanism called *atomic serialization* which allows for the execution of user-defined transactions under mutual exclusion. Conceptually, atomic serialization works by effectively serializing execution of atomic regions using a single global lock. Atomic serialization aborts a transaction which must fallback and acquires a global lock prior to re-executing the critical region protected by the user-defined transaction.

Our system thus optimistically executes all concurrency control primitives transactionally. In situations where such an execution is infeasible (e.g., eliding locks violates lock semantics), the implementation switches back to using mutual exclusion. This transition is one-directional – once execution of a critical section reverts to using mutual exclusion, it will run in this execution mode until

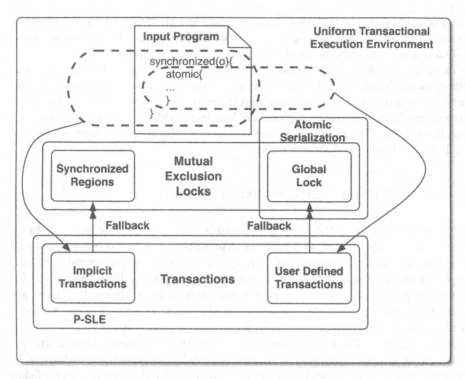

Fig. 4. Execution model for a program containing both synchronized blocks and atomic regions. The uniform execution environment utilizes both a lock-based implementation and a transactional one. Double arrows represent the fallback mechanism, while single arrows show the initial implementation underlying both concurrency control primitives.

completion. Figure 4 illustrates the system depicting both concurrency control primitives and the transitions supported by the implementation.

4 Pure-Software Lock Elision (P-SLE)

Our first step to constructing a uniform transactional execution environment for Java programs is replacing the existing implementation for Java's synchronized blocks (i.e., mutual exclusion) with P-SLE. Because in doing so we are obligated to preserve lock semantics, P-SLE must provide properties mirroring mutual exclusion, that is, both thread and memory synchronization effects of lock operations. The JMM uses these lock properties to define valid executions for Java programs.

4.1 Correctness

Clearly, in order for one implementation to be correctly replaced by the other we must define a correlation between their semantics. We do so in terms of program schedules produces by each implementation. A program schedule reflects the execution of a concurrent program on a single-processor machine and defines a total order among program operations. This notion of a schedule can be easily generalized to a multi-processor case – operations whose order cannot be determined when analyzing the execution of a program are independent and can be executed in arbitrary order. For schedules generated under a transactional implementation, only operations of the last successful execution of a transaction become part of the program schedule.

Our first step in defining the correctness property is to determine what it means for two schedules to be equivalent under the JMM. The JMM defines a *happens-before* relation (written $\xrightarrow{hb}$) among the actions performed by threads in a given execution of a program. For single-threaded executions, the happens-before relation is defined by program order. For multi-threaded executions, the happens-before relation is defined between pairs of synchronization operations, such as the begin and end of a critical section, or the write and read of the same volatile variable. The happens-before relation is transitive: $x \xrightarrow{hb} y$ and $y \xrightarrow{hb} z$ imply $x \xrightarrow{hb} z$.

The JMM uses the happens-before relation to define visibility requirements for operations in a given schedule. Consider a pair of read and write operations, r_v and w_v, accessing the same variable v and ordered by the happens-before relation ($w_v \xrightarrow{hb} r_v$). Assume further that no intervening write exists such that $w_v \xrightarrow{hb} w'_v \xrightarrow{hb} r_v$. In other words, w_v is the "latest" write to v preceding r_v in the order defined by the happens-before relation. Then, r_v is obligated to observe the effect of w_v, unless intervening writes to v unordered by the happens-before relation, exist between w_v and r_v. In this case, r_v may observe either a value produced by w_v or a value produced by any of the intervening writes. We say that two schedules are identical if all happens-before relations are preserved between the same operations in both schedules.

The JMM has been defined under an implicit assumption that critical sections are implemented using mutual exclusion locks. Given a program P, the JMM defines a set of possible schedules, S, that characterizes P's runtime behavior. Clearly, a transactional version of P, $\tau(P)$, cannot produce a schedule s such that $s \notin S$. Similarly, if $S = \{s\}$ then $\tau(P)$ can only have one unique schedule as defined by the JMM, namely s. Thus, a transactional version of a Java program cannot produce any new schedules and it must produce the exact schedule the original program produces if only one exists. However, what occurs when multiple schedules are plausible for a program P? The JMM itself does not enforce any scheduling fairness restrictions. The underlying virtual machine and its scheduler are free to provide any proper subset of schedules for P. We leverage the freedom provided by the JMM in defining correct executions for a transactionalized program. If program P produces a set of schedules S under the JMM and $\tau(P)$ produces a set of schedules S' then $\tau(P)$ is a correct execution if $S' \subseteq S$.

Table 1. A list of safety properties for isolation and ordering concerns related to shared memory accesses (* – depends on a particular incarnation)

Property	Mutual Exclusion	Weak Atomicity	Strong Atomicity	P-SLE
Repeatable Reads	*no*	*no*	*yes*	*yes/no**
Intermediate Updates	*no*	*no*	*yes*	*yes/no**
Intermediate Reads	*no*	*yes/no**	*yes*	*yes/no**
Speculation Safety	*yes*	*yes/no**	*yes*	*yes*
Publication Safety	*yes*	*yes/no**	*yes*	*yes*
Privatization Safety	*yes*	*yes/no**	*yes*	*yes*
Granular Safety	*yes*	*yes/no**	*yes*	*yes*

One could argue that a uniform transactional execution environment should only be obligated to provide correctness guarantees for transactional and lock-based executions when the program is *properly structured* [30]. Such programs do not exhibit races, have shared data protected by a consistent set of locks, etc. Unfortunately, requiring programs to be properly structured in order to leverage transactional execution is a severe restriction in practice and prevents such programming idioms as privatization [26]. Our focus is on ensuring well-defined behavior even when programs are not properly structured.

We identify a set of properties that the P-SLE implementation must satisfy in order to correctly support lock semantics. We do so by analyzing properties of existing implementations: both non-transactional (mutual exclusion) and transactional (weak atomicity and strong atomicity [1]). Our discussion is separated into two parts: one concerning problems related to isolation and ordering of operations that may lead to incorrect results being computed, and the other concerning problems related to visibility of an operation's effects that may prevent programs from making progress. Problems related to isolation and ordering have been examined in previous work [19,26] and our system builds off of such solutions.

4.2   Isolation and Ordering Concerns

Table 1 presents a classification of isolation and ordering safety properties preserved by different implementations (*yes* means that the implementation supports the property, *no* means that it does not and *yes/no* means that different incarnations of a particular implementation exist which may or may not preserve it [2].). In the following, accesses to shared variables can be either protected within critical sections or unprotected.

The first three properties described in the table concern direct interactions between protected and unprotected accesses. In order to provide some intuition

---

[1] We assume that both weak atomicity and strong atomicity use closed nesting.

[2] For example, some incarnations of weak atomicity use updates in-place while others use write buffering.

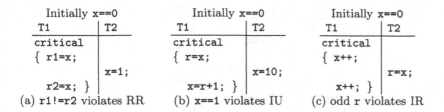

Fig. 5. Safety violations resulting from direct interactions between protected and unprotected accesses

behind their definition, Figure 5 demonstrates what happens if these properties are violated. The code samples in Figure 5 use the same shared variable x for illustration of the violations and (as well as all the remaining figures in this section) are written in "pseudo-Java" – we use the `critical` keyword to denote critical sections (instead of `synchronized` or `atomic`) to avoid implying a particular implementation of a concurrency control mechanism. We assume that if mutual exclusion is used to execute critical sections, then all threads synchronize using the same global lock.

Preservation of repeatable reads (RR) requires that protected reads of the same shared variable by one thread must return the same value despite intermediate unprotected write to the same variable by another thread being executed between the reads. The intermediate updates (IU) property is preserved if the effect of an unprotected update to some shared variable happening between a protected read of the same variable and a protected write of the same variable is not lost. Finally, preservation of the intermediate reads (IR) property requires that an unprotected read of some shared variable does not see a dirty intermediate value available between two protected writes of the same variable. Since mutual exclusion preserves none of these properties, they also do not need to be preserved by P-SLE.

The next property described in the table, speculation safety (SS)[3], concerns (possibly indirect) interactions between protected and unprotected accesses combined with the effects of speculative execution. Speculation safety prevents a protected speculative write to some variable from producing an "out-of-thin-air" value that could be observed by an unprotected read in another thread. Mutual exclusion trivially preserves speculation safety since no protected access is ever speculative under this implementation. As a result, P-SLE must preserve this property as well, but in case of transactional implementations special care needs to be taken to satisfy it – strong atomicity preserves it but weak atomicity may or may not, depending on its particular incarnation. The example in Figure 6 illustrates one possible scenario when speculation safety gets violated – under mutual exclusion, thread T2 could never observe r==1 since critical sections of threads T1 and T2 would be executed serially and thread T2 would never see

---

[3] This safety property subsumes another safety property discussed in previous work [19] – observable consistency.

T1	T2	T3
critical		
{	critical	
y++;	{	
	if(y!=z) x=1;	
		r=x;
z++;	// abort	
}	}	

Fig. 6. r==1 violates SS

values of y and z to be different from each other. When executed transaction-ally, the transaction executed by thread T2 could observe different values of y and z, and even though the transaction would be later aborted because of an inconsistent state, it would still perform an update to x producing a value out of thin air, visible to thread T3.

The following two safety properties, privatization safety (PRS) and publication safety (PUS), concern ordering of protected accesses with respect to unprotected accesses. These idioms reflect how a privatizing or publishing action can convert data from shared to private state, or vice versa. The privatization safety pattern is generalized in Figure 7(a) – some memory location is shared when accessed in S1 but private to T2 when accessed in S2. An intervening privatizing action ensures that the location is only accessible to T2 and involves execution of a memory synchronization operation to guarantee that other threads are aware of the privatization event. The publication pattern, generalized in Figure 7(b), is a reverse of the publication pattern. Both patterns have been well-researched [19,1,26,28], and the conclusion is that while mutual exclusion trivially preserves both safety properties, it is not necessarily automatically true for transactional implementations, such as P-SLE, and requires special care to provide the same memory synchronization effects.

The last property, granular safety (GS), prevents protected writes from affecting unprotected reads of adjacent data. In Java, a protected write to a field x of an object should have no effect on a read of field y of the same object. By definition, granular safety cannot be violated when using mutual exclusion

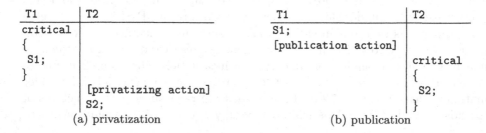

T1	T2		T1	T2
critical			S1;	
{			[publication action]	
S1;				critical
}				{
	[privatizing action]			S2;
	S2;			}
(a) privatization			(b) publication	

Fig. 7. Safety of protected vs. unprotected accesses ordering

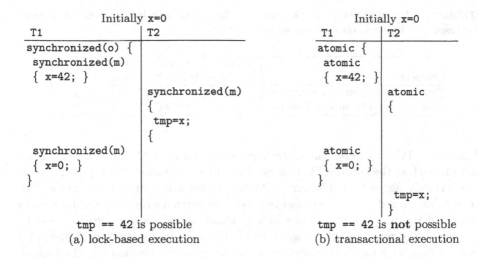

Fig. 8. Visibility in presence of inner synchronization-related operations

locks since no protected accesses ever modify adjacent data (protected reads and writes occur at the same granularity as "regular" data accesses). In order for the same guarantee to hold for transactional implementations, special care may have to be taken on how modified data is logged and written to shared memory.

Thus, P-SLE must provide at least the same level of isolation and ordering guarantees as mutual exclusion provides. At the same time, according to our correctness definition presented in Section 4.1, P-SLE can provide stronger guarantees than mutual exclusion since our obligation is to reproduce only a subset of all schedules legal under the JMM. For example, an implementation of a P-SLE system can allow or disallow violation of any of the first properties listed in Table 1, provided that the visibility properties described in the next section are satisfied.

4.3 Visibility Concerns

While the isolation and ordering properties of transactional systems have recently attracted significant attention, issues concerning mismatches between visibility properties of systems supporting mutual exclusion semantics and those supporting transactional semantics have been, with some notable exceptions [4,30], largely neglected.

Visibility issues are closely tied to progress guarantees provided by the underlying execution engine. The JMM (or, in fact, the Java Language Specification [8] or the Java Virtual Machine Specification [15]) does not require the Java execution environment to provide any guarantees with respect to application progress or scheduling fairness. As a result, a legal implementation of a JVM could attempt to execute all threads in sequential order, getting "stuck" when control dependencies among operations in these threads manifest. In other words, it is

Table 2. A list of safety properties for visibility concerns related to shared memory accesses. (* – depends on a particular incarnation).

Property	Mutual Exclusion	Weak Atomicity	Strong Atomicity	P-SLE
Symmetric Dependent Visibility	*yes*	*no*	*no*	*yes*
Asymmetric Dependent Visibility	*yes*	*yes/no**	*no*	*yes*

legal for a JVM to *never* successfully complete an inter-thread communication action, such as the coordination barrier presented in Section 2 in Figure 2. While we certainly agree that different JVM implementations are free to make their own scheduling decisions, we also believe that certain programs are intuitively expected to make progress under lock semantics, and these programs must be guaranteed to make progress regardless of the underlying execution model. This is consistent with our correctness definition presented in Section 4.1 – two schedules generated for the same program under two different execution models cannot be equal if one of them is terminating and the other is non-terminating.

In languages like Java, different locks can be used to protect different accesses to the same shared data. In other words, no concurrency control is enforced if two accesses to the same location are protected by two different locks. As a result, two critical sections protected by different locks can execute concurrently, such as an outer critical section of thread T1 and a critical section of thread T2 in Figure 8(a).

Transactions, on the other hand, make no such distinction between critical sections. All transactions will appear serialized with respect to one another. Consequently, if the critical sections in Figure 8(a) were executed transactionally, the schedule presented in this figure could not have been generated. In a transactional implementation supporting pessimistic writers [3,12], thread T1 would acquire a write lock when writing x for the first time and release it only at the end of the outer critical section, making an intermediate read of x by thread T2 impossible. One possible schedule that could be generated is presented in Figure 8(b). In accordance with isolation properties of transactions, propagation of both updates performed by thread T1 is delayed until the end of the outermost critical section executed by thread T1. Observe that the schedule presented in Figure 8(b) would still be legal under lock-based execution if the runtime system used a different thread scheduling policy.

Thus, delaying propagation of updates can often be explained as a benign change in scheduler behavior. However, additional visibility-related safety properties must be defined to guarantee that lock semantics can be correctly supported by a transactional implementation in situations where this is not true. In the following code samples, an explicit "lock" parameter is used with the `critical` keyword in order to be able to express the difference between executions using transactions and executions using mutual exclusion locks. We assume that if transactions are used to execute critical sections then the "lock" parameter is ignored.

Visibility-related safety properties can be divided into two categories summarized in Table 2: symmetric dependent visibility (SV) and asymmetric dependent
visibility (AV). Their definitions rely on the notion of control dependency between operations of different threads. We say that two operations are control
dependent if, under all lock-based executions, the outcome of the first operation
dictates whether the second one is executed.

Symmetric Dependent Visibility. Dependent symmetric visibility (SV) concerns the case when all control dependent operations are executed inside of critical sections. The SV property is satisfied if a schedule can be generated in which,
for every pair of control dependent operations, the second operation eventually
sees the outcome of the first.

Consider the following example of a handshake protocol given in Figure 9(a).
In this code the variables x, y, and z are used for communication. The two
executing threads alternate waiting on variables to be set to one by spinning in
while loops, making read and write operations on these variables control dependent. Under locks, the dependent symmetric visibility is obviously satisfied – the
updates of x, y, and z will become visible to the respective threads allowing
for the handshake to proceed. Consequently, the same visibility property must
also be satisfied by P-SLE. However, if we executed this program using strong
or weakly atomic transactions, the program would hang because transactions

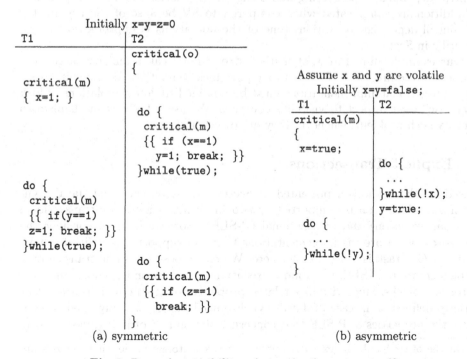

Fig. 9. Dependent visibility – is termination guaranteed?

enforce isolation of shared accesses: execution of the outer transaction in thread T2 would prevent the update of x and z from being visible to the code it protects.

Detecting potential visibility violations between critical sections is then tantamount to detecting control dependencies among data accesses executed within critical sections. We describe one solution to discovering symmetric dependent visibility violations in Section 6.

Asymmetric Dependent Visibility. Unfortunately, examining only critical sections is insufficient since visibility issues can also arise between protected and unprotected code. Dependent asymmetric visibility (AV) addresses this case.

Consider the example given in Figure 9(b). Thread T2's progress depends on making a result of thread T1s update of x available to thread T2. Since x is a volatile, lock semantics dictates that **Thread 2** must eventually see the result of thread T1's update to x. Similarly, thread T1 is guaranteed under lock semantics to see the result of thread T2's update to y. Therefore, this program is guaranteed to successfully complete execution of both threads under lock semantics. At the same time, strong atomicity and certain incarnations of weak atomicity (such as those using write buffering) would prevent a write to x from being visible to thread T2 until the end of the critical section in thread T1. If we run this program under such an implementation, the program will fail to terminate [4]. Once again we notice that the variables through which communication occurs are in fact control dependent. Discovering and remedying violations of the AV property is additionally complicated when compared to SV because of the asymmetry of control dependent operations (one of the operations is unprotected), as we describe in Section 6.

Our examples illustrate that neither strong nor weak atomicity satisfy the properties required from P-SLE to support lock semantics. As a result, existing transactional implementations must be modified to detect violations of lock semantics with respect to visibility concerns. We use a fallback mechanism to remedy such problems whenever they are discovered.

5   Explicit Transactions

Based on the discussion presented in Section 4, we observe that Java's synchronized blocks can be supported by two implementations: non-transactional (mutual exclusion) and transactional (P-SLE). Now we have to consider the opposite – what are the implementations that can support user-defined atomic regions? Our task is much simpler here. We can choose the same transactional implementation, P-SLE, to support execution of both atomic regions and synchronized blocks. Since visibility-related properties of atomic regions are not as strictly defined as in case of Java's synchronized blocks, we only need to consider the properties of P-SLE that concern isolation and ordering, described in

---

[4] On the other hand, the execution under a weakly atomic model that exposes uncommitted values to other threads could lead to violation of the speculation safety property described in Section 4.2.

Section 4.2. The analysis of required properties for P-SLE defined in the last column of Table 1 reveals that this set corresponds to a so-called SGLA (Single Global Lock Atomicity) transactional semantics [9,19]. SGLA is a middle-of-the-road semantics which is STM-implementation agnostic. SGLA provides a simple, more intuitive, semantics compared to weak atomicity, but does incur additional implementation-related constraints because it must provide stronger guarantees. By utilizing SGLA, our system is not tied to a particular underlying STM, as demonstrated in [19]. Atomic regions behave under SGLA as if they were protected by a single global lock, including treatment of entry and exit to every atomic region as a memory synchronization point for a unique lock with respect to visibility requirements defined by the JMM. This property allows us to trivially define a non-transactional implementation for atomic regions, *atomic serialization*, in which execution of atomic regions is serialized using a unique global mutual exclusion lock.

6 Implementation

Our implementation builds on an STM system using in-place updates, supporting optimistic readers and pessimistic writers, and providing strong atomicity guarantees [26]. Although our implementation leverages strong atomicity, any STM implementation that supports SGLA semantics is sufficient. We first briefly describe an implementation of the "base" transactional infrastructure, then discuss how multiple semantics can be supported within the same system, and finally describe modifications and extensions to the base transactional implementation needed to make it match properties required by P-SLE. Our implementation supports all of Java 1.4 including native method calls, class loading, reflection, dynamic thread creation, wait/notify, volatiles, etc. but does not currently support Java 1.5 extensions.

The base STM system extends the Java language into *Transactional Java* with an `atomic` primitive. Transactional Java is defined through a Polyglot [23] extension and implemented in pure Java. Our implementation utilizes the StarJIT compiler [2] to modify code of all critical sections so that they can be executed using either mutual exclusion locks or transactions. The run-time system, composed of the ORP JVM [7] and the transactional memory (TM) run-time library, provides transactional support and is tasked with handling interactions between transactions and Java monitors.

6.1 Base System

In the base STM system every access to a shared data item is "transactionalized" – mediated using a *transaction record*. In case of objects, a transaction record is embedded in the object header, and in case of static variables it is embedded in the header of an object representing the class that declares this static variable (access to all static variables of a given class is mediated through the same transaction record). The appropriate barriers implementing transactionalized accesses are automatically generated by the JIT compiler and protect accesses to data objects performed inside of transactions.

Data objects can be either exclusively write-locked or unlocked. In case a given data item is unlocked, its transaction record contains a version number. In case a given data item is write-locked, its transaction record contains a *transaction descriptor pointer* pointing to a data structure containing information about the lock owner (*transaction descriptor*). These two cases can be distinguished by checking a designated low-order *version bit*. When a transaction record contains a transaction descriptor pointer, this bit is always unset since pointers are aligned. In case a transaction record contains a version number, this bit is always set because of the way version numbers are generated. All writes performed by a transaction are recorded in a transaction-local *write set* which allows a terminating (committing or aborting) transaction to release its write locks by incrementing version numbers for locations it has updated. All reads performed by a transaction are recorded in the transaction-local *read-set* which is used at transaction commit to verify validity of all the reads performed by the committing transaction – writes are automatically valid since they are preceded by acquisition of exclusive write locks. If this validation procedure is successful, the transaction is allowed to commit, otherwise it is aborted and re-executed.

Because the base STM system supports strong atomicity, appropriate barriers are generated for non-transactional data accesses. Non-transactional reads are allowed to proceed only when a given data item is unlocked. Non-transactional writes, in order to avoid conflicts with transactional accesses, behave as *microtransactions*: they acquire a write lock, update the data item and release the write lock. Since the write is conceptually non-transactional, no explicit transaction owns the lock. Therefore, instead of a regular write lock, non-transactional writes acquire an *anonymous lock*. The anonymous lock is implemented by flipping a version bit to give the contents of the transaction record the appearance of a write lock [26].

We augment the base STM system to handle translation of both concurrency primitives (Section 6.2) and their interchangeability (Section 6.3). The STM was also extended with special types of barriers (Section 6.4) and a visibility violation detection scheme (Section 6.5). Our implementation spans all three parts of the STM system: ORP, StarJIT and the TM library.

6.2   Translating Concurrency Primitives

Both types of concurrency primitives (`synchronized` and `atomic`) are translated by the JIT compiler to use the same run-time API calls:

```
– criticalstart(Object m, ...)
– criticalend(Object m, ...)
```

Both API calls take an object as one of their parameters representing a Java monitor (i.e., a mutual exclusion lock) – either associated with the `synchronized` keyword or generated by the run-time system in case of `atomic`s. The run-time

```
                                     while (true) {
try {                                  try {
  monitorenter(m)                        criticalstart(m,..)
  ...                                      ...
  monitorexit(m)            ⟹            if (criticalend(m,...)) continue;
} catch (Throwable x) {                } catch (Throwable x) {
  monitorexit(m)                         if (criticalend(m,...)) continue;
  throw(x)                               throw(x)
}                                      }
                                       break;
                                     }
```

Fig. 10. Translation of synchronized blocks

system, thus, has the ability to choose a specific implementation for critical sections – either transactional (by instructing the TM library to start or commit a transaction) or lock-based (by acquiring or releasing a monitor passed as a parameter). The remaining parameters are used to pass additional transactional meta-data.

A typical JVM (including ORP) handles synchronized blocks and synchronized methods differently. In case of synchronized blocks, the source-to-bytecode compiler (e.g., javac) generates explicit calls to the JVM's implementation of the bytecode-level **monitorenter** and **monitorexit** primitives. The synchronized methods, on the other hand, are simply marked as such in the bytecode and the JVM is responsible for insertion of the appropriate synchronization operations during the generation of method prologues and epilogues. In order to be able to treat synchronized methods and synchronized blocks uniformly, we modify the JIT compiler to wrap the body of every synchronized method in a synchronized block (using either **this** object or the "class" object as a monitor) instead of invoking synchronization operations in the method's prologue and epilogue.

Our translation of synchronized blocks and methods in the JIT compiler mirrors the code structure of atomic blocks generated at the source level by the Polyglot compiler [3]. Figure 10 depicts this translation as a pseudo-code transformation (with **monitorenter** and **monitorexit** operations represented as method calls) – the left-hand side shows code generated for acquisition of monitor m to support Java's synchronized blocks and the right-hand side the code after transformation. The actual translation involves an additional pass in the JIT compiler which transforms the control-flow graph – the pseudo-code description of the transformation is out of necessity somewhat simplified. The intuition behind this transformation is that **monitorenter(Object m)** and **monitorexit(Object m)** operations are translated to **criticalstart(Object m, ...)** and **criticalend(Object m, ...)** method calls. The existing byte-code structure is leveraged to handle exceptions thrown inside of a transaction. Re-executions of aborted transactions are supported through an explicit loop inserted into the code stream – successful commit of a transaction is followed by a loop break.

During translation of original Java synchronization primitives, we also need to correctly disambiguate nesting. Our transactional API calls have one of two different versions selected depending on the execution context – outer (when no transaction is currently active) and inner (when executed in the context of an already active transaction). To discover the execution context, the JIT compiler performs a data flow analysis and builds a stack representation of monitor enter/exit calls for each node in the control flow graph. This allows us to identify the code fragments protected by transactions, and their nesting level. Additionally, every compiled method is marked as either transactional or non-transactional, depending on its calling context.

6.3   Coexistence of Transactions and Java Monitors

Ideally, Java monitors would be elided and all critical regions would be executed transactionally. Unfortunately, this is not possible for code that performs native method calls with side effects, triggers class loading and initialization, or contains critical regions that engage in inter-thread communication or spawn threads. In such cases, the fallback mechanism is utilized to use mutual exclusion rather than transactional execution.

The fallback operation is performed by aborting the currently running (outermost) transaction. The transaction is then restarted in *fallback mode* where concurrency is managed by acquiring and releasing Java monitors passed to transactional API calls as parameters. As a result, the implementation of the existing synchronization-related primitives, such as wait and notify operations, can be left largely untouched provided that they are only executed by *fallback transactions*.

Naturally, as a result of the fallback operation, some critical sections in the system are protected by Java monitors and others protected by transactions. In order to guarantee correct interaction between critical sections, every fallback transaction acquires transactional locks on all objects representing Java monitors it is using (to simulate transactional writes) and every regular transaction adds all its Java monitors to its read-set (simulating transactional reads). This prevents any regular transaction (translated from a Java monitor) from successfully completing if another thread is executing a critical section in fallback mode with the same monitor. The read-set of the regular transaction would become invalid, and the transaction itself would be aborted and re-executed. Notice that arbitrarily many regular transactions may execute concurrently, even if they share the same monitor.

6.4   Fallback Barriers

In the base STM system, the JIT compiler generates two versions of each method, transactional and non-transactional, containing appropriate versions of read and write barriers. The specific version of the method is then chosen at run-time depending on its invocation context. Read and write barriers occur on non

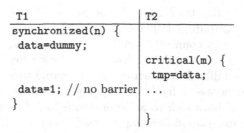

T1	T2
synchronized(n) { data=dummy;	
	critical(m) { tmp=data;
data=1; // no barrier	...
}	
	}

Fig. 11. Incorrectly eliminated barrier thread (T1 is in fallback mode, thread T2 is transactional)

transactional code since our implementation is strongly atomic. The JIT compiler eliminates unnecessary barriers where appropriate.

In our system, transactions in fallback mode behave differently than regular transactions - namely their execution must be faithful to Java monitor semantics. In order to reproduce Java monitor semantics, transactions in fallback mode have to ignore conflicts between each other while still properly interacting with regular transactions. Since concurrency control between a regular transaction and a transaction in fallback mode sharing the same monitor is mediated through this monitor, it does not need to be controlled at the level of data accesses. At the same time, according to the Java monitor semantics, no special concurrency control guarantees are provided between critical sections using different monitors. As a result, operations executed by a transaction in fallback mode should behave as if they were non-transactional, by blocking on reads of write-locked data items (to avoid speculation-related problems) and turning write operations into micro-transactions.

The read barriers for transactions executing in fallback mode can therefore be identical to non-transactional barriers. Unfortunately, turning write barriers into micro-transactions is surprisingly tricky. This is because code for fallback transactions has been compiled with regular transactional barriers. Optimizations may remove some barriers because they appear to be redundant. Consider the example shown in Figure 11 in which the second write of thread T1 executing a transaction in fallback mode should cause an abort of the regular transaction executed by thread T2. Unfortunately, the transactional barrier at the second write is dominated by the barrier at the first write (in a regular transaction the first write would acquire a lock) and would be eliminated.

One option is to have the JIT compiler generate yet another version of all methods executed by transactions in fallback mode. However, this would lead to increase in code size, complicate the method dispatch procedure, and increase compilation time. Additionally, we would lose all benefits of barrier elimination optimizations. Therefore, we adopt a dynamic solution and re-use barrier code sequences for both regular transactions and transactions executing in fallback mode. To do so, we introduce another version of the anonymous lock, the *fallback lock*. The fallback lock can be acquired only by a transaction executing in fallback mode and is held until this transaction is completed. If more than one fallback transaction wants to acquire a fallback lock for the same data item, the lock gets inflated - we need to count the number of writers and retain information about the version number. Regular transactions block when trying to access a data item locked by a fallback transaction. At the same time, non-transactional reads are allowed to access it freely, as are the non-transactional writes that additionally change fallback lock to an anonymous lock for the duration of the write operation [5]. A diagram illustrating transitions in a lock's state is given in Figure 12.

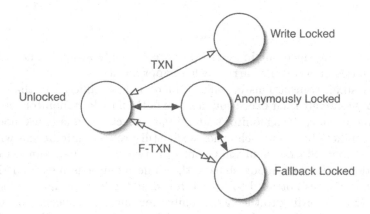

Fig. 12. Transitions made by non-transactional accesses are depicted by black arrows. White arrows represent transactional accesses – a single arrow by a bona fide transaction and a double arrow by a fallback transaction.

6.5   Detecting Dependent Visibility Violations

When dependent visibility violations occur, the observable effect is that execution becomes "stuck". We provide a mechanism to detect these situations rather than painstakingly tracking data and control dependencies between critical sections. Our specific solution differs slightly between cases of symmetric and asymmetric dependent visibility violations.

Symmetric Case. In case some transaction T is (permanently) unable to complete its execution because it expects to see results computed by a different transaction T' (such as in the example presented in Section 4.3 in Figure 9(a)), the control dependencies between data access operations that belong to these transactions must form a cycle. Otherwise, if transaction T' was independent of transaction T and allowed to complete successfully, its computation results would be eventually made available to T removing the reason for it being stuck.

---

[5] Fallback transaction must wait for anonymous lock to be released both when updating the value and when releasing the fallback locks.

This situation can be trivially generalized to the multi-transaction case. Obviously, we could employ full-fledged cycle detection to detect such situations, but because we assume these kinds of situation to be infrequent, we opt for a simpler solution and choose to utilize a time-out mechanism. If a transaction is unable to complete its data access operation after a pre-specified amount of time, it will be aborted and will re-execute in fallback mode. As a result of reverting to an implementation that is identical with Java monitors, the visibility violation cannot happen upon re-execution since Java monitor semantics prevents it automatically.

Asymmetric Case. This case is a little more subtle, because execution can get stuck in a non-transactional code region (as illustrated in Section 4.3 in Figure 9(b)). Therefore, the run-time system has no transactional context available that could be aborted and re-executed in a different mode. The solution we adopt to handle this case is for the non-transactional data access operation that failed to successfully complete its execution after a pre-specified amount of time, and to request the transaction blocking this data access to abort and re-start in fallback mode. It is guaranteed that this request will be ultimately delivered since by definition there must be a control dependency that prevents the transaction from completing. The identity of the transaction blocking the data access is readily available from the transaction record that must contain its transaction descriptor in order for the access to be forbidden. Note that non-transactional execution can only get stuck on accesses to volatile variables – otherwise no happens-before edge forcing the visibility restriction would exist. Thus, we are obligated to modify only those data accesses that concern volatile variables.

7   Performance Evaluation

Our implementation is based on an STM system that has already been shown to deliver good performance for explicitly transactional applications [26]. In this section, we consider the performance characteristics of legacy applications executed with transactions and mutual exclusion.

In order to better understand the performance implications of our system, we chose three different benchmarks representing three different locking schemes:

- OO7 [6]. This benchmark traverses and updates a shared tree-like data structure. Each each thread locks the entire shared data structure before performing a traversal (using a mixture of 80% lookups and 20% updates). This benchmark reflects a coding style that uses coarse-grain locks for concurrency control.
- SpecJBB2000 [29]. This server application involves multiple threads operating over different objects (e.g., warehouses). Because operations of different threads are protected by different locks, this benchmark reflects a coding style that uses fine-grain locks for concurrency control.
- TSP. This implementation of the traveling salesman involves threads that perform their searches independently, but share partially completed work

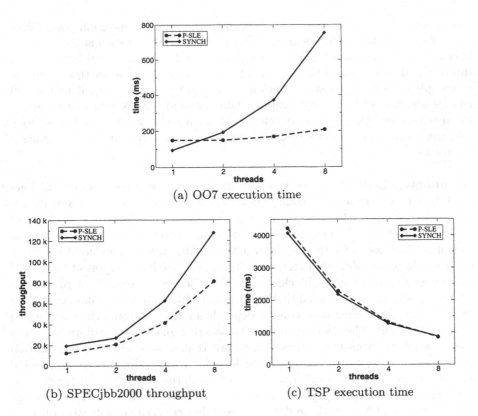

(a) OO7 execution time

(b) SPECjbb2000 throughput

(c) TSP execution time

Fig. 13. Preformance evaluation over multiple threads

and the best-answer-so-far via shared memory. It uses both fine- and coarse-grained concurrency control.

We ran all the benchmarks in two configurations: *P-SLE* which utilized our uniform transaction execution environment, transparently translating all synchronized blocks into atomic regions and dynamically falling back where necessary and *Synch* which used mutual exclusion provided by the original implementation of Java monitors. Synch represents the original benchmark without the additional overhead of transactional instrumentation and fallback. All our experiments have been performed on an Intel Clovertown system with two 2.66 GHz quad-core processors for a total of eight hardware threads and 3.25 GB of RAM running Microsoft Windows XP Professional with Service Pack 2.

The performance of our system has met our expectations. When running the lock-based version of OO7 benchmark transactionally under the P-SLE configuration, the system was able to automatically extract additional parallelism and significantly improve performance over executions using coarse-grain mutual exclusion locks (Figure 13(a)). Since our implementation is based on a strongly atomic implementation, there is a certain amount of overhead that is expected [26] when only small amount of additional parallelism is available compared to executions using mutual-exclusion locks. However, note that even though the absolute performance of SPECjbb2000 when executed transactionally does not quite match its performance when executed using mutual-exclusion locks, the scalability characteristics in both cases is virtually the same (Figure 13(b)). Finally, the performance of the TSP benchmark is almost identical, regardless of whether it is executed transactionally or using mutual-exclusion locks (Figure 13(c)).

Given that our system is based on a strongly atomic engine, our performance evaluation results reflect very similar trends to those reported in [26]. In our prior case study benchmarks were modified by hand to use explicit atomic blocks under a strong atomicity model. Using our uniform transactional execution environment we were able to avoid by hand translation and ensure safety while improving both scalability and performance.

8   Related Work

Recently there have been many proposals for Software Transactional Memory [5,11,13,14,17,18,20,22,24,26]. Such systems, unfortunately, provide limited or no support to compose transactions with locks. The Haskel STM [11] utilizes the type system to prevent any I/O actions within a transaction. Although we suspect such a restriction would allow for the *safe* composition of locks and atomic regions, it defacto limits the use of libraries that perform I/O in transactions. Other systems do not explicitly prevent composability of concurrency constructs, but they leave their interactions undefined. Interactions can vary based on the transactional implementation. Weakly atomic STMs, such as [13], suffer from subtle visibility and isolation anomalies [4], where as strongly atomic systems prevent the use wait/notify primitives. As such, program semantics vary based on the virtual machine's implementation of Java monitors as well as the guarantees provided by the STM itself. Programs must be hand-tuned for each system and virtual machine pairing.

Previous work which attempts to combine Java monitors and transactions [30,31] place restrictions on programmers. Notably, programs must be race-free, even if races are benign. Such restrictions prevent the use of programming paradigms such as privatization. In such systems, programmers are forced to examine all interactions between transactions and locks to guarantee safety.

Other approaches [27] attempt to mirror lock based semantics by providing programmers with additional primitives to break transactional properties. Potential interactions between threads are tracked through the type system and reported to the programmer. The programmer is required to establish consistency at specific points within the transaction. Unfortunately, the programmer must reason about the *transitive* effects of a given transactional region. Transactional regions maybe called from many different contexts and it is unclear if a break of isolation in one context is compatible with another.

9   Conclusions

We have presented the design and implementation of the first uniform transactional execution environment for Java programs. We have explored implications of executing *arbitrary* lock-based Java programs transactionally. We have also presented techniques that allow explicit transactional constructs, such as atomic blocks, to be seamlessly integrated into an existing programming language. We have presented performance evaluation of our system that demonstrates its ability to extract additional parallelism from lock-based applications by executing them transactionally, providing better performance when coarse-grain locks are used and providing performance approaching those of mutual-exclusion locks in case of fine-grain locking.

References

1. Abadi, M., Birrell, A., Harris, T., Isard, M.: Semantics of transactional memory and automatic mutual exclusion. In: POPL 2008 (2008)
2. Adl-Tabatabai, A.-R., Bharadwaj, J., Chen, D.-Y., Ghuloum, A., Menon, V.S., Murphy, B.R., Serrano, M., Shpeisman, T.: The StarJIT compiler: a dynamic compiler for managed runtime environments. Intel Technology Journal 7(1) (2003)
3. Adl-Tabatabai, A.-R., Lewis, B.T., Menon, V.S., Murphy, B.R., Saha, B., Shpeisman, T.: Compiler and runtime support for efficient software transactional memory. In: PLDI 2006, Ottawa, Canada (2006)
4. Blundell, C., Lewis, E.C., Martin, M.: Subtleties of transactional memory atomicity semantics. Computer Architecture Letters, 5(2) (November 2006)
5. Blundell, C., Lewis, E.C., Martin, M.: Unrestricted transactional memory: Supporting i/o and system calls within transactions. Technical Report CIS-06-09, University of Pennsylvania, Department of Comp. and Info. Science (2006)
6. Carey, M.J., DeWitt, D.J., Kant, C., Naughton, J.F.: A status report on the OO7 OODBMS benchmarking effort. In: OOPSLA (1994)
7. Cierniak, M., Eng, M., Glew, N., Lewis, B., Stichnoth, J.: Open Runtime Platform: A Flexible High-Performance Managed Runtime Environment. Intel. Technology Journal 7(1) (2003)
8. Gosling, J., Joy, B., Steele Jr., G., Bracha, G.: The Java Language Specification, 2nd edn. Addison-Wesley, Reading (2000)
9. Grossman, D., Manson, J., Pugh, W.: What do high-level memory models mean for transactions? In: MSPC 2006 (2006)
10. Harris, T., Fraser, K.: Language support for lightweight transactions. In: OOPSLA 2003 (2003)
11. Harris, T., Marlow, S., Jones, S.P., Herlihy, M.: Composable memory transactions. In: PPoPP 2005 (2005)
12. Harris, T., Plesko, M., Shinnar, A., Tarditi, D.: Optimizing memory transactions. In: PLDI 2006 (2006)
13. Herlihy, M., Luchangco, V., Moir, M., William, I., Scherer, N.: Software transactional memory for dynamic-sized data structures. In: PODC 2003 (2003)
14. Herlihy, M., Luchangco, V., Moir, M.: A flexible framework for implementing software transactional memory. In: OOPSLA 2006 (2006)
15. Lindholm, T., Yellin, F.: The Java Virtual Machine Specification. Addison-Wesley, Reading (1999)

16. Manson, J., Pugh, W., Adve, S.V.: The Java memory model. In: POPL 2005 (2005)
17. Marathe, V.J., Scherer, W.N., Scott, M.L.: Adaptive software transactional memory. In: ISDC 2005 (2005)
18. Marathe, V.J., Scherer, W.N., Scott, M.L.: Design tradeoffs in modern software transactional memory systems. In: LCR 2004 (2004)
19. Menon, V., Balensiefer, S., Shpeisman, T., Adl-Tabatabai, A.-R., Hudson, R.L., Saha, B., Welc, A.: Single global lock semantics in a weakly atomic stm. In: TRANSACT 2008 (2008)
20. Moir, M.: Hybrid hardware/software transactional memory (2005), http://www.cs.wisc.edu/ rajwar/tm-workshop/TALKS/moir.pdf
21. Moss, J.E.B., Hosking, A.L.: Nested transactional memory: model and preliminary architecture sketches. In: SCOOL 2005 (2005)
22. Ni, Y., Menon, V., Adl-Tabatabai, A.-R., Hosking, A.L., Hudson, R.L., Moss, J.E.B., Saha, B., Shpeisman, T.: Open Nesting in Software Transactional Memory. In: PPoPP 2007 (2007)
23. Nystrom, N., Clarkson, M.R., Myers, A.C.: Polyglot: an extensible compiler framework for Java. In: Bodik, R. (ed.) CC 2005. LNCS, vol. 3443. Springer, Heidelberg (2005)
24. Ringenburg, M.F., Grossman, D.: AtomCaml: first-class atomicity via rollback. In: ICFP 2005 (2005)
25. Saha, B., Adl-Tabatabai, A.-R., Hudson, R., Minh, C.C., Hertzberg, B.: McRT-STM: A high performance software transactional memory system for a multi-core runtime. In: PPoPP 2006 (2006)
26. Shpeisman, T., Menon, V., Adl-Tabatabai, A.-R., Balensiefer, S., Grossman, D., Hudson, R.L., Moore, K.F., Bratin, S.: Enforcing isolation and ordering in stm. In: PLDI 2007 (2007)
27. Smaragdakis, Y., Kay, A., Behrends, R., Young, M.: Transactions with Isolation and Cooperation. In: OOPSLA 2007 (2007)
28. Spear, M.F., Marathe, V.J., Dalessandro, L., Scott, M.L.: Privatization techniques for software transactional memory. Technical Report 915, University of Rochester, Computer Science Dept (2007)
29. Standard Performance Evaluation Corporation. SPEC JBB 2000 (2000), http://www.spec.org/jbb2000
30. Welc, A., Hosking, A.L., Jagannathan, S.: Transparently reconciling transactions with locking for Java synchronization. In: Thomas, D. (ed.) ECOOP 2006. LNCS, vol. 4067. Springer, Heidelberg (2006)
31. Welc, A., Jagannathan, S., Hosking, A.L.: Transactional monitors for concurrent objects. In: Odersky, M. (ed.) ECOOP 2004. LNCS, vol. 3086. Springer, Heidelberg (2004)

Ptolemy: A Language with Quantified, Typed Events*

Hridesh Rajan and Gary T. Leavens

[1] Iowa State University
hridesh@cs.iastate.edu
[2] University of Central Florida
leavens@eecs.ucf.edu

Abstract. Implicit invocation (II) and aspect-oriented (AO) languages provide related but distinct mechanisms for separation of concerns. II languages have explicitly announced events that run registered observer methods. AO languages have implicitly announced events that run method-like but more powerful advice. A limitation of II languages is their inability to refer to a large set of events succinctly. They also lack the expressive power of AO advice. Limitations of AO languages include potentially fragile dependence on syntactic structure that may hurt maintainability, and limits on the available set of implicit events and the reflective contextual information available. Quantified, typed events, as implemented in our language Ptolemy, solve all these problems. This paper describes Ptolemy and explores its advantages relative to both II and AO languages.

1 Introduction

> *For temperance and courage are destroyed both by excess and defect,*
> *but preserved by moderation. – Aristotle, Nicomachean Ethics*

The objective of both implicit invocation (II) [1,2,3,4,5,6] and aspect-oriented (AO) [7] languages is to improve a software engineer's ability to separate conceptual *concerns*. The problem that they address is that not all concerns are amenable to modularization by a single dimension of decomposition [8]; instead, some concerns cut across the main dimension of decomposition. For example, code implementing a visualization concern would be scattered across the classes of an object-oriented (OO) decomposition. The II and AO approaches aim to better encapsulate such crosscutting concerns and decouple them from other code, thereby easing maintenance.

However, both II and AO languages suffer from various limitations. The goal of this paper is to explain how our language Ptolemy, which combines the best ideas of both kinds of language, can solve many of these problems.

1.1 Implicit Invocation Languages and Their Limitations

The key idea in II languages is that *events* are used as a way to interface two sets of modules, so that one set can remain independent of the other. Events promote decou-

---

* Rajan was supported in part by the NSF grant CNS-0627354. Leavens was supported in part by NSF grant CCF-0429567. Both were supported in part by NSF grant CNS 08-08913.

J. Vitek (Ed.): ECOOP 2008, LNCS 5142, pp. 155–179, 2008.

```
 1 abstract class FElement extends Object{
 2   event ChangeEvent(FElement changedFE);
 3   event MoveUpEvent(FElement targetFE,
 4       Number y, Number delta);
 5 }
 6 class Point extends FElement { /* ... */
 7   Number x; Number y;
 8   FElement setX(Number x) {
 9     this.x = x;
10     announce ChangeEvent(this);
11     this
12   }
13   FElement moveUp(Number delta) {
14     announce MoveUpEvent(this,this.y,delta);
15     this.y = this.y.plus(delta); this
16   }
17   FElement makeEqual(Point other) {
18     other.x = this.x; other.y = this.y;
19     announce ChangeEvent(other); other
20   }
21 }
```

```
22 class Update extends Object { /* ... */
23   FElement last;
24   Update registerWith(FElement fe) {
25     fe.register(this, FElement.ChangeEvent);
26     fe.register(this, FElement.MoveUpEvent);
27     this
28   }
29   FElement update(FElement changedFE, Number x){
30     this.last = changedFE;
31     Display.update();
32     changedFE
33   }
34   FElement check(FElement targetFE,
35       Number y, Number delta) {
36     if (delta.lt(100)) { targetFE }
37     else{throw new IllegalArgumentException()}
38   }
39   when FElement.ChangeEvent do update
40   when FElement.MoveUpEvent do check
41 }
```

Fig. 1. Drawing Editor in an II language

pling and can be seen as direct linguistic support for the Observer pattern [9]. The mechanisms of an II language are also known as "event subscription management." [3]

With declared events, certain modules (subjects) dynamically and explicitly *announce* events. Another set of modules (observers) can dynamically *register* methods, called *handlers*. These handlers are invoked (implicitly) when events are announced. The subjects are thus independent of the particular observers.

Figure 1 illustrates the mechanisms of a hypothetical Java-like II language based on Classic Java (and thus similar to Ptolemy) for a figure editor that we will use as a running example in this paper. This code is part of a larger editor that works on drawings comprising points, lines, and other such figure elements [10,11]. The code announces two kinds of events, named ChangeEvent and MoveUpEvent (lines 2–4). The subclass Point announces these events using **announce** expressions (lines 10, 14, and 19). When an instance of the class Update is properly "registered", by calling the registerWith method on an instance of the Point class, these announcements will implicitly invoke the methods of class Update (lines 22–41). The connection between the events and methods of class Update is made on lines 39–40, where it is specified that the update method is to be called when the ChangeEvent occurs and the check method when MoveUpEvent occurs. Dynamic registration (lines 25–26) allows the receiver of these method calls to be determined (and allows unregistration and multiple registration).

The main advantage of an II language over OO languages is that it provides considerable automation of the Observer pattern [3], which is key to decoupling subject modules from observer modules. That is, modules that announce events remain independent of the modules that register methods to handle their event announcements. Compared to AO languages, as we will see, II languages also have some advantages. First, event announcement is explicit, which helps in understanding the module announcing the event, since the points where events may occur are obvious from the code. Second, event announcement is flexible; i.e., arbitrary points in the program can be exposed as events.

However, compared with AO languages, II languages also have three limitations: coupling of observers to subjects, no ability to replace event code, and lack of quantification. We describe these below.

Coupling of Observers to Subjects. While subjects need not know about observers in an II language, the observer modules still know about the subjects. In Figure 1, for example, the registration code on lines 25–26 and the binding code on lines 39–40 mentions the events declared in FElement. (Mediators, a design style for II languages, also decouple subjects and observers so that they can be changed independently [6]. However, mediator modules remain coupled to both the subject and observers.)

No Replacement of Event Code. The ability to replace the code for an event (what AO calls "around advice"), is not available, without unnecessarily complex emulation code (to simulate closures in languages such as Java and C#). Instead, to stop an action, one must have a handler throw an exception (as on line 37), which does not clearly express the idea. Similarly, throwing an exception does not support replacing actions with different actions, such as replacing a local method call with a remote method invocation.

No Quantification. In II languages describing how each event is handled, which following the AO terminology we call *quantification*, can be tedious. Indeed, such code can grow in proportion to the number of objects from which implicit invocations are to be received. For example, to register an Update instance u to receive implicit invocations when events are announced by both a point p and a line 1, one would write the following code: u.registerWith(p); u.registerWith(l). One can see that such registration code has to find all figure element instances. In this case these problems are not too bad, since all such instances have types that are subtypes of FElement, where the relevant events are declared. However, if the events were announced in unrelated classes, then the registration code (lines 25–26) and the code that maps events to method calls (lines 39–40) would be longer and more tedious to write.

1.2 Aspect-Oriented Languages and Their Limitations

In AO languages [12,13] such as AspectJ [7,10,14,15] events (called "join points") are pre-defined by the language as certain kinds of standard actions (such as method calls) in a program's execution. (We emphasize AspectJ for the maturity of its design and the availability of a workable implementation.) AO events are all implicitly announced. *Pointcut descriptions (PCDs)* are used to declaratively register handlers (called "advice") with sets of events. Using PCDs to register a handler with an entire set of events, called *quantification* [16], is a key idea in AO languages that has no counterpart in II languages. A language's set of PCDs and events form its *event model* (in AO terms this is a "join point model").

The listings in Figure 2 shows an AspectJ-like implementation for the drawing editor discussed before. (We have adapted the syntax of AspectJ to be more like our language Ptolemy, to make comparisons easier.) In this implementation the Point class is free of any event-related code (as are other figure elements such as Line).

Modularization of display update is done with an aspect. This aspect uses PCDs such as **target**(fe) && **call**(FElement+.set*(..)) to select events that change the state of figure elements. This PCD selects events that call a method matching set* on a subtype of FElement and binds the context variable fe (of type FElement) to that call's receiver.

```
1  abstract class FElement extends Object {}       15  aspect Update {
2  class Point implements FElement { /*...*/        16  FElement around(FElement fe) :
3  Number x; Number y;                              17  call(FElement+.set*(..)) && target(fe)
4  FElement setX(Number x) {                        18  || call(FElement+.makeEq*(..)) && args(fe){
5    this.x = x; this                               19  FElement res = proceed(fe);
6  }                                                20  Display.update(); res
7  FElement moveUp(Number delta) {                  21  }
8    this.y = this.y.plus(delta); this              22  FElement around(FElement fe, Number delta):
9  }                                                23    target(fe)&&(call(FElement+.move*(..))
10 FElement makeEqual(Point other) {                24    && args(delta){
11   other.x = this.x;                              25  if (delta.lt(100) { proceed(delta) }
12   other.y = this.y; other                        26  else { fe }
13 }                                                27  }
14 }                                                28 }
```

Fig. 2. Drawing editor's AO implementation

AO languages also have several advantages. Quantification provides ease of use. For example, one can select events throughout a program (and bind them to handlers) by just writing a simple regular expression based PCD, as on lines 17–18. Moreover, by not referring to the names in the modules announcing events directly, the handler code remains, at least syntactically, independent of that code. Implicit event announcement both automates and further decouples the two sets of modules, compared with II languages. This property, sometimes called *obliviousness* [16], avoids the "scattering" and "tangling" [7] of event announcement code within the other code for the subjects, which can be seen in lines 10, 14, and 19 of Figure 1. In that figure, this explicit announcement code is mixed in with other code, resulting in tangled code that makes it harder to follow the main program flow.

However, AO languages suffer from four limitations, primarily because most current event models use PCDs based on pattern matching. These languages differ by what they match. For example, AspectJ-like languages use pattern matching on names [10], LogicAJ and derivative languages use pattern matching on program structures [17,18], and, history-based pointcuts use pattern matching on program traces [19]. An example PCD in languages that match names is **call**(FElement+.set*(..)) that describes a set of call events in which the name of the called method starts with "set". An example PCD in languages that match program structures is stmt(?**if**,**if**(?**call**){??someStatements}&&fooBarCalls(?**call**) that describes a set of call events in which the name of the called method is "foo" or "bar" and the call occurs within an **if** condition [17, Fig 4.]. An example PCD in languages that match program traces would be $G(call(*Line.set(..)) \rightarrow F(call(*Point.set(..))))$ that describes every call event in which the name of the called method is "Line.set" and that is finally followed by another call event in which the name of the called method is "Point.set" [20, Fig 3.].

Fragile Pointcuts. The fragility of pointcuts results from the use of pattern matching as a quantification mechanism [21,22]. Such PCDs are coupled to the code that implements the implicit events they describe. Thus, seemingly innocuous changes break aspects. For example, for languages that match based on names, a change such as adding new methods that match the PCD, such as settled, can break an aspect that is counting on methods that start with "set" to mean that the object is changing. As pointed out by Kellens *et al.* [23], in languages that match based on program structures a simple change such as changing an **if** statement to an equivalent statement that used a conditional (?:) expression would break the aspect. For languages that match based on program traces a simple change such as to inline the functionality of "Point.set" would break the aspect that is counting on "Line.set" to be eventually followed by "Point.set" [23]. Conversely, when adding a method such as makeEqual that does not conform to the naming convention, one has to change the PCD to add the new method pattern (as shown in line 18 of Figure 2). In the same vein, when adding a new call such as foo() within a **while** statement that does not conform to the existing program structure, one has to change the PCD to accomodate the new program structure. Similar arguments apply for trace-based pointcuts. Indeed, to fix such problems PCDs must often be changed (e.g., to exclude or include added methods). Such maintenance problems can be important in real examples.

Several recent ideas such as Aspect Aware Interfaces (AAIs) [11], Crosscut Programming Interfaces (XPIs) [24,25], Model-based Pointcuts [23], Open Modules (OM) [26], etc, have recognized and proposed to address this fragile pointcut problem. Briefly, AAIs, computed using the global system configuration, allow a developer to see the events in the base code quantified by a PCD, but do not help with reducing the impact of base code changes on PCDs, which primarily causes the fragile pointcut problem. XPIs reduce the scope of fragile pointcut problem to the scope declared as part of the interface, however, within a scope the problem remains. OMs allow a class to explicitly expose the set of events, however, for quantifying such events explicit enumeration is needed, which couples the PCD with names in the base code. Such enumerations are also potentially fragile as pointed out by Kellens *et al.* [23]. A detailed discussion of these ideas is presented in Section 4.

Quantification Failure. The problem of quantification failure is caused by incompleteness in the language's event model. It occurs when the event model does not implicitly announce some kinds of events and hence does not provide PCDs that select such events [24, pp. 170]. In AspectJ-like AO languages there is a fixed classification of potential event kinds and a corresponding fixed set of PCDs. For example, some language features, such as loops or certain expressions, are not announced as events in AspectJ and have no corresponding PCDs.[1] While there are reasons (e.g., increased coupling) for not making some kinds of potential events available, some practical use cases need to handle

---

[1] Some may view that as a problem of the underlying language rather than the approach to aspects: e.g., in a language where all computation takes place in methods, this, target and args are always defined. We argue that it may not be necessary to continue to support such differentiation between means of computation, instead a unified view of all such means of computation can be provided to the aspects.

them [27,28]. This fixed set of event kinds and PCDs contributes to quantification failure, because some events cannot be announced or used in PCDs.

There are approaches such as LogicAJ that provide a finer-grained event model [17]. For example, in LogicAJ one could match arbitrary program structure in the base code, which is significantly more expressive compared to matching based on names. However, as discussed above, a problem with such technique is that the PCDs becomes strongly coupled with the structure of the base code and therefore become more fragile.

An alternative approach to solving this problem is taken by the technique used in SetPoint [29]. This technique allows a programmer to select events by attaching annotations to locations of such events. This technique is not fragile in the sense that it does not depend on names, program structure, or order of events. A problem, however, is that this technique does not allow arbitrary expressions to be selected, primarily because the underlying languages do not allow annotations on arbitrary expressions.

Limited Access to Context Information. Current AO languages provide a limited interface for accessing contextual (or reflective) information about an event [24]. For example, in AspectJ, a handler (advice) can access only fixed kinds of contextual information from the event, such as the current receiver object (**this**), a call's target, its arguments, etc. Again there are good reasons for limiting this interface (e.g., avoiding coupling), but the fundamental problem is that, in current languages, this interface is fixed by the language designer and does not satisfy all usage scenarios. For example, when modularizing logging, developers need access to the context of the logging events, including local variables. However, local variables are not available in existing AO event models.

Approaches such as LogicAJ [17] allow virtually unlimited reflective access to the program context surrounding code using meta-variables, which is more expressive than AspectJ's model; e.g., a local variable can be accessed by associating it with a meta-variable. However, as we discuss in detail below, this unlimited access is achieved with ease only in cases where the events form a regular structure.

Uniform Access to Irregular Context Information. A related problem occurs when contextual information that fulfills a common need (or role) in the handlers is not available uniformly to PCDs (and handlers). For example, in Figure 2 setX and makeEqual contribute to the event "changing a figure element," however, they are changing different figure element instances: **this** and other in the case of setX and makeEqual respectively. In this simple case, it is possible to work around this issue by writing a PCD that combines (using | |, as in lines 17–18 of Figure 2) two separate PCDs, as shown in Figure 2. Each of these PCDs accesses the changed instance differently (one using **target**, the other using **args**). However, each such PCD depends on the particular code features that it needs to access the required information.

This problem is present in even significantly more expressive approaches based on pattern matching such as LogicAJ [17]. For irregular context information, the best solution in these techniques also need to resort to explicit enumeration of base code structure to identify meta-information that need to be accessed. Note that such enumeration increases the coupling between the PCDs and the details of the base code.

1.3 Contributions

In this work, we present a new language, Ptolemy, which adds quantified, typed events to II languages, producing a language that has many of the advantages of both II and AO languages, but suffers from none of the limitations described above.

Ptolemy declares named event types independently from the modules that announce or handle these events. These event types provide an interface that completely decouples subject and observer modules. An event type p also declares the types of information communicated between announcements of events of type p and handler methods. Events are explicitly announced using **event** expressions. Event expressions enclose a body expression, which can be replaced by a handler, providing expressiveness akin to **around** advice in AO languages. Event type names can also be used in quantification, which simplifies binding and avoids coupling observers with subjects.

Key differences between Ptolemy and II languages are thus:

- separating event type declarations from the modules that announce events,
- the ability to treat an expression's execution as an event,
- the ability to override that execution, and
- quantification by the use of PCDs.

Key differences between Ptolemy and AO languages are:

- events are explicitly announced, but quantification over them does not require enumeration unlike techniques such as Open Modules [26],
- an arbitrary expression can be identified as an event (unlike Setpoint [29]) without exacerbating the fragile pointcut problem (unlike languages like LogicAJ [17]),
- events can communicate an arbitrary set of reflective information to handlers without coupling handlers to program details (cf. [23]), and
- PCDs can use declared event types for quantification.

The benefit of Ptolemy's new features over II languages is that the separation of event type declarations allows further decoupling, and that the ability to replace events completely is more powerful. The benefit over AO languages is that handler methods (advice) can uniformly access reflective information from the context of events without breaking encapsulation of the code that announces events. Furthermore, event types also permit further decoupling over AO languages, since PCDs are decoupled from the code announcing events (the "base code").

These benefits make Ptolemy an interesting point in the design space between II and AO languages. Since event announcement is explicit, announcing modules are not completely "oblivious" to the presence of handlers, and hence by some definitions [16] Ptolemy is not aspect-oriented. However, this lack of obliviousness is not fatal for investigating its utility as a language design, and indeed highlights the advantages and disadvantages of obliviousness, as we will explain Sections 3.3 and 4.

In summary, this work makes the following contributions. It presents:

- a language design with simple and flexible event model;
- a precise operational semantics and type system for the language's novel constructs;
- an implementation of the language as an extension of Eclipse's Java compiler; and,
- a detailed analysis of our approach and the closely related ideas.

2 Ptolemy's Design

> *Ptolemy (Claudius Ptolemaeus), fl. 2d cent. A.D.,*
> *celebrated Greco-Egyptian mathematician, astronomer, and geographer.*

In this section, we describe Ptolemy's design. Its use of quantified, typed events extends II languages with ideas from AO languages. Ptolemy features new mechanisms for declaring event types and events. It is inspired by II languages such as Rapide [3] and AO languages such as AspectJ [10]. It also incorporates some ideas from Eos [30] and Caesar [31]. As a small, core language, its technical presentation shares much in common with MiniMAO$_1$ [32,33]. The object-oriented part of Ptolemy has classes, objects, inheritance, and subtyping, but it does not have **super**, interfaces, exception handling, built-in value types, privacy modifiers, or abstract methods. The novel features of Ptolemy are found in its event model and type system.

Like Eos [30], Ptolemy does not have special syntax for "aspects" or "advice". Instead it has the capability to replace all events in a specified set (a pointcut) with a call to a handler method. Each handler takes an event closure as its first argument. An *event closure* [30] contains code needed to run the applicable handlers and the original event's code. An event closure is run by an **invoke** expression.

Like II languages a class in Ptolemy can register handlers for events. However, unlike II languages, where one has to write an expression for registering a handler with each event in a set, Ptolemy allows a handler to be declaratively registered for a set of events using one succinct PCD in a *binding* (which is similar to declaring AO "around advice"). At runtime, one can use Ptolemy's **register** expression to activate such relationships. The **register** expression supplies an *observer instance* (an object) that becomes the receiver in calls to its handler methods that are made when the corresponding events are announced.[2] It is thus easy to make individual observer instances that handle event announcements ("instance-level advising") [34]. Singleton "aspects" could be easily added as syntactic sugars.

2.1 Syntax

Ptolemy's syntax is shown in Figure 3 and explained below. A program in Ptolemy consists of a sequence of declarations followed by an expression. The expression can be thought of as the body of a "main" method. In Figure 4 we illustrate the syntax using the example from Section 1.

Declarations. The two top-level declaration forms, classes and event type declarations, may not be nested. A class has exactly one superclass, and may declare several fields, methods, and bindings. Bindings associate a handler method to a set of events described by a pointcut description (PCD). The binding in Figure 4, line 47 says to run `update` when events of type `FEChange` are announced. Similarly, the binding on line 48 says to run `check` when events of type `MoveUpEvent` are announced.

---

[2] In AO languages such as Eos [34] and Caesar [31] register expressions correspond to "deploying aspects."

prog ::= *decl** *e*
decl ::= *c* **evtype** *p* { *form** }
     | **class** *c* **extends** *d* { *field** *meth** *binding** }
field ::= *c f* ;
meth ::= *t m* (*form**) { *e* }
t ::= *c* | **thunk** *c*
binding ::= **when** *pcd* **do** *m*
form ::= *t var*,   **where** *var*≠**this**
pcd ::= *p* | *pcd* '|' *pcd*
e ::= **new** *c* () | *var* | **null** | *e.m* (*e**) | *e.f*
     | *e.f* = *e* | **cast** *c e* | *form* = *e*; *e* | *e*; *e*
     | **register** (*e*) | **event** *p* { *e* } | **invoke** (*e*)

where
  c, d ∈ *C*, a set of class names
  p ∈ *P*, a set of evtype names
  f ∈ *F*, a set of field names
  m ∈ *M*, a set of method names
  var ∈ {**this**} ∪ *V*, *V* is
    a set of variable names

Fig. 3. Ptolemy's abstract syntax, based on Clifton's dissertation [32, Figures 3.1, 3.7]

```
1 FElement evtype FEChange{
2   FElement changedFE;
3 }
4 FElement evtype MoveUpEvent{
5   FElement targetFE; Number y; Number delta;
6 }
7 class FElement extends Object{}
8 class Point extends FElement{ /* ... */
9   Number x; Number y;
10  FElement setX(Number x) {
11    FElement changedFE = this;
12    event FEChange{ this.x = x; this }
13  }
14  FElement moveUp(Number delta){
15    FElement movedFE = this;
16    event MoveUpEvent{
17      this.y = this.y.plus(delta); this
18    }
19  }
20  FElement makeEqual(Point other){
21    FElement changedFE = other;
22    event FEChange{
23      other.x = this.x;
24      other.y = this.y; other
25    }
26  }
27 }

28 class Update extends Object{
29   FElement last;
30   Update init(){
31     register(this)
32   }
33   FElement update(thunk FElement next,
34       FElement changedFE){
35     FElement res = invoke(next);
36     this.last = changedFE;
37     Display.update(); res
38   }
39   FElement check(thunk FElement next,
40       FElement targetFE,
41       Number y, Number delta){
42     if (delta.lt(100)){
43       FElement res = invoke(next)
44     };
45     targetFE
46   }
47   when FEChange do update
48   when MoveUpEvent do check
49 }
```

Fig. 4. Drawing Editor in Ptolemy

An event type (**evtype**) declaration has a return type (*c*), a name (*p*), and zero or more context variable declarations (*form**). These context declarations specify the types and names of reflective information exposed by conforming events. Two examples are given in Figure 4 on lines 1–6. The intention of the first event type declaration (lines 1–3) is to provide a named abstraction for a set of events, with result type FElement, that contribute to an abstract state change in a figure element, such as moving a point. This event type declares only one context variable, changedFE, which denotes the FElement instance that is being changed. Similarly, the event type MoveUpEvent (lines 4–6) declares three context variables, targetFE, which denotes the FElement instance that is moving up, y, the current Cartesian co-ordinate value for that instance, and delta, the displacement of the instance.

Quantification: Pointcut Descriptions. PCDs have two forms. The named PCD denotes the set of events identified by the programmer using event expressions with the given name. Two examples appear on lines 47–48 of Figure 4. The first, FEChange, denotes events identified with the type FEChange. The context exposed by this PCD is the subset of the lexical context named by that event type and available at event expressions that mention that type.

The disjunction (| |) of two PCDs gives the union of the sets of events denoted by the two PCDs. The context exposed by the disjunction is the intersection of the context exposed by the two PCDs. However, if an identifier I is bound in both contexts, then I's value in the exposed context is I's value from the right hand PCD's context.

Expressions. Ptolemy is an expression language, thus the syntax for expressions includes several standard object-oriented (OO) expressions [32,33,35].

There are three new expressions: **register**, **invoke**, and **event**. The expression **register**(e) evaluates e to an object o, registers o by putting it into the program's list of active objects, and returns o. The list of active objects is used in the semantics to track registered objects. Only objects in this list are capable of advising events. For example lines 30–32 of Figure 4 is a method that, when called, will register the method's receiver (**this**). The expression **invoke**(e) evaluates e, which must denote an event closure, and runs that event closure. This runs the handlers in the event closure or, if there are no handlers, the event closure's original expression.

The expression **event** p {e} announces e as an event of type p and runs any handlers of registered objects that are applicable to p, using a registered object as the receiver and passing as the first argument an event closure. This event closure contains the rest of the handlers, the original expression e, and its lexical environment. In Figure 4 the event expression on line 10 has a body consisting of a sequence expression. Notice that the body of the setX method contains a block expression, where the definition on line 11 binds **this** to changedFE, and then evaluates its body, the event expression. This definition makes the value of **this** available in the variable changedFE, which is needed by the context declared for the event type FEChange. In this figure, the event declared on line 22–25 also encloses a sequence expression. As required by the event type, the definition on line 21 of Figure 4 makes the value of other available in the variable changedFE. Thus the first and the second event expressions are given different bindings for the variable changedFE, however, code that advises this event type will be able to access this context uniformly using the name changedFE.

The II syntax "**announce** p" can be thought of as sugar for "**event** p {**null**}." Thus Ptolemy's event announcement is strictly more powerful than that in II languages.

2.2 Operational Semantics of Ptolemy

This section defines a small step operational semantics for Ptolemy. The semantics is based on Clifton's work [32,33,36], which builds on Classic Java [37].

The expression semantics relies on four expressions that are not part of Ptolemy's surface syntax as shown in Figure 5. The *loc* expression represents locations in the store. The **under** expression is used as a way to mark when the evaluation stack needs popping. The two exceptions record various problems orthogonal to the type system.

Figure 5 also describes the configurations, and the evaluation contexts in the operational semantics, most of which is standard and self-explanatory. A configuration con-

Added Syntax:

$e ::= loc \mid \textbf{under } e \mid \texttt{NullPointerException} \mid \texttt{ClassCastException}$
    where $loc \in \mathcal{L}$, a set of locations

Domains:

$\Gamma ::= \langle e, J, S, A \rangle$	"Configurations"
$J ::= \nu + J \mid \bullet$	"Stacks"
$\nu ::= \textbf{lexframe } \rho \, \Pi \mid \textbf{evframe } p \, \rho \, \Pi$	"Frames"
$\rho ::= \{j : v_k\}_{k \in K}, \quad$ where K is finite, $K \subseteq I$	"Environments"
$v ::= loc \mid \texttt{null}$	"Values"
$S ::= \{loc_k \mapsto sv_k\}_{k \in K}, \quad$ where K is finite	"Stores"
$sv ::= o \mid pc$	"Storable Values"
$o ::= [c . F]$	"Object Records"
$F ::= \{f_k \mapsto v_k\}_{k \in K}, \quad$ where K is finite	"Field Maps"
$pc ::= \textbf{eClosure}(H, \theta)(e, \rho, \Pi)$	"Event Closures"
$H ::= h + H \mid \bullet$	"Handler Record Lists"
$h ::= \langle loc, m, \rho' \rangle$	"Handler Records"
$A ::= loc + A \mid \bullet$	"Active (Registered) List"

Evaluation contexts:

$$E ::= - \mid E.m(e \ldots) \mid v.m(v \ldots E e \ldots) \mid \textbf{cast } t \, E \mid E.f \mid E ; e \mid E.f=e$$
$$\mid v.f=E \mid t \, var=E; \, e \mid E; \, e \mid \textbf{register}(E) \mid \textbf{under } E \mid \textbf{invoke}(E)$$

Fig. 5. Added syntax, domains, and evaluation contexts used in the semantics, based on [32]

tains an expression (e), a stack (J), a store (S), and an ordered list of active objects (A). Stacks are an ordered list of frames, each frame recording the static environment (ρ) and some other information. (The type environments Π are only used in the type soundness proof [35].) There are two types of stack frame. Lexical frames (**lexframe**) record an environment ρ that maps identifiers to values. Event frames (**evframe**) are similar, but also record the name p of the event type being run. Storable values are objects or event closures. Event closures (**eClosure**) contain an ordered list of handler records (H), a PCD type (θ), an expression (e), an environment (ρ), and a type environment (Π). The type θ and the type environment Π (see Figure 7) are maintained by but not used by the operational semantics; they are only used in the type soundness proof [35]. Each handler record (h) contains the information necessary to call a handler method: the receiver object (loc), a method name (m), and an environment (ρ'). The environment ρ' is used to assemble the method call arguments when the handler method is called. The environment ρ recorded at the top level of the event closure is used to run the expression e when an event closure with an empty list of handler records is used in an **invoke** expression.

Figure 6 presents the key rules. The details about standard OO rules are omitted here, however, interested reader can refer to our technical report on Ptolemy [35]. The rules all make implicit use of a fixed (global) list, CT, of the program's declarations.

The (EVENT) rule is central to Ptolemy's semantics, as it starts the running of handler methods. In essence, the rule forms a new frame for running the event, and then looks up bindings applicable to the new stack, store, and list of registered (active) objects. The resulting list of handler records (H) is put into an event closure (**eclosure**(H, θ) $(e, \rho', \Pi)))$, which is placed in the store at a fresh location. This event closure will execute the handler methods, if any, before the body of the event expression (e) is evaluated. Since a new (event) frame is pushed on the stack,

Evaluation relation: $\hookrightarrow: \Gamma \to \Gamma$

(EVENT)

$$\frac{\begin{array}{c} \rho = envOf(\nu) \quad \Pi = tenvOf(\nu) \quad (c\ \textbf{evtype}\ p\{t_1\ var_1, \ldots, t_n\ var_n\}) \in CT \\ \rho' = \{var_i \mapsto v_i \mid \rho(var_i) = v_i\} \quad \pi = \{var_i : \textbf{var}\ t_i \mid 1 \le i \le n\} \\ loc \notin dom(S) \quad \pi' = \pi \uplus \{loc : \textbf{var}\ (\textbf{thunk}\ c)\} \quad \nu' = \textbf{evframe}\ p\ \rho'\ \pi' \\ H = hbind(\nu' + \nu + J, S, A) \quad \theta = \textbf{pcd}\ c, \pi \quad S' = S \oplus (loc \mapsto \textbf{eclosure}(H, \theta)\ (e, \rho, \Pi)) \end{array}}{\langle \mathbb{E}[\textbf{event}\ p\ \{e\}], \nu + J, S, A\rangle \hookrightarrow \langle \mathbb{E}[\textbf{under}\ (\textbf{invoke}(loc))], \nu' + \nu + J, S', A\rangle}$$

(UNDER)

$$\frac{\langle \mathbb{E}[\textbf{under}\ v], \nu + J, S, A\rangle}{\hookrightarrow\ \langle \mathbb{E}[v], J, S, A\rangle}$$

(REGISTER)

$$\frac{\langle \mathbb{E}[\textbf{register}(loc)], J, S, A\rangle}{\hookrightarrow\ \langle \mathbb{E}[loc], J, S, loc + A\rangle}$$

(INVOKE-DONE)

$$\frac{\textbf{eclosure}(\bullet, \theta)\ (e, \rho, \Pi) = S(loc) \quad \nu = \textbf{lexframe}\ \rho\ \Pi}{\langle \mathbb{E}[\textbf{invoke}(loc)], J, S, A\rangle \hookrightarrow \langle \mathbb{E}[\textbf{under}\ e], \nu + J, S, A\rangle}$$

(INVOKE)

$$\frac{\begin{array}{c} \textbf{eclosure}((\langle loc', m, \rho\rangle + H), \theta)\ (e, \rho', \Pi) = S(loc) \\ [c.F] = S(loc') \quad (c_2, t\ m(t_1 var_1, \ldots, t_n var_n)\{e'\}) = methodBody(c, m) \\ n \ge 1 \quad \rho'' = \{var_i \mapsto v_i \mid 2 \le i \le n, v_i = \rho(var_i)\} \quad loc_1 \notin dom(S) \\ S' = S \oplus (loc_1 \mapsto \textbf{eclosure}(H, \theta)\ (e, \rho', \Pi)) \quad \rho''' = \rho'' \oplus \{var_1 \mapsto loc_1\} \oplus \{\textbf{this} \mapsto loc'\} \\ \Pi' = \{var_i : \textbf{var}\ t_i \mid 1 \le i \le n\} \uplus \{\textbf{this} : \textbf{var}\ c_2\} \quad \nu = \textbf{lexframe}\ \rho'''\ \Pi' \end{array}}{\langle \mathbb{E}[\textbf{invoke}(loc)], J, S, A\rangle \hookrightarrow \langle \mathbb{E}[\textbf{under}\ e'], \nu + J, S', A\rangle}$$

Fig. 6. Operational semantics of Ptolemy, based on [32]. Standard OO rules are omitted

the **invoke** expression that starts running this closure is placed in an **under** expression. The (UNDER) rule pops the stack when evaluation of its subexpression is finished.

The auxiliary function *hbind* [35] uses the program's declarations, the stack, store, and the list of active objects to produce a list of handler records that are applicable for the event in the current state. When called by the (EVENT) rule, the stack passed to it has a new frame on top that represents the current event.

The (REGISTER) rule simply puts the object being activated at the front of the list of active objects. The bindings in this object are thus given control before others already in the list. An object can appear in this list multiple times.

The evaluation of **invoke** expressions is done by the two invoke rules. The (INVOKE-DONE) rule handles the case where there are no (more) handler records. It simply runs the event's body expression (e) in the environment (ρ) that was being remembered for it by the event closure.

The (INVOKE) rule handles the case where there are handler records still to be run in the event closure. It makes a call to the active object (referred to by *loc*) in the first handler record, using the method name and environment stored in that handler record. The active object is the receiver of the method call. The first formal parameter is bound to a newly allocated event closure that would run the rest of the handler records (and the original event's body) if it used in an **invoke** expression.

2.3 Ptolemy's Type System

Type checking uses the type attributes defined in Figure 7. The type checking rules themselves are shown in Figure 8. Standard rules for OO features are omitted [35]. The

$$\theta ::= \text{OK}| \text{ OK in } c \mid \textbf{var } t \mid \textbf{exp } t \mid \textbf{pcd } \tau, \pi \qquad \text{"type attributes"}$$
$$\tau ::= c \mid \bot \qquad\qquad\qquad\qquad\qquad\qquad\qquad \text{"class type exps"}$$
$$\pi, \Pi ::= \{I : \theta_I\}_{I \in K}, \qquad\qquad\qquad\qquad\qquad\quad \text{"type environments"}$$
$$\quad \textbf{where } K \text{ is finite, } K \subseteq (\mathcal{L} \cup \{\textbf{this}\} \cup \mathcal{V})$$

Fig. 7. Type attributes

(CHECK BINDING)

$$\frac{(c_2, c' \; m \, (t_1 \; var_1, \ldots, t_n \; var_n) \, \{e\}) = methodBody(c, m) \quad \vdash pcd : \textbf{pcd } c', \pi \quad isClass(c')}{\Pi \vdash (\textbf{when } pcd \textbf{ do } m) : \text{OK in } c}$$

$$n \geq 1 \qquad t_1 = \textbf{thunk } c' \qquad (\forall i \in \{2..n\} :: isType(t_i)) \qquad \{var_2 : \textbf{var } t_2, \ldots, var_n : \textbf{var } t_n\} \subseteq \pi$$

(CHECK EVTYPE)

$$\frac{isClass(c) \qquad (\forall i \in \{1..n\} :: isType(t_i))}{\vdash c \textbf{ evtype } p \, \{t_1 \; var_1 ; \ldots t_n \; var_n ; \} : \text{OK}}$$

(EV ID PCD TYPE)

$$\frac{(c \textbf{ evtype } p \, \{t_1 \; var_1 ; \ldots t_n \; var_n ; \}) \in CT \qquad \pi = \{var_1 : \textbf{var } t_1, \ldots var_n : \textbf{var } t_n\}}{\vdash p : \textbf{pcd } c, \pi}$$

(DISJUNCTION PCD TYPE)   (UNDER EXP TYPE)

$$\frac{\vdash pcd : \textbf{pcd } \tau, \pi \quad \vdash pcd' : \textbf{pcd } \tau', \pi' \quad \tau'' = \tau \sqcap \tau' \quad \pi'' = \pi \cap \pi'}{\vdash pcd \mid\mid pcd' : \textbf{pcd } \tau'', \pi''} \qquad \frac{\Pi \vdash e : \textbf{exp } t}{\Pi \vdash \textbf{under } e : \textbf{exp } t}$$

(REGISTER EXP TYPE)   (INVOKE EXP TYPE)

$$\frac{\Pi \vdash e : \textbf{exp } c}{\Pi \vdash \textbf{register}(e) : \textbf{exp } c} \qquad\qquad \frac{\Pi \vdash e : \textbf{exp } (\textbf{thunk } c)}{\Pi \vdash \textbf{invoke}(e) : \textbf{exp } c}$$

(EVENT EXP TYPE)

$$\frac{(c \textbf{ evtype } p \, \{t_1 \; var_1 ; \ldots t_n \; var_n ; \}) \in CT}{\{var_1 : \textbf{var } t_1, \ldots, var_n : \textbf{var } t_n\} \subseteq \Pi \quad \Pi \vdash e : \textbf{exp } c' \quad c' \preccurlyeq c}{\Pi \vdash \textbf{event } p \, \{e\} : \textbf{exp } c}$$

Auxiliary Functions:

$$isClass(t) = (\textbf{class } t \ldots) \in CT$$
$$isThunkType(t) = (t = \textbf{thunk } c \land isClass(c))$$
$$isType(t) = isClass(t) \lor isThunkType(t)$$

Fig. 8. Type-checking rules for Ptolemy. Rules for standard OO features are omitted

notation $\tau' \preccurlyeq \tau$ means τ' is a subtype of τ. It is the reflexive-transitive closure of the declared subclass relationships [35].

As in Clifton's work [32,33], the type checking rules are stated using a fixed class table (list of declarations) CT, which can be thought of as an implicit (hidden) inherited attribute. This class table is used implicitly by many of the auxiliary functions. For ease of presentation, we also follow Clifton in assuming that the names declared at the top level of a program are distinct and that the extends relation on classes is acyclic.

The type checking of method and binding declarations within class c produces a type of the form OK in c, in which c can be considered an inherited attribute. Thus the rule (CHECK BINDING) works with such an inherited attribute c. It checks consistency between c's method m and the PCD. PCD types contain a return type c' and a type environment π, and all but the first formal parameter of the method m must be names defined in π with a matching type. The first formal parameter must be a thunk type that returns the same type, c', as the result type of the method.

Checking event type declarations involves checking that each type used is declared.

The type checking of PCDs involves their return type and the type environment that they make available [32,35]. The return type and typing context of a named PCD are declared where the event type named is declared. For example, the FEChange PCD has FElement as its return type and the typing context that associates changedFE to the type FElement.

For a disjunction PCD, the return type is the least upper bound of the two PCDs' return types, and the typing context is the intersection of the two typing contexts. For each name I in the domain of both contexts, the type exposed for I is the least upper bound of the two types assigned to I by the two PCDs.

Expressions are type checked in the context of a local type environment Π, which gives the types of the surrounding method's formal parameters and declared local variables. Type checking of **under** and **register** is straightforward.

In an expression of the form **invoke** (e), e must have a type of the form **thunk** c, which ensures that the value of e is an event closure. The type c is the return type of that event closure, and hence the type returned by **event** (e).

In an **event** expression, the result type of the body expression, c', must be a subtype of the result type c declared by the event type, p. Furthermore, the lexical scope available (at e) must provide the context demanded by p.

The proof of soundness of Ptolemy's type system uses a standard preservation and progress argument [38]. The details are contained in our technical report [35].

2.4 Ptolemy's Compiler

We designed an extension of Java to have quantified, event types and implemented a compiler for this extension using the Eclipse's JDT core package [39]. Our prototype compiler [40] is backwards compliant; i.e., all valid Java code is valid Ptolemy code. It also generates standard Java byte-code. In the rest of the section, we describe the extensions to the Eclipse JDT Core we used to support quantified, event types.

We modified the scanner and parser of Eclipse JDT (contained in the package org.eclipse.jdt.internal.compiler.parser) to parse Ptolemy's new constructs (namely **evtype**, **event**, **register**, and bindings). Events were added as both expressions and statements, since Java makes this distinction. These modifications were fairly modular and did not require changing the existing structure of Eclipse's Java grammar; however, for automating the (extremely manual and error prone) parser building process of Eclipse some modifications to the type-hierarchy of the parser and its parser generation tool (*jikespg*) were made.

Eclipse's Java document object model (JDOM) was extended to include EventTypeDeclaration as a new TypeDeclaration, EventStatement as a new Statement, EventExpression and RegisterExpression as new subclasses of Expression, and BindingDeclaration as a new TypeMemberDeclaration.

Standard OO type checking rules are already implemented in Eclipse JDT. The semantic analysis is organized in a style similar to the composite design pattern [9], where both the composite and the leaf nodes provide uniform interface and the operation in the composite is implemented by recursively calling the operation on components. A visitor structure (ASTVisitor) is also provided, but the internal semantic analysis and code generation process does not use this structure. To add the type-checking rules for Ptolemy described in Section 2.3, we simply implemented them in the new AST nodes. The code generation for new AST nodes was also implemented similarly. These two steps also did not require modifications to implementation of other AST nodes.

Detailed description is beyond the scope of this paper, however, briefly the code generation proceeds as follows. Corresponding to an event type a set of classes and interfaces are generated that serve to model event frames, event closures, and event handlers. A closure object containing the body of event expression or statement is created as an inner class that replaces the original expression or statement. This inner class implements the interface that represents the event type at runtime and provides an implementation of the invoke method, which contains the original event's body. The replacement of the body requires a def-use analysis [41] with respect to its original environment and some name and reference mangling to propagate side-effects.

The class representing the event frame creates a chain of linked frames during registration that are parametrized with event closures during event invocation, as in the (EVENT) and (INVOKE) rules in Figure 6. Much of this is similar to the intuition discussed in Ptolemy's operational semantics in Section 2.2.

3   Comparisons with II and AO Langauges

> *The most perfect political community must be amongst those*
> *who are in the middle rank. – Aristotle, Politics*

In this section we compare Ptolemy with II and AO languages. We start with an extended example that illuminates some differences between Ptolemy and AO languages.

3.1   An Extended Example in Ptolemy

In the extended example presented in this section, we use notations closer to a full-fledged language such as Java, such as **if** statements. Such constructs can be easily added to Ptolemy's core language.

The example shown in Figure 9 extends the example from Section 1. A set of classes are added to facilitate storing several figure elements in collections, e.g. as a linked list (FEList), as a set (FESet), and a hash table (FEHashtable). Furthermore, Counter implements the policy that whenever an FElement is added to the system a count must be incremented.

The notion of "adding an element" differs among the different types of collection. For example, calling add on a FEList always extends the list with the given element. However, calling add on a FESet only inserts the element if it is not already present, as shown on lines 16–20. Therefore, an AO-style syntactic method of selecting events such as "an FElement is being added" will need to distinguish which calls will actually add the element. In a language like AspectJ, one could use an **if** PCD. A PCD such as **call**(* FESet.add(FElement fe)) && **this**(feset) && **if**(!feset.contains(fe)) would filter out undesired call events.

```
 1 FElement evtype FEAdded {FElement addedFE;}

 3 class FEList extends Object {
 4 Node listhead;  /*head of linked list*/
 5 FElement add(FElement addedFE) {
 6   event FEAdded {
 7   Node temp = listhead;
 8   listhead = new Node();
 9   listhead.data = addedFE;
10   listhead.next = temp; addedFE
11   }
12 }
13 FElement remove(FElement fe) { /*...*/ }
14 boolean contains(FElement fe) { /*...*/ }
15 }
16 class FESet extends FEList { /* ... */
17 FElement add(FElement addedFE) {
18   if(!this.contains(addedFE)) {
19     event FEAdded {
20     Node temp = listhead;
21     listhead = new Node();
```

```
22     listhead.data = addedFE;
23     listhead.next = temp; addedFE
24     }
25   } else { null }
26 }
27 }

29 class Counter extends Object {
30 Number count;
31 Counter init() {
32   register(this)
33 }
34 FElement increment(thunk FElement next,
35     FElement addedFE) {
36   this.count = this.count.plus(1);
37   invoke(next)
38 }
39 when FEAdded do increment
40 }

42 Counter u = new Counter().init();
43 /* ... */
```

Fig. 9. Figure Element Collections in Ptolemy

However, there are two issues with using such an **if** PCD. The first issue is that it exposes the internal implementation details of FESet.add (in particular that its representation does not allow duplicates). Second, such a PCD should only be used if the expression feset.contains(fe) does not have any side-effects. (Side-effects would usually be undesirable when used solely for filtering out undesired events.)

Other possibilities for handling such events include: (1) testing the condition in the handler body and (2) rewriting the code for FESet.add to make the body of the **if** a separate method call. The first has problems that are similar to those described above with using an **if** PCD. Rewriting the code to make a separate method call obscures the code in a way that may not be desirable and may cause maintenance problems, since nothing in the syntax would indicate why the body of the called method was not used inline. There may also be problems in passing and manipulating local variables appropriately in such a body turned into a method, at least in a language like Java or C# that uses call by value.

Such workarounds are also necessary in more sophisticated AO languages such as LogicAJ [17]. These have PCDs that describe code structure, but that does not prevent undesirable exposure of internal implementation details, since the structure of the code is itself such a detail.

By contrast, Ptolemy easily handles this problem without exposing internal details of FESet's add method, since that method simply indicates the occurence of event FEAdded. In essence, Ptolemy's advantage is that it can explicitly announce the body of an **if** as an event. Doing so precisely communicates the event without the problems of using **if** PCDs or extra method calls described above.

3.2 Advance Over Implicit Invocation Languages

Consider the II implementation of our drawing editor example (Figure 1). Compared to that implementation, in Ptolemy registration is more automated (see Figure 4), so programmers do not have to write code to register an observer for each separate event.

Ptolemy's registration also better separates concerns, since it does not require naming all classes that announce an event of interest. This is because events are not considered to be attributes of the classes that announce them. Thus, event handlers in Ptolemy need not be coupled with the concrete implementation of these subclasses. Furthermore, naming an event type, such as FEChange, in a PCD hides the details of event implementation and allows succinct quantification.

Ptolemy can also replace (or override) code for an event (like AO's "around advice"). Although similar functionality can be emulated, Ptolemy's automation significantly eases the programmer's task.

3.3   Advance Over AO Languages

Some of the advantages of named event types would also be found in a language like AspectJ 5, which can advise code tagged with various Java 5 annotations. If one only advises code that has certain annotations, then join points become more explicit, and more like the explicitly identified events in Ptolemy. However, Java 5 cannot attach annotations to arbitrary statements or expressions, and in any case such annotations do not solve the problems described in the rest of this section.

Robust Quantified, Typed Events. If instead of lexical PCDs Ptolemy's event expressions are used to announce events and PCDs are written in terms of these event names, innocuous changes in the code that implements the events will not change the meaning of the PCDs. For further analysis of robustness against such changes, let us compare the syntactic version of the PCD **target**(fe) && **call**(FElement+.set*(..)) with Ptolemy's version in Figure 4. The syntactic approach to selecting events provides ease of use, i.e., by just writing a simple regular expression one can select events throughout the program. But this also leads to inadvertent selection of events: set* may select setParent, which perhaps does not change the state of a figure element. AO languages with sopisticated matching, based on program structure [17] or event history [20], have more possibilities for precise description of events, but can still inadvertently select unintended events. Ptolemy's quantified typed events do not have this problem.

Flexible Quantification. The **event** expression in Ptolemy allows one to label any expression as an event expression and all such events can be selected by using the event type name in a PCD. Significant flexibility comes from giving developers the ability to decide what expressions constitute events and making them all available for quantification purposes. This largely solves the quantification failure problem [24]. The events that can be made available to handlers are no longer limited to interface elements, and the implementations of these events are not exposed to handlers. Handlers only rely on event type declarations. In contrast to implicitly announced events in AO languages, Ptolemy's **event** expression allows one to announce any expression as an event.

Flexible Access to Context Information. The third problem that we considered in Section 1 was the difficulty of retrieving context information from a join point. Event types in Ptolemy solve this problem. To make the reflective information at the event available, a programmer only needs to define, in the lexical scope surrounding the event expression, values for the names declared in that event's type. For example, in Figure 4 in the setX method a block expression assigns **this** to changedFE. Note that this flexibility does not introduce additional coupling between events and handlers. Handlers are only aware of the context variable declaration changedFE made available by the event type FEChange and not of the concrete mapping to the variables available in the lexical scope of the event expression.

Uniform Access to Irregular Context Information. AO join point models currently do not provide uniform access to irregular contextual information. But Ptolemy's event expressions allow uniform access to such context information. For example, in Figure 4, the event expression in the setX method and in the makeEqual method are given different bindings for the context variable changedFE, yet the handler update is able to access this context information uniformly using the event type name changedFE. The implementation details are also hidden from PCDs, which can uniformly access the context provided at the event (e.g., using the event type changedFE).

Concern and Obliviousness. Both AO languages and Ptolemy have advantages for certain programming tasks. Consider first whether the concern needs to affect the code in which the events happen — the *base code* in AO terminology. "Spectator" concerns, like tracing, do not affect the base code's state [42,36,43]. Since spectators do not affect reasoning about the base code, explicit announcements in the base code give little benefit. Hence the determining factor is whether PCDs are easier to write lexically (in the AO style) or using explicitly named events (as in Ptolemy). For syntactically unrelated pieces of code, e.g., the locations of the event FEAdded in Figure 9, explicit announcement makes writing such PCDs more convenient. However, if the events occur in sections of the base code that are syntactically related (by a naming convention, placement in a common package, etc.), then lexical PCDs are preferable.

Besides the availability of uniform context (as described above) another property that affects how easy it is to write lexical PCDs is whether events in the base code are explicit at a module's interface, e.g., calls or executions of a public method. As pointed out by Aldrich [26] internal events should not be implicitly exported, hence explicit announcement should be used for such events to force negotiation about the commitments involved in having spectators rely on these events.

"Assistants" (i.e., non-spectators [42]) have handlers that affect the base code's state. Hence events handled by assistants are important for reasoning about the base code's state. With implicit announcement it is difficult to see these events and take them into account during reasoning. Furthermore, conclusions drawn about the base code will change depending on which assistants are added to the program. Thus we believe that events that are of concern to assistants should always be explicitly announced.

In conclusion, implicit announcement—obliviousness—is useful for spectator concerns when it is easy to write lexical PCDs. In other cases, Ptolemy's explicit event announcement and its event model are better.

4   Comparative Analysis with Related Work

"There is no other royal path which leads to geometry," said Euclid to Ptolemy I.

In this section, we compare Ptolemy with other mechanisms that address similar problems in AO language design. The other mechanisms we selected for analysis include

Aspect-Aware Interfaces (AAIs) [11], Open Modules (OMs) [26], and Crosscut Programming Interfaces (XPIs) [24] [25]. The next section summarizes these ideas.

4.1 Overview of Related Ideas

Aspect Aware Interfaces (AAIs) [11] show dependencies between code and handlers. The whole program's configuration, which contains all classes and bindings (including PCDs) is first used to compute dependencies between events and handlers (called the "global step" [11]). The result of this global step is similar in some ways to code in Ptolemy, since one can look at an AAI and see where events may occur that will call handlers, and what handlers may be called for such events. However, whenever the program's bindings are changed, the global step must be repeated and an entirely new set of implicitly announced events might be handled, causing new dependencies. Ptolemy's event expressions do not declare what handlers are applicable for the event they explicitly announce, but the use of explicit announcement ensures that changing a program's bindings will not advise other (previously unanticipated) program points. AAIs also give no help with the problems discussed in Section 1.

Aldrich's Open Modules (OMs) proposal [26] is closely related to this work and has similar advantages. Like our work, OMs also allows a class developer to explicitly expose the sets of events that are announced. The implementations of these events remain hidden from PCDs and handlers. As a result, the impact of code changes within the class on PCDs is reduced. However, in OMs each explicitly exposed PCD has to be enumerated when binding handlers to sets of events (i.e., when writing advice). By contrast, Ptolemy's event types provide significantly simpler quantification. In Ptolemy, instead of enumerating the events of interest, one can use the event types for more convenient non-syntactic quantification to select join points. As with OMs, a programmer using Ptolemy's event types must systematically modify modules in a system that a given concern crosscuts to expose events that are to be advised, by using **event** expressions. For example, the module *Point* in Figure 4 had to be modified to expose events of type FEChange. However, unlike OMs, once modules have incorporated such **event** expressions, no awkward enumeration of explicitly exposed join points is necessary for quantification. Instead, one simply uses the event type FEChange in a PCD. Furthermore, in Ptolemy one can expose events that are internal to a module, such as the bodies of **if** statements (Figure 9, lines 17–20), which is not possible in OMs.

Sullivan *et al.* [24] proposed a methodology for aspect-oriented design based on design rules. The key idea is to establish a design rule interface that serves to decouple the base design and the aspect design. These design rules govern exposure of execution phenomena as join points, how they are exposed through the join point model of the given language, and constraints on behavior across join points (e.g. *provides* and *requires* conditions [25]). These design rule interfaces were later called crosscut programming interface (XPI) by Griswold *et al.* [25]. XPIs prescribe rules for join point exposure, but do not provide a compliance mechanism. Griswold *et al.* have shown that at least some design rules can be enforced automatically. In Ptolemy, enforcing design rules is equivalent to type checking of programs, because Ptolemy's event types automatically provide the interfaces needed to decouple different modules.

Criteria	Description	AAIs	OMs	XPIs	Ptolemy
Abstraction	Supports abstraction?	Yes	Yes	Yes	Yes
Aspect/Base IH	Is information hiding supported for aspect / base?	Aspect	Base	Aspect + Base	Aspect + Base
Reasoning	What is the granularity of reasoning?	Join point	Module	XPI's Scope	Expression
Configuration	Requires complete system configuration?	Yes	No	No	No
Decoupling	Decouples aspects from base code?	No	Yes	Yes	Yes
Locality	Are interface definitions textually localized?	No	No	Yes	Yes
Stable	Is it stable against code changes?	Low	High	Medium	High
Pattern	Allows pattern-based quantification?	Yes	in module	in XPI's scope	No
Type	Allows quantification based on type hierarchy?	No	No	No	Yes
Scope	What is the scope of the interface?	Program	Module	User defined	User defined
Scope control	Has fine-grained control over scope?	No	No	No	Yes
Adaptation	Requires base code adaption / refactoring?	No	Yes	Yes	Yes
Oblivious	Is it purely oblivious?	No	No	No	No
Lexical hints	Provides lexical hints in a module?	Yes	Yes	No	Yes

Fig. 10. Results of comparative analysis

4.2 Criteria and Analysis Results

The criteria and the analysis results are summarized in Figure 10. The rest of this section presents our analysis in detail.

Abstraction, Information Hiding. The first criterion is whether the approach supports abstraction. All four approaches support abstraction. AAIs abstract the advice that is being executed at the join point, while providing information about the advising structures in a specific system deployment scenario. Their automatically computed abstraction is useful for the developer of the base code in hiding the details of the aspects that may come to depend on the base code. OMs abstract the join point implementation by providing an explicitly declared pointcut as part of the module description. Their abstraction is useful for the aspect code and hides the details of the base code. XPIs provide an abstraction for a set of join points to the aspects, and an abstraction for the possible cumulative behavior of all advice constructs to the base program through their requires/provides clauses. Ptolemy provides an abstraction for a set of events to the handlers. It also provide a two-way abstraction for all context information exchanged between an event expression and the handler.

Modular Reasoning and the Role of the System Configuration. All four approaches support different mechanisms for modular reasoning. AAIs are different from OMs, XPIs and Ptolemy in that they require that dependencies between base code and aspects be computed before modular reasoning can begin. This may preclude reasoning about a module until all aspects and classes are known. OMs are geared towards supporting reasoning about a change inside a module without knowing about all aspects and classes present in the system. By ensuring that no aspects come to depend upon the changeable implementation details the need to pre-compute all base-aspect dependencies is eliminated. XPIs are geared towards supporting reasoning about a change inside a scope. Ptolemy allows reasoning at the expression level; in particular, only event expressions require any special treatment compared with OO programs.

Locality. This criterion evaluates whether the AO interface definitions are textually localized. AAIs are computed for each point where advice might apply, and thus are not localized. OMs are similar in that the interface of each module explicitly specifies the join points exposed by that module. In XPIs, the AO interface definitions are localized as an abstract aspect. In Ptolemy the event expressions are not localized but the type definition that serves as an interface to the handlers is localized.

Pattern-based Quantification, Scope, and Scope Control Mechanisms. AAIs, OMs and XPIs all support pattern-based quantification. The difference lies in the scope of application of the pattern-based quantification techniques. The scope in the case of AAIs is generally the entire program, but can be limited to specific regions using lexical pointcut expressions such as **within** and **withincode**. In OMs, they are applicable to inside a module only if used to declare explicitly exposed pointcut and to the entire program if used to select interface elements of modules. XPIs have an explicit scope component that can serve to limit the effect of pattern-based quantification, which in turn is implemented using the **within** and **withincode** PCDs. In Ptolemy, one can only select program execution events that are declaratively identified. A much finer-grained scope control is available in the case of Ptolemy. In other approaches scope control depends on the language's expressiveness.

Base Code Adaptation and Obliviousness. Obliviousness is a widely accepted tenet for aspect-oriented software development [16]. In an oblivious AO process, the designers and developers of base code need not be aware of, anticipate or design code to be advised by aspects. This criterion, although attractive, has been questioned by many [26,42,43,25,11,44,24]. All four approaches limit the notion of obliviousness to some extent. In Ptolemy adapting base code is necessary.

5 Other Related Ideas

> *advertise, annunciate, broadcast, declare, proclaim, promulgate, publish*
> *– entry for "announce" in Roget's II*

In some AO langauges quantification is not based on pattern matching of lexical names. For example, in LogicAJ [17] and similar languages such as LogicAJ2, Sally [45], quantification is on program structures, in languages that support trace-based pointcuts [46], quantification is based on program traces. As mentioned before, such languages, although significantly expressive compared to the AspectJ-like languages that quantify based on names, also exhibit fragile pointcut problem. Compared to this entire class of such AO languages, which quantify based on pattern matching, Ptolemy's quantified event types in Ptolemy further decouple event handlers and the code that signals events and encapsulates the details of the signaller's code. However, upfront efforts will be required in Ptolemy to anticipate and announce events.

Explicitly labeling methods for use in quantification is not a new idea and has appeared previously in SetPoint [29] and Model-based Pointcuts [23]. In SetPoint explicitly placed annotations are used for quantification. In Model-based Pointcuts, explictly created models, which express the relationship between names in the model and the program's structure, are used for quantification. Compared to these approaches, the novelty of our approach lies in: allowing arbitrary expressions to be announced as events, in providing explicitly announced events with types, in formalizing the language's sound, static type system, and in providing access to the context of event announcements. Compared to model-based pointcuts, our technique does not require a model construction step. Furthermore, keeping such model consistent with the code can be challenging.

Steimann and Pawlitzki have independently advanced ideas that are very similar [47]. Their language has event types and explicitly announced events that contain arbitrary statements. Their event types are similar to Ptolemy's. Their language is a modification of AspectJ, and has both implicit (AO style) and explicit announcement of events, whereas Ptolemy only has explicit announcement. In their language explicit announcement passes context positionally (as in a Java constructor call), whereas in Ptolemy context is passed by name matching. Their language is also somewhat similar to Open Modules in that the event types that are exported by a class must be declared by that class. They also have a prototype implementation, but do not formally present their language's semantics or type system.

Delegates in .NET languages such as C# and Java's EventObject class are also related to our approach. They are type-safe mechanism for implementing call back functions that can also be used to abstract event declaration code; however, these mechanisms do not provide the quantification feature of Ptolemy's PCDs.

Another related area is mediator-based design styles [6]. In this design style modules tell mediators about event declarations and announcements. Other modules can register with mediators to have their methods invoked by event announcements. An invocation relation is thus created without introducing name dependencies. In our approach, event types play the role of mediators. However, in Ptolemy, one can also use event types for quantification, which simplifies registration and binding. By contrast, in mediator based designs a developer has to resort to explicit and possibly error-prone enumerations to register handlers with events.

Consider a language with closures and the ability to reflectively get the run time context of a statement or expression. In such language, one could achieve the same effect as Ptolemy's quantified event types by declaring classes to represent events, announcing events by creating a closure after reflectively accessing the event body's run time context and then looping over a set of registered handler methods, passing each a closure (that it could invoke). Ptolemy provides three advantages over this emulation:

– **Static typechecking** of bindings, which ensures that PCDs only associate handlers with events that provide the necessary context.
– A considerable amount of **automation**. Ptolemy's **register**, **event**, and **invoke** expressions hide the details of registration, announcement, and running handlers. Furthermore PCDs provide quantification, which is not easy to emulate.
– **Improved compiler optimizations**. Since Ptolemy controls the details of how registration, announcement, and running handlers are implemented, there is more potential for optimization then when these features are emulated.

6 Future Work and Conclusions

Onward and upward. — Abraham Lincoln

We designed Ptolemy to be a small core language, in order to clearly communicate its novel ability to announce arbitrary expressions as events and its use of quantified, event types, and in order to avoid complications in its theory. However, this means that many practical and useful extensions had to be omitted from the language. The most important future work in the area of Ptolemy's semantics is subtyping of event types and investigating the possible advantages of positional context exposure (instead of Ptolemy's name-based context exposure). We have already extended Ptolemy's operational semantics to include control flow ("cflow") PCDs [35], which are not discussed in this paper due to lack of space. It would also be interesting to combine Ptolemy's type system with an effect system, to limit the potential side effects of handler methods [32,36]. This might allow more efficient reasoning. One could also imagine combining specifications of handler methods into code at **event** expressions, thus allowing verification of code that uses event types to be more efficient and maintainable than directly reasoning about the compiled code's semantics. In general, a detailed investigation of specification and verification issues for Ptolemy would be very interesting.

In conclusion, the main contribution of this work is the design of a language, Ptolemy, with quantified, typed events. In addition to a precise operational semantics and formal definition of Ptolemy's type system (see our technical report for a soundness proof [35]), we have carefully examined how Ptolemy fits in the design space of languages that promote separation of concerns. The main new feature of Ptolemy is event types, which contain information about the names and types of exposed context. In Ptolemy's new event model, events are explicitly announced by event expressions, which declaratively identify the type of event being announced. These event types are used in PCDs to associate handlers with sets of events. Such PCDs are robust against code changes, since they are only affected by changes to event expressions. The event types used in PCDs make it easier for handlers to uniformly access reflective information about the events without breaking encapsulation. Ptolemy has been implemented as a compiler, and an implementation is available for free download [40].

Ptolemy's ability to announce any expression as an event, which permits one to expose internal states in a principled way, promises real value. For example, this would help the integration of components when hidden internal states and transitions must be accessed in order to achieve proper composition.

References

1. Dingel, J., Garlan, D., Jha, S., Notkin, D.: Reasoning about implicit invocation. SIGSOFT Software Engineering Notes 23(6), 209–221 (1998)
2. Garlan, D., Notkin, D.: Formalizing design spaces: Implicit invocation mechanisms. In: Prehn, S., Toetenel, H. (eds.) VDM 1991. LNCS, vol. 551, pp. 31–44. Springer, Heidelberg (1991)
3. Luckham, D.C., Vera, J.: An event-based architecture definition language. IEEE Trans. Softw. Eng. 21(9), 717–734 (1995)
4. Notkin, D., Garlan, D., Griswold, W.G., Sullivan, K.J.: Adding implicit invocation to languages: Three approaches. In: JSSST International Symposium on Object Technologies for Advanced Software, pp. 489–510 (1993)
5. Reiss, S.P.: Connecting tools using message passing in the Field environment. IEEE Softw. 7(4), 57–66 (1990)
6. Sullivan, K.J., Notkin, D.: Reconciling environment integration and software evolution. ACM Transactions on Software Engineering and Methodology 1(3), 229–268 (1992)

7. Kiczales, G., Lamping, J., Menhdhekar, A., Maeda, C., Lopes, C., Loingtier, J.M., Irwin, J.: Aspect-oriented programming. In: Aksit, M., Matsuoka, S. (eds.) ECOOP 1997. LNCS, vol. 1241, pp. 220–242. Springer, Heidelberg (1997)
8. Tarr, P., Ossher, H., Harrison, W., Sutton, S.: N degrees of separation: Multi-dimensional separation of concerns. In: ICSE 1999 (1999)
9. Gamma, E., Helm, R., Johnson, R., Vlissides, J.: Design patterns: elements of reusable object-oriented software. Addison-Wesley Publishing Co., Inc, Reading (1995)
10. Kiczales, G., et al.: An overview of AspectJ. In: Knudsen, J.L. (ed.) ECOOP 2001. LNCS, vol. 2072, pp. 327–353. Springer, Heidelberg (2001)
11. Kiczales, G., Mezini, M.: Separation of concerns with procedures, annotations, advice and pointcuts. In: Black, A.P. (ed.) ECOOP 2005. LNCS, vol. 3586, pp. 195–213. Springer, Heidelberg (2005)
12. Filman, R.E., Elrad, T., Clarke, S., Akşit, M. (eds.): Aspect-Oriented Software Development. Addison-Wesley, Boston (2005)
13. Elrad, T., Filman, R.E., Bader, A.: Aspect-oriented programming: Introduction. Commun. ACM 44(10), 29–32 (2001)
14. Laddad, R.: AspectJ in Action: Practical Aspect-Oriented Programming. Manning (2003)
15. AspectJ Team: The AspectJ programming guide. Version 1.5.3 (2006), http://eclipse.org/aspectj
16. Filman, R.E., Friedman, D.P.: Aspect-oriented programming is quantification and obliviousness. In: Workshop on Advanced Separation of Concerns (OOPSLA 2000 (October 2000)
17. Rho, T., Kniesl, G., Appeltauer, M.: Fine-grained generic aspects. In: FOAL 2006 (2006)
18. Eichberg, M., Mezini, M., Ostermann, K.: Pointcuts as functional queries. In: Chin, W.-N. (ed.) APLAS 2004. LNCS, vol. 3302, pp. 366–381. Springer, Heidelberg (2004)
19. Douence, R., Fradet, P., Sudholt, M.: Trace-based aspects. Aspect-oriented Software Development, 141–150
20. Stolz, V., Bodden, E.: Temporal assertions using AspectJ. In: Fifth Workshop on Runtime Verification (RV 2005) (2005)
21. Stoerzer, M., Graf, J.: Using pointcut delta analysis to support evolution of aspect-oriented software. In: ICSM 2005, pp. 653–656 (2005)
22. Tourwé, T., Brichau, J., Gybels, K.: On the existence of the AOSD-evolution paradox. In: SPLAT 2003, Boston (March 2003)
23. Kellens, A., Mens, K., Brichau, J., Gybels, K.: Managing the evolution of aspect-oriented software with model-based pointcuts. In: Thomas, D. (ed.) ECOOP 2006. LNCS, vol. 4067, pp. 501–525. Springer, Heidelberg (2006)
24. Sullivan, K.J., Griswold, W.G., Song, Y., Cai, Y., Shonle, M., Tewari, N., Rajan, H.: Information hiding interfaces for aspect-oriented design. In: ESEC/FSE 2005, pp. 166–175 (2005)
25. W. G. Griswold et al.: Modular software design with crosscutting interfaces. IEEE Software (January/ February 2006)
26. Aldrich, J.: Open Modules. In: Black, A.P. (ed.) ECOOP 2005. LNCS, vol. 3586, pp. 144–168. Springer, Heidelberg (2005)
27. Harbulot, B., Gurd, J.R.: A join point for loops in AspectJ. In: AOSD 2006, pp. 63–74 (2006)
28. Rajan, H., Sullivan, K.J.: Aspect language features for concern coverage profiling. In: AOSD 2005, pp. 181–191 (2005)
29. Altman, R., Cyment, A., Kicillof, N.: On the need for Setpoints. In: European Interactive Workshop on Aspects in Software (2005)
30. Rajan, H., Sullivan, K.J.: Classpects: unifying aspect- and object-oriented language design. In: Inverardi, P., Jazayeri, M. (eds.) ICSE 2005. LNCS, vol. 4309, pp. 59–68. Springer, Heidelberg (2006)
31. Mezini, M., Ostermann, K.: Conquering aspects with Caesar. In: AOSD 2003, pp. 90–99 (2003)

32. Clifton, C.: A design discipline and language features for modular reasoning in aspect-oriented programs. Technical Report 05-15, Iowa State University (July 2005)
33. Clifton, C., Leavens, G.T.: MiniMAO$_1$: Investigating the semantics of proceed. Science of Computer Programming 63(3), 321–374 (2006)
34. Rajan, H., Sullivan, K.J.: Eos: instance-level aspects for integrated system design. In: ESEC/FSE 2003, pp. 297–306 (2003)
35. Rajan, H., Leavens, G.T.: Quantified, typed events for improved separation of concerns. Technical Report 07-14c, Iowa State University, Dept. of Computer Sc. (October 2007)
36. Clifton, C., Leavens, G.T., Noble, J.: MAO: Ownership and effects for more effective reasoning about aspects. In: Ernst, E. (ed.) ECOOP 2007. LNCS, vol. 4609, pp. 451–475. Springer, Heidelberg (2007)
37. Flatt, M., Krishnamurthi, S., Felleisen, M.: A programmer's reduction semantics for classes and mixins. In: Formal Syntax and Semantics of Java, pp. 241–269. Springer, Heidelberg (1999)
38. Wright, A.K., Felleisen, M.: A syntactic approach to type soundness. Information and Computation 115(1), 38–94 (1994)
39. Eclipse Foundation, http://www.eclipse.org/
40. Rajan, H., Leavens, G.T.: Ptolemy (2007),
    http://www.cs.iastate.edu/~ptolemy/
41. Nielson, F., Nielson, H.R., Hankin, C.: Principles of Program Analysis, 2nd printing edn. Springer, Heidelberg (2005)
42. Clifton, C., Leavens, G.: Observers and assistants: A proposal for modular aspect-oriented reasoning. In: FOAL 2002, pp. 33–44 (2002)
43. Dantas, D.S., Walker, D.: Harmless advice. In: POPL 2006, pp. 383–396 (2006)
44. Steimann, F.: The paradoxical success of aspect-oriented programming. In: OOPSLA 2006, pp. 481–497 (October 2006)
45. Hanenberg, S., Unland, R.: Parametric introductions. In: AOSD 2003, pp. 80–89 (2003)
46. Douence, R., Motelet, O., Südholt, M.: A formal definition of crosscuts. In: REFLECTION 2001, pp. 170–186 (2001)
47. Steimann, F., Pawlitzki, T.: Types and modularity for implicit invocation with implicit announcement. Obtained from the first author (August 2007)

Prototyping and Composing Aspect Languages

Using an Aspect Interpreter Framework

Wilke Havinga, Lodewijk Bergmans, and Mehmet Aksit

University of Twente, P.O. Box 217, 7500 AE Enschede, The Netherlands
{w.havinga,l.m.j.bergmans,m.aksit}@ewi.utwente.nl

Abstract. Domain specific aspect languages (DSALs) are becoming more popular because they can be designed to represent recurring concerns in a way that
is optimized for a specific domain. However, the design and implementation of
even a limited domain-specific aspect language can be a tedious job. To address
this, we propose a framework that offers a fast way to prototype implementations
of domain specific aspect languages. A particular goal of the framework is to be
general enough to support a wide range of aspect language concepts, such that
existing language concepts can be easily used, and new language concepts can be
quickly created.

We briefly introduce the framework and its underlying model, as well as the
workflow used when implementing DSALs. Subsequently, we show mappings of
several domain specific aspect languages to demonstrate the framework. Since in
our approach the DSALs are mapped to a common model, the framework provides an integrating platform allowing us to compose programs that use aspects
written in multiple DSALs. The framework also provides explicit mechanisms to
specify composition of advices written in multiple DSALs.

1 Introduction

The benefits of using domain specific aspect languages (DSALs) are widely recognized
[8,16,24]. In fact, the idea of expressing each crosscutting concern using a dedicated
domain-specific language was at the very heart of the first proposals called "AOP" [12].

However, designing and implementing DSALs can be a tedious job. For example,
each aspect language has to define under which circumstances an aspect should influence the program, and implement mechanisms to facilitate this (e.g. using bytecode
weaving).

In addition, most applications will need to express concerns from different problem
domains, making it desirable to write programs using multiple DSALs. That way, each
DSAL could be used to effectively address the concerns within its specific domain.

It is not trivial to compose aspects expressed in several DSALs however, as each
language typically constructs its own model of the program; unless a lot of care is
taken, the effects of one aspect may not be reflected in the models constructed by other
DSALs. In addition, aspects written in several DSALs may interact with each other,
possibly in undesirable ways (depending on the situation).

J. Vitek (Ed.): ECOOP 2008, LNCS 5142, pp. 180–206, 2008.
© Springer-Verlag Berlin Heidelberg 2008

Our paper contributes the following to address these problems:

(1) We propose an aspect interpreter framework that can be used to prototype domain specific aspect languages. As our framework supports a wide range of aspect language concepts, it can be used to prototype diverse DSALs in a reasonable amount of time, as we will show in section 3.

(2) Using our approach, aspects written in several (domain-specific) languages are mapped to a common model. As a result, we can compose applications that are written using multiple DSALs, as we will show in section 4.1.

(3) The framework provides explicit mechanisms to specify composition of advices, even if advices are written in several DSALs. This is discussed in section 4.3.

In this paper, we show implementations of only three DSALs. However, our work is based on a thorough study of aspect oriented languages [19], as well as the modeling of their possible implementation mechanisms using an interpreter, as presented in [7].

In the next section, we briefly introduce the framework itself. Section 3 presents more details about the framework by showing the implementations of several DSALs using our framework. Section 4 discusses the composition of aspects written in multiple DSALs, including specifications to resolve the interactions between aspects. Section 5 discusses several design and implementation considerations related to our framework. We discuss related work in section 6, and conclude the paper in section 7

2   JAMI - An Aspect Interpreter Framework

One of the defining features of AOP languages is the support for "implicit invocation" of application behavior. That is, behavior can be invoked without an explicit reference (such as a *method call* statement) being visible in the (source) code at the point of invocation. Implicit invocation is a key feature of the interface between the base program and the aspect program. The framework to model aspect language mechanisms we present in this paper is strongly based on implicit invocation as the connection between the base program and the aspects (advices).

In this section, we briefly discuss the concepts used in the aspect language domain, based on a reference model proposed in [19]. We then propose a framework that provides common implementations of these concepts, while supporting variations on these concepts found in different aspect languages. The general design and architecture of the framework was first proposed in [7] and [11]. Finally, we briefly outline the workflow used to prototype DSALs using this framework.

2.1   Common Aspect Language Concepts

Aspect languages must first of all support the concept of *pointcuts*. Pointcuts define the circumstances under which an aspect influences a program – for example, at certain locations (such as entering a particular method) or under particular runtime conditions (e.g., only when a variable x equals 5). Pointcuts can be seen as predicates or conditions over the *execution state* of a program. The execution state may, in a broad sense, include information about the call stack, objects, or even the execution trace and structure of the program. As pointcuts may match at several places or moments during the execution of a program, the concept of *joinpoints* is used to model references to the relevant execution state (e.g., which method is being intercepted) whenever a pointcut matches. Pointcuts can be bound to *advices*, which may add to or replace parts of the original program behavior and/or its runtime state. Advices can use the joinpoint information to adapt their behavior based on the current runtime situation. Finally, *bindings* specify how pointcuts and advices are connected and grouped into modules (usually called aspects). In addition, bindings are also used to bind "aspect state" – data stored by aspects, such that it can be shared between advices (i.e., similar to sharing state between methods by using instance variables).

2.2   Framework Implementation

Aspect languages adopt varying implementations of the concepts listed above. We provide a framework that implements the behavior of these high-level concepts, and allows for their refinement to facilitate specific language implementations.

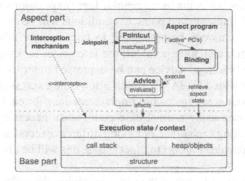

Fig. 1. The Java Aspect Metamodel Interpreter - an overview

Figure 1 shows a global overview of our framework, called the Java Aspect Metamodel Interpreter (JAMI) [1]. Basically, this framework enforces the high-level structure and control flow of aspects, while providing implementations of common concepts at an abstraction level that is appropriate when prototyping DSALs – as we intend to demonstrate in section 3. By enforcing a fixed high-level control flow, our framework provides a common platform that enables composition of aspects written in multiple DSALs, as we will show in section 4. To provide the flexibility required to model features of particular languages, each concept can be either instantiated in a dedicated configuration of framework elements, or refined (extended) when necessary. JAMI provides many of the common implementations found in different aspect languages.

Control Flow. We briefly discuss the high-level control flow within JAMI. In principle, the base program (a normal Java application) runs as it would without the interpreter. However, the *interception mechanism* (see figure 1) intercepts the control flow at any point that is of potential interest to the aspect interpreter. Our current implementation uses a regular AspectJ aspect to intercept *all* method calls and field assignments. Apart from intercepting method calls, the mechanism keeps track of *context* information that may be of interest to the framework. Currently, it keeps track of the call stack, senders, targets, and method signatures of all calls on the stack, as well as field assignments. Upon interception of the control flow, the mechanism creates a *joinpoint* object representing the current joinpoint. A refinement class exists for each different joinpoint type, such as *MethodCallJoinpoint*, *MethodReturnJoinPoint* or *AssignmentJoinpoint*. Each of these joinpoint objects keeps a reference to the relevant context information - e.g., the method that was executing upon interception, etc.

Subsequently, each *pointcut* registered with the aspect interpreter is evaluated against the current joinpoint (see figure 1). As indicated before, pointcuts are basically conditions that either match or do not match a particular joinpoint. Thus, the main *pointcut* class consists of only an *evaluate* method, which returns true or false based on whether it matches the current joinpoint. Refinement classes are provided for many common pointcut conditions; new ones can be created if necessary to implement DSAL-specific pointcut types. For example, we provide pointcuts that match based on the type of joinpoint, method signature, or target object type. In addition, there are pointcut classes that can combine other pointcuts using regular logic expressions (*and*, *or*, *not*). Many concrete examples of implemented pointcut conditions will be shown in section 3.

One or more pointcuts can be associated to one or more advices using *bindings* (see figure 1). For each matching pointcut, the interpreter looks up the corresponding *advice* through these bindings. Advice can be expressed in terms of elementary advice "building blocks" provided by JAMI, which allows the expression of many common types of advice without creating custom implementations for each advice. In addition, advice can be expressed using normal base code, when necessary. Advices may also want to share state among each other, or among different executions of the same advice. Therefore, we also provide *bindings* to aspect state; this will be discussed in more detail in section 3.1.

When several pointcuts match at the same joinpoint, the order of advice execution has to be resolved. This issue is discussed in detail in section 4.

Fur further details about the implementation, we refer to the JAMI manual and API documentation available on the JAMI website [1].

2.3   Prototyping DSALs: General Workflow

We briefly describe the steps involved in prototyping a DSAL using JAMI.

First of all, we define a grammar that can conveniently express the domain concepts of a particular DSAL, as well as the relations between those concepts. Next, a parser is needed - using a parser generator is typically the most convenient way to implement this (we use Antlr, but any Java-based parser generator could be used). Subsequently, we convert the abstract syntax trees (ASTs) obtained from the parser to an object-based version, such that the domain concepts are semantically represented by objects. This conversion can be implemented using handwritten code, or by using generated "tree walkers". The final step is to convert the object-based AST representation of domain concepts to JAMI elements. We currently implement this conversion using handwritten code.

Once an aspect written in a DSAL is (automatically) converted to JAMI elements in the way described above, the JAMI interpreter framework can run the aspect as part of a normal Java application. Typically, we write an explicit instruction to load and deploy the aspect at application startup. Once the aspect is deployed, JAMI ensures that the aspect behavior is called at the appropriate times, as described in the previous section.

In the following section, we introduce several examples to demonstrate the framework in detail. We focus on expressing each example using JAMI elements, showing the object structure of the JAMI representations of each aspect [1]. The full examples, including parsers and code that executes the mapping steps as described above, can be downloaded from the JAMI website [1].

3   Features of JAMI, Demonstrated by Example

In this section, we show 3 aspect languages optimized for a specific task, implemented using the Java Aspect Metamodel Interpreter. We first introduce a running example that we will use to demonstrate each language.

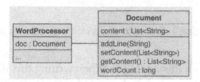

Fig. 2. Example application, used throughout the paper

Figure 2 shows the UML class-diagram of a simple word processor application. Within this application, class *Document* defines some methods to modify a document (*addLine()* and *setContent()*), a method to obtain the document content (*getContent*), as well as a method that counts the current number of words in the document (*wordCount*).

In the following subsections, we extend this example using aspects written in several domain-specific aspect languages. These extensions will allow us to: (1) create an autosave mechanism using a modularized version of the decorator pattern, (2) synchronize access to documents, such that multiple threads can access its content at the same time (for example, to run a background spellchecker), and (3) cache the results of expensive method calls, as long as variables on which the method depends are unchanged.

3.1   A Domain-Specific Language for the Decorator Pattern

Suppose we want to add autosave behavior to our word processing application. We can implement this using the decorator pattern [10] by defining a class *AutoSaveDocument*. This class implements the same methods as class *Document*, but adds the behavior to save any changes made to the document (e.g., to a file), before forwarding method calls to the original document object - see figure 3.

---

[1] In fact, the object diagrams in this paper are based on observing (using the Eclipse debugger) the actual runtime JAMI ASTs, which where automatically converted from the DSAL notations.

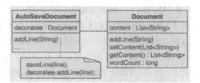

Fig. 3. Decorator pattern example

Listing 1 shows how we could use this decorator class:

```
 1  public class WordProcessor {
 2    Document doc;
 3    AutoSaveDocument autoSaveDoc;
 4
 5    public void testAutoSave() {
 6      doc = new Document();
 7      autoSaveDoc = new AutoSaveDocument(doc);
 8
 9      autoSaveDoc.addLine("AutoSaved"); // ok
10      doc.addLine("Not AutoSaved"); // bad!
11    }
12  }
```

Listing 1. Example of decorator pattern usage

There are two issues with this code. (1) When writing this in plain Java, we can still make calls to the object that is being decorated (also called the *decoratee*) - see line 10. This is almost certainly unintended, as the behavior of the decorator is not invoked this way. (2) Part of the code dealing with the decorator pattern is visible in the client (class *WordProcessor* in this example) – it is not fully modularized. We experiment with simple domain-specific extensions to Java to solve these issues.

Enforcing the Decorator Pattern. We start with the issue of enforcing the decorator pattern. Once a *decorator* is associated with a *decoratee* (listing 1, line 7), all subsequent calls should be made to the *decorator*. We define a small domain specific aspect language (DSAL) to enforce this - by automatically forwarding calls to a *decoratee* object to the *decorator*. In the first version of our language, a program in this DSAL defines which classes may act in the *decorator* and *decoratee* roles, respectively, see listing 2:

```
 1  decorate: Document -> AutoSaveDocument
```

Listing 2. An aspect language to enforce the decorator pattern

We take the specification in listing 2 to mean the following: objects of type *Document* may be decorated by objects of type *AutoSaveDocument*. However, we do not want to simply decorate every object of type *Document*. Doing so would defeat the purpose of the decorator design pattern, which is used to decide *dynamically* which objects should be decorated. Therefore, our first implementation will automatically infer the *decorator-decoratee* relationship between objects from the occurrence of constructor calls such as shown in listing 1, line 7. That is, an association is established upon calling a constructor of a class that is indicated to be a *decorator* in our DSAL specification (listing 2), of which the first argument is of the corresponding specified *decoratee* class.

Mapping to JAMI. To think of the above language in terms of an aspect language definition, we consider the aspect language concepts as shown in figure 1. The main task of programs written in this language is to intercept calls to *decoratee* objects, and forward them to the associated *decorator* object. In aspect terminology, the interception specification can be seen as a *pointcut*, whereas the forwarding part is an *advice* specification.

For the above pointcut/advice definition to make sense, the aspect program needs to know which objects are *associated* in the roles of *decoratee* and *decorator*, i.e. we need to establish and store this association as part of the aspect.

Therefore, to create the association, we intercept (using another pointcut) calls to the constructor of the type acting as *decorator*. The connected *advice* is to create an association between the object being created (the *decorator* object), and the first argument of the constructor call (which we assume to be the *decoratee* object, as discussed above). This association is stored as "aspect state", such that it can be shared between advices.

We now explain the mapping to JAMI in detail, by showing object diagrams that represent the aspect program given in listing 2. The object structures shown here consist largely of elements (classes) predefined by the JAMI framework. All these elements are described in the JAMI API documentation and reference manual, which is available online [1].

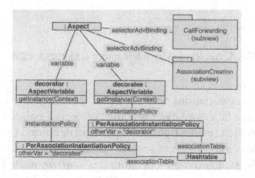

Fig. 4. Bindings between the parts of a decorator aspect

Figure 4 shows an aspect definition expressed using JAMI elements. The figure contains two subviews specifying "selector-advice-bindings", constructs connecting a particular pointcut to a particular advice. These subviews refer to figures 5 and 6, which we will discuss shortly. We model the grouping of several pointcut/advice combinations into a single aspect module to facilitate the sharing of state (data) between related advices. An "aspect" module can define its own variables, which can have different kinds of instantiation policies. For example, a "singleton" policy means that there is one instance of the variable for the entire program, a "per object" policy means there is one instance of the aspect variable for each target object (where the current target object depends on the join point context), etc. In JAMI, each variable can have its own instantiation policy, i.e. even variables within the same aspect module can have different instantiation policies.

Instantiation is usually implicit: new instances are automatically created when needed (using the default constructor of the specified variable type), i.e. on first use in a particular context. However, explicit instantiations are possible as well, as we will show in this example. Figure 4 shows two "aspect variables", *decorator* and *decoratee*, which have a 'per association' instantiation policy. This policy means that when the value of one variable is known, the value of the other one can be retrieved through it. In our implementation, this is done through the hashtable shared by the two instantiation policy objects. The associations themselves have to be explicitly instantiated, as we will show in the "AssociationCreation" subview (figure 5). The implementation of "association variables" is similar to the concept of "Association aspects" as proposed in [21].

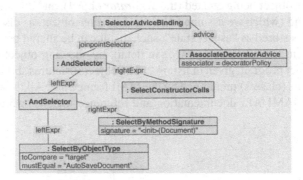

Fig. 5. Association by intercepting constructor calls

Figure 5 shows how associations between *decoratee* and *decorator* objects are created. The top element, a SelectorAdviceBinding connects a pointcut definition (on the left) to an advice definition (on the right). The pointcut definition (called "join point selector" in JAMI) in this case consists of several "primitive" selection criteria, which can be combined using the standard logic operators (i.e. *and*, *or*, *not*). The pointcut in this figure selects (a) constructor calls, (b) for which the type of the created object is "AutoSaveDocument", and (c) the constructor being called has 1 argument of type "Document". This pointcut is connected to a custom advice class – extending the framework – which explicitly creates the association between *decorator* (the constructed object) and *decoratee* (the value of the first argument). The class "AssociateDecoratorAdvice" (consisting of ca. 20 lines of code) is the only extension to JAMI needed to implement our decorator aspect language.

To finish the example, figure 6 shows the definition of the call forwarding part of the aspect. The pointcut in this figure (on the left) selects method calls for which the target object occurs as a *decoratee* value in the association table, *except* those for which the caller object is a *decorator*. Omitting this exception would make it impossible to reach

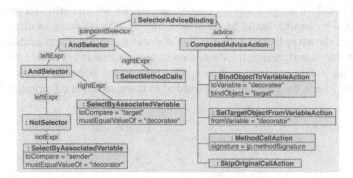

Fig. 6. Forwarding calls from decoratee to decorator

the *decoratee* object at all, and would in addition lead to an infinite loop on the first call to the *decorator* object (as the *decorator* will at some point call the *decoratee*, see figure 3).

The advice attached to this pointcut is composed of 4 predefined JAMI elements. The first, *BindObjectToVariableAction*, binds the value of the current target value to the variable *decoratee*. Next, the instruction *SetTargetObjectFromVariableAction* modifies the target object of the call to the value of the *decorator* variable, which can now be looked up through the corresponding aspect variable. Finally, we instruct the interpreter to execute the method call on the current target (in this case, set by the previous instruction). As we did not modify the signature of the called method, effectively a method with the same signature (as referred to by the current joinpoint context) is called, except on a different object (i.e. the *decorator* object instead of the *decoratee*). Finally, the instruction *SkipOriginalCallAction* instructs the interpreter not to execute the original call.

The sample program defining a JAMI-based "aspect-AST" (abstract syntax tree) as presented above can be downloaded from the JAMI website; when we initialize the aspect interpreter using this aspect, together with the "word processor" base program presented earlier, we can now write code calling the *decoratee* (as in listing 1, line 10), and still get the correct behavior. The call to the *decoratee* object (Document) is automatically forwarded to the *decorator* object (AutoSaveDocument).

Modularizing the Decorator Pattern. The simple aspect language defined above does not fully modularize the decorator pattern: associations are created in base code using explicit constructor calls to a *decorator*. If we want to fully separate the decorator from the base code, we have to find a way to specify *when* a *decorator* has to be created, and to *which decoratee* object it should apply. This is non-trivial, as the decorator pattern is (usually) to be applied selectively, i.e. not simply to all objects of a particular class.

In this section, we look at one way to specify decorator associations from an aspect. There are many possible ways to specify this, each having their own language design trade-offs. A benefit of using JAMI is that we can quickly prototype several proposals, so that we can experiment with the resulting language using real programs.

In the proposal we suggest, a programmer can specify which particular instance variable (indicated by name) should be decorated, and by which decorator class. We could specify this as shown in listing 3, line 1. The decorator is created and associated whenever a new value is assigned to the *decoratee* instance variable – variable "doc", in this case. In listing 3, this happens on line 7. The forwarding behavior stays the same as before, i.e. on line 9, the call will be forwarded to the auto-saving decorator.

```
 1  decorate: Document WordProcessor.doc -> AutoSaveDocument;
 2
 3  public class WordProcessor {
 4    Document doc;
 5
 6    public void testAutoSave() {
 7      doc = new Document();
 8
 9      doc.addLine("AutoSaved!");
10    }
11  }
```

Listing 3. Decorator example: modularized version

To implement this, we only have to replace the "association creation" part as it was shown in figure 5. Instead, we create the structure as shown in figure 7. The pointcut combines 3 criteria using the logical AND operator: the join point must be of the type *field assignment*, must be contained by class *WordProcessor*, and have the name/identifier *doc*. The advice is a custom advice class (extending the JAMI model) that associates the value assigned to the field (i.e. the *decoratee*) to a newly created and initialized *decorator* object.

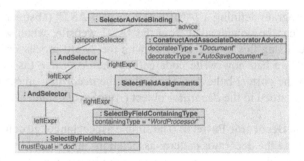

Fig. 7. Modularized creation of a decorator object

As shown above, we could implement our proposal by writing a minimal amount of (new) source code: a method constructing the (partial) aspect AST such as displayed in figure 7, as well as the custom advice class *ConstructAndAssociateDecoratorAdvice*. Everything else is already handled by the (existing) framework and interpreter. It took us 4 days to implement the entire language, enabling both the enforcement as well as modularization of the decorator pattern.

3.2   Using the D/COOL Domain-Specific Aspect Language for Synchronization

To show that JAMI can be used to conveniently accommodate more complex domain-specific languages as well, we implement a representative subset of the coordination aspect language "COOL", which is part of the D language framework. The language is documented extensively in the dissertation describing this framework [16].

Suppose we want to add a spellchecker to our word processor, which runs concurrently with the user interface by using a separate thread. To ensure correct behavior when multiple threads may access the document concurrently, we use a synchronization specification written in COOL, as shown in listing 4. By using COOL, we do not have to put any synchronization-related code in the Java source code itself.

```
1  coordinator Document {
2    selfex addLine, setContent;
3    mutex {addLine, setContent};
4
5    mutex {addLine, getContent};
6    mutex {addLine, wordCount};
7    mutex {setContent, getContent};
8    mutex {setContent, wordCount};
9  }
```

Listing 4. Using COOL to synchronize reader/writer access

Listing 4 specifies that we want to coordinate instances of class *Document*. Line 2 specifies that the methods *addLine* and *setContent* are self-exclusive; i.e. only 1 thread at a time may be running those methods. Line 3 specifies that these methods are mutually exclusive in addition; i.e. only one thread may be active in either *addLine* or *setContent* at a given time. Note that self-exclusion does not imply mutual exclusion: without mutual exclusion, it could still occur that one thread is running *addLine*, while another is running *setContent*. Vice versa, mutual exclusion does not imply self-exclusion either: although only one of the methods in a mutual exclusion specification may be running at the same time, multiple threads may be executing that one method.

Lines 5-8 also specify pairs of methods not allowed to run at the same time - *addLine* and *setContent* are writer methods, and should not run at the same time as reader methods *getContent* or *wordCount*.

By default, COOL synchronizes method access *per object*, i.e. in the above example, several threads can still run method *addLine* at the same time, as long as they do so within different object contexts. COOL also allows to specify a *per class* modifier, which makes the synchronization "global" for the specified class.

Mapping to JAMI.   We now describe a mapping of the subset of COOL described above to JAMI. First, for each method involved in a synchronization (i.e. selfex/mutex) specification, we calculate the set of methods that may not be entered while another thread is active within that method. For method *addLine*, this "exclusion set" contains *addLine* itself (because of the selfex specification on line 2), as well as methods *setContent*, *getContent* and *wordCount* (because of the mutex specifications on line 3, 5 and 6). How these exclusion sets are determined exactly is documented in [16]; we do not repeat the details here.

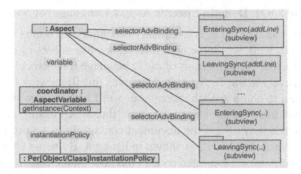

Fig. 8. Expressing COOL coordinators using JAMI concepts

A coordinator is modeled (see figure 8) as an aspect that defines one *AspectVariable* named *coordinator*. This variable has a "per object" or "per class" instantiation policy, depending on the specified granularity of the coordinator. Thus, the variable is shared between advices belonging to this coordinator, and can be used to regulate the synchronization. The instantiation policies in JAMI automatically give us the desired granularity as proscribed by the synchronization specification. Two selector-advice-bindings are defined for each method involved in a synchronization specification; one will be executed upon entering the method, one upon leaving.

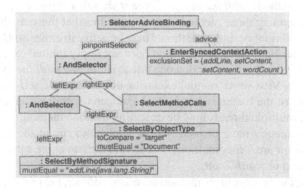

Fig. 9. Entering a synchronization context: pointcut and advice

Figure 9 shows the object diagram for the selector-advice-binding executed upon entering method *addLine*. It matches only join points of type *MethodCall*, of which the target object is of type *Document*, and of which the signature of the called method is *addLine*. Before the call is executed, we execute the advice *EnterSyncedContextAction*, an advice class specific to this language.

We show the source code of this advice in listing 5. First, the advice retrieves (line 2-4) the *coordinator* aspect variable instance belonging to this specific context (i.e. object or class, depending on the instantiation policy). This *coordinator* object ensures that the synchronization "bookkeeping" itself is properly synchronized. While the advice holds a lock on this object (line 6-21), it can safely inspect the *MethodState* objects for this coordinator. For each method (involved in synchronization), such a *MethodState* object tracks which threads are currently running that method. While other threads are active in any method in the exclusion set of the currently invoked method (line 11,12), the advice waits (releasing the lock on the *coordinator* while waiting) until this is no longer the case (line 14-16). When the loop is left, it means the method is free to run - after the advice registers the current thread with the corresponding *MethodState* object (line 20) and releases the lock on the coordinator object.

```
1   public boolean evaluate(InterpreterContext metaContext) {
2     CoordinatorImplementation coord =
3       (CoordinatorImplementation) metaContext.getAspect().
4       getDataFieldValue(metaContext, "coordinator");
5
6     synchronized(coord) {
7       boolean shouldWait;
8       do {
9         shouldWait = false;
10        // Wait while any other thread is active in any method in our exclusionset
11        for (String excludedMethod : exclusionSet)
12          shouldWait |= coord.getMethodState(excludedMethod).isActiveInOtherThread
                ();
13
14        if (shouldWait) {
15          try { coord.wait(); }
16          catch(InterruptedException e) { }
17        }
18      } while (shouldWait);
19      // This method is now allowed to run, register it
20      coord.getMethodState(myMethodName).enteringMethod();
21    }
22    return true;
23  }
```

Listing 5. Advice executed when entering a synchronized method

```
1   public boolean evaluate(InterpreterContext metaContext) {
2     CoordinatorImplementation coord = ...; //as in previous listing
3
4     synchronized(coord) {
5       // deregister this thread from running this method
6       coord.getMethodState(myMethodName).leavingMethod();
7       // Notify all threads (not just one), as potentially several may be allowed
              to continue
8       coord.notifyAll();
9     }
10    return true;
11  }
```

Listing 6. Advice executed when leaving a synchronized method

Similarly, another pointcut is created to intercept join points that occur upon *leaving* any of the methods involved in the synchronization specification. The object diagram is analogous to figure 9, except the pointcut now matches only join points of type *Method-Return*, and executes an advice of type *LeaveSyncedContextAction*. We show the source of this advice in listing 6. The advice waits until it obtains a lock on the coordinator object within the given context (object or class, as in the previous advice), allowing it to update the synchronization "bookkeeping". Once the lock is obtained, it deregisters the current thread from the *MethodState* object for this method (line 6). It then notifies all waiting threads (if any), such that they can re-evaluate their waiting conditions (line 8).

This concludes our implementation of (a subset of) COOL. The above essentially describes the same implementation mechanisms as used in [16], except using an interpreter-based implementation instead of source-code weaving. We believe that this exercise demonstrates the usefulness of JAMI in several ways. First, we successfully mapped an existing, complex language proposal to JAMI. In addition, it took minimal effort to build a functional prototype, which can be used on real base programs. It took 4 days to write the prototype, and it consists of only 500 lines of code. The advice code as shown in listings 5 and 6 comprises the majority of the actual implementation mechanism; in addition we created a parser for the subset of COOL used in this example (ca. 100 lines of code), an object-based representation of this AST (ca. 100 lines of code), as well as code to map such object-based COOL ASTs to "aspect-AST" structures such as shown in figure 8 and 9 (ca. 200 lines of code). Thus, JAMI proves useful as a "testbed" to prototype DSALs.

3.3   An Experimental DSAL to Implement Caching

As a final example, we implement an experimental language that introduces a modular way to specify caching of method return values (also called *memoization*).

Methods (or functions) to which memoization is applied, traditionally have to conform to the following conditions: (1) the method depends on its (input) parameters only; (2) given the same input parameter values, it should return the same result every time; (3) the method should have no side effects. Our implementation maintains the last two requirements. However, the first requirement is often violated in object-oriented programming, as results of a method call are often influenced by instance variables (within the same object) or specific method calls (on the same object). Therefore, our implementation extends the notion of memoization as defined above, by allowing cached results to be invalidated when the value of particular fields changes, or when particular methods are called.

In our example application from figure 2, the method *wordCount* is a good candidate for memoization, as repeatedly calculating the number of words – even when the document has not changed – can become quite time consuming on large documents. The method has no side effects, but depends on the value of instance variable *content*. This variable is written by method *setContent*, as it contains the statement "this.content = newContent;". The method *addLine*, containing the statement "content.add(line);" does not overwrite the instance variable itself; it does however modify its contained object structure. Therefore, calls to method *addLine* should also invalidate the return value of *wordCount*.

We specify the above using a domain specific aspect language as shown in listing 7.

```
1   cache Document object {
2     memoize wordCount,
3     invalidated by assigning content
4           or calling addLine(java.lang.String);
5   }
```

Listing 7. Example specification of a memoization aspect

This specification means the following: apply a caching aspect on each *Document* object (line 1). This caching aspect will memoize the return value of method *word-Count* (line 2). The cache will be invalidated when a new value is assigned to instance variable *content* within the corresponding *Document* object (line 3), or when the method *addline(..)* is called on the *Document* object (line 4).

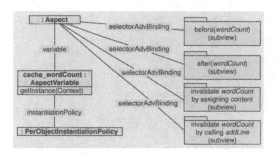

Fig. 10. Mapping a caching aspect to JAMI concepts

Mapping to JAMI. We now show how to map the specification shown in listing 7 to JAMI. As figure 10 shows, we create an aspect variable of type *Cache* for each *memoize* declaration. Its instantiation policy can again be specified as per object or per class - in the example above, we want to cache the return value of method *wordCount* for each object of type *Document*. The class *Cache* models a simple wrapper object that can store and retrieve an object, as well as clear its currently stored value.

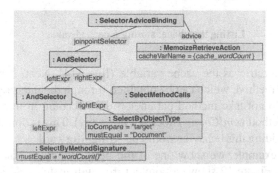

Fig. 11. Selector-advice binding for retrieving cached values

For each memoized method, we need a pointcut that intercepts calls to that method, coupled to an advice that returns the cached value (if one is stored). Another pointcut intercepts *returns* from the memoized method, coupled to an advice that stores the return value in the cache. Finally, a pointcut is needed for each cache validation specification, coupled with an advice that invalidates the cache. In this example there are two such pointcuts, corresponding to the invalidation specifications in line 3 and 4 of listing 7).

As shown in figure 11, we intercept calls to the method of which the results should be cached. The advice that is executed is shown in listing 8. First, the advice retrieves the aspect variable corresponding to this *memoize* declaration (line 2+3). If the cache currently contains a value (which means it must have been set after a previous call), we instruct the interpreter not to execute the original call after it finishes executing this advice (line 7), and instead to set the return value to the value found in the cache (line 8).

```
1   public boolean evaluate(InterpreterContext metaContext) {
2     Cache cache = (Cache)metaContext.getAspect()
3       .getDataFieldValue(metaContext, cacheVarName);
4
5     if (cache.hasValue())
6     { // Use cached value!
7       metaContext.setExecuteOriginalCall(false);
8       metaContext.setReturnValue(cache.getValue());
9     }
10    return true;
11  }
```

Listing 8. Advice: retrieving a cached value

After the method returns, the advice in listing 9 is called, which stores the return value of the method.

```
1   public boolean evaluate(InterpreterContext metaContext) {
2     Cache cache = (Cache)metaContext.getAspect()
3       .getDataFieldValue(metaContext, cacheVarName);
4
5     cache.setValue(metaContext.getReturnValue());
6     return true;
7   }
```

Listing 9. Advice: storing a cached value

First, the advice retrieves the cache variable (line 3+4). Next, it stores the return value of the called method, which can be obtained through the interpreter context (line 6). Note that we do not take method parameters into account in this implementation (fortunately, the method *wordCount()* does not have any). This is done to avoid cluttering the example; adding this behavior would be straightforward.

To finalize our example, we show one of the pointcut-advice-bindings used to invalidate the cache. Figure 12 shows a pointcut that will match field assignments, but only to the field named *content*, and when the assignment takes place within an object of type *Document*. The advice is to call the method *clearValue* on the aspect variable

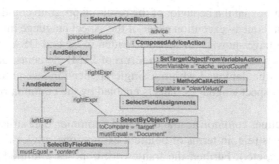

Fig. 12. Selector-advice binding for invalidating cached values

cache_wordCount. The cache can also be invalidated by particular method calls; this binding reuses the same advice, but has a pointcut selecting the specified method, in a way equivalent to many of the examples shown above, e.g. in figure 11.

It took us 3 days to implement this language, including a parser for specifications as shown in 7 and an automated mapping of the parsed structure to the JAMI object diagrams as shown in this section.

4 Composition of Multiple DSALs

As each DSAL is designed to address concerns within a particular problem domain, we would often want to combine the use of several such languages within a single application[2]. Implementing this is not straightforward however, as partial programs expressed in several languages have to be composed into a single combined, working application. Even if this is technically feasible (which is not necessarily the case), running the combined application may reveal unexpected and/or undesired results.

In this section, we discuss how several aspects written in different DSALs (all implemented using JAMI) can be composed and used within the same application. We discuss several difficulties that may occur in this case, and explain how JAMI can help to address these issues.

4.1 DSAL Composition in JAMI

In general, the composition of multiple aspect languages is far from trivial. As an example, consider the common implementation of aspect languages as transformation of the source code or byte code representation of the base program (where each of these aspect language implementations may, or may not, share a common infrastructure). This would require the sequential execution of aspect language implementations over the incrementally transformed base code. Typically, such a byte code transformation is not

---

[2] Note that the entire discussion about the composition of DSALs technically also holds for the composition of general purpose aspect languages, or a mixture of these. However, we believe composition of DSALs is much more realistic to expect, hence we focus on this.

commutative, meaning that the behavior of the resulting program could vary, according to the –normally undefined– execution order of the aspect language implementations.

In section 3, we have shown how aspects written in several DSALs are mapped to JAMI elements. Such aspects, expressed in terms of JAMI elements, or refinements of JAMI elements, can be deployed within a single application–even though they originate from different aspect languages. This is enabled by the common runtime platform provided by JAMI.

This platform defines common abstractions and a common data structure for the representation of aspects (e.g. in terms of pointcut expressions, advice-selector bindings, ordering constraints, etc.). Further, the framework imposes a unified high-level control flow for the execution of aspects, as shown schematically in figure 1. At the same time, while adopting these predefined abstractions and high-level control flow, for each language there is a large freedom to define in varying ways how e.g. pointcuts can be defined and matched.

Thus, using JAMI, it is possible to execute aspects written in different DSALs within a single application. This does not require any tailoring or design decisions that are specific to the other DSALs that are combined. However, this does not guarantee that the resulting application will show the "correct" or "desired" behavior. As is the case with aspects written in a single language, interactions or interference may also occur between aspects written in different DSALs.

This phenomenon has also been observed before: e.g. in [17], two categories of aspect interactions are distinguished[3]:

- *co-advising*: the composition of advice of multiple aspect languages at a shared join point.
- *foreign advising*: this corresponds to the notion of "aspects on aspects", where advice from one aspect language may apply to a join point associated with the execution of advice in another aspect language.

In the remainder of section 4, we first discuss the issue of co-advising, followed by an explanation of the advice composition mechanism of JAMI in section 4.3, and finally a discussion of foreign advising. These problems are all illustrated by combining the aspects shown in section 3 within the same application.

4.2 Co-advising

When multiple pointcuts match at the same join point, the order in which advices bound to these pointcuts are executed may lead to different behavior [20,9], if there are dependencies between the aspects. Reversely, in the absence of any ordering specification at shared join points, the application behavior may be non-predictable and undesirable.

The above is also true if the shared join points originate from programs written in different aspect languages. For individual languages, many mechanisms exist to deal with this.

However, when pointcuts originate from different languages, there are two additional issues:

---

[3] [17] defines these terms using a description based on weaving semantics, we reformulated these in terms of aspect execution.

198   W. Havinga, L. Bergmans, and M. Aksit

- We need improved or additional mechanisms to compose advices from different aspect languages. The reason is that we (want to) assume DSALs to be developed independently, so that aspects written in a particular DSAL are likely (and preferably) unaware of those written in another DSAL. JAMI supports a uniform constraint model (first proposed in [20]) that facilitates ordering constraints *within* as well as *between* languages. We demonstrate this below.
- There is a distinction between *language-level* and *program-level* composition [17]. In particular for DSALs, composition constraints may be specific to a combination of DSALs, and should apply to all aspects written in those DSALs (i.e. language-level constraints). However, it may –in addition– be possible that some constraints are program-specific (i.e. program level).

Example: Composing the Synchronization and Caching Aspects. When we deploy the aspects for synchronization (shown in listing 4) and caching (listing 7) within our original application (see figure 2), we observe that several shared join points occur, as most calls to methods within class *Document* are advised by both aspects. Therefore, we need to determine in what order these advices should be executed.

As an example, we consider the join point that occurs when returning from method *wordCount*.

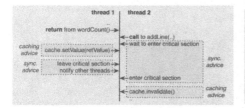
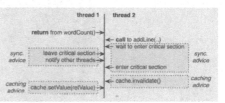

Fig. 13. Concurrent execution; correct advice ordering

Fig. 14. Incorrect advice ordering

At this join point, a caching advice will store the value that was returned by the method. The synchronization advice leaves the critical section that was entered before the method was executed, as shown in listing 6. In this case, the caching advice –at the end of a method– should be executed before the synchronization advice. This is illustrated in figure 13, whereas figure 14 illustrates a specific scenario of two threads where –in both cases– the synchronization advice precedes the caching advice. In the latter case, a different thread executing a *writer* method may invalidate the cache as soon as the critical section is left, while subsequently the caching aspect stores an (already invalidated!) value in the cache. In that case, the next call to *wordCount* would return a cached value that is incorrect.

To generalize the example, we observe that any caching advice should occur within the critical sections as imposed by the synchronization advice. Specifically, for advices executed at a shared *MethodCalljoinpoint*, the synchronization advice should have precedence, while at a shared *MethodReturnJoinpoint*, the caching advice should have precedence. This is an example of a language-level composition constraint.

Example: Composing Further with the Decorator Aspect. As a test case, we illustrate the composition of three DSALs in JAMI, including a join point where advices from all three languages must be applied. In addition to the synchronization and caching aspects discussed above, we add the decorator aspect as shown in listing 2 to our application. This means that for objects of type *Document* that are decorated, all calls to methods within *Document* will be forwarded instead to *AutoSaveDocument*. Thus, shared join points may occur where all three aspects (each originating from a different language) want to execute an advice. In this case, the desired behavior is more complex than simply ordering the advices.

When a call is redirected by a forwarding advice (as defined by a decorator aspect), the original call does no longer lead to the execution of a method –as specified by the *SkipOriginalCallAction* in figure 6. Therefore, after the execution of the advice of the decorator aspect (in this case), there is no method execution join point active. Effectively, this means that no other advices should be executed at this join point. This implies that any advice from the decorator aspect should be executed before advices specified by both other languages. After all, it would be illogical to continue and cache or synchronize the execution of a method that will not be executed at all.

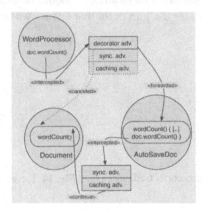

Fig. 15. Control flow combining aspects from 3 DSALs

In figure 15, we illustrate that the intended behavior is obtained by ordering the advices per language as described above. When method *Document.wordCount* is called, all three aspects match this join point. The decorator advice will be executed first, and forwards the call to *AutoSaveDoc.wordCount*, as a result canceling the original call. In addition, it ensures that no other advices are executed at this join point. Subsequently, the implementation of *AutoSaveDoc.wordCount* calls *Document.addLine* again. The decorator aspect does not match this (new!) join point, as internal calls from decorator to decoratee should not be intercepted (as defined by the pointcut expression in figure 6). The other two aspects both match this join point however, and are executed in an order such that caching takes place within the critical section of the synchronization advice.

This example illustrates that with JAMI, composition of more than two aspect languages is supported, even in the presence of delicate interdependencies; JAMI supports the expression of the necessary composition constraints such that the intended effect of each aspect is preserved.

4.3   The Advice Composition Mechanism of JAMI

JAMI offers two complementary advice composition mechanisms. First, it implements a generic ordering constraint mechanism as proposed in [19,20]. At shared join points, constraints may limit which advices are currently applicable. Such constraints may be conditional, and may for example depend on which advices where already executed (at the same join point). Even so, the application of constraints may still leave several advices eligible for execution. Second, JAMI therefore supports a "scheduling" interface to determine the further selection of advice execution. Different strategies can be implemented to disambiguate the selection of advice. Our default implementation picks an arbitrary element from the set of applicable bindings, and in addition prints a warning that the program is potentially ambiguous. In addition, the scheduler can decide to cancel further advice executions at a given join point, if requested to do so by particular advice actions[4].

Constraints are specified over selector-advice-bindings, as these are the primary elements over which we want to express ordering criteria –as opposed to ordering specified per advice, pointcut, or aspect. The reason is that advices (and pointcuts) can be reused in several bindings; the desired ordering may be different per binding. In addition, selector-advice-bindings are the most "low-level" construct within JAMI to which an ordering can be applied. Ordering between aspects can be expressed in terms of (several) constraints between selector-advice-bindings. These are examples of *program-level* constraints. *Language-level* constraints are also expressed in terms of (several) constraints between individual selector-advice-bindings. The framework could include 'convenience methods' to allow to directly express constraints between all bindings within particular aspects, or between all bindings of all aspects written in a particular language. We believe that the constraint mechanism adopted by the framework can be used as the basis of any such higher-level ordering mechanism.

Constraints are decoupled from the "aspect modules" (as shown in e.g. figure 4), and are instead kept as a separate set of entities within the aspect evaluation framework. This enables the specification of constraints between selector-advice-bindings that are part of several aspects, or that even originate from several aspect languages. It would even be possible to define a "constraint language" that can express constraints over aspects from several different DSALs, although this requires that DSALs make it possible to identify (e.g. by name) the entities to which an ordering may need to be applied.

As discussed above, for our example we want to specify language-level composition based on the originating language of each selector-advice-binding. We do not need any program-level constraints, in this case. Therefore, we simply create constraints between all selector-advice-bindings, such that caching advices occur within the critical section created by synchronization aspects (if the advices apply at the same join point), and decorator advices get even higher priority.

---

[4] This corresponds to the run-time detection and resolution of aspect interactions in [23].

Finally, we extend the "forwarding" advice of the decorator aspect (as shown in figure 6) with an advice action that instructs the scheduler to cancel any other advices at the current join point. We argue that this action should be part of the decorator language, as its "forwarding" advice effectively negates the occurrence of the join point at which it is executed. Therefore, no other advices should be executed at that join point.

A functional implementation (in JAMI) that composes aspects written in all three DSALs discussed in this paper – including the constraints as discussed in this section, is downloadable as part of the example discussed throughout this paper [1].

4.4 Foreign Advising

Another way to compose aspects, which we did not discuss so far, is the application of aspects on aspects. In particular, the application of advice written in one DSAL on another advice written in a different DSAL, is also called "foreign advising" [17].

Within JAMI, advices expressed in any DSAL are eventually executed in terms of the same kind of instructions used by the base program (e.g. using objects and method calls). Such advice instructions can again be advised, like any normal base language construct. A weaver-based approach must make sure to weave aspects (written in several DSALs) in a particular order, to ensure that the effects of one DSAL can be advised by another –or to ensure that they are *not* advised by another DSAL. As no weaving takes place within JAMI, the execution of advice is simply a runtime occurrence that can be intercepted like any other join point, if needed.

We test the application of "foreign advice" within JAMI by applying a decorator aspect to the caching aspect discussed in listing 7. Our example decorator class logs the actions of the caching aspect, which can be useful when e.g. debugging the caching aspect. We use the following decorator specification:

```
1  decorate: MemoizeRetrieveAction -> MemoizeLogDecorator
```

This specification intercepts all executions of the memoization advice, and redirects them instead to an instance of class *MemoizeLogDecorator*, which logs the activity of the caching aspect and then forwards the call back to the original advice method. Thus, it applies an advice to the caching advice.

As a final note, we remark that the advising of advice can quite easily lead to infinite interception loops. Therefore, by default, we exclude all framework classes (and extensions thereof, such as class *MemoizeRetrieveAction*) from interception by the framework. However, in cases where interception is desired, an annotation can be used to indicate that a particular class should be included for interception. On the other hand, method executions within the base language that are caused by advice executions are by default intercepted.

5   Discussion

In this section, we discuss some of the important design decisions and implementation characteristics of JAMI.

5.1 Efficiency vs. Flexibility

JAMI is designed to provide maximum flexibility while designing or testing new aspect languages or language features. As a result, in cases where we had to choose between flexibility and efficiency, we chose the former. For example, the interception of all joinpoints within an application is not very attractive from a performance point of view. However, using this mechanism makes it much simpler to experiment with pointcuts that depend on complex combinations of runtime state (including historic information). While designing a language, the developer can ignore such details as e.g. deciding which part of a pointcut can be evaluated statically, and which remaining dynamic checks have to be woven at such statically determined "shadow join points". In addition, when composing several DSALs, the effects of one DSAL may influence the static evaluation of pointcuts in other DSALs. Using JAMI, such issues do not occur, as the entire pointcut evaluation takes place at runtime.

However, when creating an efficient language implementation is a primary design goal rather than the prototyping of (new) language features, the use of other frameworks such as *abc* [2] may be more suitable.

A research framework that aims specifically at modeling efficient implementation techniques of AO mechanisms is ALIA [4]. We are currently exploring the possibility to (manually) map JAMI models to ALIA models. In this way, one could use the JAMI framework to experiment with the language design, and subsequently use the ALIA framework to implement the language to be as efficient as possible.

5.2 Modeling Different Types of Advice

JAMI does not make a distinction between different types of advice, such as *around*, *before* or *after* advice. Join points *before* and *after* method calls are simply considered different (kinds of) join points alltogether (i.e. *MethodCall* and *MethodReturn* join points). The two defining features of *around* advice (as it is known in e.g. AspectJ) are the ability (1) to share state between the *before* and *after* advice parts around a method call (using local variables within the advice definition), and (2) to decide whether or not to execute the code at the location of the current join point (determined by whether or not the advice "executes" a *proceed* construct). Both can be accomplished using JAMI as well; the first by using aspect variables with an appropriate instantiation policy, the second by using meta-advice actions that instruct the interpreter whether or not to execute the code at the current join point. For an example using both features, see section 3.3. We believe that our advice model allows more freedom over the specification of e.g. advice ordering and the semantics of particular advice actions, while it is also able to accommodate existing advice models, as indicated above.

6 Related Work

In [18], Masuhara and Kiczales propose the Aspect Sand Box, an interpreter framework to model aspect mechanisms. Using this framework, the effects of aspects are defined in terms of weaving semantics. The weaving process is modeled by extending or modifying the interpreter of a base language that models a single-inheritance OO language (which can be seen as a core subset of Java). In comparison, JAMI defines a common runtime environment for aspects, which allows us to express explicit ordering constraints between advices, and enables the deployment of multiple aspect languages within a single application. As discussed in section 4, it would be harder to define a single weaver that models the composition of multiple languages. Essentially, JAMI can be seen as an implementation of a single, parameterized (by using different predefined framework classes) aspect composition process as indicated in the future work section of [18]. In this sense, JAMI can be seen as an elaboration on the ideas proposed in the Aspect Sand Box project, thus enabling the implementation of additional features such as mentioned above.

The AspectBench Compiler (*abc*) [2] is a workbench that – like JAMI – facilitates experimentation with new (aspect) language features. Unlike JAMI however, it focuses mainly on extensions to AspectJ, and strives to provide an industrial-strength compiler architecture that facilitates efficient implementations of extensions to the AspectJ language. In contrast, while designing JAMI we specifically tried to avoid design decisions that would limit the flexibility of our framework, as discussed in section 5.1. In addition, *abc* is not designed to handle composition between multiple languages.

In [3], Bagge and Kalleberg propose to implement DSALs by creating a library that implements a program transformation system (cf. weaver), in addition to a notation that "configures" the behavior of this library. The paper does not discuss the composition of multiple DSALs, or the ordering of advices at shared joinpoints.

In [5], Bräuer and Lochmann describe how to integrate multiple DSLs based on a common semantic metamodel, using an MDA-based transformation approach. Like JAMI, this provides a model to integrate modularized specifications written in several DSLs. However, the paper aims to propose a common semantic model for the composition of multiple DSLs in general – as opposed to expressing *crosscutting* functionality (i.e. aspects) in particular, as is the focus of JAMI. Likely as a result of this, the paper does not discuss the interference issues that may result from composing multiple crosscutting specifications.

The work from Kojarski and Lorenz [17,14,13] is strongly related to ours; in particular, they also investigate the issue around the composition of multiple aspect languages.

In [14], seven interaction patterns among features of composed aspect languages are described. Some of these, such as *emergent advice ordering*, are also discussed in this paper. However, because (1) JAMI introduces its own set of *abstract features*, such as selector-advice bindings, and (2) in our interpreter-based approach, individual aspect languages are not translated into base language terminology, hence, there is never accidental interaction, not all interaction patterns are applicable. However, the proposed analysis approach could also be applied in the context of our work.

In [17,13], the AWESOME framework is described; instead of an interpreter-based approach, this adopts a weaver-based approach, that also addresses foreign advising, and language-level, but currently –according to [17] – not program level co-advising (which we presented in section 4.3).

The *Reflex* AOP kernel [24,23] is also closely related work; it is a reflection-based kernel for AOP languages, with a specific focus on the composition of aspect programs.

To this extent, it provides an (extensible) set of composition operators, which can be used when translating an aspect specification to a representation in terms of the kernel-level abstractions. Although there are many similarities with JAMI, a key difference of the current implementation is that it is weaving-based, rather than interpreter-based. Mostly due to this, the support for foreign advising is limited (as e.g. exemplified in [14]).

The XAspects project [22] implements a system to map DSALs to AspectJ source code. The approach addresses the need to compose aspects written in multiple DSAL, but does not provide explicit mechanisms to deal with interactions between aspects, other than suggesting the use of the AspectJ *declare precedence* construct. Compared to this, JAMI offers more elaborate ways to specify the composition of aspects.

In [6], Brichau et.al. propose the definition and composition of DSALs ("Aspect-Specific Languages") using Logic Metaprogramming. Although their approach is not based on a typical OO framework, it does allow the reuse and refinement of aspect languages. It is based (in [6]) on static source code weaving (by method-level wrapping). The composition of aspect languages (program level composition is not supported) is achieved by explicit composition of languages into new, combined languages. In our opinion, this is less flexible, as it requires explicit composition for each configuration of aspect DSALs that occur in an application, and the late addition of a new aspect language in a system may not be possible without restructuring the composition hierarchy.

7   Conclusion

In this paper, we introduced an aspect interpreter framework aimed at the prototyping of (domain-specific) aspect languages. We demonstrated the framework by implementating three domain-specific aspect languages, and also briefly discussed the workflow used to implement these. Using our framework, it took only 3-4 days (per language) to create functional prototypes of these diverse DSALs. Aspects written in these DSALs can be composed with regular Java programs at runtime, in an interpreted style.

We have used JAMI in a programming language course to teach the common aspect language concepts and various implementations thereof. As part of this course, students successfully developed small DSALs within limited allotted time. This supports our claim that JAMI can be used to prototype DSALs while requiring relatively little effort, even including the learning curve of the framework itself.

We contribute the effectiveness of JAMI as a framework for prototyping DSALs in large part to its flexibility and expressiveness. For example, as aspects are completely dynamically evaluated, it is easy to experiment with pointcuts that express complex selection criteria over the runtime state. In addition, our support for "aspect state" using variables that each may have different instantiation policies provides a flexible way to implement aspect language features, while requiring relatively little effort.

We have shown that our framework supports applications composed of aspects written in several DSALs. In addition, we have discussed interactions that may occur when combining multiple DSALs, and demonstrated mechanisms implemented as part of JAMI to specify aspect composition – also of aspects written in different languages.

The complete framework as well as the examples shown in this paper can be downloaded from the JAMI website [1].

Acknowledgments

This work is supported by European Commission grant IST-2-004349: European Network of Excellence on Aspect-Oriented Software Development (AOSD-Europe).

References

1. Java Aspect Metamodel Interpreter (2007), http://jami.sf.net/
2. Avgustinov, P., Christensen, A.S., Hendren, L.J., Kuzins, S., Lhoták, J., Lhoták, O., de Moor, O., Sereni, D., Sittampalam, G., Tibble, J.: abc: An extensible aspectj compiler. Transactions on Aspect-Oriented Software Development I 3880, 293–334 (2006)
3. Bagge, A.H., Kalleberg, K.T.: DSAL = library+notation: Program transformation for domain-specific aspect languages. In: Proceedings of the Domain-Specific Aspect Languages Workshop (October 2006)
4. Bockisch, C., Mezini, M.: A flexible architecture for pointcut-advice language implementations. In: VMIL 2007: Proceedings of the 1st workshop on Virtual machines and intermediate languages for emerging modularization mechanisms, ACM Press, New York (2007)
5. Bräuer, M., Lochmann, H.: Towards semantic integration of multiple domain-specific languages using ontological foundations. In: Proceedings of 4th International Workshop on (Software) Language Engineering (ATEM 2007) co-located with MoDELS 2007 (October 2007) (to appear)
6. Brichau, J., Mens, K., De Volder, K.: Building composable aspect-specific languages with logic metaprogramming. In: Batory, D., Consel, C., Taha, W. (eds.) GPCE 2002. LNCS, vol. 2487, pp. 110–127. Springer, Heidelberg (2002)
7. Brichau, J., Mezini, M., Noyé, J., Havinga, W., Bergmans, L., Gasiunas, V., Bockisch, C., Fabry, J., D'Hondt, T.: An Initial Metamodel for Aspect-Oriented Programming Languages. Technical Report AOSD-Europe Deliverable D39, Vrije Universiteit Brussel, 27 February 2006 (2006)
8. D'Hondt, M., D'Hondt, T.: Is domain knowledge an aspect? In: Lopes, C.V., Black, A., Kendall, L., Bergmans, L. (eds.) ECOOP 1999 (1999)
9. Douence, R., Fradet, P., Südholt, M.: Composition, reuse and interaction analysis of stateful aspects. In: Lieberherr [15], pp. 141–150
10. Gamma, E., Helm, R., Johnson, R., Vlissides, J.: Design Patterns: Elements of Reusable Object-Oriented Software. Addison-Wesley, Reading (1994)
11. Havinga, W.K., Staijen, T., Rensink, A., Bergmans, L.M.J., van den Berg, K.G.: An abstract metamodel for aspect languages. Technical Report TR-CTIT-06-22, Enschede (May 2006)
12. Kiczales, G., Lamping, J., Mendhekar, A., Maeda, C., Lopes, C., Loingtier, J.-M., Irwin, J.: Aspect-oriented programming. In: Aksit, M., Matsuoka, S. (eds.) ECOOP 1997. LNCS, vol. 1241, pp. 220–242. Springer, Heidelberg (1997)
13. Kojarski, S., Lorenz, D.H.: Awesome: an aspect co-weaving system for composing multiple aspect-oriented extensions. SIGPLAN Not. 42(10), 515–534 (2007)
14. Kojarski, S., Lorenz, D.H.: Identifying feature interactions in multi-language aspect-oriented frameworks. In: Proceedings of the 29th International Conference on Software Engineering ICSE 2007, Minneapolis, MN, May 20-26 2007, pp. 147–157. IEEE Computer Society Press, Los Alamitos (2007)

15. Lieberherr, K. (ed.): Proc. 3rd Int' Conf. on Aspect-Oriented Software Development AOSD 2004. ACM Press, New York (2004)
16. Lopes, C.V.: D: A Language Framework for Distributed Programming. PhD thesis, College of Computer Science, Northeastern University (1997)
17. Lorenz, D.H., Kojarski, S.: Understanding aspect interactions, co-advising and foreign advising. In: ECOOP 2007 Second International Workshop on Aspects, Dependencies and Interactions (2007)
18. Masuhara, H., Kiczales, G.: Modeling crosscutting in aspect-oriented mechanisms. In: Cardelli, L. (ed.) ECOOP 2003. LNCS, vol. 2743, pp. 2–28. Springer, Heidelberg (2003)
19. Nagy, I.: On the Design of Aspect-Oriented Composition Models for Software Evolution. PhD thesis, University of Twente (June 2006)
20. Nagy, I., Bergmans, L., Aksit, M.: Composing aspects at shared join points. In: Robert Hirschfeld, A.P., Kowalczyk, R., Weske, M. (eds.) Proceedings of International Conference NetObjectDays, NODe2005, Erfurt, Germany, September 2005. Lecture Notes in Informatics, vol. P-69, Gesellschaft für Informatik (GI) (2005)
21. Sakurai, K., Masuhara, H., Ubayashi, N., Matsuura, S., Komiya, S.: Association aspects. In: Lieberherr [15], pp. 16–25.
22. Shonle, M., Lieberherr, K., Shah, A.: XAspects: an extensible system for domain-specific aspect languages. In: OOPSLA 2003: Companion of the 18th annual ACM SIGPLAN conference on Object-oriented programming, systems, languages, and applications, pp. 28–37. ACM Press, New York (2003)
23. Tanter, É.: Aspects of composition in the Reflex AOP kernel. In: Löwe, W., Südholt, M. (eds.) SC 2006. LNCS, vol. 4089, pp. 98–113. Springer, Heidelberg (2006)
24. Tanter, É., Noyé, J.: A versatile kernel for multi-language AOP. In: Glück, R., Lowry, M. (eds.) GPCE 2005. LNCS, vol. 3676, pp. 173–188. Springer, Heidelberg (2005)

Assessing the Impact of Aspects on Exception Flows: An Exploratory Study

Roberta Coelho[1,2], Awais Rashid[2], Alessandro Garcia[2], Fabiano Ferrari[2],
Nélio Cacho[2], Uirá Kulesza[3,4], Arndt von Staa[1], and Carlos Lucena[1]

[1] Computer Science Department – Pontifical Catholic University of Rio de Janeiro, Brazil
[2] Computing Department, Lancaster University, Lancaster, UK
[3] CITI/DI/FCT - New University of Lisbon, Portugal
[4] Recife Center for Advanced Studies and Systems, Brazil
{roberta, arndt,lucena}@inf.puc-rio.br,
{marash,garciaa, ferrari.f, n.cacho}@comp.lancs.ac.ak
uira@di.fct.unl.pt

Abstract. Exception handling mechanisms are intended to support the development of robust software. However, the implementation of such mechanisms with aspect-oriented (AO) programming might lead to error-prone scenarios. As aspects extend or replace existing functionality at specific join points in the code execution, aspects' behavior may bring new exceptions, which can flow through the program execution in unexpected ways. This paper presents a systematic study that assesses the error proneness of AOP mechanisms on exception flows of evolving programs. The analysis was based on the object-oriented and the aspect-oriented versions of three medium-sized systems from different application domains. Our findings show that exception handling code in AO systems is error-prone, since all versions analyzed presented an increase in the number of *uncaught* exceptions and exceptions caught by the wrong handler. The causes of such problems are characterized and presented as a catalogue of bug patterns.

Keywords: Exception handling, aspect-oriented programs, static analysis, empirical study, uncaught exceptions, obsolete handler, unintended handler.

1 Introduction

Exception handling mechanisms aim at improving software modularity and system robustness by promoting explicit separation between normal and error handling code. It allows the system to detect errors and respond to them correspondingly, through the execution of recovery code encapsulated into handlers. The importance of exception handling mechanisms is attested by the fact they are realized in many mainstream programming languages, such as Java, C++ and C#.

The goal of Aspect-Oriented Programming (AOP) [41] is to modularize concerns that crosscut the primary decomposition of a system (e.g., functions, classes, components) through a new abstraction called aspect. Aspects use specific constructs to perform invasive modifications of programs [1], and include additional behavior at specific points in the code. AOP is being exploited to improve the modularity of

J. Vitek (Ed.): ECOOP 2008, LNCS 5142, pp. 207–234, 2008.
© Springer-Verlag Berlin Heidelberg 2008

exception handling and other equally-important crosscutting concerns, such as transaction management [31], distribution [31], and certain design patterns [13, 15]. According to some studies [5, 6, 7, 9, 20, 31], AOP has succeeded in improving the modular treatment of several exception handling scenarios. However, it is recognized that flexible programming mechanisms (e.g., inheritance and polymorphism [24]) might have negative effects on exception handling. Hence, while the invasiveness of aspect composition mechanisms may bring a realm of possibilities to software design, often allowing for more stable crosscutting designs [14, 25, 9], they might be useless for practical purposes if they make the exception handling code error prone. Aspectual refinements of base behavior can either improve abnormal behavior robustness or adversely contribute to typical problems of poorly designed error handling code, such as exception subsumption [29] and unintended handler action [24, 29].

Unfortunately, there is no systematic evaluation of the positive and negative effects of AOP on the robustness of exception handling code. Existing research in the literature has been limited to analyze the impact of aspects on the normal control flow [8, 18, 19, 27]. In addition, most of the empirical studies of AOP do not go beyond the discussion of modularity gains and pitfalls obtained when aspects are applied to exception handling [5, 6, 7] and other crosscutting concerns [9, 14, 26, 31]. For instance, these studies do not account for the consequences bearing with new exceptions and handlers that come along with the aspects' added functionality.

This paper reports a first systematic study that quantitatively assesses the error proneness of aspect composition mechanisms on exception flows of programs. The evaluation was based on an exception flow analysis tool (developed in this work) and code inspection of exception behaviors in Java and AspectJ [33] implementations of two industrial software systems – Health Watcher [14, 31] and Mobile Photo [9] – and one open-source project – JHotDraw [16][1]. For the first two systems more than one release was examined. Overall, this corresponds to 10 system releases, 41.1 KLOC of Java source code of which around 4.1 KLOC are dedicated to exception handling, and 39 KLOC lines of AspectJ source code, of which around 3.2 KLOC are dedicated to exception handling. These systems are representatives of different application domains and exhibit heterogeneous exception handling strategies. Some negative outcomes were consistently detected through the analyzed releases using AOP, such as:

- higher evidence of *uncaught exceptions* [17] when aspect advices act as exception *handlers*, thereby leading to unpredictable system crashes [34]; and
- a multitude of *exception subsumptions* [29], some of them leading to *unintended handlers* [24], .i.e, exceptions that are thrown by aspects and unexpectedly caught by existing handlers in the base code;

The causes of such increases were investigated, and are presented in the form of a bug pattern catalogue related to the exception handling code. During this study we implemented an exception flow analysis tool for Java and AspectJ programs, which was very useful when finding and characterizing these bugs. The contributions of this study are as follows:

---

[1] The source code of all systems used in this study is available on the website http://www. inf.puc-rio.br/~roberta/aop_exceptions.

- It performs the first systematic analysis which aims at investigating how aspects affect the exception flows of programs.
- It introduces a set of bug-patterns related to the exception handling code of AO programs that were characterized based on the data empirically collected.
- It presents an exception flow analysis tool for Java and AspectJ programs, which was developed to support the analysis.

The contributions of this work allow for: (i) developers of robust aspect-oriented applications to make more informed decisions in the presence of evolving exception flows, and (ii) designers of AOP languages and static analysis tools to consider pushing the boundaries of existing mechanisms to make AOP more robust and resilient to changes. The remainder of this paper is organized as follows. Section 2 describes basic concepts associated with exception handling in AO programs. Section 3 defines the hypotheses and configuration of our exploratory study, the target applications and the evaluation procedures. Section 4 reports our analysis of the empirical data collected in this study. Section 5 presents a bug catalogue for exception handling code in AO systems based on the bug patterns that actually happened in each investigated system, and Section 6 provides further discussions and lessons learned. Section 7 describes the related work. Finally, Section 8 presents our conclusions and directions for future work. Due to space limitations, throughout this article we assume that the reader is familiar with AOP terminology (i.e., aspect, join point, pointcut, and advice) and the syntax of AspectJ's main constructs.

2   Characterizing the Exception Handling Mechanism in AO Programs

In order to support the reasoning about exception flows in AO programs we present the main concepts of an exception-handling mechanism and correlate each element with the constructs available in most AO languages. An exception handling mechanism is comprised of four main concepts: the exception, the exception signaler, the exception handler, and the exception model that defines how signalers and handlers are bound [12].

Exception Raising. An exception is raised by an element - method or method-like construct, e.g., advice - when an abnormal state is detected. In most languages an exception is usually assumed as an error, and represents an abnormal computation state. Whenever an exception is raised inside an element that cannot handle it, it is signaled to the element's caller. The exception signaler is the element that detects the abnormal state and raises the exception. Thus, in AO programs the signaler can be either a method or an advice. In Figure 1, the advice a1 detects an abnormal condition and raises the exception EX. Since this advice intercepts the method mA, the exception EX comes with the additional behavior included into the affected method.

Exception Handling. The exception handler is the code invoked in response to a raised exception. It can be attached to protected regions (e.g. methods, classes and blocks of code) or specific exceptions [16]. Handlers are responsible for performing the recovery actions necessary to bring the system back to a normal state and, whenever this is not possible, to log the exception and abort the system in an expectedly safe way. In AO programs, a handler can be defined in either a method or an advice. Specific types of advice (e.g., around and after [6]) have the ability to handle the exceptions thrown by the methods they advise.

Handler Binding. In many languages, the search for the handler to deal with a raised exception occurs along the dynamic invocation chain. This is claimed to increase software reusability, since the invoker of an operation can handle it in a wider context [16, 24]. In AO programs the handler of one exception can be present: (i) in one of the methods in the dynamic call chain of the signaler; or (ii) in an aspect that advises any of the methods in the signaler's call chain. Figure 1 depicts one scenario in which one advice (a1) signals the EX exception, and the other advice (a2) is responsible for handling EX, i.e. a2 intercepts one of the methods in the dynamic call chain and handles this exception.

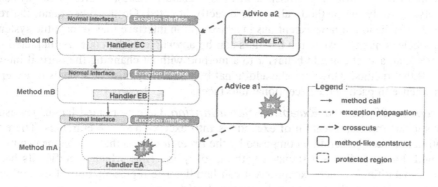

Fig. 1. Exception propagation

An *exception path* is a path in a program call graph that links the signaler and the handler of an exception. Notice that if there is no a handler for a specific exception, the exception path starts from the signaler and finishes at the program entrance point. In Figure 1, the exception path of EX is <a1→mA→mB→mC→a2>. Therefore, the *exception flow* comprises three main moments: the exception signaling, the exception flow through the elements of a system, and the moment in which the exception is handled or leaves the bounds of the system without being handled, thus becoming an uncaught exception.

Exception Interfaces [24]: The caller of a method needs to know which exceptions may cross the boundary of the called one. In this way, the caller will be able to prepare the code beforehand for the exceptional conditions that may happen during system execution. For this reason, some languages provide constructs to associate to a method's signature a list of exceptions that this method may throw. Besides providing information for the callers of such method, this information can be checked at compile time to verify whether handlers were defined for each specified exception. This list of exceptions is defined by Miller and Tripathi [24] as a method's *exception interface*. Ideally, the exception interface should provide complete and precise information for the method user. However, they are most often neither complete nor precise [4], because languages such as Java provide mechanisms to bypass this mechanism. This is achieved by throwing a specific kind of exception, called *unchecked exception*, which does not require any declaration on the method signature. For convenience, in this paper we split this concept of exception interface into two categories:

(i) the explicit exception interfaces, which are part of the method (or method-like construct) signature and explicitly declare the list of exceptions; and

(ii) the complete (de facto) exception interfaces, which capture all the exceptions signaled by a method, including the implicit (unchecked) ones not specified in the method signatures.

In the rest of this paper, unless it is explicitly mentioned, we use the expression "exception interface" to refer to a complete (de facto) exception interface. Although both the normal interface (i.e. method signature) and the exception interface of a method can evolve along a software life cycle, the impact of such a change on the system varies significantly. When a method signature varies, it affects the system locally, i.e. only the method callers are directly affected. On the other hand, the removal or inclusion of new exceptions in an exception interface may impact the system as a whole, since the exception handlers can be anywhere in the code. As depicted in Figure 1, an aspect can add behavior to a method without changing the normal interface of that method. However, the additional behavior may raise new kinds of exceptions, hence impacting the exceptional interfaces.

Exception Types and Exception Subsumption. Object-oriented languages usually support the classification of exceptions into exception-type hierarchies. The exception interface is therefore composed by the *exception types* that can be thrown by a method. Each handler is associated with an *exception type*, which specifies its handling capabilities - which exceptions it can handle. The representation of exceptions in type hierarchies allows type *subsumption* [29] to occur: when an object of a subtype can be assigned to a variable declared to be of its supertype, the subtype is said to be subsumed in the supertype. When an exception is signaled, it can be subsumed into the type associated to a handler, if the exception type associated to the handler (i.e., *the hander type*) is a supertype of the exception type being caught.

3 Evaluation Procedures

This section describes our study configuration in terms of its goals and hypotheses, the criteria used for the target systems selection (Section 3.1), methodology employed to conduct the exceptional code analyses (Section 3.2), and the actual execution of our study (Section 3.3). The goal of this case study is to evaluate the impact of AOP on exception flows of AspectJ programs, comparing them with their Java counterparts. The investigation relies on determining, in multiple Java and AspectJ versions, which exception-handling bug patterns (Section 5) are typically introduced in their original and subsequent releases. The analyzed error-prone scenarios vary from uncaught to *unintended handler actions*.

The OO and AO versions of three applications have been compared in order to observe the positive and negative effects caused by aspects on their exception flows. Specific procedures were undertaken in order to distinguish AOP liabilities for exception handling implementation from well-known intrinsic impairments of

OO mechanisms on exception handling [24]. These procedures were important to detect whether and which AO mechanisms are likely to lead to unexpected and error-prone scenarios involving exception handling. As a result, the null hypothesis (H0) for this study states that there is no difference in robustness of exception handling code in Java and AspectJ versions of the same system. The alternative hypothesis (H1) is that the impact of aspects on exception flows of programs can lead to more program flaws associated with exception flow.

3.1 Target Systems

One major decision that had to be made for our investigation was the selection of the target applications. We have selected three medium-sized systems to which there was a Java version and an AspectJ version available. Each of them is a representative of different application domains and heterogeneous realistic ways of incorporating exception handling into software systems being developed incrementally. The target systems were: Health Watcher [14, 31] (HW), Mobile Photo [9] (MP) and JHotDraw [16, 21] (JHD). The HW system [14, 31] is a Web-based application that allows citizens to register complaints regarding health issues in public institutions. MP is a software product line that manipulates photo, music and video on mobile devices. JHotdraw framework [16] is an open-source project that encompasses a two-dimensional graphics framework for structured drawing editors. It comprises a Java swing and an applet interface. In our

Table 1. Target Systems description

System	Description and Crosscutting Concerns
Health Watcher (HW)	*Version 1*: concurrency control, persistence (partially) and exception handling (partially).
	Version 9: concurrency control, transaction management, design patterns (Observer, Factory and Command), persistence (partially) and exception handling (partially).
Mobile Photo (MP)	*Version 4*: exception handling and some functional requirements comprising photo manipulation, such as to sort a list of photos, to choose the favorites, and to copy photo.
	Version 6: exception handling and some functional requirements comprising the manipulation of different kinds of media (i.e., photos and audio files), such as: to sort a list of medias, to choose the favorites, and to copy a media and sending SMS).
AJHotDraw (HD)	*Version 1*: persistence concern, design policies contract enforcement and undo command.

Table 2. Code characteristics per system

Number of:	Health Watcher V1 OO	Health Watcher V1 AO	Health Watcher V9 OO	Health Watcher V9 AO	Mobile Photo V4 OO	Mobile Photo V4 AO	Mobile Photo V6 OO	Mobile Photo V6 AO	HotDraw OO	HotDraw AO
Lines of code	6080	5742	8825	7838	2540	3098	1571	1859	21027	21123
Lines of code for exception handling	1167	854	1889	1242	474	424	356	296	320	341
Classes	88	90	132	129	46	49	30	29	288	279
Aspects	0	11	0	24	0	14	0	10	0	31
try blocks	131	118	233	173	49	40	36	24	60	61
catch blocks	285	177	481	266	69	60	52	38	67	72
throw clauses	227	182	334	229	21	18	20	17	52	56
try blocks inside classes	131	108	233	161	49	21	36	9	60	61
catch blocks inside classes	285	164	481	252	69	28	52	16	67	72
throw clauses inside classes	227	176	334	219	21	4	20	4	52	51
try blocks inside aspects	n/a	10	n/a	12	n/a	19	n/a	15	n/a	0
catch blocks inside aspects	n/a	13	n/a	14	n/a	32	n/a	22	n/a	0
throw clauses inside aspects	n/a	6	n/a	10	n/a	14	n/a	13	n/a	5
after advices	n/a	4	n/a	22	n/a	30	n/a	15	n/a	15
around advices	n/a	5	n/a	6	n/a	21	n/a	17	n/a	18
before advice	n/a	3	n/a	4	n/a	5	n/a	2	n/a	15

study, we focused on the Java Swing version of the JHotdraw. Moreover, such systems exhibit a number of crosscutting concerns in addition to exception handling. Table 1 lists the crosscutting concerns that were implemented as aspects in the AO versions of each system.

Heterogeneous, Non-Trivial Policies for Exception Handling. The target systems were also selected because they met a number of relevant additional criteria for our intended evaluation (Section 3). First, they are non-trivial software projects and particularly rich in the ways exception handling is related to other crosscutting and non-crosscutting concerns. For instance, we could find most of the typical categories of exception handlers in terms of their structure as documented in [7], including nested exception handlers and context-affecting handlers. Second, the behavior of exception handlers also significantly varied in terms of their purpose [4], ranging from error logging to application-specific recovery actions (e.g., rollback). Third, each of these systems contains a considerable amount of code dedicated to exception handling within both aspects and classes as detailed in Table 2.

Presence of Different Aspects in Incrementally-Developed Programs. Finally, AOP was applied in different ways through the system releases: (i) aspects were used to extract non-exception-handling concerns in JHotDraw, and all exception handlers are defined in the base code, (ii) aspects were used to modularize various crosscutting concerns in the Mobile Photo product line, including exception handling apart from the original release, and (iii) aspects were used to partially implement error handling in Health Watcher, where other behaviors were also aspectized. Good AOP practices were applied to structure such systems as stated in [9, 14, 31, 21]. Similar to Java releases, all the AspectJ releases were implemented and changed by developers with around three years of experience in AO design and programming. In fact, HW and MP systems have been used in the context of other empirical studies focusing on the assessment and comparison of their Java and AspectJ implementations in terms of modularity and stability [9, 14]. Alignments of Java and AspectJ versions have been undertaken in order to guarantee that both were implementing the same normal and exceptional functionalities.

3.2 Static Analysis of Exception Flow

The analysis of the exception flow can easily become unfeasible if done manually [28, 29]. In order to discover which exceptions can be thrown by a method, due to the use of unchecked exceptions, the developer needs to recursively analyze each method that can be called from such method. Moreover, when libraries are used, the developer needs to rely on their documentation, which is most often neither precise nor complete [4].

Current exception flow analysis tools [10, 11, 28] do not support AOP constructs. Even the tools which operate on Java bytecode level [11] cannot be used in a straight-forward fashion. They do not interpret the aspect-related code included on the byte-code after the weaving process of AspectJ. Hence, we developed a static analysis tool to derive exception flow graphs for AspectJ programs and support our investigation on determining flaws associated with exception flows. This tool is based on the Soot framework for bytecode analysis and transformation [32] and is composed of two main modules: the Exception Path Finder and the Exception Path Miner. Both components are described next, and more detailed information can be found at the companion website [3].

Exception Path Finder. This component uses Spark, one of the call graph builders provided by Soot. Spark is a field-sensitive, flow-insensitive and context-insensitive points-to analysis [32], also used by other static analysis tools [10, 11]. The Exception Path Finder generates the exception paths for all checked and unchecked exceptions, explicitly thrown by the application or implicitly thrown (e.g., via library method) by aspects and classes. It associates each exception path with information regarding its treatment. For instance, whether the exception was uncaught, caught by subsumption or caught by the same exception type. In this study we are assuming that only one exception is thrown at a time – the same assumption considered in [10, 11].

Exception Path Miner. This component classifies each exception path according to its signaler (i.e., class method, aspect advice, intertype or declare soft constructs) and handler. Such classification helps the developer to discover the new dependencies that arise between aspects and classes on exceptional scenarios. For instance, an exception can be thrown by an aspectual module and captured by a class or vice-versa. These different dependencies represent seeds to manual inspections whose goal is to evaluate the error proneness of the abnormal code in AO systems.

3.2.1 Inspection of Exception Handlers

The classification of the handler action for each exception path was based on a complementary manual inspection. It consisted of examining the code of each handler associated with exception paths found by the exception flow analysis tool (Section 3.2.1). Such manual inspections were also targeted at: discovering the causes for uncaught exceptions and exception *subsumptions*. It enabled us to systematically discover *bug hazards* associated with Java and AspectJ modules on the exception handling code. A bug hazard [2] is a circumstance that increases the chance of a bug to be present in the software. For instance, type coercion in C++ is a bug hazard because it depends on complex rules and declarations that may not be visible when working on a class. Each handler action was classified according to one of the categories presented in Table 3.

Table 3. Categories of handler actions and corresponding descriptions

Category	Description
swallowing	The handler is empty.
logging	Some information related to the exceptional scenario is logged.
customised message	A message describing the failure is presented to the user.
show exception message	The exception message attribute (exception.getMessage()) is presented to the user.
application specific action	An specific action is performed (e.g., rollback).
incorrect user message	A message that is not related to the failure that happened is presented to the user.
new exception	A new exception is created and thrown.
wrap	The original exception or any information associated to it is used to construct a new exception which is thrown.
convert to soft	The exception is converted into a SoftException. This action is specific to AspectJ programs and happens when the delcare soft construct is used.
framework default action	To avoid uncaught exceptions some application frameworks such as java.swing, define catch classes that handle any exception that was not caught by the application and performs a default action (e.g. kill the thread which threw the exception.).
uncaught	No handler caught the exception.

3.3 Study Operation

This study was undertaken from March 2007 to November 2007. During this period target systems were selected and the static analysis tool was implemented and executed for each target system. It was followed by the manual inspection of every exception path. The *Exception Path Finder* was used to generate the exception flow graph for every exception occurrence. Then the *Exception Path Miner* classified each exception path according to its signaler and handler (see Table 4). We discarded a few unchecked exceptions[2] that can be thrown by JVM in almost every program statement execution (e.g., IllegalMonitorStateException) and are not normally handled inside the system. The same filter was adopted by Cabral and Marques [4] in an empirical study of exception handling code in object-oriented systems. This filtering was performed on the static analysis. Then we manually inspected each one of the 2.901 exception paths presented in Table 4. The goal of this inspection was threefold: (i) to discover what caused uncaught exceptions and exception subsumptions; (ii) to specify the handler action of each exception path, and (iii) to determine the *bug hazards* associated with AspectJ constructs on certain exception handling scenarios.

4 Analysis of Exception Flows and Handler Actions

This section presents the results for each of the study stages. First, it presents evaluation of the data collected via the exception flow analysis tool (Section 4.1). The following discussion focuses on the information collected during the manual inspections of each exception path (Section 4.2). Our goal in providing such a fine-grained data analysis is to enable a detailed understanding of how aspects typically affected positively or negatively the robustness of exception handling in each target system and its different releases.

4.1 Empirical Data

Table 4 presents the number of *exception paths* identified by the exception flow analysis tool (Section 3.2.1). It presents the tally of exception paths per target system structured according to a *"Signaler-Handler"* relation. The element responsible for signaling the exception can be either a class or an aspect. When the exception is signaled by an aspect, it is signaled by one of its internal operations: an advice, a method defined as intertype declaration, or a declare soft construct[3]. An exception occurrence can be caught in two basic ways. It can be caught by a *specialized handler* when the catch argument has the same type of the caught exception type. Alternatively, it

---

[2] The discarded exceptions were the exceptions thrown by bytecode operations (NullPointerException, IllegalMonitorStateException, ArrayIndexOutOfBoundsException, ArrayStoreException, NegativeArray SizeException, ClassCastException, ArithmeticException) and exceptions specific to the AspectJ (NoAspectBoundException). Since such exceptions may be thrown by almost every operation, including those could generate too much information which could compromise the usability of the exception analysis.

[3] Declare soft is an AspectJ specific construct. It is associated to a pointcut and wraps any exception thrown on specific join points in a SoftException, and re-throws it.

can be caught by *subsumption* when the `catch` argument is a supertype of the exception being caught. It is also possible that the exception is not handled by the application and remains *uncaught*. This happens when there is no system's handler defined for the exception type in the exception flow.

Table 4. Classification of exception paths per target system

	Health Watcher V1		Health Watcher V9		Mobile Photo V4		Mobile Photo V6		HotDraw	
	OO	AO	OO	AO	OO	AO	OO	AO	OO	AO
Signaler: Class										
Uncaught	5	9	9	0	0	0	0	0	124	112
Handler on Class										
Specialized Handler	196	132	277	119	53	26	63	13	64	5
Subsumption	43	26	47	21	13	0	9	0	316	143
Handler on Aspect										
Specialized Handler	n/a	8	n/a	8	n/a	7	n/a	2	n/a	0
Subsumption	n/a	4	n/a	40	n/a	0	n/a	0	n/a	0
Signaler: Aspect										
Construct: Advice										
Uncaught	n/a	2	n/a	27	n/a	5	n/a	16	n/a	0
Handler on Class										
Specialized Handler	n/a	0	n/a	0	n/a	2	n/a	0	n/a	0
Subsumption	n/a	3	n/a	2	n/a	1	n/a	3	n/a	84
Handler on Aspect										
Specialized Handler	n/a	21	n/a	60	n/a	18	n/a	8	n/a	0
Subsumption	n/a	98	n/a	181	n/a	0	n/a	2	n/a	0
Construct: Declare Soft										
Uncaught	n/a	32	n/a	1	n/a	42	n/a	40	n/a	0
Handler on Class										
Specialized Handler	n/a	0	n/a	0	n/a	0	n/a	0	n/a	0
Subsumption	n/a	46	n/a	47	n/a	1	n/a	1	n/a	36
Handler on Aspect										
Specialized Handler	n/a	0	n/a	63	n/a	0	n/a	0	n/a	0
Subsumption	n/a	0	n/a	20	n/a	0	n/a	0	n/a	0
Construct: Intertype										
Uncaught	n/a	0	n/a	0	n/a	0	n/a	0	n/a	24
Handler on Class										
Specialized Handler	n/a	0	n/a	0	n/a	0	n/a	0	n/a	0
Subsumption	n/a	0	n/a	0	n/a	0	n/a	0	n/a	121
Handler on Aspect										
Specialized Handler	n/a	0	n/a	0	n/a	0	n/a	0	n/a	0
Subsumption	n/a	0	n/a	0	n/a	0	n/a	0	n/a	0

The next subsections analyze the *exception paths* presented in Table 4 in detail. First, Section 4.1.1 contrasts the occurrence of *subsumptions* and *uncaught* exceptions in Java and AspectJ versions of each target system. Section 4.1.2 determines the relation between certain aspect elements (as exception signalers) and higher or lower incidences of *uncaught* exceptions and *subsumptions*. Section 4.1.3 focuses the analysis on how exceptions thrown by aspects are typically treated in the target systems.

4.1.1 The Impact of Aspects on How Exceptions Are Handled

A recurring question to AO software programmers is whether it is harmful to aspectize certain behaviors in existing OO decompositions in the presence of exceptional conditions. Hence, our first analysis focused on observing how aspects affected the robustness of the original exception handling policies of the Java versions. Figure 2 illustrates the total number of exception paths on which exceptions (i) remained uncaught exceptions, (ii) were caught by *subsumption*, or (iii) by specialized handlers in each of the target systems.

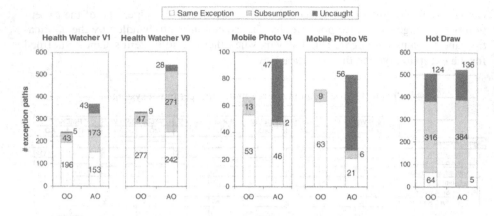

Fig. 2. Uncaught exceptions, *subsumptions*, and specialized handlers per system

Figure 2 shows a significant increase in the overall number of exception paths. Also significant is the increase in *uncaught exceptions* and *subsumptions* for the AO versions of all the three systems. This increase is a sign that the robustness of exception handling policies in AspectJ releases was affected and sometimes degraded when compared to their Java equivalents. Of course, the absolute number of exception paths is expected to vary due to design modifications, such as aspectual refactorings. However, the number of uncaught exceptions and *subsumptions* ideally should be equivalent between the Java and AspectJ implementations of a same system, since experimental procedures were undertaken to assure that both versions implemented the same functionalities (Section 3).

Figure 3 shows the percentage of occurrence for each category of handler action. We can observe that the relative number of uncaught exceptions also increased in

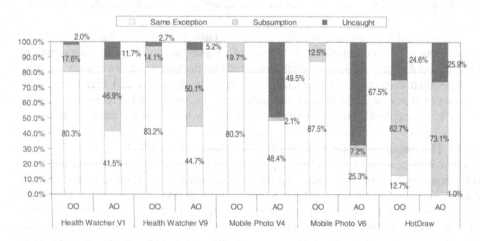

Fig. 3. Percentage of uncaught exceptions, *subsumptions*, and specialized handlers

every system, and so did the relative number of *subsumptions*. In some target systems, this increase was significant. In the Mobile Photo V6, for example, the number of uncaught exceptions represent 67.5% of the exceptions signaled on the system. In the Health Watcher V9, the percentage of exceptions caught by *subsumption* increased from 14.1% in OO version to 50.1% in the AO version. This significant increase amplifies the risk of unpredictable system crashes in AspectJ systems, caused by either uncaught exceptions or inappropriate exception handling via *subsumptions*. Correspondingly, there was a decrease in the percentage of exceptions handled by specialized handlers in all AO implementations. When the handler knows exactly which exception is caught, it can take an appropriate recovery action or show a more precise message to the user. However, this was not the typical case in the AO implementations of the investigated systems.

4.1.2 The Blame for Uncaught Exceptions and Subsumptions

After discovering that the number of *uncaught* exceptions and *subsumptions* has significantly increased in the AO implementations (Section 4.1.1), we continued our analysis, looking for the main causes of such discrepancies between AO and OO versions. The intuition here is that most of these exceptions were signaled by the aspects in the three target systems. Figure 4 presents charts that confirm this intuition; they show the participation of the exceptions signaled by aspects in the entire number of uncaught exceptions and *subsumptions* per system.

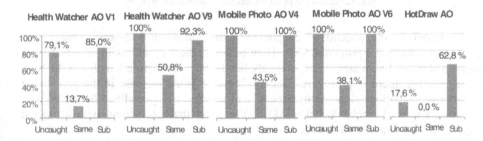

Fig. 4. Participation of aspect-signalized exceptions on the **whole** number of *subsumption*, *uncaught* and specifically-handled exceptions **per system**

In both AO versions of Health Watcher and Mobile Photo, the aspects were responsible for signaling most of the uncaught exceptions and those ones caught by *subsumption*. In Mobile Photo V4 and V6, for example, aspects were responsible for 100% of the uncaught exceptions found in this system. This means that no base class in this system signaled an exception that became uncaught. In the AO version of JHotDraw, the aspects were responsible for signaling only 17.6% of the uncaught exceptions, and the aspects participation on the number of exceptions caught by subsumption was high (62.8%). This is explained by the fact that the exception policy of the HotDraw OO was already based on exception subsumption (see Figure 2), thus the exceptions signaled by aspects were handled in the same way.

4.1.3 Are All Exceptions Signaled by Aspects Becoming Uncaught or Caught by Subsumption?

Figure 5 gives a more detailed view of what is happening with all exceptions signaled by aspects. We can observe that not all exceptions signaled from aspects become uncaught or are caught by *subsumption*. In HealthWatcher AO V9, for example, only 7% of the exceptions signaled by aspects became uncaught, but they represented 100% of the uncaught exceptions reported to this system (see Figure 3). On the other hand, in the AO versions of the MobilePhoto, the percentage of exceptions signaled by aspects that became uncaught is high (68.1% and 80%). As discussed in the next section, this system was the one that had the exception handling concern aspectized.

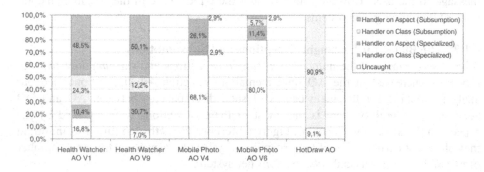

Fig. 5. Handler type of exceptions thrown by aspects

In Figure 5, the exceptions caught by *subsumption* on handlers coded inside classes characterize a *potential fault*. They may represent scenarios in which the exception signaled by an aspect is mistakenly handled by an existing handler in the base code. Another interesting thing to notice in Figure 5 is the increase in the percentage number of exceptions signaled by aspects and handled by specialized handlers from versions 1 to 9 of Health Watcher AO. It illustrates that exceptions signaled by an aspect can be adequately handled.

4.2 Detailed Inspection

In order to obtain a more fine-grained view of how exceptions were handled in AO and OO versions of the same system, we manually inspected all the 2,901 exception paths presented in Table 2. Each exception path was classified according to the action taken on its handler – following the classification presented in Section 3.2.2. Table 5 illustrates the number of each type of handler action per target system and the ratio (%) between the number of the handler action in the AO version and the corresponding value in the OO version of the same system. The ratio is expressed as the quotient of former divided by the latter.

As mentioned before, the total number of exception paths mostly increased in AO versions. During the manual inspections we discovered there were two causes for that: (i) if one exception is not caught inside a specific method (e.g., due to a fault on an aspect that acts as handler) this exception will continue to flow on the call chain, generating new exception paths; and (ii) specific design modifications bring new elements to the call graph and consequently lead to more exception paths. Figure 6 illustrates the handler actions per target system. Overall, it confirms the findings of previous sections based on the tool outputs: the aspects used to implement the cross-cutting functionalities tend to violate the exception policies previously adopted in each system. Subsequent subsections elaborate further on the data in Figure 6 and explain the causes behind AspectJ inferiority.

Table 5. Classification of *exception paths* according to their handler action

Handler Action	Health Watcher V1			Health Watcher V9			Mobile Photo V4			Mobile Photo V6			HotDraw		
	OO	AO	Ratio, %	OO	AO	Ratio, %	OO	AO	Ratio, %	OO	AO	Ratio, %	OO	AO	Ratio, %
swallowing	5	7	140.0	5	7	140.0	0	0	--	0	0	--	3	3	100.0
logging	7	1	14.3	12	10	83.3	14	6	42.9	41	13	31.7	4	11	275.0
customised message	12	43	358.3	20	73	365.0	13	4	30.8	0	0	--	0	0	--
show exception message	43	32	74.4	39	100	256.4	0	0	--	7	1	14.3	291	285	97.9
application specific action	115	121	105.2	169	160	94.7	3	5	166.7	0	0	--	8	0	0.0
incorrect user message	17	53	311.8	16	43	268.8	0	0	--	0	0	--	0	0	--
new exception	3	3	100.0	3	3	100.0	0	3	--	1	2	200.0	0	0	--
wrap	37	38	102.7	60	65	108.3	36	0	--	23	0	0.0	0	0	--
convert to soft	0	40	--	0	100	--	0	37	--	0	13	--	0	8	--
framework default action	0	0	--	0	0	--	0	0	--	0	0	--	0	0	--
uncaught	5	43	860.0	9	28	311.1	0	47	--	0	56	--	124	136	109.7
TOTAL	244	381	156.1	333	589	176.9	66	102	154.5	72	85	118.1	504	525	104.2

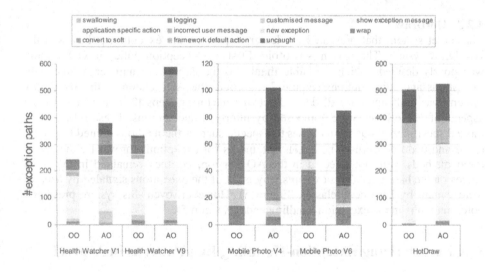

Fig. 6. The handler actions in the *exception paths* of each target system

4.2.1 Health Watcher

In the AO versions of Health Watcher, there was an increase in the number of exception paths classified as `incorrect user message` (see Table 5), in relation to the corresponding OO versions. It means that there were exception paths in such systems in which a message not related to the exception that really happened was presented to the user. This characterizes the problem known as *Unintended Handler Action,* when an exception is handled by mistake by an existing handler. The causes of such failures were diverse: (i) mistakes on the pointcut expressions of exception handling aspects in both versions; (ii) in version 9, an aspect defined to handle exceptions intercepted a point in the code in which the exception was already caught; (iii) aspects signaled exceptions and no handler was defined for such exceptions in both versions; and (iv) the wrong use of the `declare soft` statement. Each of these causes entails a bug pattern in AspectJ that will be discussed in Section 5. In the version 1, all softened exceptions became uncaught (categories `convert to soft` and `uncaught` respectively), because the `declare soft` statement was not used correctly (see *Handler Mismatch* in Section 5.3). In version 9, the misuse of the `declare soft` statement was fixed but some exceptions remained uncaught or unintended, handled by a `catch` block on the base code that presented an `incorrect user message`.

4.2.2 Mobile Photo
In all AO versions of Mobile Photo there was a significant increase in the number of uncaught exceptions. This application defined many exception handler aspects. Due to mistakes on pointcut expressions and a limitation on the use of `declare soft` many exceptions became uncaught. Differently from the exception handling policy defined in the Health Watcher system, in Mobile Photo there were no "catch all" clauses on the View layer to prevent exceptions - not handled by the handler defined for it - from becoming uncaught.

4.2.3 HotDraw
The target system that presented the lesser impact on the exception policy was the JHotDraw system. The reason is twofold. First, the exception policy in OO version was poorly defined, which is visible thanks to the expressive number of uncaught exceptions and subsumptions (Figure 2). Second, the AO version of the JHotDraw system was built upon a well defined set of refactoring steps [21], and most of the aspects of AJHotDraw were composed by intertype declarations. These refactorings moved specific methods from classes to aspects, such as the methods related to persistence and undo concerns. The `catch` statements for exceptions thrown by the refactored methods were not affected in the AO version, i.e. they remained in the same places on the base code. This explains why most of the exceptions signaled by aspects were caught by base code classes (Figure 5). However, even this system presented potential faults in the exception handling code (Section 5).

5 Characterizing Exception-Handling Bug Patterns in AspectJ

Bug patterns [2] are recurring correlations between signaled errors and underlying bugs in a program. They are related to design anti-patterns, but bug patterns are typical sources of faults at source code level. The manual inspection of the exception handling code related to the exception paths reported by the tool allowed us to identify several exception-handling bug patterns. These patterns can be classified into three categories. First, the use of *aspects as handlers* led to some scenarios in which the `catch` clauses were moved to aspects, the so-called exception handling aspects. However, these aspects did not catch the exceptions they were intended to handle. Second, the application of *aspects as signalers* often implied aspects signaling exceptions for which no handler was defined. Such exceptions flew through the system and became uncaught exceptions or were caught by an existing handler in the code (usually by *subsumption*). Third, the use of `declare soft` construct was often problematic: due to its complex semantics, almost all developers performed similar mistakes when using this construct in almost all the analyzed software releases.

In some cases, we observed that the use of `declare soft` in combination with after throwing advice generated a bytecode in which the after throwing advice were not included, what represents a bug in the AspectJ weaver. Table 6 summarizes the bug pattern distribution in relation to the analyzed systems. The next sections describe the bug patterns shown in this table. For each of them, we provide a description, but due to space constraints, only some examples based on code snippets are provided; code examples for all the bug patterns can be found on the companion website [3].

Table 6. Distribution of the bug patterns per system

Bug patterns	Health Watcher AO		Mobile Photo AO		HotDraw AO
	V1	V9	V4	V6	V1
Aspects as Handlers					
Inactive Aspect handler	✓	✓	✓	✓	
Late Binding Aspect Handler		✓			
Obsolete Handler in the Base Code					✓
Aspects as Signalers					
Solo Signaler Aspect	✓	✓			✓
Unstable Exception Interfaces	✓	✓	✓	✓	
Exception Softening					
Handler Mismatch.	✓				
Solo Declare Soft Statement.			✓	✓	
Unchecked Exception Cause					✓
The Precedence Dilemma			✓	✓	

5.1 Advice as Exception Handlers

The role of aspects as handlers can be classified into two: (1) the aspect can handle its own internal exceptions; and (2) and it can handle external exceptions thrown by other aspects or classes. Aspects can be used to modularize the handlers of external exceptions relative to other crosscutting concerns implemented as aspects. The latter occurred in both Health Watcher and Mobile Photo systems. It can also be used to modularize part of exception handling from the base code (as in Mobile Photo). Such exception handling aspects are implemented using `around` and `after throwing` advice. The first two bug patterns presented next are related to aspects that act as external exception handlers, the last one is related to aspects implementing internal handlers.

Inactive Aspect Handler. This kind of fault happens when an Aspect Handler does not handle the exception that it was intended to handle. The cause is a faulty pointcut expression. Such a fault prevents the handler from advising the join point in which an exception should be handled. This exception either becomes *uncaught* (Section 5.2) or is mistakenly caught by an existing handler (*unintended handler action* discussed in Section 5.2). Instances of this bug pattern were detected in Health Watcher and Mobile Photo systems as exception handling was not aspectized in HotDraw. The typical reasons for this bug pattern are the fragility of the pointcut language, usually based on naming conventions, and the number of different and very specific join points to be intercepted by the handler aspects.

Late Binding Aspect Handler. This bug pattern occurred in Health Watcher V9. The concurrency control was implemented within an aspect, which throws the `Transac-tionException` exception. A specific handler aspect – called `EHAspect` - was defined to handle this exception and although the pointcut expression was correctly specified, the handler intercepted a point in which the exception was already caught beforehand by a "catch all clause" on the base code. This problem is difficult to diagnose because the current IDEs will indicate to the developer of the `EHaspect` that the join points in the code (where the exception should be caught) are correctly intercepted. This explains why this fault remained until version V9 of the HW system. Moreover, even if there is no "catch all" clause between signaler and aspect handler during development, such a clause can be added in a maintenance task. If the handler was defined in the base code and it was a checked exception, the compiler would warn the developer that the handler was inactive. Figure 7 (a) presents a schematic view of this problem. In this figure, the advice a1 adds a new functionality to method mA. This additional functionality comes along with a new exception EX, which flows through the advised method call chain until it is handled. Another advice was defined to handle the exception (advice a2), which intercepts a point on the base code were the exception EX should be handled (method mC). We can observe from this schematic view that the exception EX was caught by a catch clause defined on method mB and, as a consequence, EX could not reach the point in the code where it should be handled by advice a2.

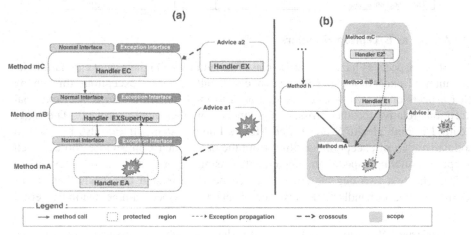

Fig. 7. Schematic view of Bug Patterns - (a) Late Binding Handler, and (b) Unstable Exception Interfaces

Obsolete (or Outdated) Handler in the Base Code. When an aspect handles or softens (Section 3.4.3) an exception previously thrown by an application method, the handler associated with this exception on the base code will become obsolete. The reason is that the exception handled by it can no longer be signaled. In this study, four exceptions handled by aspects generated obsolete handlers. Notice that an obsolete handler may lead to the consequences presented by Miller and Tripathi [24].

5.2 Aspects as Exception Signalers

During the manual inspections we found potential faults that can occur when aspects signal exceptions. They are detailed below.

Solo Signaler Aspect. Solo Signalers are the aspects that signal an exception and no handler is bound to it. Such an aspect may lead to the same failures caused by the Inactive Aspect Handler defined in the previous section: an *uncaught exception* or an *Unintended Handler Action*. The *Unintended Handler Action* [24] is usually characterized by the exception signaled by an aspect being handled by *subsumption* via classes.

Unstable Exception Interface. In this study we observed that aspects had the ability of *destabilizing the exception interface* of the advised methods. Every time a static or dynamic scope is used and the advice may signal an exception, the exception interface of the method will vary according to the scope in which a method is called. As a consequence, the same method could raise a different set of exceptions, even when the method arguments were the same, depending on the static (e.g., which class called it) or dynamic (information on the execution stack) scopes. The next code snippet, extracted from the AJHotDraw implementation, exemplifies an *unstable exception interface*.

```
pointcut commandExecuteCheckView(AbstractCommand command): this(command)

    && execution(void AbstractCommand+.execute())
    && !within(*..DrawApplication.*) && !within(*..CTXWindowMenu.*)
    && !within(*..WindowMenu.*) && !within(*..JavaDrawApp.*);

before(AbstractCommand command) : commandExecuteCheckView(command) {
        if (command.view() == null) {
            throw new JHotDrawRuntimeException("execute should NOT be
                getting called when view() == null");
        }
}
```

In this example, the `execute()` method will throw a `JHotDrawRuntimeException` if it is called from a method that is not defined on the classes specified on the pointcut expression (`DrawApplication`, `CTXWindowMenu`, `WindowMenu` and `JavaDrawApp`). As a consequence, the same method will have different behaviors depending on the scope it is called. When the exceptions that can be thrown from a method vary according to the scope it is executed, we say that such method contains an *unstable exception interface*.

Figure 7 (b) presents a schematic view of this problem. In this figure, the *advice x* adds a new functionality to *method mA* only when such method is called from *method mC* (i.e., the pointcut expression contains a dynamic scope delimiter). Therefore, this additional functionality, and the new exception E2 that comes with it, will not be part of method mA when it is called from another method such as *method h*. As a consequence, when the *method mA* is called from *method mC* it may throw E2 exception – and a handler should be defined for it. On the other hand, if it is called from *method h*, it will not throw the exception E2 (even if the method arguments are the same as the one passed on the previous scope) since *advice x* does not affect the *method mA* in this scope.

5.3 Softening Exceptions

In AspectJ an advice can only throw a checked exception if all intercepted methods can signal it (i.e. declaring it on their `throws` clause). In other words, concerning checked exceptions, an advice should follow a rule similar to the "Exception Conformance" rule [28] applied during inheritance, when methods are overridden. As a result an advice can only throw a checked exception if it is thrown by every intercepted method. To bypass this restriction, AspectJ offers the `declare soft` statement, which converts (wraps) a given checked exception (in a specific scope) into a specialized unchecked exception, named `SoftException`. The syntax is: `declare soft : <someException> : <scope>`. The `scope` is specified by a pointcut that selects the join points in which the `someException` exception will be wrapped. AspectJ is the only AO language that provides a `declare soft` construct. As detailed in Section 6.4, in Spring AOP and JBoss AOP, advices are allowed to throw any kind of exception, either checked or unchecked. It is possible because their weavers convert the exception interface of every advised method to allow every kind of exception to flow from it – including a `Throwable` in its `throws` clause. This section presents some bug patterns and also potential error-prone scenarios on the exception handling code when the `declare soft` statement is used.

Solo Declare Soft Statement. According to the AspectJ documentation [33], every time an exception is softened by an aspect, the developer should implement another aspect that will be responsible for handling the softened exception. However, this solution is very fragile. It is up to the programmer to define a new aspect to handle the exception that was softened, and no message is shown at compile time to warn the programmer in case s/he forgets to define this aspect handler. In Health Watcher and Mobile Photo, exceptions were softened and no handler was defined for them. This led to uncaught exceptions and *unintended handler actions* - exceptions caught by *subsumption* on the base code.

Unchecked Exception Cause. When a checked exception is softened, it is wrapped in a `SoftException` object. As mentioned before, in Java-like languages the type of an exception is used to make the binding between an exception and its handler. Thus, when wrapping an exception, we are also wrapping useful information in order to provide a fine-grained action for each exception. To overcome this limitation, at every point that needs to handle a softened exception, one should catch the `SoftException` and unwrap it (through its `getCause()` method) in order to compare its cause with every possible exception that may potentially be thrown inside the handler's context. Such "wrapping" solution is documented as one of the exception handling anti-patterns [22].

Handler Mismatch. Some exceptions were softened in one of the Health Watcher versions. However, handlers were defined for the exceptions' primitive types (i.e. types before being wrapped in a `SoftException`). This *Handler Mismatch* implies that almost all exceptions signaled by aspect implementations became uncaught or were caught by unintended handlers. The code snippet bellow, extracted from Health Watcher, illustrates this problem. The HWTransactionManagement aspect softens the exception, and the HWTransactionExceptionHandler aspect tries to capture the primitive exception (i.e., a TransactionException exception). This bug pattern illustrates an emergent property of a particular combination of aspects woven into the base program.

```
public aspect HWTransactionManagement {
    ...
    declare soft: TransactionException:
                 call(void IPersistenceMechanism.beginTransaction())…;
}

public aspect HWTransactionExceptionHandler {
    void around(HttpServletResponse response) :
        execution(* HWServlet+.doGet(HttpServletRequest,
    HttpServletResponse)) && args(.., response) {
        try {  proceed(response); }
        catch (TransactionException e) { ... }
    }
}
```

The Precedence Dilemma. This problem occurs when an after throwing advice is used in combination with the declare soft statement for a specific pointcut. Only the code related to the declare soft is included in the bytecode. Since both constructions work by converting one exception into another, the weaver cannot decide which one should happen first and as a consequence includes on the bytecode only the code relative to the declare soft statement. This bug in the language implementation generates a SoftException exception that will not be adequately caught.

6 Discussions and Study Constraints

This section provides further discussion of issues and lessons learned while performing this exploratory study.

6.1 Exception Handling vs. AOP Properties

The goal of exception handling mechanisms is to make programs more reliable and robust. However, we could observe that some properties of AOP may conflict with characteristics of exception mechanisms. In this study we observed that *quantification* and *obliviousness* properties pose specific pitfalls to the design of exception handling code. We explain and discuss these pitfalls in the following.

Quantification Property. Aspects have the ability to perform invasive modifications at specific join points in the program execution where a property holds – an ability also known as the *quantification property* [35]. AspectJ supports quantification via pointcuts and advice. Pointcuts are in general specified in terms of two kinds of pointcut designators: call and execution. They intercept the call and execution of methods, respectively. On exception-aware systems, such designators may cause different impact in the exceptional interfaces of methods. While the execution pointcut affects the exceptional interface of the advised methods themselves, the call advice affects the exceptional interface of the advised method's caller. Such impact can also be influenced by static and dynamic scopes associated with the pointcuts. Static scopes such as within and withincode delimit the classes or packages on which the aspects will inject a new behavior. Yet, dynamic scope constructs (i.e., cflow and cflowbelow) allow aspects to affect (or not) a specific point in the code depending on the information available on the runtime execution stack.

The main consequence of the quantification property on exception-aware AO systems was that the *exception interfaces* of methods can vary depending on where the method was called, even when the method arguments were the same. Therefore, the same method of a class could raise a different set of exceptions depending on which object called it or on some information on the execution stack (in case of cflow and cflowbelow, for example). These *unstable exception interfaces* cannot happen in OO programs since the set of exceptions thrown by a method cannot vary according to the scope where it is executed – provided that the arguments are the same. We observed in our study that in scenarios in which methods presented such *unstable exceptional interfaces*, the exceptions signaled on specific scopes by the advised method often became uncaught or were erroneously handled by an existing handler on the base code (*Unintended Handler Action* bug pattern discussed in Section 5). A possible reason is that it is more difficult for the method's user to prepare the base code to handle the exceptions that will be thrown depending on the dynamic or static scope it is executed.

Obliviousness property. The *obliviousness property* [35], which was believed to be a fundamental property for aspect-oriented programming, states that programmers of the base code do not need to be aware of the aspects which will affect it. It means that programmers do not need to prepare the base code to be affected by the aspects [35]. However, since there are no mechanisms to protect the base code from the exceptions that will flow from aspects, a new exception signaled by the aspect may flow through the system, if no handler is defined for it. This exception may become uncaught and terminate the system in an unpredictable way. Even in cases when a handler aspect is defined for each aspect that can throw an exception (as implemented in the AO versions of Health Watcher), there is no guarantee that the exception thrown by an aspect will be handled by the handler aspect defined to it. Such exceptions may be prematurely caught by a handler on the base code, as illustrated on the bug pattern *Late Binding Aspect Handler* (Section 5.1). Moreover, AspectJ and other existing AO languages allow the invasive modifications caused by aspects to happen dynamically. Although this mechanism opens a new realm of possibilities in software development, it hinders the task of preparing the base code of the exceptions that can be thrown from aspects. During system execution, it is difficult to anticipate whether any unintended handler action or uncaught exception will be caused by the aspects.

6.2 Representativeness

We have investigated other AOP technologies such as: CaesarJ [23], JBoss AOP and Spring AOP. Basically, they follow the same join point model as AspectJ, which allows an aspect to add or modify behavior on join points, potentially adding new exceptions. Table 7 summarizes our analysis regarding exception throwing and handling mechanisms available in such technologies, which was mainly based on available documentation.

228   R. Coelho et al.

Table 7. EH constructs in different AO programming languages

	declare soft	advice can signal		advice types that act as external handlers			around	moments of actuation		pointcut scope			
		checked	unchecked	handler-like	after throwing	after-all-like		call	execution	within-like	withincode-like	cflow-like	cflowbelow-like
AspectJ	yes	partially	yes	yes	yes	yes	yes	yes	yes	yes	yes	yes	yes
CaesarJ	no	partially	yes	yes	yes	yes	yes	yes	yes	yes	yes	yes	yes
JBoss AOP	no	yes	yes	no	yes	yes	yes	yes	yes	yes	yes	yes	yes
Spring AOP	no	yes	yes	no	yes	yes	yes	no	yes	yes	no	no	no

According to Table 7, only AspectJ provides a syntactic element to explicitly soften checked exceptions (2nd column). Thus, the bug patterns related to this construct (Section 5.3) are peculiar to AspectJ. Depending on the nature of exceptions that may be thrown by advice, all languages allow advice to throw runtime exceptions (4th column). In AspectJ and CaesarJ, an advice can only throw a checked exception if "every" intercepted method can throw it (declaring it on its throws clause) (3rd column). In CaesarJ, only around advice signature may throw checked exceptions. In Spring AOP and JBoss AOP languages, advice may throw checked exceptions, no matter the exceptions that can be signaled by the advised methods[4]. All languages allow the definition of pointcut scopes (11th to 14th columns), and allow the advice to intercept a method at both calls and executions (9th and 10th columns), consequently facilitating the occurrence of *unstable exceptional interfaces*. Therefore all bug patterns associated with *Advice as Signalers* (Section 5.2) may occur on systems developed in such languages. Finally, all languages allow the definition of aspects that may handle exceptions thrown by another aspect of the base code (5th to 7th columns). As a consequence, all bug patterns associated with *Advice as Handlers* (Section 5.1) can also be found on systems developed in these languages.

6.3 Study Constraints

The main benefit of an exploratory study such as this one is that it allows the effect of a new programming method to be assessed in realistic situations [42]. One may argue that evaluating the AO and OO versions in a sample of 10 releases for three different systems is a limiting factor. The needed characteristics for the target systems (i.e., medium-sized systems to which there was a Java version and an AspectJ version available) and study based on manual code inspections (a very time-consuming task) restricted the number of subjects evaluated in the study. Given such restrictions, we feel that our set is representative as it includes significant, varied policies and aspectization processes for exception handling (Section 3.1). Another factor that might influence the study results *against* aspectual decompositions could be the developers' expertise on AOP and AspectJ. However, as mentioned before (Section 3.1) all the target systems developers had significant experience in AOP and AspectJ constructs. Moreover, the fact that the AO version of each target system was developed after the OO version, could also impact in the study results, acting *in favor* or *against* AO solutions. However, most AO systems developed so far are derived from an OO

---

[4] It is possible because the exception interface of every advised method is modified to allow any kind of exception to flow from it (`throws Throwable` defines the exception interface of the intercepted methods).

version, to which AO *refactorings* [21] are typically applied. Therefore, the threats to validity in this study are not much different than the ones imposed on the other empirical studies with similar goals [6, 9, 13, 14].

6.4 Additional Lessons Learned

AO Refactoring Strategies in Exception-Aware Systems. Many AO systems nowadays are generated from an OO version in which some crosscutting concerns are detected and AO Refactoring techniques are used to convert some crosscutting concerns into aspects. Such AO Refactoring techniques should account for the consequences of aspects on the exception flow of programs. The catalogue of bug patterns presented in this study can be used by such techniques to prevent some avoidable bugs when refactoring a system.

Software Maintainability. Since it is very hard to define at the beginning of a project which exceptions should be dealt with inside the system [30], the exception handling code is often modified along the system development and maintenance tasks. As a consequence, some bugs avoided during AO refactoring, such as the *Late Binding Aspect Handler* (Section 5.1), may be included during a maintenance task - breaking an existing exception handling policy. The exception handling policy comprises a set of design rules that defines the system elements responsible for signaling, handling and re-throwing the exceptions; and the system dependability relies on the conformance to such rules. Reasoning about the excep-tional control path, looking for po-tential-faults on the exception handling code, can quickly become unfeasible if carried out manually [28]. Thus, developers need tools to support them in (i) understanding the impact of aspect weaving on the existing exception handling policy, and (ii) finding bugs on the exceptional handling code along maintenance tasks.

Finding Bugs on Exception Handling Code of AO Programs. Testing exception handling code is inherently difficult [36] due to the huge number of possible exceptional conditions to simulate in a system and the difficulty associated to the simulation of most scenarios. Hence, a valuable strategy for finding faults on the exception handling code can be to *statically* look for them [36]. The exception flow analysis tool developed in our work can detect some failures (e.g., uncaught exceptions), and support the manual inspections whose goal is to find out the cause of the failure (e.g., *bug diagnosing*[5]). Our tool could be extended in order to automatically detect some of the bug patterns described in this work. A similar strategy was adopted by Bruntink et al [36] to find faults on idiom-based exception handling code.

New Interactions between Aspects and Classes. The works presented so far on the interactions between aspects and classes focus on the normal control flow and on information extracted from data-flow analysis. In this study we could observe that new kinds of interaction, between aspects and classes, emerged from the exceptional scenarios (e.g., one class catches one exception thrown by an aspect). Such *Signaler-Handler* relationships between the elements of an AO system can be used as a

---

[5] The Bug fixing is a less complex problem after the bug was effectively diagnosed.

coupling metric that exists between these elements on exceptional scenarios. We are currently refining the categorization of the *Signaler-Handler* relationships derived from this study.

7 Related Work

Since the effects of AO composition mechanisms on the flow of exceptions on a system are still not well understood, we conducted an empirical study in order to discover these effects and their extent in AO systems. In this section, we present works we believe are directly related to our own, distributed in four categories: (i) static analysis tools; (ii) AOP and exception handling; (iii) experimental studies on exception handling code; and (iv) AO fault models and bug patterns.

Static Analysis Tools: Robillard and Murphy [29] developed a tool called Jex that analyzes the flow of exceptions in Java Programs. Based on java source code this tool performs dataflow analysis in order to find the propagation paths of checked and unchecked exception types. Jo et al. [17] present a set-based static analysis of Java programs that estimates their exception flows. This analysis is used to detect too general or unnecessary exception specifications and handlers. Fu et al. [10] developed a static analysis tool, built upon Soot framework for bytecode analysis, and Spark a call graph builder provided by Soot that generates a call graph of a higher precision compared to the works mentioned previously. This static analysis tool generates the exception paths to every exception thrown on the system. Fu et al. [11] extended their tool in order to compute chains. An exception chain is a combination of semantically-related exception paths. Our tool is similar to the previous one [10], but it works on top of AspectJ code.

AOP and Exception Handling: Lippert and Lopes [20] applied aspect constructs on a large OO framework, called JWAM, to modularize the exception handling code. In their experiment, they obtained a large reduction in the amount of exception handling code present in the application – from 11% of the total code in the OO version to 2.9% in the AO version. Castor Filho et al. [6, 7] performed a similar study but their work reports that the reuse of exception handlers is not straightforward as advocated beforehand by Lippert and Lopes [20]. Instead, it depends on a set of factors such as: the type of exceptions being handled; what the handler does; the amount of contextual information needed; what the method raising the exception returns; and what the throws clause actually specifies. Our study differs from its predecessors since it does not aim at aspectizing exception handling constructs. Actually, we aim at providing a better understanding on how programmers write exception handling code in AspectJ, and identifying possible flaws in the usage of aspects in the presence of exceptional scenarios.

Experimental Studies on Exception Handling Code: Bruno and Cabral [4] performed a quantitative study in which they examined source code samples of 32 different applications, both for Java and .NET. The goal of their study was to identify how exceptions were handled in different categories of systems. They examined the exception handlers and the respective actions taken on them. As a result of this analysis, they observed that the action handlers were very simple (e.g., logging and present a message to the user). However, Bruno and Cabral did not consider the exception paths of each system. As a consequence, they did not take into account the number of *uncaught* exceptions, and the number of exceptions treated by each handler. In our work, we performed an empirical study of how AOP constructs may influence on the way the exceptions are treated on the system.

AO Fault Models and Bug Patterns: Alexander et al. [37] proposed a candidate fault model that includes a set of fault types mostly related to AspectJ features. However, none of them is related to the exceptional scenarios. This fault model was later extended by Cecatto et al. [38], who characterized faults related to "incorrect changes in exceptional control flow." These faults may occur when an aspect signals an exception which can triggers the execution of a catch statement, either in the aspect itself or in the base program. They also argue that signaled exceptions, when declared as soft, may imply the execution of different branches in the aspectized code. Bækken [39] presents a fine-grained fault model for pointcuts and advice in AspectJ programs. Although Bækken does not describe faults related to exceptional scenarios, he discuss how control and data flows are influenced by exception throwing in order to establish necessary and collectively sufficient conditions for a fault to produce a failure. Ferrari et al. [43] summarized all the previously identified fault types and included three new ones, which were all grouped according to the AO features they are related to. In addition, Ferrari et al. proposed a set of mutation operators to model instances of most of identified fault types, including some related to exception handling code. However, none of these authors detail the consequences of possible faults nor assessed the fault density in the context of real systems. Regarding bug patterns in AO programs, Zhang and Zhao [40] presented a set of general bug patterns for AO programs based on the AspectJ language. The authors stated that a bug pattern is a *"recurring relationship between potential bugs and explicit errors in a program."* However, the authors did not conduct any observational study that could provide evidences of presence of the proposed bug patterns. The bug patterns we present in this paper are specifically related to exception handling code in AO software and are based on recurring faults found throughout a fine-grained analysis of a set of AO applications.

8 Concluding Remarks

This paper presented a quantitative study to evaluate the impact of aspects on the exception control flow of programs. We selected a set of three systems that were implemented in Java and AspectJ. For two of these systems two different releases were investigated. After that, we compared all versions of the systems in terms of the number of *uncaught* exceptions, exceptions caught by *subsumption*, and exceptions caught with specialized handlers. In all the AspectJ versions, we observed an increase in the number of uncaught exceptions and a decrease in the number of exceptions caught with specialized handlers. Such increase was less significant in AJHotdraw due to the fact that it was built through a well defined set of refactoring steps [21], and most of the aspects are composed by intertype declarations. We performed systematic code inspection of each exception path to find out what caused such negative discrepancies in AspectJ releases. The bug patterns identified came from three sources: aspects acting as *handlers*, aspects as *exception signalers*, and misuses of the `declare soft` construct. This paper also presents a catalogue of bug patterns that characterizes a set of recurring program anomalies found on the exception handling code of AspectJ programs. Our findings indicate that mechanisms of AO languages negatively affect the robustness of exception-aware software systems. As a result, there is a need for both improving the design of exception handling mechanisms in AO programming languages and building static analysis tools and testing techniques tailored to improve the reliability of the error handling code in AO programs. We are currently working on an extension of AspectJ [5] to improve modularity and robustness of exception handling. We are also currently evolving our exception flow analysis tool to support automatic finding of the bug patterns catalogue in this paper.

Acknowledgements. This research was partially sponsored by: CAPES (grants No. 3548-06-6 and 653-07-1);FAPERJ (grant No. E-26/100.061/06);FAPESP (grant No. 05-55403-6);EC Grant AOSD-Europe-European Network of Excellence on AOSD (IST-2-004349);EC Grant AMPLE - Aspect-Oriented, Model-Driven Product Line Engineering (IST-33710);and LatinAOSD/CNPq-Prosul project.

References

1. Aldrich, J.: Open Modules: Modular Reasoning about Advice. In: Black, A.P. (ed.) ECOOP 2005. LNCS, vol. 3586, pp. 144–168. Springer, Heidelberg (2005)
2. Allen, E.: Bug patterns in Java, 2nd edn. Apress (2002)
3. Assessing the Impact of Aspects on Exception Flows: An Empirical Study, http://www.inf.puc-rio.br/~roberta/aop_exceptions
4. Cabral, B., Marques, P.: Exception Handling: A Field Study in Java and.NET. In: Ernst, E. (ed.) ECOOP 2007. LNCS, vol. 4609, pp. 151–175. Springer, Heidelberg (2007)
5. Cacho, N., Castor Filho, F., Garcia, A., Figueiredo, E.: EJFlow: Taming Exceptional Control Flows in Aspect-Oriented Programming. In: Proc. of AOSD 2008 (2008)
6. Castor Filho, F., Cacho, N., Figueiredo, E., Maranhão, R., Garcia, A., Rubira, C.: Exceptions and Aspects: The Devil is in the Details. In: 13th ACM SIGSOFT (2006)
7. Castor Filho, F., Garcia, A., Rubira, C.: Extracting Error Handling to Aspects: A Cookbook. In: ICSM 2007 (2007)
8. Clifton, C., Leavens, G.T.: Observers and Assistants: A Proposal for Modular Aspect-Oriented Reasoning. In: Workshop on Foundations of Aspect Languages (2002)
9. Figueiredo, E., et al.: Evolving Software Product Lines with Aspects: An Empirical Study on Design Stability. In: Proc. of ICSE 2008 (2008)
10. Fu, C., Milanova, A., Ryder, B.G., Wonnacott, D.: Robustness Testing of Java Server Applications. IEEE Trans. Software Engineering 31(4), 292–311 (2005)
11. Fu, C., Ryder, B.G.: Exception-Chain Analysis: Revealing Exception Handling Architecture in Java Server Applications. In: ICSE 2007, pp. 230–239. ACM Press, New York (2007)
12. Garcia, A., et al.: A Comparative Study of Exception Handling Mechanisms for Building Dependable Object-Oriented Software. Journal of Systems and Software 59(6), 197–222 (2001)
13. Garcia, A., Sant'Anna, C., Figueiredo, E., Kulesza, U., Lucena, C.J.P., von Staa, A.: Modularizing Design Patterns with Aspects: A Quantitative Study. In: AOSD 2005, pp. 3–14 (2005)

14. Greenwood, P., et al.: On the Impact of Aspectual Decompositions on Design Stability: An Empirical Study. In: Ernst, E. (ed.) ECOOP 2007. LNCS, vol. 4609, pp. 176–200. Springer, Heidelberg (2007)
15. Hannemann, J., Kiczales, G.: Design Pattern Implementation in Java and AspectJ. In: OOPSLA 2002, pp. 161–173. ACM Press, New York (2002)
16. JHotDraw as Open-Source Project (accessed 19/12/2007), http://www.jhotdraw. org/
17. Jo, J., Chang, B., Yi, K., Choe, K.: An Uncaught Exception Analysis for Java. Journal of Systems and Software 72(1), 59–69 (2004)
18. Katz, S.: Aspect Categories and Classes of Temporal Properties. In: Rashid, A., Aksit, M. (eds.) Transactions on Aspect-Oriented Software Development I. LNCS, vol. 3880, pp. 106–134. Springer, Heidelberg (2006)
19. Krishnamurthi, S., Fisler, K., Greenberg, M.: Verifying Aspect Advice Modularly. In: FSE 2004, pp. 137–146. ACM Press, New York (2004)
20. Lippert, M., Lopes, C.: A Study on Exception Detection and Handling Using Aspect-Oriented Programming. In: Proc. of ICSE 2000, pp. 418–427. ACM Press, New York (2000)
21. Marin, M., Moonen, L., van Deursen, A.: An Integrated Crosscutting Concern Migration Strategy and its Application to JHotDraw. In: SCAM 2007, pp. 101–110. IEEE Comp. Soc, Los Alamitos (2007)
22. McCune, T.: Exception Handling Antipatterns (2006) (accessed 19/12/2007), http://today.java.net/pub/a/today/006/04/06/exception-handling-antipatterns.html
23. Mezini, M., Ostermann, K.: Conquering Aspects with Caesar. In: AOSD 2003, pp. 90–99 (2003)
24. Miller, R., Tripathi, A.: Issues with Exception Handling in Object-Oriented Systems. In: Aksit, M., Matsuoka, S. (eds.) ECOOP 1997. LNCS, vol. 1241, pp. 85–103. Springer, Heidelberg (1997)
25. Molesini, A., Garcia, A., Chavez, C., Batista, T.: On the Quantitative Analysis of Architecture Stability in Aspectual Decompositions. In: WICSA 2008 (2008)
26. Rashid, A., Chitchyan, R.: Persistence as an Aspect. In: AOSD 2003, pp. 120–129 (2003)
27. Rinard, M., Salcianu, A., Bugrara, S.: A Classification System and Analysis for Aspect-Oriented Programs. In: FSE 2004, pp. 147–158. ACM Pres, New York (2004)
28. Robillard, M., Murphy, G.: Static Analysis to Support the Evolution of Exception Structure in Object-Oriented Systems. ACM Trans. Softw. Eng. Methodol. 12(2), 191–221 (2003)
29. Robillard, M., Murphy., G.: Analyzing Exception Flow in Java Programs. In: Nierstrasz, O., Lemoine, M. (eds.) ESEC 1999 and ESEC-FSE 1999. LNCS, vol. 1687, pp. 322–337. Springer, Heidelberg (1999)
30. Robillard, M., Murphy., G.: Designing Robust Java Programs with Exceptions. In: Proc. of FSE 2000, pp. 2–10. ACM Press, New York (2000)
31. Soares, S., Borba, P., Laureano, E.: Distribution and Persistence as Aspects. Software Practice and Experience 36(7), 711–759 (2006)
32. The Soot Framework (accessed 19/12/2007) (2007), http://www.sable.mcgill. ca/soot
33. The AspectJ Project (accessed 19/12/2007) (2007), http://www.eclipse.org/ aspectj/
34. van Dooren, M., Steegmans, E.: Combining the Robustness of Checked Exceptions with the Flexibility of Unchecked Exceptions Using Anchored Exception Declarations. In: Proc. of OOPSLA 2005, pp. 455–471. ACM Press, New York (2005)

35. Filman, R., Elrad, T., Clarke, S., Aksit, M.: Aspect-Oriented Software Development. Addison-Wesley, Reading (2005)
36. Bruntink, M., Deursen, A., Tourwé, T.: Discovering faults in idiom-based exception handling. In: ICSE 2006, pp. 242–251 (2006)
37. Alexander, R.T., Bieman, J.M., Andrews, A.A.: Towards the Systematic Testing of Aspect-Oriented Programs. Report CS-04-105, Dept. of Computer Science, Colorado State University, Fort Collins/Colorado - USA (2004)
38. Ceccato, M., Tonella, P., Ricca, F.: Is AOP Code Easier or Harder to Test than OOP Code? In: Proc. of WTAOP 2005 (2005)
39. Bækken, J.S.: A Fault Model for Pointcuts and Advice in AspectJ Programs. Master's thesis, School of Electrical Engineering and Computer Science, Washington State University, Pullman/WA - USA (2006)
40. Zhang, S., Zhao, J.: On Identifying Bug Patterns in Aspect-Oriented Programs. In: Proc. of COMPSAC 2007, pp. 431–438. IEEE Computer Society, Los Alamitos (2007)
41. Kiczales, G., Lamping, J., Mendhekar, A., Maeda, C., Lopes, C., Loingtier, J., Irwin, J.: Aspect-Oriented Programming. In: ECOOP (1997)
42. Wohlin, C., Runeson, P., Host, M., Ohlsson, M.C., Regnell, B., Wesslen, A.: Experimentation in Software Engineering - An Introduction. Kluwer Academic Publishers, Dordrecht (2000)
43. Ferrari, F.C., Maldonado, J.C., Rashid, A.: Mutation Testing for Aspect-Oriented Programs. In: Proc. of ICST 2008. IEEE Computer Society Press, Los Alamitos (2008)

UpgradeJ: Incremental Typechecking for Class Upgrades

Gavin Bierman[1], Matthew Parkinson[2], and James Noble[3]

[1] Microsoft Research Cambridge
[2] University of Cambridge
[3] Victoria University of Wellington

Abstract. One of the problems facing developers is the constant evolution of components that are used to build applications. This evolution is typical of any multi-person or multi-site software project. How can we program in this environment? More precisely, how can language design address such evolution? In this paper we attack two significant issues that arise from constant component evolution: we propose language-level extensions that permit multiple, co-existing versions of classes and the ability to dynamically upgrade from one version of a class to another, whilst still maintaining type safety guarantees and requiring only lightweight extensions to the runtime infrastructure. We show how our extensions, whilst intuitive, provide a great deal of power by giving a number of examples. Given the subtlety of the problem, we formalize a core fragment of our language and prove a number of important safety properties.

1 Introduction

Modern programming languages typically provide support for separate compilation and dynamic linking of components. This allows for code to be developed at multiple sites and shared across multiple applications, supporting code evolution and reuse. Programmers can build applications from these components, utilizing the runtime infrastructure to dynamically link in the components as required.

Experience has shown that this style of software construction is extremely fragile: because both context code and components evolve independently, there are few guarantees a program will actually "run anywhere"—or even typecheck—when linked dynamically against the motley collections of components found in most installed systems. There are many instances of this problem—commonly known as "DLL hell" or more recently "JAR hell"—servlet engines that depend on different, incompatible versions of XML libraries; web tools that rely on rendering engines from specific versions of open-source web browsers, so upgrading the browsers breaks the associated tools; language runtimes that depend on exact versions of ActiveX code support and so on.

A number of solutions to this problem have been proposed, ranging from third-party tools, particular programming patterns, centralized management systems (e.g. RPM [4]), dynamic, reflective package infrastructures (e.g. OSGi [21]), to runtime architectural support (e.g. .NET and JVM). Most of these solutions are external to the application itself, and place a burden on the runtime infrastructure. Rather than solving the problem of evolving and incompatible programs and components, they just move it sideways, into tools, middleware, or external policies that allow flexible bindings but

J. Vitek (Ed.): ECOOP 2008, LNCS 5142, pp. 235–259, 2008.

make few guarantees about the compatibility between a program and the components to which it may be bound.

In this paper, we aim to tackle the problem of program and component upgrading and evolution head-on, giving control to the programmer. Rather than having implicit rules about how programs can be bound, we make component versions explicit: every class and type in the program has a version number. We provide language support for upgrading classes in a variety of ways, and provide an assymetrical, incremental (but not iterative) type system that checks upgrades for consistency with the currently-running program. This enables us to be explicit about component compatibility; to give guarantees about which changes to classes are at least type safe (and which are not); and so to write code that is robust against multiple upgrades of the same component.

Having decided on language support for upgrading, an immediate question is at what level of granularity do we provide such support? Unfortunately, many issues concerning programming in the large are still being resolved for Java-like languages, e.g. witness the ongoing discussions on providing modules for Java [28]. In this paper we address upgrading in the small rather than in the large.

In any case, we argue that upgrading of classes is the *essence of the problem*— even if language support is eventually provided at some higher level, matters will still boil down to class definitions in Java-like languages. As we shall see, this is a highly non-trivial problem. The issues of correctness are subtle enough that we believe that a precise approach is essential, and required prior to any implementation or software engineering issues.

The conceptual contribution of this paper is embodied in the design of UpgradeJ, a Java-like language with support for type-safe dynamic class upgrading. We extend classes to have explicit version numbers, e.g.

```
class Button[1] extends Widget[1] {
  Font[1] font = new Font[1=]();
  Colour[2] colour = new Colour[3+]();
}
```

and types declare the versions of classes they will accept (the font field stores objects compatible with Font version 1, while the colour field stores Colour instances compatible with version 2). Then, new expressions also include version numbers with the class names, but in addition they include information about instances' upgradeability. Hence the new Font object instance will remain fixed at version 1, whilst the new Colour object will be version 3 but may be upgraded later. (The exact behaviour of these annotations will be explained in more detail in §2 and formalized precisely in §4.)

Programmers can also request instances of the most evolved version of a particular class. For example, given:

```
Colour[3] latest = new Colour[3++]();
```

the instance actually stored in latest will be the most evolved version of Colour version 3 at object creation time. Moreover, it may be subsequently upgraded.

UpgradeJ then allows classes to be updated with newer versions dynamically. There are a number of ways that this could be supported; but for simplicity we model upgrading with upgrade statements of the form: upgrade. When an upgrade statement is executed the program will be upgraded if any suitable upgrades are available.

Not all upgrades make sense, or can be supported trivially. The technical contribution of the paper is exactly how we enforce the safe upgrading of classes to be *incremental*—so that any class declaration is only ever typechecked once—whilst ensuring that an upgrade can never break the type safety of a running program.

Compared to some previous work, the focus of UpgradeJ is on what we call *class upgrading*: adding in new classes to a running system, and performing minor or major upgrades of existing classes. Unlike many other approaches, UpgradeJ does *not* perform any kind of object or instance upgrading. In other words we never alter a runtime object, just perhaps its behaviour. As a result, we expect that the features of UpgradeJ should be able to be implemented efficiently: each class or method definition is checked only once when first presented to the system; and UpgradeJ never requires any (expensive) traversals, inspections or bulk modifications of the heap. Indeed, our aim in this paper is to explore the design space of upgrading mechanisms that are strictly less powerful than object updates, although we argue in §6 that object updating could be implemented in UpgradeJ by combining class upgrades with a couple of reflective primitives. For similar reasons of practicality, we do not consider any kind of functional correctness between upgrades: we work only with types, and not with behavioural specifications.

The rest of the paper is organized as follows. We give an extensive, examples-driven introduction to the support for class upgrades in UpgradeJ in §2, beginning with support for class versions, then describing three different kinds of upgrades: *new class upgrades* that introduce new subclasses; *revision upgrades* that change the code of existing classes; and *evolution upgrades* that extend existing classes (but do not change existing instances). In §3 we consider a more realistic example and show how UpgradeJ can be used to dynamically upgrade a long-running server application. In §4 we give a precise definition of a featherweight version of UpgradeJ, FUJ, and define formally its type system and operational semantics. We can prove that FUJ is type-sound. We discuss related and future work in §5 before concluding in §6.

2   An Introduction to UpgradeJ

Explicit versions and new class upgrades: UpgradeJ extends Java syntactically by requiring all class names (other than Object by convention) to be annotated by a version number in square brackets after the class name.[1] For example:

```
class Button[1] extends Object {
  Object press() { ... }
}
class AnimatedButton[1] extends Button[1] {
  Object fancyPress() { ... this.press(); ... }
}
```

UpgradeJ programs can include *upgrade statements*, written upgrade. When an upgrade statement is executed, the program waits to receive an upgrade (this could be via a command prompt or from a file). The upgrade is typechecked and if correct is applied to the program. Having explicit upgrade statements allows programmers to control the timing of upgrades to the application. UpgradeJ supports three forms of upgrade that we shall now discuss in turn.

---

[1] One can imagine tool support that would alleviate the burden of writing version numbers.

The simplest form of upgrade supported by UpgradeJ is called a *new class upgrade*. It allows new class definitions to be added (at runtime) to the class table. For clarity, a new class upgrade is written as a class definition prefixed with the keyword new. To differentiate upgrades from standard code in this paper, we present them in a shaded box. For example, in the example above the class AnimatedButton[1] could have been defined via a new class upgrade as follows:

```
new class AnimatedButton[1] extends Button[1] {
  Object fancyPress() { ... this.press(); ... }
}
```

UpgradeJ will typecheck the upgrade in the context of the current program state: if the tests pass, then the current program is upgraded to include the new definitions. An important design feature of UpgradeJ is that typechecking of upgrades is *incremental*, that is, only the new definitions in the upgrade are typechecked. Old definitions are never re-checked: the typechecker will check the correctness of each class definition only once (either when supplied as part of the initial program, or when it arrives as an upgrade).

At this point there is no way an UpgradeJ program can *use* any classes introduced by a new class upgrade: references from old classes to new classes will fail because the old classes will have been typechecked before the upgrades arrive: we call this the "*no time travel*" principle. As we shall see later, new class upgrades are still very useful as they allow new code to be installed; other upgrade forms will allow this code to be put to work.

Revision upgrades: Returning to our simple button example, let's imagine that Button has also a method bgColour which returns the colour of their background. For example, the first version of Button was clearly written around 1990:

```
class Button[1] extends Object {
  Object press(){ ... }
  Colour bgColour() { return new BeigeColour[1](); }
}
```

By the mid-90s, these buttons have begun to look dated. In UpgradeJ we can use a *revision upgrade* to provide a revision of an existing class to fix this problem. The revision upgrade is written as follows:[2]

```
new class Button[2] extends Object revises Button[1]{
  Object press(){...}
  Colour bgColour() { return new GreyColour[1](); }
}
```

To allow upgrades to affect running programs, we provide new forms of instantiation. As in Java, objects are created by calling new, however in UpgradeJ programmers must supply both a version number for the class *and* an annotation of either '+' to denote an upgradeable instance or '=' to denote a non-upgradeable (or exact) instance.

---

[2] Actually, this is sugar for two primitive UpgradeJ upgrades: first, a new class upgrade introducing the class Button[2], and second, a *revises statement* Button[2] revises Button[1]. Our formalization in §4 uses these primitive forms.

For example, new Button[2=]() creates a new instance of Button[2], the = ensures that the object will have the *exact* version 2 (in other words, if the Button class is subsequently upgraded this instance is insensitive to those upgrades). By contrast, upgradeable objects take advantage of all revisions as soon as they are supplied: after a revision upgrade, any methods sent to an upgradeable object will execute the revised method definitions.

For example, we can create two instances of Button[1], one exact and one upgradeable, both of which will have a beige background. Then, we can execute an upgrade statement (whose effect is to revise Button[1] to Button[2] as above), and ask each button for its bgColour. The exact button object will still return a BeigeColour instance, while the upgradeable button will return GreyColour.

```
Button[1] x = new Button[1=](); // exact
Button[1] u = new Button[1+](); // upgradeable
x.bgColour(); // returns BeigeColour
u.bgColour(); // returns BeigeColour

upgrade; // Button[2] revises Button[1]

x.bgColour(); // returns BeigeColour
u.bgColour(); // returns GreyColour
```

One point to note here is that the *types* of the variables storing the buttons are the same — both are just Button[1]. This is because every class introduced as a revision upgrade, just as every class introduced as a new class upgrade, is a *subtype* of the class being upgraded. A type like Button[1] will accept any Button[1] (as per usual); any subclass of Button[1] (defined either in the initial program or supplied via a new class upgrade); and any other upgrade of Button[1].[3] We discuss supporting exact annotations on types later in this section.

As fashions change, we can upgrade again:

```
new class Button[3] extends Object revises Button[2]{
  Object press(){ ... }
  Colour bgColour() { return new TransparentAquaColour[1](); }
}
```

Multiple upgrades can be hard to follow, so we draw class diagrams showing version numbers explicitly, and revision relationships with a wavy arrow. The three versions of the Button class that we have defined so far are shown as follows:

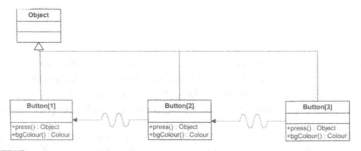

---

[3] **UpgradeJ** supports explicit syntax for this. In fact, Button[1] is shorthand for Button[1+].

To support the dynamic behaviour of upgradeable objects, however, UpgradeJ must place some restrictions on the bodies of revision upgrades: the classes must have the same name, the upgrade cannot revise a class that has already been revised, and (most importantly) the resulting revised class must have *exactly the same fields and method signature as the class it is revising*, and implement every interface. By the method signature of a class, we mean all the methods and their types that are understood by objects of that class, including inherited methods. Hence, the methods themselves need not reside in the same class; this allows for *refactoring* by upgrades (see later).

So, for example,

```
new class Button[4] extends Object revises Button[2] { ... }
```

is an invalid upgrade if Button[2] has already been revised to Button[3]; and

```
new class Button[5] extends Object revises Button[3] {
...
Integer transparency;
Integer setTransparency(Integer t){...}
...
}
```

is invalid because it includes a new field and a new method to the Button class.

The restrictions on version numbers and names are primarily there to make the type names consistent. The linear ordering on revisions (only the latest revision can itself be revised) is important to support upgradeable objects: there is a simple, nonbranching sequence of revisions, the *latest* revision of a class is always obvious, and so it's clear which methods an upgradeable object should run.

The restriction that the resulting revised class must have exactly the same fields and method signature means that revised classes can change method bodies, and omit or override methods declared concretely in ancestor classes. This restriction is necessary to support the incremental nature of UpgradeJ, and to avoid any heap inspection. A revision cannot add (or remove) fields from an object, because that would require the heap representation of every upgradeable object to be changed. Methods cannot be added into a class because they cannot be checked incrementally. We do not expect these restrictions to be too arduous in practice because they reflect the intent of revision upgrades: to *revise* an existing class, not to introduce new functionality.

Evolution upgrades: New class upgrades allow new fields and methods to be defined, but require a new class to be created: existing instances cannot take advantage of the upgrade. On the other hand, revision upgrades take immediate effect across all upgradeable instances of the class, but cannot add fields and methods. The final type of upgrade supported by UpgradeJ is the *evolution upgrade* that is, in some sense, a combination of the other two upgrade forms.

Evolution upgrades may add new methods and fields, but do not update existing objects. Rather, evolution upgrades are supported by another form of new, written new C[v++]() that creates an upgradeable object of the *latest evolution* of a class—in effect, doing a dynamic dispatch from a class to its most recent evolution upgrade.

Returning to our simple button example, we can add "2007" design and animation features to the button class with an evolution upgrade:[4]

```
new class Button[6] extends Object evolves Button[3]{
  Integer animationRate;
  void tick() {this.redraw(); }
  Colour bgColour() { return new VistaBlackColour[1](); }
  ...
}
```

Writing new Button[1++] will create a new instance of the *latest revision of the latest evolution upgrade* of the Button[1] class.

```
Button[1] e = new Button[1++]();
e.bgColour(); // returns TransparentAquaColour

upgrade; // Button[6] evolves Button[3]
e.bgColour(); // returns TransparentAquaColour

e = new Button[1++](); // latest creation
                       // now Button[6] is the latest kind of button
e.bgColour(); // returns VistaBlackColour
```

Note that this example demonstrates that, unlike revision upgrades, evolution upgrades do not upgrade the behaviour of existing instances. As with other upgrades, the types of the variables do not need to change; every upgrade is still a subtype of its target class; a variable at version n will be compatible with every subsequent version of that class.

There are restrictions on evolution upgrades. Whereas revision upgrades must preserve the same fields and method signatures of the revised class, evolution upgrades can extend both. Thus the new version of the class must include the fields and method signatures of the old version, but it can add new fields and new methods.

We also introduce a diagrammatic form for evolution upgrades. We introduce an evolution relationship between classes which is denoted using a "sawtooth" arrow (this is intended to symbolize the breaking change possible with an evolution upgrade). For example:

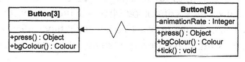

Revision, Evolution, and Inheritance: UpgradeJ has three different relationships between classes: the traditional inheritance relationship (that can be extended with new class upgrades), plus the revision and evolution relationships introduced to support upgrades. How do these relationships interact?

First, UpgradeJ permits a single class to have both revision and evolution upgrades. For example, consider the following definitions, where C[1] is revised by C[2] and, in addition, evolved into C[3]:

---

[4] Again, we use some syntactic sugar: this evolution upgrade can be decomposed into a new class upgrade and an *evolves statement* (in this case Button[6] evolves Button[3]).

```
class C[1] {
  void v() { print "one"; }
}
```

```
new class C[2] revises C[1] {
  void v() { print "two"; }
}
new class C[3] evolves C[1] {
  void v() { print "three"; }
}
```

giving the following class structure:

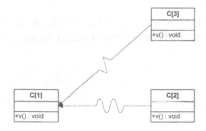

There are three forms of object creation in UpgradeJ: (1) exact creation giving a fixed object; (2) creating an upgradeable object (that follows the `revises` relationship); and (3) creating an upgradeable object of the latest version (that follows both the `evolves` relationship and then the `revises` relationship):

```
new C[1=]().v();   // outputs "one"
new C[1+]().v();   // outputs "two"
new C[1++]().v();  // outputs "three"
```

Second, inheritance (the `extends` relationship) interacts quite straightforwardly with upgrades. Message sends to upgradeable objects always take account of revision upgrades (while sends to exact objects always ignore them) so upgradeable objects also see revisions to their superclasses:

```
new class D[2] extends C[1] {}
```

```
new D[2=]().v(); // outputs "one"
new D[2+]().v(); // outputs "two"
```

while new class and evolution upgrades will only affect message sending if instances of their classes are involved directly.

Refactoring: As revision upgrades are required to preserve only the fields and method *signatures* of the classes they revise, we can move methods around the hierarchy using a combination of revision and evolution or new class upgrades. The key here is that provided a revised class has the same signatures and fields as the target class it is revising, the two classes need have no other relationship. Given a couple of simple classes:

```
class Component[1] { }
class Button[1] extends Component[1] {
 TLevel getTransparencyLevel(){...}
}
```

We can evolve the Component superclass to define a getTransparencyLevel() method, and then *revise* the Button subclass to inherit that method from the new superclass, and so *removing the method from the subclass.*

```
new class Component[2] evolves Component[1] {
    TLevel getTransparencyLevel(){...}
}

new class Button[2] extends Component[2] revises Button[1] { }
```

The resulting structure is shown below: note that, because we use a revision upgrade upon the Buttons, this change will apply dynamically to every upgradeable instance of Button[1].

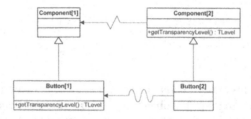

Exact version types: Sometimes programmers will need to restrict their code to a particular version of a class. For example, for historical or aesthetic reasons, a programmer might wish to write a BeigeWindow class that only uses the first beige version for its Buttons:

```
class BeigeWindow[1] extends Window {
  Button[1=] okButton, cancelButton;
  ...
}
```

To prevent the fields okButton and cancelButton from receiving more recent versions, we use *exact version types* declared with an "=" modifier.

An exact version type is compatible with only one (or a list of) explicit version(s): versions of the type outside that list are not subtypes of the exact version type. (The relationship between exact version types and version types is the same as that between exact types and subtypes in object-oriented languages [9]). An exact version type is assignable only from another exact type or an exact object creation. Hence, okButton = new Button[2](); would fail to typecheck, as Button[2] is *not* a subtype of the exact version type Button[1=], but only of the non-exact type Button[1].

In fact, our UpgradeJ language design supports a list of versions in exact types, and also allows that list to be open ended. For example, if it was known that the Button[3] upgrade introduced a bug that was subsequently removed by the Button[5] upgrade, a variable safeButton could be declared as: Button[1=,2=,5] safeButton; permitting exact Button objects of versions 1 and 2, and any exact or upgradeable Buttons of version 5 or above to be stored in the variable but not the buggy Button[3] or Button[4].

Exact types, even more than exact objects, reduce the flexibility of software which uses them: we expect that they would be used sparingly, primarily to avoid bugs in particular versions of components. This is why the default for type declarations is that the types are upgradeable, and why exact types require the "=" annotation. Nevertheless, we expect there will be situations where programmers will demand that only a particular version of a component is used to build a system, and exact version types provide this guarantee.

Summary: UpgradeJ introduces a number of novel features to Java-like programming languages: explicit versions of classes, fixed version and upgradeable version objects, an upgrade statement, new class, revision, and evolution upgrades, and exact version types.

The following table summarizes the relationships between the main features of UpgradeJ: the kinds of upgrades versus the kinds of objects and constructor calls.

		Upgrade Type		
		New Class	Revision	Evolution
Class Definitions:	Redefine existing method bodies	N/A	yes	yes
	Add new fields	yes	no	yes
	Add new methods	yes	no	yes
Creation:	Exact new C[1=]	no	no	no
	Upgradeable new C[1+]	no	yes	no
	Latest new C[1++]	no	yes	yes
Method invocation:	Exact T[1=,2=]	no	no	no
	Upgradeable T[1]	no	yes	no

Revision and evolution upgrades may redefine methods (give new method bodies such that the resulting flattened class signature does not change), while only new class and evolution upgrades may declare new fields or methods. Creating an exact object "new C[1=]" sees no upgrades, while creating an upgradeable object "new C[1+]" sees revision upgrades and using latest creation "new C[1++]" creates an instance of the most recent revision of the most recent extension. Methods sent to exact objects again see no revisions, while methods sent to upgradeable objects see revision updates.

Finally (not shown in the table), exact version types are subtypes only of the exact versions given in the type, while all subsequent versions of a type (both exact and not-exact) are subtypes of earlier non-exact versions of that type.

3   Example: Upgrading a Server Application

In this section we present a fairly realistic example of the upgrading of a long-lived server application. This example first appeared in a functional programming setting in work on dynamic software updating by Bierman et al. [5] (although updates in that setting required a run-time typecheck of the entire program state). To make the example simpler, we ignore the issues of concurrency and assume a single-threaded, event-based software architecture. In order to save space, we also only give the essential code fragments to illustrate our point, rather than giving a full program.

Initial system: The code for our server is given below. The key class is Server which contains a private field, myQ, containing a queue of events, e.g. HTTP requests from clients or responses from handlers. (We do not give details of the Queue class for lack of space.) New events are created by the NewEvent method, which either enqueues the event and returns, or blocks if the queue is empty and no new events have occured. Once an event occurs, then it is removed from the head of the queue using the remove method. All events extend the Event class, which specifies a handle method. We assume for now just two events; get_Event and upgrade_Event (the programmer has forgotten about put events; this will be added later). The upgrade_Event simply executes an upgrade statement and leaves the event queue untouched. This enables the server to be upgraded. Note that after this upgrade has taken place, the next statement is the recursive call to loop, i.e. no remaining computation exists at this point.

```
new class Server[3] evolves Server[2] {
    Queue[1] myQ = new Queue[1]();
    Log[1]  myLog = new Log[1]();
    void newEvent(){ ... }
    void handOver(Queue[1] q){ myQ=q; loop(); }
    void logv1Event(Event[1] e){ ... }
    void loop(){
     newEvent(); //Enqueues new event
     Object e = myQ.remove();
     if (e instanceof Event[2])
       (Event[2])e.handle(myQ,myLog);
     else {
       e.handle(myQ);
       logv1Event(e);
     }
     loop();
    }
}
```

The code for the main method of our application then simply creates an *upgradeable* instance of the Server class and invokes its loop method, as follows.

```
Server[1] s = new Server[1+](); // Upgradeable object!
s.loop();                       // Do the work
```

First upgrade: Handling put events: As mentioned earlier, the programmer has forgotten about put events. These are easy to add to the system *dynamically* using new class and revision upgrades. First, we use a new class upgrade (by sending an upgrade event to the server) to add the new class put_Event.

```
new class put_Event[1] extends Event[1]{
    void handle (Queue[1] q){ ... }
}
```

We will also need to change the code of the newEvent method, as it will need to create instances of the put_Event class. As the signature of this method will be unchanged, this can be captured by a revision upgrade. We add the new revised class

`Server[2]` which is identical to `Server[1]` save for the new code in the `newEvent` method.

```
new class Server[2] revises Server[1] {
    Queue[1] myQ = new Queue[1]();
    void newEvent(){ ... } //NEW CODE!
    void loop(){
    newEvent(); //Enqueues new event
    Event[1] e = (Event[1])myQ.remove();
                       // remove head of myQ
    e.handle(myQ);
    loop();
    }
}
```

Now the original instance of `Server[1]` will invoke the new code for the `newEvent` method the next time it enters `loop`.

Second upgrade: Adding a log: Now we consider a much more disruptive upgrade to our system: adding a log to the server and requiring that all events update the log when they are handled. First we need to change the Event class as follows (the classes `get_Event`, `put_Event` and `upgrade_Event` must also be changed accordingly).

```
new class Event[2] evolves Event[1] {
    void handle (Queue[1] q, Log[1] l);
}
```

Note that this is an *evolution* upgrade: the signature of the events has changed. We also need an evolution upgrade to the `Server` class, as follows.

```
new class Server[3] evolves Server[2] {
    Queue[1] myQ = new Queue[1]();
    Log[1]   myLog = new Log[1]();
    void newEvent(){ ... }
    void handOver(Queue[1] q){ myQ=q; loop(); }
    void logv1Event(Event[1] e){ ... }
    void loop(){
    newEvent(); //Enqueues new event
    Object e = myQ.remove();
    if (e instanceof Event[2])
      (Event[2])e.handle(myQ,myLog);
    else {
      e.handle(myQ);
      logv1Event(e);
    }
    loop();
    }
}
```

This new version of the `Server` class has a new field, `myLog` to contain the system log. It also contains a new method, `logv1Event` to enable the logging of a `Event[1]` object. The body of the `loop` method is similar except that we now need to inspect each event to see if it can log itself or not. The handOver method will be more apparent after the next revision upgrade. (Note here the use of co-existing revision and evolution upgrades.)

```
new class Server[2.1] revises Server[2]{
    Queue[1] myQ = new Queue[1]();
    void newEvent(){ ... }
    void loop(){
      Server[3] s = new Server[3+]();
      s.handOver(myQ);
    }
}
```

This *revision* upgrade of Server[2] changes only the body of the loop method. Recall that after the upgrade event the next call is to the latest revision of the loop method. Hence our original (version 1) instance of Server will invoke the loop method defined in version 2.1. This loop method now simply creates a fresh Server[3] object and invokes its handOver method. The handOver method accepts the state from the old Server object and executes the loop method of the Server[3] object. Hence we have elegantly transitioned from an old to a new version of the server *at runtime*, whilst both maintaining the state and guaranteeing type safety!

4   Formalizing UpgradeJ

Featherweight UpgradeJ (FUJ) is to UpgradeJ what other core calculi such as FJ [18] and MJ [7] are to Java. It is a small, but expressive subset of the language that is used to verify formal properties of the language. FUJ is slightly unusual in that it has an extremely compact form, which facilitates a very simple operational semantics, however, it is as expressive as more familiar core calculi. It is important to note that FUJ programs are syntactically correct UpgradeJ programs.

Syntax: The syntax of FUJ class definitions, types, field and method definitions, and statements is defined as follows.

$T, S, U ::=$	Type
$C[v_1=, \ldots, v_n=]$	Version list type ($n \geq 1$)
$C[v+]$	Version range type
$K, J, I ::= C[v=]$	Exact version type
$R ::=$	Runtime type
$C[v=]$	Exact type
$C[v+]$	Upgradeable type
$L ::= \text{class } I \text{ extends } J\{ \overline{T} \overline{f}; \overline{M} \}$	Class definitions
$M ::= S \, m(\overline{T} \, \overline{x})\{ B \text{ return } y; \}$	Method definition
$B ::= \overline{T} \, \overline{x}; \overline{s}$	Method block

t, s ::=		Statement
	x = y;	Assignment
	x = y.f;	Field access
	x.f = y;	Field update
	x = y.m($\overline{z}$);	Method invocation
	x = (T)y	Cast
	if(x == y){$\overline{s}$} else {$\overline{t}$}	Equality test
	if(x instanceof I){$\overline{s}$} else {$\overline{t}$}	Instance test
	x = new C[v=]() ;	Object creation
	x = new C[v+]() ;	Object creation
	x = new C[v++]() ;	Object creation
	x = new Object() ;	Object creation
	upgrade;	Upgrading
Z ::=		Upgrade definitions
	new L	New class upgrade
	C[v=] revises C[w=]	Revision upgrade
	C[v=] evolves C[w=]	Evolution upgrade

In the syntax rules we assume a number of metavariables: f ranges over field names, C over class names, m over method names, v, w over versions,[5] and x, y, z over program variables. We assume that the set of program variables includes a designated variable this, which cannot be used as an argument to a method. We follow FJ and use an 'overbar' notation to denote sequences.

FUJ types are ranged over by S, T, U and can be either an exact version type, of the form C[v=], or a version list type, written C[v_1=, ... ,v_n=], or a version range type, written C[v+]. To simplify some definitions we use the metavariables I and J to range over exact version types. As with FJ, for simplicity we do not include any primitive types in FUJ. In FUJ there is a special exact version class Object[1=] which we abbreviate to Object. We do *not* allow this class to be revised or evolved, so it remains the root of the inheritance hierarchy.

A FUJ class definition, L, contains a collection of field and method definitions. For simplicity, in this paper we shall not consider constructor methods; they do not complicate the treatment of versioning and we simply model that fields are initialised to null. A field is defined by a type and a name. A method definition, M, is defined by a return type, a method name, an ordered list of arguments—where an argument is a variable name and a type—a method block, B, and a return statement.

The real economy of FUJ is that we do not have any syntactic forms for expressions (or even promotable expressions [7]), and that the forms for statements are syntactically restricted. All expression forms appear only on the right-hand side of assignments. Moreover expressions only ever involve variables. In this respect, our form for statements is reminiscent of the A-normal form for λ-terms [17]. A statement, s, is either an assignment, a field access, a field update, a method invocation, a cast, an instance conditional, an object creation, or an upgrade statement. In spite of the heavy syntactic restrictions, we have not lost any expressivity; it is quite simple to translate FJ or MJ

---

[5] Purely for presentational simplicity, versions are restricted to be integers.

programs into FUJ. Another advantage of our approach is that we have no need for the 'stupid' rules of FJ.

In FUJ we assume a rather large amount of syntactic regularity to make the definitions compact. All class definitions must (1) include a supertype; (2) start with all the declarations of the variables local to the method (hence a method block is a sequence of local variable declarations, followed by a sequence of statements); (3) have a `return` statement at the end of every method; and (4) write out field accesses explicitly, even when the receiver is `this`.

A FUJ upgrade is either a new class upgrade (which consists of a class definition prefixed with a new modifier) or a revision upgrade (which is of the form I `revises` J) or an evolution upgrade (which is of the form I `evolves` J).

Class table and subtyping: Following FJ, we take an FUJ program to be a pair (CT, B) of a class table CT and a method block B. This method block corresponds to the `main` method. As we are interested in upgrading the class table it cannot be assumed to be fixed and implicit as in FJ.

A FUJ class table, CT, is a triple $\langle C, \textbf{revises}, \textbf{evolves} \rangle$. The first component is a map from exact version types to class definitions. The second and third are relations between exact version types. We use some shorthand and write $CT \vdash \text{I} \triangleq \{\overline{\text{T}}\,\overline{\text{f}}; \overline{\text{M}}\}$ and $CT \vdash \text{I} \textbf{ extends } \text{J}$ where $C(\text{I}) = \text{class I extends J}\{\overline{\text{T}}\,\overline{\text{f}}; \overline{\text{M}}\}$. We also write $\text{I} \in dom(CT)$ to mean $\text{I} \in dom(C)$. We write $CT \vdash \text{I} \textbf{ revises } \text{J}$ when $(\text{I}, \text{J}) \in \textbf{revises}$, and similarly $CT \vdash \text{I} \textbf{ evolves } \text{J}$ when $(\text{I}, \text{J}) \in \textbf{evolves}$. The **revises** and **evolves** relations are initially empty and are incremented by the action of upgrade definitions.

By looking at a class table, we can read off a subtype relation between types. We write $CT \vdash \text{S} <: \text{T}$ when S is a subtype of T given the class table CT. This relation is slightly more complicated than for FJ because we have three relations between types (extends, revises and evolves) and also support version list and version range types. The rules for forming valid subtyping judgements are defined as follows.

$$\frac{\text{v=} \in \overline{\text{w}}}{CT \vdash \text{C[v=]} <: \text{C[\overline{w}]}} \text{ [ST-In]} \qquad \frac{CT \vdash \text{C[v=] revises C[w=]}}{CT \vdash \text{C[v=]} <: \text{C[w+]}} \text{ [ST-RevRng]}$$

$$\frac{CT \vdash \text{C[v=] evolves C[w=]}}{CT \vdash \text{C[v=]} <: \text{C[w+]}} \text{ [ST-EvRng]} \qquad \frac{CT \vdash \text{S} <: \text{T} \quad CT \vdash \text{T} <: \text{U}}{CT \vdash \text{S} <: \text{U}} \text{ [ST-Trans]}$$

$$\frac{CT \vdash \text{C[v=] revises C[w=]}}{CT \vdash \text{C[v+]} <: \text{C[w+]}} \text{ [ST-RngRng1]} \qquad \frac{CT \vdash \text{C[v=] evolves C[w=]}}{CT \vdash \text{C[v+]} <: \text{C[w+]}} \text{ [ST-RngRng2]}$$

$$\frac{CT \vdash \text{C[v=] extends I}}{CT \vdash \text{C[v+]} <: \text{I}} \text{ [ST-Rng]} \qquad \frac{CT \vdash \text{C[v=] extends I}}{CT \vdash \text{C[v=]} <: \text{I}} \text{ [ST-Ex]}$$

$$\frac{CT \vdash \text{C[v}_1\text{=]} <: \text{T} \cdots CT \vdash \text{C[v}_n\text{=]} <: \text{T}}{CT \vdash \text{C[v}_1\text{=}, \ldots, \text{v}_n\text{=]} <: \text{T}} \text{ [ST-List]}$$

Correctness conditions: Unlike in normal fragments of Java where correctness conditions on the class table are so routine that they are traditionally omitted [18], they are *essential* in formalizing UpgradeJ. In some senses they are the very essence of

UpgradeJ as the class table can be changed at runtime and all upgrade checks are made with reference to the class table. In other words an upgrade should not be able to compromise type safety.

The first correctness condition we impose is a well-formedness property on the three relations in the class table.

Definition 1. $\vdash CT$ *wfr iff*

1. $\forall S, T.$ *If* $CT \vdash S <: T$ *and* $CT \vdash T <: S$ *then* $T = S$,
2. $\forall K, I, J.$ *If* $CT \vdash K$ **extends** I *and* $CT \vdash K$ **extends** J *then* $I = J$, $I \in dom(CT)$ *and* $K \in dom(CT)$,
3. $\forall K, I, J.$ *If* $CT \vdash I$ **revises** K *and* $CT \vdash J$ **revises** K *then* $I = J$, $I \in dom(CT)$ *and* $K \in dom(CT)$, *and*
4. $\forall K, I, J.$ *If* $CT \vdash I$ **evolves** K *and* $CT \vdash J$ **evolves** K *then* $I = J$, $I \in dom(CT)$ *and* $K \in dom(CT)$.

Condition (1) ensures that the subtyping relation induced by the class table does not include cycles. Condition (2) reflects the fact that UpgradeJ supports only single inheritance. Analogously, UpgradeJ only supports single revision (3) and single evolution (4). Note that this does not preclude a class being both revised *and* evolved.

The next two correctness conditions we impose are on the **revises** and **evolves** relations.

Definition 2.

1. $CT \vdash J$ **revises** I ok *iff* $fields(CT, I) = fields(CT, J)$ *and* $methSig(CT, I) = methSig(CT, J)$
2. $CT \vdash J$ **evolves** I ok *iff* $fields(CT, I) \subseteq fields(CT, J)$ *and* $methSig(CT, I) \subseteq methSig(CT, J)$

(The auxiliary functions *fields* and *methSig* are defined in Figure 1.)

These correctness conditions for the upgrade relations formalize the discussions of §2. Thus a class J revises a class I if (i) the fields are identical, and (ii) the *method signatures* are identical. Notice that this does *not* force class J itself to have the same methods as class I; just that they support the same methods (possibly inherited from other classes). This allows us to support the refactoring upgrades described in §2.

The correctness rule for an evolution upgrade is similar but more permissive, as it allows the evolved class to have more fields and a larger method signature.

We can now give the overall correctness condition for a class table.

Definition 3. $\vdash CT = \langle C, \textbf{revises}, \textbf{evolves} \rangle$ ok *iff*

1. $\vdash CT$ *wfr,*
2. $\forall I \in dom(C).CT \vdash I$ ok,
3. $\forall I, J.(I, J) \in \textbf{revises} \implies CT \vdash I$ **revises** J ok, *and*
4. $\forall I, J.(I, J) \in \textbf{evolves} \implies CT \vdash I$ **evolves** J ok.

Informally, a class table is correct if (1) the class table relations are well-formed, (2) every class definition in the class table is correct (the formal definition of this is given later in this section), and (3-4) the revises and evolves relations are correct (in the sense of Defn. 2).

Fields:

$$fields(CT, \texttt{Object}) \overset{\text{def}}{=} \emptyset$$
$$fields(CT, \texttt{I}) \overset{\text{def}}{=} \{\overline{\texttt{T}}\ \overline{\texttt{f}}\} \cup fields(CT, \texttt{J}) \text{ where } CT \vdash \texttt{I} \triangleq \{\overline{\texttt{T}}\ \overline{\texttt{f}};\ \overline{\texttt{M}}\}$$
$$\text{and } CT \vdash \texttt{I} \textbf{ extends } \texttt{J}$$

Field lookup:

$$ftype(CT, \texttt{I}, \texttt{f}) \overset{\text{def}}{=} \texttt{T} \qquad\qquad \text{where } CT \vdash \texttt{I} \triangleq \{\overline{\texttt{S}}\ \overline{\texttt{g}}; \texttt{T}\ \texttt{f}; \overline{\texttt{U}}\ \overline{\texttt{h}};\ \overline{\texttt{M}}\}$$
$$ftype(CT, \texttt{I}, \texttt{f}) \overset{\text{def}}{=} ftype(CT, \texttt{J}, \texttt{f}) \qquad \text{where } CT \vdash \texttt{I} \triangleq \{\overline{\texttt{S}}\ \overline{\texttt{g}};\ \overline{\texttt{M}}\}, \texttt{f} \notin \overline{\texttt{g}},$$
$$\text{and } CT \vdash \texttt{I} \textbf{ extends } \texttt{J}$$
$$ftype(CT, \texttt{C[v+]}, \texttt{f}) \overset{\text{def}}{=} ftype(CT, \texttt{C[v]}, \texttt{f})$$
$$ftype(CT, \texttt{C[}v_1, \ldots v_n\texttt{]}, \texttt{f}) \overset{\text{def}}{=} ftype(CT, \texttt{C[}v_1\texttt{]}, \texttt{f})$$

Method type lookup:

$$mtype(CT, \texttt{I}, \texttt{m}) \overset{\text{def}}{=} \overline{\texttt{T}} \to \texttt{S} \qquad\qquad \text{where } CT \vdash \texttt{I} \triangleq \{\overline{\texttt{U}}\ \overline{\texttt{f}};\ \overline{\texttt{M}}\},$$
$$\text{and } \texttt{S}\ \texttt{m}(\overline{\texttt{T}}\ \overline{\texttt{x}})\{\ \texttt{B return y;}\ \} \in \overline{\texttt{M}}$$
$$mtype(CT, \texttt{I}, \texttt{m}) \overset{\text{def}}{=} mtype(CT, \texttt{J}, \texttt{m}) \qquad \text{where } CT \vdash \texttt{I} \triangleq \{\overline{\texttt{U}}\ \overline{\texttt{f}};\ \overline{\texttt{M}}\}, \texttt{m} \notin \overline{\texttt{M}},$$
$$\text{and } CT \vdash \texttt{I} \textbf{ extends } \texttt{J}$$
$$mtype(CT, \texttt{C[v+]}, \texttt{m}) \overset{\text{def}}{=} mtype(CT, \texttt{C[v]}, \texttt{m})$$
$$mtype(CT, \texttt{C[}v_1, \ldots v_n\texttt{]}, \texttt{m}) \overset{\text{def}}{=} mtype(CT, \texttt{C[}v_1\texttt{]}, \texttt{m})$$

Method body lookup:

$$mbody(CT, \texttt{C[v=]}, \texttt{m}) \overset{\text{def}}{=} \overline{\texttt{x}}.\texttt{B return y;} \qquad \text{where } CT \vdash \texttt{C[v=]} \triangleq \{\overline{\texttt{U}}\ \overline{\texttt{f}};\ \overline{\texttt{M}}\},$$
$$\text{and } \texttt{S}\ \texttt{m}(\overline{\texttt{S}}\ \overline{\texttt{x}})\{\ \texttt{B return y;}\ \} \in \overline{\texttt{M}}$$
$$\overset{\text{def}}{=} mbody(CT, \texttt{I}, \texttt{m}) \quad \text{where } CT \vdash \texttt{C[v=]} \triangleq \{\overline{\texttt{U}}\ \overline{\texttt{f}};\ \overline{\texttt{M}}\}, \texttt{m} \notin \overline{\texttt{M}},$$
$$CT \vdash \texttt{C[v=]} \textbf{ extends } \texttt{I}$$
$$mbody(CT, \texttt{C[v+]}, \texttt{m}) \overset{\text{def}}{=} mbody(CT, \texttt{I+}, \texttt{m}) \text{ where } CT \vdash \texttt{I} \textbf{ revises } \texttt{C[v=]}$$
$$\overset{\text{def}}{=} \overline{\texttt{x}}.\texttt{B return y;} \qquad \text{where } \forall\texttt{I}.\neg(CT \vdash \texttt{I} \textbf{ revises } \texttt{C[v=]}),$$
$$\text{and } CT \vdash \texttt{C[v=]} \triangleq \{\overline{\texttt{U}}\ \overline{\texttt{f}};\ \overline{\texttt{M}}\},$$
$$\text{and } \texttt{S}\ \texttt{m}(\overline{\texttt{S}}\ \overline{\texttt{x}})\{\ \texttt{B return y;}\ \} \in \overline{\texttt{M}}.$$
$$\overset{\text{def}}{=} mbody(CT, \texttt{J+}, \texttt{m}) \text{ where } \forall\texttt{I}.\neg(CT \vdash \texttt{I} \textbf{ revises } \texttt{C[v=]})$$
$$\text{and } CT \vdash \texttt{C[v=]} \triangleq \{\overline{\texttt{U}}\ \overline{\texttt{f}};\ \overline{\texttt{M}}\},$$
$$\text{and } \texttt{m} \notin \overline{\texttt{M}},$$
$$\text{and } CT \vdash \texttt{C[v=]} \textbf{ extends } \texttt{J}$$

Method signature:

$$methSig(CT, \texttt{Object}) \overset{\text{def}}{=} \emptyset$$
$$methSig(CT, \texttt{I}) \overset{\text{def}}{=} \{\texttt{m}: mtype(CT, \texttt{I}, \texttt{m})\}^{\texttt{m} \in \overline{\texttt{M}}} \cup methSig(CT, \texttt{J})$$
$$\text{where } CT \vdash \texttt{I} \triangleq \{\overline{\texttt{U}}\ \overline{\texttt{f}};\ \overline{\texttt{M}}\}, \text{ and } CT \vdash \texttt{I} \textbf{ extends } \texttt{J}$$

Latest version:

$$latest(CT, \texttt{J}) \overset{\text{def}}{=} latest(CT, \texttt{I}) \text{ if } CT \vdash \texttt{I} \textbf{ evolves } \texttt{J}$$
$$\overset{\text{def}}{=} latest(CT, \texttt{I}) \text{ if } CT \vdash \texttt{I} \textbf{ revises } \texttt{J}, \text{ and } \forall\texttt{K}.\neg(CT \vdash \texttt{K} \textbf{ evolves } \texttt{J})$$
$$\overset{\text{def}}{=} \texttt{J} \qquad\qquad \text{otherwise}$$

Fig. 1. Auxiliary functions

Typing rules: The typing rules for statements are given below where a typing environment Γ is a finite map from variables to types.

$$\frac{CT \vdash S <: T}{CT; \Gamma, x: T, y: S \vdash x = y;\ ok}\ \text{[T-Assign]} \qquad \frac{CT \vdash ftype(CT, S, f) <: T}{CT; \Gamma, x: T, y: S \vdash x = y.f;\ ok}\ \text{[T-FAccess]}$$

$$\frac{CT \vdash S <: ftype(CT, T, f)}{CT; \Gamma, x: S, y: T \vdash y.f = x;\ ok}\ \text{[T-FAssign]} \qquad \frac{}{CT; \Gamma, x: \texttt{Object} \vdash x = \texttt{new Object();}\ ok}\ \text{[T-New1]}$$

$$\frac{CT \vdash C[v] <: T}{CT; \Gamma, x: T \vdash x = \texttt{new C[v=]();}\ ok}\ \text{[T-New2]} \qquad \frac{CT \vdash C[v+] <: T}{CT; \Gamma, x: T \vdash x = \texttt{new C[v+]();}\ ok}\ \text{[T-New3]}$$

$$\frac{CT \vdash C[v+] <: T}{CT; \Gamma, x: T \vdash x = \texttt{new C[v++]();}\ ok}\ \text{[T-New4]} \qquad \frac{CT \vdash S <: T \quad CT \vdash S <: R}{CT; \Gamma, x: T, y: R \vdash x = \texttt{(S)y;}\ ok}\ \text{[T-DCast]}$$

$$\frac{CT \vdash R <: S \quad CT \vdash S <: T}{CT; \Gamma, x: T, y: R \vdash x = \texttt{(S)y;}\ ok}\ \text{[T-UCast]} \qquad \frac{}{CT; \Gamma \vdash \texttt{upgrade;}\ ok}\ \text{[T-Upgrade]}$$

$$\frac{CT; \Gamma \vdash \overline{s}\ ok \quad CT; \Gamma \vdash \overline{t}\ ok \quad CT \vdash S <: T \ \text{ or } \ CT \vdash T <: S}{CT; \Gamma, x: S, y: T \vdash \texttt{if(x == y)}\{\overline{s}\}\ \texttt{else}\ \{\overline{t}\}\ ok}\ \text{[T-If]}$$

$$\frac{CT; \Gamma \vdash \overline{s}\ ok \quad CT; \Gamma \vdash \overline{t}\ ok \quad CT \vdash T <: S \ \text{ or } \ CT \vdash S <: T}{CT; \Gamma, x: S \vdash \texttt{if(x instanceof T)}\{\overline{s}\}\ \texttt{else}\ \{\overline{t}\}\ ok}\ \text{[T-IfInst]}$$

$$\frac{mtype(CT, S, m) = \overline{T_1} \to U \qquad CT \vdash \overline{T_0} <: \overline{T_1} \quad CT \vdash U <: V}{CT; \Gamma, x: V, y: S, \overline{z}: \overline{T_0} \vdash x = \texttt{y.m(}\overline{z}\texttt{);}\ ok}\ \text{[T-Invoke]}$$

These rules are pretty routine. The remaining typing rules for statement sequences, method blocks, method definitions, and class definitions are similarly straightforward and are as follows.

$$\frac{CT; \Gamma \vdash s_1\ ok \ \cdots \ CT; \Gamma \vdash s_n\ ok}{CT; \Gamma \vdash s_1 \cdots s_n\ ok} \qquad \frac{CT; \Gamma, \overline{x}: \overline{T} \vdash \overline{s}\ ok}{CT; \Gamma \vdash \overline{T}\ \overline{x}; \overline{s}\ ok} \qquad \frac{}{CT \vdash \texttt{Object}\ ok}$$

$$\frac{\Gamma \stackrel{\text{def}}{=} \overline{x}: \overline{T}, \texttt{this}: I \quad CT; \Gamma \vdash B\ ok \quad CT \vdash \Gamma(y) <: S \quad CT \vdash I\ \text{extends}\ J}{\text{If } mtype(CT, J, m) = \overline{T_1} \to S_1 \text{ then } \overline{T_1} = \overline{T} \text{ and } S_1 = S}{CT \vdash S\ m(\overline{T}\ \overline{x})\{\ B\ \texttt{return}\ y;\ \}\ \texttt{in}\ I\ ok}$$

$$\frac{CT \vdash I \triangleq \{\overline{T}\ \overline{f};\ \overline{M}\} \quad CT \vdash I\ \text{extends}\ J \quad CT \vdash J \triangleq \{\overline{S}\ \overline{g};\ \overline{N}\} \quad \overline{f} \cap \overline{g} = \emptyset \quad CT \vdash \overline{M}\ \texttt{in}\ I\ ok}{CT \vdash I\ ok}$$

Operational Semantics: We define the operational semantics of FUJ in terms of labelled transitions between configurations (where l ranges over the labels). A configuration is a four-tuple, written $(CT, S, H, \overline{s})$, where CT is a class table, S is a stack which is a function from program variables to values, H is a heap which is a function from object identifiers to heap objects, and $\bar{s}$ is a sequence of statements that represents the code that is being executed. Because of the restricted syntactic form of FUJ we do not need the evaluation contexts of FJ [18] or the frame stacks and scopes of MJ [7]. The operational semantics are given in Figure 2.

The transition rules are fairly routine; the ones of interest are those dealing with object creation, method invocation and upgrades. The rule for creating a non-upgradeable object creates an object with a runtime type C[v=] and the rule for creating a revision upgradeable instance produces an object with a runtime type C[v+]. The rule dealing with creating a evolution upgradeable instance (new C[v++]) is a little more subtle. First we use the auxiliary function *latest* to discover the latest version of type C[v=], which is, say, I. We then create an upgradeable instance of type I. We write this type I+, where (C[v=])+ is defined to be C[v+].

The rule for method invocation uses the auxiliary function *mbody* to return the body of method m for an object whose runtime type is R. The definition of *mbody* is given in Figure 1. Its behaviour is dependent on the runtime type of the object. If it is an exact type, then *mbody* behaves as it does for FJ. If the runtime type is C[v+], then we look to see if the class has been revised. If there has been a revision, then we recursively search the revision. If there have been no revisions to the class and the method is implemented in class C[v=] then we use this implementation. If class C[v=] does not implement the method and there has not been a revision then we recursively search the superclass of C[v=].

We have also included the transition rules that deal with erroneous situations, e.g. null pointer invocation. Rather than introduce exceptions we follow MJ [7] and define a number of "stuck states".

Now we consider the upgrade transition rules. We label the transition with the upgrade definition in the familiar way [27]. Each of the transition rules for upgrades must extend the CT while ensuring that the subtype relation is a partial order (Defn. 1.1). Each transition rule builds on the following lemma to ensure this.

Lemma 1. *If R is a partial order, $\neg(xRy)$ and $\neg(yRx)$, then $(R \cup \{(x,y)\})^*$ is also a partial order.*

We consider the three 'upgrade' transition rules in turn.

Semantics of new class upgrades First we check that the new class has not already been defined. If it hasn't then we first add the definition to the class table (we use the shorthand $CT \uplus L$ to mean that the map from class names to definitions is updated) and then check that the class definition is type correct. (It must be added first to allow for recursive uses of the class in its definition.)

The transition rule embodies the following property that follows from the definition of the typing rules.

Lemma 2. *If $\vdash CT$ ok, $I \notin dom(CT)$, $CT' \stackrel{\text{def}}{=} CT \uplus \text{class I extends J\{\overline{U} \ \overline{f}; \ \overline{M}\}}$ and $CT' \vdash I$ ok, then $\vdash CT'$ ok.*

Semantics of revision upgrades First we need to check that the revision upgrade will not introduce any cycles in the inheritance graph. Assuming that it does not we then check that the revision upgrade is type correct. Finally we extend the class table with this revision (we use the shorthand $CT \uplus (J \text{ revises } I)$ to mean that the class table's **revises** relation is extended with the pair (J, I).)

$(CT, S, H, \mathtt{x = y}; \bar{\mathtt{s}}) \longrightarrow (CT, S[\mathtt{x} \mapsto S(\mathtt{y})], H, \bar{\mathtt{s}})$

$(CT, S, H, \mathtt{x = y.f}; \bar{\mathtt{s}})$ where $S(\mathtt{y}) = o$ and $H(o) = \langle \_, F \rangle$
$\quad \longrightarrow (CT, S[\mathtt{x} \mapsto F(\mathtt{f})], H, \bar{\mathtt{s}})$

$(CT, S, H, \mathtt{x.f = y}; \bar{\mathtt{s}})$ where $S(\mathtt{x}) = o$ and $H(o) = \langle R, F \rangle$ and $F' \stackrel{\text{def}}{=} F[\mathtt{f} \mapsto S(\mathtt{y})]$
$\quad \longrightarrow (CT, S, H[o \mapsto \langle R, F' \rangle], \bar{\mathtt{s}})$

$(CT, S, H, \mathtt{x = (T)y}; \bar{\mathtt{s}})$ where $S(\mathtt{y}) = o$, $H(o) = \langle R, F \rangle$, and $CT \vdash R <: \mathtt{T}$.
$\quad \longrightarrow (CT, S[\mathtt{x} \mapsto o], H, \bar{\mathtt{s}})$

$(CT, S, H, \mathtt{if(x == y)\{\bar{s}\} else \{\bar{t}\}} \bar{\mathtt{u}})$
$\quad \longrightarrow (CT, S, H, \bar{\mathtt{s}}\, \bar{\mathtt{u}})$ if $S(\mathtt{x}) = S(\mathtt{y})$
$\quad \longrightarrow (CT, S, H, \bar{\mathtt{t}}\, \bar{\mathtt{u}})$ otherwise

$(CT, S, H, \mathtt{if(x instanceof T)\{\bar{s}\} else \{\bar{t}\}} \bar{\mathtt{u}})$
$\quad \longrightarrow (CT, S, H, \bar{\mathtt{s}}\, \bar{\mathtt{u}})$ if $S(\mathtt{x}) = o$, $H(o) = \langle R, F \rangle$, and $CT \vdash R <: \mathtt{T}$
$\quad \longrightarrow (CT, S, H, \bar{\mathtt{t}}\, \bar{\mathtt{u}})$ otherwise

$(CT, S, H, \mathtt{x = new\ Object()}; \bar{\mathtt{s}})$ where $\textit{fields}(CT, \mathtt{Object}) = \overline{T}\, \bar{\mathtt{f}}$, $o \notin dom(H)$,
$\quad \longrightarrow (CT, S[\mathtt{x} \mapsto o], H', \bar{\mathtt{s}})$ and $H' \stackrel{\text{def}}{=} H[o \mapsto \langle \mathtt{Object}, \{\bar{\mathtt{f}} \mapsto \mathtt{null}\} \rangle]$

$(CT, S, H, \mathtt{x = new\ C[v=]()}; \bar{\mathtt{s}})$ where $\textit{fields}(CT, \mathtt{C[v=]}) = \overline{T}\, \bar{\mathtt{f}}$, $o \notin dom(H)$,
$\quad \longrightarrow (CT, S[\mathtt{x} \mapsto o], H', \bar{\mathtt{s}})$ and $H' = H[o \mapsto \langle \mathtt{C[v=]}, \{\bar{\mathtt{f}} \mapsto \mathtt{null}\} \rangle]$

$(CT, S, H, \mathtt{x = new\ C[v+]()}; \bar{\mathtt{s}})$ where $\textit{fields}(CT, \mathtt{C[v=]}) = \overline{T}\, \bar{\mathtt{f}}$, $o \notin dom(H)$,
$\quad \longrightarrow (CT, S[\mathtt{x} \mapsto o], H', \bar{\mathtt{s}})$ and $H' = H[o \mapsto \langle \mathtt{C[v+]}, \{\bar{\mathtt{f}} \mapsto \mathtt{null}\} \rangle]$

$(CT, S, H, \mathtt{x = new\ C[v++]()}; \bar{\mathtt{s}})$ where $\textit{latest}(CT, \mathtt{C[v=]}) = \mathtt{I}$, $\textit{fields}(CT, \mathtt{I}) = \overline{T}\, \bar{\mathtt{f}}$,
$\quad \longrightarrow (CT, S[\mathtt{x} \mapsto o], H', \bar{\mathtt{s}})$ $o \notin dom(H)$, and $H' \stackrel{\text{def}}{=} H[o \mapsto \langle \mathtt{I+}, \{\bar{\mathtt{f}} \mapsto \mathtt{null}\} \rangle]$

$(CT, S, H, \mathtt{x_0 = y_0.m(\overline{z_0})}; \bar{\mathtt{s}})$ where $S(\mathtt{y_0}) = o$, $H(o) = \langle R, F \rangle$,
$\quad \longrightarrow (CT, S', H, (\mathtt{B}\sigma)\, \mathtt{x_0 = (y\sigma)}; \bar{\mathtt{s}})$ $\textit{mbody}(CT, R, \mathtt{m}) = \bar{\mathtt{x}}.\mathtt{B\ return\ y};$,
$\quad (\mathtt{y_1}, \overline{\mathtt{z_1}}) \cap dom(S) = \emptyset$, $\sigma = [\mathtt{this}, \bar{\mathtt{x}} := \mathtt{y_1}, \overline{\mathtt{z_1}}]$,
$\quad$ and $S' = S[\mathtt{y_1}, \overline{\mathtt{z_1}} \mapsto S(\mathtt{y_0}), S(\overline{\mathtt{z_0}})]$

$(CT, S, H, \mathtt{upgrade}; \bar{\mathtt{s}})$ where $L = \mathtt{class\ I\ extends\ J\{\ \overline{U}\,\mathtt{f}; \overline{M}\ \}}$
$\quad \xrightarrow{\mathtt{new\ L}} (CT', S, H, \bar{\mathtt{s}})$ $\mathtt{I} \notin dom(CT)$, $CT' \stackrel{\text{def}}{=} CT \uplus L$ and $CT' \vdash \mathtt{I\ ok}$

$(CT, S, H, \mathtt{upgrade}; \bar{\mathtt{s}})$ where $\neg(CT \vdash \mathtt{I} <: \mathtt{J})$, $\neg(CT \vdash \mathtt{J} <: \mathtt{I})$
$\quad \xrightarrow{\mathtt{I\ revises\ J}} (CT', S, H, \bar{\mathtt{s}})$ $CT \vdash \mathtt{I\ revises\ J\ ok}$, $\neg \exists \mathtt{K}(CT \vdash \mathtt{K\ revises\ J})$ and
$\quad CT' \stackrel{\text{def}}{=} CT \uplus (\mathtt{I\ revises\ J})$

$(CT, S, H, \mathtt{upgrade}; \bar{\mathtt{s}})$ where $\neg(CT \vdash \mathtt{I} <: \mathtt{J})$, $\neg(CT \vdash \mathtt{J} <: \mathtt{I})$
$\quad \xrightarrow{\mathtt{I\ evolves\ J}} (CT', S, H, \bar{\mathtt{s}})$ $CT \vdash \mathtt{I\ evolves\ J\ ok}$, $\neg \exists \mathtt{K}(CT \vdash \mathtt{K\ evolves\ J})$ and
$\quad CT' \stackrel{\text{def}}{=} CT \uplus (\mathtt{I\ evolves\ J})$

$\left.\begin{array}{l} (CT, S, H, \mathtt{x = y.f}; \bar{\mathtt{s}}) \\ (CT, S, H, \mathtt{y.f = x}; \bar{\mathtt{s}}) \\ (CT, S, H, \mathtt{x = y.m(\bar{z})}; \bar{\mathtt{s}}) \end{array}\right\} \longrightarrow (CT, S, H, \mathbf{NPE})$ where $S(\mathtt{y}) = \mathtt{null}$

$(CT, S, H, \mathtt{x = (T)y}; \bar{\mathtt{s}}) \longrightarrow (CT, S, H, \mathbf{CCE})$ where $S(\mathtt{y}) = o$, $H(o) = \langle R, F \rangle$ and $CT \nvdash R <: \mathtt{T}$

Fig. 2. Operational semantics of FUJ

This transition rule embodies the following property that follows from the definition of the typing rules.

Lemma 3. *If* $\vdash CT$ ok, $\neg(CT \vdash \mathtt{I} <: \mathtt{J})$, $\neg(CT \vdash \mathtt{J} <: \mathtt{I})$, $\neg \exists \mathtt{K}(CT \vdash \mathtt{K\ revises\ J})$, $CT \vdash \mathtt{I\ revises\ J}$ ok *and* $CT' \stackrel{\text{def}}{=} CT \uplus (\mathtt{I\ revises\ J})$, *then* $\vdash CT'$ ok.

Semantics of evolution upgrades This transition is similar to that for revision upgrades except that it involves the **evolves** relation. It embodies the following property.

Lemma 4. *If*⊢ CT ok, ¬(CT ⊢ I <: J), ¬(CT ⊢ J <: I), ¬∃K(CT ⊢ K **evolves** J), CT ⊢ I **evolves** J ok *and* $CT' \stackrel{\text{def}}{=} CT \uplus$ (I **evolves** J), *then* ⊢ CT' ok

Type soundness: One advantage of our formal approach is that we are able to prove important safety properties of our system. The most fundamental property is *type soundness*: this means that the upgrades permitted by the FUJ transition rules do not compromise the underlying language-based security system of Java-like languages. In this section we give only an outline of the proof of this property; the somewhat routine details can be found elsewhere [6].

As is familiar with type soundness proofs [31] we need to both extend the notion of typing to FUJ configurations ($\Gamma \vdash (CT, S, H, \bar{s})$ ok) in the obvious way and to prove various weakening lemmas; the most interesting of which is the following.

Lemma 5 (Class table weakening). *If* $CT \subseteq CT'$, ⊢ CT' ok *and* $\Gamma \vdash (CT, S, H,$ $\bar{s})$ ok, *then* $\Gamma \vdash (CT', S, H, \bar{s})$ ok.

We can then prove that the transition rules preserve type correctness as follows.

Lemma 6 (Type preservation). *If* $\Gamma \vdash (CT, S, H, \bar{s})$ ok, ⊢ CT ok, *and* $(CT, S, H, \bar{s})$ $\stackrel{l}{\rightarrow} (CT', S', H', \bar{s}')$, *then there exists* Γ' *such that* $\Gamma' \vdash (CT', S', H', \bar{s}')$ ok *and* ⊢ CT' ok.

Proof. For most transition rules the proof is identical to that for pure MJ [7]. The new cases are to handle the upgrade definitions. The type preservation of these three transition rules is essentially given by Lemmas 2, 3 and 4.

Finally we can prove that an well-typed configuration is either a value, stuck or can make a transition.

Lemma 7 (Progress). *If* $\Gamma \vdash (CT, S, H, \bar{s})$ ok *then either* $\bar{s} \equiv \epsilon$ *(ϵ denotes an empty sequence), or* $\bar{s} \equiv NPE$, *or* $\bar{s} \equiv CCE$ *or* $\exists l. (CT, S, H, \bar{s}) \stackrel{l}{\rightarrow} (CT', S', H', \bar{s}')$.

5   Future and Related Work

Future work: Clearly there is much work still to be done; a fuller description is given elsewhere [6]. In the interests of space we simply record some initial thoughts on implementation and on object-level updating.

We do not yet have an implementation of UpgradeJ, although we are currently designing a prototype based on Java. We propose a series of annotations on classes and types (@version() to specify an upgradeable version, @exact() for an exact version, and @latest() for latest version creation) and plan to produce a basic pluggable type checker to implement the type system [2]. Then, we expect that typechecked UpgradeJ programs will be translated and executed on a JVM using HotSwap[6] to implement the

---

[6] http://java.sun.com/j2se/1.4.2/docs/guide/jpda/

upgrading. As part of this process, however, we use the annotations on classes and types to drive bytecode rewritings to create several JVML classes and interfaces for each UpgradeJ class, and use name mangling to encode versions into JVML typenames.

For each UpgradeJ class we create two JVML classes, one for exact instances of the class, and one for variable instances — this means we do not need any extra per-object storage to distinguish between exact and upgradable objects. New class and evolution upgrades are implented by using HotSwap to bring in new classes, while revision upgrades additionally overwrite the upgradeable versions of the classes that are being revised. The duplicate hierarchies means we get the effect of the two behaviours of the *mbody* lookup functions without having to change the standard JVM lookup. Methods can be removed where necessary by replacing them with calls to super; exact and upgradeable objects are created by instantiating the appropriate class; and latest creation requires a reflexive call to implement the dynamic lookup for the most recent upgrade.

Finally, to translate exact and upgradeable types, we also produce two JVML interfaces for each UpgradeJ class, one for each unitary exact type, and one for each upgradeable type: variables are declared as the appropriate interface, and each JVML class we produce implements the interfaces appropriate to its type; we also produce a single JVML interface to represent exact version set types. This means that most of the UpgradeJ runtime type structure is also encoded in JVML types, but where necessary (exact version set types) we use bytecode rewriting and casts.

We have carefully restricted UpgradeJ to provide *class upgrading* rather than *object updating*: UpgradeJ does not require any heap inspection. Given class upgrading, however, it is interesting to consider how little additional support is required to provide object updates. Runtime support for a heap lookup primitive (FIND) and updating individual objects (value assignments ":=", or Smalltalk's "one way become") are sufficient for programmers to implement object updates in a library:

```
while ((Button[2] b = FIND Button[2])!=null) {b := Button[4](b.x, b.y);}
```

This code example searches for instances of Button[2] (assuming FIND returns a random instance of that class) and replaces them with new Button[4] instances. To preserve type safety, the r-value must be a subtype of the l-value (as usual in assignment), and the assignment needs to check that the l-value is quiescent (that is, check the stack so that the target object is nowhere bound to "this"). The return value could be tested to check the success of the update, but in this case, if an object is not updated it will presumably be returned sometime later from FIND.

Related work: A full comparison with related work is impossible given the space constraints—here we atttempt to provide the surrounding context for UpgradeJ. UpgradeJ supports multiple co-existing versions; an idea from our earlier work on updating ML-like modules [5]. By moving to an object-oriented setting we have found different problems, in particular, how upgrading and inheritance can be combined; how classes can be upgraded without heap inspection; and how the latest version of a class can be created.

The .NET architecture addresses versioning issues by allowing assemblies to contain version information [22,10]. It allows multiple versions to be stored on a client and lets the versioning policy select the correct version. It is unclear, however, that this can deal with the different versions interacting, as it appears that each application can only require one version of the code. The more recent OSGi framework [21] provides stronger support for multiple versioning and updating, allowing bundles to be loaded, updated, and unloaded dynamically, and supporting multiple versions of classes within the same VM. Like .Net, however, OSGi does not have a formal model of version type safety: we hope that FUJ could in the future provide the basis for such a model.

Closely related to versioning is dynamic linking. Dynamic linking also allows late updates to code to occur. Drossopoulou et al. have studied dynamic linking in detail [15,13,16]. They provide details of when linking errors will occur under changes of class definitions, paying close attention to when different phases of the compilation occur, such as field layout. In this paper we have remained at a level close to the source code to avoid the problems they highlight. To avoid directly compiling versions into the code, one might like to consider a versioned variant of polymorphic bytecode [1], which is an extension to Java bytecode that allows more flexible linking at run-time.

UpgradeJ's revision upgrades have some similarity to various forms of object re-classification; for example, Kea [19], Predicate Classes [11] and Fickle [14]. Compared with UpgradeJ, these systems are much more flexible: classes can move around the hierarchy (implicitly based on values of instance variables in Kea and Predicate classes, or via an explicit reclassification operation in Fickle), and can gain or lose fields depending on that classification. In contrast, UpgradeJ supports revision upgrades taking objects to higher versions without affecting memory layout, and new class and evolution upgrades that can introduce new fields but do not affect existing classes. All UpgradeJ upgrades are "one way" operations: our "no time travel" principle means that upgraded objects can never be downgraded to previous versions.

Object-level updating has also been studied in depth. Techniques that search-and-replace objects on the heap via user-supplied update functions are well known, but generally rely on dynamic checks; CLOS, for example, directly supports class redefinition and allows programmers to update individual instances in various ways [26]. Some recent research has investigated how objects can be updated in a typesafe manner. For example, Boyapati et al. describe how ownership types can assist in updating aggregate objects in object-oriented databases [8].

More prosaically, the idea of incrementally defining and updating the classes rather than the objects is also not new. The earliest Smalltalk systems were in practice maintained by passing around "goodies"— patches that could affect multiple classes [23]. Modular Smalltalk propsed an explicit class extension construct to support this [30]. More recently, systems like Changeboxes [20] have supported dynamic extensions to systems, with relatively flexible mechanisms for describing potential changes and run-time support for multiple coexisting versions. All these systems are checked dynamically, of course, whereas UpgradeJ is checked statically.

UpgradeJ's dynamic lookup over the `revises` and `extends` relationships has some commonality with the two-dimensional inheritance hierarchies found e.g. in New-tonScript [25]. The key difference here is that NewtonScript's secondary hierarchy follows interface widget's composition structure, while our secondary hierarchy follows dynamically upgraded versions of classes.

Open Classes [12] and Expanders [29] also allow new methods and fields to be added to pre-existing classes. Both these systems have restrictions to ensure unambiguous typesafe module composition which prevent replacing existing methods. In contrast, we can revise any method, and avoid ambiguity via incremental typechecking. Moreover, UpgradeJ allows classes to be upgraded at runtime.

Zenger [32] takes a different approach to the versioning problem. He proposes an extension of Java with an extensible module system, which allows modules to be upgraded. The main advantage of our work is that it does not require such a big leap from the original programming language.

A number of functional languages provide varying support for versioning and upgrading. Most notably, Erlang [3] is an untyped, first-order language that supports concurrency and module-level upgrading, but not multiple versions of the same module. Acute [24] is an extension of OCaml that has a rich set of version constraints and policies intended for distributed programming. It is interesting future work to see if similar support is possible in the UpgradeJ setting.

6   Conclusions

Programs, especialy long running, widely distributed programs, are no longer monolithic. Programs need to be upgraded with new features, new classes, and new methods even while they continue running. Previous work has focused on how to translate objects in the heap, in a type-safe and version-consistent way. This paper takes a different approach: in order to have a lightweight mechanism no heap update is applied, and assumptions on versions are made explicit. UpgradeJ supports *class upgrades* directly—adding new classes, revising existing classes, and evolving classes to incompatible versions—and typechecking is purely incremental. We hope UpgradeJ will provide a useful conceptual model of the core problems of software upgrading, and that it may inspire future language designs.

References

1. Ancona, D., Damiani, F., Drossopoulou, S., Zucca, E.: Polymorphic bytecode: Compositional compilation for Java-like languages. In: Proceedings of POPL (2005)
2. Andreae, C., Noble, J., Markstrum, S., Millstein, T.: A framework for implementing pluggable type systems. In: Proceedings of OOPSLA (2006)
3. Armstrong, J., Virding, R., Wikstrom, C., Williams, M.: Concurrent programming in Erlang. Prentice-Hall, Englewood Cliffs (1996)
4. Bailey, E.: Maximum RPM. Sams (1997)
5. Bierman, G., Hicks, M., Sewell, P., Stoyle, G.: Formalizing dynamic software updating. In: Proceedings of USE (2003)
6. Bierman, G., Parkinson, M., Noble, J.: UpgradeJ: Incremental typechecking for class upgrades. Technical Report 716, University of Cambridge Computer Laboratory (2008)
7. Bierman, G., Parkinson, M., Pitts, A.: MJ: An imperative core calculus for Java and Java with effects. Technical Report 563, University of Cambridge Computer Laboratory (2004)
8. Boyapati, C., Liskov, B., Shrira, L.: Lazy modular upgrades in persistent object stores. In: Proceedings of OOPSLA (2003)
9. Bruce, K.B., Foster, J.N.: LOOJ: Weaving LOOM into Java. In: Proceedings of ECOOP (2004)
10. Buckley, A.: A model of dynamic binding in.NET. In: Proceedings of FTfJP (2005)
11. Chambers, C.: Predicate classes. In: Nierstrasz, O. (ed.) ECOOP 1993. LNCS, vol. 707. Springer, Heidelberg (1993)
12. Clifton, C., Leavens, G.T., Chambers, C., Millstein, T.: MultiJava: Modular open classes and symmetric multiple dispatch for Java. In: Proceedings of OOPSLA (2000)

13. Drossopoulou, S.: Towards an abstract model of Java dynamic linking, loading and verification. In: Proceedings of TIC (2000)
14. Drossopoulou, S., Damiani, F., Dezani, M., Giannini, P.: $Fickle_{II}$ more object reclassification. ACM Transactions on Programming Languages and Systems 24(2) (2002)
15. Drossopoulou, S., Eisenbach, S., Wragg, D.: A fragment calculus—towards a model of separate compilation, linking and binary compatibility. In: Proceedings of LICS (1999)
16. Drossopoulou, S., Lagorio, G., Eisenbach, S.: Flexible models for dynamic linking. In: Degano, P. (ed.) ESOP 2003 and ETAPS 2003. LNCS, vol. 2618. Springer, Heidelberg (2003)
17. Flanagan, C., Sabry, A., Duba, B.F., Felleisen, M.: The essence of compiling with continuations. In: Proceedings of PLDI (1993)
18. Igarashi, A., Pierce, B., Wadler, P.: Featherweight Java: A minimal core calculus for Java and GJ. ACM Transactions on Programming Languages and Systems 23(3), 396–450 (2001)
19. Mugridge, W.B., Hamer, J., Hosking, J.G.: Multi-methods in a statically-typed programming language. In: Knudsen, J.L. (ed.) ECOOP 2001. LNCS, vol. 2072. Springer, Heidelberg (2001)
20. Nierstrasz, O., Denker, M., Gîrba, T., Lienhard, A.: Analyzing, capturing and taming software change. In: Proceedings of the Workshop on Revival of Dynamic Languages (2006)
21. OSGi Alliance. About the OSGi service platform (November 2005), http://osgi.org
22. Pratschner, S.: Simplifying deployment and solving DLL hell with the .NET framework (2001), http://msdn.microsoft.com
23. Putz, S.: Managing the evolution of Smalltalk-80 systems. In: Smalltalk-80: Bits of History, Words of Advice. AW (1984)
24. Sewell, P., Leifer, J., Wansbrough, K., Allen-Williams, M., Zappa Nardelli, F., Habouzit, P., Vafeiadis, V.: Acute: High-level programming language design for distributed computation. Design rationale and language definition. Technical Report 605, University of Cambridge Computer Laboratory (October 2004)
25. Smith, W.R.: Using a prototype-based language for user interface: The Newton project's experience. In: Proceedings of OOPSLA (1995)
26. Steele, G.: Common Lisp the Language. Digital Press (1990)
27. Stoyle, G., Hicks, M., Bierman, G., Sewell, P., Neamtiu, I.: Mutatis mutandis: Safe and predictable dynamic software updating. In: Proceedings of POPL (2005)
28. Strniša, R., Sewell, P., Parkinson, M.: The Java module system: core design and semantic definition. In: Proceedings of OOPSLA (2007)
29. Warth, A., Stanojević, M., Millstein, T.: Statically scoped object adaptation with expanders. In: Proceedings of OOPSLA (2006)
30. Wirfs-Brock, A., Wilkerson, B.: An overview of Modular Smalltalk. In: Proceedings of OOPSLA (1988)
31. Wright, A., Felleisen, M.: A syntactic approach to type soundness. Information and Computation 115(1), 38–94 (1994)
32. Zenger, M.: Programming Language Abstractions for Extensible Software Components. PhD thesis, EPFL, Switzerland (2004)

Integrating Nominal and Structural Subtyping

Donna Malayeri and Jonathan Aldrich

Carnegie Mellon University, Pittsburgh, PA 15213, USA
{donna, aldrich}@cs.cmu.edu

Abstract. Nominal and structural subtyping each have their own strengths and weaknesses. Nominal subtyping allows programmers to explicitly express design intent, and, when types are associated with run time tags, enables run-time type tests and external method dispatch. On the other hand, structural subtyping is flexible and compositional, allowing unanticipated reuse. To date, nearly all object-oriented languages fully support one subtyping paradigm or the other.

In this paper, we describe a core calculus for a language that integrates the key aspects of nominal and structural subtyping in a unified framework. We have also merged the flexibility of structural subtyping with statically typechecked external methods, a novel combination. We prove type safety for this language and illustrate its practical utility through examples that are not easily expressed in other languages. Our work provides a clean foundation for the design of future languages that enjoy the benefits of both nominal and structural subtyping.

1 Introduction

In a language with structural subtyping, a type U is a subtype of T if its methods and fields are a superset of T's methods and fields. The interface of a class is simply its public fields and methods; there is no need to declare a separate interface type. In a language with nominal subtyping, on the other hand, U is a subtype of T if and only if it is *declared* to be. Accordingly, structural subtyping can be considered *intrinsic*, while nominal subtyping is *declarative*. Each kind of subtyping has its merits, but a formal model has not been developed for a language that integrates the two subtyping disciplines.

Structural subtyping offers a number of advantages. It is often more expressive than nominal subtyping, as subtyping relationships do not need to be declared ahead of time. It is compositional and intrinsic, existing outside of the mind of the programmer. This has the advantage of supporting unanticipated reuse—programmers don't have to plan for all possible scenarios. Additionally, structural subtyping is often more notationally succinct. Programmers can concisely express type requirements without having to define an entire subtyping hierarchy. In nominal systems, some situations may require multiple inheritance or an unnecessary proliferation of types; in a structural system, the desired subtyping properties just arise naturally from the base cases. Finally, structural subtyping is far superior in contexts where the structure of the data is of primary importance, such as in data persistent environments or distributed computing. In contrast, nominal subtyping can lead to unnecessary versioning problems: if some class C is modified to C' (perhaps to add a method m), C' objects cannot be serialized and sent to a distributed process with the original definition C, even if C' is a strict extension of C.

J. Vitek (Ed.): ECOOP 2008, LNCS 5142, pp. 260–284, 2008.

As an example of the reuse benefits of structural subtyping, suppose class A has methods foo(), a() and b(), and class B has methods foo(), x() and y(). Suppose also that the code for A and B cannot be modified. In a language with structural subtyping, A and B share an implicit common interface { foo } and a programmer can write code against this interface. But, in a language with nominal subtyping, since the programmer did not plan ahead and create an IFoo interface and make A and B its subtypes, there is no way to write code that takes advantage of this commonality (short of using reflection). In contrast, with structural subtyping, if a class C is later added that contains method foo(), it too will share this implicit interface. If a programmer adds new methods to A, A's interface type will change automatically, without the programmer having to maintain the interface himself. If B or C also contain these new methods, the implicit combined interfaces will automatically exist.

Nominal subtyping also has its advantages. First, it allows the programmer to express and enforce design intent explicitly. A programmer's defined subtyping hierarchy serves as checked documentation that specifies how the various parts of a program are intended to work together. Second, explicit specification has the advantage of preventing "accidental" subtyping relationships, such as the standard example of cowboy.draw() and circle.draw(). Nominal subtyping also allows recursive types to be easily and transparently defined, since recursion can simply go through the declared names. Third, error messages are usually much more comprehensible, since, for the most part, every type in a type error is one that the programmer has defined explicitly. Finally, nominal subtyping enables efficient implementation of external dispatch.

External dispatch is provided by number of statically typed languages, such as Cecil [6, 7], MultiJava [8], among others. External methods increase the flexibility and evolvability of code because they do not fix in advance the set of methods of a class. Consider the example of a class hierarchy that represents AST nodes. (This motivating example is expanded further in Sec. 2.3.) Suppose this is part of a larger system, which includes an IDE for editing elements represented by this AST. Now suppose a programmer wishes to add new functionality to the IDE but cannot modify the original source code for the AST nodes. The new function provides the capability to jump from one node to a node that it references; this differs depending on what type of node is selected. Clearly, this functionality cannot be written without code that somehow performs dispatch on the AST class hierarchy.

In a language without external dispatch, the developer has limited choices. Usually, she must resort to manually writing instanceof tests, which is tedious and error-prone. In particular, if a new element is added to the AST hierarchy, the implementation will not behave correctly.

If the developers of the original class hierarchy *anticipated* this need and implemented the Visitor design pattern, it would then be easy to add new operations to the hierarchy, but then it would be difficult to add new classes. At best, Visitor trades one problem for another.

On the other hand, in a language with external dispatch, a programmer simply writes an *external method* that dispatches on the AST class hierarchy (i.e., separate from its code). External dispatch makes it easy to adapt existing code to new interfaces, since new code can be added as an external method. Exhaustiveness checking rules for external methods ensure that when a new class is added to the hierarchy, in the absence of an inherited method, a new method must be added for that class.

Nominal subtyping enables efficient external dispatch since there is a name on which to tie the dispatch. Additionally, if external dispatch were allowed on structural types, the problem of accidental subtyping would be exacerbated, since overridden methods would apply wherever there was a structural match. Further, ambiguity problems could frequently arise, which would have to be manually resolved by the programmer. Consider, for example, a method m defined on objects with a foo:int field. If m is also later defined for objects with a bar:char field, m is now ambiguous—which method is called for an object with both fields?

In our language, Unity, we sidestep this issue—nominal and structural subtyping are integrated. This makes efficient external dispatch compatible with structural subtyping, but also gives programmers the benefits of both subtyping disciplines. Nominal subtyping gives programmers the ability to express explicit design intent, while structural subtyping makes interfaces easier to maintain and reuse.

Contributions. The contributions of this paper are as follows:

- A language design, Unity, that provides user-defined and structural subtyping relationships in a novel and uniform way. Unity combines the flexibility of external dispatch with the conceptual clarity of width and depth subtyping.
- A formalization of the design of Unity, along with proofs of type safety (Sec. 5).
- Examples that illustrate the expressiveness and flexibility of the language (Sec. 2), We contrast Unity with other languages in Sec. 2.1.
- A case study (Sec. 3) and an empirical study of several Java programs (Sec. 4).

2   Motivating Examples

We give, by example, the intuition behind Unity and illustrate combining structural subtyping with external methods. In Unity, an object type is a record type tagged with a *brand*. Brands induce the nominal subtyping relation, which we call "sub-branding."[1] Brands are nominal in that the user defines the sub-brand relationship, like the subclass relation in languages like Java, Eiffel, and C++.

When a brand β is defined, the programmer lists the fields that any objects tagged with β will include. In other words, if the user defines the brand Point as having the fieldss {x : int, y : int}, then any value tagged with Point must include at least the labels x and y (with int type)—but it may also contain additional fields, due to record subtyping. For instance, a programmer could create a colored point object with the expression Point({x=0,y=1,color=blue}). Subtyping takes into account both the nominal sub-brand relationship and the usual structural subtyping relationship (width and depth) on records.

To integrate these two relationships, brand extension is constrained: the associated field types must be subtypes. In other words, a brand β_1 can be declared as a sub-brand

---

[1] The name "brand" is borrowed from Strongtalk [3], which in turn borrowed it from Modula-3.

of β_2 only if β_1's field type is a structural subtype of β_2's field type. As an example, suppose the brand 3DPoint is defined as 3DPoint({x:int, y:int, z:int}). 3DPoint can be declared as a sub-brand of Point, since {x:int, y:int, z:int} is a sub-record of {x:int, y:int}. However, a brand 1DPoint({x:int}) cannot be a sub-brand of Point (since it lacks the y field), nor can FloatingPoint(x:float, y:float}) (assuming float is not a subtype of int).

2.1   Example 1: A Window Toolkit

Fig. 1 contains a code excerpt for a windowing system and illustrates the novel features of Unity. The built-in brand Top is the root of the brand hierarchy, like Object in Java. To simplify the presentation, we include only the field title. ScrollBar is defined as a type alias using the type syntax. By default, a window does not have a scrollbar. The brands Textbox and StaticText extend Window, and also do not scroll by default.[2]

To add scrolling functionality, we have defined the function scroll, which operates on any Window (or sub-brand thereof) that has a getScrollBar() method. The type Window({getScrollBar():ScrollBar}) classifies such an object. (We suppose here that the implementation of scroll need only access the scrollbar field and the fields of Window.) Note that the structural component of this type refers to another structural type, ScrollBar; structural types may be arbitrarily nested.

Let us assume that in a non-scrolling textbox, the user can only enter a fixed number of characters. Consequently, we define the brand ScrollingTextbox in order to change textbox functionality—in particular, the behavior when inserting a character. The scroll function is applicable to ScrollingTextbox since it is automatically a subtype of Window({getScrollBar():ScrollBar}).

In Unity, methods can be either internal (defined within a brand), or external (defined outside the brand). To allow sound modular checking of external methods (see Sec. 5), only internal methods are permitted to be abstract; external methods must be concrete. The method insertChar has been defined as an external method. This method is applicable to a Textbox or ScrollingTextbox that has a getCurrentPos method. Textbox does not have an internal getCurrentPos method, so it has been added as an external method. The method getCurrentPos, in turn, is only applicable to a Textbox that has a pos:int field. This illustrates the structural constraints that can be put on a method. For a method m, a programmer can specify a set of fields and methods that must be present in m's receiver.

Since a textbox that scrolls allows the user to enter more text than the window size permits, a new sub-brand had to be defined so that its implementation of insertChar could be overridden. If other sub-brands of Window (such as StaticText) do not need to change their existing behavior when a scrollbar is added, no new sub-brands need be defined. Scrolling functionality can be added to these types by including a ScrollBar field and a getScrollBar() method, and the scroll function is then applicable.

This example demonstrates both the use of functions (i.e., lambda expressions), and methods. The difference between the two is that functions do not perform dispatch (that

---

[2] Note that all fields must be listed by the subtypes of Window; this design decision is merely to simplify our core calculus.

```
abstract brand Window ({title : string}) extends Top
concrete brand Textbox ({title : string, text : string}) extends Window
concrete brand StaticText ({title : string, text : string}) extends Window
concrete brand ScrollingTextbox({title : string, text : string, s : ScrollBar};
                 method getScrollbar() : ScrollBar = this.s)
                 extends Textbox

type ScrollBar = Top(getMaximum():int, setMaximum(x:int) : unit,
                     getValue():int, setValue(x:int) : unit)


let scroll = λw : Window({getScrollBar() : ScrollBar}) .
      ... // code that performs the scrolling operation


method insertChar Textbox({getCurrentPos() : int}) : unit =
      λc : char .  ...  // insert a character only if it will fit in the window

method insertChar ScrollingTextbox({getCurrentPos() : int}) : unit =
      λc : char .  ...  // insert the character, scrolling if necessary

method getCurrentPos(Textbox({pos:int})) : int = ...
```

Subtyping relationships

```
Window ({title : string, s : ScrollBar}) ≤ Window ({title : string})

Textbox ({...}) ≤ Window ({title : string})
ScrollingTextbox ({...}) ≤ Textbox ({...})
ScrollingTextbox({...}) ≤ Window({title : string, s : ScrollBar})

StaticText({...}) ≤ Window ({title : string})
StaticText({..., s : ScrollBar}) ≤ Window(title : string, s : ScrollBar)
```

Fig. 1. Unity code for a windowing system. Nominal subtyping allows the brand ScrollingTextbox to change the behavior of insertChar through tag dispatch, while structural subtyping allows the scroll function to apply to any window with an s : ScrollBar field. ScrollBar is defined as a type alias using the type syntax. In the subtyping relationships, some field names are elided with "....."

is, they cannot be overridden), but they can be defined at any scope. Methods can be overridden, but they can only be defined at the top-level.

These brand definitions induce subtyping relationships, shown below the code listing in Fig. 1. Interestingly, ScrollingTextbox({...}) is a subtype of both Window({getScrollBar():ScrollBar}) and of Textbox({...}), but we have avoided both multiple inheritance and the problems typically associated with it. The type Window({getScrollBar():ScrollBar}) is a conceptual interface that exists without being named.

The example illustrates the two kinds of extensibility that Unity provides: structural extensibility and brand extensibility.

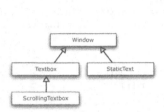

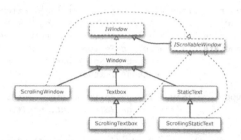

(a) The windowing example as implemented in Unity. Depicted here are the brands that must be defined in order to obtain the desired subtyping relationships.

(b) The same example implemented in Java. Dashed rectangles are interfaces; solid rectangles are classes. Dashed lines indicate the `implements` relationship and solid lines indicate `extends`.

Fig. 2. For the windowing example, the user-defined subtyping relationships necessary in Unity vs. those necessary in Java

- **Structural types** can be used to create *structural method constraints*—methods that an object must have in order to conform to that type. They can be also be used to *create a new type that adds fields to an existing brand*, without defining new behavior for the resulting type. So, a `ScrollBar` can be added to a `StaticText` object without defining a new brand, as the existing functionality of the static text box does not need to change if a scrollbar is added.
- **Brand extension** creates a new brand that can be used in dispatch; as a consequence, programs can *define new behavior for the newly defined brand*. Here, `ScrollingTextbox` is defined as an extension of `Textbox` because the behavior of `insertChar` is different depending on whether or not the text box has a scrollbar attached to it. Design intent is preserved because whenever different behavior is required (such as with `Cowboy.draw()` and `Circle.draw()`), nominal subtyping must be used.

Additionally, we see here the synergy between structural subtyping and external dispatch. Structural subtyping can be used to *specify the constraints* of a method, and external methods can be used to make existing brands *conform* to those constraints.

2.2   Comparison to Other Systems

Here we compare Unity to closely related systems. See Sec. 6 for other related work.

Java.   In Java-like languages, expressing this example would be unwieldy. A common way to express the necessary constraints would involve first defining two interfaces, `IWindow` and `IScrollableWindow`. `ScrollBar` would also have to be an interface.

If a programmer wished to allow the possibility of adding a scrollbar to a window class, even without changing any other functionality, he would have to define a subclass that also implemented `IScrollableWindow`. In this example, we would define the classes ScrollingWindow, ScrollingTextbox, and ScrollingStaticText, though only ScrollingTextbox needs to change any functionality; see the class diagram Fig. 2(b). Contrast this with the brand structure of the Unity program depicted in Fig. 2(a). In Unity, only the types associated with dispatch need to be defined, in contrast to Java.

The Java equivalent of the scroll function could be a static function of some helper class and would take an object of type IScrollableWindow. Of course, if a programmer defined a new scrolling window class with the correct getScrollBar() method, but forgot to implement IScrollableWindow, the scroll function could not be used on objects of that class. (This situation often arises in Java programs, particularly when one wishes to use library code, the developers of which are not even aware of the interface that they should implement.)

There are other oddities in the Java version. The Java class ScrollingWindow is semantically analogous to the Unity type Window(getScrollBar():ScrollBar), but ScrollingTextbox and ScrollingStaticText are *not* subclasses of ScrollingWindow, while the corresponding Unity types *are* subtypes of Window(getScrollBar():ScrollBar). To have such subtyping relationships would require multiple inheritance in a language like Java, while the Unity code works with just single inheritance. This illustrates the lack of expressiveness that is inherent in languages that require the programmer to name all relevant subtyping relationships.

Traits. A language with traits [25] would provide a much cleaner solution than that of Java, but would still lack the expressiveness of Unity's structural subtyping. This is because traits are mainly designed to solve issues of implementation inheritance (especially multiple inheritance) that are largely orthogonal to the ones we are considering. In this example, the same subtyping hierarchy would have to be created as in the Java example, but the scroll function could be written for IScrollableWindow with the appropriate dispatch. (A static method could always be written in Java, but it would not perform dispatch on subtypes.) This would enable some code reuse, but would still require creating a number of types.

Mixins. In a language with mixins [2], the programmer would create a mixin class ScrollableWindow that consists of the fields of Window along with s : ScrollBar and the code for the function scroll. The code for the ScrollableWindow would then be mixed into StaticText to create a ScrollingStaticText and into Textbox to create ScrollingTextbox. The behavior of insertChar would then be specialized for ScrollingTextbox.

With mixins, the same number of eventual classes would be created as in Java, but creating them becomes easier because of mixin construction. In contrast with Unity, the code for scroll cannot be reused unless the mixin ScrollableWindow is used, which restricts its flexibility. This can pose a problem when interoperating with classes that were created in isolation from the mixin. Mixins also require up-front planning; methods and fields cannot be added after-the-fact.

Structural subtyping. Languages which support structural subtyping, such as Moby [10], O'Caml [14], and PolyTOIL [4], would elegantly express all of the desired subtyping relationships, but these languages allow only internal dispatch—that is, all methods must be defined inside the class definition. In our language, insertChar can be an external method; it need not reside inside the definitions of Textbox and ScrollingTextbox. It would be non-trivial to add support for external dispatch or multimethods to these types of languages.

Cecil. Cecil fully supports external and multimethod dispatch [6, 7]. Cecil's powerful, but very complex, type system can express most of the necessary relationships (though new classes do need to be defined for ScrollingWindow and ScrollingStaticText). To write the scroll function, a programmer would have to use bounded quantification and a "where" clause constraint, the latter being type-checked via a constraint solver. That is, in psuedo-code, the argument to scroll would have type:

for all T where T <: Window and signature getScrollBar(T) : ScrollBar

Here, the type ScrollBar would have to be a class, rather than a structural type as in Unity, due to two major shortcomings of where clauses: they cannot be nested and can only occur on top level methods. Additionally, where clauses cannot be used to constrain the method's receiver. In Unity, on the other hand, structural types are compositional and can therefore be nested within another type (e.g., ScrollBar in Fig. 1), can occur at any level in the program (e.g., the lambda expression scroll), and can be used to constrain a method's receiver (e.g., method insertChar).

Virtual classes. Some of the required relationships could be expressed elegantly using virtual classes [15] or nested inheritance [21], but only with advance planning. To express this example, the programmer would create a class Base containing the virtual classes Window, Textbox, and StaticText. Then, she would create a subclass of Base, called Scroll, that contained its own Window. This definition of Window would add a field for a scrollbar. Additionally, Scroll would have a virtual class ScrollingTextbox which would include the new definition of insertChar. The programmer would not to create a new class ScrollingStaticText since the new definition of Window would automatically apply to StaticText (i.e., Scroll.StaticText would automatically have a scrollbar).

The virtual classes solution is elegant, but if the programmer did not plan ahead and redefine Window in the Scroll class, there would not be a way to describe this type. Essentially, virtual classes make it very easy to reuse code across related classes (an advantage of virtual classes and nested inheritance over Unity), but cannot easily express the structural types of Unity.

2.3 Example 2: AST Nodes in an IDE

In this section, we describe another example to show other ways in which Unity can be used. Suppose we have an integrated development environment that includes an editor and a compiler. The top portion of Fig. 3 contains an excerpt of a simplified version of the code for such a system. Here, the brands PlusNode, Num and Var define a simple abstract syntax tree. The internal method compile performs compilation on an AstNode.

One can use structural subtyping to create AST nodes with additional information, such as a node with a loc field specifying the file location of the code corresponding to the node. Additional functions are available for such nodes, such as the function highlightNode that highlights a node's source code in the text editor.

```
abstract brand AstNode( ;{abstract method compile : () → unit}) extends Top

concrete brand PlusNode ({n1 : AstNode(), n2 : AstNode()};
    method compile() : unit = compilePlus(this); /* compile PlusNode */)
    extends AstNode
concrete brand Num ({val : int}; method compile() : unit = ... /* compile Num*/)
    extends AstNode
concrete brand Var ({s : Symbol}; method compile() : unit = ... /* compile Var */)
    extends AstNode


// highlight the text corresponding to 'node' in the text editor,
// using the location specified by the 'loc' field
let highlightNode = λ node : AstNode(loc : Location). ...

// AST nodes with debug information
concrete brand DebugPlusNode ({n1 : AstNode(), n2 : AstNode(), loc : Location};
    method compile() : unit = compilePlus(this); outputLocation(out, this.loc))
    extends PlusNode
concrete brand DebugNum ({val : int, loc : Location};
    method compile() : unit = ... /* compile DebugNum */) extends Num
concrete brand DebugVar ({s : Symbol, loc : Location, varName : string};
    method compile() : unit = ... /* compile DebugVar */) extends Var
```

Fig. 3. Example 2: AST Nodes in an IDE. The top portion is the code before changes to add debug information to the AST. The function highlightNode makes use of structural information and the external dispatch in compile changes its behavior for the declared Debug* sub-brands.

We did not have to define a new brand for AST nodes that include file location information. Whether or not a node contains file information, functions that operate over AST nodes need not change their behavior, so in this case structural subtyping suffices.

Suppose now that the programmer wishes to add "debug" versions of these AST nodes that contain additional output information for compiling in debug mode. For example, a DebugNum has a Location field, while DebugVar includes a Location field as well as a string representation of the variable name. The newly added code is listed in the bottom portion of Fig. 3.

Since each of these brands have been defined as extensions, they may also customize the behavior of compile to output this additional information when compiling. Additionally, since all of the Debug* brands have a Location field, the function highlightNode can be used on objects of this type.

This example again illustrates the expressiveness that achieved by combining nominal and structural subtyping; highlightNode makes use of additional structural information, while compile relies on nominal dispatch to behave differently in different situations.

2.4 Real-World Examples

The following real-world examples illustrate the gains in flexibility that could be achieved through structural subtyping.

Eclipse SWT. In the Eclipse SWT (Simple Windowing Toolkit), many classes (such as Button, Label, Link, etc.) have the methods getText and setText, that set the main text for the control, such as a button's text, the text in a textbox, etc. However, there is no common IText interface. Many classes—13 in total—also support adding an image through the getImage and setImage method, but again there is no interface that captures this. A programmer may wish to write a method that sets the image of any control by retrieving the image from an image registry. Given the current API, such a method would have to rely on runtime reflection, with no guarantee of successful method invocation at compile time.

Eclipse JDT. In the JDT (Java Development Tools), there are 8 classes (including IMethod, IType, IField) that have the method getElementName, but there is no IElement interface with this method. With structural subtyping, these classes implicitly share an interface, and code could be written that is polymorphic over the exact class type. For instance, a tree view of an AST may wish to display packages, methods, and fields in a uniform way. With the current hierarchy it is not possible to simply call the getElementName of the object, since these classes do not have an explicit interface with this method.

3 Case Study: Optional Methods in Java

In this section, we describe the tradeoffs that a library designer must make when using a language that has only nominal subtyping. The design of the Java collections library illustrates that designers would rather circumvent the type system than have a proliferation of types. We believe this situation often occurs with nominal subtyping, but because of structural subtyping, such a situation need not occur in Unity.

In the Java collections library, the interface java.util.Collection has several "optional" methods: add, addAll, clear, remove, removeAll, and retainAll. Many of the abstract classes implementing Collection (e.g., AbstractCollection, AbstractList, AbstractSet) throw an UnsupportedOperationException when those methods are called. There are a total of 30 optional methods in java.util.*, and java.lang.Iterator has an additional optional method. The methods were designed this way to avoid an explosion of interfaces such as MutableCollection, ImmutableCollection, etc., and a corresponding increase in the number of sub-interfaces (e.g., MutableList, ImmutableList, etc.) [18].

Let us consider a Java collections framework without the optional methods. Figure 4 shows a relevant portion of the current Java collections hierarchy. Figure 5 show new interfaces that capture the distinction of mutability directly in the hierarchy—doing away with optional operations. The interface Collection<E> represents a collection that is modifiable, while the new interface ReadableCollection<E> represents a collection that only contains read operations. Accordingly, its iterator() method returns a ReadIterator, which is defined without a remove() operation. There are now two new ListIterator interfaces, for fixed-size lists, modifiable lists, read-only lists. These correspond to the FixedSizeList<E> and ReadableList<E> interfaces in Figure 5. (The interface FixedSizeList<E> has been added because selective overriding of methods in AbstractList would yield such a type, as noted in the documentation.) The hierarchy for Set is similar to that of List (though simpler, since there are no fixed-size sets, and no set-specific iterator).

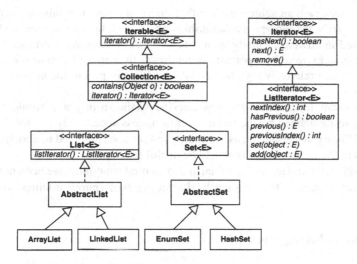

Fig. 4. A portion of the Java collections framework. A few methods are highlighted in most interfaces. Type parameters are elided in classes.

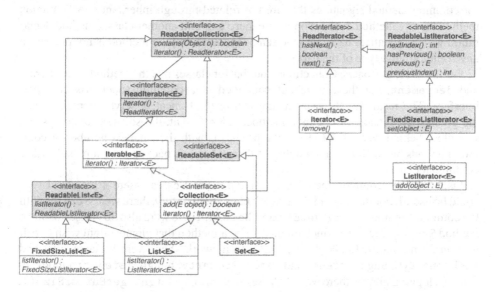

Fig. 5. Refactored `AbstractList` and `AbstractSet` classes, along with new interfaces to remove optional methods. A few methods of most interfaces are highlighted for List and Set; for iterators, all methods, except for inherited methods, are shown. New interfaces have a gray background.

In a language with structural subtyping, such as Unity, not all interesting combinations of structural types have to be declared in advance (though in a library setting they might be, for consistency's sake). For a language with type abbreviations, the key idea is that a type abbreviation would simply be syntactic sugar for a set of methods, which could be given an abbreviation with a different name in another part of the system. Additionally, the subtyping relationships between all the interfaces would not need to be defined in advance. Finally, as a side note, the notational overhead in defining type abbreviations would be potentially far lower than that of defining a Java interface, which has a relatively high notational cost (due, in part to the nominal nature of interfaces).

For this example, in Unity, the new interfaces (shown in gray), would not necessarily need to be defined by the library author, unless specifically needed. This eases the task of library development, as the library author does not need to anticipate which supertypes of the given interfaces would be useful for clients.

Thus, with a combination of nominal and structural subtyping, we need not sacrifice static type safety in order to overcome the shortcomings of a purely nominal type system.

4   Empirical Analysis

To determine if there are potential cases where structural subtyping would be useful in a real system, we ran an analysis of 15 open-source Java programs. The analysis searches for common method signatures that are not related through inheritance. A "common method" is any method declaration where there exists in another class a method declaration with an identical name and the same signature, but the method is not present in any common supertype of the two.

For instance, in Apache Collections, four buffer classes had the methods increment and decrement, but these were not contained in a common superclass or superinterface. The results of the analysis are in Fig. 6. Tomcat, a servlet container, had the greatest percentage of common methods, 28.4%. Ant, the software build system, was close behind with 28.1%. Even the programs with the smallest number of common methods had a significant number of them; Areca, a backup program, had 11.9% common methods.

Inspecting the common methods, we found several cases where a structural type could be useful. For instance, in Smack, a Jabber client library, there were 6 classes with the common method String getElementName(). There were also 30 classes with the method String toXML() which might also be a method that clients might wish to call in a uniform manner. In JHotDraw, a GUI framework, there were 9 classes that had addPropertyChangeListener and removePropertyChangeListener methods. In Log4j, a logging library, there were 4 classes with the method int getBufferSize(), and 8 classes with the method setOption. In the Apache Collections library, nearly all the common methods appeared to be potentially useful. For instance, there were 5 iterator decorator classes with getIterator and setIterator methods. 4 bag classes had a method getBag, 4 buffer classes had a method getBuffer, and 4 classes had the method getComparator. Additionally, 7 classes had the method int size() and 5 classes had the method int indexOf(Object).

Note that we did not closely examine the implementations of these methods to determine if they were semantically performing similar actions, as we were unfamiliar with the codebase. So, it is possible that the methods coincidentally had similar names but

	Total methods	Common methods	% Common	Average methods/group	Total common groups
Tomcat	14678	4172	28.4%	3.2	1288
Ant	9178	2577	28.1%	3.5	727
JHotDraw	5149	1193	23.2%	2.8	428
Smack	3921	881	22.5%	3.3	270
Struts	3783	772	20.4%	2.7	291
Apache Forrest	164	28	17.1%	2.2	13
Cayenne	9243	1545	16.7%	2.8	553
Log4j	1950	312	16.0%	3.1	102
OpenFire	8135	1300	16.0%	2.8	470
Apache Collections	3762	584	15.5%	2.8	211
Derby	24521	3575	14.6%	2.5	1402
Lucene	2472	331	13.4%	2.5	134
jEdit	5845	699	12.0%	2.6	271
Apache HttpClient	1818	217	11.9%	2.6	83
Areca	3565	423	11.9%	2.6	163

Fig. 6. Results of empirical analysis. For each program, the total number of methods, the number of common methods, the percentage of common methods compared to the total, the average number of methods in each common method group, and the number of common method groups are displayed. "Total methods" includes interface methods, abstract methods, and overriding implementations of the same method. The results suggest that many Java programs have potential uses of structural subtyping.

were performing different actions. In future work, we plan to study one application in depth to see how it can benefit from structural subtyping.

Overall, however, we found the results to be promising, and they suggest that Java programs could indeed benefit from structural subtyping. If a programmer wished to write code that called a common method, he could easily do so by using a type—which exists implicitly—consisting of that method. In contrast, in Java and other languages with nominal subtyping, programmers would have to explicitly create interfaces. And, in some cases, the interface would contain only one method, which seems an unnecessary overhead.

5   Formal System

The Unity grammar is presented in Fig. 7. The language is a lambda calculus extended with values tagged with brands. Methods can be defined on a brand and the usual dispatch semantics apply. Brand and method declarations are top-level. To define brands, the brand construct is used. A brand can be either abstract or concrete. Objects cannot be created from abstract brands (similar to Java's abstract classes). We use the metavariables β and θ to range over brand names. The metavariable M ranges over a list of (method : type) pairs.

Programs	$p ::= decl$ in $p \mid e \mid e; p$
Declarations	$decl ::= brand\text{-}decl \mid ext\text{-}decl$
Brand declaration	$brand\text{-}decl ::= mod$ brand $\beta(\tau; \overline{m\text{-}decl})$ extends β
Modifiers	$mod ::= $ abstract $\mid$ concrete
Method declaration	$m\text{-}decl ::= $ abstract method $m\ (\overline{m : \tau}) : \tau$
	$\mid$ method $m\ (\overline{m : \tau}) : \tau = e$
External method	$ext\text{-}decl ::= $ method $m\ \beta(\overline{m : \tau_m}) : \tau = e$
Expressions	$e ::= () \mid x \mid \lambda x{:}\tau.\ e \mid e\ e \mid \widehat{\beta}(e) \mid \{\overline{\ell = e}\} \mid e.\ell \mid e.m$
Types	$\tau ::= $ unit $\mid \tau \to \tau \mid \tau \wedge \tau \mid \beta(\overline{m : \tau}) \mid \{\overline{\ell : \tau}\} \mid \tau \Rightarrow \tau$
Values	$v ::= () \mid \widehat{\beta}(v) \mid \{\overline{\ell = v}\} \mid \lambda x{:}\tau.\ e \mid$
Contexts	$\Gamma ::= \cdot \mid \Gamma, x : \tau$
	$\Sigma ::= \cdot \mid \Sigma, mod\ \beta(\tau; \overline{mod\ m : \tau})$ extends β
	$\Delta ::= \cdot \mid \Delta, \widehat{\beta}(\overline{m = e})$ extends $\widehat{\beta}$

Conventions

$\widehat{\beta} \equiv$ tag value corresponding to β

$\text{fieldType}_\Sigma(\beta) = \tau$ if $\beta(\tau; \overline{m : \tau})$ extends $\beta' \in \Sigma$

$\text{modifier}_\Sigma(\beta) = mod$ if $mod\ \beta(\tau; \overline{m : \tau})$ extends $\beta' \in \Sigma$

M ranges over $\overline{m : \tau}$

Fig. 7. Unity grammar

One of the valid expression forms for a program is an expression followed by a program $(e; p)$. In this last construct, the expression is evaluated and will be type correct according to the definitions that preceded it.

When a brand is defined, a name is given for it, as well as the brand's *field type* (usually a record); this is the type of the fields of the brand. The programmer initializes the field value when an object is created.

In Unity, a method is either internal or external. In the former case, the method is defined along with the brand, like method declarations in Java-like languages. To allow modular exhaustiveness checking of external methods, external methods cannot be abstract; a method body must be provided for every external method. We have taken this rule from MultiJava [8].

When a method m is defined on a brand β, a set of methods is specified—the methods that must exist within β (either internal or external) before m can be invoked.[3] For example, in Fig. 1, the function insertChar required that its receiver have a getCurrentPos method.

---

[3] For simplicity and to support information hiding, types cannot contain field constraints as in example 1, but this is not a fundamental limitation of the system.

To simplify the formal system, methods take only one argument: the this parameter. Additional parameters may be specified using lambda expressions.[4]

If β is a brand name, then $\widehat{\beta}$ is the tag value corresponding to β. In other words, $\beta(\overline{m:\tau})$ is a type, and $\widehat{\beta}$ is its run-time analogue.

To create objects, the expression form $\widehat{\beta}(e)$ is used. This creates an object that is tagged with $\widehat{\beta}$. Methods are called using $e.m$, while function application is written $e_1 e_2$.

Our language includes a limited form of intersection types. Our motivation for including these is to make external methods available to objects that were defined before the external method was created. Section 5.1 describes this in more detail.

Σ is the subtyping context; it stores the user-declared sub-branding relationships. Δ is the corresponding run-time context. Δ contains a strict subset of the information in Σ—it does not contain whether a brand is abstract or concrete, and it does not keep track of the field type or methods associated with each brand. We assume the existence of a special brand Top that is not defined in Σ or Δ, but that may be extended by user-defined brands. Since every brand must have a super-brand, the brand subtype hierarchy is a tree rooted at Top.

Like other object calculi, Unity is purely functional so as to simplify the system. State is orthogonal to the issues we are considering; our design should be easily adaptable to a language with imperative features.

5.1 Static Semantics

Here we describe the subtyping and typing judgements shown in Figures 8, 9 and 10. Auxiliary judgements are in Fig. 11

Subtyping. Subtyping comprises two parts: the sub-brand judgement ($\sqsubseteq$) and the subtype judgement ($\leq$). The latter is shown in Fig. 8. The first judgement is not on types, but brands, which are a component of a type but not themselves a type. The sub-brand judgement is just the reflexive, transitive closure of the declared extends relation.

The subtype judgement ($\leq$) uses the sub-brand judgement in the third subtyping rule, which states that an object type $\beta_1(M_1)$ is a subtype of $\beta_2(M_2)$ when β_1 is a sub-brand of β_2 ($\beta_1 \sqsubseteq \beta_2$) and M_1 is a sub-record of M_2 ($M_1 \leq M_2$). There are additional conditions that $\beta_1(M_1)$ **type** and $\beta_2(M_2)$ **type**, which ensures that these are valid types. The relevant type formation rule here is:

$$\frac{\overline{m} \text{ distinct} \qquad \Gamma \mid \Sigma \vdash \overline{\sigma} \text{ type} \qquad \Sigma \vdash \beta \text{ extends } \beta_2 \qquad override_\Sigma(\overline{m:\sigma}, \beta_2)}{\Gamma \mid \Sigma \vdash \beta(\overline{m:\sigma}) \text{ type}}$$

This rule checks that the given labels and types are a sub-record of the required fields for the brand. This ensures that a brand type always contains at least the labels it

---

[4] Note that if the body of a method is a lambda expression, it does not perform dispatch. To perform dispatch, the body of the method should be another method call. In this way, asymmetric multimethods (multimethods where the order of parameters is used in dispatch) can easily be encoded in our system. To encode a method m with body e that dispatches on β_1 and β_2, method m in β_1 dispatches to method m in β_2, the body of which is e.

$$\boxed{\Sigma \vdash \tau_1 \leq \tau_2}$$

$$\frac{}{\Sigma \vdash \tau \leq \tau} \qquad \frac{\Sigma \vdash \tau_1 \leq \tau_2 \quad \Sigma \vdash \tau_2 \leq \tau_3}{\Sigma \vdash \tau_1 \leq \tau_3} \qquad \frac{\Sigma \vdash \beta_1 \sqsubseteq \beta_2 \quad \Sigma \vdash M_1 \leq M_2 \quad \Sigma \vdash \beta_1(M_1) \text{ type} \quad \Sigma \vdash \beta_2(M_2) \text{ type}}{\Sigma \vdash \beta_1(M_1) \leq \beta_2(M_2)}$$

$$\frac{\Sigma \vdash \sigma_1 \leq \tau_1 \quad \Sigma \vdash \tau_2 \leq \sigma_2}{\Sigma \vdash \tau_1 \to \tau_2 \leq \sigma_1 \to \sigma_2} \qquad \frac{\Sigma \vdash \tau \leq \sigma_1 \quad \Sigma \vdash \tau \leq \sigma_2}{\Sigma \vdash \tau \leq \sigma_1 \wedge \sigma_2} \qquad \frac{}{\Sigma \vdash \tau_1 \wedge \tau_2 \leq \tau_1}$$

$$\frac{}{\Sigma \vdash \tau_1 \wedge \tau_2 \leq \tau_2} \qquad \frac{\{\ell_i : \tau_i{}^{i \in 1..n}\} \text{ is a permutation of } \{\ell_j : \tau_j{}^{j \in 1..n}\}}{\Sigma \vdash \{\ell_i : \tau_i{}^{i \in 1..n}\} \leq \{\ell_j : \tau_j{}^{j \in 1..n}\}}$$

$$\frac{n > m}{\Sigma \vdash \{\ell_i : \tau_i{}^{i \in 1..n}\} \leq \{\ell_j : \tau_j{}^{j \in 1..m}\}} \qquad \frac{\Sigma \vdash \tau_i \leq \sigma_i \ (i \in 1..n)}{\Sigma \vdash \{\ell_i : \tau_i\}^{i \in 1..n} \leq \{\ell_i : \sigma_i\}^{i \in 1..n}}$$

$$\frac{\Sigma \vdash \beta_1 \sqsubseteq \beta_2}{\Sigma \vdash \beta_1(M_1) \wedge \beta_2(M_2) \leq \beta_1(M_1 \wedge M_2)}$$

$$\frac{\Sigma \vdash \beta_1 \sqsubseteq \beta_2 \quad \Sigma \vdash M_2 \leq M_1 \quad \Sigma \vdash \sigma_1 \leq \sigma_2}{\Sigma \vdash \beta_1(M_1) \Rightarrow \sigma_1 \leq \beta_2(M_2) \Rightarrow \sigma_2} \qquad \frac{\Sigma \vdash \{\overline{m : \tau}\} \leq \{\overline{n : \sigma}\}}{\Sigma \vdash \overline{m : \tau} \leq \overline{n : \sigma}}$$

Fig. 8. Unity subtyping judgement

was defined to have. There is an additional check that the methods are valid overrides (*override* is defined in Fig. 11). The rest of the rules for the type formation judgement are straightforward; the full judgement appears in Appendix A.

Our language includes a limited form of intersection types, à la Davies and Pfenning; the rules for intersection types are borrowed from their work [9].

There is also a subtyping rule for a list of (method : type) pairs; it simply applies the record subtyping rule. The remaining subtyping rules are the standard reflexivity, transitivity, and function subtyping rules.

Typing rules. Full typing rules for typechecking programs and expressions appear in Figs. 9 and 10, respectively. Auxiliary judgements are defined in Fig. 11. The interesting rules are TP-BRAND, TP-EXT-METHOD, TP-NEW-OBJ and TP-INVOKE; the others are standard.

The rule TP-BRAND (Fig. 9) ensures that a brand declaration is well-formed. The newly defined brand must contain at least the labels and fields of the supertype (possibly with refined types); this is checked via the condition $\tau \leq \text{fieldType}_\Sigma(\beta')$. Note that if a field type is a record, then subtypes must list all the labels of the parent. Aside from simplifying the calculus, this sidesteps issues of variable shadowing while allowing subtypes to refine the type of a particular label. The rule also checks that the methods given are valid overrides of the methods of the super-brand, and, in the case of concrete classes, that all methods are concrete.

$\boxed{\Sigma \vdash p \ \mathbf{ok}}$

$$\frac{\begin{array}{c} \beta \notin \Sigma \qquad \tau \le \text{fieldType}_\Sigma(\beta') \\ \Sigma \vdash \beta.\overline{m\text{-}decl} : (\overline{mod_m\, m : \tau}) \qquad \Sigma' = \Sigma, mod\ \beta(\tau; \overline{mod_m\, m : \tau})\ \text{extends}\ \beta' \\ \Sigma' \vdash \beta.(\tau; \overline{m\text{-}decl})\ \mathbf{ok} \qquad override_\Sigma(\overline{m : \tau}, \beta') \\ mod = \text{concrete implies } methods_{\Sigma'}(\beta) = \text{concrete } \overline{n : \sigma} \qquad \Sigma' \vdash p\ \mathbf{ok} \end{array}}{\Sigma \vdash mod\ \mathbf{brand}\ \beta(\tau; \overline{m\text{-}decl})\ \text{extends}\ \beta'\ \text{in}\ p\ \mathbf{ok}} \quad \text{(Tp-Brand)}$$

$$\frac{\begin{array}{c} \Sigma = \{ mod\ \beta_1(\sigma; M')\ \text{extends}\ \beta_2 \}, \Sigma_0 \\ m \notin M' \qquad \Sigma' = \{ mod\ \beta_1(\sigma; M', m : \beta_1(M) \Rightarrow \tau)\ \text{extends}\ \beta_2 \}, \Sigma_0 \\ override_\Sigma(\beta_1(M) \Rightarrow \tau, \beta_2) \\ \text{this} : \beta_1(M), \text{fields} : \sigma \mid \Sigma' \vdash e : \tau \qquad \Sigma' \vdash p\ \mathbf{ok} \end{array}}{\Sigma \vdash \mathbf{method}\ m\ \beta_1(M) : \tau = e\ \text{in}\ p\ \mathbf{ok}} \quad \text{(Tp-Ext-Method)}$$

$$\frac{\cdot \mid \Sigma \vdash e : \tau}{\Sigma \vdash e\ \mathbf{ok}} \ \text{(Tp-Expr1)} \qquad \frac{\cdot \mid \Sigma \vdash e : \tau \qquad \Sigma \vdash p\ \mathbf{ok}}{\Sigma \vdash e; p\ \mathbf{ok}} \ \text{(Tp-Expr2)}$$

Fig. 9. Unity typing judgement for programs

$\boxed{\Gamma \mid \Sigma \vdash e : \tau}$

$$\frac{x : \tau \in \Gamma}{\Gamma \mid \Sigma \vdash x : \tau} \qquad \overline{\Gamma \vdash () : \text{unit}} \qquad \frac{\Sigma \vdash \tau_1\ \text{type} \qquad \Gamma, x : \tau_1 \mid \Sigma \vdash e : \tau_2}{\Gamma \mid \Sigma \vdash \lambda x{:}\tau_1.\, e : \tau_1 \to \tau_2}$$

$$\frac{\Gamma \mid \Sigma \vdash e_1 : \tau_1 \to \tau_2 \qquad \Gamma \mid \Sigma \vdash e_2 : \tau_1}{\Gamma \mid \Sigma \vdash e_1\, e_2 : \tau_2} \qquad \frac{\Gamma \mid \Sigma \vdash e : \sigma \qquad \Sigma \vdash \sigma \le \tau}{\Gamma \mid \Sigma \vdash e : \tau}$$

$$\frac{\begin{array}{c} \text{concrete}\ \beta(\tau) \in \Sigma \\ \Gamma \mid \Sigma \vdash e : \tau' \qquad \Sigma \vdash \tau' \le \tau \qquad methods_\Sigma(\beta) = \overline{mod_m\, m : \sigma} \end{array}}{\Gamma \mid \Sigma \vdash \widehat{\beta}(e) : \beta(\overline{m : \sigma})} \quad \text{(Tp-New-Obj)}$$

$$\frac{\Gamma \mid \Sigma \vdash \overline{e} : \overline{\tau}}{\Gamma \mid \Sigma \vdash (\overline{\ell = e}) : \{\overline{\ell : \tau}\}} \qquad \frac{\Gamma \mid \Sigma \vdash e : \{\ell_i : \tau_i\ ^{i \in 1..n}\}}{\Gamma \mid \Sigma \vdash e.\ell_k : \tau_k}$$

$$\frac{\begin{array}{c} \Gamma \mid \Sigma \vdash e : \beta(M) \qquad m_k : \tau_{m_k} \in (M \wedge methods_\Sigma(\beta)) \\ \tau_{m_k} = \beta'(\overline{n : \sigma}) \Rightarrow \tau \qquad \beta(M \wedge methods_\Sigma(\beta)) \le \beta'(\overline{n : \sigma}) \end{array}}{\Gamma \mid \Sigma \vdash e.m_k : \tau} \quad \text{(Tp-Invoke)}$$

Fig. 10. Unity typing judgement for expressions

This rule and the type formation rule for brands described above illustrate the need for both a sub-brand and subtype judgement. The context Σ stores information about the fields and methods of a brand; these are retrieved via fieldType$_\Sigma$ and $methods_\Sigma$ (called by $override_\Sigma$), respectively. Additionally, without a runtime component to the nominal hierarchy, there would not be a way to perform dispatch, which we describe in Sect. 5.2.

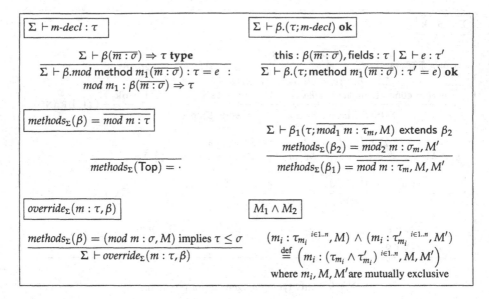

Fig. 11. Unity typechecking auxiliary judgements

The rule Tp-Ext-Method checks external method definitions. The existing brand definitions are updated by adding the new external method via the new context Σ'. The rule also checks that the method types of the external method defined on sub-brands are in the subtype relation, which ensures that the context Σ' is well-formed.

The rule Tp-New-Obj (Fig. 10) checks the correctness of the object creation expression. The rule checks that the brand has been defined as concrete, and that the given record labels are a subtype of the required record labels.

The rule Tp-Invoke typechecks method invocations. The method being called must be contained in either the set of methods in the brand's type, M, or in the set of methods of the brand ($methods_\Sigma(\beta)$). Additionally, the methods in the brand's type, combined with the methods of the brand (via intersection) must be a subtype of the method's required methods. Adding the intersection condition increases expressiveness over having the rule just consider the methods of the brand, since the type might have methods defined on a sub-brand. For example, within the body of the function $\lambda x : \text{Top}(\text{toString} : () \rightarrow string). e$, the type of x contains the method toString. If we suppose that toString is not defined for the brand Top, then x's type contains methods that are not defined in the brand itself.

5.2 Dynamic Semantics

Most of the evaluation rules for Unity are standard; the evaluation judgement is in Fig. 12 and auxiliary judgements are in Fig. 13.

The interesting evaluation rules are E-Brand-Decl and E-Ext-Decl, which evaluate brand definitions and external method definitions, respectively. To evaluate a brand

$$\boxed{p \mid \Delta \longmapsto p' \mid \Delta'}$$

$$\frac{\overline{m\text{-}decl} \longmapsto \overline{m = e}}{\text{mod brand } \beta_1(\tau; \overline{m\text{-}decl}) \text{ extends } \beta_2 \text{ in } p \mid \Delta \longmapsto} \quad \text{(E-BRAND-DECL)}$$
$$p \mid \Delta, (\beta_1(\overline{m = e}) \text{ extends } \beta_2)$$

$$\frac{\Delta = \{\beta(\overline{m = e}) \text{ extends } \beta'\}, \Delta_0}{\text{method } m_1 \, \beta(\overline{m : \tau_m}) : \sigma = e_1 \text{ in } p \mid \Delta \longmapsto} \quad \text{(E-EXT-DECL)}$$
$$p \mid \{\beta(\overline{m = e}, m_1 = e_1) \text{ extends } \beta'\}, \Delta_0$$

$$\frac{e \longmapsto_\Delta e'}{e \mid \Delta \longmapsto e' \mid \Delta} \qquad \frac{e \longmapsto_\Delta e'}{e; p \mid \Delta \longmapsto e'; p \mid \Delta} \qquad \frac{p \mid \Delta \longmapsto p' \mid \Delta'}{v; p \mid \Delta \longmapsto p' \mid \Delta'}$$

$$\boxed{e \longmapsto_\Delta e'}$$

$$\frac{e \longmapsto_\Delta e'}{e.m \longmapsto_\Delta e'.m} \qquad \frac{mbody_\Delta(m, \widehat{\beta}) = e}{\widehat{\beta}(v).m \longmapsto_\Delta [\widehat{\beta}(v)/\text{this}, v/\text{fields}] \, e} \quad \text{(E-INVOKE)}$$

$$\frac{e \longmapsto_\Delta e'}{\widehat{\beta}(e) \longmapsto_\Delta \widehat{\beta}(e')} \qquad \frac{e_1 \longmapsto_\Delta e_1'}{e_1 \, e_2 \longmapsto_\Delta e_1' \, e_2} \qquad \frac{e_2 \longmapsto_\Delta e_2'}{v_1 \, e_2 \longmapsto_\Delta v_1 \, e_2'} \qquad \frac{}{(\lambda x{:}\tau.e) \, v \longmapsto_\Delta [v/x] \, e}$$

$$\frac{e_k \longmapsto_\Delta e_k'}{\{\ldots, \ell_k = e_k, \ldots\} \longmapsto_\Delta} \qquad \frac{e \longmapsto_\Delta e'}{e.\ell \longmapsto_\Delta e'.\ell} \qquad \frac{}{\{\ell_i = v_i \stackrel{i \in 1..n}{}\}.\ell_k \longmapsto_\Delta v_k}$$
$$\{\ldots, \ell_k = e_k', \ldots\}$$

Fig. 12. Unity evaluation judgement

definition, the method definitions are evaluated to the method body and the rest of the program is evaluated with the extended context. Similarly, E-EXT-DECL updates the context with new method definitions for the brand, then evaluates the rest of the program with the new context.

The auxiliary function $mbody_\Delta(m, \widehat{\beta})$ finds the appropriate method body for a method m, starting at the tag $\widehat{\beta}$. This function is used by the rule E-INVOKE, which within the method body returned by $mbody_\Delta$, substitutes the object for this and the field value of the object for fields. Method declarations are evaluated in a straight-forward manner; all of the type information is discarded (so in the case of abstract methods, the entire declaration is discarded), leaving just the method body.

5.3 Type Safety

The full proof of type safety is provided in a companion technical report [17]. We summarize the main results here. First, we provide the definition of a well-formed context:

$$\boxed{mbody_\Delta(m,\widehat{\beta}) = e}$$

$$\frac{\widehat{\beta_1}(m_0 = e_0, \overline{m' = e'_m}) \text{ extends } \widehat{\beta_2} \in \Delta}{mbody_\Delta(m_0, \widehat{\beta_1}) = e_0} \qquad \frac{\widehat{\beta_1}(\overline{m = e}) \text{ extends } \widehat{\beta_2} \in \Delta \quad m_0 \notin \overline{m} \quad mbody_\Delta(m_0, \widehat{\beta_2}) = e_0}{mbody_\Delta(m_0, \widehat{\beta_1}) = e_0}$$

$$\boxed{m\text{-}decl \longmapsto m = e}$$

$$\overline{\text{abstract method } m(\overline{m : \sigma_m}) : \tau \longmapsto \cdot} \qquad \overline{\text{method } m(\overline{m : \sigma_m}) : \tau = e \longmapsto m = e}$$

Fig. 13. Unity evaluation auxiliary judgements

Definition 1 (Well-formed context).
The context Σ is *well-formed*, iff the following conditions hold:

1. there is exactly one entry for each brand β.
2. if $mod\ \beta_1(\tau; M)$ extends $\beta_2 \in \Sigma$, then
   (a) $\beta_2(M)$ **type**
   (b) $\tau \leq \text{fieldType}_\Sigma(\beta_2)$
   (c) if $mod = \text{concrete}$, then $methods_\Sigma(\beta_1) = \text{concrete } \overline{n : \tau}$.

Our theorems on type safety assume a correspondence between the static brand definition context Σ and the runtime context Δ. This ensures that the runtime context, which does not contain type information, is consistent with the static typing context. Formally, this correspondence is defined as follows:

Definition 2 (Models relation on contexts). The definition of $\Sigma \vdash \Delta$ (Σ *models* Δ) is given by the following inference rules:

$$\frac{}{\cdot \vdash \cdot} \qquad \frac{\Sigma \vdash \Delta \quad \Sigma' = \Sigma, mod\ \beta_1(\tau; \{\text{concrete } m_i : \beta_1(M_i) \Rightarrow \tau_i'\ ^{i\in 1..n}\}, \overline{\text{abstract } n : \sigma}) \text{ extends } \beta_2 \quad \text{this} : \beta_1(M_i), \text{fields} : \tau \mid \Sigma' \vdash e_i : \tau_i\ (i\in 1..n)}{\Sigma' \vdash \Delta, \widehat{\beta_1}(m_i = e_i\ ^{i\in 1..n}) \text{ extends } \widehat{\beta_2}}$$

Type safety is proved using the standard progress and preservation theorems. For progress, we prove a lemma that states that if we have a well-typed value whose type contains a method m_k, then a runtime context consistent with the static context must contain a method body for m_k:

Lemma 1. *If* $\Gamma \mid \Sigma \vdash \widehat{\beta}(v) : \tau$ *and* $\Sigma \vdash \tau \leq \beta'(M)$, *where* $\Sigma \vdash \Delta$ *and* $m_k \in M$, *then* $mbody_\Delta(m_k, \widehat{\beta})$ *is defined.*

The lemma is stated in this way so that the subsumption case is easy to prove. The lemma is proved by induction on the typing derivation. The interesting case is that of Tp-New-Obj, which uses the definition of a well-formed context and that of $\Sigma \vdash \Delta$.

Theorem 1 (Progress [programs]). *If* $\cdot \mid \Sigma \vdash p$ *ok, for some* Σ, *then either* p *is a value or, for* Δ *such that* $\Sigma \vdash \Delta$, *there exist* p' *and* Δ' *such that* $p \mid \Delta \longmapsto p' \mid \Delta'$.

This theorem is proved by appealing to an auxiliary lemma that proves progress for expressions and a standard canonical forms lemma. The interesting case is that of method invocation, which is proved using Lemma 1.

Preservation is slightly more difficult to prove. We first prove the following lemma by induction on the typing derivation. The lemma states that the body of a method is well-typed if the static context Σ models the runtime context Δ.

Lemma 2. *If* $\Gamma \mid \Sigma \vdash \widehat{\theta}(v) : \sigma$ *and* $\sigma \leq \beta(m_0 : \beta'(M_0) \Rightarrow \tau, M)$ *and* $\Sigma \vdash \Delta$ *and* $mbody_\Delta(m_0, \widehat{\theta}) = e_0$, *then this* $: \beta'(M_0)$, *fields* $: fieldType_\Sigma\theta \mid \Sigma \vdash e_0 : \tau$.

Theorem 2 (Preservation [programs]). *If* $\Gamma \mid \Sigma \vdash p$ *ok and* $\Sigma \vdash \Delta$ *and* $p \mid \Delta \longmapsto p' \mid \Delta'$, *then there exists a* Σ' *such that* $\Sigma' \vdash \Delta'$ *where* $\Gamma \mid \Sigma' \vdash p'$ *ok.*

We prove this theorem using of a preservation theorem on expressions, a standard substitution lemma, and Lemma 2 above.

5.4 Modularity

Our typechecking rules are modular; each rule relies only on information in the context up to the current program point, rather than requiring a global dictionary of brand definitions. Our exhaustiveness checks are modular because external method definitions cannot be abstract (enforced by the grammar); otherwise, information about all brand definitions would be required.

Since our language does not include modules, our ambiguity checks are not modular in the strictest sense of the term, as they depend on all definitions up to the current program point. However, our system could be easily extended with additional rules to support modular ambiguity checking. Millstein and Chambers have developed such rules and have also defined several levels of modular typechecking [19]. Our current system is compatible with their broadest notion of modular typechecking, the so-called "most-extending module" approach, exemplified by their language System E. To perform the most modular form of typechecking, however, we would require that all implementations of an external method be in the same module. Further, external methods would be forbidden from overriding internal methods (currently permitted in our system). These checks correspond to the restriction $M1$ in Dubious [19] and restriction $R3$ in MultiJava [8].

A related issue is that of information hiding, a form of which our language supports. A brand's field value can only be accessed by the brand's methods, effectively making them private. It would be possible to extend this further and disallow external methods from accessing fields, or allow marking some internal methods as private.

5.5 Polymorphism and Recursive Types

We have designed an extension Unity$_\alpha$ with polymorphism (described in [17]), but we have omitted this feature in this version of Unity since we discovered that polymorphism was orthogonal to the issues surrounding nominal and structural subtyping. In Unity$_\alpha$, the syntax is extended as follows:

$$brand\text{-}decl ::= mod \text{ brand } \forall \overline{T}.\ \beta\langle \overline{T}\rangle(\tau; \overline{m\text{-}decl}) \text{ extends } \beta\langle \overline{\tau}\rangle$$

$$ext\text{-}decl ::= \text{method } m\ \forall \overline{T'}.\ \beta\langle \overline{T'}\rangle(\overline{m : \tau}) : \tau = e$$

$$e ::= \dots \mid \widehat{\beta}[\overline{\tau}] \mid \Lambda T.\ e \mid e[e]$$

$$\tau ::= \dots \mid X \mid \beta\langle \overline{\tau}\rangle(\overline{m : \tau}) \mid \forall T.\ \tau$$

The sub-brand judgement is on parameterized brands (i.e. $\beta\langle\overline{\tau}\rangle$) and, aside from a new rule for $\forall T.\ \tau$ types, the subtype judgement is essentially the same.

We have also created an extension that includes structural recursive types [17]. Unity as presented in this paper supports only nominal recursive types; when defining a brand β, the name β can be used in the components of its definition. Adding structural recursive types was relatively straightforward; we simply added standard iso-recursive μ types to the language, along with a fold and unfold operation. In this system, it is possible to express types such as:

$$\mu X.\text{Top}(\texttt{clone}() : X)$$

which specifies that the result of the clone function is the type itself being defined. The advantage to structural recursive types is that structural object interfaces, such as ScrollBar in Example 1, can be specified as pure structural types (using the Top brand) while still being self-referential.

6 Related Work

Type Systems. At the FOOL/WOOD '07 workshop, we presented the predecessor of this version of Unity [16]. Here, we have extended that work by adding methods and information hiding to our core calculus, providing additional examples, and including a case study.

Researchers have recently considered the problem of integrating nominal and structural subtyping. Reppy and Turon have addressed the problem in the context of type-checking traits [24]. Their resulting type system is a hybrid of nominal and structural subtyping. However, in their system, structural types are second-class; they apply to trait functions but not to expressions or ordinary functions. Consequently, there is less expressiveness as compared with Unity: it is not possible to constrain the argument of a function to have particular members, for example.

After our initial workshop proposal, Odersky et al. independently implemented a similar language feature, validating the practical importance of our work. In Scala, type refinements allow a nominal type to include additional structural information [22]. Scala type refinements have many similarities with the language Whiteoak, an extension of Java with structural types [12]. Like Scala, in Whiteoak, by using intersection types, a type can include both structural and nominal aspects.

Scala and Whiteoak differ from Unity in that they do not have external methods, nor do they allow structural constraints to be placed on a method's receiver. Also, the language designs have neither been formalized nor proved sound.

Ostermann has designed a language that seeks to enhance the expressiveness of nominal subtyping to gain some of the benefits of structural subtyping [23]. Ostermann has identified an additional important benefit of nominal subtyping—that of blame assignment: i.e., who accepts responsibility for maintaining a subtype relation, the user or the designer of a component? The language design is much more expressive than a purely nominal system; it is possible to, for example, create subtypes of a class type without inheriting its implementation, and declare supertypes of an existing type. But, this comes at the cost of a subtyping relation that is not transitive, which may prove counter-intuitive to programmers. The programmer must manually provide a set of "witness" types so that the typechecker can apply subsumption. Therefore, it is unclear whether this approach is practical.

Bono et al. have also proposed a type system that includes both nominal and structural aspects, but their system does not fully integrate the two disciplines [1]. The system only uses structural typing when typechecking uses of the this variable, making their system considerably less expressive than ours.

The language MOBY is in many ways similar to Unity, as it supports structural subtyping and a form of tag subtyping through its inheritance-based subtyping mechanism, which is similar to our sub-branding [10, 11]. This allows expressing many useful subtyping constraints, but MOBY's class types are not integrated with object types in the same way as in Unity. For instance, in MOBY, it is not possible to express the constraint that an object should have a particular class *and* should have some particular methods (that are not defined in the class itself). Additionally, the object-oriented core of MOBY supports only internal dispatch. MOBY does include "tagtypes" that are very similar to our brands. These can be used to support downcasts or to encode multimethods, but they are disjoint from the object-oriented core of the system.

Strongtalk presents a structural type system for Smalltalk and also supports named subtyping relationships through its "brand" mechanism [3]. However, it is not possible to define subtyping on brands. Additionally, since it is a type system for Smalltalk, it supports only the single dispatch model.

Modula-3's type system has structural types with branding, but not structural sub*typing* [20]. That is, its type system will treat two record types as equivalent if they have the same structure but different type aliases, but does not recognize one as a subtype of the other if it has additional fields. The object-oriented part of the language uses nominal subtyping.

In the C++ concepts proposal, concepts can be either nominal or structural [13]. However, concepts apply only to template constraints, not to the subtyping relation.

External and Multimethod Dispatch. External and multimethod dispatch has been extensively studied, but in the context of either dynamically typed languages, or languages with a purely nominal type system. Cecil is one of the first languages to include statically checked multimethods, but performs a whole-program analysis to ensure that multimethods are exhaustive and unambiguous [6, 7]. As previously mentioned (Sect. 2.2), Cecil contains "where" clauses that can model some aspects of structural types, but they can only appear on top-level methods and cannot be nested, in contrast to Unity.

More recent work has focused on modular typechecking of external methods and multimethods, as well as the problem of integrating external methods into existing languages; this includes the Dubious calculus (System M) and MultiJava [19, 8]. We have built on these existing techniques for modular typechecking of external methods.

The language λ& [5] includes multimethod dispatch and includes structural subtyping on methods, similar to Unity. However, the subtyping hierarchy on classes uses only nominal subtyping, in contrast to Unity.

Acknowledgements. We would like to thank Karl Crary and William Lovas for helpful discussion and feedback on our language, and Kevin Bierhoff for comments on an earier version of this paper. This research was supported in part by the U.S. Department of Defense, Army Research Office grant number DAAD19-02-1-0389 entitled "Perpetually Available and Secure Information Systems," and NSF CAREER award CCF-0546550.

References

[1] Bono, V., Damiani, F., Giachino, E.: Separating Type, Behavior, and State to Achieve Very Fine-grained Reuse. In: Electronic proceedings of FTfJP (2007), http://www.cs.ru.nl/ftfjp/

[2] Bracha, G., Cook, W.: Mixin-based inheritance. In: ECOOP 1990(1990)

[3] Bracha, G., Griswold, D.: Strongtalk: typechecking Smalltalk in a production environment. In: OOPSLA 1993, pp. 215–230 (1993)

[4] Bruce, K.B., Schuett, A., Gent, R.V., Fiech, A.: PolyTOIL: A type-safe polymorphic object-oriented language. ACM Trans. Program. Lang. Syst. 25(2), 225–290 (2003)

[5] Castagna, G., Ghelli, G., Longo, G.: A calculus for overloaded functions with subtyping. Inf. Comput. 117(1), 115–135 (1995)

[6] Chambers, C.: Object-oriented multi-methods in Cecil. In: Lehrmann Madsen, O. (ed.) ECOOP 1992. LNCS, vol. 615. Springer, Heidelberg (1992)

[7] Chambers, C.: Cecil Group. The Cecil language: specification and rationale, version 3.2 (February 2004), http://www.cs.washington.edu/research/projects/cecil/

[8] Clifton, C., Millstein, T., Leavens, G.T., Chambers, C.: MultiJava: Design rationale, compiler implementation, and applications. ACM Trans. Program. Lang. Syst. 28(3), 517–575 (2006)

[9] Davies, R., Pfenning, F.: Intersection types and computational effects. In: ICFP 2000, pp. 198–208 (2000)

[10] Fisher, K., Reppy, J.: The design of a class mechanism for Moby. In: PLDI 1999, pp. 37–49 (1999)

[11] Fisher, K., Reppy, J.: Inheritance-based subtyping. Inf. Comput. 177(1), 28–55 (2002)

[12] Gil, J., Maman, I.: Whiteoak (2008), http://ssdl-wiki.cs.technion.ac.il/wiki/index.php/Whiteoak

[13] Gregor, D., Järvi, J., Siek, J., Stroustrup, B., Reis, G.D., Lumsdaine, A.: Concepts: Linguistic support for generic programming in C++. In: Proceedings of OOPSLA 2006, October 2006, pp. 291–310. ACM Press, New York (2006)

[14] Leroy, X., Doligez, D., Garrigue, J., Rémy, D., Vouillon, J.: The Objective Caml system, release 3.09 (2004), http://caml.inria.fr/pub/docs/manual-ocaml/index.html

[15] Madsen, O.L., Moller-Pedersen, B.: Virtual classes: a powerful mechanism in object-oriented programming. In: OOPSLA 1989, pp. 397–406 (1989)

[16] Malayeri, D., Aldrich, J.: Combining structural subtyping and external dispatch. In: FOOL/WOOD 2007 (January 2007), http://foolwood07.cs.uchicago.edu/program.html

[17] Malayeri, D., Aldrich, J.: Integrating Nominal and Structural Subtyping. Technical Report CMU-CS-08-120, School of Computer Science, Carnegie Mellon University (May 2008)

[18] Sun Microsystems. Java collections API design FAQ (2003), http://java.sun.com/j2se/1.4.2/docs/guide/collections/designfaq.html

[19] Millstein, T.D., Chambers, C.: Modular statically typed multimethods. Inf. Comput. 175(1), 76–118 (2002)

[20] Nelson, G. (ed.): Systems programming with Modula-3. Prentice-Hall, Inc., Upper Saddle River (1991)

[21] Nystrom, N., Chong, S., Myers, A.C.: Scalable extensibility via nested inheritance. In: OOPSLA 2004, pp. 99–115 (2004)

[22] Odersky, M.: The Scala language specification (2007), http://www.scala-lang.org/docu/files/ScalaReference.pdf

[23] Ostermann, K.: Nominal and Structural Subtyping in Component-Based Programming. Journal of Object Technology 7(1) (2008)

[24] Reppy, J., Turon, A.: Metaprogramming with traits. In: Ernst, E. (ed.) ECOOP 2007. LNCS, vol. 4609. Springer, Heidelberg (2007)

[25] Schärli, N., Ducasse, S., Nierstrasz, O., Black, A.: Traits: Composable units of behavior. In: Cardelli, L. (ed.) ECOOP 2003. LNCS, vol. 2743. Springer, Heidelberg (2003)

A Formal System

Well-formed judgement

$$\boxed{\Sigma \vdash \tau \text{ type}}$$

$$\frac{}{\Sigma \vdash \text{unit type}} \qquad \frac{\Sigma \vdash \tau_1 \text{ type} \quad \Sigma \vdash \tau_2 \text{ type}}{\Sigma \vdash \tau_1 \to \tau_2 \text{ type}} \qquad \frac{\Sigma \vdash \tau_1 \text{ type} \quad \Sigma \vdash \tau_2 \text{ type}}{\Sigma \vdash \tau_1 \wedge \tau_2 \text{ type}}$$

$$\frac{\overline{m} \text{ distinct} \quad \Sigma \vdash \overline{\sigma} \text{ type} \quad \Sigma \vdash \beta \text{ extends } \beta_2 \quad \Sigma \vdash override(\overline{m : \sigma}, \beta_2)}{\Sigma \vdash \beta(\overline{m : \sigma}) \text{ type}} \qquad \frac{\overline{\ell} \text{ distinct} \quad \Sigma \vdash \overline{\tau} \text{ type}}{\Sigma \vdash \{\overline{\ell : \tau}\} \text{ type}}$$

$$\frac{\Sigma \vdash \beta(m_i : \theta_i(\overline{n_i : \sigma_i}) \Rightarrow \tau_i'{}^{\,i\in 1..n}) \text{ type} \quad \Sigma \vdash \beta \sqsubseteq \theta_i \ (i \subset 1..n) \quad \Sigma \vdash \tau_2 \text{ type}}{\Sigma \vdash \beta(m_i : \theta_i(\overline{n_i : \sigma_i}) \Rightarrow \tau_i'{}^{\,i\in 1..n}) \Rightarrow \tau_2 \text{ type}}$$

Flow Analysis of Code Customizations

Anders Hessellund and Peter Sestoft

IT University of Copenhagen, Denmark
{hessellund,sestoft}@itu.dk

Abstract. Inconsistency between metadata and code customizations is a major concern in modern, configurable enterprise systems. The increasing reliance on metadata, in the form of XML files, and code customizations, in the form of Java files, has led to a hybrid development platform. The expected consistency requirements between metadata and code should be checked but often are not, so current tools offer surprisingly poor development support. In this paper, we adapt classical data flow analyses to detect inconsistencies and provide better static guarantees. We provide a formalization of the consistency requirements and a set of adapted analyses for a concrete case study. Our work is implemented in a fast and efficient prototype in the form of an Eclipse plugin. We validate our work by testing this prototype on actual production code; preliminary results show that this approach is worthwhile. We found a significant number of previously undetected consistency errors and have received very positive feedback from the developer community in the case study.

1 Introduction

Complex enterprise systems increasingly use metadata in the form of XML files for configuration. This facilitates maintenance and allows developers to gain a better overview by focusing on the *what* of the system rather than on the *how*. However, metadata cannot tell the whole story and especially for business logic requirements, it is often necessary to add custom code (e.g. in Java) to implement specialized functionality. This is frequently done through *code customizations*. A code customization is a small code snippet with a predefined interface that can be plugged into the base system. The relation between metadata and code customization is that metadata declares the existence of specialized business logic and the code customization provides an implementation. A code customization fulfills concrete requirements but at the same time introduces new consistency constraints on the system: Metadata and code must agree on proper use of common names and types. Current tools are surprisingly poor at managing these consistency constraints and the errors that arise from violating them.

In this paper, we claim that some of these problems can be eliminated by adapting classic data flow analyses to framework-specific code customizations. We propose a set of data flow analyses for a concrete case study: The Apache Open For Business (OFBiz) [1] enterprise resource planning (ERP) system.

J. Vitek (Ed.): ECOOP 2008, LNCS 5142, pp. 285–308, 2008.

These analyses are implemented in an Eclipse plugin and have been applied to a production quality installation of OFBiz. Our prototype has found a large number of consistency errors in this code base. In this paper, we show how our prototype can locate the source of each error and help developers increase the quality of their code customizations. The prototype has been released to the OFBiz developer community and received very positive feedback [2, 3].

The contributions of this work are:

- A formalization of the consistency constraints between metadata and code customizations in OFBiz.
- A set of framework-specific adaptions of dataflow analyses based on this formalization.
- A working implementation of these analyses in the form of an Eclipse plugin.
- An empirical validation of the tool by analyzing production code and eliciting feedback from OFBiz developers.
- A discussion of the limitations of the analyses, and the trade-off between soundness (no false negatives) and precision (only few false positives).

Section 2 below shows a motivating example from the out-of-the-box version of OFBiz, and section 3 provides more background on this case study with an emphasis on its size and complexity. Section 4 formalizes the implicit consistency requirements in OFBiz, and sections 5 and 6 describe the flow analyses used to realize these consistency requirements. Section 7 describes our prototype Eclipse plugin that implements these analyses, and section 8 presents and discusses empirical results from applying this tool to the case study. Section 9 discusses wider perspectives and implications of this work, and section 10 considers related work.

2   Motivating Example: Code Customizations in OFBiz

The OFBiz framework exposes a range of services. A service can be described in a *service definition* such as that shown in listing 1.1. A service definition contains metadata about a service, such as its name and where it is implemented, and describes the service's input and output in the form of attributes. For each attribute, it states its name and type as well as whether this attribute is mandatory or optional. Services are often implemented in Java code snippets, called *code customizations*. A code customization must conform to the service interface given by the service definition. *Conformance* is in this case defined as accepting the same input and returning the same output as specified in the service definition.

Listing 1.1 provides an actual example of the `buildPdfFromSurveyResponse` service from the `Content` module in OFBiz v.3. This service creates PDF-files based on online surveys. The actual implementation of a service is typically written in a more expressive language such as Java. As stated in line 3 of listing 1.1, the `buildPdfFromSurveyResponse` service is implemented in Java by the method `buildPdfFromSurveyResponse`, shown in listing 1.2. The service

```
1  <service name="buildPdfFromSurveyResponse" engine="java"
2         location="org.ofbiz.content.survey.PdfSurveyServices"
3         invoke="buildPdfFromSurveyResponse">
4         <description>Build Pdf From Survey
               Response</description>
5         <attribute name="surveyResponseId" type="String"
               mode="IN" optional="false" />
6         <attribute name="outByteWrapper"
               type="org.ofbiz.entity.util.ByteWrapper"
               mode="OUT" optional="false" />
7  </service>
```

Listing 1.1. The `buildPdfFromSurveyResponse` service definition states that the service is implemented in Java by the `buildPdfFromSurveyResponse` method in the `PdfSurveyServices` class. The service has a mandatory input attribute `surveyResponseId` and a mandatory output attribute `outByteWrapper`.

```
1  public static Map buildPdfFromSurveyResponse
2  (DispatchContext dctx, Map context) {
3    GenericDelegator delegator = dctx.getDelegator();
4    Map results = ServiceUtil.returnSuccess();
5    String surveyResponseId =
         (String)context.get("surveyResponseId");
6    String contentId = (String)context.get("contentId");
7    try {
8      if (UtilValidate.isNotEmpty(surveyResponseId)) {
9        GenericValue surveyResponse =
10         delegator.findByPrimaryKey("SurveyResponse",
11           UtilMisc.toMap("surveyResponseId",
               surveyResponseId));
12     }
13       ...some 45 lines of code left out ...
14     ByteWrapper outByteWrapper =
15         new ByteWrapper(baos.toByteArray());
16     results.put("outByteWrapper", outByteWrapper);
17   } catch (GenericEntityException e) {
18     ServiceUtil.returnError(e.getMessage());
19   }
20   return results;
21 }
```

Listing 1.2. The `buildPdfFromSurveyResponse` method implements the service declared in listing 1.1. The `context` map declared in line 2 contains input attributes and the `results` map in line 4 contains the output attributes. An input attribute is read in line 5 and an output attribute is set in line 16.

declares two mandatory attributes: an input attribute `surveyResponseId` of type `String` and an output attribute `outByteWrapper` of type `ByteWrapper`.

There are three expected kinds of consistency constraints between listing 1.1 and 1.2, detailed in sections 2.1 through 2.3 below. These constraints are not stated explicitly in the OFBiz documentation and are not checked until runtime where violations can lead to unpredictable behaviour.

2.1 A Java Implementation Must Exist

The service definition says that there must exist a PdfSurveyServices class with a buildPdfFromSurveyResponse method that implements the service. Checking this constraint is a prerequisite for checking the two other kinds of constraints; since this is fairly easy to do it is not discussed further.

2.2 Only Declared Input Attributes May Be Accessed

The service definition contains a mandatory input attribute surveyResponseId of type String. Input attributes are supplied to the method via the context map in line 2 in listing 1.2. The implementation code should only access keys in this map that correspond to declared input attributes, such as surveyResponseId. Lines 5 and 6 in listing 1.2 show a correct access to a declared input attribute surveyResponseId and an incorrect access to an undeclared input attribute contentId.

2.3 All Declared Output Attributes Must Be Assigned

The example service definition contains a single mandatory output attribute, outByteWrapper. Clients of this service can assume that on successful execution, this key is present in the results map. Hence the service implementation should make sure that either the key is present or an error message is returned. In listing 1.2, the outByteWrapper attribute is set in line 16. However, the findByPrimaryKey method in line 10 may throw a checked exception which would prevent the attribute from being set. The catch block in line 18 creates a map containing an error message but does not return this map and hence has no effect. This type of subtle error is hard to spot and potentially leads to erroneous output of the service.

Note that the two errors described above are genuine consistency errors found in the release version of OFBiz (November 2007).

2.4 Current Development Tools

A key concern in OFBiz development is to ensure that the definition and implementation of a service are consistent. Development is traditionally done using normal Java- and XML-editors, so there is no tool-support for checking the three above-mentioned kinds of consistency constraints. This is because traditional tools such as XML schema conformance checking and Java type checking do not reveal constraint violations that involve *both* XML and Java artifacts. This lack of tool support causes slow development, costly maintenance, and errors in deployed OFBiz products, as shown in a previous survey [4] of the OFBiz user forums, issue tracking system, and so on. That consistency is a major concern is further evidenced from the positive feedback that we have received from the OFBiz community on the release of our initial prototype [2, 3]. Before we describe analyses and tools developed, we briefly introduce the overall case study, OFBiz.

3   Case Study: Apache Open for Business (OFBiz)

The OFBiz [1] project is an open source enterprise resource planning (ERP) system. The cornerstone of the project is a J2EE-based framework. The base framework is implemented in Java and can be configured using XML files conforming to 17 different schemas. These schemas can be considered as separate domain-specific languages tailored for individual concerns in OFBiz development, such as user interface, data model, services, workflow etc. The use of these schemas is described in greater detail in [4]. Apart from XML configuration files, code customizations written as small Java code snippets can be added to realize specialized functionality that is beyond the scope of ordinary configuration. Finally, the framework uses HTML and a template engine to render user interfaces, and also uses scripting languages, such as BeanShell script [5], for minor tasks.

Fig. 1. The 3-layer architecture of OFBiz

The framework has a three layer architecture as shown in figure 1. The bottom layer is a base engine that handles loading and wiring of modules. The middle layer is a set of base modules to define business objects, services, graphical widgets and workflows. The top layer is a set of standard ERP application modules such as Inventory, Accounting, Content Management etc. Developers can add their own modules or extend existing modules so the framework is highly flexible.

To give an impression of the size and strength of OFBiz, we list the following metrics: The out-of-the-box solution consists of approximately 180 000 lines of Java code and 195 000 lines of XML. The data model consists of more than 700 domain classes designed according to patterns based on industrial practice [6]. Industrial users include large companies such as British Telecom and United Airlines [7] as well as a range of small- and medium-sized companies [8]. It is a top-level project in the Apache Software Foundation and is backed by an active community. We therefore consider it a valid case study of large scale, industrial-strength development with metadata and code customizations.

Because of the size and complexity of OFBiz, we have chosen to focus on a specific subset of code customizations. OFBiz exposes a range of services to internal and external clients. These services are located by their metadata descriptions, i.e., service definitions as exemplified in listing 1.1. A concrete service, described by a service definition, can be implemented in a variety of ways, such as SOAP, RMI, scripting languages, a custom domain-specific language for data manipulation called Minilang, or by a general-purpose language. We will focus on the last option, viz. the general-purpose language Java, since services implemented in Java are the cause of most problems. Using Java is a double-edged sword: On one hand, it gives developers great expressive power to meet their requirements; on the other hand, this is easily misused to create a whole range of new and subtle bugs.

4   Formalizing the Consistency Requirements

The OFBiz documentation does not state any consistency requirements on the relation between metadata and code customizations. The expected requirements are implicit and only enforced at runtime where a constraint violation can lead to unpredictable behaviour or system malfunction. In this section, we will formalize the *exact* consistency requirements between metadata and code customizations with respect to input and output. Later in sections 5 and 6, we will describe our analyses that are approximations of these requirements. Our formalization is based on the idea that the XML metadata files are the specification that the Java code must conform to. To formalize the consistency constraints between metadata and code, we first introduce our general formalization of metadata and code.

4.1   Formalizing Metadata

To represent a service definition from the XML metadata, we introduce the following definitions: Let Θ be the unbounded set of all possible service attributes, and let θ be an individual attribute, such as surveyResponseId. We will use the predicate *mandatory* to denote whether an attribute is mandatory or optional. We will use the predicates *in* and *out* to denote declared input and output attributes. Note that an attribute can be *both* input and output at the same time. Let Θ_{IN} be the bounded set of all *declared* input attributes. Let Θ_{OUT} be the bounded set of *declared* output attributes. Finally, let Θ_{REQ} be the bounded set of all declared, mandatory output attributes.

$$\Theta = \{\theta_1, \theta_2, \ldots\}$$
$$\Theta_{IN} = \{\theta | \theta \in \Theta \wedge \mathrm{in}(\theta)\}$$
$$\Theta_{OUT} = \{\theta | \theta \in \Theta \wedge \mathrm{out}(\theta)\}$$
$$\Theta_{REQ} = \{\theta | \theta \in \Theta_{OUT} \wedge \mathrm{mandatory}(\theta)\}$$

4.2   Formalizing Code

Code customizations of services in OFBiz always have the following signature:

```
public static Map service
            (DispatchContext dctx, Map context)
```

Input attributes are stored in the `context` map and output attributes are typically stored in a `results` map. We will use `context` and `results` as general identifiers for the sets of input and output attributes in our formalization. Furthermore, let Σ be the set of all program traces. A program trace, $\sigma = \langle \alpha_1, \alpha_2 \ldots \alpha_n \rangle$, is a sequence of executed statements.

$$\Sigma = \{\sigma_1, \sigma_2 \ldots\}$$
$$\sigma = \langle \alpha_1, \alpha_2 \ldots \alpha_n \rangle$$

4.3   Input Requirements

Service input consists of a set of input attributes, as described in section 2. The requirement on input attributes is that only declared attributes are read in the code. As an illustration, one can think of this as similar to Java's scoping rules [9, ch.6.3]. An attribute can only be used if it is in the scope of its declaration. If an attribute is required by the service definition then it is in scope in the code.

The `context` parameter contains the input attributes so we are interested in checking every use of `context`. To use an input attribute, x, one must invoke the `context.get(x)`. If this method is invoked then the service definition must state that x is indeed an input attribute. This rule can be stated more formally as follows:

$$\forall \langle \alpha_1, \alpha_2 \ldots \alpha_n \rangle \in \Sigma. \forall x \in \Theta. \forall i.\alpha_i \text{ is context.get(x)} \Rightarrow x \in \Theta_{IN}$$

The above constraint is violated if there is a statement α_i and a key $x \notin \Theta_{IN}$ such that α_i attempts to read x from `context`.

4.4   Output Requirements

Service output consist of a set of output attributes. Like input attributes, output attributes are stored in a `Map` but an output map may be returned from multiple `return` statements. The requirement on output attributes is that mandatory output attributes are *definitely assigned* at the point where they are returned. In particular, one must ensure that all mandatory output attributes have definitely been assigned for each individual `return` statement. This corresponds to the definite assignment rules of Java [9, ch.16] and checking that these rules are obeyed involves many of the same intricacies, most notably in the case of `try` statements.

Output attributes are stored in a `results` map, so we are interested in checking every use of `results`. To assign a value y to an output attribute x one must invoke `results.put(x, y)`. Such an assignment can be undone by invoking the `results.remove(x)` method. If an output attribute x is mandatory then it must be assigned when the method returns. This rule can be stated more formally like this:

$$\forall x \in \Theta_{REQ}. \forall \langle \alpha_1, \alpha_2 \ldots \alpha_n \rangle \in \Sigma. \forall i.\alpha_i \text{ is return results} \Rightarrow$$
$$\exists j.j < i.(\alpha_j \text{ is results.put(x, y)} \land \neg \exists k.j < k < i.\alpha_k \text{ is results.remove(x)})$$

The above constraint is violated if there is a mandatory output attribute x and an execution σ with a **return** statement α_i and such that *either* there is no statement α_j that sets key x before α_i *or* there is a statement α_k between α_j and α_i that removes the key x from the map.

4.5   Further Output Attribute Checks

In addition, one might require that the service implementation only attempts to set output attributes that may be needed according to the service definition. This rule can also be stated formally as follows:

$$\forall x \in \Theta. \forall \langle \alpha_1, \alpha_2 \ldots \alpha_n \rangle \in \Sigma. \forall i. \alpha_i \text{ is return results} \wedge$$
$$\exists j. j < i. \alpha_j \text{ is results.put}(x, y) \Rightarrow x \in \Theta_{OUT}$$

This constraint is violated if there is an attribute x and an execution σ with a **return** statement α_i and a key $x \notin \Theta_{OUT}$ such that α_i attempts to assign x to the returned map **results**, and x is not an output attribute.

4.6   Duality of Requirements

Interestingly, the requirement on the output in section 4.4 is the dual of the requirement on the input in section 4.3. The input requirement says that if x is used in **context.get(x)** on *some* execution path in the code then attribute x must be provided to the service according to the XML service definition. The output requirement says that if attribute x must be returned from the service according to the XML service definition then *every* execution path that leads to a **return** statement in the Java code must define x. We shall see that this duality is reflected in the analyses by the use of different *meet* operators.

5   Analysis of Service Input

In this section, we describe the individual steps performed by our analysis of service input. The analysis uses two artifacts: the service definition and the implementation code. The analysis consists of the following five steps:

1. Collect declared attributes from the XML service definition.
2. Construct a control flow graph for the Java code.
3. Perform a *reaching definitions flow analysis* on the code.
4. Construct a *def-use chain* for the code.
5. For each use of the input map, check that only declared keys are used.

5.1   Collect Declared Attributes from the XML Service Definition

The first step in the analysis is to determine which input attributes are declared. Not all service definitions are as simple as listing 1.1. Figure 2 shows the OFBiz domain classes involved in the collection of service attributes. In addition to the service's own attributes, a service can inherit attributes from other services and optionally override characteristics of these inherited attributes. For instance, the `ClearCommerce` and `CyberSource` provider services from the `Accounting` module all inherit attributes from the general OFBiz credit card and payment processing services to enable service polymorphism. Furthermore, a service can automatically collect attributes based on the fields of a business entity through the `auto-attributes` association, shown in figure 2. For instance, the `updateAgreement` service from the `Accounting` module uses all fields of the `Agreement` business entity as input attributes. The advantage of this is that whenever the `Agreement` business entity is extended with a new field, this change is automatically reflected in the `updateAgreement` service. This can be further refined such that all primary keys are mandatory attributes and all non-primary keys are optional attributes.

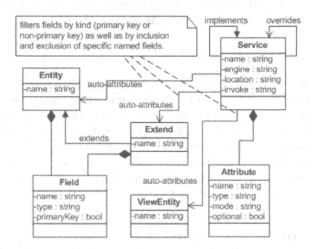

Fig. 2. The domain classes relevant for locating and collecting attributes for an OFBiz service. The collection process is described as step (1) in section 5. A service may have its own attributes, may inherit attributes from other services, and may collect automatic attributes based on fields of a set of business *entities*, *extends* and *views*.

In summary, collecting service attributes from the metadata is a non-trivial process. The collection process requires traversing the service inheritance hierarchy and checking for overridden attributes. If the service uses the `auto-attributes` association, shown in figure 2, then one must also traverse related business entities, use their fields as attributes and check whether primary or non-primary keys are filtered out and whether any named fields are included or excluded.

5.2   Construct a Control Flow Graph for the Java Code

The second step in the analysis is to construct an intraprocedural control flow graph for the service implementation to facilitate flow analysis at a later stage. The control flow graph is constructed using classical algorithms [10, ch.8.4] with graph nodes being statements. The construction process handles straightforward constructs such as conditionals and loops as well as the more complicated `try-catch-finally` construct in Java. For our prototype, described in section 7, we traverse the built-in abstract syntax tree representation of the Eclipse Java Development Tools (JDT) to build the control flow graph.

Constructing the control flow graph for the `try-catch-finally` construct requires some special considerations. The control flow must facilitate a flow analysis that can determine whether a variable is definitely assigned after a `try` statement. As the Java Language Specification [9, ch.16.2.15] shows, this is non-trivial matter since (1) `try` statements can be nested, (2) there can be several `catch` clauses, (3) the exception classes form an inheritance hierarchy that affects `catch` clause matching, and (4) one has to take any `finally` clauses into account.

The construction process proceeds in the following manner: For each statement that is in scope of one or more `try` statements, we add an edge to the next statement in the current `try` block, or if there is no such next statement, we add an edge to either the first statement in the `finally` block (if any) or else to the next statement after the `try-catch` statement. For each checked exception that the statement in question throws, we must add an edge to the corresponding `catch` clause. To do the latter, we iterate through every `catch` clause starting from the first in the innermost `try` statement to the last in the outermost `try` statement. If the innermost `try` statement does not have a relevant `catch` clause, we must add an edges to any intermediate `finally` clauses (in the case of nested `try` statements). In principle, almost every statement in the `try` block can throw an unchecked exception, but our analysis only takes checked exceptions into account. Taking unchecked exceptions into account would lead to too many edges on the graph and render the results of the final flow analysis less interesting because the final result would contain too many false positives.

5.3   Perform a Reaching Definitions Flow Analysis on the Code

The third step in our analysis is to perform a classic *reaching definitions flow analysis* [10, ch.9.2.4]. The purpose of this flow analysis is to determine which definitions reach each statement in the code. A definition is represented as a pair of a variable and its defining statement's location (its AST node). Specifically, for each statement we determine which variable definitions reach this point. This is done by solving the following equations where *entry(stmt)* is the set of definitions reaching a statement, *stmt*. The set *exit(stmt)* contains the definitions that may be exposed to the successors of *stmt* in the control flow graph. The gen_{stmt} and $kill_{stmt}$ sets are the definitions that are generated and killed by the statement *stmt*. The *init* node is the starting point of the graph [10, p.605-6].

$$exit(init) = \emptyset$$
$$exit(stmt) = gen_{\text{stmt}} \cup (entry(stmt) - kill_{\text{stmt}})$$
$$entry(stmt) = \cup_{\text{pred is a predecessor of stmt}} exit(pred)$$

The analysis is monotonic and the result is the least fixpoint of the equations. An important part of the equations is the use of union as the *meet* operator. The significance is that a definition reaches a statement if there is *some* path from a definition to the statement on the control flow that does not kill the definition.

5.4   Construct a Def-Use Chain for the Code

The control flow graph and the results of the reaching definitions analysis enable us to build *def-use* chains for every variable in the code. A def-use chain ties a definition of a variable together with the statements where the variable is being used. For the purposes of our analysis, we are specifically interested in the **defToUse** function which given a definition, **def**, returns the set of statements, **stmt**, where this definition is being used. The **use** predicate expresses whether a statement uses a variable and the **entry(stmt)** set is the previously computed set of definitions reaching *stmt* [11].

$$defToUse(def) = \{stmt | use(stmt, def) \wedge def \in entry(stmt)\}$$

5.5   For Each Use of the Input Map, Check That Only Declared Keys Are Used

The final step in our service input analysis is to check that only declared input attributes are actually being used. This is the consistency requirement on service input described in section 4.3. The analysis as implemented provides an approximation to this exact requirement, primarily because the control flow graph generates a superset of the set Σ of possible program traces. The analysis may deem a statement **context.get(x)** reachable although no actual computation could execute it.

Furthermore, the analysis checks whether the attribute is being cast to the correct type, such as when **surveyResponseId** is cast to the String type in line 5 in listing 1.2. The idiom **(C)context.get(x)** is used for casting input attributes so the analysis performs the type check simply by checking whether the declared type of **x** is assignable to type C.

A constraint violation is flagged as an error called *Use of undeclared input attribute*. In some cases, the key, **x**, is an expression or a variable whose value is computed by an expression at an earlier program statement. Then the analysis fails and the statement is annotated with a warning that the analysis is unable to determine whether this attribute is declared in the service definition. Using such computed keys can be considered metaprogramming on top of the OFBiz framework. An example of this practice is for instance the **updateOrRemove** service in the Content Management Module. This service can change the structure of business entities at runtime. This practice is used in less than 10 places in our version of the framework so we consider it beyond the scope of our current analysis requirements.

6   Analysis of Service Output

In this section, we will describe the steps performed in the service output analysis. The analysis uses the service definition and the implementation code.

1. Collect declared attributes from the XML service definition.
2. Construct a control flow graph for the Java code.
3. Perform an *available map keys flow analysis* on the code.
4. For each return statement, check that each mandatory output attribute has definitely been assigned before that statement.
5. For each use of the output map, check that only declared keys are used.

6.1   Collect Declared Attributes from the XML Service Definition

The collection of output attributes is completely analogous to the collection of input attributes, described in section 5.1.

6.2   Construct a Control Flow Graph for the Java Code

The control flow graph from the previous section is reused.

6.3   Perform an Available Map Keys Flow Analysis on the Code

The third step in the analysis is to determine which keys are put into the map of output attributes during different traces of the program. The analysis is a flow analysis which shares some characteristics with the classical *available expressions flow analysis* [10, ch.9.2.6]. The purpose of the analysis is to compute the domain of each defined map for each statement in the implementation code. By domain, we here mean the set of keys that have definitely been assigned. The analysis results are represented as a pair of the AST node defining the map and a set of those map keys. Where the *available expressions flow analysis* determines whether an expression is definitely available at a given program point, our available map keys analysis determines whether a key in a given map is definitely available at a given program point. The main difference is that in our analysis map entries are treated as variables instead of merely runtime values. This difference is reflected in the **gen** and **kill** functions.

Analysis of output attributes is a bit more complicated than input attributes because an output attribute can be set in several different but equivalent ways. The most common approach is to instantiate a **HashMap** and invoke the put(x, y) method on that map to set the output attribute x to the value y. Another approach is to use the framework-provided method **UtilMisc.toMap** which takes a number of keys and values and returns a map containing those keys and values as entries, i.e., a batch of `put` invocations. A third approach is to programmatically invoke another service, e.g., the `someService` service, which returns a map using the method `dctx.runSynch("someService",inputMap)`. Each of these different approaches generates a key at the statement where it occurs and plays a part in the gen_{stmt} function. Examples of the corresponding $kill_{stmt}$ function would be invocations of methods such as `clear()` or `remove(x)` on the map of output attributes.

The analysis is performed similarly to the available expressions analysis with the main difference being different `gen` and `kill` functions. Specifically, we solve the following set of equations [10, p.612]:

$$exit(init) = \emptyset$$

$$exit(stmt) = gen_{\text{stmt}} \cup (entry(stmt) - kill_{\text{stmt}})$$

$$entry(stmt) = \bigcap_{\text{pred is a predecessor of stmt}} exit(pred)$$

An important part of the analysis is the use of intersection as the *meet* operator in these equations as opposed to union in the reaching definitions analysis in section 5.3. This reflects the duality of the consistency requirements on input and output discussed in section 4.6. The significance of using intersection here is that a map key only definitely reaches a `return` statement if every path leading to this `return` sets the map key. This means that if a map key is in the entry set of a `return` statement, the output attribute is definitely assigned at that statement. Another difference between the two analyses is that where the reaching definitions analysis starts by initializing every statement to have empty exit sets, the available map keys analysis initializes the exit set of every statement, except the starting node, to the universe of all possible keys. This is a direct consequence of using the intersection operator and in terms of execution of the analysis, it requires a pre-pass to compute the universe.

6.4 For Each Return Statement, Check That Each Mandatory Output Attribute has Definitely been Assigned Before That Statement

The fourth step in the analysis is to check that mandatory output attributes have definitely been assigned on return. This is the consistency requirement on service output described in section 4.4. A constraint violation is flagged as an error called *Missing mandatory output attribute, x*. This is because there is some path leading to this statement that does not set the key x in the returned map.

6.5 For Each Use of the Output Map, Check That Only Declared Keys Are Used

Finally, similar to the previous analysis in section 5.5 we check that only declared keys are used. Violations of this constraint do not cause the system to malfunction but indicate an attribute spelling error or other programmer error or misunderstanding. Setting an undeclared output attribute is somewhat similar to declaring a local variable in Java and never making use of it. It is not an error but a redundancy that indicates a possible problem in the code.

7   Prototype Implementation

Eclipse is a commonly used tool among OFBiz developers, so our implementation approach has aimed to extend Eclipse and make the previously described analyses available in that environment. Our prototype is an Eclipse plugin that provides an OFBiz model browser, as shown in figure 3, that allows developers to browse the logical structure of an OFBiz installation to manage entities and services rather than XML- and Java-files. From the browser, one can navigate to service definitions and service implementations in a single click. From the browser one can also initiate an analysis of either a single service or the entire installation.

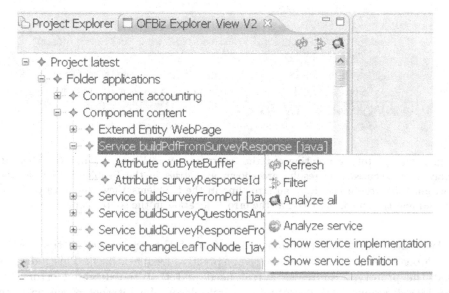

Fig. 3. Our prototype extends Eclipse with a browser for the logical model of an OFBiz installation. Here, the `buildPdfFromSurveyResponse` service in the Content Management component is selected and the two attributes of the service are shown. The context menu offers the choice of navigating to the service implementation or service definition.

The prototype uses a standard XML parser to parse and load all relevant XML files and relies on the Eclipse Java Development Tools (JDT) to parse and build abstract syntax trees for the corresponding Java code. The analyses are performed by traversing these XML- and Java-representations. The result of each analysis is reported as errors and warnings in the Problems View and marked in XML and Java editors as well, as shown in figure 4. The prototype is therefore integrated into the regular OFBiz development experience in a non-invasive way. Developers can quickly navigate from an error in the Problems View to the cause of the error in a Java editor, and repair it there.

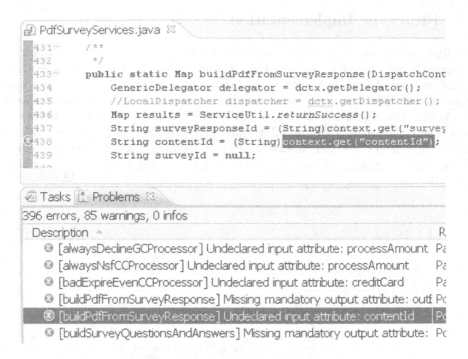

Fig. 4. Our prototype pointing out the inconsistency in listing 1.1 line 6. When an analysis is executed, the results are shown as entries in the Problems View at the bottom. When the user selects an error line in the Problems View, the Java editor is opened and the cursor is placed at the error's location in the source code.

We have released a preliminary version of the prototype to the OFBiz developer community and received very positive feedback [2, 3]. This indicates that the prototype addresses a real need and that the detected errors are considered serious. The prototype is available on the Internet along with an online Flash-demo of its capabilities [12]. In the next section, we will describe the results of applying this prototype to actual OFBiz production code.

8 Empirical Results

In order to validate our claims, we have applied our prototype on the out-of-the-box version of OFBiz (November 2007). This version contains some 2000 services of which 550 are implemented using Java code customizations. Our test setup is an Intel Core 2 CPU, 1.83 GHz, laptop with 2 GB of RAM. Running a complete analysis of the entire OFBiz installation (see section 3) took 22.3 seconds and used an average of 105 MB of heap space. In another setup with constrained memory, the complete analysis took 65.2 seconds but used only an average of 55 MB of heap space. This indicates that the prototype is fast enough to be used in a real industrial scenario.

Table 1. Overview of the 133 errors and 122 warnings detected in the out-of-the-box version of OFBiz. This version is already deployed in several industrial settings so these errors and warnings are present in *live* installations.

Severity	Type	No. of
Error	Undeclared input attribute	77
Error	Missing mandatory output attribute	56
Warning	May be missing mandatory output attribute	16
Warning	Unable to analyze expression	12
Warning	Unable to analyze complex returns	27
Warning	Unable to analyze interprocedural call	67

Our analysis found 133 errors and 122 warnings in our OFBiz installation. The tested OFBiz installation is a relatively stable version that is currently being used in several industrial settings. This means that the errors and warnings we have detected are present in several deployed OFBiz products. An overview of these errors and warnings can be found in table 1.

The two classes of errors in table 1 are the most serious problems. Use of an undeclared input attribute can potentially lead to `NullPointerExceptions` since reading an undeclared attribute from the map of input attributes typically returns `null`. An attempt to call a method on this attribute will therefore throw a `NullPointerException` and cause the OFBiz application to fail. A missing mandatory output attribute is quite simply a breach of the contract specified in the service definition. Clients of the service in question will expect this contract to be fulfilled. Closer examination of these errors has shown that it is often an exception handling control flow path that does not assign all mandatory output attributes. In some special cases, the analysis indicates that a mandatory output attribute *might* not be assigned. This happens when irregular use of certain framework-provided utility methods is detected. The last three classes of warnings are all caused by limitations in the analysis. If a variable is assigned the value of an expression and later used as key in the map of output attributes, it is typically part of some metaprogramming on top of the framework.

```
int j = computeFieldNo();
String key = "field" + j;
results.put(key, "someValue");
return results;
```

These parts of the code are beyond the scope of the analysis, and this is indicated by the *unable to analyze expression* warning.

If a `return` statement returns the value of an expression then the analysis issues a warning since we are unable to determine the value of that expression.

```
return isEmpty() ? new HashMap() : results;
```

Finally, the largest class of warnings are those caused by interprocedural calls that have not been incorporated into the analysis. The analysis has been adapted to handle most framework-provided utility methods. However, certain customizations introduce idiosyncratic utility methods that the analysis is unable to handle.

```
Map results = new HashMap();
otherObject.foo(results);
return results;
```

Where `otherObject.foo` is a custom method not provided by the framework and hence not included in the analysis.

9 Discussion

Several questions arise from our analysis and examination of the OFBiz framework. In this section, we will discuss four central ones. First, what are the limitations of our analysis? Second, can our approach be applied to other areas of OFBiz? Third, are the code customization described in this paper particular for OFBiz or do they appear in other frameworks as well? Fourth, is the OFBiz idiom of using maps to store input and output attributes really an internal domain-specific language, embedded in Java? If so, our input and attribute analyses are really standard compiler checks for consistency of this domain-specific language.

9.1 Limitations of the Analysis

Our analyses compute approximations of the constraints outlined in section 4. To discuss the sources of approximation, let us say that a "positive" is an actual consistency error, and a "negative" is the absence of such an error. A "true positive" is when an analysis discovers and reports an actual consistency error; a "false positive" is when an analysis reports a consistency error but there actually is none: the service will always execute without failure. Conversely, "true negative" is when an analysis reports no consistency error and there is none; a "false negative" is when an analysis reports no consistency error, but actually there is one: the service may fail.

Using an analogy from logic, we may say that an analysis without false positives is *complete* and that one without false negatives is *sound*. An analysis with neither false positives nor false negatives is exact.

For computability reasons, our analyses are necessarily incomplete and have false positives: they may report a consistency error where there is none. The main reason for this is that the control flow graph built in sections 5.2 and 6.2 is an approximation of the set Σ of actual program traces. Consider:

```
if (... complex expression, always false ...)
   context.get("thisAttributeIsNotDefined");
```

Moreover, our analyses are unsound and have false negatives: they may report no consistency error although the service may fail at runtime. Some people would consider such an analysis flawed and useless, but our point of view is that making the analysis sound (by eliminating all false negatives) would increase the number of false positives to an extent that would make the analysis uninteresting.

There are two sources of unsoundness:

(a) We perform no alias analysis [10, ch.12.4]
(b) We consider only checked exceptions when building the control flow graph for `try-catch-finally` statements

The lack of alias analysis affects the analysis of both input and output attributes. For input attributes, it means that we get a false negative in this case, where `thisAttributeIsNotDefined` is not an input attribute:

```
Map inputMapAlias = context;
inputMapAlias.get("thisAttributeIsNotDefined");
```

Our analysis will not discover that `inputMapAlias` is an alias of the input attribute may `context`, and hence will not flag the `get`-method call as a violation of the input attribute constraint.

For output attributes, the lack of alias analysis means that we get a false negative in this case:

```
Map results = new HashMap();
results.put("x", 1);
Map outputMapAlias = results;
outputMapAlias.remove("x");
return results;
```

Our analysis would not report that the output attribute `x` is missing from the `results` map.

It would be fairly easy to add an alias analysis step and hence remove this source of unsoundness, but we believe that it will only marginally affect the practical utility of the analysis, because there is no reason for service implementations to define aliases of input and output maps.

Considering only checked exceptions is the other main source of unsoundness. The construction of the control flow graph does not take unchecked (runtime) exceptions into account. Almost every Java statement may throw a runtime exception. Taking such exceptions into account would give significantly more control flow edges, which would cause a large number of false positives in the analysis without contributing any significant new useful error messages. We have therefore omitted runtime exceptions to get a simpler graph, fewer false positives, and an analysis that is overall more useful.

Finally, a further source of approximation in our analyses is that they are intraprocedural only. Hence if an input or output map is passed to a method the analysis will issue a warning, corresponding to "don't know" rather than give a positive or negative answer:

```
Map results = new HashMap();
doSomething(results);
return results;
```

Since the doSomething method may manipulate the entries in the results map, and the analysis is intraprocedural only, it cannot know the state of results after the method call.

The analysis *does* understand the effect of a small number of framework-provided utility methods, such as UtilMisc.toMap, that perform batch assignment of values to attributes. User-defined utility methods are, however, beyond the scope of our analysis.

9.2   Other Areas of Application in OFBiz

The OFBiz framework contains several other areas where our analysis may be applicable. Service implementations in Java account for only 25% of the service implementations in the entire framework. The remaining OFBiz service implementations are written in a domain-specific language called Minilang, see listing 1.3 for an example. Minilang is a simple, imperative, data manipulation language with a concrete syntax in XML. One can express operations on primitive types, Strings and OFBiz entities as well as conditionals and simple error handling.

```
1   <simple-method method-name="createWorkEffortCostCalc"
2   short-description="Create a WorkEffortCostCalc entry">
3       <make-value entity-name="WorkEffortCostCalc"
            value-name="newEntity"/>
4       <set-pk-fields map-name="parameters"
            value-name="newEntity"/>
5       <set-nonpk-fields map-name="parameters"
            value-name="newEntity"/>
6       <if-empty field-name="newEntity.fromDate">
7           <now-timestamp-to-env env-name="newEntity.fromDate"/>
8       </if-empty>
9       <create-value value-name="newEntity"/>
10  </simple-method>
```

Listing 1.3. The implementation of the createWorkEffortCostCalc service in the Minilang DSL. The code creates a WorkEffortCostCalc entity and initializes its fields from a map of input attributes called parameters.

Minilang is much less expressive than Java so it should be fairly easy to adapt our analyses to this language. This adaptation would involve two steps: (1) changing our parser from the Eclipse JDT parser to a standard XML parser, and (2) changing the gen and kill functions to include the syntactical constructs of Minilang. The reason that we focused on Java is that if the analysis can handle

Java with all its complexity then we claim that it is a trivial matter to extend the analysis to other implementation languages in OFBiz.

9.3 Code Customizations in Other Frameworks

An obvious question that arise from this work is whether these analyses are restricted to OFBiz. One of the main points of the paper is that exactly by adapting classic flow analyses to a framework-specific setting can we reap extra benefits. As it turns out, code customizations *are* found in other frameworks than OFBiz. Request processing in J2EE web applications provides good examples, such as servlet filters [13, ch.11] and Actions in Struts [14]. The Spring Framework [15] is an open source, J2EE-based webapplication framework with widespread industry adoption. Listing 1.4 shows an excerpt from one of the Spring sample applications. In this code we can identify the exact same patterns as in OFBiz. In line 3, an input attribute is accessed, and in lines 6 and 7 output attributes are assigned. In this case the metadata are split between Spring configuration files and the client-side HTML, and standard tools do not enforce consistency with the `handleRequest` code.

```
1  public ModelAndView handleRequest
2  (HttpServletRequest request , HttpServletResponse response)..{
3          String itemId = request.getParameter("itemId");
4          Item item = this.petStore.getItem(itemId);
5          Map model = new HashMap();
6          model.put("item", item);
7          model.put("product", item.getProduct());
8          return new ModelAndView("Item", model);
9  }
```

Listing 1.4. The `handleRequest` method from the `ViewItemController` class in the JPetStore sample application from the Spring Framework version 2.5. The code follows the same idiom as OFBiz code customizations by accepting a map, in this case the `request`, and returning another map, in this case the `model`.

Our prototype could be adapted to the Spring framework merely by changing the `gen` and `kill` functions in the available map keys analysis. The code in listing 1.4 uses `getParameter(x)` instead of OFBiz's `get(x)` to access an input attribute named `x`. Similarly, the output analysis would also only need a little tweaking. Further work, however, must be done in order to determine how easy it is to capture this kind of variability in the prototype.

9.4 An Internal Domain-Specific Language

It seems that the OFBiz style approach is common, especially in the context of Java web application frameworks. We do, however, want to further extend our claim about this approach. The use of attributes stored in maps can be thought of as an internal domain-specific language (DSL) hosted in the Java language. Let us call this language the *Attribute DSL*. The Attribute DSL contains the following five language constructs:

Construct	Meaning
`java.util.Map.get(x)`	reads an attribute x
`java.util.Map.put(x, y)`	assigns value y to attribute x
`java.util.Map.remove(x)`	deletes an attribute x
`org.ofbiz.base.util.UtilMisc.toMap(...)`	batch assignment of values
`java.util.Map.clear()`	batch deletion of attributes

The Attribute DSL is weakly typed in contrast to Java. So by using this DSL within Java, we lose static guarantees. Reading an attribute is a good example of this loss; the existence of the `Customer` attribute is checked only at runtime, and the type of the attribute value is checked only at runtime. The introduction of generic types in Java 5.0 does not solve this problem since a single input map may contain attributes of type String, Customer and Integer. The most specific `java.util.Map` type that can hold these attribute is `Map<String,Object>`, which means that all attributes will have compile-time type Object.

```
Customer customer = (Customer) context.get("Customer");
```

Fortunately, OFBiz provides us with the metadata needed by our analysis to re-establish the previously lost static guarantees:

```
<attribute name="Customer" type="dk.itu.Customer" ../>
```

The existence of these metadata may explain why OFBiz developers feel confident leaving out the explicit runtime checks that one would expect in the above code.

The analyses that we have provided in the previous sections provide the static guarantees of definedness and type correctness that are missing from the Attribute DSL. The input attribute analysis is really a standard compiler check for variables being in scope when used, and the output attribute analysis is a standard compiler check for definite assignment.

10   Related Work

This work is influenced mainly by two areas of research: framework-completion and static semantic checking of weakly typed languages.

10.1   Framework-Completion

Framework-completion code is similar to code customizations in the sense that they conform to predefined interfaces and makes use of framework-provided methods. The code customizations that we have described are a bit more monolithic than framework-completion code which typically is split between multiple methods and relies heavily on framework callbacks.

Fairbanks et al. [16] have investigated framework-completion code in the Eclipse and the Java Applet framework and identified API complexity as a key problem in development. To help developers they propose *design fragments*, a kind of framework-completion recipes expressed in XML. These design fragments are similar to OFBiz service definitions in the sense that they contain extra metadata. The tool support for design fragments is of a more syntactic nature than our plugin which on the other hand relies more on semantics in the form of data flow. Other related work in this category is recent papers on framework-specific modelling languages that synthesize metadata and code in a higher-level language [17, 18].

10.2   Static Semantic Checking of Weakly Typed Languages

The idiom of storing attributes in maps has, as described in section 9, the unfortunate consequence that the type system is weakened. Our flow analyses are a way of providing static guarantees in spite of this weakened type system. There are several pieces of related work in area of weakly typed languages. Wright and Cartwright [19] have suggested the concept of *soft typing* based on work in Scheme. The main idea is to provide type information for the compiler by relying on a generalization of Hindley-Milner type inference. This work has been extended to other languages such as JavaScript [20] and Erlang [21]. Our work has a similar purpose but can be distinguished by the fact that we rely on two artifacts: metadata and code as opposed to merely code. Another related approach which relies heavily on data flow analysis is Christensen et al. [22]. Their focus is on dynamically generated string expressions such as SQL queries but the goal is similar to ours.

11   Conclusion

The use of XML and Java as a hybrid development platform for configurable enterprise systems leads to inconsistencies between metadata and code customizations. We have formalized the consistency constraints for a concrete platform, viz. OFBiz, and provided a set of dataflow analyses adapted to this platform. The analyses are implemented in the a tool that we have successfully applied to OFBiz. Using the tool, we have detected a large number of errors as well as elicited very positive feedback from the OFBiz community. Our overall contributions in this paper are:

- A formalization of the consistency constraints between metadata and code customizations in OFBiz.

- A set of framework-specific adaptions of dataflow analyses based on this formalization.
- A working implementation of these analyses in the form of an Eclipse plugin.
- An empirical validation of the tool by analyzing production code and eliciting feedback from OFBiz developers.
- A discussion of the limitations of the analyses, and the trade-off between soundness (no false negatives) and precision (only few false positives).

Acknowledgement

The authors would like to thank Kasper Østerbye, Andrzej Wąsowski and Steen Brahe for their valuable comments on an earlier draft of the paper.

References

1. The Apache Software Foundation: The Apache Open for Business Project (2007) March 8 (2007), http://ofbiz.apache.org/
2. Franck, D.: Personal correspondance (2008)
3. Chen, S.: Personal correspondance (2008)
4. Hessellund, A., Czarnecki, K., Wasowski, A.: Guided Development with Multiple Domain-Specific Languages. In: Engels, G., Opdyke, B., Schmidt, D.C., Weil, F. (eds.) MODELS 2007. LNCS, vol. 4735, pp. 46–60. Springer, Heidelberg (2007)
5. BeanShell: Lightweight Scripting for Java (2007), http://www.beanshell.org/
6. Jones, D., Schuessler, E.: Apache OFBiz: Real-World Open Source Java Platform ERP. Presented at the 2007 JavaOne Conference (2007)
7. Chen, S.: Opening Up Enterprise Software: Why Enterprises are Adopting Open Source Applications (2006), http://www.opensourcestrategies.com/slides/
8. Various: Apache OFBiz User List (2007), http://docs.ofbiz.org/display/ OFBIZ/Apache+OFBiz+User+List
9. Gosling, J., Joy, B., Steele, G.L., Bracha, G.: The Java Language Specification, 3rd edn. Sun Microsystems (2005)
10. Aho, A.W., Lam, M.S., Sethi, R., Ullman, J.D.: Compilers: Principles, Techniques, & Tools. 2 edn. Pearson Education, Inc (2007)
11. Fuhrer, R.M.: Static Analysis for Java in Eclipse, Lecture slides from the tutorial Static Analysis for Java in Eclipse at the ACM SIGPLAN 2005 Programming Language Design and Implementation (PLDI), Chicago, Illinois, USA. (2005), http://www.cs.purdue.edu/homes/jv/plditut/eclipse/index.html
12. Hessellund, A.: OFBiz Explorer v2 (2007), http://www.itu.dk/people/ hessellund/smartemf/ofbizexplorer.htm
13. Bodoff, S., Armstrong, E., Ball, J., Carson, D., Evans, I., Green, D., Haase, K., Jendrock, E.: J2EE Tutorial, 2nd edn. Prentice-Hall, Englewood Cliffs (2004)
14. The Apache Software Foundation: The Struts Framework (2007), http://struts. apache.org/
15. Spring Source: The Spring Framework (2007), http://www.springframework.org/
16. Fairbanks, G., Garlan, D., Scherlis, W.L.: Design fragments make using frameworks easier. In: Tarr, P.L., Cook, W.R. (eds.) OOPSLA, pp. 75–88. ACM, New York (2006)

17. Antkiewicz, M., Czarnecki, K.: Framework-specific modeling languages with round-trip engineering. In: Nierstrasz, O., Whittle, J., Harel, D., Reggio, G. (eds.) MoDELS 2006. LNCS, vol. 4199, pp. 692–706. Springer, Heidelberg (2006)
18. Antkiewicz, M., Bartolomei, T.T., Czarnecki, K.: Automatic extraction of framework-specific models from framework-based application code. In: ASE 2007: Proceedings of the twenty-second IEEE/ACM international conference on Automated software engineering, pp. 214–223. ACM, New York (2007)
19. Wright, A.K., Cartwright, R.: A practical soft type system for scheme. In: LISP and Functional Programming, 250–262 (1994)
20. Thiemann, P.: Towards a type system for analyzing javascript programs. In: Sagiv, S. (ed.) ESOP 2005. LNCS, vol. 3444, pp. 408–422. Springer, Heidelberg (2005)
21. Marlow, S., Wadler, P.: A practical subtyping system for erlang. In: ICFP 1997: Proceedings of the second ACM SIGPLAN international conference on Functional programming, pp. 136–149. ACM, New York (1997)
22. Christensen, A.S., Møller, A., Schwartzbach, M.I.: Precise Analysis of String Expressions. In: Cousot, R. (ed.) SAS 2003. LNCS, vol. 2694, pp. 1–18. Springer, Heidelberg (2003)

Online Phase-Adaptive Data Layout Selection[*]

Chengliang Zhang[1] and Martin Hirzel[2]

[1] Microsoft in Redmond, WA
(C. Zhang was a student at the U. of Rochester when doing this work.)
chengzh@microsoft.com
[2] IBM in Hawthorne, NY
hirzel@us.ibm.com

Abstract. Good data layouts improve cache and TLB performance of object-oriented software, but unfortunately, selecting an optimal data layout a priori is NP-hard. This paper introduces layout auditing, a technique that selects the best among a set of layouts online (while the program is running). Layout auditing randomly applies different layouts over time and observes their performance. As it becomes confident about which layout performs best, it selects that layout with higher probability. But if a phase shift causes a different layout to perform better, layout auditing learns the new best layout. We implemented our technique in a product Java virtual machine, using copying generational garbage collection to produce different layouts, and tested it on 20 long-running benchmarks and 4 hardware platforms. Given any combination of benchmark and platform, layout auditing consistently performs close to the best layout for that combination, without requiring offline training.

1 Introduction

Cache and TLB misses often cause programs to run slowly. For example, we estimate that pseudojbb05 spends 34% of its time stalled in misses on a 4-processor AMD machine [17]. Cache and TLB misses often stem from a mismatch between

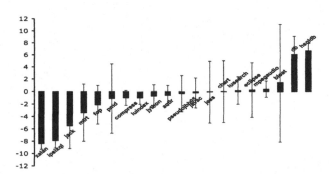

Fig. 1. Percent speedup of *HI* data layout, compared to *BF*, on an 8-processor AMD at 4× the minimum heap size. Section 5 explains *HI* and *BF*, and Section 6 explains the methodology. The error bars show 95% confidence intervals from Student's t-test.

[*] This research was funded in part by DARPA contract No. NBCH30390004.

J. Vitek (Ed.): ECOOP 2008, LNCS 5142, pp. 309–334, 2008.
© Springer-Verlag Berlin Heidelberg 2008

data layout and data access order. For example, Fig. 1 shows that the same layout can degrade or improve runtime depending on how well it matches the program's data accesses, and on how expensive the layout is to apply.

Results like those in Fig. 1 are typical: optimizations that improve performance for some programs often risk degrading performance for other programs. The results depend on tradeoffs between optimization costs and rewards, and on interactions between complex software and hardware systems. Picking the best data layout a priori is difficult. Petrank and Rawitz showed that even with perfect knowledge of the data access order, finding the optimal data placement, or approximating it within a constant factor, is NP-hard [32]. Zhang et al. showed that finding a general affinity-hierarchy layout is also NP-hard [45]. While these hardness results were shown for fairly regular scientific code, reliance on pointers and dynamic dispatch exacerbate the problem further for object-oriented code. Practically, picking a data layout before the program starts would require training runs and command line arguments, both of which impede user acceptance.

This paper proposes *layout auditing*, a framework for picking the best data layout online without requiring any user input. Layout auditing optimizes data layouts with a *try-measure-decide* feedback loop: use a data reorganizer to try one of several data layouts, use a profiler to measure the impact of the data layout on performance, and use a controller to decide which layout to try next.

The data reorganizer *tries* a layout for the program's data. The data reorganizer can reorder data arrays or index arrays for scientific programs [11]; or it can copy objects in a specific order during garbage collection for object-oriented programs [13]; or it can even remap addresses using special-purpose hardware [46]. Layout auditing works with off-the-shelf data reorganizers [24], and the engineers who implement them need not be aware that the layouts get picked based on profile information.

The profiler *measures* the reward of the layout of the program's current data. The reward is high iff the program spends little physical time per virtual time. Virtual time is a data layout-independent measure of program progress, such as loop iterations, allocated bytes, or instructions. Physical time (seconds) depends on the data layout. The profiler can either simply obtain physical time from the CPU clock, or it can derive physical time from other information sources. The profiler reports not just the reward of a data layout in terms of program performance, but also the cost of the data reorganizer, profiler, and controller.

The controller *decides* the layout for the next data reorganization, and also decides how much, if any, time to spend on profiling. If the controller is confident about which layout is best, it picks that layout to exploit its good performance characteristics. If the controller is uncertain, it picks a layout it is curious about, to explore its reward. The controller uses off-the-shelf reinforcement learning techniques [41]. It turns the reward and curiosity for each data layout into a probability, and then picks randomly from its repertoire of layouts using those probabilities. To adapt to phase shifts, the profiler never allows probabilities to drop to zero, so that it always performs a minimal amount of exploration.

Selecting one of several layouts is a *multi-armed bandit* problem [33]. The analogy is that of a slot machine (one-armed bandit), but with more than one arm. Each arm is a data layout, and the reward is improved program performance. The controller repeatedly tries different arms, and hones in on the best ones. Layout auditing subscribes to the philosophy of *blind justice*. The controller is a fair and impartial judge who decides based on hard evidence only, and gives each candidate the benefit of the doubt. In fact, the judge is not only fair, but also merciful: even when a layout performs badly, it still gets sampled occasionally to check for phase changes.

Layout auditing combines the advantages of two strands of prior work. First, like online profile-directed locality optimizations, it adapts to platforms, programs, and phases to achieve better performance than what offline optimization can achieve. Second, like performance auditing [26], it separates optimization concerns from controller concerns, it requires no correct model of complex hardware interaction, and it does not get fooled by misleading access patterns where finding the optimal data layout is NP-hard [32]. Unlike performance auditing, this paper addresses data layouts, not code optimization, and adapts to phases. This paper differs from prior profile-directed locality optimizations as well as from performance auditing in that it uses a uniform controller for not just performance rewards, but also optimization costs.

We evaluated layout auditing for 20 long-running Java programs on 4 hardware platforms. The layouts were produced by copying generational garbage collection changing the relative placement of heap objects in memory. Given any combination of benchmark and platform, layout auditing consistently performs close to the best layout for that combination.

Section 2 presents layout auditing as a framework, and Sections 3 to 5 present one concrete implementation that is evaluated in Sections 6 and 7. Section 8 sketches alternative implementations of the framework, Section 9 discusses related work, and Section 10 concludes.

2   Layout Auditing Framework

Fig. 2 illustrates the try-measure-decide feedback loop of layout auditing. The data reorganizer tries a data layout, the profiler measures its reward, and the controller decides the next actions of the data reorganizer and the profiler.

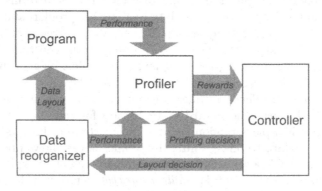

Fig. 2. Feedback loop

2.1 Program

What: The program performs some calculation on behalf of the user. It is oblivious to the layout auditing feedback loop that surrounds it. The layout of the program's data in memory is determined by the data reorganizer, and the program's performance is monitored by the profiler.

How: Section 6 describes a suite of 20 large Java programs from a wide range of application domains. They run unperturbed on a product language runtime system with JIT compilation, a popular operating system, and stock hardware.

2.2 Data Reorganizer

What: The data reorganizer executes a layout decision by placing the program's data in a specific order in memory. The layout affects program performance; in addition, the performance of the data reorganizer itself is monitored by the profiler.

How: Garbage collection is widely used to support robust object-oriented software. Section 5 uses copying garbage collection to implement the data reorganizer. This paper is based on high-performance implementations of two well-known collectors [7,44] that ship with a product language runtime system, and some experimental collectors [17].

2.3 Profiler

What: The profiler monitors the performance of the program and the data reorganizer. It reports rewards for each data layout to the controller. Rewards measure physical time per virtual time. Virtual time is a metric of program progress that is independent of the data layout, such as loop iterations, allocated bytes, or executed instructions.

How: Section 4 describes the minimalist profiler. It simply looks at the machine clock to obtain physical time in seconds, and counts bytes allocated as virtual time. The minimalist profiler uses the most authoritative model of the interaction of data layouts with the hardware: concrete measurements of unperturbed execution.

2.4 Controller

What: The controller turns rewards of data layouts into decisions for which layout to try next, and how much profiling to do. The controller is responsible for optimizing overall performance, even when the program has phase changes.

How: Section 3 describes the softmax controller. It uses a simple reinforcement learning policy [41] to turn rewards into probabilities. The controller remembers historical rewards to avoid unstable decisions when there is noise, but it decays old rewards to adapt to phase changes.

3 Softmax Controller

The controller turns data layout rewards from the profiler into layout decisions for the data reorganizer, and profiling decisions for the profiler. It does so by first turning rewards into probabilities, then deciding randomly based on those probabilities. The two main challenges for the controller are noise and phase changes: noise is random jitter in program behavior that the controller should ignore, and phase changes are systematic transitions in program behavior that the controller should adapt to. The controller in this section solves both challenges for a small fixed number of layouts while remaining reasonably simple.

3.1 Layout Decision

In reinforcement learning, functions that map rewards to probabilities are known as *policies*. The softmax controller is named for the *softmax* policy [41]:

$$\Pr(\ell) = \frac{e^{reward(\ell)/\tau}}{\sum\limits_{\ell'} e^{reward(\ell')/\tau}} \tag{1}$$

Equation 1 calculates $\Pr(\ell)$, the probability with which the controller will decide on layout ℓ for the next data reorganization. Layouts with higher rewards receive higher probabilities, since $e^{reward(\ell)/\tau}$ is larger. Before exponentiation, each reward is divided by a temperature τ. A high τ makes probabilities of different rewards more similar. A low τ emphasizes the reward differences in the probabilities; at low temperatures, controller decisions "freeze". The division in Equation 1 normalizes the probabilities such that they add up to 1.

Depending on the temperature, layout auditing will spend additional time exploring other layouts besides the best layout. Spending time on exploration is only justified if the information so far is too unreliable to exploit. To make this tradeoff, the controller computes the pooled standard error of the rewards of all layouts, and uses that as a *curiosity* value. The intuition for using error as curiosity is that when the error is high, the controller is curious to learn more, whereas additional data points will satisfy curiosity by shrinking the error. The controller sets the temperature such that the expected reward of the chosen layout differs from the reward of the best layout only by a small constant k times the curiosity. Given a temperature τ, the expected reward of a randomly chosen layout is

$$expectedReward(\tau) = \sum_{\ell} \left\{ \Pr_{\tau}(\ell) \cdot reward(\ell) \right\} \tag{2}$$

The controller tries different values for τ using binary search until the absolute difference between the maximum reward and the expected reward matches the desired target value $k \cdot curiosity$:

$$k \cdot curiosity = \left| \max_{\ell} \left\{ reward(\ell) \right\} - expectedReward(\tau) \right| \tag{3}$$

We chose $k = 1\%$ to ensure performance close to the best layout.

Curiosity is the pooled standard error of historical rewards for different layouts. To adapt to changes in program behavior, it should weigh recent results more heavily than old results that might come from a different phase. The controller achieves this with exponential decay. In other words, the weight of a reward is $decay^{age}$, where the base $decay$ can be for example 0.95, and the exponent age is the number of data reorganizations since the reward was measured. Because the statistical formula for pooled standard error does not directly accommodate weighing values, the controller implements exponential decay with a trick: it duplicates values with higher weights, then computes the statistics on a larger population.

To adapt to phase changes and to admit redemption after miscarriages of justice (if any), the controller shows mercy to layouts that seemed to perform badly in the past. It achieves this by assigning each layout a probability of at least 5%, regardless of its reward. The price of mercy is degraded performance compared with the best layout. The controller blindly assumes that all unexplored layouts, for which there is no data yet, initially have infinite rewards.

3.2 Profiling Decision

Some profilers incur overhead, and should only be activated when their benefits (information gain) outweigh their costs (overhead). This paper uses a zero-overhead profiler, so the profiler is always active, without controller decisions. Nevertheless, this section offers a technique to the interested reader for controlling profiling overhead with layout auditing. The decision to profile ($p = \top$) or not ($p = \bot$) is a two-armed bandit problem, which the controller can decide with reinforcement learning analogously to the multi-armed layout decision.

The reward of profiling, $reward(p = \top)$, is the reward of satisfied curiosity, which Section 3.1 defined as the pooled standard error of layout costs. The reward of not profiling, $reward(p = \bot)$, is avoiding two overheads: profiling overhead incurred during program execution, plus overhead incurred when the profiler processes raw measurements to compute layout rewards.

The controller computes $reward(p = \top)$, and relies on the profiler to report its own overhead in the form of $reward(p = \bot)$. The controller then decides whether or not to profile during the next execution interval using the softmax policy

$$\Pr(p) = \frac{e^{reward(p)/\tau}}{\sum_{p'} e^{reward(p')/\tau}} \tag{4}$$

The temperature τ is the same as in Equation 3.

4   Minimalist Profiler

The profiler monitors the performance of the program and the data reorganizer, and turns them into rewards for each data layout for the controller. The main challenge for any profiler used in online optimization is maximizing truthfulness while ignoring noise and minimizing overhead and Heisenberg effects. If the controller should be a blind judge, then the profiler should be a reliable witness.

The measurements of the minimalist profiler are very simple: seconds and allocated bytes. Both can be obtained truthfully at negligible overhead. This section discusses how the minimalist profiler turns seconds and bytes into rewards for each layout. Internally, the minimalist profiler computes costs, which are negative rewards, so low costs correspond to high rewards and vice versa. A cost is a seconds-per-byte ratio, and has the advantage of being additive when there are different costs from different system components. Formally, the reward of a data layout ℓ is

$$reward(\ell) = -cost(\ell) \tag{5}$$

The cost of a layout ℓ is the sum of its execution time cost $cost_e(\ell)$ and its data reorganization cost $cost_r(\ell)$:

$$cost(\ell) = cost_e(\ell) + cost_r(\ell) \tag{6}$$

The quantities in Equation 6 represent averages of ratios of corresponding historical measurements. To explain what that means, we first introduce some notation. Let e_i be the physical time of the program execution interval that follows reorganization i; let v_i be the virtual time in number of bytes allocated between reorganizations i and $i + 1$; and let ℓ_i be the layout of reorganization i. The minimalist profiler calculates

$$cost_e(\ell) = \mathrm{avg}\left\{\frac{e_i}{v_i} \mid \ell_i = \ell\right\} \tag{7}$$

In words: to compute the programs's execution time cost for layout ℓ, average the set of historical seconds per bytes ratios e_i/v_i that used layout ℓ. Likewise, given the physical time r_i of data reorganization number i, the formula for data reorganizer cost is

$$cost_r(\ell) = \mathrm{avg}\left\{\frac{r_i}{v_{i-1}} \mid \ell_i = \ell\right\} \tag{8}$$

The minimalist profiler assumes that reorganizer time r_i is proportional to the allocation volume v_{i-1} of the preceding execution interval, and that execution time e_i reflects the layout ℓ_i of the preceding data reorganization.

Averaging over historical values (Equations 7 and 8) reduces noise. To reduce noise further, the averages omit outliers. The averages are weighted toward recent data using an exponential decay curve, to adapt when program behavior changes over time.

In addition to rewards for layouts, profilers also report their own cost to the controller in the form of $reward(p = \bot)$, which is the reward of not profiling. Since the minimalist profiler incurs no overhead, there is no reward for not profiling, hence $reward(p = \bot)$ is always 0.

To summarize, the minimalist profiler uses only information that is trivially available on any platform: seconds and allocated bytes. The disadvantage is that layout auditing will settle slowly when there is too much noise. Another drawback is the assumption that program execution time reflects the data layout of the previous data reorganization only, which plays down the effect of data in a different memory area that was unaffected by that reorganization, and thus has a different layout. On the positive side, the minimalist profiler is cheap, portable, and direct.

5   Data Reorganization with Garbage Collection

The data reorganizer tries a layout for the program's data. There are many possible implementations for data reorganizers; this paper chose to use off-the-shelf garbage collection algorithms [24]. This section reviews background on copying collectors, and describes some common data layouts.

5.1   Copying Garbage Collection

Copying garbage collection divides heap memory into two semispaces. Only one semispace is active for allocation at a time. Garbage collection starts when the active semispace is full. The collector traverses pointers from program variables to discover reachable objects, which it copies to the other semispace (from from-space to to-space). It updates all pointers to refer to the to-space copies, and discards the from-space originals. When the program resumes, it uses to-space as the active semispace for allocation. An example for a copying garbage collector is Fenichel and Yochelson's algorithm, which traverses objects with a recursive procedure [13].

Most language runtime systems today use generational garbage collectors, because they tend to yield the best throughput. Generational collectors segregate objects by age into generations [27,42]. Younger generations are collected more often than older generations, which reduces overall collector work, because most objects become unreachable while they are still young. This paper is based on a

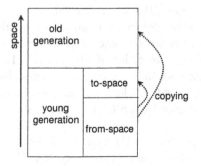

Fig. 3. Generational copying garbage collection

generational garbage collector with two generations, a copying young generation and a mark-sweep old generation. The collector also implements numerous other techniques, among others, parallelism [16] and tilted semi-spaces [28].

Fig. 3 shows the two kinds of copying: between the semi-spaces of the young generation, and from the young generation to the old generation. Each garbage collection can independently choose a copy order. Each set of objects allocated between the same two collections starts out in allocation order, and may then experience different layouts as it gets copied within the young generation. When the objects reach an age threshold, they get copied into the old generation (tenured), where they come to rest with a final layout.

The repeated data reorganizations when copying objects give layout auditing the opportunity to find the best layout.

5.2   Data Layouts

This section briefly surveys some common data layouts; for a more comprehensive survey and evaluation, see [17].

Fenichel and Yochelson's recursive algorithm uses variables on the call stack to keep track of already copied objects that may contain pointers to not-yet copied objects [13]. Using a LIFO-stack leads to copying objects in depth-first (DF) order. Other DF copying collectors are not recursive, but maintain the stack as an explicit data structure and share it between parallel collector threads [8]. The DF layout is good for locality if the program often accesses a parent object together with a child object that it points to.

When the collector keeps objects in a FIFO-queue during the reachability traversal, it copies them in breadth-first (BF) order. Cheney's BF copying algorithm [7] uses the to-space copies of the objects themselves as an implicit queue. The BF layout is good for locality if the program often accesses sibling objects together.

An algorithm designed to achieve both the parent $\rightarrow$ child locality of the depth-first layout and the sibling locality of the breadth-first layout is hierarchical (HI) garbage collection by Moon and Wilson et al. [30,44]. It works by copying a subtree to the same block as its root whenever possible.

Most of this paper uses layout auditing (LA) to choose between parallel implementations of the BF and HI layouts [22,38].

Compacting collectors do not reserve an entire semispace for copying, instead they move objects toward one end of just one space. Sliding compaction aims at preserving the relative order of objects [24, Lisp 2 collector, Section 5.4]; [1,14,25]. When used as the sole copying mechanism, sliding compaction preserves allocation order (AO), which yields good locality when the program touches objects in the same order it allocated them, and can also facilitate stride prefetching [2,23].

Segregating objects by *type* (TY) may yield better locality if the program tends to access objects of the same type together. This data layout also has potential benefits in reducing object header sizes, and has been used for reducing data reorganizer cost [19,36].

6 Methodology

Table 1 shows the benchmark suite, consisting of 20 Java programs: pseudojbb05, which runs SPECjbb2005[1] for a fixed number of transactions; the 7 SPECjvm98 programs[2]; the 11 DaCapo benchmarks version 2006-10 [4]; and ipsixql[3]. Except for Fig. 4, all numbers in this paper are averages of nine JVM process invocations. Within each JVM invocation, the layout auditor starts with a clean slate, learning the best layout online as it goes. As is common practice for these benchmarks, each run contains several iterations (application invocations within one JVM process invocation), see Column "Command line arguments". Timings measure the entire run of the JVM process, and thus include any overheads incurred by layout auditing, such as initially making wrong decisions. Furthermore, all numbers in this paper are checked for statistical confidence using Student's t-test. Wherever the t-test indicates that performance differences are too small to be relevant at 95% confidence, we report a "0" value instead.

Table 1. Benchmark programs

Name	Suite	Command line arguments	Description	PT	MB
antlr	DaCapo	-s large -n 16	parser generator	1	2.0
bloat	DaCapo	-s large -n 4	bytecode optimizer	1	16.1
chart	DaCapo	-s large -n 8	pdf graph plotter	1	14.3
compress	jvm98	-a -m72 -M72 -s100	Lempel-Ziv compressor	1	7.0
db	jvm98	-a -m24 -M24 -s100	in-memory database	1	11.2
eclipse	DaCapo	-s small -n 4	development environment	>1	14.0
fop	DaCapo	-s large -n 60	XSL-FO to pdf converter	1	9.1
hsqldb	DaCapo	-s large -n 12	in-memory JDBC database	20	173.8
ipsixql	Colorado	80 7	in-memory XML database	1	2.5
jack	jvm98	-a -m164 -M164 -s100	parser generator	1	1.3
javac	jvm98	-a -m92 -M92 -s100	Java compiler	1	20.5
jess	jvm98	-a -m228 -M228 -s100	expert shell system	1	2.1
jython	DaCapo	-s large -n 4	Python interpreter	1	1.9
luindex	DaCapo	-s large -n 32	text indexing for search	1	2.2
lusearch	DaCapo	-s large -n 8	keyword search in text	32	7.1
mpegaudio	jvm98	-a -m156 -M156 -s100	audio file decompressor	1	1.0
mtrt	jvm98	-a -m232 -M232 -s100	multi-threaded raytracer	2	8.7
pmd	DaCapo	-s large -n 4	source code analyzer	1	15.7
pseudojbb05	jbb05	SPECjbb-4x200000.props	business benchmark	4	123.9
xalan	DaCapo	-s large -n 16	XSLT processor	1	27.5

---

[1] http://www.spec.org/jbb2005/

[2] http://www.spec.org/osg/jvm98/

[3] http://www-plan.cs.colorado.edu/henkel/projects/colorado_bench/

Column "PT" in Table 1 shows the number of program threads. The JVM also has some service threads that run concurrently with the program. Garbage collection is parallel with itself, but not concurrent with program execution. Column "MB" gives, in megabytes, the minimum heap size in which the program runs without throwing an OutOfMemoryError. Most experiments in this paper provision each program with 4× its minimum heap size; garbage collection kicks in when the heap size is exhausted.

Table 2. Memory hierarchy parameters per core

	L1 Cache		L2 Cache		TLB	
	AMD	Intel	AMD	Intel	AMD	Intel
Associativity	2	8	16	8	4	8
Block size	64 B	64 B	64 B	64 B	4 KB	4 KB
Capacity/blocks	1,024	256	16K	16K	512	64
Capacity/bytes	64K	16K	1,024K	1,024K	2,048K	256K

The experiments in this paper ran on one 2-processor Linux/IA32 machine, and on three different Linux/AMD machines with 2, 4, and 8 processors. We used the default run level of Linux (not single-user mode) to demonstrate that layout auditing can make correct decisions even in the presence of noise. The Intel machine was a Pentium 4 clocked at 3.2GHz with SMT, so the 2 physical processors correspond to 4 virtual processors. The AMD machines had Opteron 270 cores clocked at 2GHz, with 2 cores per chip. Table 2 shows the data caches and TLBs for each core. We implemented layout auditing in J9, which is IBM's high-performance product Java virtual machine. The experiments in this paper are based on an internal development release of J9.

7 Results

This section evaluates data layout auditing using the concrete component instantiations from earlier sections: softmax policy, minimalist profiler, and data reorganization by copying garbage collection.

7.1 A Control Theoretic Approach to Controller Evaluation

Layout auditing employs an online feedback loop to control a system. Such feedback loops have been extensively studied in control theory. Control theory commonly talks about *SASO* properties: Stability, Accuracy, Settling, and Overshoot. A good controller is a controller that is stable, accurately makes the right decisions, settles on that decision quickly, and does not overshoot the range of acceptable values. In the context of layout auditing, *stability* means sticking with a data layout once the controller picks one; *accuracy* means picking the data layout that yields the best performance; and *settling* is the time from the start or from a phase shift until the controller has made a decision. Overshoot does not apply in this context, because all layout decisions are in the range of acceptable values by definition. This is common for discrete, rather than continuous, control systems.

In addition to the SASO properties, layout auditing strives to achieve another desirable property: low overhead. Since the minimalist profiler treats the time for data reorganization as part of the reward of a data layout, there is no separate overhead for data reorganization. The minimalist profiler just reads the clock and counts bytes, so it does not incur any overhead on its own. This leaves controller *overhead*: time spent doing the statistical calculations in the softmax controller. On average, each control decision takes on the order of 0.1ms. Compared to data reorganization times, which are on the order of 10ms to 100ms, controller overhead is negligible in most cases.

Phase adaptivity is the ability of the controller to change its decision if the program changes its behavior such that a different data layout becomes the best data layout. Phase adaptivity is another way to look at settling, accuracy, and stability. The minimalist profiler and the softmax controller achieve phase adaptivity by using exponential decay to forget old profile information. The decay factor determines how well layout auditing can adapt to phase changes.

Overall, layout auditing can make investments, such as profiling overhead, data reorganization cost, or time spent exploring data layouts it is curious about. For these investments, it reaps rewards, such as improved program execution time or improved data reorganization time due to reduced cache and TLB misses. The success of layout auditing depends on its ability to make the right tradeoff between the different investments and rewards.

7.2 Accuracy

This section explores the accuracy of the layout auditor presented in this paper. Accuracy is the ability of the controller to accurately pick the correct data layout. If it does, then the bottom-line performance of a program when run with layout auditing should match the performance of that program with its best statically chosen layout. In terms of Fig. 1, layout auditing should get all the speedups for programs at the right side of the bar chart, while avoiding all the slowdowns for programs at the left side of the bar chart. To evaluate accuracy, this section ran all 20 benchmark programs from Table 1 using the breadth-first (BF) and hierarchical (HI) data layout, both with and without layout auditing (LA).

Table 3 shows the results. For each of the 4 runtime platforms (2-processor Intel and 2-, 4-, and 8-processor AMD), there is one column for each of the data layouts BF and HI and one for layout auditing LA. All the numbers are percent slowdowns compared to the best runtime of the given benchmark/platform combination. For example, for ipsixql on the 2-processor Intel machine, BF was best, HI caused a 12% slowdown compared to BF, and LA matched the performance of BF. A "0" in Table 3 means that the results of the 9 runs with that data layout were indistinguishable from the results of the 9 runs with the best data layout for that benchmark and platform, using Student's t-test at 95% confidence. The bottom of Table 3 shows summary rows: "Average" is the

Table 3. Percent slowdown compared to best, on varying platforms at heap size 4×

Benchmark	Intel-2 BF	HI	LA	AMD-2 BF	HI	LA	AMD-4 BF	HI	LA	AMD-8 BF	HI	LA
antlr	0	1.1	2.1	1.4	0	2.2	0	0	0	0	0	0
bloat	0	0	0	0	0	0	0	0	0	0	0	0
chart	0	0	0	0	0	0	0	0	0	0	0	0
compress	0	1.2	0	0	0	0	0	0	0	0	0	0
db	5.2	0	2.9	6.0	0	1.9	0	0	0	6.5	0	0
eclipse	0	0	0	0	0	0	0	0	0	0	0	0
fop	0	0	0	0	0	0	0	0	0	0	0	0
hsqldb	0	0	0	0	0	0	2.8	0	0	7.2	0	0
ipsixql	0	12.0	0	0	10.7	1.9	0	10.4	0	0	7.9	1.4
jack	0	0	0	0	2.4	0	0	0	0	0	5.5	0
javac	0	1.5	0	0	1.3	0	0	0	0	0	0	0
jess	0	1.4	2.2	0	3.6	3.1	0	0	0	0	0	0
jython	0	0	0	0	0	0	0	0	0	0	0	0
luindex	0	0	0	0	0	0	0	0	0	0	1.0	1.0
lusearch	0	0	0	0	0	0	0	2.7	0	0	0	0
mpegaudio	0	1.8	0	0	0	0	0	0	0	0	0	0
mtrt	0	0	0	0	0	0	0	0	0	0	0	0
pmd	0	0	0	0	0	0	8.4	0	0	0	0	0
pseudojbb05	2.1	0	1.2	1.6	0	0	0	0	0	0	0	0
xalan	0	0	0	0	0	0	0	4.0	0	0	8.4	4.3
Average	0.4	0.9	0.4	0.5	0.9	0.5	0.6	0.9	0.0	0.7	1.1	0.3
# not 0	2	6	4	3	4	4	2	3	0	2	4	3
Worst	5.2	12.0	2.9	6.0	10.7	3.1	8.4	10.4	0.0	7.2	8.4	4.3

arithmetic mean of the slowdowns of the layout compared to the best layout for each benchmark, "# not 0" counts benchmarks for which the layout was not the best, and "Worst" is the maximum slowdown of the layout compared to the best.

Table 3 demonstrates that on all four platforms, online layout selection performs almost as well as an oracle that would pick the best layout for each program offline. Note that Petrank and Rawitz have shown conclusively that building such an offline oracle would be impractical [32]. Layout auditing usually, but not always, matches the performance of the best data layout for a program and platform; sometimes the program finishes executing too quickly for LA to settle on the best layout and recoup its exploration costs. However, layout auditing has the most benign worst cases. Statically picking the wrong layout can slow down execution by up to 12.0%, but dynamically picking with layout auditing never causes slowdowns exceeding 4.3%.

As noted in prior work [20,38], some benchmarks, such as db and ipsixql, are unusually sensitive to data layouts. For those programs, layout auditing has the largest benefits. But it is equally important that for benchmarks that are mostly insensitive to data layouts, layout auditing does not degrade performance appreciably. Except for antlr and jess, this is usually the case. The reliable accuracy of layout auditing over a large range of programs and platforms gives it an edge over traditional locality optimizations.

To summarize, layout auditing is accurate. It makes good on its promise of requiring no model of the complex hardware/software interaction: it works equally well with no user tuning on four platforms.

7.3   Settling, Stability, and Phase Adaptivity

This section investigates how long our implementation of layout auditing takes to settle, whether it is stable once it reaches a decision, and whether it can adapt to phase changes. This section answers these questions with a layout auditing experiment designed to illustrate phase changes, while still being realistic. Let T be the time in seconds since the start of the run, then the experiment first executes benchmark db from $T = 0$ to $T = 155$, then executes benchmark mtrt from $T = 155$ to $T = 320$, and finally goes back to db from $T = 320$ to $T = 475$. The softmax controller decides between the breadth-first data layout BF and the hierarchical data layout HI.

Benchmark db is much more data layout sensitive than mtrt. This constitutes a challenging scenario for settling, stability, and phase adaptivity. The two data layouts BF and HI have been shown to exhibit among the largest performance differences between common data layouts [17, Figure 4]. The experiment ran on the 2-processor AMD machine, and used heap size 44.8MB, which is $4\times$ the minimum for db and $5.1\times$ the minimum for mtrt. This setup models what happens when a server machine changes to a different workload that exercises different code.

Fig. 4 shows the results. There are three columns: Column (a/d/g) is based on a run where the minimalist profiler and the softmax controller use decay 0.9, Column (b/e/h) uses decay 0.95, and Column (c/f/i) did not decay historical values (decay=1.0). The x-axis of all graphs is the same. physical time in seconds. Row (a/b/c) shows rewards as reported by the minimalist profiler, Row (d/e/f) shows the controller's current probability of BF, and Row (g/h/i) shows the cumulative number of decisions for HI and against BF. Each time the controller chooses HI for a data reorganization, the choice curve increases by one; each time the controller chooses BF, the choice curve decreases by one.

Rewards are physical time per virtual time, where lower is better. The reward graphs (Figures 4(a/b/c)) use a logarithmic y-axis, because data layout rewards are an order of magnitude higher in db than in mtrt. The phase transitions at around $T = 155$ and $T = 320$ are clearly visible. With a decay value of 0.9, the minimalist profiler quickly forgets earlier data, and therefore computes a reward that closely follows each spike in the data. Zooming in closely on the first phase in Fig. 4(a) reveals that the rewards for HI are higher than the rewards for BF, but the difference is lower than the amplitude of the program's own performance behavior over time. Fig. 4(c) shows that when the decay is 1.0,

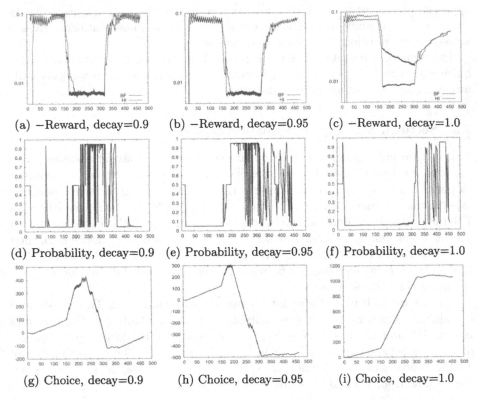

(a) −Reward, decay=0.9   (b) −Reward, decay=0.95   (c) −Reward, decay=1.0

(d) Probability, decay=0.9   (e) Probability, decay=0.95   (f) Probability, decay=1.0

(g) Choice, decay=0.9   (h) Choice, decay=0.95   (i) Choice, decay=1.0

Fig. 4. Controller behavior over time for db/mtrt/db run, on AMD-2

the profiler never forgets, and the curve becomes smooth over time. This means that without decay, the profiler can not adapt to phases: by the last phase, the rewards of *BF* and *HI* are indistinguishable. Figures 4(a/b/c) show that the controller faces a tough challenge: it has to learn the best layout despite the fact that the difference between the layouts is dwarfed by the difference between program phases.

The probability graphs (Figures 4(d/e/f)) illustrate *settling*. For decay 0.9, the controller settles on the best data layout for each phase at approximately $T = 20$, $T = 220$, and $T = 370$, which is 20, 75, and 50 seconds after the phase transitions. For decay 0.95, the controller settles on the best data layout for each phase at approximately $T = 15$, $T = 200$, and $T = 445$, which is 15, 45, and 125 seconds after the phase transitions. For decay 1.0, the controller settles on *HI* for the first phase, but then takes the entire second phase to discover that *HI* is no longer the best, and is then unstable during the last phase. This illustrates that decay is necessary for *phase adaptivity*.

The probability graphs (Figures 4(d/e/f)) also illustrate *stability*. Fig. 4(d) shows that for decay 0.9, the controller is mostly stable during the first and the third phase, but has some spikes indicating instability. During the second phase, it is less stable, but Fig. 4(g) shows that it still chooses the correct layout most of the time. Fig. 4(e) shows that for decay 0.95, the controller is more stable during the first and second phases than with decay 0.9, but takes so long to settle that it only becomes stable again at the very end of the third phase. Fig. 4(f) shows that decay 1.0 leads to the best stability for stationary programs, at the cost of sacrificing settling after phase changes.

The choice graphs (Figures 4(g/h/i)) follow the probability graphs (Figures 4(d/e/f)), in the sense that when the probability is 50/50, the choice forms a horizontal line; when the probability for *HI* is high, the line rises; and when the probability for *BF* is high, the line falls. Figure 4(i) may look unexpected at first. During the second phase, *BF* is the best layout, yet the choice curve rises even more steeply than during the first phase where *HI* was the best layout. The reason why it rises is that the controller makes wrong decisions: without decay, it fails to adapt to the phase change. The explanation why the curve rises more steeply is that there are more data reorganizations per second. That is caused by the fact that mtrt has a higher alloc/live ratio than db (see Table 4 in [4]). That also explains the increased gradients in Figure 4(g/h).

To summarize, this section showed settling times ranging from 15s to 125s for decay values of 0.9 and 0.95. Lower decay values lead to less stable controller decisions; when the decay is too small, the controller gets confused by noise in the program behavior. But in the other extreme, when the decay is too high or when there is no decay, the controller can not adapt to phase changes. This motivates why we designed the controller the way we did. With decay, the softmax controller adapts to phase changes by accurately picking the best data layout for each phase.

7.4   Cache and TLB Behavior

This section explores whether the performance improvements of layout auditing come from reducing the program's data cache and TLB miss rates. The cache and TLB misses are measured in the same experiments as those for Section 7.2, by using PAPI [5] and then accumulating the counts for all program threads but excluding the data reorganizer.

Table 4 shows the results. The columns and rows are the same as in Table 3, and the numbers show percent miss rate increases compared to the layout with the best miss rate for a given program and platform. It turns out that layout auditing does **not** always achieve the lowest miss rate. We did not expect that it would: we already saw that layout auditing achieves the best performance, but program cache and TLB miss rates are only one factor in that. They have to be weighed against other performance factors, such as data reorganization time, hardware prefetching effects, instruction level parallelism, bus bandwidth, etc. Layout auditing does prevent the worst-case miss rates that occur for some programs; without layout auditing, those miss rate increases can easily amount to 100% and more. But more importantly, no matter how complex the performance effects of a particular hardware, layout auditing consistently and reliably optimizes the bottom-line performance.

Table 4. Percent miss rate increase compared to best, at heap size 4×

Benchmark	L2:Intel-2			L2:AMD-2			L2:AMD-4			L2:AMD-8		
	BF	HI	LA	BF	HI	LA	BF	HI	LA	BF	HI	LA
antlr	0	0	0	5.2	0	1.9	2.5	0	3.0	2.6	0	2.5
bloat	0	0	0	12.9	0	5.8	13.2	0	0	12.7	0	5.4
chart	0	0	0	0	0	0	0	0	0	0	0	0
compress	0	0	0	0	0	0	0	0	0	0	0	0
db	0	20.9	10.3	0	0	0	0	0	0	0	0	0
eclipse	0	0	0	0	0	0	0	0	0	0	0	0
fop	0	0	0	3.7	0	0	3.7	0	0	11.2	0	0
hsqldb	0	0	0	0	0	0	0	2.5	0	0	0	0
ipsixql	0	11.7	0	0	46.5	0	0	61.3	3.3	0	62.3	7.0
jack	0	0	0	0	0	13.5	0	0	0	0	14.2	0
javac	0	0	0	7.3	0	6.3	5.8	0	0	6.0	0	0
jess	0	0	0	0	0	0	0	7.2	5.2	0	9.1	3.7
jython	0	0	0	0	0	0	0	0	0	0	0	0
luindex	0	0	0	4.2	0	2.5	0	2.1	0	0	1.9	2.0
lusearch	0	0	0	0	0	0	0	12.5	0	0	0	0
mpegaudio	0	0	0	0	0	29.2	0	0	0	0	0	0
mtrt	7.0	0	0	0	0	7.9	7.1	0	0	0	0	0
pmd	0	0	0	0	0	0	0	0	0	10.2	0	0
pseudojbb05	0	0	0	9.2	0	4.8	8.7	0	5.5	8.2	0	5.0
xalan	0	0	0	4.1	0	2.3	3.4	0	0	0	0	0
Average	0.4	1.7	0.5	2.5	2.4	3.9	2.3	4.5	0.9	2.5	5.0	1.5
# not 0	1	2	1	7	1	9	7	5	4	6	5	7
Worst	7.0	20.9	10.3	12.9	46.5	29.2	13.2	61.3	5.5	12.7	62.3	7.0

Benchmark	TLB:Intel-2			TLB:AMD-2			TLB:AMD-4			TLB:AMD-8		
	BF	HI	LA	BF	HI	LA	BF	HI	LA	BF	HI	LA
antlr	0	0	0	2.0	0	0	0	0	0	0	0	0
bloat	10.1	0	0	0	0	0	5.7	0	0	0	0	0
chart	0	0	0	0	0	0	0	0	0	18.1	0	9.1
compress	0	0	0	0	0	1.1	0	0	0	0	0	0
db	134.2	0	59.7	163.3	0	46.2	167.3	0	65.3	177.6	0	94.3
eclipse	0	0	0	0	0	0	0	0	0	0	0	0
fop	0	0	0	1.7	0	2.0	4.0	3.9	0	0	0	0
hsqldb	13.5	0	0	12.6	0	0	11.0	0	0	0	0	0
ipsixql	20.5	22.9	0	31.2	0	0	0	0	0	0	11.4	0
jack	0	0	0	0	0	0	0	0	0	0	0	0
javac	15.9	0	13.3	14.9	0	9.4	11.0	0	12.1	9.0	0	0
jess	3.2	0	0	3.1	0	0	0	0	0	0	0	0
jython	10.4	0	0	0	0	0	0	0	0	0	0	0
luindex	9.3	0	0	0	0	0	0	0	0	0	0	0
lusearch	0	0	0	0	0	0	2.6	0	0	9.2	0	0
mpegaudio	0	0	0	0	0	0	0	2.9	2.1	0	0	0
mtrt	31.9	0	14.8	25.0	0	16.6	22.8	0	9.6	15.4	0	0
pmd	0	0	0	10.2	0	9.7	0	0	0	22.9	0	0
pseudojbb05	6.1	0	0	11.7	0	7.5	13.4	0	7.7	11.5	0	7.4
xalan	12.0	0	6.7	7.1	0	6.3	5.7	0	0	9.5	0	0
Average	14.1	1.2	5.0	14.9	0.0	5.2	12.8	0.4	5.1	13.7	0.6	5.5
# not 0	11	1	4	11	0	8	9	2	5	8	1	3
Worst	134.2	22.9	59.7	163.3	0.0	46.2	167.3	3.9	65.3	177.6	11.4	94.3

7.5   Data Reorganization Cost and Heap Sizes

Switching between data layouts changes not just program performance, but also data reorganizer performance. In addition, if the data reorganizer is a garbage collector, its performance is also affected by the heap size: in a large heap, the program can allocate more memory before triggering a garbage collection. This

Table 5. Percent slowdown compared to best, on AMD-2 at varying heap sizes

Benchmark	2× heap			4× heap			10× heap		
	BF	HI	LA	BF	HI	LA	BF	HI	LA
antlr	0	1.0	2.9	1.4	0	2.2	0	0	2.1
bloat	0	0	0	0	0	0	0	0	0
chart	0	0	0	0	0	0	0	0	0
compress	0	0	0.7	0	0	0	0	0	0
db	5.3	0	2.6	6.0	0	1.9	6.4	0	2.5
eclipse	0	0	0	0	0	0	0	0	0
fop	0	0	0	0	0	0	0	0	0
hsqldb	0	0	0	0	0	0	0	0	0
ipsixql	0	10.6	3.9	0	10.7	1.9	0	13.8	6.5
jack	0	2.3	0	0	2.4	0	0	0	0
javac	0	3.3	0	0	1.3	0	0	0	0
jess	0	2.1	4.1	0	3.6	3.1	0	0	0
jython	0	0	0	0	0	0	0	0	0
luindex	0	0	0	0	0	0	0	0	0
lusearch	0	0	0	0	0	0	0	0	0
mpegaudio	0	0	0	0	0	0	0	0	0
mtrt	0	0.7	0	0	0	0	0	0	0
pmd	0	0	0	0	0	0	0	0	0
pseudojbb05	0	0	0	1.6	0	0	0	0	0
xalan	0	1.0	0	0	0	0	0	0.8	0
Average	0.3	1.1	0.7	0.5	0.9	0.5	0.3	0.7	0.6
# not 0	1	7	5	3	4	4	1	2	3
Worst	5.3	10.6	4.1	6.0	10.7	3.1	6.4	13.8	6.5

usually means that objects have more time to die, and thus garbage collection is cheaper, since it has to run less frequently and processes relatively fewer survivors.

Layout auditing takes data reorganization cost into account, as described in Section 4. It should therefore always find the right performance tradeoff irrespective of heap size and garbage collection cost. The experiments in this section provision each program with 2×, 4×, or 10× the minimum heap size in which the program runs without throwing an OutOfMemoryError. The tight heap size 2× (50% utilization) frequently triggers garbage collection; the standard heap size 4× (25% utilization) is what most of the rest of this paper uses; and the roomy heap size 10× (10% utilization) infrequently triggers garbage collection. Table 5 shows the relative overall performance of the different data layouts in different heap sizes. Table 5 is organized similarly to Table 3, with which it shares the AMD-2 / 4× heap columns. Remember that "0" values indicate that whatever performance degregation there may be compared to the best layout is too small to be deemed statistically relevant. The 10× heap makes benchmarks less layout sensitive, since that heap size deemphasizes data reorganizer cost, one of the factors in performance differences. Conversely, the 2× heap makes benchmarks more layout sensitive. The slightly worse results in the 10× heap might be caused by fewer garbage collections offering fewer trials. Even so, in all three heap sizes, layout auditing picks the best layout most of the time.

7.6   Bandits with More Than Two Arms

The results so far are based on layout auditing chosing between two layouts BF and HI. These are the only two high-performance layouts implemented in our infrastructure. So in order to explore chosing between three layouts, we had to resort to slow experimental garbage collectors. We use the algorithms from [17], but whereas that paper focuses on program time excluding data reorganization cost only, here we look at the total cost including data reorganization. We use the layouts BF_s, DF_s, and TY_s, where the subscript denotes slow implementations. Note in particular that $BF_s \neq BF$.

Table 6, which is formatted similarly to Table 3, shows the results. Despite running in a loose heap, the slow data reorganizer of TY_s causes high overheads compared to the other two reorganizers. Layout auditing successfully avoids the risk of degrading performance nearly as much as TY_s, and comes close to BF_s and DF_s. In fact, for most programs, layout auditing performs close to the best

Table 6. Multi-layout percent slowdown compared to best, at heap size 10×

Benchmark	AMD-2				AMD-8			
	BF_s	DF_s	TY_s	LA_s	BF_s	DF_s	TY_s	LA_s
antlr	4.8	0	24.3	4.4	3.3	0	20.1	2.7
bloat	0	0	18.3	0	0	0	26.4	0
chart	0	0	10.3	0	0	0	79.9	0
compress	0	0	0	0	0	0	1.2	0
db	8.1	0	22.7	3.4	10.1	0	21.8	7.0
eclipse	0	0	18.2	7.2	0	0	24.5	8.8
fop	0	0	10.4	0	0	0	18.5	0
hsqldb	10.2	0	214.0	24.5	17.0	0	253.1	22.5
ipsixql	19.8	0	144.3	7.4	32.9	0	158.6	4.3
jack	0	2.4	14.7	0	0	0	13.4	0
javac	8.4	0	90.3	3.9	11.5	0	92.5	0
jess	0	0	17.6	2.4	0	0	16.4	4.6
jython	0	0	0	0	2.2	0	1.9	0
luindex	0	0	9.1	0	0	0	8.4	1.7
lusearch	0	0	5.9	0	0	0	13.5	7.0
mpegaudio	0	1.5	0	0	1.8	0	0	0
mtrt	0	0	151.6	0	0	0	212.4	0
pmd	0	0	35.3	0	0	0	39.2	5.5
pseudojbb05	2.6	0	74.9	9.3	9.4	0	113.6	18.9
xalan	5.5	0	15.8	6.9	8.5	0	47.6	4.9
Average	3.0	0.2	43.9	3.5	4.8	0.0	58.2	4.4
# not 0	7	2	17	9	9	0	19	11
Worst	19.8	2.4	214.0	24.5	32.9	0	253.1	22.5

of the three layouts. We do not expect layout auditing to perform well with tens or hundreds of layouts, because the settling time would grow unreasonably long.

8   Alternative Layout Auditing Components

This section discusses alternative data reorganizers, profilers, and controllers that fit in the layout auditing framework from Section 2.

8.1   Alternative Data Reorganizers

Layout auditing is designed to accommodate a variety of off-the-shelf data reorganization techniques. Section 5 already mentioned several data layouts (depth-first, breadth-first, hierarchical, allocation order). Other garbage collectors segregate objects by size, type, or allocating thread. One could even consider a random data layout; while random layouts are unlikely to perform best, they are equally unlikely to perform worst, and can thus effectively prevent pathological interference situations.

While layout auditing works with profile-oblivious data layouts, it can be applied just as easily to decide whether or not to use profile-directed approaches, such as Huang et al.'s online object reordering [20] or the locality optimizations by Chen et al. [6].

As mentioned earlier in this paper, layout auditing is not confined to garbage collection; a variety of other data reorganizers has been proposed. One technique is to reorder data arrays or index arrays for scientific programs [11]. Zhang et al. present and simulate a piece of hardware that can remap data to a different layout [46]. Another possibility is to change the data layout during allocation, for example, by using different alignments, or by profile-directed techniques [37].

8.2   Alternative Profilers

In the easiest case, the profiler just measures seconds by looking at the clock. The advantage is that this causes no overhead, but the disadvantage is that it makes it hard to isolate the impact of the data layout from the impact of extraneous effects. To complicate things further, it is often desirable to isolate the impact of the layout of some memory subspace from the impact of the layout of other subspaces. This challenge could be addressed with a *subspace locality profiler*.

For example, if the data reorganizer is a generational garbage collector (like in Section 5), each collection of the young generation copies some objects within the young generation, and others from the young to the old generation. Over time, a situation like in Fig. 5 arises. The left column shows the heap spaces: an old generation, and a young generation with two semispaces. The middle column further divides spaces into groups of objects, annotated by the last time they were copied; e.g., "survivors (T-3)" were tenured 3 collections ago, whereas the "newest" objects were allocated after the last collection and have yet to be copied for the first time. Column "layout" shows which copy order, and hence which data layout, the corresponding objects have. It is easy to keep

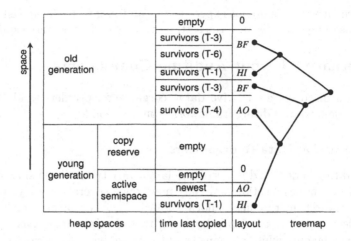

heap spaces			time last copied	layout	treemap

Fig. 5. Mapping from addresses to layouts

track of the mapping from addresses to memory areas and their data layouts; a subspace locality profiler could do so with a treemap. What is needed, then, is a measurement of locality for specific data addresses.

One possibility for this is PEBS (precise event based sampling), where hardware counter overflows generate interrupts, and the interrupt handler can inspect parts of the machine state. Adl-Tabatabai et al. used PEBS on Itanium to identify objects that cause cache misses [2]. Similarly, one could count misses separately for memory subspaces with different data layouts. Unfortunately, on IA32 and AMD, the PEBS machine state does not contain the data address, and each interrupt costs several thousand cycles.

Another possibility for a subspace locality profiler is trace-driven cache simulation. To accommodate layout auditing, the tracing and simulation must occur online and automatically. Bursty tracing [3,18] can produce a memory access trace at low overhead. Online cache simulation has been reported by Zhao et al. [48]. To use online trace-driven simulation for layout auditing, map simulated accesses and misses to data layouts via the treemap from Fig. 5.

A drawback of more sophisticated profilers is that they make more assumptions about how the software and hardware interact. Such assumptions can be misleading: for example, more cache misses do not necessarily imply worse performance if instruction-level parallelism overlays them with useful computation.

8.3   Alternative Controllers

Layout auditing is designed to accommodate a variety of off-the-shelf machine learning techniques. The authors come from a systems background, and have to refer the reader to the relevant literature for details [41]. This paper uses a softmax policy. Other possibilities include sequential analysis and reinforcement computation.

Also, there are alternatives for dealing with phase changes. This paper uses exponential decay of historical profile information. Another possibility is to remember a sliding window of values. There are also more sophisticated stand-alone phase detectors [31,35].

9   Related Work

Layout auditing uses an online feedback loop that first tries different data layouts, then evaluates their performance, and based on that, changes data layout decisions later in the same run. This section reviews other online try-measure-decide feedback loops.

Lau et al. proposed performance auditing [26], which first tries different ways to optimize a method using a JIT compiler, then evaluates their performance, and finally decides which one to use. Performance auditing addresses measurement noise by continuing to collect information until it reaches statistical confidence for a decision. Our work is also performance auditing, but we apply it to data, not code, and we extend it to adapt when program behavior changes over time.

We picked copying garbage collection as the mechanism for executing data layout decisions. Our controller switches between different copying collectors for the young generation. Soman et al. showed how to switch between a more diverse set of collectors, including both generational and non-generational, copying and non-copying algorithms [40]. But whereas we decide to switch to another collector based on online measurements of application performance, Soman et al. decide based on heap size thresholds.

Chen et al. try a data layout optimization in a garbage collector, measure whether it reduces miss rates, and throttle it if it does not [6]. Whereas Chen et al. use online feedback to throttle an optimization in one collector, we use online feedback to pick between multiple alternative collectors. Chen et al.'s throttling mechanism is woven into the collector, and this tightly integrated design compromises desirable features for both: the collector is not parallel, and the controller does not use statistical or machine learning techniques to deal with noise or with changes in program behavior.

Besides changing the data layout, an alternative technique for improving locality is prefetching. Some papers propose online try-measure-decide feedback loops for picking the best prefetch distance [34,47].

Zhang et al. use an online try-measure-decide feedback loop for picking the largest memory footprint that does not yet cause paging [45]. Unlike our work, they change the heap size, not the data layout, and focus on paging, not on cache and TLB locality.

A number of papers show how to pick between differently optimized versions of scientific code at runtime [12,15,43]. Unlike our work, and unlike Lau et al.'s performance auditing [26], they pay little attention to dealing with noise. Also, they focus on code, we focus on data.

Other online data layout optimizations do not use a try-measure-decide feedback loop [9,10,20,21]. Instead, they use online profile data to predict which layout will benefit performance, without checking later whether the prediction came true. Petrank and Rawitz showed that these predictions can be easily fooled by misleading data access patterns [32]. This is exacerbated by the fact that the predictions rely on a model of hardware/software interactions, which change and become more complex over time.

Reinforcement learning has been used for programming language optimizations in the past (e.g., [29]), and different machine learning techniques have been used for selecting garbage collectors [39]. But unlike layout auditing, these approaches require offline training runs, and their benefits only become available by providing learned information to a second production run.

10   Conclusions

Layout auditing is an approach for picking the best among a set of data layouts by trying them and measuring their performance. It handles noise with a continuous feedback loop, and with a controller based on reinforcement learning. It smoothly adapts when program behavior changes over time. It controls its own profiling and exploration overheads by tuning them in the same way it tunes data layout decisions. This paper demonstrates that layout auditing achieves close to the best performance for all programs we tried it on, and avoids pathological worst cases that can happen with any statically chosen layout. Layout auditing successfully reevaluates its decisions after phase changes during program execution.

The trend towards multicore machines is likely to increase the importance of locality optimizations in the near future, as more CPUs compete for limited memory subsystem resources. At the same time, hardware complexity is on the rise, and the unpredictability of hardware behavior calls for approaches like layout auditing that optimize regardless of the detailed instruction-level behavior.

Acknowledgements. We thank Matthew Arnold, Jeremy Lau, Rodric Rabbah, Erik Altman, Priya Nagpurkar, and the anonymous reviewers for their feedback.

References

1. Abuaiadh, D., Ossia, Y., Petrank, E., Silbershtein, U.: An efficient parallel heap compaction algorithm. In: Object-Oriented Programming, Systems, Languages, and Applications (OOPSLA) (2004)
2. Adl-Tabatabai, A.-R., Hudson, R.L., Serrano, M.J., Subramoney, S.: Prefetch injection based on hardware monitoring and object metadata. In: Programming Language Design and Implementation (PLDI) (2004)
3. Arnold, M., Ryder, B.G.: A framework for reducing the cost of instrumented code. In: Programming Language Design and Implementation (PLDI) (2001)
4. Blackburn, S.M., Garner, R., Hoffman, C., Khan, A.M., McKinley, K.S., Bentzur, R., Diwan, A., Feinberg, D., Frampton, D., Guyer, S.Z., Hirzel, M., Hosking, A., Jump, M., Lee, H., Moss, J.E.B., Phansalkar, A., Stefanović, D., VanDrunen, T., von Dincklage, D., Wiedermann, B.: The DaCapo benchmarks: Java benchmarking development and analysis. In: Object-Oriented Programming, Systems, Languages, and Applications (OOPSLA) (2006)

5. Browne, S., Dongarra, J., Garner, N., London, K., Mucci, P.: A scalable cross-platform infrastructure for application performance tuning using hardware counters. In: IEEE SuperComputing (SC) (2000)
6. Chen, W.K., Bhansali, S., Chilimbi, T., Gao, X., Chuang, W.: Profile-guided proactive garbage collection for locality optimization. In: Programming Language Design and Implementation (PLDI) (2006)
7. Cheney, C.J.: A nonrecursive list compacting algorithm. Communications of the ACM (CACM) (1970)
8. Cheng, P., Blelloch, G.E.: A parallel, real-time garbage collector. In: Programming Language Design and Implementation (PLDI) (2001)
9. Chilimbi, T.M., Larus, J.R.: Using generational garbage collection to implement cache-conscious data placement. In: International Symposium on Memory Management (ISMM) (1998)
10. Courts, R.: Improving locality of reference in a garbage-collecting memory management system. Communications of the ACM (CACM) (1988)
11. Ding, C., Kennedy, K.: Improving cache performance in dynamic applications through data and computation reorganization at run time. In: Programming Language Design and Implementation (PLDI) (1999)
12. Diniz, P., Rinard, M.: Dynamic feedback: An effective technique for adaptive computing. In: Programming Language Design and Implementation (PLDI) (1997)
13. Fenichel, R.R., Yochelson, J.C.: A LISP garbage-collector for virtual-memory computer systems. Communications of the ACM (CACM) (1969)
14. Flood, C.H., Detlefs, D., Shavit, N., Zhang, X.: Parallel garbage collection for shared memory multiprocessors. In: Java Virtual Machine Research and Technology Symposium (JVM) (2001)
15. Fursin, G., Cohen, A., O'Boyle, M., Temam, O.: A practical method for quickly evaluating program optimizations. In: Conte, T., Navarro, N., Hwu, W.-m.W., Valero, M., Ungerer, T. (eds.) HiPEAC 2005. LNCS, vol. 3793. Springer, Heidelberg (2005)
16. Halstead Jr., R.H.: Multilisp: A language for concurrent symbolic computation. Transactions on Programming Languages and Systems (TOPLAS) (1985)
17. Hirzel, M.: Data layouts for object-oriented programs. In: Measurement and Modeling of Computer Systems (SIGMETRICS) (2007)
18. Hirzel, M., Chilimbi, T.M.: Bursty tracing: A framework for low-overhead temporal profiling. In: Feedback-Directed and Dynamic Optimizations (FDDO) (2001)
19. Hirzel, M., Diwan, A., Hertz, M.: Connectivity-based garbage collection. In: Object-Oriented Programming, Systems, Languages, and Applications (OOPSLA) (2003)
20. Huang, X., Blackburn, S.M., McKinley, K.S., Moss, J.E.B., Wang, Z., Cheng, P.: The garbage collection advantage: improving program locality. In: Object-Oriented Programming, Systems, Languages, and Applications (OOPSLA) (2004)
21. Ibrahim, A., Cook, W.R.: Automatic prefetching by traversal profiling in object persistence architectures. In: Thomas, D. (ed.) ECOOP 2006. LNCS, vol. 4067. Springer, Heidelberg (2006)
22. Imai, A., Tick, E.: Evaluation of parallel copying garbage collection on a shared-memory multiprocessor. IEEE Transactions on Parallel and Distributed Systems (1993)
23. Inagaki, T., Onodera, T., Komatsu, H., Nakatani, T.: Stride prefetching by dynamically inspecting objects. In: Programming Language Design and Implementation (PLDI) (2003)

24. Jones, R., Lins, R.: Garbage collection: Algorithms for automatic dynamic memory management. John Wiley, Chichester (1996)
25. Kermany, H., Petrank, E.: The Compressor: Concurrent, incremental, and parallel compaction. In: Programming Language Design and Implementation (PLDI) (2006)
26. Lau, J., Arnold, M., Hind, M., Calder, B.: Online performance auditing: Using hot optimizations without getting burned. In: Programming Language Design and Implementation (PLDI) (2006)
27. Lieberman, H., Hewitt, C.: A real-time garbage collector based on the lifetimes of objects. Communications of the ACM (CACM) (1983)
28. McGachey, P., Hosking, A.L.: Reducing generational copy reserve overhead with fallback compaction. In: International Symposium on Memory Management (ISMM) (2006)
29. McGovern, A., Moss, J.E.B., Barto, A.G.: Building a basic block instruction scheduler with reinforcement learning and rollouts. Machine Learning 49(2-3) (2002)
30. Moon, D.A.: Garbage collection in a large Lisp system. In: LISP and Functional Programming (LFP) (1984)
31. Nagpurkar, P., Hind, M., Krintz, C., Sweeney, P., Rajan, V.: Online phase detection algorithms. In: Code Generation and Optimization (CGO) (2006)
32. Petrank, E., Rawitz, D.: The hardness of cache conscious data placement. In: Principles of Programming Languages (POPL) (2002)
33. Robbins, H.E.: Some aspects of sequential design of experiments. Bulletin of the American Mathematical Society (58), 527–535 (1952)
34. Saavedra, R.H., Park, D.: Improving the effectiveness of software prefetching with adaptive execution. In: Parallel Architectures and Compilation Techniques (PACT) (1996)
35. Sherwood, T., Perelman, E., Calder, B.: Basic block distribution analysis to find periodic behavior and simulation points in applications. In: Malyshkin, V.E. (ed.) PACT 2001. LNCS, vol. 2127. Springer, Heidelberg (2001)
36. Shuf, Y., Gupta, M., Bordawekar, R., Singh, J.P.: Exploiting prolific types for memory management and optimizations. In: Principles of Programming Languages (POPL) (2002)
37. Shuf, Y., Gupta, M., Franke, H., Appel, A., Singh, J.P.: Creating and preserving locality of Java applications at allocation and garbage collection times. In: Object-Oriented Programming, Systems, Languages, and Applications (OOPSLA) (2002)
38. Siegwart, D., Hirzel, M.: Improving locality with parallel hierarchical copying GC. In: International Symposium on Memory Management (ISMM) (2006)
39. Singer, J., Brown, G., Watson, I., Cavazos, J.: Intelligent selection of application-specific garbage collectors. In: International Symposium on Memory Management (ISMM) (2007)
40. Soman, S., Krintz, C., Bacon, D.F.: Dynamic selection of application-specific garbage collectors. In: International Symposium on Memory Management (ISMM) (2004)
41. Sutton, R.S., Barto, A.G.: Reinforcement Learning: An Introduction. MIT Press, Cambridge (1998)
42. Ungar, D.: Generation scavenging: A non-disruptive high performance storage reclamation algorithm. In: Software Engineering Symposium on Practical Software Development Environments (SESPSDE) (1984)
43. Voss, M.J., Eigenmann, R.: High-level adaptive program optimization with ADAPT. In: Principles and Practice of Parallel Programming (PPoPP) (2001)

44. Wilson, P.R., Lam, M.S., Moher, T.G.: Effective "static-graph" reorganization to improve locality in a garbage-collected system. In: Conference on Programming Language Design and Implementation (PLDI) (1991)
45. Zhang, C., Ding, C., Ogihara, M., Zhong, Y., Wu, Y.: A hierarchical model of data locality. In: Principles of Programming Languages (POPL) (2006)
46. Zhang, L., Fang, Z., Parker, M., Mathew, B.K., Schaelicke, L., Carter, J.B., Hsieh, W.C., McKee, S.A.: The Impulse memory controller. IEEE Transactions on Computers (2001)
47. Zhang, W., Calder, B., Tullsen, D.M.: A self-repairing prefetcher in an event-driven dynamic optimization framework. In: Code Generation and Optimization (CGO) (2006)
48. Zhao, Q., Rabbah, R., Amarasinghe, S., Rudolph, L., Wong, W.-F.: Ubiquitous memory introspection. In: Code Generation and Optimization (CGO) (2007)

MTM^2: Scalable Memory Management for Multi-tasking Managed Runtime Environments

Sunil Soman[1], Chandra Krintz[1], and Laurent Daynès[2]

[1] Computer Science Department
University of California, Santa Barbara
{sunils,ckrintz}@cs.ucsb.edu
[2] Sun Microsystems Inc.
laurent.daynes@sun.com

Abstract. Multi-tasking, managed runtime environments (MREs) for modern type-safe, object-oriented programming languages enable isolated, concurrent execution of multiple applications within a single operating system process. Multi-tasking MREs can potentially extract high-performance on desktop and hand-held systems through aggressive sharing of classes and compiled code, and by exploiting high-level dynamic program information.

We investigate the performance of a state-of-the-art multi-taking MRE for *concurrent program execution*. We find that due to limited support for multi-tasking and performance isolation in the memory management subsystem, multi-tasking performs poorly compared to a production-quality, single-tasking MRE. We present MTM^2: a comprehensive memory management system for concurrent multi-tasking. MTM^2 facilitates performance isolation and efficient heap space usage through on-demand allocation of application-private regions. MTM^2 mitigates fragmentation using a novel hybrid garbage collector that combines mark-sweep with opportunistic copying. Our evaluation shows that MTM^2 improves overall performance, scalability, and footprint for concurrent workloads over state-of-the-art, multi- and single-tasking MREs.

1 Introduction

As desktop and hand-held platforms become more capable (faster multicore CPUs, larger memories, etc.), users increasingly expect more from the software they execute. In particular, users that once executed a single program at a time, now demand that these systems *multi-task*, i.e, seamlessly and simultaneously execute multiple applications (such as, instant messaging, calendar and email clients, audio player, Internet browsers, office suite, etc.). Concurrently, developers of these applications commonly employ high-level, type-safe, portable programming languages (e.g. Java^{TM} and the Microsoft .Net^{TM} languages) for their implementation, since these languages offer high programmer productivity, portability, rapid deployment, and support for verification of safety properties.

J. Vitek (Ed.): ECOOP 2008, LNCS 5142, pp. 335–361, 2008.
© Springer-Verlag Berlin Heidelberg 2008

Programs in these languages are encoded by a source compiler into an architecture neutral format that can be executed on any system with a managed runtime environment (MRE) for the format. To address both of these demands and to better utilize the underlying resources on modern desktops and hand-held systems, modern MREs have emerged with multi-tasking extensions [5,4,26,28].

Multi-tasking MREs address isolation and resource management for multi-application workloads and provide application developers with a first-class representation of an isolated program execution (e.g., the *isolate* in [15,5] and the *application domain* in *.Net* [19]). This representation provides the necessary functionality to launch and control the life cycle of multiple, isolated execution units (programs).

MREs have access to high-level program information, can potentially monitor time-varying program behavior and resource requirements, and can dynamically optimize programs as well as the runtime based on prior information. Therefore, they offer potential for more intelligent scheduling and resource management of programs. Prior work has shown that multi-tasking is more effective at enabling cross-program sharing of dynamically loaded and compiled code, and at achieving smaller memory footprint and faster startup times [4,6] than traditional MREs that rely on process-based isolation. Yet, little attention has been directed at the *performance of multi-tasking MREs for simultaneous program execution*, i.e., concurrent workloads, compared to a more common scenario in which each program runs in its own process.

Figure 1 shows the results from a set of experiments that we have conducted to compare MVM [4,26], a state-of-the art multi-tasking JVM from Sun Microsystems, with the single-tasking JVM (the Sun Microsystems HotSpot virtual machine version 1.5.0) from which the MVM is derived. The programs are a subset of the benchmarks that we use for our evaluation (that we describe in detail in Section 4) that exhibit significant garbage collection (GC) activity for the old generation (the longer-lived region). The figure shows that the MVM significantly degrades execution performance for concurrent workloads (2, 5, and 10 concurrent program instances in this graph), despite the significant opportunity for sharing (i.e. multiple versions of the same program are executing concurrently).

The MVM prototype that we use in this study is based on prior work [26] and achieves partial performance isolation across applications, reclamation of an application's heap memory upon task termination without having to perform GC, per-application accounting of heap usage, and per-application control of heap size settings. However, our results indicate that the prior state-of-the-art fails to perform favorably compared to its single-tasking counterpart for concurrent workloads that fully exercise the memory management system. The key impediment to scalability is the lack of GC performance isolation and a poorly performing full-heap GC algorithm.

To address these issues, we propose a novel memory management approach, which we call *multi-tasking memory manager (MTM^2)*. MTM^2 provides better GC performance isolation between programs while preserving other benefits

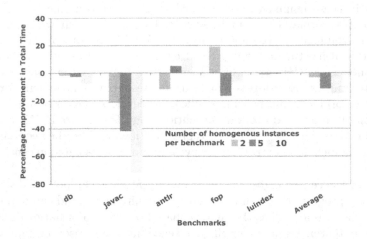

Fig. 1. Performance of a state-of-the-art multi-tasking MRE (MVM) versus multiple instances of the Java^{TM} HotSpot virtual machine for *concurrent* execution of five community benchmarks. No prior work has performed such an evaluation. Our analysis of MVM reveals that the key bottleneck to multi-tasking performance is memory management. MVM enables significant sharing and fewer OS processes, but this benefit does not outweigh the lack of performance isolation in the garbage collection subsystem.

of multi-tasking (small aggregate footprint, fast startup and sharing of classes and dynamically compiled code). MTM^2 is a generational GC system [29] that employs per-application young generation collection from [26] and introduces a novel *hybrid* approach to old generation collection that (i) maintains the constraint that all live objects within a region belong to the same application (which is key to GC isolation and the accuracy of tracking per-application heap usage), (ii) ensures that the aggregate footprint of the multi-tasking MRE is small for concurrent workloads, and (iii) enables space reclaimed through opportunistic evacuation of objects from sparsely populated regions of one program to be made available to other programs. To achieve these goals, MTM^2 performs full collection of a single program's heap in isolation with co-located concurrent programs by combining fast, space-efficient, mark-sweep collection for regions with little fragmentation, with copying collection for regions with significant garbage and fragmentation. MTM^2 combines and extends a large body of recent GC research [8,26,25,2,20] to facilitate scalability via hybrid collection of independent applications in a multi-tasking MRE.

We have integrated MTM^2 with a prototype of MVM described in [26], and have used it to compare the execution of multiple programs executed using a single multi-tasking MRE versus using multiple concurrent instances of single-tasking MREs (one per program). Two metrics are particularly interesting with respect to the scalability of the two approaches: the overall footprint when executing multiple programs, and the execution times of programs. We demonstrate that on average, MTM^2 achieves better overall execution times and footprint versus its single-tasking counterpart, for concurrent workloads using a number of community benchmarks. Moreover, MTM^2 is able to do so while maintaining the other benefits of running with a multi-tasking MRE. MTM^2 outperforms the HotSpot single-tasking MRE by up to 14% on average for concurrent instances of the same program (homogeneous), and by up to 16% on average for workloads with a mix of programs (heterogeneous). MTM^2 achieves up to 41% reduction in footprint on average for homogeneous workloads, and by up to 33% on average for heterogeneous workloads over the single-tasking MRE. Finally, we show that MTM^2 outperforms an extant state-of-the-art multi-tasking MRE by 10% to 22% for concurrent workloads.

In summary, we contribute the following:

- the first study that compares multi-instance JVM execution vs multi-tasking execution for concurrent program execution;
- a complete memory management system that provides full GC performance isolation for multi-tasking MREs;
- the design and implementation of a hybrid, multi-tasking aware GC that combines GC approaches that are well understood, i.e., mark-sweep and copying, to balance GC performance and memory footprint. Hybrid GC reuses reclaimed space across multiple isolated program executions; this design achieves footprint-aware memory management that facilitates runtime efficiency for concurrent workloads;
- an empirical evaluation that shows that multi-tasking MREs when equipped with appropriate mechanisms for GC performance isolation, compare favorably to single-tasking MREs with respect to footprint and program execution time for concurrent workloads. This result further strengthens the case for multi-tasking MREs.

In the sections that follow, we first detail the design and implementation of MTM^2. We then present our experimental framework and empirical results in Section 4. We compare and contrast related work in Section 5. Finally, we conclude with a summary of our findings and contributions in Section 6.

2   Multi-tasking Memory Management

MTM^2's design enables GC to be performed for a given application in isolation, and concurrently with respect to the mutators (threads modifying heap objects) of other applications.

MTM^2 follows the generational design [29] and each application is provided with a private two-generation heap. As with prior versions of MVM, a third generation, called the permanent generation, is shared across applications. The permanent generation is used to allocate long-lived meta-data, such as the runtime representation of classes (including method byte codes, constant pools, etc.), symbols and interned strings, and data structures of the MRE itself, all of which may be transparently shared across programs. The meta-data stored in the permanent generation may survive the execution of many programs, and is rarely collected.

The permanent generation is a single contiguous area. Memory for the young and old generations of applications originates from two pools of fixed-size regions managed by MTM^2. Each pool uses its own region size. The two pools and the shared permanent generation are contiguous in virtual space, such that old regions are in between the young regions pool and the permanent generation.

Memory for the young generation of a program is allocated at program startup, by provisioning a region from the young generation pool. Memory for a program's old generation is allocated on demand, on a per-region basis, from an *old region pool*. Thus, old and young generations are both made of one or more regions, that are possibly disjoint in virtual space. Regions are made of an integral number of operating system virtual pages and aligned to page boundaries to enable on-demand allocation/deallocation of the physical pages allocated to regions by the operating system[1]. Backing storage for the virtual pages of a region is allocated only upon allocation of the region to a program. Conversely, when a region is returned to the pool, the backing storage for its virtual memory pages is freed immediately.

A region can only contain objects allocated by the same program, i.e., a region is always private to a program. This constraint facilitates both tracking of program memory usage and instantaneous, GC-less, reclamation of space upon program-termination [26]. It also helps performance isolation since GC only needs to synchronize with the threads of a single application (instead of all applications).

Following standard generational GC practice, programs allocate primarily from their young generation. Threads of a program are each assigned a thread local allocation buffer (TLAB) [14,9,16] from the corresponding program's young generation. TLABs satisfy most allocation requests with a simple, non-atomic, increment of a pointer of the TLAB's allocation hand (bump-pointer).

Tracking of cross-generation references uses a card-marking scheme [3,12,11,1]. Old regions are card-aligned and consist of an integral number of cards, so that young generation collection of an application only needs to scan the dirty cards that correspond to the old regions allocated to the application. These are maintained by MTM^2 in a per-application list ordered by increasing virtual address. Each application is also associated with a *current* old region, which identifies the region used to allocate tenured space for the applications. Tenured space is allocated primarily during young generation collection, when promoting young objects, and occasionally, directly by mutator threads of the application to allocate space for large objects.

MTM^2 initiates a young generation collection for an application when the application's young generation is full, and an old generation collection when the application reaches its maximum heap size limit, or when allocation of a region from the pool of old region fails. Minor collection for an application is

---

[1] E.g., using map/unmap system calls on the Solaris^{TM} OS.

performed concurrently with respect to other applications using mechanisms described previously [26].

Collection of the old generation of an application's heap space follows a *hybrid* approach that combines fast, space-efficient, mark-sweep for regions of the old generation with little fragmentation or garbage, with a copying collection for regions of the old generation with either significant fragmentation or with a significant amount of garbage. Old generation collection is on a per-application basis, i.e., only the old generation of the application that triggers GC is collected.

MTM^2 also exploits MVM's representation of classes to organize the permanent generation in a way to limit tracing, during young and old generation collection, to objects of the application that initiated the collection (henceforth called the *GC initiator*). The MVM separates the application-dependent part of the runtime representation of classes from the rest of the class representation. When a class is sharable across applications, a *task table* is interposed between the class representation and its application-dependent part, the latter being allocated in the old generation of the corresponding application. The task table for a class has an entry for every application executing in the MRE, and each application is assigned, upon startup, a unique number (*the task identifier*) which is used to index these tables. The entry of a task table holds a reference to the object that holds the application-dependent part of the class when the application associated with that entry loads the class, or a null pointer otherwise [4]. Classes whose representation cannot be shared across programs (e.g., classes defined by program-defined class loaders) refer directly to the application-dependent part. All data structures that directly reference application-dependent data are clustered in a specific area of the permanent generation, which is the only area that needs to be traced during collection of younger generations. When an application does not use program-defined class loaders, tracing is limited to a single entry in every task table (the entry assigned to the GC trigger).

Other data-structures that reference application-dependent data (e.g., JNI Handles) are organized either in a per-application pool or in tables with one entry per application, similar to the task table. MTM^2 is aware of this organization and exploits it to *scan only those pools or table entries associated with the GC initiator*. Further, only stacks of threads of the GC initiator are scanned for roots.

3 MTM^2's Mark-Evacuate-Sweep Garbage Collector

Our experiments with prototypes of MVM suggest that efficient GC is key to making the concurrent execution of multiple programs using multi-tasking a viable alternative to running the same programs using one instance of a single-task MRE per application.

MTM^2's old generation design is constrained by the need to ensure that an old region contains only objects from the same application, for performance isolation, as well as for efficient and accurate tracking of heap resources. This implies that dead space within an old region allocated to an application cannot be reused by another application. This can potentially lead to significant fragmentation and substantially increase footprint for multi-tasking. Copying GC is effective at mitigating fragmentation, but at the cost of excessive copying of live objects, and the necessity of a copy reserve area. In place compaction requires multiple passes over the heap (although recent work has significantly optimized compaction [20]). Mark-sweep, however, is fast, and involves a single pass over live data, but may result in poor space utilization [17].

MTM^2 combines two relatively simple and well-understood techniques: mark-sweep and copying. We use copying to evacuate live objects from only those regions that are fragmented or are sparsely populated, and mark-sweep for the remaining regions. The goal is to maintain a low footprint, but without the overhead of copying of all live objects and a copy reserve for every GC. Space reclaimed via sweeping can only be used by the GC initiator, since the free space may be co-located with live data in the same region. Evacuated regions, on the other hand, can be returned to the old region pool where the backing storage for their virtual pages is freed until the regions are re-assigned to an application.

Candidate regions for evacuation are selected based on the amount of fragmentation the GC *is likely to cause* in the region. Before the collection begins, MTM^2 suspends all the threads of the GC initiator at a GC *safepoint*. The threads are restarted when GC completes.

The collection itself is performed in four phases: marking, selecting candidate regions for evacuation, evacuation (copying), and sweeping and adjustment of regions (performed in the same pass). The first two phases gather information (liveness, connectivity, occupancy, and estimated fragmentation) necessary for the last two phases. Evacuation and adjustment are optional, and occurs only if the second phase selects regions for evacuation.

Figure 2 illustrates with an example the main phases of MTM^2's hybrid collection. The following sub-sections detail each of the four phases.

3.1 Marking Phase

The marking phase begins a collection and produces two data structures as output: a *mark bitmap* that records live objects of the GC initiator; and a *connectivity matrix* that records connectivity information between old generation regions. Together, these are used to determine regions to evacuate, sweep and adjust.

Storage for the mark bitmap and the connectivity matrix is allocated for the duration of the hybrid GC cycle. The mark bitmap has one bit for every word of heap memory. Marking starts with the roots of live objects for the GC initiator: the stacks of the application's threads; the entry corresponding to the GC initiator in each task table for the runtime representation of shared classes in the permanent generation, and entries in global tables maintained by the multi-tasking MRE (such as JNI handles).

Marking then traverses the object graph from these roots. Because isolation is strictly enforced between applications through application-private regions, the marking phase will never access an object allocated by another application nor traverse a region allocated to another application.

The connectivity matrix is updated when a yet unmarked object is traversed. The matrix is encoded as a two-dimension boolean array, so that an entry (i, j) set to *true* indicates that there exists *at least* one reference from region i to region j. The matrix is initially zero-filled.

Testing whether each reference crosses a region boundary can be expensive. We have observed that inter region object references in the old generation are clustered, and that the distance between the referencing (source) object and the object being referenced (destination) in an old region is often small. Therefore, given an old region size that is large enough, the source and destination objects are likely to reside in the same region. If region size is a power of two, and regions are aligned, testing whether two addresses are in the same region can be inexpensively performed as follows [2]:

```
to == *from;
if (to ∧ from) >> LOG_REGION_SIZE) != 0 {
    // Not in the same region.
    update_connectivity_matrix(to,from);
}
```

When the test fails, a slow path is taken in order to update the connectivity matrix. The choice of an appropriate region size contributes to confine clusters of connected objects to a single region, which has two benefits: reducing the overhead of tracking inter-region connectivity (i.e., the fast path will be taken more often); and limiting the number of regions that needs to be inspected for potential pointer adjustment after regions are evacuated. We have empirically identified an old region size of 256KB that works well.

In summary, tracking of connectivity information helps to reduce the amount of live data that needs to be scanned during pointer adjustment if any region is evacuated.

3.2   Selecting Regions for Evacuation

The decision to evacuate a region attempts to balance the cost of evacuation (copying and pointer adjustment) and heap fragmentation (consequently, footprint). To maintain a low cost for evacuation we evacuate sparsely populated regions, while to maintain a low footprint, we evacuate regions with fragmentation.

That is, our evacuation policy evacuates a region unconditionally if the ratio of the live to dead space (*live ratio*) is less than a certain minimum live ratio (*MinLiveRatio*). The region is also evacuated if it is estimated to be fragmented. This is done by comparing the average size of each contiguous fragment of dead space to a threshold (*MinFragmentSize*). That is, given L, the amount of live

---

[2] This test for cross-region object references is similar to the test in the write barrier of the Beltway framework [2] except that, in our case, the test is performed at marking-time.

data in the region, F, the number of contiguous areas of dead objects in the region, and R the size of the region, a region is selected for evacuation if:

$$(L/R)<MinLiveRatio \vee ((L/R)<K \wedge (F>1) \wedge ((R{-}L)/F) < MinFragmentSize)$$

We empirically chose $MinLiveRatio$ to be 0.25, i.e., a region is always evacuated if it contains over 75% of garbage. When the pool of old regions is closed to exhaustion, this parameter is increased up to 0.9 to aggressively evacuate all but the almost full regions. K is the occupancy threshold and chosen to be 0.9, i.e., we look for fragmentation in regions that are at least 90% full. $MinFragmentSize$ is set to 50 bytes by default.

In order to realize this policy, MTM^2 needs to determine the ratio of live to dead data and the number of contiguous fragments of dead space in each region. This is done following the completion of the marking phase, by scanning the mark bitmap. For each region belonging to the GC initiator, MTM^2 walks over the region's objects, using the mark bitmap to determine their liveness and the objects' header to obtain their size. In addition, in this pass, adjacent dead objects are coalesced into a single dead area to reduce scanning time for future passes.

3.3   Evacuation, Sweeping and Adjustment of Old Regions

Live objects in regions selected for evacuation are relocated to new regions allocated from the old regions pool. Evacuation traverses the region being evacuated for live objects using the mark bitmap. Live objects are copied to the new region, and a forwarding pointer is installed in the header of the (old) copied object. Forwarding pointers are necessary for pointer adjustment. This, however, prevents the evacuated regions from being freed before adjustment is complete.

New regions used to store evacuated objects are added to the set of regions that need adjustment, i.e., we assume that the a region is likely to contain objects that point to other objects in the same region.

Once evacuation is complete, sweeping and adjustment of pointers can be performed in the same pass. For each region that was not evacuated, the mark bitmap corresponding to the region is used to build lists of live and free areas within the region. The connectivity matrix is also checked to determine if the region contains objects that reference objects in evacuated regions. If so, the live objects in the region are scanned to adjust references. Finally, the free and live lists of areas are combined into a list of live old generation areas used by the application. The live list is used to account for the old generation usage of the application, as well as during young generation collection to limit the amount of work that is done during card scanning, i.e., we only need to scan dirty cards that correspond to the application's list of old generation regions. The application's free list that was constructed during sweeping can only be used to satisfy allocation requests for that application (cf. Section 2).

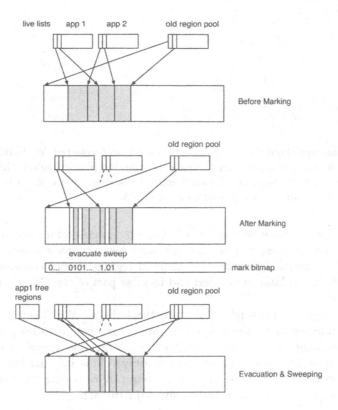

Fig. 2. Marking, Evacuation and Sweeping of Old Regions. Each application has a corresponding list of live areas. Marking traverses live objects for an application and marks live objects in the mark bitmap. After marking, candidate regions for evacuation (or sweeping) are selected based on the amount of live data and fragmentation. Regions selected for evacuation are then evacuated, regions selected for sweeping are swept and free areas in these added to a per-application free list. Pointer adjustment for swept regions is also performed during this pass, if necessary.

If any region is evacuated, in addition to adjustment of some old regions, we also need to adjust objects in the young generation of the application, the permanent generation, and outside the heap (globals) that reference objects in the evacuated region(s).

The young generation is typically small (the default is 2MB) and can therefore be scanned in its entirety without significant overhead. However, performing an object graph traversal beginning from the roots to identify globals and permanent generation pointers that need to be adjusted can be prohibitively expensive. Instead, we keep track of the locations of these pointers during the marking phase, and update them during pointer adjustment. The space overhead required to keep track of these locations is small, and is reported as part of the total footprint of MTM^2 in Section 4.

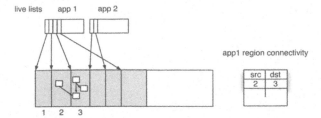

Fig. 3. Adjustment of old regions. Application 1 is being collected. We build the region connectivity matrix for application 1 during the marking phase. Region 2 has outgoing pointers to Region 3, therefore, Region 2 must be scanned if Region 3 is evacuated. However, Region 1 and 4 do not need to be scanned.

Once all regions have been adjusted, the evacuated regions are returned to the pool of free regions, and backing physical memory corresponding to their virtual address pages is unmapped, i.e., freed regions do not consume physical memory and can be later re-mapped and used as part of the old generations for *any* application.

Objects larger than a single region are treated specially. They are assigned an integral number of contiguous old regions large enough to hold the object. MTM^2 notes whether a region is part of a single large object region and whether that object contains no references (scalars only). This information is used to reclaim space when these large objects die (e.g., by returning their regions immediately to the pool, without waiting for adjustment).

4 Evaluation

The design of MTM^2 was motivated by the poor behavior of extant approaches to multi-tasking for concurrent application workloads, especially when compared to running the same concurrent workload using one instance of a single-tasking MRE per application as noted in Section 1.

In this section, we report our assessment of how well a multi-tasking MRE using MTM^2 fares when facing similar workloads. We first compare the performance of the most recent prototype of MVM (described in [26]) to that of an MVM modified to integrate MTM^2. We then compare MTM^2 to a single-tasking MRE. We use the Java^{TM} HotSpot virtual machine, version 1.5.0-03 [14], a production quality, high-performance virtual machine from Sun Microsystems (which we will refer to as HSVM from now on). Both MVM and MTM^2 derive their implementation from HSVM and share a significant amount of code, which facilitates comparison. MVM and MTM^2 differ only in their memory management sub-systems and modification to the runtime to achieve GC performance isolation. All other mechanisms to support multi-tasking and sharing of the runtime representation of classes, byte code and compiled code (see [4,5] for detailed descriptions) as well as other virtual machine implementation aspects inherited from HSVM are identical.

The main metrics of interest for our comparison are execution time and the aggregate memory footprint necessary to run concurrent workloads.

We begin with a description of our experimental setup, including hardware, benchmark, and methodology.

Benchmark	Description
compress	SpecJVM98 compression utility (input 100)
jess	SpecJVM98 expert system shell benchmark: Computes solutions to rule based puzzles (input 100)
db	SpecJVM98 database access program (input 100)
javac	SpecJVM98 Java to bytecode compiler (input 100)
mtrt	SpecJVM98 multi-threaded ray tracing implementation (input 100)
jack	SpecJVM98 Java parser generator based on the Purdue Compiler
antlr	Dacapo antlr: Parses grammar files and generates a parser and lexical analyzer for each (default input)
fop	Dacapo fop: XSL-FO to PDF parser/converter (default input)
luindex	Dacapo luindex: uses lucene to index the works of Shakespeare and the King James Bible (default input)
ps	Dacapo ps: Postscript interpreter (default input)
opengrok	Open source code browser and cross reference tool (input: Source files in HSVM "memory" subdirectory, 118 files)
jruby	Ruby interpreter written in Java (uses small scripts as input: beer song, fibonacci numbers, number parsing, thread test)
groovy	Groovy interpreter written in Java (input: unsigns, i.e., strips MANIFESTs) for a number of jar files from Apache ant)
antlr-mixed	mixed workload consisting of antlr, fop and opengrok
luindex-mixed	mixed workload consisting of luindex, fop and ps
javac-mixed	mixed workload consisting of javac, jess, mtrt and jack
scripts-mixed	mixed workload consisting of groovy and jruby

Fig. 4. Benchmarks and workloads used in the empirical evaluation of MTM^2

4.1   Experimental Methodology

We ran our experiments on a dedicated dual CPU 1.5GHz UltraSPARC IIIi system, with 2GB physical memory, 32KB instruction and 64KB data cache running the Solaris^{TM} Operating System version 10.

Figure 4 describes the benchmarks and workloads we used for our experiments.

Programs used in our concurrent workloads are selected from community programs from the SpecJVM98 [27] and Dacapo [7] benchmark suites [3], as well as two commonly used open-source scripting applications, jruby [18] and groovy [10], and an open-source source code browser and cross reference tool called opengrok [23]. We exclude *mpegaudio* from SpecJVM98 (as is commonly done) since it does not exercise the GC.

We experimented with two types of workloads: *homogeneous* and *heterogeneous*. A homogeneous workload consists of multiple concurrent instances of the same program. For instance, 10 instances of javac implies that 10 instances of this program are launched simultaneously. A heterogeneous workload consists of concurrent instances of different programs.

---

[3] We used version 2006-10-MR2 version of the Dacapo benchmarks, and ps from Dacapo version beta-05022004.

| Bmark | Number of instances | | | | | |
| | 2 | | 5 | | 10 | |
	Exec time (sec)	Footprint (MB)	Exec time (sec)	Footprint (MB)	Exec time (sec)	Footprint (MB)
compress	10.96	139.44	27.60	351.16	56.41	650.80
jess	4.93	19.82	12.33	33.18	24.54	55.12
db	20.84	35.95	52.50	74.05	105.10	141.00
javac	10.40	49.51	26.78	109.85	53.97	261.03
mtrt	3.39	20.46	8.47	62.27	16.24	114.26
jack	4.21	30.84	10.75	59.53	20.89	104.78
antlr	9.17	67.51	20.95	114.23	39.86	219.61
fop	6.00	51.84	14.31	87.45	28.53	148.49
luindex	40.08	76.68	89.45	173.35	169.42	333.43
ps	27.18	16.63	68.37	23.91	136.80	37.02
opengrok	10.44	101.50	25.40	230.85	51.35	429.77
groovy	10.15	138.06	21.54	366.63	50.92	544.25
jruby	2.58	34.80	5.66	49.67	10.67	73.47
Average	12.33	60.23	29.55	133.55	58.82	239.46

| Bmark | Number of instances | | | |
| | 1 | | 2 | |
	Exec time (sec)	Footprint (MB)	Exec time (sec)	Footprint (MB)
antlr-mixed	12.64	79.52	24.43	148.06
luindex-mixed	34.44	77.04	42.47	132.76
javac-mixed	13.28	31.97	23.58	63.57
scripts-mixed	8.28	68.68	11.30	118.95
Average	17.16	64.30	25.45	115.84

Fig. 5. Total execution time (in seconds) and footprint (in MB) data with MTM^2 for concurrent homogeneous (multiple instances of same application), and heterogeneous (multiple instances of different applications). The benchmarks are described in Figure 4. All relative performance improvement results for execution time as well footprint in this paper use these values.

We refer to the heterogeneous workload as *mixed* in Figure 4. We present results for 1 and 2 instances each of an application in a heterogeneous workload. For example, 2 instances each for antlr-mixed implies that we launch 2 instances each of antlr, fop and opengrok simultaneously, i.e., 6 concurrent instances.

We report total execution time by reporting the time elapsed since the applications in a workload were launched and until the last application completes. We use a harness that executes each application as an *isolate* [15] using reflection and we report total elapsed time using System.nanoTime(). To measure footprint, we use the UNIX pmap utility, which we execute as an external process in a tight loop and report the maximum of the total RSS (resident segment size) value reported by executing pmap -x on the MRE process. Footprint and execution times are reported using independent runs. In case of single-tasking, we sum the RSS values returned by pmap for each individual MRE process (since to execute concurrent workloads, we must launch a single-tasking MRE process for each application).

We perform all HSVM experiments using the *client* compiler and the default serial GC (sliding mark-compact) used for client configuration (i.e., using the -client -XX:+UseSerialGC command line flags). HSVM and MTM^2 both use copying GC for collecting the young generation. For all results, we present the average of 5 executions.

4.2 MTM^2 Versus MVM

We first present performance results that compare MTM^2 to MVM. MVM provides performance isolation for the young generation only, per-application resource accounting, and immediate, GC-less reclamation of heap space upon program termination. However, as seen earlier, this MVM performs poorly for concurrent workloads relative to executing the same concurrent workload with multiple instances of HSVM (cf Figure 1).

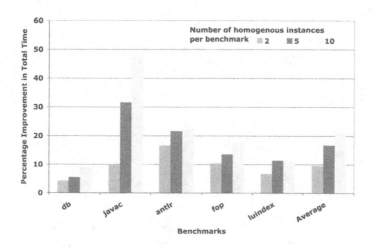

Fig. 6. Percentage improvement in execution time enabled by MTM^2 versus a state-of-the-art implementation of MVM for concurrent workloads that show significant old generation GC activity. MTM^2 enables better performance due to a more efficient old generation GC and performance isolation.

Figure 6 shows the performance improvement enabled by MTM^2 over this MVM. The results indicate that MTM^2 outperforms MVM by 10%, 15%, and 22% on average when running 2, 5, and 10 concurrent instances, respectively. For this experiment, we only present results for applications that show significant old generation GC activity. This performance improvement is possible due to the hybrid old generation GC in MTM^2 that enables performance isolation, as well as improved GC performance.

Figure 7 shows the old generation GC times for MTM^2 versus MVM. MTM^2's hybrid GC significantly improves GC performance over MVM. MVM uses a stop-the-world mark-compact GC for the old generation that performs three passes over the entire old generation (for all applications), with cost proportional to the size of the heap. With more concurrent instances, the cost of old generation GC in MVM increases.

	Number of instances								
	2			5			10		
Bmark	MVM (sec)	MTM^2 (sec)	% imp	MVM (sec)	MTM^2 (sec)	% imp	MVM (sec)	MTM^2 (sec)	% imp
db	0.57	0.28	**51.95**	2.92	0.70	**76.05**	5.47	1.38	**74.81**
javac	3.24	2.51	**22.47**	8.95	3.48	**61.06**	40.10	7.93	**80.23**
antlr	2.44	0.48	**80.17**	4.11	1.29	**68.69**	6.23	1.39	**77.75**
fop	1.18	0.67	**42.96**	2.29	1.11	**51.58**	4.98	2.54	**49.00**
luindex	4.27	1.51	**64.73**	8.36	2.86	**65.82**	14.35	8.24	**42.60**
Average	2.34	1.09	**52.46**	5.32	1.89	**64.64**	14.22	4.29	**64.88**

Fig. 7. Old generation GC times (total) for MTM^2 versus a prior state-of-the-art implementation of multi-tasking (MVM). GC times are presented in seconds along with percentage improvement in GC time enabled by MTM^2 vs MVM. MTM^2 's per-application hybrid old generation GC outperforms MVM's mark-compact old generation GC.

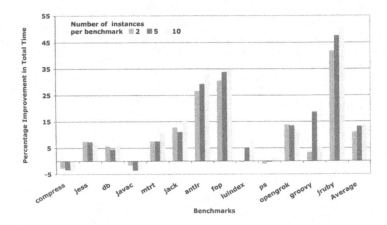

Fig. 8. Percentage improvement in execution time enabled by MTM^2 over HSVM (default initial heap size = max heap size = 64MB) for homogeneous concurrent workloads (multiple instances of the same application). Benchmarks are described in Figure 4.

In addition, unlike MVM, MTM^2 never pauses tasks to perform GC and all allocation and collection for any application is isolated with respect to other applications. MTM^2 scales better over MVM overall due to performance isolation as the number of instances is increased, as seen in Figure 6. The impact of performance isolation is especially evident in the case of javac. For instance, when 10 concurrent instances of javac execute, the total old generation GC time for MVM is about 40 seconds. The cost of old generation GC is higher since mark-compact GC needs to scan a larger heap in case of MVM. Further, since *all* applications are paused during old generation GC, MVM significantly degrades execution time for javac. In the case of *db* and *luindex*, GC time does not dominate total execution time, and consequently, the improvement enabled by MTM^2 versus MVM is less significant.

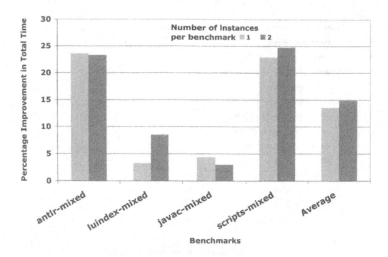

Fig. 9. Percentage improvement in execution time enabled by MTM^2 versus HSVM (default initial heap size = max heap size = 64MB) for heterogeneous concurrent workloads (multiple instances of different applications). Benchmarks are described in Figure 4.

4.3 MTM^2 Versus HSVM

We next compare the execution time and footprint of MTM^2 to HSVM. HSVM allows users to specify an initial heap size (32MB by default) and a maximum heap size (64MB by default) when launching an application. The initial heap size controls the heap limit, the point at which a full GC is triggered. The initial heap size grows (or shrinks) after a full GC, if required. For results in Figures 8, 9, 10, and 11, we set the initial heap size for HSVM equal to the maximum heap size. With this setting, HSVM performs less frequent GC and achieves better overall performance (total execution time), compared to when the initial heap size is at the default value. This setting allows single-tasking to perform at its best potential since the application heap is not restricted. We also present results for the other case, i.e., when the initial heap size for HSVM is not set to the maximum initially (the default behavior), thereby allowing HSVM to achieve a smaller footprint (Figures 14, 15, 12 and 13). MTM^2 does not restrict the initial heap size, or use a "soft limit" for applications, yet *we always ensure that we never exceed the maximum heap size setting for an application* (which is set to the HSVM default maximum heap size of 64MB in order to ensure a fair comparison).

Figure 8 shows percentage improvement in total execution time when homogeneous workloads are executed with MTM^2 versus the HSVM virtual machine, i.e., concurrent instances of the same application. We present results for 2, 5 and 10 concurrent instances for each application. Multi-tasking allows sharing of compiled code and classes between applications resulting in reduced overall execution time. MTM^2 enables an improvement of 11%, 13% and 14% for 2, 5

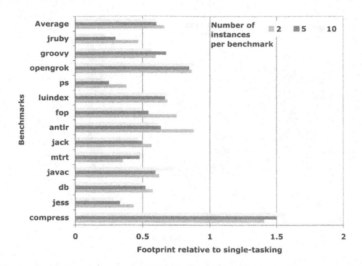

Fig. 10. Percentage improvement in footprint enabled by MTM^2 versus HSVM (default initial heap size = max heap size = 64MB) for homogeneous concurrent workloads (2, 5, and 10 instances of the same application).

and 10 concurrent applications on average for homogeneous workloads. MTM^2 allows complete application isolation and space reclaimed by evacuating old generation regions for an application to be reused by other applications. Scripting and parsing applications such as antlr and jruby are commonly used on desktop systems and particularly show a significant benefit due to sharing of compiled code.

For some applications, such as compress, javac and ps multi-tasking does not outperform single-tasking. For compress in particular, multi-tasking performance lags single tasking due to the fact that it allocate large objects (byte arrays) in the old generation which leads to fragmentation and worse GC performance in a shared old generation address space, and also due to the overhead due to a level of indirection to access static variables [4]. However, MTM^2 attempts to mitigate the adverse impact of fragmentation and achieves a significant benefit for these worst-case applications over the state-of-the-art multi-tasking MRE implementation, as shown earlier (cf Figure 6), while achieving performance that is close to the performance of these applications with single-tasking (within 3%). On average, MTM^2 significantly outperforms single-tasking.

Figure 9 shows the percentage improvement in total execution time for heterogeneous workloads, i.e., concurrent instances of different applications for 1 instances of each application, and 2 instances of each application for every heterogeneous workload (see Figure 4). For example, *antlr-mixed* with two instances indicates that 2 instances each of antlr, fop, opengrok are executed concurrently (6 concurrent applications). On average, MTM^2 improves performance by up to 16%, with improvements ranging from 3% to 25% in individual cases. As seen earlier, scripting workloads in particular perform very well with multi-tasking.

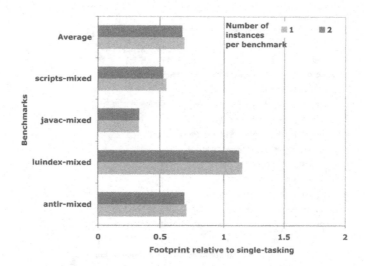

Fig. 11. Percentage improvement in footprint enabled by MTM^2 versus HSVM (default initial heap size = max heap size = 64MB) for heterogeneous concurrent workloads. 1 denotes 1 instance each of the mix of applications that constitute a heterogeneous workload. 2 indicates 2 instances of each application in the mix.

Figures 10 and 11 compare the total process footprint for MTM^2 versus HSVM for the same set of applications as in the previous figures. Each bar represents the ratio of the footprint for MTM^2 versus HSVM. The value 1 indicates that MTM^2 and HSVM have identical footprint for a given workload. Values less than 1 indicate that MTM^2 has a lower footprint.

MTM^2 shows a better footprint compared to HSVM and on average, MTM^2 achieves 34% to 41% reduction in footprint for homogeneous workloads, and 31% to 33% benefit for heterogeneous workloads. These savings are possible due to sharing of classes and compiled code in a multi-tasking MRE.

However, `compress` shows worse footprint (around 50% or 1.5x). The worse footprint for `compress` can be attributed to large scalar objects (objects that do not hold references, such as byte arrays). As noted earlier, `compress` allocates a significant number of large byte arrays which are directly allocated in the old generation. Since our old generation is non-contiguous, and since we allocate large scalar objects in a separate region, which we can safely skip during pointer adjustment, allocation of very large (> minimum region size, which is 256KB by default), byte arrays leads to excess fragmentation. A new region needs to be allocated for each such large byte array, and this region needs to be aligned to the region boundary for correctness. However, the number and size of these is unknown at runtime, without a priori profiling. Therefore, we cannot preallocate a suitable sized region. As part of future work, we plan to address the allocation of large objects, by providing a per-application large object region that is sized differently and collected separately from the old generation. Note

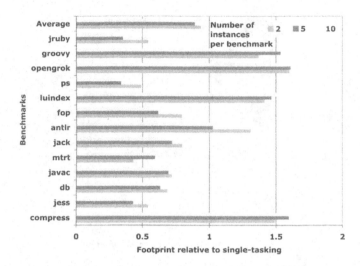

Fig. 12. Percentage improvement in footprint enabled by MTM^2 versus HSVM (default initial heap size = 32MB) for homogeneous concurrent workloads (2, 5, and 10 instances of the same application)

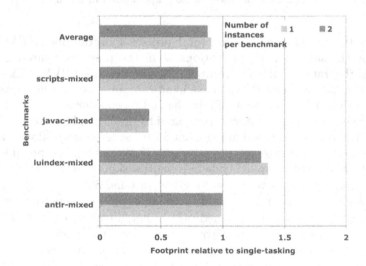

Fig. 13. Percentage improvement in footprint enabled by MTM^2 versus HSVM (default initial heap size = 32MB), heterogeneous workloads, i.e., multiple concurrent instances of different applications. 1 denotes 1 instance each of the mix of applications that constitute a heterogeneous workload. 2 indicates 2 instances of each application in the mix.

that **compress** is a numerical computation benchmark and does not represent typical MRE workloads.

Figures 12 and 13 compare the process footprint for MTM^2 versus HSVM, when the initial heap size for HSVM is restricted and increased gradually. In this

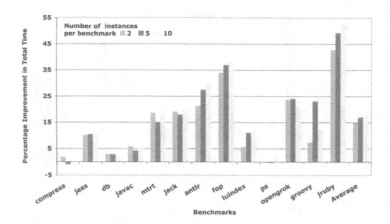

Fig. 14. Percentage improvement in execution time enabled by MTM^2 versus HSVM (default initial heap size = 32MB) homogeneous concurrent workloads. Benchmarks are described in Figure 4.

configuration, HSVM gradually increases the heap (if required), starting from an initial default (32MB), in order to achieve smaller footprint. As expected, HSVM runs in a much smaller heap and consequently, the process footprint is lower. On average, MTM^2 shows a footprint improvement of 6% to 14% for homogeneous workloads, and 12% to around 15% for heterogeneous workloads. Note that these values are smaller compared to the earlier configuration of HSVM, i.e. when the initial heap size for HSVM is not restricted. However, if we look at the execution time for MTM^2 versus HSVM (Figures 14 and 15) when the initial heap size for HSVM is restricted, MTM^2 outperforms HSVM by a *greater margin* than when we do not restrict the initial heap size for HSVM. On average, MTM^2 shows an improvement of 15% to over 17% for homogeneous workloads, and 19% to 21% for heterogeneous workloads.

In summary, by controlling heap growth the single-tasking HSVM virtual machine can achieve a better footprint when the heap is not restricted, however, MTM^2 shows a comparable or better footprint on average across concurrent workloads that we looked at. Further, MTM^2 outperforms HSVM by a larger margin, since there is a reduction in performance for the single-tasking MRE due to more frequent GC. There exists a tradeoff between execution time and footprint by choosing the threshold at which GC is triggered. We believe that manually having to select an appropriate per-application heap size in a context of a multi-tasking VM is counter-productive. On average, MTM^2 significantly outperforms HSVM and has a better footprint without having to manually select an appropriate initial per-application heap size.

We next examine the performance of MTM^2 versus HSVM as the heapsize is varied from the minimum that an application requires to execute in MTM^2, to 4 times the minimum for that application (Figure 16). We only consider benchmarks that show significant old generation GC activity. The minimum

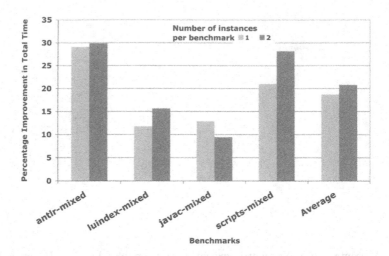

Fig. 15. Percentage improvement in execution time enabled by MTM^2 versus HSVM (default initial heap size = 32MB) for heterogeneous concurrent workloads (multiple instances of different applications). Benchmarks are described in Figure 4.

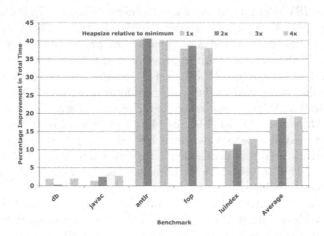

Fig. 16. Percentage improvement in execution time enabled by MTM^2 over HSVM for 1 through 4 times the minimum heap size that each benchmark needs to execute in MTM^2.

heap size selected is 45MB for `luindex` and 22MB for the rest. Across heap sizes, MTM^2 outperforms HSVM by 18 – 19% on average.

However, HSVM is able to execute programs in a smaller heap compared to MTM^2 (i.e., < 45MB for `luindex` and < 22MB for other benchmarks). HSVM uses in-place sliding compacting GC, which is more space efficient than MTM^2's hybrid GC for small heaps. This is due to the fact that evacuation, although it is partial and selective, requires a copy reserve for the duration of the GC to copy live objects. For highly memory constrained scenarios, HSVM's GC may be a

Bmark	Number of instances														
	2					5					10				
				% imp vs					% imp vs					% imp vs	
	MTM² (KB)	MTM² MS (KB)	MTM² CP (KB)	MS	CP	MTM² (KB)	MTM² MS (KB)	MTM² CP (KB)	MS	CP	MTM² (KB)	MTM² MS (KB)	MTM² CP (KB)	MS	CP
javac	49.5	127.7	65.4	**61.2**	**24.3**	109.9	297.5	117.7	**63.1**	**6.6**	261.0	602.1	261.7	**56.6**	**0.3**
luindex	76.7	128.4	83.5	**40.3**	**8.2**	173.4	302.9	182.0	**42.8**	**4.7**	333.4	589.5	351.9	**43.4**	**5.2**

Bmark	Number of instances									
	1					2				
				% imp vs					% imp vs	
	MTM² (KB)	MTM² MS (KB)	MTM² CP (KB)	MS	CP	MTM² (KB)	MTM² MS (KB)	MTM² CP (KB)	MS	CP
antir-mixed	79.5	86.1	80.6	**7.6**	**1.3**	148.1	156.6	148.2	**5.5**	**0.1**
javac-mixed	32.0	51.9	41.6	**38.4**	**23.2**	63.6	91.3	87.5	**30.4**	**27.4**
scripts-mixed	68.7	94.8	104.5	**27.5**	**34.3**	119.0	127.0	140.3	**6.4**	**15.2**

Fig. 17. Footprint for MTM^2 with hybrid GC (mix of mark-sweep and copying) versus mark-sweep (MS) only and copying GC (CP) only for a set of homogeneous (instances of the same application) and heterogeneous (different applications) concurrent workloads. Hybrid GC achieves a footprint that is lower than always choosing mark-sweep or always choosing copying.

more suitable choice compared to evacuation. We are investigating mechanisms to perform in-place compaction across disjoint regions as part of future work.

4.4 Sensitivity Analysis

In the next set of results, we examine how MTM^2 with selective evacuation (copying) and mark-sweep compares to only mark-sweep and only copying. Our hybrid GC can operate as a mark-sweep only GC (by setting the $MinLiveRatio$ threshold described in Section 3 to 0), or as a copying only GC (by setting the $MinLiveRatio$ threshold to 1, i.e., 100%).

In particular, in Figure 17 we present total process footprint for MTM^2 with hybrid GC versus MTM^2 with mark-sweep only, and MTM^2 with copying only, for a subset of benchmark programs. We only present results for benchmarks that show significant change in footprint compared to either mark-sweep or copying ($> 5\%$). For all other benchmarks, we did not find a significant change in the footprint (however, MTM^2 with hybrid GC never shows a worse footprint compared to either mark-sweep or copying).

For javac, luindex, javac-mixed and scripts-mixed, hybrid GC has a much smaller footprint compared to mark-sweep. We believe this is due to fragmentation due to using mark-sweep only without any compaction. For javac-mixed and scripts-mixed, copying has a higher footprint, since always copying all live data requires a larger copy reserve space during GC. While performing evacuation, the old as well as the new (copied to) regions need to be occupied (mapped) for the duration of the GC cycle.

We next examine the effect of using hybrid GC, mark-sweep only, and copying only, on execution time for javac, which shows a significant difference in performance (Figure 18). Using mark-sweep only results in excess fragmentation. Fragmentation has an interesting effect on execution time for javac – an increase in young generation GC time by 8% on average (or 0.51 sec, 0.66 sec and 1.17 sec for 2, 5 and 10 instances respectively) due to an increase in card scanning time, since more cards need to be scanned. Using copying alone results in excess copying and adjustment, and consequently, performance suffers due to an increase in old generation GC time by around 6% (or 0.07 sec, 0.16 sec and 0.70 sec for 2, 5 and 10 instances respectively).

	Number of instances														
		2		% imp vs			5		% imp vs			10		% imp vs	
Bmark	MTM^2 (sec)	MTM^2 MS (sec)	MTM^2 CP (sec)	MS	CP	MTM^2 (sec)	MTM^2 MS (sec)	MTM^2 CP (sec)	MS	CP	MTM^2 (sec)	MTM^2 MS (sec)	MTM^2 CP (sec)	MS	CP
javac	10.40	10.82	10.57	**3.9**	**1.6**	26.78	28.14	27.29	**4.8**	**1.9**	53.97	56.48	55.25	**4.4**	**2.3**

Fig. 18. Execution time MTM^2 with hybrid GC (mix of mark-sweep and copying) versus mark-sweep (MS) only and copying GC (CP) only for the javac benchmark

For other benchmarks, we did not encounter a significant change in execution time (however, in all cases, hybrid GC never performs worse than using mark-sweep or copying alone).

To summarize, hybrid GC achieves a lower footprint in many cases for benchmarks that show significant old generation GC activity, while maintaining performance that is on-par or better than using mark-sweep or copying alone.

5 Related Work

Our work relates directly to other multi-tasking implementations of MREs. To our knowledge, no prior work conclusively demonstrates that multi-tasking has the ability to outperform a single-tasking MRE in terms of execution time, as well as overall footprint for concurrent workloads (multiple applications executing simultaneously). MVM is the most well-known, state-of-the-art implementation of a multi-tasking MRE. Prior work on MVM reports substantial improvement for startup, footprint and execution time compare to a corresponding single-tasking JVM [4,5]. However, execution times were measured for serial execution of programs, and footprint of concurrently running programs were obtained when applications were quiescent, and do not reflect the footprint of programs when they are actually running concurrently and are exercising the memory management system. Recent attempts at improving GC performance isolation for MVM [26] only address young generation GC and GC-less instantaneous reclamation of the heap space of terminated programs, and demonstrates only provision of performance isolation for short-lived programs that do not stress the GC. Sun Microsystems' CLDC HotSpot Implementation, aimed at small hand-held devices, supports multi-tasking in a way that is similar to MVM, but uses a single heap shared by all tasks [28], with no provision for GC performance isolation. We were not able to find any information about GC performance isolation for .NET application domains.

Our work also builds upon and extends a large body of important contributions to memory management for single-tasking MREs.

Our hybrid GC bears some similitude to incremental copying GCs that divide the heap into equally sized regions that can be evacuated independently of others. In our case, heap space partitioning is primarily motivated by the need to allocate private tenured space to isolated applications on demand. Like our hybrid GC, Garbage First [8] only evacuates regions that can be reclaimed with little copying. Information regarding the amount of live data in regions is provided by a concurrent marker (as opposed to a synchronous marking phase in our case). Bidirectional remembered sets between regions are maintained by mutators (with help from the concurrent marker) to allow any set of regions to be collected independently of the others. In the case of our hybrid GC, this property is achieved by gathering cross-regions connectivity information during marking. The Mature Object Space (MOS) collector of Hudson and Moss [13] is another region-based incremental copying GC. It uses unidirectional remembered sets, which requires regions to be evacuated in order. MOS cannot therefore pick an arbitrary region to evacuate based on cost-related criteria (e.g., amount of live data). Both Garbage First and MOS are evacuation-only GC.

Lang and Dupont [21] describes a hybrid mark-sweep and copy similar to ours. The heap is divided into equal size segments. During GC, a single segment is compacted, while others are swept. Like our hybrid mark-sweep-evacuate GC, the collector is primarily mark-sweep. The cost of compaction is bounded since a single segment is collected. However, the segment compacted at each GC is chosen arbitrarily. By contrast, we use copying opportunistically, only to evacuate sparsely populated regions or highly fragmented one. We may thus evacuate several regions during a single GC, or none if the regions are densely populated with little fragmentation.

MC^2 [25] and its predecessor, Mark-Copy [24] describe an incremental copying GC that uses a marking phase to precisely annotate equal size regions of the old generation of the heap with the amount of live data in them, like our GC, and then build uni-directional remembered set to update pointers to evacuated objects. MC^2 builds precise remembered sets, whereas we build an imprecise connectivity matrix that only records regions that references other regions. MC^2 aims at achieving good throughput and low pause times for memory constrained devices.

Beltway [2] provides incremental and generational GC by partitioning the heap into *belts* and collecting a single belt during GC. Garbage cycles larger than a belt cannot be reclaimed by collecting a single belt. However, Beltway has a provision for performing full GC by providing a separate belt with a single region and collecting this when it occupies half the heap space. Our per-application GC is complete and reclaims all garbage for that application. We, therefore, do not require precise remembered sets between regions or need mechanisms to ensure completeness.

McGachey et al [22] present a scheme that uses a generational GC with a reduced copy reserve, with the ability to dynamically switch to a compacting GC if necessary.

Page unmapping as well as compaction has been used to reduce application memory footprint in prior work, such as the Compressor [20]. However, Compressor is a concurrent, parallel compacting GC that achieves low pause times. Our goal is different: to provide a relative simple, per-application GC that achieves good footprint and overall performance for desktop or small client applications, while allowing other applications to execute concurrently, without interference.

6 Conclusion

Multi-tasking has been proposed as a means to enable sharing of code and classes between applications in order to enable better startup performance, footprint and for faster overall execution compared to single-tasking, i.e., executing each application in a separate MRE process. While prior implementations of multi-tasking have demonstrated the above for serial execution of programs, and for execution of multiple programs with little simultaneous activity, we show that the prior state-of-the-art performs poorly for concurrent workloads. We attribute this to lack of performance isolation and a poor performing garbage collector for full garbage collection (GC).

We have described MTM^2, a scalable approach to memory management for multi-tasking managed runtime environments. MTM^2 enables complete performance isolation with respect to GC, provides each application with a private heap, and employs generational GC with a hybrid GC for old generation collection. MTM^2's hybrid GC combines mark-sweep with copying collection in the same GC cycle along with fast adjustment for copied objects, to achieve good performance and a low footprint while avoiding the overhead of full copying GC. The hybrid GC uses marking to gather information (liveness, connectivity, occupancy, and estimated fragmentation) necessary to determine regions of the old generation to evacuate (if any) and to sweep and to identify which regions need to be scanned for pointer adjustment.

We have integrated MTM^2 with MVM, a multi-tasking implementation of the JVM, and a compare it to a widely used, production-quality, single-tasking MRE for concurrent application workloads. Our results show that MTM^2 enables significant performance, as well as footprint improvement compared to single-tasking for concurrent workloads. MTM^2 outperforms single-tasking by up to 14% on average for homogeneous workloads (instances of the same application) and up to 16% on average for heterogeneous workloads (mix of different applications). MTM^2 achieves up to 41% reduction in footprint on average for homogeneous workloads, and up to 33% on average improvement for heterogeneous workloads over single-tasking. In addition, MTM^2 achieves better performance for concurrent workloads over the extant state-of-the-art multi-tasking implementation, outperforming it by 10% to 22%. These results indicate that multi-tasking is a viable approach for executing concurrent applications and strengthens the case for multi-tasking MREs.

Trademarks

Sun, Sun Microsystems, Inc., Java, JVM, HotSpot, and Solaris are trademarks or registered trademarks of Sun Microsystems, Inc., in the United States and other countries. SPARC and UltraSPARC are trademarks or registered trademarks of SPARC International, Inc., in the United States and other countries.

References

1. Blackburn, S., McKinley, K.: In or Out? Putting Write Barriers in Their Place. In: International Symposium on Memory Management (ISMM) (2002)
2. Blackburn, S.M., Jones, R., McKinley, K.S., Moss, J.E.B.: Beltway: Getting around garbage collection gridlock. In: Conference on Programming Language Design and Implementation (June 2002)
3. Chambers, C.: The Design and Implementation of the SELF Compiler, an Optimizing Compiler for an Objected-Oriented Programming Language. PhD thesis, Stanford University (March 1992)
4. Czajkowski, G., Daynès, L.: Multitasking without Compromise: A Virtual Machine Evolution. In: Conference on Object-Oriented Programming, Systems, Languages, and Applications (OOPSLA) (October 2001)
5. Czajkowski, G., Daynès, L.: A Multi-User Virtual Machine. In: USENIX 2003 Annual Technical Conference (June 2003)
6. Czajkowski, G., Daynès, L., Nystrom, N.: Code Sharing among Virtual Machines. In: European Conference on Object-Oriented Programming (ECOOP) (June 2002)
7. The Dacapo Benchmark Suite, version beta050224, http://www-ali.cs.umass.edu/DaCapo/gcbm.html
8. Detlefs, D., Flood, C., Heller, S., Printezis, T.: Garbage-First Garbage Collection. In: International Symposium on Memory Management (ISMM) (October 2004)
9. Garthwaite, A., Dice, D., White, D.: Supporting per-processor local-allocation buffers using lightweight user-level preemption notification. In: First International Conference on Virtual Execution Environments (June 2005)
10. Groovy: An agile dynamic language for the Java Platform, http://groovy.codehaus.org/
11. Hölzle, U.: A Fast Write Barrier for Generational Garbage Collectors. In: OOPSLA/ECOOP Workshop on Garbage Collection in Object-Oriented Systems (October 1993)
12. Hosking, A.L., Moss, J.E.B., Stefanović, D.: A Comparative Performance Evaluation of Write Barrier Implementations. In: Conference on Object-Oriented Programming, Systems, Languages, and Applications (OOPSLA) (October 1992)
13. Hudson, R.L., Moss, J.E.B.: Incremental Garbage Collection for Mature Objects. In: International Workshop on Memory Management (IWMM) (1992)
14. Sun Microsystems Inc.: The Java Hotspot Virtual Machine white paper, http://java.sun.com/products/hotspot/docs/whitepaper/Java_HotSpot_WP_Final_4_30_01.html

15. Java Community Process. JSR-121: Application Isolation API Specification, http://jcp.org/jsr/detail/121.jsp
16. Jones, R., King, A.C.: A Fast Analysis for Thread-Local Garbage Collection with Dynamic Class Loading. In: Fifth International Workshop on Source Code Analysis and Manipulation (SCAM 2005) (2005)
17. Jones, R.E., Lins, R.: Garbage Collection: Algorithms for Automatic Dynamic Memory Management, July 1996. Wiley, Chichester (1996)
18. JRuby: Java powered Ruby implementation, http://jruby.codehaus.org/
19. Kennedy, A., Syme, D.: Combining generics, pre-compilation and sharing between software-based processes. In: Proceedings of the Second Workshop on Semantics, Program Analysis and Computing Environments for Memory Management (SPACE 2001) (2001)
20. Kermany, H., Petrank, E.: The Compressor: concurrent, incremental, and parallel compaction. Proceedings of the, ACM SIGPLAN conference on Programming language design and implementation (2006)
21. Lang, B., Dupont, F.: Incremental Incrementally Compacting Garbage Collection. In: Symposium on Interpreters and Interpretive Techniques (1987)
22. McGachey, P., Hosking, A.L.: Reducing Generational Copy Reserve Overhead with Fallback Compaction. In: International Symposium on Memory Management (ISMM) (June 2006)
23. OpenSolaris Project: OpenGrok. http://opensolaris.org/os/project/opengrok/
24. Sachindran, N., Eliot, J., Moss, B.: Mark-copy: Fast Copying GC with less Space Overhead. In: Conference on Object-Oriented Programming, Systems, Languages, and Applications (OOPSLA) (October 2003)
25. Sachindran, N., Eliot, J., Moss, B.: MC^2: high-performance garbage collection for memory-constrained environments. In: Conference on Object-Oriented Programming, Systems, Languages, and Applications (OOPSLA) (October 2004)
26. Soman, S., Daynès, L., Krintz, C.: Task-Aware Garbage Collection in a Multi-Tasking Virtual Machine. In: International Symposium on Memory Management (ISMM) (June 2006)
27. SpecJVM'98 Benchmarks, http://www.spec.org/osg/jvm98
28. Sun Microsystems Inc. CLDC HotSpot^{TM} Implementation, http://java.sun.com/javame/reference/docs/cldc-hi-2.0-web/
29. Ungar, D.: Generation Scavenging: A Non-disruptive High Performance Storage Recalamation Algorithm. In: Software Engineering Symposium on Practical Software Development Environments (April 1992)

Externalizing Java Server Concurrency with CAL

Charles Zhang[1] and Hans-Arno Jacobsen[2]

[1] Department of Computer Science and Engineering
The Hong Kong University of Science and Technology
charlesz@cse.ust.hk

[2] Department of Electrical and Computer Engineering
and Department of Computer Science
University of Toronto
jacobsen@eecg.toronto.edu

Abstract. One of the most important design decisions about a server program is regarding its concurrency mechanisms. However, good concurrency models for general-purpose server programs are increasingly difficult to conceive as the runtime conditions are hard to predict. In this work, we advocate that the concurrency code is to be decoupled from server programs. To enable such separation, we propose and evaluate CAL, — the Concurrency Aspect Library. CAL provides uniform concurrency programming abstractions and mediates the intrinsic differences among concurrency models. Through CAL, a server program is not tied to any particular concurrency model and framework. CAL can be configured without modifications to use concurrency frameworks of fundamentally different natures. The concurrency code based on CAL is simpler and looks closer to the design. Leveraging the customizability of CAL, we show that a commercial middleware server, refactored to use CAL, outperforms its original version by as much as 10 times.

1 Introduction

A common definition of concurrency is the perceived simultaneous executions of multiple sets of program instructions within the same address space. Concurrency mechanisms, particularly in relation to I/O, are vital to the functionality of today's general-purpose server programs, such as databases, web servers, application servers, and middleware systems. Since the trend of multi-core architectures no longer focuses on the clock speed, server programs increasingly rely on concurrency for performance improvements. The current research on the design of concurrency models is characterized by the pattern-based concurrency designs [2,18,20,21]. These approaches primarily focus on achieving high, scalable and fair server throughput, assuming specific runtime conditions such as hardware concurrency capabilities and characteristics of incoming requests. As the nature of today's network-based applications continues to diversify, such concurrency models will become increasingly hard, if not completely impossible, to design due to the difficulties in predicting the runtime conditions for general

J. Vitek (Ed.): ECOOP 2008, LNCS 5142, pp. 362–386, 2008.

purpose server programs. Let us first exemplify this problem through a simple design exercise.

The goal of our design exercise is to allow a simple server program, presented in Figure 1(A), to provide a generic upload service to simultaneously connected clients. Despite its simplicity, the server performs some of the typical operations of Java server programs: binding to a server-side socket and waiting for incoming connections (Line 9), decoding the application frame from the incoming socket (Line 4), and processing the received frame such as storing it in a database (Line 5). This server, as shown, can only serve one client for the duration of request processing.

```
  class Server{
2     public boolean dispatch(Socket s){
          InputStream in = s.getInputStream();
4         Frame buf = decodeData(in);
          database.store(buf);
6     }

8     public void start(){
          socket = serverSocket.accept();
10        dispatch(socket);
      }
12 }
```

```
class Server{
2  ... ...
   public void start(){
4      socket = serverSocket.accept();
       new Thread(new Runnable(){
6        public void run(){
             dispatch(socket);
8        }
       };
10     }
}
```

Fig. 1. (A) Upload server (B) Thread-per-connection

First solution. Our first attempt is to implement the "thread-per-connection" concurrency model (Figure 1(B)), common in tutorials, textbooks, and industrial practices. We evaluate our improved design through quantifying the server throughput measured as number of processed requests per unit time[1]. In Figure 3, we plot the number of frames received by the server within a fixed duration against the number of concurrent clients. We measure two types of client/server connections: *long*, i.e., the clients keep their connections alive for the entire duration (upload(L)); and *short*, i.e., the clients repeatedly connect to the server, send a piece of data, and disconnect (upload(S)). Figure 3(A) shows that our solution works well as the server throughput only degrades around 20% to 30% for both types of connections even for a high number of clients. We now introduce an evolutionary change to the example server by adding a new service: factorizing big integers, as illustrated in Figure 2(A). The measurements for this new service are plotted in Figure 3(A) with labels factor(L) and factor(S). We immediately observe that, when the number of concurrent clients gets large (> 1000), the throughput of the constant connections (factor(L)) degrades as much as 90%, and the periodic connections also suffers from significant throughput oscillations. Seasoned concurrency programmers can quickly point out that the use of Java threads in our factor server does not scale to the large

---

[1] We also measure the fairness of the services. However, for motivation purposes here we omit the relevant discussions. We come back to the fairness issue in Section 4.

```
   class Server{                              public void start(){
2     public boolean dispatch(Socket s){    2     final SocketChannel channel = ssc_.accept();
         InputStream in = s.getInputStream();        channel.configureBlocking(false);
4        Frame buf = decodeData(in);        4     /* notify me if data are ready on channel*/
         switch(buf.jobtype){                      final SelectionKey key = channel.register(
6           case CPUJOB:                      6        reactor.getSelector(), SelectionKey.OP_READ);
              factor.doFactorization(buf);          class Handler implements IAsyncWorker{
8           break;                            8        public void doAsyncWork() {
            case IOJOB:                                  dispatch(channel);
10            database.store(buf);           10        }
            break;                                 }
12       }                                   12   /* reactor executes the handler if the READ
         return true;                               * event is fired */
14    }                                      14   reactor.registerWorker(key, new Handler());
   }                                            }
                                             16
```

Fig. 2. (A) Evolved server (B) Reactor-based event multiplexing

number of concurrent clients due to contention of the CPU resources between the thread-level context switches and the factorization work itself.

Modified solution. The availability of asynchronous I/O in the Java platform allows concurrency to be supported using the event multiplexing model, hence, avoiding the thread-level context switches. Figure 2(B) illustrates a modified implementation of the server using the *Reactor* [18] design pattern, in which each incoming connection is registered with a key (Line 5). The key is used by the reactor (Line 16) to invoke the corresponding handler when data from the network is ready to be processed. The stream-based sockets are also replaced by the channel-based counterparts. Figure 3(B) plots the measurements for the reactor-based server regarding both the factorization and the upload services. The factorization service scales very well for both connection types. However, the upload service suffers from around 63% degradation when admitting 5000 clients. This is because, when the dispatch table used by the reactor becomes large, frequent I/O event triggering and dispatching become costly for both OS and the VM when a large amount of network data arrive.

We now run the same server program on a dual-core CPU machine as quantified in Figure 4. For the number of connections lower than 2000, the event-dispatch model is once again significantly costly to use even for the CPU-bound requests that have low I/O dispatch overheads, due to the performance boost to the multi-threaded concurrency model by the multi-core CPU. Our modified solution, in spite of significant design and code-level alterations, is still not general enough for both types of connections.

Based on this example, we argue that, if designing a general concurrency model for our simplistic example server is not straightforward, it would be even more difficult to do so for servers of much more sophisticated semantics. The difficulty lies in the fact that concurrency designs are dependent upon both the deployment and the runtime conditions of the server programs such as the load characteristics and the hardware capabilities. More specifically, these deployment and runtime conditions are subject to the following design uncertainties:

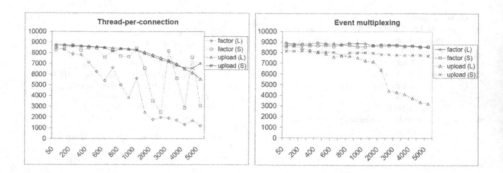

Fig. 3. (A) Thread-per-connection (B) Reactor-based event multiplexing. Data is collected on JRockit JVM version R27.3.1-jre1.6.0_01. Programs are hosted on two Intel Single CPU Xeon 2.5GHz machines with 512KB cache and 2GB physical memory connected by a 100MB switched network. Both machines run Fedora 2 with the 2.6.10 kernel. Uploads are in 80KB chunks. The integer factored is 22794993954179237141472. Each data point is measured three times for a duration of 60 seconds. The median value is chosen for the plot.

I: *Unforeseeable platform capabilities.* The computing resources of the hardware are not known until deployment time. Java programs are separated further from both the hardware and the operating system due to the virtual machine model. However, concurrency mechanisms are sensitive to hardware profiles such as the number of processors, the size of the physical memory, and execution privileges regarding the number of allowed open files or active OS-level threads.

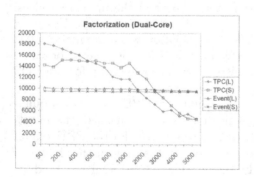

Fig. 4. Event-based factorization server on dual-core CPU

II: *Diversified load characteristics.* General-purpose server programs exert little control over how they are actually used, hence, they are often subject to diversified and yet specialized load characteristics. Browsing requests seen by Web servers are usually I/O-bound and short in duration, while providing services like YouTube needs to support longer I/O-bound requests of both outbound (viewing) and inbound (uploading) traffic. client-server interactions in services such as online interactive games are typically CPU-bound and long in duration, while services for computing driving routes usually serve shorter CPU-bound requests.

III: *Unanticipated evolution.* Our server example demonstrates a case of unanticipated evolution of the server semantics. The recent push towards multi-core architectures, for example, makes it attractive for many legacy server architecture to parallelize their operations. Another kind of unanticipated evolution concerns with concurrency frameworks and libraries. The I/O and concurrency facilities of the Java platform is a very good example. Java servers on early JVMs only had synchronous I/O and the "thread" primitive at their disposal. More powerful concurrency and event-driven I/O support later came from third party libraries such as the util.concurrent library[2], the aio4j library[3], and the NBIO package[4]. The latest Java platforms introduce both more sophisticated concurrency primitives and the support for the asynchronous I/O. During this period of fast evolution, leveraging platform advances would require repeated and "deep" modifications to the server code even if the server semantics do not change.

IV: *Different correctness requirements.* It is important and often very difficult to maintain the safety and liveness [15] properties in complex concurrent systems. Most concurrency primitives, as those in JDK, rely on the experience of the programmers to guard against concurrency hazards such as race conditions, deadlocks, or livelocks. For some domains, the transient faults produced by concurrency bugs can be tolerated through sophisticated schemes such as replication [3]. But it is often important for the concurrency implementation to be provably correct. Verifiable concurrency models such as CSP [9] or the Actor model [1] have been proposed for decades. However, as far as Java programs are concerned, these models use very different abstractions and operating semantics, which are constitute barriers to popular adoption.

Conventional wisdom tells us that the effective way to treat the afore-mentioned uncertainties, or unanticipated changes in general, is through modularity and proven software decomposition principles such as information hiding [17] or design by contract [16]. However, due to the strong coupling of concurrency mechanism and application semantic, concurrency implementation and synchronization primitives are usually tightly integrated and entangled with the application code. For example, locks can appear as class variables of any class that need to be re-entrant. Inheritance is usually the only choice for a class type to use the primitives of concurrency libraries. The conventional concurrency code is typically invasive and not aligned with respect to the modular boundaries of the server logic. For this reason, concurrency is often referred to as a type of crosscutting concerns [13,4,14,22] which is best treated by the aspect-oriented programming (AOP) [13] paradigm.

We are not the first to examine the suitability of AOP to the support of concurrency. Earlier studies [4,14] drew opposite conclusions regarding the possibilities of both the syntactic and the semantic separation of concurrency design from the application logic. We take the mid-ground. We believe that we should only abolish both the design-time and the code-level coupling between server code and *specific* concurrency models. However, the server code should stay amenable to the common characteristics of different concurrency models. We

---

[2] The util.concurrent package. URL: http://gee.cs.oswego.edu/dl/classes/
EDU/oswego/cs/dl/util/concurrent/intro.html
[3] IBM NIO package. URL: http://www.alphaworks.ibm.com/tech/aio4j
[4] NBIO Package. URL: http://www.eecs.harvard.edu/~mdw/proj/seda/

term this property "concurrency awareness". Its purpose is to make the coding structures of concurrent parts of the server logic explicit for allowing external manipulations. We formulate "concurrency awareness" as a set of programming invariants, encoding commonly observed design practices. In combination with these invariants, we create high-level abstractions for programmers to work with the differences of concurrency models through a uniform API and the associated Concurrency Aspect Library, CAL. CAL functions as a mediator between the "concurrency-aware" server logic and the diversified abstractions of concurrency libraries. We show that the use of CAL not only simplifies the coding effort but also makes concurrency implementations more explicit in terms of design. Due to the effective mediation capabilities of CAL, we can compose the same server code with a variety of different concurrency models purely by changing the compilation configurations. CAL not only incurs no observable performance overhead, but also significantly improves the performance of a commercial middleware implementation by as much as ten times through changing concurrency models according to the runtime conditions.

The contributions of our work are as follows:

1. We present the concept of "concurrency awareness" as the foundation of decoupling concurrency models from the server logic. We describe a set of programming invariants as the guiding principles for creating "concurrency awareness" in server programs.
2. We describe the design of CAL, the Concurrency Aspect Library, which allows programmers to work with concurrent frameworks of very different genders through a uniform API. CAL also effectively decouples these frameworks from the server logic at the code level. We make CAL publicly available at: http://www.cse.ust.hk/~charlesz/concurrency for inspections and experiments.
3. We present the quantification of our approach in terms of both the coding effort and performance measurements. We show that programming concurrency with CAL, especially against different concurrency models, can be simplified and be structurally explicit. CAL can support a complex commercial middleware system with no runtime penalty and, through adaptations, dramatically improve its performance.

The rest of the paper is organized as follows: Section 3 describes the "concurrency-aware" architecture principles and the implementation of CAL and Section 4 presents the evaluation of our approaches.

2   Related Work

In this section, we present the related research on enabling the architecture-level customization of concurrency mechanisms. Please refer to [20] for a good summary of the different types of concurrency mechanisms themselves. We first present research in the code-level separation of concurrency mechanisms using AOP-like approaches, i.e., those based on aspect-oriented programming and other meta-programming approaches such as the use of annotations. We then present approaches for enabling the flexible compositions of concurrency models in server applications, not limited to Java applications. We last discuss the difference of our work compared to the AOP treatment of design patterns in general.

Java concurrency externalization. The work closest related to our approach is the assessment of concurrency and failure in distributed systems conducted by Kienzle and Guerraoui [14]. They have focused on investigating the semantic separation of concurrency and failure through the use of AspectJ in the context of transaction processing. The conclusion was that a separation is not possible. We agree that the server logic cannot be made entirely semantically oblivious to concurrency semantics. However, we demonstrate that, through making the server code concurrency-aware, it can be made semantically and syntactically oblivious to lower-level details of specific concurrency models. We delay the study of our approach in treating transaction-based concurrency to future work. Douence et al [6] introduced a generative approach to synthesize and to coordinate concurrency mechanisms defined in aspect modules. Their approach is complementary to our effort in verifying the correctness of concurrency model compositions.

D [4] is a language system for separating the distribution code from Java programs. D consists of a simplified Java language, the Cool language for composing the synchronization of threads, and the Ridl language for composing the communication between threads. The D aspect weaver is responsible for merging three language systems to produce the transformed Java sources. The main objective of D is to provide one of the first evaluations of the benefit of using AOP-like languages to compose distribution.

JAC [8] uses annotation-based hints in Java programs and the accompanied Java pre-compiler to separate the concurrency code from the operational logic of the server. The pre-compiler modifies the Java source by inserting both synchronization and concurrency code based on the annotations. We think that annotation-based approaches, despite sharing many similarities to the aspect-oriented approach, do not achieve the source-level detachment of concurrency models compared to our approach. The server implementation is hardwired to JAC-based concurrency support. With respect to our work, it is not clear how different concurrency models and the composition of these models can be supported by JAC annotations. The evaluation of the JAC approach on complex distributed systems is not reported.

Java concurrency can be entirely externalized for Java programs hosted by application servers. For example, Java server programs written as Enterprise Java Beans (EJB) can be free of concurrency and synchronization concerns and, instead, have them configured as runtime policies understood by the EJB containers. Our work is concerned with the concurrency models used by application containers themselves. It is possible to build server programs on top of containers such as Spring[5] and have the container control the concurrency mechanisms.

---

[5] The Spring framework. URL: www.springframework.org

Due to the fact that containers typically utilize reflection to enable object invocations, we choose not to evaluate such approaches because of their significant performance overhead compared to the bytecode transformation of the AspectJ compiler.

Customizable concurrency. Many conventional approaches give server applications the flexibility of choosing the best concurrency models according to the specific server needs. SEDA [20] proposed and evaluated an architecture for Java servers utilizing asynchronous events and thread pools to partition server data flows into multi-staged pipelines. From the software engineering point of view, SEDA enables the server application to compose the most appropriate concurrency models by changing the topology and the depth of the pipeline as well as the control parameters of pipeline stages. Similarly, the ACE framework allows C++ servers to choose concurrency models adaptively through the use of C++ templates. The components of the ACE network library are in the form of parameterized templates so that the internal implementation mechanisms can be changed without affecting the user code. This is an instance of the open implementation principles [12]. The architecture adaptation of concurrency in these approaches is confined within the provided frameworks themselves. The applications are hardwired and subject to the framework capabilities, which is the exact problem we address in this work.

Aspect-oriented treatment of patterns. There have been numerous recent approaches on externalizing the implementation of design patterns with aspect-oriented programming by Kendall [10], Hannemann and Kiczales [7], and Cunha et al [5]. The externalization of patterns are realized by reusable pattern libraries implementing the roles of patterns as mix-in types and role interactions as retargetable abstract pointcuts. Our work, inspired by this line of research, reasons about the common characteristics of concurrency patterns in general and takes the application-aspect co-design approach. As shown by our examples later in the paper, it is possible to support complex design patterns through composition of basic modules using the CAL library APIs.

3 Concurrency Externalization

For the virtue of reuse and customizability, the afore-presented design uncertainties mandate the dismantling of both the design-time and the code-level coupling of server code to particular concurrency models or libraries. We achieve this goal first by making the observation that there exist common interaction assumptions which the different concurrency models make towards the server logic. The server code needs to be compatible with these assumptions and become "concurrency-aware". The main utility of an aspect concurrency library is essentially to facilitate programmers in capturing these assumptions in the server code through a uniform API. In this section, we introduce these concepts in detail.

3.1   Concurrency-Aware Servers

We loosely define the *concurrency-aware* server programs as programs not concurrent themselves but having salient properties about their structures and execution flows that are compatible to the common interaction assumptions of concurrency models. Finding a comprehensive list of these assumptions for all concurrency models is not an easy task. We present our initial findings which we have found to be effective as follows:

I. Captivity assumption. The primary interaction assumption of concurrency models is that certain parts of the server logic can be captured as units of concurrent activities and submitted to a concurrent executor. Popular concurrency libraries identify such parts of the server logic as instances of classes. For Java programs, a unit of concurrent activity is typically cast as an instance of Thread, Runnable[6], Handler [20], or Task in the util.concurrent package.

II. Execution context assumption. Each concurrent activity has an execution context that has control over the life-cycle of the activity: creation, modification, and termination. The context can be exclusive to each activity or shared among all activities. For example, creating a thread in Java through extending the Thread class type causes each thread to have independent object states. Creating threads through inner classes allows all threads to share the same object state.

III. Data flow assumption. Concurrent activities might have an immediate incoming data flow dependency upon their execution contexts. The context, however, typically does not have the same dependency upon the activities. For example, activities supported by thread-pools might rely on the context to perpetually supply data that are to be processed. These activities are usually continuously active and do not return control to the context until they terminate, hence, have no immediate outgoing data flow, such as passing a return value to the context.

IV. Execution mode assumption. The mode of the execution flow of the server logic can be active, with instructions executed in loops, or passive, completely subject to external activations. The execution mode is assumed to be consistent with the currency models of use. For example, for the *reactive* concurrency model [18], the concurrent activity is typically passive since it only reacts to events. Concurrent activities in models based on the abstraction of "thread" are in general active, i.e., executing in a proactive manner.

V. Synchronization assumption. The usages of synchronization primitives also need to be kept consistent with the concurrency models of use. For example, concurrent activities in the reactive model are usually unsynchronized because they are always executed in a serialized manner. However, they need to be carefully synchronized for thread-based concurrency schemes. Inconsistent synchronization policies incur either runtime overhead or incorrect program behaviours.

One of the essential goals of *concurrency awareness* is to preserve these interaction assumptions in the server code. We therefore formulate concurrency awareness as a set of programming invariances as follows:

---

[6] Both Thread and Runnable are documented in the Java 5 Documentation. URL:http://java.sun.com/j2se/1.5.0/docs/api/

Rule 1: Group concurrent activities within concurrency-aware procedures. A concurrency-aware procedure usually satisfies three minimum requirements: (1) It has well defined termination conditions that are known to the caller; (2) It does not contain active execution controls such as persistent loops or regularly scheduled executions; (3) It does not return a value that is to be used later by the caller.

Rule 2: Localize data inflow at either invocations or instantiations. One of the major functions of concurrent activities in server programs is to process a continuous inflow of data or requests. We advocate that the data in-flow is in form of parameter passing at the time of initializing a concurrent activity or of invoking its procedures.

Rule 3: Make the concurrent activities of the server logic "synchronizable". The choices of synchronization mechanisms should be considered in conjunction with the chosen concurrency models. To protect the shared program state, we advocate making the relevant server logic synchronizable (not synchronized) by making critical regions structurally explicit, e.g., having procedural boundaries.

These structural rules are syntactic with no semantic connotations, hence, generally applicable. The first two rules are also common practices in the eyes of a veteran concurrency programmer. The last rule is to avoid any critical regions within undistinguishable code structures, which are problematic to have synchronization policies applied externally. Server code following these structural rules generally satisfies the common assumptions of many concurrency models. The physical composition between the server code and the concurrency libraries is facilitated by CAL, the Concurrency Aspect Library, presented in the next section.

3.2   Concurrency Aspect Library

The core of our externalization approach is the Currency Aspect Library CAL. CAL aims at providing high level abstractions to hide the details of concurrency models and to enable a closer correspondence between the concurrency design and the code. We design CAL with the following specific goals in mind:

1. **Oblivious.** The library should allow concurrency implementors to focus on expressing concurrency in terms of application semantics while remaining oblivious to the details of the concurrency frameworks, as long as the server code remains concurrency-aware. This is a crucial requirement for achieving the separation of server semantics from concurrency mechanisms.
2. **Versatile.** The library should be capable of supporting concurrency frameworks of very different mechanisms and type abstractions. Neither design alteration nor coding changes are required for the server code if we choose to switch from one framework, such as a reactive model, to another, such as one based on threads.
3. **Uniform.** The library should provide simple and uniform programming interfaces to facilitate the implementation of concurrency. The programming effort required to use Framework A should not differ significantly from the

use of Framework B. Otherwise the library is not effective in capturing common interaction assumptions.

4. **Efficient.** The library should only incur acceptable runtime overhead as a trade-off for the structural flexibility. For server programs, performance, more specifically, throughput and fairness, is the vital quality metric not to be significantly compromised.

We now describe our library from two perspectives: the static perspective of dealing with the diversification of types in concurrency libraries through "type mediation", and the dynamic perspective of integrating concurrency mechanisms with the server execution flow through "activity capture". We believe the first two design goals can be validated after the design of the library is presented in detail. The quantitative evaluations of these design goals are deferred until Section 4.

Type mediation: We have previously argued that the common interaction assumptions of concurrency models center around "activities" and "contexts of activities". In CAL, we use the entities `Activity` and `WorkingContext` to represent these two concepts. These two concepts mediate between the server-specific concepts and concurrency models through a two-step type-space adaptation process accomplished by the CAL user. The first step adapts towards the abstract data types in the concurrency frameworks, and the second to the server class types. The automatic adaptation is performed by the library if the activities are mapped to the call-sites of methods. We term this type of activity an *auto activity*. Auto activities might share the same working context if the mapped method invocations are made by the same caller. This simple scheme decouples the direct type-space wiring between the server code and concurrency frameworks. The liability lies with the generality of the library concepts in representing the interaction assumption of concurrency models. As we will show in our evaluation, we have found that our existing concepts are quite adequate with respect to a broad range of different concurrency schemes.

We illustrate the type mediation process in Figure 5, which depicts three sets of domain models. The concurrency models are exemplified by three popular schemes on the top of the drawing: *reactive, thread-per-task*, and *thread pooling*. The outer box with dotted borders represents the state of the program with respect to the concurrent executions. The inner light-shaded boxes represent concurrent activities (the "wired" box denotes the "thread" abstraction). The consistent shading and arrows across the concurrency and the library models signify the "representation" relationship. Arrows with bold lines represent the "mapping" relationship between library models and server domain models are represented as UML diagrams on the bottom of the graph.

Activity capture: The primary purpose of the type mediation is to flexibly integrate multiple concurrency libraries into a unified type space. To integrate the dynamic execution flow of the server logic into these libraries, we provide programming APIs for the users of the library to identify, based on domain knowledge, the appropriate dynamic execution points in the server program where the

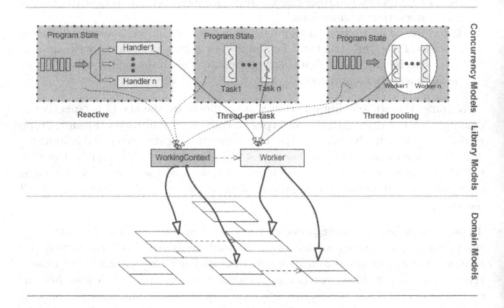

Fig. 5. Concept mediation

concurrent activities can be "captured" by the library. These APIs are in the forms of AspectJ [11] pointcuts:

captureOnInstantiation is a `call`-based pointcut used to identify the *instantiation* relationship between the `WorkingContext` and the `Activity`. The pointcut is typically mapped to constructor calls or factory methods. This entails that one class type is associated with one particular concurrency model with its concurrency-aware method adapted by the generic library interface. If the adapted concurrency-aware method of the class is invoked somewhere in the server code, the invocation needs to be canceled. The invocation can be canceled because, by our definition of concurrency-awareness, there is no data dependencies between the concurrency-aware procedures and their calling stacks. We provide the `cancelCall` pointcut to automate this action.

captureOnInvocation is a `call`-based pointcut used to identify the *invocation* relationship instead. In this case, method invocations are created as the new concurrent activities. Compared to **captureOnInstantiation**, one advantage of this finer granularity of activity capturing is that it allows one class to have a different concurrency scheme per method, if the method is invoked by different callers. Our implementation of the method-level activity captivity essentially creates a Java inner class per method invocation, which, in spite of incurring no runtime overhead in our experiments, can be an expensive operation.[7]

---

[7] Java duplicates the runtime state of the parent class for each inner class created.

In Figure 6, we show a simplified version of an AspectJ module in CAL, which supports the activity capture on method invocations for the Java 5 executor framework. Line 5 is the abstract pointcut, part of the library API, to be mapped to the invocation of a concurrency-aware procedure in the server code. Lines 10-16 execute in place of the procedure invocation by the **around** advice. The inner class (Lines 10-13) performs the type-space adaptation of the library native type, IExecutorActivity, to the Java executor interface type, **Runnable**. Line 15 submits method executions as inner classes of type **Runnable** to the executor framework.

```
   public abstract aspect DynaConcurrency<T extends IExecutorActivity> {
2          private IWorkingContext.executor_ = Executors.newCachedThreadPool();

4          /* This is the method(s) to be detached as a thread.*/
           public abstract pointcut captureOnInvocation();
6
           /* The generic activity creation on a method call.*/
8          boolean around(final IWorkingContext context):captureOnInvocation()&&this(context){
                  /* * Here we use inner class to wrap the method call captured by the joinpoint. */
10                class T implements Runnable{
                      public void run(){
12                            while(proceed(context));
                      }
14            }
              context.executor_.execute(new T());
16            return true;
           }
18 }
```

Fig. 6. Implementation of Concurrency Aspect Library

3.3   The CAL Implementation

To verify the fundamental concepts of our aspect oriented approach, we have created an aspect library consisting of the support for four types of representative and dramatically different concurrency models. All implementations assume that the concurrency-aware procedure uses a Boolean return value to signal the termination condition.

Reactive. Central to our reactive concurrency library is a simpler version of the Reactor [18] event multiplexer using the Java nio package. The server processes client requests in a single thread of execution, demultiplexing I/O events to a collection of IAsyncWorkers. In addition to the *type mediation* and *activity capture* functionalities, our library enables the automatic and seamless socket replacement for creating the asynchronous counterparts of the synchronous Java sockets and I/O stream classes. The replacement is realized by intercepting the creation process for synchronous sockets and streams using AspectJ advices. Our library implementation is capable of supporting 10K simultaneous connections on a 2GHZ commodity PC[8].

---

[8] The C10K problem. URL: http://www.kegel.com/c10k.html

Executor framework. We have implemented the mediation and the capture capabilities leveraging the new Java 5 Executor concurrency framework[9]. Among many capable concurrency models provided in the executor framework, we chose to implement support for the thread-per-activity and the pooled-thread models.

JCSP framework. JCSP [19][10] is a Java framework implementing the concepts of the Communication Sequential Process [9]. JCSP facilitates the creation of "verifiable" concurrent programs for which the model-checking techniques can be used to check for concurrency problems such as race conditions, deadlocks, or livelocks. Our JCSP aspect library executes concurrent activities as JCSP processes. The pooling model is implemented leveraging the inherent synchronizing capabilities of JCSP Channels. Special support is needed for common synchronization mechanisms such as *locks* and *synchronized regions* due to the lack of these primitives in the CSP vocabulary.

Native Java thread. We have also implemented support for the native Java thread class as a representation of the conventional approach to multi-threading. The *thread pool* model is implemented as a fixed number of threads feeding on an *activity* queue.

3.4 Example

We now go back to our simple server, presented in Section 1, to illustrate how users of CAL can compose different concurrency models without code modifications. We present two examples. The first example shows how CAL APIs are used to support the Java 5 executor framework. We then showcase the composition capabilities of CAL by building a multi-staged hybrid concurrency model from two basic ones: the executor framework and the event-driven model, again requiring no changes to the server code.

Java executor framework. The Java executor framework is a new addition to the Java platform that offers improved support for concurrency. We first present an abbreviated version of the server code in Figure 7(A). We identify, with dotted rectangles, two activities that can be executed concurrently: the establishment of a new connection (Line 14) and the persisting of uploaded data (Line 7). The concurrency implementation is given in Figure 8. Given some degree of familiarity with the AspectJ syntax, one can see that this implementation looks very close to an actual design blueprint. The user first determines that the type Server encapsulates some concurrent activities, represented by dotted rectangles (declare Server as the *WorkingContext* at Line 4). She then explicitly specifies two method invocations to be executed concurrently ("concretize" the abstract pointcut at Lines 7-9). Lines 11-14 are not part of the library usage, however, they are necessary to switch the server into the active execution mode.

---

[9] Java Executor. http://java.sun.com/j2se/1.5.0/docs/api/
   java/util/concurrent/Executor.html
[10] Communicating Sequential Processes for Java
   URL:http://www.cs.kent.ac.uk/projects/ofa/jcsp/

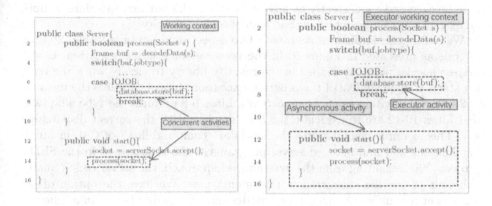

Fig. 7. (A) Analysis for Executor (B) Analysis for Hybrid

The example shows that the most important difference of our library approach, compared to conventional ways of concurrency programming, is that the concurrency perspective of the server program is not only *modularized* but also more *explicit* and *descriptive*.

```
public privileged aspect EXConcurrency extends DynaConcurrency<IExecutorActivity> {
2       /* Type adaptation */
        declare parents: Server implements IWorkingContext;
4
        /* Capture two method calls as concurrent activities*/
6       public pointcut captureOnInvocation():
            call(* Server.process(..)) || call(* Database.store(..));
8
        Object around():call(* Server.start()){
10          /* Switch into the active execution mode*/
            while(true)
12              proceed();
        }
14 }
```

Fig. 8. Implementing the executor framework through CAL

Multi-staged concurrency model. In reality, complex server programs often use a combination of concurrency models to maximize the processing efficiency. For our simple server example, it could be more efficient to provide the data uploading service by using the event-based model to accept new incoming connections and the executor framework to dispatch the database operations in separate threads. In this way, we avoid the threading overhead for a higher number of clients and pipeline the incoming data towards the database service. Figure 7(B) depicts our design: The entire **start** method definition is identified as a unit of asynchronous activity and the call to the **Database.store** method is to be executed concurrently by Java executors. The Server, therefore, is both an executor working context and an asynchronous activity[11].

We realize this implementation with two aspect modules in less than 20 lines of code as presented in Figure 9. In the reactive stage implementation, Line 3 maps a special pointcut defined in the reactive library to signify when the reactor starts to gain control of the program execution. Line 4 captures the instance of Server at creation as an *async activity*. Lines 6-8 perform the type adaption, and Lines 10-12 are to associate the Server class with the correct dispatching key. This example demonstrates the modular "composability" of CAL in building complex and multi-staged server programs as those described in the SEDA project [20]. Benefiting from the externalized approach, the server code remains oblivious to specific concurrency implementations. We have the option of using an entirely different concurrency model that is possibly better in a different service context.

```
   public privileged aspect AsyncConcurrency extends ReactiveServer{
2      declare parents: Server implements IAsyncActivity;
       public pointcut startPoint():call(* Server.start());
4      public pointcut captureOnInstantiation():call(Server.new(..));

6      public void Server.doWork(){
           start();
8      }

10     public SelectionKey Server.getSelectionKey(){
           return getSelectionKey(serverSocket);
12     }
   }
14

16 public privileged aspect ExecutorConcurency extends
                          DynaConcurrency<IExecutorActivity> {
18     declare parents: Server implements IExecutorWorkingContext;
       public pointcut captureOnInvocation():call(* Database.store(..));
20 }
```

Reactive Stage

Executor Stage

Fig. 9. Implementing the hybrid model through CAL

3.5 Synchronization

The externalization of synchronization is a challenging topic. In the context of this paper, we present the synchronization externalization as an implementation issue and delay further discussion to future work. We address synchronization in Java programs via two simple rewriting rules: (1) For methods to be declared with the synchronized keywords, we use around advices with execution

---

[11] Note that in this case Server is not a working context because we identify its method definition as the activity.

pointcuts to enclose the method body within the **synchronized** blocks. (2) For block-level, i.e., intra-method, critical regions, we factor the block into a method, if necessary, and enclose the call-site of the method with either **synchronized** blocks or other synchronization primitives, such as **wait/notify** pairs, through the **call**-based **around** advices.

Special implementation concern is given to the JCSP library for its lack of common Java synchronization operations such as *synchronized regions* and *wait/notify/notifyAll* operations. These Java primitives are supported, with the exception of the *notifyAll* semantics, by the JCSP concept of **Channel** as we emulate mutual exclusion as the exclusive communication between the executing thread and an oracle. The *notifyAll* semantics is supported by the JCSP concept of **Bucket** for its capability of releasing multiple threads simultaneously. Our implementations support the correct operations of the systems that we have evaluated with negligible runtime overhead. The functional evaluation is presented in Section 4.

4   Evaluation

We intend to achieve four design objectives with our aspect-oriented library approach to concurrency externalization: *obliviousness, versatility, uniformity,* and *efficiency*. To evaluate these design objectives, we have used the CAL library on two server programs: our simple server presented earlier as a micro-benchmark, and ORBacus[12], a commercial middleware implementation. With respect to these two server programs, our evaluation aims at answering two questions:

1. How effective is the concurrency awareness concept and the CAL API in simplifying concurrency implementations when working with diversified concurrency models?
2. What is the runtime cost of the CAL-based server implementations as a trade-off for the configuration flexibility compared to conventional approaches?

We answer the first question through the static quantification regarding the structures of the CAL user code. We provide insights to the second question by extensive runtime simulations. The rest of the section proceeds as follows. We first describe the relevant physical attributes of the CAL implementation and the applications of CAL to both the micro benchmark and ORBacus. We then present the quantification of the coding quality of the CAL-based implementations, followed by the metric-based runtime evaluations.

4.1   The CAL Implementations

As aforementioned, the CAL library consists of support for four different types of concurrency models: Java thread, event-driven, Java executor framework, and JCSP framework. Each model is supported by CAL types extended from the

---

[12] ORBacus URL:http://www.iona.com/orbacus

generic `Activity` and `WorkingContext` interfaces. For instance, the `Runnable` interface of the *thread* and the *executor* models are adapted by `IThreadActivity` and `IExecutorActivity` interfaces in the library, respectively. For each concurrency model, we implemented both the bounded and unbounded versions with respect to the number of concurrently executed tasks. The unbounded version admits as many concurrency activities as possible and the bounded version uses a "thread" pool that feeds on a queue of CAL *activities*.[13] The library is fairly light weight, consisting of 84KB in total bytecode size. We prove by implementation that the concepts such as `Context` and `Activity` are compatible to the chosen concurrency models.

We implemented the four concurrency models for both the example server presented throughout the paper and the ORBacus[14] object request broker (ORB) using CAL. ORBacus is implemented in Java. It supports the full CORBA 2.4 specification[15] and is being commercially deployed. It consists of around 2000 Java classes and 200K lines of code. The network communication components of ORBacus use the thread-per-connection model to serve the incoming clients. Refactoring was first performed to remove the native concurrency implementation from these components. We then make them concurrency-aware by removing the loop structures and the synchronization code. The relevant method definitions in the original implementation do not have data dependencies over the callers. They also have well defined termination conditions defined by state variables. These variables are accessible by AspectJ constructs and checked in the library user code. Applying CAL to the simple server allows us to better assess the performance characteristics of CAL without being influenced by the operational complexity of the server. ORBacus, on the other hand, serves as an experimentation of how our concurrency externalization approach benefits non-trivial and sophisticated server programs.

4.2   Coding Effort

To assess the coding effort of the concurrency implementation using CAL, we examine the static code structures of the CAL user code for both the micro-benchmark and ORBacus. Our hypothesis is that, if CAL effectively supports model variations, the effectiveness can be reflected in two ways: (1) One does not need to write a lot of code to use a concurrency model and (2) one does not need to change the code dramatically to switch to a different concurrency model. Note that the server code stays the same for all of the models.

In Table 1, we enumerate the AspectJ language elements used in the user code of CAL as a way of reflecting the coding effort as well as the structural similarity in dealing with the four concurrency models. Each model, including the pool

---

[13] Due to the technical difficulty of sharing `Selector` across threads, we implemented the pool version of the event-driven model essentially as to balancing the load among concurrently running `Selector` event loops.

[14] The ORBacus ORB.
  URL: http://www.iona.com/products/orbacus.htm?WT.mc_id=1234517

[15] CORBA 2.4 URL: http://www.omg.org/corba

version, is supported by one aspect module, corresponding to a row in the table. For ORBacus, we also report the aspect-oriented synchronization implementations for both the thread-based models and the JCSP model[16]. We observe that for both cases, in addition to the light coding effort[17], the coding structure among the bounded as well as the unbounded (pool) versions are almost identical. In fact, the actual code only differs from each other for extending different interface types. Interested readers are invited to verify this themselves by obtaining a copy of our implementation[18]. The simplified coding effort reflects the effectiveness of the high-level abstractions provided by CAL in matching code with design. The similarity of the coding structures shows that the CAL abstractions capture the common characteristics of the chosen concurrency models.

Table 1. Structural comparison for the micro-benchmark (MB) and ORBacus (ORB). LOC:lines of code. ITD: inter-type declaration.

Model	LOC		pointcut		type ITD		method ITD		advice	
	MB	ORB	MB	ORB	MB	ORB	MB	ORB	MB	ORB
event	47	37	3	3	1	4	3	6	1	0
executor	10	46	2	3	1	3	0	3	1	1
thread	9	46	2	3	1	3	0	3	1	1
csp	9	46	2	3	1	3	0	3	1	1
exe.pool	12	50	2	3	1	3	1	4	1	1
thread.pool	12	50	2	3	1	3	1	4	1	1
csppool	12	50	2	3	1	3	1	4	1	1
thread sync	N/A	37	N/A	1	N/A	1	N/A	0	N/A	2
csp sync	N/A	39	N/A	1	N/A	1	N/A	0	N/A	2
Ave.	16	45	2	3	1	3	1	3	1	1

4.3   Runtime Assessment

To assess the runtime overhead of concurrency through CAL, we measure the server throughput as well as the client-side fairness on server machines based on both single-core and multi-core CPUs. To benchmark the two servers, we simulate four types of client/server communication patterns: the sustained (CPU) or the periodic (CPU short) connections for CPU-bound factorization requests, and the sustained (IO) or the periodic connections (IO short) for sending data chunks of 80K bytes. In all experiments, we use the thread-per-connection model, implemented in vanilla Java as the baseline for comparison. For each server, we

---

[16] Recall that the synchronization semantics in JCSP is based on channels.

[17] The event-driven model needs more coding effort to associate asynchronous activities with dispatching keys as illustrated in Figure 9.

[18] The examples can be downloaded from
http://www.cse.ust.hk/~charlesz/concurrency

produce 8 runs. Due to space limits, we selectively report 4 runs for each case. The fairness is calculated from the average, m, and the standard deviation, δ, of the number of messages sent by each client as follows: $fairness = (m - \delta)/m$. It is a measure of how much clients deviate from the mean in successfully being serviced by the server.

Micro benchmark: The measurements for the micro-benchmark are reported in Figure 10. The first conclusion we draw from our observations is that CAL does not incur noticeable performance overhead because the baseline performance is not consistently better than any CAL implementations in any case. For long CPU-bound connections, the event-driven model (async) significantly outperforms the other models when the number of clients increases on the single CPU server. This is not true on the dual-core machine (CPU(Multi)), as the single-threaded event-driven model (async) becomes significantly more costly to use when the number of connections is less than 2000. This is because thread-based models can be boosted by the dual-CPU configuration. The problem is solved by our load-balanced event-driven version (asyncpool). For the I/O-bound periodic connections (IO Short (Single)), the baseline is at par with other models except the executor framework . The sustained I/O-bound connections on the dual-core machine (IO (Multi)) are well serviced by thread-based models, whereas the event-driven models, whether load balanced or not, suffer severely.

In summary, our experiments confirm that, for this simple server, none of the concurrency models we chose to implement scales well for all connection types and processor profiles. Fortunately, due to the externalized approach, we are able to flexibly choose the most appropriate concurrency implementations and always outperform the baseline.

ORBacus: For the performance evaluation of ORBacus, we created two CORBA server objects, one performing the factorization task and the other simply receiving the inbound data chunks. We observe that, in accordance to the case of the micro-benchmark, the CAL-based approaches do not incur perceivable performance overhead. For the I/O-bound measurements (IO (Single) and IO Short (Multi)), the server throughput generally degrades as the number of client ORBs increases. This behavior is different compared to the micro-benchmark version in which case the server scales well. This is due to a particular demarshalling mechanism used in the request broker. The demarshalling process is a CPU-bound operation carried out for each incoming data chunk for decoding the middleware frames from the network data. The demarshalling process is in contention with the thread context switches on the CPU resources. The sustained CPU-bound connections (CPU (Multi)), in accordance to the case of the micro-benchmark, are well serviced by the load balanced event-dispatching model. In the case of CPU Short (Single), we observe that the thread pooling is very effective in servicing periodic short CPU-bound requests as all of the three pooling versions have near constant throughput. The event-driven model is most suitable for both kinds of CPU-bound connections. As for the fairness measures, the Executor and JCSP frameworks have consistently the worst fairness

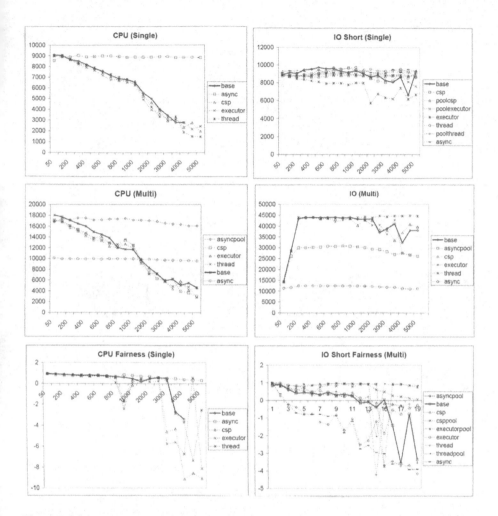

Fig. 10. Measurements of the example server for the CPU intensive connections on both types of servers, the short I/O connections on the single CPU server, and the sustained I/O connections on the dual-core server. In all charts, the baseline measurements are plotted as thick solid lines for the ease of visual comparison. The technical settings of the single-core experiments are identical to the ones presented in the introduction section. The multi-core experiments are conducted on two server machines with Intel Xeon dual core CPUs clocked at 1.8GHz with 4MB on-chip cache and 3GB physical memory. These two servers are both running Linux 2.6 kernels and connected by a 1Gbps switched network. All experiments are carried out by the JRockit R27.3.1-jre1.6.0_01 JVMs with 1M memory limitations (Xmx flag) and 156K maximum stack size (Xss). The pool size is fixed at 100.

measures compared to all other versions. We suspect this is due to the intrinsic mechanisms of these frameworks not to the use of CAL because the fairness of the baseline is not consistently better than the rest of the models.

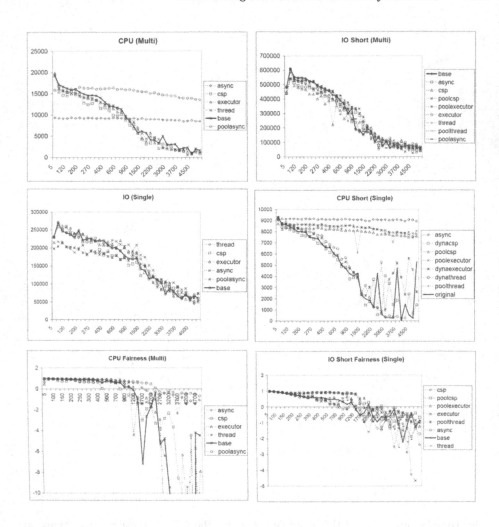

Fig. 11. Measurements of ORBacus: Sustained CPU-bound (CPU (Multi)) and periodic I/O-bound (IO Short (Multi)) requests on dual-core servers; Sustained I/O-bound (IO (Single)) and periodic CPU-bound (CPU Short (Single)) requests on single-core servers. For fairness measures, we present the plots for the sustained dual-core CPU-bound and the periodic single-CPU I/O-bound. The technical settings are identical to the previous case except that the Xss flag is not used.

In summary, our experiments reveal that we made significant improvements over the original implementation for the continuous and periodic CPU-bound requests by changing the concurrency models to either the event-based or the pool-based. The improvements range from around 50% on the single CPU server to about 4-10 times on the dual-core CPU. The benefit of changing concurrency models for the I/O-bound requests, however, is not significant compared to the original implementation of ORBacus. On the one hand this shows that the use of CAL achieves the same performance as the conventional approach and, at the same time, exhibits the customization flexibilities. On the other hand, it poses new challenges for us to improve processing for requests that are both I/O and CPU intensive. Our future work will address this issue.

5   Conclusions

The ubiquitous trend of network-based computations require the architecture of concurrency in today's server programs to adapt to the large variations of runtime conditions. Consequently, server programs often need to employ multiple concurrency models that can be very different in nature. In this work we propose CAL, the Concurrency Aspect Library, as a way of both raising the level of abstraction for programming concurrency and, more importantly, separating the specific semantics of concurrency models from the server architecture.

We have presented CAL as both a design methodology and a prototype implementation. Server programs leveraging CAL must maintain a set of coding invariants to become "concurrency-aware". This is an effective compromise between the conventional approach of invasive concurrency programming and the semantic obliviousness of concurrency that is highly desired but difficult to achieve. Concurrency-aware server programs are amenable to the basic interaction assumptions of many intrinsically different concurrency models. CAL provides a uniform programming interface consisting of both static type and dynamic execution abstractions for programmers to work with the concurrency-aware server code and CAL hides the semantic details of individual concurrency models.

Our general conclusion is that the externalization of concurrency mechanisms using CAL is effective. The effectiveness of the CAL approach is based on two factors: the imposed programming invariants need to give applications the customization and performance advantages; the API abstractions of CAL need to reduce the programming effort in coding architecture customizations for the concurrency libraries. To evaluate these design objectives, we implemented the CAL support for four different concurrency models and applied CAL on two server programs. Our observation is that even for a sophisticated server program the coding effort of programming concurrency with CAL is both light and consistent in spite of model differences. The server code, without being modified, can be composed with the four concurrency libraries either individually or in combination. We have also shown that the code written based on CAL has closer correspondence to the design of concurrency as compared to conventional approaches.

We presented the evaluation of the performance of the CAL-based concurrency on both single and multi-core CPU hardware platforms. We conclude that CAL does not incur observable runtime overhead on both kinds of platforms while enabling customization and flexibility. Compared to conventional approaches, the CAL-based concurrency customization can produce speedups as much as ten fold. The load-time transformation capability of AspectJ allows us to make very delayed concurrency customization decisions for servers after gathering sufficient information about how the servers are being used in deployment.

We are only at the initial stage of the concurrency externalization research. We plan to continuously gain experience with the applications of CAL by evaluating more broader types of server programs including Web servers and database servers. We will continue to validate our design by enriching the concept of concurrency awareness and the capabilities of CAL. In particular, we plan to focus on the externalization of synchronization and intend to explore the meaning of "synchronizable code" as well as the structure of a synchronization aspect library. We also plan to study more sophisticated load characteristics and think about how concurrency customizations can help with server loads that are not exclusively CPU or I/O bound.

References

1. Agha, G.: ACTORS: A Model of Concurrent Computation in Distributed Systems. MIT Press, Cambridge (1986)
2. Buschmann, F., Meunier, R.: A System of Patterns. John Wiley, Chichester (1997)
3. Castro, M., Liskov, B.: Practical byzantine fault tolerance. In: USENIX OSDI, Berkeley, CA, USA, pp. 173–186. USENIX Association (1999)
4. Kiczales, G., Lopes, C.V.D.: A Language Framework for Distributed Programming. TR SPL97-010, P9710047 Xerox PARC
5. Cunha, C.A., Sobral Jo, a.L., Monteiro, M.P.: Reusable aspect-oriented implementations of concurrency patterns and mechanisms. In: AOSD, ACM, New York (2006)
6. Douence, R., Botlan, D.L., Noyé, J., Südholt, M.: Concurrent aspects. In: GPCE, pp. 79–88. ACM Press, New York (2006)
7. Hannemann, J., Kiczales, G.: Design Pattern Implementation in Java and AspectJ. In: ACM OOPSLA, pp. 161–173. ACM Press, New York (2002)
8. Haustein, M., Löhr, K.-P.: JAC: Declarative Java Concurrency. Concurrurrent Computing: Practice & Experience 18(5), 519–546 (2006)
9. Hoare, C.A.R.: Communicating Sequential Processes. Prentice-Hall, Englewood Cliffs (1985)
10. Kendall, E.A.: Role model designs and implementations with aspect-oriented programming. In: ACM OOPSLA, pp. 353–369. ACM Press, New York (1999)
11. Kiczales, G., Hilsdale, E., Hugunin, J., Kersten, M., Palm, J., Griswold, W.G.: An overview of AspectJ. In: Knudsen, J.L. (ed.) ECOOP 2001. LNCS, vol. 2072, pp. 327–355. Springer, Heidelberg (2001)
12. Kiczales, G., Lamping, J., Lopes, C.V., Maeda, C., Mendhekar, A., Murphy, G.C.: Open implementation design guidelines. In: IEEE ICSE, pp. 481–490 (1997)
13. Kiczales, G., Lamping, J., Menhdhekar, A., Maeda, C., Lopes, C., Loingtier, J.-M., Irwin, J.: Aspect-oriented programming. In: Aksit, M., Matsuoka, S. (eds.) ECOOP 1997. LNCS, vol. 1241, pp. 220–242. Springer, Heidelberg (1997)
14. Kienzle, J., Guerraoui, R.: AoP – does it make sense? the case of concurrency and failures. In: Magnusson, B. (ed.) ECOOP 2002. LNCS, vol. 2374, pp. 37–54. Springer, Heidelberg (2002)
15. Lamport, L.: Proving the correctness of multiprocess programs. IEEE Transaction of Software Engineering 3(2), 125–143 (1977)
16. Meyer, B.: Design by contract. In: Advances in Object-Oriented Software Engineering, pp. 1–50 (1991)

17. Parnas, D.L.: On the Criteria To Be Used in Decomposing Systems into Modules. Communications of the ACM 15(12), 1053–1058 (1972)
18. Schmidt, D., Stal, M., Rohnert, H., Buschmann, F.: Pattern-Oriented Software Architecture Patterns for Concurrent and Networked Objects, 1st edn. Software Design Patterns, vol. 2. John Wiley, Chichester (1999)
19. Welch, P.H., Brown, N.C., Moores, J., Chalmers, K., Sputh, B.: Integrating and Extending JCSP. In: McEwan, A.A., Ifill, W., Welch, P.H. (eds.) CPA, July 2007, pp. 349–369 (2007)
20. Welsh, M., Culler, D., Brewer, E.: Seda: an architecture for well-conditioned, scalable internet services. In: ACM SOSP, pp. 230–243. ACM Press, New York (2001)
21. Welsh, M., Gribble, S.D., Brewer, E.A., Culler, D.: A design framework for highly concurrent systems. UC Berkeley Technical Report UCB/CSD-00-1108
22. Zhang, C., Jacobsen, H.-A.: Refactoring Middleware with Aspects. IEEE Transactions on Parallel and Distributed Systems 14(11), 1058–1073 (2003)

Regional Logic
for Local Reasoning about Global Invariants

Anindya Banerjee[1,*], David A. Naumann[2,**], and Stan Rosenberg[2,**]

[1] Kansas State University, Manhattan KS 66506 USA and
Microsoft Research, Redmond WA 98052 USA
[2] Stevens Institute of Technology, Hoboken NJ 07030 USA

Abstract. Shared mutable objects pose grave challenges in reasoning, especially for data abstraction and modularity. This paper presents a novel logic for error-avoiding partial correctness of programs featuring shared mutable objects. Using a first order assertion language, the logic provides heap-local reasoning about mutation and separation, via ghost fields and variables of type 'region' (finite sets of object references). A new form of modifies clause specifies write, read, and allocation effects using region expressions; this supports effect masking and a frame rule that allows a command to read state on which the framed predicate depends. Soundness is proved using a standard program semantics. The logic facilitates heap-local reasoning about object invariants: disciplines such as ownership are expressible but not hard-wired in the logic.

1 Introduction

The potential for interference between supposedly independent program phrases or components due to shared mutable objects is the bane of formal reasoning and static analysis of software. This paper charts new territory, combining two simple and well known ideas —regions and ghost state— in a new way. We formulate a logic that needs only classical, first-order assertions, though inductively defined predicates are compatible. The key novelty is "modifies" specifications expressed in terms of state-dependent region expressions. Together with judicious static analysis of the "footprints" of formulas, this makes it possible to achieve the kinds of modularity associated with ownership methodologies and separation logic, in a flexible way that is compatible with widely used specification languages and tools.

Various notions of regions have been used in static analysis to abstract sets of objects of interest [28]. Separation logic [23] owes its success in specifying and verifying pointer algorithms at least in part to its ability to manifest the "footprint" or region of heap relevant to a particular predicate (and thereby the footprint of a command). At a coarser level, ownership systems and separation logic ideas have been critical to advances in data abstraction [11,2], especially for object invariants [18,5].

In this paper, instead of abstracting from regions and expressing separation via logical connectives or ownership types, we make regions explicit in a way similar to work

---

* Partially supported by US NSF awards CNS-0627748, ITR-0326577.
** Partially supported by US NSF awards CNS-0627338, CRI-0708330, CCF-0429894.

J. Vitek (Ed.): ECOOP 2008, LNCS 5142, pp. 387–411, 2008.

of Amtoft et al [1]. Most importantly, we follow Kassios [14] in using regions to directly represent footprints. We augment a Java-like language with type **rgn** ranging over finite sets of (allocated) references. Following Kassios, we instrument programs with assignments to ghost variables and fields, so assertions can refer explicitly to regions. Whereas Kassios works in the setting of a relational refinement theory and higher order logic, we develop a Hoare logic using first class regions in the "modifies" clause, often the most useful part of a program specification. Asserting the disjointness of regions helps delimit effects and facilitate heap-local reasoning.

It is no surprise that it is possible to reason in terms close to the semantic model [8]. If one's aim is to prove functional correctness of, say, a garbage collector then at the very least, the specification involves reachability, inductive definitions, quantification over paths, etc. But to specify and prove weaker properties, e.g., that an application program does not stray beyond its intended resources, what we achieve is promising. Without the need for inductive predicates or quantification over predicates to hide all but their footprint, we reason directly in terms of footprints. In particular we get "frame rules" that account for modular reasoning about representation invariants.

Notions like ownership [11] support encapsulation of state on which a single object's invariant depends. A precursor to our work is the use of ghost state to encode ownership [16,22] in a way that allows transfer of objects between clients and abstractions (as in low level memory management and higher level OO design patterns like connection pools and layered I/O abstractions). Unlike ownership type systems or programming disciplines, and unlike static analyses using regions, we avoid commitment to a fixed use of regions. On the contrary, regions as ghost state can encode such disciplines but can also combine them in uniform or ad hoc ways.

A benefit of treating regions as ghost state is that it can be done using first-order specification languages based on classical logic with modest use of set theory. Thus it fits with mostly-automated tools based on verification condition generation and it fits with conventional means of program structuring such as scope-based encapsulation. In this foundational study we expose the issues and formalize the ideas in terms of a simple object-based language and Hoare-style proof system which we prove sound using a standard program semantics. There is a major difficulty: "modifies" specifications using region expressions dependent on mutable state are susceptible to a kind of interference: The effect of a command can alter the meaning of the effect specification of another command! This issue has appeared before, in Kassios' dissertation and in the work of Leino and Nelson [17]; we explicitly focus on modifies specifications and offer a novel and flexible solution.

Our first contribution is the logic: its rules and subsidiary judgements together with proof of soundness. Various subtleties made it difficult to correctly design the details of our logic, but we find most of the rules and soundness proofs to be elegant.

Our second contribution is to show how the logic serves as a basis for encapsulating object invariants and invariants for clusters of objects (peers, friends and beyond). Remarkably, our approach can be formalized by a second order frame rule like that of separation logic. Soundness of the second order frame rule in separation logic is challenging [23,7]. Our version is an admissible rule, but the technical result is the subject of another paper [21]. In this paper, we propose an approach to developing sound and flexible disciplines for modular reasoning about invariants, inspired by the work of Kassios, the Boogie team, and many others.

Outline. Sec. 2 sketches an example to illustrate features of the logic. Sec. 3 formalizes an illustrative, object-based programming language and Sec. 4 presents the assertion language. Sec. 5 formalizes effects using regions and Sec. 6 gives a static analysis for the separation of a formula from a write effect. Sec. 7 defines correctness statements and gives the proof rules and soundness theorem. Sec. 8 wraps up the running example and Sec. 9 applies the logic to modular reasoning about invariants. Sec. 10 discusses related work. More examples and proofs are in the online appendix [3].

2 A Small Example

We give a step-by-step correctness proof of a command acting on variable x of type *Node*. A *Node* has three fields: *item* of type **int** and *left*, *rt* of type *Node*. The command sets the *item* field of x's *left* node to zero. The precondition is $P \wedge Q$ and the postcondition is Q where

$$P \qquad \hat{=}\ x \neq \textbf{null} \wedge x.left \in r_1 \wedge x.rt \in r_2 \wedge r_1 \# r_2 \wedge closed$$
$$closed \ \hat{=}\ r_1.left \subseteq r_1 \wedge r_1.rt \subseteq r_1 \wedge r_2.left \subseteq r_2 \wedge r_2.rt \subseteq r_2$$
$$Q \qquad \hat{=}\ \forall x : Node \in r_2 \mid x.item > 0$$

The specification uses two region variables, r_1 and r_2. Precondition P expresses that x is non-null and the object denoted by $x.left$ is in r_1 (and $x.rt$ is in r_2). Furthermore, regions r_1, r_2 are disjoint which in our syntax is denoted by $r_1 \# r_2$. Regions are finite sets of object references, of any type. Since null is not a reference, $x.left \in r_1$ implies $x.left \neq \textbf{null}$. Formula *closed* says that both r_1 and r_2 are closed under both *left* and *rt*: If $o \in r_1$ and $o.left \neq \textbf{null}$ then $o.left \in r_1$, etc.

In general, for region expressions G, G' and field name f, the formula $G.f \subseteq G'$ says that the f-image of region G is contained in G'. For reasons discussed later, "$G.f$" is not a region expression.

In summary, the precondition P states that the left "subtree" of x is in r_1 and the right "subtree" of x is in r_2. (But these "subtrees" need not be trees, nor even dags.)

The formula Q plays the role of an invariant. It says that for any node o in r_2, o's item field is positive. Finally, since the command writes to the *item* field, we will show that its write effect is at most the *item* field of objects residing in r_1, denoted by $\textbf{wr}\ r_1.item$. The complete correctness statement is

$$\{\ P \wedge Q\ \}\ \textbf{var}\ y : Node\ \textbf{in}\ y := x.left;\ y.item := 0\ \textbf{end}\ \{\ Q\ \}\ [\textbf{wr}\ r_1.item] \qquad (1)$$

One can prove a stronger postcondition but this is enough for expository purposes.

We now turn to the proof. Here is a specification for the first assignment:

$$\{\ x \neq \textbf{null}\ \}\ y := x.left\ \{\ y = x.left\ \}\ [\textbf{wr}\ y]$$

This is a *small* specification in that it only mentions entities that are relevant to the assignment. Since $y := x.left$ only writes y, and since neither P nor Q mention y, their truth value is not changed by the assignment. So we conjoin $P \wedge Q$ to both pre- and post-condition:

$$\{ P \wedge Q \} \; y := x.left \; \{ y = x.left \wedge P \wedge Q \} \, [\mathbf{wr} \, y]$$

This step is an instance of the *Frame* rule (Fig. 9), cf. [23]. We will be more precise later, but for now we say that $x, r_1, r_2, \langle x \rangle.left, r_1.left, r_2.left, \langle x \rangle.rt, r_1.rt, r_2.rt$ constitute a "frame" of P because modifications to the frame may affect the truth value of P, but no other modifications can. Notice that y, the variable modified by the command, is not in the frame. Similarly, $r_2, r_2.item$ constitute the frame of Q. Again, y is absent. This separation between the write effect of the command and the frames licenses conjoining $P \wedge Q$ to the pre- and postconditions above.

Recall that $x.left \in r_1$ implies $x.left \neq \mathbf{null}$ which together with $y = x.left$ implies that $y \neq \mathbf{null}$ and $y \in r_1$. The last assertion implies a weaker one: $\langle y \rangle \subseteq r_1$, where $\langle y \rangle$ denotes the singleton region iff y is non-null, and otherwise the empty region. Thus by the standard rule of Consequence we get

$$\{ P \wedge Q \} \; y := x.left \; \{ P \wedge y \neq \mathbf{null} \wedge \langle y \rangle \subseteq r_1 \wedge Q \} \, [\mathbf{wr} \, y] \qquad (2)$$

Here is a small specification for $y.item := 0$:

$$\{ y \neq \mathbf{null} \} \; y.item := 0 \; \{ y.item = 0 \} \, [\mathbf{wr} \, \langle y \rangle.item]$$

The write effect, $\mathbf{wr} \, \langle y \rangle.item$, records the fact that the *item* field of the singleton region, $\langle y \rangle$, may have changed. Now we would like to conjoin Q to pre/post of the above specification, so it could be sequenced with (2). However, doing so appears to be unsound, since Q reads *item* whereas the command writes *item*. We shall refine the above specification to obtain a stronger precondition, which will imply that Q is separated from the write. First, we use the Frame rule to conjoin $P \wedge \langle y \rangle \subseteq r_1$, whose frame is clearly separated from $\langle y \rangle.item$ because a write to $y.item$ leaves y, r_1, and r_2 unchanged and *item* is not in the frame of P. This yields

$$\{ y \neq \mathbf{null} \wedge P \wedge \langle y \rangle \subseteq r_1 \} \; y.item := 0 \; \{ y.item = 0 \wedge P \wedge \langle y \rangle \subseteq r_1 \} \, [\mathbf{wr} \, \langle y \rangle.item]$$

Now, to apply the Frame rule to Q we need that $r_2.item$ is separated from the write of $\langle y \rangle.item$. It suffices to show that $\langle y \rangle$ is a region disjoint from r_2. This follows from $\langle y \rangle \subseteq r_1$ and the fact that $P \Rightarrow r_1 \# r_2$. So Frame yields

$$\{ y \neq \mathbf{null} \wedge P \wedge \langle y \rangle \subseteq r_1 \wedge Q \} \; y.item := 0 \; \{ y.item = 0 \wedge P \wedge \langle y \rangle \subseteq r_1 \wedge Q \} \, [\mathbf{wr} \, \langle y \rangle.item]$$

whence by the rule of Consequence we obtain

$$\{ y \neq \mathbf{null} \wedge P \wedge \langle y \rangle \subseteq r_1 \wedge Q \} \; y.item := 0 \; \{ Q \} \, [\mathbf{wr} \, \langle y \rangle.item] \qquad (3)$$

Now we are ready to sequence (2) followed by (3). But what should the effects be? Simply unioning the effects $\mathbf{wr} \, y$ and $\mathbf{wr} \, \langle y \rangle.item$ is unsound because effects are interpreted in the *pre-state*: the y in $\mathbf{wr} \, y.item$ does not have the same meaning as in the pre-state of the sequence, because y is modified by the first command. So the write to

$$x, y, r \in VarName \qquad f, g \in FieldName \qquad K \in DeclaredClassNames$$
$$T ::= \mathbf{int} \mid K \mid \mathbf{rgn}$$
$$E ::= x \mid c \mid \mathbf{null} \mid E \oplus E \qquad \text{where } c \text{ is in } \mathbb{Z} \text{ and } \oplus \text{ is in } \{=, +, -, *, >, \ldots\}$$
$$G ::= x \mid x.f \mid \langle E \rangle \mid \mathbf{emp} \mid \mathbf{alloc} \mid G \otimes G \qquad \text{where } \otimes \text{ is in } \{\cup, \cap, -\}$$
$$F ::= E \mid G$$
$$C ::= x := F \mid x := \mathbf{new}\ K \mid x := x.f \mid x.f := F$$
$$\mid\ \mathbf{if}\ x\ \mathbf{then}\ C\ \mathbf{else}\ C \mid \mathbf{while}\ x\ \mathbf{do}\ C \mid C; C \mid \mathbf{var}\ x : T\ \mathbf{in}\ C\ \mathbf{end}$$

Fig. 1. Programming language. We confuse category names with typical elements (e.g., T).

the *item* field must be recorded by some other expression. Precondition $\langle y \rangle \subseteq r_1$ of (3) implies that $\mathbf{wr}\,\langle y \rangle \centerdot item$ is a sub-effect of $\mathbf{wr}\,r_1 \centerdot item$, so by weakening we obtain

$$\{\, y \neq \mathbf{null} \wedge P \wedge \langle y \rangle \subseteq r_1 \wedge Q \,\}\ y.item := 0\ \{\, Q \,\}\ [\mathbf{wr}\,r_1 \centerdot item]$$

Now we can apply the rule of sequential composition to obtain

$$\{\, P \wedge Q \,\}\ y := x.left; y.item := 0\ \{\, Q \,\}\ [\mathbf{wr}\,y, \mathbf{wr}\,r_1 \centerdot item]$$

The rule for local blocks lets us remove the effect $\mathbf{wr}\,y$ and conclude the proof of (1).

3 Programming Language

This section presents an illustrative language for which we formalize the programming logic. A program consists of a command C in the context of some class declarations. The grammar for commands etc. is in Fig. 1. A class declaration **class** $K\ \{\ \overline{T}\,\overline{f}\ \}$ introduces a type name K; values of this type are **null** and references to mutable objects with typed fields $\overline{f} : \overline{T}$. Here and throughout, identifiers with an overline range over lists. As in Java, an assignment $x := y.f$ implicitly dereferences the value in y and reads field f in the heap. Equality test, written $=$, is for reference equality.

In addition to **int** and reference types, there is type **rgn** with values ranging over finite sets of references (excluding null). Region expressions include set operations like subtraction $(-)$. Region expressions cannot influence control flow or the value of non-region fields/variables, so they can only serve as ghosts for reasoning.

Ordinary expressions (E in Fig. 1) do not depend on the heap: $y.f$ is not an expression but rather part of the primitive command $x := y.f$ for reading a field. There is also a primitive formula for reading a field (see Fig. 3). This restriction serves, as in separation logic, to simplify rules for reasoning about assignments. We also gain some simplification in the framing rules to come (Fig. 7). Region expressions (G in Fig. 1) do include a form that reads a single step into the heap, namely $x.g$ when g has type **rgn** (in which case $x.g.f$ is not well formed). The form $x.g$ is essential for our purposes, but allowing multi-step heap dependence would cause complications, e.g., in the framing rules. This is why the form "$G.f$" which appears in effects and assertions is not a region expression. Of course syntax sugars can be added for practical purposes, with derived rules.

There is an ambient class table comprising a well formed collection of class declarations. We write fields(K) for the field declarations $\overline{f}:\overline{T}$ of class K. The judgement $\Gamma \vdash F:T$ says that region or ordinary expression F has type T in context Γ that assigns types to variable names. Similarly, $\Gamma \vdash C$ says C is a well formed command. For programs we assume the standard rules that prevent "field not defined" errors. For brevity we omit a boolean type. The guard for an if- or while-command has type **int**; the semantics interprets any non-zero value as true.

We omit most of the rules since they are straightforward, but note that **int** is separated from reference types: there is no pointer arithmetic. The typing rules make some distinctions between region expressions G and those of other type. The rule for singleton region $\langle E \rangle$ enforces that E is of reference type. Field dereferencing in expressions is allowed only for fields of type **rgn**, as per: $\dfrac{(g:\mathbf{rgn}) \in \text{fields}(K)}{\Gamma, x:K \vdash x.g:\mathbf{rgn}}$. Recall that metavariable K ranges over class names; only classes have fields. Here and throughout the paper, rules are only permitted to be instantiated when the consequent as well as the antecedent are well formed. For example, the rule for context extension is $\dfrac{\Gamma \vdash F:T'}{\Gamma, x:T \vdash F:T'}$ and it cannot be used with x that is in dom(Γ), because the comma in $\Gamma, x:T$ denotes the union of disjoint partial functions.

The concrete syntax $x := y.f$ has an ambiguity that is resolved by typing: If $f:\mathbf{rgn}$ then it is read as $x := F$ with $F \equiv y.f$ —and in case y is null, the value is the empty region, for convenience in reasoning. If f is any other type, it is read as a primitive command —and of course there is a runtime error if y is null.

Semantics. We use a straightforward denotational semantics where commands denote deterministic state transformers, which fits well with pre/post specifications. The details are adapted and simplified from a machine-checked semantics of CoreJML encoded in PVS and including hooks to add types like **rgn** and operations on ghost state [15].

We are given a set, Ref, of reference values and a distinguished value, null, not in Ref or $\mathbb{Z}$ or 2^{Ref}. The values denoted by a reference type K include null as well as all references that have been allocated for objects of type K, and the values of type **rgn** are finite sets of allocated references (of any type).

A *state* for context Γ has the form (r, h, s) where: r is a *ref context*, i.e., a partial function mapping the allocated references to their types; h is a *heap* that maps each allocated reference to its object state (i.e., map from field names to values); and s is a *store* that maps each variable x in Γ to its value. Throughout the paper, states are assumed to be well typed and have no dangling references. The semantics is parameterized on the allocator, i.e., a deterministic function of the state that yields fresh references but is otherwise arbitrary.

Following separation logic and program verifiers like ESC/Java, correctness judgements specify error-free partial correctness. So we use a denotational semantics in which $[\![\Gamma \vdash C]\!]\sigma$, for Γ-state σ, is either ⋔ (fault), $\bot$ (divergence), or a Γ-state σ' (normal termination). The only faults are null dereference, since we consider programs that satisfy usual Java-style typing rules and therefore there are no dangling references (and we assume the arithmetic operators are error-avoiding, to avoid complications about definedness). The compound commands like sequence and loops are strict in ⋔ as well

$$\llbracket y \rrbracket \sigma \quad = \sigma(y) \qquad\qquad\qquad\qquad \llbracket G_1 \cup G_2 \rrbracket \sigma = \llbracket G_1 \rrbracket \sigma \cup \llbracket G_2 \rrbracket \sigma$$
$$\llbracket x.g \rrbracket \sigma = \sigma(x.g) \text{ if } \sigma(x) \neq \text{null, else } \varnothing \qquad \llbracket G_1 \cap G_2 \rrbracket \sigma = \llbracket G_1 \rrbracket \sigma \cap \llbracket G_2 \rrbracket \sigma$$
$$\llbracket \langle E \rangle \rrbracket \sigma = \{ \llbracket E \rrbracket \sigma \} \text{ if } \llbracket E \rrbracket \sigma \neq \text{null, else } \varnothing \qquad \llbracket G_1 - G_2 \rrbracket \sigma = \llbracket G_1 \rrbracket \sigma - \llbracket G_2 \rrbracket \sigma$$
$$\llbracket \mathbf{alloc} \rrbracket \sigma = \text{alloc}(\sigma) \qquad\qquad\qquad\qquad \llbracket \mathbf{emp} \rrbracket \sigma \quad = \varnothing$$

Fig. 2. Semantics of region expressions (eliding $\Gamma \vdash \ldots : \mathbf{rgn}$). Here y and g have type $\mathbf{rgn}$.

as in $\bot$. The semantics of loops is given by fixpoint as usual, where we order outcomes by $\bot \leq \text{\reflectbox{h}}$ and $\bot \leq \sigma$ for any state σ (but distinct states are incomparable and not comparable with \reflectbox{h}).

We use the following abbreviations, for state $\sigma = (r, h, s)$
$\sigma(x)$ for $s(x)$ —variable lookup
$\sigma(x.f)$ for $h(s(x))(f)$ —field of object referenced by variable x
$\sigma(o.f)$ for $h(o)(f)$ —field of reference value o
$\text{alloc}(\sigma)$ for $\text{dom}(r)$ —set of all allocated references
$\text{type}(o, \sigma)$ for $r(o)$ —type of an allocated reference
$\text{update}(\sigma, x, v)$ for (r, h, s'), where s' overrides s to map x to v
$\text{extend}(\sigma, x, v)$ for (r, h, s'), where s' extends s to map x to value v, for $x \notin \text{dom}(s)$
$\text{update}(\sigma, o.f, v)$ for (r, h', s), where h' overrides h to map field f of o to v.

Here metavariables x, y, z range over variable names, whereas we use o, p, q for elements of Ref. We write $\text{fields}(o, \sigma)$ for $\text{fields}(\text{type}(o, \sigma))$. Less obviously, we write $f \in \text{refields}(o, \sigma)$ to say that f is of some reference type, i.e., there is K such that $(f : K) \in \text{fields}(o, \sigma)$.

Semantics for expressions and commands are routine and omitted. Note that $\llbracket E \rrbracket \sigma$ depends on the store but not the heap and is always a value (of appropriate type), never \reflectbox{h} or $\bot$. As one would expect, $x.f := E$ faults if x is **null**, and the same for $x := y.f$ —except in case f has type $\mathbf{rgn}$. As mentioned earlier, that case is actually parsed as $x := G$ and uses the semantics of region expressions given in Fig. 2.

4 Assertion Language

Fig. 3 gives the grammar for assertions. Quantification is over **int** and reference types only, and in the latter case a bounding region is required as in $(\forall x : K \in \mathbf{alloc} \mid P)$ where the quantification is over all allocated objects as is usual [25,9] and important for certain global invariants. There are also atomic formulas for inclusion and disjointness of regions. The formula $G_1.f \subseteq G_2$ says that for every object in G_1, if it has field f with non-null value then that value is in G_2. The formula $x.f = E$ says that x is non-null and the value of its f field is E. The semantics is two-valued and classical. So *false* can be defined as $1 = 0$, $\vee$ and $\exists$ by DeMorgan, etc. Another syntax sugar is $E \in G \,\hat{=}\, E \neq \mathbf{null} \wedge \langle E \rangle \subseteq G$. Officially, we cannot write "$x.f \in G$" because $x.f$ is not an expression (unless $f : \mathbf{rgn}$, but then $\in$ does not make sense). But it is safe to abbreviate $x.f \in G \,\hat{=}\, x.f \neq \mathbf{null} \wedge \langle x \rangle.f \subseteq G$. Another convenient feature is the ability to refer to all fields, as in $G.\text{any} \subseteq G$; we use it in examples but omit the formalization. Finally, we abbreviate $x \,\mathbf{is}\, K$ for $\mathbf{type}(K, \langle x \rangle)$.

$$P ::= E = E \mid x.f = F \mid G \subseteq G \mid G \# G \mid \textbf{type}(K, G)$$
$$\mid G.f \subseteq G \mid G.f \# G \mid (\forall x : \textbf{int} \mid P) \mid (\forall x : K \in G \mid P) \mid P \wedge P \mid \neg P$$

$\sigma \models x.f = F$	iff $\sigma(x) \neq$ null and $\sigma(x.f) = \llbracket F \rrbracket \sigma$
$\sigma \models G_1 \# G_2$	iff $\llbracket G_1 \rrbracket \sigma \cap \llbracket G_2 \rrbracket \sigma = \varnothing$
$\sigma \models G_1.f \subseteq G_2$	iff $\sigma(o.f) =$ null or $\sigma(o.f) \in \llbracket G_2 \rrbracket \sigma$
	for all $o \in \llbracket G_1 \rrbracket \sigma$ with $f \in$ refields(o, σ)
$\sigma \models G_1.f \# G_2$	iff $\sigma(o.f) \notin \llbracket G_2 \rrbracket \sigma$ for all $o \in \llbracket G_1 \rrbracket \sigma$ with $f \in$ refields(o, σ)
$\sigma \models \textbf{type}(K, G)$	iff type$(o, \sigma) \leq K$ for all $o \in \llbracket G \rrbracket \sigma$
$\sigma \models^\Gamma \forall x : \textbf{int} \mid P$	iff extend$(\sigma, x, v) \models^{\Gamma, x : \textbf{int}} P$ for all $v \in \mathbb{Z}$
$\sigma \models^\Gamma \forall x : K \in G \mid P$	iff extend$(\sigma, x, o) \models^{\Gamma, x : K} P$ for all o in $\llbracket G \rrbracket \sigma$ with type$(o, \sigma) \leq K$

Fig. 3. Formulas: grammar and selected semantics. The boolean connectives are standard.

The well-formedness judgement $\Gamma \vdash P$ has straightforward rules, but note:

$$\frac{\Gamma \vdash G : \textbf{rgn} \quad \Gamma \vdash G' : \textbf{rgn} \quad (f : K) \in \text{fields}(K')}{\Gamma \vdash G.f \subseteq G'} \qquad \frac{\Gamma, x : K \vdash P \quad \Gamma \vdash G : \textbf{rgn}}{\Gamma \vdash \forall x : K \in G \mid P}$$

The first rule (like that for $\Gamma \vdash G.f \# G'$) ensures that f is of class type. The second disallows quantification over regions and demands that the bound variable x not appear in the bound, G, of the quantification where G is a region expression. This facilitates framing.

To streamline the treatment of local variables and quantifiers, we assume a hygiene condition: no identifier should occur both bound and free in any context, nor bound more than once.

The semantics of a well-formed formula $\Gamma \vdash P$ is given as a satisfaction relation, written $\sigma \models^\Gamma P$ and defined for all Γ-states σ. The definition is in Fig. 3. In most cases we elide Γ since it is unchanged throughout. A formula in context Γ is called *valid* iff it is true in all states.

Example. The recursive predicate $List(o, r)$ defined below expresses that o points to *null*-terminated list and that the region r is exactly the set of all nodes of the list. Our running example involves a subject together with its list of observers. Thus variable o and field nxt have type *Observer*.

$$List(o : Observer, \; r : \textbf{rgn}) \; \hat{=} \; (\langle o \rangle . nxt = \textbf{emp} \Rightarrow r = \langle o \rangle) \wedge$$
$$(\langle o \rangle . nxt \neq \textbf{emp} \Rightarrow o \in r \wedge List(o.nxt, r - \langle o \rangle))$$

Note that in the case that o is null, $\langle o \rangle$ is empty and so is $\langle o \rangle . nxt$. If o is non-null but its nxt field is null, then $\langle o \rangle . nxt$ is empty and $\langle o \rangle$ is the singleton set $\{o\}$.

We do not formalize recursively defined predicates. There is no difficulty with *List* since its occurrences on the right side are in monotonic positions (with respect to the subset ordering on state-sets); such recursions have least fixpoints in the complete lattice of state-sets. (A small complication is that *List* has parameters.) Note that "$o.nxt$" is not in the syntax for expressions; we write $List(o.nxt, r - \langle o \rangle)$ to abbreviate the formula $o.nxt \in r \wedge \forall p : Observer \in r \mid p = o.nxt \Rightarrow List(p, r - \langle o \rangle)$.

```
class Subject{                                    class Observer{
    Observer obs; int val; rgn O;                     Subject sub; int cache;
                                                      Observer nxt;
    Subject(){
        self.obs := null;  self.val := 0;  self.O := emp; }    Observer(Subject s){
                                                          self.sub := s;  s.register(self); }
    void register(Observer o){
        self.add(o);  o.notify(); }                   void notify(){
                                                          self.cache := self.sub.get(); }
    void update(int n){
        self.val := n;  Observer o := self.obs;       int val(){return self.cache; }
        while (o! = null){o.notify();  o := o.nxt; }}  }

    int get(){return self.val; }

    void add(Observer o){
        self.O := self.O∪⟨o⟩;
        o.nxt := self.obs;  self.obs := o;
}
```

Fig. 4. Subject/Observer implementation

5 Effects

The "frames" described in Sec. 2 are formalized as read effects. For commands, we focus in this paper on write effects. But the full logic includes read effects for commands; these are useful for reasoning about method calls in assertions as well as for program transformations. An *effect set* is a comma-separated list $\overline{\varepsilon}$ of *effects*, ε, with grammar

$$\varepsilon ::= \mathbf{rd}\, x \mid \mathbf{rd}\, G.f \mid \mathbf{wr}\, x \mid \mathbf{wr}\, G.f \mid \mathbf{rd\,alloc} \mid \mathbf{wr\,alloc} \mid \mathbf{fr}\, G$$

The idea is that $\mathbf{rd}\, x$ allows variable x to be read, $\mathbf{rd}\, G.f$ allows read of the f field of objects in G, $\mathbf{wr}\, x$ allows update of variable x, $\mathbf{wr}\, G.f$ allows update of the f field of objects in G. The region expression $\mathbf{alloc}$ is like a variable that holds the set of all allocated references and is automatically updated by the allocator, so $\mathbf{wr\,alloc}$ allows allocation and $\mathbf{rd\,alloc}$ allows dependence on the set of allocated objects. Finally, $\mathbf{fr}\, G$ says that all elements of G in the final state are freshly allocated.

Freshness is used to mask updates to fresh objects in sequences. For example, consider the sequence $x := \mathbf{new}\ Node; x.rt := 0$ in using class $Node$ from Sec. 2, By itself, the field update has effect $\mathbf{wr}\, \langle x \rangle.rt$. But in the pre-state of the sequence, $\langle x \rangle$ cannot possibly contain the updated object. Indeed, no pre-existing object is updated. In the proof rules, the effect of $x := \mathbf{new}\ Node$ includes $\mathbf{fr}\, \langle x \rangle$ which by the sequence rule (in Fig. 8) annihilates the write effect.

Before delving into the technicalities of effects, we give, in Fig. 4, code that we will use as a running example, $Subject/Observer$. Fig. 5 gives the specifications. Note that $notify$ is called on an observer from within the $update$ method but this results in a callback to the $Subject$'s get method via $\mathbf{self}.sub.get()$.

Method	Pre-condition	Post-condition
Subject()	true	$SubObs(\mathbf{self}, 0)$
register(o)	$o \neq \mathbf{null} \wedge SubObs(\mathbf{self}, val) \wedge o \notin O$	$SubObs(\mathbf{self}, val) \wedge o \in O$
update(n)	$SubObs(\mathbf{self}, val)$	$SubObs(\mathbf{self}, n)$
get	$Sub(\mathbf{self}, val)$	$Sub(\mathbf{self}, val) \wedge res = val$
add(o)	$o \neq \mathbf{null} \wedge Sub(\mathbf{self}, val) \wedge o \notin O$	$Sub(\mathbf{self}, val) \wedge o \in O$
Observer(s)	$SubObs(s, s.val)$	$SubObs(s, s.val) \wedge \mathbf{self} \in s.O$
notify	$Sub(sub, sub.val)$	$Sub(sub, sub.val)$
	$\wedge\, Obs(\mathbf{self}, sub, cache)$	$\wedge\, Obs(\mathbf{self}, sub, sub.val)$
val	$SubObs(sub, sub.val) \wedge \mathbf{self} \in sub.O$	$SubObs(sub, sub.val) \wedge res = sub.val$

Method	Effects
Subject()	
register(o)	$\mathbf{wr}\,\mathbf{self}.O\bullet nxt, \langle\mathbf{self}\rangle\bullet O, \langle o\rangle\bullet nxt, \langle o\rangle\bullet cache, \langle\mathbf{self}\rangle\bullet obs$
update(n)	$\mathbf{wr}\,\langle\mathbf{self}\rangle\bullet val, \mathbf{self}.O\bullet cache$
get	
add(o)	$\mathbf{wr}\,\mathbf{self}.O\bullet nxt, \langle\mathbf{self}\rangle\bullet O, \langle o\rangle\bullet nxt, \langle\mathbf{self}\rangle\bullet obs$
Observer(s)	$\mathbf{wr}\,s.O\bullet nxt, \langle s\rangle\bullet O, \langle s\rangle\bullet obs$
notify	$\mathbf{wr}\,\langle\mathbf{self}\rangle\bullet cache$
val	

Fig. 5. Specifications for Subject/Observer example based on Parkinson [24]

For the specifications of the methods of Fig. 4, the predicates $SubObs$, Sub, Obs are used (following Parkinson [24]). The predicate $List$ used in Sub is defined in Sec. 4.

$$SubObs(s, v) \;\hat{=}\; Sub(s, v) \wedge \forall o\colon Observer \in s.O \mid Obs(o, s, v)$$
$$Sub(s, v) \;\hat{=}\; s.val = v \wedge List(s.obs, s.O)$$
$$Obs(o, s, v) \;\hat{=}\; o.cache = v \wedge o.sub = s$$

$SubObs$ is an invariant for the entire aggregate structure comprising an instance of $Subject$ together with its $Observers$. $SubObs$ holds when the subject's invariant, Sub, holds and for each observer in the subject's list of observers, that observer's invariant, Obs, holds. The invariant $Sub(s, v)$ says that the current internal state of subject s is v and all observers of s are in a list whose nodes lie in region $s.O$. The invariant $Obs(o, s, v)$ says that o is an observer of subject s and that o's view of s's internal state is v.

With the above definitions, the method specifications in Fig. 5 are self-explanatory so we move on to explaining the effects. The effect for *notify* records that a call to it will result in the writing of an observer's *cache*. The effect for *add* records that O was written to when an observer o was added to the existing list of observers of a subject. The effect for *register* takes into account the effects of *add* and *notify*. The effect for *update* records that the subject's *val* field is updated and also takes into account the effects accrued as a result of calling *notify*. The constructor for $Subject$ has no effects that need be recorded; we are only concerned with the write effects of pre-existing objects. Similarly, note the absence of effects $\mathbf{wr}\,\langle\mathbf{self}\rangle\bullet sub$, $\mathbf{wr}\,\langle\mathbf{self}\rangle\bullet nxt$ and $\mathbf{wr}\,\langle\mathbf{self}\rangle\bullet cache$ in the effects of the constructor for $Observer$.

Technicalities. Effects must be well formed (wf) for the context Γ in which they occur: $\mathbf{rd}\,x$ and $\mathbf{wr}\,x$ are wf if $x \in \mathrm{dom}(\Gamma)$; $\mathbf{rd}\,G.f$, $\mathbf{wr}\,G.f$, and $\mathbf{fr}\,G$ are wf if G is wf in Γ. We say σ' *extends* σ provided $\mathrm{alloc}(\sigma) \subseteq \mathrm{alloc}(\sigma')$ and $\mathrm{type}(o,\sigma) = \mathrm{type}(o,\sigma')$ for all $o \in \mathrm{alloc}(\sigma)$. The semantics has the property that σ' extends σ whenever $\sigma' = [\![C]\!]\sigma$.

Definition 1 (allows transition). Let effect set $\bar{\varepsilon}$ be well formed in Γ and let σ, σ' be Γ-states. We say $\bar{\varepsilon}$ *allows transition from* σ *to* σ', written $\sigma \to \sigma' \models \bar{\varepsilon}$, iff σ' extends σ and the following all hold:

(a) for every y in $\mathrm{dom}(\Gamma)$ we have either $\sigma(y) = \sigma'(y)$ or $\mathbf{wr}\,y$ is in $\bar{\varepsilon}$
(b) for every $o \in \mathrm{alloc}(\sigma)$ and every $f \in \mathrm{fields}(o,\sigma)$, either $\sigma(o.f) = \sigma'(o.f)$ or there is $\mathbf{wr}\,G.f$ in $\bar{\varepsilon}$ such that $o \in [\![G]\!]\sigma$
(c) if $\mathrm{alloc}(\sigma') \neq \mathrm{alloc}(\sigma)$ then $\mathbf{wr\,alloc}$ is in $\bar{\varepsilon}$.
(d) for each $\mathbf{fr}\,G$ in $\bar{\varepsilon}$, $[\![G]\!]\sigma' \subseteq \mathrm{alloc}(\sigma') - \mathrm{alloc}(\sigma)$.

Definition 2 (agreement on read effects). Let $\bar{\varepsilon}$ be an effect set and σ, σ' be states such that σ' extends σ. Say that σ and σ' *agree on* $\bar{\varepsilon}$, written $\sigma \sim_{\bar{\varepsilon}} \sigma'$, provided the following hold:

(a) for all $\mathbf{rd}\,x$ in $\bar{\varepsilon}$, we have $\sigma(x) = \sigma'(x)$
(b) if $\mathbf{rd\,alloc}$ in $\bar{\varepsilon}$ then $\mathrm{alloc}(\sigma) = \mathrm{alloc}(\sigma')$
(c) for all $\mathbf{rd}\,G.f$ in $\bar{\varepsilon}$, for all $o \in [\![G]\!]\sigma$ with $f \in \mathrm{fields}(o,\sigma)$, we have $\sigma(o.f) = \sigma'(o.f)$

For Def. 2(c), note that because σ' extends σ, we have $o \in \mathrm{alloc}(\sigma')$ and $\mathrm{type}(o,\sigma) = \mathrm{type}(o,\sigma')$, hence $f \in \mathrm{fields}(o,\sigma')$. But it need not be the case that $o \in [\![G]\!]\sigma'$. Were we to consider **alloc** as a variable, (b) would be subsumed by (a); but it is not an ordinary variable.

Often, as discussed following Eqn. (3) in Sec. 2, we need to subsume an effect by a weaker one when the effect refers to a local variable in a different context. An effect set $\bar{\varepsilon}, \varepsilon$, with ε added to $\bar{\varepsilon}$, allows at least the effects allowed by $\bar{\varepsilon}$. In the case of an effect like $\mathbf{wr}\,G.f$ there is also the possibility of more liberal effect $\mathbf{wr}\,G'.f$ in case $G \subseteq G'$. Since regions can be state-dependent, inclusions like the above are state-dependent, so we use a judgement $P \vdash \bar{\varepsilon} \leq \bar{\varepsilon}'$ to express that the writes/reads in a bigger effect are more permissive. Subsumption for freshness effects is treated separately, since such effects are interpreted in the post-state. Rules for sub-effecting are defined in Fig. 6. Note that the relation is reflexive, since in the weakening rule $\vdash \bar{\varepsilon} \leq \bar{\varepsilon}, \varepsilon$ one may choose ε to be some element of the set $\bar{\varepsilon}$.

Lemma 1 (write sub-effect). Suppose $P \vdash \bar{\varepsilon}_1 \leq \bar{\varepsilon}_2$ and $\bar{\varepsilon}_1$ allows transition from σ to σ'. If $\sigma \models P$ then $\bar{\varepsilon}_2$ allows transition from σ to σ'.

Lemma 2 (read sub-effect). Suppose $P \vdash \bar{\varepsilon}_1 \leq \bar{\varepsilon}_2$ and σ and σ' agree on $\bar{\varepsilon}_2$. If $\sigma \models P$ then σ, σ' agree on $\bar{\varepsilon}_1$.

$$G_1 \subseteq G_2 \vdash \mathbf{wr}\, G_1{\cdot}f \leq \mathbf{wr}\, G_2{\cdot}f \qquad G_1 \subseteq G_2 \vdash \mathbf{rd}\, G_1{\cdot}f \leq \mathbf{rd}\, G_2{\cdot}f \qquad true \vdash \overline{\varepsilon} \leq \overline{\varepsilon}, \varepsilon$$

$$true \vdash \mathbf{wr}\, G_1{\cdot}f, \mathbf{wr}\, G_2{\cdot}f \lessgtr \mathbf{wr}\,(G_1 \cup G_2){\cdot}f \qquad true \vdash \mathbf{rd}\, G_1{\cdot}f, \mathbf{rd}\, G_2{\cdot}f \lessgtr \mathbf{rd}\,(G_1 \cup G_2){\cdot}f$$

$$\dfrac{P \vdash \overline{\varepsilon}_1 \leq \overline{\varepsilon}_2 \quad P \vdash \overline{\varepsilon}_2 \leq \overline{\varepsilon}_3}{P \vdash \overline{\varepsilon}_1 \leq \overline{\varepsilon}_3} \qquad \dfrac{P' \Rightarrow P \quad P \vdash \overline{\varepsilon} \leq \overline{\varepsilon}'}{P' \vdash \overline{\varepsilon} \leq \overline{\varepsilon}'} \qquad \dfrac{P \vdash \varepsilon_1 \leq \varepsilon_2}{P \vdash \varepsilon_1, \overline{\varepsilon} \leq \varepsilon_2, \overline{\varepsilon}}$$

Fig. 6. Selected sub-effect rules. We write $\lessgtr$ to abbreviate two inclusion rules.

6 Framing and Separators

This section defines a judgement, $P \vdash \overline{\varepsilon}$ **frm** P', that says the truth or falsity of predicate P' depends only on the state read according to $\overline{\varepsilon}$, i.e., $\overline{\varepsilon}$ covers the footprint of P' in P-states. This is one of the two critical ingredients in the Frame rule (Sec. 7). The other is the notion of *separator*, which applies to the read effects of a formula and the write effects of a command. Their separator is a conjunction of region disjointness formulas sufficient to ensure that in any transition from state σ to σ' allowed by the write effects, σ, σ' agree on the read effects.

6.1 Framing

First, we define a syntax-directed analysis that computes a precise "footprint" of ordinary expressions, region expressions and primitive assertions. Intuitively, the footprint is all reads needed to evaluate a given expression or primitive assertion whereas the frame of an assertion is an over-approximation of these requisite reads. We want $true \vdash \mathsf{ftpt}(P)$ **frm** P to hold for any primitive assertion P.

For any expression F, define the set of read effects of F, written $\mathsf{ftpt}(F)$, as follows: If F is an ordinary expression, E, define $\mathsf{ftpt}(E) = \{\mathbf{rd}\, x \mid x \in \mathit{Vars}(E)\}$. For a region expression G, define $\mathsf{ftpt}(G)$ as:

$$
\begin{aligned}
\mathsf{ftpt}(x) &= \{\mathbf{rd}\, x\} & \mathsf{ftpt}(x.g) &= \{\mathbf{rd}\, x, \mathbf{rd}\, \langle x \rangle{\cdot}g\} \\
\mathsf{ftpt}(\mathbf{alloc}) &= \{\mathbf{rd\, alloc}\} & \mathsf{ftpt}(\mathbf{emp}) &= \varnothing \\
\mathsf{ftpt}(G_1 \cup G_2) &= \mathsf{ftpt}(G_1) \cup \mathsf{ftpt}(G_2) & \mathsf{ftpt}(G_1 \cap G_2) &= \mathsf{ftpt}(G_1) \cup \mathsf{ftpt}(G_2) \\
\mathsf{ftpt}(G_1 - G_2) &= \mathsf{ftpt}(G_1) \cup \mathsf{ftpt}(G_2) & \mathsf{ftpt}(\langle E \rangle) &= \mathsf{ftpt}(E)
\end{aligned}
$$

For primitive assertions P, define $\mathsf{ftpt}(P)$ as follows:

$$
\begin{aligned}
\mathsf{ftpt}(E = E') &= \mathsf{ftpt}(E) \cup \mathsf{ftpt}(E') \\
\mathsf{ftpt}(x.f = F) &= \{\mathbf{rd}\, x, \mathbf{rd}\, \langle x \rangle{\cdot}f\} \cup \mathsf{ftpt}(F) \\
\mathsf{ftpt}(G_1 \subseteq G_2) &= \mathsf{ftpt}(G_1 \# G_2) = \mathsf{ftpt}(G_1) \cup \mathsf{ftpt}(G_2) \\
\mathsf{ftpt}(G_1{\cdot}f \subseteq G_2) &= \mathsf{ftpt}(G_1{\cdot}f \# G_2) = \mathsf{ftpt}(G_1) \cup \mathsf{ftpt}(G_2) \cup \{\mathbf{rd}\, G_1{\cdot}f\}
\end{aligned}
$$

Fig. 7 specifies the judgement $P \vdash \overline{\varepsilon}$ **frm** P'. The rule for framing a conjunction $P_1 \wedge P_2$ with $\overline{\varepsilon}$ allows P_1 to be used as hypothesis in showing that $\overline{\varepsilon}$ frames P_2. This is sound because in a state where P_1 is false, the conjunction's value is independent from the

$$\frac{P \text{ is primitive}}{true \vdash \text{ftpt}(P) \textbf{ frm } P}$$

$$\frac{P \vdash \overline{\varepsilon}_1 \textbf{ frm } P' \quad P \vdash \overline{\varepsilon}_1 \leq \overline{\varepsilon}_2 \quad Q \Rightarrow P}{Q \vdash \overline{\varepsilon}_2 \textbf{ frm } P'}$$

$$\frac{P_1 \Leftrightarrow P_2 \quad P \vdash \overline{\varepsilon} \textbf{ frm } P_1}{P \vdash \overline{\varepsilon} \textbf{ frm } P_2}$$

$$\frac{P \vdash \overline{\varepsilon} \textbf{ frm } P_1 \quad P \wedge P_1 \vdash \overline{\varepsilon} \textbf{ frm } P_2}{P \vdash \overline{\varepsilon} \textbf{ frm } P_1 \wedge P_2}$$

$$\frac{P \vdash \overline{\varepsilon}, \textbf{rd } x \textbf{ frm } P'}{P \vdash \overline{\varepsilon} \textbf{ frm } \forall x : \textbf{int} \mid P'}$$

$$\frac{\text{ftpt}(G) \subseteq \overline{\varepsilon} \quad P \wedge x \in G \vdash \overline{\varepsilon}, \textbf{rd } x, \textbf{rd } \langle x \rangle.\overline{f} \textbf{ frm } P'}{P \vdash \overline{\varepsilon}, \textbf{rd } G.\overline{f} \textbf{ frm } \forall x : K \in G \mid P'}$$

$$\frac{\text{ftpt}(G) \subseteq \overline{\varepsilon} \quad \text{ftpt}(G') \subseteq \overline{\varepsilon}}{P \Rightarrow \forall x \in G \mid x.g \subseteq G' \quad P \wedge x \in G \vdash \overline{\varepsilon}, \textbf{rd } x, \textbf{rd } \langle x \rangle.\overline{f}, \textbf{rd } x.g.\overline{g} \textbf{ frm } P'}{P \vdash \overline{\varepsilon}, \textbf{rd } G.\overline{f}, \textbf{rd } G'.\overline{g} \textbf{ frm } \forall x : K \in G \mid P'}$$

Fig. 7. Inductive definition of the frames judgement

value of P_2. It is very helpful in subsuming local effects by more global effects. For example, suppose $\overline{\varepsilon} = \textbf{rd } o, \textbf{rd } p, \textbf{rd } r, \textbf{rd } r.nxt$ and we wish to establish that $\overline{\varepsilon}$ frames the formula $o \in r \wedge p = o.nxt$. It is clear that $\overline{\varepsilon}$ frames $o \in r$. But the frame of $p = o.nxt$ must include $\langle o \rangle.nxt$, and this is missing from $\overline{\varepsilon}$. However, because of $o \in r$ we have $\textbf{rd } \langle o \rangle.nxt \leq \textbf{rd } r.nxt$ using the second rule in Fig. 6. Note that $\wedge$ is commutative —it has standard semantics. The rule for $\wedge$ can be use for either conjunct, owing to the rule to its left which allows use of a valid $P_1 \Leftrightarrow P_2$.

To frame a quantification $\forall x : K \in G \mid P'$ in context P, observe that because P' might refer to x, we are likely to need $\textbf{rd } x, \textbf{rd } \langle x \rangle.\overline{f}$ and $x.g.\overline{g}$ (i.e., the read effects of the pivot field $x.g$) to frame P'. The frame of the quantification cannot mention x. However, read effects $\textbf{rd } \langle x \rangle.\overline{f}$ may be subsumed by $\textbf{rd } G.\overline{f}$ because $x \in G$. Similarly if we are able to establish that for all x the pivot expressions $x.g$ are all bounded by the region G', the effect $x.g.\overline{g}$ can be subsumed by $G'.\overline{g}$. The first rule in Fig. 7 for quantification of a reference variable $(x : K)$ applies when there are no pivot regions, the second when P' uses only a single pivot region, $x.g$. The generalization to multiple pivots is straightforward but notationally messy.

For our running examples one can derive the following:

$$true \vdash \textbf{rd } o, r, r.nxt \textbf{ frm } List(o, r)$$
$$true \vdash \textbf{rd } o, s, v, \langle o \rangle.cache, \langle o \rangle.sub \textbf{ frm } Obs(o, s, v)$$
$$true \vdash \textbf{rd } s, v, \langle s \rangle.val, \langle s \rangle.obs, \langle s \rangle.O, s.O.nxt \textbf{ frm } Sub(s, v)$$
$$true \vdash \textbf{rd } s, v, \langle s \rangle.val, \langle s \rangle.obs, \langle s \rangle.O, s.O.nxt, s.O.cache, s.O.sub \textbf{ frm } SubObs(s, v)$$

Lemma 3 (footprint agreement). For any states, σ, σ', for any expression F, suppose that σ, σ' agree on $\text{ftpt}(F)$. Then $[\![F]\!]\sigma = [\![F]\!]\sigma'$.

Lemma 4 (frame agreement). For any σ, σ', any predicates P, P', and any set of effects $\overline{\varepsilon}$, suppose $P \vdash \overline{\varepsilon} \textbf{ frm } P'$ and $\sigma \models P$ and $\sigma \sim_{\overline{\varepsilon}} \sigma'$. Then $\sigma \models P'$ iff $\sigma' \models P'$.

Proof. By induction on a derivation of $P \vdash \overline{\varepsilon} \textbf{ frm } P'$. We consider the case for conjunction. Suppose $P \models \overline{\varepsilon} \textbf{ frm } P_1 \wedge P_2$ because $P \models \overline{\varepsilon} \textbf{ frm } P_1$ and $P \wedge P_1 \models \overline{\varepsilon} \textbf{ frm } P_2$.

Assume that σ, σ' agree on $\overline{\varepsilon}$ and $\sigma \models P$. By induction on judgement of P_1 we obtain $\sigma \models P_1$ iff $\sigma' \models P_1$. Case $\sigma \models P_1$: Then $\sigma \models P \wedge P_1$. Hence by induction on judgement of P_2 we obtain $\sigma \models P_2$ iff $\sigma' \models P_2$. Thus $\sigma \models P_1 \wedge P_2$ and $\sigma' \models P_1 \wedge P_2$. Case $\sigma \not\models P_1$: Then $\sigma' \not\models P_1$. Hence, in either case, $\sigma \models P_1 \wedge P_2$ iff $\sigma' \models P_1 \wedge P_2$.   □

6.2   Separators

Given effect sets $\overline{\varepsilon}_r$ and $\overline{\varepsilon}_w$, we define the *separator* formula $\overline{\varepsilon}_r \star \overline{\varepsilon}_w$ to be a conjunction of certain disjointnesses. In a state where $\overline{\varepsilon}_r \star \overline{\varepsilon}_w$ holds, nothing that the read effects in $\overline{\varepsilon}_r$ allow to be read can be written according to the write effects in $\overline{\varepsilon}_w$. Note that $\overline{\varepsilon}_w$ (resp. $\overline{\varepsilon}_r$) may contain read (resp. write) effects but these do not influence the separator.

Definition 3 (separator). Define separator $\overline{\varepsilon}_r \star \overline{\varepsilon}_w$ by recursion on the effect sets:

$$
\begin{aligned}
\mathbf{rd}\, G_1.f \,\star\, \mathbf{wr}\, G_2.g &= \text{ if } f \equiv g \text{ then } G_1 \# G_2 \text{ else } \textit{true} \\
\mathbf{rd}\, y \,\star\, \mathbf{wr}\, x &= \text{ if } x \equiv y \text{ then } \textit{false} \text{ else } \textit{true} \\
\mathbf{rd}\,\mathbf{alloc} \,\star\, \mathbf{wr}\,\mathbf{alloc} &= \textit{false} \\
\varepsilon \star \varepsilon' &= \textit{true} \quad \text{otherwise (for all other single effects)} \\
(\varepsilon, \overline{\varepsilon}) \star \overline{\varepsilon}_1 &= (\varepsilon \star \overline{\varepsilon}_1) \wedge (\overline{\varepsilon} \star \overline{\varepsilon}_1) \\
\varepsilon \star (\varepsilon', \overline{\varepsilon}) &= (\varepsilon \star \varepsilon') \wedge (\varepsilon \star \overline{\varepsilon})
\end{aligned}
$$

In Sec. 2, to get Eqn. (3) we needed to use a separator. We can now restate that condition as $\langle y \rangle \subseteq r_1 \wedge r_1 \# r_2 \Rightarrow \mathbf{rd}\, r_2.item \star \mathbf{wr}\, \langle y \rangle.item$. By definition of $\star$, it is immediate that the consequent is equal to $r_2 \# \langle y \rangle$ so the implication is valid.

Lemma 5 (separator agreement). Consider any effect sets $\overline{\varepsilon}_1$ and $\overline{\varepsilon}_2$. Suppose $\sigma \rightarrow \sigma' \models \overline{\varepsilon}_2$ and $\sigma \models \overline{\varepsilon}_1 \star \overline{\varepsilon}_2$. Then $\sigma \sim_{\overline{\varepsilon}_1} \sigma'$.

On separating conjunction. In separation logic, $P_1 * P_2$ says that P_1 and P_2 are both true and their truth is supported by disjoint regions of the heap. We can approximate the intuitionistic version that allows there to be objects outside the footprint of P_1 and P_2. Suppose $\overline{\varepsilon}_1$ **frm** P_1 and $\overline{\varepsilon}_2$ **frm** P_2. Obtain $\overline{\varepsilon}_2'$ from $\overline{\varepsilon}_2$ by discarding reads of variables and replacing each region read **rd** $G.f$ by **wr** $G.f$. Then the separation logic formula $P_1 * P_2$ amounts to $P_1 \wedge P_2 \wedge (\overline{\varepsilon}_1 \star \overline{\varepsilon}_2')$.

There is a significant difference, however. The semantics of $*$ is that there exists a partition of the heap, and there may be more than one partition in case P_1 and P_2 do not have unique semantic footprints. Our use of explicit footprints and ghost variables can be seen as skolemizing the existential implicit in $*$, since $\overline{\varepsilon}_1 \star \overline{\varepsilon}_2'$ typically refers to regions involving ghost variables assigned in the (instrumented) program. For example, define $P(r) \;\hat{=}\; \forall x : Node \in r \mid x.item \leq 0$ and $Q(r) \;\hat{=}\; \forall x : Node \in r \mid x.item \geq 0$. Let $R \;\hat{=}\; P(r) \wedge Q(\mathbf{alloc} - r)$. Then we have both $\{R\}\, x := \mathbf{new}\, K; x.n := 0\, \{R\}\, [\mathbf{wr}\, x, r]$ and $\{R\}\, x := \mathbf{new}\, K; x.n := 0; r := r \cup \langle x \rangle\, \{R\}\, [\mathbf{wr}\, x, r]$. But the reasoner must choose between these two commands. Issues with nondeterminacy could arise if we allowed bound region variables, e.g., $\exists r \mid P(r) \wedge Q(\mathbf{alloc} - r)$. Such matters are discussed further in [21].

6.3 Immunity

Recall from Sec. 2 the sequence $y := x.left; y.item := 0$. The individual effects, write of y and write of $\langle y \rangle.item$, cannot just be unioned to give the effect of the sequence, because write effects are interpreted in the pre-states (Def. 1(b)). The y in $\mathbf{wr}\,\langle y \rangle.item$ is not the same y as in the pre-state of the entire composition. The proof rule for sequential composition in Fig 8 must therefore ensure that the effect of the field update is *immune* from (or does not interfere with) the effect of the assignment. In this particular case we saw that the effect $\mathbf{wr}\,\langle y \rangle.item$ can be subsumed by a bigger effect, $\mathbf{wr}\,r_1.item$. The footprint of the region r_1 in the write effect is separate from the footprint of y and this permits the combined write effects to be $\mathbf{wr}\,y, \mathbf{wr}\,r_1.item$.

Definition 4 ($P/\overline{\varepsilon}$-**immune**). Region expression G is said to be $P/\overline{\varepsilon}$-immune provided $P \Rightarrow \mathrm{ftpt}(G) \star \overline{\varepsilon}$ is valid. Effect set $\overline{\varepsilon}_2$ is $P/\overline{\varepsilon}_1$-immune provided that for all G, f such that $\mathbf{wr}\,G.f$ occurs in $\overline{\varepsilon}_2$, it is the case that G is $P/\overline{\varepsilon}_1$-immune. □

For example, $\mathbf{alloc}$ is $P/\overline{\varepsilon}$-immune provided $\mathbf{wr}\,\mathbf{alloc}$ is not in $\overline{\varepsilon}$. Also, $\mathbf{wr}\,x$ is $true/\mathbf{wr}\,x$-immune (vacuously), but $\mathbf{wr}\,\langle x \rangle.f$ is not $true/\mathbf{wr}\,x$-immune because $\mathrm{ftpt}(\langle x \rangle) \star \mathbf{wr}\,x = false$ by Def. 3.

The key property of immunity is that if $\{P\}\,C_1\,\{P_1\}\,[\overline{\varepsilon}_1]$ and $\{P_1\}\,C_2\,\{P'\}\,[\overline{\varepsilon}_2]$ are valid, and $\overline{\varepsilon}_2$ is $P/\overline{\varepsilon}_1$-immune, then $\overline{\varepsilon}_1, \overline{\varepsilon}_2$ is a valid effect for the sequence $C_1; C_2$. This is part of the proof of soundness for the [Seq] rule, see Thm. 1.

Lemma 6. Let G be $P/\overline{\varepsilon}$-immune. Then $[\![G]\!]\sigma = [\![G]\!]\sigma'$ for any σ, σ' such that $\sigma \to \sigma' \models \overline{\varepsilon}$ and $\sigma \models P$.

Proof. Since G is $P/\overline{\varepsilon}$-immune, $P \Rightarrow \mathrm{ftpt}(G) \star \overline{\varepsilon}$. So by $\sigma \models P$, we have $\sigma \models \mathrm{ftpt}(G) \star \overline{\varepsilon}$. Then from $\sigma \to \sigma' \models \overline{\varepsilon}$ we have by Lemma 5 that σ, σ' agree on $\mathrm{ftpt}(G)$. Then by Lemma 3 we have $[\![G]\!]\sigma = [\![G]\!]\sigma'$. □

7 Program Correctness

A *correctness statement* takes the form $\{P\}\,C\,\{P'\}\,[\overline{\varepsilon}]$. The intended meaning is that from any initial state that satisfies P, C does not fault (terminate with error), and if it terminates then the final state satisfies P'. Moreover any allocation and update effects are allowed by $\overline{\varepsilon}$ (Def. 1). The statement is *well-formed in* Γ provided that P, P', C, and $\overline{\varepsilon}$ are well-formed in Γ.

The notation $\vdash^\Gamma$ is used for provability of statements that are well formed in Γ, so the proof system derives judgements of the form $\vdash^\Gamma \{P\}\,C\,\{P'\}\,[\overline{\varepsilon}]$. The semantics is used to define *valid* correctness statements, for which we use notation $\models^\Gamma$.

Definition 5 (**validity**). For state transformer φ of type Γ, define $\varphi \models^\Gamma \{P\} - \{P'\}\,[\overline{\varepsilon}]$ iff for all Γ-states σ, σ' such that $\sigma \models P$ we have $\varphi(\sigma) \neq \pitchfork$ and if $\varphi(\sigma) = \sigma'$ then $\sigma' \models P'$ and $\sigma \to \sigma' \models \overline{\varepsilon}$.

Let $\{P\}\,C\,\{P'\}\,[\overline{\varepsilon}]$ be well-formed in Γ. The correctness statement is *valid*, written $\models^\Gamma \{P\}\,C\,\{P'\}\,[\overline{\varepsilon}]$, if and only if $[\![\Gamma \vdash C]\!] \models^\Gamma \{P\} - \{P'\}\,[\overline{\varepsilon}]$. □

$$\text{ALLOC} \quad \cfrac{\text{fields}(K) = \overline{f} : \overline{T}}{\vdash \{\,true\,\}\; x := \mathbf{new}\; K\; \{\,x\,\mathbf{is}\,K \wedge x.\overline{f} = \overline{default(\overline{T})}\,\}\, [\mathbf{wr}\,x, \mathbf{wr}\,\mathbf{alloc}, \mathbf{fr}\,\langle x \rangle]}$$

$$\text{FIELDACC} \quad \cfrac{z \not\equiv x}{\vdash \{\,y \neq \mathbf{null} \wedge z = y\,\}\; x := y.f\; \{\,x = z.f\,\}\, [\mathbf{wr}\,x]}$$

$$\text{FIELDUPD} \quad \vdash \{\,x \neq \mathbf{null} \wedge y = F\,\}\; x.f := F\; \{\,x.f = y\,\}\, [\mathbf{wr}\,\langle x \rangle\bullet f]$$

$$\text{SEQ} \quad \cfrac{\begin{array}{c} \vdash \{P\}\; C_1\; \{P_1\}\, [\overline{\varepsilon}_1, \mathbf{fr}\,G] \\ \vdash \{P_1\}\; C_2\; \{P'\}\, [\overline{\varepsilon}_2, \mathbf{wr}\,\overline{G}\bullet\overline{f}] \qquad \overline{\varepsilon}_1 \text{ is } \mathbf{fr}\text{-free} \qquad \overline{\varepsilon}_2 \text{ is } P/\overline{\varepsilon}_1\text{-immune} \\ G \text{ is } P_1/(\overline{\varepsilon}_2, \mathbf{wr}\,\overline{G}\bullet\overline{f})\text{-immune} \qquad P_1 \Rightarrow \overline{G}_i \subseteq G \text{ for every } \mathbf{wr}\,\overline{G}_i\bullet\overline{f}_i \end{array}}{\vdash \{P\}\; C_1\,;C_2\; \{P'\}\, [\overline{\varepsilon}_1, \overline{\varepsilon}_2, \mathbf{fr}\,G]}$$

$$\text{VAR} \quad \cfrac{\vdash^{\Gamma,x:T} \{\,P \wedge x = default(T)\,\}\; C\; \{P'\}\, [\mathbf{wr}\,x, \overline{\varepsilon}]}{\vdash^{\Gamma} \{P\}\; \mathbf{var}\; x:T\; \mathbf{in}\; C\; \mathbf{end}\; \{P'\}\, [\overline{\varepsilon}]}$$

Fig. 8. Selected correctness rules and axioms for commands

$$\text{FRAME} \quad \cfrac{\vdash \{P\}\; C\; \{P'\}\, [\overline{\varepsilon}_C] \qquad P \vdash \overline{\varepsilon}_Q \; \mathbf{frm}\; Q \qquad P \Rightarrow \overline{\varepsilon}_Q \star \overline{\varepsilon}_C}{\vdash \{P \wedge Q\}\; C\; \{P' \wedge Q\}\, [\overline{\varepsilon}_C]}$$

$$\text{SUB EFF} \quad \cfrac{\vdash \{P\}\; C\; \{P'\}\, [\overline{\varepsilon}] \qquad P \vdash \overline{\varepsilon} \leq \overline{\varepsilon}'}{\vdash \{P\}\; C\; \{P'\}\, [\overline{\varepsilon}']} \qquad\qquad \text{CONTEXT} \quad \cfrac{\vdash^{\Gamma} \{P\}\; C\; \{P'\}\, [\overline{\varepsilon}]}{\vdash^{\Gamma,x:T} \{P\}\; C\; \{P'\}\, [\overline{\varepsilon}]}$$

$$\text{NO UPDATE} \quad \cfrac{\vdash \{P\}\; C\; \{P'\}\, [\mathbf{wr}\,\langle x \rangle\bullet f, \overline{\varepsilon}] \qquad \mathbf{rd}\, x \star \overline{\varepsilon} \qquad \mathbf{rd}\, y \star \overline{\varepsilon} \qquad P \vee P' \Rightarrow x.f = y}{\vdash \{P\}\; C\; \{P'\}\, [\overline{\varepsilon}]}$$

Fig. 9. Selected structural rules. Rules of Consequence, Conjunction, etc. are as usual.

Fig. 8 gives selected syntax-directed proof rules and axioms. In axiom [FieldUpd], one step of dereferencing is allowed since F in the rule can be of the form $x.f$ in the case that $f : \mathbf{rgn}$. But if we allowed command $x.f := y.f.g$, the rule would yield postcondition $x.f = y.f.g$ which is unsound due to possible sharing.

Fig. 9 gives selected structural rules. Rule [No Update] illustrates how assertional reasoning can be used to eliminate effects.

Theorem 1. If $\vdash \{P\}\; C\; \{P'\}\, [\overline{\varepsilon}]$ then $\models \{P\}\; C\; \{P'\}\, [\overline{\varepsilon}]$, for any $C, P, P', \overline{\varepsilon}$.

Proof. By induction on the derivation of $\vdash \{P\}\; C\; \{P'\}\, [\overline{\varepsilon}]$. This boils down to showing soundness for each rule. For brevity we focus on the case of normal termination. Recall that $\sigma, \sigma', \sigma_1$ range over proper states (non-$\Uparrow$).

Case [Frame]: To prove $\models \{P \wedge Q\}\; C\; \{P' \wedge Q\}\, [\overline{\varepsilon}_C]$, suppose $\sigma \models P \wedge Q$ and $[\![C]\!]\sigma = \sigma'$. Then $\sigma \models P$. From $\vdash \{P\}\; C\; \{P'\}\, [\overline{\varepsilon}]$ we get $\models \{P\}\; C\; \{P'\}\, [\overline{\varepsilon}]$ by induction, hence $\sigma' \models P'$ and $\sigma \to \sigma' \models \overline{\varepsilon}_C$. Using $\sigma \models P$ and $P \Rightarrow \overline{\varepsilon}_Q \star \overline{\varepsilon}_C$, we get $\sigma \models \overline{\varepsilon}_Q \star \overline{\varepsilon}_C$. Now by Lemma 5 we can conclude that σ, σ' agree on $\overline{\varepsilon}_Q$. So we have $P \vdash \overline{\varepsilon}_Q$ **frm** Q and σ, σ' agree on $\overline{\varepsilon}_Q$ and $\sigma \models P$. Thus from Lemma 4 we can conclude that $\sigma \models Q$ iff $\sigma' \models Q$. But $\sigma \models Q$ because $\sigma \models P \wedge Q$. Hence $\sigma' \models Q$ and so $\sigma' \models P' \wedge Q$.

Case [Seq]: Let σ be any Γ-state such that $\sigma \models P$. Suppose $[\![C_1]\!]\sigma = \sigma_1$ and $[\![C_2]\!]\sigma_1 = \sigma'$. By validity of the antecedent correctness statements we get $\sigma_1 \models P_1$ and $\sigma' \models P'$; moreover $\sigma \to \sigma_1 \models \overline{\varepsilon}_1, \mathbf{fr}\ G$ and $\sigma_1 \to \sigma' \models \overline{\varepsilon}_2, \mathbf{wr}\ \overline{G.f}$. To prove $\sigma \to \sigma' \models \overline{\varepsilon}_1, \overline{\varepsilon}_2, \mathbf{fr}\ G$, we argue by cases on the parts of Def. 1.

Part (a): Consider any x such that $\sigma(x) \neq \sigma'(x)$. If $\sigma_1(x) \neq \sigma'(x)$ then $\mathbf{wr}\ x$ is in $\overline{\varepsilon}_2$, by $\sigma_1 \models P_1$ and $\sigma_1 \to \sigma' \models \overline{\varepsilon}_2, \mathbf{wr}\ \overline{G.f}$ (from above). If $\sigma_1(x) = \sigma'(x)$ then $\sigma(x) \neq \sigma_1(x)$ so then $\mathbf{wr}\ x$ is in $\overline{\varepsilon}_1$, by $\sigma \models P$ and $\sigma \to \sigma_1 \models \overline{\varepsilon}_1, \mathbf{fr}\ G$ (from above).

Part (b): Consider any $p \in \mathsf{alloc}(\sigma)$ and f such that $\sigma(p.f) \neq \sigma'(p.f)$.

- Case $\sigma_1(p.f) \neq \sigma'(p.f)$: Owing to $\sigma_1 \models P_1$ and $\sigma_1 \to \sigma' \models \overline{\varepsilon}_2, \mathbf{wr}\ \overline{G.f}$, we have one of two cases:
  - There is $\mathbf{wr}\ G'.f \in \overline{\varepsilon}_2$ such that $p \in [\![G']\!]\sigma_1$. By antecedent of [Seq], $\overline{\varepsilon}_2$ is $P/\overline{\varepsilon}_1$-immune, so G' is $P/\overline{\varepsilon}_1$-immune. Thus by Lemma 6, $p \in [\![G']\!]\sigma$. Thus this update is allowed in virtue of $\mathbf{wr}\ G'.f$.
  - There is i such that $p \in [\![\overline{G}_i]\!]\sigma_1$ and $\overline{f}_i$ is f. Since $\sigma_1 \models P_1$, antecedent $P_1 \Rightarrow \overline{G}_i \subseteq G$ of [Seq] yields $p \in [\![G]\!]\sigma_1$. And since we have $\sigma \to \sigma_1 \models \overline{\varepsilon}_1, \mathbf{fr}\ G$, we have that $[\![G]\!]\sigma_1 \subseteq \mathsf{alloc}(\sigma') - \mathsf{alloc}(\sigma)$, which contradicts the assumption that $p \in \mathsf{alloc}(\sigma)$ —so this case cannot happen.
- Case $\sigma_1(p.f) = \sigma'(p.f)$: Then $\sigma(p.f) \neq \sigma_1(p.f)$, so by $\sigma \to \sigma_1 \models \overline{\varepsilon}_1, \mathbf{fr}\ G$ there is some $\mathbf{wr}\ G'.f \in \overline{\varepsilon}_1$ with $p \in [\![G']\!]\sigma$.

Part (c): Consider any $p \in \mathsf{alloc}(\sigma')$ such that $p \notin \mathsf{alloc}(\sigma)$. Case $p \in \mathsf{alloc}(\sigma_1)$: then $\mathbf{wr}\ \mathbf{alloc}$ is in $\overline{\varepsilon}_1$. Case $p \notin \mathsf{alloc}(\sigma_1)$: then $\mathbf{wr}\ \mathbf{alloc}$ is in $\overline{\varepsilon}_2$.

Part (d): For any $\mathbf{fr}\ G'$ in $\overline{\varepsilon}_2$, we have $[\![G']\!]\sigma' \subseteq \mathsf{alloc}(\sigma') - \mathsf{alloc}(\sigma_1)$ from $\sigma_1 \to \sigma' \models \overline{\varepsilon}_2, \mathbf{wr}\ \overline{G.f}$. Since σ_1 extends σ (by semantics), we thus have $[\![G']\!]\sigma' \subseteq \mathsf{alloc}(\sigma') - \mathsf{alloc}(\sigma)$. Finally, since $\overline{\varepsilon}_1$ is $\mathbf{fr}$-free it remains to justify the final effect $\mathbf{fr}\ G$: Using the antecedent that G is $P_1/(\overline{\varepsilon}_2, \mathbf{wr}\ \overline{G.f})$-immune, and $\sigma_1 \models P_1$, we have by Lemma 6 and $\sigma_1 \to \sigma' \models \overline{\varepsilon}_2, \mathbf{wr}\ \overline{G.f}$ that $[\![G]\!]\sigma_1 = [\![G]\!]\sigma'$. By $\sigma \models P$ and $\sigma \to \sigma_1 \models \overline{\varepsilon}_1, \mathbf{fr}\ G$ we have $[\![G]\!]\sigma_1 \subseteq \mathsf{alloc}(\sigma_1) - \mathsf{alloc}(\sigma)$ and hence since σ' extends σ_1 we have $[\![G]\!]\sigma_1 \subseteq \mathsf{alloc}(\sigma') - \mathsf{alloc}(\sigma)$. Using $[\![G]\!]\sigma_1 = [\![G]\!]\sigma'$ we get $[\![G]\!]\sigma' \subseteq \mathsf{alloc}(\sigma') - \mathsf{alloc}(\sigma)$. □

Substitution and ghost elimination rules. In order to connect initial and final states, we often use variables that occur in pre- and post-conditions but not the program. Substitution for such variables is sound, but it takes a bit of work to formulate that they do not occur in the program. This is made straightforward by the inclusion of read effects in command specifications. Then we can formulate the substitution rule as follows. We use Reynolds' notation for substitution in formulas, writing $P/x{\to}F$ for substitution of F for x in P.

$$\frac{\vdash \{P\}\ C\ \{P'\}\ [\overline{\varepsilon}] \qquad (P/x{\to}F) \Rightarrow \mathsf{ftpt}(F) \star (\overline{\varepsilon}/x{\to}F) \qquad \mathbf{rd}\ x \notin \overline{\varepsilon} \qquad \mathbf{wr}\ x \notin \overline{\varepsilon}}{\vdash \{P/x{\to}F\}\ C\ \{P'/x{\to}F\}\ [\overline{\varepsilon}/x{\to}F]}$$

In accord with our convention on well formed rule instantiations, the result of substitution must be well formed here, e.g., $(x.g \subseteq r)/x{\to}\mathbf{null}$ is not. The proof uses routine techniques but it requires the semantics of read effects of commands which we omit from this paper for brevity. There is also an auxiliary elimination rule (cf. Owicki-Gries), needed since local variables of type **rgn** are used as ghosts for reasoning.

8 Examples

We conclude the Subject/Observer example by verifying a simple client program using the specifications in Fig. 5. Method call and constructor rules are omitted from the technical formalization but are straightforward and we use them here. Here is the client program: $o := \mathbf{new}\ Observer(s);\ s.update(n);\ i := o.val();$. Here is its specification: requires $SubObs(s, s.val)$, ensures $i = n$, effects $\overline{\varepsilon_1}, \overline{\varepsilon_2}, \mathbf{wr}\ i$ where: $\overline{\varepsilon_1} = \mathbf{wr\ alloc}, o, s.O.nxt, \langle s \rangle.O, \langle s \rangle.obs, \mathbf{fr}\ \langle o \rangle$, and $\overline{\varepsilon_2} = \mathbf{wr}\ \langle s \rangle.val, s.O.cache$. Our first step uses the (omitted) rule for allocation with constructor call. Informally, the rule says that we can use constructor's pre/postconditions by adapting them to the calling context. The effects are those of the constructor with **self** replaced by LHS of the assignment.

$$\{ SubObs(s, s.val) \}\ o := \mathbf{new}\ Observer(s)\ \{ SubObs(s, s.val) \wedge o \in s.O \}\ [\overline{\varepsilon_1}] \quad (4)$$

The method call rule yields $\{ SubObs(s, s.val) \}\ s.update(n)\ \{ SubObs(s, n) \}\ [\overline{\varepsilon_2}]$. Now we can apply Frame to conjoin $o \in s.O$ since $true \vdash \mathbf{rd}\ o, s, \langle s \rangle.O$ **frm** $o \in s.O$ and $true \Rightarrow (\mathbf{rd}\ o, s, \langle s \rangle.O) \star (\mathbf{wr}\ \langle s \rangle.val, s.O.cache)$.

$$\{ SubObs(s, s.val) \wedge o \in s.O \}\ s.update(n)\ \{ SubObs(s, n) \wedge o \in s.O \}\ [\overline{\varepsilon_2}] \quad (5)$$

Next, we have by the method call rule, and [Conseq]

$$\{ SubObs(o.sub, o.sub.val) \wedge o \in o.sub.O \}\ i := o.val()\ \{ i = o.sub.val \}\ [\mathbf{wr}\ i]$$

Let $Q \mathrel{\hat{=}} o.sub = s \wedge s.val = n$. Framing the above with Q we obtain

$$\{ SubObs(o.sub, o.sub.val) \wedge o \in o.sub.O \wedge Q \}\ i := o.val()\ \{ i = o.sub.val \wedge Q \}\ [\mathbf{wr}\ i]$$

First, $i = o.sub.val \wedge Q$ implies $i = n$. Next, we can show that the postcondition of (5) implies $SubObs(o.sub, o.sub.val) \wedge o \in o.sub.O \wedge Q$ by unfolding the definition of $SubObs$ using $o \in o.sub.O$. Thus we get by [Conseq]

$$\{ SubObs(s, n) \wedge o \in s.O \}\ i := o.val()\ \{ i = n \}\ [\mathbf{wr}\ i] \quad (6)$$

Now using [Seq] on (4), (5), (6) we obtain the desired correctness judgement at the beginning of the section.

For examples that use separation without any inductive predicates, we have verified the standard list copy and in-situ reversal algorithms with respect to the following specifications. For *reversal*: requires $x \in r \wedge r.nxt = r$, ensures $res \in r \wedge r.nxt = r$, effect $\mathbf{wr}\ r.nxt$. That is, r remains closed, the result is in r, and there is no allocation. Our specification for *copy* says the copy is disjoint from the original: requires $x \in r_1 \wedge r_1.nxt = r_1$, ensures $res \in r_2 \wedge r_2.nxt = r_2 \wedge r_1 \# r_2$, effect $\mathbf{wr}\ r_2$, **alloc**.

9 Framing Module Invariants

The previous section focused on framing in the small: using effect specifications to reason about commands in terms of specifications of their constituent commands. This section addresses framing at a higher level, in particular, reasoning about invariants for encapsulated state [13]. The idea is that the implementation of an abstract data type can maintain an invariant that pertains to its encapsulated data representation, without exposing the invariant to clients (or subclasses). This creates a mismatch between the client's view of a method call, say $\{ P/\textbf{self} \rightarrow x \}$ $x.m()$ $\{ P'/\textbf{self} \rightarrow x \}$ $[\ldots]$, using the specification P, P' of m, and the proof obligation for the implementation C_m of m: $\{ P \wedge Inv(\textbf{self}) \}$ C_m $\{ P' \wedge Inv(\textbf{self}) \}$ $[\ldots]$.

Sec. 9.1 considers ownership confinement, the idea that a client-visible object that represents, say, a Collection can encapsulate its internal representation as a region disjoint from the reps of other collections and from clients. If the invariant is framed by the owned reps, and disjointness is maintained as a confinement invariant, and client effects are disjoint from the reps, then the mismatched proof obligations [13] are sound.

We treat confinement as an explicit invariant that pertains to all instances of some class (or subclasses, though we refrain from emphasizing that dimension). We treat the object invariant in terms of a single invariant that pertains to all instances. This treatment allows an encapsulation discipline to be expressed on a per-module basis, rather than being globally imposed on all code. Moreover, it allows the mismatch to be formalized as a second order frame rule like that of separation logic [23], with a confinement invariant and client effect bound carried through the part of a proof in which an invariant is hidden. The rule is admissible [21], which amounts to saying that the mismatch can always be fixed by augmenting the proof with explicit uses of our ordinary Frame rule.

Sec. 9.2 returns to the Subject/Observer example, again in terms of a global invariant that describes disjointness of encapsulated islands, albeit not based on hierarchical ownership.

9.1 Ownership and Object Invariants

The following classes illustrate a scenario like a set represented by a linked list that may contain duplicate elements.

class $Coll$ $\{\textbf{rgn } rep;\ Node\ lst;\ \textbf{int } size;\}$ **class** $Node$ $\{T\ item;\ \textbf{int } len;\ Node\ nxt;\}$

The $size$ of a collection is part of its external interface. For the sake of an example, we choose an object invariant that relates $size$ to the internal representation:

$CollI(c) \; \hat{=} \; c \neq null \wedge c \textbf{ is } Coll \wedge c.lst \in c.rep \wedge c.rep.nxt \subseteq c.rep \wedge c.lst.len \geq c.size$

Recall that $c.lst \in c.rep$ abbreviates $c.lst \neq \textbf{null} \wedge \langle c \rangle.lst \subseteq c.rep$. Field rep serves to delimit the encapsulated representation or owned objects. The following can be derived:

$$true \vdash \textbf{rd } c, \langle c \rangle.(rep, lst, size), c.rep.(len, nxt) \; \textbf{frm } CollI(c) \qquad (7)$$

Let $d: Collection$, to consider a call $d.m()$ that relies on invariant $CollI(d)$. Methodologies based on ownership can be described as a way to ensure that a client command, say $\{P\}\ C\ \{P'\}\ [\bar{\varepsilon}]$, can be lifted by the Frame rule to $\{P \wedge CollI(d)\}\ C\ \{P' \wedge CollI(d)\}\ [\bar{\varepsilon}]$ because the frame of $CollI(d)$ is necessarily separate from the client effect. If specifications for all parts of the client code are thus lifted, they match the hidden precondition $CollI(d)$.

An object invariant is intended to apply *separately* to *each instance* of the class. It is easy to say it applies to each instance: $\forall c\colon Coll \in \mathbf{alloc}\mid CollI(c)$. To illustrate the flexibility of our logic, let us instead suppose there is a global region variable $CollS$ that holds some or all instances of $Coll$. (In practice this would be a static field of class $Coll$.) The "component" of interest to clients is the pool of objects in $CollS$. We want each of these collections to satisfy its invariant: $\forall c \in CollS\mid CollI(c)$. To frame this formula, suppose global variable $CollR$ holds the union of the reps of $CollS$, i.e.

$$CollC_0 \triangleq \forall c \in CollS\mid c.rep \subseteq CollR$$

This serves to derive, from (7), a frame for $\forall c \in CollS\mid CollI(c)$, to wit

$$CollC_0 \vdash \mathbf{rd}\ CollS, CollR, CollS\bullet(rep, lst, size), CollR\bullet len\ \mathbf{frm}\ \forall c \in CollS\mid CollI(c)$$

Formula $CollC_0$ says that the module's internal representation objects are in $CollR$. We can express the "package confinement" condition that clients don't reach reps:

$$CollC_1 \triangleq (\mathbf{alloc} - (CollS \cup CollR))\bullet\mathbf{any} \# CollR$$

If package confinement holds at call sites, then we can use the Frame rule to lift client code to get it to match with

$$\{P \wedge \forall c \in CollS\mid CollI(c)\}\ d.m()\ \{P' \wedge \forall c \in CollS\mid CollI(c)\}\ [\ldots] \qquad (8)$$

(Doing this once and for all is the point of the second order frame rule [21].)

The precondition of (8) is certainly strong enough to verify the implementation of m, since it implies $CollI(d)$. The postcondition appears very strong. But recall that an object invariant is supposed to apply "separately" to each instance. Besides separating clients from representations, with $CollC_1$, we can also use an "island confinement" condition to say that distinct collections have disjoint reps:

$$CollC_2 \triangleq \forall c, c'\colon Coll \in CollS\mid c = c' \vee c.rep \# c'.rep$$

Confinement conditions like $CollC_0$, $CollC_1$, and $CollC_2$ can be enforced by ownership type systems and other pointer analyses.[1] Such enforcement mechanisms typically ensure that confinement holds in all reachable states.[2]

---

[1] For example, if we represent an ownership hierarchy using a ghost field *owner*, and impose the dominator property of Ownership Types, then $CollC_2$ will be an easy consequence. If instead we allow some references, for read-only use as in Universe Types, then a weaker confinement condition holds; but the story can still play out, as we distinguish between read and write effects of commands.

[2] Making these conditions explicit in program annotations might be a high cost, compared with getting them as global invariants "for free" from a separate static analysis. On the other hand, making them explicit would be one way to show soundness of the result of a particular analysis, and also provide a means to work around restrictions due to approximations made by static analysis. For now we set that issue aside and simply assume they are all-states invariants.

Let us return to the problem of establishing the postcondition of (8) in the implementation of method m. To focus on **self**, we can rewrite $\forall c \in CollS \mid CollI(c)$ as $P_C \wedge CollI(\textbf{self})$ where

$$P_C \;\hat{=}\; \forall c \in CollS - \langle\textbf{self}\rangle \mid CollI(c)$$

In light of the frame we found for $\forall c \in CollS \mid CollI(c)$, we can frame P_C as

$$CollC_0 \vdash \textbf{rd self}, CollS, CollR, (CollS - \langle\textbf{self}\rangle)\textbf{.}(rep, lst, size), CollR\textbf{.}len \;\textbf{frm}\; P_C$$

Further, we can remove $\textbf{self}.rep.len$ from the effect **rd** $CollR\textbf{.}len$ owing to the island confinement $CollC_2$.

In short, we should verify the implementation with respect to just $CollI(\textbf{self})$. Owing to confinement, the footprint of the implementation is disjoint from the frame of $\forall c \in CollS - \langle\textbf{self}\rangle \mid CollI(c)$, so the frame rule will yield $\forall c \in CollS \mid CollI(c)$.

Making confinement an all-states invariant is sufficient but not necessary. The confinement conditions are necessary at those points where the frame rule is used to lift a local correctness property, like preserving $CollI(\textbf{self})$, to a stronger property like preserving $\forall c \in CollS \mid CollI(c)$. Confinement may also be exploited for reasoning within the implementation, e.g., at outgoing method calls —more on that below.

In summary, we suggest that method implementations maintain module invariants, which may include module-wide conditions for resource management etc, together with object invariants in global form, like $\forall c \in CollS \mid CollI(c)$.

On reentrant callbacks. Through cyclic references, it is possible for some module operation to invoke a method that leads to a *re-entrant callback*. That is, an invocation on some object o at a point when another operation is already in progress and which may thus have temporarily falsified the invariant. In some cases, re-entrant callback can be shown to be impossible simply in virtue of the graph of which method implementations invoke which (disambiguated) methods. Another technique is the "visible state semantics" [18] in which invariants are required to hold on every method call boundary; so in particular the module operation is required to re-establish the object invariant before making any call. In some cases, pointer analysis can determine the absence of cyclic references by which a chain of calls can lead back to an instance. Using the Frame requires separation and thus prevents hiding invariants in cases where the effects of callbacks are not disjoint from the invariants' footprints.

Sometimes reentrant callbacks are desirable, of course. The Subject/Observer code is an example where the relevant methods belong together in a module and therefore hiding the invariant is not an issue. In cases where hiding is important, such as other Subject/Observer scenarios where the Observer cannot be expected to be responsible for the Subject's invariants, a typical solution is to designate the intended callback methods as not assuming the hidden invariant.

Hierarchical ownership. *Coll* relies on *Node* operations. If *Node* is in a different module, it may rely on invariants that are hidden from *Coll*. For example, if *Coll* requires that the actual number of values in the list is at most $lst.len$, then *Node* takes care of that when a new item is inserted. On the other hand, that will make $self.lst.len$ out of sync with $self.size$; restoring that is *Coll*'s responsibility.

Our idea is that a module, say the module for *Node*, has some confinement policy and its clients are checked for conformance. The code of *Node* can thereby rely on its object invariant. This can be hidden from *Coll*, which is a client of *Node*. In turn, by encapsulating its list nodes, possibly by a different discipline, *Coll* ensures that operations on nodes of *c.reps* only happen when methods of *Coll* have control.

9.2   Beyond Ownership to Cluster Invariants

In this section let us say an *abstract component* is one or more *interface objects* that serve to represent some data abstraction, together with their representation objects which are meant for internal use. For example, a collection together with its iterators are an abstract component that provides a set with stateful enumerations. Ownership is suited to situations where there is a single interface object. Perhaps the most obvious way to express an invariant for this example is as a predicate that involves an instance of *Coll* together with all its associated *Iterators*. A number of techniques have been proposed to treat such a "cluster invariant" as one or more object invariants whose dependencies are constrained but not by ownership [22]. There are several reasons to try to reduce cluster invariants to object invariants. On the other hand, notions like peer dependencies and friendship are very limited in applicability. It is worthwhile to develop disciplines tailored to design patterns in wide use, such as Subject/Observer and Iterator. But it is also desirable to have a setting in which ad hoc reasoning patterns can be devised for very specific situations, yet still achieving modular and economic reasoning based on encapsulated invariants.

The client of a cluster with multiple interface objects has the potential to interfere with the invariant via those multiple handles, and thus the specifications of operations on particular interface objects —like adding to the collection, or advancing one of its iterators— must surely expose a holistic view of the cluster. In the paper [24] from which we borrow the Subject/Observer example, Parkinson uses a cluster invariant *SubObs* that appears in preconditions of methods of both Subject and Observer.

First, we imagine *Subject* and *Observer* are together in a module, with methods *register* and *add* given module scope while others are public. The module-scope methods are verified in the same context and without need to hide the invariant; it can simply be made explicit in their specifications. Now we factor apart the *Sub* predicate into a condition, *SubX*, suited to public (external) specifications, and another, *SubH*, suited to be a hidden invariant. (In a more realistic example, *val* would be a model field.)

$$SubX(s,v) \mathrel{\hat{=}} s.val = v \qquad SubH(s,v) \mathrel{\hat{=}} List(s.obs, s.O)$$
$$SubObsX(s,v) \mathrel{\hat{=}} SubX(s,v) \wedge \forall o: Observer \in s.O \mid Obs(o,s,v)$$
$$SubObsH(s,v) \mathrel{\hat{=}} SubH(s,v) \wedge SubX(s,v)$$

Whereas the X-versions of the invariant are left in the method specifications, the H-versions are used only for verification of the implementations of the methods of Subject and Observer. Specifically, a global invariant like this is used:

$$SOI \mathrel{\hat{=}} \quad (\forall s: Subject \in \mathbf{alloc} \mid SubObsH(s, s.val))$$
$$\wedge (\forall o: Observer \in \mathbf{alloc} \mid o.sub \neq \mathbf{null} \Rightarrow o \in o.sub.O)$$

Given precondition SOI for a method of $Observer$, the verifier can instantiate the second conjunct with **self** for o, and the first conjunct with **self**.sub for s, to obtain the invariant for its cluster. Confinement invariants can be used to separate clusters so that the $Observer$ method is responsible for restoring the invariant, $SubObsH$, for its cluster but then restores SOI for all others simply by framing. In particular, the separation of clusters would look similar to $CollC_2$, though in this case the islands are not as isolated from clients since both $Subject$s and $Observer$s are accessible.

10   Discussion

The genesis of this work is our ongoing work on secure information flow analysis, combining verification and type checking [4]. We are developing a relational logic that lets us specify fine grained declassification policies. Amtoft et al [1] achieve precise, modular reasoning about information flow using regions. In order to extend their work to declassification policies, which may depend on complex program state conditions, we needed to enrich the assertion language, which led to dropping their abstract interpretation of heap locations in favor of explicit regions.

State of the art verifiers use intricate reasoning about the heap, often based on variants of ownership régimes. Our approach is inspired by the Boogie methodology [5,16], which is explicitly based on all-states invariants that use ghost fields to express an encapsulation régime (though not focused on confinement). Boogie also combines instance invariants into a global condition akin to our example $\forall c: Coll \in \textbf{alloc} \mid CollI(c)$.

Another inspiration is the work of Kassios [14], showing how explicit use of ghost state can be effective without global imposition of a fixed programming discipline. Kassios uses a ghost field to hold the footprint of an object's invariant, a means to specify the footprint, and a means to specify that a procedure touches only that footprint. Kassios works directly with the semantics of "frames" as a second order predicate, quantifying over all global program states. By contrast, we work out a first order assertion-based logic. But there are similarities, e.g., Metatheorem 5.4.1 in his thesis is related to our notion of immunity, as is the swinging pivots restriction of Leino and Nelson [17, Sec. 8.3].

Smans et al [26] investigate Kassios' approach to framing in the setting of pre / post / modifies specifications, focusing on reasoning with pure method calls in assertions. Like us they use explicit regions in modifies specifications, expressed as pure methods. Their approach has been implemented in a prototype verifier and applied to examples like observer and iterator.

Smith [27] uses regions denoted by ownership contexts to formulate a simple, type based frame rule that resembles ours.

Recent work on ownership has addressed the need for clusters without a single dominating owner. Cameron et al [10] give a good survey of ownership systems. They adapt Ownership Types to a system of "boxes" (clusters) that describes rather than restricts program structure. Thus it does not ensure encapsulation, but they provide and prove sound an effect system for disjointness of boxes. Müller and Rudich [19] extend Universe Types, which provides encapsulation and has been adopted by JML for invariants, to solve the difficult problem of ownership transfer. Drossopoulou et al [12] provide a general theory to account for a variety of invariant disciplines, focusing on visible state semantics. Ownership type systems cater for hierarchical ownership, with the benefit of uniformity and a fixed semantics of when invariants hold. We propose the use of second order framing with module-specific disciplines, in hopes of more flexible deployment of these and even earlier and simpler ownership systems.

The influence of separation logic on our work is clear. The separating conjunction hides the heap and expresses separation in the heap implicitly. Becauses footprints are shadows of predicates, specifications require full functional descriptions using inductive definitions, or else quantification over predicates. Parkinson's position paper [24] clearly articulates the case for specifications at the level of object clusters. In higher order separation logics [7] and Hoare type theory [20], one can quantify predicates to get multi-instance abstractions at the cost of intricate semantics and sometimes the loss of the [Conj] rule. Various works articulate the view that the second order frame rule pertains to static, single-instance modules, e.g., this motivated Parkinson's technique for hiding invariants by opaque naming, which can be understood as second order existentials [6].

Now we turn to future work. The Boogie discipline can be viewed as a proof outline logic; it would be interesting to show that the invariants specified in the discipline hold in that logic by using reasoning similar to the one developed in this paper. More generally, the logic may be of use in connecting and even unifying various disciplines for ownership and beyond. To that end we are investigating better means to abstract from field names than the crude "any" used here in examples. Another question is whether effects can be made conditional, or even subsumed in two-state postconditions, while retaining effective generation of framing conditions as in Sec. 6.

The proof rules of our logic are formulated in a way that shows how reasoning works. An automated verifier will likely not apply such rules directly but will rather transform the code and generate verification conditions. Experiments with the logic are underway, by translating into BoogiePL, and the third author is investigating decision procedures for quantifier-free assertions. Another avenue to explore is use of the logic as translation target from higher level static analyses; instead of metatheory to justify that analysis and its use, it just creates verification conditions (c.f. runtime verification).

Acknowledgements. We are grateful for encouragement and helpful suggestions from people including Mike Barnett, Sophia Drossopoulou, Manuel Fähndrich, Peter Müller, James Noble, Peter O'Hearn, Matthew Parkinson, and anonymous reviewers for POPL and ECOOP.

References

1. Amtoft, T., Bandhakavi, S., Banerjee, A.: A logic for information flow in object-oriented programs. In: ACM Symposium on Principles of Programming Languages (POPL) (2006)
2. Banerjee, A., Naumann, D.A.: Ownership confinement ensures representation independence for object-oriented programs. Journal of the ACM 52(6), 894–960 (2005)
3. Banerjee, A., Naumann, D., Rosenberg, S.: Regional logic for local reasoning about global invariants, www.cs.stevens.edu/~naumann/pub/rllrgi.pdf

4. Banerjee, A., Naumann, D., Rosenberg, S.: Towards a logical account of declassification. In: ACM Workshop on Programming Languages and Analysis for Security (2007)
5. Barnett, M., DeLine, R., Fähndrich, M., Leino, K.R.M., Schulte, W.: Verification of object-oriented programs with invariants. Journal of Object Technology 3(6), 27–56 (2004)
6. Bierman, G., Parkinson, M.: Separation logic and abstraction. In: ACM Symposium on Principles of Programming Languages (POPL), pp. 247–258 (2005)
7. Birkedal, L., Torp-Smith, N., Yang, H.: Semantics of separation-logic typing and higher-order frame rules. In: IEEE Symp. on Logic in Computer Science (LICS) (2005)
8. Bornat, R.: Proving pointer programs in Hoare logic. In: MPC (2000)
9. Calcagno, C., O'Hearn, P., Bornat, R.: Program logic and equivalence in the presence of garbage collection. Theoretical Comput. Sci. 298(3), 557–581 (2003)
10. Cameron, N.R., Drossopoulou, S., Noble, J., Smith, M.J.: Multiple ownership. In: OOPSLA (2007)
11. Clarke, D., Drossopoulou, S.: Ownership, encapsulation and the disjointness of type and effect. In: OOPSLA, pp. 292–310 (November 2002)
12. Drossopoulou, S., Francalana, A., Müller, P.: A unified framework for verification techniques for object invariants. In: FOOL (2008)
13. Hoare, C.A.R.: Proofs of correctness of data representations. Acta. Inf. 1, 271–281 (1972)
14. Kassios, I.T.: Dynamic framing: Support for framing, dependencies and sharing without restriction. In: Formal Methods: International Conference of Formal Methods Europe (2006)
15. Leavens, G.T., Naumann, D.A., Rosenberg, S.: Preliminary definition of core JML. Technical Report CS Report 2006-07, Stevens Institute of Technology (2006)
16. Leino, K.R.M., Müller, P.: Object invariants in dynamic contexts. In: Odersky, M. (ed.) ECOOP 2004. LNCS, vol. 3086, pp. 491–516. Springer, Heidelberg (2004)
17. Leino, K.R.M., Nelson, G.: Data abstraction and information hiding. ACM Trans. Prog. Lang. Syst. 24(5), 491–553 (2002)
18. Müller, P.: Modular Specification and Verification of Object-Oriented Programs. In: Müller, P. (ed.) Modular Specification and Verification of Object-Oriented Programs. LNCS, vol. 2262. Springer, Heidelberg (2002)
19. Müller, P., Rudich, A.: Ownership transfer in Universe Types. In: ACM Conf. on Object-Oriented Programming Languages, Systems, and Applications (OOPSLA) (2007)
20. Nanevski, A., Morrisett, G., Birkedal, L.: Polymorphism and separation in Hoare type theory. In: ICFP (2006)
21. Naumann, D.A.: An admissible second order frame rule in region logic. Technical Report CS Report 2008-02, Stevens Institute of Technology (2008)
22. Naumann, D.A., Barnett, M.: Towards imperative modules: Reasoning about invariants and sharing of mutable state. Theoretical Comput. Sci. 365, 143–168 (2006)
23. O'Hearn, P., Yang, H., Reynolds, J.: Separation and information hiding. In: ACM Symposium on Principles of Programming Languages (POPL), pp. 268–280 (2004)
24. Parkinson, M.: Class invariants: the end of the road. In: International Workshop on Aliasing, Confinement and Ownership (2007)
25. Pierik, C., de Boer, F.S.: A proof outline logic for object-oriented programming. Theoretical Comput. Sci. 343, 413–442 (2005)
26. Smans, J., Jacobs, B., Piessens, F., Schulte, W.: An automatic verifier for java-like programs based on dynamic frames. In: FASE (2008)
27. Smith, M., Drossopoulou, S.: Cheaper reasoning with ownership types. In: International Workshop on Aliasing, Confinement and Ownership (2003)
28. Tofte, M., Talpin, J.-P.: Implementation of the Typed Call-by-Value lambda-Calculus using a Stack of Regions. In: POPL (1994)

A Unified Framework for Verification Techniques for Object Invariants

S. Drossopoulou[1], A. Francalanza[2], P. Müller[3], and A.J. Summers[1]

[1] Imperial College London
[2] University of Southampton
[3] Microsoft Research, Redmond

Abstract. Object invariants define the consistency of objects. They have subtle semantics because of call-backs, multi-object invariants and subclassing. Several visible-state verification techniques for object invariants have been proposed. It is difficult to compare these techniques and ascertain their soundness because of differences in restrictions on programs and invariants, in the use of advanced type systems (*e.g.*, ownership types), in the meaning of invariants, and in proof obligations.

We develop a unified framework for such techniques. We distil seven parameters that characterise a verification technique, and identify sufficient conditions on these parameters which guarantee soundness. We instantiate our framework with three verification techniques from the literature, and use it to assess soundness and compare expressiveness.

1 Introduction

Object invariants play a crucial role in the verification of object-oriented programs, and have been an integral part of all major contract languages such as Eiffel [25], the Java Modeling Language JML [17], and Spec# [2]. Object invariants express consistency criteria for objects, ranging from simple properties of single objects (for instance, that a field is non-null) to complex properties of whole object structures (for instance, the sorting of a tree).

While the basic idea of object invariants is simple, verification techniques for practical OO-programs face challenges. These challenges are made more daunting by the common expectation that classes should be verified without knowledge of their clients and subclasses:

Call-backs: Methods that are called while the invariant of an object o is temporarily broken might call back into o and find o in an inconsistent state.

Multi-object invariants: When the invariant of an object p depends on the state of another object o, modifications of o potentially break the invariant of p. In particular, when verifying o, the invariant of p may not be known and, if not, cannot be expected to be preserved.

Subclassing: When the invariant of a subclass D refers to fields declared in a superclass C then methods of C can break D's invariant by assigning to these fields. In particular, when verifying a class, its subclass invariants are not known in general, and so cannot be expected to be preserved.

J. Vitek (Ed.): ECOOP 2008, LNCS 5142, pp. 412–437, 2008.
© Springer-Verlag Berlin Heidelberg 2008

Several verification techniques address some or all of these challenges [1, 3, 14, 16, 18, 23, 26, 27, 31]. They share many commonalities, but differ in the following important aspects:

1. *Invariant semantics:* Which invariants are expected to hold when?
2. *Invariant restrictions:* Which objects may invariants depend on?
3. *Proof obligations:* What proofs are required, and where?
4. *Program restrictions:* Which objects' methods/fields may be called/updated?
5. *Type systems:* What syntactic information is used for reasoning?
6. *Specification languages:* What syntax is used to express invariants?
7. *Verification logics:* How are invariants proved?

These differences, together with the fact that most verification techniques are not formally specified, complicate the comparison of verification techniques, and hinder the understanding of why these techniques satisfy claimed properties such as soundness. For these reasons, it is hard to decide which technique to adopt, or to develop new sound techniques.

In this paper, we present a unified framework for verification techniques for object invariants. This framework formalises verification techniques in terms of seven parameters, which abstract away from differences pertaining to language features (type system, specification language, and logics) and highlight characteristics intrinsic to the techniques, thereby aiding comparisons. Subsets of these parameters describe aspects applicable to all verification techniques; for example, a generic definition of *soundness* is given in terms of two framework parameters, expressivity is captured by three other parameters.

We concentrate on techniques that require invariants to hold in the pre-state and post-state of a method execution (often referred to as *visible states* [27]) while temporary violations between visible states are permitted. These techniques constitute the vast majority of those described in the literature.

Contributions. The contributions of this paper are:

1. We present a unified formalism for object invariant verification techniques.
2. We identify conditions on the framework that guarantee soundness of a verification technique.
3. We separate type system concerns from verification strategy concerns.
4. We show how our framework describes some advanced verification techniques for visible state invariants.
5. We prove soundness for a number of techniques, and, guided by our framework, discover an unsoundness in one technique.

Our framework allows the extraction of comparable data from techniques that were presented using different concepts, terminology and styles. Comparative value judgements concerning the techniques are beyond the scope of our paper.

Outline. Sec. 2 gives an overview of our work, explaining the important concepts. Sec. 3 formalises program and invariant semantics. Sec. 4 describes our framework and defines soundness. Sec. 5 instantiates our framework with existing verification techniques. Sec. 6 presents sufficient conditions for a verification

technique to be sound, and states a general soundness theorem. Sec. 7 discusses
related work. Proofs and more details are in the companion report [8]. This paper
follows our FOOL paper [7], but provides more explanations and examples.

2   Example and Approach

Example. Consider a scenario, in which a Person holds an Account, and has a
salary. An Account has a balance, an interestRate and an associated DebitCard.
This example will be used throughout the paper. We give the code in Fig. 1.

```
class Account {                           class Person {
  Person holder;                            Account account;
  DebitCard card;                           int salary;
  int balance, interestRate;
                                            // invariant I4:
  // invariant I1: balance < 0 ==>          //    account.balance + salary > 0;
      interestRate == 0;
  // invariant I2: card.acc == this;        void spend(int amount)
                                              { account.withdraw(amount); }
  void withdraw(int amount) {
    balance -= amount;                       void notify()
    if (balance < 0) {                          { ... }
      interestRate = 0;                      }
      this.sendReport();
    }                                     class DebitCard {
  }                                         Account acc;
                                            int dailyCharges;
  void sendReport()
    { holder.notify(); }                    // invariant I5:
  }                                         //    dailyCharges <= acc.balance;
                                          }
class SavingsAccount
        extends Account {
  // invariant I3: balance >= 0;
  }
```

Fig. 1. An account example illustrating the main challenges for the verification of
object invariants. We assume that fields hold non-null values.

Account's interestRate is required to be zero when the balance is negative (I1).
A further invariant (the two can be read as conjuncts of the full invariant for
the class) ensures that the DebitCard associated with an account has a consistent
reference back to the account (I2). A SavingsAccount is a special kind of Account,
whose balance must be positive (I3). Person's invariant (I4) requires that the
sum of salary and account's balance is positive. Finally, DebitCard's invariant (I5)

requires dailyCharges not to exceed the balance of the associated account. Thus, I2, I4, and I5 are multi-object invariants.

To illustrate the challenges faced by verification techniques, suppose that p is an object of class Person, which holds the Account a with DebitCard d:

Call-backs: When p executes its method spend, this results in a call of withdraw on a, which (via a call to sendReport) eventually calls back notify on p; the call notify might reach p in a state where I4 does not hold.

Multi-object invariants: When a executes its method withdraw, it may temporarily break its invariant I1, since its balance is debited before any corresponding change is made to its interestRate. This violation is not important according to the visible state semantics; the if statement immediately afterwards ensures that the invariant is restored before the next visible state. However, by making an unrestricted reduction of the account balance, the method potentially breaks the invariants of other objects as well. In particular, p's invariant I4, and d's invariant I5 may be broken.

Subclassing: Further to the previous point, if a is a SavingsAccount, then calling the method withdraw may break the invariant I3, which was not necessarily known during the verification of class Account.

These points are addressed in the literature by striking various trade-offs between the differing aspects listed in the introduction.

Approach. Our framework uses seven parameters to capture the first four aspects in which verification techniques differ, *i.e.*, invariant semantics, invariant restrictions, proof obligations and program restrictions. To describe these parameters we use two abstract notions, which we call *regions* and *properties*. A *region* (when interpreted semantically) describes a set of objects (e.g., those on which a method may be called), while a property describes a set of invariants (e.g., the invariants that have to be proven before a method call). We deal with the aspects identified in the previous section as follows:

1. *Invariant semantics:* The property $\mathbb{X}$ describes the invariants expected to hold in visible states. The property $\mathbb{V}$ describes the invariants *vulnerable* to a given method, *i.e.*, those which may be broken while the method executes.
2. *Invariant restrictions:* The property $\mathbb{D}$ describes the invariants that may depend on a given heap location. This also characterises indirectly the locations an invariant may depend on.
3. *Proof obligations:* The properties $\mathbb{B}$ and $\mathbb{E}$ describe the invariants that must be proven to hold before a method call and at the end of a method body, respectively.
4. *Program restrictions:* The regions $\mathbb{U}$ and $\mathbb{C}$ describe the permitted receivers for field updates and method calls, respectively.
5. *Type systems:* We parameterise our framework by the type system. We state requirements on the type system, but leave abstract its concrete definition. We require that types are formed of a region-class pair so that we can handle types that express heap topologies (such as ownership types).

6. *Specification languages:* Rather than describing invariants concretely, we assume a judgement that expresses that an object satisfies the invariant of a class in a heap.
7. *Verification logics:* We express proof obligations via a special construct prv p, which throws an exception if the invariants in property p cannot be proven, and has an empty effect otherwise. We leave abstract how the actual proofs are constructed and checked.

Fig. 2 illustrates the parameters of our framework by annotating the body of the method withdraw. $\mathbb{X}$ may be assumed to hold in the pre- and post-states of the method. Between these visible states, some object invariants may be broken (so long as they fall within $\mathbb{V}$), but $\mathbb{X} \setminus \mathbb{V}$ is known to hold throughout the method body. Field updates and method calls are allowed if the receiver object (here, this) is in $\mathbb{U}$ and $\mathbb{C}$, respectively. Before a method call, $\mathbb{B}$ must be proven. At the end of the method body, $\mathbb{E}$ must be proven. Finally, $\mathbb{D}$ (not shown in Fig. 2) constrains the effects of field updates on invariants. Thus, assignments to balance and interestRate affect at most $\mathbb{D}$.

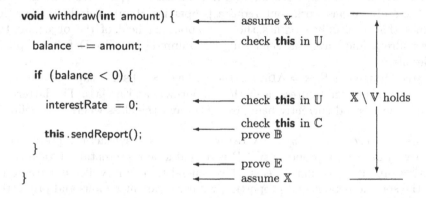

Fig. 2. Role of framework parameters for method withdraw from Fig. 1

The number of parameters reflects the variety of concepts used by verification techniques, such as accessibility of fields, purity, helper methods, ownership, and effect specifications. For instance, $\mathbb{V}$ would be redundant if all methods were to re-establish the invariants they break; in such a setting, a method could break invariants only through field updates, and $\mathbb{V}$ could be derived from $\mathbb{U}$ and $\mathbb{D}$. However, in general, methods may break but not re-establish invariants.

The seven parameters capture concepts explicitly or implicitly found in all verification techniques, defined either through words [27, 14, 16, 31] or typing rules [23]. For example, $\mathbb{V}$ is implicit in [27], but is crucial for their soundness argument. $\mathbb{X}$ and $\mathbb{V}$ are explicit in [23], while $\mathbb{U}$ and $\mathbb{C}$ are implicitly expressed as constraints in their typing rules. Subsets of these seven parameters characterise verification technique concepts e.g., soundness (through $\mathbb{X}$ and $\mathbb{V}$), expressiveness ($\mathbb{D}$, $\mathbb{X}$ and $\mathbb{V}$), proof obligations ($\mathbb{B}$ and $\mathbb{E}$).

3   Invariant Semantics

We formalise invariant semantics through an operational semantics, defining at which execution points invariants are required to hold. In order to cater for the different techniques, the semantics is parameterised by properties to express proof obligations and which invariants are expected to hold. In this section, we focus on the main ideas of our semantics and relegate the less interesting definitions to App. A. We assume sets of identifiers for class names CLS, field names FLD, and method names MTHD, and use variables $c \in$ CLS, $f \in$ FLD and $m \in$ MTHD.

Runtime Structures. A *runtime structure* is a tuple consisting of a set of heaps HP, a set of addresses ADR, and a set of values VAL $=$ ADR $\cup$ {null}, using variables $h \in$ HP, $\iota \in$ ADR, and $v \in$ VAL. A runtime structure provides the following operations. The operation $dom(h)$ represents the domain of the heap. $cls(h, \iota)$ yields the class of the object at address ι. The operation $fld(h, \iota, f)$ yields the value of a field f of the object at address ι. Finally, $upd(h, \iota, f, v)$ yields the new heap after a field update, and $new(h, \iota, t)$ yields the heap and address resulting from the creation of a new object of type t. We leave abstract how these operations work, but require properties about their behaviour, for instance that upd only modifies the corresponding field of the object at the given address, and leaves the remaining heap unmodified. See Def. 9 in App. A for details.

A stack frame $\sigma \in$ STK $=$ ADR $\times$ ADR $\times$ MTHD $\times$ CLS is a tuple of a receiver address, an argument address, a method identifier, and a class. The latter two indicate the method currently being executed and the class where it is defined.

Regions, Properties and Types. A region $\mathrm{r} \in$ R is a syntactic representation for a set of objects; a property $\mathrm{p} \in$ P is a syntactic representation for a set of assertions about particular objects. It is crucial that our syntax is parametric with the specific regions and properties; we use different regions and properties to model different verification techniques.[1]

We define a type $t \in$ TYP, as a pair of a region and a class. The region allows us to cater for types that express the topology of the heap, without being specific about the underlying type system.

Expressions. In Fig. 3, we define source expressions $e \in$ EXPR. In order to simplify our presentation (but without loss of generality), we restrict methods to always have exactly one argument. Besides the usual basic object-oriented constructs, we include proof annotations e prv p. As we will see later, such a proof annotation executes the expression e and then imposes a proof obligation for the invariants characterised by the property p. To maintain generality, we avoid being precise about the actual syntax and checking of proofs.

In Fig. 3, we also define runtime expressions $e_r \in$ REXPR. A runtime expression is a source expression, a value, a nested call with its stack frame σ, an

---

[1] For example, in Universe types, rep and peer are regions, while in ownership types, ownership parameters such as X, and also this, are regions (more in Sec. 5).

$$
\begin{array}{llll}
e ::= \text{this} & (this) & \mid x & (variable) & \mid \text{null} & (null) \\
\mid \text{new } t & (new\ object) & \mid e.f & (access) & \mid e.f = e\ (assignment) \\
\mid e.m(e) & (method\ call) & \mid e\ \text{prv}\ \mathrm{p}\ (proof\ annotat.) & \\
\end{array}
$$

$$
\begin{array}{llll}
e_r ::= \ldots & (as\ source\ exprs.) & \mid v & (value) & \mid \text{verfExc}\ (verif\ exc.) \\
\mid \text{fatalExc} & (fatal\ exc.) & \mid \sigma \cdot e_r & (nested\ call) & \mid \text{call } e_r\ (launch) \\
\mid \text{ret } e_r & (return) & \\
\end{array}
$$

Fig. 3. Source and runtime expression syntax

exception, or a decorated runtime expression. A verification exception verfExc indicates that a proof obligation failed. A fatal exception fatalExc indicates that an expected invariant does not hold. Runtime expressions can be decorated with call e_r and ret e_r to mark the beginning and end of a method call, respectively.

In Def. 10 (App. A), we define evaluation contexts, $E[\cdot]$, which describe contexts within one activation record and extend these to runtime contexts, $F[\cdot]$, which also describe nested calls.

Programming Languages. We define a programming language as a tuple consisting of a set PRG of programs, a runtime structure, a set of regions, and a set of properties (see Def. 11 in App. A). Each $\Pi \in$ PRG comes equipped with the following operations. $\mathcal{F}(c, f)$ yields the type of field f in class c as well as the class in which f is declared (c or a superclass of c). $\mathcal{M}(c, m)$ yields the type signature of method m in class c. $\mathcal{B}(c, m)$ yields the expression constituting the body of method m in class c as well as the class in which m is declared. Moreover, there are operators to denote subclasses and subtypes (<:), inclusion of regions ($\sqsubseteq$), and interpretation ($[\![\cdot]\!]$) of regions and properties.

The interpretation of a region produces a set of objects. We characterise each invariant by an object-class pair, with the intended meaning that the invariant specified in the class holds for the object.[2] Therefore, the interpretation of a property produces a set of object-class pairs, specifying all the invariants of interest. Regions and properties are interpreted w.r.t. a heap, and from the *viewpoint* of a "current object"; therefore, their definitions depend on heap and address parameters: $[\![\ldots]\!]_{h,\iota}$.

Each program also comes with typing judgements $\Gamma \vdash e : t$ and $h \vdash e_r : t$ for source and runtime expressions, respectively. An environment $\Gamma \in$ ENV is a tuple of the class containing the current method, the method identifier, and the type of the sole argument.

Finally, the judgement $h \models \iota, c$ expresses that in heap h, the object at address ι satisfies the invariant declared in class c. We define that the judgement trivially holds if the object is not allocated ($\iota \notin dom(h)$) or is not an instance of c ($cls(h, \iota) \not<: c$). We say that the property p is *valid* in heap h w.r.t. address ι if all invariants in $[\![\mathrm{p}]\!]_{h,\iota}$ are satisfied. We denote validity of properties by $h \models \mathrm{p}, \iota$:

$$
h \models \mathrm{p}, \iota \iff \forall(\iota', c) \in [\![\mathrm{p}]\!]_{h,\iota}.\ h \models \iota', c
$$

---

[2] An object may have different invariants for each of the classes it belongs to [18].

$$\text{(rThis)} \quad \frac{\sigma = (\iota, \_, \_, \_)}{\sigma \cdot \text{this}, h \longrightarrow \sigma \cdot \iota, h} \qquad \text{(rVar)} \quad \frac{\sigma = (\_, v, \_, \_)}{\sigma \cdot x, h \longrightarrow \sigma \cdot v, h}$$

$$\text{(rNew)} \quad \frac{\sigma = (\iota, \_, \_, \_) \quad h', \iota' = new(h, \iota, t)}{\sigma \cdot \text{new } t, h \longrightarrow \sigma \cdot \iota', h'}$$

$$\text{(rDer)} \quad \frac{v = fld(h, \iota, f)}{\iota.f, h \longrightarrow v, h} \qquad \text{(rAss)} \quad \frac{h' = upd(h, \iota, f, v)}{\iota.f = v, h \longrightarrow v, h'} \qquad \text{(rCxtFrame)} \quad \frac{e_r, h \longrightarrow e'_r, h'}{\sigma \cdot e_r, h \longrightarrow \sigma \cdot e'_r, h'}$$

$$\text{(rCall)} \quad \frac{\mathcal{B}(m, cls(h, \iota)) = e, c \quad \sigma = (\iota, v, c, m)}{\iota.m(v), h \longrightarrow \sigma \cdot \text{call } e, h} \qquad \text{(rCxtEval)} \quad \frac{\sigma \cdot e_r, h \longrightarrow \sigma \cdot e'_r, h'}{\sigma \cdot E[e_r], h \longrightarrow \sigma \cdot E[e'_r], h'}$$

$$\text{(rLaunch)} \quad \frac{\sigma = (\iota, \_, c, m) \quad h \models \mathbb{X}_{c,m}, \iota}{\sigma \cdot \text{call } e, h \longrightarrow \sigma \cdot \text{ret } e, h}$$

$$\text{(rLaunchExc)} \quad \frac{\sigma = (\iota, \_, c, m) \quad h \not\models \mathbb{X}_{c,m}, \iota}{\sigma \cdot \text{call } e, h \longrightarrow \sigma \cdot \text{fatalExc}, h}$$

$$\text{(rFrame)} \quad \frac{\sigma = (\iota, \_, c, m) \quad h \models \mathbb{X}_{c,m}, \iota}{\sigma \cdot \text{ret } v, h \longrightarrow v, h}$$

$$\text{(rFrameExc)} \quad \frac{\sigma = (\iota, \_, c, m) \quad h \not\models \mathbb{X}_{c,m}, \iota}{\sigma \cdot \text{ret } v, h \longrightarrow \text{fatalExc}, h}$$

$$\text{(rPrf)} \quad \frac{\sigma = (\iota, \_, \_, \_) \quad h \models \mathbb{p}, \iota}{\sigma \cdot v \text{ prv } \mathbb{p}, h \longrightarrow \sigma \cdot v, h}$$

$$\text{(rPrfExc)} \quad \frac{\sigma = (\iota, \_, \_, \_) \quad h \not\models \mathbb{p}, \iota}{\sigma \cdot v \text{ prv } \mathbb{p}, h \longrightarrow \sigma \cdot \text{verfExc}, h}$$

Fig. 4. Reduction rules of operational semantics

Operational Semantics. The framework parameter $\mathbb{X}$ describes which invariants are expected to hold at visible states. Given a program Π and a set of properties $\mathbb{X}_{c,m}$, each characterising the property that needs to hold at the beginning and end of a method m of class c, the *runtime semantics* is the relation $\longrightarrow \subseteq$ (REXPR $\times$ HP) $\times$ (REXPR $\times$ HP) defined in Fig. 4.

The first eight rules are standard for object-oriented languages. Note that in rNew, a new object is created using the function *new*, which takes a type as parameter rather than a class, thereby making the semantics parametric w.r.t. the type system: different type systems may use different regions and definitions of *new* to describe heap-topological information. Similarly, *upd* and *fld* do not fix a particular heap representation. Rule rCall describes method calls; it stores the class in which the method body is defined in the new stack frame σ, and introduces the "marker" call e_r at the beginning of the method body.

Our reduction rules abstract away from program verification and describe only its effect. Thus, rLaunch, rLaunchExc, rFrame, and rFrameExc check whether $\mathbb{X}_{c,m}$ is valid at the beginning and end of any execution of a method m defined in class c, and generate a fatal exception, fatalExc, if the check fails. This represents the visible state semantics discussed in the introduction. Proof obligations e prv $\mathbb{p}$ are verified once e reduces to a value (rPrf and rPrfExc); if $\mathbb{p}$ is not found to be valid, a verification exception verfExc is generated.

Verification using visible state semantics amounts to showing all proof obligations in some program logic, based on the assumption that expected invariants hold in visible states. Informally then, a specific verification technique described in our framework is sound if it guarantees that a fatalExc is never encountered. Verification technique soundness does allow verfExc to be generated, but this will never happen in a correctly verified program. We give a formal definition of soundness at the end of the next section.

This semantics allows us to be parametric *w.r.t.* the syntax of invariants and the logic of proofs. We also define properties that permit us to be parametric *w.r.t.* a sound type system (*cf.* Def. 15 in App. A). Thus, we can concentrate entirely on verification concerns.

4   Verification Techniques

A verification technique is essentially a 7-tuple, where the *components* of the tuple provide instantiations for the seven parameters of our framework. These instantiations are expressed in terms of the regions and properties provided by the programming language. To allow the instantiations to refer to the program (for instance, to look up field declarations), we define a verification technique as a mapping from programs to 7-tuples.

Definition 1. *A* verification technique $\mathcal{V}$ *for a programming language is a mapping from programs into a tuple:*

$$\mathcal{V} \; : \; \text{PRG} \to \text{eXP} \times \text{VUL} \times \text{DEP} \times \text{PRE} \times \text{END} \times \text{UPD} \times \text{CLL}$$

where

$$
\begin{array}{llll}
\mathbb{X} \in & \text{eXP} = \text{CLS} \times \text{MTHD} \to \text{P} & \mathbb{V} \in & \text{VUL} = \text{CLS} \times \text{MTHD} \to \text{P} \\
\mathbb{D} \in & \text{DEP} = \text{CLS} \to \text{P} & \mathbb{B} \in & \text{PRE} = \text{CLS} \times \text{MTHD} \times \text{R} \to \text{P} \\
\mathbb{E} \in & \text{END} = \text{CLS} \times \text{MTHD} \to \text{P} & \mathbb{C} \in & \text{CLL} = \text{CLS} \times \text{MTHD} \times \text{CLS} \to \text{R} \\
\mathbb{U} \in & \text{UPD} = \text{CLS} \times \text{MTHD} \times \text{CLS} \times \text{MTHD} \to \text{R}
\end{array}
$$

To describe a verification technique applied to a program, we write the application of the components to class, method names, etc., as $\mathbb{X}_{c,m}$, $\mathbb{V}_{c,m}$, $\mathbb{D}_c$, $\mathbb{B}_{c,m,\mathbf{r}}$, $\mathbb{E}_{c,m}$, $\mathbb{U}_{c,m,c'}$, $\mathbb{C}_{c,m,c',m'}$. The meaning of these components is:

$\mathbb{X}_{c,m}$: the property expected to be valid at the beginning and end of the body of method m in class c. The parameters c and m allow a verification technique to expect different invariants in the visible states of different methods. For instance, JML's helper methods [17] do not expect any invariants to hold.

$\mathbb{V}_{c,m}$: the property vulnerable to method m of class c, that is, the property whose validity may be broken while control is inside m. The parameters c and m allow a verification technique to require that invariants of certain classes (for instance, c's subclasses) are not vulnerable.

$\mathbb{D}_c$: the property that may depend on fields declared in class c. The parameter c can be used, for instance, to prevent invariants from depending on fields declared in c's superclasses [16, 27].

$\mathbb{B}_{c,m,\mathbf{r}}$: the property whose validity has to be proven before calling a method on a receiver in region $\mathbf{r}$ from the execution of a method m in class c. The parameters allow proof obligations to depend on the calling method and the ownership relation between the caller and the callee.

$\mathbb{E}_{c,m}$: the property whose validity has to be proven at the end of method m in class c. The parameters allow a technique to require different proofs for different methods, e.g., to exclude subclass invariants.

$\mathbb{U}_{c,m,c'}$: the region of allowed receivers for an update of a field in class c', within the body of method m in class c. The parameters allow a technique, for instance, to prevent field updates within pure methods.

$\mathbb{C}_{c,m,c',m'}$: the region of allowed receivers for a call to method m' of class c', within the body of method m of class c. The parameters allow a technique to permit calls depending on attributes (e.g., purity or effect specifications) of the caller and the callee.

The class and method identifiers used as parameters to our components can be extracted from an environment Γ or a stack frame σ in the obvious way. Thus, for $\Gamma = (c, m, \_)$ or for $\sigma = (\iota, \_, c, m)$, we use $\mathbb{X}_\Gamma$ and $\mathbb{X}_\sigma$ as shorthands for $\mathbb{X}_{c,m}$; we also use $\mathbb{B}_{\Gamma,\mathbf{r}}$ and $\mathbb{B}_{\sigma,\mathbf{r}}$ as shorthands for $\mathbb{B}_{c,m,\mathbf{r}}$.

Well-Verified Programs. The judgement $\Gamma \vdash_{\mathcal{V}} e$ expresses that expression e is *well-verified* according to verification technique $\mathcal{V}$. It is defined in Fig. 5.

$$
\begin{array}{cccccc}
\text{(vs-null)} & \text{(vs-var)} & \text{(vs-this)} & \text{(vs-new)} & \text{(vs-fld)} & \text{(vs-ass)} \\[4pt]
& & & & \dfrac{\Gamma \vdash_{\mathcal{V}} e}{\Gamma \vdash_{\mathcal{V}} e.f} & \dfrac{\Gamma \vdash e : \mathbf{r}\,c' \quad \mathcal{F}(c',f) = \_, c \quad \mathbf{r} \sqsubseteq \mathbb{U}_{\Gamma,c} \quad \Gamma \vdash_{\mathcal{V}} e \quad \Gamma \vdash_{\mathcal{V}} e'}{\Gamma \vdash_{\mathcal{V}} e.f = e'}
\end{array}
$$

$$\overline{\Gamma \vdash_{\mathcal{V}} \text{null}} \quad \overline{\Gamma \vdash_{\mathcal{V}} x} \quad \overline{\Gamma \vdash_{\mathcal{V}} \text{this}} \quad \overline{\Gamma \vdash_{\mathcal{V}} \text{new}\, t}$$

$$
\begin{array}{cc}
\text{(vs-call)} & \text{(vs-class)} \\[4pt]
\dfrac{\Gamma \vdash e : \mathbf{r}\,c' \quad \mathcal{B}(c',m) = \_, c \quad \mathbf{r} \sqsubseteq \mathbb{C}_{\Gamma,c,m} \quad \Gamma \vdash_{\mathcal{V}} e \quad \Gamma \vdash_{\mathcal{V}} e'}{\Gamma \vdash_{\mathcal{V}} e.m(e'\ \text{prv}\ \mathbb{B}_{\Gamma,\mathbf{r}})} & \dfrac{\left.\begin{array}{l} \mathcal{B}(c,m) = e, c \\ \mathcal{M}(c,m) = t, t' \end{array}\right\} \Rightarrow \left\{\begin{array}{l} e = e'\ \text{prv}\ \mathbb{E}_{c,m} \\ c, m, t \vdash_{\mathcal{V}} e' \end{array}\right.}{\vdash_{\mathcal{V}} c}
\end{array}
$$

Fig. 5. Well-verified source expressions and classes

The first five rules express that literals, variable lookup, object creation, and field lookup do not require proofs. The receiver of a field update must fall into $\mathbb{U}$ (vs-ass). The receiver of a call must fall into $\mathbb{C}$ (vs-call). Moreover, we require the proof of $\mathbb{B}$ before a call. Finally, a class is well-verified if the body of each of its methods is well-verified and ends with a proof obligation for $\mathbb{E}$ (vs-class). Note that we use the type judgement $\Gamma \vdash e : t$ without defining it; the definition is given by the underlying programming language, not by our framework.

Fig. 9 in App. A defines the judgement $h \vdash_{\mathcal{V}} e_r$ for verified runtime expressions. The rules correspond to those from Fig. 5, with the addition of rules for values and nested calls.

A program Π is well-verified w.r.t. $\mathcal{V}$, denoted as $\vdash_{\mathcal{V}} \Pi$, iff *(1)* all classes are well-verified and *(2)* all class invariants respect the dependency restrictions dictated by $\mathbb{D}$. That is, the invariant of an object ι' declared in a class c' will be preserved by an update of a field of an object of class c if it is not within $\mathbb{D}_c$.

Definition 2. $\vdash_{\mathcal{V}} \Pi \Leftrightarrow$

    (1) $\forall c \in \Pi. \vdash_{\mathcal{V}} c$

    (2) $\mathcal{F}(cls(h,\iota),f) = \_, c, (\iota',c') \notin \llbracket D_c \rrbracket_{h,\iota}, h \models \iota',c' \Rightarrow upd(h,\iota,f,v) \models \iota',c'$

Valid States. The properties X and $X \setminus V$ characterise the invariants that are expected to hold in the visible states and between visible states of the current method execution, respectively. That is, they reflect the local knowledge of the current method, but do not describe globally all the invariants that need to hold in a given state.

For any state with heap h and execution stack $\overline{\sigma}$, the function $vi(\overline{\sigma}, h)$ yields the set of *valid invariants*, that is, invariants that are expected to hold :

$$vi(\overline{\sigma}, h) = \begin{cases} \emptyset & \text{if } \overline{\sigma} = \epsilon \\ (vi(\overline{\sigma_1}, h) \cup \llbracket X_\sigma \rrbracket_{h,\sigma}) \setminus \llbracket V_\sigma \rrbracket_{h,\sigma} & \text{if } \overline{\sigma} = \overline{\sigma_1} \cdot \sigma \end{cases}$$

The call stack is empty at the beginning of program execution, at which point we expect the heap to be empty. For each additional stack frame σ, the corresponding method m may assume X_σ at the beginning of the call, therefore we add $\llbracket X_\sigma \rrbracket_{h,\sigma}$ to the valid invariants. The method may break V_σ during the call, and so we remove $\llbracket V_\sigma \rrbracket_{h,\sigma}$ from the valid invariants.

A state with heap h and stack $\overline{\sigma}$ is *valid* iff:

(1) $\overline{\sigma}$ is a valid stack, denoted by $h \vdash_{\mathcal{V}} \overline{\sigma}$ (Def. 12 in App. A), and meaning that the receivers of consecutive method calls are within the respective $\mathbb{C}$ regions.

(2) The valid invariants $vi(\overline{\sigma}, h)$ hold.

(3) If execution is in a visible state with σ as the topmost frame of $\overline{\sigma}$, then the expected invariants X_σ hold additionally.

These properties are formalised in Def. 3. A state is determined by a heap h and a runtime expression e_r; the stack is extracted from e_r using function *stack*, given by Def. 13 in App. A.

Definition 3. *A state with heap h and runtime expression e_r is valid for a verification technique $\mathcal{V}$, $e_r \models_{\mathcal{V}} h$, iff:*

    (1) $h \vdash_{\mathcal{V}} stack(e_r)$ *(2)* $h \models vi(stack(e_r), h)$

    (3) $e_r = F[\sigma \cdot call\, e]$ *or* $e_r = F[\sigma \cdot ret\, v] \Rightarrow h \models X_\sigma, \sigma$

Soundness. A verification technique is *sound* if verified programs only produce valid states and do not throw fatal exceptions. More precisely, a verification technique $\mathcal{V}$ is sound for a programming language PL iff for all well-formed and verified programs $\Pi \in PL$, any well-typed and verified runtime expression e_r executed in a valid state reduces to another verified expression e_r' with a resulting valid state. Note that a verified e_r' contains no fatalExc (see Fig. 9).

Well-formedness of program Π is denoted by $\vdash_{\mathbf{wf}} \Pi$ (Def. 14, App. A). Well-typedness of runtime expression e_r is denoted by $h \vdash e_r : t$ and required as part of a sound type system in Def. 11, App. A. These requirement permits separation of concerns, whereby we can formally define verification technique soundness *in isolation*, assuming program well-formedness and a sound type system.

Definition 4. *A verification technique* $\mathcal{V}$ *is sound for a programming language* *PL iff for all programs* $\Pi \in PL$:

$$\left. \begin{array}{lll} \vdash_{wf} \Pi, & h \vdash e_r : \_, & \vdash_{\mathcal{V}} \Pi, \quad e_r \models_{\mathcal{V}} h, \\ h \vdash_{\mathcal{V}} e_r, & e_r, h \longrightarrow e'_r, h' \end{array} \right\} \Rightarrow e'_r \models_{\mathcal{V}} h', \quad h' \vdash_{\mathcal{V}} e'_r$$

5 Instantiations

In our earlier paper [7], we discuss six verification techniques from the literature in terms of our framework, namely those by Poetzsch-Heffter [31], Huizing & Kuiper [14], Leavens & Müller [16], Müller *et al.* [27], and Lu *et al.* [23]. In this paper we concentrate on the techniques based on heap topologies [27, 23], because those benefit most from the formalisation in our framework.

Müller *et al.* [27] present two techniques for multi-object invariants, called ownership technique and visibility technique (*OT* and *VT* for short), which use the hierarchic heap topology enforced by Universe types [6]. Their distinctive features are: (1) Expected and vulnerable invariants are specified per class. (2) Invariant restrictions take into account subclassing (thereby addressing the subclass challenge). (3) Proof obligations are required before calls (thereby addressing the call-back challenge) and at the end of calls. (4) Program restrictions are uniform for all methods[3], and are based on the relative object placement in the hierarchy.

Lu *et al.* [23] define *Oval*, a verification technique based on ownership types, which support owner parameters for classes [5], thus permitting a more precise description of the heap topology. The distinctive features of *Oval* are: (1) Expected and vulnerable invariants are specific to every method in every class through the notion of *contracts*. (2) Invariant restrictions do not take subclassing into account. (3) Proof obligations are only imposed at the end of calls. (4) To address the call-back challenge, calls are subject to "subcontracting", a requirement that guarantees that the expected and vulnerable invariants of the callee are within those of the caller.

OT, *VT*, and *Oval* are discussed in more detail in our companion report [8]. In the remainder of this section, we introduce these techniques and summarise them in Fig. 6. We explain the notation from Fig. 6 informally, and define it formally in the appendix. This section (without the appendix) gives an overall intuition, aimed at the reader who is not interested in all of the formal details.

To sharpen our discussion w.r.t. structured heaps, we will be adding annotations to the example from Fig. 1, to obtain a topology where the Person p owns the Account a and the DebitCard d.

5.1 Instantiation for *OT* and *VT*

Universe types associate reference types with *Universe modifiers*, which specify ownership relative to the current object. The modifier rep expresses that an

---

[3] However, both *OT* and *VT* have special rules for pure (side-effect free) methods. We ignore pure methods here, but refer the interested reader to [7].

	Müller *et al.* (*OT*)	Müller *et al.* (*VT*)	Lu *et al.*(*Oval*)
$\mathbb{X}_{c,m}$	own ; rep$^+$	own ; rep$^+$	I ; rep*
$\mathbb{V}_{c,m}$	super$\langle c\rangle$ ⊔ own$^+$	peer$\langle c\rangle$ ⊔ own$^+$	E ; own*
$\mathbb{D}_c$	self$\langle c\rangle$ ⊔ own$^+$	peer$\langle c\rangle$ ⊔ own$^+$	self ; own*
$\mathbb{B}_{c,m,\mathbf{r}}$	super$\langle c\rangle$ if intrsPeer($\mathbf{r}$) emp otherwise	peer$\langle c\rangle$ if intrsPeer($\mathbf{r}$) emp otherwise	emp
$\mathbb{E}_{c,m}$	super$\langle c\rangle$	peer$\langle c\rangle$	self if I = E emp otherwise
$\mathbb{U}_{c,m,c'}$	self	peer	self if I = E emp otherwise
$\mathbb{C}_{c,m,c',m'}$	rep$\langle c\rangle$ ⊔ peer	rep$\langle c\rangle$ ⊔ peer	⊔$_{\mathbf{r},\text{ with } SC(\mathsf{I},\mathsf{E},\mathsf{I}',\mathsf{E}',\mathcal{O}_{\mathbf{r},c})}$ $\mathbf{r}$

Fig. 6. Components of verification techniques. For *Oval*, $\mathcal{O}_{\mathbf{r},c}$ is the owner of $\mathbf{r}$; we use shorthands $\mathsf{I} = \mathsf{I}(c,m)$, and $\mathsf{E} = \mathsf{E}(c,m)$, and $\mathsf{I}' = \mathbf{r} ; \mathsf{I}(c',m')$, and $\mathsf{E}' = \mathbf{r} ; \mathsf{E}(c',m')$.

object is owned by the current object; peer expresses that an object has the same owner as the current object; any expresses that an object may have any owner. Fig. 7 shows the Universe modifiers for our example from Fig. 1, which allow one to apply *OT* and *VT*.

```
class Account {              class Person {              class DebitCard {
    peer DebitCard card;         rep  Account account;        peer Account acc;
    any Person holder;           ...                          ...
    ...                      }                            }
}
```

Fig. 7. Universe modifiers for the Account example from Fig. 1

To address the subclass challenge, *OT* and *VT* both forbid rep fields f and g declared in different classes c_f and c_g of the same object o to reference the same object. This *subclass separation* can be formalised in an ownership model where each object is owned by an object-class pair (see [18] for details).

Regions and Properties. For *OT* and *VT*, we define the sets of regions and properties to be:

$$\mathbf{r} \in \mathsf{R} \quad ::= \quad \text{emp} \mid \text{self} \mid \text{rep}\langle c\rangle \mid \text{peer} \mid \text{any} \mid \mathbf{r} \sqcup \mathbf{r}$$
$$\mathbf{p} \in \mathsf{P} \quad ::= \quad \text{emp} \mid \text{self}\langle c\rangle \mid \text{super}\langle c\rangle \mid \text{peer}\langle c\rangle \mid \text{rep} \mid \text{own} \mid \text{rep}^+ \mid \text{own}^+ \mid \mathbf{p} \sqcup \mathbf{p} \mid \mathbf{p}; \mathbf{p}$$

In our framework, Universe modifiers intuitively correspond to regions, since they describe areas of the heap. For example, peer describes all objects which share the owner (object-class pair) with the current object. However, because of the subclass separation described above, it is useful to employ richer regions of the form rep$\langle c\rangle$, describing all objects owned by the current object *and* class c. For regions (and properties) we also include the "union" of two regions (properties). The predicate intrsPeer(r) checks whether a region intersects the peer region.

For properties, self$\langle c \rangle$ represents the singleton set containing a pair of the current object with the class c. The property super$\langle c \rangle$ represents the set of pairs of the current object with all its classes that are superclasses of c. The property peer$\langle c \rangle$ represents all the objects (paired with their classes) that share the owner with the current object, provided their class is visible in c. There are also properties to describe the invariants of an object's owned objects, its owner, its transitively owned objects, and its transitive owners. A property of the form $p_1; p_2$ denotes a composition of properties, which behaves similarly to function composition when interpreted. The formal definitions of the interpretations of these regions and properties can be found in App. B.

Ownership Technique. As shown in Fig. 6, OT requires that in visible states, all objects owned by the owner of this must satisfy their invariants ($\mathbb{X}$).

Invariants are allowed to depend on fields of the object itself (at the current class), as in I1 in Fig. 1, and all its rep objects, as in I2. Other client invariants such as I4 and I5) and subclass invariants that depend on inherited fields (such as I3) are not permitted. Therefore, a field update potentially affects the invariants of the modified object and of all its (transitive) owners ($\mathbb{D}$).

A method may update fields of this ($\mathbb{U}$). Since an updated field is declared in the enclosing class or a superclass, the invariants potentially affected by the update are those of this (for the enclosing class and its superclasses, which addresses the subclass challenge) as well as the invariants of the (transitive) owners of this ($\mathbb{V}$).

OT handles multi-object invariants by allowing invariants to depend on fields of owned objects ($\mathbb{D}$). Therefore, methods may break the invariants of the transitive owners of this ($\mathbb{V}$). For example, the invariant I2 of Person (Fig. 1) is legal only because account is a rep field (Fig. 7). Account's method withdraw need not preserve Person's invariant. This is reflected by the definition of $\mathbb{E}$: only the invariants of this are proven at the end of the method, while those of the transitive owners may remain broken; it is the responsibility of the owners to re-establish them, which addresses the multi-object challenge. As an example, the method spend has to re-establish Person's invariant after the call to account.withdraw.

Since the invariants of the owners of this might not hold, OT disallows calls on references other than rep and peer references ($\mathbb{C}$). For instance, the call holder.notify() in method sendReport is not permitted because holder is in an ancestor ownership context.

The proof obligations for method calls ($\mathbb{B}$) must cover those invariants expected by the callee that are vulnerable to the caller. This intersection contains the invariant of the caller, if the caller and the callee are peers because the callee might call back; it is otherwise empty (reps cannot callback their owners).

Visibility Technique. VT relaxes the restrictions of OT in two ways. First, it permits invariants of a class c to depend on fields of peer objects, provided that these invariants are visible in c ($\mathbb{D}$). Thus, VT can handle multi-object structures that are not organised hierarchically. For instance, in addition to the invariants permitted by OT, VT permits invariants I4 and I5 in Fig. 1. Visibility is transitive, thus, the invariant must also be visible wherever fields of c are updated. Second, VT permits field updates on peers of this ($\mathbb{U}$).

These relaxations make more invariants vulnerable. Therefore, $\mathbb{V}$ includes additionally the invariants of the peers of this. This addition is also reflected in the proof obligations before peer calls ($\mathbb{B}$) and before the end of a method ($\mathbb{E}$). For instance, method withdraw must be proven to preserve the invariant of the associated DebitCard, which does not in general succeed in our example.

5.2   Instantiation for *Oval*

Fig. 8 shows our example in *Oval* using ownership parameters [5] to describe heap topologies. The ownership parameter o denotes the owner of the current object; p denotes the owner of o and specifies the position of holder in the hierarchy, more precisely than the any modifier in Universe types.

```
class Account[o,p] {                      class Person[o] {
  DebitCard⟨o⟩ card;                        Account⟨this⟩ account;
  Person⟨p⟩ holder;                          ...
  ...                                       void spend(int amount)⟨this,this⟩
  void withdraw(int amount)⟨this,this⟩         { account.withdraw(amount); }
    { ... }                                 void notify ()⟨bot,top⟩
  void sendReport()⟨bot,p⟩                     { ... }
    { ... }                               }
}
```

Fig. 8. Ownership parameters and method contracts in *Oval*

Method Contracts. Ownership parameters are also used to describe expected and vulnerable invariants, which are specific to each method. Every *Oval* program extends method signatures with a contract $\langle I, E \rangle$: the expected invariants at visible states ($\mathbb{X}$) are the invariants of the object characterised by I and all objects transitively owned by this object; the vulnerable invariants ($\mathbb{V}$) are the object at E and its transitive owners. These properties are syntactically characterised by Ls in the code (and Ks in typing rules), where:

$$L ::= \mathsf{top} \mid \mathsf{bot} \mid \mathsf{this} \mid X \qquad\qquad K ::= L \mid K\,; \mathsf{rep}$$

and where X stands for the class' owner parameters.[4] An ordering $L \preceq L'$ is defined, expressing that at runtime the object denoted by L will be transitively owned by the object denoted by L'. This is used to formally specify various restrictions in the technique, for example that for all method contracts, $I \preceq E$ must hold.

---

[4] We discuss a slightly simplified version of *Oval*, where we omit the existential owner parameter '*', and *non-rep* fields, a refinement whereby only the current object's owners depend on such fields. Both enhance the expressiveness of the language, but are not central to our analysis.

In class Account (Fig. 8), withdraw() expects the current object and the objects it transitively owns to be valid (I=this) and, during execution, this method may invalidate the current object and its transitive owners (E=this). The contract of sendReport() does not expect any objects to be valid at visible states (I=bot) but may violate object p and its transitive owners (E=p).

Subcontracting. Call-backs are handled via *subcontracting*, which is defined using the order $L \preceq L'$. To interpret *Oval*'s subcontracting in our framework, we use $SC(I, E, I', E', K)$, which holds iff:

$$I \prec E \Rightarrow I' \preceq I \qquad I = E \Rightarrow I' \prec I \qquad I' \prec E' \Rightarrow E \preceq E' \qquad I' = E' \Rightarrow E \preceq K$$

where I, E characterise the caller, I', E' characterise the callee, and K stands for the callee's owner. The first two requirements ensure that the caller guarantees the invariant expected by the callee. The other two conditions ensure that the invariants vulnerable to the callee are also vulnerable to the caller. For instance, the call holder.notify() in method sendReport satisfies subcontracting because caller and callee do not expect any invariants, and the callee has no vulnerable invariants. In particular, the receiver of a call may be owned by any of the owners of the current receiver, provided that subcontracting is respected ($\mathbb{C}$).

Given that $I \preceq E$ for all well-formed methods, and that $\mathbb{B}_{c,m,r}$ =emp, the first two requirements of subcontracting exactly give *(S1)*, while the latter two exactly give *(S3)* from Def. 5 in the next section – more in [8].

Regions and Properties. To express *Oval* in our framework, we define regions and properties as follows (see App. B for their interpretations):

$$r \in R ::= \mathsf{emp} \mid \mathsf{self} \mid c\langle \overline{K} \rangle \mid r \sqcup r \qquad p \in P ::= \mathsf{emp} \mid \mathsf{self} \mid K \mid K; \mathsf{rep}^* \mid K; \mathsf{own}^*$$

As already stated, expected and vulnerable properties depend on the contract of the method and express $\mathbb{X}$ as I; rep* and $\mathbb{V}$ as E; own* (see Fig. 6). Similarly to OT, invariant dependencies are restricted to an object and the objects it transitively owns ($\mathbb{D}$). Therefore, I1 and I4 are legal, as well as I3, which depends on an inherited field. *Oval* imposes a restriction on contracts that the expected and vulnerable invariants of every method intersect at most at this. Consequently, at the end of a method, one has to prove the invariant of the current receiver, if $I = E = $ this, and nothing otherwise ($\mathbb{E}$). In the former case, the method is allowed to update fields of its receiver; no updates are allowed otherwise ($\mathbb{U}$). Therefore, spend and withdraw are the only methods in our example that are allowed to make field updates. *Oval* does not impose proof obligations on method calls ($\mathbb{B}$ is empty), but addresses the call-back challenge through subcontracting. Therefore, call-backs are safe because the callee cannot expect invariants that are temporarily broken. With the existing contracts in Fig. 8, subcontracting permits spend to call account.withdraw(), and withdraw to call this.sendReport(), and also sendReport to call holder.notify(). The last two subcalls may potentially lead to callbacks, but are safe because the contracts of sendReport and notify do not expect the receiver to be in a valid state (I=bot).

Subclassing and Subcontracting. *Oval* also requires subcontracting between a superclass method and an overriding subclass method. As we discuss later, this does not guarantee soundness [22], and we found a counterexample (*cf.* Sec. 6). Therefore, we require that a subclass expects no more than the superclass, and vice versa for vulnerable invariants, and that if an expected invariant in the superclass is vulnerable in the subclass, then it must also be expected in the subclass:[5]

$$I' \preceq I \preceq E \preceq E' \qquad I = E' \Rightarrow I' = E'$$

where I, E, I′, E′ characterise the superclass, resp. subclass, method. This requirement gives exactly *(S5)* from Def. 5. It allows I′ = I = E = E′ which is forbidden in Oval. We refer to the verification technique with the above requirement for method overriding as *Oval′*.

5.3 Summary

In spite of differences in, *e.g.*, the underlying type systems and the logics used, our framework allows us to extract comparable information about these three techniques. We summarise here the commonalities and differences in the results.

1. *Invariant semantics:* In *OT* and *VT*, the invariants expected at the beginning of withdraw are I1, I2, and I3 for the receiver, as well as I5 for the associated DebitCard (which is a peer). For withdraw in *Oval*, I=this, therefore the expected invariants are I1, I2, and I3 for the receiver.
2. *Invariant restrictions:* Invariants I2 and I5 are illegal in *OT* and *Oval*, while they are legal in *VT* (which allows invariants to depend on the fields of peers). Conversely, I3 is illegal in *OT* and *VT* (it mentions a field from a superclass), while it is legal in *Oval*.
3. *Proof obligations:* In *OT*, before the call to this.sendReport() and at the end of the body of withdraw, we have to establish I1 and I2 for the receiver. In addition to these, in *VT* we have to establish I5 for the debit card. In *Oval*, the same invariants as for *OT* have to be proven, but only at the end of the method because call-backs are handled through subcontracting. In addition, I3 is required.[6] In all three techniques, withdraw is permitted to leave the invariant I4 of the owning Person object broken. It has to be re-established by the calling Person method.
4. *Program restrictions:* OT and VT forbid the call holder.notify() (reps cannot call their owners), while *Oval* allows it. On the other hand, if method sendReport required an invariant of its receiver (for instance, to ensure that holder is non-null), then *Oval* would prevent method withdraw from calling it, even though the invariants of the receiver might hold at the time of the call. The proof obligations before calls in *OT* and *VT* would make such a call legal.

---

[5] Note, that we had erroneously omitted the latter requirement in [7].
[6] This means that verification of a class requires knowledge of a subclass. The *Oval* developers plan to solve this modularity problem by requiring that any inherited method has to be re-verified in the subclass [22].

6   Well-Structured Verification Techniques

We now identify conditions on the components of a verification technique that are sufficient for soundness, state a general soundness theorem, and discuss soundness of the techniques presented in Sec. 5

Definition 5. *A verification technique is* well-structured *if, for all programs in the programming language:*

$$(S1)\ \mathbf{r} \sqsubseteq \mathbb{C}_{c,m,c'm'} \Rightarrow (\mathbf{r} \triangleright \mathbb{X}_{c',m'}) \setminus (\mathbb{X}_{c,m} \setminus \mathbb{V}_{c,m}) \subseteq \mathbb{B}_{c,m,\mathbf{r}}$$
$$(S2)\ \mathbb{V}_{c,m} \cap \mathbb{X}_{c,m} \subseteq \mathbb{E}_{c,m}$$
$$(S3)\ \mathbb{C}_{c,m,c',m'} \triangleright (\mathbb{V}_{c',m'} \setminus \mathbb{E}_{c',m'}) \subseteq \mathbb{V}_{c,m}$$
$$(S4)\ \mathbb{U}_{c,m,c'} \triangleright \mathbb{D}_{c'} \subseteq \mathbb{V}_{c,m}$$
$$(S5)\ c' <: c \Rightarrow \mathbb{X}_{c',m} \subseteq \mathbb{X}_{c,m} \land \mathbb{V}_{c',m} \setminus \mathbb{E}_{c',m} \subseteq \mathbb{V}_{c,m} \setminus \mathbb{E}_{c,m}$$

In the above, the set theoretic symbols have the obvious interpretation in the domain of properties. For example *(S2)* is short for $\forall h, \iota : \ [\![\mathbb{V}_{c,m}]\!]_{h,\iota} \cap ([\![\mathbb{X}_c]\!]_{h,\iota} \subseteq [\![\mathbb{E}_{c,m}]\!]_{h,\iota}$. We use *viewpoint adaptation* $\mathbf{r} \triangleright \mathbf{p}$, defined as:

$$[\![\mathbf{r} \triangleright \mathbf{p}]\!]_{h,\iota} = \bigcup_{\iota' \in [\![\mathbf{r}]\!]_{h,\iota}} [\![\mathbf{p}]\!]_{h,\iota'}$$

meaning that the interpretation of a viewpoint-adapted property $\mathbf{r} \triangleright \mathbf{p}$ *w.r.t.* an address ι is equal to the union of the interpretations of $\mathbf{p}$ *w.r.t.* each object in the interpretation of $\mathbf{r}$.

The first two conditions relate proof obligations with expected invariants. *(S1)* ensures for a call within the permitted region that the expected invariants of the callee $(\mathbf{r} \triangleright \mathbb{X}_{c',m'})$ minus the invariants that hold throughout the calling method $(\mathbb{X}_{c,m} \setminus \mathbb{V}_{c,m})$ are included in the proof obligation for the call $(\mathbb{B}_{c,m,\mathbf{r}})$. *(S2)* ensures that the invariants that were broken during the execution of a method, but which are required to hold again at the end of the method $(\mathbb{V}_{c,m} \cap \mathbb{X}_{c,m})$ are included in the proof obligation at the end of the method $(\mathbb{E}_{c,m})$.

The third and fourth condition ensure that invariants that are broken by a method m of class c are actually in its vulnerable set. Condition *(S3)* deals with calls and therefore uses viewpoint adaptation for call regions $(\mathbb{C}_{c,m,c',m'} \triangleright \ldots)$. It restricts the invariants that may be broken by the callee method m', but are not re-established by the callee through $\mathbb{E}$. These invariants must be included in the vulnerable invariants of the caller. Condition *(S4)* ensures for field updates within the permitted region that the invariants broken by updating a field of class c' are included in the vulnerable invariants of the enclosing method, m.

Finally, *(S5)* establishes conditions for subclasses. An overriding method m in a subclass c may expect fewer invariants than the overridden m in superclass c'. Moreover, the subclass method must leave less invariants broken than the superclass method.

Note that the five soundness conditions presented here are slightly weaker than those in the previous version of this work [7]. [7]

Soundness Results. The five conditions from Def. 5 guarantee soundness of a verification technique (Def. 4), provided that the programming language has a sound type system (see Def. 15 in App. A).

Theorem 6. *A well-structured verification technique, built on top of a programming language with a sound type system, is sound.*

This theorem is one of our main results. It reduces the complex task of proving soundness of a verification technique to checking five fairly simple conditions.

Unsoundness of Oval. The original *Oval* proposal [23] is unsound because it requires subcontracting for method overriding. As we said in the previous section, subcontracting corresponds to our *(S1)* and *(S3)*. This gives, for $c' <: c$, the requirements that $\mathbb{X}_{c',m'} \subseteq \mathbb{X}_{c,m} \setminus \mathbb{V}_{c,m}$, and $\mathbb{V}_{c',m'} \setminus \mathbb{E}_{c',m'} \subseteq \mathbb{V}_{c,m}$, which do not imply *(S5)*. We were alerted by this discrepancy, and using only the $\mathbb{X}$, $\mathbb{E}$ and $\mathbb{V}$ components (no type system properties, nor any other component), we constructed the following counterexample.

```
class D[o] {                          class C1[o]{
                                          void mm() <this,this> {...}
    C1<this> c = new C2<this>();      }
    void m() <this,o> { c.mm() }      class C2[o] extends C1<o> {
                                          void mm() <bot,this> {...}
}                                     }
```

The call c.mm() is checked using the contract of C1::mm; it expects the callee to re-establish the invariant of the receiver (c), and is type correct. However, the body of C2::mm may break the receiver's invariants, but has no proof obligations ($\mathbb{E}_{C2,mm} = emp$). Thus, the call c.mm() might break the invariants of c, thus breaking the contract of m. The reason for this problem is, that the—initially appealing—parallel between subcontracting and method overriding does not hold. The authors confirmed our findings [22].

Soundness of the Presented Techniques

Theorem 7. *The verification techniques OT, VT, and Oval' are well-structured.*

Corollary 8. *The verification techniques OT, VT, and Oval' are sound.*

---

[7] Namely, *(S3)* and *(S5)* are weaker, and thus less restrictive, here. In [7], instead of *(S3)* we required the stronger version $\mathbb{C}_{c,m,c',m'} \triangleright (\mathbb{V}_{c',m'} \setminus \mathbb{X}_{c',m'}) \subseteq \mathbb{V}_{c,m}$, and a similarly stronger version for *(S5)*. However, the two versions are equivalent when $\mathbb{E}_{c,m}$ is the minimal set allowed by *(S2)*, i.e., when $\mathbb{E}_{c,m} = \mathbb{V}_{c,m} \cap \mathbb{X}_{c,m}$ for all c and m. In all techniques presented here, $\mathbb{E}_{c,m}$ is minimal in the above sense.

Our proof of Corollary 8 confirmed soundness claims from the literature. We found that the semi-formal arguments supporting the original soundness claims at times missed crucial steps. For instance, the soundness proofs for OT and VT [27] do not mention any condition relating to *(S3)* of Def. 5; in our formal proof, *(S3)* was vital to determine what invariants still hold after a method returns. We relegate proofs of the theorems to the companion report [8].

7   Related Work

Object invariants trace back to Hoare's implementation invariants [12] and monitor invariants [13]. They were popularised in object-oriented programming by Meyer [24]. Their work, as well as other early work on object invariants [20, 21] did not address the three challenges described in the introduction. Since they were not formalised, it is difficult to understand the exact requirements and soundness arguments (see [27] for a discussion). However, once the requirements are clear, a formalisation within our framework seems straightforward.

The idea of regions and properties is inspired from type and effects systems [33], which have been extremely widely applied, *e.g.*, to support race-free programs and atomicity [10].

The verification techniques based on the Boogie methodology [1, 3, 18, 19] do not use a visible state semantics. Instead, each method specifies in its precondition which invariants it requires. Extending our framework to Spec# requires two changes. First, even though Spec# permits methods to specify explicitly which invariants they require, the default is to require the invariants of its arguments and all their peer objects. These defaults can be modelled in our framework by allowing method-specific properties $\mathbb{X}$. Second, Spec# checks invariants at the end of expose blocks instead of the end of method bodies. Expose blocks can easily be added to our formalism.

In separation logic [15, 32], object invariants are generally not as important as in other verification techniques. Instead, predicates specifying consistency criteria can be assumed/proven at *any* point in a program [28]. Abstract predicate families [29] allow one to do so without violating abstraction and information hiding. Parkinson and Bierman [30] show how to address the subclass challenge with abstract predicates. Their work as well as Chin *et al.*'s [4] allow programmers to specify which invariants a method expects and preserves, and do not require subclasses to maintain inherited invariants. The general predicates of separation logic provide more flexibility than can be expressed by our framework.

We know of only one technique based on visible states that cannot be directly expressed in our framework: Middelkoop *et al.* [26] use proof obligations that refer to the heap of the pre-state of a method execution. To formalise this technique, we have to generalise our proof obligations to take two properties; one for the pre-state heap and one for the post-state heap. Since this generality is not needed for any of the other techniques, we omitted a formal treatment in this paper.

Some verification techniques exclude the pre- and post-states of so-called helper methods from the visible states [16, 17]. Helper methods can easily be expressed in our framework by choosing different parameters for helper and non-helper methods. For instance in JML, X, B, and E are empty for helper methods, because they neither assume nor have to preserve any invariants.

Once established, strong invariants [11] hold throughout program execution. They are especially useful to reason about concurrency and security properties. Our framework can model strong invariants, essentially by preventing them from occurring in V.

Existing techniques for visible state invariants have only limited support for object initialisation. Constructors are prevented from calling methods because the callee method in general requires all invariants to hold, but the invariant of the new object is not yet established. Fähndrich and Xia developed delayed types [9] to control call-backs into objects that are being initialised. Delayed types support strong invariants. Modelling these in our framework is future work.

8   Conclusions

We presented a framework that describes verification techniques for object invariants in terms of seven parameters and separates verification concerns from those of the underlying type system. Our formalism is parametric w.r.t. the type system of the programming language and the language used to describe and to prove assumptions. We illustrated the generality of our framework by instantiating it to describe three existing verification techniques. We identified sufficient conditions on the framework parameters that guarantee soundness, and we proved a universal soundness theorem. Our unified framework offers the following important advantages:

1. It allows a simpler understanding and separation of verification concerns. In particular, most of the aspects in which verification techniques differ are distilled in terms of subsets of the parameters of our framework.
2. It facilitates comparisons since relationships between parameters can be expressed at an abstract level (e.g., criteria for well-structuredness in Def. 5), and the interpretations of regions and properties as sets allow formal comparisons of techniques in terms of set operations.
3. It expedites the soundness analysis of verification techniques, since checking the soundness conditions of Def. 5 is significantly simpler than developing soundness proofs from scratch.
4. It captures the design space of *sound* visible states based verification techniques.

We are currently using our framework in developing verification techniques for static methods, and plan to use it to develop further, more flexible, techniques.

Acknowledgements.   We thank Rustan Leino, Matthew Parkinson, Ronald Middelkoop, John Potter, Yi Lu, as well as the POPL, FOOL and ECOOP referees for their feedback. This work was funded in part by the Information Society Technologies program of the European Commission, Future and Emerging Technologies under the IST-2005-015905 MOBIUS project.

References

1. Barnett, M., DeLine, R., Fähndrich, M., Leino, K.R.M., Schulte, W.: Verification of object-oriented programs with invariants. JOT 3(6), 27–56 (2004)
2. Barnett, M., Leino, K.R.M., Schulte, W.: The Spec# programming system: An overview. In: CASSIS. LNCS, pp. 49–69. Springer, Heidelberg (2005)
3. Barnett, M., Naumann, D.: Friends need a bit more: Maintaining invariants over shared State. In: Kozen, D. (ed.) MPC 2004. LNCS, vol. 3125, pp. 54–84. Springer, Heidelberg (2004)
4. Chin, W.-N., David, C., Nguyen, H.H., Qin, S.: Enhancing modular OO verification with separation logic. In: POPL, pp. 87–99. ACM Press, New York (2008)
5. Clarke, D.G., Potter, J.M., Noble, J.: Ownership types for flexible alias protection. In: OOPSLA, vol. 33(10), pp. 48–64. ACM Press, New York (1998)
6. Dietl, W., Müller, P.: Universes: Lightweight ownership for JML. JOT 4(8), 5–32 (2005)
7. Drossopoulou, S., Francalanza, A., Müller, P.: A unified framework for verification techniques for object invariants. In: FOOL (2008)
8. Drossopoulou, S., Francalanza, A., Müller, P., Summers, A.J.: A unified framework for verification techniques for object invariants. In: Vitek, J. (ed.) ECOOP 2008. LNCS, vol. 5142, pp. 412–437. Springer, Heidelberg (2008), http://www.doc.ic.ac.uk/~ajs300m/papers/frameworkFull.pdf
9. Fähndrich, M., Xia, S.: Establishing object invariants with delayed types. In: OOPSLA, pp. 337–350. ACM Press, New York (2007)
10. Flanagan, C., Qadeer, S.: A Type and Effect System for Atomicity. In: PLDI, pp. 338–349. ACM Press, New York (2003)
11. Hähnle, R., Mostowski, W.: Verification of safety properties in the presence of transactions. In: Barthe, G., Burdy, L., Huisman, M., Lanet, J.-L., Muntean, T. (eds.) CASSIS 2004. LNCS, vol. 3362, pp. 151–171. Springer, Heidelberg (2005)
12. Hoare, C.A.R.: Proofs of correctness of data representation. Acta Informatica 1, 271–281 (1972)
13. Hoare, C.A.R.: Monitors: an operating system structuring concept. Commun. ACM 17(10), 549–557 (1974)
14. Huizing, K., Kuiper, R.: Verification of object-oriented programs using class invariants. In: Maibaum, T.S.E. (ed.) ETAPS 2000 and FASE 2000. LNCS, vol. 1783, pp. 208–221. Springer, Heidelberg (2000)
15. Ishtiaq, S.S., O'Hearn, P.W.: BI as an assertion language for mutable data structures. In: POPL, pp. 14–26. ACM Press, New York (2001)
16. Leavens, G.T., Müller, P.: Information hiding and visibility in interface specifications. In: ICSE, pp. 385–395. IEEE Computer Society Press, Los Alamitos (2007)
17. Leavens, G.T., Poll, E., Clifton, C., Cheon, Y., Ruby, C., Cok, D.R., Müller, P., Kiniry, J., Chalin, P.: JML Reference Manual. Department of Computer Science, Iowa State University (February 2007), http://www.jmlspecs.org
18. Leino, K.R.M., Müller, P.: Object invariants in dynamic contexts. In: Odersky, M. (ed.) ECOOP 2004. LNCS, vol. 3086, pp. 491–516. Springer, Heidelberg (2004)
19. Leino, K.R.M., Schulte, W.: Using history invariants to verify observers. In: De Nicola, R. (ed.) ESOP 2007. LNCS, vol. 4421, pp. 316–330. Springer, Heidelberg (2007)
20. Liskov, B., Guttag, J.: Abstraction and Specification in Program Development. MIT Press, Cambridge (1986)
21. Liskov, B., Wing, J.: A behavioral notion of subtyping. ACM ToPLAS 16(6), 1811–1841 (1994)

22. Lu, Y., Potter, J.: Soundness of Oval. Priv. Commun. (June 2007)
23. Lu, Y., Potter, J., Xue, J.: Object Invariants and Effects. In: Ernst, E. (ed.) ECOOP 2007. LNCS, vol. 4609, pp. 202–226. Springer, Heidelberg (2007)
24. Meyer, B.: Object-Oriented Software Construction. Prentice-Hall, Englewood Cliffs (1988)
25. Meyer, B.: Eiffel: The Language. Prentice-Hall, Englewood Cliffs (1992)
26. Middelkoop, R., Huizing, C., Kuiper, R., Luit, E.J.: Invariants for non-hierarchical object structures. Electr. Notes Theor. Comput. Sci. 195, 211–229 (2008)
27. Müller, P., Poetzsch-Heffter, A., Leavens, G.T.: Modular invariants for layered object structures. Science of Computer Programming 62, 253–286 (2006)
28. Parkinson, M.: Class invariants: the end of the road? In: International Workshop on Aliasing, Confinement and Ownership (2007)
29. Parkinson, M., Bierman, G.: Separation logic and abstraction. In: POPL, pp. 247–258. ACM Press, New York (2005)
30. Parkinson, M., Bierman, G.: Separation logic, abstraction and inheritance. In: POPL, pp. 75–86. ACM Press, New York (2008)
31. Poetzsch-Heffter, A.: Specification and verification of object-oriented programs. Habilitation thesis, Technical University of Munich (1997)
32. Reynolds, J.C.: Separation logic: A logic for shared mutable data structures. In: LICS, pp. 55–74. IEEE Computer Society Press, Los Alamitos (2002)
33. Talpin, J.P., Jouvelot, P.: The Type and Effect Discipline. In: LICS, pp. 162–173. IEEE Computer Society Press, Los Alamitos (1992)

A   Appendix—The Framework

Definition 9. *A runtime structure is a tuple*

$$\text{RStruct} = (\text{Hp}, \text{Adr}, \simeq, \preceq, dom, cls, fld, upd, new)$$

where Hp, *and* Adr *are sets, and where*

$$\simeq\ \subseteq\ \text{Hp}\times\text{Hp} \qquad \preceq\ \subseteq\ \text{Hp}\times\text{Hp} \qquad dom : \text{Hp} \to \mathcal{P}(\text{Adr})$$
$$cls : \text{Hp}\times\text{Adr} \rightharpoonup \text{Cls} \qquad\qquad new : \text{Hp}\times\text{Adr}\times\text{Typ} \rightharpoonup \text{Hp}\times\text{Adr}$$
$$fld : \text{Hp}\times\text{Adr}\times\text{Fld} \rightharpoonup \text{Val} \qquad upd : \text{Hp}\times\text{Adr}\times\text{Fld}\times\text{Val} \to \text{Hp}$$

where $\text{Val}=\text{Adr}\cup\{null\}$ *for some element* $null \notin \text{Adr}$. *For all* $h \in \text{Hp}$, $\iota, \iota' \in \text{Adr}$, $v \in \text{Val}$, *we require:*

(H1) $\iota \in dom(h) \Rightarrow \exists c.cls(h,\iota) = c$

(H2) $h \simeq h' \Rightarrow dom(h) = dom(h'),\quad cls(h,\iota) = cls(h',\iota)$

(H3) $h \preceq h' \Rightarrow dom(h) \subseteq dom(h'),\quad \forall\iota \in dom(h).cls(h,\iota) = cls(h',\iota)$

(H4) $upd(h,\iota,f,v) = h' \Rightarrow \begin{cases} h \simeq h' & fld(h',\iota,f) = v, \\ \iota \neq \iota' \text{ or } f \neq f' \Rightarrow fld(h',\iota',f') = fld(h,\iota',f') \end{cases}$

(H5) $new(h,\iota,t) = h',\iota' \Rightarrow h \preceq h',\quad \iota' \in dom(h')\backslash dom(h)$

Definition 10. $E[\cdot]$ *and* $F[\cdot]$ *are defined as follows:*

$$E[\cdot] ::= [\cdot] \mid E[\cdot].f \mid E[\cdot].f = e \mid \iota.f = E[\cdot] \mid E[\cdot].m(e) \mid \iota.m(E[\cdot]) \mid E[\cdot]\,\text{prv}\,\mathbb{p} \mid \text{ret}\,E[\cdot]$$
$$F[\cdot] ::= [\cdot] \mid F[\cdot].f \mid F[\cdot].f = e \mid \iota.f = F[\cdot] \mid F[\cdot].m(e) \mid \iota.m(F[\cdot]) \mid F[\cdot]\,\text{prv}\,\mathbb{p} \mid \sigma\cdot F[\cdot]$$
$$\mid \text{call}\,F[\cdot] \mid \text{ret}\,F[\cdot]$$

Definition 11. *A programming language is a tuple*

$$PL = (\text{PRG}, \text{RSTRUCT}, \text{R}, \text{P})$$

where R *and* P *are sets, and* PRG *is a set where every* $\Pi \in$ PRG *is a tuple*

$$\Pi = \begin{pmatrix} \mathcal{F}, \mathcal{M}, \mathcal{B}, <: \text{(class definitions)} & \sqsubseteq, [\![\cdot]\!] \text{ (inclusion and interpretations)} \\ \models, \vdash & \text{(invariant and type satisfaction)} \end{pmatrix}$$

with signatures:

$$\mathcal{F} \; : \; \text{CLS} \times \text{FLD} \rightharpoonup \text{TYP} \times \text{CLS} \qquad \mathcal{M} \; : \; \text{CLS} \times \text{MTHD} \rightharpoonup \text{TYP} \times \text{TYP}$$
$$\mathcal{B} \; : \; \text{CLS} \times \text{MTHD} \rightharpoonup \text{EXPR} \times \text{CLS}$$
$$<: \; \subseteq \; \text{CLS} \times \text{CLS} \cup \text{TYP} \times \text{TYP} \qquad \sqsubseteq \; \subseteq \; \text{R} \times \text{R}$$
$$[\![\cdot]\!] \; : \; \text{R} \times \text{HP} \times \text{ADR} \rightarrow \mathcal{P}(\text{ADR}) \qquad [\![\cdot]\!] \; : \; \text{P} \times \text{HP} \times \text{ADR} \rightarrow \mathcal{P}(\text{ADR} \times \text{CLS})$$
$$\models \; \subseteq \; \text{HP} \times \text{ADR} \times \text{CLS} \qquad \vdash \; \subseteq \; (\text{ENV} \times \text{EXPR} \cup \text{HP} \times \text{REXPR}) \times \text{TYP}$$

where every $\Pi \in$ PRG *must satisfy the constraints:*

(P1) $\mathcal{F}(c, f) = t, c' \Rightarrow c <: c'$ (P2) $\mathcal{B}(c, m) = e, c' \Rightarrow c <: c'$

(P3) $\mathcal{F}(cls(h, \iota), f) = t, \_ \Rightarrow \exists v. \text{fld}(h, \iota, f) = v$ (P4) $\text{r}_1 \sqsubseteq \text{r}_2 \Rightarrow [\![\text{r}_1]\!]_{h,\iota} \subseteq [\![\text{r}_2]\!]_{h,\iota}$

(P5) $[\![\text{r}]\!]_{h,\iota} \subseteq \text{dom}(h)$ (P6) $h \preceq h' \Rightarrow [\![\text{p}]\!]_{h,\iota} \subseteq [\![\text{p}]\!]_{h',\iota}$

(P7) $\text{r}\,c <: \text{r}'\,c' \Rightarrow \text{r} \sqsubseteq \text{r}', \; c <: c'$

Definition 12. *Stack* $\bar{\sigma}$ *is valid w.r.t. heap* h *in a verification technique* $\mathcal{V}$, *denoted by* $h \vdash_{\mathcal{V}} \bar{\sigma}$, *iff:*

$$\bar{\sigma} = \overline{\sigma_1} \cdot \sigma \cdot \sigma' \cdot \overline{\sigma_2} \Rightarrow \sigma' = (\iota, \_, c', m), \quad h, \sigma \vdash \iota : \text{r}\_, \quad c' <: c, \quad \text{r} \sqsubseteq \mathbb{C}_{\sigma, c, m}$$

Definition 13. *The function* stack : REXPR $\rightarrow$ STK* *yields the stack of a runtime expression:*

$$\text{stack}(E[e_r]) = \begin{cases} \sigma \cdot \text{stack}(e_r') & \text{if } e_r = \sigma \cdot e_r' \\ \epsilon & \text{otherwise} \end{cases}$$

Definition 14. *For every program, the judgement:*

$$\vdash_{wf} \; : \; (\text{HP} \times \text{STK} \times \text{STK} \times \text{R}) \; \cup \; (\text{ENV} \times \text{HP} \times \text{STK}) \; \cup \; \text{PRG} \; \text{ is defined as:}$$

$$- \vdash_{wf} \Pi \Leftrightarrow \begin{cases} (F1) & \mathcal{M}(c, m) = t, t' \Rightarrow \exists e. \, \mathcal{B}(c, m) = e, \_, \; c, m, t \vdash e : t' \\ (F2) & c <: c', \, \mathcal{F}(c', f) = t, c'' \Rightarrow \mathcal{F}(c, f) = t', c'', \; t' = t \\ (F3) & c <: c', \, \mathcal{M}(c, m) = t, t', \, \mathcal{M}(c', m) = t'', t''' \Rightarrow t = t'', \; t' = t'''' \\ (F4) & c <: c', \, \mathcal{B}(c', m) = e', c'' \Rightarrow \exists c'''. \, \mathcal{B}(c, m) = e, c''', \; c''' <: c'' \end{cases}$$

$$- \; h, \sigma \vdash_{wf} \sigma' : \text{r} \quad \Leftrightarrow \quad \sigma' = (\iota, \_, \_, \_), \; h, \sigma \vdash \iota : \text{r}\_$$

$$- \; \Gamma \vdash_{wf} h, \sigma \quad \Leftrightarrow \quad \begin{cases} \exists c, m, t, \iota, v. \quad \Gamma = c, m, t, \; \sigma = (\iota, v, c, m), \\ cls(h, \iota) <: c, \; h, \sigma \vdash v : t \end{cases}$$

Definition 15. *A programming language* PL *has a sound type system if all programs* $\Pi \in$ PL *satisfy the constraints:*

(T1) $\Gamma \vdash e : t, \; t <: t' \Rightarrow \Gamma \vdash e : t'$ (T2) $h \vdash e_r : t, \; t <: t' \Rightarrow h \vdash e_r : t'$

(T3) $h \vdash e_r : t, \; h \simeq h' \Rightarrow h' \vdash e_r : t$ (T4) $h \vdash \sigma \cdot \iota : \_c \Rightarrow cls(h, \iota) <: c$

(T5) $h \vdash \sigma \cdot \iota. m(v) : t \Rightarrow h \vdash \sigma \cdot \iota : \text{r}\,c \, \mathcal{M}(c, m) = t', t, \; h \vdash \sigma \cdot v : t'$

(T6) $\sigma = (\iota, \_, \_, \_), \; h \vdash \sigma \cdot \iota' : \text{r}\_ \Rightarrow \iota' \in [\![\text{r}]\!]_{h,\iota}$

(T7) $\Gamma \vdash e : \text{r}\,c, \; \Gamma \vdash h, \sigma \Rightarrow h \vdash \sigma \cdot e : \text{r}\,c$

(T8) $\vdash_{wf} \Pi, \; h, \sigma \vdash e_r : t \; e_r, h \longrightarrow e_r', h' \Rightarrow h', \sigma \vdash e_r' : t$

(ad-null)   (ad-addr)   (ad-new)   (ad-Var)   (ad-this)   (ad-verEx)

$$\frac{}{h \vdash_\mathcal{V} \sigma \cdot \mathsf{null}} \qquad \frac{\iota \in dom(h)}{h \vdash_\mathcal{V} \sigma \cdot \iota} \qquad \frac{}{h \vdash_\mathcal{V} \sigma \cdot \mathsf{new}\, t} \qquad \frac{}{h \vdash_\mathcal{V} \sigma \cdot x} \qquad \frac{}{h \vdash_\mathcal{V} \sigma \cdot \mathsf{this}} \qquad \frac{}{h \vdash_\mathcal{V} F[\mathsf{verfExc}]}$$

(ad-ass)

$$\frac{\begin{array}{c} h, \sigma \vdash e_r : \mathtt{r}\, c' \\ \mathcal{F}(c', f) = \_, c \\ \mathtt{r} \sqsubseteq \mathsf{U}_{\sigma,c} \\ h \vdash_\mathcal{V} \sigma \cdot e_r \\ h \vdash_\mathcal{V} \sigma \cdot e_r' \end{array}}{h \vdash_\mathcal{V} \sigma \cdot e_r.f = e_r'}$$

(ad-fld)

$$\frac{h \vdash_\mathcal{V} \sigma \cdot e_r}{h \vdash_\mathcal{V} \sigma \cdot e_r.f}$$

(ad-end)

$$\frac{h \vdash_\mathcal{V} \sigma' \cdot v}{h \vdash_\mathcal{V} \sigma \cdot \sigma' \cdot \mathsf{ret}\, v}$$

(ad-call)

$$\frac{\begin{array}{c} h, \sigma \vdash e_r : \mathtt{r}\, c' \\ \mathcal{B}(c', m) = \_, c \\ \mathtt{r} \sqsubseteq \mathsf{C}_{\sigma,c,m} \\ h \vdash_\mathcal{V} \sigma \cdot e_r \\ h \vdash_\mathcal{V} \sigma \cdot e_r' \end{array}}{h \vdash_\mathcal{V} \sigma \cdot e_r.m(e_r'\ \mathsf{prv}\ \mathbb{B}_{\sigma,\mathtt{r}})}$$

(ad-call-2)

$$\frac{\begin{array}{c} h, \sigma \vdash v : \mathtt{r}\, c' \\ \mathcal{B}(c', m) = \_, c \\ h \models \mathbb{B}_{\sigma,\mathtt{r}}, \sigma \\ \mathtt{r} \sqsubseteq \mathsf{C}_{\sigma,c,m} \\ h \vdash_\mathcal{V} \sigma \cdot v \\ h \vdash_\mathcal{V} \sigma \cdot v' \end{array}}{h \vdash_\mathcal{V} \sigma \cdot v.m(v')}$$

(ad-start)

$$\frac{h \vdash_\mathcal{V} \sigma' \cdot e}{h \vdash_\mathcal{V} \sigma \cdot \sigma' \cdot \mathsf{call}\, e\ \mathsf{prv}\ \mathbb{E}_{\sigma'}}$$

(ad-frame)

$$\frac{h \vdash_\mathcal{V} \sigma' \cdot e_r}{h \vdash_\mathcal{V} \sigma \cdot \sigma' \cdot \mathsf{ret}\, e_r\ \mathsf{prv}\ \mathbb{E}_{\sigma'}}$$

Fig. 9. Well-verified runtime expressions

B   Appendix—The Instantiations

Müller et al. We assume an additional heap operation, which gives an object's owner: $own : \mathrm{HP} \times \mathrm{ADR} \to \mathrm{ADR} \times \mathrm{CLS}$.
Regions are interpreted as follows:

$$[\![\mathsf{self}]\!]_{h,\iota} = \{\iota\} \qquad\qquad\qquad [\![\mathsf{any}]\!]_{h,\iota} = dom(h)$$
$$[\![\mathsf{rep}\langle c\rangle]\!]_{h,\iota} = \{\iota' \mid own(h, \iota') = \iota\, c\} \qquad [\![\mathsf{emp}]\!]_{h,\iota} = \emptyset$$
$$[\![\mathsf{peer}]\!]_{h,\iota} = \{\iota' \mid own(h, \iota') = own(h, \iota)\} \qquad [\![\mathtt{r}_1 \sqcup \mathtt{r}_2]\!]_{h,\iota} = [\![\mathtt{r}_2]\!]_{h,\iota} \cup [\![\mathtt{r}_2]\!]_{h,\iota}$$

Properties are interpreted as follows:

$$[\![\mathsf{self}\langle c\rangle]\!]_{h,\iota} = \{(\iota, c) \mid cls(h, \iota) <: c\} \qquad [\![\mathsf{emp}]\!]_{h,\iota} = \emptyset$$
$$[\![\mathsf{peer}\langle c\rangle]\!]_{h,\iota} = \{(\iota', c') \mid own(h, \iota') = own(h, \iota) \wedge vis(c', c)\}$$
$$[\![\mathsf{rep}]\!]_{h,\iota} = \{(\iota', c') \mid own(h, \iota') = \iota\, \_\} \qquad [\![\mathsf{rep}^+]\!]_{h,\iota} = [\![\mathsf{rep}]\!]_{h,\iota} \cup [\![\mathsf{rep}; \mathsf{rep}^+]\!]_{h,\iota}$$
$$[\![\mathsf{own}]\!]_{h,\iota} = \{own(h, \iota)\} \qquad [\![\mathsf{own}^+]\!]_{h,\iota} = [\![\mathsf{own}]\!]_{h,\iota} \cup [\![\mathsf{own}; \mathsf{own}^+]\!]_{h,\iota}$$
$$[\![\mathsf{super}\langle c\rangle]\!]_{h,\iota} = \{(\iota, c') \mid c <: c'\} \qquad [\![\mathsf{p}_1; \mathsf{p}_2]\!]_{h,\iota} = \bigcup_{(\iota', c) \in [\![\mathsf{p}_1]\!]_{h,\iota}} [\![\mathsf{p}_2]\!]_{h,\iota'}$$

The predicate $\mathsf{intrsPeer}(\mathtt{r})$, is defined as:
$$\mathsf{intrsPeer}(\mathsf{emp}) = \mathsf{intrsPeer}(\mathsf{rep}\langle c\rangle) = false$$
$$\mathsf{intrsPeer}(\mathsf{self}) = \mathsf{intrsPeer}(\mathsf{peer}) = \mathsf{intrsPeer}(\mathsf{any}) = true$$
$$\mathsf{intrsPeer}(\mathtt{r}_1 \sqcup \mathtt{r}_2) = \mathsf{intrsPeer}(\mathtt{r}_1) \mathbin{\|} \mathsf{intrsPeer}(\mathtt{r}_2)$$

Lu et al. We interpret regions as follows:

$$[\![\mathsf{emp}]\!]_{h,\iota} = \emptyset \qquad [\![\mathsf{self}]\!]_{h,\iota} = \{\iota\} \qquad [\![\mathtt{r} \sqcup \mathtt{r}']\!]_{h,\iota} = [\![\mathtt{r}]\!]_{h,\iota} \cup [\![\mathtt{r}']\!]_{h,\iota}$$
$$[\![c\langle \overline{K}\rangle]\!]_{h,\iota} = \{\iota' \mid h \vdash \iota' : c\langle \overline{\iota}\rangle, \forall i.\, \iota_i \in \{\!\{K_i\}\!\}_{h,\iota}\}$$

As usual in ownership systems, $h \vdash \iota : c\langle \bar{\iota} \rangle$ describes that ι points to an object of a subclass of $c\langle \bar{\iota} \rangle$, while $h \vdash \iota' \preceq \iota$ expresses that ι' is owned by ι, and $h \vdash \iota' \preceq^* \iota$ is the transitive closure. We interpret properties as follows:

$$[\![\mathsf{emp}]\!]_{h,\iota} = [\![\mathsf{top}]\!]_{h,\iota} = [\![\mathsf{bot}]\!]_{h,\iota} = \emptyset \quad [\![\mathsf{self}]\!]_{h,\iota} = \{(\iota, c) \mid \dots\}$$

$$[\![K]\!]_{h,\iota} = \{(\iota', c) \mid \iota' \in \{\!\{K\}\!\}_{h.\iota}, \; cls(h, \iota') <: c\}$$

$$[\![K; \mathsf{p}]\!]_{h,\iota} = \begin{cases} all(h) & K = \mathsf{top}, \mathsf{p} = \mathsf{rep}^* \vee K = \mathsf{bot}, \mathsf{p} = \mathsf{own}^* \\ \bigcup_{(\iota', c) \in [\![K]\!]_{h,\iota}} [\![\mathsf{p}]\!]_{h,\iota'} & \mathsf{p} \in \{\mathsf{rep}^*, \mathsf{own}^*\} \end{cases}$$

$$[\![\mathsf{rep}^*]\!]_{h,\iota} = \{\iota' \mid h \vdash \iota' \preceq^* \iota\} \qquad [\![\mathsf{own}^*]\!]_{h,\iota} = \{\iota' \mid h \vdash \iota \preceq^* \iota'\}$$

$$\{\!\{X\}\!\}_{h,\iota} = \{\iota_i \mid h \vdash \iota : c\langle \bar{\iota} \rangle, \; c \text{ has formal parameters } \bar{X}, \; X = X_i\}$$

The owner extraction function $\mathcal{O}$ is defined as:

$$\mathcal{O}_{\mathsf{r},c} = \begin{cases} K_1, & \text{if } \mathsf{r} = c\langle \overline{K} \rangle \\ X_1, & \text{if } \mathsf{r} = \mathsf{self}, \text{ class } c \text{ has formal parameters } \bar{X}. \\ \bot & \text{otherwise} \end{cases}$$

Extensible Universes for Object-Oriented Data Models

Achim D. Brucker[1] and Burkhart Wolff[2]

[1] SAP Research, Vincenz-Priessnitz-Str. 1, 76131 Karlsruhe, Germany
achim.brucker@sap.com
[2] Universität des Saarlandes, 66041 Saarbrücken, Germany
wolff@wjpserver.cs.uni-sb.de

Abstract. We present a datatype package that enables the shallow embedding technique to object-oriented specification and programming languages. This datatype package incrementally compiles an object-oriented
data model to a theory containing object-universes, constructors, accessors functions, coercions between dynamic and static types, characteristic
sets, their relations reflecting inheritance, and the necessary class invariants. The package is conservative, i. e., all properties are derived entirely
from axiomatic definitions. As an application, we use the package for an
object-oriented core-language called IMP++, for which correctness of a
Hoare-Logic with respect to an operational semantics is proven.

1   Introduction

While object-oriented programming is a widely accepted programming paradigm, theorem proving over object-oriented programs or object-oriented specifications is far from being a mature technology. Classes, inheritance, subtyping, objects and references are deeply intertwined and complex concepts that
are quite remote from the platonic world of first-order logic or higher-order
logic (HOL). For this reason, there is a tangible conceptual gap between the verification of functional and imperative programs on the one hand and imperative
and object-oriented programs on the other.

Among the existing implementations of proof environments dealing with subtyping and references, two categories can be distinguished: 1) *pre-compilation* into
standard logic, and 2) *deep-embeddings* into a meta-logic. As pre-compilation tools,
for example, we consider Boogie for Spec# [2, 14] and tools based on the Java
Modeling Language (JML) such as Krakatoa [15]. The underlying idea is to compile object-oriented programs into standard imperative ones and to apply a verification condition generator on the latter. While technically sometimes very advanced, the foundation of these tools is quite problematic: The compilation in itself
is not verified, and it is not clear if the generated conditions are sound with respect
to the (usually complex) operational semantics. Among the tools based on deep-
embeddings, there is a sizable body of literature on formal models of Java-like languages (e. g., [5, 10, 11, 21, 25]). In a deep embedding of a language semantics, syntax and types are represented by free datatypes. As a consequence, derived calculi

J. Vitek (Ed.): ECOOP 2008, LNCS 5142, pp. 438–462, 2008.
© Springer-Verlag Berlin Heidelberg 2008

inherit a heavy syntactic bias in form of side-conditions over binding and typing issues. This is unavoidable if one is interested in meta-theoretic properties such as type-safety; however, when reasoning over applications and not over language tweaks, this advantage turns into a major obstacle for efficient deduction. Thus, while proofs for type-safety, soundness of Hoare-Calculi and even soundness of verification condition generators are done, none of the mentioned deep embeddings has been used for substantial proof work in applications.

In contrast, the *shallow embedding* technique has been used for semantic representations such as HOL itself (in Isabelle/Pure), for HOLCF (in Isabelle/HOL) allowing reasoning over Haskell-like programs [17] or, for HOL-Z [7]. These embeddings have been used for substantial applications (e. g., [3]). The essence of a shallow embedding is to represent object-language binding and typing directly in the binding and typing machinery of the meta-language. Thus, many side-conditions are simply unnecessary; type-safety, for example, has been proven implicitly when deriving computational rules from semantic definitions. Since implicit side-conditions are "implemented" by built-in mechanisms, they are handled orders of magnitude faster compared to an explicit treatment.

At first sight, it seems impossible to apply the shallow embedding technique to object-oriented languages in HOL. In this technique, an expression E of type T in some object-oriented language must be translated into some HOL-expression E of HOL-type T. The translation should preserve well-typedness in both ways. However, by "translation" we do not mean a simple one-to-one conversion; rather, the translation might use the object-oriented type system for a pre-processing step, making, for example, implicit coercions between subtypes and supertypes explicit. Still, this requires a representation where subtyping is embedded into parametric polymorphism.

The type representation problem becomes apparent when defining the most fundamental concept of an object-oriented language, namely its underlying *state* called *object structure*. *Objects* are abstract representations of pieces of memory that are linked via references (object identifiers, oid) to each other. Objects are tuples of class attributes, i. e., elementary values like Integers or Strings or references to other objects. The type of these tuples is viewed as the type of the class they are belonging to. Obviously, object structures are maps of type oid $\Rightarrow \mathscr{U}$ relating references to objects living in a universe $\mathscr{U}$ of all objects.

Instead of constructing such a universe globally for all data-models (which is either untyped or "too large" for (simply) typed HOL, where all type sums must be finite), one could think of generating an object universe only for each given system of classes. Ignoring subtyping and inheritance for a moment, this would result in a universe $\mathscr{U}^0 = A + B$ for some class system with the classes A and B. Unfortunately, such a construction is not extensible: If we add a new class to an existing class system, say D, then the "obvious" construction $\mathscr{U}^1 = A + B + D$ results in a *different* type to $\mathscr{U}^0$, making their object structures logically incomparable. Properties, that have been proven over $\mathscr{U}^0$ will not hold over $\mathscr{U}^1$. Thus, such a naive approach rules out an incremental construction of class systems, which makes it clearly unfeasible.

As contributions of this paper, we will present a novel universe construction which represents subtyping within parametric polymorphism in a preserving manner *and* which is extensible. This construction is used in a novel kind of datatype-package (implemented for Isabelle/HOL), i. e., a kind of logic compiler that generates for each class system and its extensions (for example, given as class models in a standardized format like XMI) various conservative definitions representing an object-oriented data theory. This includes the definition of constructors and accessors, coercions between types, tests, characteristic sets of objects. On this basis, properties reflecting subtyping and proof principles like class invariants are automatically derived. Further, we apply this datatype-package for a small imperative language with object-oriented features and show the soundness of a Hoare-Calculus.

2 Formal and Technical Background

Isabelle [20] is a generic, LCF-style theorem prover implemented in SML. For our objects-oriented datatype package, we use the possibility to build SML programs performing symbolic computations over HOL formulae in a logically safe way. Isabelle/HOL offers support for checks for conservatism of definitions, datatypes, primitive and well-founded recursion, and powerful generic proof engines based on rewriting and tableaux provers.

Higher-order logic (HOL) [1] is a classical logic with equality enriched by total polymorphic higher-order functions. It is more expressive than first-order logic, e. g., induction schemes can be expressed inside the logic. HOL is based on the typed λ-calculus, i. e., the *terms* of HOL are λ-expressions. The *application* is written by juxtaposition $E\ E'$, and the *abstraction* is written $\lambda x.\,E$. Types may be built from *type variables* (like α, β, optionally annotated by *type classes*, e. g., $\alpha :: order$) or *type constructors* (e. g., bool). Type constructors may have arguments (e. g., α list). The type constructor for the function space is written infix: $\alpha \Rightarrow \beta$; multiple applications like $\tau_1 \Rightarrow (\ldots \Rightarrow (\tau_n \Rightarrow \tau_{n+1})\ldots)$ are also written as $[\tau_1, \ldots, \tau_n] \Rightarrow \tau_{n+1}$. HOL is centered around the extensional logical equality $\_ = \_$ with type $[\alpha, \alpha] \Rightarrow$ bool, where bool is the fundamental logical type. The logical connectives $\_ \wedge \_$, $\_ \vee \_$, $\_ \rightarrow \_$ of HOL have type $[$bool, bool$] \Rightarrow$ bool, $\neg\_$ has type bool $\Rightarrow$ bool. The quantifiers $\forall \_.\_$ and $\exists \_.\_$ have type $[\alpha$ set, $\alpha \Rightarrow$ bool$] \Rightarrow$ bool. Quantifiers may range over higher order types, i. e., functions.

The type discipline rules out paradoxes such as Russels paradox in untyped set theory. Sets of type α set can be defined isomorphic to functions of type $\alpha \Rightarrow$ bool; the element-of-relation $\_ \in \_$ has the type $[\alpha, \alpha$ set$] \Rightarrow$ bool and corresponds basically to the application; in contrast, the set comprehension $\{\_|\_\}$ has type $[\alpha$ set, $\alpha \Rightarrow$ bool$] \Rightarrow \alpha$ set and corresponds to the λ-abstraction.

Isabelle supports conservative theory extensions schemes; this means that a theory (viewed as a pair of a signature Σ and a set of axioms Φ) can only by extended by type-declarations, constant-declaration and axioms with a particular form. For example, the conservative extensions of a *constant definition* is constrained to a constant declaration $c :: \tau$ and an axiom $c = E$ where c is fresh, i. e., not contained in the previous signature, E does neither contain free (type) variables nor c (these syntactic conditions are checked by Isabelle). For conservative extension schemes such as constant definitions, the extended theory is consistent ("has models") if the original theory is consistent [12].

For our work, we assume a type class $\alpha :: \text{bot}$ for all types α that provide an exceptional element $\bot$; for each type in this class a test for definedness is available via $\text{def } x \equiv (x \neq \bot)$. The HOL type constructor $\tau_\bot$ assigns to each type τ a type *lifted* by $\bot$. Thus, each type $\alpha_\bot$ is member of the class bot. The function $\lfloor \_ \rfloor : \alpha \to \alpha_\bot$ denotes the injection, the function $\lceil \_ \rceil : \alpha_\bot \to \alpha$ its inverse for defined values.

3 Typed Object Universes in an Object Store

In this section, we focus on the map associating an expression E of type T to a HOL expression E of type T. The cornerstones of this map are the (functional) constructors,[1] selectors, tests for dynamic type and kind as well as cast operations between objects along the class hierarchy.

As a pre-requisite, we have to define the families $\mathscr{U}^i$ of object universes. Each $\mathscr{U}^i$ comprises all *value types* and an extensible *class type representation* induced by a class hierarchy. To each class, a *class type* (like Node or Object) is associated which represents the set of *object instances* or *objects*. The extensibility of a universe type is reflected by "holes" (polymorphic variables), that can be filled when "adding" extensions to a class. Our construction ensures that $\mathscr{U}^{i+1}$ is just a type instance of $\mathscr{U}^i$ (where $\mathscr{U}^{(i+1)}$ is constructed by adding new classes to $\mathscr{U}^i$). Thus, properties proven over object systems over $\mathscr{U}^i$ remain valid with respect to $\mathscr{U}^{i+1}$, see Figure 1 for an illustration of the main ideas of the construction we present in the following.

A Formal Framework of Object Structure Encodings. We will present the framework of our object encoding together with a small example: assume a class Node with an attribute i of type integer and two attributes left and right of type Node, and an inherited class Cnode (i. e., Cnode is a subtype of Node) with an attribute color of type Boolean.

In the following we define several type sets which all are subsets of the types of the HOL type system. These sets, although denoted in usual set-notation, are a meta-theoretic construct, i. e., they cannot be formalized in HOL. For the class attributes we define:

Definition 1 (Attribute Types). *The set of* attribute types $\mathfrak{A}$ *is defined inductively as follows:*
1. $\{\text{Boolean}, \text{Integer}, \text{Real}, \text{String}, \text{oid}\} \subset \mathfrak{A}$, *and*
2. $\{a \text{ Set}, a \text{ Sequence}, a \text{ Bag}\} \subset \mathfrak{A}$ *for all* $a \in \mathfrak{A}$.

---

[1] These constructors only create a value, in contrast to constructors in object-oriented languages that additionally bind this value to a fresh oid in the memory.

$$\mathcal{U}^1_{(\alpha^A, \beta^{\text{Object}})} = A \times \alpha^A_\perp + \beta^{\text{Object}}$$

(a) A single class A represented by the type sum $A \times \alpha^A_\perp + \beta^{\text{Object}}$. The type variable $\alpha^A_\perp$ allows for introducing subclasses of A and the type variable β^{Object} allows for introducing new top-level classes.

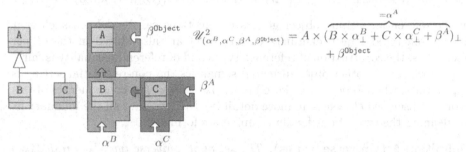

$$\mathcal{U}^2_{(\alpha^B, \alpha^C, \beta^A, \beta^{\text{Object}})} = A \times \overbrace{(B \times \alpha^B_\perp + C \times \alpha^C_\perp + \beta^A)_\perp}^{= \alpha^A} + \beta^{\text{Object}}$$

(b) Extending the previous class model simultaneously with two direct subclasses of A is represented by instantiating the type variable α^A of $\mathcal{U}^1_{(\alpha^A, \beta^{\text{Object}})}$.

Fig. 1. Assume we have a model consisting only of one class A which "lives" in the universe $\mathcal{U}^1_{(\alpha^A, \beta^{\text{Object}})}$ that we want to extend simultaneously with two new subclasses, namely B and C. As both new classes are derived from class A, we construct a local type polynomial $B \times \alpha^B_\perp + C \times \alpha^C_\perp + \beta^A$. This type polynomial is used for instantiating type variable α^A. This process results in the universe $\mathcal{U}^2_{(\alpha^B, \alpha^C, \beta^A, \beta^{\text{Object}})}$ for the final class hierarchy. In particular, the universe $\mathcal{U}^2_{(\alpha^B, \alpha^C, \beta^A, \beta^{\text{Object}})}$ is a type instance of $\mathcal{U}^1_{(\alpha^A, \beta^{\text{Object}})}$. Thus, properties that have been proven over the initial universe $\mathcal{U}^1_{(\alpha^A, \beta^{\text{Object}})}$ are still valid over the extended universe $\mathcal{U}^2_{(\alpha^B, \alpha^C, \beta^A, \beta^{\text{Object}})}$.

In principle, classes are Cartesian products of its attribute types extended by an abstract type ensuring uniqueness.

Definition 2 (Tag Types). *For each class C a tag type $t \in \mathfrak{T}$ is associated. The set $\mathfrak{T}$ is called the set of tag types.*

Tag types allow for building a strongly typed universe (with regard to the object-oriented type system), e. g., for class Node we assign an abstract datatype Node_t with the only element Node_{key}. For each class, we introduce a base class type:

Definition 3 (Base Class Types). *The set of base class types $\mathfrak{B}$ is defined as follows:*

1. *classes without attributes are represented by $(t \times \text{unit}) \in \mathfrak{B}$, where $t \in \mathfrak{T}$ and unit is a special HOL type denoting the empty product.*
2. *if $t \in \mathfrak{T}$ is a tag type and $a_i \in \mathfrak{A}$ for $i \in \{0, \ldots, n\}$ then $(t \times a_0 \times \cdots \times a_n) \in \mathfrak{B}$.*

Thus, the base object type of class Node is $\text{Node}_t \times \text{Integer} \times \text{oid} \times \text{oid}$ and of class Cnode is $\text{Cnode}_t \times \text{Boolean}$.

Without loss of generality, we assume in our object model a common supertype of all objects. In the case of OCL, this is OclAny, in the case of Java this is Object. This assumption is no restriction because such a common supertype can always be added to a given class structure.

Definition 4 (Object). *Let* $\text{Object}_t \in \mathfrak{T}$ *be the tag of the common supertype* Object *and* oid *the type of the object identifiers,*

1. *in the* non-referential *setting, we define* $\alpha\,\text{Object} := (\text{Object}_t \times \alpha_\perp)$.
2. *in the* referential *setting, we define* $\alpha\,\text{Object} := ((\text{Object}_t \times \text{oid}) \times \alpha_\perp)$.

In the referential setting, object generator functions can be defined such that freshly generated object-identifiers to an object are also stored in the object itself; thus, the construction of reference types and of referential equality is fairly easy. However, for other object-oriented semantics the non-referential setting is appropriate, where objects are viewed more like values. The consequences of this choice is discussed elsewhere in more detail [8]. Now we have all the foundations for defining the type of our family of universes formally:

Definition 5 (Universe Types). *The set of all universe types* $\mathfrak{U}_{ref}$ *resp.* $\mathfrak{U}_{nref}$ *(abbreviated* $\mathfrak{U}_x$*) is inductively defined by:*

1. $\mathscr{U}_\alpha^0 \in \mathfrak{U}_x$ *is the initial universe type with one type variable (hole)* α.
2. $\mathscr{U}_{(\alpha_0,\ldots,\alpha_n,\beta_1,\ldots,\beta_m)} \in \mathfrak{U}_x$, $n, m \in \mathbb{N}$, $i \in \{0,\ldots,n\}$ *and* $c \in \mathfrak{B}$ *then*

$$\mathscr{U}_{(\alpha_0,\ldots,\alpha_n,\beta_1,\ldots,\beta_m)}\left[\alpha_i := \left((c \times (\alpha_{n+1})_\perp) + \beta_{m+1}\right)\right] \in \mathfrak{U}_x$$

3. $\mathscr{U}_{(\alpha_0,\ldots,\alpha_n,\beta_1,\ldots,\beta_m)} \in \mathfrak{U}_x$, $n, m \in \mathbb{N}$, $i \in \{0,\ldots,n\}$, *and* $c \in \mathfrak{B}$ *then*

$$\mathscr{U}_{(\alpha_0,\ldots,\alpha_n,\beta_1,\ldots,\beta_m)}\left[\beta_i := \left((c \times (\alpha_{n+1})_\perp) + \beta_{m+1}\right)\right] \in \mathfrak{U}_x$$

Here, item 2 covers the special case of introducing the first subtype by instantiating the α-variable and item 3 covers the general case of introducing further subtypes by instantiating the corresponding β-variable.

The initial universe $\mathscr{U}_\alpha^0$ represents the common supertype (i. e., Object) of all classes, i. e., a simple definition would be $\mathscr{U}_\alpha^0 = \alpha\,\text{Object}$. However, we will need the ability to also store value types: $Values = \text{Real}+\text{Integer}+\text{Boolean}+\text{String}$. Therefore, we define the initial universe type by $\mathscr{U}_\alpha^0 = \alpha\,\text{Object} + Values$. Continuing our example we extend the initial universe $\mathscr{U}_{(\alpha)}^0$, in parallel, with the classes Node and Cnode. This extension leads to the following successor universe type:

$$\mathscr{U}_{(\alpha_C,\beta_C,\beta_N)}^1 \equiv \Big((\text{Node}_t \times \text{Integer} \times \text{oid} \times \text{oid})$$
$$\times \left((\text{Cnode}_t \times \text{Boolean}) \times (\alpha_C)_\perp + \beta_C\right)_\perp + \beta_N\Big)\,\text{Object} + Values$$

We pick up the idea of a universe representation without values for a class with all its extensions (subtypes). For each class we construct a type that describes this class and all its subtypes. They can be seen as paths in the tree-like structure of universe types, collecting all attributes in Cartesian products and pruning the type sums and β-alternatives.

Definition 6 (Class Type). *The set of* class types $\mathfrak{C}$ *is defined as follows: Let* $\mathcal{U}$ *be the universe covering, among others, class* C_n, *and let* $C_0, \ldots, C_{n-1}$ *be the supertypes of* C, *i. e.,* C_i *is inherited from* C_{i-1}. *The class type of* C *is defined as:*

1. $C_i \in \mathfrak{B}, i \in \{0, \ldots, n\}$ *then*

$$\mathscr{C}_\alpha^0 = \Big(C_0 \times \Big(C_1 \times (C_2 \times \cdots \times (C_n \times \alpha_\perp)_\perp)_\perp \Big)_\perp \Big)_\perp \in \mathfrak{C},$$

2. $\mathfrak{U}_\mathfrak{C} \supset \mathfrak{C}$, *where* $\mathfrak{U}_\mathfrak{C}$ *is the set of universe types with* $\mathcal{U}_\alpha^0 = \mathscr{C}_\alpha^0$.

Thus in our example we construct for the class type of class Node the type abbreviation:

(α_C, β_C) Node $=$

$\Big((\text{Node}_t \times \text{Integer} \times \text{oid} \times \text{oid}) \times \big((\text{Cnode}_t \times \text{Boolean}) \times (\alpha_C)_\perp + \beta_C)_\perp \big) \Big)$ Object.

Here, α_C allows for extension with new classes by inheriting from Cnode while β_C allows for direct inheritance from Node.

Alternatively, one could omit the lifting of the base types of the supertypes in the definition of class types. This would lead to:

$$\mathscr{C}_\alpha^0 = \Big(C_0 \times \Big(C_1 \times (C_2 \times \cdots \times (C_n \times \alpha_\perp)) \Big) \Big)_\perp$$

We see our definition as the more general one, since it allows for "partial objects" potentially relevant for other object-oriented semantics for programming languages. For example Java, for which partial class objects may occur during construction. This paves the way for establishing the definedness of an object step by step.

Furthermore, since the injections and projections are only built to define attribute accessors, partial objects are hidden in our language.

In both cases the outermost $\cdot_\perp$ reflect the fact that class objects may also be undefined, in particular after projecting them from some term in the universe or failing type casts. This choice has the consequence that constructor arguments may be undefined.

Handling Instances. For each class we provide injections and projects for each class. In the case of Object these definitions are quite easy, e. g., using the constructors Inl and Inr for type sums we can easily insert an Object object into the initial universe via

$$\text{mk}_{\text{Object}}\, o \equiv \text{Inl}\, o \qquad \text{with type } \alpha\, \text{Object} \to \mathcal{U}_\alpha^0$$

and the inverse function for constructing an Object object out of an universe can be defined as follows:

$$\text{get}_{\text{Object}}\, u \equiv \begin{cases} k & \text{if } u = \text{Inl}\, k \\ \varepsilon\, k.\, \text{true} & \text{if } u = \text{Inr}\, k \end{cases} \qquad \text{with type } \mathcal{U}_\alpha^0 \to \alpha\, \text{Object}.$$

In the general case, the definitions of the projections are a little bit more complex, but follows the same schema: for the injections we have to find the "right" position in the type product and insert the given object into that position. Further, we define in a similar way projections for all class attributes. For example, we define the projections for accessing the left attribute of the class Node:

$$obj.\,\text{left}^{(l)} \equiv (\text{fst} \circ \text{snd} \circ \text{snd} \circ \text{fst}) \ulcorner\text{base}\ obj\urcorner$$

with type (α_1, β) Node $\rightarrow$ oid$_\perp$ and where base is a variant of snd over lifted tuples:

$$\text{base}\,x \equiv \begin{cases} b & \text{if } x = \lfloor(a,b)\rfloor, \\ \perp & \text{otherwise.} \end{cases}$$

This construction is not yet type-safe. Nevertheless, this can be easily extended to a type-safe one by adding a unique abstract type for each class type (see Section 4 for details).

In a next step, we define type test functions; for universe types we need to test if an element of the universe belongs to a specific type, i.e., we need to test which corresponding extensions are defined. This is done for Object via

$$\text{isUniv}_{\text{Object}}\,u \equiv \begin{cases} \text{true} & \text{if } u = \text{Inl}\,k \\ \text{false} & \text{if } u = \text{Inr}\,k \end{cases} \qquad \text{with type } \mathscr{U}_\alpha^0 \rightarrow \text{bool.}$$

For class types we define two type tests, an exact one that tests if an object is exactly of the given *dynamic type* and a more liberal one that tests if an object is of the given type or a subtype thereof. Testing the latter one, which is called *kind* in the OCL standard, is quite easy. We only have to test that the base type of the object is defined, e.g., not equal to $\perp$:

$$\text{isKind}_{\text{Object}}\,o \equiv \text{def}\,o \qquad \text{with type } \alpha\,\text{Object} \rightarrow \text{bool.}$$

An object is exactly of a specific dynamic type, if it is of the given kind and the extension is undefined, e.g.:

$$\text{isType}_{\text{Object}}\,o \equiv \text{isKind}_{\text{Object}} \wedge \neg\big((\text{def} \circ \text{base})\,o\big) \quad \text{with type } \alpha\,\text{Object} \rightarrow \text{bool.}$$

The type tests for user defined classes are defined in a similar way by testing the corresponding extensions for definedness.

Finally, we define coercions, i.e., ways to type-cast classes along their subtype hierarchy. Thus we define for each class a cast to its direct subtype and to its direct supertype. We need no conversion on the universe types where the subtype relations are handled by polymorphism. Therefore we can define the type casts as simple compositions of projections and injections, e.g.:

$$\text{Node}_{[\text{Object}]} \equiv \text{get}_{\text{Object}} \circ \text{mk}_{\text{Node}} \text{ with type } (\alpha_1, \beta)\,\text{Node} \rightarrow (\alpha_1, \beta_1)\,\text{Object,}$$
$$\text{Object}_{[\text{Node}]} \equiv \text{get}_{\text{Node}} \circ \text{mk}_{\text{Object}} \text{ with type } (\alpha_1, \beta_1)\,\text{Object} \rightarrow (\alpha_1, \beta_1)\,\text{Node.}$$

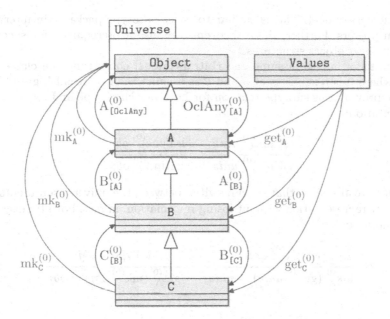

Fig. 2. The type casts, e. g., $B_{[C]}$ allow for the conversion of a type to its direct successor or predecessor in the type hierarchy. The injections, e. g., mk_B convert a class type to the universe type and the projections, e. g., get_B, convert a universe type to a concrete class type. For a universe without values, the class type and the universe type of the top most class are identical. Here, the package **Universe** represents the universe, i. e., the top level class (**Object**) and the primitive types (**Values**).

These type-casts are changing the *static type* of an object, while the *dynamic type* remains unchanged. Figure 2 summarizes this construction for the three classes A, B, and C.

Note, for a universe construction without values, e. g., $\mathscr{U}_\alpha^0 = \alpha$ **Object**, the universe type and the class type for the common supertype are the same. In that case there is a particular strong relation between class types and universe types on the one hand and on the other there is a strong relation between the conversion functions and the injections and projections function. In more detail, one can understand the projections as a cast from the universe type to the given class type and the injections are inverse.

Now, if we build theorems over class invariants (based finally on these projections, injections, casts, characteristic sets, etc.), it will remain valid even if we extend the universe via α and β instantiations.

3.1 Properties of Elementary Objects

Based on the presented definitions, our object-oriented datatype package proves that our encoding of object-structures is a faithful representation of object-oriented (e. g., in the sense of language like Java or Smalltalk or the UML standard [22]). These theorems are proven for each model, e. g., during loading a specific class model. This is similar to other datatype packages in interactive theorem provers. Further, these theorems are also a prerequisite for successful reasoning over object structures.

In the following, we assume an arbitrary model comprising the classes A, B and C where B is a subclass of A and C is a subclass of B (recall Figure 2). We start by proving this subtype relation for both our class type and universe type representation:

$$\frac{\text{isUniv}_A^{(0)} \; univ}{\text{isUniv}_B^{(0)} \; univ} \qquad \frac{\text{isType}_B^{(0)} \; obj}{\text{isKind}_A^{(0)} \; obj}$$

Moreover, we also show that we can switch between the universe representations and object representation without losing information, in fact, both type systems are isomorphic:

$$\frac{\text{isUniv}_A^{(0)} \; univ}{\text{mk}_A^{(0)}(\text{get}_A^{(0)} \; univ) = univ} \qquad \frac{\text{isType}_A^{(0)} \; obj}{\text{get}_A^{(0)}(\text{mk}_A^{(0)} \; obj) = obj}$$

$$\frac{\text{isType}_B^{(0)} \; obj}{\text{isUniv}_A^{(0)}(\text{mk}_A^{(0)} \; obj)} \qquad \frac{\text{isUniv}_A^{(0)} \; univ}{\text{isType}_A^{(0)}(\text{get}_A^{(0)} \; univ)}$$

Moreover, we can "re-cast" an object safely, i.e., up and down casts are idempotent. However, casting an object deeper in the subclass hierarchy than its dynamic type results in undefinedness:

$$\frac{\text{isType}_A^{(0)} \; obj}{obj_{[B]}^{(0)} = \bot} \qquad \frac{\text{isType}_B^{(0)} \; obj}{\left((obj_{[A]}^{(0)})_{[B]}^{(0)}\right) = obj}$$

and also, the cast operations are strict and transitive, e.g.:

$$\frac{}{\bot_{[A]}^{(0)} = \bot} \qquad \frac{\text{isType}_C^{(0)} \; obj}{\left(obj_{[B]}^{(0)}\right)_{[A]}^{(0)} = obj_{[A]}^{(0)}}$$

Further, for all class types c, both $\text{isType}_c^{(0)} \bot = \texttt{false}$ and $\text{isKind}_c^{(0)} \bot = \texttt{false}$ are valid. Summarizing, these derived rules show that our encoding of inheritance establishes a subtype relation. Moreover, the (informal) relations between classes one would expect from languages like UML, Java, or Spec#, also hold in our encoding.

Our datatype package also derives similar properties for the injections and projections into attributes automatically. For example, assume the class A has two attributes a and b then we derive among others:

$$\frac{obj \neq \bot}{(obj.\text{set}_a^{(0)} \; x).a^{(0)} = x} \qquad \frac{}{(obj.\text{set}_a^{(0)} \; x).b^{(0)} = obj.b^{(0)}}$$

$$\overline{(obj.\,\mathrm{set}_a^{(0)}\ x).\,\mathrm{set}_a^{(0)}\ y = obj.\,\mathrm{set}_a^{(0)}\ y}$$

$$\overline{(obj.\,\mathrm{set}_a^{(0)}\ x).\,\mathrm{set}_b^{(0)}\ y = (obj.\,\mathrm{set}_b^{(0)}\ y).\,\mathrm{set}_a^{(0)}\ x}$$

As we use a shallow embedding of object-oriented data-structures into HOL, these properties cannot be proven as meta-theoretic property of our encoding. Instead, our datatype package proves these properties, fully automatically, during the import of an object-oriented data models.

4   The Package

The previously described construction is the foundation of the datatype package of HOL-OCL [9, 6, 8]. For a given class system, described as UML class model, the datatype package of HOL-OCL generates may definitions (the subset of definitions presented in the previous section is marked by $\_ \equiv \_$). Technically, our datatype package supports the standardized XMI format as input (see [8] for implementation details). Besides, it proves automatically several theorems over the imported specification; these theorems are proven for each class, e. g., during loading a specific class model. This includes properties of the object structure, e. g., that our conversion between universe representations and object representation is lossless. This property is characterized by the following two properties, which are, among others, proven automatically by our datatype package:

$$\mathrm{isKind}_C\,o \implies \mathrm{get}_C(\mathrm{mk}_C\,o) = o \quad \text{and} \quad \mathrm{isUniv}_C\,u \implies \mathrm{mk}_C(\mathrm{get}_C\,u) = u\,.$$

Our construction works also for the encoding of *recursive* object structures, including the support for class invariants. First we must introduce some basic notion: for arbitrary binary HOL operations op, we write $\sigma \vDash P\ op\ Q$ for $\ulcorner P\,\sigma \urcorner op \ulcorner Q\,\sigma \urcorner$. Moreover, we write $\sigma \vDash \partial\ x$ ("x is defined in state σ") for $\mathrm{def}(x\,\sigma)$, and $\sigma \vDash \not{\partial}\ x$ for the contrary. For constant symbols we will simplify the presentation: for example, we will write 5 for $\lambda\,\sigma.\,5$, $\lfloor\mathrm{true}\rfloor$ for $\lambda\,\sigma.\,\lfloor\mathrm{true}\rfloor$, etc.

Now we approach our main goal to provide a type-safe embedding of the accessors, and, consequently, of the whole assertion language.

We define the *store* as a partial map based on the concept of object universes:

$$\alpha\,\mathrm{St} := \mathrm{oid} \rightharpoonup \mathscr{U}_\alpha\,.$$

Since all operations over our object store will be parametrized by $\alpha\,\mathrm{St}$, we introduced the following type synonym:

$$V_\alpha(\tau) := \alpha\,\mathrm{St} \Rightarrow \tau\,.$$

Thus we can define type-safe accessor functions, i. e., object identifiers (references) are completely encapsulated. For example, the function for accessing the left attribute of an object of class Node in a system state σ is defined as follows:

$$obj.\,\text{left} \equiv \lambda\,\sigma.\ \begin{cases} \text{get}_{\text{Node}}\,u & \text{if } \sigma(obj.\,\text{left}^{(l)}) = \llcorner u \lrcorner \\ \bot & \text{otherwise.} \end{cases}$$

For accessor with type set or sequence, we provide definitions that de-reference each element of, e. g., a set of object identifiers and build a set of typed objects.

The object-language accessor .left of type Node, which is in fact a function of type Node $\rightarrow$ Node, is now represented by our construction as follows:

$$\_.\,\text{left} :: V_{(\alpha_C,\beta_C)}((\alpha_C,\beta_C)\,\text{Node}) \Rightarrow V_{(\alpha_C,\beta_C)}((\alpha_C,\beta_C)\,\text{Node}).$$

Thus, the representation map is injective on types; subtyping is represented by type-instantiation on the HOL-level. However, due to our universe construction, the theory on accessor, casts, etc. is also extensible.

All other operations like casting, type- or kind-check are lifted equivalently; in the following, we will always assume these lifted versions since due to our typing discipline, no confusion may arise. These definitions are also generated by our package and "lifted" versions of the theorems are derived.

We turn now to our construction of characteristic sets and the derivation of class invariant theorems. Recall our previous example, where the class Node describes a potentially infinite recursive object structure. Assume that we want to constrain the attribute i of class Node to values greater than 5. This is expressed by the following function approximating the set of possible instances of the class Node and its subclasses:

$$\text{NodeKindF} :: \mathscr{U}^1_{(\alpha_C,\beta_C,\beta_N)}\,\text{St} \Rightarrow \mathscr{U}^1_{(\alpha_C,\beta_C,\beta_N)}\,\text{St} \Rightarrow (\alpha_C,\beta_C)\,\text{Node set}$$
$$\Rightarrow \mathscr{U}^1_{(\alpha_C,\beta_C,\beta_N)}\,\text{St} \Rightarrow (\alpha_C,\beta_C)\,\text{Node set}$$

$$\text{NodeKindF} \equiv \lambda\,\sigma.\ \lambda\,X.\ \{\,obj \mid \sigma \vDash \partial\,obj.\text{i} \wedge \sigma \vDash obj.\text{i} > 5$$
$$\wedge\ \sigma \vDash \partial\,obj.\text{left} \wedge \sigma \vDash (obj.\text{left}) \in X$$
$$\wedge\ \sigma \vDash \partial\,obj.\text{right} \wedge \sigma \vDash (obj.\text{right}) \in X\,\}$$

In a setting with subtyping, we need two characteristic type sets, a more liberal one, the *characteristic kind set*, and narrower one, the *characteristic type set*. By adding the conjunct $\sigma \vDash obj$ isTypeOf(Node) (essentially a notation for the previously defined type tests), we can construct another approximation function (which has obviously the same type as NodeKindF):

$$\text{NodeTypeF} \equiv \lambda\,\sigma.\ \lambda\,X.\ \{\,obj \mid (obj \in (\text{NodeKindF}\ \sigma\ X))$$
$$\wedge\ \sigma \vDash obj\ \text{isTypeOf(Node)}\,\}$$

Thus, the characteristic kind set for the class Node can be defined as the greatest fixed-point over the function NodeKindF:

$$\text{NodeKindSet} :: \mathscr{U}^1_{(\alpha_C,\beta_C,\beta_N)}\,\text{St} \Rightarrow \mathscr{U}^1_{(\alpha_C,\beta_C,\beta_N)}\,\text{St} \Rightarrow (\alpha_C,\beta_C)\,\text{Node set}$$
$$\text{NodeKindSet} \equiv \lambda\,\sigma.\ (\text{gfp(NodeKindF}\ \sigma)).$$

For the characteristic type set we proceed analogously. We infer a *class invariant theorem*:

$$\sigma \vDash obj \in \text{NodeKindSet} = \sigma \vDash \partial\, obj.\mathrm{i} \wedge \sigma \vDash obj.\mathrm{i} > 5$$
$$\wedge\, \sigma \vDash \partial\, obj.\text{left} \wedge \sigma \vDash (obj.\text{left}) \in \text{NodeKindSet}$$
$$\wedge\, \sigma \vDash \partial\, obj.\text{right} \wedge \sigma \vDash (obj.\text{right}) \in \text{NodeKindSet}$$

and prove automatically by monotonicity of the approximation functions and their point-wise inclusion:

$$\text{NodeTypeSet} \subseteq \text{NodeKindSet}$$

This kind of theorem remains valid if we add further classes in a class system.

Now we relate class invariants of subtypes to class invariants of supertypes. Here, we use coercion functions described in the previous section; we write $o_{[\text{Node}]}$ for the object o converted to the type Node of its superclass. The trick is done by defining a new approximation for an inherited class Cnode on the basis of the approximation function of the superclass:

$$\text{CnodeF} \equiv \lambda\sigma.\, \lambda X.\, \big\{ obj \mid obj_{[\text{Node}]} \in (\text{NodeKindF}\, \sigma\, (\lambda o.\, o_{[\text{Node}]})\, {}^{`} X)) \wedge \cdots \big\}$$

where the ... stand for the constraints specific to the subclass.

Similar to [23] we can handle mutual-recursive datatype definitions by encoding them into a type sum. However, we already have a suitable type sum together with the needed injections and projections, namely our universe type with the make and get methods for each class. The only requirement is that a set of mutual recursive classes must be introduced "in parallel," i. e., as *one* extension of an existing universe.

These type sets have the usual properties that one associates with object-oriented type systems. Let $\mathfrak{C}_N$ ($\mathfrak{K}_N$) and be the characteristic type set (characteristic kind set) of a class N and $\mathfrak{C}_C$ and $\mathfrak{K}_N$ the corresponding type sets of a direct subclass of N, then our encoding process proves formally that the characteristic type set is a subset of the kind set, i. e.:

$$\sigma \vDash obj \in \mathfrak{C}_N \longrightarrow \sigma \vDash obj \in \mathfrak{K}_N$$

and that the kind set of the subclass is (after type coercion) a subset of the type set (and thus also of the kind set) of the superclass:

$$\sigma \vDash obj \in \mathfrak{K}_C \longrightarrow \sigma \vDash obj_{[\text{Node}]} \in \mathfrak{C}_N\,.$$

These proofs are based on co-inductions and involve a kind of bi-simulation of (potentially) infinite object structures. Further, these proofs depend on theorems that are already proven over the pre-defined types, e. g., Object. These proofs were done in the context of the initial universe $\mathscr{U}^0$ and can be instantiated directly in the new universe without replaying the proof scripts; this is our main motivation for an *extensible* construction.

The Underlying Method. Our object-oriented datatype package also supports a special analysis and verification method based on the idea of providing several versions of invariants that restrict the type and kind sets with different grades. For example, the discussed type sets and kind sets are of major importance when resolving overloading and late-binding: If we can infer from a class invariant that some object must be of a particular *type*, then late-binding method invocation can be reduced to a straight-forward procedure call with simplified semantics.

As a default we generate for each class three different type sets and kind sets:

1. a set based on the user-defined invariant,
2. a set allowing undefined references, i.e., all accessor to attributes of type oid are or-ed with a corresponding $\emptyset$-statement, and
3. one allowing undefined references *and* undefined value types, i.e., all accessor to attributes are or-ed with a corresponding $\emptyset$-statement.

This enumeration is ordered ascending with respect to the number of instances that fulfill the conditions, i.e., every object that is in the first set, is also in the other two. Such an hierarchy of invariants allows for formally specifying the circumstances which invariants should hold.

In practice we assume the need for an even more fine-grained graduation of invariants. Whereas at the moment one has to reproduce the encoding process of our package to introduce new invariant types, we intend to provide an automatic mechanism for defining new invariant types, i.e., an interface to our package that defines new type sets and also automatically proves the basic properties, including the inclusion relation with respect to the already defined type sets.

5   A Modular Proof-Methodology for Object-Oriented Modeling

In the previous sections, we discussed a technique to build *extensible* object-oriented data models. Now we turn to the wider goal of a *modular* proof methodology for object-oriented systems and explore achievements and limits of our approach with respect to this goal. Two aspects of modular proofs over object-oriented models have to be distinguished:

1. the modular construction of theories over object-data models and
2. a modular way to represent dynamic type information or storage assumptions underlying object-oriented programs.

With respect to the former, the question boils down to what degree extensions of class models and theories built over them can be merged. With respect to the latter, we will show how co-inductive properties over the store help to achieve this goal.

5.1   Non-overlapping Merges

The positive answer to the modularity question is that object-oriented data-model theories can be merged provided that the extensions to the underlying object-data models are non-overlapping. Two extensions are *non-overlapping*, if

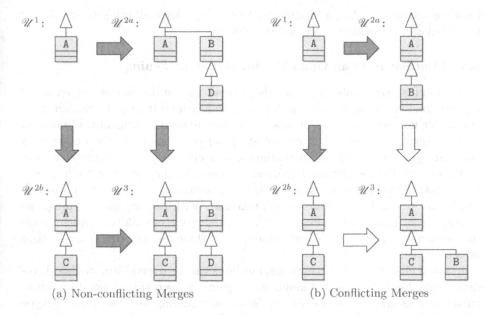

(a) Non-conflicting Merges   (b) Conflicting Merges

Fig. 3. Merging Universes

their set of classes including their direct parent classes are disjoint (see Figure 3a). In these cases, there exists a most general type instance of the merged object universe $\mathscr{U}^3$ (the type unifier of both extended universes $\mathscr{U}^{2a}$ and $\mathscr{U}^{2b}$); thus, all theorems built over the extended universes are still valid over the merged universe (see Figure 3a). We argue that the non-overlapping case is the pragmatically more important one; for example, all libraries of the HOL-OCL system [8] are linked to the examples in its substantial example suite this way. Without extensibility, the datatype package would have to require the recompilation of the libraries, which takes in the case of the HOL-OCL system about 20 minutes.

5.2 Handling Overlapping Merges

Unfortunately, one pragmatically important case in object-oriented modeling is considered as an overlap in our package. Consider the case illustrated in Figure 3b. Here, the parent class A is in the class set of both extensions (*including* parent classes). The technical reason for the conflict is that the order of insertions of sub-classes into a parent class is relevant since the type sum $\alpha + \beta$ is not a commutative type constructor.

In our encoding scheme of object-oriented data models, this scenario of extensions represents an overlap that the user is forced to resolve. One pragmatic possibility is to arrange an order of the extensions by changing the import hierarchy of theories producing overlapping extensions. This worst-case results in re-running the proof scripts of either B or C—usually a matter of a minute. Another option is to introduce an empty class B' and inherit B from there. A further option consists in adding a mechanism into our package allowing to specify for a child-class the position in the insertion-order.

5.3   Modularity in an Open-World: Dynamic Typing

Our notion of extensible class models generalizes the distinction "open-world assumption" vs. "closed-world assumption" widely used in object-oriented modeling. Our universe construction is strictly "open-world" by default; the case of a "closed-world" results from instantiating all α,β-"holes" in the universe by the unit type. Since such an instantiation can also be partial, there is a spectrum between both extremes. Furthermore, one can distinguish α-*finalizations*, i.e., instantiation of an α- variable in the universe by the unit type, and β-*finalizations*. The former close a class hierarchy with respect to subtyping, the latter prevent that a parent class may have further direct children (which makes the automatic derivation of an exhaustion theorem for this parent class possible).

In usual object-oriented languages, methods can be overridden, method invocations like in object-oriented languages require an overridden resolution mechanism such as *late binding* as used in Java. Late binding uses the dynamic type isType$_X$ *obj* of *obj*. The late-binding method invocation is notorious for its difficulties for modular proof. Consider the case of an operation:

```
method Node::m()::Bool
pre:   P
post:  Q
```

Furthermore assume that the implementation of m invokes itself recursively, e. g., by `self.left.m()`. Based on an open-world assumption, the postcondition Q cannot be established in general since it is unknown which concrete implementation is called at the invocation.

Based on our universe construction, there are two ways to cope with this underspecification. First, finalizations of all child classes of Node results in a *partial* closed-world assumption allowing to treat the method invocation as case switch over dynamic types and direct calls of method implementations. Second, similarly to the co-inductive invariant example in Section 4 which ensures that a specific dereferentiation is in fact defined, we can specify that a specific dereferentiation *obj*. left has a given dynamic type. An analogous invariant $\text{Inv}_{\text{left}}(obj)$ can be defined co-inductively. From this invariant, we can directly infer facts like isType$_{\text{Node}}^{(1)}$ (obj. left), and isType$_{\text{Node}}^{(1)}$ (obj. left. left), i. e., in an object graph satisfying this invariant, the left "spine" must consist of nodes of dynamic type Node. Strengthening the precondition P by $\text{Inv}_{\text{left}}(obj)$ consequently allows to establish postcondition Q—in a modular manner, since only the method implementation above has to be considered in the proof. Invoking the method on an object graph that does not satisfy this invariant can therefore be considered as a breach of the contract.

5.4 Modularity in an Open-World: Storage Assumptions

Similarly to co-inductive invariants, it is possible via co-recursive functions to map an object to the set of objects that can be reached along a particular path set. The definition must be co-recursive, since object structures may represent a graph. However, the presentation of this function may be based on a primitive-recursive approximation function depending on a factor k :: nat that computes this object set only up to the length k of the paths in the path set.

$$\text{ObjSetA}_{\text{left}}\ 0\ obj\ \sigma = \{\}$$
$$\text{ObjSetA}_{\text{left}}\ k\ obj\ \sigma = \text{if}\ \sigma \models \partial\ obj\ \text{then}\{\}$$
$$\text{else}\ \{obj\} \cup \text{ObjSetA}_{\text{left}}\ (k-1)\ (obj.\,\text{left}\ \sigma)\ \sigma$$

The function $\text{ObjSet}_{\text{left}}\ obj\ \sigma$ can then be defined as limit

$$\bigcup\nolimits_{n \in \text{Nat}} \text{ObjSetA}_{\text{left}}\ n\ obj\ \sigma\,.$$

On the other hand, we can add a *state invariant* on our concept of state per type definition $\alpha\,\text{St} = \{\sigma :: \text{oid} \rightharpoonup \mathscr{U}^\alpha.\ \text{Inv}\ \sigma\}$. Here, we require for *inv* that each oid points to an object that contains itself:

$$\forall\,\text{oid} \in \text{dom}\ \sigma.\ \text{OidOf}(\text{the}(\sigma\ \text{oid})) = \text{oid}$$

As a consequence, there exists a one-to-one correspondence between objects and their oid in a state. Thus, sets of objects can be viewed as sets of references, too, which paves the way to interpret these reference sets in different states and specify that an object did not change during a system transition or that there are no references from one object-structure into some critical part of another object structure.

6 Application: A Shallow Embedding of IMP++

In the following, we integrate the operations derived from an object-oriented data model into assertions in a derived Hoare-Calculus for a small, imperative language. This language is pretty much in the spirit of Featherweight Java [13], in the sense that it is reduced to the absolute minimum. IMP++does not even comprise the concept of a method invocation or a procedure call; on the other hand, it provides a "generic slot" for these concepts via the CMD-construct, that allows for an arbitrary transition over the entire program state. Given the dynamic type tests of the data model, it is straight-forward to *define* an arbitrary overload resolution within this language; demonstrating how this definitions scale up with the presented machinery to a modular proof method, however, is a far more evolved subject that we consider beyond the scope of this paper.

Instead, we focus on how our type-safe framework pays off by not further complicating its rules by side-conditions related to well-formedness of objects, the syntactic admissibility of attribute accesses to an object or reasoning along the class hierarchy as in the deep embedding of, e. g., NanoJava [25]. We will show that compact calculi for denotational, operational and axiomatic semantics can be derived in a standard exercise.

We follow deliberately the standard presentation of IMP [19], a canonical imperative core language, in the Isabelle/HOL library; this language has been inspired by a standard textbook on program semantics [26]. We will extend IMP with object-oriented typedness, creation, update, selection and a simple form for exceptional computation (motivated by illegal memory accesses). In a small example, we sketch how to apply it for reasoning on weak and strong data invariants on tree-like structures.

In contrast to the previous sections where definitions and proofs were done automatically for all classes and attributes—the proof presented here are done interactively. However, we emphasize that a large part of it (e. g., the core Hoare-Calculus and the rules for update and create) could be mechanically derived, too.

6.1 Syntax

The syntax of IMP++is introduced via a datatype definition:

α com = SKIP	EXN
| CMD α cmd	| IF α bexp THEN α com ELSE α com
| α com ; α com	| WHILE α bexp DO α com

SKIP denotes the empty, successfully terminating command, EXN the program that raises the exception (IMP++ possesses only one). The generic command CMD takes as argument a function α cmd which is a synonym for a function α state $\Rightarrow \alpha$ state$_\perp$. Thus, a α cmd is allowed to raise an exception; in our context, this will be used to react operationally on undefined argument oid's of creation and update operations. The sequential composition, the conditional and the while loop are the conventional constructs of the language. The latter two are controlled by a Boolean expression α bexp which is a synonym for α state $\Rightarrow$ bool$_\perp$. Any assertion has a type which is an instance of α bexp, thus, it can be used as control expression in IMP++.

6.2 Denotational Semantics

In general, the denotational semantics of an imperative language is a relation on states; since uncaught exceptions may occur on the command level, we have also *error states* denoted by $\perp$. Thus, the type of the relation is $(\alpha :: \text{bot state}_\perp \times \alpha \text{ state}_\perp)set$. As a consequence, we need as prerequisite the "strict extension" $\_ \circ_\perp \_$ of type $(\beta_\perp \times \gamma_\perp)$ set $\Rightarrow (\alpha_\perp \times \beta_\perp)$ set $\Rightarrow (\alpha_\perp \times \gamma_\perp)$ set on relations:

$$r \circ_\perp s \equiv \{(\perp, \perp)\} \cup \{(x, z).\ \text{def } x \land (\exists y.\ \text{def } y \land (x, y) \in s \land (y, z) \in r)\}$$
$$\cup \{(x, z).\ \text{def } x \land (\exists y. \neg \text{def } y \land (x, y) \in s \land z = \perp)\}$$

The definition of the semantic function C is a primitive recursion over the syntax:

$$C(\text{SKIP}) = \text{Id}$$
$$C(\text{EXN}) = \{(s,t).\, t = \bot\}$$
$$C(\text{CMD } f) = \{(s,t).\, s = \bot \wedge t = \bot\} \cup \{(s,t).\, \text{def } s \wedge t = f\ulcorner s\urcorner\}$$
$$C(c_0; c_1) = C(c_1) \circ_\bot C(c_0)$$

$$C(\text{IF } b \text{ THEN } c_1 \text{ ELSE } c_2) = \{(s,t).\, (s = \bot \vee b\ulcorner s\urcorner = \bot) \wedge t = \bot\}$$
$$\cup \{(s,t).\, \text{def } s \wedge b\ulcorner s\urcorner = \lfloor \text{true}\rfloor \wedge (s,t) \in C\, c_1\}$$
$$\cup \{(s,t).\, \text{def } s \wedge b\ulcorner s\urcorner = \lfloor \text{false}\rfloor \wedge (s,t) \in C\, c_2\}$$
$$C(\text{WHILE } b \text{ DO } c) = \text{lfp}(\Gamma\, b\, (C\, c))$$

where Γ is the usual approximation functional for the least fixed-point operator lfp, enriched by the cases for undefined states:

$$\Gamma\, b\, cd \equiv (\lambda\, \phi.\, \{(s,t).\, (s = \bot \vee b\ulcorner s\urcorner = \bot) \wedge t = \bot\} \cup$$
$$\{(s,t).\, \text{def } s \wedge b\ulcorner s\urcorner = \lfloor \text{true}\rfloor \wedge (s,t) \in (\phi \circ_\bot cd)\} \cup$$
$$\{(s,t).\, \text{def } s \wedge b\ulcorner s\urcorner = \lfloor \text{false}\rfloor \wedge s = t\})$$

6.3 Hoare Semantics

In our setting, assertions are functions $\alpha :: \text{bot state}_\bot \Rightarrow \text{bool}$. The validity of a Hoare triple is stated as traditional:

$$\models \{P\}c\{Q\} \equiv \forall s\, t.\, (s,t) \in C(c) \longrightarrow P\, s \longrightarrow Q\, t$$

Based on the definition for C, we can derive a Hoare calculus for IMP++. Since we focus on correctness proof and not completeness, we present the rules for validity $\models$ directly, avoiding a detour via a derivability notion $\vdash$. Moreover, we use the abbreviation $\odot\, P$ for $\lambda\sigma.\, \text{def } \sigma \wedge P\sigma$. Thus, assertions like $\models \{\odot\, P'\}c\{\odot\, Q'\}$ relate "non-exception" states allowing inference of normal behavior. The derived calculus is then surprisingly standard (see Table 1).

6.4 Data-Model Specific Hoare Rules

Recall our running example with the classes Node and CNode. Besides the type-safe accessor functions, we need families of store-related (i. e., level 1) update and creation operations on objects. For example, the lifting of update operations to the level of the assertion language is straight-forward:

$$obj.\, \text{set}_{\text{left}}^{(1)}\, E \equiv \lambda\sigma.\sigma(\text{OidOf } obj := obj\, \sigma.\, \text{set}_{\text{left}}^{(0)}\, (E\, \sigma))$$

Here, the operation $\_(\_ := \_)$ denotes the usual update on functions. Instead of $\text{CMD}(obj.\, \text{set}_{\text{left}}^{(1)}\, E)$ we write $obj.\, \text{left} := E$.

Table 1. The Hoare Calculus for IMP++

$$\frac{\forall s.\, P'\, s \longrightarrow P\, s \quad \vDash \{P\}c\{Q\} \quad \forall s.\, Q\, s \longrightarrow Q'\, s}{\vDash \{P'\}c\{Q'\}} \qquad \overline{\vDash \{\odot P\}\, \mathtt{SKIP}\,\{\odot P\}}$$

$$\frac{\vDash \{\odot P\}c\{\odot Q\} \quad \vDash \{\odot Q\}d\{\odot R\}}{\vDash \{\odot P\}c;d\{\odot R\}} \qquad \frac{\vDash \{\odot\,\lambda\sigma.\, P\sigma \wedge (\ulcorner\sigma\urcorner \vDash b)\}c\{\odot P\}}{\vDash \{\odot P\}\{\mathtt{WHILE}\}b\{\mathtt{DO}\}c\{\odot\,\lambda\sigma.\, P\sigma \wedge (\ulcorner\sigma\urcorner \vDash \neg b)\}}$$

$$\overline{\vDash \{\lambda\sigma.\,\sigma = \bot\}\,c\,\{\lambda\sigma.\,\sigma = \bot\}} \qquad \overline{\vDash \{\odot\,\lambda\sigma.\,\ulcorner\sigma\urcorner \vDash \partial f \wedge Q(f\ulcorner\sigma\urcorner)\}\,\mathtt{CMD}\, f\{\odot Q\}}$$

$$\frac{\vDash \{\odot\,\lambda\sigma.\,(P\sigma) \wedge (\ulcorner\sigma\urcorner \vDash b) \wedge (\ulcorner\sigma\urcorner \vDash \partial b)\}d\{\odot Q\}}{\vDash \{\odot\,\lambda\sigma.\,(P\sigma) \wedge (\ulcorner\sigma\urcorner \vDash \neg b) \wedge (\ulcorner\sigma\urcorner \vDash \partial b)\}d\{\odot Q\}}{\vDash \{\odot P\}\{\mathtt{IF}\}b\{\mathtt{THEN}\}c\{\mathtt{ELSE}\}d\{\odot Q\}}$$

With respect to the creation operations, we define:

$$\mathrm{newOid}\,\sigma \equiv \varepsilon\, x.\, x \notin \mathrm{dom}\,\sigma$$

where $\varepsilon\, x.\, P\, x$ is the Hilbert-operator that chooses an arbitrary x satisfying P.

$$\mathrm{new}_{\mathrm{Node}}\; oid \equiv \llcorner((\mathrm{Object}_t,\, oid),\llcorner((\mathrm{Node}_t, \bot, \bot, \bot, \bot))\lrcorner)\lrcorner$$

The creation operation generates a new object of some type and stores the reference to it in a given attribute of obj:

$$obj.\,\mathrm{new}^{(1)}_{\mathrm{left}} \equiv \lambda\,\sigma.\,\mathrm{let}\,\sigma' = \sigma(\mathrm{newOid}\,\sigma := \mathrm{new}_{\mathrm{Node}}\,(\mathrm{newOid}\,\sigma))$$

$$\mathrm{in}\; obj.\,\mathrm{set}^{(1)}_{\mathrm{left}}\,(\mathrm{new}_{\mathrm{Node}}\,(\mathrm{newOid}\,\sigma))\sigma'$$

Instead of $\mathtt{CMD}(obj.\,\mathrm{new}^{(1)}_{\mathrm{left}})$ we write $obj.\,\mathrm{left} := \mathrm{new}(\mathrm{Node})$.

From these definitions, the following family of class model-specific Hoare-rules is derived (as usual, we pick the case for attribute left):

$$\overline{\vDash \{\odot\,\lambda\sigma.\,x(\ulcorner\sigma\urcorner \vDash (\partial\,self)) \wedge Q(obj.\,\mathrm{set}^{(1)}_{\mathrm{left}}\,E\ulcorner\sigma\urcorner)\}\,obj.\,\mathrm{left} := E\{\odot Q\}}$$

The analogous case for the creation is a special case of this rule.

6.5 An Example in IMP++

A program that produces the smallest possible object system satisfying the CNode invariant looks in a fictive language as follows:

```
method Node m();
var   H1:CNode;
var   H2:CNode;
begin
    H1:= New(CNode);
    H2:= New(CNode);
    H1.i:= 7;
    H1.color:=true;
    H1.left:=H2;
    H1.right:=H2;
    H2.i:= 9;
    H2.color:=false;
    H2.left:=H1;
    H2.right:=H1;
    return H1
end
```

Well, the method call as such cannot be represented in IMP++ because we did not provide syntax for that. However, we can represent the local variables by extending the underlying class model by a *stack object class for method m* (a terminology also used in the Java language specification), and express pre and post conditions for the body called m_{body}.

The stack-object class class m_{so} has the form:

```
self   : Node
return : CNode
H1 : CNode
H2 : CNode
```

i. e., it comprises attributes for the local variables H1 and H2 with the previously described types as well as a **return** attribute of type **CNode**. The package will then generate the usual update functions for this class and give semantics to the corresponding assignments in our example program (the return statement is viewed as an update to the **return** attribute).

We want to specify that the program establishes by a sequence of creation and update steps the global invariant verification of the body is stated as follows, assuming that the stack object is defined when the method is called:

$$\vDash \{\odot \lambda \sigma.\, \sigma \vDash \partial(m_{\text{so}})\}\, m_{\text{body}}\, \{\odot\, \sigma \vDash m_{\text{so}}.\,\text{return}^{(1)} \in \text{CNodeKindSet}\}$$

The proof for this statement proceeds in essentially two phases: First, by several applications of the consequence rule and the update-rule, we accumulate an equation system as assertion:

$$\sigma \models \partial(m_{so}.\,H1^{(1)})$$
$$\wedge \quad \sigma \models \partial(m_{so}.\,H2^{(1)})$$
$$\wedge \quad \sigma \models m_{so}.\,H1.\,i^{(1)} = 7 \wedge \sigma \models m_{so}.\,H1.\,color^{(1)} = \lfloor true \rfloor$$
$$\wedge \quad \sigma \models m_{so}.\,H1.\,left^{(1)} = H2 \wedge \sigma \models m_{so}.\,H1.\,right^{(1)} = H2$$
$$\wedge \quad \sigma \models m_{so}.\,H2.\,i^{(1)} = 9 \wedge \sigma \models m_{so}.\,H2.\,color^{(1)} = \lfloor false \rfloor$$
$$\wedge \quad \sigma \models m_{so}.\,H2.\,left^{(1)} = H1 \wedge \sigma \models m_{so}.\,H2.\,right^{(1)} = H1$$
$$\wedge \quad \sigma \models m_{so}.\,return^{(1)} = H1$$

(Recall that we overload 7, 9, ... with $\lambda\,\sigma.7$, $\lambda\,\sigma.7$, ... to simplify notation). This assertion must imply the postcondition, which is reduced to:

$$\sigma \models m_{so}.\,return^{(1)} \in gfp\ CnodeKindF$$

The gap is bridged by the application of the derived fixed-point-induction:

$$\frac{[\sigma \models m_{so}.\,return^{(1)} \in X]}{\vdots}$$
$$\frac{\bigwedge X. \quad \sigma \models m_{so}.\,return^{(1)} \in CnodeKindF\ X}{\sigma \models m_{so}.\,return^{(1)} \in gfp\ CnodeKindF}$$

The example also shows how liberal invariants (a freshly generated object only satisfies such an invariant since the .left and .right attribute are uninitialized) can be used to establish stronger ones. In [14] local flags in objects are suggested to switch on and off parts of static class invariants. Our approach does not need such flags (while it can mimic them), rather, we would generate versions of invariants and relate them via co-induction automatically.

7   Conclusion

We presented an extensible universe construction supporting object-oriented datatype theories including subtyping and (single) inheritance. On the theoretical side, this proves that object-oriented datatype theories can be represented in typed λ-calculus with Hindley-Milner Polymorphism. As a by-product, the construction also gives insight into the representation of open-world and closed-world assumptions in types. The achievement on the practical side is three-fold: First, we show that the core of object-oriented reasoning can be made amenable to off-the-shelf HOL theorem provers (no Isabelle specific features are inherently necessary for this) in form of a shallow embedding. Second, this can be done in a conservative way: provided that the 9 axioms of HOL are consistent (on which the large majority of logicians agree), the generated datatype theory will also be consistent. Third, albeit the underlying complexity, deriving automatically the datatype theory from the basic definitions is still technically feasible: [6, 8] report on an example suite of class models. The computation time for each of these models is below 2 minutes on recent hardware.

One might object that the universe construction described in Section 3 and Section 4 is entirely meta-theoretic, thus not verifiable; and principles like conservative definitions are not applicable on this level. However, this is not entirely true. While concepts like "the set of all HOL-types" or "the set of class types" are indeed not formalized in HOL, for each concrete type resulting from the construction a consistent theory is generated. If our construction or our implementation has an error, Isabelle will refuse to accept these definitions or the proofs.

Related Work. Work on object-oriented semantics based on deep embeddings has been discussed earlier. For shallow embeddings, to the best of our knowledge, there is only [24]. In this approach, however, emphasis is put on a universal type for a *classes* comprising method tables. This results in local "universes" for input and output types of methods and the need for reasoning on class isomorphisms. Subtyping on *objects* must be expressed implicitly via refinement. With respect to extensibility of data-structures, the idea of using parametric polymorphism is partly folklore in HOL research communities; for example, extensible records and their application for some form of subtyping has been described in HOOL [18]. Since only α-extensions are used, this results in a restricted form of class types with no coercion mechanism to α Object.

Datatype packages have been considered mostly in the context of HOL or functional programming languages. Going back to ideas of Milner in the 70ies, systems like [16, 4] build over an S-expression like term universe (co)-inductive sets which are abstracted to (freely generated) datatypes. Paulson's inductive package [23] also uses subsets of the ZF set universe i.

Even systems like Spec# [2, 14] or Krakatoa [15], which are clearly more advanced with respect to the degree of automation for *program verification* as a whole, might profit from guaranteed consistent data-models: at present, a quite substantial axiomatization of a given object-oriented memory model is generated in these systems. The second author witnessed several logical inconsistencies in the data model underlying Spec#. We believe that the properties of our object-oriented data model, even if taken axiomatically, could provide assurance. If required, our system can generate for given class system proofs of consistency.

Future Work. We see the following lines of future research:

- *Multiple Inheritance.* Our approach is strictly limited to single inheritance. However, it is easy to extend our package with support for multiple subtyping based on *interfaces*.
- *Modular Verification of Recursive Methods.* The presented language does not comprise method invocation—it remains to be shown how the presented machinery can be used for an extensible program theory comprising these crucial features.
- *Support for Inductive Constraints.* By introducing measure-functions over object-structures, inductive datatypes can be characterized for defined

measures of an object. This paves the way for the usual structural induction and well-founded recursion schemes,

– *Support of built-in Co-recursion.* Co-recursion can be used to define e. g., deep object equalities.
– *Deriving VCG.* Similar to the IMP-theory, verification condition generators for IMP++programs can be proven sound and complete. This leads to effective program verification techniques based entirely on derived rules.

References

[1] Andrews, P.B.: Introduction to Mathematical Logic and Type Theory: To Truth through Proof, 2nd edn. Kluwer Academic Publishers, Dordrecht (2002)
[2] Barnett, M., Leino, K.R.M., Schulte, W.: The Spec# programming system: An overview. In: Barthe, G., Burdy, L., Huisman, M., Lanet, J.-L., Muntean, T. (eds.) CASSIS 2004. LNCS, vol. 3362, pp. 49–69. Springer, Heidelberg (2005)
[3] Basin, D.A., Kuruma, H., Takaragi, K., Wolff, B.: Verification of a signature architecture with HOL-Z. In: Fitzgerald, J.S., Hayes, I.J., Tarlecki, A. (eds.) FM 2005. LNCS, vol. 3582, pp. 269–285. Springer, Heidelberg (2005)
[4] Berghofer, S., Wenzel, M.T.: Inductive Datatypes in HOL – Lessons Learned in Formal-Logic Engineering. In: Bertot, Y., Dowek, G., Hirschowitz, A., Paulin, C., Théry, L. (eds.) TPHOLs 1999. LNCS, vol. 1690. Springer, Heidelberg (1999)
[5] Bierman, G.M., Parkinson, M.J.: Effects and effect inference for a core Java calculus. Electronic Notes in Theoretical Computer Science 82(7), 1–26 (2003)
[6] Brucker, A.D.: An Interactive Proof Environment for Object-oriented Specifications. Ph.d. thesis, ETH Zurich, 2007. ETH Dissertation No. 17097
[7] Brucker, A.D., Rittinger, F., Wolff, B.: HOL-Z 2.0: A proof environment for Z-specifications. Journal of Universal Computer Science 9(2), 152–172 (2003)
[8] Brucker, A.D., Wolff, B.: The HOL-OCL book. Tech. Rep. 525, ETH Zurich (2006)
[9] Brucker, A.D., Wolff, B.: HOL-OCL – A Formal Proof Environment for UML/OCL. In: Fiadeiro, J., Inverardi, P. (eds.) Fundamental Approaches to Software Engineering FASE 2008, vol. 4961, pp. 97–100. Springer, Heidelberg (2008)
[10] Drossopoulou, S., Eisenbach, S.: Describing the semantics of Java and proving type soundness. In: Alves-Foss, J. (ed.) Formal Syntax and Semantics of Java. LNCS, vol. 1523, pp. 41–82. Springer, Heidelberg (1999)
[11] Flatt, M., Krishnamurthi, S., Felleisen, M.: A programmer's reduction semantics for classes and mixins. In: Alves-Foss, J. (ed.) Formal Syntax and Semantics of Java. LNCS, vol. 1523, pp. 241–269. Springer, Heidelberg (1999)
[12] Gordon, M.J.C., Melham, T.F.: Introduction to HOL: a theorem proving environment for higher order logic. Cambridge University Press, New York (1993)
[13] Igarashi, A., Pierce, B.C., Wadler, P.: Featherweight Java: a minimal core calculus for Java and GI. ACM Transactions on Programming Languages and Systems 23(3), 396–450 (2001)
[14] Leino, K.R.M., Müller, P.: Modular verification of static class invariants. In: Fitzgerald, J.S., Hayes, I.J., Tarlecki, A. (eds.) FM 2005. LNCS, vol. 3582, pp. 26–42. Springer, Heidelberg (2005)
[15] Marché, C., Paulin-Mohring, C.: Reasoning about Java programs with aliasing and frame conditions. In: Hurd, J., Melham, T. (eds.) TPHOLs 2005. LNCS, vol. 3603, pp. 179–194. Springer, Heidelberg (2005)

[16] Melham, T.F.: A package for inductive relation definitions in HOL. In: Archer, M., Joyce, J.J., Levitt, K.N., Windley, P.J. (eds.) International Workshop on the HOL Theorem Proving System and its Applications (TPHOLs), pp. 350–357. IEEE Computer Society Press, Los Alamitos (1992)

[17] Müller, O., Nipkow, T., von Oheimb, D., Slotosch, O.: HOLCF = HOL + LCF. Journal of Functional Programming 9(2), 191–223 (1999)

[18] Naraschewski, W., Wenzel, M.: Object-Oriented Verification Based on Record Subtyping in Higher-Order Logic. In: Grundy, J., Newey, M. (eds.) TPHOLs 1998. LNCS, vol. 1479, pp. 349–366. Springer, Heidelberg (1998)

[19] Nipkow, T.: Winskel is (almost) right: Towards a mechanized semantics textbook. Formal Aspects of Computing 10(2), 171–186 (1998)

[20] Nipkow, T., Paulson, L.C., Wenzel, M.: Isabelle/HOL. LNCS, vol. 2283. Springer, Heidelberg (2002)

[21] Nipkow, T., von Oheimb, D.: Java$_{light}$ is type-safe—definitely. In: ACM Symp. Principles of Programming Languages POPL, pp. 161–170. ACM Press, New York (1998)

[22] Unified modeling language specification (version 1.5) (2003), Available as OMG document formal/03-03-01

[23] Paulson, L.C.: A fixedpoint approach to (co)inductive and (co)datatype definitions. In: Plotkin, G., Stirling, C., Tofte, M. (eds.) Proof, Language, and Interaction: Essays in Honour of Robin Milner, pp. 187–211. MIT Press, Cambridge (2000)

[24] Smith, G., Kammüller, F., Santen, T.: Encoding Object-Z in Isabelle/HOL. In: Bert, D., P. Bowen, J., C. Henson, M., Robinson, K. (eds.) B 2002 and ZB 2002. LNCS, vol. 2272, pp. 82–99. Springer, Heidelberg (2002)

[25] von Oheimb, D., Nipkow, T.: Hoare logic for NanoJava: Auxiliary variables, side effects, and virtual methods revisited. In: Eriksson, L.-H., Lindsay, P.A. (eds.) FME 2002. LNCS, vol. 2391, pp. 89–105. Springer, Heidelberg (2002)

[26] Winskel, G.: The Formal Semantics of Programming Languages. MIT Press, Cambridge (1993)

Programming with Live Distributed Objects

Krzysztof Ostrowski[1], Ken Birman[1], Danny Dolev[2], and Jong Hoon Ahnn[1]

[1] Cornell University, and
[2] The Hebrew University of Jerusalem
{krzys, ken, ja275}@cs.cornell.edu, dolev@cs.huji.ac.il

Abstract. A component revolution is underway, bringing developers improved productivity and opportunities for code reuse. However, whereas existing tools work well for builders of desktop applications and client-server structured systems, support for other styles of distributed computing has lagged. In this paper, we propose a new programming paradigm and a platform, in which instances of distributed protocols are modeled as "live distributed objects". Live objects can represent both protocols and higher-level components. They look and feel much like ordinary objects, but can maintain shared state and synchronization across multiple machines within a network. Live objects can be composed in a type-safe manner to build sophisticated distributed applications using a simple, intuitive drag and drop interface, very often without writing any code or having to understand the intricacies of the underlying distributed algorithms.

1 Motivation

It has become common to build applications in a component-oriented manner, composing reusable building blocks by binding strongly-typed interfaces. At runtime, an underlying object-oriented managed environment, such as Java/J2EE or .NET provides further checking and support. The paradigm has numerous benefits: it promotes clean, modular architectures, facilitates extensions, enables collaborative development and code reuse, and by making contracts between components explicit and their code more isolated, reduces the risk of bugs resulting from badly documented or implicit assumptions such as cross-component behavior or side effects.

Unfortunately, distributed systems developers are only able to exploit these tools in limited ways, typically wedded to client-server programming styles. Moreover, the most widely used technologies can be awkward and inflexible. For example, a developer uses different methods to access a system depending on whether it is hosted on a single remote server [6], cloned for load-balancing on a cluster [37], or using state machine replication [52]. Yet even as the available tools have standardized on these limited options, the research community is creating a wave of powerful new technologies that includes peer-to-peer and gossip protocols, multicast with various levels of consistency, ordering and timing, Byzantine state replication, distributed hash tables, credential management services, naming services, content distribution networks, etc.

Our goal is to break through this barrier by treating protocols as components in the same sense as in .NET or COM. We propose a technology in which application components and protocols are unified within a single object-oriented paradigm. Our "live

J. Vitek (Ed.): ECOOP 2008, LNCS 5142, pp. 463–489, 2008.

distributed objects" represent running instances of distributed protocols, but they have types and support composition, much like "ordinary" objects. While ours is certainly not the first approach to unify distributed protocols with object-oriented environments, we innovate in ways that make the solution uniquely powerful:

• *We leverage the type system without being language-specific.* Our platform offers mechanisms such as reflection and dynamic type checking, previously seen only in systems closely tied to an underlying language, such as Smalltalk, Java, ML or IOA. In our interactive GUI, type-checking prevents users from dropping objects in inappropriately. Down the road, we'll use type checking to ensure that replicated application objects use a protocol with sufficiently strong properties.

• *It can be incrementally deployed, and supports legacy applications,* including Excel spreadsheets, Oracle databases, and web services. For example, we can import data from a database, multicast it, and export it back into a set of desktop spreadsheets.

• *Our object-oriented embedding can support any distributed protocol as a reusable component.* Existing systems are protocol-agnostic only in the limited sense that users can choose among several different protocols to implement communication. For us, protocols are objects; a small shift in perspective with broad implications.

• *The approach extends from the UI to the hardware level,* whereas prior systems focused on one class of application objects, e.g. shared data structures or UI components[1]. Jini has a vision similar to ours, but is tightly bound to the client-server paradigm, whereas our model is focused on distributed multi-party protocols.

• *We support composition of behavioral protocol types.* Prior composition toolkits either lacked types, or used a limited form of typing, where the protocol type was the type of the implementing class, and composition was achieved via inheritance.

• *Our model is replication-centric.* Although many live objects don't replicate state, the handling of replication and scalability sets our solution apart from prior ones. We're able to support various replication (multicast) models, and to express this in a type system.

• *Our system may be the first drag and drop tool for type-safe protocol composition.* Drag and drop mechanisms are easy to use and yet can support sophisticated applications. For many applications, no new code is needed at all. Prior systems (including some from which we took inspiration, such as Ensemble [33], BAST [20], x-Kernel [45], and I/O automata [36]) were programmer-intensive.

Although the current system is quite usable, live objects raise a number of questions, only some of which have been addressed. The technology requires a scalable multicast layer capable of supporting very large groups, and in which a single node can join large numbers of object-groups. In work reported elsewhere, we describe *Quicksilver,* a high-performance, scalable communication layer that achieves these goals [46,47,48]. We're also collaborating with a group at INRIA/IRISA on a gossip-based infrastructure compatible with live objects; we expect this to be useful for discovering and tracking system configuration information. Looking further out, we're extending Quicksilver to support a range of reliability models (expressed in a new protocol scripting language [47]), and are implementing a new security architecture based on reflection. We also have ideas for WAN and mobile applications, debugging, performance tuning, system management, and object state persistence. However, all of these questions lie beyond the scope of the present paper.

---

[1] Demos of this functionality and a prototype of our platform are available on our website [34].

2 Prior Work

While we believe our work to be innovative in the ways just described, we're not the first to integrate the object-oriented and distributed programming models.

There are many language abstractions for distributed protocols, including remote objects [17, 20], fault-tolerant objects [24], multicast objects [19], asynchronous collections [9], tuple spaces [6, 38], and replicated objects driven by multicast [25, 37] or two-phase commit [34]. None matches the requirements described above. First, these abstractions are all specialized to support specific protocols. For example, asynchronous collections cannot easily be used to express two-phase commit or leader election. Second, most lack the notion of a distributed type, and in those that do, this notion is shallow, e.g. the type of a multicast object [19] is determined by the type of transmitted events, and the type of an asynchronous collection [9] is the type of the implementing class. The former definition can't convey information about subtle behaviors of protocols such as virtual synchrony [5], while the latter severely restricts reusability. Finally, most lack support for composition.

The idea of defining object types in terms of their *behaviors* is not new [55]. CSP [24] and π-calculus [41] were some of the first protocol specifications, and these early process calculi serve as a basis for recent specification efforts, such as BPEL [3], SSDL [49], and WSCL [4]. As recently noted [19], the weakness of process calculi, and specifications based on them, is that they can't express the semantics of replication or the behavior of protocols such as consensus in a clean way. For example, while BPEL is clearly strong enough to express business processes, the language defines protocols in terms of sets of participants fixed at the outset, and can't model dynamic join or leave events. It would be very hard to express replication properties, such as *"once any group member does X, eventually all operational members do too"* [12].

On the other hand, while *state-based* approaches such as I/O automata [36], CFSM [7], interface automata [1], and others [18] are very expressive, they combine functional descriptions of protocol behaviors with the specifics of their implementations expressed through state transitions. This is useful in correctness proofs, but it may be a weakness in the context of a type system. Two protocols implemented using different data structures and states can exhibit the same external behavior, e.g. *"messages are totally ordered and delivered atomically with respect to failures"*. We believe that protocols that behave equivalently should be considered to have the same distributed type; state transition representations can easily obscure such relationships [27].

Live objects support an extensible style of formal behavioral specifications for group and multicast protocols [2, 12, 22, 26]. As one composes protocols, a constructive distributed type system is obtained. The type checking mechanism is itself componentized, and can be extended by developers.

The idea of building protocols from simpler components dates to the x-Kernel [45] and to systems like Ensemble [33], which constructed replication protocols from microprotocols. Among such systems, BAST [20] is closest to ours in terms of the diversity of protocols it can express, but lacks a behavioral notion of a protocol type: protocol types in BAST are determined by the types of the implementing classes, and composition is achieved by inheritance. The creators of BAST observed that in retrospect, inheritance wasn't the right mechanism for this task. We've drawn lessons from these experiences and created a model in which inheritance isn't used at all: we treat protocols as black boxes and connect them with typed event channels in a visual designer. Our protocol objects interact via events, much as in Smalltalk [21].

Jini [57], the widely used Java-based platform in which clients access services by dynamically loading proxy code, is highly relevant prior work. The strongest contrast is that Jini has a pervasive client-server bias, making it very hard to express object replication, particularly in applications that use strong consistency or (at the other extreme) peer-to-peer protocols.

This client-server bias is visible in many ways. First, Jini lacks a rigorous notion of a group [43], and it is hard to implement consistency across a set of group members, state replication within the group, coordination, leader-election, etc. Jini's lookup, join, and discovery specifications lack membership views (needed to assign tasks to group members) and synchronized state transfer (used to initialize new group members). Moreover, Jini doesn't guarantee consistent failure detection. Thus, while services in Jini can be grouped, the mechanism lacks expressive power to facilitate building systems that use stronger forms of replication. Additionally, abstractions such as notification and transactional protocols can't be directly modeled as objects in Jini. Finally, Jini lacks distributed types and protocol composition mechanisms.

Live objects are replication-centric, with a strong notion of protocol types and composition. This makes live objects particularly appropriate for building applications in which users collaborate, share content, or engage in other kinds of peer-to-peer behaviors, (obviously we can also support traditional non-replicated and client-server behaviors). Complex protocols can be modeled as objects, in a manner that separates behavior of the protocol from its implementation.

Many of these same issues distinguish our work from WS-* standards. Elsewhere [48], we discuss issues that arise if one tries to use WS-Notification or WS-Eventing to implement live objects. We concluded that the relevant WS-* standards are tightly bound to specific protocol implementations; as written, they cannot accommodate commercially important protocols such as peer-to-peer video streaming, BitTorrent, or Byzantine replication. We've proposed an extended WS-based eventing standard matched to the work described here, and able to overcome this problem [48].

JXTA [57] is probably the most sophisticated existing collaboration technology for peer-to-peer systems, but it doesn't support stronger replication and consistency models. While JXTA does have notions such as a group and a membership view, members can have inconsistent views. Researchers have struggled to layer reliable multicast on these mechanisms [35]. Groupware toolkits, such as Croquet [53], Groove [39], and group communication [5] toolkits all support replication, and some support strong forms of consistency. However, unlike Jini, JXTA and our work, none of these is positioned as a general-purpose interoperability platform.

3   Model

3.1   Objects and Their Interactions

A *live distributed object* (or *live object*) is an instance of a distributed protocol: programming logic executed by a set of components that may reside on different nodes and communicate by sending messages over the network. For flexibility, we won't assume that the machines running the protocol "know" about one-another or that they share any common state. Thus, a live object could be a Byzantine fault-tolerant replicated state machine, but it could also be an entity with purely local state, one that uses gossip to share data, or an IP multicast channel.

Live objects have *behavioral types*. Suppose that object A logs messages on the nodes where it runs, using a reliable, totally ordered multicast to ensure consistency between replicas. Object B might offer the same functionality, but be implemented differently, perhaps using a gossip protocol. As long as A and B offer the same interfaces and equivalent properties (consistency, reliability, etc), we consider A and B to be implementations of the same type. The concept of behavioral equivalence is the key here; we define it more carefully in section 3.2.

When node Y executes live object X, we'll say that a *proxy* of live object X is running on Y. Thus, a live object is executed by the group of its proxies (Figure 1). A proxy is a functional part of the object running on a node. When two objects have proxies on overlapping sets of nodes, their respective proxies may interact. We can think of the live objects as interacting through their proxies.

A *reference to a live object X* is a complete set of instructions for constructing and configuring a proxy of X on a node. Thus, when node Y wants to access live object X, node Y uses a reference to X as a recipe with which it can create a new proxy for X that will run locally on Y. The proxy then executes the protocol associated with X. For example, it might seek out other proxies for X, transfer the current distributed state from them, and connect itself to a multicast channel to receive updates. Unlike proxies, which can have state, references are just passive, stateless, portable recipes.

The instructions in a reference must be complete, but need not be self-contained. Some of their parts can be stored inside online repositories, from which they need to be downloaded. These repositories are themselves live objects, referenced by the objects that use them. Thus, given a reference, a node can dereference it without prior "knowledge" of the protocol. An exception is thrown if dereferencing fails (for example, if a repository containing a part of the reference is unavailable).

We model proxies in a manner reminiscent of I/O automata. A proxy runs in a virtual context consisting of a set of *endpoints:* strongly-typed bidirectional event channels, through which the proxy can communicate with other software on the same node (Figure 1). Unlike in I/O automata, a proxy can use external resources, such as local network connections, clocks, or the CPU. These interactions are not expressed in our

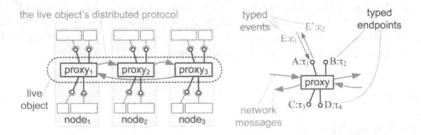

Fig. 1. To access a live object (protocol), a node starts a *proxy:* a software component that runs the protocol on the node, and may communicate with proxies on other nodes by sending messages over the network. On a given node, proxies for different objects communicate via *endpoints:* strongly-typed, bidirectional event channels.

model and they are not limited in any way. However, interactions of a live object's proxy with any other component of the distributed system must be channeled through the proxy's endpoints.

All proxies of the same live object run that live object's *code*. Unlike in state machines [37, 52], we need not assume that proxies run in synchrony, in a deterministic manner, or that their internal states are identical. We do assume that each proxy of a live object X interacts with other components of the distributed system using the same set of endpoints, which must be specified as part of X's type. To avoid ambiguity, we sometimes use the term *instance of endpoint E at proxy P* to explicitly refer to a running event channel *E*, physically connected to and used by *P*.

Because our model is designed to facilitate component integration, we shall adopt a somewhat radical perspective, in which the entire system, all applications and infrastructure are composed of live objects. Accordingly, endpoints of a live object's proxy will be connected to endpoints exposed by proxies of other live objects running on the same node (Figure 2). When proxies of two different objects X and Y are connected through their endpoints on a certain node Z, we'll say that *X* and *Y* are connected on *Z*.

Example (a). Consider a distributed collaboration tool that uses reliable multicast to propagate updates between users (Figure 2). Let **a** be an application object in this system that represents a collaboratively edited document. Proxies of **a** have a graphical user interface, through which users can see the document and submit updates. Updates are disseminated to other users over a reliable multicast protocol, so that everyone can see the same contents. The system is designed in a modular way, so instead of linking the UI code with a proprietary multicast library, the document object **a** defines a typed endpoint **reliable_channel_client**, with which its proxies can submit updates to a reliable multicast protocol (event **send**) and receive updates submitted by other proxies and propagated using multicast (event **receive**). Multicasting can then be implemented by a separate object **r**, which has a matching endpoint **reliable channel**. Proxies of **a** and **r** on all nodes are connected through their matching endpoints.   ■

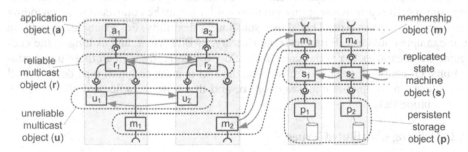

Fig. 2. Applications in our model are composed of interconnected live objects. Objects are "connected" if endpoints of a pair of their proxies are connected. Connected objects can affect one-another by having their proxies exchange events through endpoints. A single object can be connected to multiple other objects. Here, a reliable multicast object **r** is simultaneously connected to an unreliable multicast object **u**, a membership object **m**, and an application object **a**. The same object can be accessed by different machines in different ways. For example, **m** is used in two contexts: by the multicast object **r**, and by replicas of a membership service. The latter employs a replicated state machine **s**, which persists its state through a storage object **p**.

Similarly, object **r** may be structured in a modular way: rather than being a single monolithic protocol, **r** could internally use object **u** for dissemination and object **m** for membership tracking [12]. Additional endpoints **unreliable channel** and **membership** would serve as contracts between **r** and its internal parts **u** and **m**.

Figure 2 illustrates several features of our model. First, a pair of endpoints can be connected multiple times: there are multiple connections between different instances of the **reliable channel** endpoint of object **r** and the **reliable_channel_client** endpoint of **a**, one connection on each node where **a** runs. Since objects are distributed, so are the control and data flows that connect them. If different proxies of **r** were to interact with proxies of **a** in an uncoordinated manner, this might be an issue. To prevent this, each endpoint has a type, which constrains the patterns of events that can pass through different instances of the endpoint. These types could specify ordering, security, fault-tolerance or other properties. The live objects runtime won't permit connections between **a** and **r**, unless their endpoint types declare the needed properties.

A single object could also define multiple endpoints. One case when this occurs is when the protocol involves different roles. For example, the membership object **m** has two endpoints, for clients and for service replicas. The role of the proxy in the protocol depends on which endpoint is connected. In this sense, endpoints are like interfaces in object-oriented languages, giving access to a subset of the object's functionality. Another similarity between endpoints and interfaces is that both serve as contracts and isolate the object's implementation details from the applications using it. We also use multiple endpoints in object **r**, proxies of which require two kinds of external functionality: an unreliable multicast, and a membership service. Both are obligatory: **r** cannot be activated on a platform unless both endpoints can be connected.

Earlier, we commented that not all live objects replicate their state. We see the latter in the case of the persistent store **p**. Its proxies present the same type of endpoint to the state machine **s**, but each uses a different log file and has its own state.

Our model promotes reusability by isolating objects from other parts of the system via endpoints that represent strongly typed contracts. If an object relies upon external functionality, it defines a separate endpoint by which it gains access to that functionality, and specifies any assumptions about the entity it may be connected to by encoding them in the endpoint type. This allows substantial flexibility. For example, object **u** in our example could use IP multicast, an overlay, or BitTorrent, and as long as the endpoint that **u** exposes to **r** is the same, **r** should work correctly with all these implementations. Of course this is conditional upon the fact that the endpoint type describes all the relevant assumptions **r** makes about **u**, and that **u** does implement all of the declared properties.

3.2 Defining Distributed Types

The preceding section introduced endpoint types, as a way to define contracts between objects. We now define them formally and give examples of how typing can be used to express reliability, security, fault-tolerance, and real time properties of objects.

Formally, the type Θ of a live object is a tuple of the form $\Theta = (E, C, C')$. E in this definition is a set of named endpoints, $E = \{(n_1, \tau_1), (n_2, \tau_2), ..., (n_k, \tau_k)\}$, where n_i is the name and τ_i is the type of the ith endpoint. C and C' represent sets of constraints describing security, reliability, and other characteristics of the object (C), and of its environment (C'). C models constraints *provided* by the object, such as semantics of the protocol: guarantees that the object's code delivers to other objects connected to it. C' models constraints *required*, which are prerequisites for correct operation of the object's code. Constraints can be described in any formalism that captures aspects of object and environment behavior in terms of endpoints and event patterns. Rather than trying to invent a new, powerful formalism that subsumes all the existing ones, we build on the concepts of aspect-oriented programming [28], and we define C to be a finite function from some set A of aspects to predicates in the corresponding formalisms. For example, constraints $C = \{(a_1, \varphi_1), (a_2, \varphi_2), ..., (a_m, \varphi_m)\}$ would state that in formalism a_1 the object's behavior satisfies formula φ_1, and so on. We'll give examples of various practically useful formalisms and constraints later in this section.

Type τ of an endpoint is a tuple of the form $\tau = (I, O, C, C')$. I is a set of *incoming events* that a proxy owning the endpoint can receive from some other proxy, O is a set of *outgoing events* that the proxy can send over this endpoint, and C and C' represent constraints provided and required by this endpoint, defined similarly to constraints of the object, but expressed in terms of event patterns, not in terms of endpoints (for example, an endpoint could have an event of type *time*, and with a constraint that time advances monotonically in successive events). Each of the sets I and O is a collection of named events of the form $E = \{(n_1, \varepsilon_1), (n_2, \varepsilon_2), ..., (n_k, \varepsilon_k)\}$, where n_i is event name and ε_i is its type. Event types can be value types of the underlying type system, such as .NET or Java primitive types and structures, or types described by WSDL [13] etc., but not arbitrary object references or addresses in memory. We assume that events are serializable and can be transmitted across the network or process boundaries. References to live objects are also serializable, hence they can also be passed inside events. The subtyping relation on the event types is inherited from the underlying type system.

The purpose of creating endpoints is to connect them to other, matching endpoints, as described in Section 3.1 and illustrated on Figure 2. **Connect** is the only operation possible on endpoints. We say that endpoint types τ_1 and τ_2 *match*, denoted $\tau_1 \propto \tau_2$, when the following two conditions hold.

1. For each output event n of type ε of either endpoint, its counterpart must have an input event with the same name n, and with either type ε, or some supertype of ε. This guarantees that all events can be delivered between the two connected proxies.

2. The provided constraints of each of the endpoints must imply (be no weaker than) the required constraints of the other. This ensures that the endpoints mutually satisfy each other's requirements.

Formally, for $\tau_1 = (I_1, O_1, C_1, C_1')$ and $\tau_2 = (I_2, O_2, C_2, C_2')$ we define:

$$\tau_1 \propto \tau_2 \Leftrightarrow O_1 \to^* I_2 \wedge O_2 \to^* I_1 \wedge C_1 \Rightarrow^* C_2' \wedge C_2 \Rightarrow^* C_1'. \tag{1}$$

Relation $\to^*$ between two sets of named events expresses the fact that events from the first can be understood as events from the second. Formally, we express it as follows:

$$E \to^* E' \Leftrightarrow \forall (n, \varepsilon) \in E \,\exists\, (n, \varepsilon') \in E' \text{ such that } \varepsilon \leq \varepsilon'. \tag{2}$$

Operator "$\leq$" on types always represents the relation of subtyping in this paper.

Relation $\Rightarrow^*$ between two sets of constraints expresses the fact that the constraints in the first set are no weaker than constraints in the second. Formally, we write this as:

$$C \Rightarrow^* C' \Leftrightarrow \forall \, (a, \varphi') \in C' \; \exists \, (a, \varphi) \in C \text{ such that } \varphi \Rightarrow_a \varphi'. \tag{3}$$

Relation $\Rightarrow_a$ is simply a logical consequence in formalism **a**. Intuitively, this definition states that if **C'** defines a constraint defined in some formalism, then **C** must define a constraint that is no weaker than that, in the same formalism. For example, if **C'** defines some reliability constraint expressed in temporal logic, then **C** must define an equivalent or stronger constraint, also in temporal logic, in order for **C** $\Rightarrow^*$ **C'** to hold.

For a pair of endpoint types τ_1 and τ_2, the former is a subtype of the latter if it can be used in any context in which the latter can be used. Since the only possible operation on an endpoint is connecting it to another, matching one, hence $\tau_1 \leq \tau_2$ holds iff τ_1 matches every endpoint that τ_2 matches, i.e. $\tau_1 \leq \tau_2$ iff $\forall_{\tau'} \, (\tau_2 \propto \tau') \Rightarrow (\tau_1 \propto \tau')$, which after expanding the definition of "$\propto$" can be formally expressed as follows:

$$\tau_1 \leq \tau_2 \Leftrightarrow O_1 \rightarrow^* O_2 \wedge I_2 \rightarrow^* I_1 \wedge C_1 \Rightarrow^* C_2 \wedge C_2' \Rightarrow^* C_1'. \tag{4}$$

Intuitively, $\tau_1 \leq \tau_2$ if (a) τ_1 defines no more output events and no fewer input events than τ_2, (b) the types of output events of τ_1 are subtypes and the types of input events of τ_1 are supertypes of the corresponding events of τ_2, and (c) the provided constraints of τ_1 are no weaker and the required constraints of τ_1 are no stronger than those of τ_2.

Subtyping for live object types is defined in a similar manner. Type Θ_1 is a subtype of Θ_2, denoted $\Theta_1 \leq \Theta_2$, when Θ_1 can replace Θ_2. Since the only thing that one can do with a live object is connect it to another object through its endpoints, this boils down to whether Θ_1 defines all the endpoints that Θ_2 defines, and whether the types of these endpoints are no less specific, and whether Θ_1 guarantees no less and expects no more than Θ_2. Formally, for two types $\Theta_1 = (E_1, C_1, C_1')$ and $\Theta_2 = (E_2, C_2, C_2')$, we define:

$$\Theta_1 \leq \Theta_2 \Leftrightarrow E_1 \leq^* E_2 \wedge C_1 \Rightarrow^* C_2 \wedge C_2' \Rightarrow^* C_1'. \tag{5}$$

Relation $\leq^*$ between sets of named endpoints used above is defined as follows:

$$E \leq^* E' \Leftrightarrow \forall \, (n, \tau') \in E' \; \exists \, (n, \tau) \in E \text{ such that } \tau \leq \tau'. \tag{6}$$

The use of types in our platform is limited to checking whether the declared object contracts are compatible, to ensure that the use of objects corresponds to the developer's intentions. The live objects platform performs the following checks at runtime:

1. When a reference to an object of type Θ is passed as a value of a parameter that is expected to be a reference to an object of type Θ', the platform verifies that $\Theta \leq \Theta'$.

2. When an endpoint of type τ is to be connected to an endpoint of type τ', either programmatically or during the construction of composite objects described in Section 4.2, the platform verifies that the two endpoints are compatible i.e. that $\tau \propto \tau'$.

We believe that in practice, this limited form of type safety is sufficient for most uses. For provable security, the runtime could be made to verify that live object's code implements the declared type prior to execution. Techniques such as proof-carrying code [44] and domain-specific languages with limited expressive power could facilitate this.

3.3 Constraint Formalisms

We conclude this section with a discussion of different formalisms that can be used to express the constraints in the definition of objects and endpoints. The issue is subtle because on the one hand, a type system won't be very helpful if it has nothing to check, but on the other hand, there are a great variety of ways to specify protocol properties. It isn't much of an exaggeration to suggest that every protocol of interest brings its own descriptive formalism to the table! As noted earlier, many prior systems have effectively selected a single formalism, perhaps by defining types through inheritance. Yet when we consider protocols that might include time-critical multicast, IPTV, atomic broadcast, Byzantine agreement, transactions, secure key replication, and many others, it becomes clear that no existing formalism could possibly cover the full range of options.

A further issue is the incompleteness of many specifications, in a purely formal sense. For example, one popular formalism is temporal logic [22,12]. Here, we assume a global time and a set of locations, and a function that maps from time to events that occur at those locations. In the context of endpoint constraints, we can think of instances of the endpoint as locations, and the endpoint's incoming and outgoing events, and explicit connect/disconnect events, as the events of the temporal logic. Constraints would be expressed as formulas over these events, identifying the legal event sequences within the (infinite) set of possible system histories.

Example (b). Consider the **reliable channel** endpoint, exposed by the reliable channel **r** in the example in Section 3.1. The endpoint's type might define one incoming event **send(m)** and one outgoing event **receive(m)**, parameterized by message body **m**. Constraints provided by the channel object **r** might include a temporal logic formula stating that if event **receive(m)** is delivered by **r** through some of the instances of the endpoint sooner than **receive(m′)**, then for any other instance of the endpoint, if both events are delivered, they are delivered in the same sequence.   ∎

Example (b) illustrates a safety property of a type for which temporal logic is especially convenient. Chockler et. al. use temporal logic to specify a range of reliable multicast protocols in [12]. However, the FLP impossibility result establishes that these protocols cannot guarantee liveness in traditional networks. Thus, while we can express a liveness constraint in such a logic, no protocol could achieve it – in effect, such a protocol type would be useless in real systems!

Temporal logic is just one of many useful formalisms. In our work on a security architecture, still underway, we're looking into using a variant of the BAN logic [9] to define security properties provided by live objects or expected from their environment. Real-time and performance guarantees are conveniently expressed as probabilistic guarantees on event occurrences, e.g. in terms of predicates such as *"at least* **p** *% of the time,* **receive(m)** *occurs at all endpoint instances at most* **t** *seconds following* **send(m)**," or *"at least* **p** *% of the time,* **receive(m)** *occurs at all different endpoint instances in a time window of at most* **t** *seconds"*.

Yet another useful formalism would be a version of temporal logic that talks about the number of instances of different endpoints in time. For example, constraints of the sort *"at most one instance of the* **publisher** *endpoint may be connected at any given time"* could describe single-writer semantics or similar assumptions made by the protocol designer. Constraints of this sort could also express fault-tolerance properties, e.g. define the minimum number of proxies to maintain a certain replication level etc.

In general, with formalisms like those listed above, type-checking might involve a theorem prover, and hence may not always be practical. In practice, however, the majority of object and endpoint types would choose from a relatively small set of standard constraints, such as best-effort, virtually-synchronous, transactional, or atomic dissemination, total ordering of events etc. Predicates that represent common constraints could be indexed, and stored as macros in a standard library of such predicates, and the object and endpoint types would simply list such macros. The runtime would perform type-checking by comparing such lists, and using cached known facts, such as that a virtually synchronous channel is also best-effort reliable etc. By taking advantage of late binding and reflection, features of .NET and of most Java platforms, it is easy to make these mechanisms extensible in a "plug and play" manner. This will allow developers to introduce additional formalisms down the road.

3.4 Group Types

Readers familiar with group communication [5,11] may be concerned that although our model is fundamentally about creating and working with groups of entities (live object proxies), the type system itself lacks a rigorous notion of a group. This actually makes our model simpler and more generic, without preventing us from expressing group properties. For example, to model a virtually synchronous group, we can define a pair of endpoints **channel** and **membership**, and specify constraints on the occurrences of events on the two endpoints, as in group communication specifications [12]. Within groups of endpoints, one can use temporal logic formulas with operators such as *everywhere* and *everywhere within a membership view*, much as in [2,12,22]. To bind to such a group an object would define two matching endpoints. This approach has the advantage of generality: we can potentially express a range of group semantics.

4 Language Embeddings and Support for Composition

4.1 Language Embeddings

Our model has a good fit with modern object-oriented programming languages. There are two aspects of this embedding. On one hand, live object code can be written in a language like Java and C# (we will demonstrate this in Section 4.2). On the other hand, live objects, proxies, endpoints, and connections between them are first-class entities that can be used within C# or Java code. Their distributed types build upon and extend the set of non-distributed types in the underlying managed environment. In this section, we'll discuss each of the new programming language entities we introduce: *references to live objects, references to proxies, references to endpoint instances*, and *references to connections between endpoints*. An example of their use is shown in Code 1. We will conclude this section with a discussion of two more advanced mechanisms, *template object references* and *casting operator extensions*.

Code 1. An example piece of code in a language similar to C#, but with a simplified syntax for legibility. Here, "ReceiveObject" is a handler of an incoming event of a live object proxy. The event is parameterized by a live object reference "ref_object". If the reference is to a shared folder, the code launches a new proxy to connect to the folder's protocol and attaches a handler to event "AddedElement" generated by this protocol, in order to monitor this folder's contents.

```
01  void ReceiveObject(ref<liveobject> ref_object) // code of an event handler
02  {
03      if (referenced_type(ref_object) is SharedFolder)
04      {
05          ref<SharedFolder> ref_folder := (ref<SharedFolder>) ref_object;
06          SharedFolder folder := dereference(ref_folder); // creates a proxy
07          external<FolderClient> folder_ep := endpoint(folder, "folder");
08          internal<FolderClient> my_ep := new_endpoint<FolderClient>();
09          my_ep.AddedElement += ...; // here's a code that registers an event handler
10          connection my_connection := connect(folder_ep, my_ep);
11          // some code to store the newly created proxy and endpoint connection references
12      }
13  }
```

A. References to Live Objects. Operations that can be performed on these references include reflection (inspecting the referenced object's type), casting, and dereferencing (the example uses are shown in Code 1, in lines 03, 05, and 06 accordingly). Dereferencing results in the local runtime launching a new proxy of the referenced object (recall from Section 3.1 that references include complete instructions for how to do this). The proxy starts executing immediately, but its endpoints are disconnected A reference to the new proxy is returned to the caller (in our example it is assigned to a local variable **folder**). This reference controls the proxy's lifetime. When it is discarded and garbage collected, the runtime disconnects all of the proxy's endpoints and terminates it. To prevent this from happening, in our example code we must store the proxy reference before exiting (we would do so in line 11).

Whereas a proxy must have a reference to It to remain active, a reference to a live object is just a pointer to a recipe for constructing a proxy for that object, and can be discarded at any time. An important property of object references is that they are serializable, and may be passed across the network or process boundaries between proxies of the same or even different live objects, as well as stored on in a file etc. The reference can be dereferenced anywhere in the network, always producing a functionally equivalent proxy – assuming, of course, that the node on which this occurs is capable of running the proxy. In an ideal world, the environmental constraints would permit us to determine whether a proxy actually can be instantiated in a given setting, but the world is obviously not ideal. Determining whether a live object can be dereferenced in a given setting, without actually doing so, is probably not possible.

The types of live object references are based on the types of live objects, which we will define formally below. To avoid ambiguity, if Θ is a live object type, and **x** is a reference to an object of type Θ, we will write **ref<Θ>** to refer to the type of entity **x**.

The semantics of casting live object references is similar to that for regular objects. Recall that if a regular reference of type **IFoo** points to an object that implement **IBar**, we can cast the reference to **IBar** even if **IFoo** is not a subtype of **IBar**, and while as a result the type of the reference will change, the actual referenced object will not. In a similar manner, casting a live object reference of type **ref<Θ>** to some **ref<Θ'>** produces a reference that has a different type, and yet dereferencing either of these references, the original one or the one obtained by casting, result in the local runtime creating the same proxy, running the same code, with the same endpoints. A reference can be cast to **ref<Θ>** for as long as the actual type of the live object is a subtype of Θ.

B. References to Proxies. The type of a proxy reference is simply the type of the object it runs, i.e. if the object is of type Θ, references to its proxies are of type Θ. Proxy references can be type cast just like live object references. One difference between the two constructs is that proxy references are local and can't be serialized, sent, or stored. Another difference is that they have the notion of a lifetime, and can be disposed or garbage collected. Discarding a proxy reference destroys the locally running proxy, as explained earlier, and is like assigning **null** to a regular object reference in a language like Java. The live object is not actually destroyed, since other proxies may still be running, but if all proxy references are discarded (and proxies destroyed), the protocol ceases to run, as if it were automatically garbage collected.

Besides disposing, the only operation that can be performed on a proxy reference is accessing the proxy endpoints for the purpose of connecting to the proxy. An example of this is seen in line 07, where we request the proxy of the shared folder object to return a reference to its local instance of the endpoint named "folder".

C. References to Endpoint Instances. There are two types of references to endpoint instances, *external* and *internal*. An external endpoint reference is obtained by enumerating endpoints of a proxy through the proxy reference, as shown in line 07. The only operation that can be performed with an external reference is to connect it to a single other, matching endpoint (line 10). After connecting successfully, the runtime returns a connection reference that controls the connection's lifetime. If this reference is disposed, the two connected endpoints are disconnected, and the proxies that own both endpoints are notified by sending explicit **disconnect** events.

An internal endpoint reference is returned when a new endpoint is programmatically created using operator **new** (line 08). This is typically done in the constructor code of a proxy. Each proxy must create an instance of each of the object's endpoints in order to be able to communicate with its environment. The proxy stores the internal references of each of its endpoints for private use, and provides external references to the external code per request, when its endpoints are being enumerated. Internal references are also created when a proxy needs to dynamically create a new endpoint, e.g. to interact with a proxy of some subordinate object that it has dynamically instantiated.

An internal reference is a subtype of an external reference. Besides connecting it to other endpoints, it also provides a "portal" through which a proxy that created it can send or receive events to other connected proxies. Sending is done simply by method calls, and receiving by registering event callbacks (line 09).

An important difference between external and internal endpoint references is that the former could be serialized, passed across the network and process boundaries, and then connected to a matching endpoint in the target location. The runtime can implement this e.g. by establishing a TCP connection to pass events back and forth between proxies communicating this way. This is possible because events are serializable.

Internal endpoint references are not serializable. This is crucial, for it provides isolation. Since any interaction between objects must pass through endpoints, and events exchanged over endpoints must be serializable, this ensures that an internal endpoint reference created by a proxy cannot be passed to other objects or even to other proxies of the same object. Only the proxy that created an endpoint has access to its portal functionality of an endpoint, and can send or receive events with it.

D. References to Connections. Connection references control the lifetime of connections. Besides disposing, the only functionality they offer is to register callbacks, to be invoked upon disconnection. These references are not strongly typed. They may be created either programmatically (as in line 10 in Code 1), or by the runtime during the construction of a composite proxy. The latter is discussed in detail in Section 4.2.

E. Template Object References. Template references are similar to generics in C# or templates in C++. Templates are parameterized descriptions of proxies; when dereferencing them, their parameters must be assigned values. Template types do not support subtyping, i.e. references of template types cannot be cast or assigned to references of other types. The only operation allowed on such references is conversion to non-template references by assigning their parameters, as described in Section 4.2.

Template object references can be parameterized by other types and by values. The types used as parameters can be object, endpoint, or event types. Values used as parameters must be of serializable types, just like events, but otherwise can be anything, including *string* and *int* values, live object references, external endpoint references etc.

Example (c). A channel object template can be parameterized by the type of messages that can be transmitted over the channel. Hence, one can e.g. define a template of a reliable multicast stream and instantiate it to a reliable multicast stream of video frames. Similarly, one can define a template dissemination protocol based on IP multicast, parameterized with the actual IP multicast address to use. A template shared folder containing live objects could be parameterized by the type of objects that can be stored in the folder and the reference to the replication object it uses internally. ■

F. Casting Operator Extensions. This is a programmable reflection mechanism. Recall that in C# and C++, one can often cast values to types they don't derive from. For example, one can assign an integer value to a floating-point type. Conversion code is then automatically generated by the runtime, and injected into this assignment. One can define custom casting operators for the runtime to use in such situations. Our model also supports this feature. If an external endpoint or an object reference is cast to a mismatching reference type, the runtime can try to generate a suitable wrapper.

Example (d). Consider an application designed to use encrypted communication. The application has a user interface object **u** exposing a **channel** endpoint, which it would like to connect to a matching endpoint of an encrypted channel object. But, suppose that the application has a reference to a channel object **c** that is not encrypted, and that exposes a **channel** endpoint of type lacking the required security constraints. When the application tries to connect the endpoints of **u** and **c**, normally the operation would fail with a type mismatch exception. However, if the **channel** endpoint of **c** can be made compatible with the endpoint of **u** by injecting encryption code into the connection, the compiler or the runtime might generate such wrapper code instead. Notice that proxies for this wrapper would run on all nodes where the channel proxy runs, and hence could implement fairly sophisticated functionality. In particular, they could implement an algorithm for secure group key replication. In effect, we are able to wrap the entire distributed object: an elegant example of the power of the model. ■

The same can be done for object references. While casting a reference, the runtime may return a description of a composite reference that consists of the old proxy code, plus the extra wrapper, to run side by side (we discuss composite references in Section 4.2). In addition to encryption or decryption, this technique could be used to automatically inject buffering code, code that translates between push and pull interface, code that persists or orders events, automatically converts event data types, and so on.

Currently, our platform uses casting only to address certain kinds of binary incompatibilities, as explained in Section 5.2. In future work, we plan to extend the platform to support more sophisticated uses of casting, e.g. as in the example above, and define rules for choosing casting operators when more that one is available.

4.2 Construction and Composition

As noted in Section 4.1, a live object *exists* if references to it exist, and it *runs* if any proxies constructed from these references are active. Creating new objects thus boils down to creating references, which are then passed around and dereferenced to create

Code 2. An example live object reference, based on a shared document template, parameterized by a reliable communication channel. The channel is composed of a dissemination object and a reliability object, connected to each other via their "UnreliableChannel" endpoints, much like **r** and **u** in Figure 2. The "ReliableChannel" endpoint of the reliability object is exposed by the channel. The dissemination object reference is to be found as an object named "MyChannel", of type "Channel", in an online repository ("Id" and "Channel" are predefined types). The reference to the repository is to be found, as an object named "QuickSilver", of type "Folder", i.e. containing channels, in another online repository, the "registry" object (see Section 0).

```
01   parameterized object // an object based on a parameterized template
02     using template primitive object 3 // the id of a "shared document" template
03   {
04     parameter "Channel" :
05       composite object // a complex object built from multiple component objects
06       {
07         component "DisseminationObject" :
08           external object "MyChannel" as Channel
09             from external object "QuickSilver" as Folder<Id, Channel>
10               from primitive object 2 // the id of a predefined "registry" object
11         component "ReliabilityObject" :
12           ... // specification of some loss recovery object, omitted for brevity
13         connection // an internal connection between a pair of component endpoints
14           endpoint "UnreliableChannel" of "DisseminationObject"
15           endpoint "UnreliableChannel" of "ReliabilityObject"
16         export // endpoints of the components to be exposed by the composite object
17           endpoint "ReliableChannel"  of "ReliabilityObject"
18       }
19   }
```

running applications. Object references are hierarchical: references to complex objects are constructed from references to simpler objects, plus logic to "glue" them together. The construction can use four patterns, for constructing *composite, external, parameterized,* and *primitive* objects. We shall now discuss these, illustrating them with an example object reference that uses each of these patterns, shown in Code 2.

A. Composite References. A composite object consists of multiple internal objects, running side by side. When such an object is instantiated, the proxies of the internal objects run on the same nodes (like objects **r** and **u** in Figure 2). A composite proxy thus consists of multiple embedded proxies, one for each of the internal objects. A composite reference contains embedded references for each of the internal proxies, plus the logic that glues them together. In the example reference shown in lines 05 to 18 in Code 2, there is a separate section "**component** *name* : *reference*" for each of the embedded objects, specifying its internal name and reference. This is followed by a section of the form "**connection** *endpoint1 endpoint2*", for each internal connection. Finally, for every endpoint of some embedded internal object that is to be exposed by the composite object as its own, there is a separate section "**export** *endpoint*".

When a proxy is constructed from a composite reference, the references to any internal proxies and connections are kept by the composite proxy, and discarded when the composite proxy is disposed of (Figure 3). The lifetimes of all internal proxies are thus connected to the lifetime of the composite. Embedded objects and their proxies thus play the role analogous to member fields of a regular object.

B. External References. An external reference is one that has not been embedded and must be downloaded from somewhere. It is of the form "**external object** *name* **as** *type* **from** *reference*", where *reference* is a reference to the live object that represents some online repository containing live object references, and *name* is the name of the object, the reference to which is to be retrieved from this repository. The type Θ of the retrieved object is expected to be a subtype of *type*, and the type of the external reference is **ref**<*type*>. One example of such a reference is shown in lines 08 to 10, and another (embedded in the first one) in lines 09 to 10.

The repository could be any object of type $\Theta \leq$ **folder**, where type **folder** is a built-in type of objects with a simple dictionary-like interface. Objects of this type have an endpoint with input event **get(n)** and with output events **item(n, r)** and **missing(n)**. To retrieve an external reference, the runtime creates a repository object proxy from the embedded reference, runs it, connects to its folder endpoint, submits the **get** event, and awaits response. Once the response arrives, the repository proxy can be discarded.

The "**as** *type*" clause allows the runtime to statically determine the type of the reference without having to engage in any protocol. In case of composite, parameterized, or primitive references, the runtime can derive the type right from the description. The "**as** *type*" clause can still be used in the other categories of references as an explicit type cast, in case it is necessary e.g. to hide some of the object's endpoints.

The types in the reference (such as **Channel** in line 08 or **Folder<Id, Channel>** in line 09) could either refer to the standard, built-in types, or they could be described explicitly using a language based on the formalisms in Section 3.2. To keep our example simple, we assume that all types are built-in, and we refer to them by names.

C. Parameterized References. These references are based on template objects introduced in Section 4.1. They include a section "**using template** *reference*", where *reference* is an embedded template object reference, and a list of assignments to parameter values, each in a separate section of the form "**parameter** *name* : *argument*", where the *argument* could be a type description or a primitive value, e.g. an embedded object reference. For example, the reference in Code 2 is parameterized with a single parameter, **Channel**. The type of the parameter needn't be explicitly specified, for it is determined by the template. In our example, the template expects a live object reference to a reliable communication channel. The specific reference used here to instantiate this template is the composite reference in lines 05 to 18.

D. Primitive References. The types of references mentioned so far provide a means for recursively constructing complex objects from simple ones, but the recursion needs to terminate somewhere. Hence, the runtime provides a certain number of built-in protocols that can be selected by a known 128-bit identifier (lines 02 and 10 in Code 2). Of course even a 128-bit namespace is finite, and many implementations of the live objects runtime could exist, each offering different built-in protocols. To avoid chaos, we reserve primitive references only for objects that either cannot be referenced using other methods, or where doing so would be too inefficient. We will discuss two such objects: the *library* template and the *registry* object.

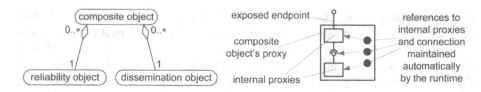

Fig. 3. A live object class diagram for the composite object in Code 2 (left) and the structure of the composite proxy (right). When constructing a composite proxy, the runtime automatically constructs all the internal proxies and the internal connections between them, and stores their references in the composite proxy. Embedded proxies and connections are destroyed together with the composite proxy. The latter can expose some of the internal endpoints as its own.

Code 3. An example live object reference for a custom protocol, implemented in a library that can be downloaded from http://www.mystuff.com/mylibrary.dll. Objects running this protocol are of type "MyType1", and can be found in the library under name "MyProtocol1". The library template provides the folder abstraction introduced in Section 0.

```
01   external object "MyProtocol1" as MyType1 // my own, custom implementation
02     from parameterized object // an instance of the library template
03       using template primitive object 1 // an id of a built-in library template
04     {
05       parameter "URL" : http://www.mystuff.com/mylibrary.dll
06     }
```

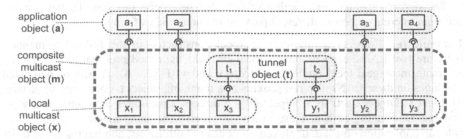

Fig. 4. An example of a hybrid multicast object m, constructed from two local protocols x, y that disseminate data in two different regions of the network, e.g. two LANs, combined using a tunnel object t that acts as a repeater and replicates messages between the two LANs. Different proxies of the composite object **m**, running on different nodes, are configured differently, e.g. some use an embedded proxy of object **x**, while others use an embedded proxy of object **y**.

Code 4. A portable reference to the "hybrid" object **m** from Figure 4 built using the registry.

```
01  external object "MyChannel" as Channel
02    from external object "MyPlatform" as Folder<Id, Channel>
03      from primitive object 2 // the registry
```

Code 5. An example of a "proper" use of the registry, to specify a locally configured multicast platform, which could then be used by external references like the one in Code 4. Here, the local instance of the communication platform is configured with the address of a node that controls a region of the Internet, from which other objects can be bootstrapped.

```
01  parameterized object
02    using template external object "MyPlatform" as Folder<Id, Channel>
03      from parameterized object // from a binary downloaded from the url below
04        using template primitive object 1 // the library template
05        { parameter "URL" : http://www.mystuff.com/mylibrary.dll }
06  { parameter "LocalController" : tcp://192.168.0.100:60000 }
```

D.1 Library. A library is an object of type **folder**, representing a binary containing executable code, from which one can retrieve references to live objects implemented by the binary. The library template is parameterized by URL of the location where the binary is located (see Code 3, lines 02 to 06). The binary can be in any of the known formats that allow the runtime to locate proxy code, object and type definitions in it, either via reflection, or by using an attached manifest (we show one example of this in Section 5.2). After a proxy of a library is created, the proxy downloads the binary and loads it. When an object reference retrieved from a library is dereferenced, the library locates the corresponding constructor in the binary, and invokes it to create the proxy.

D.2 Registry. The registry object is again a live object of type **folder**, i.e. a mapping of names to object references. The registry references are stored locally on each node, can be edited by the user, and in general, the mapping on each node may be different. Proxies respond to requests by returning the locally stored references.

The registry enables construction of complex heterogeneous objects that can use different internal objects in different parts of the network, as follows

Example (e). Consider a multicast protocol constructed in the following manner: there are two LANs, each running a local IP multicast based protocol to locally disseminate messages: local multicast objects **x** and **y** (Figure 4). A pair of dedicated machines on these LANs also run proxies of a tunneling object **t**, connected to proxies of **x** and **y**. Object **t** acts as a "repeater", i.e. it copies messages between **x** and **y**, so that proxies running both of these protocols receive the same messages. Now, consider an application object **a**, deployed on nodes in both LANs, and having some of its proxies connected to **x**, and some to **y**. From the point of view of object a, the entire infrastructure consisting of **x**, **y**, and **t** could be thought of as a single, composite multicast object **m**. Object **m** is heterogeneous in the sense that its proxies on different machines have a different internal structure: some have an embedded object **x** and some are using **y**. Logically, however, **m** is a single protocol and we'd like to be able to fully express it in our model. The problem stems from the fact that on one hand, references to **m** must be complete descriptions of the protocol, so they should have references to **x** and **y** embedded, yet on the other hand, references containing local configuration details are not portable. The registry object solves this problem by introducing a level of indirection (Code 4).   ∎

The reader might be concerned that the portability of live objects is threatened by use of the registry. References that involve registry now rely on all nodes having properly configured registry entries. For this reason, we use the registry sparingly, just to bootstrap the basic infrastructure. Objects placed in the registry would represent the entire products, e.g. "the communication infrastructure developed by company XYZ", and would expose the **folder** abstraction introduce earlier, whereby specific infrastructure objects can be loaded. An example of such proper use is shown in Code 5.

5 System

5.1 Embedding Live Objects into the Operating System Via Drag and Drop

Our implementation of the live object runtime runs on Microsoft Windows[2] with .NET Framework 2.0. The system has two major components: an embedding of live objects into Windows drag and drop technologies, discussed here, and embedding of the new language constructs into .NET, discussed in Section 5.2.

Our drag and drop embedding is visually similar to Croquet [53] and Kansas [54], and mimics that employed in Windows Forms, tools such as Visual Studio (or similar ones for Java), and in the Object Linking and Embedding (OLE) [8], XAML [40], and ActiveX standards used in Microsoft Windows to support creation of compound documents with embedded images, spreadsheets, drawings etc. The primary goal is to enable non-programmers to create live collaborative applications, live documents, and business applications that have complex, hierarchical structures and non-trivial internal logic, just by dragging visual components and content created by others from toolbars, folders, and other documents, into new documents or design sheets.

---

[2] Porting our system from C#/.NET to Mono, to run under Linux, or building a Java/J2EE version of the runtime, shouldn't be a problem, but we haven't yet undertaken this task.

Our hope is that a developer who understands how to create a web page, and understands how to use databases and spreadsheets as part of their professional activities, would use live objects to glue together these kinds of components, sensors capturing real-world data, and other kinds of information to create content-rich applications, which can then be shared by emailing them to friends, placing them in a shared repository, or embedding them into standard productivity applications.

Live object references are much like other kinds of visual components that can be dragged and dropped. References are serialized into XML, and stored in files with a ".liveobject" extension. These ".liveobject" files can easily be moved about. Thus, when we talk about emailing a live application, one can understand this to involve embedding a serialized object reference into an HTML email. On arrival the object can be activated in place. This involves deserializing the reference (potentially running online repository protocols to retrieve some of its parts), followed by analysis of the object's type. Live objects can also be used directly from the desktop browser interface. We configured the Windows shell to interpret actions such as doubleclick on ".liveobject" files by passing the XML content of the file to our subsystem, which processes it as described above. Note that although our discussion has focused on GUI objects, the system also supports services that lack user interfaces.

We have created a number of live object templates based on reliable multicast protocols, including 2-dimensional and 3-dimensional desktops, text notes, video streams, live maps, and 3-dimensional objects such as airplanes and buildings. These can be mashed up to create live applications such as the ones on our web site (Figure 5).

Although the images in Figure 5 are evocative of multi-user role-playing systems such as Second Life, Live Objects differ in important ways. In particular, live objects can run directly on the user nodes, in a peer-to-peer fashion. In contrast, systems such as Second Life are tightly coupled to the data centers on which the content resides and is updated in a centralized manner. In Second Life, the state of the system lives in that data center. Live objects keep state replicated among users. When a new proxy joins, it must obtain some form of a checkpoint to initialize itself, or starts in a **null** state.

As noted earlier, live objects support drag and drop. The runtime initiates a drag by creating an XML to represent the dragged object's reference, and placing it in a clipboard. When a drop occurs, the reference is passed on to the application handling the drop. The application can store it as XML, or it can deserialize it, inspect the type of the dropped object, and take the corresponding action based on that. For example, the spatial desktop on Figure 5, only supports objects with a 3-dimensional user interface. Likewise, the only types of objects that can be dropped onto airplanes are those that represent textures or streams of 3-dimensional coordinates. The decision in each case is made by the application logic of the object handling the drop.

Live objects can also be dropped into OLE-compliant containers, such as Microsoft Word documents, emails, spreadsheets, or presentations. In this case, an OLE component is inserted with an embedded XML of the dragged object's reference. When the OLE component is activated (e.g. when the user opens the document), it invokes the live objects runtime to construct a proxy, and attaches to its user interface endpoint (if there is one). This way, one can create documents and presentations, in which instead of static drawings, the embedded figures can display content powered by any type of a distributed protocol. Integration with spreadsheets and databases is also possible, although a little trickier because these need to access the data in the object, and must trigger actions when a new event occurs.

As mentioned above, one can drag live objects into other live objects. In effect, the state of one object contains a reference to some other live object. This is visible in the desktop example on Figure 5. This example illustrates yet another important feature. When one object contains a reference to another (as is the case for a desktop containing references to objects dragged onto it), it can dynamically activate it: dereference, and connect to the proxy of the stored object, and interact with the proxy. For example, the desktop object automatically activates references to all visual objects placed on it, so that when the desktop is displayed, so are all objects, the references of which have been dragged onto the desktop.

Fig. 5. Screenshots of our platform running live objects with an attached user interface logic. The 3-dimensional space, the area map embedded in this space, as well as each of the airplanes and buildings (left) is a separate live object, with its own embedded multicast channel. Similarly, the green desktop, and the text notes and images embedded in it are independent live objects. Each of these objects can be viewed and accessed from anywhere on the network, and separately embedded in other objects to create various web-style mash-ups, collaborative editors, online multiplayer games, and so on. Users create these by simply dragging objects into one another. Our download site includes a short video demonstrating the ease with which applications such as these can be created.

By now, the reader will realize that in the proposed model, individual nodes might end up participating in large numbers of distributed protocol instances. Opening a live document of the sort shown on Figure 5 can cause the user's machine to join hundreds of instances of a reliable, totally ordered multicast protocol with state transfer, which support the objects embedded in the document. This might lead to scalability concerns. In our prior work we demonstrated that this problem is not a showstopper. Our Quicksilver Scalable Multicast (QSM) system [46], can support thousands of overlapping multicast groups, communicating at network speeds with low overhead.

5.2 Embedding Live Object Language Constructs into .NET Via Reflection

Extending a platform such as .NET to support the new constructs discussed in Section 4.1 would require extending the underlying type system and runtime, thus precluding incremental deployment. Instead, we leverage the .NET reflection mechanism to implement dynamic type checking. This technique doesn't require modifications to the

.NET CLR, and it can be used for other managed environments, such as Java. The key idea is to use ordinary .NET types as "aliases" representing our distributed types. Whenever such an alias type is used in a .NET code, the live objects runtime "understands" that what is "meant" by the programmer is actually the distributed type. Aliases are defined by decorating .NET types with attributes, as in Code 6 and Code 7.

Example (f). Consider a template object type **channel** for multicast channels, parameterized by the .NET type of the messages that can be transmitted. One defines an alias type as a .NET interface annotated with **ObjectTypeAttribute** (Code 6, line 01). When a library object (of Section 4.2) loads a new binary, the runtime scans the binary for .NET types annotated this way and registers them on its internal list of aliases.

Code 6. A .NET interface can be associated with a live object type using an "ObjectType" attribute (line 01). The interface may then be used anywhere to represent the represented live object type. The live objects runtime uses reflection to parse such annotations in binaries it loads and build a library of built-in objects, object types and templates. Object and type templates are defined by specifying and annotating generic arguments (line 03).

```
01  [ObjectTypeAttribute] // annotates "IChannel" as an alias for a live object type
02  interface IChannel<
03     [ParameterAttribute(ParameterClass.ValueClass)] MessageType>
04  {
05     [EndpointAttribute("Channel")] EndpointTypes.IDual<
06        Interfaces.IChannel<MessageType>,
07        Interfaces.IChannelClient<MessageType>>
08     ChannelEndpoint { get; } // returns an external reference to endpoint "Channel"
09  }
```

Parameters of the represented live object type are modeled as generic parameters of the alias. Each generic parameter is annotated with **Parameter Attribute** (line 03), to specify the kind of parameter it represents. The classes of parameters supported by the runtime include *Value*, *ValueClass*, *ObjectClass*, *EndpointClass*, and others we won't discuss here. *Value* parameters are simply serializable values, including .NET types or references to live objects, The others represent the types of values, types of live objects and types of endpoints. For example, we could define a live object type template parameterized by the type of another live object. A practical use of this is a typed folder template, i.e. a folder that contains only references to live objects of a certain type. For example, an instance of this template could be a folder that contains reliable communication channels of a particular type. Another good example is a factory object that creates references of a particular type, e.g. an object that configures new reliable multicast channels in a multicast platform.

An alias interface for a live object type is expected to specify only .NET properties, each annotated with **EndpointAttribute** (line 05). Each property defines one named endpoint for all live objects of this type. The property can only have a getter (line 08), which must return a value of a .NET type that is an alias for some endpoint type. The example in Code 6 uses alias **EndpointTypes.IDual<Interface1, Interface2>**. This is an alias template built into the runtime, but parameterized by two .NET interfaces.

Code 7. A live object template is defined by decorating a generic class definition (line 01), its generic class parameters (line 03), and constructor parameters (line 08) with .NET attributes. To specify the template live object's type, the class must implement an interface that is annotated to represent a live object type (line 04 referencing the definition shown in Code 6). In the body of the class, we create endpoints to be exposed by the proxy (created in lines 11-12, exposed in lines 19-25), handle incoming events (line 27) and send events through its endpoints.

```
01 [ObjectAttribute("89BF6594F5884B6495F5CD78C5372FC6")]
02 sealed class MyChannel<
03    [ParameterAttribute(ParameterClass.ValueClass)] MessageType>
04 : ObjectTypes.IChannel<MessageType>, // specifies the live object type
05    Interfaces.IChannel // we implement handlers to all incoming events, see line 12
06 {
07    public MyChannel(
08       [Parameter(ParameterClass.Value)] // also a parameter of the template
09       ObjectReference<ObjectTypes.IMembership> membership_reference)
10    {
11       this.myendpoint = new Endpoints.Dual<
12          Interfaces.IChannel, Interfaces.IChannelClient>(this);
13       ... // the rest of the constructor would contain code very similar to that in Code 1
14    }
15    // this is our internal reference to the channel endpoint, the endpoint's "backdoor"
16    private Endpoints.Dual<
17       Interfaces.IChannel, Interfaces.IChannelClient> myendpoint;
18
19    EndpointTypes.IDual<
20       Interfaces.IChannel<MessageType>,
21       Interfaces.IChannelClient<MessageType>>
22    ObjectTypes.IChannel.ChannelEndpoint
23    {
24       get { return myendpoint; } // returns an external endpoint reference
25    }
26    // this is a handler for one of the incoming events of the channel endpoint
27    Interfaces.IChannel.Send(MessageType message) { ... } // details omitted
28    ... // the rest of the alias definition, containing all the other event handlers etc.
29 }
```

The methods defined by these interfaces, again accordingly annotated, are used by the runtime to compile the list of this endpoint's incoming and outgoing events, and similar annotations can be used to express its constraints. When the alias defined this way is used in some context with its generic parameters assigned (lines 05-07), the runtime treats it as an alias for the specific endpoint type, with the specific events defined by those interfaces.

Having defined the object's type, we can define the object itself. This is again done via annotations. An example definition of a live object template is shown in Code 7.

A live object template is defined as a .NET class, the instances of which represent the object's proxies. The class is annotated with **ObjectAttribute** (line 01) to instruct the runtime to build a live object definition from it. This template has two parameters: the type parameter representing the type of messages carried by the channel (line 03), and a "value" parameter - the reference to the membership object that this channel should use (lines 08-09). To specify the type of the live object, line 03 inherits from an alias. This forces our class to implement properties returning the appropriate endpoints (lines 19-25). The actual endpoints are created in the constructor (lines 11-12). While creating endpoints, we connect event handlers for incoming events (hooking itself up, in line 12, and implementing these handlers, as in line 27).   ∎

While the use of aliases is convenient as a way of specifying distributed types, alias types are, of course, not distributed, and the .NET runtime doesn't understand subtyping rules we defined in Section 3.2. The actual type checking is done dynamically. When the programmer invokes a method of a .NET alias to request a type cast, or to create a connection between endpoints, the runtime uses its internal list of aliases to identify the distributed types involved and performs type checking by itself. The physical .NET types of aliases are irrelevant. Indeed, if the runtime determines that two different .NET types are actually aliases for the same distributed type, it will inject a wrapper code, as demonstrated below.

Example (g). Suppose that binary **Foo.dll** defines an object type alias **IChannel** as in Code example 6, and an object template alias **MyChannel** as in Code example 7. Now, suppose that a different, unrelated binary **Bar.dll** also defines an alias **IChannel** in exactly the same way, as in Code 6, and then uses this alias, e.g. in the definition of an application object that could use channels of the corresponding distributed type. If both binaries are loaded by the live objects runtime, we will end up with two distinct, binary-incompatible .NET aliases **IChannel**, representing the same distributed type. Whenever the programmer makes an assignment between these two types, the runtime dynamically creates, compiles, and injects the appropriate wrapper to forward method calls between the incompatible interfaces, to make the assignment legal in .NET.   ∎

6 Conclusions

Our paper described the architecture and implementation of a system supporting live distributed objects, a strongly typed, object-oriented platform in which distributed protocols are treated as first-class objects. The platform is working and quite versatile, but is still a work in progress. Future challenges include implementing our security and WAN architectures (designed but not yet operational), providing runtime monitoring and debugging tools, and automated self-configuration and tuning.

Acknowledgements. Our work was funded by AFRL/IF, AFOSR, NSF, I3P and Intel. We'd like to thank Mahesh Balakrishnan, Kathleen Fisher, Paul Francis, Lakshmi Ganesh, Rachid Guerraoui, Chi Ho, Maya Haridasan, Annie Liu, Tudor Marian, Greg Morrisett, Andrew Myers, Anil Nerode, Robbert van Renesse, Yee Jiun Song, Einar Vollset, and Hakim Weatherspoon for the feedback they provided.

References

1. de Alfaro, L., Henzinger, T.: Interface automata. SIGSOFT Softw. Eng. Notes 26, 5 (2001)
2. Anceaume, E., Charron-Bost, B., Minet, P., Toueg, S.: On the Formal Specification of Group Membership Services. Cornell University Tech. Report TR95-1534 (August 1995)

3. Andrews, T., et al.: Business Process Execution Language for Web Services v1.1. May (2003), http://download.boulder.ibm.com/ibmdl/pub/software/dw/specs/ws-bpel/ws-bpel.pdf
4. Banerji, A., et al.: Web Services Conversation Language (WSCL), http://www.w3.org/TR/wscl10
5. Birman, K.: The Process Group Approach to Reliable Distributed Computing. Communications of the ACM 36(12), 37–53 (1993)
6. Birrell, A., Nelson, G., Owicki, S., Wobber, W.: Network Objects. In: SOSP 1993
7. Brand, D., Zafiropulo, P.: On communicating finite-state machines. JACM, 30(2) (1983)
8. Brockschmidt, K.: Inside OLE. Microsoft Press (1995)
9. Burrows, M., Abadi, M., Needham, R.: A Logic of Authentication. TOCS 8(1), 18–36 (1990)
10. Carriero, N., Gelernter, D.: Linda in Context. CACM 32(4), 444–458 (1989)
11. Cheriton, D., Zwaenepoel, W.: Distributed Process Groups in the V Kernel. ACM Transactions on Computer Systems 3(2), 77–107 (1985)
12. Chockler, G., Keidar, I., Vitenberg, W.: Group Communication Specifications: A Comprehensive Study. ACM Computer Surveys 33(4):1, 43 (2001)
13. Christensen, E., Curbera, F., Meredith, G., Weerawarana, S.: Web Services Description Lan-guage (WSDL). W3C Note 15 March (2001), http://www.w3.org/TR/wsdl
14. Eugster, P., Guerraoui, R.: On Objects and Events. In: OOPSLA 2001, pp. 254–269 (2001)
15. Eugster, P., Guerraoui, R.: Distributed Programming with Typed Events. IEEE Software 21(2), 56–64 (2004)
16. Eugster, P., Damm, H., Guerraoui, R.: Towards Safe Distributed Application Development. In: ICSE 2004, pp. 347–356 (2004)
17. Eugster, P., Guerraoui, R., Sventek, J.: Distributed Asynchronous Collections: Abstractions for Publish/Subscribe Interaction. In: Bertino, E. (ed.) ECOOP 2000. LNCS, vol. 1850, pp. 252–276. Springer, Heidelberg (2000)
18. Fu, X., Bultan, T., Su, J.: Conversation Specification: A New Approach to Design and Anal-ysis of E-Service Composition. In: WWW 2003, Budapest, Hungary, May 20-24 (2003)
19. Fuzzati, R., Nestmann, U.: Much Ado About Nothing. In: Algebraic Process Calculi, the First Twenty Five Years and Beyond. Process algebra, http://www.brics.dk/NS/05/3/
20. Garbinato, B., Guerraoui, R.: Using the Strategy Pattern to Compose Reliable Distributed Protocols. In: Proceedings of 3rd USENIX COOTS, Portland, Oregon (June 1997)
21. Goldberg, A., Robson, D.: Smalltalk-80: the language and its implementation. Addison-Wesley Longman Publishing Co., Inc., Boston (1983)
22. Halpern, J., Fagin, R., Moses, Y., Vardi, M.: Reasoning about Knowledge. MIT Press, Cambridge (1995)
23. Hickey, J., Lynch, N., van Renesse, R.: Specifications and proofs for Ensemble layers. In: Cleaveland, W.R. (ed.) ETAPS 1999 and TACAS 1999. LNCS, vol. 1579, Springer, Heidelberg (1999)
24. Hoare, C.: Communicating sequential processes. CACM 21(8), 666–677 (1978)
25. Jul, E., Levy, H., Hutchinson, N., Black, A.: Fine-Grained Mobility in the Emerald System. ACM TOCS 6(1), 109–133
26. Karr, D.: Specification, Composition, and Automated Verification of Layered Communication Protocols. Ph.D. Thesis. Cornell University (1997)

27. Keidar, I., Khazan, R., Lynch, N., Shvartsman, A.: An inheritance-based technique for building simulation proofs incrementally. ACM Trans. Soft. Eng. Methodol. 11(1), 63–91 (2002)
28. Kiczales, G., Lamping, J., Mendhekar, A., Maeda, C., Lopes, C., Loingtier, J.-M., Irwin, J.: Aspect-Oriented Programming. In: Aksit, M., Matsuoka, S. (eds.) ECOOP 1997. LNCS, vol. 1241, pp. 220–242. Springer, Heidelberg (1997)
29. Krumvieda, C.: Distributed ML: Abstractions for Efficient and Fault-Tolerant Prgramming. Technical Report, TR93-1376, Cornell University (1993)
30. Lamport, L.: The Temporal Logic of Actions. ACM Toplas 16(3), 872–923 (1994)
31. Liskov, B.: Distributed Programming in Argus. CACM 31(3), 300–312 (1988)
32. Liskov, B., Schieffler, R.: Guardians and Actions: Linguistic Support for Robust, Distributed Programs. ACM TOPLAS 5, 3 (1983)
33. Liu, X., Kreitz, C., van Renesse, R., Hickey, J., Hayden, M., Birman, K., Constable, R.: Building Reliable, High-Performance Communication Systems from Components. In: SOSP (1999)
34. Live Objects at Cornell, http://liveobjects.cs.cornell.edu/
35. Loesing, K., Wirtz, G.: An Implementation of Reliable Group Communication Based on the Peer-to-Peer Network JXTA. In: AICCSA 2005 (2005)
36. Lynch, N., Tuttle, M.: Hierarchical correctness proofs for dist.ributed algorithms. In: PODC 1987 (1987)
37. Maffeis, S., Schmidt, D.: Constructing Reliable Distributed Communication Systems with CORBA. IEEE Communications Magazine 14 (February 1997)
38. Makpangou, M., Gourhant, Y., Le Narzul, J.-P., Shapiro, M.: Fragmented Objects for Distri-buted Abstractions, pp. 170–186. IEEE Computer Society Press, Los Alamitos (1994)
39. Microsoft. Microsoft Office Groove, http://office.microsoft.com/en-us/groove/
40. Microsoft. XAML Overview, http://msdn2.microsoft.com/en-us/library/ms752059.aspx
41. Milner, R., Parrow, J., Walker, D.: A Calculus of Mobile Processes, parts I and II. LFCS Report 89-85. University of Edinburgh (June 1989)
42. Miranda, H., Pinto, A., Rodrigues, L.: Appia, a Flexible Protocol Kernel Supporting Multiple Coordinated Channels. In: Proc. of 21st ICDCS, Phoenix, Arizona, pp. 707–710 (2001)
43. Montresor, A., Davoli, R., Babaoglu, O.: Enhancing Jini with group communication. In: ICDCS Workshop, April 2001, pp. 69–74 (2001)
44. Necula, G.: Proof-Carrying Code. ACM SIGPLAN-SIGACT POPL 1997 (1997)
45. O'Malley, S., Peterson, L.: A Dynamic Network Architecture. TOCS 10(2), 110–143 (1992)
46. Ostrowski, K., Birman, K., Dolev, D.: Quicksilver Scalable Multicast. In: 7th IEEE International Symposium on Network Computing and Applications (IEEE NCA 2008) (to appear, 2008)
47. Ostrowski, K., Birman, K., Dolev, D.: Declarative Reliable Multi-Party Protocols. Cornell University Technical Report, TR2007-2088 (March 2007)
48. Ostrowski, K., Birman, K., Dolev, D.: Extensible Architecture for High-Performance, Scalable, Reliable Publish-Subscribe Eventing and Notification. JWSR v. 4, no 4 (October- December 2007)
49. Parastatidis, S., Webber, J., Woodman, S., Kuo, D., Greenfield, P.: SOAP Service Description Language (SSDL). Technical Report, University of Newcastle, CS-TR-899 (2005)
50. Reiter, M., Birman, K.: How to securely replicate services. In: TOPLAS, vol. 16(3), pp. 986–1009 (1994)

51. van Renesse, R., Birman, K., Hayden, M., Vaysburd, A., Karr, D.: Building Adaptive Systems Using Ensemble. Software Practice and Experience. 28(9), pp. 963-979 (August 1998)
52. Schneider, F.: Implementing Fault-Tolerant Services Using the State Machine Approach: a Tutorial. ACM Computng Surveys 22(4), 299–319 (1990)
53. Smith, D., Kay, A., Raab, A., Reed, D.: Croquet: a collaboration system architecture. Creating, Connecting and Collaborating Through Computing, C5 2003, p. 2–9 (2003)
54. Smith, R., Wolczko, M., Ungar, D.: From Kansas to Oz: Collaborative Debugging When a Shared World Breaks. CACM, 72–78 (1997)
55. Snyder, A.: Encapsulation and Inheritance in Object-Oriented Programming Languages. In: OOPLSA 1986
56. van Steen, M., Homburg, P., Tanenbaum, A.: Globe: A Wide Area Distributed System. IEEE Concurrency 7(1), 70–78 (1999)
57. Sun Microsystems, Inc. JXTA v2.0 Protocols Specification, http://www.jxta.org
58. Waldo, J.: The Jini architecture for network-centric computing. CACM 42(7), 76–82 (1999)

Bristlecone: A Language for Robust Software Systems

Brian Demsky and Alokika Dash

University of California, Irvine

Abstract. We present Bristlecone, a programming language for robust software systems. Bristlecone applications have two components: a high-level organization description that specifies how the application's conceptual operations interact, and a low-level operational description that specifies the sequence of instructions that comprise an individual conceptual operation. Bristlecone uses the high-level organization description to recover the software system from an error to a consistent state and to reason how to safely continue the software system's execution after the error.

We have implemented a compiler and runtime for Bristlecone. We have evaluated this implementation on three benchmark applications: a web crawler, a web server, and a multi-room chat server. We developed both a Bristlecone version and a Java version of each benchmark application. We used injected failures to evaluate the robustness of each version of the application. We found that the Bristlecone versions of the benchmark applications more successfully survived the injected failures.

1 Introduction

Software faults pose a significant challenge to developing reliable, robust software systems. The current approach to addressing software faults is to work hard to minimize the number of software faults through development processes, automated tools, and testing. While minimizing the number of software faults is a critical component in the development process for reliable software, it is not sufficient: the faults that inevitably slip through the development and testing processes will still cause deployed systems to fail.

The Lucent 5ESS telephone switch, the Ericsson AXD301 ATM switch, and the IBM MVS operating system are examples of critical systems that use recovery routines to automatically recover from software failures [1,2]. The software in these systems contains a set of manually coded recovery procedures that detect errors and then take actions to automatically recover from the errors. The reported results indicate that the recover routines can provide an order of magnitude increase in the reliability of these systems [3]. This additional reliability comes at a significant additional development cost — the recovery routines for the Lucent 5ESS telephone switch constitute more than 50% of the switch's software [4]. As a result of these high costs, recovery procedures have been primarily relegated to the domain of critical infrastructure software that can justify the cost. A wide range of other applications including desktop applications such as web browsers, office applications, games, servers, and control systems could potentially benefit from lower-cost automated recovery. The goal of Bristlecone is to

J. Vitek (Ed.): ECOOP 2008, LNCS 5142, pp. 490–515, 2008.

provide a lower-cost approach to software recovery that will enable a larger class of applications to benefit from this technique.

The key inspiration for this research is the observation that many software errors propagate through software systems to cause further damage either through data structure corruption or control-flow–induced coupling between conceptual operations. We have developed Bristlecone, a programming language for robust software systems, to address the error propagation problem. The basic idea is to address error propagation by having developers write software systems as a set of decoupled tasks with each task encapsulating an individual conceptual operation. The developer also provides specifications that describe how these decoupled tasks interact and optionally what consistency properties should hold for data structures. The runtime checks for data structure consistency violations and monitors for illegal operations (such as illegal memory accesses or arithmetic errors) to detect software errors. If the runtime detects an error in the execution, the runtime rolls back the data structures to their state at the beginning of the task's execution, and then uses the task specifications to adapt the execution of the software system to avoid re-executing the same error and make forward progress.

Alternatively, we can view Bristlecone as a programming language that allows for a large space of possible execution paths for any given software system with an implicit ordering of how desirable any given path is. If the most desirable path results in an error, the runtime rolls back the execution enough to follow a different path thereby avoiding the error. The result is a robust software system that can continue to successfully provide service even in the presence of errors.

1.1 Bristlecone Language

Figure 1 gives an overview of the components in the Bristlecone system. We can view software systems as a composition of thousands of conceptual operations — in practice, the correct execution of any conceptual operation is likely to be independent of many of the other conceptual operations. However, many traditional programming languages force developers to linearize the conceptual operations of a software system. This linearization tightly couples these conceptual operations: if one conceptual operation fails, it becomes unclear how to safely execute any future conceptual operations.

Bristlecone avoids artificially coupling operations by providing the developer with the *task* program construct. The developer uses a task to encompass a single conceptual operation. Tasks are represented in Figure 1 as rectangles. A set of task specifications loosely couple the tasks together. Each task contains a task specification that the runtime uses to determine (1) when to execute the task, (2) what data the task needs, and (3) how the task changes the role this data plays in the computation. If a task fails, the runtime uses the task specifications to reason how to adapt the future execution of the software system so that the execution does not depend on the failed task.

Bristlecone contains the following components (represented by rounded boxes in the figure):

- **Bristlecone Compiler:** The Bristlecone compiler compiles the tasks and task specifications into C code. Our implementation then uses the gcc C compiler to generate executables. The ellipse labeled `Compiled Tasks` represents the compiled tasks.

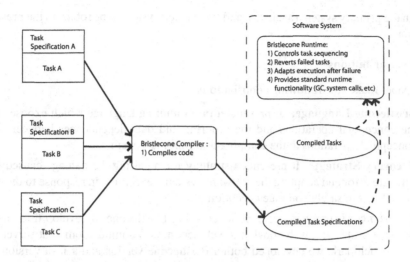

Fig. 1. Overview of the Bristlecone System

- **Runtime:** The runtime uses the compiled code and compiled specifications generated by the compilers (represented by the ellipses in the figure) to execute the software system. It uses the consistency checker to detect errors that silently corrupt
  data structures. The runtime then uses rollback to recover consistent data structures
  if it detects a software error. Finally, it uses the task specifications to determine
  when to execute the tasks and how to recover from errors.

1.2   Scope

Bristlecone is not suitable for all software systems. Certain computations, such as some
scientific simulations, are inherently tightly coupled. While Bristlecone may detect errors in such software systems, it is unlikely to enable these systems to recover in any
meaningful way. For other computations, it may be desirable for a software system to
shut down rather than deviate from a specific designed behavior or produce a partial
result.

Bristlecone is designed for software systems that place a premium on continued
execution and that can tolerate some degradation from a specific designed behavior.
For example, we expect that Bristlecone will be useful for financial server software,
e-commerce systems, office applications, web browsers, online game servers, sensor
networks, and control systems for physical phenomena. For applications like finance,
Bristlecone can be used to develop software systems that only process error-free transactions and back out all changes that corrupt data structures, while still ensuring that
cosmetic errors do not cause potentially expensive downtime. Ultimately, the software
developer must decide whether using this approach is reasonable for a given software
system.

This decision could depend on the environment in which a system is deployed. For
example, in systems with redundant backup systems, we expect that developers would

design the primary system to fail-fast and the backup system to be robust in the presence of errors.

1.3 Contributions

This paper makes the following contributions:

- **Bristlecone Language:** It presents a programming language which exposes both the conceptual operations and the ordering and data dependences between these conceptual operations to the compiler and runtime system.

- **Recovery Strategy:** It presents a strategy for repairing the damage caused by a software error and adapting the software system's execution in response to the error to enable it to safely continue execution.

- **Experience:** It presents our experience using Bristlecone to develop three robust software systems: a web crawler, a web server, and a multi-room chat server. For each benchmark, we developed both a Bristlecone version and a Java version. We designed the Java versions to be resilient: they use threads to tolerate failures. Our experience indicates that the Bristlecone versions are able to successfully recover from significantly more of the injected failures.

The remainder of the paper is structured as follows. Section 2 presents an example that illustrates our approach. Section 3 presents the Bristlecone languages. Section 4 presents the runtime system. Section 5 presents our experience using Bristlecone to develop several robust software applications. Section 6 discusses related work; we conclude in Section 7.

2 Example

We next present a web server example that illustrates the operation of Bristlecone. This web server has specialized e-commerce functionality and maintains state to track inventory.

As the example web server executes, the conceptual state or role of objects in the computation evolves. This evolution changes the way that the software system uses the object and can change the functionality that the object supports. For example, the Java connect method changes the functionality of a Socket object in a computation: after the connect method is invoked, data can be written to or read from that Socket object.

The Bristlecone language provides *flags* to track the conceptual state of an object. The runtime uses the conceptual state of the object as indicated by the object's flag to determine which conceptual operations or *tasks* to invoke on the given object. When a task exits, it can change the values of the flags of its parameter objects.

2.1 Classes

Figure 2 gives part of the WebRequest class definition. The web server example uses instances of the WebRequest class to manage connections to the web server. The WebRequest class definition declares three flags: the initialized flag, which

```
class WebRequest {
  /* This flag indicates that the WebRequest object is in its
     initial state. */
  flag initialized;

  /* This flag indicates that the system has received a request
     to send a requested file. */
  flag file_req;

  /* This flag indicates that the connection should be logged.*/
  flag write_log;
  ...
}
```

Fig. 2. WebRequest Class Declaration

indicates whether the connection is in the initial state; the file_req flag, which indicates that the server has received a file request from this client connection; and the write_log flag, which indicates whether the connection information is available for logging.

In many cases, the developer may need to invoke a task on multiple objects that are related in some way. Bristlecone provides a tag construct, which the developer can use to group objects together. New tag instances are created using tag allocation statements of the form tag tagname=new tag(tagtype). Such a tag allocation statement allocates a new tag instance of type tagtype and assigns the variable tagname to this tag instance. The developer can tag multiple objects with a tag instance to group them, and then use that tag instance to ensure that the runtime invokes a task on two or more objects in the group defined by the tag instance. The developer can tag an object by including the statement add tagname in an object allocation site to tag the newly allocated object or in a taskexit statement to tag a parameter object. The example uses the connection tag to group a WebRequest object with the corresponding Socket object that provides the TCP connection for that web request. Tag instances can be added to objects when the object is allocated, and they can be added or removed to or from a task's parameter objects when the task exits.

2.2 Tasks

Bristlecone software systems consist of a collection of interacting tasks. The key difference between tasks and methods is that the runtime invokes a task when the heap contains objects with the specified flag settings to serve as the task's parameters. Note that while the runtime controls task invocation, tasks can call methods. The runtime uses a task's specification to determine which objects serve as the task's parameters and when to invoke the task.

Each task declaration consists of the keyword task, the task's name, the task's parameters, and the body of the task. Figure 3 gives the task declarations for the web server example. We indicate the omission of the Java-like imperative code inside the task declarations with ellipses. The first task declaration declares a task named

```
/* This task starts the web server */
task startup(StartupObject start in initialstate) {
  ...
  ServerSocket ss=new ServerSocket(80);
  Logger l=new Logger() (initialized:=true);
  taskexit(start: initialstate:=false);
}

/* This task accepts incoming connection requests and creates a
   Socket object. */
task acceptConnection(ServerSocket ss in pending_socket) {
  ...
  tag t=new tag(connection);
  WebRequest w=new WebRequest(...)(initialized:=true, add t);
  ss.accept(t);
  ...
}

/* This task reads a request from a client. */
task readRequest(WebRequest w in initialized with connection t,
    Socket s in IO_Pending with connection t) {
  ...
  if (received_complete_request)
    taskexit(w: initialized:=false, file_req:=true,
      write_log:=true);
}

/* This task sends the request to the client. */
task sendPage(WebRequest w in file_req with connection t,
    Socket s with connection t) {
  ...
  taskexit(w: file_req:=false);
}

/* This task logs the request. */
task logRequest(WebRequest s in write_log, Logger l in
    initialized) {
  ...
  taskexit(s: write_log:=false);
}
```

Fig. 3. Flag Specifications for Tasks

startup that takes a StartupObject object as a parameter and points the parameter variable start to this object. The declaration also contains a guard that states
that the StartupObject object must have its initialstate flag set before the
runtime can invoke this task. The runtime invokes the task when there exist parameter objects in the heap that satisfy the parameters' guard expressions. Before exiting,

the `taskexit` statement in the `startup` task resets the `initialstate` flag in the `StartupObject` to false to prevent the runtime from repeatedly invoking the `startup` task.

Task declarations can contain constraints on tag bindings to ensure that the parameter objects are related. A tag binding constraint contains the keyword `with` followed by the type of the tag and the tag variable. For example, the task declaration `task readRequest(WebRequest w in initialized with connection t, Socket s in IO_Pending with connection t)` ensures that the runtime only invokes the `readRequest` task on a set of parameter objects in which the first parameter object is bound to an instance of a `connection` tag and the second parameter object is bound to the same `connection` tag instance. When the task executes, the tag variable `t` is bound to that `connection` tag instance.

2.3 Error-Free Execution

Figure 4 gives a diagram of the dependences between tasks in the web server example. The ellipses in the diagram represent tasks and the edges represent the control and data dependences between the tasks. The rectangle labeled `Runtime initialization` represents the initialization performed by the Bristlecone runtime. From this diagram, we can see that the web server performs the following operations in an error-free execution (although not necessarily in this order):

1. **Startup:** When a Bristlecone program is executed, the Bristlecone runtime creates a `StartupObject` object and then sets its `initialstate` flag to true. Setting this flag causes the runtime to invoke the `startup` task in our example. Note that the code never explicitly calls a task. Instead, the runtime keeps track of the status of the flags of objects in the heap and invokes a task when the heap contains objects with the specified flag settings to serve as parameters.

   When the runtime invokes the `startup` task, the `startup` task creates a `ServerSocket` object to accept incoming connections to the web server. Next, it creates a `Logger` object to manage logging web page requests and sets its `initialized` flag to indicate that the object is ready to provide logging functionality. Finally, it resets the `StartupObject` object's `initialstate` flag to false to prevent the runtime from repeatedly invoking the `startup` task.

2. **Accepting an Incoming Connection:** At some point, the web server will receive an incoming connection request from a web browser. This causes the runtime to set the `ServerSocket` object's `pending_socket` flag to true, which in turn causes the runtime to invoke the `acceptConnection` task with this `ServerSocket` object as its parameter. The `acceptConnection` task creates a `WebRequest` object to store the connections state and calls the accept method on the `ServerSocket` to create a `Socket` object to manage communication with the web browser. Note that the `acceptConnection` task creates a new `connection` tag instance to group the `Socket` object and `WebRequest` object together by binding this tag instance to the `WebRequest` object and then passing this tag instance into the `accept` method to bind the newly created `Socket` object.

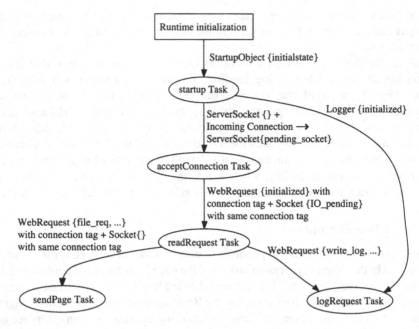

Fig. 4. Task Diagram for the Web Server

3. **Reading a Request:** After a connection is established, the client web browser sends a web page request to the server. In response to this incoming web page request, the runtime sets the Socket object's IO_pending flag to true[1], which in turn causes the runtime to invoke the readRequest task. The readRequest task checks whether the server has received the complete request.[2] If it has received the complete request, it sets both the file_req flag and the write_log flag to true and resets the initialized flag to false. These flag changes cause the runtime to eventually invoke both the sendPage and the logRequest tasks and prevents repeated invocations of the readRequest task on the same object.

4. **Sending the Page:** The runtime invokes the sendPage task when the WebRequest object's request_processed flag is set to true. The sendPage task then reads the requested file and sends the contents of the file to the client browser. The sendPage task then resets the received_request flag to false to prevent repeated invocations of the sendPage task.

5. **Logging the Request:** The runtime invokes the logRequest task when both the WebRequest object's write_log flag is set to true and the Logger object's

---

[1] The IO_pending flag is declared with the external keyword to indicate that the runtime manages setting and clearing this flag. The current runtime implementation of Bristlecone is single-threaded and, therefore, uses non-blocking I/O. Future runtime implementations will support multiple concurrent tasks and (transactional) blocking I/O [5].

[2] Note that it is possible for a client browser to split a long request across multiple packets and therefore it may be necessary to invoke the readRequest task multiple times to receive a single request.

initialized flag is set to true. The logRequest task writes a log entry to record which web page was requested. The logRequest task then resets the write_log flag to false to prevent repeated invocations of the logRequest task.

2.4 Error Handling

The Bristlecone runtime uses task specifications to automatically recover from errors. For example, suppose that the logRequest task fails while updating the Logger object. If the web server were written in a traditional programming language, it could be difficult to recover from such a failure. While some traditional languages provide exceptional handling mechanisms, using them effectively is challenging — the developer must both identify which failures are likely to occur and reason about how to recover from those failures. Alternatively, the program could simply ignore the failure. Unfortunately, if the web server were to simply ignore the failure, it could easily leave the Logger object in an inconsistent state, possibly eventually causing a catastrophic failure later.

To address this issue Bristlecone tasks have transactional semantics — upon failure, the Bristlecone runtime aborts the enclosing transaction to return the affected objects, including the Logger object, to consistent states. The runtime then records that the logRequest task failed when invoked on the combination of those specific WebRequest and Logger objects. The runtime uses this record to avoid re-executing the same specific failure. At this point, the Bristlecone runtime has returned the web server to a known consistent state and must now determine how to safely continue the web server's execution.

The traditional problem with using transactions to recover from deterministic software faults is that after aborting a transaction the software system cannot make forward progress — retrying the same transaction will cause the system to repeat the same failure. Bristlecone solves this problem by using the flags, tags, and task specifications to determine which other tasks are safe to execute after the error. Although the software fault prevents the system from logging this request, since the file_req flag is set to true, the task specification for the sendPage task allows the runtime to invoke the sendPage task. Therefore, the runtime can still safely serve the web page request.

The end result is that the software system is able to safely continue to execute even in the presence of software errors. Bristlecone is able to successfully isolate the effects of the error to a minimal part of the web server's execution — only a single task is aborted and the abort is logged. Without Bristlecone, the web server could potentially leave the Logger object in an inconsistent state, possibly causing the web server to fail to log future requests. If the web server written in a conventional language was designed to log request before serving a request, corruption of the log data structure could even cause the server to stop serving requests.

3 Language Design

The Bristlecone language includes a task specification language that describes how to orchestrate task execution. Bristlecone introduces object flags to store the conceptual

$$flagdecl := \mathbf{flag}\,flagname; \mid \mathbf{external\ flag}\,flagname;$$
$$tagdecl := tagtype\ tagname;$$
$$taskdecl := \mathbf{task}\ name(taskparamlist)$$
$$taskparamlist := taskparamlist, taskparam \mid taskparam$$
$$taskparam := type\ name\ \mathbf{in}\,flagexp \mid type\ name\ \mathbf{in}\,flagexp\ \mathbf{with}\ tagexp$$
$$flagexp := flagexp\ \mathbf{and}\,flagexp \mid flagexp\ \mathbf{or}\,flagexp \mid !flagexp \mid (flagexp) \mid flagname \mid \mathbf{true} \mid \mathbf{false}$$
$$tagexp := tagexp\ \mathbf{and}\ tagtype\ tagname \mid tagtype\ tagname$$
$$statements := \dots \mid \mathbf{taskexit}(flagactionlist) \mid \mathbf{tag}\ tagname\ =\ \mathbf{new\ tag}(tagtype) \mid$$
$$\mathbf{new}\ name(params)(flagortagactions) \mid \mathbf{assert}(expression)$$
$$flagactionlist := flagactionlist;\ name\ :\ flagortagactions \mid name\ :\ flagortagactions$$
$$params := \dots \mid \mathbf{tag}\ tagname$$
$$flagortagactions := flagortagactions, flagortagaction \mid flagortagaction$$
$$flagortagaction := flagaction \mid tagaction$$
$$flagaction := flagname := boolliteral$$
$$tagaction := \mathbf{add}\ tagname \mid \mathbf{clear}\ tagname$$

Fig. 5. Task Grammar

state of the object. Each task contains a corresponding task specification that describes which objects the task operates on, when the task should execute, and how the task affects the conceptual state of objects.

Bristlecone is an object-oriented, type-safe language with syntax similar to Java. Figure 5 presents the grammar for Bristlecone's task extensions to Java. We omit the Java-like imperative component of Bristlecone from the grammar to save space. The developer includes a flag declaration inside a class declaration to declare that objects of that class contain the declared flag. Flag declarations use the `flag` keyword followed by the flag's name. The developer may optionally use the `external` keyword to specify that the flag is set and reset by the runtime system. External flags are intended to handle asynchronous events such as communication over the Internet or mouse clicks. External flags are intended to be declared in library code with the corresponding runtime component setting and clearing the external flag.

The developer can use tags to enforce relations between the parameters of a task. The developer can create new tag instances with the `new tag` statement and a tag type. Note that there may be many instances of a given type of tag. Each different instance of that tag is distinct — objects labeled by two different instances of the same tag type are not grouped together. The developer can bind tags to objects when an object is allocated or bind or unbind tags to or from parameter objects at the task's exit.

The developer declares a task using the `task` keyword followed by the task's name, the task's parameters, and the task's code. Each task parameter declaration contains the parameter's name, the parameter's type, a flag guard expression that specifies the state of the parameter's flags, and an (optional) tag guard expression that specifies the tags the object has. The task may be executed when all of its parameters are available. A parameter is available if the heap contains an object of the appropriate type, that object's flags satisfy the parameter's guard expression, and that object contains the tag instances that the parameter's guard expression specifies. Bristlecone adds a modified `new` statement that specifies the initial flag settings and tag bindings for a newly allocated object. These take effect when the task exits. Bristlecone contains a `taskexit` statement that specifies how the task changes the state of the flags or tag bindings of its parameter objects at that task exit point.

Bristlecone contains an `assert` statement that can be used to specify correctness properties that must hold. The goal of assert statements is to provide a mechanism to detect higher-level errors that do not cause low-level exceptions. The compiled application uses the assert statements to detect errors at runtime— if it detects an error, the runtime system will invoke the recovery algorithm. These assertion statements can be used with data structure consistency checking tools [6,7], JML assertions [8], or design by contract methodologies [9]. In many cases, the assertions can be generated automatically using dynamic invariant detection tools [10,11,12].

4 Runtime System

The Bristlecone runtime is responsible for dispatching tasks, detecting errors, and recovering from errors.

4.1 Task Execution

Recall that the task specification contains guard expressions for all of the task's parameters and that the runtime executes a task when parameter objects are available that satisfy these guards. We next discuss how our implementation efficiently performs task dispatch. A naive approach to task dispatch could potentially be very inefficient — a parameter's guard expression is quantified over all objects in the heap!

Parameter Sets. The runtime maintains a *parameter set* for each parameter of each task. A parameter set contains all of the objects that satisfy the corresponding parameter's guard. For each object type, the runtime precomputes a list of parameter sets that objects of this type can potentially be a member of. When a task exit changes an object's flag settings or tag bindings, the runtime updates that object's membership in the parameter sets by traversing the precomputed list of possible parameter sets for the class and evaluating whether the object satisfies the guard expression to be a member of the parameter set.

Bristlecone also uses the parameter sets as root sets for garbage collection. Objects in Bristlecone are garbage collected if (1) the object is unreachable from any potential parameter objects and (2) the object cannot be a parameter object of any task as determined by membership in a parameter set. Note that it is possible to write incorrect programs that leave objects in task queues (e.g consider a two parameter task with tagged parameters, the program might only change one parameter object's flags leaving the other parameter object in the queue). We have developed a static analysis that the developer can use to automatically identify this type of memory leak [13].

Task Queue. A *task invocation* is a tuple that includes both a task and bindings for that task's object parameters and tag parameters. An *active task invocation* is a task invocation that satisfies all of the task specification's guards and can therefore safely be invoked by the runtime. The runtime maintains the *task queue* of all active task invocations and executes task invocations from this task queue.

Our implementation maintains a conservative approximation of the task queue — our implementation's task queue may contain a number of non-active task invocations in addition to all of the active task invocations. When an object is added to a parameter set, the implementation generates all active task invocations that bind that object to the corresponding parameter and then adds these active task invocations to the task queue. When an object is removed from a parameter set, our implementation does not remove task invocations from the task queue. Instead, before the implementation executes a task invocation in the queue, the implementation verifies that the task invocation is still active.

Iterators. We next describe how our implementation efficiently generates all active task invocations. Note that tag bindings restrict how parameter objects can be grouped together into a task invocation, and therefore, a naive implementation can needlessly explore many task invocations that do not satisfy tag guards. For example, the sendPage task in a web server may require both a WebRequest object and a Socket object tagged with the same connection instance as parameters. An efficient implementation must prune the search space of possible task invocations to avoid the overhead of exploring many task invocations that do not satisfy the tag guards.

Our implementation searches the parameter binding space using a sequence of iterators. It uses two iterator types: *object instance iterators* and *tag instance iterators*. Object instance iterators iterate over the objects in the corresponding parameter set that are compatible with all tag variable bindings made by previous iterators. In general, we expect that relatively few objects will be bound to a given tag instance and relatively few tag instances will be bound to a given object. Our implementation uses this expectation to optimize the object iterators: if the parameter has a tag guard with a tag variable that was bound by a previous tag iterator, the implementation optimizes the object iterator to only iterate over the objects bound to that tag instance. Tag iterators iterate over tag instances that are bound to an object. Tag iterators bind the tag variables in tag guards to tag instances.

As described above, our iterators use the constraints provided by the tag guards to prune the search space. Note that the order of the iterators can affect the size of the search space that the implementation explores to generate all active task invocations. Our implementation precomputes iterator orderings for each parameter of each task. The implementation uses the following ordering priority:

1. Tag iterators for tags bound to parameter objects that have already been iterated over have the highest priority. We expect that the set of iterated tag instances will be small and, therefore, tag bindings will substantially prune subsequent object iterations for parameters bound to the same tag variable.

2. Object iterators for parameters with tags that are bound by previous tag iterators.

3. Object iterators for parameters with tags that have not yet been iterated over.

4. Remaining object iterators have the lowest priority.

Task Execution Semantics. Tasks may fail either as a result of software errors, hardware failures, or user errors. If a task fails, it may leave data structures in inconsistent states. Further computation using these inconsistent data structures will likely have un-predictable and potentially catastrophic results. To avoid this problem, tasks in Bristle-cone have transactional semantics — if a task fails, the Bristlecone runtime aborts the task's transaction.

Recall that a potential issue with the use of transactions in traditional programming languages is that after the system recovers to the previous point, the system may simply re-execute the same deterministic fault and that fault will cause the system to fail repeat-edly in the same way. Bristlecone addresses this issue by using the flexibility provided by the task-based language to avoid re-executing the same failure. The Bristlecone run-time records the combination of task and parameter assignments that caused the failure and uses this record to avoid re-executing the failed combination task and parameter assignments. Instead, the runtime executes other tasks to avoid retriggering the same underlying fault.

4.2   Error Detection

Errors can cause the computation to produce incorrect results and corrupt data struc-tures, potentially eventually causing the software system to perform unacceptably. Bristlecone uses runtime checks to detect errors, enabling the software system to adapt its execution. The Bristlecone runtime uses error detection routines to trigger recovery actions.

Bristlecone uses checks to detect many software errors. For example, the Bristlecone compiler generates array bounds checks. These checks verify that the software system does not read or write past the end of arrays. The Bristlecone compiler also generates the necessary type checks for array operations and cast operations. These checks ensure that the dynamic types of objects do not violate type safety.

The runtime uses hardware page protection to perform null pointer checks. This is implemented by catching the segmentation fault signal from the operating system. These checks ensure that the software system does not attempt to dereference a null pointer or write values to the fields of a null pointer. The runtime also uses hardware exceptions to detect arithmetic errors including division by zero. Native library routines also signal errors to the runtime. For example, if a software systems attempts to send data over a closed network connection, the runtime will signal an error. Software errors can also cause a program to loop. Looping can prevent the software system from pro-viding services. It is straightforward to support developer-provided task time-outs that the runtime can use to detect looping tasks.

Bristlecone includes a runtime assertion mechanism to ensure that the execution is consistent with respect to specified properties. The developer can simply write im-perative code to check properties or can use the assertion mechanism to call exter-nal consistency checking code. This mechanism is intended to be used to ensure data structure consistency or to use techniques such as design by contract to detect higher-level errors. The mechanism can be used in conjunction with JML assertions [8], data structure consistency specifications languages [6,7], or other runtime checkable specifications.

4.3   Error Recovery

Bristlecone was designed to support reasoning about failures using the high-level task abstraction. In Bristlecone, a task either successfully completes execution or does not execute at all. The Bristlecone runtime uses a straightforward checkpointing-based transaction approach to implement this failure abstraction. Because a task can only access the part of the heap that is reachable from the task's parameter, it suffices to create a snapshot of all objects reachable from the task's parameters.

While the current prototype implementation uses a naive checkpointing-based approach, it is conceptually straightforward for future Bristlecone implementations to leverage the large body of work on efficiently implementing software or hardware transactional memory. A second issue with the current implementation is transactionalizing I/O. One solution is to use a transactional I/O API that delays the effects of I/O operations until a task commits.

If Bristlecone detects an error, it simply fails the entire task and uses this stored checkpoint to rollback the state affected by the failed task. This recovery strategy greatly simplifies reasoning about the state of the software system after a failure. Restoring state from the previous checkpoint ensures that a failure does not leave partially updated data structures in inconsistent states.

Many software errors are deterministic. If Bristlecone re-executes a failed task on the same parameters in the same state, it is likely that the task will fail again due to the same error. Bristlecone addresses this issue by maintaining a record of failures. For each failure, this record contains the combination of the failed task and the parameter assignments that failed. Bristlecone uses this record to avoid re-executing the same failures by checking reference equality of the task's parameters. The Bristlecone runtime then uses the object flags to determine which tasks can be executed even though part of the computation has failed. To better handle non-deterministic failures, the approach can be extended to automatically retry failed task executions a few times. We note that after a failure, a failed object can remain in task queue and never be garbage collected. We expect that in practice, software systems will be mostly correct and therefore a failure will be a rare occurrence and only small amounts of memory will be leaked due to failures.

4.4   Debugging and Error Logging

While it is desirable for deployed Bristlecone software systems to make every effort to avoid failures, during the development phase this behavior can mask failures and therefore complicate the debugging process. To facilitate debugging, Bristlecone can be configured to fail-fast. The fail-fast mode ensures that developers will notice software errors during the development process. Moreover, it would be straightforward to have the runtime record the state of the objects that caused the task failure by using the stored checkpoints. This information could help with debugging many software errors.

Furthermore, both developers and system administrators often want to be aware of failures in deployed systems so that the underlying software faults, if any, can be fixed. Bristlecone contains a logging mechanism that records both the task that failed and the type of error. This log ensures that developers and system administrators are aware of failures in Bristlecone software systems and gives the developers a starting point for diagnosing the cause of the failure. In some cases, developers may wish to create a custom framework to communicate failure data. It would be possible to provide an API that applications could use to query the runtime system about failures.

5 Experience

We next discuss our experiences using Bristlecone to develop three robust software systems: a web crawler, a web server, and a multi-room chat server.

5.1 Methodology

We have implemented the Bristlecone compiler. Our implementation consists of approximately 22,400 lines of Java code and C code for the Bristlecone compiler and runtime system. The Bristlecone compiler generates C code that runs on both Linux and Mac OS X. The Bristlecone runtime uses precise stop-and-copy garbage collection. The source code for our compiler and runtime is available at http://demsky.eecs.uci.edu/bristlecone/. We ran the benchmarks on a MacBook with a 2 GHz Intel Core Duo processor, 1 GB of RAM, and Mac OS X version 10.4.8.

For each benchmark, we developed two versions: a Bristlecone version and a Java version. We designed the Java versions to tolerate faults by isolating components of the computation using threads. Without the use of threads to provide fault tolerance, the Java versions would have halted with the first failure.

Our evaluation was designed to evaluate how robust each version of the benchmark applications was to the large class of faults that cause the faulty thread or task to perform an illegal operation. This fault class includes faults that cause null pointer dereferences, out of bound array index errors, failed assertions, failed data structure consistency checks, library usage errors, and arithmetic exceptions. Our evaluation simulated the effects of this fault class by randomly injecting halting failures.

We used the Bristlecone compiler to automatically insert failure injection code after each instruction. We used the Java frontend of our compiler framework to compile and instrument the Java versions. The failure injection code takes three parameters at runtime: the number of instructions to execute before considering injecting a failure, the probability that a failure will be injected, and the total number of failures to inject. For each benchmark, we selected the number of failures and then set the failure probability to ensure that the normal execution of the benchmark would reach the set number of failures.

5.2 Web Crawler

The web crawler takes an initial Uniform Resource Locator (URL) as input, visits the web page referenced by the URL, extracts the hyperlinks from the page, and then repeats this process to visit all of the URLs transitively reachable from the initial URL.

The Bristlecone version contains four tasks. The Startup task creates a Query object to store the initial URL that was specified on the command line and creates a QueryList object to store the list of URLs that the web crawler has extracted. The requestQuery task takes a newly created Query object as input, contacts the web server specified by the Query object, and then requests the URL specified by the Query object. The readResponse task reads the data that is currently available on the connection and then checks if the task has received the complete web page. The processPage task extracts URLs from the web page, checks the QueryList object to see if the crawler has seen this URL before, and then creates a Query object if the URL has not been seen before.

The Java version uses a pool of three threads to crawl web pages. Each thread dequeues a URL from a global list of pages to visit, downloads the corresponding web page, extracts URLs from the web page, and then stores any URLs it has not seen before into the global list of pages to visit.

We evaluated the robustness of the web crawler by developing both a workload and a failure injection strategy. Our workload consisted of a set of 100 web pages that each contain 3 hyperlinks to other web pages in the set. We used randomized failure injection to inject failures into the executions of the web crawlers. We injected 3 failures into each execution with each instruction having a 1 in 426,000 chance of failing.

We performed 100 trials of the experiment on each of the two versions. For each trial, we measured how many web pages the crawler downloaded. Figure 6 presents the results of the web crawler experiments. Without the injected failures, both versions download 100 web pages. With the injected failures, on average the Bristlecone version downloaded 91 out of 100 web pages and the Java version downloaded 6 out of 100 web pages. While most of the injected failures in the Bristlecone version only affect crawling a single web page, failures that are injected into either the startup task or the processing of the initial web page can affect crawling many web pages. Such failures prevent the Bristlecone version from discovering the URLs of any further pages and significantly lowered the Bristlecone version's average number of crawled pages.

	Java	Bristlecone
Web Pages Crawled (out of 100)	6	91

Fig. 6. Summary of Web Crawler Benchmark Results

5.3 Web Server

The web server benchmark contains features that are intended to model an e-commerce server. The web server maintains an inventory of merchandise and supports requests to perform commercial transactions on this inventory, including adding new items, selling items, and printing the inventory.

The Bristlecone version contains six tasks. The StartUp task creates a ServerSocket object to accept incoming connections, creates a Logger object to log the connections, and creates an Inventory object to keep track of the current inventory of merchandise. The AcceptConnection task processes incoming connections and creates a WebSocket objects to manage each connection. The

`ProcessRequest` task reads the data that is currently available from the incoming connection and then checks if the task has received the complete request. When the complete request is available, the `ProcessRequest` task parses the request to determine whether the request is an e-commerce transaction or a simple file request.

The `Transaction` task processes e-commerce transaction requests. It first inspects the request to determine whether the request is to add new items to the inventory, to make a purchase, or to display inventory and then performs the requested operation. For example, after receiving a purchase request the task looks up the price of the item in the `Inventory` object, verifies that the item is available, and if so, decrements the inventory count for the item and adds the price of the item to the sales figure.

The `SendFile` task processes file requests. It opens the requested file, reads the file's contents, and writes the file's contents to the socket. The `LogRequest` task logs all of the requests to the log file.

The Java version of the web server uses a thread to monitor for incoming connections. When a new connection arrives, the server spawns a separate connection thread for that incoming connection. The server uses a global object to store the inventory values. We used this design to isolate failures in connection threads to that specific request as much as possible. Note that failures can potentially corrupt the shared state. Note that unlike the Bristlecone version of the web server, a failure in a connection thread will prevent the server from performing any further operations for that connection including logging the request.

We evaluated the robustness of both versions of the web server by developing both a workload and a failure injection strategy. Our workload simulated web traffic to the server. Our workload consisted of a sequence of 4,400 transaction requests. Our failure injection strategy utilized the failure injection code described in the previous section.

We used failure injection to randomly inject 50 failures into the execution with a probability of injecting a failure after a given instruction of 1 in 2,100,000. We performed 200 trials on each of the two versions. For each trial we recorded whether the final inventory request was served, whether the final inventory was consistent, how many requests each version failed to serve, and how many request each version failed to log.

Figure 7 summarizes the results of the fault injection experiments with the web server. The Java version failed to serve the inventory request in 4.5% of the trials while the Bristlecone version failed to serve the inventory request in 1.5% representing a three-fold reduction in the number of failures to serve inventory requests. More importantly, while the Java version served correct inventory responses only 68.6% of the time, the Bristlecone version served the correct inventory response 100% of the time.

	Java	Bristlecone
Failures to serve Inventory Responses	4.5%	1.5%
Correct Inventory Responses	68.6%	100%
Failures to Serve Request	3.8%	2.2%
Failures to Log Request	3.9%	2.6%

Fig. 7. Summary of Web Server Benchmark Results

The Java version failed to serve 3.8% of the web requests and Bristlecone version failed to serve 2.2% of the web requests, representing a 42% reduction in the failure rate. The Java version failed to log 3.9% of the web requests and Bristlecone version failed to log 2.6% of the web requests, representing a 33% reduction in the failure rate.

5.4 Chat Server

The multi-room chat server benchmark accepts incoming connections, asks the user to create a new room or select an existing room, and then allows users to chat with other users in the same chat room. The Bristlecone version contains six tasks. The StartUp task creates a ServerSocket object to accept incoming connections and a RoomObject to manage the chat rooms. The AcceptConnection task processes incoming chat connections. It creates a ChatSocket object to manage this connection and then sends a message to ask the user to select a chat room.

The ReadRequest task reads the user's chat room selection. It reads the currently available data from the incoming connection and checks if the chat server has received the complete chat room selection. When the complete room request has been received, the ProcessRoom task processes the request. If the requested room does not exist, it creates the requested chat room. It then adds the user to the requested chat room. The chat server stores the mapping of chat room names to the set of chat room participants and for each room, maintains a list of participants in the corresponding room.

The Message task processes incoming chat messages and stores these message in a Message object. The SendMessage task then reads these Message objects, parses the messages, and then sends the messages to all of the participants in the chat room. Note that a problematic message or other error condition that causes the SendMessage task to fail will not prevent the server from processing future messages from the same connection.

The Java version of the chat server uses a thread to monitor for incoming connections. When a new connection arrives, the server spawns a separate connection thread for that incoming connection. The server uses a global object to store the set of chat rooms. Unless a failure corrupts the room list, this design isolates failures in connection threads to the specific connection. Note that unlike the Bristlecone version of the chat server, a single failure in a connection thread will prevent the server from relaying any further messages from that connection.

We evaluated the robustness of both versions by developing both a workload and a failure injection strategy. Our workload simulated multiple users chatting on the server. Our workload sent a total of 800 messages. Our failure injection strategy utilized the failure injection code described in the previous section.

We used failure injection to randomly inject 10 failures into the execution with a probability of injecting a failure after a given instruction of 1 in 270,000. We performed 100 trials on each of the two versions. For each trial we recorded how many messages were successfully transmitted.

In the presence of the injected failures, the Java version failed to deliver 39.9% of the messages and the Bristlecone version failed to deliver 19.3% of the messages, representing a factor of two reduction in the failure rate.

5.5   Experiences Writing Bristlecone Applications

We have developed Bristlecone and Java versions of three different benchmark applications. In general, we found writing Bristlecone applications to be straightforward. Typically, writing the Bristlecone version of an application simply requires reorganizing the application's code.

The Bristlecone versions of the benchmarks were approximately the same size as the Java versions. The Bristlecone version of the web crawler contained 20% fewer lines of code than the Java version, the Bristlecone version of the web server contained 2% more lines of code than the Java version, and the Bristlecone version of the chat server contained 5% more lines of code. The Bristlecone version of the web crawler was shorter because it did not require an auxiliary data structure to store queries.

One potential concern with Bristlecone is that developers may make mistakes writing the high-level task specifications that Bristlecone requires. In our experience, we have found that task declarations were in general simpler than the lower-level imperative code and therefore easy to write correctly. However, we have developed an analysis that can analyze the task specification to extract state transition diagrams for each class [13]. Developers can use these state transition diagrams to quickly visually verify that their task specifications have the desired behaviors.

5.6   Performance

Although Bristlecone uses standard compilation techniques for the body of methods and tasks, it incurs extra overheads supporting transactions and task invocation. Our current runtime implements transactions using a combination of checkpointing and single-threaded execution. We have measured the current implementation's checkpointing and task invocation overhead to be 4.7 microseconds per task invocation on a 3 GHz Pentium-D machine for a microbenchmark. Researchers have developed efficient hardware or software transactional memory implementations [14,15,16,17,18,19,20,21] that could be used to lower the transaction overhead. Static task scheduling could also be used to statically schedule a sequence of task invocations to further reduce the task invocation overhead.

5.7   Discussion

Our experience indicates that software systems developed using Bristlecone can recover from many otherwise fatal failures. The Bristlecone versions of all three benchmarks were able to recover from many more injected failures and provided a higher of quality of service than the hand-designed Java versions.

Note that these results only hold for software faults that can be automatically detected. These results can be generalized to include faults that cause the application to silently perform an incorrect action, if the developer provides Bristlecone with a runtime-checkable correctness specification the detects the error. Examples of such specifications include runtime assertions or data structure consistency specifications.

6 Related Work

We survey related work in testing, static analysis, exception mechanisms, fault toler-ance, programming languages, and software architectures.

6.1 Approaches to Reliable Software

The standard approach to dealing with software failures is to work hard to find and eliminate software faults. Approaches such as extensive testing [22], static analy-sis [23,24,25], software model checking [26], error correction codes [27], and software isolation mechanisms [28] are all designed, in part, to eliminate as many potential er-rors as possible. We expect that Bristlecone will complement these other techniques: Bristlecone will enable software systems to recover from software errors that the other techniques miss.

Many programming languages, including Java, provide an exception handling mech-anism [29]. Writing exception handlers requires developers to reason about what parts of the computation are effected by the failure and how to recover the computation from a failure — note that the failed operation may leave critical data structures in inconsis-tent, partially updated states.

Fault tolerance researchers have developed many methods to address software fail-ures. Recovery blocks allow a developer to provide multiple implementations of an al-gorithm and an acceptance test for these implementations [30]. This technique requires the developer to expend the effort to develop multiple implementations and acceptance tests. Furthermore, the recovery block technique may fail if the algorithms share a com-mon defect or if there is an error in the acceptance test.

Backward recovery uses a combination of checkpointing and acceptance tests (or error detection) to prevent a software system from entering an incorrect state [31,32,33,34]. Unfortunately, it can be difficult to handle deterministic failures us-ing backward recovery as the same software error will likely cause the software system to repeatedly fail. Forward recovery uses multiple copies of a computation to recover from transient errors [35]. Forward recovery is designed to handle intermittent failures — it cannot help deterministic errors that affect all copies of the computation.

Databases utilize transactions to ensure that the database is never left in a half-updated state by a partially completed sequences of operations [3].

In N-version programming, the developer constructs a software system out of mul-tiple, independent implementations and a decision algorithm to decide which result to use in the event of a disagreement [36]. However, N-version programming may be prohibitively expensive — it requires developers to perform the difficult task of imple-menting multiple versions that are independent enough to not share failure modes but similar enough to be comparable.

The Recovery-Oriented Computing project has explored integrating an undo operation into software systems [37] and constructing systems out of a set of individ-ually rebootable components [38]. Failure oblivious computing is designed to address memory errors in C programs [39]. It detects erroneous memory operations and discards illegal write operations and manufactures values for invalid read operations. DieHard handles similar memory errors by using replication and randomization of the memory layout [40]. Randomization probabilistically ensures that illegal memory operations can only damage data structures in one of the replicants.

Specification-based data structure repair automatically generates repair algorithms from declarative specifications [7] and imperative consistency checking code [41]. This technique enables software systems to recover from data structure consistency errors.

Researchers have used meta-languages to decompose numerical computations into parallelizable tasks [42]. This technique is applicable to parallelizable numerical computations that compute many subproblems and then combine the subproblem results to compute an overall result. If one of the subcomputations executes slowly, this approach can ignore the subcomputation. Bristlecone is designed to handle a broader class of software systems including servers, control systems, and office applications. Bristlecone can provide stronger correctness guarantees.

6.2 Related Languages

A key component of Bristlecone is decoupling unrelated conceptual operations and tracking data dependences between these operations. Bristlecone's approach contains common elements with many parallel programming paradigms [43]. Dataflow computation was one of the earlier computational models that keeps track of data dependences between operations so that the operations can be parallelized [44]. Note that dataflow languages are not designed to handle failures — a failure in a data flow program will likely cause an operation to fail to place a value in a queue, which would likely cause the application to fail catastrophically because operations that operate on multiple queues would pair the wrong values for the rest of the computation. Bristlecone ensures that failures cannot cause the wrong parameter objects to be paired together or prevent a task from operating on parameter objects that were not affected by the error.

Tuple-space languages, such as Linda [45], decouple computations to enable parallelization. The threads of execution communicate through a set of primitives that manipulate a global tuple space. While these systems were not designed to address software errors as errors in these systems can permanently halt the execution of threads, Bristlecone implements a similar technique to decouple the execution of its tasks.

The orchestration language Orc [46] specifies how work flows between tasks. Orc is designed to decouple operations and expose parallelism. Note that if an operation fails, any work (and any corresponding data) flowing through the task may be lost. Since the goal of Orc is not failure recovery, it was not designed to contain mechanisms to recover data from failed tasks. Therefore, errors can cause critical information to disappear, eventually causing the software system to fail. Bristlecone uses flags to keep track of the conceptual states (or roles) that objects are in, enabling software systems to recover data from software errors and to continue to execute successfully.

Actors communicate through messages [47,48]. Actors were originally designed as a concurrent programming paradigm. Failures may cause actors to drop messages and corrupt or lose their state. Bristlecone's objects persist across task failures and can still be used by other tasks. Moreover, state corruption in actors can cause actors to permanently crash. Since Bristlecone's tasks are stateless, a previous failure of a task does not affect future invocations of that task on different inputs.

Argus is a distributed programming language that organizes processes under guardians and isolates a process failure to the guardian under which it executes [49]. Inconsistencies could potentially cause the enclosing guardian to shut down. Argus supports failure recover through an exception handling mechanism. This approach is complementary to Bristlecone: a developer can write exception handlers for anticipated failures and Bristlecone can be used to recover from unexpected failures.

Oz is a concurrent, functional language that organizes computations as a set of tasks [50,51]. Tasks are created and destroyed by the program. A task becomes reducible (executable) once the constraint store satisfied the task's guard. Task reducibility is monotonic — once a task is reducible it is always reducible. Task activation in Bristlecone is not monotonic — the developer can temporarily disable a task when other tasks have placed objects into states that are incompatible with the task or when the effect of a task is no longer desirable. Non-monotonicity makes it straightforward for a Bristlecone application to use multiple implementations of the same functionality for redundancy. Moreover, since task creation is controlled by the program in Oz, it is more difficult to reason statically about tasks.

Concurrent Prolog is logic-based language that uses unification to prove a goal [52,53]. The proof corresponds to the execution of the program. Concurrent Prolog's guarded notation is similar to Bristlecone's flag expressions, but Concurrent Prolog's evaluation strategy starts from an end goal and reasons backwards. Concurrent Prolog programs may be able to recover from some failures by finding a different execution that reaches the same end goal. The downside is that if a failure prevents the program from completely achieving its end goal, the program will be unable to make partial progress. Bristlecone works forward and therefore can make progress even if a failure prevents the system from completely achieving its goal.

Erlang has been used to implement robust systems using a set of supervisors and a hierarchy of increasingly simple implementations of the same functionality [54]. The supervisors monitor the computation for errors. If an error is detected, the system falls back to a simpler implementation in the hierarchy. Ericsson has taken this approach in their telephone switches. Bristlecone is complementary to the supervisor approach — while the supervisor approach gives the developer complete control of the recovery process, the downside of this approach is that it requires the developer to manually develop multiple implementations of the same functionality. Bristlecone requires minimal development effort and could potentially make recovery cost effective for a larger set of applications. Furthermore, while a shared but minor fault could cause the entire Erlang implementation hierarchy to fail, in many cases Bristlecone may be able to execute around the fault and still provide nearly complete functionality.

Several research projects use type state-based approaches to automatically check that an API is used correctly [55,56]. Puntigam proposes tokens as a synchronization mechanism for object-oriented languages [57]. Bristlecone flags are similar to these mechanisms with one significant difference — Bristlecone uses flags to determine the execution of a program while these mechanisms only check (or synchronize) the actions of traditional imperative programs.

6.3 Related Software Architectures

The staged event-driven architecture (SEDA) pushes events through stages [58]. Note that this architecture was been designed for high-performance computation and not fault tolerance. An error in a stage can prevent relaying the event and cause information to be lost. Stages also have local state, therefore, corruption of this state will cause that stage to shutdown until reboot. It appears difficult to specify that an application should either execute one sequence of operations or a second sequence, but not both.

7 Conclusion

We have successfully developed several robust software systems using Bristlecone. Bristlecone software systems consist of a set of interacting tasks with each task implementing one of the conceptual operations in the software system. The developer specifies how these tasks interact using task specifications. Bristlecone uses transaction to recover data structures from task failures. Bristlecone then uses task specifications to reason about how to continue execution in the presence of a failed task. The key results in this paper include the Bristlecone language, the Bristlecone compiler and runtime, and our experience using the Bristlecone language. Our experience indicates that the task-based approach used in Bristlecone can effectively enable software systems to recover from otherwise fatal errors. Bristlecone promises to increase the robustness of software systems and to decrease the cost of developing many classes of robust software systems.

Acknowledgments. We would like to thank the anonymous referees for their insightful feedback on our paper. This work was funded in part by NSF Grant CCF-0725350 and NSF Grant CNS-0720854.

References

1. Haugk, G., Lax, F., Royer, R., Williams, J.: The 5ESS(TM) switching system: Maintenance capabilities. AT&T Technical Journal 64(6 part 2), 1385–1416 (1985)
2. Mourad, S., Andrews, D.: On the reliability of the IBM MVS/XA operating system. IEEE Transactions on Software Engineering (September 1987)
3. Gray, J., Reuter, A.: Transaction Processing: Concepts and Techniques. Morgan Kaufmann, San Francisco (1993)
4. Baker, W.O., Ross, I.M., Mayo, J.S., Stanzione, D.C.: Bell labs innovations in recent decades. Bell Labs Technical Journal 5(1), 3–16 (2000)
5. Harris, T.: Exceptions and side-effects in atomic blocks. Science of Computer Programming 58(3), 325–343 (2005)
6. Demsky, B., Cadar, C., Roy, D., Rinard, M.C.: Efficient specification-assisted error localization. In: Proceedings of the Second International Workshop on Dynamic Analysis (2004)

7. Demsky, B., Rinard, M.: Data structure repair using goal-directed reasoning. In: Proceedings of the 2005 International Conference on Software Engineering (May 2005)

8. Leavens, G.T., Leino, K.R.M., Poll, E., Ruby, C., Jacobs, B.: JML: notations and tools supporting detailed design in Java. In: OOPSLA 2000 Companion, pp. 105–106 (2000)

9. Meyer, B.: Applying Design by Contact. Computer 23(10), 40–51 (1992)

10. Demsky, B., Ernst, M.D., Guo, P.J., McCamant, S., Perkins, J.H., Rinard, M.: Inference and enforcement of data structure consistency specifications. In: Proceedings of the 2006 International Symposium on Software Testing and Analysis (2006)

11. Burdy, L., Cheon, Y., Cok, D., Ernst, M., Kiniry, J., Leavens, G.T., Leino, K.R.M., Poll, E.: An overview of JML tools and applications. International Journal on Software Tools for Technology Transfer 7(3), 212–232 (2005)

12. Ernst, M.D., Czeisler, A., Griswold, W.G., Notkin, D.: Quickly detecting relevant program invariants. In: Proceedings of the 22nd International Conference on Software Engineering (June 2000)

13. Demsky, B., Sundaramurthy, S.: Static analysis of task interactions in bristlecone for program understanding. Technical Report UCI-ISR-07-7, Institute for Software Research, University of California, Irvine (October 2007)

14. Shavit, N., Touitou, D.: Software transactional memory. In: Proceedings of the 14th ACM Symposium on Principles of Distributed Computing (August 1995)

15. Ananian, C.S., Asanović, K., Kuszmaul, B.C., Leiserson, C.E., Lie, S.: Unbounded transactional memory. In: 11th International Symposium on High Performance Computer Architecture (February 2005)

16. Harris, T., Plesko, M., Shinnar, A., Tarditi, D.: Optimizing memory transactions. In: Proceedings of the 2006 Conference on Programming Language Design and Implementation (June 2006)

17. Spear, M.F., Marathe, V.J., Schereer, W.N., Scott, M.L.: Conflict detection and validation strategies for software transactional memory. In: Proceedings of the Twentieth International Symposium on Distributed Computing (2006)

18. Harris, T., Plesko, M., Shinnar, A., Tarditi, D.: Optimizing memory transactions. In: Proceedings of the 2006 ACM SIGPLAN conference on Programming Language Design and Implementation, pp. 14–25. ACM Press, New York (2006)

19. Herlihy, M., Moss, J.E.B.: Transactional memory: Architectural support for lock-free data structures. In: Proceedings of the Twentieth Annual International Symposium on Computer Architecture (1993)

20. Kumar, S., Chu, M., Hughes, C.J., Kundu, P., Nguyen, A.: Hybrid transactional memory. In: Proceedings of the Eleventh ACM SIGPLAN symposium on Principles and Practice of Parallel Programming (2006)

21. Hammond, L., Wong, V., Chen, M., Hertzberg, B., Carlstrom, B., Prabhu, M., Wijaya, H., Kozyrakis, C., Olukotun, K.: Transactional memory coherence and consistency (tcc). In: Proceedings of the 11th Intl. Symposium on Computer Architecture (June 2004)

22. Boyapati, C., Khurshid, S., Marinov, D.: Korat: Automated testing based on java predicates (2002)

23. Ghiya, R., Hendren, L.J.: Is it a tree, a dag, or a cyclic graph? a shape analysis for heap-directed pointers in c. In: Proceedings of the 23rd ACM SIGPLAN-SIGACT symposium on Principles of Programming Languages (1996)

24. Wies, T., Kuncak, V., Lam, P., Podelski, A., Rinard, M.: Field constraint analysis. In: Proceedings of the International Conference on Verification, Model Checking, and Abstract Interpretation (2006)

25. Sagiv, M., Reps, T., Wilhelm, R.: Parametric shape analysis via 3–valued logic. In: Symposium on Principles of Programming Languages, pp. 105–118 (1999)

26. Corbett, J.C., Dwyer, M.B., Hatcliff, J., Laubach, S., Pasareanu, C.S., Robby, Zheng, H.: Bandera: Extracting finite-state models from Java source code. In: Proceedings of the 2000 International Conference on Software Engineering (2000)

27. Shirvani, P.P., Saxena, N.R., McCluskey, E.J.: Software-implemented EDAC protection against SEUs. IEEE Transactions on Reliability 49(3), 273–284 (2000)

28. Accetta, M., Baron, R., Bolosky, W., Golub, D., Rashid, R., Tevanian, A., Young, M.: Mach: A new kernel foundation for UNIX development. In: Proceedings of the USENIX Summer Conference (1986)

29. Goodenough, J.B.: Structured exception handling. In: POPL 1975: Proceedings of the 2nd ACM SIGACT-SIGPLAN symposium on Principles of programming languages (1975)

30. Anderson, T., Kerr, R.: Recovery blocks in action: A system supporting high reliability. In: Proceedings of the 2nd International Conference on Software Engineering, pp. 447–457 (1976)

31. Zhang, Y., Wong, D., Zheng, W.: User-level checkpoint and recovery for LAM/MPI. ACM SIGOPS Operating Systems Review 39(3), 72–81 (2005)

32. Plank, J.S., Beck, M., Kingsley, G., Li, K.: Libckpt: Transparent checkpointing under Unix. In: Usenix Winter Technical Conference, January 1995, pp. 213–223 (1995)

33. Chandy, K.M., Ramamoorthy, C.: Rollback and recovery strategies. IEEE Transactions on Computers C-21(2), 137–146 (1972)

34. Young, J.W.: A first order approximation to the optimum checkpoint interval. Communications of the ACM 17(9), 530–531 (1974)

35. Huang, K., Wu, J., Fernandez, E.B.: A generalized forward recovery checkpointing scheme. In: Proceedings of the 1998 Annual IEEE Workshop on Fault-Tolerant Parallel and Distributed Systems (April 1998)

36. Avizienis, A.: The methodology of n-version programming (1995)

37. Patterson, D., Brown, A., Broadwell, P., Candea, G., Chen, M., Cutler, J., Enriquez, P., Fox, A., Kcman, E., Merzbacher, M., Oppenheimer, D., Sastry, N., Tetzlaff, W., Traupman, J., Treuhaft, N.: Recovery-oriented computing (ROC): Motivation, definition, techniques, and case studies. Technical Report UCB//CSD-02-1175, UC Berkeley Computer Science (March 15, 2002)

38. Candea, G., Fox, A.: Recursive restartability: Turning the reboot sledgehammer into a scalpel. In: HotOS-VIII, May 2001, pp. 110–115 (2001)

39. Rinard, M., Cadar, C., Dumitran, D., Roy, D.M., Leu, T., William, S., Beebee, J.: Enhancing server availability and security through failure-oblivious computing. In: Proceedings of the 6th Symposium on Operating Systems Design and Implementation (December 2004)

40. Berger, E., Zorn, B.: Diehard: Probabilistic memory safety for unsafe languages. In: Proceedings of the ACM SIGPLAN 2006 Conference on Programming Language Design and Implementation (June 2006)

41. Khurshid, S., García, I., Suen, Y.L.: Repairing structurally complex data. In: Proceedings of the 12th International SPIN Workshop on Model Checking of Software (August 2005)

42. Rinard, M.: Probabilistic accuracy bounds for fault-tolerant computations that discard tasks. In: Proceedings of the 20th ACM International Conference on Supercomputing (2006)

43. Benton, N., Cardelli, L., Fournet, C.: Modern concurrency abstractions for C#. In: Proceedings of the 16th European Conference on Object-Oriented Programming (2002)

44. Johnston, W.M., Hanna, J.R.P., Millar, R.J.: Advances in dataflow programming languages. ACM Comput. Surv. 36(1) (2004)

45. Gelernter, D.: Generative communication in Linda. ACM Transactions on Programming Languages and Systems 7(1), 80–112 (1985)

46. Cook, W.R., Patwardhan, S., Misra, J.: Workflow patterns in Orc. In: Proceedings of the 2006 International Conference on Coordination Models and Languages (2006)

47. Hewitt, C., Baker, H.G.: Actors and continuous functionals. Technical report, Massachusetts Institute of Technology, Cambridge, MA, USA (1978)
48. Agha, G., Mason, I.A., Smith, S.F., Talcott, C.L.: A foundation for actor computation. Journal of Functional Programming 7(1), 1–72 (1997)
49. Liskov, B., Day, M., Herlihy, M., Johnson, P., Leavens, G., Scheifler, R., Weihl, W.: Argus reference manual. Technical Report MIT-LCS-TR-400, Massachusetts Institute of Technology (November 1987)
50. Smolka, G.: The Oz programming model. In: Proceedings of the European Workshop on Logics in Artificial Intelligence, p. 251. Springer, London (1996)
51. Mehl, M.: The Oz Virtual Machine - Records, Transients, and Deep Guards. PhD thesis, Technische Fakultät der Universität des Saarlandes (1999)
52. Shapiro, E.: The family of concurrent logic programming languages. ACM Computing Surveys 21(3), 413–510 (1989)
53. Shapiro, E.: Concurrent Prolog: A progress report. Computer 19(8), 44–58 (1986)
54. Armstrong, J.: Making Reliable Distributed Systems in the Presence of Software Errors. PhD thesis, Swedish Institute of Computer Science (November 2003)
55. DeLine, R., Fahndrich, M.: Typestates for objects. In: Proceedings of the 18th European Conference on Object-Oriented Programming (2004)
56. Bierhoff, K., Aldrich, J.: Modular typestate checking of aliased objects. In: Proceedings of the 22nd Annual ACM SIGPLAN Conference on Object-Oriented Programming Systems and Applications, pp. 301–320 (2007)
57. Puntigam, F.: Internal and external token-based synchronization in object-oriented languages. In: Modular Programming Languages, Proceedings of the 7th Joint Modular Languages Conference, pp. 251–270 (2006)
58. Welsh, M., Culler, D.E., Brewer, E.A.: SEDA: An architecture for well-conditioned, scalable internet services. In: Proceedings of the Eighteenth Symposium on Operating Systems Principles (October 2001)

Session-Based Distributed Programming in Java

Raymond Hu[1], Nobuko Yoshida[1], and Kohei Honda[2]

[1] Imperial College London
[2] Queen Mary, University of London

Abstract. This paper demonstrates the impact of integrating session types and object-oriented programming, through their implementation in Java. Session types provide high-level abstraction for structuring a series of interactions in a concise syntax, and ensure type-safe communications between distributed peers. We present the first full implementation of a language and runtime for session-based distributed programming featuring asynchronous message passing, delegation, and session subtyping and interleaving, combined with class downloading and failure handling. The compilation-runtime framework of our language effectively maps session abstraction onto underlying transports and guarantees communication safety through static and dynamic session type checking. We have implemented two alternative mechanisms for performing distributed session delegation and prove their correctness. Benchmark results show session abstraction can be realised with low runtime overhead.

1 Introduction

Communication in object-oriented programming. Communication is becoming a fundamental element of software development. Web applications increasingly combine numerous distributed services; an off-the-shelf CPU will soon host hundreds of cores per chip; corporate integration builds complex systems that communicate using standardised business protocols; and sensor networks will place a large number of processing units per square meter. A frequent pattern in communication-based programming involves processes interacting via some structured sequence of communications, which as a whole form a natural unit of *conversation*. In addition to basic message passing, a conversation may involve repeated exchanges or branch into one of multiple paths. Structured conversations of this nature are ubiquitous, arising naturally in server-client programming, parallel algorithms, business protocols, Web services, and application-level network protocols such as SMTP and FTP.

Objects and object-orientation are a powerful abstraction for sequential and shared variable concurrent programming. However, objects do not provide sufficient support for high-level abstraction of distributed communications, even with a variety of communication API supplements. Remote Method Invocation (RMI), for example, cannot directly capture arbitrary conversation structures; interaction is limited to a series of separate send-receive exchanges. More flexible interaction structures can, on the other hand, be expressed through lower-level

J. Vitek (Ed.): ECOOP 2008, LNCS 5142, pp. 516–541, 2008.

(TCP) socket programming, but communication safety is lost: raw byte data communicated through sockets is inherently untyped and conversation structure is not explicitly specified. Consequently, programming errors in communication cannot be statically detected with the same level of robustness as standard type checking protects object type integrity.

The study of *session types* has explored a type theory for structured conversations in the context of process calculi [27,12,13] and a wide variety of formal systems and programming languages. A session is a conversation instance conducted over, logically speaking, a private channel, isolating it from interference; a session type is a specification of the structure and message types of a conversation as a complete unit. Unlike method call, which implicitly builds a synchronous, sequential thread of control, communication in distributed applications is often interleaved with other operations and concurrent conversations. Sessions provide a high-level programming abstraction for such communications-based applications, grouping multiple interactions into a logical unit of conversation, and guaranteeing their communication safety through types.

Challenge of session-based programming. This paper demonstrates the impact of integrating session types into object-oriented programming in Java. Preceding works include theoretical studies of session types in object-oriented core calculi [10,8], and the implementation of a systems-level object-oriented language with session types for shared memory concurrency [11]. We further these works by presenting the first full implementation of a language and runtime for session-based distributed programming featuring asynchronous message passing, delegation, and session subtyping and interleaving, combined with class downloading and failure handling. The following summarises the central features of the proposed compilation-runtime framework.

1. *Integration of object-oriented and session programming disciplines.* We extend Java with concise and clear syntax for session types and structured communication operations. Session-based distributed programming involves specifying the intended interaction protocols using session types and implementing these protocols using the session operations. The session implementations are then verified against the protocol specifications. This methodology uses session types to describe interfaces for conversation in the way Java interfaces describe interfaces for method-call interaction.

2. *Ensuring communication safety for distributed applications.* Communication safety is guaranteed through a combination of static and dynamic validations. Static validation ensures that each session implementation conforms to a locally declared protocol specification; runtime validation at session initiation checks the communicating parties implement compatible protocols.

3. *Supporting session abstraction over concrete transports.* Our compilation-runtime framework maps application-level session operations, including delegation, to runtime communication primitives, which can be implemented over a range of concrete transports; our current implementation uses TCP. Benchmark results show session abstraction can be realised over the underlying transport with low runtime overhead.

A key technical contribution of our work is the implementation of distributed session delegation: transparent, type-safe endpoint mobility is a defining feature that raises session abstraction above the underlying transport. We have designed and implemented two alternative mechanisms for performing delegation, and proved their correctness. We also demonstrate how the integration of session types and objects can support extended features such as eager remote class loading and eager class verification.

Paper summary. Section 2 illustrates the key features of session programming by example. Section 3 describes the design elements of our compilation-runtime framework. Section 4 discusses the implementation of session delegation and its correctness. Section 5 presents benchmark results. Section 6 discusses related work, and Section 7 concludes. The compiler and runtime, example applications and omitted details are available at [26].

2 Session-Based Programming

This section illustrates the central ideas of programming in our session-based extension of Java, called SJ for short, by working through an example, an online ticket ordering system for a travel agency. This example comes from a Web service usecase in WS-CDL-Primer 1.0 [6], capturing a collaboration pattern typical to many business protocols [3,28]. Figure 1 depicts the interaction between the three parties involved: a client (Customer), the travel agency (Agency) and a travel service (Service). Customer and Service are initially unknown to each other but later communicate directly through the use of *session delegation*. Delegation in SJ enables dynamic mobility of sessions whilst preserving communication safety. The overall scenario of this conversation is as follows.

1. Customer begins an *order session s* with Agency, then requests and receives the price for the desired journey. This exchange may be repeated an arbitrary number of times for different journeys under the initiative of Customer.
2. Customer either accepts an offer from Agency or decides that none of the received quotes are satisfactory (these two possible paths are illustrated separately as adjacent flows in the diagram).
3. If an offer is accepted, Agency opens the session s' with Service and *delegates* to Service, through s', the interactions with Customer remaining for s. The particular travel service contacted by Agency is likely to depend on the journey chosen by Customer, but this logic is external to the present example.
4. Customer then sends a delivery address (unaware that he/she is now talking to Service), and Service replies with the dispatch date for the purchased tickets. The transaction is now complete.
5. Customer cancels the transaction if no quotes were suitable and the session terminates.

The rest of this section describes how this application can be programmed in SJ. Roughly speaking, session programming consists of two steps: specifying the intended interaction protocols using session types, and implementing these protocols using session operations.

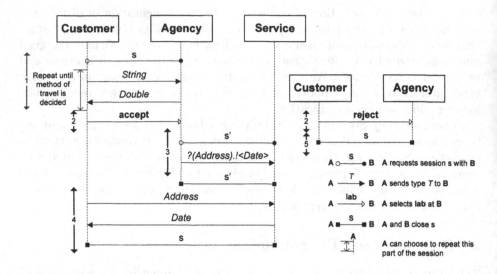

Fig. 1. A ticket ordering system for a travel agency

Protocol specification. In SJ, session types are called *protocols*, which are declared using the `protocol` keyword. The protocols for the order session (between Customer and Agency) are specified below as `placeOrder`, which describes the interactions from Customer's side, and `acceptOrder`, from Agency.[1]

```
protocol placeOrder {              protocol acceptOrder {
  begin.    // Commence session.     begin.
  ![           // Can iterate:       ?[
    !<String>. // send String          ?(String).
    ?(Double)  // receive Double       !<Double>
  ]*.                                 ]*.
  !{        // Select one of:        ?{
    ACCEPT: !<Address>.?(Date),        ACCEPT: ?(Address).!<Date>,
    REJECT:                            REJECT:
  }                                   }
}                                  }
```

Order protocol: Customer side.   Order protocol: Agency side.

We first look at `placeOrder`: the first part says Customer can repeat as many times as desired (expressed by `![..]*`), the sequence of sending a String (`!<String>`) and receiving a Double (`?(Double)`). Customer then selects (`!{...}`) one of the two options, ACCEPT and REJECT. If ACCEPT is chosen, Customer sends an Address and receives a Date, then the session terminates; if REJECT, the session terminates immediately. The `acceptOrder` protocol is *dual* to `placeOrder`, given by inverting

---

[1] SJ also supports an alternative syntax for protocols (session types) that replaces the symbols such as '!' and '?' with keywords in English [26].

the input '?' and the output '!' symbols in placeOrder, thus guaranteeing a precise correspondence between the actions of each protocol.

Session sockets. After declaring the protocols for the intended interactions, the next step is to create *session sockets* for initiating sessions and performing session operations. There are three main entities:

- *Session server socket* of class SJServerSocket, which listens for session requests, accepting those compatible with the specified protocol.
- *Session server-address* of class SJServerAddress, which specifies the address of a session server socket and the type of session it accepts; and
- *Session socket* of class SJSocket, which represents one endpoint of a session channel, through which communication actions within a session are performed. Clients use session sockets to request sessions with a server.

SJ uses the terminology from standard socket programming for familiarity. The *session sockets* and *session server sockets* correspond to their standard socket equivalents, but are enhanced by their associated session types. Client sockets are bound to a session server-address at creation, and can only make requests to that server. Session server sockets accept a request if the type of the server is compatible with the requesting client; the server will then create a fresh session socket (the opposing endpoint to the client socket) for the new session. Once the session is established, messages sent through one socket will be received at the opposing endpoint. Static type checking ensures that the sent messages respect the type of the session; together with the server validation, this guarantees communication safety. The occurrences of a session socket in a SJ program clearly delineate the flow of a conversation, interleaved with other commands.

Session server sockets. Parties that offer session services, like Agency, use a session server socket to accept session requests:

```
SJServerSocket ss_ac = SJServerSocketImpl.create(acceptOrder,port);
```

After opening a server socket, the server party can accept a session request by,

```
s_ac = ss_ac.accept();
```

where s_ac is an uninitialised (or null) SJSocket variable. The accept operation blocks until a session request is received: the server then validates that the protocol requested by the client is compatible with that offered by the server (see § 3 for details) and returns a new session socket, i.e. the server-side endpoint.

Session server-address and session sockets. A session server-address in the current SJ implementation identifies a server by its IP address and TCP port. At the Customer, we set:

```
SJServerAddress c_ca = SJServerAddress.create(placeOrder, host, port);
```

A server-address is typed with the session type seen from the client side, in this case placeOrder. Server-addresses can be communicated to other parties, allowing them to request sessions with the same server. Customer uses c_ca to create a session socket:

```
SJSocket s_ca = SJSocketImpl.create(c_ca);
```

and request a session with Agency:

```
s_ca.request();
```

Assuming the server socket identified by c_ca is open, `request` blocks until Agency performs the corresponding accept. Then the requesting and accepting sides exchange session types, independently validate compatibility, and if successful the session between Customer and Agency is established. If incompatible, an exception is raised at both parties (see 'Session failure' below).

Session communication (1): send and receive. After the session has been successfully established, the session socket `s_ca` belonging to Customer (respectively `s_ac` for Agency) is used to perform the actual session operations according to the protocol `placeOrder`. Static session type checking ensures that this contract is obeyed modulo session subtyping (see § 3.2 later).

The basic message passing operations, performed by `send` and `receive`, asynchronously communicate typed objects. The opening exchange of `placeOrder` directs Customer to send the details of the desired journey (`!<String>`) and receive a price quote (`?(Double)`).

```
s_ca.send("London to Paris, Eurostar"); // !<String>.
Double cost = s_ca.receive(); // ?(Double)
```

In this instance, the compiler infers the expected receive type from the `placeOrder` protocol; explicit receive-casts are also permitted.

Session communication (2): iteration. Iteration is abstracted by the two mutually dual types written `![...]*` and `?[...]*` [10,8]. Like regular expressions, `[...]*` expresses that the interactions in `[...]` may be iterated zero or more times; the `!` prefix indicates that this party controls the iteration, while its dual party, of type `?[...]*`, follows this decision. These types are implemented using the `outwhile` and `inwhile` [10,8] operations, which can together be considered a distributed version of the standard while-loop. The opening exchange of `placeOrder`, `![!<String>.?(Double)]*`, and its dual type at Agency can be implemented as follows.

```
boolean decided = false;             s_ac.inwhile() {
... // Set journey details.             String journeyDetails
s_ca.outwhile(!decided) {                   = s_ac.receive();
  s_ca.send(journeyDetails);            ... // Calculate the cost.
  Double cost = agency.receive();        s_ac.send(price);
  ... // Set decided to true or       }
  ... // change details and retry
}
```

Like the standard while-statement, the `outwhile` operation evaluates the boolean condition for iteration (`!decided`) to determine whether the loop continues or terminates. The key difference is that this decision is implicitly communicated to the session peer (in this case, from Customer to Agency), synchronising the control flow between two parties.

Agency is programmed with the dual behaviour: inwhile does not specify a loop-condition because this decision is made by Customer and communicated to Agency at each iteration. These explicit constructs for iterative interaction can greatly improve code readability and eliminate subtle errors, in comparison to ad hoc synchronisation over untyped I/O.

Session communications (3): branching. A session may branch down one of multiple conversation paths into a sub-conversation. In placeOrder, Customer's type reads !{ACCEPT: !<Address>.?(Date), REJECT: }, where ! signifies the selecting side. Hence, Customer can select ACCEPT, proceeding into a sub-conversation with two communications (send an Address, receive a Date); otherwise, selecting REJECT immediately terminates the session.

The branch types are implemented using outbranch and inbranch. This pair of operations can be considered a distributed switch-statement, or one may view outbranch as being similar to method invocation, with inbranch likened to an object waiting with one or more methods. We illustrate these constructs through the next part of the programs for Customer and Agency.

```
if (want to place an order) {              s_ac.inbranch() {
  s_ca.outbranch(ACCEPT) {                   case ACCEPT: {
    s_ca.send(address);                        ...
    Date dispatchDate = s_ca.receive();      }
  }                                          case REJECT: { }
} else { // Don't want to order.           }
  s_ca.outbranch(REJECT) { }
}
```

The condition of the if-statement in Customer (whether or not Customer wishes to purchase tickets) determines which branch will be selected at runtime. The body of ACCEPT in Agency is completed in 'Session delegation' below.

Session failure. Sessions are implemented within *session-try* constructs:

```
try (s_ac, ...) {
    ... // Implementation of session 's_ac' and others.
} catch (SJIncompatibleSessionException ise) {
    ... // One of the above sessions could not be initiated.
} catch (SJIOException ioe) {
    ... // I/O error on any of the above sessions.
} finally { ... } // Optional.
```

The session-try refines the standard Java try-statement to ensure that multiple sessions, which may freely interleave, are consistently completed within the specified scope. Sessions may fail at initiation due to incompatibility, and later at any point due to I/O or other errors. Failure is signalled by propagating terminal exceptions: the failure of one session, or any other exception that causes the flow of control to leave the session-try block, will cause the failure of all other ongoing sessions within the same scope. This does not affect a party that has successfully completed its side of a session, which will asynchronously leave its session-try scope. Nested session-try statements offer programmers the choice to fail the outer session if the inner session fails, or to consume the inner exception and continue normally.

Session delegation. If Customer is happy with one of Agency's quotes, it will select ACCEPT. This causes Agency to open a second session with Service, over which Agency delegates to Service the remainder of the conversation with Customer, as specified in acceptOffer. After the delegation, Agency relinquishes the session and Service will complete it. Since this ensures that the contract of the original order session will be fulfilled, Agency need not perform any further action for the delegated session; indeed, Agency's work is finished after delegation.

At the application-level, the delegation is exposed to only Agency and Service; Customer will proceed to interact with Service unaware that Agency has left the session, which is evidenced by the absence of any such action in placeOrder. The session between Agency and Service is specified by the following mutually dual protocols:

```
protocol delegateOrderSession {        protocol receiveOrderSession {
    begin.!<?(Address).!<Date>>             begin.?(?(Address).!<Date>)
}                                      }
```

Delegation is abstracted by *higher-order session types* [10,13,8], where the specified message type is itself a session type; in this example, ?(Address).!<Date>. The message type denotes the unfinished part of the protocol of the session being delegated; the party that receives the session will resume the conversation, according to this partial protocol.

In terms of implementation, delegation is naturally represented by sending the session socket of the session to be delegated. Continuing our example, Agency can delegate the order session with Customer to Service by

```
case ACCEPT: {
    SJServerAddress c_as = ... // delegateOrderSession.
    SJSocket s_as = SJSocketImpl.create(c_as);
    s_as.request();
    s_as.send(s_ac); // Delegation: Agency has finished with s_ac.
}
```

and Service receives the delegated session from Agency by

```
SJServerSocket ss_sa = SJServerSocketImpl.create(..., port)
SJSocket s_sa = ss_sa.accept();
SJSocket s_sc = s_sa.receive(); // Receive the delegated session.
```

Service then completes the session with Customer.

```
Address custAddr = s_sc.receive();
Date dispatchDate = ... // Calculate dispatch date.
s_sc.send(dispatchDate);
```

The SJ runtime incorporates two alternative mechanisms for delegation: § 4 discusses in detail the protocols by which these mechanisms coordinate the session parties involved a delegation.

The example covered in this section illustrates only the basic features of SJ. The full source code, compiler and runtime are available at [26], as well as further SJ programs featuring more complex interactions, including the implementation of business protocols from [6].

3   Compiler and Runtime Architecture

3.1   General Framework

The compilation-runtime framework of SJ works across the following three layers, in each of which session type information plays a crucial role.

Layer 1 SJ source code.
Layer 2 Java translation and session runtime APIs.
Layer 3 Runtime execution: JVM and SJ libraries.

By going through these layers, transport-independent session operations at the application-level are compiled into more fine-grained communication actions on a concrete transport. Layer 1 is mapped to Layer 2 by the SJ compiler: session operations are statically type checked and translated to the communication primitives that are supported by the session runtime interface. Layer 3 implements the session runtime interface over concrete transports and performs dynamic session typing. The compiler comprises approximately 15 KLOC extension to the base Polyglot framework [21]. The current implementation of the session runtime over TCP consists of approximately 3 KLOC of Java.

A core principle of this framework is that explicit declaration of conversation structures, coupled with the static and dynamic type-based validations, provides a basis for well-structured communication programming. We envisage programmers working on a distributed application first agree on the protocols, specified as session types, through which the components interact, and against which the implementation of each component is statically validated. Dynamic type checking, performed at runtime when a session is initiated, then ensures that the components are correctly composed: session peers must implement compatible protocols in order to conduct a conversation. The mechanisms encapsulated by the session runtime, which realise the major session operations (initiation, send/receive, branch, loop, delegation) as well as additional features (eager class downloading, eager class verification), are discussed in § 3.3 and § 4.

3.2   The SJ Compiler and Type-Checking

The SJ compiler type-checks the source code according to the constraints of both standard Java typing and session typing. Then using this type information, it maps the SJ surface syntax to Java and the session runtime APIs. Type-checking

```
begin            c.request(), ss.accept()        // Session initiation.
!<C>             s.send(obj)                      // Object 'obj' is of type C.
!<S>             s1.send(s2)                      // 's2' has remaining contract S.
?(T)             s.receive()                      // Type inferred from protocol.
!{L: T,..}       s.outbranch(L){...}              // Body of case L has type T, etc.
?{L: T,..}       s.inbranch(){...}                // Body of case L has type T, etc.
![T]*            s.outwhile(boolean expr){...}    // Outwhile body has type T.
?[T]*            s.inwhile(){...}                 // Inwhile body has type T.
```

Fig. 2. Session operations and their types

for session types starts from validating the linear usage of each session socket, preventing aliasing and any potential concurrent usage. On the basis of linearity, the type-checker verifies that each session implementation conforms to the specified protocol with respect to the message types and conversation structure, according to the correspondence between session operations and type constructors given in Figure 2. As we discuss below, protocol declarations include all the information required for static type-checking of higher-order session communication (delegation).

We illustrate some of the notable aspects of static session verification. Firstly, when session sockets are passed via session delegation and as arguments to a method call (the latter is an example of integrating session and object types), the typing needs to guarantee a correct transfer of responsibility for completing the remainder of the session being passed. For this purpose, a method that accepts a session socket argument simply specifies the expected session type in place of the usual parameter type, e.g.

```
void foobar(!<int>.?(String) s, ...) throws SJIOException {
    ... // Implementation of 's' according to !<int>.?(String).
}
```

Session passing is also subject to linearity constraints. For example, the same session socket cannot be passed as more than one parameter in a single method call. Similarly the following examples are ill-typed since they delegate the outer session s2 multiple times.

```
while(...) { s1.send(s2); }        s1.inwhile() { s1.send(s2); }
```

However, delegation of nested sessions within an iteration is typable.

The type checking in SJ fully incorporates *session subtyping*, which is an important feature for practical programming, permitting message type variance for send and receive operations as well as structural subtyping for branching and selection [12,4]. Message type variance follows the object class hierarchy, integrating object types into session typing; intuitively, a subtype can be sent where a supertype is expected. Structural session subtyping [12,3] has two main purposes. Firstly, an outbranch implementation only selects from a subset of the cases offered by the protocol, and dually for inbranch; secondly, inbranch

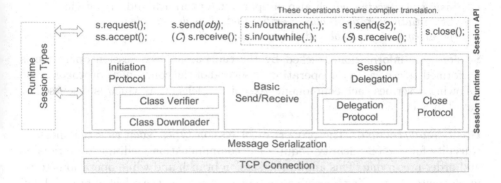

Fig. 3. The structure of the SJ session runtime

(server) and outbranch (client) types are compatible at runtime if the former supports a superset of the all cases that the latter may require. The following demonstrates these two kinds of session subtyping.

```
protocol thirstyPerson {              protocol vendingMachine {
  begin.!{                              begin.?{
    COFFEE: !<Euros>,                      COFFEE: ?(Money),
    TEA: !<Euros>                          TEA: ?(Money),
  }                                        CHOCOLATE: ?(Money)
}                                        }
...                                    }
if (...) { // Implemented...          ...
  s.outbranch(COFFEE) { ... };        s.inbranch() {
}                                       case COFFEE: { ... }
else { // ...a coffee addict.           case TEA: { ... }
  s.outbranch(COFFEE) { ... };          case CHOCOLATE: { ... }
}                                     }
```

This example demands the use of subtyping at both compilation and runtime. Message subtyping is augmented by remote class loading, discussed in § 3.3.

3.3   The Session Runtime

The structure of the session runtime is illustrated in Figure 3. The SJ compiler translates the session operations, depicted as the upper-most layer of the figure, into the communication primitives of the session APIs. The session runtime implements these primitives through a set of interdependent protocols that together model the semantics of the translated operations: these protocols effectively map the abstract operations to lower-level communication actions on a concrete transport. In this way, the session APIs and runtime cleanly separate the transport-independent session operations from specific network and transport concerns. The main components of the session runtime include:

- *basic send/receive*, which also supports in/outbranch and in/outwhile;
- the *initiation protocol*, *class verifier* and *class downloader*;
- the *delegation protocol* and *the close protocol*.

Session type information, tracked by the runtime as each session operation is performed, is crucial to the operation of several of the component protocols. The following describes each component, except for delegation which is discussed in detail in § 4.

Basic send/receive. The properties of session types, such as strict message causality for session linearity, require the communication medium to be reliable and order preserving. This allows the session branch and while operations to be implemented by sending/receiving a single message, i.e. the selected branch label or loop condition value. Basic send/receive is also asynchronous, meaning a basic send does not block on the corresponding receive; however, receive does block until a (complete) message has been received. As depicted in Figure 3, our current implementation uses TCP: each active session is supported by a single underlying TCP connection. Session messages, either Java objects or primitive types, are transmitted through the TCP byte stream using standard Java serialization. Logically, we can use other transports; little modification would be required for transports that also support the above properties, such as SCTP.

Session initiation and dynamic type checking. Session initiation takes place when the `accept` and `request` operations of a server and client interact. The initiation protocol establishes the underlying TCP connection and then verifies session compatibility. The two parties exchange the session types which they implement and which have already been statically verified, and each independently validates compatibility modulo session subtyping. If successful, the session is established, otherwise both parties raise an exception and the session is aborted. The runtime also supports monitoring of received messages against the expected type. The initiation protocol can perform eager class downloading and/or eager class verification, depending on the parameters set on each session socket.

Class downloader and class verifier. Our runtime supports a remote class loading feature similar to that of Java RMI. Remote class loading is designed to augment message subtyping, enabling the communication of concrete message types that implement the abstract types of a protocol specification. Session peers can specify the address of a HTTP class repository (codebase) from which additional classes needed for the deserialization of a received message object can be retrieved. By default, remote class loading is performed *lazily*, i.e. at the time of deserialization, as in RMI. Alternatively, a party may choose to *eagerly* load, at session initiation, all potentially needed classes as can determined from the session type of the session peer (although, due to subtyping, lazy class loading may still be required during the actual session). Similarly, session peers may choose to perform eager class verification for all shared classes at session initiation; class verification is currently implemented using the standard `SerialVersionUID` checks for serializable classes.

The close protocol. SJ does not have an explicit session close operation in its surface syntax; instead, a session is implicitly closed when a session terminates. There are essentially three ways for this to happen. The first case is when both parties finish their parts in a conversation and the session terminates normally. The second is when an exception is raised at one or both sides in an enclosing session-try scope, signalling session failure. In this case, the close protocol is responsible for propagating a failure signal to all other active sessions within the same scope, maintaining consistency across such dependent sessions. The third, more subtle, case arises due to asynchrony: it is possible for a session party to complete its side of a session before or whilst the peer is performing a delegation. § 4 discusses how the delegation and close protocols interact in this case.

4   Protocols for Session Delegation

Session delegation is a defining feature of session-based programming; transparent, type-safe endpoint mobility raises session abstraction above ordinary communication over a concrete transport. This means that a conversation should continue seamlessly regardless of how many times session peers are interchanged at any point of the conversation. Consequently, each session delegation involves intricate coordination among three parties, or even four if both peers simultaneously delegate the same session. This section examines implementation strategies for delegation, focusing on the protocols for two alternative mechanisms that realise the above requirements, and presents key arguments for their correctness.

In the rest of this section, we use the following terminology. The *s-sender* stands for session-sender; the *s-receiver* for session-receiver; and the *passive-party* for the peer of the s-sender in the session being delegated. Recall that delegation is transparent to the passive party. Our design discussions assume a TCP-like connection-based transport, in accordance with the communication characteristics of session channels: asynchronous, reliable and order-preserving.

4.1   Design Strategies for Delegation Mechanisms

Indefinite redirection and direct reconnection. One way to implement delegation is for the s-sender to indefinitely redirect all communications of the session, in both directions, between the s-receiver and passive-party. This is similar to Mobile IP [16]. The merit of this approach is that no extra actions are required on the part of the runtime of the passive-party. At the same time, communication overhead for the indirection can be expensive, and the s-sender is needed to keep the session alive even after it has been logically delegated. Thus, the s-sender is prevented from terminating, even if it has completed its own computation, and a failure of the s-sender also fails the delegated session.

An alternative strategy is to reconnect the underlying transport connections so that they directly reflect the conversation dynamics: we first close the original connection for the session being delegated, and then replace it with a connection between the new session peers (the s-receiver and the passive-party). This mechanism demands additional network operations on the part of the runtime of the passive-party: at the same time, it frees the s-sender from the obligation to indefinitely take care of the delegated session. Reconnection precludes (long-running) rerouting of messages, which can have significant cost if many message exchanges are expected after the delegation or the session is further delegated.

While indefinite redirection is relevant for fixed and reliable hosts, its design characteristics discussed above make it unsuitable for dynamic network environments such as P2P networks, Web services and ubiquitous computing, where the functionality of delegation would be particularly useful. Direct reconnection gives a robust and relatively efficient solution for such environments, and treats resources and failure in a manner that respects the logical conversation topology. For these reasons, we focus on designs based on direct reconnection in our implementation framework for delegation.

Reconnection strategy and asynchrony. The crucial element in the design of a reconnection-based delegation mechanism is its interplay with asynchronous communication (i.e. send is non-blocking). We illustrate this issue by revisiting the Travel Agency example in § 2 (see Figure 1): if Customer selects ACCEPT, Agency delegates to Service the active order session with Customer, and then Customer should send the Address to Service, its new peer. Now Customer, operating concurrently, may asynchronously dispatch the Address before or during the delegation, so that the message will be incorrectly delivered to Agency. We call such messages *"lost messages"*: because Customer and Service may have inconsistent session states at the point of delegation, performing reconnection naively can break communication safety. Thus, a reconnection-based delegation requires careful coordination by a *delegation protocol* that resolves this problem.

Two reconnection-based protocols: key design ideas. Below we outline the key design ideas of the two reconnection-based protocols implemented in the SJ runtime. They differ in their approach to resolving the issue of lost messages.

Resending Protocol: (resend lost messages after reconnection) Here lost messages are cached by the passive-party and are resent to the s-receiver after the new connection is established, explicitly re-synchronising session state before resuming the delegated session. In Travel Agency, after the original connection is replaced by one between Customer and Service, Customer first resends the Address to Service before resuming the conversation.

Forwarding Protocol: (forward lost messages before reconnection) Here the s-sender first forwards all lost messages (if any) received from the passive-party, and then the delegated session is re-established. In our example, the Address is forwarded by Agency to Service and then the original connection is replaced by the new connection between Customer and Service.

4.2 Correctness Criteria for Delegation Protocols

For a delegation protocol to faithfully realise the intended semantics of session delegation, it needs to satisfy at least the following three properties. Below

Case 1: A is performing an input operation (i.e. `receive`, including higher-order receive, `inbranch` or `inwhile`), waiting for a value, a session or a label.

Case 2: A has finished its side of s, and is waiting (in the separate close thread) for the acknowledgement.

Case 3: A is attempting to delegate another session s'' to B via s, where s'' is with the fourth party D.

Case 4: A is also delegating the session s, to the fourth party D. This case is called *simultaneous delegation*.

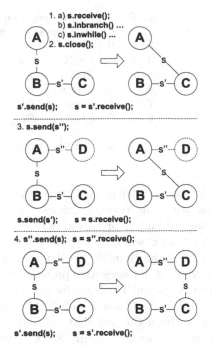

Fig. 4. The scenarios of session delegation

"control message" means a message created by the delegation protocol, as opposed to the actual "application messages" of the conversation.

P1: Linearity For each control message sent, there is always a unique receiver waiting for that message. Hence, each control message is delivered deterministically without confusion.

P2: Liveness Discounting failure, the delegation protocol cannot deadlock, i.e.:
- (Deadlock-freedom) No circular dependencies between actions.
- (Readiness) The server side of the reconnection is always ready.
- (Stuck-freedom) The connection for the session being delegated is closed only after all lost messages can be correctly identified.

P3: Session Consistency The delegation protocol ensures no message is lost or duplicated, preserving the order and structure of the delegated session.

4.3   General Framework for Reconnection-Based Protocols

We first describe the structure shared by the two delegation protocols, introducing the common notation and terminology along the way. We write A for the passive-party, B for the s-sender; and C for the s-receiver. B will delegate the session s to C via s'. In each protocol, B will inform A that s is being delegated s via a *delegation signal* containing the address of C. Eventually the original connection for s is closed and A reconnects to the delegation target C. Henceforth, we say "A" to mean the "runtime for A" if no confusion arises.

1. B→C: "Start delegation"
2.   C: open server socket on free port p_C, accept on p_C
3. C→B: p_C
4. B→A: $DS_A^B(C) = \langle ST_A^B, IP_C, p_C \rangle$
5. A→B: ACK_{AB}

6.	A:	close s	6'. B:	close s
7.	A:	connect to $IP_C : p_C$		
8.	A→C:	$LM(ST_B^A - ST_A^B)$		

Fig. 5. Operation of the resending protocol for Case 1

We assume each delegation protocol uses the same (TCP) connection for both application and control messages, as in our actual implementation. Since this means ordering is preserved between the two kinds of messages, the delegation signal from B will only be detected by the runtime of A when blocked expecting some message from B, as dictated by the session type of s. The subsequent behaviour of the delegation protocols depends on what A was originally expecting this input to be. There are four cases, as illustrated in Figure 4 (the first picture corresponds to Cases 1 and 2, the second Case 3 and the third Case 4). Case 3 comes from the fact that delegating a session is a compound operation that contains a blocking input. Since A has to be waiting for an input to detect the delegation signal, we need not consider the cases where A is performing an atomic output operation (ordinary send, outbranch or outwhile).

As an illustration, we return to Travel Agency: Customer is attempting to receive a Date (from Agency) when it detects the delegation signal, hence this is an instance of Case 1. Taking Case 1 as the default case for the purposes of this discussion, we shall illustrate the operation of the resending and forwarding protocols in § 4.4 and § 4.5. The remaining three cases are outlined in § 4.6.

4.4 Resending Protocol

The operation of the resending protocol for Case 1, as implemented given our existing design choices, is given in Figure 5. The key feature of this protocol is the use of session types at runtime to track the progress of the two peers of the delegated session: this makes it possible to exactly identify the session view discrepancy ("the lost messages") and re-synchronise the session.

The first phase of the protocol runs from Step 1 to Step 5, which delivers the information needed for reconnection and resending to the relevant parties. In Step 1, B informs C that delegation is happening. In Step 2, C binds a new ServerSocket to a fresh local port p_C for accepting the reconnection, and in Step 3, C tells B the value of p_C. In Step 4, B sends the delegation signal (for target C), denoted $DS_A^B(C)$, to A. As stated, this signal contains the runtime session type of the session being delegated, from B's perspective, denoted ST_A^B. As a result A can now calculate the difference between its view and B's view for this session. The delegation signal also contains the IP address and open port of the

1. B→C: "Start delegation"
2.   C: *open server socket on free port* p_C
3. C→B: p_C
4. B→A: $DS_A^B(C) = \langle IP_C, p_C \rangle$
5. A→B: ACK_{AB} 5'.   B: enter f/w mode
6.   A: close s 6'. B→C: $\tilde{V}{::}ACK_{AB}$
7.   A: connect to $IP_C{:}p_C$ 7'.   B: exit f/w mode   7". C: buffer $\tilde{V}$
                            8'.   B: close s 8". C: accept on p_C

Fig. 6. Operation of the forwarding protocol for Case 1

delegation target, IP_C and p_C. In Step 5, A sends an acknowledgement ACK_{AB} to B. This concludes the first phase.

The second phase performs the actual reconnection and lost message resending. Firstly, in Step 6 and Step 6', A (immediately after sending ACK_{AB}) and B (after receiving it) close their respective socket endpoints for the original session connection: any lost messages at B are simply discarded. In Step 7, A connects to C to establish the new connection for the delegated session (C has been waiting for reconnection at p_C since Step 2). In Step 8, A resends the lost messages, denoted $LM(ST_B^A - ST_A^B)$, to C based on the session type difference calculated above (after Step 4). A retrieves the lost messages from its cache of previously sent messages (maintained by each party), and C buffers them. In our running example, the runtime type ST_A^B (the view from B) is $\ldots!\{\texttt{ACCEPT}{:}!\texttt{<Address>}\}$, and the runtime type ST_B^A (the view from A) is $\ldots?\{\texttt{ACCEPT}{:}\ \}$. Hence the difference $ST_A^B - ST_B^A$ is $!\texttt{<Address>}$, and the corresponding message is resent after the reconnection. After Step 8, A and C can resume the session as normal.

4.5   Forwarding Protocol

In the forwarding protocol, A does not have to concern itself about lost messages as they are automatically forwarded from B (the old endpoint of the delegated session) to C (the new endpoint). The protocol works as listed in Figure 6.

The first phase of the protocol (Step 1 to Step 5) is precisely as in the resending protocol, except that the delegation signal in Step 4 no longer needs to carry the runtime session type ST_A^B.

In the second phase, reconnection is attempted in parallel with the lost message forwarding. In Step 5', which immediately follows Step 4 (sending the delegation signal to A), B starts forwarding to C all messages that have arrived or are newly arriving from A. The actual delivery is described in Step 6' where $\tilde{V}$ denotes all messages received by B from A up to ACK_{AB}, i.e. the "lost messages". The delegation acknowledgment ACK_{AB} sent by A in Step 5 signifies end-of-forwarding when it is received and forwarded by B to C in Step 6': B knows that A aware of the delegation and will not send any more messages (to B), and hence ends forwarding in Step 7'. $\tilde{V}$ is buffered by C to be used when the delegated session is resumed.

In Step 6, A closes its endpoint to the connection with B after sending ACK_{AB} in Step 5; since B may still be performing the forwarding at this point, the opposing endpoint is not closed until Step 8'. In Step 7, A requests the new connection to C using the address and port number received in Step 4. However, C does not accept the reconnection until Step 8" (p_C is open so A blocks) after receiving all the forwarded messages in Step 7". As in the resending protocol, after the session is resumed C first processes the buffered messages $\tilde{V}$ before any new messages from A, preserving message order. Note Steps 5-7, Steps 5'-8' (after Step 4) and Steps 7"-8" (after Step 6') can operate in parallel with two cross-dependencies, 6' on 5 and 8" on 7.

4.6   Outline of Delegation Cases 2, 3 and 4

We summarise how the two protocols behave for the remaining three cases of the description in § 4.3. The full protocol specifications are found at [26]. In both protocols, each of the remaining cases is identical to Case 1 in most parts: the key idea is that the role of the delegation acknowledgement ACK_{AB} in Case 1 is now played by some other control signal in each case.

In *Case 2*, A sends a special signal FIN_{AB} (due to the close protocol) to let B know that it has completed its side of the session. Basically FIN_{AB} signifies to B (instead of ACK_{AB}) that the original session connection can be closed immediately (hence Step 5 is not needed).

In *Case 3*, A is the s-sender for another session s'' between A and the fourth party D (the passive-party of s''). In this case, B receives a "Start delegation" signal (for the delegation of s'') from A. In the resending protocol, this signal is resent with $LM(ST_B^A - ST_A^B)$ at Step 8 to C in order to start the subsequent run of the delegation protocol between A and D. In the forwarding protocol, this message simply replaces ACK_{AB} as an end-of-forwarding signal after being forwarded by B, and at the same time alerts C to the subsequent delegation.

In *Case 4*, instead of ACK_{AB} at Step 5, B receives $DS_B^A(D)$ from A. In the resending protocol, C then buffers the lost messages from A, closes this intermediate connection, and reconnects to the port at which D is waiting (C gets the address of D from A). In the the forwarding protocol, the behaviour is similar to that for *Case 3*.

4.7   Correctness of the Delegation Protocols

Below we briefly outline the key arguments for the correctness of our delegation protocols with respect to the three properties **P1-3** in § 4.2, focusing on *Case 1* of the resending protocol. For details and the remaining cases, see [26].

Property **P1** is obvious from the description of the protocol. For **P2**, we first observe concurrent executions only exist between Step 6-8 and Step 6'. Note that deadlock arises only when a cycle (like A→B and B→A) is executed concurrently, which is impossible from the protocol definition. Readiness holds since the connection to p_C (Step 7) takes place after its creation (as Step 2). Stuck-freedom holds since Steps 6 and 6' take place after all operations are completed between A and B, ensured by ACK_{AB}. The key property for the correctness argument is **P3**. This holds since the sending action from C takes place after the lost messages from Step 8 are stored at C, which in turn holds since the sending action from C uses the same port p_C. Hence the order of session messages is preserved before and after the protocol.

5   SJ Runtime Performance

The current implementation of SJ [26] supports all of the features presented in this paper, including implementations of both the forwarding and resending protocols in § 4, called SJFSocket and SJRSocket. This section presents some performance measurements for the current SJ runtime implementation, focusing on micro benchmarking of session initiation and the session communication primitives. Although the current implementation is as yet unoptimised, these preliminary benchmark results demonstrate the feasibility of session-based communication and the SJ runtime architecture: SJFSocket communication incurs little overhead over the underlying transport, and SJRSocket, despite additional costs, is competitive with RMI. The full source code for the benchmark applications and the raw benchmark data are available from the SJ homepage [26].

The micro benchmark plan. The benchmark applications measure the time to complete a simple two-party interaction: the protocols respectively implemented by the 'Server' and 'Client' sides of the interaction are

```
begin.?[!<MyObject>]*              begin.![?(MyObject)]*
```

which basically specify that the Server will repeatedly send objects of type MyObject for as long as the Client wishes. Recall that session-iteration involves the implicit communication of a boolean primitive from the outwhile party (here, the Client) to its peer. Although this protocol does not feature branching, the SJ branch operations (communication of the selected label) are realised as the send/receive of an ordinary object (String), hence perform accordingly.

The implementation of these protocols in SJ is straightforward, and similarly for the "untyped" TCP socket implementation in standard Java (referred to as Socket), which mimics the semantics of the session-iteration operations using while-loops (with explicit communication of the boolean control value). Socket serves as the base case (i.e. direct usage of the underlying transport) for comparison with the SJ sockets. For the RMI implementation (RMI), the session-iteration is simulated by making consecutive calls to a remote server method with signature MyObject getMyObject(boolean b) (the boolean is passed to attain the same communication pattern). Henceforth, a session of *length* n means that the session-iteration is repeated n times; for RMI, n remote calls.

The benchmark applications specifically measure the time taken for the Client to initiate a session with the Server and finish the session-iteration. For Socket, session initiation simply means establishing a connection to the server. For RMI, the connection is established implicitly by the first remote call (RMI "reuses" a

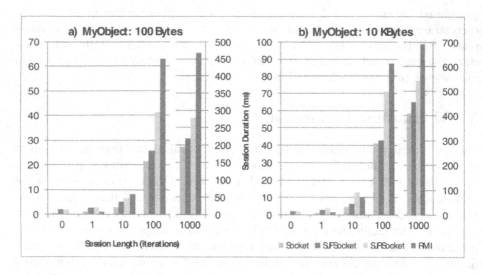

Fig. 7. Benchmark results for MyObject sizes 100 Bytes and 10 KBytes

server connection for subsequent calls), but we do not include the cost of looking up the remote object in the RMI registry. Each run of a session is preceded by a dummy run of length one: this helps to stabilise the Server and Client processes before the actual benchmark run, and removes certain factors from the results such as class loading and verification. The RMI dummy run calls an instance of the remote object hosted on the local machine, to avoid creating a connection to the Server before the actual benchmark run.

The benchmarks were conducted using MyObject messages of serialized size 100 Bytes (for reference, an Integer serializes to 81 Bytes) and 10 KBytes for sessions of length 0, 1, 10, 100 and 1000. We recorded the results from repeating each benchmark configuration 1000 times in low ($\sim$0.1ms) and higher latency ($\sim$10ms) environments. Nagle's algorithm was disabled (TCP_NODELAY is set to true) for these benchmarks, for both the standard and SJ sockets. RMI was run using the default settings for each platform. Runtime state tracking is disabled (as a default) for SJFSocket.

The low latency environment consisted of two physically neighbouring PCs (Intel Pentium 4 HT 3 GHz, 1 GB RAM) connected via gigabit Ethernet, running Ubuntu 7.04 (Linux 2.6.20.3) with Java compiler and runtime (Standard Edition) version 1.6.0. Latency between the two machines was measured using ping (56 Bytes) to be on average 0.10 ms. The higher latency benchmarks were recorded using one of the above machines as the Client (the timer) and a Windows XP PC (SP2, Intel Core Duo 3 GHz, 2 GB RAM) with an average communication latency (56 Byte ping) of 8.70 ms.

Results. We first look at the low latency results: minimising the latency factor emphasises the internal overheads of the SJ runtime. Graphs a) and b) in Figure 7 compare the results from the four benchmark applications over each session length for each of the two MyObject sizes.

The results show that SJFSocket exhibits low runtime overhead in relation to Socket, decreasing for longer sessions. Shorter sessions increase the relative cost of SJ session initiation, roughly 2ms in the measured environment. Note session initiation for both Socket and the session sockets involve establishing a TCP connection, but the SJ sockets do extra work to check session compatibility. SJRSocket is slower than SJFSocket: the cost for session initiation is the same for both, but SJRSocket employs (1) runtime state tracking and (2) a different routine for serialization and communication (in order to retain serialized messages for the sent message cache, § 4). In fact, comparison of SJFSocket and SJRSocket using sessions that communicate only primitive data types [26] show that most of the overhead comes from (2) with runtime state tracking incurring little overhead. Despite these additional overheads, SJRSocket performs better than RMI for longer sessions.

The results from the higher latency benchmarks [26] also support these observations. We note a few additional points. The cost of session initiation, which involves sending an extra message, increases accordingly. As before, the relative overheads of the SJ sockets become smaller for longer sessions, although higher communication latency appears to ameliorate these costs at a higher rate. This means that the latency factor dominates the overheads of SJ, from both internal computation and additional communication costs (such as SJ message headers and extra control messages), under the present benchmark parameters. Indeed, the differences in performance over the longer sessions are minimal.

Travel Agency benchmarks. Preliminary performance evaluation of session delegation has also been conducted based on the Travel Agency example (§ 2). We measured the time required to complete the transaction (10 iterations of the order-quote exchange and Customer always accepts the quote) from the point of view of Customer. For comparison, a purely forwarding-based (i.e. no reconnection) equivalent was implemented using standard sockets. Unlike the above benchmarks, we now include the time needed to create the SJ socket objects and close the session (in the SJ runtime, close involves spawning a new thread, § 4). The results for Socket, SJFSocket and SJRSocket using three machines in the low latency environment (same specifications) were 3.8, 7.3 and 9.1 ms respectively. We believe these figures are reasonable, given the overheads of delegation (extra control messages and coordination, the cost of reconnection, resending by SJRSocket, and others), and that the delegation mechanisms, like much of the current runtime implementation, are as yet unoptimised. Note that Travel Agency is in fact close to a worst case scenario for this kind of delegation benchmark: as discussed in § 4, reconnection-based protocols are advantageous when there are a substantial number of communications after the delegation and/or when the session is further delegated, especially if latency is high.

Potential optimisations. Firstly, many optimisations are possible exploiting the information on conversation structure and message types given by session types, including session-typed message batching (possibly based on the size of the underlying transport unit), the promotion of independent send types (pushing asynchronous sends earlier), tuning of I/O buffer sizes, and others. Knowing the expected message types in advance can also be used to reduce the amount of meta data (e.g. SJ message headers, class tags embedded by serialization) for basic message passing. Secondly, sessions peers can exchange extra runtime information at session initiation; for example, no delegation means SJRSocket would not need to cache sent messages. We also envisage situations where the duality check may only be needed whilst an application is being developed and tested: once the application has been deployed in some trusted environment (e.g. a company using an internal messaging system), this check can be disabled.

6   Related Work

Language design for session types. An application of session types in practice is found in Web services. Due to the need for static validation of the safety of business protocols, the Web Services Choreography Description Language (WS-CDL) is developed by a W3C standardisation working group [24] based on a variant of session types. WS-CDL descriptions are implemented through communications among distributed end-points written in languages such as Java or WS4-BPEL. [3,6,14] studied the principles behind deriving sound and complete implementations from CDL descriptions. Session types are also employed as a basis for the the standardisation of financial protocols in UNIFI (ISO20022) [28]. We plan to use our language and compiler-runtime framework as part of the implementation technologies for these standards.

An embedding of session programming in Haskell is studied in [18]. More recently, [22] proposed a Haskell monadic API with session-based communication primitives, encoding session types in the native type system. A merit of these approaches is that type checking for session types can be done by that for Haskell. Type inference for session types without subtyping has been implemented for C++ [7]. In these works, a session initiation (compatibility check) for open and distributed environments are not considered, and session delegation is not supported; type-safe delegation may be difficult to realise since their encoding does not directly type I/O channels.

Fähndrich et. al [11] integrate a variant of session types into a derivative of C♯ for systems programming in shared memory uni/multiprocessor (non-distributed) environments, allowing interfaces between OS-modules to be described as message passing conversations. Their approach is based on a combination of session types with ownership types to support message exchange via a designated heap area (shared memory): session communication becomes basic pointer rewriting, obtaining efficiency suitable for low-level system programming. From the viewpoint of abstraction for distributed programming, their design lacks essential dynamic type checking elements and support for delegation, and other features such as session subtyping. In spite of differences between the target environments and design directions, our works both demonstrate the significant impact the introduction of session types can have on abstraction and implementation in objected-oriented languages.

A framework based on F# for cryptographically protecting session execution from both external attackers and malicious principals is studied in [9]. Their session specifications model communication sequences between two or more network peers (*roles*). The description is given as a graph whose nodes represent the session state of a role, and edges denote a dyadic communication and control flow. Their aim is to use such specifications for modelling and validation rather than direct programming; their work does not consider features such as delegation or the design of a session runtime architecture.

Language design based on process calculi. The present work shares with many recent works its direction towards well-structured communication-based programming using types. Pict [20] is a programming language based on the π-calculus with linear and polymorphic types. Polyphonic C♯ [2] is based on the Join-calculus and employs a type discipline for safe and sophisticated object synchronisation. Acute [1] is an extension of OCaml for coherent naming and type-safe version change of distributed code. The Concurrency and Coordination Runtime (CCR) [5] is a port-based concurrency library for C♯ for component-based programming, whose design is based on Poly♯.

Occam-pi [19,29] is a highly efficient concurrent language based on channel-based communication, with syntax based on both Hoare's CSP (and its practical embodiment, Occam) and the π-calculus. Designed for systems-level programming, Occam-pi supports the generation of more than million threads for a single processor machine without efficiency degradation, and can realise various locking and barrier abstractions built from its highly efficient communication primitives. DirectFlow [17] is a domain specific language which supports stream processing with a set of abstractions inspired by CSP, such as filters, pipes, channels and duplications. DirectFlow is not a stand-alone programming language, but is used via an embedding into a host language for defining data-flow between components. In both languages, typing of a communication unit larger than a series of individual communications or compositions is not guaranteed.

X10 [30] is a typed concurrent language based on Java, and designed for high-performance computing. Its current focus is on global, distributed memory, with sharing carefully controlled by X10's type system. A notable aspect is the introduction of distributed locations into the language, cleanly integrated with a disciplined thread model. The current version of the language does not include first-class communication primitives.

None of the above works use conversation-based abstraction for communication programming, hence neither typing disciplines that can guarantee communication safety for a conversation structure, nor the associated runtime for realising the abstraction are considered. The interplay between session types and the design elements of the above works is an interesting future topic.

7 Conclusion and Future Work

There is a strong need to develop structured, higher-level and type-safe abstractions and techniques for programming communications and interaction. This paper has presented the design and implementation of an extension of Java to support session-based, distributed programming. Building on the preceding theoretical studies of session types in object-oriented calculi [10,8], our contribution furthers these and other works on session types with a concrete, practical language that supports the wide range of session-programming features presented. Communication safety for distributed applications is guaranteed through a combination of static and dynamic type checking. We implemented two alternative mechanisms for performing type-safe session delegation, with correctness arguments, and showed that session types can be used to augment existing features such as remote class loading.

We believe our language exhibits a natural and practical integration of session type principles and object-oriented programming. The session-programming constructs and accompanying methodology, based on explicit specification of protocols followed by implementation through these constructs (with static type checking), aid the writing of communications code and improve readability. Our experience so far indicates that session types can describe a diverse range of structured interaction patterns [6,28]; further examples, such as file-transfer and chat applications, are available from [26]. Future work includes detailed analysis of how session-based programming can impact on the development of more complicated and large-scale applications. Integration of session-based programming with such languages as [30,19,17,25] is also an open subject.

Preliminary benchmark results demonstrate the feasibility of session-based communication and our session runtime architecture. Static and dynamic performance optimisations that utilise session type information (see §5) are a topic for future investigation. Other interesting directions include the incorporation of transports other than TCP into the session runtime, possibly coupled with the design of alternative abstractions to (session) socket. Session parties can dynamically monitor messages received against the expected type according to agreed protocol: however, our current work does not yet tackle deeper security issues involving malicious peers [9].

This work and future directions, combined with theories from [3,15], are being developed as a possible foundation for public standardisations of programming and execution for Web services [6] and financial protocols [28,23].

Acknowledgements. We thank the reviewers and Susan Eisenbach for their useful comments, Fred Van Den Driessche for his contributions to the implementation, and our academic and industry colleagues for their stimulating conversations. The work is partially supported by EPSRC GR/T04724, GR/T03208, GR/T03215, EP/F002114 and IST2005-015905 MOBIUS.

References

1. Acute homepage, http://www.cl.cam.ac.uk/users/pes20/acute
2. Benton, N., Cardelli, L., Fournet, C.: Modern concurrency abstractions for C#. ACM Trans. Program. Lang. Syst. 26(5), 769–804 (2004)

3. Carbone, M., Honda, K., Yoshida, N.: Structured Communication-Centred Programming for Web Services. In: De Nicola, R. (ed.) ESOP 2007. LNCS, vol. 4421, pp. 2–17. Springer, Heidelberg (2007)

4. Carbone, M., Honda, K., Yoshida, N., Milner, R., Brown, G., Ross-Talbot, S.: A theoretical basis of communication-centred concurrent programming. Published in [6] (2006)

5. CCR: An Asynchronous Messaging Library for C#2.0, http://channel9.msdn.com/wiki/default.aspx/Channel9.ConcurrencyRuntime

6. W3C Web Services Choreography, http://www.w3.org/2002/ws/chor/

7. Collingbourne, P., Kelly, P.: Inference of session types from control flow. In: FESCA. ENTCS. Elsevier, Amsterdam (to appear, 2008)

8. Coppo, M., Dezani-Ciancaglini, M., Yoshida, N.: Asynchronous Session Types and Progress for Object-Oriented Languages. In: Bonsangue, M.M., Johnsen, E.B. (eds.) FMOODS 2007. LNCS, vol. 4468, pp. 1–31. Springer, Heidelberg (2007)

9. Corin, R., Denielou, P.-M., Fournet, C., Bhargavan, K., Leifer, J.: Secure Implementations for Typed Session Abstractions. In: CFS 2007. IEEE-CS Press, Los Alamitos (2007)

10. Dezani-Ciancaglini, M., Mostrous, D., Yoshida, N., Drossopoulou, S.: Session Types for Object-Oriented Languages. In: Thomas, D. (ed.) ECOOP 2006. LNCS, vol. 4067, pp. 328–352. Springer, Heidelberg (2006)

11. Fähndrich, M., Aiken, M., Hawblitzel, C., Hodson, O., Hunt, G.C., Larus, J.R., Levi, S.: Language Support for Fast and Reliable Message-based Communication in Singularity OS. In: EuroSys 2006. ACM SIGOPS, pp. 177–190 (2006)

12. Gay, S., Hole, M.: Subtyping for Session Types in the Pi-Calculus. Acta Informatica 42(2/3), 191–225 (2005)

13. Honda, K., Vasconcelos, V.T., Kubo, M.: Language primitives and type disciplines for structured communication-based programming. In: Hankin, C. (ed.) ESOP 1998 and ETAPS 1998. LNCS, vol. 1381, pp. 22–138. Springer, Heidelberg (1998)

14. Honda, K., Yoshida, N., Carbone, M.: Web Services, Mobile Processes and Types. The Bulletin of the European Association for Theoretical Computer Science February(91), 165–185 (2007)

15. Honda, K., Yoshida, N., Carbone, M.: Multiparty Asynchronous Session Types. In: POPL 2008, pp. 273–284. ACM Press, New York (2008)

16. IETF. Mobility for IPv4, http://dret.net/rfc-index/reference/RFC3344

17. Lin, C.-K., Black, A.P.: DirectFlow: A domain-specific language for information-flow systems. In: Ernst, E. (ed.) ECOOP 2007. LNCS, vol. 4609, pp. 299–322. Springer, Heidelberg (2007)

18. Neubauer, M., Thiemann, P.: An Implementation of Session Types. In: Jayaraman, B. (ed.) PADL 2004. LNCS, vol. 3057, pp. 56–70. Springer, Heidelberg (2004)

19. Occam-pi homepage, http://www.occam-pi.org/

20. Pierce, B.C., Turner, D.N.: Pict: A programming language based on the pi-calculus. In: Plotkin, G., Stirling, C., Tofte, M. (eds.) Proof, Language and Interaction: Essays in Honour of Robin Milner. MIT Press, Cambridge (2000)

21. Polyglot homepage, http://www.cs.cornell.edu/Projects/polyglot/

22. Sackman, M., Eisenbach, S.: Session types in Haskell, draft (2008)

23. Scribble Project homepage, http://www.scribble.org

24. Sparkes, S.: Conversation with Steve Ross-Talbot. ACM Queue 4(2) (March 2006)
25. Spring, J.H., Privat, J., Guerraoui, R., Vitek, J.: StreamFlex: high-throughput stream programming in Java. In: OOPSLA, pp. 211–228. ACM Press, New York (2007)
26. SJ homepage, http://www.doc.ic.ac.uk/~rh105/sessionj.html
27. Takeuchi, K., Honda, K., Kubo, M.: An Interaction-based Language and its Typing System. In: Halatsis, C., Philokyprou, G., Maritsas, D., Theodoridis, S. (eds.) PARLE 1994. LNCS, vol. 817, pp. 398–413. Springer, Heidelberg (1994)
28. UNIFI. International Organization for Standardization ISO 20022 UNIversal Financial Industry message scheme (2002), http://www.iso20022.org
29. Welch, P., Barnes, F.: Communicating Mobile Processes: introducing occam-pi. In: Abdallah, A.E., Jones, C.B., Sanders, J.W. (eds.) Communicating Sequential Processes. LNCS, vol. 3525, pp. 175–210. Springer, Heidelberg (2005)
30. X10 homepage, http://x10.sf.net

ReCrash: Making Software Failures Reproducible by Preserving Object States

Shay Artzi, Sunghun Kim, and Michael D. Ernst

MIT Computer Science and Artificial Intelligence Laboratory
Cambridge, MA, 02139, USA
{artzi, hunkim, mernst}@csail.mit.edu

Abstract. It is very hard to fix a software failure without being able to reproduce it. However, reproducing a failure is often difficult and time-consuming. This paper proposes a novel technique, ReCrash, that generates multiple unit tests that reproduce a given program failure. During every execution of the target program, ReCrash stores partial copies of method arguments in memory. If the program fails (e.g., crashes), ReCrash uses the saved information to create unit tests reproducing the failure.

We present ReCrashJ, an implementation of ReCrash for Java. ReCrashJ reproduced real crashes from Javac, SVNKit, Eclipsec, and BST. ReCrashJ is efficient, incurring 13%–64% performance overhead. If this overhead is unacceptable, then ReCrashJ has another mode that has negligible overhead until a crash occurs and 0%–1.7% overhead until the crash occurs for a second time, at which point the test cases are generated.

Keywords: Fault, bug, crash, failure, object, reproducing, capture, replay, test generation.

1 Introduction

It is difficult to find and fix a software problem, and to verify the solution, without the ability to reproduce it. As an example, consider bug #30280 from the Eclipse bug database (Figure 1). A user found a crash and supplied a back-trace, but neither the developer nor the user could reproduce the problem. Two days after the bug report, the developer finally reproduced the problem; four minutes after reproducing the problem, the developer fixed it.

Our work aims to reduce the amount of time it takes a developer to reproduce a problem. Suppose that the user had been using a ReCrash-enabled version of Eclipse. As soon as the Eclipse crash occurred, ReCrash would have generated a set of unit tests (Figure 2), each of which reproduces the problem. The user could have sent these test cases with the initial bug report, eliminating the two-day delay for the developer to reproduce the problem.

Upon receiving the test cases, the developer could run them under a debugger to examine fields, step through execution, or otherwise investigate the cause of failure. (The readability of the test case is secondary to reproducibility; a test need not be readable, nor end-to-end, to be useful.) The developer can use the same test to verify the bug fix.

J. Vitek (Ed.): ECOOP 2008, LNCS 5142, pp. 542–565, 2008.

2003-01-27 08:01 U: I found crash (here is the back-trace)
2003-01-27 08:26 D: Which build are you using?
                                  Do you have a test-case to reproduce?
2003-01-27 08:39 D: Which JDK are you using?
2003-01-28 13:06 U: I'm running eclipse 2.1, ...
                                  I was not able to reproduce the crash
2003-01-29 04:28 D: Thanks for clarification ...
2003-01-29 04:33 D: Reproduced
2003-01-29 04:37 D: Fixed ...

Fig. 1. An excerpt of comments (`https://bugs.eclipse.org/bugs/show_bug.cgi?id=30280`) between the user (U) who reported Eclipse bug #30280 and the developer (D) who fixed it

Reproducing failures (in Java, these often result from un-handled exceptions) can be difficult for the following reasons.

Nondeterminism. A problem that depends on timing (e.g., context switching), memory layout (e.g., hash codes), or random number generators will manifest itself only rarely. Reproducing the problem requires replacing the sources of nondeterminism with specific choices that reproduce previous behavior. As an example, consider the (somewhat contrived) RandomCrash program [30] of Figure 5.

Remote detection. A problem that is discovered by someone other than the developer who can fix it may depend on local information such as user GUI actions, environment variables, the state of the file system, operating system behavior, and other explicit or implicit program inputs. Not all dependences may be apparent to the developer or the user; many users are not sophisticated enough to gather this information; some of the information may be confidential; and the effort of collecting it may be too burdensome for the user, the developer (during interactions with the user), or both.

Test case complexity. Even if a problem can be reproduced deterministically, the exposing execution might be complex, and the buggy method might be called multiple times before the bug is triggered. A simpler test case, such as a unit test, is often faster and easier to run and understand than the execution that triggered the failure.

We propose a technique, ReCrash, that addresses these problems in many cases. ReCrash automatically converts a failing program execution into a set of deterministic and self-contained unit tests. Each of the unit tests reproduces the problem that caused the program to fail. ReCrash has two phases: monitoring and test case generation.

monitoring. During an execution of the target program, ReCrash maintains a shadow stack with an n-deep copy of the receiver and arguments to each method. From depth n on, these objects refer to the original objects on the heap (see Section 2.2.1). Thus, ReCrash exploits the object-oriented nature of the program by using objects as the unit of granularity for including or excluding values from the stored shadow stack. When the program fails (i.e., crashes), ReCrash serializes the shadow stack contents, including all heap objects referred to from the shadow stack. Heap data that was not copied to the shadow stack might have been side-effected between the point of the call and the point of the failure; this is a cause of imprecision for the ReCrash technique.

```
1  // Generated by reCrash
2  // Eclipse 2.1M4/JDK 1.4
3  //-- The original crash stack back trace for java.lang.NullPointerException:
4  //    org...QualifiedAllocationExpression.resolveType
5  //    org...Expression.resolve
6  //    ...
7  public class EclipseTest extends TestCase {
8    protected void setUp() throws Exception {
9      ShadowStackReader.readTrace("eclipse.trace");
10   }
11
12   public void test_resolveType() throws Throwable {
13     ShadowStackReader.setMethodStackItem(0);
14
15     // load receiver
16     // rec = i.new Y()
17     QualifiedAllocationExpression rec =
18       (QualifiedAllocationExpression)ShadowStackReader.readReceiver(0);
19
20     // load arguments
21     // arg_1 = Scope-locals: java.lang.String;
22     BlockScope arg_1 = (BlockScope)ShadowStackReader.readArgument(1);
23
24     // Method invocation
25     rec.resolveType(arg_1);
26   }
27
28   public void test_resolve() throws Throwable {
29     ShadowStackReader.setMethodStackItem(1);
30
31     // load receiver
32     // rec = i.new Y()
33     Expression rec = (Expression)ShadowStackReader.readReceiver(0);
34
35     // load arguments
36     // arg_1 = Scope-locals: java.lang.String;
37     BlockScope arg_1 = (BlockScope)ShadowStackReader.readArgument(1);
38
39     // Method invocation
40     rec.resolve(arg_1);
41   }
42 }
```

Fig. 2. Two test cases (out of eight) generated by ReCrash to reproduce Eclipse bug #30280. Each test case comes with a serialized representation of method arguments in file `eclipse.trace` (line 9). Lines 16, 21, 32, 36 show the `toString` representation of the object being read from the serialized trace.

test generation. ReCrash generates candidate tests by calling each method that was on the shadow call stack with the de-serialized receiver and arguments from the shadow stack. ReCrash outputs all candidate tests that reproduce the original failure. ReCrash outputs multiple tests because a test that calls only the method at top of the call stack may not provide enough context to find the error. A test calling a method closer to the bottom of the stack provides more context, but is less likely to reproduce the original failure.

ReCrash is effective, despite recording only partial information about the program state in-memory. For many failures, it is possible to reproduce them with *only* some of the information available on entry to the methods on the stack at the time of the failure. This may be due to the following characteristics of object-oriented programs.

– Many bugs are dependent on small parts of the heap (also the premise of unit testing).
– Good object-oriented style encapsulates important state nearby.
– Good object-oriented style avoids excessive use of globals. Furthermore, ReCrash has access to and will store any parts of the global state or environment that are passed as method arguments.

ReCrash's monitoring phase can be made efficient by reducing the amount of monitoring. For example, objects that are not changed by the code need not be monitored. As another example, ReCrash has an optimization mode called *second chance* in which the monitoring phase initially records only stack back-traces when the program fails. On subsequent runs, ReCrash monitors only the methods that were in the stack back-trace of failures. If the same problem reappears, it will be captured and might be reproduced. Second chance allows a vendor to use ReCrash in a similar way to an anti-virus program which frequently updates the virus profile data. When one client discovers a failure and sends the produced back-trace to the vendor, the vendor will send an update containing a list of additional methods to monitor, to all other clients. When ReCrash is used remotely (not by the developer who is debugging a failure), the test generation phase may be performed either remotely or by the developer.

ReCrashJ is an implementation of the ReCrash technique for Java. In a case study of real applications, ReCrashJ reproduced failures from Javac-jsr308, SVNKit, Eclipse Java Compiler, and BST with little performance overhead.

This paper makes the following contributions:

– The ReCrash technique efficiently captures and reproduces failures using in-memory storage of method arguments.
– Optimizations give the ReCrash technique low enough overhead to enable routine use, by monitoring only relevant parts of a program.
– The second chance mode operates with almost no overhead.
– ReCrashJ is a practical implementation of ReCrash for Java.
– Case studies show that ReCrashJ effectively and efficiently reproduces failures for several real applications.

The remainder of this paper is organized as follows. Section 2 describes the ReCrash technique. Section 3 presents the ReCrashJ implementation. Section 4 describes our experimental evaluation. Section 5 discusses some of ReCrash's limitations. Section 6 surveys related work, and Section 7 concludes.

2   ReCrash Technique

The ReCrash technique has two parts. Monitoring is done during program execution (Section 2.1), and test generation is done after the program fails (Section 2.3). Section 2.2 discusses several optimizations to the monitoring phase.

2.1   Monitoring Phase

In the monitoring phase, ReCrash maintains in memory a shadow version of the call stack with copies of the receiver and arguments to each method. Figure 3 presents pseudo-code for the monitoring phase.

On entry to method m with arguments $args$, ReCrash generates a unique id id for the invocation of m, then pushes $\langle id, m, rec_{copy}, args_{copy} \rangle$ onto the ReCrash shadow stack, where rec_{copy} contains copies of the method's receiver and $args_{copy}$ contains a copy of the method's arguments.

ReCrash can use different copy strategies. It can make a deep copy of each argument, store only a reference, or use hybrid strategies (see Section 2.2.1). If m exits normally, ReCrash removes the method call data $\langle id, m, rec_{copy}, args_{copy} \rangle$ from the top of its shadow stack.

If an un-handled exception is thrown out of main, ReCrash outputs the un-handled exception and a deep copy of the current ReCrash shadow stack. The methods that ReCrash stores include at least the methods on the virtual machine call stack at the time of the failure. In cases where a method catches an exception and then throws a different uncaught exception, the ReCrash shadow stack contains additional methods (those that were on the shadow stack when the original exception was thrown). This additional information can improve the reproducibility of failures.

2.2   Optimizations to the Monitoring Phase

ReCrash's time and space overhead is dominated by the cost of copying the methods arguments at method entry. We have considered two orthogonal ways to reduce overhead: reducing the depth of copied state for the method's arguments, and monitoring fewer methods. Recording less information might reduce the chances of reproducing a failure. Section 4 discusses tradeoffs between the performance overhead and the ability to reproduce failures.

2.2.1   Depth of Copying Arguments

In order to recreate the state of the method's arguments at the time of the failure, ReCrash copies the arguments to the shadow stack on the method entry. However, a deep copy of the shadow stack is only stored when an exception is not caught by the program. Thus, any part of an argument's state that is not copied into the shadow stack may change between the method entry and the time of the failure. This change might prevent ReCrash from reproducing the failure.

This section considers different strategies for copying arguments (including the receiver) at the method entry. In each strategy a different amount of the argument state is copied to the shadow stack and the rest of the argument state uses references to the original objects (that might get side-effected). The different copying strategies, in order of increasing overhead, are:

reference (depth-0). Copying only the reference to the argument.
shallow (depth-1). Copying the argument itself. Each of the fields in the copy contains whatever the original argument did, a primitive or a reference. Shallow copying is more resilient to direct side effects on the top-level primitive fields of the arguments.

Input: copy - a function that copies arguments (see Section 2.2.1)
Output: file - containing deep copy of the shadow stack

s : shadow stack of the current method on the call stack and their arguments

On program start:
begin
  $s \leftarrow$ new empty stack
end

On entry to method m in the call rec.m(args):
begin
  $rec_{copy} \leftarrow$ copy(rec)
  $args_{copy} \leftarrow$ copy(args)
  $id \leftarrow$ generate unique id for current execution of m
  push tuple $\langle id, m, rec_{copy}, args_{copy} \rangle$ into s
end

On non-exceptional exit from method m:
begin
  $id \leftarrow$ lookup id for current execution of m
  pop from s until $\langle id, \_, \_, \_ \rangle$ is popped
end

On top-level (main) uncaught exception e:
begin
  $file \leftarrow$ new output file
  store e to $file$
  foreach $\langle id, m, rec_{copy}, args_{copy} \rangle$ in s **do**
    store $\langle id, m, $ deepCopy(rec_{copy}), deepCopy$(args_{copy}) \rangle$ to $file$
  end
end

Fig. 3. Pseudo-code for the ReCrash technique. If an exception is uncaught by the program (main), ReCrash stores the exception and a deep copy of the current shadow stack to the output file. The technique uses two auxiliary functions: deepCopy which copies all the reachable state of an object, and copy which is a parameter to this technique. The exact semantics of copy depends on the chosen copy strategy (see Section 2.2).

depth-i. Copying an argument to a specified depth: all the state reachable with i or fewer dereferences.
deep copy. Copy the entire state. This strategy gives ReCrash the best chance of reproducing the same method execution, since it preserves the object state at the time of the method entry.

ReCrash has an additional copying option, **used-fields**, applicable to all copying strategy except reference. When the used-fields option is selected, ReCrash performs deeper copying on fields that are used (read or written) in the method. For example, supposed that ReCrash is using shallow (depth-1) copying with used-fields, x is an argument to a method m, and x.a is used in m. Then ReCrash will perform shadow copying on x and x.a. The used fields are the fields that the method is likely to depend on, and therefore copying them increases the chance of reproducing the failure.

It is possible to use different strategies for different arguments. For instance, shallow copying the receiver and reference copying of all other arguments. ReCrash always uses the reference strategy for immutable parameters. A method's parameter p is immutable if the method never changes the state reachable from p. Therefore, an object passed to an immutable parameter will have the same state at the method entry and at the time of the failure.

2.2.2 Monitoring Fewer Methods

ReCrash need not monitor methods that are unlikely to expose or reveal problems, or cannot be used in the generated tests. Those include empty methods, non-public methods, and simple methods such as getters and setters.

second-chance mode It would be most efficient to monitor only methods that will fail. However, it is impossible to compute this set of methods in advance. One way of approximating this set is to create a set of methods that already failed, updating the set each time a new method fails.

This is the underlying idea behind *second chance*, a mode of operating ReCrash that only monitors methods that have failed at least once. In second chance mode, ReCrash initially monitors no method calls. Each time a failure occurs, ReCrash enables method argument monitoring for all methods found on the (real) stack back-trace at the time of the failure.

This mode is efficient, but requires a failure to be repeated twice (possibly with other failures in between) before ReCrash can reproduce it. Second chance mode has no impact on the reproducibility of a failure (the second time the failure appears).

2.2.3 Which Optimizations to Use

When using ReCrash, a developer needs to decide which optimizations to use. Which copying strategy should ReCrash use for the arguments? Should ReCrash use the used-fields option on the arguments? Should ReCrash use the second-chance mode?

The answers depend on the developer's needs and the subject program. For example, if the developer doesn't mind missing the first time a failure happens, and the failure occurs relatively often, the second chance mode is a good fit. If one wants ReCrash to reproduce all possible failures and can suffer the performance hit, then deep copy might be the right mode. We found that using the copying strategy shallow copying (depth-1) with used-fields enabled ReCrash to reproduce most failures with acceptable performance overhead.

2.3 Test Generation Phase

The test generation phase of ReCrash attempts to generate a unit test for each method invocation $\langle id, m, rec_{copy}, args_{copy} \rangle$ in the ReCrash shadow stack. The pseudo-code for the test generation phase is presented in Figure 4.

ReCrash generates a test for each of the method frame in the shadow stack (s). ReCrash restores the state of the arguments (module the shadow stack) that were passed to m in execution id, and then invokes m the same way it was invoked in the original execution. Only tests that end with the same exception as the original failure are saved. Storing more than one test that ends with the same failure is useful because it is possible

Input: *inFile*- containing deep copy of the shadow stack
Output: *outFile*- containing tests reproducing the failure
begin
    e : exception, the original exception resulting in the failure
    testSuite : Collection of test sources, each test reproducing the original failure
    outFile : output file for the generated tests
    testSuite ← empty test suite
    e ← load exception from *inFile*
    len ← get length of shadow stack from *inFile*

    for *i* =1 *to len* **do**
        t : test source
        t ← generateTest(*inFile*, *i*)
        if execution of *t* ends with *e* **then**
            add *t* to *testSuite*
        end
    end
    store *testSuite* into *outFile*
end

generateTest(File *file*, int *i*)
begin
    $\langle id, m, rec_{copy}, args_{copy} \rangle$ ← pop i^{th} tuple from *file*
    output("test *m.id*")
    output("rec = load i^{th} receiver from *file*")
    output("args = load i^{th} arguments from *file*")
    output("rec.m(args)");
end

Fig. 4. Pseudo-code for ReCrash test generation. ReCrash generates a test for every method on the original stack at the time of the failure, using the saved copy of the arguments. ReCrash outputs each test whose executions results in the same exception. The `generateTest` subroutine creates the source for a test. Each test loads the appropriate receiver and arguments from the file containing the shadow stack, and then calls the method on the receiver with the arguments.

that some tests reproduce a failure, but would not help the developer understand, fix, or check her solution. See Section 3.2 for an example of such a case.

3   Implementation

We have implemented the ReCrash technique for Java. This section describes the implementation, ReCrashJ, using as an example the program in Figure 5. ReCrashJ has two phases: monitoring (Section 3.1) and test generation (Section 3.2). Section 3.3 discusses implementation details of the optimizations of Section 2.2.

3.1   Implementation of the Monitoring Phase

ReCrashJ instruments an existing program (in Java class file format, using the ASM instrumentation tool [23]) to perform the monitoring phase of the ReCrash technique

```
 1 class RandomCrash {
 2   public String hexAbs(int x) {
 3     String result = null;
 4     if (x > 0)
 5       result = Integer.toHexString(x);
 6     else if (x < 0)
 7       result = Integer.toHexString(-x);
 8     return toUpperCase(result);
 9   }
10
11   public String toUpperCase(String s) {
12     return s.toUpperCase();
13   }
14
15   public static void main(String args[]) {
16     RandomCrash rCrash = new RandomCrash();
17     rCrash.hexAbs(random.nextInt());
18   }
19 }
```

Fig. 5. This program, taken from [30], will crash with a null pointer exception in the toUpperCase method, when the argument x to the method hexAbs is 0. Since the value of x is randomly chosen (line 17), this crash is not deterministically repeatable. Figure 6 presents the instrumented version of the program.

(Section 2.1). The instrumented program can be deployed in the field instead of the original program. Figure 6 shows the instrumented version of the program in Figure 5.

The instrumentation has four parts, one for each of the tasks in Figure 3.

on program start. The shadow stack is implemented using static fields in the Shadow-Stack class. When the program starts, the requested copy strategies for the receiver and the arguments is set (Lines 33 and 34). The different copy strategy classes implement the strategies of Section 2.2.1.

on entry to method *m.* The receiver and the arguments to the method are stored on the shadow stack at the beginning of each method. In addition, ReCrashJ generates an id for the invocation of *m*. The id is stored as a local variable (*id*) in the method. This is demonstrated by lines 3–5 and 18–20 of Figure 6. The specific behavior of the methods addReceiver and addArgument is determined by the type of the ShadowStack (see Section 3.3 for more details).

on non-exceptional exit from method *m.* If the method successfully returns without a crash, ReCrashJ removes all the data (arguments and receiver) about the method execution from the shadow stack. ReCrashJ uses the unique identifier *id* to perform this cleanup (lines 13, 23).

on top-level uncaught exception. In order to react to a thrown exception that is not caught by main, ReCrashJ replaces the original main by a new main as shown in lines 27–37 in Figure 6. The new main invokes the original main in a try-catch block and handles exceptions. When an exception is caught by the new try-catch block (line 36), ReCrashJ serializes the information on the shadow stack, and stores it to the output file (line 36).

```
 1 class RandomCrash {
 2   public String hexAbs(int x) {
 3     int _id = ShadowStack.push("hexAbs");
 4     ShadowStack.addReceiver(this);
 5     ShadowStack.addArgument(x);
 6     String result = null;
 7     if (x > 0)
 8       result = Integer.toHexString(x);
 9     else if (x < 0)
10        result = Integer.toHexString(-x);
11
12     String ret = toUpperCase(result);
13     ShadowStack.popUntil(_id);
14     return ret;
15   }
16
17   public String toUpperCase(String s) {
18     int _id = ShadowStack.push("toUpperCase");
19     ShadowStack.addReceiver(this);
20     ShadowStack.addArgument(s);
21
22     String ret = s.toUpperCase();
23     ShadowStack.popUntil(_id);
24     return ret;
25   }
26
27   public static void _original_main_(String args[]){
28     RandomCrash rCrash = new RandomCrash();
29     rCrash.hexAbs(random.nextInt());
30   }
31
32   public static void main(String args[]) {
33     ShadowStack.setReceiverCopyingStrategy(new ShallowCopy());
34     ShadowStack.setArgumentsCopyingStrategy(new ReferenceCopy());
35     try _original_main_(args);
36       catch (Throwable e)  StackDataWriter.writeStackData(e);
37   }
38 }
```

Fig. 6. The instrumented program of Figure 5. Instrumentation code is bold.

3.1.1 Serialization

To serialize objects and store the serialized objects into a file, ReCrashJ uses the XStream framework [6] rather than Java serialization. Java serialization is limited to classes implementing the java.io.Serializable interface, and in which all fields must be of Serializable types. XStream does not have this limitation. ReCrash should be similarly applicable to any language with a library for marshalling/unmarshalling data. It may be that an advantage of Java is that Java has libraries that represent external resources, such as files, as Java objects. It may be that at language like Eiffel that uses opaque pointers would be at a disadvantage.

3.1.2 Alternatives to the Shadow Stack

The instrumented program is deployable. No other program or configuration is needed in order to run it. Both the Java Platform Debugger Architecture (JPDA) [2] and the Java Virtual Machine Tool Interface (JVMTI) [3] provide features to access Java objects in the stack with low overhead. However, in order to use these tools, we would have to deploy a separate program (in addition to the instrumented program) to communicate with either JVM or JPDA.

```
1 public void processList(List inputList) {
2     List minimizedList = minimizeList(inputList);
3
4     // minimizedList should not be null
5     if (minimizedList == null) {
6         StackDataWriter.writeStackData(); // record this state
7         minimizedList = inputList;
8     }
9
10    ...
11 }
```

Fig. 7. A manually written ReCrash annotation helps record a program state and reproduce errors that do not results in uncaught exceptions

3.1.3 Reproducing Non-crashing Failures

A developer may wish to reproduce failures other than crashes, for example exceptions that are caught by an exception handler or errors that do not result in an exception. In this case, the vendor can add calls to writeStackData wherever the program becomes aware of a failure—for example, in a catch-all handler or where an invariant is found to be false in an invariant validation routine.

As an example, consider the method processList in Figure 7. This method processes large lists. It first tries to minimize the input list by removing duplicates before processing it (call in line 2). However, if due to a bug, the minimization method fails and returns null, it is possible to process the entire list without minimization. Thus, the processing method is able to recover from the bug in the minimization method and continue. However, the developer will probably be interested in debugging the problem in the minimization method. In this case, the developer can signal to ReCrash (using the annotation in Line 6) that it should reproduce the state of the method in this case.

3.2 Implementation of the Test Generation Phase

ReCrashJ uses the stored shadow stack to generate a JUnit testSuite. Figure 8 shows the tests that ReCrashJ generated for the crash in Figure 5. Figure 2 shows two of the tests generated for the Eclipse compiler crash reported in Figure 1. Each test in the suite loads the receiver and the method arguments for one method from the serialized shadow stack, and then calls that method, which results in the same exception as the original crash. To facilitate debugging, for each argument (including receiver) that has a custom toString method, ReCrashJ write the argument's string representation as a comment (Lines 16, 21, 32, 36 of Figure 2).

Not every object is dynamically read from the stored shadow stack when a test is executed. ReCrashJ writes the values of primitives, strings, and null objects directly into the tests. For example, see lines 8 and 18 of Figure 8.

3.2.1 Generating Multiple Tests for Each Crash

The tests in Figure 8 demonstrate a reason to create multiple tests that reproduce the crash, one for each method on the stack. The first test in Figure 8 is useless in detecting and solving the problem, because the developer is unable to understand the source of the null argument. This test would also continue to fail even when the problem is solved.

```
 1 public void test_toUpperCase() {
 2    ShadowStackReader.setMethodStackItem(2);
 3
 4    // load receiver
 5    RandomCrash rec = (RandomCrash)ShadowStackReader.readReceiver(0);
 6
 7    // Method invocation
 8    rec.toUpperCase(null);
 9 }
10
11 public void test_hexAbs() {
12    ShadowStackReader.setMethodStackItem(1);
13
14    // load receiver
15    RandomCrash rec = (RandomCrash)ShadowStackReader.readReceiver(0);
16
17    // Method invocation
18    rec.hexAbs(0);
19 }
```

Fig. 8. Tests generated by ReCrash for the program of Figure 5

On the other hand, the second test captures a value that is not handled correctly by the hexAbs method. This test is useful in determining and verifying a solution for the problem.

3.2.2 Extra Information

When instrumenting a subject program, developers can embed an identifier, such as a version number, in the subject program. This identifier will appear in the generated test cases, as shown in line 2 of Figure 2. This identifier can help the developers to identify which version of their program failed.

3.3 Optimizations

In order to implement the different copying strategies of Section 2.2.1, ReCrashJ uses the Java Cloneable interface. ReCrashJ automatically adds the clone method to all classes that do not already implement it. The added clone method copies primitive fields and the references of non-primitive fields. Parameter immutability classification can be found statically [27] or by a combination of static and dynamic analysis [8]. ReCrashJ currently uses [8].

ReCrashJ approximates simple methods (i.e., getters and setters) as methods with no more than six opcodes. We use six opcodes as the bound since the standard getter (getX() {return x}) has 4 opcodes and setter (setX(int x) {this.x=x}) has 6 opcodes without debug information.

4   Experimental Study

We evaluated ReCrashJ by performing experiments with crashes of real applications. We designed the experiments around the following research questions:

Q1 How reliably can ReCrashJ reproduce crashes?
Q2 What is the size of the stored deep copy of the shadow stack?

program	crash name	exception type	# of candidate tests	# of reproducible tests			serialized shadow stack size
				reference	used-fields	copy	
Javac-jsr308	j1	null pointer	17	5	5	5	374
	j2	illegal argument	23	11	11	11	448
	j3	null pointer	8	1	1	1	435
	j4	index out of bounds	28	11	11	11	431
SVNKit	s1	index out of bounds	3	3	3	3	36
	s2	null pointer	2	2	2	2	34
	s3	null pointer	2	2	2	2	33
Eclipsec	e1	null pointer	13	0	1	8	62
BST	b1	class cast	3	3	3	3	5
	b2	class cast	3	3	3	3	5
	b3	unsupported encoding	3	3	3	3	25

Fig. 9. Subject programs and crashes used in our experimental study. For each crash, ReCrashJ generates multiple test cases that aim to reproduce the original crash. In the used-fields column ReCrashJ used the shallow (depth-1) copying strategy with the used-fields option. The serialized shadow stack size is in gzipped KB.

Q3 Are the tests generated by ReCrashJ useful for debugging?
Q4 What is the overhead (time and memory) of running ReCrashJ?

Our results indicate that ReCrashJ can reproduce many crashes, that it generates useful tests, that it incurs low overhead, and that the size of the stored data (serialized shadow stack) is small. We present the analysis of two real crashes in detail and show that the tests generated by ReCrashJ help to locate the source of the problem. In addition, the developers of one subject program found the generated test cases helpful. Overall, the experimental results indicate ReCrashJ is effective, scalable, and useful.

4.1 Subject Systems and Methodology

We use the following subject programs in our experiments:

- **Javac-jsr308**[1] is the OpenJDK Java compiler, extended with the implementation of JSR308 ("Annotations on Java Types") [17]. We used four crashes that were provided to us by the developers. Javac-jsr308 version 0.1.0 has 5,017 methods in 86 kLOC.
- **SVNKit**[2] is a subversion[3] client. We used three crash examples for SVNKit bug reports #87 and #188. SVNKit version 0.8 has 2,819 methods in 22 kLOC.
  Eclipsec[4] is a Java compiler included in the Eclipse JDT. We used the crash from bug #30280 found in the Eclipse bug database. In version 2.1 of Eclipse, Eclipsec has 4,700 methods in 83 kLOC.

---

[1] http://groups.csail.mit.edu/pag/jsr308/
[2] http://svnkit.com/
[3] http://subversion.tigris.org
[4] http://www.eclipse.org

– **BST**[5] is a toy subject program used by Csallner in evaluating CnC [11,12]. We used three BST crashes found by CnC. BST has 10 methods in 0.2 kLOC.

We used the following experimental procedure. We ran the ReCrashJ-instrumented versions of the subject programs on inputs that made the subject programs crash. We counted how many test cases reproduced each crash. We repeated this process for the different argument copying strategies introduced in Section 2.2.1, and with and without the second chance mode of Section 2.2.2. For the required parameter immutability classification (see Section 2.2.2) ReCrashJ runs PIDASA [8] one time for each subject program. It took less than half an hour to calculate the parameter immutability classification for each of the subject programs.

4.2 Reproducibility

Q1 How reliably can ReCrashJ reproduce crashes?

ReCrashJ was able to reproduce the crash in all cases (Figure 9). For some crashes (b1, b2, b3, s1, s2, and s3), every candidate test case reproduces the crash. For other crashes (e1, j1, j2, j3, and j4), only a subset of the generated test cases reproduces the crash.

In most cases, simply copying references is enough to reproduce crashes ('reference' column). However, in some cases an argument is side-effected, between the method entry and the point of the failure in the method, in such a way that will prevent the crash if the modified argument had been supplied on the method entry. In those cases (e.g., e1), using at least the shallow copying strategy with used-fields (Section 2.2.1) was necessary to reproduce the crash.

4.3 Stored Deep Copy of the Shadow Stack Size

Q2 What is the size of the stored deep copy of the shadow stack?

If ReCrashJ is deployed in the field, and a crash happens, the user will need to send the serialized deep copy of the shadow stack to the program developers. For each crash, the last column of Figure 9 presents the size of the serialized deep copy of the shadow stack for each of the inspected crashes. The size can be further reduced if the tests are generated and executed locally. In this case ReCrash could trim the data from frames whose candidate test cases were discarded, or perform other minimization of the test cases.

4.4 Usability Study

Q3 Are the tests generated by ReCrashJ useful for debugging?

To learn whether ReCrashJ's test cases help developers to find errors, we analyzed the generated test cases for each crash. We present a detailed analysis of two crashes, e1 and j4. We also present developers' comments about the utility of the generated tests for j1-4.

---

[5] http://www.cc.gatech.edu/cnc/index.html

```
1 public Void visitMethodInvocation (MethodInvocationTree node, Void p) {
2   List<AnnotatedClassType> parameters = method.getAnnotatedParameterTypes();
3
4   List<AnnotatedClassType> arguments = new LinkedList<AnnotatedClassType>();
5   for (ExpressionTree arg : node.getArguments())
6     arguments.add(factory.getClass(arg));
7
8   for (int i = 0; i < arguments.size(); i++) {
9     if (!checker.isSubtype(arguments.get(i), parameters.get(i)))
10       ...
11   }
12 }
```

Fig. 10. A code snippet that illustrates a Javac-jsr308 crash (j4). The crash (in line 9) happens when the parameters list is shorter then the arguments list.

```
1 public void test_visitMethodInvocation() throws Throwable {
2   // load receiver
3   // rec = ...
4   SubtypeVisitor rec = (SubtypeVisitor) ShadowStackReader.readReceiver(0);
5
6   // load arguments
7   // arg_1 = test("foo", "bar", "baz");
8   MethodInvocationTree arg_1 = (MethodInvocationTree)
9                               ShadowStackReader.readArgument(1);
10
11   // Method invocation
12   rec.visitMethodInvocation(arg_1, null);
13 }
```

Fig. 11. Test case generated for a Javac-jsr308 crash (j4)

Eclipsec bug (e1): Figure 12 presents the bug resulting in crash e1. Eclipsec crashes in method canBeInstantiated (line 19) because an earlier if statement in lines 9–11 failed to set the hasError to true. Using the generated tests (Figure 2) the developer would have been led to the buggy code. The developer would fix this problem by adding hasError=true on line 11. Notice that the test case for method canBeInstantiated (not shown in the figure) will reproduce the crash, but is not helpful in understanding it as the state of the parameter is already corrupted. Also, note that just looking at the backtrace does make the problem obvious: stepping through will be more useful (the error is far removed from the crash, but is in a method on the stack.) This is an example of why it is important to generate tests for multiple methods on the stack.

Javac-jsr308 bug (j4): Using Javac-jsr308 to compile source code with an annotation with too many arguments results in an index-out-of-bounds exception. Figure 10 shows the erroneous source code. The compiler assumes that the parameters and arguments lists are of the same size (line 9), but may not be.

ReCrashJ generates multiple test cases that reproduce the crash; one test is shown in Figure 11.

Note that the generated test does not require the whole source code and encodes only the necessary minimum to reproduce the crash. This makes ReCrashJ especially useful

```
 1  public class QualifiedAllocationExpression {
 2    public TypeBinding resolveType(BlockScope scope) {
 3      TypeBinding receiverType = null;
 4      boolean hasError = false;
 5      if (anonymousType == null) {
 6        if ((enclosingInstanceType =
 7              enclosingInstance.resolveType(scope)) == null){
 8          hasError = true;
 9        } else if (enclosingInstanceType.isArrayType()) {
10          ...
11          //hasError = true; Missing and causing the error
12        } else if ((this.resolvedType =
13              receiverType = ...)) == null) {
14          hasError = true;
15        }
16        ...
17        // limit of fault-tolerance
18        if (hasError) return receiverType;
19        if (!receiverType.canBeInstantiated()) ...
20        ...
21      }
22  }
```

Fig. 12. Buggy source code from Eclipsec (Eclipse Java compiler) causing bug #30280. The program crashes with a NullPointerException in the canBeInstantiated method (line 19). This case happens when the positive path of the if in line 9 is taken. In which case hasError is not set to false (line 11).

in scenarios where the compiler crash happens in the field, and the user cannot provide the entire possibly proprietary source code for debugging.

Developer testimonials. We gave the tests for j1-4 to two Javac-jsr308 developers and asked for comments about the tests' usefulness. We received positive responses from both developers.

Developer 1: "I often have to climb back up through a stack trace when debugging. ReCrash seems to generate a test method for multiple levels of the stack, which would make it useful." "I find the fact that you wouldn't have to wait for the crash to occur again useful."

Developer 2: "One of the challenging things for me in debugging is that when I set a break point, the break point maybe be executed multiple times before the actual instance where the error is cased, [...] Using ReCrash, I was able to jump (almost directly) to the necessary breakpoint."

4.5 Performance Overhead

Q4 What is the runtime overhead (time and memory) of ReCrashJ?

We compared the time and memory usage of the original and instrumented versions of the subject programs, while performing the following tasks (the first three Java classes were taken from the /samples/nio/server directory in JDK 1.7):

task	execution time			
	original	reference	shallow w/used-fields	deep copy
SVNKit checkout	1.17	1.62 (38%)	1.75 (50%)	1657 (142,000%)
SVNKit update	0.56	0.62 (11%)	0.63 (13%)	657 (118,000%)
Eclipsec Content	0.95	1.08 (13%)	1.12 (15%)	114 (12,000%)
Eclipsec String	1.07	1.36 (27%)	1.39 (31%)	1656 (155,000%)
Eclipsec Channel	1.27	1.72 (34%)	1.74 (37%)	8101 (638,000%)
Eclipsec JLex	3.45	4.93 (42%)	5.51 (60%)	> 2 days

task	second-chance execution time			
	original	reference	shallow w/used-fields	deep copy
SVNKit checkout	1.17	1.17 (0.0%)	1.18 (0.8%)	1.42 (21%)
SVNKit update	0.56	0.56 (0.0%)	0.56 (0.3%)	0.56 (0.8%)
Eclipsec Content	0.95	0.97 (1.5%)	0.96 (0.9%)	3.98 (317%)
Eclipsec String	1.07	1.09 (1.7%)	1.08 (0.8%)	8.99 (742%)
Eclipsec Channel	1.27	1.27 (0.1%)	1.27 (0.0%)	16.6 (1,210%)
Eclipsec JLex	3.45	3.47 (0.7%)	3.48 (1.1%)	1637 (47,000%)

Fig. 13. Execution times of the original and instrumented programs in seconds. Slowdowns from the baseline appear in parentheses. The columns are described in Section 2.2.1.

SVNKit checkout:	Checking out a project[6], 880 files, 44Mb
SVNKit update:	Updating a project, 880 files, 44Mb
Eclipsec Content:	Compiling `Content.java` (48 LOC)
Eclipsec String:	Compiling `StringContent.java` (99 LOC)
Eclipsec Channel:	Compiling `ChannelIOSecure.java` (642 LOC)
Eclipsec JLex:	Compiling JLex version 1.2.4 (7,841 LOC)[7]

Figure 13 compares the execution time of the original subject programs and the instrumented ones, measured using the UNIX `time` command. Because of variability in network, disk, and CPU usage, there is some noise in the measurements, but the trend is clear. Our deep copy version is completely unusable, except possibly in second chance mode, where it might be usable for in-house testing. A more optimized implementation could be more efficient, but will probably still be impractical.

Even copying only the references can be expensive, 11%–42% run-time overhead. The shallow copying strategy with used-fields has a very similar overhead, 13%–60% overhead. These values are probably usable for in-house testing.

Second chance mode, however, is where our system shines. It reduces the overhead to a barely noticeable 0%–1.7% — and that is *after* a crash has already been observed, before which the overhead is negligible (essentially 0%). Second chance mode obtains these benefits by monitoring only a very small subset of all the methods in the program. This simple idea is sufficient, effective, and efficient.

---

[6] http://amock.googlecode.com/svn/trunk

[7] http://www.cs.princeton.edu/~appel/modern/java/JLex/

task	maximum memory usage (MB)		
	original	shallow w/used-fields	overhead%
SVNKit checkout	8.7	9.3	6.9
SVNKit update	7.6	7.8	2.6
Eclipsec Content	4.8	8.4	75.0
Eclipsec String	5.3	9.5	79.2
Eclipsec Channel	5.2	9.9	90.3
Eclipsec JLex	9.1	11.1	21.9

Fig. 14. Memory use overhead of the instrumented programs, as measured by JProfiler

For the memory usage comparison, we used JProfiler[8] to measure the maximum memory used in performing each task. Figure 14 shows the memory usage — in our experiments, ReCrashJ adds 0.2M–4.7M memory overhead for the effective shallow copying strategy with the used field option. The memory overhead for the same copying strategy in the second-chance mode was negligible.

5   Discussion

This section discusses limitations of our technique and threats to the validity of our experiments.

5.1   Limitation in Reproducing Failures

ReCrash cannot necessarily reproduce all failures. The following list contains some cases that might prevent ReCrash from reproducing a failure:

failures dependent on timing. This category of failures includes concurrency-related failures such as failures resulting from a race condition in a multi-threaded application. Monitoring concurrency timing dependent failures and reproducing them is future work.

failures dependent explicitly on external resources. ReCrash may be unable to reproduce a failure that depends on external resources such as file system, network, hardware devices, etc. For example, a failure might depend on loading a file that no longer exists. ReCrash could be combined with tracing tools for calls that access external resource. This would be less expensive than performing full tracing.

failures dependent implicitly on external resources. Failures may depend implicitly on external resources. For instance, an argument such as a socket or GUI object, cannot be serialized.

failures dependent on global state, or side-effected argument state. Failures may depend on global state that is not serialized. Or a failure might depend on a part of the argument state that is not stored to the shadow stack (due to the copy strategy) and is side-effected between the method entrance and the time of the failure.

---

[8] http://www.ej-technologies.com/products/jprofiler/overview.html

```
1  public class SVNCommandLine {
2    private list myURLs;
3
4    public String getURL(int index) {
5      return (String) myURLs.get(index);
6    }
7
8    protected void init(String[] arguments) throws SVNException {
9      myURLs = new ArrayList();
10     for(int i = 0; i < arguments.length; i++) {
11       ...
12     }
13   }
14 }
```

Fig. 15. A code snippet from SVNKit illustrating crash s1. The method causing the crash (init) will not be on the stack at the time of the crash.

We believe that not storing global state is not a great limitation for Java, as noted in Section 1, and validated by our experiments. Evaluating the effect of storing global state on reproducibility is future work.

ReCrash might still be able to reproduce a failure that depends on one of these cases. This may occur if the method call that ReCrash cannot reproduce results in a legal state that triggers a failure later in the execution. In this case the developer might be able to find, understand, and fix the failure even without understanding the exact condition that led to the state exposing it.

5.2 Buggy Methods not in the Stack at Time of the Failure

It is possible that a failure is caused by a method that is not on the call stack at the time of the failure. For example, consider the code in Figure 15. This figure contains the source of crash s1 (SVNKit bug #87). An index-out-of-bounds exception is thrown if the user omits the URL from the check out command. When no URL is supplied, the method init should set a default URL or throw an exception about a missing URL, but it does neither.

The program in Figure 15 will crash on Line 5, and at the time of the crash the call stack will contain the method getURL but will not contain the method init. The test case ReCrash creates for method getURL calls the method getURL with 0 as a parameter, and the exception is thrown. This test does not help the developer to find the reason for the illegal state of myURLs. However, ReCrash generates test cases for each frame in the call stack. Thus, ReCrash will generate a test for the run method (not shown), which calls init. Debugging using the test for the run method will expose the real bug.

5.3 Reusing ReCrash Generated Tests

The ReCrash generated tests are not intended to be added as is to the program test suite. The reason is that the tests de-serialize objects. If the structure of a class changes, the de-serialization will stop working. However, the generated test cases provide the skeleton of tests, and developers can replace the de-serialization with normal code.

Developers are not intended to examine the JUnit code of the generated tests to find a bug. Rather, a developer can use a debugger to examine the test's execution, revealing the cause of the failure.

5.4 Privacy

One of the problems with debugging deployed applications is that users may be reluctant to send data to the developers for fear of exposing proprietary data. For instance, a user who discovers a bug in Eclipse might be unable to send proprietary source files to the developer.

While we have not solved this problem, using ReCrash might be seen as an intermediate solution. Sending only the parts of the shadow stack that are used in selected tests is less likely to contain proprietary data. In addition, it should be possible for a client to prevent ReCrash from storing sensitive data by marking it (i.e., via program annotations). Another possible solution is to provide a shadow stack reader to the client, so that the client can review the encoded data and decide which parts of it (or which tests) are safe to send to the developers.

5.5 Threats to Validity

We identify the following key threats to validity.

Systems and crashes examined might not be representative. We might have a system or crash selection bias. Our experiments use every crash we considered. However, we examined only 11 crashes from 4 subject systems. It is time-consuming to find a real bug (by studying bug reports), download an older version of the software, compile it, and reproduce the bug. We may have accidentally chosen systems or crashes that have better (or worse) than average ReCrash reproducibility.

All failures are runtime exceptions. Our experiments use failures that manifest as runtime exceptions, such as null pointer or index out of bounds exceptions. However, ReCrashJ can monitor user-annotated exceptions or errors as discussed in Section 3.1.3. Evaluating the usefulness of the ReCrash annotation requires a user study. Future experiments and user studies should consider other types of failures including user-annotated non-exception points.

6   Related Work

6.1   Record and Replay

Many existing record and replay techniques for postmortem analysis and debugging [10,14,19,9,21,18,31,15] are based on three components: checkpoints, logging, and replay. The checkpoint provides a snapshot of the full state of the program at specific times, while the log records events between snapshots. The replay component uses the log to replay the events between checkpoints. By contrast, ReCrash performs a checkpoint at each method entry and has no log of events, only an in-memory record of stack elements. ReCrash does not replay the entire execution, instead ReCrash allows the developer to observe the system in several states before the failure, then run the original program until the failure is reproduced. ReCrash's logging simplicity allows it to be deployed remotely with relatively low overhead. Most of the previous techniques are designed for in-house testing or debugging, and have unreasonable overhead for deployed applications.

BugNet [21], ReVirt [15], and FlashBack [28] require changes to the host operating system while FDR [31] uses a proprietary hardware recorder. ReCrash, on the other hand, can be deployed in any environment, and can be used to reproduce a recorded failure in different environments.

Choi et al. [9], Instant Replay [19], BugNet [22], and many others emphasize the ability to deterministically replay an execution of a non-deterministic program. They are able to reproduce race conditions and other non-deterministic failures. In order to achieve this goal, these techniques either impose a large space and time overhead [9,19], or they only allow replaying a narrow window of time [22]. Similar to BugNet [22], ReCrash only allows replaying a part of the execution before the failure. ReCrash is only able to deterministically reproduce a non-deterministic failure if one of the generated tests captures the state after the non-determinism. ReCrash could be combined with other monitoring tools (storing only some of the environment dependencies) to create an efficient technique that can reproduce non-deterministic failures.

jRapture [29], test factoring [26], test carving [16], and ADDA [10] capture the interactions between the program and the environment to create smaller test cases or enable reproducing failures. These techniques capture a trace, and then run the subject code in a special harness, such as a mock object representing all interactions with the rest of the system, that reads values out of the trace whenever the subject code would have interacted with its environment. Test factoring does this at the level of method calls; ADDA does it at the level of file operations and C standard library functions. By contrast, our approach does not record a trace; it sets up the system in a particular start state, and then the system runs unassisted. However, ReCrash can be viewed as writing mock objects in the method call data. The objects recorded are a faithful representation of the actual objects down to a given depth. At lower depths their fields contain values that are possibly incorrect, but that in practice are effective in reproducing program behavior.

6.2 Test Generation

Contract Driven Development [20] generates test cases using contracts (pre- and post-conditions) written by developers. If a contract is violated during the execution of an application in debug mode, CDD captures the transitive state of the arguments to one method (often the failing method). CDD then attempts to use the captured state to generate a test case that reproduces the violation. Since the arguments' state is captured after the violation, it is equal to ReCrash's reference copying strategy. ReCrash might generate more useful tests and reproduce more failures because ReCrash can store arguments' state before a violation occurs, and because ReCrash generates multiple tests, one for each method on the shadow stack at the time of the failure. CDD is designed to be used in the development process, whereas ReCrash can be used either in-house or in-field. ReCrash monitors the stack and generates a test case without the need for special IDE support.

CnC [12], JCrasher [11], Eclat [24], Randoop [25], and DSDCrasher [13] use random inputs to find program crash points. Their generated tests may not be representative of actual use, whereas ReCrash generates tests that reproduce real crashes. Palulu's [7] model-based test generation similarly attempt to generates tests based on values observed during an actual program execution.

6.3 Remote Data Collection

Crash reporting systems such as Dr. Watson [4], Apple's Crash Reporter [1], and Talkback [5] send a stack back-trace or program core-dump to the vendor. The vendor uses the stack back-trace to correlate the report to known problems. If several reports share similar characteristics, the vendor may try to reproduce the original failure. However, reproducing the original failure requires non-trivial human effort. The core-dump provides one snapshot of the program state at the end of time (after the crash). ReCrash provides several partial snapshots and enables execution of each of them, using a test. ReCrash stored data is smaller than a core-dump and thus is easier to send to the vendor.

7 Conclusion

We have introduced the ReCrash technique for generating unit tests that reproduce a software failure. The tests utilize partial snapshots of the program state that ReCrash captures on each execution and records in the case of a failure. ReCrash is simple to implement, it is scalable, and it generates simple, helpful test cases that effectively reproduce failures. Our ReCrashJ tool implements the technique for Java.

We have evaluated ReCrashJ with real crashes from Javac-jsr308, SVNKit, Eclipsec, and BST. ReCrashJ created tests that reproduced every crash we have inspected, and developers found the generated tests useful for debugging. The performance overhead of programs instrumented by ReCrashJ was 13%–64% for the shallow copying strategy with used-fields and 0%–1.7% for all copying strategies in the second-chance mode. In our experiments, ReCrashJ increases memory usage when using the effective shallow copying strategy with used-fields, by 0.2M–4.7M, and the size of the stored snapshots, the serialized shadow stack, is manageable (0.5k—448k). ReCrashJ is usable in real software deployment.

The ReCrashJ tool described in this paper is publicly available for download from http://pag.csail.mit.edu/ReCrash.

Acknowledgements. We thank Matthias Hauswirth and the anonymous reviewers for their comments.

References

1. Apple Crash Reporter (2007), http://developer.apple.com/technotes/tn2004/tn2123.html
2. Java Platform Debugger Architecture (2007), http://java.sun.com/javase/technologies/core/toolsapis/jpda/

3. JVMTI Tool Interface (JVM TI) (2007), http://java.sun.com/j2se/1.5.0/docs/guide/jvmti/index.html
4. Microsoft Online Crash Analysis (2007), http://oca.microsoft.com
5. Talkback Reports (2007), http://talkback-public.mozilla.org
6. XStream Project Homepage (2007), http://xstream.codehaus.org/
7. Artzi, S., Ernst, M.D., Kieżun, A., Pacheco, C., Perkins, J.H.: Finding the needles in the haystack: Generating legal test inputs for object-oriented programs. Technical Report MIT-CSAIL-TR-2006-056, MIT Computer Science and Artificial Intelligence Laboratory, Cambridge, MA, September 5 (2006)
8. Artzi, S., Kieżun, A., Glasser, D., Ernst, M.D.: Combined static and dynamic mutability analysis. In: ASE 2007: Proceedings of the 22nd Annual International Conference on Automated Software Engineering, Atlanta, GA, USA, November 7-9 (2007)
9. Choi, J.-D., Srinivasan, H.: Deterministic replay of Java multithreaded applications. In: SPDT 1998: Proceedings of the SIGMETRICS symposium on Parallel and distributed tools, pp. 48–59 (1998)
10. Clause, J., Orso, A.: A technique for enabling and supporting debugging of field failures. In: ICSE 2007, Proceedings of the 29th International Conference on Software Engineering, Minneapolis, MN, USA, May 23–25, 2007, pp. 261–270 (2007)
11. Csallner, C., Smaragdakis, Y.: JCrasher: an automatic robustness tester for Java. Software: Practice and Experience 34(11), 1025–1050 (2004)
12. Csallner, C., Smaragdakis, Y.: Check 'n' Crash: Combining static checking and testing. In: Inverardi, P., Jazayeri, M. (eds.) ICSE 2005. LNCS, vol. 4309, pp. 422–431. Springer, Heidelberg (2006)
13. Csallner, C., Smaragdakis, Y.: DSD-Crasher: A hybrid analysis tool for bug finding. In: ISSTA 2006, Proceedings of the 2006 International Symposium on Software Testing and Analysis, Portland, ME, USA, July 18–20, 2006, pp. 245–254 (2006)
14. de Oliveira, D.A.S., Crandall, J.R., Wassermann, G., Wu, S.F., Su, Z., Chong, F.T.: ExecRecorder: VM-based full-system replay for attack analysis and system recovery. In: ASID 2006: Proceedings of the 1st workshop on Architectural and system support for improving software dependability, pp. 66–71 (2006)
15. Dunlap, G.W., King, S.T., Cinar, S., Basrai, M.A., Chen, P.M.: Revirt: enabling intrusion analysis through virtual-machine logging and replay. SIGOPS Oper. Syst. Rev., 211–224 (2002)
16. Elbaum, S., Chin, H.N., Dwyer, M.B., Dokulil, J.: Carving differential unit test cases from system test cases. In: Proceedings of the ACM SIGSOFT 14th Symposium on the Foundations of Software Engineering (FSE 2006), pp. 253–264 November 7-9 (2006)
17. Ernst, M.D.: Annotations on Java types: JSR 308 working document. November 12 (2007), http://pag.csail.mit.edu/jsr308/
18. Geels, D., Altekar, G., Shenker, S., Stoica, I.: Replay debugging for distributed applications. In: USENIX-ATC 2006: Proceedings of the Annual Technical Conference on USENIX 2006 Annual Technical Conference, Boston, MA, p. 27 (2006)
19. LeBlanc, T.J., Mellor-Crummey, J.M.: Debugging parallel programs with instant replay. IEEE Trans. Comput. 36(4), 471–482 (1987)
20. Leitner, A., Ciupa, I., Fiva, A.: Contract Driven Development = Test Driven Development – Writing Test Cases. In: Proc. of the 12th European Software Engineering Conference (ESEC/FSE), September 2007, pp. 425–434 (2007)
21. Narayanasamy, S., Pokam, G., Calder, B.: BugNet: Continuously recording program execution for deterministic replay debugging. In: ISCA 2005: Proceedings of the 32nd annual international symposium on Computer Architecture, pp. 284–295 (2005)
22. Narayanasamy, S., Pokam, G., Calder, B.: BugNet: Recording application-level execution for deterministic replay debugging. IEEE Micro. 26(1), 100–109 (2006)

23. ObjectWeb Consortium. ASM - Home Page (2007), http://asm.objectweb.org/
24. Pacheco, C., Ernst, M.D.: Eclat: Automatic generation and classification of test inputs. In: Black, A.P. (ed.) ECOOP 2005. LNCS, vol. 3586, pp. 504–527. Springer, Heidelberg (2005)
25. Pacheco, C., Lahiri, S.K., Ernst, M.D., Ball, T.: Feedback-directed random test generation. In: ICSE 2007, Proceedings of the 29th International Conference on Software Engineering, Minneapolis, MN, USA, May 23–25 (2007)
26. Saff, D., Artzi, S., Perkins, J.H., Ernst, M.D.: Automatic test factoring for Java. In: ASE 2005: Proceedings of the 20th Annual International Conference on Automated Software Engineering, Long Beach, CA, USA, November 9–11, 2005, pp. 114–123 (2005)
27. Sălcianu, A., Rinard, M.C.: Purity and side-effect analysis for Java programs. In: Cousot, R. (ed.) VMCAI 2005. LNCS, vol. 3385, pp. 199–215. Springer, Heidelberg (2005)
28. Srinivasan, S.M., Kandula, S., Andrews, C.R., Zhou, Y.: Flashback: A lightweight extension for rollback and deterministic replay for software debugging. In: ATEC 2004: Proceedings of the USENIX Annual Technical Conference 2004 on USENIX Annual Technical Conference, Boston, MA, p. 3 (2004)
29. Steven, J., Chandra, P., Fleck, B., Podgurski, A.: jRapture: A capture/replay tool for observation-based testing. In: ISSTA 2000: Proceedings of the 2000 ACM SIGSOFT international symposium on Software testing and analysis, pp. 158–167 (2000)
30. Tomb, A., Brat, G., Visser, W.: Variably interprocedural program analysis for runtime error detection. In: ISSTA 2007, Proceedings of the 2007 International Symposium on Software Testing and Analysis, London, UK, July 10–12 (2007)
31. Xu, M., Bodik, R., Hill, M.D.: A "flight data recorder" for enabling full-system multiprocessor deterministic replay. In: ISCA 2003: Proceedings of the 30th annual international symposium on Computer architecture, pp. 122–135 (2003)

An Extensible State Machine Pattern for Interactive Applications

Brian Chin and Todd Millstein

Computer Science Department
University of California, Los Angeles
{naerbnic, todd}@cs.ucla.edu

Abstract. The *state design pattern* is the standard object-oriented programming idiom for implementing the state machine logic of interactive applications. While this pattern provides a number of advantages, it does not easily support the creation of extended state machines in subclasses. We describe the *extensible state design pattern*, which augments the traditional state pattern with a few additional constraints that allow subclasses to easily add both new states and new events. Further, we observe that *delimited continuations*, a well-known construct from functional programming languages, supports *state refinement* in subclasses as well as the modular expression of control flow in the presence of interaction. We illustrate our pattern in the context of Java, leveraging its generics to obviate the need for dynamic typecasts and employing a small library that implements delimited continuations. We have used our pattern to simplify and modularize a widely used application written by others.

1 Introduction

Interactive applications are those that repeatedly accept input from and produce output to an external entity. Typically the output produced depends upon the current input along with the current state of the application, and this output may in turn affect the next input. Many common application domains are fundamentally interactive, including servers, user interface programs, and computer games. In addition, more traditional applications often include an interactive component. For example, a program whose behavior is configured by an XML file might interactively parse the file through the event-driven Simple API for XML (SAX) [17].

The logic of an interactive application essentially takes the form of a state machine, and the standard way to implement this logic in an object-oriented (OO) language is with the *state design pattern* [9]. This pattern reifies each state as a distinct class, which has one method for each possible external event. The state machine class maintains a field containing the current state, and all external events are forwarded to the current state to be handled appropriately. Handling an event may result in some output and additionally update the current state.

J. Vitek (Ed.): ECOOP 2008, LNCS 5142, pp. 566–591, 2008.
© Springer-Verlag Berlin Heidelberg 2008

The state design pattern has a number of advantages. Because the current state is represented explicitly as an object, there is no need to manually test the current state of the machine when an event occurs. Instead, the state object is sent an ordinary message send upon an event, and each state "knows" how to appropriately respond to each kind of event. Further, each state class can naturally encapsulate its own data (i.e., fields), which is less error prone than storing all necessary data in the state machine itself.

While the state design pattern simplifies the creation of a *new* state machine, even simple ways in which one might want to extend an existing state machine in a subclass are difficult to implement without code duplication and/or unsafe features like type casts. State logic is inherently difficult to reuse via standard mechanisms like method overriding, since the logic of the machine is fragmented across multiple cooperating event handlers. The state design pattern exacerbates this problem by fragmenting the application logic across several interdependent classes. As a result, the traditional benefits of object-oriented software reuse mechanisms are not readily applicable to interactive applications.

In this paper, we present an extension of the state design pattern that we call the *extensible state design pattern* (Section 2). In addition to the requirements of the basic state pattern, we impose new rules on how state machines and state classes should be structured. Obeying the rules allows subclasses to modularly and safely extend the original state logic in a variety of desirable ways. This pattern is implemented within vanilla Java 1.5, however, the pattern is not Java-specific and could be implemented in other OO languages. The pattern relies on the *generics* found in both Java and C#; an implementation in C++ is possible using templates but would have weaker type-correctness guarantees.

Using our pattern, subclasses of a state machine can easily add new states to the machine and override existing states to have new behaviors (Section 2.1), as well as add new kinds of events that the extended state machine can accept (Section 2.2). These tasks are similar to those in the *expression problem* identified originally by Reynolds [16] and named by Wadler [20]. Torgersen [19] provides several solutions to the expression problem in Java, which make heavy use of generics. Our solution borrows ideas from his "data-centered" solution but is specialized for the domain of the state design pattern, which allows for a simpler solution without loss of functionality. For example, since states are not a recursive datatype, we do not require the sophistication of F-bounded polymorphism [3].

The state pattern additionally has several extensibility requirements that have no analogue in the expression problem. For example, we would like to allow a subclass to easily "interrupt" the existing state logic, insert some additional logic, and later resume the original state logic. This natural idiom can be seen as the interactive equivalent of a subroutine call. It can also be used to express a form of hierarchical state machines, whereby a state of the superclass is implemented in the subclass as its own state machine. Further, traditional control flow logic such as subroutines and loops are difficult to express modularly even within a single state machine, due to the need to pass control back to the environment. For instance, if a state machine must wait for an event in the middle of a loop,

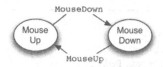

Fig. 1. The Base State Machine

that loop must be unrolled and split between multiple classes, obfuscating the original intent and introducing new possibilities for error.

We observe that *delimited continuations* [7], a well-studied language feature from the functional programming community, naturally supports modular expression of traditional control flow in the presence of interaction. We have implemented a form of delimited continuations as a small Java library with a simple API (Section 4), and we incorporate the usage of this API as constraints in our extensible state design pattern. We illustrate how this API and the associated constraints overcome all of the difficulties described above and provide several other benefits (Sections 2.3 and 3).

To validate our design pattern, we have used it to refactor a widely used application written by others (Section 5). This application, JDOM [12], is an XML parser that creates a DOM tree by using a SAX model parser. JDOM was originally implemented as a monolithic class that used several fields to encode properties of its current state. We refactored its implementation to employ our design pattern, which greatly simplified the logic and made it significantly more readable. Further, we demonstrate the extensibility benefits of our pattern by structuring the refactored code as two state machines: a class that supports basic XML parsing and a subclass that supports more advanced features of XML and has the same functionality as the original JDOM implementation.

2   The Extensible State Pattern

In this section we build up our extensible state machine pattern in stages, beginning with the standard state design pattern [9]. As a running example we consider a state machine for a simple user interface, along with several desired extensions to this state machine. Each stage in our discussion will refine the design pattern to obey new constraints necessary to enable a particular kind of extensibility. Our example sometimes sacrifices realism for simplicity, but it represents the kinds of tasks which are needed in UIs in general.

In our first user interface, there is a window containing a single button. The state machine logic should simply cause a function `triggerButton` to be invoked whenever the button is clicked. The `InputState` interface at the top of Listing 1 shows the three events that can occur based on a user's actions. Clicking a button actually consists of two events, a mouse down followed by a mouse up, both of which need to occur inside the bounds of the button. The diagram for this state machine is depicted in Figure 1.

```java
interface InputState {
    void MouseUp(Point at);
    void MouseDown(Point at);
    void MouseMotion(Point from, Point to);
}

class InputStateMachine {
 // standard currState members
 private InputState currState = new MouseUpState();
 public InputState getCurrState() {
   return currState;
 }
 protected void setCurrState(InputState newState) {
   currState = newState;
 }

 // state class definitions
 protected class MouseUpState implements InputState {
   public void MouseDown(Point at) {
     if (buttonShape.contains(at)) {
       setCurrState(new MouseDownState());
     }
   }

   public void MouseUp(Point at) {}
   public void MouseMotion(...) {}
 }

 protected class MouseDownState implements InputState {
   public void MouseUp(Point at) {
     if (buttonShape.contains(at)) {
       setCurrState(new MouseUpState());
       triggerButton();
     }
   }

   public void MouseDown(Point at) {}
   public void MouseMotion(...) {}
 }

 // forwarding methods and other members...
}
```

Listing 1. The base code for the UI example

Fig. 2. Adding the Drag State

The rest of the code in Listing 1 uses the standard state design pattern to implement the desired functionality. The `InputStateMachine` class maintains a field `currState` representing the current state of the machine. There is one state class per state in our machine. The `MouseUpState` represents the situation when the mouse is currently up, and similarly for `MouseDownState`. We define these classes as inner classes to allow them access to the state machine's members. Forwarding methods (not shown) pass signaled events to `currState`, which does the main work of the state machine.

In the rest of this section, we illustrate how to sequentially extend our example in three stages:

1. We will add basic drag-and-drop capabilities, allowing the user to click-drag the button in order to move it around. Releasing the mouse after a drag will not trigger the button.
2. We will add an event to handle keyboard presses, which can change the button's color. The user may modify the button's color while dragging it.
3. We will add a feature to hit a designated button during a drag, which will bring up a dialog box with information about the dragged object. When the dialog box is dismissed, the drag will continue.

2.1 Adding and Overriding States

As the diagram in Figure 2 shows, implementing drag-and-drop functionality requires the creation of a new state, to represent the situation when we are in the middle of a drag. The state machine should move to this state upon a `MouseMotion` event when the mouse is down on the button, and subsequent `MouseMotion` events should be used to move the dragged button.

The state design pattern makes adding new states straightforward: a subclass `DragStateMachine` of `InputStateMachine` can simply contain a new inner class `DragState` to represent the `DragState`. `DragStateMachine` can similarly contain a subclass `DragMouseDownState` of `MouseDownState`, which overrides the implementation of `MouseMotion` to move to the dragging state as appropriate.

Unfortunately, these changes alone will not affect the state machine logic, since the state machine is still creating instances of `MouseDownState` rather than `DragMouseDownState`. We can of course solve this problem by code duplication,

```
class InputStateMachine {
  // standard currState members
  private InputState currState = makeMouseUpState();
  // ...

  // factory methods
  protected InputState makeMouseUpState() {
    return new MouseUpState();
  }

  protected InputState makeMouseDownState() {
    return new MouseDownState();
  }

  // state class definitions
  protected class MouseUpState implements InputState {
    public void MouseDown(Point at) {
      if (buttonShape.contains(at)) {
        setCurrState(makeMouseDownState());
      }
    }
    public void MouseUp(Point at) {}
    public void MouseMotion(Point from, Point to) {}
  }

  // ...
}
```

Listing 2. The base state machine with factory methods added

for example by creating a subclass `DragMouseUpState` of `MouseUpState`, which reimplements the `MouseDown` method to instantiate `DragMouseDownState`. However, this approach is tedious, error prone, and non-modular. This problem leads to the first new constraint for our design pattern:

> *Constraint*: There must exist a consistent way of creating states that will allow future extensions to override the implementation of a state class.

To satisfy the constraint, we introduce *factory methods* [9] in the base state machine, as shown in Listing 2. The state machine logic must never directly instantiate state classes, but instead always go through the factory methods. For example, the `MouseUpState`'s `MouseDown` method now invokes `makeMouseDownState` to create the new state.

Given this extension to the state design pattern, implementing drag-and-drop functionality is straightforward, as shown in Listing 3. We define a new class `DragState` as well as a subclass `DragMouseDownState` of `MouseDownState`. To incorporate `DragMouseDownState` into the state machine logic, we simply override the corresponding factory method for that state. We also create a new

```
class DragStateMachine extends InputStateMachine {
  // overridden factory methods
  protected InputState makeMouseDownState() {
    return new DragMouseDownState();
  }

  // new factory methods
  protected InputState makeDragState() {
    return new DragState();
  }

  // subclassed state classes
  protected class DragMouseDownState extends MouseDownState {
    public void MouseMotion(Point from, Point to) {
      setCurrState(makeDragState());
    }
  }

  // new state classes
  protected class DragState implements InputState {
    public void MouseUp(Point at) {
      setCurrState(makeMouseUpState());
    }

    public void MouseMotion(Point from, Point to) {
      buttonShape.move(from, to);
    }

    public void MouseDown(Point at) {}
  }
}
```

Listing 3. The drag-and-drop extension

factory method for the dragging state, so that `DragStateMachine` itself satisfies our constraint. In this way, the new state machine can itself be seamlessly extended by future subclasses. We will maintain this *hierarchical* nature of the design pattern throughout.

To summarize, we add the following rules to the standard state design pattern, in order to support new states:

– Each state class should have an associated factory method in the state machine class.
– State objects must always be instantiated through their factory method.

2.2 Adding Events

As the diagram in Figure 3 shows, in order to implement our second extension we need to respond to a new kind of event, representing a keyboard press. It is

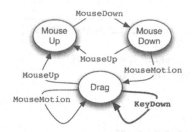

Fig. 3. Adding the KeyDown Event

natural to incorporate this event through an extension to the `InputState` event interface:

```
public interface KeyState extends InputState {
  public void KeyDown(Key key);
}
```

Now a subclass `KeyStateMachine` of `DragStateMachine` can subclass each state class to add a `KeyDown` method and implement this new interface. However, all of the factory methods are declared to return an `InputState`, as is the `currState` field. Therefore, the `KeyStateMachine` will have to use type-unsafe casts from `InputState` to `KeyState` whenever it needs to make use of the new `KeyDown` method. If the implementer forgets to subclass one of the state classes appropriately, this error will only manifest as a runtime `ClassCastException`.

The underlying problem is that the state interface is set in stone in the base state machine. To be able to update the state interface without typecasts, our pattern should obey the following constraint:

> *Constraint*: Each state machine must abstract over the events it responds to. While it may require that certain events exist, it may not limit what events can be added by future extensions.

Generics provide a natural way to satisfy this constraint. Rather than hardcoding the interface for events as `InputState`, we use a type variable to represent the eventual interface to be used, as shown in Listing 4. The `State` type variable replaces all previous occurrences of `InputState`. The `State` type variable is declared to extend `InputState`, so the implementation of the state machine can assume that at least the three events in `InputState` will be handled.

Since the factory methods no longer know which concrete class will actually meet the abstract interface `State`, they can no longer have a concrete implementation and are instead declared `abstract` (making the entire class abstract as well). As a result, the `InputStateMachine` class can no longer be instantiated directly. Rather, we must *concretize* the state machine, as shown in Listing 5; this new class is identical in behavior to our original version of the UI from Listing 1. Concretization serves two purposes. First, it fixes the set of events by instantiating the `State` type variable with an interface. Second, it fills in all of

```
abstract class InputStateMachine<State extends InputState> {
  // standard currState members
  private State currState = makeMouseUpState();
  public State getCurrState() {
    return currState;
  }
  protected void setCurrState(State newState) {
    currState = newState;
  }

  // factory methods
  protected abstract State makeMouseUpState();
  protected abstract State makeMouseDownState();

  // ...
}
```

Listing 4. `InputStateMachine` modified for adding events

the factory methods by instantiating classes that meet this interface. Because
`ConcreteInputStateMachine` explicitly defines the state interface, it effectively
terminates future extensions being made from it. Of course this does not prevent
further extensions derived off of `InputStateMachine`.

The entire logic of the state machine is still contained within the abstract state
machine class. For example, the class in Listing 4 will contain the definitions
of the `MouseUpState` and `MouseDownState` classes that we have seen earlier.
The uniform usage of factory methods and the `State` type variable allow the
definitions of these state classes to remain unchanged. For example, a call of the
following form is the idiomatic way to change states and requires no typecasts
within the context of the class in Listing 4:

```
setCurrState(makeMouseUpState())
```

Extending the state machine is now accomplished by subclassing from the
abstract state machine class. Listing 6 contains an updated version of our drag-
and-drop state machine. The body of this class is identical to that of Listing 3,
except that the `State` variable is used in place of `InputState` and the factories
are abstract. Keeping this class abstract allows it to be uniformly extended, as
we will do next. Naturally, the concretized drag-and-drop state machine would
instantiate the `State` variable as `InputState` and add the necessary implementations of the factory methods.

Finally, Listing 7 shows how to use our pattern to easily add new events. The
`State` variable is given the new bound `KeyState`, which indicates that the state
machine must handle the `KeyDown` event in addition to the others. Accordingly,
the existing state classes are subclassed in order to provide appropriate `KeyDown`
implementations. The concretized version of this state machine (not shown) will
instantiate `State` with `KeyState` and override all of the factory methods to

```
class ConcreteInputStateMachine extends
InputStateMachine<InputState> {
  protected InputState makeMouseUpState() {
    return new MouseUpState();
  }

  protected InputState makeMouseDownState() {
    return new MouseDownState();
  }
}
```

Listing 5. The concretized `InputStateMachine`

```
abstract class DragStateMachine<State extends InputState>
  extends InputStateMachine<State>
{
  // new factory methods
  protected abstract State makeDragState();
  // ...
}
```

Listing 6. The `DragStateMachine` extension modified for adding events

```
abstract class KeyStateMachine<State extends KeyState>
  extends DragStateMachine<State>
{
  public class KeyDragState extends DragState implements KeyState {
    public void KeyDown(Key key) {
      if(key.equals(COLOR_KEY))
        changeButtonColor(key);
    }
  }

  // default implementation
  public class KeyMouseUpState
    extends MouseUpState implements KeyState
    { public void KeyDown(Key key) {} }
  // same for others ...
}
```

Listing 7. Adding a new event in a state machine extension

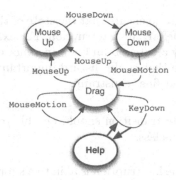

Fig. 4. Interrupting the Drag

instantiate the new state classes. Unlike with the original pattern, no type casts are necessary, and the Java typechecker will signal an error if one of the state classes is not properly handling the new event.

To summarize, we add the following rules to our design pattern, in order to support new events:

- A state machine must define a type variable that is bound by the currently known state interface.
- This type variable must be used uniformly in place of any particular state interface.
- All factory methods are declared abstract.
- A state machine must be concretized before it can be used, by fixing the state interface type and implementing the factory methods.

2.3 Adding "Subroutines"

With the above modifications to our pattern, we can modularly add both new states and new events. While these abilities allow essentially arbitrary modifications to the base state machine, there is a common extensibility idiom that deserves special support. It is often useful to "interrupt" an existing state machine at some point, insert some new state logic, and later "resume" the original state machine where it left off. Intuitively, this is the interactive equivalent of a subroutine call, and it also naturally represents a form of hierarchical state refinement, in which a state of the superclass is implemented as its own state machine in the subclass.

A case in point is our final extension, shown pictorially in Figure 4. While dragging an object, a user can press a specified key to bring up a dialog box about the entity being dragged. Another key press will dismiss the dialog box, at which point the drag should be resumed. Effectively, the drag state is being hierarchically refined. We could implement this extension using the above techniques, but manually interrupting and resuming the drag is tedious. Further, that approach requires care to ensure that the state of the drag upon resumption is identical to the state before the interruption. For example, in general it may not be sufficient to simply create a brand new instance of DragState with which to resume the drag, since that could discard important state from the original drag. This brings us to our final constraint:

> *Constraint*: Each state transition should be able to be interrupted and later resumed by a subclass.

As mentioned above, the interruption is akin to a subroutine call in traditional program logic. We might therefore attempt to satisfy our constraint by allowing the base state machine to include a call to a dummy method interruptKeyDown within each KeyDown method:

```
public void KeyDown(Key key) {
  // ...
  interruptKeyDown(key)
  // ...
}
```

The location for this call is decided in the superclass. Now, we can override interruptKeyDown in subclasses in order to perform the interruption. Unfortunately, such an interruption would be forced to complete entirely within the current state transition, before control is returned to the event sender. Therefore, such an approach does not allow interruptions that require further user interaction, as is required in our example.

One way around this problem is to capture the part of the KeyDown method after the interrupt as an explicit function that can be called at will by subclasses. Java's Runnable interface provides a solution:

```
public void KeyDown(Key key) {
  // ...
  interruptKeyDown(key, new Runnable() {
    public void run() {
      // ... rest of the transition after the interrupt
    }
  });
}

public void interruptKeyDown(Key key, Runnable next) {
  next.run();
}
```

By default, interruptKeyDown simply invokes the given Runnable immediately, thereby executing the rest of the transition. However, a subclass can override the method to properly perform the interruption:

```
public void interruptKeyDown(Key key, Runnable next) {
  if(key.equals(HELP_KEY)) {
    setCurrState(makeHelpState(next));
  } else {
    super.interruptKeyDown(key, next);
  }
}
```

In the above code, if the help key is pressed, then we move to the new help
state (not shown). That state is passed the given Runnable, so it can properly
resume the original transition when the dialog box is dismissed by the user. If
a key other than the help key is pressed, then a super call is used to perform
the original transition as usual. With this approach, a state machine designer
can easily declare points in each state transition that are interruptible, allowing
future extenders to insert arbitrary state logic without breaking the original
state machine's invariants.

There are two problems that need to be addressed in this approach. First, the
above code still requires the subclass to explicitly set the state back to the drag
state upon a resumption of the original transition. To address this problem, we
require each event handler to always end by setting its state appropriately, *even
if the state does not change*. With this rule, we can be sure that the original
code will set its state appropriately upon being resumed. To satisfy our rule, the
original code for KeyDown will be modified as follows:

```
public void KeyDown(Key key) {
  // ...
  interruptKeyDown(key, new Runnable() {
    public void run() {
      // ... rest of the transition after the interrupt
      setCurrState(this);
    }
  });
}
```

The call to setCurrState ensures that we always return to the original drag
state after the dialog box subroutine completes.

Second, the use of simple functions (i.e., Runnables) to capture the code after
the interruption has a number of limitations. Since a runnable can only capture
the code within a single method, it has to be created in the top-level event
handler method, rather than in some auxiliary method. Similarly, these interrupt
points cannot easily occur within control structures like loops or conditionals,
since the resulting runnable would be stuck in a particular scope and therefore
unable to capture the entire rest of the computation. What we need is a uniform
way to save the entire state of the computation after an arbitrary interrupt point.

We discovered that *delimited continuations* [7,2,8], a language feature developed in the functional programming community, does exactly this. Programmers
can declare a *reset point* at any point in the code, which has no semantic effect.
However, if a *shift* is later executed, then the entire execution stack up to the

```
public void KeyDown(Key key) {
  reset {
    // ...
    shift (continuation) {
      interruptKeyDown(key, continuation);
    }
    // ...
    setCurrState(this);
  }
}

public void interruptKeyDown(Key key, Continuation cont) {
  cont.execute();
}
```

Listing 8. Example use of delimited continuations

most recent reset is popped off and saved as a continuation. A block of code provided with the shift is subsequently executed and is passed the continuation, which can be invoked to restore the original computation.

For example, the shift-reset version of our KeyDown method is shown in Listing 8. It has the same semantics as the earlier code, but it avoids the limitations mentioned above. The shift can occur anywhere in our code, even in methods called by KeyDown or inside of control structures. Further, the "rest" of the computation can be nicely kept outside of the shift block, unlike with runnables.

We have created a simple Java library that implements delimited continuations, which is discussed in Section 4. The library allows the code to be written essentially as shown above, except that reset and shift are method calls into the library. For ease of presentation, we continue to use the prettier syntax.

Listing 9 shows how to use delimited continuations to implement our final state-machine extension. The relevant portion of the KeyStateMachine has been modified to satisfy the new constraint. The KeyDown method properly ends by setting the state. The getThis factory method is necessary in order to satisfy the typing constraints introduced by abstracting on the State type variable; the concretization of this class will implement getThis appropriately. The KeyDown method uses a shift to support interruption by subclasses. As mentioned earlier, the state machine forwards each event to currState. Therefore, it is natural to put a *reset* in each such forwarding method, as shown at the bottom of the figure, thereby alleviating the need for resets within the state classes.

Listing 10 shows our final state machine extension. We override interrupt-KeyDown in the dragging state in order to move to the new help state, rather than simply calling the continuation. The new state stores the continuation and opens up the dialog box. When any key is pressed subsequently, the dialog box is closed and the continuation is invoked, in order to resume the drag.

To summarize, we add the following rules to our state design pattern, in order to support state-logic interruptions:

```
abstract class KeyStateMachine<State extends KeyState>
  extends DragStateMachine<State>
{
  public abstract class KeyDragState extends DragState implements KeyState {
    public abstract State getThis();

    public void KeyDown(Key key) {
      if (key.equals(COLOR_KEY)) {
        changeButtonColor(key);
      }
      shift (continuation) {
        interruptKeyDown(key, continuation);
      }
      setCurrState(this.getThis());
    }

    protected interruptKeyDown(Key key, Continuation cont) {
      cont.execute();
    }
  }

  public void KeyDown(Point at) {
    reset {
      this.getCurrState().KeyDown(at);
    }
  }
}
```

Listing 9. The Key state machine with inserted interrupt-point

- The last command on each path through an event handler must either be a setCurrState call or an invocation of a continuation.
- Each forwarding method in a state machine class should set a reset before forwarding an event to the current state.
- An *interrupt point* consists of a shift placed anywhere inside code that is part of an event handler. The associated code block contains a call to an interrupt method, to which it passes the created continuation as well as any auxiliary information.
- The default behavior for an interrupt method is to immediately call the continuation which it is passed.

3   Interrupt Points Explored

This section discusses how our novel notion of interrupt points may be used in our pattern to gain even more flexibility, giving several examples to illustrate their expressiveness in a variety of dimensions.

```
abstract class HelpStateMachine<State extends InputState>
  extends KeyStateMachine<State>
{
  // new factory methods
  public abstract State makeHelpState(Continuation cont);

  public abstract class HelpDragState extends KeyDragState {
    public void interruptKeyDown(Key key, Continuation cont) {
      if (key.equals(HELP_KEY)) {
        setCurrState(makeHelpState(cont));
      } else {
        super.interruptKeyDown(key, cont);
      }
    }
  }


  // new state class
  public abstract class HelpState implements KeyState {
    private Continuation cont;

    public HelpState(Continuation cont) {
      showHelpWindow();
      this.cont = cont;
    }

    public void KeyDown(Key key) {
      closeHelpWindow();
      cont.execute();
    }
    // other events with the default body ...
  }
}
```

Listing 10. Our extension using the added interrupt-point

3.1 Returning Values from Interrupt Points

So far shifts have been used only as control structures, copying the stack into a continuation to return in the future. Our library also allows a shift to return a value. The following code illustrates a simple example:

```
String name = shift(Continuation<String> k) {
    k.execute("Hello World!");
}
```

As usual, the shift saves the current execution state in the continuation k and executes its body. The type of the continuation indicates that it expects a String as an argument. Accordingly, the continuation is invoked with a string literal in the shift block. This argument becomes the value of the entire `shift` expression, so the above code causes `name` to have the value `"Hello World!"`.

The ability for "interrupters" to easily pass values back to the interrupted state logic is often extremely useful. Such values can be used to change the behavior of the original state logic or to allow that logic to declaratively gather necessary data from its extensions. Our case study in the next section uses this feature of shifts to good effect.

3.2   A Stack of Interrupted States

Since any state that stores a continuation from an interrupt point may itself be interrupted, it is easy to form an arbitrarily long chain of states, each of which has been interrupted by the next state on the chain. In essence, this is the interactive equivalent of a run-time call stack. Executing a shift that transitions to a new state and passes the current continuation to that state has the effect of pushing that new state onto the call stack. Invoking a continuation has the effect of popping the top state off the call stack. This ability makes the state machine powerful enough to declaratively encode a pushdown system. Our case study in the next section relies on this technique to handle parsing of arbitrarily nested XML data.

Similar functionality could be implemented by having each state keep a reference to the previous state, given to it at creation time, forming a reference stack that does not use delimited continuations. When a machine wants to transition back to a previous state, it just calls `setCurrState()` with the stored state pointer. In the pure state machine case, where the only purpose of state transitions is to end up in the specified state, this would work fine. In real-world cases, when state transitions can have general Turing-complete code on them, delimited continuations allow clean-up code to be run after the interrupt point is returned to, such as that which may be desired in a locking protocol. Further, the clean-up code could even be used to decide which state should come next, based on the current context.

3.3   After-the-fact Interrupt Points

In our example in the previous section, the implementer of the base state machine anticipated the need for an interrupt point in the `KeyDown` event handler. However, subclasses can easily add new interrupt points after the fact, for use both within that subclass and within any future extensions. Since our pattern requires that the base state machine wrap each event handler call with a reset, any shifts within the dynamic extent of an event handler are always well defined. For example, if `KeyDown` did not contain a shift, a subclass could simply override `KeyDown` and add one. We make use of this ability in our case study in the next section.

3.4   Interrupt Points and Information Hiding

In the traditional state design pattern the current state object must maintain all of the data associated with the current execution state. If any data is needed

```
public void KeyDown(Key key) {
  DelimitedContinuation.Reset(new ResetHandler() {
    public void doReset() {
      // ...
      DelimitedContinuation.Shift(new ShiftHandler<Unit>() {
        public void doShift(Continuation<Unit>() cont) {
          interruptKeyDown(key, cont);
        }
      });
      // ...
      setCurrState(this);
    }
  });
}

public void interruptKeyDown(Key key, Continuation<Unit> cont) {
  cont.execute(null);
}
```

Listing 11. Version of Listing 8 using our API

in future states, it must be explicitly passed along to a new state whenever a state transition occurs. Thus states may have to store data that they don't need in order to pass it on to states that may use it later. Aside from being tedious, this also results in a loss of modularity, since data has to be available where it logically should never be manipulated.

Interrupt points provide a convenient solution to this problem. A continuation uniformly stores all current data (indeed, all data on the stack up to the recent reset) and encapsulates it as a single value. Therefore, a state need only accept a continuation in order to maintain all of the data potentially needed in the future, and the state only needs to explicitly maintain the data that it actually manipulates. When the continuation is eventually invoked, the data in the continuation is restored and made available to the state logic that has been resumed.

4 Implementation

As previously mentioned, we implemented delimited continuations as a Java library. Each continuation is implemented as a thread, which is a simple way to save the current execution state. A continuation thread waits on itself until it is invoked. At that point the continuation thread is notifyed so it can run, and the calling thread in turn waits on the continuation thread. When the continuation thread is to return, the reverse logic happens. In this way we ensure a deterministic handoff of control between threads.

Our library has a simple API. Listing 11 shows how Listing 8 looks using the API. Reset is a static method on the DelimitedContinuation class. It takes a

ResetHandler as an argument, whose doReset method provides the implementation of the reset block. Shift is handled analogously. The ShiftHandler is parameterized by the type of the result, as discussed in Section 3.1. The Unit type admits only the value null, thereby acting similar to void. The doShift method is provided the continuation thread as an argument. When the continuation is eventually invoked, the Shift method returns the value the continuation was passed, and the code proceeds as usual.

Our library approach to implementing delimited continuations has a few limitations. First, a continuation cannot be invoked more than once, and doing so results in a dynamic error. Second, resets prevent exceptions from continuing up the stack, thereby violating normal exception semantics. Others have considered direct support for continuations in the Java virtual machine [5], which could resolve these limitations.

5   Experience

JDOM [12] is a Java implementation of the Document Object Model (DOM) for XML, which represents XML data as a tree of objects. Clients can then use this tree to easily access the XML data from within Java programs. JDOM's implementation parses XML files using a SAX parser, which reads an XML file and reports events to an instance of JDOM's SAXHandler class, such as the start of a new element, one by one. The SAXHandler object incrementally builds the DOM tree in response to each event from the parser. As such, SAXHandler is a real-world example of an interactive software component.

The original SAXHandler implementation is written as a single monolithic class, rather than using the state design pattern. We refactored the code to use our extensible state design pattern, creating explicit state classes. To illustrate the extensibility provided by our pattern, we implemented the functionality of SAXHandler in two stages. First we implemented a base state machine that can build the DOM tree for basic XML documents. Then we created a subclass of this state machine to handle more advanced features of XML, including entities, Document Type Definitions (DTDs), and CDATA blocks. This class has the same functionality as the original SAXHandler class.

5.1   Base State Machine

The original SAXHandler class implements four interfaces, which contain the various parsing events that must be handled. Our basic refactored version of SAXHandler implements only the ContentHandler interface, which provides events for, among other things, the beginning and end of the XML document, the beginning and end of an XML element, and character data within an element.

This state machine (depicted in Figure 5) is fairly simple. There are three main states: The first is the initial state. On a startDocument event, it enters the main parsing state. When the document is done, it gets sent the endDocument event which causes it to enter the Document Complete state. There is one more

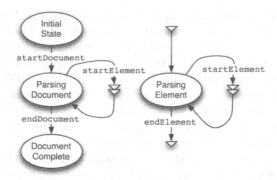

Fig. 5. The State Machine for the Simple SAX Handler

state devoted to parsing XML elements, which we will describe in more detail shortly.

Implementing this state machine in our pattern was straightforward. The most interesting part is the need to handle arbitrarily nested elements. Effectively, the state machine needs to maintain a stack of elements that are currently in the process of being parsed. In the original code, this stack was maintained explicitly, and integer fields were used to keep track of the current nesting depth during parsing.

Our use of interrupt points provides a much more natural solution. We employ our aforementioned "subroutine" idiom to parse a single element. This pattern is indicated in Figure 5. The interrupt point (represented by the double triangle) is the entrance to the subroutine that begins at the small triangle at the top, entering the "Parsing Element" state. When this state receives an `endElement` event, it will exit the subroutine environment and return the constructed element, allowing the remainder of the "calling" code to complete (in this case, adding the returned element to the document). The parsing element state will also enter into the same subroutine upon receiving the `startElement` event, causing a recursive call. This recursion is what gives rise to the implicit stack-like nature of this idiom.

Listings 12 and 13 show the code that implements this approach. When a `startElement` event occurs, we invoke the `readElement` method shown in Listing 12. This method shifts the event handler's execution, stores it into a continuation k, and transitions into a `ParsingElementState` object, which stores the continuation (in field `prevCont`) for later use. Recall that our pattern places a reset at the beginning of each event handler, so this shift is well defined. The `ParsingElementState` builds up the current element (in field `currElement`) as it receives `characters` events. If it receives a `startElement` event, then it invokes `readElement` to recursively interrupt execution in order to parse the nested element. Finally, as shown in Listing 13, when the `ParsingElementState` receives the `endElement` event it invokes the stored continuation in order to resume execution of the interrupted state machine, passing the parsed element back. This value becomes the return value of the shift from `readElement`.

```
public Element readElement(String name) {
   return shift (Continuation<Element> k) {
      setCurrState(makeParsingElementState(name, k));
   }
}
```

Listing 12. The `readElement()` method

```
public void endElement(String name) {
   prevCont.execute(currElement);
}
```

Listing 13. The `endElement()` event handler for the `ParsingElementState`

In addition to methods representing possible events, the `ContentHandler` interface contains a method `getDocument`. This method should return the root of the DOM tree if parsing has completed and `null` otherwise. This method does not update any local state and hence is not part of the state logic of the machine. Therefore, it is safe to implement it as a regular method, which does not conform to the rules of our design pattern. For instance, it does not begin with a reset nor end by updating the state. Our design pattern naturally accommodates such methods, which query the state of the machine but do not update it.

5.2   Extended State Machine

Our subclass of the above state machine class adds support for the events in the `DeclHandler`, `DTDHandler`, and `LexicalHandler` interfaces. These interfaces respectively add support for XML entities, DTDs, and CDATA blocks. With the addition of support for these events, our version of `SAXHandler` implements all of the functionality of the original class. While for brevity's sake we implemented these aspects in a single extension, we could just as easily have created one extension for each of these aspects.

In total, we added four new states and support for 12 new events. We also used four interruption points to insert "subroutines" in the original logic. Our extensible state design pattern made these additions straightforward. The most inconvenient part was the addition of the new events, which required subclassing each of the existing state classes in order to add the new methods. If Java had multiple inheritance, we could create a class `DefaultState` which contains default handlers for the new events, and each new state class could then inherit from both the appropriate old state class as well as `DefaultState`. Because Java lacks multiple inheritance, each new state class instead has its own implementation of each of the new events, thereby incurring some code duplication.

```
//...
if (atRoot) {
  document.setRootElement(element);
  atRoot = false;
} else {
  factory.addContent(getCurrentElement(), element);
}
currentElement = element;
```

Listing 14. A snippet of `startElement()` from the original `SAXHandler` implementation

We briefly discuss each of the three new pieces of functionality in turn. XML entities are names that can be given to a block of XML data. When the name is later referenced, it has the effect of inserting the associated data at the current point, similar to a `#include` directive in C. Accordingly, when the SAX parser encounters a reference to an entity, it sends events that correspond to the entity's associated data.

The original implementation of `SAXHandler` allowed the client code to decide whether to handle entities properly or to simply ignore them. This was accomplished via a boolean field `suppress`, which was consulted within each event handler to determine whether to handle the current event or not. Our implementation uses a more declarative approach. When we receive a `startEntity` event in the `ParsingElementState`, we check the `suppress` field once. If the client has configured us to expand all entities, we simply continue as usual. Otherwise, we transition to a new `SuppressedState`, which simply ignores all events.

When the `SuppressedState` receives an `endEntity` event, we must transition back to the state we were in before the most recent `startEntity` event. Effectively, the logic for suppressing entities interrupts the ordinary flow of the state machine and later resumes it. Therefore, an interrupt point is the natural approach for implementing this extension. Accordingly, the `ParsingElementState`'s `startEntity` method uses a `shift` to transition to the `SuppressedState`:

```
shift (Continuation<Unit> cont) {
    setCurrState(makeSuppressedState(cont));
}
setCurrState(this.getThis());
```

Upon an `endEntity` event, the `SuppressedState` invokes the given continuation in order to resume the original state logic. After invoking the continuation, the last statement above is executed, in order to return the state machine to the proper state before returning control to the SAX parser.

Both DTDs (inline declarations of the XML schema) and CDATA blocks (inline escaped text) were parsed in a similar manner. A new state was defined for each, which was able to accept the events necessary to parse their respective structure. The parsing of a CDATA block produces a value, so we implemented a `readCDATA` method in the same mold of the `readElement` method shown in Listing 12.

5.3 Comparison

It is instructive to compare our refactored version of `SAXHandler` with the original one. The original class maintained its state through many fields, including seven boolean variables and an explicit stack for keeping track of the incomplete elements. The event handlers were typically rife with `if` statements dispatching on the aforementioned boolean fields to implement state-like behavior. For instance, Listing 14 shows a snippet from the `startElement` event handler which used the `atRoot` field to decide which implementation to use. Thus implementation for two states was put into the same method, making it hard to understand. In contrast, our pattern allowed us to separate out code associated with different states, with each state class maintaining its own fields. For example, our version of Listing 14 has each branch as an event handler in a distinct state.

Our code was longer than the original code. Some of this was due to boilerplate code that, to a practiced eye, could be quickly understood. Some of it was due to the extra classes and methods which our pattern requires. The base class in our version has 388 non-comment non-whitespace lines and the extension has 600, while the original JDOM code has 424 non-comment non-whitespace lines. Excluding boilerplate (forwarding methods, empty event handlers, and factory declarations), our numbers are 270 for the base and 330 for the extension.

We believe that the improved readability and extensibility of the reimplemented code outweighs the increase in code length. The mental overhead of the pattern could be reduced by using a static checking framework such as Java-COP [1] to automatically ensure that the pattern's constraints are obeyed. It could also be possible to automatically generate much of the boilerplate code, given a high-level description of the state machine.

6   Related Work

The *expression problem* [16,20] highlights the difficulty of adding both new operations and new classes to an inheritance hierarchy in a statically typesafe manner, and many solutions have been proposed. Our work borrows from solutions proposed in Java [19] and in Scala [14], both of which use the idea of concretizing a generic abstract class with a trivial concrete subclass that instantiates the type parameters. Our pattern additionally introduces interrupt points via delimited continuations as a form of extensibility and modular control flow in the face of interactive logic.

Family polymorphism [6] is an inheritance scheme that allows a group of classes to be extended simultaneously, enabling each of the extensions to explicitly use the new features of the other extended classes. This allows for much more powerful interrelationships between the classes in the group as compared to our state class extensions. Several languages such as gbeta [10] and Scala [18] implement a version of it. Family polymorphism could be used to make our pattern more lightweight. For instance, some forms of family polymorphism can obviate the need for factory methods by making constructors virtual. Even so, our pattern remains simple and can be implemented in vanilla Java 1.5.

Delimited continuations [7] are a language feature derived from classic continuations that limit the amount of remaining execution they save and can be called without losing the current state of execution. A great deal of work has been done in the functional community detailing properties and implementation issues of delimited continuations [2,8] . To our knowledge, the use of delimited continuations to achieve a common form of extensibility for state machines has not previously been investigated.

The PLT Scheme web server [13] uses continuations to store the state of HTTP sessions. This allows them to maintain state while transferring information over the otherwise stateless HTTP. This approach is similar to our implicit stack approach. We additionally identify the synergy between delimited continuations and inheritance in OO languages, in order to support natural forms of state machine extensibility, and we codify this idiom in a general design pattern.

Others have recently added direct support for various forms of continuation in the Open Virtual Machine [15] for Java [5]. By leveraging their work, we may be able to avoid the overhead of switching thread contexts in our implementation, thus improving our performance and making our delimited continuation library more powerful.

We previously described *ResponderJ* [4], an extension to Java that allows state logic to be implemented as ordinary control flow interspersed with coroutine-like event-dispatch blocks called `eventloops`. *Actors* [11] implement a similar mechanism using the closures and pattern matching in Scala. Both features are primarily targeted at improving the state logic of a single state machine rather than at easily creating new state machines from old ones. However, careful planning and leverage of ordinary method overriding can be used to achieve the forms of extensibility that our pattern supports. For example, encapsulating each `eventloop` in ResponderJ in its own method allows subclasses to override this method in order to achieve the effect of replacing an existing state. ResponderJ is a fairly large language extension, while our new pattern is implementable in vanilla Java.

7   Conclusion

We have defined the extensible state design pattern, which adds a small number of requirements onto the traditional state design pattern. By requiring a state machine to obey extra constraints, we make it possible for subclasses to easily and flexibly extend the state machine in several dimensions. Our pattern is implementable in Java, and we have also shown how a library based on the notion of delimited continuations can give the pattern more power. Our experience indicates that our pattern's new requirements are easy to respect and that the pattern provides commonly desired forms of extensibility in a practical manner.

Acknowledgements

This material is based upon work supported by the National Science Foundation under Grant Nos. CCF-0427202 and CCF-0545850, as well as by a generous gift from Microsoft Research. Thanks to Robby Findler and the anonymous reviewers for useful feedback on this work.

References

1. Andreae, C., Noble, J., Markstrum, S., Millstein, T.: A framework for implementing pluggable type systems. ACM SIGPLAN Notices 41(12), 57–74 (2006)
2. Biernacki, D., Danvy, O., Shan, C.: On the static and dynamic extents of delimited continuations. Sci. Comput. Program 60(3), 274–297 (2006)
3. Canning, P., Cook, W., Hill, W., Olthoff, W., Mitchell, J.C.: F-bounded polymorphism for object-oriented programming. In: Proc. of 4th Int. Conf. on Functional Programming and Computer Architecture, FPCA 1989, London, September 11-13, 1989, pp. 273–280. ACM Press, New York (1989)
4. Chin, B., Millstein, T.D.: Responders: Language support for interactive applications. In: Thomas, D. (ed.) ECOOP 2006. LNCS, vol. 4067, pp. 255–278. Springer, Heidelberg (2006)
5. Dragos, I., Cunei, A., Vitek, J.: Continuations in the java virtual machine. In: Proceedings of the Second Workshop on Implementation, Compilcation, Optimization of Object-Oriented Languages, Programs and Systems (ICOOOLPS 2007) (2007)
6. Ernst, E.: Family polymorphism. In: Knudsen, J.L. (ed.) ECOOP 2001. LNCS, vol. 2072, pp. 303–326. Springer, Heidelberg (2001)
7. Felleisen, M.: The theory and practice of first-class prompts. In: POPL, pp. 180–190 (1988)
8. Flatt, M., Yu, G., Findler, R.B., Felleisen, M.: Adding delimited and composable control to a production programming environment. In: Proceedings of the ACM SIGPLAN International Conference on Functional Programming (ICFP 2007) (2007)
9. Gamma, E., Helm, R., Johnson, R.E., Vlissides, J.: Design Patterns: Elements of Reusable Object-Oriented Software. Addison-Wesley, Massachusetts (1995)
10. GBeta home page, http://www.daimi.au.dk/~eernst/gbeta
11. Haller, P., Odersky, M.: Event-based programming without inversion of control. In: Lightfoot, D.E., Szyperski, C.A. (eds.) JMLC 2006. LNCS, vol. 4228, pp. 4–22. Springer, Heidelberg (2006)
12. JDOM home page, http://www.jdom.org
13. Krishnamurthi, S., Hopkins, P.W., McCarthy, J., Graunke, P.T., Pettyjohn, G., Felleisen, M.: Impelementation and Use of the PLT Scheme Web Server. In: Higher-Order and Symbolic Computation (2007)
14. Odersky, M., Zenger, M.: Independently extensible solutions to the expression problem. In: Proc. FOOL 12 (January 2005)
15. Ovm home page, http://www.ovmj.org
16. Reynolds, J.C.: User-defined types and procedural data structures as complementary approaches to type abstraction. In: Schuman, S.A. (ed.) New Directions in Algorithmic Languages, pp. 157–168. IRIA, Rocquencourt (1975)

17. The Simple API for XML (SAX) home page, http://sax.sourceforge.net
18. The Scala language home page, http://scala.epfl.ch
19. Torgersen, M.: The expression problem revisited. In: Odersky, M. (ed.) ECOOP 2004. LNCS, vol. 3086, pp. 123–146. Springer, Heidelberg (2004)
20. Wadler, P.: The expression problem. Email to the Java Genericity mailing list (December 1998)

Practical Object-Oriented Back-in-Time Debugging

Adrian Lienhard, Tudor Gîrba, and Oscar Nierstrasz

Software Composition Group, University of Bern, Switzerland
{lienhard, girba, oscar}@iam.unibe.ch

Abstract. Back-in-time debuggers are extremely useful tools for identifying the causes of bugs. Unfortunately the "omniscient" approaches that try to remember *all* previous states are impractical because they consume too much space or they are far too slow. Several approaches rely on heuristics to limit these penalties, but they ultimately end up throwing out too much relevant information. In this paper we propose a practical approach that attempts to keep track of only the relevant data. In contrast to other approaches, we keep object history information together with the regular objects in the application memory. Although seemingly counter-intuitive, this approach has the effect that data not reachable from current application objects (and hence, no longer relevant) is garbage collected. We describe the technical details of our approach, and we present benchmarks that demonstrate that memory consumption stays within practical bounds. Furthermore, the performance penalty is significantly less than with other approaches.

1 Introduction

When debugging object-oriented systems, the hardest task is to find the actual root cause of the failure as this can be far from where the bug actually manifests itself [1]. In a recent study, Liblit *et al.* examined bug symptoms for various programs and found that in 50% of the cases the execution stack contains essentially no information about the bug's cause [2].

Classical debuggers are not always up to the task, since they only provide access to information that is still in the run-time stack. In particular, the information needed to track down these difficult bugs includes (1) how an object reference got here, and (2) the previous values of an object's fields. For this reason it is helpful to have previous object states and object reference flow information at hand during debugging. Techniques and tools like back-in-time debuggers, which allow one to inspect previous program states and step backwards in the control flow, have gained increasing attention recently [3,4,5,6].

The ideal support for a back-in-time debugger is provided by an *omniscient* implementation that remembers the complete object history, but such solutions are impractical because they generate enormous amounts of information. Storing the data to disk instead of keeping it in memory can alleviate the problem, but it only postpones the end, and it has the drawback of further increasing the runtime overhead. Current implementations such as ODB [3], TOD [4] or Unstuck [5] can incur a slowdown of factor 100 or more for non-trivial programs.

The common strategy for discarding data is to delete the oldest data first, which inevitably leads to the problem that bugs that have their cause located far enough from

J. Vitek (Ed.): ECOOP 2008, LNCS 5142, pp. 592–615, 2008.
© Springer-Verlag Berlin Heidelberg 2008

their effect cannot be tracked down anymore [3]. Another strategy to address the memory problem is to generate less data by only instrumenting parts of the application [4]. In this case, however, the programmer must know upfront where the potential source of the problem is. This approach produces less data, but it still presents the problem that the data grows over time making it necessary to discard old data at some point.

In this paper, we attempt to answer the question: *How can we make back-in-time debugging practical, while still preserving all relevant information?* Our approach is to track historical information at the level of the virtual machine, and to keep the tracked information (*i.e.*, the object flows) in the same memory space as the regular application objects. A direct consequence of this approach is that information no longer reachable from the objects of the running application will be automatically garbage collected.

We extend the object memory model of conventional object-oriented virtual machines (such as Java or Smalltalk VMs) by representing object references as real objects on the heap. In this way we seamlessly integrate historical execution data into the object model of the virtual machine. The created object references and their mutual relationships capture side effects and the flow of objects through the system. This design provides the following benefits:

– The relevance of a datapoint is determined by the reachability of an object in the memory graph. Which history and how much of it is retained depends on the interconnectivity of the objects that capture historical execution data.
– Garbage collection of historical data comes "for free" since we can employ the usual garbage collector without any modifications to incrementally and efficiently delete no longer reachable data.

As our evaluation shows (Section 4), how much memory is consumed with our approach largely depends on the characteristics of the application. In some cases the data recorded does not grow indefinitely and hence in these cases recording can be turned on all the time. However, our approach does *not* guarantee that the virtual machine will never run out of memory — it only makes it less likely. In case the recorded data continues to accumulate over time, we run out of memory much later than with conventional approaches. In the latter case, we provide means to configure the recording to capture and remember less data, which can lead to a dramatic decrease in memory consumption.

To make back-in-time debugging truly practical, it is important not only to manage memory consumption, but also to keep the runtime overhead within reasonable limits. A slowdown of 100 can make a program unusable even for debugging. Unlike many other back-in-time debuggers, which rely on bytecode manipulation techniques and application-level logging, our implementation is at the virtual machine level and because of that the performance is significantly improved. From our experiments the worst case scenario led to a slowdown of only a factor of 7 compared to the original virtual machine.

The contributions of this paper are:

– An object model for object-oriented virtual machines with an explicit notion of references to capture and introspect historical execution data for back-in-time debuggers.
– An approach to capture past object state and object flow and to incrementally discard no longer relevant information by employing the garbage collector.

– Benchmarks for a modified Smalltalk virtual machine implementing our approach and an evaluation of the execution overhead and memory characteristics for real world applications.

Outline. In the following section we describe our approach to incorporate historical information into a high-level language virtual machine. In Section 3 we discuss our implementation, in Section 4 we present our evaluation and in Section 5 we discuss the results. We present the related work in Section 6 and conclude in Section 7.

2   Approach

Most back-in-time debuggers are based on tracing events emitted at the application level. This technique is commonly based on transforming bytecode to introduce sensors that emit events. We take a radically different approach by modifying the virtual machine to add the program's execution history to the object model. The model used to store the execution history is based on our previous works on analyzing dynamic data flows in the context of program comprehension [7,8,9].

2.1   The Basis: Representing Object References as Objects

The memory layout of objects in object-oriented virtual machines typically consists of a header for the class pointer, hash bits, GC flags, size etc. and a fixed number of fields containing object references and primitive values. In many virtual machines, object references are implemented as direct pointers, that is, an object reference is just the address of that object in memory. Examples are the Sun HotSpot VM, Jikes RVM (formerly known as the Jalapeño VM [10]), and the Squeak Smalltalk VM [11].

In the proposed object model we add a level of indirection by representing object references by so-called *alias* objects. We chose the term *alias* to discern it from an *object reference*, the concept it represents.

Figure 1.a illustrates the typical approach where an object reference is represented by a pointer, and Figure 1.b shows how in our object memory model the object reference is substituted by an alias object. Thus, the pointer stored in field_1 points to the alias and the alias has a pointer to the actual object. Aliases cannot be nested, that is, the object reference of an alias is always a direct pointer to a non-alias object. Aliases cannot only substitute reference values but also the undefined value and primitive values. In this case field_1 contains the primitive value (*e.g.*, tagged pointer for small integers).

Aliases have the following key properties that distinguish them from common objects:

– **Transparency.** Aliases are completely invisible at the application level. This means that the semantics of the language are not altered. For instance, method lookup, field access, or primitive operations are performed as if the actual object were referenced directly. To make the information of an alias accessible at the application level we use the concept of Mirrors [12].
– **Optionality.** The conventional direct pointer reference model (Figure 1.a) is still supported. This allows the recording of aliases to be switched on only when required (Section 2.2).

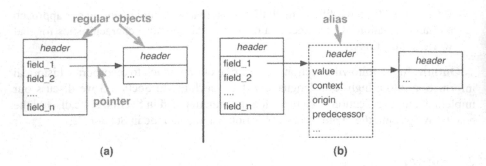

Fig. 1. (a) Typical object format with references as direct pointers and (b) proposed extension with references being optionally represented by alias objects

- **History.** Apart from the object pointer, an alias carries information about the object reference it represents. Through the relationship with other aliases, two main dimensions of object-oriented runtime behavior are captured: historical object state (Section 2.3) and object flow (Section 2.4).

Representing aliases directly as conventional objects allocated on the heap simplifies the internal object model of the virtual machine and allows us to use the standard garbage collector without needing to adapt it. For the same reason, many virtual machines represent classes and methods as internal objects.

2.2 Capturing Object References

In order to track object flow and reconstitute program states, we create an alias object whenever an object is:

1. allocated (referred to as *allocation alias*),
2. passed as parameter (*parameter alias*),
3. returned from a method invocation (*return alias*),
4. read from a field (*field read alias*),
5. read from an array (*array read alias*),
6. written into a field (*field write alias*), and
7. written into an array (*array write alias*).

The rationale is to capture all situations in which an object is made visible in a method invocation (1-5) or wherever a side effect is produced (6,7). Furthermore, we also capture the initialization of fields with the undefined value (referred to as *init alias*). By representing exceptions as objects, an allocation alias is created when an exception is thrown. Like this, also the propagation of exceptions is captured and can be traced.

Figure 2 illustrates the relationships among the entities Alias, MethodInvocation, and Value. With Value we refer to any type of value of the language (namely, objects, arrays, and primitive values, including the undefined value). A MethodInvocation represents a frame on the execution stack and also is a real object on the heap.

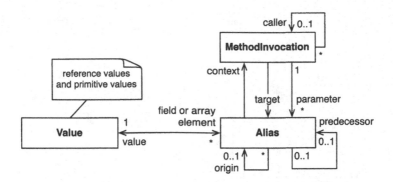

Fig. 2. Conceptual object model with aliases capturing historical execution data

In contrast to other back-in-time debugging approaches, which typically collect and store data centrally as a trace of events, aliases are part of the object model. Like events, aliases capture historical execution data, but instead of ordering them in a temporal trace they are attached to object references. For example, in the case of writing to a field the alias objects are directly pointed to from the corresponding field of the object. For each value there can exist many aliases, whereas an alias always points to exactly one value.

Parameter aliases are referred to from the method invocation in which they replace the pointer to the actual parameter objects. The context of an alias is used to navigate to the method invocation in which the alias was created. To model the call stack, each method invocation holds onto its caller. In case of object allocation, return value, field read and array read, the aliases are used on the operand stack of the method invocation the same way as the objects they point to would be.

The predecessor of a field write alias is the field write alias of the value previously stored in the field (respectively the array write alias previously stored in the slot of the array). Only field and array write aliases have a predecessor.

The origin of an alias is the alias that was used to create the alias. For instance, the origin of a field read alias always is a field write alias because going back one step in the flow of an object from a field read alias always leads to the field write alias. Any alias can be the origin of potentially many other aliases. Allocation aliases and init aliases are the only aliases without an origin.

In the following two sections we discuss the predecessor and origin relationships among aliases in more depth. Those two orthogonal relationships among aliases are key to our approach as they capture object state changes and as they track the flow of objects.

2.3 Remembering Historical Object State

An important historical dimension to capture is how the state of an object evolves. This allows a back-in-time debugger to answer the question: *What were the previous values of a field and where in the control flow were they assigned?* More precisely, we want to capture data that allows us to later determine which value was stored in a field of an object (or at a specific index of an array) at a particular point in time.

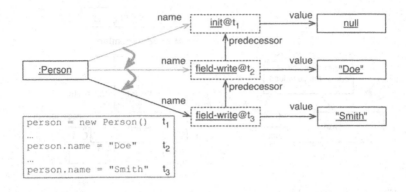

Fig. 3. Capturing historical object state through predecessor aliases

Figure 3 illustrates an example of a person object with the attribute name. When the object is allocated at the point in time t_1, the field is initially undefined. Later, at t_2, the string "Doe" is written into the field and at t_3 it is renamed to "Smith".

In our model, the initial undefined value is captured by an alias of type *init* and all subsequent stores into the field are captured by aliases of type *field write* (or *array write* respectively). In the example the field first points to the alias of null, then to the alias of "Doe" and lastly to the alias of "Smith". The key idea is that each alias keeps a reference to its predecessor, that is, to the alias that was stored in the field beforehand. In this way, the alias pointed to from a field is the head of a linked list of aliases that constitute the history of that field.

Looking into the past. To go back in time, a selected process can be put into a state in which it "sees" the system as it happened to exist at a certain point in the past. Like this, accessing a historical value of a field is straightforward because when accessing a field (or array), the historical value is returned directly — just like the current value is normally returned.

Figure 4 shows pseudocode for the implementation of field access in the virtual machine. In case the current process has an activated back-in-time view, the predecessor list of the currently referenced alias is traversed backwards to the alias that was present in the field at the selected point in time.

In the example of Figure 3, accessing person.name at timestamp t_3 directly returns the alias of the string "Smith" whereas at t_1 an alias of the undefined value is returned.

```
then
    return x.f
else
    alias := x.f
    while alias.timestamp > process.timestamp and alias.predecessor is defined
        alias := alias.predecessor
    return alias
end if
```

Fig. 4. VM implementation of field access x.f with back-in-time capability

With this model previous object state can be accessed very quickly (depending on
the number of state changes of the field, which is typically a small number). Compared
to other approaches, which need to reconstitute previous object state from a log or
database, this is significantly faster (see Section 4).

2.4   Remembering the Flow of Objects

In addition to the historical object state dimension discussed above, we want to capture how objects propagate at runtime. The goal is to answer the second key question,
which is: *How was this object passed here?* This means, for any object accessible in
the debugger, we want to be able to inspect all origins up until the allocation of the object. This also allows us to find out where a particular value of a variable comes from.
Furthermore, we also want to track the flow of the undefined value and any primitive
values. Tracking the undefined value is important as null pointer exceptions can be hard
to debug.

The way we track the flow of objects is similar to that of tracking past object states
discussed above. In our model, all transfers of object references in the system are captured by the creation of aliases (when recording is turned on). Each alias in the system
originates from an existing one, except for the allocation and init aliases, which are created when instantiating a class. Therefore, to capture how an object is passed through
the system, each alias maintains a link to the alias from which it originates.

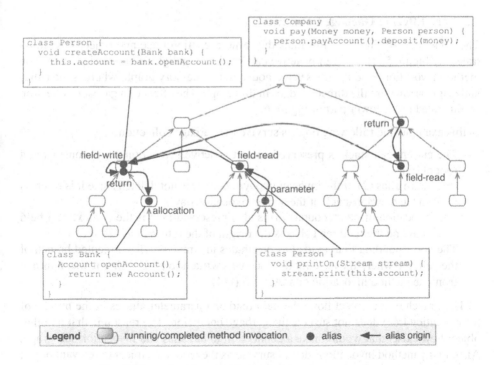

Fig. 5. Flow of an Account instance through an execution tree

Figure 5 illustrates the flow of an account object in an execution trace (represented as a tree of method invocations where the callee points to the caller). A point represents an alias. An arrow from one alias to another shows the origin of the alias. Note that the actual flow of the object reference is opposite to the direction of the origin arrows.

Each alias is created in the context of the method invocation in which the object reference becomes visible. This means that for return values this is the calling method rather than the returning method. The parameter aliases are created at the callee site.

By means of the origin link of an alias we can track back how an object was passed to a method invocation in which a failure occurred. This helps one to understand how and why a possibly incorrect object reference has been propagated — even and especially if its flow spans the whole program execution and goes through fields and arrays.

Introspecting object flows. Aliases are completely invisible at the application level because they forward all messages to the actual objects. Therefore, we have to provide other means to access object flow information than to send messages to an alias instance. We employ the concept of Mirrors [12] to introspect aliases. For each object reference that is represented by an alias instance, a mirror can be obtained through a primitive. A mirror is an object that provides an interface to access for example the origin and the predecessor of an alias, which in both cases returns a new mirror of the corresponding alias. In the same way we can access the method invocation context of an alias to get information about where in the control flow the alias was created. Our prototype implementation of the enhanced debugger uses this mechanism to navigate backwards in time.

2.5   The Effect of Garbage Collection

The upper part of Figure 6 illustrates the same execution trace and object flow illustrated by Figure 5. The currently active call stack is highlighted on the right side. The method invocations and the aliases are nodes in the memory graph, whereas the caller and origin arrows are the directed edges in this graph. The effect of a garbage collection is illustrated in the lower part of Figure 6.

In this example, the following objects survive the garbage collection:

- The current call stack is preserved since the active invocation (1) is considered a root object.
- The return alias (2) of the invocation payAccount() is not deleted since it is referred to from the operand stack of the active invocation pay().
- The invocation of payAccount() (3) is also preserved as it is the context of a field read alias and the field read alias is the origin of the return alias (2).
- The corresponding field read alias originates in a much earlier executed branch of the call tree where the account instance was written to a field after it was returned from the method invocation openAccount() (4).

The branch of the object flow (the field read and parameter aliases in the middle of the execution tree) does not survive the garbage collection. The reason is that no other object flow exists that would make a connection to the alias and invocation sub-graph. Also, many method invocations do not survive as they are not subject to relevant object flows and as they are not in the caller chain of a relevant invocation.

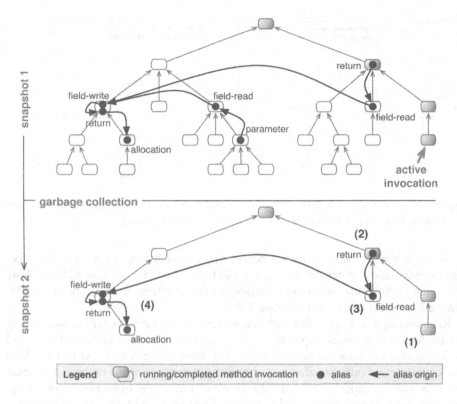

Fig. 6. Flow of an object through an execution tree and the effect of garbage collection

Figure 7 shows memory statistics from the execution of the Squeak bytecode compiler. In regular intervals we measured how many aliases have been allocated in total (solid line) and how many of those aliases still exist in memory (dashed line) over time. The effect of the garbage collection over the whole execution is a reduction of data by 70%. Both statistics in Figure 7 show the same run of the compiler, but with different garbage collector settings. On the left side, there are fewer GC cycles. For instance between 50ms and 120ms there is no GC activity and therefore both lines increase at the same rate. On the right side, between almost all sample steps there is a GC cycle.

3   Implementation

We have extended the Smalltalk Squeak VM [11] with the recording capability and representation of the execution history in the object model as described in Section 2. The majority of the Squeak VM is implemented in a subset of Squeak Smalltalk, named Slang. The Slang source code is then translated to C to compile and link with the low-level, platform-specific C code. The Squeak VM implementation closely follows the specification given in the Smalltalk-80 Blue Book [13], except for the object memory format. Like most modern virtual machines, Squeak implements references as direct pointers rather than using an object table.

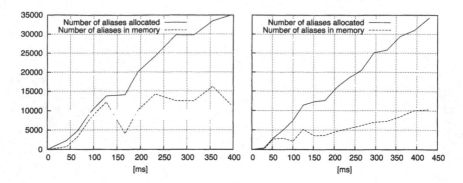

Fig. 7. Garbage collection discards 70% of the aliases in a run of the compiler. The right side shows the same execution but with a flatter curve due to more GC activity.

We implemented aliases as real objects of a new class Alias that has the fields value, context, origin and predecessor as illustrated in Figure 1 and Figure 2. In addition, Alias has an integer field that encodes information like the timestamp and the type of the alias (one of the 8 types described in Section 2.2).

Representing aliases as ordinary objects in memory has the advantage of simplifying the implementation. Most importantly, no changes to the object memory layout and to the garbage collector are necessary. The two main changes to the virtual machine are to allocate and initialize aliases, and to forward message sends to the actual target object in case the object is aliased. Aliases are created in the bytecode routines (*e.g.*, read and write aliases), on method invocation (parameter and return aliases) or when instantiating a class. There exist a few exceptional classes for which no aliases are created to simplify the implementation where aliasing is not important. Those classes are Process, Semaphore, MethodContext, BlockContext, and CompiledMethod.

Since method invocations are already represented as objects in Squeak (instances of the class MethodContext), to implement the model as illustrated in Figure 2, no further changes were required.

To optimize performance and space we implemented Alias as a compact class. That is, the object header of its instances consists of only a single 32-bit word and contains the index of its class in the compact classes table. This spares one word per alias instance, but more importantly, it allows the virtual machine to check whether an object is an alias or a real object by looking at the object header alone. The efficiency of this check is especially important because not every object reference is represented as an alias and hence this check has to be performed very frequently.

To generate the different kind of aliases when tracing is enabled, we extended various bytecode routines (*e.g.*, the store and fetch bytecodes), the method invocation behavior, and the class instantiation primitives. Small modifications had to be applied to many other primitives and bytecode routines that operate on the actual object rather than on the alias. In those cases the receiver and objects popped from the operand stack need to be unwrapped, for instance in arithmetic operations or the jump bytecode routines.

Overall, about 200 methods of the Slang implementation were modified or created. In comparison, the core of the virtual machine is implemented with about 750 methods (not counting platform specific code directly written in C and plugin code). Half of our changes were necessary due to the need of unwrapping aliases. Other parts of the virtual machine, for instance the memory format, method lookup, and the garbage collector, are not modified.

At the application level only very few extensions in system classes are required to support recording, to allow the user to control recording, and to introspect the execution history. First, the class Alias has to be loaded. It implements no methods and cannot be instantiated by the user. Second, the class Process is extended to allow the user to control recording at runtime. We added a field to Process which specifies the recording mode as well as the timestamp of its back-in-time point of view. At runtime, the behavior of the virtual machine then depends on these settings of the active process.

In addition, we implemented the class AliasMirror, which can be loaded to introspect the execution history. Mirrors are used by the graphical debugger, which we modified to be capable of moving backwards in time and to navigate backwards in the flow of objects. The debugger accesses information about the flow or history of an object by requesting a mirror for the reference through which the object is made visible in the selected method invocation. There is no need to traverse the heap or perform a lookup in a trace to get the flow or history of an object, since this information is available through direct object references. A mirror on an object reference is created by the virtual machine through a primitive call. Using a mirror on an alias, the fields of the alias can be accessed. This behavior is implemented with a set of primitives in the virtual machine because any direct access to the alias would be performed on the actual object rather than on the alias instance.

4   Evaluation

In this section we evaluate our implementation from the point of view of the execution overhead (Section 4.1) and of the memory usage (Section 4.2). All experiments were performed on a MacBook Pro, 2.4GHz Intel Core 2 Duo, 4GB RAM, with Mac OS X 10.5.2.

4.1   Execution Overhead

Setup. To evaluate the execution overhead, we compare the performance of the modified Squeak virtual machine to the original virtual machine by means of several standard benchmarks. As a reference, we first executed the benchmarks in an original Squeak virtual machine (version 3.9-10), which we compiled using gcc 4.0.1. Then, we executed the same benchmarks using our modified virtual machine, which had been compiled under identical conditions. First, we took the benchmarks with the recording of historical data being turned off, and second with recording turned on. For each of the three cases the five benchmarks were executed 30 times, and before each execution we forced a full heap garbage collect.

Overview. The results of this comparison are shown in Table 1. The first three columns show the results of the benchmarks executed on our modified virtual machine without historical data recording, that is, no aliases are created. The remaining columns to the right show the results obtained from running the benchmarks with recording turned on. These overheads include the time that is needed to allocate and initialize alias instances, the additional time to forward message sends from aliases to normal objects and the additional time spent in the garbage collector.

The most important numbers are shown in the two Δ columns, which indicate the execution overhead of the benchmarks compared to the reference run of the unmodified standard virtual machine. The column *time* is the runtime of the benchmark and *%GC* indicates how much of this time is consumed by the garbage collector. The last two columns of the table show how many alias objects respectively method invocation objects are created (k indicates that both figures are given in 1000 objects). The figures in Table 1 are computed using the arithmetic mean of the 30 runs of each benchmark.

Table 1. In comparison with the original VM, the execution overhead of the modified VM averaged 15% when recording is disabled and the average slowdown when recording is turned on is 3.84 (see column Δ)

Benchmark	Recording OFF			Recording ON				
	Δ	time[s]	%GC	Δ	time[s]	%GC	aliases	methods
Tiny benchmark (bytecodes)	**1.02**	1.03	0.0	**2.26**	2.29	16.1	13773 k	8 k
Tiny benchmark (sends)	**1.20**	1.39	0.0	**2.06**	2.39	7.1	7881 k	11406 k
STones80 (low-level)	**1.12**	0.51	5.6	**1.53**	0.70	8.4	21600 k	4960 k
STones80 (medium-level)	**1.27**	0.38	0.4	**6.43**	1.91	46.0	59478 k	17077 k
Squeak macro benchmark	**1.16**	0.38	2.0	**6.91**	2.23	60.7	5532 k	669 k
Average	**1.15**	0.74	1.6	**3.84**	1.91	27.6	21653 k	6824 k

Benchmarks. We used five different benchmarks[1]. The first two rows show the results of two *Tiny benchmarks*, which measure how many bytecodes and message sends can be executed per second. The bytecode benchmark is based on a bytecode-heavy implementation of the "Sieve of Eratosthenes" whereas the message send benchmark is based on a send-heavy recursive calculation of Fibonacci numbers. The second and third rows show the results of the *STones80 benchmarks*, which are available for many different Smalltalk dialects. Whereas the low-level version mainly involves arithmetic operations, array operations, and object allocation, the medium-level version also performs recursive calls, collection and stream operations. The last row of Table 1 shows the results of the *Squeak macro benchmark*, which measures decompiling and then recompiling methods.

Discussion. The results of the benchmarks taken with disabled recording averaged 15%. These numbers are a good indication of the performance penalty caused by our virtual machine modifications. When recording is turned off, no aliases are allocated and hence no message sends have to be forwarded and no additional time is spent in the garbage collector. Interestingly, the overhead of the Tiny bytecodes benchmark is very low with an overhead of only 2%, while the overheads of the other benchmarks average between

---

[1] The Tiny benchmarks can be found in the standard Squeak distribution. The STones80 and the Squeak macro benchmarks can be found in the Benchmarks package on http://map.squeak.org/

12% and 27%. To find out whether this difference is significant or whether our modifications have no measurable influence on the performance of the bytecode benchmark, we performed the following statistical analysis.

We formulate the null hypothesis H_0 that the average runtime of the Tiny bytecode benchmark is not slower when executed on our modified VM (M) compared to the original VM (O), formally: $\mu_O \geq \mu_M$. The alternative hypothesis H_1 postulates that the average runtime of the benchmark is slower when being executed on our modified VM compared to the original VM, formally: $\mu_O < \mu_M$.

To test the hypotheses we apply the independent one-sided two-sample t-test [14] with an α value of 1% and 58 degrees of freedom. The variance requirement is fulfilled and both data sets are normally distributed (verified with the Kolmogorov-Smirnov test). We calculated a t value of -16, which means that we can clearly reject the null hypothesis H_0 and accept the alternative hypothesis H_1 (the t distribution tells us that the probability that $t \leq -2.4$ is 1%). Therefore, we can conclude that the 2% slowdown of this benchmark is due to our modifications of the VM. Using the same method, we can draw the analogous conclusion for all other benchmarks. This result is not surprising as those runtimes are clearly distinct from the reference runtimes.

In the case of recording switched on, particularly noticeable are the big differences between the overheads of the first three low-level benchmarks compared to the other higher-level benchmarks. The overheads of the medium-level STones80 benchmark (factor 6.43) and the Squeak macro benchmark (factor 6.91) are more than three times as big as the overheads of the low-level benchmarks. One reason for this is that those benchmarks spend a significant percentage of their runtime in the garbage collector (46.0% and 60.7%). The high pressure on the garbage collector cannot be explained entirely by the higher rate by which alias and method invocation objects are created (31 million aliases/s for medium-level STones80 and 2.5 million for the macro benchmark). For instance, the low-level STones80 benchmark produces 30.7 million aliases/s but incurs a relatively low overhead. Rather, it is likely that the high pressure is due to the different memory usage characteristics, e.g., how fast aliases can be garbage collected.

Summary. These benchmarks suggest that a significant overhead incurs because of the additional pressure on the garbage collector, which depends on the characteristics of memory usage. (Memory usage characteristics are further discussed in Section 4.2.) In turn, instantiating and initializing aliases seems to contribute not as much as the garbage collector to the overhead.

Without much optimization effort the overhead of our implementation when recording is switched off is just 15%. This suggests that with more aggressive performance optimizations a virtual machine enhancement for capturing execution history could potentially be incorporated into a standard distribution. This would allow users to switch recording on and off as required without needing to recompile code and restart the application with a different virtual machine.

4.2   Memory Usage

To further evaluate the practicality of our approach, we also investigated the characteristics of larger applications with respect to the amount of memory consumed. Of particular interest is whether the retained historical data increases steadily over time, or whether the amount of data is bounded by an upper value.

We expected this characteristic to be dependent on the type of application. For example, in applications with persistent objects that undergo many state changes, this is obviously not possible as all previous object states are retained until the objects themselves are garbage collected. In contrast, in applications where objects are used only temporarily it is possible that long running programs can be recorded without running out of memory.

To study different types of memory usages we chose the following three programs:

- *A program that allocates a large number of temporary objects that get garbage collected after some time.* We selected the Squeak bytecode compiler which we ran on 1000 classes. We expected that the history of objects generated to represent tokens, AST nodes and intermediate representation objects can be garbage collected after the bytecode of a class has been successfully emitted.
- *A program with a stable number of objects that undergo a large number of state changes.* We selected a gas tank simulator shipped as a Squeak demo. Each molecule in the tank is represented by an object and on each GUI update the position of the molecules, their velocities and directions are recalculated and changed. Since all previous positions of the molecules are remembered, we expected a lower effect of the garbage collector in comparison to the bytecode compiler.
- *A program with an existing object graph that is heavily accessed and modified.* We chose a commercial web content management system (CMS). The history of modifications of the object model and the behavior leading to it cannot be discarded after some time because the object model of the CMS is completely kept in memory.

Bytecode Compiler. Figure 8 shows virtual machine statistics taken from sampling the execution of the Squeak bytecode compiler. We compiled 1000 classes from the Squeak Smalltalk system which took 652 seconds when recording was turned on (compared to 168s when recording was disabled). In total the execution produced more than 2 billion aliases (solid line in Figure 8) and 443 million method invocations (not shown). On average, 3 million aliases are created per second. The actual number of aliases in memory was relatively low at an average of 2.9 million (notice the different scales of the left and right Y-axes). The maximum amount of memory allocated by the virtual machine was 317MB.

The temporal development of the number of regular objects (excluding alias objects) is similar to one of the number of aliases. The reoccurring pattern of growth and decline is caused by incremental and full garbage collect cycles.

The analysis of this application showed the expected behavior. The historical data kept in memory does not grow without limit because the compiling history of a class is discarded after the bytecode has been generated and emitted.

Gas tank simulation. Figure 9 shows the analysis of the following usage scenario of the gas tank simulation. First we started one instance of the simulator and paused it after

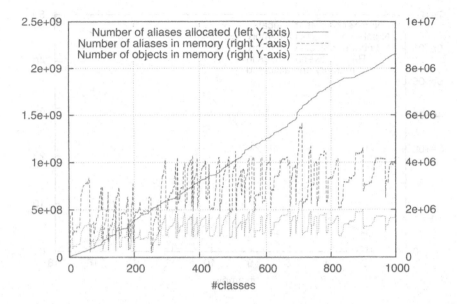

Fig. 8. Compiling 1000 classes (X-axis) produces more than 2 billion aliases, however, the number of aliases in memory stays below 6 million. Please note that because of the large differences between the number of allocated aliases (solid line) and the aliases and objects in memory (dashed and dotted lines), we use two scales: one for the solid line to the left and one for the dashed and dotted lines to the right

the sample step #5. Then we started a second simulator with twice the number of molecules. The higher rate of aliases allocated from this time on is reflected in Figure 9. At step #10 we quit the second simulator and resumed the first one.

Quitting the second simulator has a big effect on the number of aliases retained in memory (see decline between steps #10 and #11). Since the objects of the second simulator are not accessible anymore, the remaining execution history is garbage collected. The same happens after quitting the simulator at the end of the analysis, where the number of aliases in memory drops to zero.

A striking difference to the case of the bytecode compiler is that the number of aliases in memory grows with respect to the number of aliases allocated over time. As Figure 9 shows, the ratio is constantly 22% in the first half of the analysis up until the event where the second simulator instance was quit. This means, that for this application 78% of the aliases are garbage collected but the rest adds up in memory and eventually the virtual machine will run out of memory for long runs.

The execution history retained by our approach allows one to revert the state of objects that are currently accessible (or that are accessible through a past field reference of an accessible object). In case of the simulator this means that we can move back in time as long as the simulator user interface has not been closed. For instance we can set the point of view of its GUI process to a past point in time. This has the effect that the molecules are displayed where they were positioned at that time, and that also all

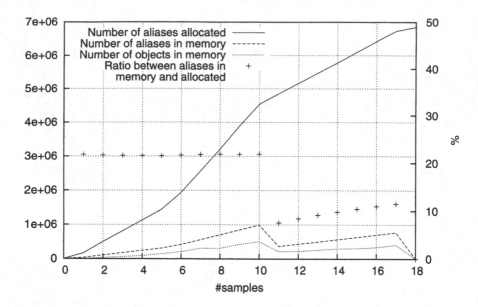

Fig. 9. Analysis of a gas tank simulator shows that 22% of the aliases allocated are retained in memory (19 samples with an interval of 3s each)

settings of the simulator are reverted to their previous states. To find out how a position was calculated, we can follow back the flow of the corresponding point object to where it was allocated.

Content Management System. Figure 10 illustrates an analysis of a user session in Cmsbox[2], a commercial web content management system. The session consists of 26 user actions such as login, editing content, drag and drop, copy and paste elements, publish page etc.

We chose Cmsbox as a case study, because it stores all objects in memory rather than in a database, which makes it a worst case scenario for our approach. Indeed, as the figure shows, the aliases do increase steadily over time, the main reason being that more objects are added and retained in the model and in memory.

This experiment shows the limits of our approach. However, as described in Section 5.1 we can limit the effect of this phenomenon through selective recording of aliases.

5   Discussion

Memory consumption and performance can be further tuned by adjusting the level of detail of information gathered. We now look at several ways this can be done, and we discuss difficulties, limitations and potential optimizations of our implementation.

---

[2] http://www.cmsbox.com/

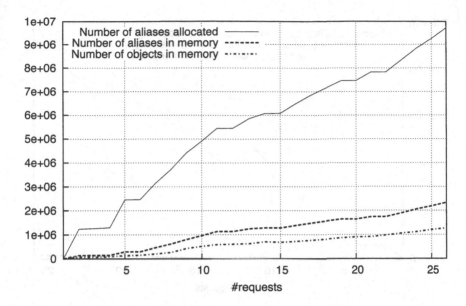

Fig. 10. Analysis of a user session in a Content Management System. After 26 requests, 24% of the allocated aliases are still in memory.

5.1 Capturing and Remembering Less Data

Depending on the usage of the back-in-time debugger, for instance in a testing or production environment, it can be necessary to further decrease memory consumption and lower the execution overhead. A common solution to reduce the amount of data recorded is to not instrument all code, for instance by excluding libraries and framework code. The effect is that in the code that is out of scope, no side effects are captured and the links of objects being passed through this code are lost.

We experimented with an alternative approach that is not based on structural scoping but on tuning how fast recorded data is discarded. In particular, in our implementation the user can change the behavior of the virtual machine by (a) disabling tracking of predecessor aliases, (b) disabling tacking of origin aliases, and (c) selecting which types of aliases are created. By default, all predecessor and origin aliases and all types of aliases are recorded.

For example by not tracking predecessors, we can reduce the consumed memory but still benefit from being able to inspect object flows. By means of such configurations we can provide the same functionality as the following two debugger extensions that have been proposed recently. They are specialized to a particular debugging task and hence only need to track a fraction of the whole execution history.

Reverse watchpoint, an approach proposed by Maruyama *et al.*, analyses the execution and moves the debugger to the last write access of a selected variable by re-executing the program from the beginning [6]. This technique automates the task of finding where a variable was erroneously written and then moves the debugger to that point. With our approach, finding where a variable was written means to move one step

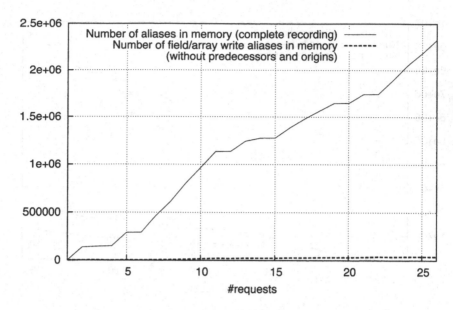

Fig. 11. Comparison of the number of aliases retained in memory with the default configuration compared to the configuration where only the last write alias of each field and array slot is remembered (same run of the CMS as in Figure 10)

back in the object flow from a field read alias to its origin, which is the field write alias. If we want to gather exactly this information, we can disable predecessors, and restrict the recording to create only field write and array write aliases. The effect is that for each field the most recent write alias is available with the execution stack in which it was created. When writing to a field, the previous write alias of the field or array can be discarded immediately because it is not referenced as a predecessor or origin alias.

Our benchmarks show that with this minimal configuration, we achieve a very low execution overhead that is only insignificantly higher than the base slowdown of 15%, which the virtual machine incurs when recording is turned off completely. In comparison, Maruyama report a slowdown of their technique of about 400% [6]. Figure 11 shows that with this reduced configuration only a fraction of the aliases are remembered, compared to the aliases remembered using the standard configuration as illustrated in Figure 10.

Origin tracking of null values, proposed by Bond *et al.*, is a very efficient technique to track the method in which an undefined values originates to support debugging the well-known problem of null pointer exceptions [15]. We can do the same by only tracking aliases of type *undefined*, which again incurs a similar overhead to the configuration discussed above. In comparison, the approach of Bond *et al.* adds an overhead of only 4%. The low overhead is made possible by only tracking undefined values, which allows for "value piggybacking", a technique to store origin information directly in pointers (in this case in null pointers).

5.2 Remembering Control Flow Dependencies

With the default configuration our approach retains information about the flow of objects and previous states of objects. In contrast, conventional back-in-time debuggers typically record and store the complete execution history (until they run out of memory). While our approach records the same data, it discards most of it within a very short time and only remembers what is relevant for the object flow and historical states of objects that are accessible at the current point of execution. To provide enough context, with each alias, the method invocation where it is used is retained, including the execution stack with all target objects and objects passed as parameters.

Still, depending on the kind of bug, it is possible that relevant information is missing. In particular, no links between aliases exist to represent the fact that the value of a variable influences the value of another variable. For example, in the statement "if x.f then y.f = 1" there is no dependency link between the field read alias x.f and the field write alias y.f. In case the value of y.f turns out to be incorrect because of the unexpected execution of a branch, it is possible that x.f has already been discarded. However, this does not happen if x is the target object of the method or one of its parameters. In this case it is referenced from the method invocation which in turn is referenced as the context of the field write alias stored in y.f. (How exactly aliases and method invocations refer to each other is illustrated in Figure 2.)

We decided not to explicitly capture such control flow dependencies because we believe that the most difficult bugs in object-oriented programs are caused by subtle inconsistencies in object graphs and by the propagation of unexpected object references. However, it would be possible to extend our approach to also include dependency relationships among aliases. Each alias would need to maintain a list of other aliases it depends on, similar to the predecessor and origin relationships. The dependence information could be computed by an intra-procedural static analysis. An inter-procedural analysis would not be necessary since this dependency is indirectly captured by the link of an alias to the target of the invocation in which it is created (alias → context → target).

5.3 Limitations and Potential Optimizations of the Implementation

Not freed memory. Using our back-in-time debugger we noticed a couple of times that parts of the history were unexpectedly not garbage collected. The reason turned out to be that the program execution in those cases produced subtle side effects on global state. The effect is that the part of the execution history that produced the side effect is not garbage collected as long as the global state that was modified exists. We observed three cases of this problem: singletons, caches and writing to a log console (strings passed from the application are stored in the console stream and hence retain links to the execution history where they originate). While in some cases this can be the desired behavior (in case of the cache or singleton), it may be undesired in other cases (the console). To remedy the undesired cases we can simply disable recording of the appropriate methods or classes. The real difficulty, however, is to first find the cause of such a problem. What is missing are high-level views to inspect and navigate the recorded data.

Capturing non-word size data. A limitation of our implementation is that the history of values stored as non-word data are not captured. For instance, in a byte array where four bytes are stored per word, we cannot use the approach of exchanging a value with an alias indirection because the alias pointer requires 4 bytes. Typically this is not problematic since Squeak uses non-word fields in most cases to represent internal data of objects only, such as float objects, large integer objects, or strings.

Potential optimizations of our implementation. As our benchmarks show, the slowdown is mainly caused by the additional garbage collector activity. An optimization of the garbage collector to better cope with the special characteristics of our virtual machine would improve the performance but is not straightforward to realize.

A different optimization that would also improve the performance of the virtual machine when tracing is turned off is to use different sets of bytecode routines. The current implementation uses conditionals in bytecode routines and primitives to execute code depending on the tracing state of the current thread. Implementing two sets of bytecode routines would allow the virtual machine to switch jump tables when recording is toggled.

The memory consumption of our implementation could be slightly optimized by distinguishing between field/array write aliases and the other types of aliases. Field write and array write aliases require the predecessor field to hold onto historical state, whereas the other aliases do not need this field. Using two different classes of aliases would be simple to implement and would save one word per non-historical alias instance.

6 Related Work

Logging-based approaches. The most common approach to implementing back-in-time debuggers has been to create a trace log of the program execution. ZStep95 is a reversible debugger for Lisp that provides animated views but does not address performance and scalability issues [16]. Lewis proposed ODB [3], a back-in-time debugger for Java, and Hofer proposed Unstuck [5], a similar proof of concept implementation for Squeak Smalltalk. Both approaches have in common that they keep the log history in memory and hence can only record and store the complete history for a short period of time. ODB allows one to set a fixed limit on the number of events and it then discards older events when the limit is reached.

A more scalable approach has recently been proposed by Pothier *et al.* [4]. Their back-in-time debugger, TOD, addresses the space problem by storing execution events in a distributed database. While this approach has the benefit that no data is lost, its drawback is that it requires extensive hardware power, which is not available for many developers today. To cope with the data generated by a CPU-intensive program, 10 database nodes in a server cluster are required. Also, the approach has a performance overhead of a factor 113 in the worst case, which is approximately the same as the one of ODB for the same benchmark [4].

In comparison, the performance of our approach is about one order of magnitude better. On the one hand, this is because our approach is implemented at the virtual machine level, whereas all previously mentioned approaches are based on bytecode instrumentation. On the other hand, as our approach stores historical data directly in the application memory, it does not require any additional logging facility to gather and store data. As a side effect, our representation of historical information is also very space efficient. For example, there is no need to assign identifiers to objects or to serialize objects since they exist in memory and can be referred to directly by pointers.

Outside of research, back-in-time debuggers have unfortunately not been widely adopted yet. An example of a commercial back-in-time debugger is Omnicore's Code-Guide[3]. It is also based on bytecode instrumentation and its execution history, which is kept in memory, is limited to the few last thousand events. An interesting aspect of CodeGuide is that only methods containing breakpoints and methods close to them in the control flow are instrumented to keep the runtime overhead low.

Related to logging-based back-in-time debugging is *query-based debugging*. In those approaches the user formulates a query in a higher-level language that is then applied to the logged data [17,18,19,20]. Queries can test complex object interrelationships and sequences of related events. Approaches exist that execute the query at runtime, which can improve performance because no history has to be stored [21]. Our approach, like other back-in-time debugging approaches, does not support querying for complex relationships in the history, but in return it incurs a much smaller execution overhead.

Replay-based approaches. A different approach for implementing back-in-time debuggers is to replay the debugged program until a desired point in the past. To optimize the time required to reach a particular point in the past, many approaches take periodic state snapshots, for instance Bdb [22] and Igor [23]. The main advantage of replay-based approaches over logging-based approaches is their low performance overhead (roughly 2 times for Bdb and 4 times for Igor). The disadvantage of those kinds of approaches is that moving backwards in time can be very slow because the program has to be partly re-executed. This issue has been addressed in a recent publication by Xu *et al.* [24]. Our approach can access past object state almost instantly because it only needs to look up the appropriate alias in the predecessors chain (as described in Section 2.3). An open issue of replay-based approaches is that of deterministic replay, which cannot be guaranteed by all approaches if the program depends on external resources or if it is multithreaded.

The approach of taking (incremental) memory snapshots and replaying has also been used in the Leonardo virtual machine [25], a virtual machine based approach for assembly-like languages that features reversing program state. Similar to our approach, programs slow down by a factor of 6 in the worst case. However, the Leonardo virtual machine does not support inspecting object flows and it does not provide a strategy to discard data.

7   Conclusions and Future Work

In this paper we tackle the problem of how to make back-in-time debugging practical by (1) keeping memory consumption within reasonable bounds by only keeping track of still-relevant past data, and (2) reducing the run-time overhead by implementing

---

[3] http://www.omnicore.com/

recording at the virtual machine level. Our approach does not store all data, but instead it focuses on remembering the history of the objects that are still referenced in the current program state. Our solution makes use of the garbage collector to release the objects that are not referenced anymore in the program and that are not relevant anymore in the program's history.

Benchmarks have shown significant improvements over existing approaches. First, the memory consumption is confined to an upper bound limit in the best case, or grows slowly in the worst case. However, for the worst case scenario, we can configure the recording to capture and remember less data, which can lead to a dramatic decrease in memory consumption (*e.g.*, 55 times fewer aliases when just remembering the last field write alias). Second, performance is in the worst case 7 times slower than a regular execution. Furthermore, the modified virtual machine with tracing switched off introduces only modest overhead (*e.g.*, in our benchmarks, it introduces an average of 15%) as compared with a regular one.

The results we obtained are very promising and we envision several paths to improve them. First, we want to provide more control for adjusting the level of detail depending on the static structure. For instance, we can gather more data in code that is young and hence is more likely to have defects. Second, we want to experiment with instrumentation mechanisms that can be adapted at runtime. For example, we can increase the recording detail when an error is detected for the followup runs, or we can decrease recording detail when memory gets low. Lastly, we want to further investigate the effectiveness of our approach, for instance to identify potential limitations of its usability due to missing control flow dependencies.

Acknowledgments

We gratefully acknowledge the financial support of the Swiss National Science Foundation for the project "Analyzing, capturing and taming software change" (SNF Project No. 200020-113342, Oct. 2006 - Sept. 2008), and the financial support of ESUG. We would like to thank Stéphane Ducasse and David Röthlisberger for their help in reviewing drafts of this paper.

References

1. Zeller, A.: Why Programs Fail: A Guide to Systematic Debugging. Morgan Kaufmann, San Francisco (2005)
2. Liblit, B., Naik, M., Zheng, A.X., Aiken, A., Jordan, M.I.: Scalable statistical bug isolation. In: Proceedings of the 2005 ACM SIGPLAN conference on Programming language design and implementation (PLDI 2005), pp. 15–26. ACM, New York (2005)
3. Lewis, B.: Debugging backwards in time. In: Proceedings of the Fifth International Workshop on Automated Debugging (AADEBUG 2003) (October 2003)
4. Pothier, G., Tanter, E., Piquer, J.: Scalable omniscient debugging. In: Proceedings of the 22nd Annual SCM SIGPLAN Conference on Object-Oriented Programming Systems, Languages and Applications (OOPSLA 2007). ACM, New York (to appear, 2007)
5. Hofer, C., Denker, M., Ducasse, S.: Design and implementation of a backward-in-time debugger. In: Proceedings of NODE 2006, September 2006. Lecture Notes in Informatics, vol. P-88, pp. 17–32. Gesellschaft für Informatik (GI) (2006)

6. Maruyama, K., Terada, M.: Debugging with reverse watchpoint. In: Proceedings of the Third International Conference on Quality Software (QSIC 2003), p. 116. IEEE Computer Society, Washington (2003)

7. Lienhard, A., Greevy, O., Nierstrasz, O.: Tracking objects to detect feature dependencies. In: Proceedings International Conference on Program Comprehension (ICPC 2007), June 2007, pp. 59–68. IEEE Computer Society, Washington (2007)

8. Lienhard, A., Ducasse, S., Gîrba, T.: Object flow analysis — taking an object-centric view on dynamic analysis. In: Proceedings of the 2007 International Conference on Dynamic Languages (ICDL 2007), pp. 121–140. ACM Digital Library, New York (2007)

9. Lienhard, A., Gîrba, T., Greevy, O., Nierstrasz, O.: Test blueprints – exposing side effects in execution traces to support writing unit tests. In: 12th European Conference on Software Maintenance and Reengineering (CSMR 2008), pp. 83–92. IEEE Computer Society Press, Los Alamitos (2008)

10. Alpern, B., Attanasio, C.R., Cocchi, A., Lieber, D., Smith, S., Ngo, T., Barton, J.J., Hummel, S.F., Sheperd, J.C., Mergen, M.: Implementing jalapeño in java. In: Proceedings of the 14th ACM SIGPLAN conference on Object-oriented programming, systems, languages, and applications (OOPSLA 1999), pp. 314–324. ACM, New York (1999)

11. Ingalls, D., Kaehler, T., Maloney, J., Wallace, S., Kay, A.: Back to the future: The story of Squeak, a practical Smalltalk written in itself. In: Proceedings of the 12th ACM SIGPLAN conference on Object-oriented programming, systems, languages, and applications (OOPSLA 1997), November 1997, pp. 318–326. ACM Press, New York (1997)

12. Bracha, G., Ungar, D.: Mirrors: design principles for meta-level facilities of object-oriented programming languages. In: Proceedings of OOPSLA 2004, ACM SIGPLAN Notices, pp. 331–344. ACM Press, New York (2004)

13. Goldberg, A., Robson, D.: Smalltalk 80: the Language and its Implementation. Addison-Wesley, Reading (1983)

14. Kanji, G.K.: 100 Statistical Tests. SAGE Publications, Thousand Oaks (1999)

15. Bond, M.D., Nethercote, N., Kent, S.W., Guyer, S.Z., McKinley, K.S.: Tracking bad apples: reporting the origin of null and undefined value errors. In: Proceedings of the 22nd annual ACM SIGPLAN conference on Object oriented programming systems and applications (OOPSLA 2007), pp. 405–422. ACM, New York (2007)

16. Lieberman, H., Fry, C.: ZStep 95: A reversible, animated source code stepper. In: Stasko, J., Domingue, J., Brown, M.H., Price, B.A. (eds.) Software Visualization — Programming as a Multimedia Experience, pp. 277–292. MIT Press, Cambridge (1998)

17. Martin, M., Livshits, B., Lam, M.S.: Finding application errors and security flaws using pql: a program query language. In: Proceedings of Object-Oriented Programming, Systems, Languages, and Applications (OOPSLA 2005), pp. 363–385. ACM Press, New York (2005)

18. Lencevicius, R., Hölzle, U., Singh, A.K.: Query-based debugging of object-oriented programs. In: Proceedings of the 12th ACM SIGPLAN conference on Object-oriented programming (OOPSLA 1997), pp. 304–317. ACM, New York (1997)

19. Potanin, A., Noble, J., Biddle, R.: Snapshot query-based debugging. In: Proceedings of the 2004 Australian Software Engineering Conference (ASWEC 2004), p. 251. IEEE Computer Society, Washington (2004)

20. Ducasse, S., Gîrba, T., Wuyts, R.: Object-oriented legacy system trace-based logic testing. In: Proceedings of 10th European Conference on Software Maintenance and Reengineering (CSMR 2006), pp. 35–44. IEEE Computer Society Press, Los Alamitos (2006)

21. Lencevicius, R., Hölzle, U., Singh, A.K.: Dynamic query-based debugging. In: Guerraoui, R. (ed.) ECOOP 1999. LNCS, vol. 1628, pp. 135–160. Springer, Heidelberg (1999)

22. Feldman, S.I., Brown, C.B.: Igor: a system for program debugging via reversible execution. In: Proceedings of the 1988 ACM SIGPLAN and SIGOPS workshop on Parallel and distributed debugging (PADD 1988), pp. 112–123. ACM, New York (1988)
23. Boothe, B.: Efficient algorithms for bidirectional debugging. In: Proceedings of the ACM SIGPLAN 2000 conference on Programming language design and implementation (PLDI 2000), pp. 299–310. ACM, New York (2000)
24. Xu, G., Rountev, A., Tang, Y., Qin, F.: Efficient checkpointing of java software using contextsensitive capture and replay. In: Proceedings of the the the 6th joint meeting of the European software engineering conference and the ACM SIGSOFT symposium on The foundations of software engineering (ESEC-FSE 2007), pp. 85–94. ACM, New York (2007)
25. Demetrescu, C., Finocchi, I.: A portable virtual machine for program debugging and directing. In: Proceedings of the 2004 ACM symposium on Applied computing (SAC 2004), pp. 1524–1530. ACM, New York (2004)

Inference of Reference Immutability

Jaime Quinonez, Matthew S. Tschantz, and Michael D. Ernst

MIT Computer Science and Artificial Intelligence Lab
Cambridge, MA, USA
{jaimeq, tschantz, mernst}@csail.mit.edu

Abstract. Javari is an extension of Java that supports reference immutability constraints. Programmers write **readonly** type qualifiers and other constraints, and the Javari typechecker detects mutation errors (incorrect side effects) or verifies their absence. While case studies have demonstrated the practicality and value of Javari, a barrier to usability remains. A Javari program will not typecheck unless all the references in the APIs of libraries it uses are annotated with Javari type qualifiers. Manually converting existing Java libraries to Javari is tedious and error-prone.

We present an algorithm for inferring reference immutability in Javari. The flow-insensitive and context-sensitive algorithm is sound and produces a set of qualifiers that typecheck in Javari. The algorithm is precise in that it infers the most **readonly** qualifiers possible; adding any additional **readonly** qualifiers will cause the program to not typecheck. We have implemented the algorithm in a tool, Javarifier, that infers the Javari type qualifiers over a set of class files.

Javarifier automatically converts Java libraries to Javari. Additionally, Javarifier eases the task of converting legacy programs to Javari by inferring the mutability of every reference in a program. In case studies, Javarifier correctly inferred mutability over Java programs of up to 110 KLOC.

1 Introduction

An immutability reference constraint, such as a **readonly** type qualifier, prevents a reference from being used to modify its referent objects (including their transitive state). Immutability constraints have many benefits: programmers can formally express intended properties of their code; explicit, machine-checked documentation enhances program understanding; static or dynamics checkers can detect errors or guarantee their absence; and analyses and transformations depending on compiler-verified properties are enabled. In practice, immutability constraints have been shown to be practical and to find errors in software.

Writing reference immutability annotations to obtain these benefits can be tedious and error-prone. An even more important motivation for immutability inference is the need to annotate the signatures of all used libraries. Otherwise, a sound reference immutability type checker would be forced to assume that all methods in these libraries modify their arguments. In particular, passing a **readonly** reference to any library method would be a type error.

J. Vitek (Ed.): ECOOP 2008, LNCS 5142, pp. 616–641, 2008.

```
┌────── Java ──────┐   ┌────────── Javari ──────────┐
│ class Event {     │   │ class Event {                │
│   Date date;      │   │   /*this-mutable*/ Date date; │
│                   │   │                              │
│   Date getDate() {│   │   polyread Date getDate() polyread {│
│     return Date;  │   │     return Date;             │
│   }               │   │   }                          │
│                   │   │                              │
│   void setDate(Date d) {│ │   void setDate(/*mutable*/ Date d) /*mutable*/ {│
│     this.date = d;│   │     this.date = d;           │
│   }               │   │   }                          │
│ }                 │   │ }                            │
└───────────────────┘   └──────────────────────────────┘
```

Fig. 1. A Java class (left) and the corresponding Javari class (right) that is automatically produced by Javarifier. Underlines indicate added immutability qualifiers. The figure shows default qualifiers in comments for clarity (Javarifier adds nothing in such cases). A qualifier after the parameter list and before the opening curly brace annotates that method's receiver, similar to annotations on other parameters. The qualifiers are explained in Section 2.

We have created an algorithm that soundly calculates reference immutability. Although our framework can accomidate other notions of reference immutability, for concreteness, this paper uses the reference immutability constraints of Javari [29]. Javari is an extension of Java with reference immutability type qualifiers (see Section 2).

This algorithm computes all the references (including local variables, method parameters, and static and instance fields) that may have Javari's readonly, polyread, or ? readonly keywords added to their declarations. Figure 1 shows an example Java class and the corresponding inferred Javari class.

Our algorithm targets a realistic and fully-featured implementation of reference immutability, Javari. The algorithm infers the multiple annotations that are needed for an expressive language, including readonly, an extension to wildcards (? readonly), non-generics polymorphism (polyread), and containing-object context this-mutable. [1] Javari provides reference immutability guarantees over the abstract state of an object (see Section 2.1). The algorithm handles the complexities of the Java language, including subtyping, generics, arrays, and unseen code. The algorithm is sound and precise.

Javarifier is a scalable tool that implements this algorithm. Javarifier's input is a Java (or partially annotated Javari) program in classfile format, because programmers may wish to convert library code whose source is unavailable. The Javarifier toolset can insert the inferred qualifiers in source or class files, or present them to a user for inspection. If the user wants to refine the results, the user can insert any number of annotations in the program and run Javarifier in

---

[1] As a pre-pass, the algorithm heuristically recommends fields to exclude from the abstract state of a class via the assignable or mutable field annotations; the user may accept some or all of the recommendations. Page limits prohibit an explanation of these heuristics [28,22], though they are implemented in the Javarifier tool.

Type qualifiers	
readonly	The reference cannot be used to modify its referent
/*mutable*/	The reference may be used to modify its referent
polyread	Polymorphism (for parameters and return types) over mutability
? readonly	The reference has a readonly upper bound and mutable lower bound

Field annotations	
/*this-mutable*/	The field inherits its mutability from the reference through which it is reached
assignable	The field may be reassigned through a readonly reference
mutable	The field may be mutated through a readonly reference

Fig. 2. Javari keywords: type qualifiers and field annotations. Default keywords that are not written in a program are shown in comments.

the presence of these annotations (see Section 3.3). All of the tools use the JSR 308 [10] extension to Java annotations, which is backward-compatible and which is planned for inclusion in Java 7.[2]

The rest of this paper is organized as follows. Section 2 provides an overview of the Javari language for reference immutability. Sections 3–5 describe the algorithm: sound inference of reference immutability for ordinary readonly references (Section 3), arrays and generic types (Section 4), and polyread polymorphic references (Section 5). Section 6 reports experience using Javarifier. Section 7 discusses related work. Finally, Section 8 concludes.

2   The Javari Language: Java with Reference Immutability

Javari extends Java's type system to allow programmers to specify and statically enforce reference immutability constraints. This section briefly explains Javari's keywords, as listed in figure 2. The language is fully defined elsewhere [29,28].

For every Java type T, Javari also has the type readonly T, with T being a subtype of readonly T. A reference declared to have a readonly type cannot be used to mutate the object it references:

```
readonly Date d = new Date();
d.setHours(9);                 // compile-time error
```

Mutation is any modification to an object's abstract state (see Section 2.1). References that are not readonly can be used to modify their referent and are said to be *mutable*. By Java's subtyping rules, a mutable reference can be used anywhere a readonly reference is expected, but a readonly reference cannot be treated as a mutable reference.

Javari handles generic type parameters in a natural way to account for the fact that every type now specifies its mutability. Below are four declarations of type List. The mutability of the parameterized type List does not affect the mutability of the type argument.

---

[2] To avoid explaining JSR 308, this paper uses keywords rather than annotations for the Javari type qualifiers.

```
/*mutable*/ List</*mutable*/ Date> ld1;  // List: may add/remove; Date: may mutate
/*mutable*/ List<readonly    Date> ld2;  // List: may add/remove
readonly    List</*mutable*/ Date> ld3;  // Date: may mutate
readonly    List<readonly    Date> ld4;  // (no side effects allowed)
```

As in Java, subtyping is invariant in terms of type arguments. Javari expresses the common supertype of `List</*mutable*/ Date>` and `List<readonly Date>` as `List<? readonly Date>`. The `? readonly` wildcard keyword is an extension to Java's wildcard mechanism. It specifies that `readonly Date` is the type argument's upper bound and `/*mutable*/ Date` is its lower bound. Elements are read from this type of list as `readonly`, but must be written to it as `mutable`. This type would be written as `List<? extends readonly Date super /*mutable*/ Date>`, except Java does not allow the declaration of both a lower and an upper bound on a wildcard.

The mutability wildcard is useful for the same reasons Java wildcards are. For example, a method that prints all the `Dates` in an input `List` can have a `List<? readonly Date>` parameter. If the parameter were declared as `List<readonly Date>`, a `List<mutable Date>` argument could not be passed in.

Javari keywords, inclusindg `? readonly`, apply to arrays analogously to parameterized types; each level of an array has its own mutability, and Javari arrays are invariant with respect to mutability.

The `polyread` keyword (see Figure 3) expresses parametric polymorphism over mutability. (`polyread` was previously named "romaybe" [29,28].) The type checker conceptually duplicates any method containing a `polyread` keyword. In the first version of the method, all instances of `polyread` are replaced by `readonly`. In the second version, all instances of `polyread` are removed, so the references are mutable. Clients may use either version. `polyread` may occur on fields of method-local classes, and Javarifier inferred such annotations in our case studies. `polyread` is critical for precision; in the JDK, `polyread` is needed 70% as often as `readonly` [19]. `polyread` is not expressible in terms of Java generics; Neither of `polyread` and `? readonly` subsumes the other [28].

2.1   Abstract State

By default, the abstract state of an object is its transitively reachable state, which is the state of the object and all state reachable from it by following references. Javari's deep reference immutability is achieved by giving each field the default annotation of `this-mutable`, which means the field inherits its mutability from the reference (`this`) through which it is accessed. Since it is the default, `this-mutable` is never written in a program.

The `assignable` and `mutable` keywords enable a programmer to exclude specific fields from an object's abstract state. The `assignable` keyword specifies that the field may always be reassigned, even through a `readonly` reference; Java's `final` keyword plays a related role, specifying that a field may not be reassigned at all through any reference once it has been set. The `mutable` keyword specifies that a field has mutable type (its own fields may be reassigned or mutated) even

```
class Bicycle {
  private Seat seat;
  polyread Seat getSeat() polyread { return seat; }
}

static void lowerSeat(/*mutable*/ Bicycle b) {
  /*mutable*/ Seat s = b.getSeat();
  s.height = 0;
}

static void printSeat(readonly Bicycle b) {
  readonly Seat s = b.getSeat();
  System.out.println(s);
}
```

Fig. 3. The `polyread` keyword expresses polymorphism over mutability without polymorphism over the Java type. `lowerSeat` uses the mutable version of `getSeat` and takes a mutable `Bicycle` parameter. `printSeat` uses the readonly version of `getSeat` and can take a readonly `Bicycle` parameter. Without `polyread`, all the underlined annotations would be `/*mutable*/`. In particular, `printSeat` would take a mutable `Bicycle` parameter, and this imprecision could propagate through the rest of the program.

when referenced through a `readonly` reference. A `mutable` field's abstract value is not a part of the abstract state of the object (but the field's identity may be). Assignability and mutability of fields are orthogonal notions. Both are necessary to express code idioms such as caches, logging, and benevolent side effects, where not every field is part of the object's abstract state. For example, in the following class, the value of the `log` field is excluded from the abstract state of the object:

```
public class NetworkRouter {
  mutable List<String> log;

  // The readonly keyword indicates that the method does not modify its receiver
  public void selectRoute(String destination) readonly {
    log.add("selecting route to: " + destination);
  }
}
```

The (implicit, default) `mutable` type qualifier denotes that a reference may be used to modify its referent. The (explicit) `mutable` field annotation denotes that the field may always be used to modify its referent— it is excluded from the abstract state of the object.

3   Inferring Reference Immutability

Javarifier uses a flow-insensitive and context-sensitive algorithm to infer reference immutability. The algorithm determines which references may be declared

$$Q ::= \texttt{class } \{\overline{\texttt{f}}\ \overline{\texttt{M}}\}\quad \text{class def}$$
$$M ::= \texttt{m}(\overline{\texttt{x}})\{\overline{\texttt{s};}\}\qquad \text{method def}$$
$$s ::= \texttt{x} = \texttt{x}\qquad\qquad \text{statements}$$
$$\mid\ \texttt{x} = \texttt{x.m}(\overline{\texttt{x}})$$
$$\mid\ \texttt{return x}$$
$$\mid\ \texttt{x} = \texttt{x.f}$$
$$\mid\ \texttt{x.f} = \texttt{x}$$

Fig. 4. Grammar for core language used during constraint generation. $\overline{\texttt{x}}$ is shorthand for the (possibly empty) sequence $\texttt{x}_1 \ldots \texttt{x}_n$. The special variable $\texttt{this}_\texttt{m}$ is the receiver of method $\texttt{m}$; it is treated as a normal variable, except that any program that attempts to reassign $\texttt{this}_\texttt{m}$ is malformed.

with `readonly` or other Javari keywords; other references are left as the default (`this-mutable` for fields, `mutable` for everything else). The algorithm is sound: Javarifier's recommendations type check under Javari's rules. Furthermore, the algorithm is precise: declaring any references in addition to Javarifier's recommendations as `readonly` — without other modifications to the code — will result in the program not type checking.

Section 3.1 describes the core inference algorithm. The algorithm extends to handle subtyping (Section 3.2); unseen code and pre-existing constraints including assignable and mutable fields (Section 3.3); arrays (Section 4.1); Java generics (Section 4.2); and mutability polymorphism (Section 5).

3.1 Core Algorithm

Given as input a program, Javarifier generates, then solves, a set of mutability constraints. A mutability constraint states when a given reference must be declared `mutable`. The core algorithm uses two types of constraints: unguarded and guarded. (Section 5 introduces a third variety of constraints, *double-guarded constraints*.) An unguarded constraint such as "$\texttt{x}$" states that a reference is unconditionally mutable. $\texttt{x}$ is a *constraint variable* that refers to a Java reference or other entity in the code. A guarded constraint such as "$\texttt{y} \rightarrow \texttt{x}$" states that if $\texttt{y}$ is mutable, then $\texttt{x}$ is mutable; again, $\texttt{x}$ and $\texttt{y}$ are constraint variables.

Constraint Generation. The first phase of the algorithm generates constraints for each statement in a program. Unguarded constraints are generated when a reference is used to modify an object. Guarded constraints are generated by assignments and field dereferences.

We present constraint generation using a simple three-address core language (Figure 4). Control flow constructs are not modeled, because the flow-insensitive algorithm is unaffected by such constructs. Java types are not modeled because the core algorithm does not use them. Constructors are modeled as regular methods returning a mutable reference to $\texttt{this}_\texttt{m}$. Static members are omitted because they do not illustrate any interesting properties. Without loss

$$x = y : \{x \to y\} \; (\text{ASSIGN})$$

$$\frac{\text{this}(m) = \text{this}_m \qquad \text{params}(m) = \overline{p} \qquad \text{retVal}(m) = \text{ret}_m}{x = y.m(\overline{y}) : \{\text{this}_m \to y, \; \overline{p} \to \overline{y}, \; x \to \text{ret}_m\}} \; (\text{INVK})$$

$$\frac{\text{retVal}(m) = \text{ret}_m}{\text{return } x : \{\text{ret}_m \to x\}} \; (\text{RET})$$

$$x = y.f : \{x \to f, \; x \to y\} \; (\text{REF})$$

$$x.f = y : \{x, \; f \to y\} \; (\text{SET})$$

Fig. 5. Constraint generation rules for the statements of Figure 4. Auxiliary functions `this(m)` and `params(m)` return the receiver reference (this_m) and parameters of method m, respectively. `retVal(m)` returns ret_m, the constraint variable that represents the reference to m's return value. *type*(x) returns the static type of x.

of generality, all references and methods have globally-unique names. (While this paper's formalism is simplified, the Javarifier implementation handles the full Java language.)

Each statement from Figure 4 has a constraint generation rule (Figure 5):

Assign. The assignment of variable y to x causes the guarded constraint $x \to y$ to be generated because, if x is a mutable reference, y must also be mutable for the assignment to be valid.

Invk. The constraints are extensions of the ASSIGN rule when method invocation is viewed as pseudo-assignments or framed in terms of operational semantics: the receiver, y, is assigned to this_m, each actual argument is assigned to the method's corresponding formal parameter, and the return value, ret_m, is assigned to x.

Ret. The return statement `return x` adds the constraint $\text{ret}_m \to x$ because, if the return type of the method is found to be mutable, all references returned by the method must be mutable.

Ref. The assignment of y.f to x generates two constraints. The first, $x \to f$, is required because, if x is mutable, then the field f cannot be readonly. The second, $x \to y$, is needed because, if x is mutable, then y must be mutable to yield a mutable reference to field f. (The core algorithm assumes all fields are `this-mutable`. Fields that have been manually annotated as `mutable` can override this behavior, as discussed in Section 3.3.)

Set. The assignment of y to x.f causes the unguarded constraint x to be generated because x has just been used to mutate the object to which it refers. The constraint $f \to y$ is added because if f, which is `this-mutable`, is ever read as `mutable` from a `mutable` reference, then a mutable reference must be assigned to it. If f is never mutated, the algorithm infers that it is `readonly`, in which case y is not constrained to be `mutable`.

```
                                                       class C {
                                                         readonly F f;
  class C {                                              readonly Y foo(P p)
    F f;                      field declaration            /*mutable*/ {
    Y foo(P p) {                                            /*mutable*/ X x = p;
      X x = p;               ASSIGN: {x→p}                  readonly   Y y = x.f;
      Y y = x.f;             REF: {y → f, y→x}              readonly   Z z = x.foo(y);
      Z z = x.foo(y);        INVK: {this_foo→x,
                                    p→y, z→ret_foo}
      this.f = y;            SET: {this_foo, f→y}          this.f = y;
      return y;              RET: {ret_foo→y}              return y;
    }                                                    }
    void doNothing(P p)                                  void doNothing(readonly P p)
    {                        no constraints to generate    readonly {
    }                                                    }
  }                                                    }
                            Simplified program constraints:
                            {this_foo, x, p}
```

Fig. 6. Example of constraint generation and solving. The left part of the figure shows the original code. The center shows, for each line of code, the constraint generation rule used, the constraints generated, and the simplified program constraints — the references that may not be declared readonly. All the other references (y, z, ret_{foo}, and f) can be declared readonly, as shown in the Javarifier output on the right side of the figure.

The constraint set for a program is the union of the constraints generated for each line of the program. Figure 6 shows constraints for a sample program.

Constraint Solving. The second phase of the algorithm solves the constraints by simplifying the constraint set. If any unguarded constraint satisfies (i.e., matches) the guard of a guarded constraint, then the guarded constraint is "fired" by removing it from the constraint set and adding its consequent to the constraint set as an unguarded constraint. Once no more constraints can be fired, constraint simplification terminates. If the guarded constraints are viewed as graph edges, then the core algorithm can be viewed as graph reachability starting at the unguarded constraints. This approach can be implemented with linear time complexity in the number of constraints [22], and the Javarifier tool does so.

The unguarded constraints in the simplified constraint set must be declared mutable (or this-mutable in the case of instance fields). All other references may safely be declared readonly, since the algorithm propagated unguarded constraints to every reference that those constraints could reach. Thus, the algorithm excludes the maximum number of constraint variables from the unguarded constraint set when there are no field annotations. (Section 3.3 discusses how the assignable and mutable field annotations change the constraint generation rules, but they do not change the constraint solving step.) For a fixed set of field annotations, constraint solving therefore results in the maximum number of readonly references in the program. (Section 4.1 expands this argument to the other Javari qualifiers.) Constraint solving cannot fail because the algorithm always terminates [22] and in the worst case, every reference is mutable when the algorithm terminates.

Figure 6 shows the result of applying the algorithm to an example program.

3.2 Subtyping

Java and Javari allow subtyping polymorphism, which enables multiple implementations of a method to be specified through overriding[3]. Javari requires that overriding methods have covariant return mutability types and contravariant parameter mutability types (including the receiver, the implicit this parameter). To enforce these constraints, the algorithm adds the appropriate guarded constraints for every return and parameter of an overriding method. If a parameter is mutable in an overriding method, it must be mutable in the overridden method. If the return type is mutable in an overridden method, it must be mutable in the overriding method. For simplicity, a previous formalism [28] forced the mutabilities of overriding methods to be identical to the overriden method, but that is not required for correctness.

3.3 Pre-existing Annotations and Unanalyzed Code

This section extends the inference algorithm to incorporate pre-existing annotations. These are useful for un-analyzable code such as native methods; for missing code, such as clients of a library, which might have arbitrary effects; and to permit users to override inferred annotations, such as when a reference is not currently used for mutation, but its specification permits it to be. Furthermore, user-provided annotations enable the algorithm to recognize which fields should be excluded from the abstract state of a class [28,22].

This section first discusses pre-existing annotations that specify that a reference is either readonly or mutable. Then, it discusses annotations that exclude a field from the abstract state of the object.

Mutability Annotations. A readonly annotation causes the algorithm, upon finishing, to check whether the reference may be declared readonly. If not, the algorithm issues an error. (Alternately, the algorithm can recommend code changes that permit the reference to be declared readonly [28,22].)

A mutable type qualifier (not field annotation) or a field this-mutable annotation causes the algorithm to add an unguarded constraint that the reference is not readonly.

The algorithm has two modes. In *closed-world*, or whole-program, mode, the algorithm may change the type qualifiers of returned/escaped references, such as public method return types and types of public fields. This yields more precise results — that is, more readonly references. In *open-world* mode, the algorithm marks as mutable (i.e., adds an unguarded constraint for) every non-private field

---

[3] We use the term *overriding* both for overriding a concrete method, and for implementing an abstract method or a method from an interface. For brevity and to highlight their identical treatment, we refer to both abstract methods and interface methods as *abstract methods*.

$$\frac{\neg\texttt{assignable(f)}}{\texttt{x.f} = \texttt{y} : \{\texttt{x, f} \rightarrow \texttt{y}\}} \;(\text{Set-N}) \qquad \frac{\texttt{assignable(f)}}{\texttt{x.f} = \texttt{y} : \{\texttt{f} \rightarrow \texttt{y}\}} \;(\text{Set-A})$$

$$\frac{\texttt{mutable(f)}}{\{\texttt{f}\}} \;(\text{Mutable})$$

$$\frac{\neg\texttt{mutable(f)}}{\texttt{x} = \texttt{y.f} : \{\texttt{x} \rightarrow \texttt{f, x} \rightarrow \texttt{y}\}} \;(\text{Ref-N}) \qquad \frac{\texttt{mutable(f)}}{\texttt{x} = \texttt{y.f} : \{\}} \;(\text{Ref-M})$$

Fig. 7. Modified constraint generation rules for assignable and mutable fields. The SET and REF rules of Figure 5 are replaced by those of this figure. MUTABLE is new.

and non-private method return value. The open-world assumption is required when analyzing partial programs or library classes with unknown clients, because an unseen client may mutate a field or return value.

Assignable and Mutable Fields. Javarifier handles fields annotated as `mutable` or `assignable` by extending the constraint generation rules to check the assignability and mutability of fields before adding constraints. The auxiliary function `assignable(f)` returns true if and only if `f` is declared to be `assignable`; likewise for `mutable(f)`. The changes to the constraint generation rules are shown in Figure 7 and are described below.

To handle `assignable` fields, the SET rule is divided into two rules, SET-A and SET-N, that depend on the assignability of the field. If the field is not `assignable`, SET-N proceeds as normal. If the field is `assignable`, SET-A does not add the unguarded constraint that the reference used to reach the field must be mutable: an `assignable` field may be assigned through either a `readonly` or a `mutable` reference.

Constraint generation rule MUTABLE adds an unguarded constraint for each `mutable` field.

The REF rule is divided into two rules depending on the mutability of the field. If the field is not `mutable`, then REF-N proceeds as normal. If the field is `mutable`, then REF-M does not add any constraints because, when compared to the original REF rule, (1) the consequence of the first constraint, $\texttt{x} \rightarrow \texttt{f}$, has already been added to the constraint set via the MUTABLE rule, and (2) the second constraint, $\texttt{x} \rightarrow \texttt{y}$, is eliminated because a `mutable` field is mutable regardless of how it is reached.

4   Arrays and Generics

This section discusses how to infer immutability for arrays and generic classes. (Javarifier also handles generic methods [28], but the details are omitted here for brevity.) The key difficulty is inferring the `?` `readonly` type, which requires

s ::= ...	T, S ::= A | C	*types*	T, S ::= C$<\overline{T}>$ | X	*types*
| x[x] = x	A, B ::= T[]	*array types*	C, D	*class names*
| x = x[x]	C, D	*class names*	X, Y	*type variables*

Fig. 8. Core language grammar (Figure 4) extended for arrays (left). Constraint generation type meta-variables extended for arrays (center) and parametric types (right).

inferring two types (an upper and a lower bound) for each array/generic class. If the bounds are different, then the resulting Javari type is `? readonly`.

4.1 Arrays

This section extends the algorithm to handle arrays. First, we extend the core language grammar to allow storing to and reading from arrays (Figure 8).

A non-array reference has a single immutability annotation; therefore, a single constraint variable per reference suffices. Arrays need more constraint variables, for two reasons. First, an array reference's type may have multiple immutability annotations: the element type can be annotated in addition to the array itself. Second, Javari array elements have two-sided bounded types (Section 2). For example, the type (`? readonly Date`)[] has elements with upper bound `readonly Date` and lower bound `mutable Date`, and (`readonly Date`)[] has elements with identical upper bound and lower bound `readonly Date`.

Javarifier constrains each *part* of a type using a separate constraint variable. An array has parts for the top-level array type and for the upper and lower bounds of the element type. If the elements are themselves arrays, then there are parts for the upper and lower bounds of elements of the elements, and so on. For example, the type `Date[][]` has seven type parts: `Date[][]`, the top-level type; `Date[]`$_\triangleleft$, the upper bound of the element type, and `Date[]`$_\triangleright$, the lower bound of the element type; and four `Date` types corresponding to the upper/lower bound of the upper/lower bound[4].

We subscript upper bounds with $_\triangleleft$ and lower bounds with $_\triangleright$. This matches the conventional ordering: in the declaration `List<? extends readonly Date super /*mutable*/ Date>`, the upper bound is on the left and the lower bound is on the right. We assume that within a program, textually different instances of the same type are distinguishable. The type meta-variables are shown in Figure 8. As usual, T and S range over types, and C and D over class names. We add A and B to range over array types.

The type constraint generation rules use the auxiliary function *type*, which returns the declared type of a reference, similar to the less intuitively named Γ type environment used in other work.

---

[4] An alternate approach of treating arrays as objects with fields of the same type as the array element type would not allow inferring different mutabilities on the different levels of the array. This alternate approach would not be able to infer the `? readonly` qualifier.

$$\frac{S[] \to T[] \qquad T \sqsubset: S}{T[] <: S[]} \qquad \frac{D \to C}{C <: D} \qquad \frac{T_\lhd <: S_\lhd \qquad S_\rhd <: T_\rhd}{T \sqsubset: S}$$

Fig. 9. Simplified subtyping (<:) rules for mutability in Javari. These simplified rules only check the mutabilities of the types, because we assume the program being converted type checks under Java. An array element's type, T, is said to be contained by another array element's type, S, written $T \sqsubset: S$, if the set of types denoted by T is a subset of the types denoted by S. Each rule states an equivalence between subtyping and guarded constraints on types, so each rule can be replicated with predicates and consequents swapped. Java arrays are covariant. Javari arrays are invariant in respect to mutability (see Section 2); therefore, we use the contains relationship as Java's parametric types do.

$$x = y : \{type(y) <: type(x)\} \ (\text{ASSIGN})$$

$$\frac{this(m) = this_m \qquad params(m) = \bar{p} \qquad retVal(m) = ret_m}{x = y.m(\bar{y}) : \{type(y) <: type(this_m), \ type(\bar{y}) <: type(\bar{p}), \ type(ret_m) <: type(x)\}} \ (\text{INVK})$$

$$\frac{retVal(m) = ret_m}{return \ x : \{type(x) <: type(ret_m)\}} \ (\text{RET})$$

$$x = y.f : \{type(f) <: type(x), \ type(x) \to type(y)\} \ (\text{REF})$$

$$x.f = y : \{type(x), \ type(y) <: type(f)\} \ (\text{SET})$$

$$x = y[z] : \{type(y[z]) <: type(x)\} \ (\text{ARRAY-REF})$$

$$x[z] = y : \{type(x), \ type(y) <: type(x[z])\} \ (\text{ARRAY-SET})$$

Fig. 10. Constraint generation rules extended for arrays. These rules replace the constraint generation rules of Figure 5, where the $type()$ function was not needed.

Constraint Generation. The constraint generation rules are extended to enforce subtyping constraints. For the assignment $x = y$, where x and y are arrays, the extension must enforce that y is a subtype of x. Simplified subtyping rules for Javari are given in Figure 9.

The constraint generation rules now use types as constraint variables and enforce the subtyping relationship across assignments including the implicit pseudo-assignments that occur during method invocation. The extended rules are shown in Figure 10.

Type Well-Formedness Constraints. In addition to the constraints generated for each line of code, the algorithm adds constraints to the constraint set to ensure that every array type is well-formed. Array well-formedness constraints enforce that an array element's lower bound is a subtype of the element's upper bound.

Constraint Solving. Before the constraint set can be simplified as before, subtyping ($<:$) and containment ($\subset:$) constraints must be reduced to guarded ($\rightarrow$) constraints. To do so, the algorithm replaces each subtyping or containment constraint by the corresponding guarded constraints and simplified subtyping or contains constraint (see Figure 9). This step is repeated until only guarded and unguarded constraints remain in the constraint set. For example, the statement x = y, where x and y have the types T[] and S[], respectively, would generate and reduce constraints as follows:

$$
\begin{aligned}
\text{x = y} : &\ \{type(\text{y}) <: type(\text{x})\} \\
: &\ \{\text{S[]} <: \text{T[]}\} \\
: &\ \{\text{T[]} \rightarrow \text{S[]},\ \text{S} \subset: \text{T}\} \\
: &\ \{\text{T[]} \rightarrow \text{S[]},\ \text{S}_\triangleleft <: \text{T}_\triangleleft,\ \text{T}_\triangleright <: \text{S}_\triangleright\} \\
: &\ \{\text{T[]} \rightarrow \text{S[]},\ \text{T}_\triangleleft \rightarrow \text{S}_\triangleleft,\ \text{S}_\triangleright \rightarrow \text{T}_\triangleright\}
\end{aligned}
$$

In the final result, the first guarded constraint enforces that y must be a mutable array if x is a mutable array, while the second and third constraints constrain the bounds on the arrays' element types. $\text{T}_\triangleleft \rightarrow \text{S}_\triangleleft$ requires the upper bound of y's elements to be mutable if the upper bound of x's elements is mutable. This rule is due to covariant subtyping between upper bounds. $\text{S}_\triangleright \rightarrow \text{T}_\triangleright$ requires the lower bound of x's elements to be mutable if the lower bound y's elements is mutable. This rule is due to contravariant subtyping between lower bounds.

After reducing all subtyping and containment constraints, the remaining guarded and unguarded constraint set is simplified as before. A subtype or containment constraint on an array type only leads to one guarded constraint for the top-level type and two guarded constraints for the lower and upper bounds. Compared to the non-array algorithm, the total number of constraints only increases by a constant factor. Therefore, the constraint simplification algorithm remains linear-time.

Applying Results. Finally, the results must be mapped back to the initial Java program. Top-level types are annotated the same way they were before. However, for element types, the constraints on the type upper bound and type lower bound must map back to a single Javari type. Figure 11 illustrates this mapping.

As in Section 3.1, given a fixed set of field annotations, the algorithm excludes the maximum number of constraint variables from the unguarded constraint set. After the mapping of mutabilities on constraint variables to Javari types, no reference that is `? readonly` could be `readonly` because a mutable lower bound implies the reference cannot be `readonly` (since only `mutable` references can be assigned to it). Therefore, the algorithm infers the maximum number of references that do not need to be `mutable`, and each of these references is either `readonly` or `? readonly`.

Upper bound ($\triangleleft$)	Lower bound ($\triangleright$)	Javari type
mutable	mutable	mutable
readonly	readonly	readonly
readonly	mutable	? readonly

Fig. 11. The inferred mutability of the upper and lower bounds on array element types are mapped to a single Javari type. The case that the upper bound is `mutable` and the lower bound is `readonly` cannot occur due to the well-formedness constraints.

$$asType_\Delta(\texttt{C<}\overline{\texttt{T}}\texttt{>}, \texttt{C}) = \texttt{C<}\overline{\texttt{T}}\texttt{>}$$

$$\frac{\texttt{class C<}\overline{\texttt{X}}\ \overline{\texttt{V}}\texttt{>} \triangleleft \texttt{C}'\texttt{<}\overline{\texttt{U}}\texttt{>} \qquad \texttt{S} = asType_\Delta([\overline{\texttt{T}}/\overline{\texttt{X}}]\texttt{C}'\texttt{<}\overline{\texttt{U}}\texttt{>}, \texttt{D})}{asType_\Delta(\texttt{C<}\overline{\texttt{T}}\texttt{>}, \texttt{D}) = \texttt{S}}$$

Fig. 12. *asType* returns $\texttt{C<}\overline{\texttt{T}}\texttt{>}$'s supertype of class D

4.2 Parametric Types (Java Generics)

Parametric types (Java generics) are handled similarly to arrays. For a parametric type, constraint variables are created for the upper and lower bound of each type argument to a parametric class. As with arrays, type parts serve as constraint variables.

The following meta-syntax represents parametric types. Figure 8 shows the type meta-variable definitions. As with arrays, $\triangleleft$ denotes type arguments' upper bounds and $\triangleright$ denotes their lower bounds.

Auxiliary Functions. The subtyping rules use the auxiliary function $bound_\Delta$. $bound_\Delta(\texttt{T})$ returns the declared upper bound of T if T is a type variable; if T is not a type variable, T is returned unchanged. In this formulation, there is a global type environment, Δ, that maps type variables to their declared bounds. *bound* ignores any upper bound ($\triangleleft$) or lower bound ($\triangleright$) subscripts on the type.

As with arrays, the type constraint generation rules use the auxiliary function *type*, which returns the declared type of a reference.

The subtyping rules use the $asType_\Delta(\texttt{C<}\overline{\texttt{T}}\texttt{>}, \texttt{D})$ function (Figure 12) to return C's supertype of class D[5]. *asType* is used when a value is assigned to a reference that is a supertype of the value's type. In such a case, *asType* converts the value's type to have the same class as the reference. For example, consider

```
class Foo<T> extends List<Date> { ... }

Foo<Integer> f;
List<Date> lst = f;
lst.get(0).setMonth(JUNE);
```

---

[5] We call $\texttt{C<}\overline{\texttt{T}}\texttt{>}$ a type because its type arguments are present. We call D a class because type arguments are not provided.

$$x = y : \{type(y) <: type(x)\} \ (\text{ASSIGN})$$

$$\frac{\texttt{this}(m) = \texttt{this}_m \quad \texttt{params}(m) = \overline{p} \quad \texttt{retVal}(m) = \texttt{ret}_m}{x = y.m(\overline{y}) : \{type(y) <: type(\texttt{this}_m), \ type(\overline{y}) <: type(\overline{p}), \ type(\texttt{ret}_m) <: type(x)\}} \ (\text{INVK})$$

$$\frac{\texttt{retVal}(m) = \texttt{ret}_m}{\texttt{return } x : \{type(x) <: type(\texttt{ret}_m)\}} \ (\text{RET})$$

$$x = y.f : \{type(f) <: type(x), \ type(x) \rightarrow type(y)\} \ (\text{REF})$$

$$x.f = y : \{type(x), \ type(y) <: type(f)\} \ (\text{SET})$$

Fig. 13. Constraint generation rules in the presence of parametric types

$$\frac{D \rightarrow C \quad \overline{T''} \sqsubset : \overline{S'}}{T <: S \ \textbf{where} \ bound_\Delta(T) = C{<}\overline{T'}{>} \ \textbf{and} \ bound_\Delta(S) = D{<}\overline{S'}{>} \ \textbf{and}}$$
$$asType_\Delta(C{<}\overline{T'}{>}, D) = D{<}\overline{T''}{>}$$

$$\frac{T_\lhd <: S_\lhd \quad S_\rhd <: T_\rhd}{T \sqsubset : S}$$

Fig. 14. Simplified subtyping rules for mutability in the presence of parametric types

On the assignment of `f` to `lst`, *asType* converts `f`'s type from `Foo<Integer>` to `List<Date>` with the call: $asType_\Delta$(`Foo<Integer>`, `List`). This conversion ensures that constraints placed on the type of `lst` elements affect `f` indirectly through the type of `lst` rather than the type of `f`, so the final inference result is `class Foo<T> extends List</*mutable*/ Date>` rather than the incorrect `Foo</*mutable*/ Integer> f`.

Constraint Generation. As with arrays, the constraint generation rules (shown in Figure 13) use subtyping constraints. However, the subtyping rules (shown in Figure 14) are extended to handle type variables. In Javari, a type variable is not allowed to be annotated as `mutable`; therefore, type variables cannot occur in the constraint set. In the case of a type variable appearing in a subtyping constraint, *bound* is used to calculate the upper bound of the type variable, and the mutability constraints are applied to the type variable's bound. Therefore, mutation of a reference whose type is a type variable results in the type variable's bound being constrained to be mutable. An example of this behavior is shown in Figure 15.

Type Well-Formedness Constraints. As with arrays, in addition to the constraints from the constraint generation rules, well-formedness constraints are added to the constraint set. As before, a constraint is added that a type argument's lower bound must be a subtype of the type argument's upper bound. Parametric types, additionally, introduce the well-formedness constraint that a

```
class Week<X extends /*mutable*/ Date> {
  X f;
  void startWeek() {
    f.setDay(Day.SUNDAY);
  }
}
```

Fig. 15. The result of applying type inference to a program containing a mutable type variable bound. Since the field f is mutated, X's upper bound is inferred to be /*mutable*/ Date. The mutable annotation may not be applied directly to f's type because in Javari, a type parameter cannot be annotated as `mutable`.

type argument's upper bound (and, therefore, by transitivity, lower bound) is a subtype of the corresponding type variable's declared upper bound.

Constraint Simplification and Applying Results. As with arrays, subtyping (and containment) constraints are simplified into guarded constraints by removing the subtyping constraint from the constraint set and replacing it with the subtyping rule's predicate. The results of the solved constraint set are applied in the same manner as with arrays. Javari does not allow raw types, and this analysis is incapable of operating on code that contains raw types. In particular, this algorithm does not account for the required casts when using raw types.

5 Inferring Mutability Polymorphism

This section extends the inference algorithm to infer the `polyread` keyword (previously named "romaybe" [29]). As described in Section 2 and illustrated in Figure 3, `polyread` enables more precise and useful immutability annotations to be expressed than if methods could not be polymorphic over mutability.

5.1 Approach

Methods that have at least one `polyread` parameter or return type have two contexts. In the first context, all `polyread` references are `mutable`. In the second context, all `polyread` references are `readonly`. Javarifier creates both contexts for every method. If a parameter/return type has an identical mutability in both contexts, then that parameter/return type should have that mutability. If a parameter/return type is `mutable` in the `mutable` context and `readonly` in the `readonly` context, then that parameter/return type should be `polyread`.

To create two contexts for a method, Javarifier creates two constraint variables for every method-local reference (local variables, return value, and parameters, including the implicit `this` parameter). To distinguish each context's constraint variables, we superscript the constraint variables from the readonly context with `ro` and those from the mutable context with `mut`. Constraint variables for fields are not duplicated: `polyread` may not be applied to fields and, thus, only a single context exists.

Section 5.3 demonstrates that inferring `polyread` only requires increasing the number of constraints (and the time complexity of the algorithm) by a constant factor.

5.2 Constraint Generation Rules

With the exception of INVK, all the constraint generation rules are the same as before, except now they generate (identical) constraints for constraint variables from both the readonly and mutable versions of the methods. For example, x = y now generates the constraints $\{x^{ro} \rightarrow y^{ro}, x^{mut} \rightarrow y^{mut}\}$.

Thus, there are now two constraint variables for every reference, one for when it is in a mutable context and one for when it is in a readonly context. For shorthand, we write constraints that are identical with the exception of constraint variables' contexts by superscripting the constraint variables with "?". For example, the constraints generated by x = y can be written as: $\{x^? \rightarrow y^?\}$.

The method invocation rule (shown in Figure 16) must be modified to invoke the `mutable` version of a method when a `mutable` return type is needed, and to invoke the `readonly` version otherwise. This restriction can be represented using double-guarded constraints. For example, consider the code in Figure 3, in which the `Bicycle.getSeat()` method has a `polyread` return type and a `polyread` parameter. In the `lowerSeat()` method, the returned reference is mutated, so the `mutable` version of `getSeat()` must be used. In the `printSeat()` method, the returned reference is indeed `readonly`, so the `readonly` version of `getSeat()` can be used.

The first constraint in the invocation rule of Figure 16 thus states that if the returned reference s is `mutable`, then the reference b on which (the `mutable` version of) `getSeat()` is called must be `mutable` if the receiver of `getSeat()` is `mutable` inside the `mutable` version of `getSeat()`. (Recall that the receiver inside a `readonly` method is `readonly` in both the `mutable` and `readonly` versions of that method, whereas the receiver of a `polyread` method is `mutable` only in the `mutable` version of the method.)

In matching Figure 3 to the invocation rule of Figure 16, note that the ? superscripts would be on the references s and b local to `lowerSeat()` (or `printSeat()`), whereas the explicit ᵐᵘᵗ superscript would only occur on references local to `getSeat()`. In particular, since the `lowerSeat()` and `printSeat()` methods are static, they only have one context so the different versions of duplicated constraint variables will always be the same. The ? superscripts demonstrate that after fixing the explicit ᵐᵘᵗ contexts, these constraints are generalized with ? in the same fashion all other constraints are generalized.

The last constraint in the invocation rule states that if the reference s is later mutated, then the return type of `getSeat()` must be `mutable` in the `mutable` version of `getSeat()`. The RET rule for return types and REF rule for field references in Figure 5 together generate the constraint that if the return type of `getSeat()` is mutable (in whichever version of the method is called), then the receiver of `getSeat()` is mutable (in that version of the method). Since the method invocation rule in Figure 16 only generates the constraint that the return

$$\frac{\mathtt{this}(m) = \mathtt{this}_m \qquad \mathtt{params}(m) = \overline{p} \qquad \mathtt{retVal}(m) = \mathtt{ret}_m}{x = y.m(\overline{y}) : \{x^? \to \mathtt{this}_m^{\overline{mut}} \to y^?,\ x^? \to \overline{p^{mut}} \to \overline{y^?},\ x^? \to \mathtt{ret}_m^{mut}\}} \quad (\textsc{Invk-polyread})$$

Fig. 16. The core algorithm's INVK rule (Figure 5) is replaced by INVK-POLYREAD, which is used for method invocation in the presence of **polyread** references. Each superscript denotes the contexts of the method in which the variable is declared. All of the $^?$ contexts refer to the method containing the references x and y, whereas the explicit ^{mut} contexts refer to context inside method m.

type of `getSeat()` is `mutable` in the `mutable` version of `getSeat()`, the return type and receiver of `getSeat()` are `mutable` only in the `mutable` version of the method, and thus they are both inferred to be `polyread`.

5.3   Constraint Solving

The algorithm for solving the constraint set is an extension to the algorithm briefly described in Section 3.1 in order to account for double-guarded constraints. For clarity, we now provide the full algorithm and demonstrate that it has linear time complexity.

There are three constraint sets: the unguarded constraint set ($\mathcal{U}$) which contains constraints of the form a, the guarded constraint set ($\mathcal{G}$) which contains constraints of the form $a \to b$, and the double-guarded constraint set ($\mathcal{D}$) which contains constraints of the form $a \to b \to c$. The following pseudocode illustrates how the algorithm processes constraints using a work-list ($\mathcal{W}$):

```
initialize W with all the constraints from U
while W is not empty
  pop a constraint a from W
  for each constraint g in G that has a as its guard
    let c be the consequent of g
    if c is not in U, add c to W and to U

  for each double-guarded constraint d in D that has a as its first guard
    let b → c be the consequent of d
    if b is in U
      if c is not in U, add c to W and to U
    else, add b → c to G
```

The algorithm maintains linear time complexity if the sets $\mathcal{G}$ and $\mathcal{D}$ are implemented as hash tables. For $\mathcal{G}$, the table maps a guard to the constraint variable it guards. For $\mathcal{D}$, the table maps the first guard to a set of the consequents (which are single-guarded constraints) that it guards. That is, given constraints $a \to b_1 \to c_1$ and $a \to b_2 \to c_2$, the hash table maps a to the set $\{b_1 \to c_1, b_2 \to c_2\}$. This allows looking up all single-guarded constraints that are guarded by the same guard in a double-guarded constraint to take constant time, in expectation. Since every constraint is read from either $\mathcal{G}$ or $\mathcal{D}$ at most once, and each double-guarded constraint only adds one single-guarded constraint to

$\mathcal{G}$, the constraint-solving algorithm has linear time complexity in the total number of constraints. The number of constraints is linear in the size of the program under analysis as measured in the three-address core language of Figure 4.

5.4 Interpreting the Simplified Constraint Set

Once the constraint set is solved, the results are applied to the program. For method-local references, the two constraint variables from the readonly and mutable method contexts must be mapped to a single method-local Javari type: readonly, mutable, or polyread.

A reference is declared mutable if both the mutable and readonly contexts of the reference's constraint variable are in the simplified, unguarded constraint set. A reference is declared readonly if both mutable and readonly contexts of the reference's constraint variable are absent from the constraint set. Finally, a reference is declared polyread if the mutable context's constraint variable is in the constraint set but the readonly constraint variable is not in the constraint set, because the mutability of the reference depends on which version of the method is called.[6] Thus, in the example of Figure 3, after the constraints have been solved, the receiver of getSeat() is known to be mutable in a mutable context but not known to be mutable in a readonly context, so it is annotated as polyread. The reference returned by getSeat() is similarly known to be mutable in a mutable context but not known to be mutable in a readonly context, so it is also annotated as polyread.

It is possible for a method to contain polyread references but no polyread parameters. For example, below, x and the return value of getNewDate could be declared polyread.

```
Date getNewDate() {
  Date x = new Date();
  return x;
}
```

However, polyread references are only useful if the method has a polyread parameter. Thus, if none of a method's parameters (including the receiver) are polyread, all the method's polyread references are converted to mutable references.

6 Evaluation

We have implemented the inference algorithm described in Sections 3–5 as a tool, Javarifier, that reads a set of classfiles, determines the mutability of every reference in those classfiles, and inserts the inferred Javari annotations in either

---

[6] The case that the readonly constraint variable is found in the constraint set, but the mutable context's constraint variable is not, cannot occur by the design of the INVK-POLYREAD constraint generation rule.

Program	Size		Time	Annotatable references					
	lines	classes		Total	readonly	mutable	this-mut.	polyread	?readonly
JOlden	6223	57	9	1580	927	553	52	48	0
tinySQL	30691	119	47	5606	2227	2964	175	240	0
htmlparser	63780	238	45	4596	1623	2740	72	144	17
ejc	110822	320	1410	24899	8887	14774	690	548	0

Fig. 17. Subject programs used in our case studies. Inference time is in seconds on a Pentium 4 3.6GHz machine with 3GB RAM. The right portion tabulates the number of annotatable references for each inference result (in Javarifier's closed-world mode). When counting annotatable references, each type argument counts separately; for example, List<Date> is counted as two references.

class files or Java source files. Javarifier is publicly available for download at http://pag.csail.mit.edu/javari/javarifier/.

To verify that Javarifier infers correct and maximally precise Javari qualifiers we performed two types of case studies. The first variety (Section 6.1) compared Javarifier's output to manually written Javari code that had been type-checked by the Javari type-checker. The second variety (Section 6.2) compared Javarifier to another tool for inferring immutability. For both varieties of case study, we examined every difference among the annotations. The case studies revealed no errors in Javarifier. It is possible that errors in Javarifier were masked by identical errors in the other tools and the manual annotations, but we consider this unlikely.

Figure 17 gives statistics for the subject programs used in our case studies:

- JOlden benchmark suite (http://osl-www.cs.umass.edu/DaCapo/benchmarks. html)
- tinySQL database engine (http://www.jepstone.net/tinySQL/)
- htmlparser library for parsing HTML (http://htmlparser.sourceforge.net/)
- ejc compiler for the Eclipse IDE (http://www.eclipse.org/)

The JOlden benchmark suite is written using raw types, so we first converted the source code to use generics. We also renamed some identically named but distinct classes in the different benchmarks within JOlden.

6.1   Comparison to Manual Annotations

Before the Javarifier implementation was complete, a developer (not one of the authors of this paper) manually annotated the JOlden benchmark suite and verified the correctness of the annotations by running the Javari type-checker. We compared the manually-written and automatically-verified annotations with Javarifier's inference results.

There were 74 differences between the manual annotations and Javarifier's output. 58 are human errors, and 16 disappear when using Javarifier's inference of assignable fields.

Program	inheritance	polyread	this-mutable	arrays
tinySQL	0	3	6	0
htmlparser	12	6	0	2
ejc	1	0	17	31

Fig. 18. Reasons for differences between Javarifier and Pidasa inference results. None of the differences indicates an error in Javarifier.

The programmer omitted 22 `readonly` qualifiers, such as on the receiver of `toString()`. Tool support while the programmer was annotating the program would have both eased the annotation task and prevented these errors.

Javarifier inferred 36 private fields to be `readonly`, while the developer accepted the default of `this-mutable`, meaning that the fields are part of the abstract state of the object. However, all 36 of these fields are either never read or are only used to store intermediate values that do not need to be mutated. Thus, Javarifier pointed out that these fields can be excluded from the abstract state, or even removed altogether, without affecting the rest of the program.

The remaining 16 annotations that differed between the manual annotations and Javarifier's results do not represent any conceptual errors, and when we enabled heuristics for inferring `assignable` fields [22], Javarifier's results were identical to the manual annotations. The developer had marked 4 fields as `assignable`. Each of these fields is a placeholder for the current element in an `Enumeration` class. The `assignable` annotation allowed the `nextElement()` method, which reassigns the field, to have a `polyread` receiver and return type. In other words, the manual annotations differentiate the abstract state from the concrete state of an object. When run without inference of assignable fields, Javarifier inferred that the return type is `readonly` and the receiver is `mutable`, and this mutability propagated to other methods, for a total of 16 differences in annotations.

6.2 Comparison to Another Mutation Inference Tool

Pidasa [3] is a combined static and dynamic immutability inference tool for parameters and receivers. Pidasa uses a different but closely related definition of reference immutability. We compared Javarifier's results to Pidasa's results on four randomly-selected classes from each of tinySQL, htmlparser, and ejc (for more details, see Artzi et al. [4]). We manually analyzed each difference to verify the correctness of Javarifier's results.

All of the differences can be attributed to four causes, as tabulated in Figure 18. The first three causes are conservatism in the Javari type system which makes it impossible to express that a particular reference is not mutated. The last cause is inflexibility in Pidasa that prevents it from expressing different mutabilities on arrays and their elements.

```
class TagNode {
  private List<Attribute> mAttributes;
  public /*mutable*/ List<Attribute> getAttributes() /*mutable*/ {
    return mAttributes;
  }
  public String toHtml() /*mutable*/ {
    String s = "";
    for(Attribute attr : getAttributes()) {
      s += attr.toHtml();
    }
    return s;
  }
}

class LazyTagNode extends TagNode {
  public /*mutable*/ List<Attribute> getAttributes() /*mutable*/ {
    // Actually mutates the abstract state of the object,
    // in accordance to the specification for this class.
  }
}
```

Fig. 19. Inheritance conservatism in the Javari type system, as observed in simplified code from the htmlparser program. The method `LazyTagNode.getAttributes()` is inferred to have a `mutable` receiver (line 16) because it may change the state of its receiver. The method subtyping rule thus forces `TagNode.getAttributes()` to have a `mutable` receiver (line 3). Since `TagNode.toHtml()` calls `getAttributes()` (line 8), it must also have a `mutable` receiver (line 6), even though not every call to `toHtml()` can cause a mutation.

Inheritance: In 13 cases, Javarifier inferred a method receiver to be mutable due to contravariant receiver mutability in Javari, even though Pidasa was able to recognize contexts in which the receiver could not be mutated. Figure 19 gives an example.

`polyread:` In 9 cases, Javarifier inferred a parameter to be `mutable` due to the type rules of the `polyread` qualifier, but Pidasa inferred the parameter to be readonly. A method such as `filter(polyread Date)` cannot mutate its `polyread` parameter because the method would not typecheck when all `polyread` qualifiers are replaced with `readonly`. However, when `filter` is called from anoter method (from the same class) that has a `mutable` receiver, the type of `this` is `mutable` and thus Javari requires that the program typecheck as if the `filter` method took a `mutable` parameter.

`this-mutable:` In 23 cases, Javarifier inferred a `mutable` parameter due to Javari's type rule that `this-mutable` fields are always written to as `mutable`, but Pidasa inferred the parameter to be readonly. For example, if a method stores a parameter into a `this-mutable` field, that parameter must be declared `mutable`, even if no mutations occur to it.

Arrays: In 33 cases, Javarifier correctly inferred an array type to be partly immutable, but Pidasa was conservative and marked the whole array as mutable. For example, htmlparser used two readonly arrays of mutable objects. Javarifier correctly inferred the outer level of the arrays to be `readonly` and the inner level to be `mutable`. Pidasa infers a single mutability for all levels of the array. Ejc contained examples of mutable arrays of readonly objects.

In conclusion, we found differences among the tools' definitions, but in every case Javarifier inferred correct Javari annotations, even where the results are not immediately obvious — another advantage of a machine-checked immutability definition such as that of Javari.

7 Related Work

Our full inference algorithm, and experience with a preliminary Javarifier implementation, first appeared as part of Tschantz's thesis [28]. This paper builds upon that work with an extensive experimental evaluation.

In subsequent work, JQual [14] cites Tschantz's thesis and adopts our approach. JQual's core rules are essentially identical to Javarifier's. Like Javarifier, JQual uses syntax-directed constraint generation, then solves the constraints using graph reachability, and reports limited experimental results. However, there are some differences in the approaches. (1) Polymorphism: JQual discards our support for Java generics, and with it any hope for compatibility with the Java language. Instead, JQual generalizes our mutability polymorphism. Whereas polyread introduces exactly one mutability parameter into a method definition, JQual supports an arbitrary number. Given support for Java generics, we have not yet found a need for multiple mutability parameters. (2) Expressiveness: JQual generalizes Javarifier by being able in theory to infer any type qualifier, not just ones for reference immutability. This generality comes with a cost. JQual is tuned to simple "negative" and "positive" qualifiers that induce subtypes and supertypes of the unqualified type; it appears too inexpressive for richer type systems. JQual was used to create an inference tool for a @ReadOnly qualifier, but it lacks support for every other Javarifier keyword, for qualifiers on different levels of an array, for immutable classes, and for various other features of Javari. Additionally, it has a limitation on inheritance that ignores qualifiers in determining method overriding: it does not enforce the constraint, required for backward compatibility with Java, that mutability qualifiers do not affect overriding. (3) Scalability: Context- and flow-sensitive variants of the JQual algorithm exist, but the authors report that they are unscalable, so in their experiments they hand-tuned the application of these features. Even so, JQual has not been run on substantial codebases, andm, , except for JOlden, crashed on all of our subject programs. By contrast, both Javarifier's algorithm and its implementation are scalable. (4) Evaluation: JQual's output and input languages differ (e.g., it has no surface syntax for its parametric polymorphism), so its analysis results do not type check even in JQual. Artzi et al. [4] report that JQual's recall (fraction of truly immutable parameters that were inferred to be immutable) was 67%, compared to 94% recall for a version of Javarifier without inference of assignable or mutable fields. JQual misclassifies a receiver as mutable in method m if m reads a field f that is mutated by any other method. JQual also suffered a few errors in which it misclassified a mutable reference as immutable.

Javarifier and JQual can be viewed as extensions of the successful CQual [12,13] type inference framework for C to the object-oriented context.

Constraint-based type inference has also been used for inferring atomicity annotations to detect races [7,11], inferring non-local aliasing [1], and supporting type qualifiers dependent on flow-sensitivity (like read, write, and open) [13].

Pidasa [3] is a combined static and dynamic analysis for inferring parameter reference immutability. Pidasa uses a pipeline of (intra- and interprocedural) stages, each of which improves the results of the previous stage, and which can leave a parameter as "unknown" for a future stage to classify. This results in a system that is both more scalable and precise than previous work. Pidasa has both a sound mode and also unsound heuristics for applications that require higher precision and can tolerate unsoundness. By contrast, our work is purely static, making it sound but potentially less precise. Another contrast is that our definition is more expressive: our inference determines reference immutability for fields and for Java generics/arrays. Artzi et al. [4] compare both the definitions and the implementations of several tools including Javarifier, Pidasa, and JQual.

JPPA [27] is a previous reference immutability inference implementation. (Sălcianu also provides a formal definition of parameter safety, but JPPA implements reference immutability rather than parameter safety.) JPPA uses a whole-program pointer analysis, limiting scalability. Earlier work by Rountev [24] takes a similar approach but computes a coarser notion of side-effect-free methods rather than per-parameter mutability.

Reference immutability is distinct from the related notions of object immutability and of parameter "safety" [27]; none of them subsumes the others. They are useful for different purposes; for example, reference immutability is effective for specifying interfaces that should not modify their parameters (even though the caller may do so), and for a variety of other purposes [29]. A method parameter is safe if the method never modifies the object passed to the parameter during method invocation. Effect analyses [8,26,23,25,17,16] can be used to compute safety or object immutability, often with the assistance of a heavyweight context-sensitive pointer analysis to achieve reasonable precision. (Like type qualifier inference, points-to analysis aims to determine the flow of objects or values through the program.) Our algorithm is much more scalable — the algorithm is flow-insensitive, and the base algorithm is context-insensitive — but is tuned to take advantage of the parametric polymorphism offered by both Java and Javari.

Porat et al. [21] and Liu and Milanova [15] propose immutability inference for fields in Java, the latter in the context of UML, but their definitions differ from ours.

Our focus in this paper is on inference of reference immutability. For reasons of space, we cannot review the extensive literature proposing different variants of immutability. We briefly mention type checkers for closely related notions of reference immutability. Birka built a type-checker for an earlier dialect of Javari that lacked support for Java generics, and wrote 160,000 lines of code in Javari [6]. Correa later wrote a complete Javari implementation using the Checkers Framework [20] and did case studies involving 13,000 lines of Javari [19]. The JQual inference system [14] (discussed above) can be treated as a type checker. JavaCOP [2] is a framework for writing pluggable type systems for Java. Like JQual, JavaCOP aims for generality rather than practicality. Also like JQual, JavaCOP has been used to write a type checker for a small subset of Javari. The checker handles only one keyword (readonly) and cannot verify even that one in the presence of method overriding. Neither the checker nor any example output is publicly available, so it is difficult to compare to our work. Other frameworks that could be used for writing pluggable type systems include JastAdd [9], JACK [5], and Polyglot [18].

8 Conclusion

This paper presents an algorithm for statically inferring the reference immutability qualifiers of the Javari language. Javari extends the full Java language (including generics, wildcards, and arrays) in a rich and practical way: for example, it includes parametric polymorphism over mutability and permits excluding fields from an object's abstract state. To the best of our knowledge, ours is the first inference algorithm for a practical definition of reference immutability.

The algorithm is both sound and precise. Its correctness has been experimentally confirmed. The experiments also show that, like any conservative static type system, the Javari language's definition sometimes requires a reference to be declared mutable even when no mutation can occur at run time.

The Javarifier tool infers immutability constraints and inserts them in either Java source files or class files. Javarifier solves two important problems for programmers who wish to confirm that their programs are free of (a large class of) mutation errors. First, it can annotate existing programs, freeing programmers of that burden or revealing errors. Second, it can annotate libraries; because the Javari checker conservatively assumes any unannotated reference is mutable, use of any unannotated library makes checking of a program that uses it essentially impossible. Together, these capabilities permit programmers to obtain the many benefits of reference immutability at low cost.

Javarifier is publicly available for download at http://pag.csail.mit.edu/javari/javarifier/.

References

1. Aiken, A., Foster, J.S., Kodumal, J., Terauchi, T.: Checking and inferring local non-aliasing. In: PLDI, June 2003, pp. 129–140 (2003)
2. Andreae, C., Noble, J., Markstrum, S., Millstein, T.: A framework for implementing pluggable type systems. In: OOPSLA, October 2006, pp. 57–74 (2006)
3. Artzi, S., Kieżun, A., Glasser, D., Ernst, M.D.: Combined static and dynamic mutability analysis. In: ASE (November 2007)
4. Artzi, S., Quinonez, J., Kieżun, A., Ernst, M.D.: A formal definition and evaluation of parameter immutability, December 2007 (under review)
5. Barthe, G., Burdy, L., Charles, J., Grégoire, B., Huisman, M., Lanet, J.-L., Pavlova, M., Requet, A.: JACK: A tool for validation of security and behaviour of Java applications. In: FMCO (October 2006)
6. Birka, A., Ernst, M.D.: A practical type system and language for reference immutability. In: OOPSLA, October 2004, pp. 35–49 (2004)

7. Cooper, K.D., Kennedy, K.: Interprocedural side-effect analysis in linear time. In: PLDI, June 1988, pp. 57–66 (1988)
8. Cooper, K.D., Kennedy, K.: Interprocedural side-effect analysis in linear time. In: PLDI, June 1988, pp. 57–66 (1988)
9. Ekman, T., Hedin, G.: The JastAdd extensible Java compiler. In: OOPSLA, October 2007, pp. 1–18 (2007)
10. Ernst, M.D.: Annotations on Java types: JSR 308 working document (November 12, 2007), http://pag.csail.mit.edu/jsr308/
11. Flanagan, C., Freund, S.N.: Type inference against races. In: Static Analysis Symposium, pp. 116–132 (2004)
12. Foster, J.S., Fähndrich, M., Aiken, A.: A theory of type qualifiers. In: PLDI, June 1999, pp. 192–203 (1999)
13. Foster, J.S., Terauchi, T., Aiken, A.: Flow-sensitive type qualifiers. In: PLDI, June 2002, pp. 1–12 (2002)
14. Greenfieldboyce, D., Foster, J.S.: Type qualifier inference for Java. In: OOPSLA, October 2007, pp. 321–336 (2007)
15. Liu, Y., Milanova, A.: Ownership and immutability inference for UML-based object access control. In: ICSE, May 2007, pp. 323–332 (2007)
16. Milanova, A., Rountev, A., Ryder, B.G.: Parameterized object sensitivity for points-to and side-effect analyses for Java. In: ISSTA, July 2002, pp. 1–11 (2002)
17. Nguyen, P.H., Xue, J.: Interprocedural side-effect analysis and optimisation in the presence of dynamic class loading. In: ACSC, February 2005, pp. 9–18 (2005)
18. Nystrom, N., Clarkson, M.R., Myers, A.C.: Polyglot: An Extensible Compiler Framework for Java. In: Hedin, G. (ed.) CC 2003 and ETAPS 2003. LNCS, vol. 2622, pp. 138–152. Springer, Heidelberg (2003)
19. Papi, M.M., Ali, M., Correa Jr., T.L., Perkins, J.H., Ernst, M.D.: Pluggable type-checking for custom type qualifiers in Java. Technical Report MIT-CSAIL-TR-2007-047, MIT CSAIL (September 17, 2007)
20. Papi, M.M., Ali, M., Correa Jr., T.L., Perkins, J.H., Ernst, M.D.: Practical pluggable types for Java. In: ISSTA (July 2008)
21. Porat, S., Biberstein, M., Koved, L., Mendelson, B.: Automatic detection of immutable fields in Java. In: CASCON (November 2000)
22. Quinonez, J.: Inference of reference immutability in Java. Master's thesis, MIT Dept. of EECS (May 2008)
23. Razafimahefa, C.: A study of side-effect analyses for Java. Master's thesis, School of Computer Science, McGill University, Montreal, Canada (December 1999)
24. Rountev, A.: Precise identification of side-effect-free methods in Java. In: ICSM, September 2004, pp. 82–91 (2004)
25. Ryder, B.G., Rountev, A.: Points-to and Side-Effect Analyses for Programs Built with Precompiled Libraries. In: Wilhelm, R. (ed.) CC 2001 and ETAPS 2001. LNCS, vol. 2027, pp. 20–36. Springer, Heidelberg (2001)
26. Ryder, B.G., Landi, W.A., Stocks, P.A., Zhang, S., Altucher, R.: A schema for interprocedural modification side-effect analysis with pointer aliasing. ACM TOPLAS 23(2), 105–186 (2001)
27. Sălcianu, A., Rinard, M.C.: Purity and Side Effect Analysis for Java Programs. In: Cousot, R. (ed.) VMCAI 2005. LNCS, vol. 3385, pp. 199–215. Springer, Heidelberg (2005)
28. Tschantz, M.S.: Javari: Adding reference immutability to Java. Master's thesis, MIT Dept. of EECS (August 2006)
29. Tschantz, M.S., Ernst, M.D.: Javari: Adding reference immutability to Java. In: OOPSLA, October 2005, pp. 211–230 (2005)

Computing Stack Maps with Interfaces

Frédéric Besson[1], Thomas Jensen[2], and Tiphaine Turpin[3]

[1] Inria
[2] CNRS
[3] Université de Rennes I
first.last@irisa.fr

Abstract. Lightweight bytecode verification uses stack maps to annotate Java bytecode programs with type information in order to reduce the
verification to type checking. This paper describes an improved bytecode
analyser together with algorithms for optimizing the stack maps generated. The analyser is simplified in its treatment of base values (keeping
only the necessary information to ensure memory safety) and enriched
in its representation of interface types, using the Dedekind-MacNeille
completion technique. The computed interface information allows to remove the dynamic checks at interface method invocations. We prove
the memory safety property guaranteed by the bytecode verifier using
an operational semantics whose distinguishing feature is the use of untagged 32-bit values. For bytecode typable without sets of types we show
how to prune the fix-point to obtain a stack map that can be checked
without computing with sets of interfaces i.e., lightweight verification is
not made more complex or costly. Experiments on three substantial test
suites show that stack maps can be computed and correctly pruned by
an optimized (but incomplete) pruning algorithm.

1 Introduction

The Java bytecode verifier, which is part of the Java Virtual Machine (JVM) [13],
is a central component of Java security. At load time, the verifier checks that the
bytecode conforms to the JVM typing policy. Together with additional dynamic
checks this enables the virtual machine to run safely untrusted bytecodes such
as web applets or mobile phone midlets. While the standard bytecode verifier
performs a dataflow analysis on the bytecode the lightweight bytecode verifier [4]
only checks the analysis result (which is called a *stack map*) that is shipped with
the bytecode. It was originally designed for resource-constrained devices but the
mainstream Java 2 Standard Edition (J2SE) is now moving towards lightweight
bytecode verification, with slightly enhanced stack maps (see JSR 202 [9]).

A particular issue for the type inference performed in bytecode verification is
the possibility for a class to implement several interfaces. The problem arises as
soon as the language has multiple inheritance (only for interfaces, in the case
of Java). This implies that the type hierarchy is not a lattice and prevents the
computation of a unique most precise type for some variables, unless using sets
of types. For simplicity, the choice made in the original verifiers (both standard

J. Vitek (Ed.): ECOOP 2008, LNCS 5142, pp. 642–666, 2008.

```
void foo(boolean b) {
    if (b) {
(1)    i:=new A() ;
    } else
(2)    i:=new B();
(3) }
(4) i.m1();
(5) i.m2();
}
```

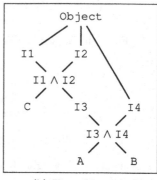

(a) Main method   (b) Type hierarchy

Fig. 1. A Java bytecode program and its type hierarchy

and lightweight) was to ignore interfaces in bytecode verification and to make the necessary checks dynamically. This choice has been maintained in JSR 202.

We propose to extend the bytecode analysis to check interfaces statically, using conjunctions of types, and then to prune the result to get a stak map without conjunctions that can be fed to an almost unmodified checker. This does not work for every bytecode, but it applies to bytecode obtained by compilation of Java programs. As a result, the dynamic checks on interface methods may be safely removed for free. We describe the case of (idealised) Java bytecode, but the solution would apply to a more general use of multiple inheritance.

In this paper, the term analysis refers to the typing process that produces stack maps, checking is the validation of those stack maps on the consumer's side, and verification encompasses analysing, possibly pruning, and checking.

Motivating Example. Figure 1 provides a small example which illustrates the existing verification and its extension to conjunctive types. Figure 1a represents a bytecode program written in pseudo Java, without type information. We suppose a type hierarchy with three classes A, B and C and four interfaces Ii ($i \in [1, \ldots, 4]$) where C implements and I3 extends I1 and I2, and A and B implements I3 and I4. Each interface Ii declares a method mi. Figure 1b shows the completion of the type hierarchy that is used by our enhanced analyser, which adds the elements I1 ∧ I2 and I3 ∧ I4 to the type hierarchy.

The standard bytecode verifier ignores interfaces. Thus, in method foo, the variable i at program point 3 is given as type the first common super-class of A and B, i.e., Object. Note also that the call to each method mi is in fact a call to the method of interface Ii, where it is declared. When analysing those calls, the bytecode verifier only checks statically that the variable i contains an object type. At run-time, the JVM dynamically checks whether the object referenced by i implements I1 and I2, before doing a lookup with respect to the dynamic type of i. If it is not the case, a run-time exception is thrown.

Our extended analizer will type the example program using conjunctions of types, and in particular, the variable i at program point 3 will have type I3 ∧ I4, which is propagated at program points 4 and 5. As this is a sub-type of both I1 and I2, this ensures that the two method calls are safe. However, for the purpose of lightweight bytecode verification, it is desirable to avoid annotating the variables with conjunctions. The backtracking pruning algorithm proposed in Section 4 detects that in the above conjunction, only I3 is needed to type the subsequent method invocations, hence it removes I4. In the resulting stack map, the variable i has therefore the type I3 at program points 3, 4 and 5.

The example also shows that opting for a backward program analysis does not simplify the problem. An analyser which starts from the invocation sites and propagates these "uses" of a variable to the point of definition would still require the use of conjunctions and lead to a back-tracking algorithm. With such a technique, the variable i at program point 5 would get the type I2. The problem arises when typing i at program point 4: it must be the intersection of I1 and I2, which requires either to introduce the conjunction I1 ∧ I2, or to choose one of the types C and I3. The right choice can only be made knowing the creation sites 1 and 2, hence the need for a backtraking algorithm.

Organisation of the Paper. The formal development of these ideas is done in Sections 2–4. We define the intraprocedural part of a small-step operational semantics with big-step calls for a subset of the Java bytecode (Section 2), with a low-level treatment of values that allows for a convincing definition of the memory safety property (which is the base for all other security properties). The analysis is presented in Section 3 in terms of an abstract interpretation [5]. We define the notions of stack maps and lightweight verification for a method, and state the main soundness theorem of the stack maps produced by the analysis. Section 4 describes the pruning algorithms that remove conjunctive types from those stack maps. We give an efficient algorithm that works in all but some well-identified, pathological cases, that do not seem to occur in average Java programs. We report on some experiments on verifying Soot, Eclipse and a suite of Java MIDP applets for mobile phones with a prototype implementation in Section 5. Related work is discussed in Section 6 and Section 7 concludes.

Notations. Sets have long *italic* names, other constants and constants functions are in roman, with the exception of bytecode instructions for which we use sans serif. Meta-variables have short lowercase *italic* names, except that we write $C, I, F^\sharp$ for classes, interfaces and abstract transfer functions, respectively.

For sets a and b, we write $a \rightharpoonup b$ for the set of partial functions from a to b. If f is a partial function, $\mathrm{dom}(f)$ is the domain of f, and any boolean expression e containing a sub-expression $f(e')$ implicitly means: $e' \in \mathrm{dom}(f) \wedge e$. We note $|x|$ for the cardinal of the set x, or the cardinal of its domain if x is a function. If f is a function (or a partial function), we note $f[x \leftarrow v]$ the function that maps x to v and any $y \neq x$ to $f(y)$.

Cartesian product takes precedence over other set operations: $\times \prec \cup, \rightarrow, \rightharpoonup$.

2   Intraprocedural Semantics and Memory Safety

In this section we define formally our bytecode language and its semantics, and state the memory safety property that we ensure. We define the semantics (and safety) of one single method, parameterised by the semantics of the (direct) method calls it may involve. The interprocedural part of the semantics (which is essentially defined as a least fix-point of the intraprocedural semantics) and the proof that the safety property can be lifted to whole programs are omitted for space reasons. Details can be found in section 4 of a companion technical report [2].

2.1   The Java Bytecode Language

We present a minimal subset of the language, abstracting away irrelevant features (such as the operand stack) while keeping the main aspects (objects, interface methods) that are relevant to typing. The subset is sufficiently representative for the results to extend to the whole Java bytecode. We list some features that are absent from our language. The local operand stack is a feature of the bytecode that has no impact on the abstract domain used for the verification. For this reason, we replace actual bytecode instructions by three-address style instructions that directly operate on local variables. Constant fields and static or interface members, exceptions, void methods, basic types others than int, sub-routines, threads, class and objects initialisation, access control (visibility), as well as explicit type checks (the checkcast instruction) are not considered. We discuss their impact on this study in Section 5.1. Also, for conciseness we use less specialised instructions than the real JVM (for example, we merge iaload and aaload, ireturn and areturn).

Let *ident* be the set of fully qualified Java identifiers. We assume a set *class* $\subset$ *ident* of class names with a distinguished element Object, and a disjoint set *interface* $\subset$ *ident* of interface names. We define the set of types recursively as:

$$type ::= \text{int} \quad | \quad C \quad | \quad I \quad | \quad t[]$$

where $C \in class$, $I \in interface$, and $t \in type$.

The class hierarchy is modeled by the following three functions:

$$
\begin{array}{lll}
\text{super} & : class \setminus \{\text{Object}\} \to & class \\
\text{implements} : & class & \to \mathcal{P}(interface) \\
\text{extends} & : & interface & \to \mathcal{P}(interface)
\end{array}
$$

The function super must be the ancestor function of a tree with root Object:

$$\forall C \in class \quad \exists i \geq 0 \quad \text{super}^i(C) = \text{Object}.$$

A method signature is made of an object type, an identifier and a list of parameter types. We assume a subset *msig* of such signatures which represents the methods that are declared in the program being verified:

$$msig \subset \{t.m(t_1, \ldots, t_n) \mid t \in type \setminus \{\text{int}\}, m \in ident, t_i \in type\}$$

Note that we have a virtual method signature if t is a class or an array type, and an interface method signature otherwise. We let $\text{arity}(t.m(t_1, \ldots, t_n)) = n$. Each method signature has a return type given by the function result : $msig \rightarrow type$.

A field signature is made of a class name, an identifier and a type. We assume a subset $fsig$ of such signatures:

$$fsig \subset \{C.f : t \mid C \in class, f \in ident, t \in type\}$$

Note that $C.f : t$ represents a field declared in class C, and consequently, the set of fields that are relevant for a given class of objects must be looked for in its super-classes too (see the function fields in Section 2.2).

As stated in the introduction, we only consider the verification of one "current" method. We write var for the set of local variables of the method to verify and $arg \subseteq var$ for its set of formal parameters, whose types are described by the function $t_{\text{arg}} : arg \rightarrow type$. The return type of the current method is denoted by $t_{\text{ret}} \in type$. Program points are represented by the interval $ppoint = [0, |ppoint| - 1]$. Expressions and instructions are defined as follows. Here, C ranges over classes, t over types, ms over method signatures, fs over field signatures, x, y, z, x_i over local variables, and p over program points.

$$
\begin{aligned}
expr ::=\ &n \qquad n \in [-2^{31}, 2^{31} - 1] \\
&\mid\ null \quad\mid\quad y + z \quad\mid\quad new\ C \quad\mid\quad y.fs \quad\mid\quad new\ t[y] \quad\mid\quad y[z] \\
&\mid\ y.ms(x_1, \ldots, x_{\text{arity}(ms)})
\end{aligned}
$$

$$
\begin{aligned}
instr ::=\ &x := e \qquad e \in expr \\
&\mid\ x.fs := y \quad\mid\quad x[y] := z \quad\mid\quad goto\ p \quad\mid\quad if\ x < y\ p \quad\mid\quad return\ x
\end{aligned}
$$

The method code is represented by the function code : $ppoint \rightarrow instr$ mapping program points to instructions. The last instruction code$(|ppoint| - 1)$ must be either goto p for some p or return x for some x.

These last definitions enforce some well-formedness constraints on the code: the execution remains within the bounds of the code and cannot fall through the end, only valid local variables are referred to, and methods are always called with the right number of arguments. These properties are normally checked by the bytecode verifier prior to the type verifications.

2.2 Semantics

The operational semantics is defined as a small-step transition relation between program states (except for method calls which are big-step). A distinguishing feature of our semantic model is that we use a single data type of 32-bit values both for signed integer values and memory locations (note that objects and arrays are still annotated with their dynamic type in the heap, as in actual JVM implementations). This differs from most other formalisations where a disjoint set of locations is used (or equivalently, values are tagged with their type), this choice being only informally justified, as e.g. by Pusch [14]:

> *"[...] the type information is not used to determine the operational semantics of (correct) JVM code."*

Barthe, Dufay, Jakubiec and de Sousa [1] formalized this intuition by considering the actual virtual machine (which is called offensive) as an abstraction of the tagged (defensive) machine, and proving that the former correctly abstracts the latter, whenever the latter does not raise a type error (which is true for verifiable bytecode). Working directly with an untagged semantics immediately frees us from the risk of making unwanted implicit typing assumptions.

A precise model of the memory layout of objects and arrays is however not necessary. It is enough to use functions, state explicitly their domain and not use them outside of it; any concrete representation, for example that maps these domains to sets of offsets, will conform to this model, if the allocator keeps track of the range of objects and does not make them overlap.

Errors. We make an important distinction between two kinds of errors:

- Runtime errors that are checked for dynamically and cause the JVM to raise an exception, such as accessing an array out of bounds or putting an element of the wrong type in it, are represented by the absence of transition.
- Actual type errors (called linking errors in the JVM specification) that violate the assumptions that a virtual machine implementation is allowed to make about the code (see [13]), such as dereferencing an integer, or accessing a non-existing field of an object, are represented by a transition to the special state error. This second kind of errors must be correctly handled by the bytecode verification, as the behavior of the virtual machine is unspecified for those cases, and in practice this can result in a crash (in the optimistic case) or the by-passing of access controls.

In the current JVM, the `invokeinterface` instruction raises the exception `IncompatibleClassChangeError` if the receiver of the method does not implement the interface. Because our enhanced bytecode verifier will also type-check interfaces, we shift this exception from the class of runtime errors to the class of type errors. In our semantics, interface calls are dealt with like virtual calls and it is a type error if the receiver of an interface call does not implement the desired interface. Remark that the runtime errors raised in the explicit cast instruction (which we don't consider) are not removed by this technique.

Objects, Arrays and States. We write *word* for the set of 32-bit values. Values are used to represent signed integers as well as memory locations. We let fields : *class* $\rightarrow$ $\mathcal{P}(fsig)$ be the function that returns the set of (transitively inherited) fields of a class:

$$\text{fields}(C) = \{C.f : t \in fsig\} \cup \begin{cases} \text{fields(super}(C)) & \text{if } C \neq \text{Object} \\ \emptyset & \text{otherwise} \end{cases}$$

An object is a pair $\langle C, o \rangle$ where $C \in class$ and $o : \text{fields}(C) \rightarrow word$ gives the value of the relevant fields. We write *object* for the set of objects. We let *array* be the set of arrays, annotated with their element type (which can be an array type). We define *heap* as the sets of partial mappings from non-zero values to objects and arrays. The memory allocator is represented by a partial function alloc : *heap* $\rightharpoonup$ *word* \ {0} that maps a heap h to a value that is not defined in h (the absence of value represent the failure of the allocation)[1]: $\forall h \in heap$ alloc(h) = $v \implies v \notin$ dom(h). A program state $s = \langle h, l, p \rangle$ consists of a heap, a (total) mapping from variables to values, and a program point.

$$
\begin{aligned}
object &= \{\langle C, o \rangle \mid C \in class, o : \text{fields}(C) \rightarrow word\} \\
array &= \{\langle t, a \rangle \mid t \in type, a : [0, n-1] \rightarrow word, n \geq 0\} \\
heap &= word \setminus \{0\} \rightharpoonup (object \cup array) \\
state &= heap \times (var \rightarrow word) \times ppoint
\end{aligned}
$$

Dynamic Typing. We first recall the standard sub-typing order $\preceq \subseteq type \times type$ induced by the functions super, implements and extends. Note that, in J2SE, every array type is a sub-type of the two interfaces Cloneable and Serializable.

$$
\frac{}{t \preceq t} \qquad \frac{t \preceq t' \quad t' \preceq t''}{t \preceq t''} \qquad \frac{t \preceq t'}{t[] \preceq t'[]}
$$

$$
\frac{}{C \preceq \text{super}(C)} \qquad \frac{I \in \text{implements}(C)}{C \preceq I} \qquad \frac{I' \in \text{extends}(I)}{I \preceq I'}
$$

$$
\frac{}{I \preceq \text{Object}} \qquad \frac{}{t[] \preceq \text{Cloneable}} \qquad \frac{}{t[] \preceq \text{Serializable}}
$$

The key properties that are actually used in the following are i) that $\preceq$ is a partial order ii) the existence of the maximum element (which is called Object in this case) iii) the covariant ordering of array types (third rule in the first line) and of course the link with the functions super, implements and extends, for the language that we consider.

The dynamic typing relation $h \vdash v : t$ between heaps, 32-bit values and types is defined as follows:

$$
\frac{}{h \vdash v : int} \qquad \frac{}{h \vdash 0 : t}
$$

$$
\frac{h(v) = \langle C, o \rangle \in object \quad C \preceq t}{h \vdash v : t} \qquad \frac{h(v) = \langle t, a \rangle \in array \quad t[] \preceq t'}{h \vdash v : t'}
$$

It is worth noting that dynamic types can be checked efficiently by at most a heap access and a sub-typing check. This is important as such an operation is used by the concrete semantics of array assignment.

Method Calls. Let *bigstep* be the type of big-step semantics for methods.

$$
bigstep = \mathcal{P}\left(\bigcup_{n \geq 0} ((heap \times word \times word^n) \times (heap \times word \cup \{error\}))\right)
$$

---

[1] This is not completely accurate, as the allocation also depends on the needed size.

Let $bs \in bigstep$ and $\langle\langle h, this, args\rangle, r\rangle \in bs$. *this* represents the object on which the method is to be invoked, and *args* represents the list of the arguments. The result r is either the error constant or a pair $\langle h', v\rangle \in heap \times word$ where v is the returned value and h' is the heap obtained by running the method from the initial heap h. The direct method calls that may arise during the execution of the current method are represented by associating a big step transition relation

$$\xrightarrow{ms} \in bigstep$$

to each method signature ms (note that the relation for one method signature may correspond to several methods due to dynamic binding). As the relation is supposed to represent every possible call without any assumption on the arguments, is must be defined even for ill-typed ones, possibly with the result error. Also, we make no hypothesis on the correctness of the invoked method yet, thus the error state may be returned even for arguments of the right type. The absence of transition from a particular list of arguments represents non-termination or a runtime exception.

Transition Relation. The semantics itself is given in Figure 2 by the transition relation

$$\rightarrow \subseteq state \times (state \cup heap \times word \cup \{\text{error}\})$$

A couple of features in this semantics merit explanation: Writing to a field (see Figure 2b) always succeeds (provided the field exists for the target object), even if the value that is written is not of the right type. This is not a safety violation in itself; only a future misuse of this bad value would be error. Writing to an array always triggers a dynamic check[2] and the execution is stuck if the value stored in the array is not a sub-type of the array's own type, or if the index is out of bounds. Remember that a run-time exception of virtual machine is modelled

$$
\begin{aligned}
[\![n]\!]_{h,l} &= n \quad \text{(32-bit signed encoding)} \\
[\![\text{null}]\!]_{h,l} &= 0 \\
[\![y + z]\!]_{h,l} &= l(y) + l(z) \\
[\![y.fs]\!]_{h,l} &= \begin{cases} o(fs) & \text{if } h(l(y)) = \langle C, o\rangle \in object \wedge fs \in fields(C) \\ \bot & \text{if } l(y) = 0 \\ \text{error} & \text{if } \quad l(y) \neq 0 \wedge l(y) \notin dom(h) \\ & \qquad \vee\, h(l(y)) \notin object \\ & \qquad \vee\, h(l(y)) = \langle C, o\rangle \in object \wedge fs \notin fields(C) \end{cases} \\
[\![y[z]]\!]_{h,l} &= \begin{cases} a(l(z)) & \text{if } h(l(y)) = \langle t, a\rangle \in array \wedge 0 \le l(z) < |a| \\ \bot & \text{if } l(y) = 0 \vee h(l(y)) = \langle t, a\rangle \in array \wedge \neg\, 0 \le l(z) < |a| \\ \text{error} & \text{if } l(y) \neq 0 \wedge l(y) \notin dom(h) \vee h(l(y)) \notin array \end{cases}
\end{aligned}
$$

(a) Semantics $[\![e]\!]_{h,l} \in word \cup \{\text{error}, \bot\}$ of a side-effect free expression e in context h, l

Fig. 2. Semantics of Java bytecode

---

[2] This is unavoidable with the covariant arrays of the Java type system.

$$[\![x := e]\!](h, l) = \begin{cases} h, l[x \leftarrow [\![e]\!]_{h,l}] \\ \quad \text{if } [\![e]\!]_{h,l} \notin \{\bot, \text{error}\} \\ \bot \quad \text{if } [\![e]\!]_{h,l} = \bot \\ \text{error if } [\![e]\!]_{h,l} = \text{error} \end{cases} \quad \begin{array}{l} \text{if } e \notin \{y.ms(\cdots), \\ \text{new } C, \\ \text{new } t[y]\} \end{array}$$

$$[\![x := \text{new } C]\!](h, l) = \begin{cases} h[v \leftarrow \langle C, \lambda fs \in \text{fields}(C).0\rangle], l[x \leftarrow v] \\ \quad \text{if } alloc(h) = v \\ \bot \quad \text{if } h \notin \text{dom}(alloc) \end{cases}$$

$$[\![x := \text{new } t[y]]\!](h, l) = \begin{cases} h[v \leftarrow \langle t, \lambda i \in [0, l(y) - 1].0\rangle], l[x \leftarrow v] \\ \quad \text{if } l(y) \geq 0 \wedge alloc(h) = v \\ \bot \quad \text{if } l(y) < 0 \vee h \notin \text{dom}(alloc) \end{cases}$$

$$[\![x.fs := y]\!](h, l) = \begin{cases} h[l(x) \leftarrow \langle C, o[fs \leftarrow l(y)]\rangle], l \\ \quad \text{if } h(l(x)) = \langle C, o\rangle \in object \wedge fs \in \text{fields}(C) \\ \bot \quad \text{if } l(x) = 0 \\ \text{error if } \quad l(x) \neq 0 \wedge l(x) \notin \text{dom}(h) \\ \qquad\quad \vee h(l(x)) \notin object \\ \qquad\quad \vee h(l(x)) = \langle C, o\rangle \in object \wedge fs \notin \text{fields}(C) \end{cases}$$

$$[\![x[y] := z]\!](h, l) = \begin{cases} h[l(x) \leftarrow \langle t, a[l(y) \leftarrow l(z)]\rangle], l \\ \quad \text{if } \quad h(l(x)) = \langle t, a\rangle \in array \\ \qquad \wedge h \vdash l(z) : t \wedge 0 \leq l(y) < |a| \\ \bot \quad \text{if } \quad l(x) = 0 \\ \qquad \vee \quad l(x) = \langle t, a\rangle \in array \\ \qquad\quad \wedge \neg (h \vdash l(z) : t \wedge 0 \leq l(y) < |a|) \\ \text{error if } \quad l(x) \neq 0 \wedge l(x) \notin \text{dom}(h) \vee h(l(x)) \notin array \end{cases}$$

(b) Semantics $[\![i]\!] : heap \times (var \rightarrow word) \rightarrow (heap \times (var \rightarrow word) \cup \{\text{error}, \bot\})$ of a non-branching intraprocedural instruction i

$$\frac{i \notin \{\text{goto } p, \text{if} \cdots, \text{return } x, x := y.ms(\cdots)\} \quad [\![i]\!](h, l) \neq \bot}{h, l \xrightarrow{i} [\![i]\!](h, l)} \qquad \frac{}{h, l \xrightarrow{\text{return } x} h, l(x)}$$

$$\frac{h, l(y), l(x_1), \ldots, l(x_n) \xrightarrow{ms} h', v}{h, l \xrightarrow{x := y.ms(x_1, \ldots, x_n)} h', l[x \leftarrow v]} \qquad \frac{h, l(y), l(x_1), \ldots, l(x_n) \xrightarrow{ms} \text{error}}{h, l \xrightarrow{x := y.ms(x_1, \ldots, x_n)} \text{error}}$$

(c) Semantics $\xrightarrow{\;\;} \subseteq (heap \times (var \rightarrow word)) \times (heap \times (var \rightarrow word) \cup heap \times word \cup \{\text{error}\})$ of a non-branching instruction i

$$\frac{\text{code}(p) \notin \{\text{goto } p', \text{if} \cdots\} \quad h, l \xrightarrow{\text{code}(p)} r \quad r \in heap \times word \cup \{\text{error}\}}{\langle h, l, p\rangle \rightarrow r}$$

$$\frac{\text{code}(p) \notin \{\text{goto } p', \text{if} \cdots\} \quad h, l \xrightarrow{\text{code}(p)} h', l'}{\langle h, l, p\rangle \rightarrow \langle h', l', p + 1\rangle} \qquad \frac{\text{code}(p) = \text{goto } p'}{\langle h, l, p\rangle \rightarrow \langle h, l, p'\rangle}$$

$$\frac{\text{code}(p) = \text{if } x < y \; p' \quad l(x) < l(y)}{\langle h, l, p\rangle \rightarrow \langle h, l, p'\rangle} \qquad \frac{\text{code}(p) = \text{if } x < y \; p' \quad l(x) \geq l(y)}{\langle h, l, p\rangle \rightarrow \langle h, l, p + 1\rangle}$$

(d) Small step transition relation $\rightarrow \subseteq state \times (state \cup heap \times word \cup \{\text{error}\})$

Fig. 2. Semantics of Java bytecode (continued)

in our setting by the execution being stuck. Finally, in Figure 2c, it is important to remember that a method call can occur with ill-typed arguments, and that the invoked method itself can be ill-typed, hence the rule for propagating the error state.

2.3 Memory Safety

We give a modular definition of memory safety that is stronger than what is actually needed for a complete program: it includes the preservation of the well-typedness of the heap, and the fact that the heap is only extended, which is needed to ensure a global safety. This property requires some prior definitions to express those accurate invariants about the heap.

Well Typed Heaps. The following relation expresses that a heap is consistent.

$$
\cfrac{
\forall v \in word \setminus \{0\} \quad
\begin{cases}
v \notin \mathrm{dom}(h) \\
\vee \quad h(v) = \langle C, o \rangle \in object \\
\quad \wedge \; \forall C'.f : t \in \mathrm{fields}(C) \quad h \vdash o(C'.f : t) : t \\
\vee \quad h(v) = \langle t, a \rangle \in array \\
\quad \wedge \; \forall i \in [0, |a| - 1] \quad h \vdash a(i) : t
\end{cases}
}{
h \vdash h
}
$$

Ordering on Heaps. The relation $\Subset$ expresses the preservation of existing objects between two heaps.

$$
\cfrac{
\forall v \in word \setminus \{0\} \quad
\begin{cases}
v \notin \mathrm{dom}(h) \\
\vee \; h(v) = \langle C, o \rangle \in object \; \wedge \; h'(v) = \langle C, o' \rangle \in object \\
\vee \; h(v) = \langle t, a \rangle \in array \; \wedge \; h'(v) = \langle t, a' \rangle \in array
\end{cases}
}{
h \Subset h'
}
$$

Modular Memory-Safety. Definition 1 introduces the general safety property for the transition relation associated with a method. We need to give two variants of it since we use slightly different formalisations for the transition relation of the current method and the relations representing method calls. As errors are immediately propagated in the semantics, it is sound to define the safety as the unreachability of error in the outermost invocation.

Definition 1. *The relation* $\rightarrow \; \subseteq state \times (state \cup (heap \times word) \cup \{error\})$ *is safe with respect to* t_{arg} *and* t_{ret} *if for all* h, l *such that* $h \vdash h \; \wedge \; \forall x \in arg \quad h \vdash l(x) : t_{arg}(x)$ *then* $\langle h, l, 0 \rangle \not\rightarrow^* error$ *and* $\langle h, l, 0 \rangle \rightarrow^* h', v \implies h \Subset h' \; \wedge \; h' \vdash h' \; \wedge \; h' \vdash v : t_{ret}$.

Similarly, a transition relation $\xrightarrow{ms} \; \in bigstep$ *is safe with respect to the signature* $ms = t.m(t_1, \ldots, t_n)$ *if for all* $h, v, v_1, \ldots, v_n$ *such that* $h \vdash h \; \wedge \; h \vdash v : t \; \wedge \; \forall i \leq n \quad h \vdash v_i : t_i$ *then* $h, v, v_1, \ldots, v_n \not\xrightarrow{ms} error$ *and* $h, v, v_1, \ldots, v_n \xrightarrow{ms} h', v' \implies h \Subset h' \; \wedge \; h' \vdash h' \; \wedge \; h' \vdash v' : \mathrm{result}(ms)$.

Memory Safety and Security. In this paper we focus on memory safety which is just one aspect of the security of Java bytecode. Memory safety ensures that the virtual machine will not crash when executing the program but the secure execution of untrusted bytecode requires stronger properties. A common (informal) security requirement is that a program should not be able to forge a pointer to a heap location that it is not supposed to have access to; this is not easy to define formally without instrumenting the semantics. With the semantics defined in this section we can prove that a method whose return type is a reference type will return a heap location that is either unallocated in the initial heap or reachable through the (reference) arguments with which the method was invoked. This is ensured by the analysis of Section 3 without any modification: only the proofs must be extended by strengthening the concretisation function for the abstract domain. This is still too simplistic, as it does not distinguish between private or public fields, nor does it account for the fact that an untrusted program can be given controlled access to some (private) objects through the invocation of trusted methods from the API. Nevertheless, even though the memory safety defined here does not in itself imply any access restriction property, the analysis by which we ensure memory safety represents a large part of what is needed to ensure security, as shown by Leroy and Rouaix [12] who formalize such stronger security properties and give sufficient conditions, in addition to well-typedness, for an applet to be safe with respect to these properties.

3   Extended Bytecode Typing

In this section we present an extended abstract domain for bytecode verification and prove it sound with respect to the semantics. The main difference with the standard verifier is the use of interfaces in types, which make the runtime check in the "invokeinterface" instruction unnecessary. Another difference is that integers are abstracted by $\top_v$. This simplifies the presentation and the stack maps.

3.1   Abstract Domain

The abstract domain elements are called *stack maps* in the context of Java bytecode verification, as they normally map program points to abstract operand stacks. We keep this name even though the stack is absent in our setting. Our abstract domain associates a type to each variable at each program point. This type is either $\top_v$ (for non-reference values), null, or a conjunction of object (or array) types.

$$
\begin{aligned}
value^\sharp \quad &::= \text{null} \quad | \quad \top_v \\
&\quad | \; t_1 \wedge \cdots \wedge t_n \quad n \geq 1, t_i \in type \setminus \{\text{int}\}, \\
&\qquad\qquad\qquad\qquad \forall i, j \leq n \quad t_i \preceq t_j \implies i = j \\
state^\sharp \quad &= \; var \rightarrow value^\sharp \\
map \quad &= \; ppoint \rightarrow state^\sharp \\[6pt]
state^{\sharp\,\top_s}_{\;\bot_s} &= \; state^\sharp \cup \{\bot_s, \top_s\}
\end{aligned}
$$

The two special abstract states $\perp_s$ and $\top_s$ indicate respectively an unreachable program point and the possibility of the (concrete) error state being reachable. We also define the abbreviation $state^{\sharp\top_s}_{\perp_s}$. Conjunctions are defined up to the order, i.e., $t \wedge t' = t' \wedge t$.

A conjunction is to be interpreted as the set of objects that are a member of every atomic type in it. Note that we only consider conjunctions of unordered atomic types. This is necessary to be able to define an order on abstract values and not just a pre-order, and also to make the concretisation (almost) injective (as adding a super-type of another conjunct does not change the concretisation of a conjunction). Another isomorphic solution is to consider upward-closed (with respect to $\preceq$) sets of atomic types. We choose the first representation which is more compact and hence allows us to compute least upper bounds efficiently (see below).

The following definition identifies a subset of stack maps in which we want to choose a "certificate" to send with the current method.

Definition 2. *A stack map $m \in map$ is conjunction-free if all of its conjunctions $t_1 \wedge \cdots \wedge t_n$ are reduced to one element (i.e., $n = 1$).*

Concretisation. We define the concretisation functions $\gamma_h : value^{\sharp} \rightarrow \mathcal{P}(word)$, $h \in heap$, $\gamma_p : state^{\sharp\top_s}_{\perp_s} \rightarrow \mathcal{P}(state \cup \{error\})$, $p \in ppoint$ and $\gamma : (value^{\sharp} \cup \{\top_s\}) \rightarrow \mathcal{P}((heap \times word) \cup \{error\})$ by

$$
\begin{aligned}
\gamma_h(\top_v) &= word \\
\gamma_h(\text{null}) &= \{0\} \\
\gamma_h(t_1 \wedge \cdots \wedge t_n) &= \{v \in word \mid \forall i \leq n \quad h \vdash v : t_i\}
\end{aligned}
$$

$$
\begin{aligned}
\gamma_p(\perp_s) &= \emptyset \\
\gamma_p(\top_s) &= state \cup \{error\} \\
\gamma_p(l^{\sharp}) &= \{\langle h, l, p\rangle \in state \mid h \vdash h \wedge \forall x \in var \quad l(x) \in \gamma_h(l^{\sharp}(x))\}
\end{aligned}
$$

$$
\begin{aligned}
\gamma(\top_s) &= heap \times word \cup \{error\} \\
\gamma(v^{\sharp}) &= \{h, v \mid h \vdash h \wedge v \in \gamma_h(v^{\sharp})\}.
\end{aligned}
$$

Partial Order, Least Upper Bound and Transfer Function. The partial orders $\sqsubseteq_v \subseteq value^{\sharp} \times value^{\sharp}$ and $\sqsubseteq \subseteq state^{\sharp\top_s}_{\perp_s} \times state^{\sharp\top_s}_{\perp_s}$ are defined by the following rules:

$$
\frac{}{\text{null} \sqsubseteq_v v^{\sharp}} \qquad \frac{}{v^{\sharp} \sqsubseteq_v \top_v} \qquad \frac{\forall j \leq n' \quad \exists i \leq n \quad t_i \preceq t'_j}{t_1 \wedge \cdots \wedge t_n \sqsubseteq_v t'_1 \wedge \cdots \wedge t'_{n'}}
$$

$$
\frac{}{\perp_s \sqsubseteq s^{\sharp}} \qquad \frac{}{s^{\sharp} \sqsubseteq \top_s} \qquad \frac{\forall x \in var \quad l^{\sharp}(x) \sqsubseteq l'^{\sharp}(x)}{l^{\sharp} \sqsubseteq l'^{\sharp}}
$$

The (commutative) least upper bound operators $\sqcup_v : value^\sharp \times value^\sharp \to value^\sharp$ and $\sqcup : state^\sharp{}_{\bot_s}^{\top_s} \times state^\sharp{}_{\bot_s}^{\top_s} \to state^\sharp{}_{\bot_s}^{\top_s}$ are defined by

$$
\begin{aligned}
\text{null} \sqcup_v v^\sharp &= v^\sharp \\
v^\sharp \sqcup_v \top_v &= \top_v \\
\begin{array}{c} t_1 \wedge \cdots \wedge t_n \\ \sqcup_v \; t'_1 \wedge \cdots \wedge t'_{n'} \end{array} &= \begin{cases} \text{let } \mathcal{T} = \{t \in type \mid \exists i \leq n, j \leq n' \;\; t_i \preceq t \wedge t'_j \preceq t\} \\ \text{in } \bigwedge \{t \in \mathcal{T} \mid \forall t' \in \mathcal{T} \;\; t' \preceq t \implies t' = t\} \end{cases} \\[1em]
\bot_s \sqcup s^\sharp &= s^\sharp \\
s^\sharp \sqcup \top_s &= \top_s \\
l^\sharp \sqcup l'^\sharp &= \lambda x. l^\sharp(x) \sqcup_v l'^\sharp(x).
\end{aligned}
$$

The least upper bound of two (non-empty) conjunctions is always defined (and non-empty), because Object is a super type of all reference types (including interfaces and array types). The second line in the least upper bounds of two conjunctions ensures that we keep only maximal atoms. The actual computation of the least upper bound of two conjunctions can be performed efficiently: as only minimal types $t \in \mathcal{T}$ will be kept, it is sufficient to find the first superclass and/or super-interfaces of each pair t_i, t'_j, which is done by traversing the hierarchy above t_i and t'_j. Figure 3 defines the abstract semantics as two relations:

$$
\begin{aligned}
\longrightarrow &\subseteq ppoint \times (state^\sharp \to state^\sharp{}_{\bot_s}^{\top_s}) \times ppoint \\
\longrightarrow &\subseteq ppoint \times (state^\sharp \to value^\sharp)
\end{aligned}
$$

3.2   Correctness of the Abstraction

Lemma 1 ensures the consistency of the partial order with respect to the concretisation, which is crucial for the correctness of the verification.

Lemma 1. *For all $h \in heap$ and $v^\sharp, v'^\sharp \in value^\sharp$, if $v^\sharp \sqsubseteq_v v'^\sharp$ then $\gamma_h(v^\sharp) \subseteq \gamma_h(v'^\sharp)$. For all $p \in ppoint$ and $s^\sharp, s'^\sharp \in state^\sharp{}_{\bot_s}^{\top_s}$, if $s^\sharp \sqsubseteq s'^\sharp$ then $\gamma_p(s^\sharp) \subseteq \gamma_p(s'^\sharp)$. For all $v^\sharp, v'^\sharp \in value^\sharp \cup \{\top_s\}$, if $v'^\sharp = \top_s \vee v^\sharp \sqsubseteq_v v'^\sharp$ then $\gamma(v^\sharp) \subseteq \gamma(v'^\sharp)$.*

The least upper bound operator is used during the fix-point computation and must be correct for the analyser to be correct (but not for the checker).

Lemma 2. *For all $v^\sharp, v'^\sharp \in value^\sharp$, $v^\sharp \sqcup_v v'^\sharp \sqsupseteq_v v^\sharp$ and $v^\sharp \sqcup_v v'^\sharp \sqsupseteq_v v'^\sharp$. For all $s^\sharp, s'^\sharp \in state^\sharp{}_{\bot_s}^{\top_s}$, $s^\sharp \sqcup s'^\sharp \sqsupseteq s^\sharp$ and $s^\sharp \sqcup s'^\sharp \sqsupseteq s'^\sharp$.*

The core of the correctness of the checker (and of the analyser) resides in Lemma 3 which says that the concrete transition relation is correctly approximated.

Lemma 3. *Suppose that for every signature ms the relation $\overset{ms}{\longrightarrow}$ is safe with respect to ms (see Definition 1). Let $s \in state$, $r \in state \cup (heap \times word) \cup \{error\}$, $p \in ppoint$ and $l^\sharp \in state^\sharp$ such that $s \to r$ and $s \in \gamma_p(l^\sharp)$. Then one of the following holds:*

$$\llbracket n \rrbracket_{l^\sharp}^\sharp = \top_v$$
$$\llbracket \text{null} \rrbracket_{l^\sharp}^\sharp = \text{null}$$
$$\llbracket y + z \rrbracket_{l^\sharp}^\sharp = \top_v$$
$$\llbracket \text{new } C \rrbracket_{l^\sharp}^\sharp = C$$
$$\llbracket \text{new } t[y] \rrbracket_{l^\sharp}^\sharp = t[]$$
$$\llbracket y.fs \rrbracket_{l^\sharp}^\sharp = \begin{cases} t & \text{if } fs = C.f : t \wedge l^\sharp(y) \sqsubseteq_v C \\ \top_s & \text{otherwise} \end{cases}$$
$$\llbracket y[z] \rrbracket_{l^\sharp}^\sharp = \begin{cases} t & \text{if } l^\sharp(y) = t[] \quad t \in type \\ \bot_s & \text{if } l^\sharp(y) = \text{null} \\ \top_s & \text{if } l^\sharp(y) \notin \{\text{null}\} \cup \{t[] \mid t \in type\} \end{cases}$$
$$\llbracket y.ms(x_1, \ldots, x_n) \rrbracket_{l^\sharp}^\sharp = \begin{cases} \text{result}(ms) \\ \quad \text{if} \quad ms = t.m(t_1, \ldots, t_n) \\ \qquad \wedge \; l^\sharp(y) \sqsubseteq_v t \wedge \forall i \le n \quad l^\sharp(x_i) \sqsubseteq_v t_i \\ \top_s \; \text{otherwise} \end{cases}$$

(a) Abstract semantics $\llbracket e \rrbracket_{l^\sharp}^\sharp \in value^\sharp \cup \{\bot_s, \top_s\}$ of an expression e in the abstract context $l^\sharp$

$$\llbracket x := e \rrbracket^\sharp(l^\sharp) = \begin{cases} l^\sharp[x \leftarrow \llbracket e \rrbracket_{l^\sharp}^\sharp] \\ \quad \text{if } \llbracket e \rrbracket_{l^\sharp}^\sharp \notin \{\bot_s, \top_s\} \\ \bot_s \; \text{if } \llbracket e \rrbracket_{l^\sharp}^\sharp = \bot_s \\ \top_s \; \text{if } \llbracket e \rrbracket_{l^\sharp}^\sharp = \top_s \end{cases}$$
$$\llbracket x.fs := y \rrbracket^\sharp(l^\sharp) = \begin{cases} l^\sharp & \text{if} \quad fs = C.f : t \\ \quad \wedge \; l^\sharp(x) \sqsubseteq_v C \wedge l^\sharp(y) \sqsubseteq_v t \\ \top_s \; \text{otherwise} \end{cases}$$
$$\llbracket x[y] := z \rrbracket^\sharp(l^\sharp) = \begin{cases} l^\sharp & \text{if } l^\sharp(x) = t[] \quad t \in type \\ \bot_s & \text{if } l^\sharp(x) = \text{null} \\ \top_s & \text{if } l^\sharp(y) \notin \{\text{null}\} \cup \{t[] \mid t \in type\} \end{cases}$$

(b) Abstract semantics $\llbracket i \rrbracket^\sharp : state^\sharp \to state^{\sharp \top_s}_{\bot_s}$ of a non-branching instruction i ($i \ne \text{return } x$)

$$\frac{code(p) \notin \{\text{return } x, \text{goto } p', \text{if} \cdots\}}{p \overset{\llbracket code(p) \rrbracket^\sharp}{\longrightarrow} p + 1} \qquad \frac{code(p) = \text{goto } p'}{p \overset{\lambda l^\sharp.l^\sharp}{\longrightarrow} p'}$$

$$\frac{code(p) = \text{if } x < y \; p'}{p \overset{\lambda l^\sharp.l^\sharp}{\longrightarrow} p'} \qquad \frac{code(p) = \text{if } x < y \; p'}{p \overset{\lambda l^\sharp.l^\sharp}{\longrightarrow} p + 1}$$

$$\frac{code(p) = \text{return } x}{p \overset{\lambda l^\sharp.l^\sharp(x)}{\longrightarrow}}$$

(c) Abstract transition relations $\longrightarrow \; \subseteq ppoint \times (state^\sharp \to state^{\sharp \top_s}_{\bot_s}) \times ppoint$ and $\longrightarrow \; \subseteq ppoint \times (state^\sharp \to value^\sharp)$

Fig. 3. Abstract semantics of Java bytecode

1. $p \xrightarrow{F^\sharp} p'$ and $r \in \gamma_{p'}(F^\sharp(l^\sharp))$ for some p' and $F^\sharp$, or
2. $p \xrightarrow{F^\sharp}$ and $r \in \gamma(F^\sharp(l^\sharp))$ for some $F^\sharp$.

Furthermore, the functions $F^\sharp$ are monotone.

Formal proofs can be found in the technical report [2].

3.3   Analysis and Checking

The following definition introduce the notion of witness of the current method whose signature is given by t_{arg} and t_{ret}.

Definition 3. *A witness is a stack map $m \in map$ such that*

1. $\forall x \in var \quad m(0)(x) \sqsupseteq_v \begin{cases} t_{arg}(x) & \text{if } x \in arg \\ \top_v & \text{otherwise} \end{cases}$

2. $\forall p, p' \in ppoint \quad p \xrightarrow{F^\sharp} p' \implies F^\sharp(m(p)) \sqsubseteq m(p')$

3. $\forall p \in ppoint \quad p \xrightarrow{F^\sharp} \implies F^\sharp(m(p)) \sqsubseteq_v t_{ret}$

Note that by definition of stack maps, witnesses contain no $\top_s$ or $\perp_s$. This correspond respectively to the assumptions that the code should type without error, and that even dead code should be typable. This second condition is necessary for the pruning to work.

The following lemma shows that the memory safety property can be ensured by simply checking that some given stack map is a witness, and shows how to compute the least witness. The next section will show that, for Java programs, the least witness can be pruned resulting in a witness without conjunction.

Theorem 1. *Suppose that every relation $\xrightarrow{ms}$ is safe with respect to ms (see Definition 1). If there exists a witness m then the relation $\rightarrow$ is safe with respect to t_{arg} and t_{ret}. Moreover, the least witness[3] (if there exists a witness) can be computed by fixpoint iteration.*

The proof can be found in the technical report [2].

4   Lightweight Verification by Fix-Point Pruning

In the previous section we formalised a bytecode analysis extended to interfaces, using conjunctions of types in the abstract domain. The drawback of this extension is its computational cost, especially in terms of memory, that could make it unapplicable on the smallest Java capable devices. We will now present an additional step to the lightweight verification setting that removes the need for computations of sets of types on the consumer side by computing a witness without conjunction, if the safety of the program does not rely on them. This is the case for programs compiled from Java in particular.

---

[3] The abstract state $\perp_s$ is not a witness by definition, but the state $\lambda x \in var.\mathsf{null}$ is a minimum of $state^\sharp$. Thus, if the set of witnesses is not empty, it has a least element.

```
public static void main(String [] args) {
    I3 ∧ I4 i = args.length > 0 ? new A() : new B();
    i.m3();
    i.m4();
}
```

Fig. 4. A safe Java bytecode program that has no conjunction-free witness

4.1   Stack Map Checking without Conjunctions

We first present an algorithm, which when possible, computes a conjunction-free witness from the least fix-point. The key hypothesis of this algorithm is therefore the existence of a witness without conjunction. This is not the case of all bytecode programs. Figure 4 shows a method that has no such witness (I3, I4, A and B are defined as in Section 1). It is shown in pseudo Java (with a conjunction of types) but has to be written directly in bytecode.

As explained in the previous section, the checking of bytecode mainly consist in the verification of the conditions of Definition 3, which reduces to computations of the functions $F^\sharp$ of the abstract semantics, and ordering checks $\sqsubseteq$ between abstract states. As the $F^\sharp$s never "create" a conjunction of types (this is easily verified on the definition), we can see that the checking of a conjunction-free witness can be performed without manipulating conjunctions[4]. So the technique of pruning removes the need for conjunction computations.

Fix-Point Pruning. The algorithm of Figure 5 optimistically searches for such a witness. It starts from the least witness (if it exists)

$$\mathrm{lfp} \in map$$

computed by direct analysis, and traverses the set of conjunction-free stack maps that are greater than lfp, until a witness is reached or the search space is exhausted. If there exists a witness without conjunction, it must belong to this set, by definition of the least fix-point. Moreover, the finite ascending chain condition satisfied by the lattice ensures that the search space is finite so the exploration terminates (which is interesting in case there is no such witness). Therefore this algorithm is complete in the sense that if a solution exists, it will find it.

More precisely, the idea is to start from $\top_v$ at each program point and each variable and replace those values by lesser ones until a witness is reached. The non-deterministic instruction "choose" is to be interpreted as follows: if the choice fails at any point (*i.e.*, there is no $v^\sharp$ satisfying the required conditions) then we backtrack to a previous choice. The algorithm can terminate either by returning a witness, or by returning nothing, if every combination of choices

---

[4] In the real process, the value of the witness is only sent for some program points and the remaining values are reconstructed at checking time, but no least upper bound is involved, thus the property still holds.

let $w = \lambda p \in ppoint.\lambda x \in var.\top_v$ and $W = ppoint$
while $W \neq \emptyset$ do
$\quad$ take $p \in W$ (and remove it)
$\quad$ choose a maximal $l^\sharp \in state^\sharp$ such that
$\quad\quad l^\sharp$ is without conjunction and $\mathrm{lfp}(p) \sqsubseteq l^\sharp \sqsubseteq w(p)$

$\quad\quad$ and $\quad \forall p' \in ppoint \quad p \xrightarrow{F^\sharp} p' \implies$
$$F^\sharp(l^\sharp) \neq \top_s$$
$$\wedge\ F^\sharp(l^\sharp) \sqsubseteq w(p')$$
$$\wedge\ p \xrightarrow{F^\sharp} \implies F^\sharp(l^\sharp) \sqsubseteq_v t_{ret}$$
$\quad$ if $l^\sharp \neq w(p)$ then
$\quad\quad w := w[p \leftarrow l^\sharp]$
$$W := W \cup \{p' \mid p' \xrightarrow{F^\sharp} p\}$$
$\quad$ end if
done
return w

Fig. 5. Naive (complete) pruning algorithm

eventually gets stuck. As for the strategy used to implement the work-set (instruction "take"), we found that a stack without duplicates was an efficient and simple heuristic. Note that this second sort of choice is never undone and does not cause further backtracking.

The following theorem formalizes the fact that the algorithm of Figure 5 is sound and complete (when a witness without conjunction exists).

Theorem 2. *The complete pruning algorithm always terminates, either by returning a stack map w or by a failure in the choice of $l^\sharp$. If it terminates by returning some w, then w is a conjunction-free witness. Furthermore, if a conjunction-free witness w exists, the algorithm will return such a witness.*

The proof can be found in the technical report [2].

Java Programs. In the Java language, all variables are declared with a fixed type $t \in type$ (actually, the basic types are not exactly the same between Java and bytecode: the smaller integer types are merged with int in the latter). This type satisfies the same constraints that are expressed by the abstract semantics in the previous section (including the ones for interfaces) and can therefore be considered as a witness for each method, where the type of every variable is the same regardless of the program point. The difference is that the variables are the source variables, not the bytecode local variables and stack positions.

If the compiler does not transform the structure of the program too much, more precisely if each variable of the source program is mapped to a (bytecode) local variable in a given subset of the (bytecode) program points, without overlapping, then we see that the witness representing the typing of the source code can be renamed to a corresponding witness on the bytecode. This witness has an interesting feature: it does not contain any conjunction (because variables are

```
public static void main(String [] args) {
    I3 i3 = args.length > 0 ? new A() : new B();
    I4 i4 = args.length > 0 ? new A() : new B();
    i3.m3();
    i4.m4();
    Object i = args.length > 0 ? i3 : i4;
    i.toString();
}
```

Fig. 6. A Java program for which a conjunction-free witness cannot be build from the atomic types of the least fix-point

declared with a single type). Therefore, for bytecode compiled from Java with a "natural" compiler, there exists a conjunction-free witness for every method (and thus the algorithm of the previous section will find it).

An alternative solution for introducing the verification of interfaces in a light-weight verification process in the case of Java (source) programs is to generate a stack map from the type annotations present in the source code. Indeed, as the lightweight verification paradigm is being generalized to J2SE Java [9], the task of generating stack maps is moving from a dedicated "preverifier" program to the compiler itself. One disadvantage of this technique is that all the tools that manipulate bytecode (notably the compiler) must take care of stack maps consistently, which complicates their design. Instead, we extract a witness without conjunction directly from the bytecode (given that there exists one).

4.2   Efficient Fix-Point Pruning

Although the first algorithm is complete, it takes potentially a very long time, since the search space is the product over program points and local variables of the part of the type hierarchy that is greater than the corresponding value type in the least fix-point. In fact, it is rarely necessary, for a given variable and program point, to consider the entire type hierarchy above the type given by the least fix-point. Most of the time it is enough to choose one of its conjuncts (if it is a conjunction). The resulting pruning algorithm still has an exponential complexity, but it performs reasonably fast in practice.

Reducing the Branching Factor. In most cases, the following holds: there exists a witness $w \in map$ without conjunction such that the atomic types that appear in w are atoms of the corresponding conjunctions in the least fix point.

$$\forall p \in ppoint \quad \forall x \in var \quad w(p)(x) = t \in type \implies lfp(p)(x) = t \wedge \cdots$$

This is not true for the program in Figure 6 (I3, I4, A and B are defined as in Section 1). In this example, we build two variables i3 and i4 with most precise type I3 $\wedge$ I4. The variable i is then defined as the "union" of the two, and its type is therefore I3 ∧ I4. However, in a stack map without conjunction, the type of i3 must be I3, and the type of i4 must be I4 (because we call m3 and m4, respectively). Therefore, the type of i must be greater than the least upper bound of I3 and I4, *i.e.*, java.lang.Object, which is not an atom of I3 ∧ I4. Nevertheless, this seems to be a pathological example and in practise the above hypothesis holds for all our (substantial) benchmarks, which indicates that it's applicability is very general.

Algorithm. Taking into account the hypothesis of section 4.2, we proceed by searching for a witness satisfying this hypothesis. The optimized algorithm is obtained by replacing the condition

$$l^\sharp \text{ is without conjunction and lfp} \sqsubseteq l^\sharp$$

by the stronger condition

$$\forall x \in var \quad l^\sharp(x) = \top$$
$$\vee \ l^\sharp(x) = t \in type \ \wedge \ \text{lfp}(p)(x) = t \ \wedge \cdots$$
$$\vee \ l^\sharp(x) = \text{null} = \text{lfp}(p)(x)$$

in the algorithm of Figure 5.

Correctness As the complete version, the new algorithm is sound and terminates and, though it is incomplete (see the above counter-example), it will succeed in finding a witness if the optimistic hypothesis holds. If not, the search will fail and the complete algorithm presented before should then be run instead.

5   Experiments

We have implemented our ideas in a verifier for real Java bytecode that adds the stack maps as method attributes, as defined in the JVM specification.

5.1   Extensions and Limitations

The bytecode language presented so far is considerably simplified. We had to address a few more issues to deal with real bytecode. First, the Java bytecode uses an operand stack in addition to local variables. This complicates the abstract states, as they now have another list of abstract values, of variable length. Of course, this adds more reasons for the verification to fail, namely, (operand) stack overflow or underflow, or the possibility to have different stack heights at some program point. Second, in addition to 32-bit integers, Java bytecode has floats, longs and doubles. floats are easily abstracted by $\top_v$, and the 64-bit types by two $\top_v$s. Note that, although 32-bit integers are not distinguished from shorter integers at the bytecode level (they are in the source code), this is not the case for arrays of such types. Therefore, to ensure that the array bounds checks performed at runtime correctly interpret the length field, the size of elements must be known. This implies that arrays of floats or ints must not be confused with arrays of shorts. However, individual float and int values can still be merged, since the instruction for accessing arrays are typed. The last additional feature is throwing and catching exceptions. From the verification point of view, exceptions just add some more transitions in the control flow graph, with a semantics that empties the stack and then push some constant reference type (the type that is caught by the corresponding handler). They pose no particular difficulty.

While analysing real bytecode, we have omitted some aspects of the verification in the concrete implementation. In particular, we do not address the issue of verifying sub-routines. Also, a byte code verifier should verify that any object is initialized before being used. The benchmarks presented here do not include this phase. Finally, note that the semantics that we gave to the bytecode used big-step calls, which prevents us to consider even a simplified (interleaving) version of concurrency, which would require explicit call stacks. Therefore, in principle, all the results presented here only applies to single-threaded programs. However, the scheme of the proof (an invariant that holds at each state of a small-step semantics) does not seem to rely on sequentiality, and we believe that there is no issue in extending it to threads.

5.2   Stack Maps and Checking

The stack maps that are attached to the bytecode are not exactly a representation of conjunction-free witnesses, but only of the value of such witnesses for a subset of the program points. These points correspond basically to the basic blocks of the control flow graph. This reduces the size of stack maps, while still allowing a very simple checking algorithm that evaluates program points in order. We will not detail this aspect, as we used the same subset of program points and the same checking algorithm as Sun's lightweight bytecode verifier. The resulting stack maps are encoded in the class files either as StackMap attributes in the same format as the lightweight bytecode verifier, or with a new attribute using a sparse representation. In the latter, we just replaced an array of value types by an array of bits (to indicate which values are not $\top_v$) followed by the list of non-$\top_v$ values. In order for the comparison to be fair, the sparse representation uses the same verbose encoding of value types as the stack map representation.

5.3   Results

Three test suites were used to experiment with the analysis, pruning and checking with interfaces. The first one consists of 433 old midlets (Java applets for mobile phones) downloaded from midlet.org. The second one is Soot 2.2.4, a framework for analysing Java bytecode. The last test case is Eclipse SDK 3.2.2

All methods have been successfully analysed, pruned and checked except those that contained sub-routines, referred to unavailable libraries, contained dead code (because the pruning algorithm does not apply if the least fix-point is $\bot_s$ for some program points) or referred to classes that existed in different versions in the same program. This last case happens in Eclipse and we built conservatively the complete hierarchy of the distributed classes, by taking the union[5]. In all cases, a stack map without conjunction could be obtained from the atoms of the least fix-point, thanks to the heuristic presented in Section 4.2.

The first table shows the main interesting computing times for the three case

	jar size	analysis + pruning	analysis	pruning	checking
midlets	11M	5m54	23%	77%	0m23
Soot	4.4M	3m40	17%	83%	0m11
Eclipse	96M	24m43	26%	74%	1m55

studies. The first column gives the size of the benchmarks (jar files). The second one shows the total time taken by the complete stack map generation procedure (on the producer's side). This time is then divided into analysis phase (third column) and the pruning phase (fourth column). The last column correspond to the checking time (consumer's side). Clearly, most of the time is spent in pruning, but even this time remains acceptable (three to six times the cost of the analysis), especially since this operation only needs to be performed once, by the code producer. The checking time is short and could be further reduced with a reasonably optimised implementation.

The second table estimates the size of witnesses before and after pruning, in

proportion of non-$\top_v$ in	lfp	pruned stack map	ratio
midlets	44%	34%	77%
Soot	67%	42%	63%
Eclipse	58%	39%	66%

terms of the proportion of pairs p, x for which the value is not $\top_v$. The last column shows the proportion of "positions" (of pairs p, x) that are kept with a non-$\top_v$ value by pruning. We see that the "initial" proportion of non-$\top_v$ is greater in Soot and Eclipse, which indicates that objects (or arrays) are used more often in Eclipse than in midlets (remember that base types are abstracted by $\top_v$). Also, the pruning removes more values in Soot and Eclipse than in midlets (which is not surprising since there are more non-$\top_v$ values to remove, in proportion). In the end, the numbers of non-$\top_v$ in the stack maps are very close for the three test cases.

The first four sub-columns of the last table give the space saved by pruning, both for the class files and the jar files (compressed archives). The numbers correspond to the difference in size with respect to the same file format without stack map. For example, the total jar size for Eclipse with pruned stack maps included is 3.0% greater than the original jar files (without stack maps). In the two columns for the fix-point, since only conjunction-free witnesses can be encoded in class files, we did not include any stack map for the methods whose least fix-point had conjunctions (which is actually quite rare). Note that we can only underestimate the benefit of pruning by doing this. In the case of midlets,

---

[5] Some classes even exist with different super-classes. In this case we just choose one, which is definitely not safe.

witness	fix-point	pruned witness			
representation	extensive	extensive		sparse	
format	.class	.jar	.class	.jar	.class	.jar
midlets	19.8%	7.3%	17.4%	6.8%	16.0%	7.0%
Soot	14.0%	7.2%	11.5%	6.5%	11.5%	7.3%
Eclipse	11.8%	3.3%	9.5%	3.0%	9.6%	3.2%

for example, the size of the stack maps is reduced from 19.8% to 17.4% of the total initial class files, or from 7.3% to 6.8% of the initial jar files. Therefore there is no significant improvement here since the size of what is shipped (*i.e.*, the jar files with stack maps) is only reduced by less that one percent.

The last two sub-columns of the figure show the effect of a sparse representation of the stack maps obtained after pruning. We see that a sparse representation has little impact on the size, and that the small savings that we get for (some) class files are canceled by the compression phase, and tend to yeld larger jar files (even if the eight-byte alignment of the class files is kept).

We have not tried to encode our stack maps with the new StackMapTable attribute defined by JSR202, which was designed to factorize most of the information. The results would probably be quite different since this format relies on the assumption that the type of variables do not change too often, while the pruning may for example set any variable to T_v even if it was not modified, as soon as the type information for this variable is not needed anymore.

6   Related Work

The formalisation of Java byte code verification has received a lot of attention. Freund and Mitchell [7] prove the soundness of a type system for a very large subset of the Java bytecode with respect to a small-step operational semantics (with explicit stacks). Their model of states is close to ours, but instrumented by tags that keep track of the type of every value. They do not address the problem of inferring types in presence of interfaces. A survey of bytecode verification techniques and solutions to various known difficulties (interfaces, object initialisation, sub-routines) can be found in [11].

The concept of lightweight verification, which is now used in J2ME, was introduced by Rose [16]. Several algorithms were given, with enhancements that allow to reduce the number of program points for which a stack map is necessary, more than what is done in Sun's lightweight bytecode verifier. The issue of verifying interfaces was not considered.

Using sets of types to verify interfaces has been explored by Knoblock and Rehof [10] who analyse an SSA form of the Java bytecode in the Dedekind-MacNeille completion of the type hierarchy. They show that this minimal completion achieves an optimal precision, *i.e.*, every program typable in the power set completion is typable in the Dedekind-MacNeille completion. The analysis presented in section 3 is therefore very similar to their work. Our representation of the domain differs, though: we use conjunctions of types rather than disjunctions (in both cases, upward/downward-closed sets are not represented in extension). The lattice that we use to abstract values is close to the ideal completion of the type hierarchy (it is a super-set of the ideal completion because the latter further requires that conjunctions be "not empty", in the sense that they must have a lower bound in the hierarchy). Furthermore, our analysis only uses the subset of $value^{\sharp}$ that is obtained by taking upper bounds of atomic types, which is isomorphic to the Dedekind-MacNeille completion of $type \setminus \{int\}$. See [6] for an account on completion techniques for posets. Knoblock and Rehof do not prove the correctness of their analysis with respect to a concrete semantics and safety property. Qian [15] proposes a type system for Java bytecode that uses arbitrary disjunctions of reference types to allow the static verification of interfaces. Several safety properties are proved for typable programs (type preservation, possible uses of uninitialized objects, of sub-routines return addresses). The actual inference of types is not detailed. Push [14] has formalised a variant of Qian's bytecode verifier in HOL and proved its correctness with respect to a small-step operational semantics. Again, concrete values are tagged with their type. Goldberg [8] focuses on dynamic loading of classes and proposes a framework for verifying Java class files out of order, while ensuring the global soundness of typing. Class files are verified by a data-flow analysis that uses disjunctions of types (which solves the problem of not knowing the type hierarchy) and yields the minimal set of ordering constraints between types under which the class is type-safe. These constraints are added to a global typing context that is transmitted across invocations of the verifier, and the global safety is defined as the consistency of this context.

We have previously proposed a pruning algorithm for getting weaker abstract interpretation witnesses [3]. Such pruning algorithms were independently studied by Seo, Yang, Yi and Han [17]. The problem that we consider here is different: the goal is not to get a maximal witness in a given lattice, but to get a witness without conjunction, a property that is not monotone. Therefore, directly applying one of the algorithms from [3] would not necessarily help in getting such a witness. The backward computation that we proposed in the same work for distributive analyses (which is the case of the bytecode verification) does not apply either, as shown in the introduction: the backward algorithm performs greatest lower bound operations, which in the present setting introduce conjunctions.

7   Conclusion

We have shown how the notion of pruning provides a viable means of integrating the verification of interfaces into lightweight bytecode verification. This is achieved by combining an extended bytecode analyser and an algorithm for removing conjunctions from the result of the analysis which, together, allows to compute stack maps where interfaces are treated on a par with other types.

The bytecode analysis that we have proposed here adds sets of types to the abstract domain in order to verify interfaces. The ensuing pruning step optimises the typing found by the analyser, reducing all such sets to a singleton, and removing as many typing information as possible while still ensuring the memory safety, *i.e.*, that all memory accesses will be to existing fields of objects. The resulting stack maps can be checked without any overhead compared to existing lightweight bytecode verification and will ensure statically the safety of interface method calls. We also show that it is possible to simplify several aspects of the BCV when constructing an abstract domain that is specific to the memory safety property. In particular, there is no need to distinguish between base types and it is even possible to identify these base type with the $\top_v$ element of the domain (which allows a program to use an address as an integer).

In terms of semantic correctness, we have shown that it is possible to reason directly with an untyped concrete semantics rather than a defensive virtual machine. Both techniques are equally sound, but the latter requires an additional abstraction step that explains the link between the raw state model that we use and the tagged memory objects used in the instrumented semantics. In other words, we use a notion of state that is closer to the actual implementation and, hence, more convincing. In order to complete the picture, the semantics with big-step calls that we used should be related to a small-step semantics with a call stack, but we leave this for further work.

In terms of experiments, we have shown that the technique works well in practice, as we could successfully analyse a large set of Java class files. Furthermore, the idea is not relevant just for Java, but should apply to other object oriented languages with multiple inheritance, since it only relies on the transformation of the poset representing a type hierarchy into a lattice. The results show that it is feasible to compute efficiently conjunction-free stack maps with interfaces ; however, they are disappointing in terms of reducing the stack map size: even though a significant number of variables are set to $\top_v$ by pruning, this is not enough for a sparse coding to be more efficient than a naive coding of stack maps, especially as class files are eventually compressed.

As we said before, in this study we considered one aspect of the security of Java bytecode, *viz.*, the memory safety. Further work should extend the formalisation proposed here to prove that for example access control properties are also ensured by the verifier. In another direction, our stack map generator should be extended to produce stack maps in the StacMapTable format proposed for Java.

References

1. Barthe, G., Dufay, G., Jakubiec, L., Melo de Sousa, S.: A formal correspondence between offensive and defensive javacard virtual machines. In: Cortesi, A. (ed.) VMCAI 2002. LNCS, vol. 2294, pp. 32–45. Springer, Heidelberg (2002)
2. Besson, F., Jensen, T., Turpin, T.: Computing stack maps with interfaces. Technical Report 1879, Irisa (2007)
3. Besson, F., Jensen, T., Turpin, T.: Small witnesses for abstract interpretation-based proofs. In: De Nicola, R. (ed.) ESOP 2007. LNCS, vol. 4421, pp. 268–283. Springer, Heidelberg (2007)
4. Bracha, G., Lindholm, T., Tao, W., Yellin, F.: CLDC Byte Code Typechecker Specification. Sun Microsystems (2003)

5. Cousot, P., Cousot, R.: Abstract interpretation: A unified lattice model for static analysis of programs by construction of approximations of fixpoints. In: Proc. of the 4th ACM Symp. on Principles of Programming Languages (POPL 1977), pp. 238–252. ACM Press, New York (1977)
6. Davey, B.A., Priestley, H.A.: Introduction to Lattices and Order, 2nd edn. Cambridge University Press, Cambridge (1990)
7. Freund, S.N., Mitchell, J.C.: A type system for the java bytecode language and verifier. Journal of Automated Reasoning 30(3-4), 271–321 (2003)
8. Goldberg, A.: A specification of java loading and bytecode verification. In: Proc. of the 5th ACM conference on Computer and Communications Security (CCS 1998), pp. 49–58. ACM Press, New York (1998)
9. JSR 202 Expert Group. Java Class File Specification Update, Sun Microsystems (2006)
10. Knoblock, T.B., Rehof, J.: Type elaboration and subtype completion for java bytecode. ACM Transactions on Programming Languages and Systems 23(2), 243–272 (2001)
11. Leroy, X.: Java bytecode verification: algorithms and formalizations. Journal of Automated Reasoning 30(3-4), 235–269 (2003)
12. Leroy, X., Rouaix, F.: Security properties of typed applets. In: Proc. of the 25th ACM Symp. on Principles of Programming Languages (POPL 1998), pp. 391–403. ACM Press, New York (1998)
13. Lindholm, T., Yellin, F.: The Java Virtual Machine Specification, 2nd edn. Prentice-Hall, Englewood Cliffs (1999)
14. Pusch, C.: Proving the soundness of a java bytecode verifier specification in isabelle/hol. In: Cleaveland, W.R. (ed.) TACAS 1999. LNCS, vol. 1579, pp. 89–103. Springer, Heidelberg (1999)
15. Qian, Z.: A formal specification of java virtual machine instructions for objects, methods and subroutines. In: Formal Syntax and Semantics of Java, pp. 271–312 (1999)
16. Rose, E.: Lightweight bytecode verification. Journal of Automated Reasoning 31(3-4), 303–334 (2003)
17. Seo, S., Yang, H., Yi, K., Han, T.: Goal-directed weakening of abstract interpretation results. ACM Transactions on Programming Languages and Systems 29(6), 39 (2007)

How Do Java Programs Use Inheritance?
An Empirical Study of Inheritance in Java Software

Ewan Tempero[1], James Noble[2], and Hayden Melton[1]

[1] Department of Computer Science, University of Auckland, Auckland, New Zealand
ewan,hayden@cs.auckland.ac.nz
[2] School of Mathematics, Statistics, and Computer Science, Victoria University of Wellington,
Wellington, New Zealand
kjx@mcs.vuw.ac.nz

Abstract. Inheritance is a crucial part of object-oriented programming, but its use in practice, and the resulting large-scale inheritance structures in programs, remain poorly understood. Previous studies of inheritance have been relatively small and have generally not considered issues such as Java's distinction between classes and interfaces, nor have they considered the use of external libraries.

In this paper we present the first substantial empirical study of the large-scale use of inheritance in a contemporary OO programming language. We present a suite of structured metrics for quantifying inheritance in Java programs. We present the results of performing a corpus analysis using those metrics to over 90 applications consisting of over 100,000 separate classes and interfaces. Our analysis finds higher use of inheritance than anticipated, variation in the use of inheritance between interfaces and classes, and differences between inheritance within application types compared with inheritance from external libraries.

1 Introduction

Since the introduction of the object-oriented paradigm, much has been written on the notion of "inheritance" [1]. To some, the very idea of "object-orientedness" is bound up in inheritance [2,3]. Inheritance does appear to be very prominent in discussions about good design. All the design patterns have it [4], frameworks depend on it [5] and it's even in UML [6].

Some presentations of the object-oriented paradigm (in textbooks for example) place so much importance on inheritance that the implication is that any design without "lots of inheritance" is not a good one (or certainly not "object-oriented"). At the same time, there is a considerable amount of advice urging caution with respect to use of inheritance, such as "Favor object composition over class inheritance" [4]. There have also been studies providing conflicting answers as to its benefits [7,8,9], but also suggesting that "too much" inheritance is detrimental.

The aim of this paper is to answer a simple question: *"How do programs use inheritance?"*. To make this question concrete, we address this question to Java, thus: "How do Java™ programs use inheritance?".

To answer this question, we first consider how Java supports inheritance. Compared with earlier object-oriented languages such as Smalltalk, Eiffel, or C++, Java distinguishes between *extends* and *implements* relationships. To understand how Java (and

J. Vitek (Ed.): ECOOP 2008, LNCS 5142, pp. 667–691, 2008.

other languages making this distinction, such as C♯) actually use inheritance, we need to consider each relationship individually. We also consider other issues regarding inheritance — for example, we treat inheritance from one of the library classes as being different to inheritance from another class defined for the system. Our work is grounded in a systematic consideration of all these issues, resulting in a structured suite of metrics for measuring the various kinds and usages of inheritance in Java programs.

The suite of inheritance metrics we propose provides a sensitive instrument for characterising various types of inheritance in a particular program. To give an overall answer to our question — how do Java programs *in general* use inheritance — we gathered a substantial corpus of 93 open-source Java applications, including over 100,000 user-defined types. Then we applied our metrics to this corpus, with the resulting distribution of metrics values characterising the use of inheritance in that corpus, and hopefully getting as close to *accepted practice* in Java programs as possible.

A key point about the methodology we use here is that it is primarily *descriptive*: our research question asks simply "what do Java programs do?" We are interested in understanding "Java as she is spoke" — that is, in the way Java programs are actually structured in the real world — rather than how we fondly imagine Java programs should be written. As our terminology suggests, we draw on the established methodology of corpus linguistics. Our corpus is collected from large, well-known, widely-used Java programs (such as Eclipse, Open Office, Spring, Tomcat) — programs that are apparently well regarded by other Java programmers, and that we believe constitute as much a representative sample of Java programs "in the wild" as any other.

In evaluating individual programs (from the corpus or outside it) we can discuss whether their use of inheritance is *typical* or *extreme* with respect to the corpus, that is whether their use of inheritance seems relatively close to accepted practice embodied by the corpus, or whether and how it diverges. This is not to say we are uninterested in questions of how inheritance could or should be used in the abstract — just that those questions are separate from the questions about how inheritance is actually used in accepted Java practice, and we do not address them in this paper.

The paper makes the following contributions:

- A fine grained, structured suite of inheritance metrics for Java-like languages.
- A corpus analysis applying these metrics to 93 Java applications containing over 100,000 user-defined types.

Based on the corpus analysis, we demonstrate some important features of the accepted practice regarding inheritance in Java programs:

- most classes in Java programs are defined using inheritance from other "user-defined" types.
- classes and interfaces are used in stereotypically different ways, with approximately one interface being declared for every ten classes.
- client metrics have truncated curve distributions while supplier metrics have power law-like distributions.
- most types (classes and interfaces) are relatively shallow in the inheritance hierarchy.
- almost all types have fewer than two types inheriting from them: however for some very popular types, the bigger the programs, the more types will inherit from them.

- larger (or older) systems make proportionally more use of inheritance from user-defined classes, and less use of standard library or third-party library classes.

The rest of this paper is organised as follows. In the next section, we summarise the related work. Section 3 discusses various issues regarding the characterisation of inheritance that need to be considered when measuring it. Section 4 presents the metrics we used in our study; our results from collecting these metrics are presented in section 5. Section 6 presents a discussion of our results, and finally we give our conclusions and discuss future work in section 7.

2 Background and Related Work

The most often mentioned inheritance related metrics are Chidamber and Kemerer's DIT and NOC metrics [10,11]. DIT for a class is defined as the length of the longest path from the class to the root of the inheritance hierarchy it is in. The authors argue that the deeper the class, the more complex it would be as it would inherit from more ancestors, but also the more potential reuse there could be. NOC for a class is defined as the number of immediate subclasses of that class. The authors suggested that more children means more reuse, but also the greater the likelihood of improper abstraction. They also observed that NOC gives an idea of the influence a class has on the design.

DIT and NOC were introduced in 1991 but it was not until the 1994 publication that Chidamber and Kemerer presented measurements using them. The measurements were of two sites. One site consisted of two graphical user interface libraries with 634 C++ classes. The other consisted of class libraries used in the implementation of a computer aided manufacturing system for the production of VLSI circuits and had 1459 Smalltalk classes.

For DIT, the C++ site had a median value of 1 and maximum of 8, whereas the Smalltalk site had a median of 3 and maximum of 10. However, it was noted that for Smalltalk, all classes are subclasses of the class "Object", meaning that only "Object" could have a DIT measurement of 0. For NOC, 73% of the C++ classes and 68% of the Smalltalk classes had no children. The maximum NOC measurements reported were 42 for C++ and 50 for Smalltalk. It is worth noting that the results in this paper were presented as a frequency distribution. This presentation means that we can determine such things as for the C++ site about 200 classes had a DIT of 0 (meaning about 400 classes had a non-zero DIT) and just under 300 classes in the Smalltalk site had a DIT of 1 (and so 1100-1200 classes had a DIT of more than 1).

There have been various efforts to establish the veracity of Chidamber and Kemerer's thinking or similar claims about inheritance. We report only the most relevant to our work.

Daly et al. carried out an investigation on the impact of depth of inheritance on maintenance as measured by the amount of time taken to perform a maintenance task [7]. Their results suggested that inheritance had a negative effect on maintenance time. This study was later replicated, with the results suggesting the opposite effect — that inheritance had a positive effect on maintenance time [8]. That these two studies could get such different results suggests there may be more to inheritance than just "depth," although both were sufficiently small that it is possible that some effect other than inheritance was observed.

Another replication was carried out by Harrison et al. [9]. They studied two C++ systems, each with two versions. One system had a version without inheritance consisting of 360 LOC and a version with 290 LOC with maximum DIT of 3. The other system had one version with 1200 LOC and the other with 900 LOC and maximum DIT of 5. Their results suggest that inheritance made it harder to modify systems, but that size and functionality of a system may affect understandability more than the "amount of inheritance" used. The authors observed that an external threat to the validity of their results was the small size of their system. They claimed that the levels of inheritance investigated were "typical of those found in larger systems." Our interest is in whether DIT is sufficient to characterise "amount of inheritance", and whether the systems used in this and earlier studies really can be considered "typical."

On the question of "how inheritance is used", there appears to be little in the way of published results. Manel et al. [12] try to determine differences in maintainability of code written in the OO paradigm vs the structured programming paradigm, which included use of metrics for inheritance. The two inheritance metrics they use are "number of derived classes", and the number of lines of code in the classes a derived class inherits from (in order to try and gauge the degree of reuse via inheritance). They look at 5 versions of one "medium sized" application from the telecommunications domain. The first version had 20 derived classes out of 57, while the 5th version had 87 derived classes out of 225 (39%).

One of the largest studies that we are aware of is by Succi et al. [13]. They applied the metrics suite by Chidamber and Kemerer to 100 Java and 100 C++ applications. They were investigating the statistical properties of the CK metrics but our interest is in the metric values they report. The Java applications ranged from 28 to 936 classes in size (median 83.5) and the C++ applications ranged from 30 to 2520 classes (median 59). The actual applications were not identified. Interpreting their box plots, the DIT measurements for the Java applications were mostly in the range 2-5, with outliers at 10. For the C++ applications, most measurements were in the range 5-6 with outliers both above and below, and a maximum of 9. For NOC, the Java measurements were almost entirely less than 10, although there were outliers larger than 150, and for the C++ measurements, the range was similar, although there appear to be more outliers.

In another large study, Collberg et al. analysed 1132 Java jar files collected from the Internet [14]. According to their statistics they analyse a total of 102,688 classes and 12,188 interfaces. While no information was given as to what applications were analysed, this paper is good for the amount of data it provides. Much of it is not directly relevant to our study, but they did produce histograms of "inheritance graph height per application" finding a maximum of 10, a median of 4 and a minimum of 1, and also "number of user-class extenders per application" finding a maximum of 641, a median of 5, and a minimum of 0.

Other studies involving measuring DIT and NOC have judged the measurements to be "low", but consisted of quite small samples. Chidamber et al. studied three systems, one with 45 C++ classes, one with 27 Objective C classes, and one identifying 25 classes in design documents [15]. The largest values they report are DIT of 3 and NOC of 11 (both from the design documents).

Basili et al. investigated the Chidamber and Kemerer metric suite as predictors of fault-prone classes [16]. Their study consisted of 8 teams of 3 students building a "medium-sized" video rental system, resulting in 8 C++ applications consisting of 180 classes in total. The maximums they observed were 4 for DIT and 5 for NOC. However it should be noted that with 180 classes spread over 8 applications, each application must be fairly small.

Briand et al. carried out a study to determine to what extent various metrics are useful for detecting the probability of detecting faulty classes using the same applications as that by Basili et al. [17]. In addition to DIT and NOC, they also considered, number of parents (NOP), number of descendants (NOD), and number of ancestors (NOA). The maximums were 1 for NOP, 9 for NOD, and 4 for NOA.

Having a measurement by itself is of limited use. We also need what Kitchenham et al. refer to as the *entity population model*, which identifies the "normal values" of what is being measured under specific conditions [18]. They observe that without knowledge of such models, we cannot interpret what a measurement means. A starting point to developing such models for a metric is to apply it to "real" code, that is, code written as part of a software application, rather than code written to demonstrate the metrics, and, most importantly, *report the results*.

3   Characterising Inheritance

The starting point for our work was to determine a meaningful answer to the question "How much inheritance is being used in this application?" There are several reasons why having an answer to this question would be useful. This question is fundamental to evaluate any claims made about its benefits. If we cannot reliably measure inheritance use, then we cannot be sure that any changes that observed are due to (or just due to) inheritance. For example, in the studies on the effect of inheritance on maintenance described in the previous section, inheritance was characterised by just one measurement (DIT), whereas other inheritance metrics have been proposed (e.g. NOC).

Given the advice against overuse of inheritance, it would be useful to know to what extent this advice has been followed. We have previously seen a case where reality does not match theory [19]. Such situations may indicate problems with the theory, problems with its application (e.g., lack of appropriate tool support), or perhaps problems with training. We cannot determine which without appropriate metrics, and knowledge of how to interpret the measurements produced by the metrics.

To illustrate these points, consider the report by Chidamber and Kemerer on the Smalltalk site. They reported it consisted of about 1450 classes and had a maximum DIT of 10. How should we interpret this value of "10"? Chidamber and Kemerer characterised it as "rather small." But as we observed, other studies suggest that systems with measurements of 10 would have maintainability issues, implying it should be rare, which is what the study by Succi et al. suggests.

Another view of the meaning of a DIT value can be gained by considering a complete binary tree with the maximum number of nodes possible while also having a maximum

DIT of 10. Such a hierarchy would have $2^{11} - 1 = 2047$ nodes in it, which is comfortably more than the 1450 classes of the Smalltalk application. While we should not expect a realistic inheritance hierarchy to look like a binary tree, it does give an indication as to what the hierarchy must look like in order to get DIT measurements greater than 10. Its shape would have to somewhat more "tall and skinny". Our key observation is, we do not know what maximum DIT value we should *expect* for an application with 1450 classes.

In the complete binary tree hierarchy, the maximum NOC would be 2, and all but one class would inherit from some other class. Yet many variations on this are obviously possible: fewer classes could inherit from other classes while still having a maximum DIT of 10 and NOC of 2, the maximum DIT could be much greater than 10 while the NOC is no more than 2, the NOC can be much greater than 2 while the DIT is less than 10. On this basis we argue that it is not sufficient to characterise the inheritance hierarchy of an application by just one (or two) metrics.

Chidamber and Kemerer observed that the Smalltalk distribution is somewhat "top heavy", with the frequencies for DIT measurements 1-3 being around 300, and those for 4 and 5 being around 200. The Smalltalk distribution could be explained by the presence of the class library that is standard for any Smalltalk distribution. We speculate that many DIT distributions for Smalltalk software would be dominated by the library classes, meaning all distributions would look very similar. This raises the question as to how such standard libraries should be handled when defining metrics.

As we noted, Chidamber and Kemerer originally provided distributions of these metrics, and from these we can answer such questions as "how many classes have DIT or NOC of 0". The proportion of classes with DIT of 0 is the proportion of classes that do not use inheritance in their definition. Knowing whether this proportion is 70% rather than 90% would seem to give us some reasonable idea of the degree to which the application uses inheritance to define classes. Similarly it would be useful to know the proportion of classes with NOC of 0, that is, not providing inheritance relationships with other classes. Rather than rely on determining these values from frequency distributions, we will define such metrics directly.

Classes can be involved in inheritance in a number of different ways. For example, in Smalltalk, all classes except "Object" can be said to use inheritance. Perhaps we should distinguish those that inherit from "Object" from those that inherit from other classes. Taking this further, perhaps we should distinguish classes that inherit from any standard library class from those that are defined in the application. Those that inherit from a library class could be considered to be benefiting the most from reuse (since the library class doesn't have to be written) albeit restricted to what the library provides. A user-defined class inheriting from another user-defined class benefits less from reuse, but the designs of both classes are under the control of the software developer, and so this relationship could better represent the "quality" of the design.

The issue with measuring some kind of "DIT" metric in Java is the distinction between `extends` and `implements`. This distinction allows for a certain kind of "multiple" inheritance. The issue of measuring DIT in the context of multiple inheritance was defined by Chidamber and Kemerer to be the length of the longest path to the root [11]. However, if we are measuring a class that extends another class and implements an interface, it's not clear that paths that follow the extends relationship are the same as those that follow the implements relationship. Rather than make a judgement, we will consider all variations.

Another issue in measuring DIT in Java is dealing with the situation where a type defined in the application inherits from a type for which we do not have the definition. For example, we create a new class MyVector that extends java.util.Vector. Since Vector has 3 ancestors, DIT (MyVector) should be 4. If we did not know Vector's ancestry (or at least its DIT value), then we would not be able to measure DIT for MyVector. It is a limitation of our study that the corpus we use does not have the complete external libraries, making it impossible to determine the "true" DIT values in all cases. We will note that as far as the developer is concerned Vector (and any other type that is not part of the application) can usually be treated as if it were a "flattened" type. In the case of our example, we know MyVector extends Vector, but in terms of reasoning about MyVector it is not so relevant what Vector's true structure is. For this reason we will define a variant of DIT (and similar metrics) that considers only the user-defined inheritance structure.

4 Inheritance Metrics for Java

4.1 Modelling Inheritance

In order to unambiguously define metrics for inheritance in Java we need to specify a model of Java inheritance. What we have been colloquially calling the inheritance "hierarchy" is really a directed acyclic graph (DAG), where the vertices are Java reference types and edges are inheritance relationships. For the purposes of the definition we always assume that java.lang.Object is in the graph, and that any classes without explicit superclasses have an edge to Object. To do otherwise would mean that some metrics change values if a programmer explicitly includes extends Object.

There are two kinds of edges, one for extends and one for implements. If A extends B then A is the *child* and B is the *parent*, similarly if A implements B. When we "follow an edge", we traverse the edge from child to parent.

The Java Language rules mean that at most one type of edge can connect any pair of vertices, and in some cases both may be disallowed. For example, an implements edge cannot occur between two class vertices. Practically speaking, the most common connections will be between pairs of classes, pairs of interfaces, or class-interface pairs. All others are very unlikely (e.g. enum implements annotation) or at least very rare (e.g. class implements annotation). Table 1 shows all the possibilities.

We have different kinds of vertices to distinguish different kinds of types, that is, *classes* (C), *interfaces* (I), *enums* (E), *annotations* (A) and *exceptions* (Ex). We distinguish classes and interfaces as they have quite different inheritance relationships with each other and play different roles in an inheritance hierarchy. We distinguish enums and annotations because, although they are respectively implemented as specialised classes and interfaces, their roles are somewhat different. Furthermore, they are in fact implemented in terms of inheritance (extending java.lang.Enum and java.lang.annotation.Annotation respectively), something that is evident at the bytecode level, although for the purposes of our metrics we will ignore these

Table 1. Allowable type inheritance relationships

	Class	Interface	Enum	Annotation	Exception
Class	extends	implements		implements	
Interface		extends		extends	
Enum		implements		implements	
Annotation					
Exception		implements		implements	extends

relationships. Finally, exceptions are distinguished from classes as they also have specialised roles, and furthermore are explicitly defined in terms of inheritance (extending java.lang.Exception). Combining exceptions with other classes when trying to determine the amount of inheritance may therefore give misleading results.

As well as ignoring the implicit inheritance relationships with Annotation and Enum we also ignore inheritance relationships with marker interfaces, specifically java.io.Serializable and java.lang.Cloneable.

For each kind of type there are 3 different kinds of vertices: user-defined (that come from the application we are measuring) standard library (from the Java Standard API), and third party (any remaining types from neither user code nor the standard library).

Each vertex has a "nesting level" attribute that indicates the level of nesting of the type represented by the vertex, where 0 indicates a top-level type, and the nesting level of any nested type (e.g., inner class or interface) is 1 more than its enclosing type.

4.2   Scalar Inheritance Metrics

The first set of metrics are what we refer to as "scalar" metrics — they all produce a single scalar value for a user-defined type, such as the original DIT and NOC metrics do. All the metrics are defined in terms of paths (following edges) in the DAG and for the purpose of this paper we only present these metrics for classes or interfaces (that is, neither enums, annotations, nor exceptions). All paths consist of either all extends edges, in which case all the vertices are represent either classes or interfaces, or at most a single implements edge, which will have only vertices represent classes before it and vertices representing interfaces after it. In all cases, we do *not* count java.lang.Object.

There are roughly 4 categories of metrics — one category involves paths going from the type being measured to a root ("depth in tree" — DIT), one involves the number of other types reachable from the type either directly ("number of parents" — NOP) or transitively ("number of ancestors" – NOA), one is the number of other types from which the type being measured is reachable either directly ("number of children" — NOC) or transitively ("number of descendants" — NOD), and the last involves paths from a leaf to the type being measured ("height in tree" – HIT), however we do not consider this last category in this study.

Within each category, we can specify different metrics by specifying the allowable vertices and edges in the paths we consider. Some distinctions include: paths that only begin at classes and only follow extends edges ("CC"), paths that only begin at

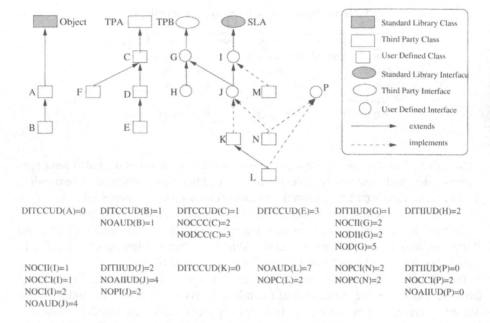

DITCCUD(A)=0   DITCCUD(B)=1   DITCCUD(C)=1   DITCCUD(E)=3   DITIIUD(G)=1   DITIIUD(H)=2
                   NOAUD(B)=1   NOCCC(C)=2   NOCII(G)=2
                                    NODCC(C)=3   NODII(G)=2
                                                                          NOD(G)=5

NOCII(I)=1   DITIIUD(J)=2   DITCCUD(K)=0   NOAUD(L)=7   NOPCI(N)=2   DITIIUD(P)=0
NOCCI(I)=1   NOAIIUD(J)=4   NOPC(L)=2   NOPC(N)=2   NOCCI(P)=2
NOCI(I)=2   NOPI(J)=2   NOAIIUD(P)=0
NOAUD(J)=4

Fig. 1. Example of scalar metrics

interfaces and only follow extends edges ("II"), paths that only begin at a class and must begin with an implements edge ("CI"), paths that begin at classes and follow any edges ("C"), similarly for interfaces ("I"), or paths that begin at any type and follow any edges.

The name of a metric indicates its category and the kinds of edges allowed. Thus, for example, DITCC (DIT category, CC edges) is the length of the longest path starting at a class and following only extends edges to the root, NOCII is the number of interfaces incident (via extends edges) on an interface, and NOPCI is the number of interface vertices reachable from the type via an implements edge.

Following our discussion in section 3, we have two variants of DIT relating to whether or not the paths consist only of user-defined (UD) types or not. So, DITCCUD considers only paths that end at a non user-defined class. If the last class is Object, then DITCCUD is one less than the length of the path, otherwise it is the length of the path. DITCCUD is undefined for anything other than classes. DITIIUD is the equivalent for interfaces.

NOCI is a metric that applies only to interfaces and measures the indegree of the corresponding vertex. As we will see, this is useful as an interface with NOCI of zero is one that is neither implemented nor extended. NOPC only applies to classes and is the outdegree of the vertex. This tells us how many parents, following both extends and implements edges.

There are 2 NOA variants and 3 NOD variants. NOA has the same problem as DIT with respect to external libraries so we define metrics that refer only to user-defined types. NOAIIUD, NODCC, and NODII follow the conventions established above (NOACCUD is equivalent to DITCCUD). NOAUD and NOD do not restrict the paths when determining what is an ancestor or descendant. NOAUD for a type X is then the number of variables with different user-defined types than X to which values of type X can be assigned. NOD for a type X is then the number of values with types different to X that can be assigned to a variable of type X.

Figure 1 gives examples of a number of the metrics. All metrics are also summarised in Appendix A.

4.3 Inheritance Summary Metrics

Inheritance Summary metrics apply to applications, that is, they produce values that are measurements of an application rather than an individual type as the scalar metrics do. These metrics report the proportion of *user-defined* types that fall into different categories. In the following, "DUI" (Defined Using Inheritance) denotes metrics that consider the types that occupy the child end of an edge in the inheritance DAG and "IF" (Inherited From) denotes metrics that consider types at the parent end. We can focus on what kinds of types participate in an inheritance relationship, with "CC" indicating class–class relationships (i.e., extends), "CI" indicating class–interface relationships (i.e., implements), "II" indicating interface–interface relationships (i.e., extends), and so on. As indicated above, we divide the user-defined types involved in an application into 3 subsets according to their origins, which we denote UD (user-defined), TP (third-party), and SL (standard library).

We begin with two metrics that give an overall idea of how much inheritance exists in an application.

DUI. The proportion of types that either implement an interface or extend another type other than Object, or, the proportion of types that occupy a child end of an edge in the inheritance DAG.
IF. The proportion of types that are either extended or implemented, or, the proportion of types that occupy a parent end of an edge in the inheritance DAG.

While these two metrics give us the proportion of user-defined types that participate in an inheritance relationship, we must keep in mind the interface/class distinction. For example, it seems reasonable to expect that all user-defined interfaces will be implemented, and thus boost the DUI measurement, so we have more refined metrics.

CCDUI. The proportion of user-defined *classes* that *extend* some other class.
CIDUI. The proportion of user-defined *classes* that *implement* some other interface.
IIDUI. The proportion of user-defined *interfaces* that *extend* some other interface.
CCIF. The proportion of user-defined *classes extended by* some other (user-defined) class.
CIIF. The proportion of user-defined *interfaces implemented by* some (user-defined) class.
IIIF. The proportion of user-defined *interfaces extended by* some other (user-defined) interface.

We can specify more refined metrics for the "DUI" category by classifying the types being extended. For each of the possible type relationships (table 1), we can consider the proportion of those relationships that have parents in SL, TP, or UD. We name these metrics by indicating which parent subset, which relationship, and the fact that we are measuring proportions at the child end of the relationship. So, for example, the proportion of classes that inherit from standard library classes is SLCCDUI, the proportion of classes that implement third-party interfaces is TPCIDUI, and the proportion of interfaces that extend user-defined annotations is UDIADUI.

Finally, we can specify metrics for types at a given nesting level, indicated by a subscript denoting the nesting level. So $SLIIDUI_1$ is the proportion of level-1 nested interfaces that extend standard library interfaces.

The metrics are also summarised in Appendix A.

5   Results

We have created a standard corpus of software to use for these kinds of studies [20]. For this study we analysed a total of 239 different codesets from 93 different open-source Java applications from the corpus. We list the latest version of each application in Appendix B. Considering only the latest version of each application, we measured 96,302 classes and 12,665 interfaces (108,967 types in total). The instrument we used for measuring looks at the bytecode version of the codeset.

In the previous section we described over 50 metrics (not counting nesting level distinctions). Due to space constraints, we present here just those measurements that seem most interesting. In particular, we provide only measurements relating to all classes and interfaces regardless of nesting level (leaving out those for enums, annotations, and exceptions). The full dataset is available on request.

5.1   Scalar Inheritance Metrics

We begin with the scalar metrics. Table 2 shows the maximum values we saw of each of these metrics, together with the applications that had types with those maximum measurements.

Some measurements are unsurprising, as are the applications that have the maximum measurements. For example, the maximum DITCCUD measurement is 10, which is consistent with other studies. Also, eclipse is one of the larger applications in our study (17622 classes, 1926 interfaces), and so it is unsurprising that it has many of the maximum values, although that one class has 795 children is noteworthy. Yet the much smaller openoffice (1320 classes, 1617 interfaces) has an interface with even more interface children. Trove's NOPCI (number of interfaces a class implements) value of 56 also seems rather extreme. The class with that value is gnu.trove.SerializationProcedure, which does not extend anything (other than Object) and so the NOPC maximum is the same.

Figure 2 shows frequency distributions for various tree depth metrics, summing all applications across the whole corpus, and reporting results in absolute values of metrics (x axis) for absolute number of classes with that metric value (y axis) on a log-log scale.

Table 2. Maximum values for scalar metrics

Metric	max Applications
DITCCUD	10 netbeans-5.5-beta
DITIIUD	8 scala-1.4.0.3,netbeans-5.5-beta
NOCCC	795 eclipse_SDK-3.1.2-win32
NOCCI	279 eclipse_SDK-3.1.2-win32
NOCII	878 openoffice-2.0.0
NOCI	878 openoffice-2.0.0
NOPCI	56 trove-1.1b5
NOPC	56 trove-1.1b5
NOPI	13 luxor-1.0-b9
NODCC	983 eclipse_SDK-3.1.2-win32
NODII	1244 openoffice-2.0.0
NOD	1873 eclipse_SDK-3.1.2-win32
NOACCUD	11 netbeans-5.5-beta
NOAIIUD	18 glassfish-9.0-b15
NOAUD	57 trove-1.1b5

The first four graphs concern the "client" side of the inheritance relationship, that is, how a class relates to other classes that it inherits from. The first graph shows DITCCUD, that is the number of transitive superclasses (ancestors) of each class (not counting `Object`). The graph shows, for example, that over 10,000 classes have precisely 2 transitive superclasses not including `Object`, for example `Vector` extends `AbstractList` which extends `AbstractCollection` which extends `Object`, while only 100 classes across our corpus have 7 transitive superclasses. The second graph, DITIIUD, is similar to the first but for interfaces, and counts the length of the longest chain of transitive superinterfaces of each interface. The shape of the distributions are similar, except that there are far fewer interfaces than classes in the corpus — roughly one interface for every ten classes. The third graph, NOPC, shows the number of parents (classes and interfaces) that each class extends or implements; while the fourth graph, NOAUD, shows all ancestors, that is the transitive closure of all classes and interfaces contribution to a definition by any kind of inheritance.

These four client graphs have the same shape, which we have previously described in software as a "*truncated curve*" distribution [21]. Truncated curves are most likely log normal or stretched exponential distributions, and so quite different from normal distributions. Truncated curve distributions are highly skewed: almost every class will have a metric value of at least one, but this then decreases rapidly. Truncated curve distributions also have a maximum value (as their name suggests, they are truncated where they meet the x axis) that tends not to depend upon the size of the underlying data set — for depth (DITCCUD and DITIIUD) this is around 10; for parents (NOPC) 10 and for ancestors (NOAUD) around 12 for most applications. The maximum values for the parents and ancestors metrics are from `trove`, a library rather than an application, which is a clear outlier.

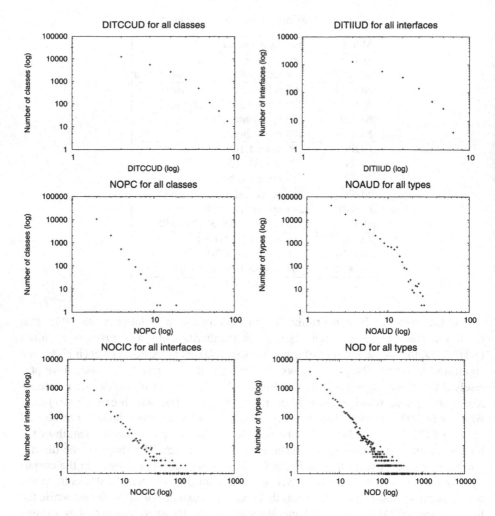

Fig. 2. Frequency distributions for scalar metrics over entire corpus (log-log)

These distributions mean that most inheritance is *shallow* — although most classes use inheritance, they are generally only a few levels down in the inheritance tree. Because of the skewed, truncated curve distributions, there will still be some classes that are quite deep in the inheritance hierarchy, but this is bounded — the number of ancestors contributing to each class' definition, and the depth of classes in the inheritance tree, does *not* increase with program size.

The other graphs in figure 2 concern the "supplier" side of the inheritance relationship, that is, how a class relates to other classes that inherit from it. The first supplier graph, NOCCI, shows for each interface, the number of classes that implement that interface (a partial complement to NOPC), while the second supplier graph, NOD, shows the total number of types (classes and interfaces) that directly or transitively inherit from that class or implement that interface (a complement to NOA).

These two supplier graphs show the classic signature of a power-law distribution: a straight line on a log-log plot. In the centre of the data, a power law behaves quite similarly to a truncated curve, so that, for example, 1,000 classes implement 2 interfaces, but only 100 classes implement 10 interfaces (NOCCI); or 10,000 types have *no* descendants, 5,000 types have only one descendant, and around 100 types have 11 descendants (NOD). The key difference between a truncated curve and a power law occurs on the right hand-side — while the absolute metric values in a truncated curve distributions are, well, truncated, power laws are unbounded. This is visible towards the bottom right of the NOCCI and NOD graphs, which show that the corpus contains one or two classes with large values for these metrics, and in the maxima for the power law metrics (279 for NOCCI, 1895 for NOD, both from `eclipse`, one of the largest applications in our corpus).

Compared with normal distributions, power law distributions are counter-intuitive: most classes are not used as suppliers in inheritance relationships, while a few classes are used very commonly. Because power law distributions are unbounded, we can expect that as programs get larger, the numbers of implementations of popular interfaces and the number of descendants of popular classes will grow without limit.

In general, these graphs confirm the results of our smaller and much more coarse-grained study of general dependency topologies in software [21]: client relationships are truncated curves, while supplier relationships are power laws. Specifically with respect to inheritance, we see that most classes are defined using some form of inheritance — either extending another class or implementing at least one interface. Although inheritance is used pervasively to help define classes, it is also shallow: we found no class with more than ten parents, and very few with more twelve or thirteen ancestors (both classes inherited from, or interfaces implemented). For programmers reading or writing new class definitions, this means that they only need to consider a limited number of classes to understand their new classes.

On the other hand, relatively few classes and interfaces participate in the definitions of other types, but a few of those that do are used very widely indeed — this is the asymmetry inherent in power law and truncated curve networks. For programmers learning libraries or applications, this is good news: it means that there will be a few crucial types that they need to understand in order to implement or subclass to extend applications, or to use libraries. Furthermore, querying codesets to find the most frequently extended or implemented classes will likely be a good strategy to use when encountering an unfamiliar problem. On the other hand, for maintenance programmers, this is mixed blessing. Most types do not participate in much inheritance as suppliers, so they can be changed with little effect on the application. There will be some classes and interfaces, however, that are used very widely throughout a program, and as the program gets bigger (as more functionality, or more classes are added) these core classes and interfaces will be used more and more often. Maintaining or extending such classes or interfaces will be very difficult indeed, and only get harder as the size of programs increases.

5.2   Inheritance Summary Metrics

We now turn to the metrics that apply to whole applications. Figure 3 shows the DUI and IF results. It shows the number of applications having a given measurement, remembering that a measurement is a proportion of some kind. Looking at figure 3, the tallest bar (mode) for DUI is at 72% and has height 7, indicating that 7 applications had 72% of their types defined using inheritance in some way.

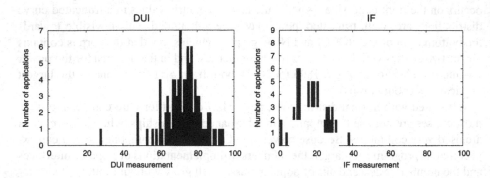

Fig. 3. Frequency distributions for DUI and IF

The striking feature of the DUI results is that the lowest is 29% (mvnforum), and that is very much an outlier. The next smallest value is 49% (openxchange, quilt). The median is 74%, that is, half the applications in our study have 74% or more of their user-defined types defined using some form of inheritance. For IF, the minimum was 2% (ireport,rssowl), the maximum was 39% (scala), the median was 17%, and mode was at 14% (9 applications).

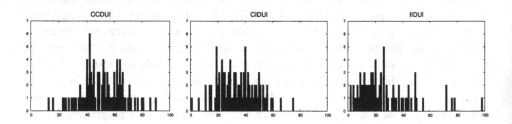

Fig. 4. Frequency distributions for CCDUI, CIDUI, and IIDUI

A class contributes to the DUI measurement by either extending another class or implementing an interface. The first is measured by CCDUI and the second by CIDUI. An interface contributes to DUI only by extending another interface (IIDUI). Their

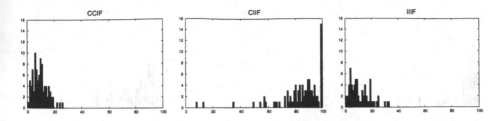

Fig. 5. Frequency distributions for CCIF, CIIF, and IIIF

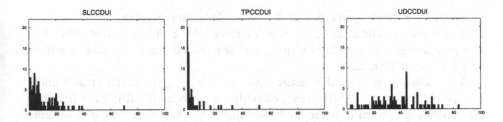

Fig. 6. Frequency distributions for SLCCDUI, TPCCDUI, and UDCCDUI

frequency distributions are shown in figure 4. For CCDUI, the minimum value is 14% (mvnforum), the median is 52%, the maximum is 91% (jparse), and the mode is 43% (6). For CIDUI, the minimum is 2% (fitjava), the median 34%, the maximum 76% (scala), and the mode 41% (5). Generally a lower proportion of classes inherit from an interface than extend another class. For IIDUI the minimum is 3% (roller), the median is 21% (ganttproject, xalan, hibernate, lucene), the maximum is 99% (scala), and the mode is at 27% (5).

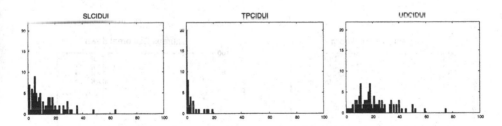

Fig. 7. Frequency distributions for SLCIDUI, TPCIDUI, and UDCIDUI

Considering figure 4, we can see that there was a wide distribution in the use of inheritance to define classes and interfaces across our corpus. So it is not the case that the distribution in figure 3 is due to (for example) just classes implementing interfaces, but each of CC, CI, and II relationships make significant contributions. In fact, applications

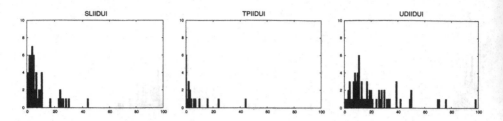

Fig. 8. Frequency distributions for SLIIDUI, TPIIDUI, and UDIIDUI

generally have a lower proportion of classes implementing interfaces than classes extending classes, and interfaces extending interfaces is lower still (note that a class both extending another class and implementing one or more interfaces will show in both the CCDUI and CIDUI results).

A type contributes to the IF measurement by either being an interface that is implemented (CIIF) or extended (IIIF) or a class that is extended (CCIF). Their frequency distributions are shown in figure 5. We see that rarely are more than 20% of either classes or interfaces extended, and most of the time more than 80% of interfaces are implemented. The latter is somewhat surprising — we would expect that if an interface is created then it would be implemented, but this is true for only 15 of the applications. One possible explanation is that some interfaces are only extended, hence it is worth looking at how many children an interface has (NOCI). The lowest CIIF value is 9% for `openoffice`, but recall that `openoffice` had the largest NOCI value.

A class can extend either a standard library class (SLCCDUI), a third-party class (TPCCDUI), or a user-defined class (UDCCDUI). Figure 6 shows their distributions. It would appear that most of the CCDUI distribution can be explained by the UDCCDUI distribution, that is, by and large, classes that extend another class tend to extend user-defined classes. Figures 7 and 8 shows the distributions for the CI and II relationships.

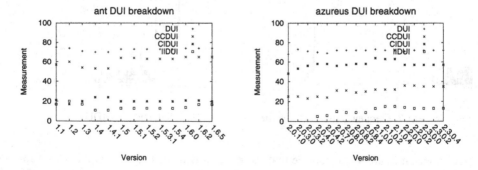

Fig. 9. DUI and its breakdown for 13 versions of ant

Fig. 10. DUI and its breakdown for 17 versions of azureus

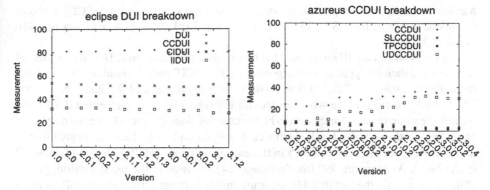

Fig. 11. DUI and its breakdown for 13 versions of eclipse

Fig. 12. CCDUI and its breakdown for 17 versions of azureus

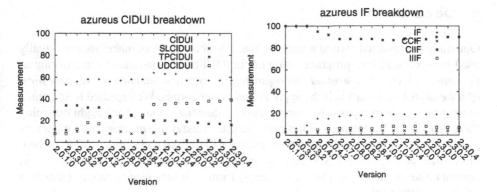

Fig. 13. CIDUI and its breakdown for 17 versions of azureus

Fig. 14. IF and its breakdown for 17 versions of azureus

5.3 Longitudinal

Another view of our data is to consider how the various metrics change over time for an application. Figures 9, 10, and 11 show DUI and its breakdown (CCDUI, CIDUI, IIDUI) on one chart each for `ant`, `azureus`, and `eclipse` respectively. What is particularly interesting about these figures is how consistent the values are, especially given the changes in size of the three applications: the number of user-defined types for `ant` goes from 102 for `ant-1.1` to 1014 for `ant-1.6.5`, for `azureus` it is from 163 for `azureus-2.0.1.0` to 2130 for `azureus-2.3.0.4`, and for `eclipse` it is from 6522 for `eclipse_SDK-1.0-win32` to 19674 for `eclipse_SDK-3.1.2-win32`.

Figures 12 and 13 show the longitudinal views of CCDUI and CIDUI for `azureus`. We note that the x-axis is not a linear scale, and that generally the size (in number of types) of `azureus` increases over the period shown. For example, for SLCCDUI, the earliest version has 15 classes whereas the latest has 42, so the absolute number has increased but the proportion is declining. On the other hand, UDCCDUI shows a marked increase, from 8%, 13 out 158 (version 2.0.1.0) to 27%, 647 out of 2410 (version 2.3.0.4).

Figure 14 shows the IF results and the breakdown for `azureus`. IF shows an initial increase and then an apparent convergence to 19%. CCIF ends up holding steady at 4% from about version 2.0.7.0, but that version has 860 classes and the final version has 2410. As a general rule we would expect all interfaces to be implemented (CIIF). As we noted earlier, reasons for this not to be the case include interfaces that exist only to be extended by others, or dead code. In this case only around 90% of interfaces are directly implemented, but there were only 5 in the earliest version and 492 (444 implemented) in the latest. As there are 492 interfaces and 2410 classes in the latest version, giving 2902 types overall, the fact that 444 are implemented accounts for 15% overall, or most of the IF measurement (19%). However, from the IIIF data we find that 35 interfaces appear not be used at all.

6 Discussion

Our study has revealed several interesting features about the way inheritance is actually used in practice in Java programs. We find the DUI results particularly interesting: as presented in section 5.2, *around three-quarters of user-defined classes use some form of inheritance* in at least half the applications in our corpus. We expected to see much lower proportions of types using some form of inheritance. Our first thought on seeing these results was that the high values could be due to heavy use of interfaces, or perhaps significant use of frameworks from the standard API or third party libraries. Refinement of our measurements (figures 4 and 6) show that neither are the case, instead the most common (but by no means the predominant) form of inheritance is classes extending other user-defined classes.

One possible explanation of our observations is that some amount of the inheritance we see is "bad inheritance" in some sense. It could be that there is so much advice around advocating avoiding inheritance where possible because it is mainly being used inappropriately. We cannot rule this out, although various checks we performed on the accuracy of our tool involved looking at the source code, and these casual observations did not reveal anything obviously wrong with the use of inheritance we saw, and our corpus is made up of well-known applications mostly written by professional Java programmers. So we interpret our data to mean that defining most classes by inheritance is accepted practice in Java programming.

Our observations thus provide a useful benchmark for managers of Java programmers — applications with significantly less than 75% of types defined using inheritance, or more than 17% are inherited from, or in other ways significantly differ from what we have observed, are applications that probably need investigation.

While a large proportion of types are defined using inheritance, rarely are more than 20% of classes or interfaces extended. While we have not shown the figures here, it also turns out that the proportion of interfaces is rarely more than 20% of the total types, and usually around 10%. This points towards a significant fan-out in the inheritance relationships, and the NOC category of scalar metrics supports this view.

We have noted the NOC frequency distributions appear to have a classic *power-law* shape we have seen in other software relationships [22,21]. If the NOC metrics do have a power-law distribution, then it follows that the larger the application, the larger the NOC values we will see, and statistical measures such as mean and standard deviations will have no useful purpose. This may explain why our NOC results are so different from the previously published data — our study is so much larger.

Other distributions such as the NOD and NOP categories also appear to be power-laws (although the NOP could be an artifact due to the small number of data points). We have also noted the appearance of the "truncated curve" distribution (figure 2) we have observed in dependency metrics in a previous study [21].

Examination of the longitudinal results also reveals a surprising feature, namely how constant the use of inheritance is across application evolution and application size. While 3 data points is hardly a strong trend, the fact that any exist is noteworthy. There is no obvious reason for why such consistency should occur. Given the significant changes in size (for example ant grows an order of magnitude across the versions we studied), it seems unlikely that it is due to something about the delivered functionality, as the delivered functionality will have changed significantly. It is possible that this application is biased by some feature of its problem domain, or the programming style used by the development team, however it is equally likely that this level of use of inheritance is simply a standard feature of accepted Java programming practice.

Another interesting feature is how much the component parts of DUI vary despite DUI itself being so constant. For example in azureus (figure 10) the proportion of classes implementing interfaces noticeably increases and then decreases without a change in DUI and without similar differences in the proportion of classes or interfaces using inheritance.

Looking at the breakdown of CCDUI for azureus (figure 12) we see that the proportion of classes extending other user-defined classes steadily increases while the proportion extending standard library or third-party classes steadily decreases, while (not shown in the figure) the overall size of azureus grows (although we again note that the x-axis is not a linear scale). This suggests that applications become more inwards looking as they age, relying on their own definitions. If externally-provided functionality is required (by inheritance), it may be more likely to be accessed via user defined classes that either themselves inherit or delegate to external code.

We note that the largest application in our study (netbeans, 19666 classes and 1830 interfaces) only has one maximum scalar measurement, and several different applications of quite different sizes are represented in the maximum scalar metric measurements. This suggests that our metrics are not simply measuring application size (at least as measured by number of types), but are actually capturing other features of programming style or practice.

There are many other points of interest in the data we have collected that we do not have space to discuss. But for example, we mentioned earlier interfaces that are neither implemented nor extended (NOCI measurement of 0). There are in fact over 2000 such interfaces. Some provide only constants, some indicate variation points of frameworks, and some seem to be just dead code. This raises the question as to how much dead code is being distributed. We also wonder what other peculiarities we might find in our data, and in other kinds of similar measurements that could be made of code.

The most likely threat to the validity of our conclusions is the corpus we used, which consists entirely of successful open-source Java applications, many of small to medium size. Our results do apply to at least these applications, many of which (`openoffice`, `eclipse`, `ant`) are some of the most used Java programs worldwide. It does however raise the question as to whether our results indicate something specific to the open-source development model. We note that the few other similar studies that have been published [11,7,8,9,12,13,16] generally indicate different results, although their small size, the lack of data they present, the lack of clarity about what they are measuring, and the coarse granularity of their metrics makes it difficult to tell. In the scientific tradition, we hope we have provided sufficient details about our corpus and metrics to allow other researchers to replicate our study: independent replication will give the best grounds to claim generalisability.

7 Conclusions

Like all programming language designs, Java is an experiment. Unlike most language designs, the general adoption of Java, and the resulting widespread availability of substantial "real-world" Java programs means that we are finally able to evaluate that experiment, in ways that are simply not possible for most other languages.

In this paper, we have introduced a new structured suite of metrics to evaluate, quantitatively, how Java programs use inheritance. More importantly, we have applied these and some more traditional "scalar" metrics in a large-scale empirical study. We believe such studies are important to establishing and understanding trends in software development.

Our results show surprisingly high levels of use of inheritance in defining types, with about 3 out of 4 types in our study being defined using inheritance in one form or other. In contrast, most types make only a small contribution to other definitions via inheritance; however a few types will be very well used, being inherited or implemented by many other classes or interfaces. We have also seen evidence that levels of inheritance are somewhat constant over the lifetime of an application. Our corpus study indicates that an apparently high use of inheritance is a characteristic of accepted Java programming practice.

The overarching methodological contribution implied by our results is that metrics for inheritance must distinguish between classes and interfaces, and between extends and implements relationships. To do otherwise obscures important data about program structure, because our results show that different kinds of inheritance are used in different ways. Furthermore, distinguishing between user code and "other" code (both standard libraries or third party components) is also important to give a true picture of the use of inheritance. So far, our results show that programmers treat standard libraries and third-party code in the same way — at least as far as inheritance is concerned — while user-defined classes are treated differently, primarily by being used more often to define other user-defined classes.

We emphasise that we make no claims as to whether our results are indicative of "good design". Without reliable data about such things as development effort, presence of faults, and other quality attributes, we cannot make such an assessment. As others before us have observed, gathering such data is crucial to understanding the impact of such things as inheritance structure on software quality. The contribution of this research is a crucial prerequisite to doing such studies: first, being able to understand and measure the various uses of inheritance in Java programs in a well-founded manner; and second, being able to use those measures to quantify the accepted Java programming practice.

There are many directions this work can take. We have collected, but have not yet analysed, data on the use of nested classes, including static nested classes, in inheritance relationships. Java also distinguishes abstract from concrete classes, and it would be interesting to determine how they are used. Others have discussed examining the number of methods inherited, and other such "internal" inheritance relationships [23,12]. Steimann has identified various roles that interfaces can play, and extending his study to our corpus may prove interesting [24]. As we noted at the end of the previous section, independent replication of our results would give more support for generalisation across other Java programs. Replication of our studies in other OO languages would help determine how much our results depend on features Java, and how much they are in some sense intrinsic to object-orientation.

Given enough data, it is often possible to find some kind of pattern, and we certainly have plenty of data. Nevertheless we suggest that the patterns we have observed are indeed an indication of significant structures in software design, and faithfully capture large-scale aspects of the use of inheritance in accepted Java programming practice. In other words, we have shown how Java programs use inheritance.

Acknowledgements

We would like to thank the anonymous referees for their comments and suggestions for improving this paper and the suggestions for new studies.

References

1. Taivalsaari, A.: On the notion of inheritance. Comp. Surv. 28(3), 438–479 (1996)
2. Meyer, B.: Reusability: the case for object-oriented design. IEEE Software, 50–64 (March 1987)
3. Snyder, A.: Inheritance and the development of encapsulated software components. In: Research Directions in Object Oriented Programming, pp. 165–188. MIT Press, Cambridge (1987)
4. Gamma, E., Helm, R., Johnson, R., Vlissides, J.: Design Patterns. Addison Wesley Publishing Company, One Jacob Way, Reading, Massachusetts 01867 (1994)
5. Johnson, R.E., Foote, B.: Designing reusable classes. Journal of Object-Oriented Programming (June/July 1988)
6. Rumbaugh, J., Jacobson, I., Booch, G.: Unified Modeling Language Reference Manual, 2nd edn. Addison-Wesley, Reading (2004)
7. Daly, J., Brooks, A., Miller, J., Roper, M., Wood, M.: Evaluating inheritance depth on the maintainability of object-oriented software. Empirical Software Engineering 1(2), 109–132 (1996)

8. Cartwright, M.: An empirical view of inheritance. Information and Software Technology 40, 795–799 (1998)
9. Harrison, R., Counsell, S., Nithi, R.: Experimental assessment of the effect of inheritance on the maintainability of object-oriented systems. Journal of Systems and Software 52, 173–179 (2000)
10. Chidamber, S.R., Kemerer, C.F.: Towards a metrics suite for object oriented design. In: ACM SIGPLAN International Conference on Object-Oriented Programming, Systems, Languages, and Applications, pp. 197–211 (1991)
11. Chidamber, S.R., Kemerer, C.F.: A metrics suite for object oriented design. IEEE Trans. Softw. Eng. 20(6), 476–493 (1994)
12. Manel, D., Havanas, W.: A study of the impact of C++ on software maintenance. In: International Conference on Software Maintenance, pp. 63–69 (1990)
13. Succi, G., Pedrycz, W., Djokic, S., Zuliani, P., Russo, B.: An empirical exploration of the distributions of the Chidamber and Kemerer object-oriented metrics suite. Empirical Softw. Engg. 10(1), 81–104 (2005)
14. Collberg, C., Myles, G., Stepp, M.: An empirical study of Java bytecode programs. Softw. Pract. Exper. 37(6), 581–641 (2007)
15. Chidamber, S., Darcy, D., Kemerer, C.: Managerial use of metrics for object-oriented software: an exploratory analysis. IEEE Trans. Software Engineering 24(8), 629–639 (1998)
16. Basili, V.R., Briand, L.C., Melo, W.L.: A validation of object-oriented design metrics as quality indicators. IEEE Trans. Softw. Eng. 22(10), 751–761 (1996)
17. Briand, L.C., Daly, J., Porter, V., Wüst, J.K.: A comprehensive empirical validation of design measures for object-oriented systems. In: METRICS 1998: Proceedings of the 5th International Symposium on Software Metrics, pp. 246–257. IEEE Computer Society Press, Los Alamitos (1998)
18. Kitchenham, B., Pfleeger, S.L., Fenton, N.: Towards a framework for software measurement validation. IEEE Trans. Softw. Eng. 21(12), 929–944 (1995)
19. Melton, H., Tempero, E.: An empirical study of cycles among classes in Java. Empirical Software Engineering 12(4), 389–415 (2007)
20. Qualitas Research Group: Qualitas corpus (June 2007), http://www.cs.auckland.ac.nz/~ewan/corpus/
21. Baxter, G., Frean, M., Noble, J., Rickerby, M., Smith, H., Visser, M., Melton, H., Tempero, E.: Understanding the shape of Java software. In: Cook, W. (ed.) ACM SIGPLAN International Conference on Object-Oriented Programming, Systems, Languages, and Applications, Portland, OR, U.S.A, October 2006, pp. 397–412 (2006)
22. Potanin, A., Noble, J., Frean, M., Biddle, R.: Scale-free geometry in OO programs. Commun. ACM 48(5), 99–103 (2005)
23. Benlarbi, S., Melo, W.L.: Polymorphism measures for early risk prediction. In: ICSE 1999: Proceedings of the 21st international conference on Software engineering, pp. 334–344. IEEE Computer Society Press, Los Alamitos (1999)
24. Steimann, F., Mayer, P.: Patterns of interface-based programming. Journal of Object Technology 4(5), 75–94 (2005), http://www.jot.fm/issues/issue_2005_07/article1

Appendix A: Metric Summaries

Scalar Metrics

These metrics provide measurements for individual types in alphabetical order. In these definitions, A is an *ancestor* of X if, A is not Object and there is a path from X to A where all the vertices, with the possible exception of A, are user-defined types, and D is a *descendent* of Y if there is a path from D to Y.

DITCCUD. Length of path from a class and consisting only of extends edges to the first non user-defined class other than Object, or one less than the length of the path that ends with Object.

DITIIUD. Length of path from an interface and consisting only of extends edges to the first non user-defined class.

NOACCUD. Number of ancestors a class has (extends edges only).

NOAIIUD. Number of ancestors an interface has (extends edges only).

NOAUD. Number of all ancestors a type has (both implements and extends edges).

NOCCC. Number of classes inheriting from a given class (via extends edges).

NOCCI. Number of classes implementing a given interface (via implements edges).

NOCII. Number of interfaces inheriting from a given interface (via extends edges).

NOCI. Total number of classes that implement a given interface and interfaces that extend that interface (both implements and extends edges).

NODCC. Number of descendants a class has (extends edges only).

NODII. Number of descendants an interface has (implements edges only).

NOD. Number of all descendants a type has (both implements and extends edges).

NOPCI. Number of interface parents a class has (via implements edges).

NOPC. Number of parents a class has (both classes and interfaces).

NOPI. Number of parents an interface has (via extends edges).

Summary Metrics

These metrics provide measurements over an application. The first set (given in alphabetical order) do not consider the source of the types participating in a given relation (see the table below for that).

CCDUI. The proportion of user-defined *classes* that *extend* some other class.

CCIF. The proportion of user-defined *classes extended by* some other (user-defined) class.

CIDUI. The proportion of user-defined *classes* that *implement* some other interface.

CIIF. The proportion of user-defined *interfaces implemented by* some (user-defined) class.

DUI. The proportion of types Defined Using Inheritance, that is, those types that either implement an interface or extend another type other than Object, or, the proportion of types that occupy a child end of an edge in the inheritance DAG.

IF. The proportion of types Inherited From, that is, those types that are either extended or implemented, or, the proportion of types that occupy a parent end of an edge in the inheritance DAG.

IIDUI. The proportion of user-defined *interfaces* that *extend* some other interface.

IIIF. The proportion of user-defined *interfaces extended by* some other (user-defined) interface.

The table below lists the most refined summary metrics. Each row is one of the 7 relationships identified (whether it is extends or implements is implied by the combination of kinds of type). The columns show the two directions of the relationship. The cells of the "using" relation have the metrics in the order of: using Standard Library, using Third Party, or using User Defined.

	Defined Using Inheritance (Using)	Inherited From (Used)
Class-Class	SLCCDUI, TPCCDUI, UDCCDUI	CCIF
Class-Interface	SLCIDUI, TPCIDUI, UDCIDUI	CIIF
Interface-Interface	SLIIDUI, TPIIDUI, UDIIDUI	IIIF
Interface-Annotation	SLIADUI, TPIADUI, UDIADUI	IAIF
Enum-Interface	SLEIDUI, TPEIDUI, UDEIDUI	EIIF
Exception-Interface	SLExIDUI, TPExIDUI, UDExIDUI	ExIIF
Exception-Exception	SLExExDUI, TPExExDUI, UDExExDUI	ExExIF

Appendix B: Applications from Qualitas Corpus

We believe it is important to provide as complete information as possible regarding the applications used in our study, although space constraints cramp our presentation somewhat. The format is *application name-version id*.

aglets-2.0.2, ant-1.6.5, antlr-2.7.6, aoi-2.2, argouml-0.20, axion-1.0-M2, azureus-2.3.0.4, c_jdbc-2.0.2, colt-1.2.0, columba-1.0, compiere-251e, derby-10.1.1.0, displaytag-1.1, drawswf-1.2.9, drjava-20050814, eclipse_SDK-3.1.2-win32, exoportal-v1.0.2, findbugs-1.0.0, fitjava-1.1, fitlibraryforfitnesse-20050923, freecol-0.6.0, freecs-1.2.20060130, galleon-1.8.0, ganttproject-1.11.1, geronimo-1.0-M5, glassfish-9.0-b15, gt2-2.2-rc3, heritrix-1.8.0, hibernate-3.1-rc2, hsqldb-1.8.0.4, htmlunit-1.8, infoglue-2.3Final, informa-0.6.5, ireport-0.5.2, itext-1.4, ivatagroupware-0.11.3, j_ftp-1.48, jag-5.0.1, jaga-1.0.b, james-2.2.0, jasperreports-1.1.0, javacc-3.2, jboss-4.0.3-SP1, jchempaint-2.0.12, jedit-4.2, jeppers-20050607, jetty-5.1.8, jfreechart-1.0.1, jgraph-5.9.2.1, jhotdraw-6.0.1, jmeter-2.1.1, joggplayer-1.1.4s, jparse-0.96, jrat-0.6, jrefactory-2.9.19, jspwiki-2.2.33, jtopen-4.9, jung-1.7.1, junit-4.1, log4j-1.2.13, lucene-1.4.3, luxor-1.0-b9, megamek-2005.10.11, mvnforum-1.0-ga, nekohtml-0.9.5, netbeans-5.5-beta, openjms-0.7.7-alpha-3, openoffice-2.0.0, openxchange-0.8.0.6, oscache-2.3-full, pmd-3.3, poi-2.5.1, proguard-3.6, quartz-1.5.2, quickserver-1.4.7, quilt-0.6-a-5, roller-2.1.1-incubating, rssowl-1.2, sablecc-3.1, sandmark-3.4, scala-1.4.0.3, sequoiaerp-0.8.2-RC1-all-platforms, servicemix-3.0-SNAPSHOT, soot-2.2.3, springframework-1.2.7, squirrel_sql-2.4, struts-1.2.9, tomcat-5.5.17, trove-1.1b5, webmail-0.7.10, xalan-j_2_7_0, xerces-2.8.0, xmojo-5.0.0.

Author Index

Lecture Notes in Computer Science

Sublibrary 2: Programming and Software Engineering

For information about Vols. 1– 4523
please contact your bookseller or Springer

Vol. 4829: M. Lumpe, W. Vanderperren (Eds.), Software Composition. VIII, 281 pages. 2007.

Vol. 4824: A. Paschke, Y. Biletskiy (Eds.), Advances in Rule Interchange and Applications. XIII, 243 pages. 2007.

Vol. 4821: J. Bennedsen, M.E. Caspersen, M. Kölling (Eds.), Reflections on the Teaching of Programming. X, 261 pages. 2008.

Vol. 4807: Z. Shao (Ed.), Programming Languages and Systems. XI, 431 pages. 2007.

Vol. 4799: A. Holzinger (Ed.), HCI and Usability for Medicine and Health Care. XVI, 458 pages. 2007.

Vol. 4789: M. Butler, M.G. Hinchey, M.M. Larrondo-Petrie (Eds.), Formal Methods and Software Engineering. VIII, 387 pages. 2007.

Vol. 4767: F. Arbab, M. Sirjani (Eds.), International Symposium on Fundamentals of Software Engineering. XIII, 450 pages. 2007.

Vol. 4765: A. Moreira, J. Grundy (Eds.), Early Aspects: Current Challenges and Future Directions. X, 199 pages. 2007.

Vol. 4764: P. Abrahamsson, N. Baddoo, T. Margaria, R. Messnarz (Eds.), Software Process Improvement. XI, 225 pages. 2007.

Vol. 4762: K.S. Namjoshi, T. Yoneda, T. Higashino, Y. Okamura (Eds.), Automated Technology for Verification and Analysis. XIV, 566 pages. 2007.

Vol. 4758: F. Oquendo (Ed.), Software Architecture. XVI, 340 pages. 2007.

Vol. 4757: F. Cappello, T. Herault, J. Dongarra (Eds.), Recent Advances in Parallel Virtual Machine and Message Passing Interface. XVI, 396 pages. 2007.

Vol. 4753: E. Duval, R. Klamma, M. Wolpers (Eds.), Creating New Learning Experiences on a Global Scale. XII, 518 pages. 2007.

Vol. 4749: B.J. Krämer, K.-J. Lin, P. Narasimhan (Eds.), Service-Oriented Computing – ICSOC 2007. XIX, 629 pages. 2007.

Vol. 4748: K. Wolter (Ed.), Formal Methods and Stochastic Models for Performance Evaluation. X, 301 pages. 2007.

Vol. 4741: C. Bessière (Ed.), Principles and Practice of Constraint Programming – CP 2007. XV, 890 pages. 2007.

Vol. 4735: G. Engels, B. Opdyke, D.C. Schmidt, F. Weil (Eds.), Model Driven Engineering Languages and Systems. XV, 698 pages. 2007.

Vol. 4716: B. Meyer, M. Joseph (Eds.), Software Engineering Approaches for Offshore and Outsourced Development. X, 201 pages. 2007.

Vol. 4709: F.S. de Boer, M.M. Bonsangue, S. Graf, W.-P. de Roever (Eds.), Formal Methods for Components and Objects. VIII, 297 pages. 2007.

Vol. 4680: F. Saglietti, N. Oster (Eds.), Computer Safety, Reliability, and Security. XV, 548 pages. 2007.

Vol. 4670: V. Dahl, I. Niemelä (Eds.), Logic Programming. XII, 470 pages. 2007.

Vol. 4652: D. Georgakopoulos, N. Ritter, B. Benatallah, C. Zirpins, G. Feuerlicht, M. Schoenherr, H.R. Motahari-Nezhad (Eds.), Service-Oriented Computing ICSOC 2006. XVI, 201 pages. 2007.

Vol. 4640: A. Rashid, M. Aksit (Eds.), Transactions on Aspect-Oriented Software Development IV. IX, 191 pages. 2007.

Vol. 4634: H. Riis Nielson, G. Filé (Eds.), Static Analysis. XI, 469 pages. 2007.

Vol. 4620: A. Rashid, M. Aksit (Eds.), Transactions on Aspect-Oriented Software Development III. IX, 201 pages. 2007.

Vol. 4615: R. de Lemos, C. Gacek, A. Romanovsky (Eds.), Architecting Dependable Systems IV. XIV, 435 pages. 2007.

Vol. 4610: B. Xiao, L.T. Yang, J. Ma, C. Muller-Schloer, Y. Hua (Eds.), Autonomic and Trusted Computing. XVIII, 571 pages. 2007.

Vol. 4609: E. Ernst (Ed.), ECOOP 2007 – Object-Oriented Programming. XIII, 625 pages. 2007.

Vol. 4608: H.W. Schmidt, I. Crnković, G.T. Heineman, J.A. Stafford (Eds.), Component-Based Software Engineering. XII, 283 pages. 2007.

Vol. 4591: J. Davies, J. Gibbons (Eds.), Integrated Formal Methods. IX, 660 pages. 2007.

Vol. 4589: J. Münch, P. Abrahamsson (Eds.), Product-Focused Software Process Improvement. XII, 414 pages. 2007.

Vol. 4574: J. Derrick, J. Vain (Eds.), Formal Techniques for Networked and Distributed Systems – FORTE 2007. XI, 375 pages. 2007.

Vol. 4556: C. Stephanidis (Ed.), Universal Access in Human-Computer Interaction, Part III. XXII, 1020 pages. 2007.

Vol. 4555: C. Stephanidis (Ed.), Universal Access in Human-Computer Interaction, Part II. XXII, 1066 pages. 2007.

Vol. 4554: C. Stephanidis (Ed.), Universal Acess in Human Computer Interaction, Part I. XXII, 1054 pages. 2007.

Vol. 4553: J.A. Jacko (Ed.), Human-Computer Interaction, Part IV. XXIV, 1225 pages. 2007.

Vol. 4552: J.A. Jacko (Ed.), Human-Computer Interaction, Part III. XXI, 1038 pages. 2007.

Vol. 4551: J.A. Jacko (Ed.), Human-Computer Interaction, Part II. XXIII, 1253 pages. 2007.

Vol. 4550: J.A. Jacko (Ed.), Human-Computer Interaction, Part I. XXIII, 1240 pages. 2007.

Vol. 4542: P. Sawyer, B. Paech, P. Heymans (Eds.), Requirements Engineering: Foundation for Software Quality. IX, 384 pages. 2007.

Vol. 4536: G. Concas, E. Damiani, M. Scotto, G. Succi (Eds.), Agile Processes in Software Engineering and Extreme Programming. XV, 276 pages. 2007.

Vol. 4530: D.H. Akehurst, R. Vogel, R.F. Paige (Eds.), Model Driven Architecture - Foundations and Applications. X, 219 pages. 2007.